The **Rough Guide** to

The Caribbean

written and researched by

Robert Coates, Joe Fullman, Sean Harvey, Sara Humphreys, Stephen Keeling, Lesley McCave, Matt Norman, Lisa Risher, Rebecca Strauss, Alex Robertson Textor, Polly Thomas

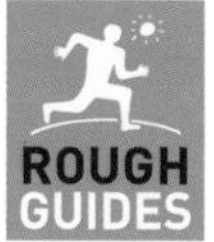

NEW YORK • LONDON • DELHI

www.roughguides.com

Contents

◀◀ Sunset over Antigua's south coast ◀ Fishing boat, Six Men's Bay, Barbados

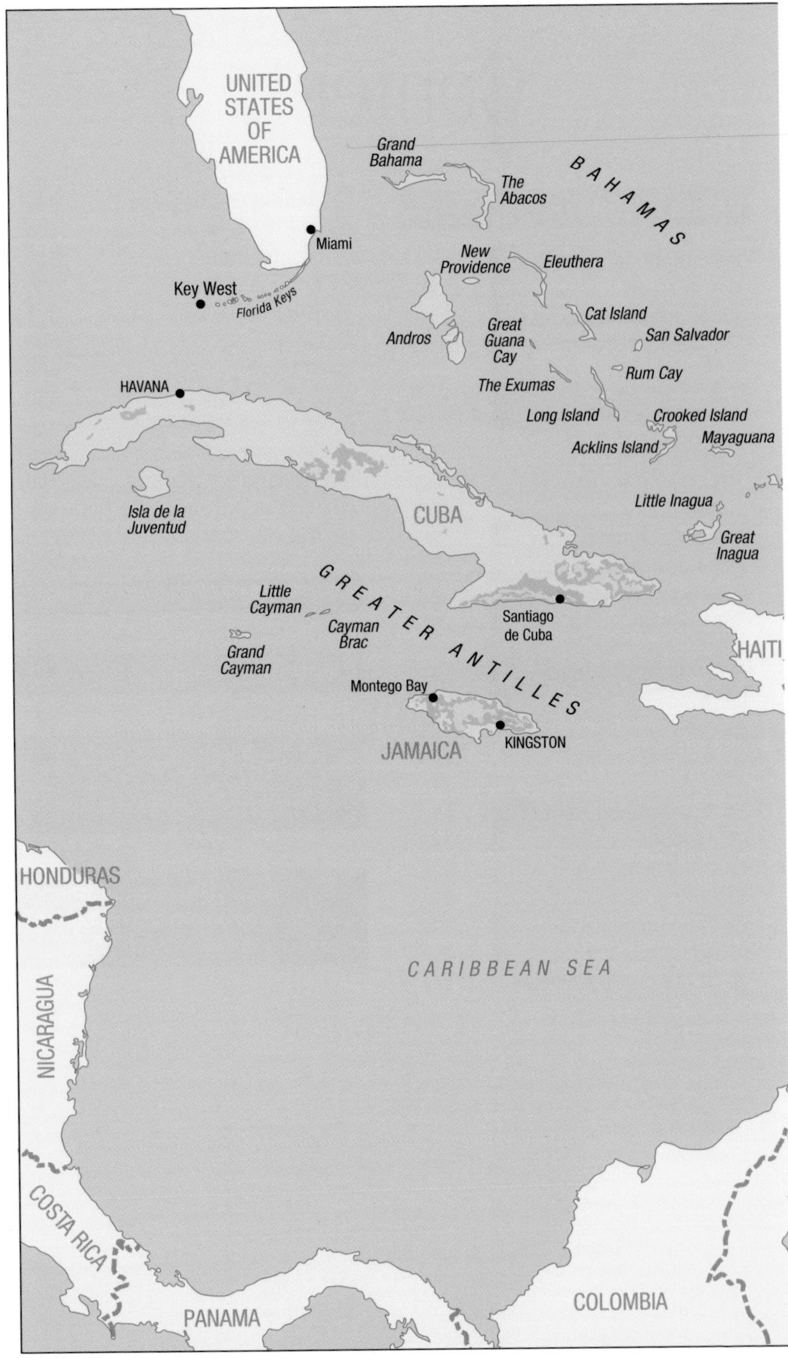
UNITED STATES OF AMERICA
Miami
Key West
Florida Keys
Grand Bahama
The Abacos
BAHAMAS
New Providence
Eleuthera
Andros
Cat Island
Great Guana Cay
San Salvador
Rum Cay
The Exumas
Long Island
Crooked Island
Acklins Island
Mayaguana
Little Inagua
Great Inagua
HAVANA
Isla de la Juventud
CUBA
Santiago de Cuba
GREATER ANTILLES
Little Cayman
Cayman Brac
Grand Cayman
Montego Bay
KINGSTON
JAMAICA
HAITI
HONDURAS
NICARAGUA
CARIBBEAN SEA
COSTA RICA
PANAMA
COLOMBIA

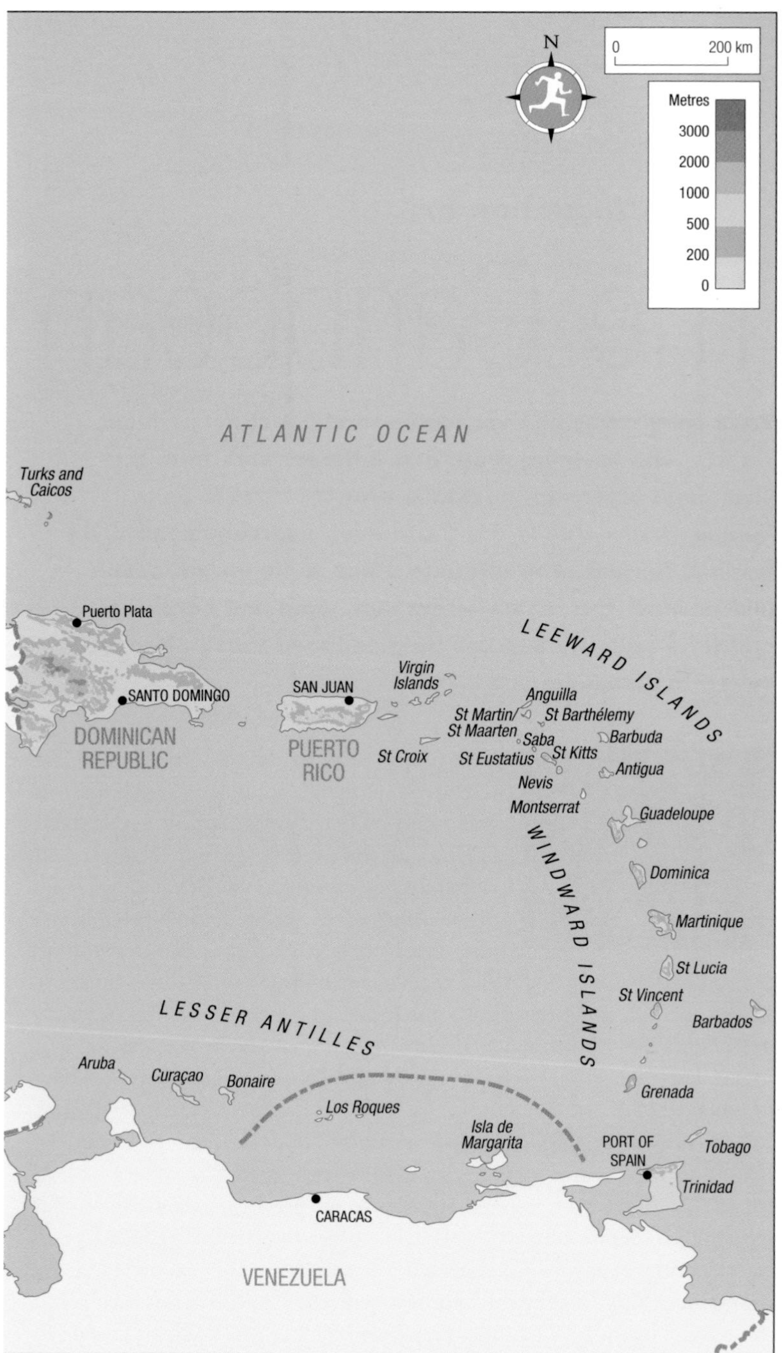
N
0
200 km
Metres
3000
2000
1000
500
200
0
ATLANTIC OCEAN
Turks and Caicos
Puerto Plata
SANTO DOMINGO
DOMINICAN REPUBLIC
SAN JUAN
PUERTO RICO
Virgin Islands
St Croix
LEEWARD ISLANDS
Anguilla
St Martin/ St Maarten
St Barthélemy
Saba
Barbuda
St Eustatius
St Kitts
Antigua
Nevis
Montserrat
Guadeloupe
WINDWARD ISLANDS
Dominica
Martinique
St Lucia
St Vincent
Barbados
Grenada
LESSER ANTILLES
Aruba
Curaçao
Bonaire
Los Roques
Isla de Margarita
PORT OF SPAIN
Tobago
Trinidad
CARACAS
VENEZUELA

Introduction to

The Caribbean

Palm trees swaying over white-sand beaches, pellucid waters with teeming reefs just a flipper kick from the shore and killer rum cocktails brought right to your lounge chair – this is the Caribbean, everyone's favourite tropical fantasy. The ultimate place to lie on the beach and unwind, the region offers sun, sand and corporeal comforts aplenty, and has long seduced those after life's sybaritic pleasures.

Given these obvious draws, a holiday in the Caribbean – anywhere in the Caribbean – is commonly proffered as the ultimate getaway. But buying into this postcard-perfect stereotype and failing to recognize the individual idiosyncrasies of the islands that make up the archipelago is the biggest mistake a visitor can make. Drawing on the collective traditions of Africa, together with those brought here by Spain, Britain, France, the Netherlands and India, no other area in the Americas exhibits such a diverse range of cultural patterns and social and political institutions: there's a lot more on offer here than sun, sea, sand and learning to limbo.

Culturally, this relatively small, relatively impoverished collection of islands has had an impact quite out of tune with its size, from the Jamaican sound-system DJs who inspired hip-hop, to the pre-Lenten bacchanalia that has come to define carnivals worldwide. Over the last five hundred years, each country or territory has carved out and maintained its own identity (some much more recently than others, with the onset of mass tourism and the advent of the all-inclusive resort), and it's hard to think of worlds so near and yet so disparate as the sensual *son* and *salsa* of Cuba compared to the dancehall and Rasta militancy of neighbouring Jamaica or the poppy *zouk* of Martinique and Guadeloupe. **Sport** rivals music as a Caribbean obsession, and though golf is well represented by the scores of world-class courses and basketball is increasingly popular amongst the youth, the region's game of choice has traditionally been cricket, introduced by the British and raised to great heights by the West Indies team, which led the world for much of the 1970s and 1980s. Wins are rather less common these days, but cricket remains central to the Caribbean psyche, with international matches known to bring their host islands to a complete standstill. Other popular spectator sports include soccer and baseball, firmly entrenched in the Dominican Republic, Puerto Rico and Cuba.

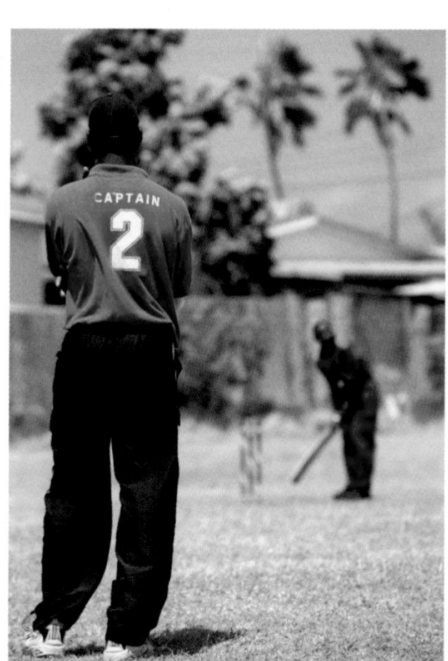

▲ Cricket

Fact file

- The combined **population** of the Caribbean islands is over 38 million; Great Inagua in the Bahamas has a human population of less than 1000 but is home to 80,000 pink flamingos, spoonbills and ducks.
- **Tourism** is by far the region's biggest business, with around 22.5 million visitors each year. With over three million annual visitors, the Dominican Republic is the most popular destination; Montserrat, with around 7000, is the least visited.
- The Caribbean Sea is the **fifth largest body of water** in the world, with a total area of 2.5 million square kilometres (slightly bigger than the Mediterranean).
- The **highest point** in the region is the Dominican Republic's Pico Duarte, at 3125m above sea level – it even gets some snow in winter. The DR also holds the Caribbean's **lowest point:** Lago Enriquillo, some 39m below sea level.
- With an estimated 230,000 people diagnosed HIV-positive, **HIV/AIDS infection rates** in the Caribbean are among the highest in the world, second only to sub-Saharan Africa.
- St Lucia has produced two **Nobel Prize winners**, the poet Derek Walcott and the economist Sir Arthur Lewis, while Trinidad has produced one, the novelist V.S. Naipaul.

Each island has a strong **culinary** tradition, too, and while you might come here to sample Caribbean classics such as Trinidadian roti, Grenadian "oil-down" or Dominican mountain chicken (actually a very big frog), you can also enjoy croissants and gourmet dinners in the French islands or Dutch delicacies in the Netherlands Antilles – and on every island with a fair-sized tourism industry, you'll find "international" restaurants of every ilk alongside hole-in-the-wall shacks selling local specialities.

The Caribbean's natural attractions are equally compelling, its **landscapes** ranging from teeming rainforest, mist-swathed mountains and volcanic peaks to lowland mangrove swamps, lush pastureland and savannah plains. The entire region is incredibly abundant in its **flora**, despite the sometimes volcanic or scrubby interiors on some islands. Heliconias and orchids flower almost everywhere, while hibiscus and ixoras brighten up the hedgerows, and the green of forest canopies are enlivened by flowering trees such as poinsettia and poui. Not surprisingly, eco-tourism abounds, whether it be hiking through the waterfall-studded rainforest of Dominica or St Lucia, high-mountain treks in Jamaica or birding in Trinidad, which has one of the highest concentrations of **bird species** in the world. The sea is as bountiful as the land; besides taking in excellent **diving** and **snorkelling** around multicoloured reefs and sunken ships that play host to technicolour marine life, you can turtle-watch on innumerable beaches that see nesting leatherbacks and hawksbills, go whale-spotting from St Lucia, Dominica and the Dominican Republic or frolic with giant manta rays offshore from Tobago and stingrays in the Caymans.

Beyond their cultural and physical richness, the Caribbean islands share a similar history of **colonization**. The first known inhabitants, farming

◀ Pelicans, Dickenson Bay, Antigua

Haiti

Truly historic as the Americas' first black republic, world-renowned centre for arts and music, and home to a continuous heritage of syncretic African religious practices, Haiti is one of the most culturally interesting countries in the region. We have, however, chosen not to cover Haiti in this edition of the Guide due to continuing political instability and violence. Of particular concern is an ongoing rash of kidnappings that have targeted returning expatriates and others who appear to have access to money. The successful slave rebellion that overthrew the colonial government some two centuries ago did not solve all political woes; military dictatorships and "presidents-for-life" have followed in modern times, as has the occasional contested election. The country remains, furthermore, in the economic doldrums, its teeming capital **Port-au-Prince** comprised of many depressed neighbourhoods, and much of its green and lovely countryside not at all set up for the casual traveller. Prospective visitors to Haiti are strongly encouraged to consult recent **travel advisories** put out by the British Foreign Office (@www.fco.gov.uk) and the US State Department (@travel.state.gov/travel/warnings.html).

and fishing Amerindians who travelled from South America by way of dugout canoes around 500 BC, were swiftly displaced by **Christopher Columbus**, the Italian explorer who "discovered" the region for Spain in the late fifteenth century, touching down on the Bahamas, Puerto Rico, Cuba, Hispaniola (modern-day Haiti and the Dominican Republic) and Jamaica, and mistakenly assuming that he had found the outlying islands of India, bestowing the title "West Indies" to the region. Seduced by fantasies of innumerable riches, the **British**, **French** and **Dutch** soon followed the Spanish, and the colonizers squabbled over their various territories for most of the sixteenth century. Colonization efforts were hindered by **pirates** and state-licensed **privateers** who plundered settlements and vessels without mercy.

Nonetheless European colonies were planted throughout the region, and by the seventeenth century, the islands had begun to be developed in earnest. The British (and later the Spanish and the French) established huge **sugar cane** plantations, which required large numbers of labourers to operate. They satisfied this need by engaging in the **slave trade**, an appalling tragedy of immense proportions. Between twelve and fifteen million people were transported to the region from Africa, many of whom died during the passage over. Plantation life for slaves was one of unimaginable barbarity, and eighteenth-century **rebellions**, combined with Christian tenets of humanity and charity, engendered the first moves toward emancipation – between 1833 and 1888, slavery was abolished in the Caribbean.

After emancipation, conditions for all but the planter elite remained abysmal, and the formation of unions and subsequent labour strikes led, by the 1930s, to the creation of political parties throughout the region. This in turn nudged the islands to call for **independence** from their colonial rulers, increasingly so after World War II. The early twentieth century also saw **tourism** start to take root. Wealthy British and North Americans had patronised palatial resorts here since the late nineteenth century, and the glitterati followed in the footsteps of Errol Flynn to Jamaica and Ernest Hemingway to Cuba, thus creating the air of exclusivity that remains inextricably tied to the Caribbean. With the introduction of long-haul air travel in the 1960s, tourists began to arrive en masse. While fenced-off all-inclusive enclaves are still going strong today, the region now has as many budget-oriented bolt holes as it does luxury resorts, and as many possibilities for adventurous travel as it does for staid beach holidays.

How to pick a beach

Finding a beach that suits your tastes shouldn't be hard, given that Caribbean shores can be as varied as the islands themselves. Spectacular swathes of beach are ten-a-penny here, but for the archetypal stretch of powdery white sand, lapped by warm clear water and generously endowed with coconut palms, you'll want to head to low-lying corraline islands such as Antigua (said to boast 365 beaches – one for every day of the year), the Bahamas (which has pink sand as well as white) or, in no particular order, Barbados, Aruba, Cayman Islands, Virgin Islands, Anguilla and the Turks and Caicos. If you're after desert-island solitude, you'll need to be willing to go off the beaten track: the best spots were snapped up long ago by developers who've added everything from hotels, bars and restaurants to watersports, and usually charge a fee for use of the facilities.

Those willing to dig a bit deeper might consider checking out the Caribbean's stunning grey- or black-sand beaches (the happy result of age-old volcanic activity), many of which are relatively undeveloped and surrounded by lush tropical foliage – St Lucia, Grenada, Dominica, St Vincent, Guadeloupe and Martinique are all solid contenders, while the larger of the Windward Islands have all types of beaches.

Remember that many islands have coastline on the Atlantic Ocean as well as the Caribbean Sea; beaches on the Atlantic side typically have rougher waves and cooler, green-tinged depths, while those on the Caribbean are usually calmer, warmer and properly conform to the classic "white-sand-and-palms" image.

Where to go

Spanning an arc from southern Florida to Venezuela on the South American coast, the islands of the Caribbean are made up of two main chains which form a 3200 kilometre breakwater between the Caribbean Sea to the south and the Atlantic Ocean to the north. Running south from Florida, the mostly limestone **Greater Antilles** (Cuba, Jamaica, Cayman Islands, Dominican Republic, Haiti, Puerto Rico and the Virgin Islands) comprise the largest and most geographically varied of the two chains, with white-sand beaches aplenty as well as rainforest-smothered peaks, which are remnants of submerged ranges related to the Central and South American mountain systems. Drier, somewhat flatter and boasting as many black-sand beaches as white, the volcanic **Lesser Antilles** can be further subdivided into the **Leeward Islands** (Anguilla, St Martin/St Maarten, St Barts, Saba, St Eustatius, St Kitts, Nevis, Antigua, Barbuda, Montserrat and Guadeloupe) and **Windward Islands** (Dominica, Martinique, St Lucia, Barbados, St Vincent, the Grenadines and Grenada). North of the Greater Antilles, the Bahamas and Turks and Caicos islands sit alone, as do Trinidad and Tobago and the "ABC islands" (Aruba, Bonaire

Rum

Tipple of choice for the region, **rum** is an integral part of Caribbean life – even the smallest village has a rum shop where old men nurse glasses of overproof "whites" mixed with water and put the world to rights. Everyone has their favourite brew, ranging from home-brewed firewaters such as Tobago's babash or Jamaica's jancro batty (strictly for masochists), to weaker, cocktail-friendly whites from Puerto Rico or sweet, rich, oak-aged concoctions like Cuba's Matusalem – best drunk after dinner, and never to be adulterated with a mixer.

Rum-making has remained much the same over the centuries. Yeast is added to sugar cane juice or molasses to kick-start fermentation (which converts the sucrose to alcohol); this "dead wash" is then boiled, and the evaporating alcohol is collected. After a little blending and the addition of water, the white rums are ready to bottle; smoother brown rums are aged in oak barrels, which colour the spirit to varying shades of brown. It's a simple process, but consider that it takes some ten to twelve tonnes of sugar cane to produce half a bottle of pure alcohol, and you'll understand the prevalence of those endless fields of swaying cane.

Carnival

Celebrated throughout the region, Caribbean **carnival** is an elaborate spectacle, when your senses are assaulted by the best in Caribbean culture and camaraderie. It has its roots in the pre-Lenten *carne vale* (literally "farewell to flesh") of early Italian Roman Catholicism, a time when Catholics were meant to finish up the meat in their pantries in preparation for the fasting period of Lent, but which became a wild costume festival. The Caribbean's carnival has grown from a two-day festival into a season of hedonism and debauchery between January and August, depending on the island. Unlike Carnival in Brazil, Caribbean carnival is a participatory celebration, making it a great way to fully experience the exuberance and joy of the festivities. Anyone can join in simply by signing up to "play mas" with a costume band, which can be arranged online before you arrive (see *Parties in paradise* colour section and individual chapters for island-specific details).

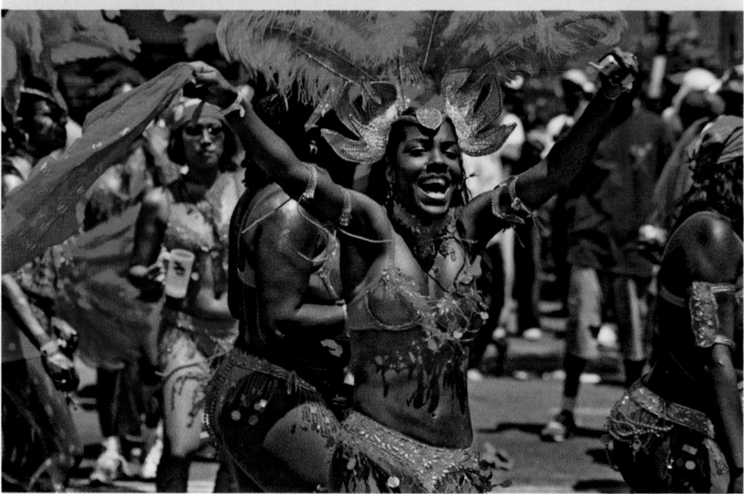

and Curaçao) in the south, just off the Venezuelan coast. The latter are an autonomous part of the Kingdom of the Netherlands and together with Saba, St Eustatius and St Maarten are collectively known as the **Netherlands Antilles**.

Deciding which of the islands to visit, however, is the fifty-million-dollar question. Obviously, you'll need to consider what you want from your holiday. If you're after two weeks of sunbathing and swimming and don't plan on doing any exploring, then you've the freedom to allow a travel agent to pick the cheapest deal available – or just flip through this guide and pick whichever resort sounds the most appealing. If variety is on your agenda, bigger islands which boast a diversity of landscapes – Cuba, Jamaica and the Dominican Republic – offer more scope for adventurous travel, with possibilities for hiking, rafting, eco-pursuits and cultural tours as well as beachlife; these probably demand a single-island trip. However, as **island-hopping** can be relatively easy, either by short plane trips or the occasional ferry, it's well worth seeing more than one island, especially if you've picked a destination in the close-set Lesser Antilles.

When to go

As visitors mainly flock to the Caribbean to swap snow, rain and wind back home for the sun and warm waters of the tropics, it should come as no surprise to find that the region's busiest time is the northern hemisphere's **winter** (roughly Nov–Feb). During this high season, the daytime heat doesn't reach blistering proportions, and is tempered by cool breezes and balmy evenings, while rain is generally restricted to brief early-afternoon showers. The downside, however, is that the beaches and attractions are busy, hotels are often full and flights can get overbooked, with fares at a premium. Prices for almost everything may decrease in the slow **summer** season, but it's not an ideal time to visit the Caribbean: days are oppressively hot and humid and nights are muggy. Late summer also sees the start of the **hurricane season** (see p.54), which

▲ Sugar mill ruins, Betty's Hope

runs roughly from July to November, and even if there's no big blow, this usually means a lot of **rain**. While there's never really a bad time to holiday in the region, the Caribbean is best enjoyed in the **shoulder seasons** (early Nov and Feb through June), when flights and hotels are plentiful (and less expensive) and the weather dependable. **Spring** is also the season for catching one of the Caribbean's many pre-Lenten carnivals.

Maximum daily temperatures and monthly rainfall

	Jan	Feb	Mar	Apr	May	Jun	July	Aug	Sept	Oct	Nov	Dec
San Juan, Puerto Rico												
Max °C	27	27	27	28	29	29	29	29	30	29	29	27
Max °F	81	81	81	82	84	84	84	84	86	84	84	81
Rain mm/in	109/4	69/3	74/3	104/4	150/6	137/5	145/6	160/6	158/6	142/6	160/6	137/5
Nassau, Bahamas												
Max °C	25	25	26	27	29	31	31	32	31	29	27	26
Max °F	77	77	79	81	84	88	88	90	88	74	71	79
Rain mm/in	26/1	38/2	36/2	64/3	117/5	163/6	147/6	135/5	175/7	165/7	71/3	33/2
Havana, Cuba												
Max °C	25	25	27	29	29	30	32	32	30	29	27	25
Max °F	77	77	81	84	84	86	90	90	86	84	81	77
Rain mm/in	71/3	46/2	46/2	58/2	119/5	165/7	125/5	135/5	150/6	173/7	79/3	58/2
Kingston, Jamaica												
Max °C	30	30	30	31	31	32	32	32	32	31	31	31
Max °F	86	86	86	88	88	90	90	90	90	88	88	88
Rain mm/in	23/1	15/.5	23/1	20/1	102/4	86/3	86/3	89/3	97/4	178/7	76/3	36/2
Bridgetown, Barbados												
Max °C	28	28	29	30	31	31	30	31	31	30	29	28
Max °F	82	82	84	86	88	88	86	88	88	86	84	82
Rain mm/in	66/3	28/1	33/2	36/2	58/2	112/4	147/6	147/6	170/7	178/7	206/8	97/4
Port of Spain, Trinidad												
Max °C	31	31	32	32	32	32	31	31	32	32	32	31
Max °F	88	88	90	90	90	90	88	88	90	90	90	88
Rain mm/in	69/3	41/2	46/2	53/2	94/4	193/7	218/8	246/10	193/7	170/7	183/7	125/5
Santo Domingo, Dominican Republic												
Max °C	29	29	29	30	30	31	31	31	31	31	30	29
Max °F	84	84	84	86	86	88	88	88	88	88	86	84
Rain mm/in	51/2	44/2	44/2	68/3	187/7	152/6	179/7	157/6	165/7	170/7	96/4	70/3

things not to miss

It's not possible to see everything that the Caribbean has to offer in one trip – and we don't suggest you try. What follows is a selective and subjective taste of the islands' highlights: spectacular natural attractions, thrilling ocean activities and rich cultural traditions. They're arranged in five colour-coded categories to help you find the very best things to see, do, eat and experience. All highlights have a page reference to take you straight into the Guide, where you can find out more.

01 Beach bumming Page **536** • Flop down on your own patch of sand, like these sun-worshippers in Antigua, and savour the freedom of not having to do anything at all.

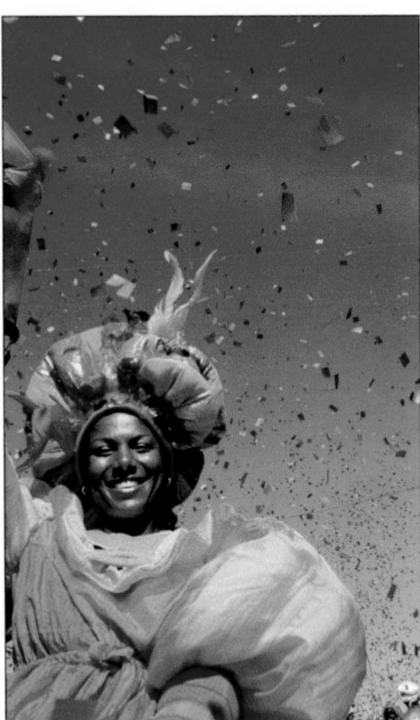

02 Trinidad Carnival Page **752** • The original Caribbean Carnival, easily the biggest and best in the islands, culminates in two days of fabulous costumed parades.

03 Sea kayaking in the Exumas Page **112** • Kayaking around this island chain – stopping off at whichever deserted beach strikes your fancy – is a compelling adventure for first-time paddlers and experienced explorers alike.

04 Boiling Lake, Dominica Page **617** • If the island's ultimate hike leading to the lake fails to impress, the eerie sight of its steam-enshrouded waters most certainly will.

05 Bonefishing in the Bahamas Page **101** • Enjoy some of the best fishing in the Caribbean at welcoming lodges on Andros, the archipelago's "big back yard".

06 The Pitons, St Lucia Page **650** • Towering over Soufrière, St Lucia's oldest town, these distinctive twin peaks are, rightfully, the island's most photographed sight.

07 Street food Page **751** • Be sure to visit food stalls in places like Trinidad and Tobago for *roti*, fresh seafood and the like – they're often the top spots to sample local cuisine and rub elbows with the islanders.

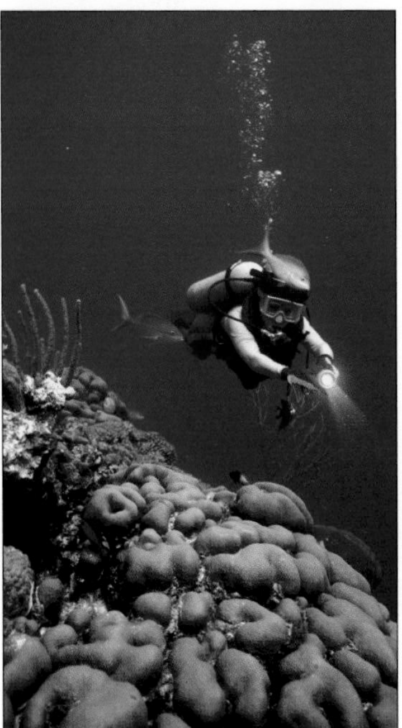

08 Bonaire Marine Park Page **817** • Home to everything from angelfish to moray eels, and just one of the Caribbean's spectacular marine habitats.

09 Willemstad, Curaçao Page **822** • One of the Caribbean's most colourful capitals, Willemstad's Dutch heritage is apparent along its narrow winding streets and attractive waterfront.

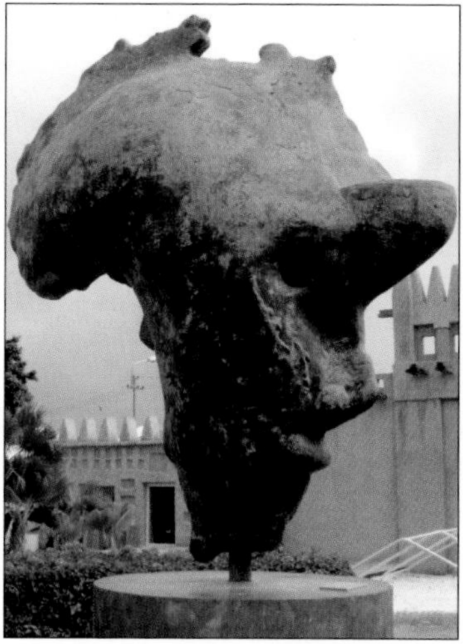

10 Kura Hulanda Museum, Willemstad, Curacao Page **823** • The Caribbean's finest exhibition on slavery and African civilisations, with exhibits that include a robe owned by Haile Sellassie himself.

11 Windsurfing Page **341** • With its brisk trade winds and a plethora of schools and rental centres, the Caribbean is one of the best places to windsurf in the Western Hemisphere.

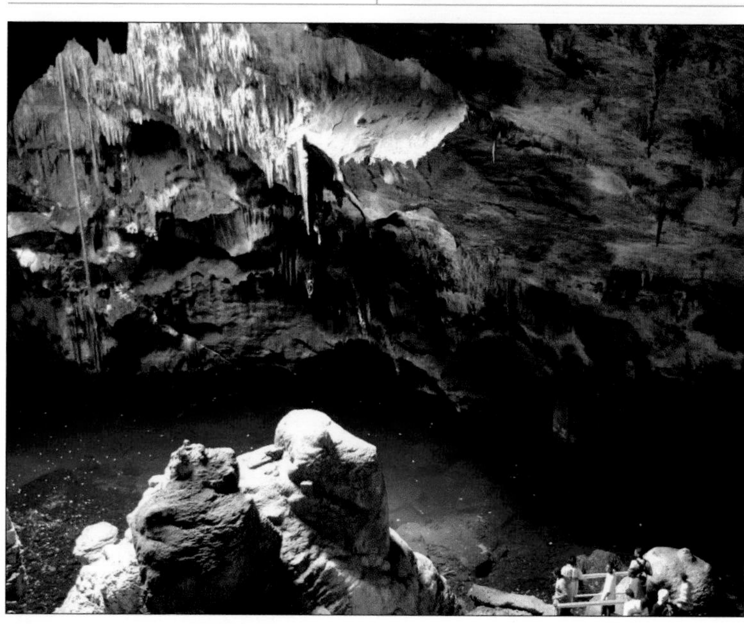

12 Caves Page **766** The limestone of many Caribbean islands has produced a multitude of caves – like Trinidad's Gasparee Cave – which boast intricate formations of stalactites and stalagmites.

13 Places you've never heard of Page **496** • Far off the beaten track lie islands like tranquil Saba, one of the unspoiled gems of the Caribbean.

14 Swimming with dolphins, the Bahamas Page **79** • Swim, feed and frolic among dolphins off the coast of Grand Bahama.

15 Plantation inns, St Kitts Page **515** • Exuding old-world ambience, inventive inns across the island – most housed in former sugar cane plantations – are a refreshing break from the usual beachside accommodation.

16 Jamaican nightlife Page **245** • From sweaty dancehalls to laid-back jam sessions or star-studded stage shows, the island's phenomenal music scene is bound to keep you busy night after night.

17 Cuban music Page **152** • The sounds of the Caribbean are every bit as important as the sights – be sure to check out some *salsa* and *son* in Cuba's dance halls, or even on its streets.

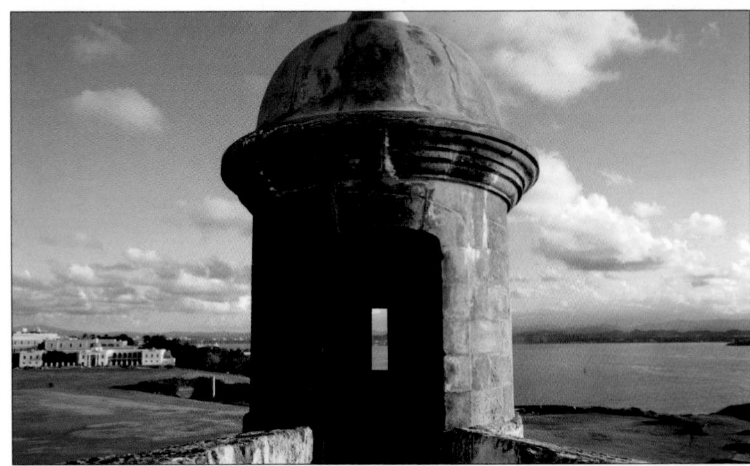

18 Old San Juan, Puerto Rico Page **366** • The preserved colonial buildings of the city make for excellent wandering, amid old fortresses, convents and the odd historic museum.

19 Fresh seafood Page **41** • Don't miss the region's countless seafood options, including succulent fresh lobster and fish, a mainstay of menus everywhere from high-end restaurants to charming beachside shacks.

20 Seven Mile Beach, Grand Cayman Page **225** • Lovely strands of coast like this lengthy one help make the Cayman Islands known for more than just offshore banking.

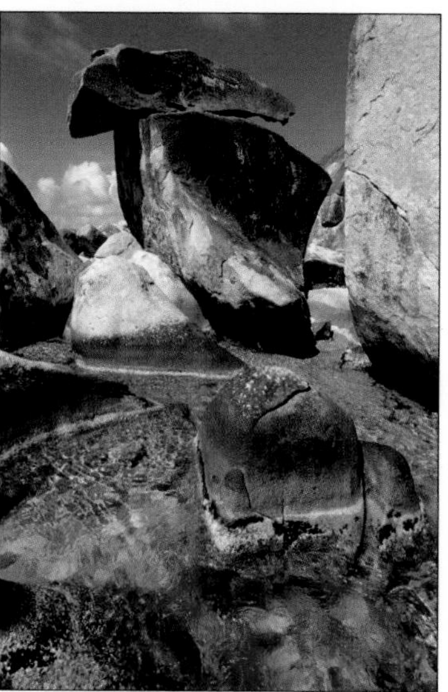

21 The Baths, Virgin Islands Page **445** • Clamber about in this otherworldly landscape, where gigantic boulders form striking grottoes, pools and underwater caves.

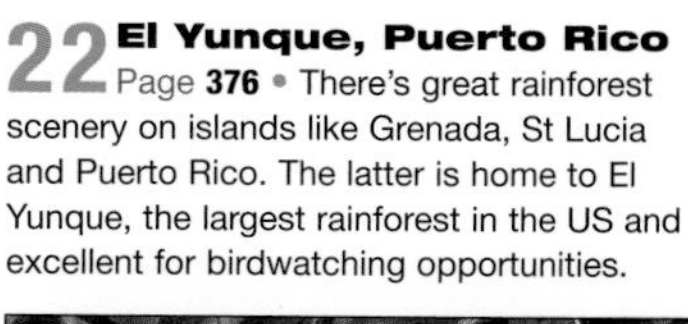

22 El Yunque, Puerto Rico Page **376** • There's great rainforest scenery on islands like Grenada, St Lucia and Puerto Rico. The latter is home to El Yunque, the largest rainforest in the US and excellent for birdwatching opportunities.

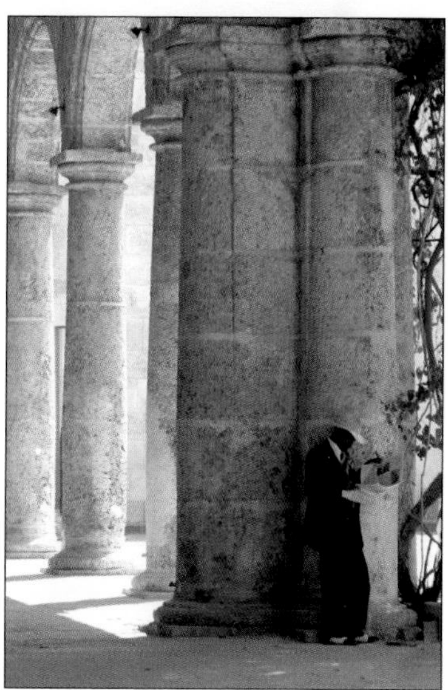

23 Habana Vieja, Cuba Page **165** • Untouched for years by tourism, the faded grandeur of Havana's old town is unmatched in the region.

24 Snorkelling Page **43** • Often as rewarding as diving, snorkelling through the Caribbean's underwater world can be far cheaper, especially if you bring your own gear.

25 Soufrière Hills Page **532** • Witness first-hand the terrible power of Montserrat's active volcano, which last erupted in 1995 and destroyed half the island, including the now-abandoned capital of Plymouth.

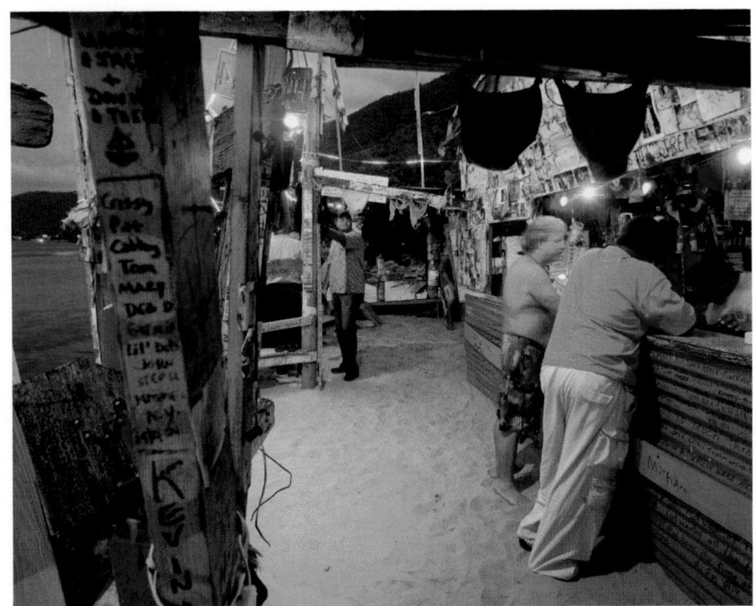

26 Bomba's shack, Virgin Islands Page **441** • Quiet and unassuming most of the time, this ramshackle bar comes alive every full moon to host an all-out bash.

Basics

Basics

Getting there

Given the ocean-bound nature of the Caribbean, **flying** is the only viable option for many visitors. Flights either operate through major US hubs – Miami, say, or New York, sometimes through Puerto Rico – or direct from European cities like London, Paris and Amsterdam. Most **cruises** to the region depart from the US East Coast, making a flight to the US an inevitable part of the itinerary for those from elsewhere.

Air fares always depend on the season. In the Caribbean, **high season** is from mid-December to April, with fares peaking during the holiday season. Fares drop during the **"shoulder" seasons** – May to July – and you'll get the best prices during the **low, wet season**, which runs from August to November (though from the UK, prices during the school summer holidays can be high). Of course, prices vary wildly depending on your destination and inevitably much cheaper deals are available to islands hosting flights from multiple **tour operators**, such as Puerto Rico, the Dominican Republic, Jamaica, Barbados and Aruba. Note also that flying at weekends is more expensive; price ranges quoted below assume midweek travel.

You can often cut costs by going through a **specialist flight agent** – either a **consolidator**, who buys up blocks of tickets from the airlines, or a **discount agent**, who may also offer special student and youth fares and a range of other travel-related services such as insurance, car rentals, tours and the like. Some agents specialize in **charter flights**, which are cheaper but departure dates are fixed and withdrawal penalties are high. Booking flights well in advance, or taking advantage of Web-only offers and airline frequent-flyer programmes, can often knock a couple of hundred dollars off the price of your flight. Another way to vastly reduce the price of your Caribbean holiday – especially if you book last-minute, accept charter flights and don't insist upon particular accommodation – is to book with a tour operator who can put together a **package deal** including flights and accommodation at an especially arranged price, and perhaps tours of the island or even a wedding ceremony as well.

Useful websites for booking flights online

Ⓦ **www.travel.yahoo.com** Incorporates a lot of Rough Guides material in its coverage of destination countries and cities across the world, with information about places to eat and sleep.

Ⓦ **www.cheapflights.co.uk** Bookings from the UK and Ireland only; for the US, visit Ⓦ www.cheapflights.com; for Canada, Ⓦ www.cheapflights.ca; for Australia and New Zealand, Ⓦ www.cheapflights.com.au. All offer flight deals, and links to other travel agent sites.

Ⓦ **www.cheaptickets.com** Hawaii-based discount flight specialists (US departures only) whose search engine claims to dig up the lowest possible fares worldwide, though the one drawback is its cumbersome log-in procedure.

Ⓦ **www.etn.nl/discount.htm** A hub of consolidator and discount agent Web links, maintained by the nonprofit European Travel Network.

Ⓦ **www.expedia.com** Discount air fares, all-airline search engine and daily deals (US only; for the UK Ⓦ www.expedia.co.uk; for Canada Ⓦ www.expedia.ca).

Ⓦ **www.hotwire.com** Return bookings from the US only. Last-minute savings of up to forty percent on regular published fares. Travellers must be at least 18 and there are no refunds, transfers or changes allowed. Log-in required. If you're looking for the cheapest possible scheduled flight, this is probably your best bet.

Ⓦ **www.lastminute.com** Offers good last-minute UK holiday package and flight-only deals; in Australia Ⓦ www.lastminute.com.au.

Ⓦ **www.qixo.com** A comparison search that trawls through other ticket sites – including agencies and airlines – to find the best deals.

Ⓦ **www.skyauction.com** Bookings from the US only. Auctions tickets and travel packages using a "second bid" scheme, just like eBay. You state the maximum you're willing to pay, and the system will bid only as much as it takes to outbid others, up to your stated limit.

Ⓦ www.travelocity.com and Ⓦ www.travelocity.co.uk Destination guides, hot Web fares and best deals for car rental, accommodation and lodging. Provides access to the travel agent system SABRE, the most comprehensive central reservations system in the US.

Flights from the US and Canada

Most airlines operate their Caribbean flights from the **East Coast** of the US (New York, Boston, Miami, Philadelphia etc) and **Toronto**, except American Airlines, which flies from most major US cities to their Caribbean hub in San Juan with connecting onward services. Other direct flights include Northwest's service from Detroit to San Juan and Montego Bay, Continental's wide range of Caribbean services from Houston, and USA3000's services from Chicago, Detroit and Pittsburgh. In Canada you can fly direct from Toronto to most Caribbean destinations. Flights from New York and Toronto average around four hours, while flights from Miami are about two hours.

Air fares peak around Christmas and New Year, when they can reach up to US$900–1000/Can$1380–1535 from the East Coast of the US and Toronto. From **January to April** you can expect to get the best weather and pay US$100–200 less. Amounts drop during the **shoulder season**, when you'll pay anything up to US$700/Can$1125. The best prices are available during the (**wet**) **low season** from August to November – you should be able to get a regular fare for around US$600/Can$700. Count on paying an extra US$300 or so to fly from the **West Coast** of the US. Note also that flying at weekends ordinarily adds at least US$50 to the round-trip fare.

Package tours can often be the most economical option and range from combined flight and accommodation deals to specialist tours. For details on **scuba-diving** tours see p.44.

Airlines

Unless otherwise specified all phone numbers work in both the US and Canada.

Air Canada Ⓣ 1-888/247-2262, Ⓦ www.aircanada.ca.

Air France US Ⓣ 1-800/237-2747, Ⓦ www.airfrance.com; Canada Ⓣ 1-800/667-2747, Ⓦ www.airfrance.ca.

Air Jamaica US Ⓣ 1-800/523-5585, Canada Ⓣ 416/229-6024; Ⓦ www.airjamaica.com.

Air Sunshine US Ⓣ 1-800/327-8900, Ⓦ www.airsunshine.com.

AirTran Airways Ⓣ 1-800/247-8726, Ⓦ www.airtran.com.

Air Transat Ⓣ 1-877/872-6728, Ⓦ www.airtransat.ca

American Airlines Ⓣ 1-800/433-7300, Ⓦ www.aa.com.

Bahamas Air US Ⓣ 1-800/222-4262, Ⓦ www.bahamasair.com.

Caribbean Airlines Ⓣ 1-800/538-2942, Ⓦ www.caribbean-airlines.com.

Cayman Airways US Ⓣ 1-800/422-9626, Ⓦ www.caymanairways.com.

Chalk's Ocean Airways US Ⓣ 1-800/424-2775, Ⓦ www.flychalks.com.

Continental Airlines domestic Ⓣ 1-800/523-3279, international Ⓣ 1-800/231-0856, Ⓦ www.continental.com.

Delta Air Lines domestic Ⓣ 1-800/221-1212, international Ⓣ 1-800/241-4141, Ⓦ www.delta.com.

Gulfstream International Airlines Ⓣ 954/226-3000 or 1-800/231-0856, Ⓦ www.gulfstreamair.com.

JetBlue Ⓣ 1-800/538-2583, Ⓦ www.jetblue.com.

Lynx Air International US Ⓣ 1-888/596-9247 or 954/772-9808, Ⓦ www.lynxair.com.

Mexicana Ⓣ 1-800/531-7921, Ⓦ www.mexicana.com.

North American Airlines Ⓣ 718/656-6250 or 1-800/359-6222, Ⓦ www.northamair.com.

Northwest/KLM Royal Dutch Airlines domestic Ⓣ 1-800/225-2525, international Ⓣ 1-800/447-4747, Ⓦ www.nwa.com, Ⓦ ww.klm.com.

Spirit Airlines Ⓣ 1-800/772-7117, Ⓦ www.spiritair.com.

United Airlines domestic Ⓣ 1-800/241-6522, international Ⓣ 1-800/538-2929, Ⓦ www.united.com.

US Airways Ⓣ 1-800/622-1015, Ⓦ www.usairways.com.

USA3000 Airlines Ⓣ 1-877/USA-3000, Ⓦ www.usa3000.com.

WestJet Ⓣ 1-888/WESTJET, Ⓦ www.westjet.com.

Travel agents and tour operators

Air Brokers International Ⓣ 1-800/883-3273, Ⓦ www.airbrokers.com. Consolidator.

Airtech Ⓣ 212/219-7000, Ⓦ www.airtech.com. Standby seat broker; also deals in consolidator fares and courier flights.

Educational Travel Center ⓣ1-800/747-5551 or 608/256-5551, ⓦwww.edtrav.com. Student/youth discount agent.
Global Exchange ⓣ415/225-7296, ⓦwww.globalexchange.org. Cultural "reality tours" to Cuba, Haiti and Jamaica.
STA Travel US ⓣ1-800/781-4040, Canada 1-888/427-5639; ⓦwww.statravel.com. Worldwide specialists in independent travel, student IDs, travel insurance, car rental, rail passes etc.
Student Flights ⓣ1-800/255-8000 or 480/951-1177, ⓦwww.isecard.com. Student/youth fares, student IDs.
Travel Cuts Canada ⓣ1-866/246-9762, US ⓣ1-800/952-2887; ⓦwww.travelcuts.com. Canadian student-travel organization.
Travelers Advantage ⓣ1-877/259-2691, ⓦwww.travelersadvantage.com. Discount travel club; annual membership fee required (currently $1 for two months' trial).
Worldtek Travel ⓣ1-800/243-1723, ⓦwww.worldtek.com. Comparison site.

Specialist tour operators

American Express Vacations ⓣ1-800/335-3342, ⓦwww.americanexpressvacations.com. Luxury vacations to various Caribbean islands.
Caribbean Concepts ⓣ206/575-0907 or 1-800/777-0977, ⓦwww.caribbeanconcepts.com. Caribbean specialists offering tours and packages all over the region.
Caribbean Journey ⓣ1-888/236-1924, ⓦwww.caribbeanjourney.com. Personalized trips to most Caribbean islands, with all categories of accommodation, as well as trips built around festivals and weddings/honeymoons.
Cheap Caribbean ⓣ1-800/915-2322, ⓦwww.cheapcaribbean.com. Flight and accommodation deals throughout the Caribbean.
Delta Vacations ⓣ1-800/654-6559, ⓦwww.deltavacations.com. Vacations in most Caribbean islands from major US cities.
Leisure Time Travel ⓣ352/795-3474 or 1-800/771-2202, ⓦwww.leisuretimetravel.com. Tour operator specializing in fly fishing and light tackle vacations to the Bahamas, Cayman Islands and Costa Rica.
TourScan Inc ⓣ1-800/962 2080, ⓦwww.tourscan.com. This Caribbean specialist offers discounted vacations all over the region.

Cruises from the US and Canada

Cruises are a popular way to visit multiple islands in a very short time. Trips can last anywhere from a few days up to a week or more and ships usually stop for a day at each port. Plenty of corporate cruise lines ply the Caribbean, offering **all-inclusive** cruises that can scale the heights of luxury (and costs) but can also be relatively affordable: a seven-day spin from Florida on a not-so-swanky ship could set you back just US$700 for the Western Caribbean, US$800 for the Eastern region and slightly more for the southern islands. The major drawback of cruises is that you only get to visit the tourist ports, making it difficult to know what the island is like in anything more than a superficial sense – and as a result, not contributing much to local communities either.

Websites such as ⓦwww.cruise.com, ⓦwww.cruisereviews.com and ⓦwww.cruisediscounters.com are helpful resources for deciding which cruise is best for you, taking into account price range, boat size and length of trip. While some companies offer cruises only, there are still many others that negotiate rates with major airlines allowing for fly/cruise options from most major airports in the US and the rest of the world. Seven-night cruises with the companies listed below range from US$500 for the Southern Caribbean (often starting in Barbados or Puerto Rico), or US$600 and US$650 for the Western and Eastern Caribbean respectively – most often starting in Florida – to US$4000 or more for the luxury liners. Prices are outside of the high season, when prices can jump by US$300–500, and are also exclusive of **port charges**, which add an extra US$200 or so.

Carnival ⓣ1-866/299-5968, ⓦwww.carnival.com. A youthful cruise line with a big emphasis on fun, offering seven nights from Miami, Orlando or Fort Lauderdale.
Disney ⓣ1-800/951-3532, ⓦwww.disneycruise.disney.go.com. Packages include seven nights from Key West, including a trip to Disney's own Bahamian island. Other ports of call include St Maarten, Grand Cayman, St Thomas/St John and Nassau.
Holland America ⓣ1-877/724-5425, ⓦwww.hollandamerica.com. Family cruise line, with hefty scheduled entertainment for both adults and kids.
Norwegian ⓣ1-800/327-7030, ⓦwww.ncl.com. Top-quality luxury fleet offering seven-day cruises from Florida to the western Caribbean.
Princess ⓣ1-800/PRINCESS, ⓦwww.princesscruises.com. Seven-day luxury cruises (including spas and scuba diving) from Florida.

Radisson Seven Seas ⓣ1-877/505-5370, ⓦwww.rssc.com. Seven-day cruises from Florida to LA via the Caribbean and South America, starting at US$5000.

Royal Caribbean ⓣ1-800/389-9819, ⓦwww.royalcaribbean.com. Caribbean specialists offering great deals for trips from Florida to destinations all over the region, and ships with such facilities as rock-climbing walls.

Silversea ⓣ1-877/760-9052, ⓦwww.silversea.com. Top-notch nine-day all-inclusive cruises and fly/cruise options from all over the world.

Flights from the UK and Ireland

Most **British** and **Irish** visitors to the Caribbean are on some form of **package tour**. This is usually the simplest way of going about things, and even if you plan to travel independently and organize your own accommodation, a seat on a charter is almost always the cheapest way to reach your destination (XL are currently leading the way with Caribbean services). But charters have their drawbacks, especially if your plans don't fit exactly into their usual two-week straitjacket. As an alternative, several airlines fly direct scheduled **flights** from London to many Caribbean destinations, and you can find comparable fares with other carriers that require a stopover in the US. For former **Dutch colonies** Aruba, Bonaire, Curaçao, Saba, St Eustatius and St Maarten, try KLM via Amsterdam, or for Guadeloupe and Martinique – both **colonies of France** – you can fly from London with Air France via Paris.

There are **no direct flights** from Ireland to the islands, but there are good connections via London, New York or Miami (see "Flights from the US and Canada").

If your holiday plans include little more than to stay in one place to soak up the sun, then a package holiday might be your best option; many specialist companies can arrange flights as well as accommodation ranging from self-catering apartments to all-inclusive hotels. Many operators offer specialized tours geared towards a wide range of interests: from couples wishing to get married in the Caribbean to diving enthusiasts and spa-seekers.

Airlines

Unless otherwise specified, all phone numbers work within the UK only.

Fly less – stay longer! Travel and Climate Change

Climate change is perhaps the single biggest issue facing our planet. It is caused by a build-up in the atmosphere of carbon dioxide and other greenhouse gases, which are emitted by many sources – including planes. Already, **flights** account for three to four percent of human-induced global warming: that figure may sound small, but it is rising year on year and threatens to counteract the progress made by reducing greenhouse emissions in other areas.

Rough Guides regard travel as a **global benefit**, and feel strongly that the advantages to developing economies are important, as are the opportunities for greater contact and awareness among peoples. But we also believe in travelling responsibly, which includes giving thought to how often we fly and what we can do to redress any harm that our trips may create.

We can travel less or simply reduce the amount we travel by air (taking fewer trips and staying longer, or taking the train if there is one); we can avoid night flights (which are more damaging); and we can make the trips we do take "climate neutral" via a carbon offset scheme. **Offset schemes** run by climatecare.org, carbonneutral.com and others allow you to "neutralize" the greenhouse gases that you are responsible for releasing. Their websites have simple calculators that let you work out the impact of any flight – as does our own. Once that's done, you can pay to fund projects that will reduce future emissions by an equivalent amount. Please take the time to visit our website and make your trip climate neutral, or get a copy of the *Rough Guide to Climate Change* for more detail on the subject.

www.roughguides.com/climatechange

Aeroflot UK ⓣ020/7355 2233, ⓦwww.aeroflot.com.
Air France UK ⓣ0870/142 4343, ⓦwww.airfrance.co.uk, Republic of Ireland ⓣ01/605 0383, ⓦwww.airfrance.ie.
Air Jamaica UK ⓣ020/8570 7999, ⓦwww.airjamaica.com.
American Airlines UK ⓣ0845/7789 789, Republic of Ireland ⓣ01/602 0550; ⓦwww.aa.com.
British Airways UK ⓣ0870/850 9850, Republic of Ireland ⓣ1890/626747; ⓦwww.ba.com.
Caribbean Airlines ⓣ0870/499 2942, Republic of Ireland ⓣ01/201 3915; ⓦwww.caribbean-airlines.com.
Continental UK ⓣ0845/607 6760, Republic of Ireland ⓣ1890/925 252; ⓦwww.continental.com.
Cubana UK ⓣ020/7537 7909, ⓦwww.cubana.co.cu.
KLM Royal Dutch Airlines ⓣ0870/5074074, Republic of Ireland ⓣ1850/747 400; ⓦwww.klm.com.
Lufthansa UK ⓣ0845/7737 747, Republic of Ireland ⓣ01/844 5544; ⓦwww.lufthansa.co.uk.
United Airlines UK ⓣ0845/8444 777, ⓦwww.united.com.
Virgin Atlantic Airways UK ⓣ01293/747747, ⓦwww.virgin-atlantic.com.

Charter flight operators

British Midland (BMI) UK ⓣ0870/607 0555 or ⓣ0870/607 0222, Republic of Ireland ⓣ01/407 3036; ⓦwww.flybmi.com.
First Choice ⓣ0870/850 3999, ⓦwww.firstchoice.co.uk.
My Travel ⓣ0870/241 5333, ⓦwww.mytravel.com.
Thomas Cook UK ⓣ0870/750 5711, ⓦwww.flythomascook.com.
Thomsonfly UK ⓣ0870/190 0737, ⓦwww.thomsonfly.com.
XL UK ⓣ01792/601820, Ireland 0818 220 220, ⓦwww.xl.com.

Travel agents

Apex Travel Republic of Ireland ⓣ01/241 8000, ⓦwww.apextravel.ie. Specialists in flights to Australia, Africa, Far East, US and Canada.
Aran Travel International Republic of Ireland ⓣ091/562 595, ⓦhomepages.iol.ie/~arantvl/aranmain.htm. Good-value flights to all parts of the world.
ebookers UK ⓣ0800/082 3000, ⓦwww.ebookers.com Republic of Ireland ⓣ01/488 3507, ⓦwww.ebookers.ie. Low fares on an extensive selection of scheduled flights and package deals.
Joe Walsh Tours Republic of Ireland ⓣ01/241 0888, ⓦwww.joewalshtours.ie. General budget fares agent.
North South Travel UK ⓣ&ⓕ01245/608 291, ⓦwww.northsouthtravel.co.uk. Friendly, competitive travel agency, offering discounted fares worldwide. Profits are used to support projects in the developing world, especially the promotion of sustainable tourism.
Premier Travel Derry ⓣ028/7126 3333, ⓦwww.premiertravel.uk.com. Discount flight specialists.
Rosetta Travel Northern Ireland ⓣ028/9064 4996, ⓦwww.rosettatravel.com. Flight and holiday agent.
STA Travel UK ⓣ0870/2300 040, ⓦwww.statravel.co.uk. Worldwide specialists in independent travel; also student IDs, travel insurance, car rental, rail passes, and more. Good discounts for students and under-26s.
Trailfinders UK ⓣ0845/0585 858, Republic of Ireland ⓣ01/677 7888; ⓦwww.trailfinders.com. One of the best-informed and most efficient agents for independent travellers.
usit Republic of Ireland ⓣ01/602 1600, Northern Ireland ⓣ028/9032 7111, ⓦwww.usit.ie. Student and youth specialists for flights.

Specialist tour operators

British Airways Holidays ⓣ0870/850 2145, ⓦwww.baholidays.co.uk. Using British Airways and other quality international airlines, offers an exhaustive range of package and tailor-made holidays.
Caribbean Expressions ⓣ020/7433 2610, ⓦwww.expressionsholidays.co.uk. Specializing in hotel holidays to most Caribbean islands, including diving packages to St Lucia, Tobago and the Cayman Islands, and yacht charters in the Virgin Islands.
Caribtours ⓣ020/7751 0660, ⓦwww.caribtours.co.uk. Long-established operator offering tailor-made breaks – including trips designed for families, spa-seekers, island hoppers and honeymooners – using scheduled flights to the Caribbean.
Complete Caribbean ⓣ01423/531031, ⓦwww.completecaribbean.co.uk. Tailor-made holidays on most islands for families, couples and adventure seekers, with accommodation in villas and hotels.
Hayes & Jarvis UK ⓣ0870/366 1636, ⓦwww.hayesandjarvis.co.uk. Specialists in long-haul holidays, particularly with diving destinations. Exotic weddings organized.
Journey Latin America UK ⓣ020/8747 3108, ⓦwww.journeylatinamerica.co.uk. Specialists in flights, packages and tailor-made trips all over the Caribbean.

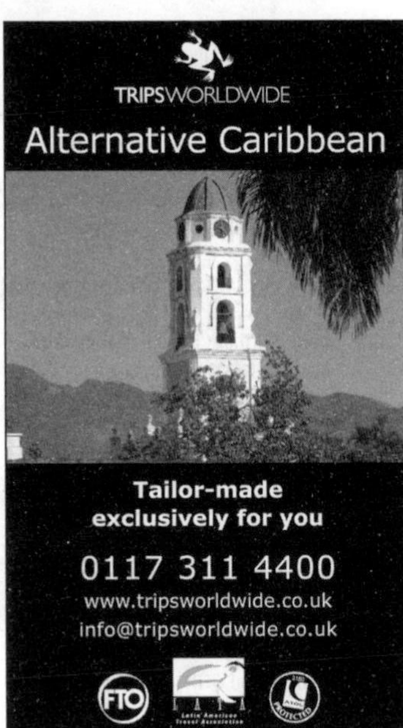

Just Grenada ⓣ01373/814214, ⓦwww.justgrenada.co.uk. The only company focusing exclusively on holidays in Grenada, with knowledgeable staff who have stayed at most properties and know the area well.
Kuoni Travel UK ⓣ01306/744 442, ⓦwww.kuoni.co.uk. Flexible package holidays with extensive presence in the Caribbean and good family offers.
Thomas Cook UK ⓣ0870/750 5711, ⓦwww.thomascook.co.uk. Long-established one-stop 24hr travel agency for package holidays or scheduled flights.
Trips Worldwide ⓣ0117/311 4400, ⓦwww.tripsworldwide.co.uk. Tailor-made holidays to the "alternative Caribbean" include rainforests, culture, birdwatching and plenty of activities. Website lets you create your own itinerary.
Tropic Breeze ⓣ01752/873 377, ⓦwww.tropicbreeze.co.uk. Holidays ashore and afloat in St Kitts and Nevis, Antigua, the Grenadines, Tobago, Barbados, St Lucia and the British Virgin Islands. Includes two-week yacht charters with flight, in low season, from as little £1000 per person.

Cruises from the UK and Ireland

Cruises aren't as good value an option from outside of the US, as you will have to **fly stateside** before getting on a boat, but several cruise operators work with major airlines to offer all-in **package deals**.
Celebrity UK ⓣ0800/018 2525, US ⓣ1-800/722-5941, ⓦwww.celebritycruises.com. Cruises with an emphasis on high-end pampering, including spas and art classes. Seven nights from Fort Lauderdale, Baltimore or San Juan.
Fred Olsen UK ⓣ01473/742 424, ⓦwww.fredolsencruises.com. An extensive range of Caribbean cruises; fourteen nights from £2400, including a flight from London or Manchester.

Flights from Australia and New Zealand

There are **no direct flights** from Australasia to the Caribbean. The best option for travellers is to fly to the US, the UK or the Netherlands to access the best possible selection of routes and fares. The most straightforward routes involve flying to the US West Coast or Canada and then transferring to Houston, Miami, or to the American Airlines hub in San Juan, for onward transportation. **Fares** tend not to vary much year-round, so expect to pay up to Aus$2000/NZ$2173 from Sydney to Miami, more at Christmas and New Year; add around Aus$500/NZ$590 to fly from Darwin or Perth. A viable alternative, if you have the time, is to buy a **Round-the-World ticket** (**RTW**); with stops in the US, Venezuela, Trinidad, Jamaica, England, Greece and Thailand could cost around Aus$6000/NZ$7055. For RTW travel specialists, see "Specialist agents", opposite.

For more on cruises, see the US section, p.29.

Airlines

Air Canada Australia ⓣ1300/655 767, New Zealand ⓣ0508/747 767; ⓦwww.aircanada.ca.
Air France Australia ⓣ1300/390 190, New Zealand ⓣ09/308 3352; ⓦwww.airfrance.com.au.
Air New Zealand Australia ⓣ13 24 76, New Zealand ⓣ0800/737000; ⓦwww.airnz.co.nz.
Air Pacific Australia ⓣ1800/230 150, New Zealand ⓣ0800/800 178; ⓦwww.airpacific.com.
Alitalia Australia ⓣ1300/0361 400, New Zealand ⓣ09/308 3357; ⓦwww.alitalia.com.
American Airlines Australia ⓣ1800/673 486, New Zealand ⓣ0800/445 442; ⓦwww.aa.com.
British Airways Australia ⓣ1300/767 177, New Zealand ⓣ09/966 9777; ⓦwww.ba.com.
Cathay Pacific Australia ⓣ13 17 47, New Zealand ⓣ09/379 0861; ⓦwww.cathaypacific.com.

Continental Airlines Australia ⓣ02/9244 2242, New Zealand ⓣ09/308 3350; ⓦwww.continental.com.
Delta Air Lines Australia ⓣ1-300/302 849, New Zealand ⓣ09/9772232; ⓦwww.delta.com.
KLM Royal Dutch Australia ⓣ1300/392 192, New Zealand ⓣ09/921 6040; ⓦwww.klm.com.
Northwest Airlines Australia ⓣ1300/767 310, ⓦwww.nwa.com.
Qantas Australia ⓣ13 13 13, New Zealand ⓣ0800/808 767; ⓦwww.qantas.com.
Singapore Airlines Australia ⓣ13 10 11, New Zealand ⓣ0800/808 909; ⓦwww.singaporeair.com.
United Airlines Australia ⓣ13 17 77, New Zealand ⓣ0800/508 648; ⓦwww.united.com.
Virgin Atlantic Airways Australia ⓣ1300/727 340, ⓦwww.virgin-atlantic.com.

Travel agents

Flight Centre Australia ⓣ13 31 33, ⓦwww.flightcentre.com.au; New Zealand ⓣ0800 243 544, ⓦwww.flightcentre.co.nz. Long-established independent travel agent that books everything from cheap flights to cruise ship specials.
STA Travel Australia ⓣ134 STA, ⓦwww.statravel.com.au; New Zealand ⓣ0800/474, ⓦwww.statravel.co.nz. Student/youth travel agent offering discounted fares.
Trailfinders Australia ⓣ1300/780 212, ⓦwww.trailfinders.com.au. Discount flights, car rental, tailor-made tours, rail passes and RTW tours, especially for the independent traveller.

Specialist agents

Caribbean Bound Australia ⓣ02/9267 2555 or 1300/786 637, ⓦwww.caribbean.com.au. Flights and packages to all the Caribbean islands, plus specialized honeymoon and wedding trips.
Caribbean Destinations Australia ⓣ03/9813 5258, ⓦwww.caribbeanislands.com.au. Specializing in hotel accommodation throughout the Caribbean, as well as holidays geared towards festivals and cricket.
Cruiseworld ⓣ08/9322 2914, ⓦwww.cruiseworld.com.au. Agents for the American Express range of cruise holidays.

Inter-island transport

One of the joys of Caribbean travel is the ease with which travellers can journey between islands, taking in two or three different cultures in one trip. Most islands are well connected by local and international airlines, although some – Cuba, for example, or Dominica – are less well served than most.

If you plan simply to travel between groups of islands – the Caymans, for example, the Virgin Islands, Leewards, or the Grenadines – the many small airline companies operating there run a regular and reasonable service, and some offer multi-islands tickets. While **airpasses** for unlimited Caribbean travel are no longer available from LIAT or Caribbean Airlines (the largest of the regional networks), there are some good deals on single flights still available by booking online.

Alternatively, you might consider travelling by **ferry**: there is a high-speed service between St Lucia, Martinique, Dominica and Guadeloupe and another between St Barts, Saba, St Maarten and Anguilla. Full details of inter-island ferry services are given on p.34.

Airlines

Abaco Air ⓣ242/367-2266, ⓦwww.abacoaviationcentre.com. Flights between the Bahamian islands; scheduled seats cost US$50–110 each way; one comp flight for every 10 purchased.
Air America Inc ⓣ787/276-5669, ⓦwww.airamericacaribbean.com. Private charters serving Puerto Rico and all surrounding islands.
Air Caraibes ⓣ0820/835 835, US ⓣ1-877/722-1005; ⓦwww.aircaraibes.com. Serves St Barts, St Martin, St Lucia, Cuba, Haiti, the Dominican Republic, Guadeloupe, Martinique, and Guyane.

Air Jamaica ⓣ876/922-3460, ⓦwww.airjamaica.com. Scheduled flights to Barbados, Bonaire, Curaçao, Grand Cayman, Grenada, Cuba, the Bahamas and St Lucia, from Jamaica.
Air Sunshine ⓣ954/434-8900, North America ⓣ1-800/327-8900, ⓦwww.airsunshine.com. Fort Lauderdale to the Bahamas, Puerto Rico, US and British Virgin Islands, Guantanamo Bay, Jamaica, flights between the above islands and charters beyond.
Air Turks and Caicos ⓣ649/941-5481 or 509/431-8173 (Haiti), ⓦwww.airturksandcaicos.com. Flights throughout Turks and Caicos, and to Haiti and Dominican Republic.
American Eagle ⓣ1-800/433-7300, ⓦwww.aa.com. Service between American Airlines' San Juan hub and most Caribbean destinations.
Bahamas Air ⓣ242/377-8451, ⓦwww.bahamasair.com. Flights from Nassau to most Bahamian islands, Turks and Caicos, several Florida destinations, and Cuba.
Carib Aviation ⓣ268/462-3147, UK ⓣ01895/450 710; ⓦwww.candoo.com/carib/. Charter flights between Antigua, St Kitts and Nevis and surrounding islands.
Caribbean Airlines ⓣ868/625-7200, ⓦwww.caribbean-airlines.com. Flights between Trinidad, Tobago, Barbados, Antigua, St Maarten, Jamaica, as well as Caracas, Guyana, Surinam and Miami.
Cayman Airways ⓣ345/949-2311, ⓦwww.caymanairways.com. Scheduled flights between several US cities and the Cayman Islands, Cuba and Jamaica.
Cubana ⓣ05/255-3776, ⓦwww.cubana.cu. Flights from Cuba to all over Latin America, Canada, Jamaica and the Dominican Republic.
Divi Divi Air ⓣ5999/839-1515, ⓦwww.flydivi.com. Best rates from Curacao to Bonaire, plus charters elsewhere.
Fly BVI ⓣ284/495-1747, US ⓣ1-866/819-3146, Canada ⓣ1-800/465-5955; ⓦwww.fly-bvi.com. Operates charter flights between most eastern Caribbean islands and Puerto Rico.
Insel Air ⓣ599/9737-0444, ⓦwww.fly-inselair.com. Curacao-based airline serving Aruba, Bonaire, St Maarten, Haiti, Dominican Republic, Trinidad, as well as Brazil, Venezuela and Surinam.
LIAT in the Caribbean ⓣ1-888/844-5428, elsewhere ⓣ268/480-5601, ⓦwww.liatairline.com. Huge range of services with hubs in Antigua and Barbados; covers Dominican Republic, Puerto Rico, St Thomas, St Croix, Tortola, Anguilla, St Maarten, St Kitts, Nevis, Guadeloupe, Dominica, Martinique, St Lucia, St Vincent, Grenada, Trinidad, Tobago, Curacao and Guyana.
Mustique Air ⓣ784/458-4380, US ⓣ718/618-4492, Canada ⓣ519/488-0542, UK ⓣ01202/233875; ⓦwww.mustique.com. Scheduled and charter flights between Barbados, St Vincent, the Grenadines and Grenada.
Sky King Air ⓣ649/941-3136, ⓦwww.skyking.tc. Turks and Caicos based airline serving local islands plus Bahamas, Dominican Republic and Haiti.
SVG Air ⓣ784/457-5124, ⓦwww.svgair.com. Offers scheduled service between St Vincent and the Grenadines, Barbados and Grenada, plus charters to Martinique, Dominica, Antigua, St Barts, Trinidad and St Lucia.
Tiara Air ⓣ297/582-0901, ⓦwww.tiara-air.com. Aruban airline serving Curacao, Bonaire and Venezuela.
Tortug' Air ⓣ509/250-2555 or 954/696-3327, ⓦwww.tortugair.com. Airline serving Haiti nationwide as well as Dominican Republic and Bahamas.
Trans Island Air 2000 ⓣ246/418-1650, ⓦwww.tia2000.com. Barbados-based airline with scheduled services to the Grenadines and charters beyond.
Vieques Air Link ⓣ787/741-8331, ⓦwww.vieques-island.com/val/. Services around Puerto Rico and to the US Virgin Islands.
Winair ⓣ599/545-4237, ⓦwww.fly-winair.com. St Maarten-based company with scheduled flights to Anguilla, St Barts, Saba, St Eustatius, St Kitts, Nevis, and charters beyond. Multi-island tickets available.
Windward Express Airlines ⓣ599/545-2001, ⓦwww.windwardexpress.com. Charter airline serving St Barts, Anguilla, Saba, St Eustatius and St Maarten.

Ferries

Some of the more useful inter-island services are listed below; note that there are no ferries between the ABC islands, or departing from Jamaica or Cuba. Ferries between islands within the same country are covered in their respective chapters.

Between St Maarten, Saba and St Barts

The Edge (ⓣ599/514-2640) is a high-speed ferry leaving Wed–Sun; the crossing takes one hour and costs US$40 one-way or US$60 return.
The Voyager (ⓣ590/87 10 68, ⓦwww.voyager-st-barths.com) travels between the islands every day. The round-trip fare is €83 (€58 one-way) and the journey takes 1hr 15min.

Between the Dominican Republic and Puerto Rico

Ferries del Caribe DR ⓣ809/688-4400, San Juan ⓣ787/725-2643; ⓦwww.ferriesdelcaribe.com. Vehicle/passenger ferry connecting Mayaguez, Puerto Rico and Santo Domingo, departs 8pm Mon, Wed & Fri from Mayaguez, and 8pm Tues, Thurs &

Car rental and driving permits

Car rental is straightforward on most Caribbean islands, with major companies vying with local outfits in terms of price. On many of the islands you will need to buy a local, temporary **driving permit**, usually valid for three to six months and costing US$15–25 (see individual chapters). Car rental costs US$240–350 per week for a compact automatic with air conditioning. Be prepared to be refused, or at least charged a hefty surcharge – sometimes as much as the regular rate again – if you are under 25. On most Caribbean islands vehicles **drive on the left**, with the exceptions being the ABC islands, St Maarten/St Martin, Cuba, Dominican Republic, Haiti, Puerto Rico, The French West Indies, Saba and St Eustatius.

Driving conditions and local driving patterns vary widely. Many roads are narrow or winding, signs may not be in English or simply non-existent, some routes may be little more than dust tracks and inaccessible after rain or without a four-wheel-drive vehicle, and in some places domestic animals roam freely. Defensive driving, therefore, is a must. Be prepared to use your horn – and hand gestures – liberally.

Sun from Santo Domingo (12 hours; from US$130 one-way).

Between Guadeloupe, Dominica, Martinique, Marie Galante, Les Saintes and St Lucia

Brudey Frères Guadeloupe ⓣ502/90 04 48, Martinique ⓣ596/70 08 50, Marie Galante ⓣ590/97 77 82; ⓦwww.brudey-freres.fr. Serves all the above destinations.

Channel Shuttles/Maritime West Indies ⓣ758/452-8757. Operates a small ferry between St Lucia and Le Marin in Martinique. Return fare €89.

Express-des-Isles ⓣ0825/359-000, ⓦwww.express-des-iles.com. High-speed catamaran operating daily in the Windward Islands. Return fares €70-100.

Between Anguilla and St Martin

The Link Ferries ⓣ264/497-2231, ⓦwww.link.ai. Ferries depart daily from Anguilla beginning at 8.40am at 45 minute intervals. The day ferry costs US$10 plus US$2 departure tax. There is one evening ferry that departs Anguilla at 5.30pm, returning at 7pm.

Health

In general, travelling in the more developed areas of the Caribbean won't raise many **health concerns.** You can count on food being well and hygienically prepared, and tap water in hotels and restaurants that's safe to drink (if heavily chlorinated and not very palatable). The preventive measures you need to take elsewhere will depend on the areas you visit but some general advice is given below.

Note, however, that the quality of medical care and facilities varies widely throughout the Caribbean. While it is excellent and readily available in places such as Aruba, the Bahamas, Barbados, the Cayman Islands, Martinique and Guadeloupe, others – particularly in rural areas on islands like the Dominican Republic – may consist of only a small, poorly equipped clinic. In any event, it's a good idea to make sure that your medical insurance covers you abroad or else take out an insurance policy that includes medical coverage (see p.51 for more on insurance).

Inoculations

No specific **inoculations** are required to enter any of the Caribbean islands, unless you're arriving from a country where yellow fever is endemic, in which case you'll need a vaccination certificate. (Consult your doctor or a travel clinic for advice on specific shots.) Islands that require yellow fever inoculations include Antigua, Bahamas, Cayman Islands, Cuba, Grenada, Guadeloupe, Jamaica, St Kitts and Nevis, St Lucia, St Vincent, and Trinidad and Tobago.

It's also worth making sure that you're up to date with **polio**, **tetanus** and **typhoid** protection; the latter is particularly recommended for those planning to visit rural areas of Puerto Rico, Cuba, Dominica and the Dominican Republic. Inoculations against **hepatitis A and B** are also strongly advised.

Malaria and dengue fever

The Caribbean is not a malarial zone, but cases of **malaria** have been reported in Haiti, the Dominican Republic (mainly along the Haitian border) and a handful of cases in Kingston, Jamaica (in 2007 only). While the risk to travellers is small, if you intend to travel in these areas it's a good idea to take a course of prophylactics (usually **chloroquine**), available from a doctor or travel clinic.

There are slightly higher rates of **dengue fever**, another mosquito-borne illness whose symptoms resemble those of malaria but include extreme aches and pains in the bones and joints, along with fever and dizziness. The only cure for dengue fever is rest and painkillers, and the only precaution you can take is to avoid mosquito bites (for details, see below).

Stomach problems

The most common food-related illness for travellers is **diarrhoea**, possibly accompanied by **vomiting** or a **mild fever**. Its main cause is a change in diet, whereby bacteria you're not used to are introduced into your system. In many cases, the condition will pass within a few days without treatment. In the meantime, rest up and replace the fluids you've lost by drinking plenty of water, coconut water, or – for persistent diarrhoea – an oral rehydration solution, readily available from your home pharmacy, should do the trick. Barring that, you can make a home-made rehydration solution by dissolving half a teaspoon of salt and eight teaspoons of sugar in a litre of boiling water. If symptoms last more than four or five days, or if you are too ill to drink, seek medical help immediately.

Travellers should note that dairy products and fruit aggravate diarrhoea and should be avoided.

Food and water

While stomach disorders aren't likely to be a big problem in the Caribbean, taking a few **common-sense precautions** will lessen the chances greatly. Steer clear of unpasteurized dairy products and unrefrigerated food, and wash and peel fresh fruit and vegetables. When buying street food, stick to obviously popular food vendors and restaurants, and wash your hands before you eat.

Although tap water is often safe to drink (the main exceptions being Haiti and the Dominican Republic), locals often boil it before drinking just to be on the safe side and to get rid of the taste of chlorine – you may prefer to stick to bottled water for this reason. Be wary of drinking tap water after heavy rain (when supplies can become contaminated), or in remote areas; you can make water safer by both passing it through an "absolute 1-micron or less" filter as well as adding iodine tablets to the filtered water. Filters and tablets are available from travel clinics and outdoor equipment stores.

Swimming or bathing in rivers and lakes has risks as well, particularly **giardia**, a bacterium that causes stomach upset, fever and diarrhoea, and **schistosomiasis**, a freshwater flatworm found in parts of Antigua, Haiti, the Dominican Republic, Guadeloupe, Martinique, Puerto Rico and St Lucia that can penetrate unbroken skin; both are treatable with **antibiotics**. If you suspect that you have either of these, seek medical help.

Ciguatera

Ciguatera is a rare form of poisoning caused by eating infected reef fish, and sporadic outbreaks have been reported throughout the Caribbean. Symptoms include nausea, numbness, diarrhoea, abdominal pains, muscular weakness and vomiting, and can last up to two weeks. As infected fish are indistinguishable from healthy ones, the only way to remove the risk is by avoiding common fish like grouper, snapper, and barracuda in particular – though this seems an extreme precaution. Travellers who suspect that they have ciguatera should seek immediate medical assistance.

Bites and stings

Bites and **stings** can lead to infection, so keep wounds clean and wash with antiseptic soap. It's inevitable that you will get some bites but there are steps you can take to avoid them. Use a heavy-duty **insect repellent** (preferably containing **DEET**) on exposed areas of skin at all times, especially from dusk until dawn, when mosquitoes are most active. Try to ensure that your hotel room has **screened windows,** and a **mosquito net** over the bed; if you don't have these, cocoon yourself in your bedsheets; constant air from a fan will also keep the bugs at bay.

Often present on beaches at dusk and so small that they're practically impossible to see, **sand flies** cause a painful, incredibly itchy and long-lasting bite; they ignore most repellents but can typically be avoided if you use Avon Skin-so-Soft, a moisturizer that's renowned for its unintentional bug-repelling power.

There are some **snakes** in the Caribbean, but very few are poisonous. One notable exception is the **fer-de-lance**, found on Martinique, St Lucia and Trinidad, and identifiable by its pointed head, yellow underside and chin, and orangish-brown triangular markings. Fortunately, most snakes, including the fer-de-lance, will slither away before you know they are there. To be safe you should wear thick socks and boots when hiking through undergrowth or rainforest. If you do get bitten, note the snake's appearance, immobilize the bitten limb as much as possible and seek medical help immediately.

You're more likely to encounter the many spiny black **sea urchins** that inhabit reefs and bays; if you tread on one, remove as much of the spine as possible, douse the area in vinegar (or even urine) and see a doctor. Take care to avoid the purple **Portuguese man o' war**, a rare but toxic jellyfish whose trailing tendrils leave red welts. Similarly, **never touch coral**; you'll kill the organism on contact and come away with a painful, slow-healing rash. In both instances, washing with vinegar or iodine will help; again urine can be used if nothing else is available. Should pain persist in the event you come in contact with any of the above, consult a doctor. For **stingray** and **stonefish stings**, alleviate the pain by immersing the wound in very hot water – just under 50°C – while waiting for medical help.

Manchineel trees

Take care to avoid **manchineel trees**, which grow to around twelve metres tall and are recognizable by their small dark green leaves and tiny apple-like fruit. Both the fruit and its milky sap are **poisonous**. Don't touch any part of the tree and avoid taking shelter under its boughs in the rain: the sap will cause blisters if it drips on you. On the more popular beaches manchineel trees have notices nailed to their trunks warning visitors of the potential danger. However, caution is advised on quieter beaches where these trees are less likely to be identified.

Heat trouble

The Caribbean's proximity to the **equator** means that the sun's rays here are very strong – use a good **sunblock** (minimum SPF 15) and apply it liberally at least every two hours and after swimming or exercise. Keep sun exposure to a minimum, especially between the hours of 11am and 4pm; wear a hat and a shirt, drink plenty of water and make sure children are well covered up. If you do **burn**, it's well worth getting hold of a couple of leaves of **aloe vera**, which grows throughout the region and is incredibly soothing; it also reduces the likelihood of peeling. To use it, split open the leaf and spread the gel liberally over your skin, taking care not to let it touch your clothes until dry as it leaves a marked yellow or purple stain; some stores sell the gel.

Dizziness, headache and nausea are symptoms of **dehydration** and should be treated by lying down in a shaded place and sipping water or other hydrating fluids. Should symptoms persist, or if you are suffering from hot, dry (but not sweaty) skin – potentially a sign of **heatstroke** – seek medical assistance immediately.

AIDS and HIV

The Caribbean has the highest regional prevalence of **AIDS** and **HIV** outside of sub-Saharan Africa. Haiti is the worst affected area, with Tobago, the Bahamas and the Dominican Republic close behind. With regard to sex, the same common-sense rule applies here as anywhere else; condomless sex is a serious health risk, and it's worth **bringing condoms** from home as those sold in some areas (eg Cuba and the Dominican Republic) are of poor quality.

Prescriptions

Be aware that even on islands with good medical facilities and well-stocked pharmacies you may not be able to find the exact **medication** that you take at home, or even a viable alternative. To be safe, bring any prescribed medicine in its original container and make sure you have enough for the length of your trip, as well as a copy of the prescription itself. The US State Department also advises bringing a letter from the prescribing doctor explaining why the drugs are needed.

Medical resources for travellers

Websites

Ⓦ**www.cdc.gov/travel** US Department of Health site, listing precautions, diseases and preventive measures by region, as well as a summary of cruise ship sanitation levels.
Ⓦ**www.fitfortravel.scot.nhs.uk** UK NHS website carrying information about travel-related diseases and how to avoid them.
Ⓦ**www.istm.org** Website of the International Society for Travel Medicine, with a full list of clinics specializing in international travel health.
Ⓦ**www.masta.org** Comprehensive website for Medical Advisory service for travellers abroad (see also listing in next column).
Ⓦ**www.tmvc.com.au** Contains a list of all Travellers' Medical and Vaccination Centres throughout Australia, New Zealand and Southeast Asia, plus general information on travel health.
Ⓦ**www.tripprep.com** Travel Health Online provides a comprehensive database of necessary vaccinations for most countries, as well as destination and medical service provider information.

In the US and Canada

Canadian Society for International Health Ⓦwww.csih.org. Extensive list of travel health centres.
CDC Ⓣ1-877/394-8747, Ⓦwww.cdc.gov/travel. Official US government travel health site.
International Society for Travel Medicine Ⓣ1-770/736-7060, Ⓦwww.istm.org. Has a full list of travel health clinics.

In the UK and Ireland

British Airways Travel Clinics Ⓣ0845/600 2236, Ⓦwww.britishairways.com/travel/healthclinintro/public/en_gb for nearest clinic.
Glasgow Travel Clinic 3rd floor, 90 Mitchell St, Glasgow G1 3NQ Ⓣ0141/221 4224. Advice and vaccinations; walk-in clinics.
Hospital for Tropical Diseases Travel Clinic Ⓣ0845/155 5000 or Ⓣ020/7387 4411, Ⓦwww.thehtd.org.
Liverpool School of Tropical Medicine Pembroke Place, Liverpool L3 5QA Ⓣ0151/708 9393 or premium-rate helpline Ⓣ09067/010 095, Ⓦwww.liv.ac.uk/lstm. Walk-in clinic.
MASTA (Medical Advisory Service for Travellers Abroad) Ⓦwww.masta.org or Ⓣ0870/606 2782 for the nearest clinic.
Tropical Medical Bureau Republic of Ireland Ⓣ1850/487 674, Ⓦwww.tmb.ie.
Travel Medicine Services Belfast Ⓣ028/9031 5220. Offers medical advice and treatment.

In Australia and New Zealand

Travellers' Medical and Vaccination Centres Ⓦwww.tmvc.com.au. Vaccination and general travel health advice, and disease alerts; call Ⓣ1300/658 844 for details of travel clinics countrywide.

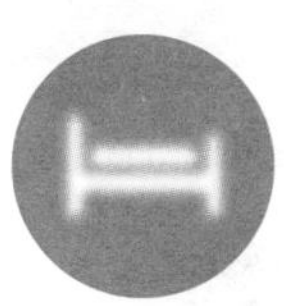

Accommodation

Accommodation choices in the Caribbean include basic guesthouses with no hot water; genteel bed-and-breakfasts and boutique hotels – usually slightly away from the cruise ship ports and main tourist drag; to moderately priced family resorts; beachside all-inclusives for couples or families; and luxury hotels with spa facilities and ultra-exclusive remote eco-resorts serving five-star cuisine.

True **budget** accommodation in much of the Caribbean is hard to come by, especially in the more exclusive islands. If you don't have large funds in your budget for accommodation then Cuba, the Dominican Republic, Haiti and the rural parts of Jamaica and Trinidad and Tobago are cheaper options with some of the lowest costs of living and accommodation in the region. Be aware, also, that **hostels** and **camping facilities** are a rarity, and private rooms in local houses are usually not an option, except in Cuba and the Dominican Republic.

Most **tourist offices** will happily provide a list of accommodations but bear in mind that establishments often have to pay to be included on these lists and consequently they often don't include the true budget options. Tourist boards generally will not recommend specific accommodation, nor will they book it – for this, you either have to go through a travel agent or do it yourself. The website of the **Caribbean Tourism Organisation**, ⓦwww.caribbeantravel.com, is a good place to start your independent search.

Prices are much cheaper off-season, and many establishments will give a reduced price for longer stays. It's worth asking around and bargaining a little, as desperate hoteliers will sometimes upgrade rooms or drop the hefty accommodation tax in order to fill beds. The more popular destinations may, however, have a seven-night minimum stay, especially in the high season.

Hotels

The range of Caribbean **hotel accommodation** is astounding, not only within islands but often within resorts themselves. Be aware that if you seem to be getting an extraordinary deal for a top-name resort, you may well end up in a small room far from the beach and other amenities – ask to see the room, or at least ask for a description in writing, before you sign anything or pay. Hotel buildings themselves range from modern, purpose-built resorts to old plantation mansions, and the most basic hotel rooms will usually have a mosquito net and possibly a sink; prices increase with minor amenities such as a bathroom, air-conditioning, or cable TV and a phone, and increase exponentially with the range of extras available: plunge pools, fridges stocked with drinks, mountain or sea views, beachfront access and outdoor showers and hammocks.

All-inclusives

Pioneered in Jamaica, **all-inclusive hotels** are resorts where a single price covers the room, all meals, snacks and tips, and often all drinks and non-motorized sports (though scuba diving can be an exception). It's worth bearing in mind that all-inclusives often do little for the **local economy**; the chains are invariably foreign, much of the food served is imported and guests don't frequent local businesses – or get a feel for local culture. At the smaller resorts, especially, the appeal of having everything provided in one place can wear off quickly. Nonetheless, the advantages are the product offered, which can be excellent value, along with the convenience of not having to reach for your wallet all the time.

Apartments and villas

One of the best ways to save money if you're travelling as a family or in a group is to rent a **villa** or **apartment** for the length of your stay. Accommodation ranges from secluded one-bedroom apartments on a remote stretch

Accommodation price codes

All accommodation listed in this guide has been graded according to the following price categories:

❶ up to US$30	❹ $91–$130	❼ $251–$300
❷ $31–$70	❺ $131–$180	❽ $301–$350
❸ $71–$90	❻ $181–$250	❾ $351 and up

of beach to palatial villas built for parties and group weekends. They are typically self-catering, with well-equipped kitchens or kitchenettes (though a cook can almost always be supplied), and can stand alone or as part of a "holiday village" where you share amenities such as a laundry, restaurant and shop with other holiday-makers but retain the privacy and independence of your own cottage. Independently leased apartments can **cost** anything from US$250 per week for a beachfront one-bedroom in the Dominican Republic to US$1500 per week for a two-bedroom, two-bathroom property on St Lucia or US$1500 per night for a five-bedroom waterfront estate with decks and a huge pool in Barbados. Property owners sometimes allow additional people to stay for a fee and extras can include anything from a maid (often included in the price of the more exclusive places) to discounted car rental.

Caribbean villa rental agencies

Caribbean Way 740 Notre Dame W, suite 1305, Montreal, Quebec H3C 3X6 ⓣ514/393-3003 or 1-877/953-7400, ⓦwww.caribbeanway.com. Representing over 800 villa properties, some on private islands, with photos, information and booking available online.

Island Hideaways ⓣ703/378-7840 or 1-800/832-2302, ⓦwww.islandhideaways.com. Agents representing private island hideaways throughout the Caribbean with an emphasis on luxurious, unique properties.

The Owners' Syndicate 3 Calico Row, Plantation Wharf, Battersea, London SW11 3TY ⓣ020/7401 1088, ⓦwww.ownerssyndicate.com. Villa specialists with properties on Anguilla, Antigua, Barbados, Grenada, Jamaica, Nevis, St Lucia, Tobago and the Virgin Islands.

Villa Connections ⓣ01625/855 851, ⓦwww.prestburytravelgroup.co.uk. Established for twenty years and offering a choice of over 300 villas all over the Caribbean. Several properties are available on private islands.

Guesthouses

Locally owned Guesthouses or **bed-and-breakfast** operations range from basic rooms with shared bathrooms to small, intimate and luxurious miniature hotels. They make a lovely alternative to large-scale resorts and, while they might not be the most private places in the region, they are often friendly, accommodating and sometimes very stylish. They can also be a welcome bargain option for Caribbean travellers on a budget, some costing as little as US$30/night – especially in areas where there are no campsites and little choice of private rooms in family homes.

Alternative accommodation

Unregulated **camping** is illegal, or else strictly controlled on many Caribbean islands, in an effort to protect the beauty and wildlife of the region's indigenous rainforests. Islands most accessible for camping holidays are **Puerto Rico**, the **Virgin Islands**, and **Martinique**, and there's a smattering of options across the English-speaking islands. See individual country chapters.

In **Cuba**, visitors have the option of "camping" in rudimentary cabins set in countryside areas called *campisimos*; there is at least one in every province, and at under US$10 per cabin they are excellent value.

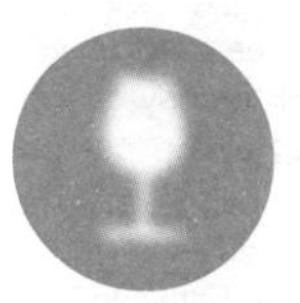

Food and drink

Caribbean food and drink can be a delight and a shock to the Western palate, with its polar extremes of heavily fried foods and fresh fruit, but it's a varied cuisine that's well worth seeking out. A blend of African, Indian, Arab, Chinese, Spanish, French, Dutch and British influences, Caribbean cooking draws on a wide range of ingredients: African groundnuts, yams, okra and oxtail; East Indian curries and rotis; French Creole and bouillabaisse; and Spanish sofritos and citrus fruits.

Fruits and vegetables

Amongst the many **fruits** on offer, some of the best are the familiar favourites, which taste sweeter and juicier than at home. Of the regional favourites, you'll find the carambola or star fruit which is de-seeded and then eaten whole, sliced in salads or as a garnish for drinks; guava is often used to make breakfast jelly; and coconuts, which produce milk when ripe and a refreshing, healthy coconut-flavoured water and jelly when green.

Vegetables tend to be versatile and filling, like the yucca, breadfruit or callaloo – a spinach-type vegetable in Jamaica, where it is used like greens, and the leaves of the dasheen tuber in the Eastern Caribbean, where they are often cooked with okra. Plantains, sweet when ripe and mealy when green, are prepared as a side dish to rice and beans or fried and made into chips, a delicious accompaniment to a beer or a cocktail at sunset. Also popular is christophene, whose pale green and crisp flesh is much used in Chinese, Latin American and West Indian cooking; calabaza, a generic term for West Indian pumpkin, which is often similar in texture to butternut squash; cassava, a root vegetable that comes in bitter and sweet forms; and okra, a finger-shaped vegetable that is often added to soups and stews.

Meat, seafood and stews

Meat – with the exception of goat – is expensive and most islanders survive on vegetables and delicious variations of chicken and fish; in Cuba, however, pork is a major feature of most cooking.

Unsurprisingly, the region's **seafood** is excellent, cheap and easy to come by, including lobster, crab, shrimp, blue marlin, kingfish, red snapper and flying fish – all of which should be sampled at a local weekend **fish fry** while soaking up the atmosphere, music and local rum. Fish are barbecued, steamed, fried or grilled and served with various types of hot cakes or grilled patties of unleavened bread.

Soups and stews are generally based on what's available at the local market on a given day, and then spiked with onions and peppers and bulked out with "hard food" (often called "provisions") or root vegetables. No meal would be complete without **pepper sauce**, developed by the Caribs and Arawaks who combined scotch bonnet peppers, cassava juice, brown sugar, cloves and cinnamon to produce a thick, tangy sauce for sprinkling over stews, barbecued fish and chicken.

Cooking styles

Cooking styles in the Caribbean islands are as heterogeneous as the various nations that populated the region. Generally, French and Spanish styles predominate, with lots of garlicky, tomato sauces served over fish, and meat cooked simply in an oven or on an open grill. Vegetables usually come on the side, as do rice and beans.

Despite similarities in cuisine, most of the islands have distinct leanings that show through in the most local of dishes and from top-notch restaurants to street-side stalls. **Criollo** cooking is popular on Spanish-speaking islands such as Puerto Rico, Cuba and the Dominican Republic, and makes liberal use of cilantro and mixed seasonings like *adobo*. Chefs in the Netherlands affiliates add **Indonesian** touches such as soy sauce, satay and nasi goreng, while old **French** colonies have a tendency to cook in a Creole style where chives, bouquet garni and tomato are made into a delicious, thick sauce and applied liberally to fish and chicken.

Jerk cooking is also common, originating with the African slaves who were brought to Jamaica in the 1600s and began to coat meat in spice mixtures such as ginger, thyme, pimento, hot peppers and green onion – before cooking it very slowly in a smoke pit or on a barbecue grill. Often spicy too are the foods of **Indian** origin such as Caribbean curry, dhal, rotis and mango souse – most notably found in Trinidad but also throughout the region.

Drinking

Rum is the liquor of choice in the Caribbean, and most islands have their own brands, distilleries and museums, with the most famous brand, Bacardi, originating in Cuba and long since made in Puerto Rico. Rum is made from fermented **sugar cane** juice (*rhum agricole* in the French islands) or molasses, and comes in various forms: **white**, the base, unmatured drink usually mixed with fruit juices in cocktails such as the French *Ti-Punch*, and including the more lethal "overproof" or "puncheon" varieties taken with water by elderly men in the region's rum shops; **ambered**, which is white rum aged in oak barrels sometimes brought from the bourbon industry in the US and with a denser flavour (often also used to make spiced rum); and the richest rums – **dark** or **red**, aged for upwards of three years usually in barrels of oak (or French brandy casks), sometimes blended, and which carry a caramely, molasses-type flavour.

Caribbean **beers** are refreshing and moderately light, somewhere between their European and American counterparts. Particularly good are Jamaica's Red Stripe, St Lucia's Piton lager and the ubiquitous regional favourite Carib, which is brewed on Trinidad and Tobago. Others include Antigua's pale lager Wadadli, Barbadian and Bahamian Banks and Kalik beers, and Dominican Kubuli, made with fresh springwater.

Fantastic **fruit juice** concoctions are a great alcohol-free alternative and widely available. Visit roadside stands for juices or **coconut water** – vendors chop off the top of the nut with a machete to get to the delicious sweet water inside (avoid the hull as it will stain your clothes). You'll also find a cranberry-coloured beverage made from the flowers of the slightly sour sorrel plant, and the almost creamy, milky-white juice of the prickly and dark-skinned soursop (guanabana).

Tea and **coffee** are readily available with Jamaican Blue Mountain coffee the region's king – but aside from the rich roast from Dominica, they tend to be of negligible quality; instead, some islanders will drink a cup of milky hot chocolate made from the shavings of local cocoa sticks with their breakfast.

There are also some local forms of **soda**: the ubiquitous Tang, which comes in various different flavours, refreshing grapefruit Ting in Jamaica, and both bottled and home-made ginger beer – for which Jamaica especially is justly famous. Carbonated **malt** drinks are also sold throughout the region, and are surprisingly good.

Sports and outdoor activities

The biggest **spectator sports** down this way are cricket, football (soccer), athletics (track and field) and, in certain cases like Cuba, Puerto Rico and the Dominican Republic, baseball. If you're game, plenty of resorts have top-notch golf courses, tennis and other leisure activities. Most islands also have, if not mountainous or rainforested interiors, at least a few good areas to explore on **hikes**; bike trips and horseriding are other enjoyable options.

Cricket

Cricket is respected and exalted throughout much of the Caribbean, with the Cricket World Cup staged here in 2007, and despite declining fortunes, the West Indies team was the very best on the planet during the 1970s and 1980s. Those interested in the game should check out official site Ⓦwww.windiescricket.com or Ⓦwww.caribbeancricket.com. Regular inter-island tournaments also take place, aside from West Indies **test matches**, and the top islands for watching the sport are Jamaica, Trinidad, Antigua and Barbados. Even if you're not a fan of the game, a day watching cricket can be tremendous fun, with music pumping from speakers between overs, free-flowing rum and a party atmosphere.

Baseball

In the **Dominican Republic** baseball is the national spectator sport. Many of the top American major league players came from the island, including Alex Rodríguez, Sammy Sosa and Pedro Martínez. The winter season runs from mid-November to mid-February, followed by the Caribbean Series. In addition to the professional season, amateur winter seasons take place notably in San Francisco de Macorís, San Juan de la Maguana, and San Cristóbal.

The **Cuban** national league, the Serie Nacional de Béisbol, takes place over a regular season that begins in October and finishes with the playoffs in March and April. Provincial capitals also have stadiums with local teams playing five times a week, even during the summer months.

Like the Dominican Republic, **Puerto Rico** has produced many ballplayers who've succeeded in the US, among them the great Roberto Clemente. The island competes in the Caribbean Series; the season runs from November to March.

Hiking

An excellent way to see untouched, and often protected, indigenous wildlife, as well as enjoying the fresh air and sunshine, is to go **hiking**. The lush rainforests of Puerto Rico, Dominica, Antigua, Trinidad and Tobago, the Dominican Republic, Jamaica and St Lucia, the coastal hikes of St Croix or the huge national park that constitutes most of St John in the US Virgin Islands are all highly recommended. For more detailed information about hiking, see the individual island chapters. Bear in mind that **camping** is illegal on many Caribbean islands (see accommodation p.39).

Plan to start very early in the morning and cover plenty of distance before the midday heat, or else choose a hike that goes through forest. Check with guides and relevant tourist authorities about conditions and marked trails before you head off, and be sure to tell someone where you are going. There are also plenty of **private tour companies** offering group trips. Many Caribbean trails have waterfalls and swimming holes along the way, so wear a bathing suit if a dip might be on the agenda.

Scuba diving and snorkelling

Wall dives, wreck dives, coral gardens, pinnacles, muck dives, drift dives and slopes all await the scuba diver in the Caribbean. The most famous site of all is off **Virgin Gorda** where the wreck of the HMS *Rhone* has lain since 1867. Other famous **wrecks** are to be found off St Croix and St Lucia; Stingray City on Grand Cayman is renowned for the scores of ray fish that populate the site and are willing to be fed by hand; while Speyside in Tobago is known for its population of friendly giant manta rays. Also highly regarded are Saba's underwater lava flows and black sand, or the amazingly accessible shore **reefs** of Bonaire and St Lucia. **Bonaire** is perhaps the finest of all the dive islands, as its entire perimeter has been protected as a marine park since 1979 and eco-friendly regulation is very much enforced.

Each of the islands famous for diving is well equipped in terms of **instruction courses** and diving **package deals** (see the list below and individual chapters). Dive operators also often take **snorkellers** on their trips. Most resorts provide free snorkelling gear; if yours doesn't, it's worth bringing your own as buying equipment in the Caribbean can be expensive.

Scuba holiday operators

Scuba Safari ⓣ01342/823 222, ⓦwww.scuba-safaris.com. UK-based company offering diving holidays to Turks and Caicos, Saba, St Kitts and the Cayman Islands.

Scuba Voyages ⓣ1-800/544-7631, ⓦwww.scubavoyages.com. USA company providing all-inclusive diving packages to Bonaire, Curacao, Dominica, Saba, St Lucia, St Vincent and Tobago.

Snooba Travel Ltd ⓦwww.snooba.com. UK; snorkelling and diving trips all over the Caribbean.

US Dive Travel ⓣ1-888/741-3483, ⓦwww.caribbeandivers.com. Family-run operation offering Caribbean-wide diving holidays.

Fishing

The Caribbean boasts some good **sport fishing**, an expensive though potentially dramatic pastime. The waters around the Bahamas and the Turks and Caicos especially offer countless fishing opportunities, among them deep-sea fishing for wahoo, tuna and marlin and shark; bottom-fishing for reef fish such as grouper, snapper and parrotfish; and fly-fishing for bonefish. Also recommended is big-game fishing along the southern coast of the Dominican Republic, around Trinidad and Tobago, and off the northern coast of Cuba. Throughout these islands you'll find plenty of charter boat operators offering **fishing excursions** as well as fully equipped boats for rent. Most boats take groups of up to six, and can cost anywhere from US$400 to 1000/day.

Sailing

Needless to say, the Caribbean is a major sailing destination. Those not fortunate enough to visit the region on their own boat will find a slew of charter operators offering all manner of trips, from rum-soaked party cruises and luxurious yacht charters to relaxed day-trips of island-hopping. Resorts, too, often rent out small sailing boats for use close to shore. For details on specific islands refer to the individual chapters.

Travel essentials

The **US dollar** is widely accepted in the Caribbean along with local currencies – albeit at less-than-favourable exchange rates. In fact, the US dollar is the official currency in the Virgin Islands, Turks and Caicos and Puerto Rico. Many of the former British colonies use the East Caribbean dollar (exceptions include Jamaica and Trinidad and Tobago), and the French islands of Guadeloupe and Martinique use **euros**.

Money

As the majority of Caribbean islands are fairly developed, at least in the touristed areas, **traveller's cheques** and **credit cards** are accepted. **ATMs** accept debit and credit cards linked to the Cirrus, Plus and Visa networks (cash is most often given in local currency), while most hotels will change money, though at less favourable rates than banks. In less developed areas, you will need to carry local currency – though even many rural towns now have ATMs (see individual chapters for information specific to the islands.)

Wiring money

Having money **wired** from home using one of the companies listed below can be convenient – funds can be collected within minutes of the transaction being made in your home country. Hefty commissions, however, (at the time of writing roughly £14/$21 on top of the first £100/$150 sent, with larger sums charged according to a sliding scale) mean that the amount you eventually receive may be considerably less than what you actually pay.

It's possible to have money wired directly from a bank in your home country to a bank in the Caribbean, although this is somewhat less reliable because it involves two separate institutions. If you go this route, your home bank will need the address of the branch bank where you want to pick up the money and the address and telex number of its main island office. Money wired this way normally takes two working days to arrive, and costs around US$40/£25 per transaction.

Money-wiring companies

Moneygram
Ⓦwww.moneygram.com.

Thomas Cook
Ⓦwww.thomascook.com.

Western Union
UK Ⓦwww.westernunion.co.uk.
US, New Zealand, Republic of Ireland Ⓦwww.westernunion.com.
Australia Ⓦwww.westernunion.com.au.
Canada Ⓦwww.westernunioncanada.ca.

Costs

Your **daily budget** in the Caribbean depends, of course, on where you are travelling and how comfortable you want to be. The **cheapest destinations** are likely to be Haiti and the Dominican Republic, with Cuba, Dominica and the rural parts of Trinidad and Jamaica somewhere behind. Even so, travelling in the Caribbean is not cheap by any standard; sleeping in the cheapest accommodation, travelling by bus, eating food from street stalls and supermarkets, and limiting yourself to free activities is still likely to set you back at minimum US$50/day, and mostly only on the cheaper islands listed above. A more realistic figure for most islands will be US$150/day, with a few – such as Aruba and St Barts – setting you back US$200/day or more. Remember that **incidentals** such as car rental, room and departure taxes, local driving permits and guides – never mind island-hopping, whale-watching, fine dining or scuba diving – really add up, though these are some of the most enjoyable facets of a Caribbean holiday.

Crime and personal safety

With a total of 35 countries making up the region, each with different levels of population, development and standards of living, it's difficult to do anything but generalize about safety standards in the Caribbean. On the whole, though, the region is politically stable and safe, and not troubled by the potential for terrorist acts. If you don't venture outside the resorts and heavily touristed areas, you might also believe that it is economically prosperous – though this is not the case for many islands, as the region is heavily reliant on tourist trade for survival and large pockets of poverty exist on the majority of islands.

Certain common-sense measures should be observed when travelling in the Caribbean. For tourists, the most common hazards are **bag-snatching** and **pickpocketing**, so always make sure you sling bags across your body rather than letting them dangle from one shoulder; keep cameras concealed whenever possible; don't carry valuables in easy-to-reach places or wear heaps of expensive jewellery; and always take a minimum of cash/cards out with you. Needless to say, don't leave bags and possessions unattended anywhere, especially at the beach. Most resorts and hotels in the Caribbean are very safe; guests should nonetheless use room safes when available. Also avoid leaving possessions on view in a rental car, even in the boot, as these are a prime target, and, depending on the island, think twice before venturing out for that romantic moonlit walk on an undeveloped beach.

Violent crime against tourists – such as assault and even rape – while rare on all islands has been reported throughout the region. Incidents tend to take place at weekend "jump-ups" or street parties, where locals and tourists mingle freely and many visitors make the mistake of ostentatiously displaying their wealth or make themselves vulnerable via their rum- or ganja-induced inebriation. Visitors should take extra care at street parties and during carnival, when everything seems like one big heady mix of music, alcohol and people.

Criminals can attack at any time, and are more likely to do so at night; women especially should take care after dusk and try not to wander through unpopulated areas alone at any time. Avoid deserted beaches or poorly lit areas at night, and make sure that any taxi you take is officially licensed – look for identification, take down the licence number and check the plates for the identifying "H" symbol (if there is one – see individual chapter entries for details of taxi travel). For advice to **women travellers**, see p.58.

As an additional precaution, visitors should know that **car theft** has been on the increase, so be sure to check all documentation carefully – sometimes vehicle leases or rentals may not be fully covered by local insurance, and car thieves often target rental cars. If you are unlucky enough to be a victim, report the incident immediately.

Visitors should also be aware that heavy **drug trafficking** and production is a major problem in many Caribbean countries – the Bahamas and the Dominican Republic have been included on the US government's list of narcotics producers. Penalties for committing a crime in the Caribbean can be extremely harsh, and those for drug use, possession and trafficking are severe and usually include jail sentences and heavy fines.

Certain islands in the Caribbean – especially Cuba, Jamaica and the Dominican Republic – are known for both their potent **marijuana** and the lax attitude of the authorities regarding recreational marijuana use. However, the consumption or possession of marijuana is not legal on any of the islands, and as governments of individual countries try to crack down on drug trafficking in general, penalties are likely to be harsh.

Electricity

Most islands in the Caribbean use 110V (US) sockets, some have 220/240V (UK) only and some have both. Larger hotels will usually be able to provide you with an adaptor, but you should bring your own just in case. (See box.)

Entry requirements

Island-specific advice about **visas** and **entry requirements** is covered at the beginning of each chapter, where necessary. As a general guide, citizens of the US, **Canada** and **Great Britain** do not need a visa for stays of less than thirty days; however, nearly every country requires that your passport be valid for at least six months from your date of entry.

As all visa requirements, prices and processing times are subject to change, it's always worth double-checking with the embassies before you leave home.

Caribbean embassies and consulates abroad

Anguilla

The UK handles consular responsibilities.

Australia British High Commission, Commonwealth Ave, Yarralumla, ACT 2600 ⓣ02/6270 6666, ⓦwww.britaus.net.

Canada British High Commission, 80 Elgin St, Ottawa ON K1P 5K7 ⓣ613/237-1530, ⓦwww.britainincanada.org.

Ireland British Embassy, 29 Merrion Rd, Ballsbridge, Dublin 4 ⓣ01/205 3822, ⓦwww.britishembassy.ie.

New Zealand British High Commission, 44 Hill St, Thorndon, Wellington ⓣ04/924 2888, ⓦwww.britain.org.nz/general/ukterra.html.

UK Foreign and Commonwealth Office, Old Admiralty Building, London SW1A 2PA ⓣ020/7008 1500, ⓦwww.fco.gov.uk.

US British Embassy, 3100 Massachusetts Ave, Washington DC 20008 ⓣ202/588-6500, ⓦwww.britainusa.com.

Antigua and Barbuda

Australia handles consular responsibilities.

Canada High Commission for the Eastern Caribbean States, 130 Albert Street, Suite 700, Ottawa, Ontario K1P 5G4 ⓣ613/236-8952, ⓦwww.oecs.org/ottawa.

UK and Ireland High Commission of Antigua and Barbuda, 15 Thayer St, London W1U 3JT ⓣ020/7486 7073, ⓦwww.antigua-barbuda.com.

US Embassy of Antigua and Barbuda, 3216 New Mexico Ave NW, Washington DC 20016, ⓣ202/362-5122, ⓔembantbar@aol.com.

Aruba, Bonaire and Curaçao

The Netherlands handles consular responsibilities.

Australia Consulate General of the Netherlands, PO Box 261, Bondi Junction NSW 1355 ⓣ02/9837 6644, ⓦwww.netherlands.org.au.

Canada Royal Netherlands Embassy, Constitution Square Building, 350 Albert St, Suite 2020, Ottawa ON K1R 1A4 ⓣ613/237-5030, ⓦwww.netherlandsembassy.ca.

Ireland Royal Netherlands Embassy, 160 Merrion Rd, Dublin 4 ⓣ01/269 3444, ⓦwww.netherlandsembassy.ie.

New Zealand Royal Netherlands Embassy, PO Box 840, Ballance at Fetherston St, Wellington ⓣ04/471 6390, ⓦwww.netherlandsembassy.co.nz.

UK Netherlands Diplomatic Mission, 38 Hyde Park Gate, London SW7 5DP ⓣ020/7590 3200, ⓦwww.netherlands-embassy.org.uk.

US Netherlands Embassy, 4200 Linnean Ave, Washington DC 20008 ⓣ202/244-5300, ⓦwww.netherlands-embassy.org.

Bahamas

Canada Bahamas High Commission, Metropolitan Life Centre, 50 O'Connor St, suite 1313, Ottawa ON K1P 6L2 ⓣ613/232-1724, ⓔottawa-mission@bahighco.com.

Electricity

Anguilla	110v
Antigua and Barbuda	110/220v
Aruba	110v
Bahamas	120v
Barbados	110v/220v adaptors
Bonaire	120v
British Virgin Islands	110v
Cayman Islands	110v
Cuba	110v, some 220v
Curaçao	110/220v
Dominica	220v
Dominican Republic	110v
Grenada	220/240v
Guadeloupe	110/220v
Jamaica	110/220v
Martinique	220v
Puerto Rico	110v
Saba	110v
St Barts	220v
St Eustatius	110/220v
St Kitts and Nevis	230v
St Lucia	110/220v
St Martin/St Maarten	110/220v
St Vincent and the Grenadines	220/240v
Trinidad and Tobago	115/220v
Turks and Caicos	110v
US Virgin Islands	120v

UK and Ireland Bahamas High Commission, 10 Chesterfield St, London W1X 8AH ⓣ7408 4488, ⓔinfo@bahamashclondon.net.
US The Embassy of the Commonwealth of the Bahamas, 2220 Massachusetts Ave NW, Washington DC 20008 ⓣ202/319-2667, ⓕ319-2668.

Barbados

Australia Consulate-General, 4 Warren Rd, Double Bay NSW 2028 ⓣ02/9327 7009.
Canada High Commission for Barbados, 130 Albert St, Suite 1204, Ottawa ON K1P 5G4 ⓣ03/236-9517, ⓕ230-4362.
UK and Ireland Barbados High Commission, 1 Great Russell St, London WC1B 3ND ⓣ020/7631 4975, ⓔlondon@foreign.gov.bb.
US Embassy of Barbados, 2144 Wyoming Avenue N.W. Washington D.C. 20008ⓣ202/939 9200, ⓔwashington@foreign.gov.bb.

British Virgin Islands

The UK handles consular responsibilities. See Anguilla, above.

Cayman Islands

The UK handles consular responsibilities. See Anguilla, above.

Cuba

Australia Consulate General of the Republic of Cuba, IPI House, ground floor, 128 Chalmers St, Surrey Hills NSW 2010 ⓣ02/9698 9797, ⓦembacuba.cubaminrex.cu/australiaing.
Canada Embassy of the Republic of Cuba, 388 Main St, Ottawa ON K1S 1E3 ⓣ613/563-0141, ⓦembacu.cubaminrex.cu.
UK Embassy of the Republic of Cuba, 167 High Holborn, London WC1V 6PA ⓣ020/7240 2488, ⓦcuba.embassyhomepage.com.
US Cuban Interests Section, 2639 16th St NW, Washington DC 20009 ⓣ202/797-8518, ⓦembacu.cubaminrex.cu.

Dominica

Australia handles consular responsibilities.
Australia Department of Foreign Affairs and Trade, R.G. Casey Building, John McEwen Crescent, Barton ACT 0221 ⓣ02 6261 1111, ⓦwww.dfat.gov.au.
UK and Ireland Dominican High Commission, 1 Collingham Gardens, London SW5 0HW ⓣ020/7370 5194, ⓔhighcommission@dominica.co.uk.
US Embassy of the Commonwealth of Dominica, 3216 New Mexico Ave NW, Washington DC 20016 ⓣ202/364-6781, ⓔembdomdc@aol.com.

Dominican Republic

Australia Consulate of the Dominican Republic, 343A Edgecliff Rd, Edgecliff NSW 2027 ⓣ02/9363 5891, ⓔconsudom@bigpond.net.au.
Canada Embassy of the Dominican Republic, 2727 Steeles Ave W, suite 301, Toronto, ON M3J 3G9 ⓣ416/739-1237, ⓦwww.drembassy.org.
UK and Ireland Embassy of the Dominican Republic, 139 Inverness Terrace, Bayswater, London W2 6JF ⓣ020/7727 6285, ⓦwww.dominicanembassy.org.uk.
US Embassy of the Dominican Republic, 1715 22nd St NW, Washington DC 20008 ⓣ202/332-6280, ⓦwww.domrep.org.

Grenada

Canada Consulate of Grenada, 439 University Ave, suite 930, Toronto, ON M5G 1Y8 ⓣ416/595-1339, ⓦwww.grenadaconsulate.com.
UK and Ireland Grenada High Commission, The Chapel, Archel Rd, West Kensington, W14 9QH ⓣ020/7385 4415, ⓦwww.grenadahighcommission.com.
US Embassy of Grenada, 1701 New Hampshire Ave NW, Washington DC 20009 ⓣ265-2561, ⓦwww.grenadaembassyusa.org.

Guadeloupe

France handles consular responsibilities.
Australia Embassy of France, 6 Perth Ave, Yarralumla, ACT 2600 ⓣ02/6216 0100, ⓦwww.ambafrance-au.org.
Canada Embassy of France, 42 Promenade St, Sussex, Ottawa, ON K1M 2C9 ⓣ613/789-1795, ⓦwww.ambafrance-ca.org.
Ireland Chancery, 36 Ailesbury Rd, Dublin 4 ⓣ01/277 5000, ⓦwww.ambafrance.ie.
New Zealand Embassy of France, 34-42 Manners St, Wellington ⓣ04/802 1590, ⓦwww.ambafrance-nz.org.
UK Embassy of France, 58 Knightsbridge, London SW1X 7JT ⓣ020/7201 1000, ⓦwww.ambafrance.org.uk.
US Embassy of France, 4101 Reservoir Rd NW, Washington DC 20007-2172 ⓣ202/944-6200 or 6187, ⓦwww.ambafrance-us.org.

Haiti

Canada Consulate of Haiti, 1801 Ave. McGill College, Suite 1335, H3A 2N4, Montreal, ⓣ514/499-1919, ⓦwww.haiti-montreal.org.

US Embassy of the Republic of Haiti, 2311 Massachusetts Avenue, NW, 20008, Washington DC, ⓣ 202/332-4090, ⓦ www.haiti.org.

Jamaica

Canada Jamaican High Commission, Standard Life Building, 275 Slater St, suite 402, Ottawa, ON KIP 5H9 ⓣ 613/233-9311, ⓦ www.jhcottawa.ca
UK and Ireland Jamaica High Commission, 1-2 Prince Consort Rd, London SW7 2BQ ⓣ 020/7823 9911, ⓦ jhcuk.org.
US Embassy of Jamaica, 1520 New Hampshire Ave NW, Washington DC 20036 ⓣ 202/452-0660, ⓦ www.embassyofjamaica.org.

Martinique

France handles consular responsibilities. See Guadeloupe, above.

Montserrat

The UK handles consular responsibilities. See Anguilla, above.

Puerto Rico

The US handles consular responsibilities.
Australia US Embassy, Moonah Place, Yarralumla ACT 2600 ⓣ 02/6214 5970, ⓦ canberra .usembassy.gov.
Canada Embassy of the United States of America, 490 Sussex Drive, Ottawa, ON K1N 1G8 ⓣ 613/238-5335, ⓦ canada.usembassy.gov.
Ireland US Embassy, 42 Elgin Rd, Ballsbridge, Dublin 4 ⓣ 01/668 8777, ⓦ dublin.usembassy.gov.
New Zealand US Embassy, 29 Fitzherbert Terrace, Thorndon, Wellington ⓣ 04/462 6000, ⓦ newzealand.usembassy.gov.
UK US Embassy, 24 Grosvenor St, London W1A 1AE ⓣ 020/7499 9000, ⓦ www.usembassy.org.uk.
US US Department of State, 2201 C St NW, Washington DC 20520 ⓣ 202/647-4000, ⓦ www .state.gov.

Saba and St Eustatius

The Netherlands handles consular responsibilities. See Aruba, above.

St Barts

France handles consular responsibilities. See Guadeloupe, above.

St Kitts and Nevis

Australia Australian Department of Foreign Affairs and Trade, R.G. Casey Building, John McEwen Crescent, Barton ACT 0221 ⓣ 02/6261 1111, ⓦ www.dfat.gov.au.
Canada High Commission for the Eastern Caribbean States 130 Albert Street, Suite 700, Ottawa, Ontario K1P 5G4 ⓣ 613/236-8952, ⓦ www.oecs.org/ottawa.
UK and Ireland St Kitts and Nevis High Commission, 10 Kensington Court, London W8 5DL ⓣ 020/7460 6500, ⓔ sknhighcomm@btconnect .com.
US Embassy of St Kitts and Nevis, 3216 New Mexico Ave NW, Washington DC 20016 ⓣ 202/686-2636, ⓦ www.stkittsnevis.org.

St Lucia

Australia Australian Department of Foreign Affairs and Trade, R.G. Casey Building, John McEwen Crescent, Barton ACT 0221 ⓣ 02/6261 1111, ⓦ www.dfat.gov.au.
Canada High Commission for the Eastern Caribbean States 130 Albert Street, Suite 700, Ottawa, Ontario K1P 5G4 ⓣ 613/236-8952, ⓦ www.oecs.org/ottawa.
UK and Ireland 1 Collingham Gardens, London SW5 0HW ⓣ 020/7370 7123, ⓔ hcslu@btconnect .com.
US Embassy of St Lucia, 3216 New Mexico Ave NW, Washington DC 20016 ⓣ 202/364-6792, ⓕ 364-6723.

St Maarten/Martin

The Netherlands and France handles consular responsibilities for respective halves of the island. See Aruba and Guadeloupe, above.

St Vincent and the Grenadines

Australia Australian Department of Foreign Affairs and Trade, R.G. Casey Building, John McEwen Crescent, Barton ACT 0221 ⓣ 02/6261 1111, ⓦ www.dfat.gov.au.
Canada Consulate of St Vincent and the Grenadines, 333 Wilson Ave, suite 601, Toronto, ON M3H 1T2 ⓣ 416/398-4277, ⓔ ebjohn@svgconsulate.org.
UK and Ireland St Vincent Diplomatic Mission, 10 Kensington Ct, London W8 5DL ⓣ 020/7937 2874, ⓔ svghighcom@clara.co.uk.
US Embassy of St Vincent and the Grenadines, 3216 New Mexico Ave NW, Washington DC 20016 ⓣ 202/364-6730.

Trinidad and Tobago

Australia Consulate-General of the Republic of Trinidad and Tobago, PO Box 109, Rose Bay, NSW 2029 ⓣ 612/9337 4391.

Canada Trinidad and Tobago High Commission, 200 First Ave, 3rd level, Ottawa, ON K1S 2G6 ⓣ613/232-2418, ⓦwww.ttmissions.com.
New Zealand Honorary Consul of Trinidad and Tobago, Level 25, 151 Queen St, PO Box 105-042, Auckland ⓣ09/302 1860.
UK and Ireland Trinidad & Tobago High Commission, 42 Belgrave Sq, London SW1X 8NT ⓣ020/7245 9351, ⓦwww.tthighcommission.co.uk.
US Embassy of Trinidad and Tobago, 1708 Massachusetts Ave NW, Washington DC 20036 ⓣ202/467-6490, ⓔinfo@ttembwash.com.

Turks and Caicos

The UK handles consular responsibilities. See Anguilla, above.

US Virgin Islands

The US handles consular responsibilities. See Puerto Rico, above.

Gay and lesbian travellers

Like any other large region, attitudes towards homosexuality in the Caribbean differ from place to place. The Bahamas take the lead in terms of positive attitude, with the government openly condemning homophobia, although there still isn't much of a gay scene. Trinidad and Tobago has had a gay rights group since 1994, and the fairly sizeable community is quite visible, especially during Carnival; in Puerto Rico, gay and lesbian visitors are not only accepted but sustained by a lively gay social scene. On many islands, such as Aruba, Bonaire and Curaçao, there is no organized gay life as such, but because of the free-thinking Dutch influence on these islands, a live-and-let-live attitude prevails. Barbados, the British Virgin Islands and Saba operate in a similar fashion. Martinique has an emergent and fairly open gay community and St Lucia has several gay-friendly resorts, though attitudes in towns and cities may be less friendly.

Other islands, however, are much **less tolerant**: in the Cayman Islands, a gay cruise ship was turned away from the port; attitudes in Dominica and the US Virgin Islands – with the exception of St John's nude beach – are fairly intolerant. In Cuba and Jamaica, public displays of affection between gays are very much frowned upon, although there are nascent, mostly underground gay scenes.

Contacts for gay and lesbian travellers

On the Web

Gay Dive ⓦwww.gay-dive.com. Provides summaries about attitudes on individual islands as well as information on dive sites and gay-friendly accommodation.
Gay Places to Stay ⓦwww.gayplaces2stay.com/caribbean.html. Information about accommodation in Aruba, Bonaire, Curacao, Jamaica, Puerto Rico, Saba, St Martin, Virgin Islands, Antigua and Dominican Republic.
Gay Travel ⓦwww.gaytravel.com. The site for trip planning, bookings and general information about gay and lesbian international travel.

In the US and Canada

Alyson Adventures ⓦwww.alysonadventures.com. Adventure holidays all over the world, including gay scuba diving packages to the Caribbean.
Aqua Terra Travel ⓣ1-800/376-3784, ⓦwww.envoytravel.com/rainbow.html. Gay-specific information and travel services, including gay cruise ship bookings.
Damron Company ⓦwww.damron.com. Publisher of the *Men's Travel Guide*, and *Women's Traveller*, pocket-sized yearbooks full of listings of hotels, bars, clubs and resources for gays and lesbians; and *Damron Accommodations*, with 1000 options worldwide.
International Gay & Lesbian Travel Association ⓣ954/630-1637, ⓦwww.iglta.org. Trade group that can provide a list of gay- and lesbian-owned or -friendly travel agents, accommodation and other travel businesses.
Out and About Travel ⓣ1-800/842-4753, ⓦwww.outandaboutravel.com. Gay- and lesbian-oriented cruises, tours and travel packages.

In the UK

Gay Travel ⓦwww.gaytravel.co.uk Online gay and lesbian travel agent, offering good deals on all types of holidays. Also lists gay- and lesbian-friendly hotels around the world.
Madison Travel ⓣ01273/202 532, ⓦwww.madisontravel.co.uk. Established travel agents specializing in packages to gay- and lesbian-friendly mainstream destinations.

In Australia and New Zealand

Gay and Lesbian Travel ⓦwww.galta.com.au. Directory and links for gay and lesbian travel in Australia and worldwide.

Parkside Travel 70 Glen Osmond Rd, Parkside, SA 5063 ⓣ08/8274 1222 or 1800/888 501, ⓔhwtravel@senet.com.au. Gay travel agent associated with local branch of Harvey World Travel; covers all aspects of gay and lesbian travel.
Tearaway Travel ⓣ03/9827 4232, ⓦwww.tearaway.com. Gay-specific business dealing with international and domestic travel.

Insurance

It is always sensible to take out an **insurance** policy before travelling to cover against theft, loss and illness or injury. Before buying a new policy, however, it's worth checking whether you are already covered; some all-risks home insurance policies may cover your possessions when overseas, and many private medical schemes include cover when abroad.

In **Canada**, provincial health plans usually provide partial cover for medical mishaps overseas, while holders of official **student/teacher/youth cards** in Canada and the US are entitled to meagre accident coverage and hospital in-patient benefits. Students will often find that their student health coverage extends during the vacations and for one term beyond the date of last enrolment.

After exhausting the possibilities above, you might want to contact a **specialist travel insurance company**, or consider the travel insurance deal we offer (see box). A typical travel insurance policy usually covers the loss of baggage, tickets and – up to a certain limit – cash or cheques, as well as cancellation or curtailment of your journey. Most exclude so-called **dangerous sports** unless an extra premium is paid: in the Caribbean this can mean scuba diving, whitewater rafting, windsurfing and trekking, though probably not kayaking or jeep safaris. Many policies can be chopped and changed to exclude coverage you don't need – for example, sickness and accident benefits can often be excluded or included at will. If you do take medical coverage, ascertain whether benefits will be paid as treatment proceeds or only after return home, and whether there is a 24hr medical emergency number.

When securing **baggage coverage**, make sure that the per-article limit – typically under US$730/£500 – will cover your most valuable possession. If you need to make a claim, you should **keep receipts** for medicines and medical treatment, and in the event that you have anything **stolen**, you must obtain an official statement from the police.

Living in the Caribbean

With the Caribbean being a diverse set of islands ranging from independent countries to dependant territories of the UK and USA as well as being actual "regions" of Holland and France – and with populations communicating in English, French, Spanish, Dutch as well as local languages – there are few generalizations that can be made regarding long-term stays and opportunities for foreigners. There are certainly **English teaching** opportunities available in the French West Indies and the Dominican Republic, for example, and those interested should contact relevant embassies; or there are organizations and government departments in France that facilitate work programmes.

A variety of organizations also organize **volunteer work**, often as part of social development or environmental conservation programmes; a few are listed below.

Rough Guides Travel Insurance

Rough Guides has teamed up with Columbus Direct to offer travel insurance that can be tailored to suit your needs. Products include a low-cost **backpacker** option for long stays; a **short break** option for city getaways; a typical **holiday package** option; and others. Annual **multi-trip** policies are also available for those who travel regularly. Different sports and activities (trekking, skiing, etc) can be usually be covered if required.

See our website (ⓦwww.roughguides.com/website/shop) for eligibility and purchasing options. Alternatively, UK residents should call ⓣ0870/033 9988; Australians should call ⓣ1300/669 999 and New Zealanders should call ⓣ0800/55 9911. All other nationalities should call ⓣ+44 870/890 2843

Study and work programmes

AFS Intercultural Programs US ⓦwww.afs.org. Intercultural exchange organization with a programme in the Dominican Republic.
Council on International Educational Exchange (CIEE) ⓦwww.ciee.org. Leading NGO offering study programmes and volunteer projects, including in the Dominican Republic and Bonaire.
CUSO ⓦwww.cuso.org. Canadian development agency placing long-term volunteers in Jamaica.
Earthwatch Institute ⓦwww.earthwatch.org. Scientific and environmental volunteer projects in the Bahamas, Virgin Islands and Trinidad.
Progressio ⓦwww.progressio.org.uk. UK development organization placing long-term volunteers in Haiti and the Dominican Republic.

Getting married

The Caribbean is one of the most popular wedding destinations in the world, as well as one favoured by many honeymooning couples. You can't, however, simply turn up and expect to be married straight away – islands have different requirements about the length of stay prior to the ceremony. Some require a notarized letter declaring the single status of the bride and groom or an affidavit for couples under the age of 18. Residency requirements can be anything from newly arrived to fifteen days. Island tourist offices will give information on their marriage requirements; many of the classier establishments will arrange everything for you. If in doubt, contact the tourist office of your chosen destination or check their website for details.

Phones

Country codes as well as details on public phones are listed for each country in the appropriate chapter.

Mobile phones

Any dual- through to quad-band **mobile phone** that is primed for roaming can work on most Caribbean mobile networks. If you have an "unlocked" cellphone that works in the region, the cheapest way to make **calls** is to pay a nominal fee (US$10–20) for a local SIM card (or "chip") which you can insert into a phone brought from home and use to make local and international calls; you add credit by way of a pay-as-you-go system. SIM cards are widely available from independent mobile phone shops and Cable and Wireless/Digicel outlets throughout the region. The main **service providers** in the Caribbean are *b*mobile (in most of the English-speaking West Indies operated by Cable and Wireless; ⓦwww.cwwionline.com, except Trinidad & Tobago; ⓦwww.bmobile.co.tt), and rapidly expanding Digicel (all of the Caribbean islands and much of the Caribbean rim, except Cuba, Dominican Republic, Puerto Rico, the Virgin islands, St Martin, St Barts, St Eustatius and Saba; ⓦwww.digicelgroup.com). Phones from either network roam in all of the countries they serve, though adding new credit to your account can be a pain across different currencies, eg a Trinidad & Tobago Digicel sim has to be topped up in $TT rather than, say, $EC in St Lucia or € in Martinique – best to take a number of top-up cards with you, or else buy a series of SIM cards in the different currencies as you travel.

Time

All islands in the Caribbean are on Atlantic Time, one hour ahead of Eastern Standard Time and four hours behind Greenwich Mean Time. Be aware that not all islands adjust for Daylight Savings Time.

Tourist Information, media and websites

Advance **information** on all of the Caribbean islands can be obtained from the tourist information offices abroad listed below. Once you've arrived at your destination, you'll find most major towns have visitor centres of some description.

There is also a wealth of information about the Caribbean on the **Web**. For the latest information on **safety issues** in the region, check out either the British Foreign & Commonwealth Office website (ⓦwww.fco.gov.uk) or the US State Department Travel Advisories (ⓦtravel.state.gov/travel_warnings.html).

BBC Caribbean ⓦwww.bbc.co.uk/caribbean. Essential site with Caribbean news reports plus arts, entertainment and sports coverage.
CANA On-Line ⓦwww.cananews.com. Daily sports, news, and features on the English-speaking Caribbean.

Codes needed to call home from abroad

To **phone abroad** from the following islands, you must first dial the international direct dialling or IDD code listed below, followed by your home country code, the area code and then the phone number.

International direct dialling codes

Anguilla ⓣ011
Antigua ⓣ011
Aruba ⓣ00
Bahamas ⓣ011
Barbados ⓣ011
Bonaire ⓣ00
British Virgin Islands ⓣ011
Cayman Islands ⓣ011
Cuba ⓣ119
Curaçao ⓣ00
Dominica ⓣ011
Dominican Republic ⓣ011
Grenada ⓣ011
Guadeloupe ⓣ00
Jamaica ⓣ011
Martinique ⓣ00
Nevis ⓣ011
Puerto Rico ⓣ011
Saba ⓣ00
St Barts ⓣ00
St Eustatius ⓣ00
St Kitts ⓣ011
St Lucia ⓣ011
St Maarten/St Martin ⓣ00
St Vincent and the Grenadines ⓣ011
Trinidad and Tobago ⓣ011
Turks and Caicos ⓣ011
US Virgin Islands ⓣ011

International country codes

Australia ⓣ61
New Zealand ⓣ64
Republic of Ireland ⓣ353
UK ⓣ44
US and Canada ⓣ1

Caribbean Beat ⓦcaribbean-beat.blogspot.com. The weblog of the renowned lifestyle publication, otherwise distributed as Caribbean Airlines in-flight magazine.
Caribbean Information Office ⓦwww.caribbeans.com. Information on travelling to the region, accommodation, packages and airlines.
Caribbean On Line ⓦwww.caribbean-on-line.com. Extensive coverage of airlines, car rental, restaurant reviews and accommodation.
Caribbean Travel and Life ⓦwww.caribbeantravelmag.com. Comprehensive Web version of the print magazine, with reader forums, custom trip planning, classifieds and resort information.
Cruise Critic ⓦwww.cruisecritic.com. Detailed reviews of cruise ships serving the Caribbean.

Tourist offices abroad

Local tourist information offices are discussed in the individual chapters. Note that in some cases public relations firms handle tourist requests from abroad.

Anguilla

ⓦwww.anguilla-vacation.com
Canada 1875 Old Waterdown Road, Burlington, Ontario Canada, L7R 3X5, ⓣ905/689-7697, ⓔdpusching@anguillacanada.ca.
UK CSB Communications, 7a Crealock St, London SW18 2BS ⓣ020/8871 0012, ⓔanguilla@tiscali.co.uk.
US Anguilla Tourist Board, 246 Central Ave, White Plains, NY 10606 ⓣ914/287-2400, ⓔmwturnstyle@aol.com.

Antigua and Barbuda

ⓦwww.antigua-barbuda.org
Canada 60 St Claire Ave E, suite 304, Toronto, ON M4T 1N5 ⓣ416/961-3085, ⓔinfo@antigua-barbuda-ca.com.
UK 2nd Floor, 45 Crawford Place, London W1H 4LP ⓣ020/7258 0070, ⓔtourisminfo@antigua-barbuda.com.
US 3 Dag Hammarskjold Plaza, 305 E. 47th Street - 6A, New York, 10017, ⓣ212/541 4117, ⓔinfo@antigua-barbuda.org.

Aruba

ⓦwww.aruba.com
Canada and US 100 Plaza Drive, First floor, Secaucus, NJ 07094 ⓣ800-TO-ARUBA or ⓣ201/558-1110, ⓔata.newjersey@aruba.com.
UK The Copperfields, 25 Copperfield St, London SE1 0EN ⓣ020/7928 1600, ⓔgeoff@saltmarshpr.co.uk.

Bahamas

ⓦwww.bahamas.com

Canada 6725 Airport Road, Suite 202, Mississauga, ON L4V 1V2, ⓣ905/672-9017, ⓔBMOTCA@bahamas.com.

UK and Ireland Bahamas House, 10 Chesterfield St, London W1J 5JL ⓣ020/7355-0800, ⓔinfo@bahamas.co.uk.

US 1200 Cornerstone, South Pine Island Rd, suite 770, Plantation, FL 33324 ⓣ954/236-9292, ⓔBMOTFL@bahamas.com.

Barbados

ⓦwww.barbados.org

Canada suite 1010, 105 Adelaide St W, Toronto, ON M5H 1P9 ⓣ416/214-9880, ⓦbarbados.org/canada.

UK 263 Tottenham Court Rd, London W1P 9AA ⓣ020/7636 9448, ⓦwww.barbados.org/uk.

US 800 Second Ave, New York, NY 10017 ⓣ212/986-6516 or 1-800/221-9831, ⓔbtany@barbados.org.

Bonaire

ⓦwww.infobonaire.com

Europe Basis Communicatie BV, Wagenweg 252, PO Box 472, NL-2000 AL Haarlem, The Netherlands ⓣ23/5430 705, ⓔeurope@tourismbonaire.com.

US and Canada 80 Broad Street, 32nd Floor, Suite 3202, New York, 10004, ⓣ212/956-5912, ⓔusa@tourismbonaire.com.

British Virgin islands

ⓦwww.bvitouristboard.com

UK BVI Tourist Board, 15 Upper Grosvenor St, London W1K 7PS ⓣ020/7355 9587, ⓔinfouk@bvi.org.uk.

US BVI Tourist Board, 1 West 34th Street, Suite 302, New York, NY 10001, ⓣ212/696-0400, ⓔinfo@bvitourism.com.

Cayman Islands

ⓦwww.caymanislands.ky

Canada 2 Bloor Street West, Suite 700, Toronto, ON M4W 3R1, ⓣ416/485-1550 or 1-800/263-5805, ⓦwww.caymanislands.ky/canada.

UK 6 Arlington St, London SW1 1RE ⓣ020/7491 7771, ⓦwww.caymanislands.co.uk.

US 3 Park Ave, 39th floor, New York, NY 10170 ⓣ212/889-9009, ⓕ986-5123.

Cuba

ⓦwww.cubatravel.cu

Canada Cuba Tourist Board, 1200 Bay St, suite 305, Toronto ON M5R 2A5 ⓣ416/362-0700, ⓦwww.gocuba.ca.

Hurricane watch

Though **hurricanes** are a rather nasty fact of life for residents of the Caribbean, relatively few big blows have swept through the region in the last few decades. 2004, however, was an exception, when the deadliest season in fifty years saw no less than four hurricanes batter the region. Packing windspeeds of up to 200mph, category 5 **Ivan** pretty much obliterated the Cayman Islands and Grenada, destroying 90 percent of homes in the latter, while less than two weeks later, flooding as a result of **Jeanne** led to the deaths of more than 3000 people in Haiti; Charley and Frances, meanwhile, pummelled the Bahamas, Cuba and Jamaica. Assisted by emergency relief funds from all over the world, the Caribbean recovered remarkably quickly – by the start of the 2004 winter tourist season, many hotels in even the worst affected islands were open for business.

The hurricane season begins around June or July, lasts four to five months and is most threatening between August and October. If a **hurricane watch** is posted, it means hurricane conditions are possible within the next 36 hours; if a **warning** is posted, conditions are expected usually within 24 hours. Advice is usually posted in hotels and guesthouses, but should you be away from your accommodation, get indoors and stay away from windows. Be aware, too, that a tornado will often follow a hurricane. For more on hurricanes, visit the sites below.

ⓦ**www.nhc.noaa.gov** The US's main hurricane site, with info on ongoing storms as well as tracking charts and satellite images.

ⓦ**ww2010.atmos.uiuc.edu/(Gh)/guides/mtr/hurr/home.rxml** Easy-to-follow background on hurricanes, from how they get their names to forecasts of current conditions, including a great tropical storm tracker.

Caribbean Tourism Development Company

Responsible for ensuring a cohesive Caribbean brand and driving forward regional hotel business, the PR gurus at the **Caribbean Tourism Development Company** (CTDC; ⓦwww.caribbeantravel.com) have a very helpful website with information on the region's history and cultures as well as details of accommodation and sights. CTDC is affiliated to the **Caribbean Tourism Organisation** (CTO; ⓦwww.onecaribbean.org), a trade organization promoting sustainable tourism throughout the region, and whose website is a good source of regional statistics, papers on anything from climate change to air transport, as well as discussion forums on regional issues.

CTDC can be contacted through the CTO's office at 80 Broad St, 32nd floor, New York, NY 10004 ⓣ212/635-9530.

UK Cuba Tourism Office, 154 Shaftesbury Ave, London WC2H 8JT ⓣ020/7240 6655 ⓔtourism@cubasi.info.

Curaçao

ⓦwww.curacao-tourism.com

Europe Curaçao Tourist Board, Vastland 82–84, 3011 BP Rotterdam, The Netherlands ⓣ10 414 2639, ⓦwww.curacaoinfo.nl.

UK Axis Sales & Marketing Ltd, Curaçao Representation UK, 421a Finchley Rd, London NW3 6HJ ⓣ020/7431 4045, ⓔcuracao@axissm.com.

US Curaçao Tourist Board 3361 SW 3rd Ave, Suite 201, Miami, FL 33145, ⓣ305/285-0511, ⓔnorthamerica@curacao.com.

Dominica

ⓦwww.ndcdominica.dm

UK The Copperfields, 25 Copperfield St, London SE1 0EN ⓣ020/7928 1600, ⓔdominica@saltmarshpr.co.uk.

US and Canada Dominica Tourist Office, 110-164 Queens Blvd, PO Box 427, Forest Hills, New York, NY 11375 ⓣ866/522 4057, ⓔdominicany@dominica.dm.

Dominican Republic

ⓦwww.godominicanrepublic.com

Canada 26 Wellington Street East Suite 201, Toronto, Ontario, M5E-1S2, ⓣ416/361-2126/27 or 1-888/494-5050, ⓔtoronto@sectur.gov.do.

UK 18-22 Hand Court, High Holborn, London WC1V 6JF ⓣ020/7242 7778, ⓔdominican.rep@btconnect.com.

US 136 E. 57 St. Suite 803, New York, 10022, ⓣ212/588-1012 or 1-888/374-6361, ⓔdrtourismboardny@verizon.net.

Grenada

ⓦwww.grenadagrenadines.com

Canada Grenada Board of Tourism, Phoenix House, 439 University Ave, suite 930, Toronto ON M5G 1Y8 ⓣ416/595-1339, ⓔtourism@grenadaconsulate.com.

UK Grenada Board of Tourism, 11 Blades Court, 121 Deodar Raod, London SW15 2NU, ⓣ020/8877-4516, ⓔgrenada@representationplus.co.uk.

US Grenada Board of Tourism, Grenada Board of Tourism
PO Box 1668, Lake Worth, FL 33460, ⓣ561/588-8176 or 800/927-9554, ⓔcnoel@grenadagrenadines.com.

Guadeloupe

ⓦwww.antilles-info-tourisme.com

Canada Maison de la France, 1981 Ave McGill College, suite 490, Montreal PQ 3A2 2W9 ⓣ514/288-4264, ⓕ514/845-4868.

UK Maison de la France, 187 Piccadilly, London W1V 0AL ⓣ020/7493-6694, ⓕ020/7493-6594.

US Maison de la France, 825 Third avenue, 29th floor, New York, 10022, ⓣ212/838-6887.

Haiti

ⓦwww.haititourisme.org

ⓦwww.travelinghaiti.com

US Haitian Consulate and Tourism Office, 71 Madison Ave., 17th Floor, New York, NY 10016; ⓣ212/697-9767, ⓦwww.haitianconsulate-nyc.org.

Jamaica

ⓦwww.visitjamaica.com

Canada 303 Eglinton Ave E, suite 200, Toronto, ON M4P 1L3 ⓣ416/482-7850 or 1-800/465-2624, ⓔjtb@visitjamaica-ca.com.

UK 1–2 Prince Consort Rd, London SW7 2BZ ⓣ020/7224 0505, ⓔmail@visitjamaica.uk.com.

US 5201 Blue Lagoon Drive, Suite # 670, Miami, Florida 33126, ⓣ305/665-0557 or 800/233-4JTB, ⓔinfo@visitjamaica-usa.com.

Martinique

ⓦwww.martinique.org
Canada Martinique Tourist Office, 4000 rue Saint Ambroise, bureau 265, Montreal, H4C 2C7, ⓣ514/844-8566.
UK Maison de la France, 178 Piccadilly, London WIJ 9AL ⓣ020/7399 3500, ⓕ020/7493-6594.
US Martinique Promotion Bureau, 825 Third avenue, 29th floor, New York, 10022, t212/838-6887, ⓔinfo@martinique.org.

Puerto Rico

ⓦwww.gotopuertorico.com
Canada Sunny Montgomery & Kerry Richards, 6-295 Queen Street East, Suite 465, Brampton, On, L6W 4S6, ⓣ416/368-2680.
US 666 Fifth Ave, 15th floor, New York, NY 10103 ⓣ212/586-6262 or 1-800/866-7827, ⓕ212/586-1212.

Saba

ⓦwww.sabatourism.com
Netherlands Netherlands Kabinet van de Gevolmachtigde Minister van de Nederlandse Antillen, Badhuisweg 173–175, 2597 JP's-Gravenhage ⓣ70/351-2811, ⓕ70/351-2722.

St Barts

ⓦwww.st-barths.com
See Guadeloupe, above.

St Eustatius

ⓦwww.statiatourism.com
See under St Maarten.

St Kitts and Nevis

ⓦwww.stkitts-tourism.com
Canada St Kitts Tourism Authority, 133 Richmond St W, suite 311, Toronto, ON M5H 2L3 ⓣ416/368-6707 or 1-888/395-4887, ⓔcanada @stkittstourism.kn.
UK St Kitts Tourism Authority, 10 Kensington Ct, London W8 5DL ⓣ020/7376 0881, ⓔuk @stkittstourism.kn.
US 414 E 75th St, suite 5, New York, NY 10021 ⓣ212/535-1234 or 1-800/582-6208, ⓔnewyork @stkittstourism.kn.

St Lucia

ⓦwww.stlucia.org
Canada 8 King St E, suite 700, Toronto, ON M5C 1B5 ⓣ416/362-4242 or 1-800/869 0377, ⓕ416/362-7832.
UK 421a Finchley Road, London NW3 6HJ ⓣ020/7431-3675.
US 800 Second Ave, 9th floor, New York, NY 10017 ⓣ212/867-2950 or 1-800/456-3984.

St Maarten

ⓦwww.st-maarten.com/tb
Canada St. Maarten Tourist Office, 2810 Matheson Blvd., E, Suite 200, Toronto, L4W 4X7, Canada, ⓣ416/622-4300.
US 675 Third Ave, suite 1806, New York, NY 10017 ⓣ212/953-2084 or 1-800/786-2278, ⓕ212/953-2145.

St Martin

ⓦwww.st-martin.org
Canada Maison de la France, 1981 Ave McGill College, suite 490, Montreal PQ 3A2 2W9 ⓣ514/288-4264, ⓕ514/845-4868.
US St Martin Tourist Office, 675 Third Ave, suite 1807, New York, NY 10017 ⓣ646/227-9440, ⓔnyoffice@st-martin.org.

St Vincent and the Grenadines

ⓦwww.svgtourism.com
Canada 333 Wilson Avenue, Suite 601, Toronto, M3H 1T2, ⓣ416/398-4277, ⓔsvgtourismtoronto @rogers.com
UK 10 Kensington Ct, London W8 5DL ⓣ020/7937 6570, ⓔsvgtourismeurope@aol.com.
US 801 Second Ave, 21st floor, New York, NY 10017 ⓣ212/687-4981 or 1-800/729-1726, ⓔsvgtony@aol.com.

Trinidad and Tobago

ⓦwww.gotrinidadandtobago.com
UK Tourism Information Office, Albany House, Albany Crescent, Claygate, Surrey KT10 OPF, ⓣ01372/469-818, ⓔtrinbago@ihml.com.
US and Canada Tourism Solutions, 2400 East Commercial Blvd., Suite # 412, Fort Lauderdale, Florida 33308, ⓣ954/776-9595, ⓔjbgrossman @aol.com.

Turks and Caicos

ⓦwww.turksandcaicostourism.com
UK 42 Westminster Palace Gardens, 1 – 7 Artillery Row, London, SW1P 1RR, t020/7222-9024, ⓔj.shankland@tcilondon.org.uk.
US and Canada Earl Higgs, Manager, Suite 2817, The Lincoln Building, 60 East 42nd Street, New York 10165, ⓣ646/375-8830, ⓔehiggs@tcigny .com.

US Virgin Islands

Ⓦwww.usvi.net
Canada 703 Evans Ave, suite 106, Toronto, ON M9C 5E9 Ⓣ416/622-7600, Ⓕ416/622-3431.
UK Power Road Station, 114 Power Road, Chadwick, London W4 5PY, Ⓣ020/8994-0978, Ⓔusvi@destination-marketing.co.uk.
US 1270 Avenue of the Americas, suite 2108, New York, NY 10020 Ⓣ212/332-2222 or 1-800/372-USVI, Ⓕ212/332-2223.

Travel bookshops and map outlets

The most detailed map of the Caribbean is the *World Map: Caribbean*, published by GeoCenter International.

In the US and Canada

Book Passage 51 Tamal Vista Blvd, Corte Madera, CA 94925 Ⓣ1-800/999-7909, Ⓦwww.bookpassage.com.
Distant Lands 56 S Raymond Ave, Pasadena, CA 91105 Ⓣ1-800/310-3220, Ⓦwww.distantlands.com.
Elliot Bay Book Company 101 S Main St, Seattle, WA 98104 Ⓣ1-800/962-5311, Ⓦwww.elliottbaybook.com.
Globe Corner Bookstore 28 Church St, Cambridge, MA 02138 Ⓣ1-800/358-6013, Ⓦwww.globecorner.com.
Map Link 30 S La Patera Lane, unit 5, Santa Barbara, CA 93117 Ⓣ805/692-6777 or 1-800/962-1394, Ⓦwww.maplink.com.
Rand McNally Ⓣ1-800/333-0136, Ⓦwww.randmcnally.com. Three US stores; check the website for the nearest location.
The Travel Bug Bookstore 3065 W Broadway, Vancouver V6K 2G2 Ⓣ604/737-1122, Ⓦwww.travelbugbooks.ca.
World of Maps 1235 Wellington St, Ottawa, ON K1Y 3A3 Ⓣ1-800/214-8524, Ⓦwww.worldofmaps.com.

In the UK and Ireland

Blackwell's Map and Travel Shop Ⓦmaps.blackwell.co.uk/index.html. Branches all over the UK; check the website for details.
Easons Bookshop 40 Lower O'Connell St, Dublin 1 Ⓣ01/858 3800, Ⓦwww.eason.ie. Call or check the website for details of other branches around Ireland.
John Smith & Son Glasgow Caledonian University Bookshop, 70 Cowcaddens Rd, Glasgow G4 0BA Ⓣ0141/332 8173, Ⓦwww.johnsmith.co.uk. For details of other branches in Scotland and England, call or check the website.
National Map Centre 22–24 Caxton St, London SW1H 0QU Ⓣ020/7222 2466, Ⓦwww.mapstore.co.uk.
Ordnance Survey Ireland Phoenix Park, Dublin 8 Ⓣ01/8025 300, Ⓦwww.irlgov.ie/osi.
Ordnance Survey of Northern Ireland Colby House, Stranmillis Ct, Belfast BT9 5BJ Ⓣ028/9025 5755, Ⓦwww.osni.gov.uk.
Stanfords 12–14 Long Acre, London WC2E 9LP Ⓣ020/7836 1321, Ⓦwww.stanfords.co.uk. For details of branches in Manchester and Bristol, call or check the website.
The Travel Bookshop 13–15 Blenheim Crescent, London W11 2EE Ⓣ020/7229 5260, Ⓦwww.thetravelbookshop.co.uk.

In Australia and New Zealand

The Map Shop 6–10 Peel St, Adelaide, SA 5000 Ⓣ08/8231 2033, Ⓦwww.mapshop.net.au.
Mapland 372 Little Bourke St, Melbourne, Victoria 3000, Ⓣ03/9670 4383, Ⓦwww.mapland.com.au.
MapWorld 173 Gloucester St, Christchurch Ⓣ03/374 5399 or 0800/627 967, Ⓦwww.mapworld.co.nz.

Travellers with disabilities

Cruise lines and top Caribbean resorts have made big steps over the course of the

Measurements and distances

You'll notice that there's a kind of schizophrenia when it comes to **measurements** in many Caribbean islands; Jamaica, for example, officially uses imperial measurements, but all of the country's road signs are metric, giving both distances and speed limits in kilometres rather than miles. A few helpful conversions are listed below.
1 mile = 1.6093 kilometres
1 metre = 1.0936 yards
1 stone (14lbs) = 6.3503 kilograms
1 kilogram = 2.2046 pounds

last decade towards catering for disabled travellers, with many cruise ships now offering cabins that have been fitted out for wheelchairs and the number of wheelchair-accessible cabins having increased by 60 percent between 1999 and 2002.

Of course, a lot remains to be done, and some islands have few facilities, accommodation or restaurants that cater to travellers with disabilities, save in the top resorts. Remember that while Caribbean **legislation** is nowhere near as stringent as American or European law when it comes to accessibility for all, after the tourism downturn in the post-9/11 climate, most of the larger resorts started ensuring that their premises accommodate most special needs in order to fill beds. At the top end of the market, it shouldn't be too difficult to find accommodation and operators who can cater for your particular needs, though at the budget end, it still remains problematic. The important thing is to check beforehand with tour companies, hotels and airlines that they can accommodate you specifically.

Contacts for travellers with disabilities

On the Web

Access-Able Ⓦwww.access-able.com. Online resource for travellers with disabilities, including detailed information on cruise lines that cater for disabled travellers.
Jim Lubin's Disability Resource Ⓦwww.makoa.org/index.html. Extensive database of links for disabled travel around the world.

In the US and Canada

Empress Directions Unlimited Ⓦwww.empressusa.com, Ⓣ1-800/533-5343 or 914/241-1700. Travel agency with staff specializing in bookings for people with disabilities.
Mobility International USA Ⓦwww.miusa.org. Information and referral services, access guides, tours and exchange programmes. Donations enable annual membership, including a quarterly newsletter.
Society for Accessible Travel and Hospitality (SATH) Ⓣ212/447-7284, Ⓦwww.sath.org. Nonprofit educational organization that has actively represented travellers with disabilities since 1976.

In the UK and Ireland

Access Travel Ⓦwww.access-travel.co.uk, Ⓣ01942/888844. UK-based travel agent specializing in holidays for people with disabilities.
Irish Wheelchair Association Ⓣ01/818 6400, Ⓦwww.iwa.ie. Useful information provided about travelling abroad with a wheelchair.
RADAR (Royal Association for Disability and Rehabilitation) Ⓣ020/7250 3222, minicom Ⓣ020/7250 4119, Ⓦwww.radar.org.uk. A good general source of advice on holidays and travel for people with disabilities.

In Australia and New Zealand

Disabled Persons Assembly Ⓣ04/801 9100 (also TTY), Ⓦwww.dpa.org.nz. Resource centre with lists of travel agencies and tour operators for people with disabilities.
National Disability Services Ⓣ02/6283 3200 (also TTY), Ⓦwww.nds.org.au. Provides lists of travel agencies and tour operators for people with disabilities.

Women travellers

Though violent attacks against women travellers are rare, many women find that the constant barrage of hisses, hoots and comments in parts of the Caribbean (Puerto Rico, Cuba, Jamaica, the Dominican Republic and the French-influenced islands, for instance) comes close to spoiling their holiday; unless, of course, you're visiting the region with romance in mind, as many women are. If you are not interested, don't be afraid to firmly communicate as much – even to the extent of seeming rude, as the mildest polite response will be interpreted as interest on your part. Be aware too that a woman on her own in a restaurant or bar will attract attention; usually a firm "no" works in deterring unwanted advances. In any event, never be afraid to ask for help if you feel lost or threatened.

Travelling with children

While many people see the Caribbean as an adult-oriented honeymoon and cruise ship destination, it's also a great place for children – the calm, shallow waters are ideal for new swimmers, and there are no worries about inoculations. With welcome attitudes towards children, the Caribbean is an easy place for families to travel independently, and an increasing number of all-inclusive resorts cater to children, offering kids' meals, water-sports, evening discos and arts and crafts. Be sure to check with your accommodation about bringing children as some hotels prefer couples only.

Guide

Guide

1

Bahamas

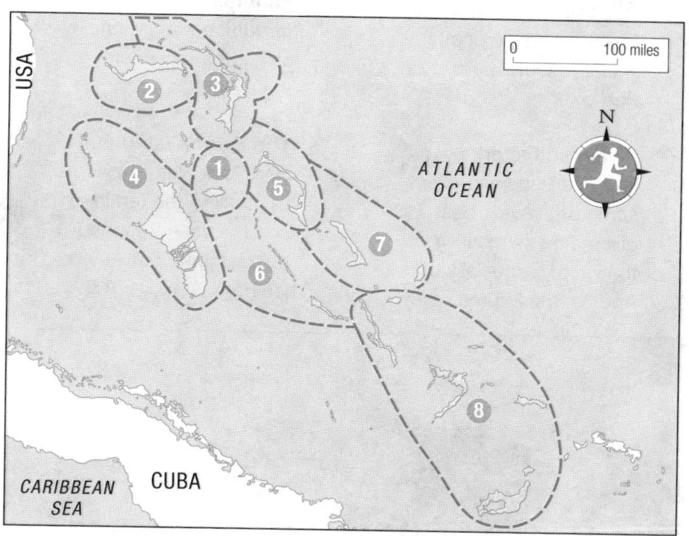
USA
0 100 miles
N
ATLANTIC
OCEAN
CARIBBEAN
SEA
CUBA
1
2
3
4
5
6
7
8

Bahamas highlights

* **Junkanoo Festival** Thousands of masquerading revellers take to the streets for this hedonistic Christmas celebration in Nassau. See p.67

* **The Cat Island Music Festival** Traditional rake 'n' scrape music, lots of food and an excuse to socialize Out Island style. See p.68

* **Diving and snorkelling** The Bahamas offer some of the very best diving and snorkelling in the world, especially off Andros, the Exumas, New Providence and Grand Bahama. See p.78 & 91

* **Out Island Regatta** Sloops from all over the Bahamas gather in April for George Town's main event. See p.110

* **Sea kayaking in the Exumas** Glide through turquoise waters, and stop for a picnic along the way. See p.112

* **The Exuma Land and Sea Park** Nature lovers will thrill to the fertile coral reefs, untouched beaches and native wildlife here. See p.113

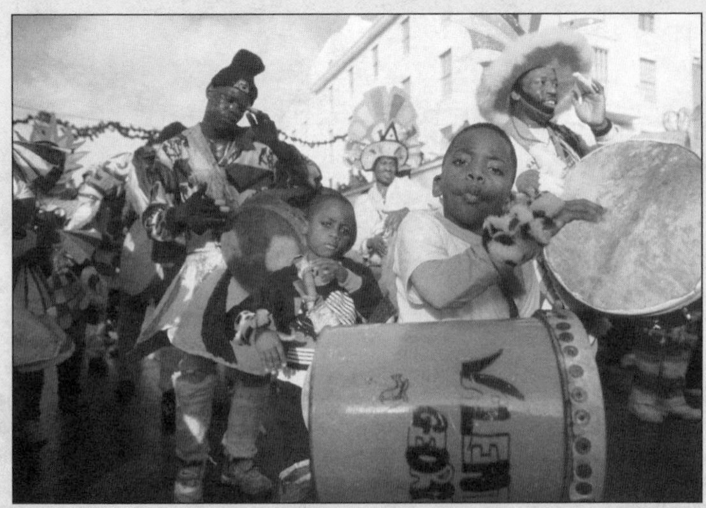

▲ Junkanoo Festival

Introduction and basics

Graced with beautiful beaches of soft pink and white sand, evocative wind-swept panoramas, abundant sunshine and countless opportunities for diving, snorkelling and fishing, the islands of **the Bahamas** are well established as one of the world's top draws for both intrepid explorers and casual holiday makers. An island chain beginning a mere 55 miles east of Miami, Florida, the Bahamas offer an array of tourist hotels, all-inclusive resorts, rustic lodges and cottage rentals. More than three million travellers each year choose the islands as their holiday destination for watersports, sun worship, casino gambling and, on some of the slightly more remote spots, eco-tourism.

The Bahamas encompass approximately seven hundred mostly uninhabited islands, cays (pronounced "keys") and rock outcroppings, strewn in a wide arc extending from just off Florida's Atlantic coast to the waters surrounding Cuba, where Great Inagua sits only sixty miles from shore. Although deep oceanic troughs surround some of the islands, most are encircled by shallow, crystalline water that is turquoise and jade-hued during the day and glows with purple luminescence at night. This combination of shallow and deep water makes diving and snorkelling both challenging and intriguing, with numerous reefs, blue holes and underwater canyons waiting to be explored just beyond the surf.

Where to go

The islands' most popular destinations are **New Providence** where the capital **Nassau** and the resort areas of **Cable Beach** and **Paradise Island** are found, and **Grand Bahama** with its vacation towns of **Freeport** and **Lucaya**. Both New Providence and Grand Bahama offer glamorous accommodations in high-rise hotels and boutique inns as well as budget motels, nightclubs, fine restaurants, shopping and plenty of beaches. Some travellers, however, may prefer the quiet, remote charms of one of the so-called **Out Islands** such as **Abaco**, **Andros**, **Eleuthera**, **Harbour Island** or **the Exumas**, or even further off the beaten track on **Cat Island** or **Long Island**, where the accommodations can be equally luxurious but rustic and the beaches and reefs virtually deserted. While all the islands of the Bahamas share the spectacular setting in a warm blue-green sea, each has its own distinctive character and pace, which makes **island-hopping** a pleasure as well as an adventure.

When to go

The southern Atlantic high-pressure system and constant trade winds make Bahamian weather consistent throughout the year, with temperatures averaging 24ºC (75ºF) during the **dry winter season** from December to May, and 5–8 degrees warmer in the **summer rainy season**. Just as a steady cooling breeze moderates the hottest hours of the day, nights in the Bahamas are temperate and, in the northern islands, even cool. Late summer and autumn comprise **hurricane season**, delivering the occasional menacing tempest as well as less destructive tropical storms. While the northern Bahamas got hit with a double whammy from Hurricanes Jeanne and Frances in the autumn of 2004, historically, the Bahamas are rarely in the direct paths of hurricanes, which usually bypass the islands to the south.

Predictably, **winter travel** is a major draw, and from December-to-May prices can be as much as 25 percent higher than during the rest of the year. **Late spring** and **early summer travel** are popular with bargain hunters, divers, and anglers and sailors drawn by the summer round of fishing tournaments, regattas and clear, still water. Travelling during the **Christmas holiday season** can be hectic and wearisome, with tourists thick on the ground and many locals taking trips to the North American mainland. Likewise, college students often crowd

Websites

ⓦ **www.bahamas.com** The Bahamas Ministry of Tourism site, covering everything from travel info, watersports and accommodation to local cuisine.

ⓦ **www.bahamasdiving.com** Includes lists of diving operators and live-aboard operators, information on diving training and links to dive-specific features.

ⓦ **www.bahamasflyfishingguide.com** Has tips for where to fish in the Bahamas, what flies you should use, and listings for fishing guides and fishing lodges in the islands.

ⓦ **www.bahamasnet.com** and ⓦ **www.myoutislands.com** Comprehensive websites with details on accommodation, activities, restaurants and a calendar of events.

ⓦ **www.thenassauguardian.com** Website of one of the two leading dailies, with the usual departments plus links to other local papers.

the major resorts during **spring break** in February and March, while other travellers escape to the Bahamas during late summer and autumn to enjoy a respite in that relatively tranquil period, the odd hurricane notwithstanding.

Getting there

The major international **airports** of the Bahamas are located in **Nassau** and **Freeport**, and are often reached via connecting flights from North American cities. Although a few carriers offer flights from Miami or Fort Lauderdale to Out Island airports, and some hotels offer charter connections to the island's resorts, most Out Island travellers fly through Nassau, or take ferries and boats to the more remote destinations.

Cruise lines such as Disney and Carnival call at Freeport and Nassau, where visitors can do some shopping and exploring for a day or two.

Information

The best source of **information** on the Bahamas is the Bahamas Ministry of Tourism; you can contact the branch nearest you before you leave home. Once in the Bahamas, you can visit the local tourist offices at the Nassau and Grand Bahama airports or in the main towns.

Information on the Out Islands is available from the Bahamas Out Island Promotion Board (ⓣ305/931-6612 or 1-800/688-4752, ⓦwww.bahama-out-islands.com), which distributes small **maps** of each Out Island as well. All major bookstores carry maps of the Bahamas. The best tourist maps of Grand Bahama and New Providence are the Trail Blazer series produced by Dupuch Publications, available through ⓦwww.bahamasnet.com or free throughout Nassau and Freeport/Lucaya. Detailed maps of each of the Out Islands have been locally produced and are available on several of the Out Islands, as noted in the relevant sections below.

Money and costs

The local **currency** is the Bahamian dollar (B$), divided into 100 cents. Coins come in denominations of 5, 10, 15, 20 and 50 cents, as well as $1 and $2. Notes are issued in denominations of $1, $3, $5, $10, $20, $50 and $100. The Bahamian dollar is on a par with the US dollar, and both currencies are accepted throughout the country; as such, there is little need to formally change US dollars before arriving. Big islands like New Providence, Grand Bahama and Abaco have major **banks** and financial institutions near the tourist centres, and have numerous **ATMs** as well.

Many **Out Islands** have few, if any, banks and most have no ATMs, so it's best to visit these more remote islands with credit cards, travellers' cheques and some cash. Note that **credit cards** are widely accepted at resorts and are almost always required to reserve and rent cars. You can use credit cards pretty much everywhere in Nassau and Freeport, Harbour Island and the Abacos, but you will need cash to pay for anything other than your hotel on the Out Islands.

Costs on the major islands are comparable to US prices. Hotels, save for motel-style lodges in downtown areas of major cities, average at least US$95–125 per night for a double room, while luxury resorts charge up to 25 percent more. Note that all hotel rooms in the Bahamas are subject to a 10–15 percent **resort tax**, and some slap on an energy surtax and a mandatory service fee on top of that. Most places do not include these fees in their advertised prices. Some Out Island lodges are less expensive, though the costs of food and transportation in the Out Islands are greater because goods and services are imported. Many resorts and hotels offer **all-inclusive packages** or **three- or seven-day rates**, which can reduce costs considerably. At least a few hotels at every destination offer **self-catering** options, which may also lower costs, especially for longer-term stays.

Getting around

In general, **island-hopping** through the Bahamas is easy, though it can be costly. The Out Islands are well linked to Nassau by daily inter-island flights and ferries several times a week but travelling from one Out Island to another generally requires returning to Nassau first. This means on average a $70–$110 **air fare** for each leg of the journey. Due to flight schedules, island-hopping will sometimes require an overnight stop in Nassau, adding another $100 or so to transit costs. Check out national carrier Bahamasair (Ⓣ242/377-5505 or 1-800/222-4262) flies regular routes between Nassau and the Out Islands; smaller, Nassau-based carriers offer charter services to the Out Islands and other destinations.

Ferry tickets are generally about half the price of flying, but most do not make daily runs, meaning you will almost certainly need to stop over in Nassau for a night or two, or use a combination of flight and ferry to get around and schedules vary depending upon the season. That said, exploring the Bahamas by ferry or mailboat is interesting and unique. The Bahamas government operates nineteen mailboats, which also carry cargo and passengers between Nassau and all the Out Islands – trips can vary from a few hours to several days. Call the dockmaster on Potter's Cay, Nassau (Ⓣ242/393-1064) for up-to-date details and schedules. The very efficient Bahamas Fast Ferry (Ⓣ242/323-2166; Ⓦwww.bahamasferries.com) runs from Nassau to Harbour Island, Eleuthera, Georgetown in the Exumas, Abaco, and Andros. Individual boat rental is also a good option for inter-island transit, with many marinas featuring choice spots for anchorage.

Nassau and Freeport both have excellent and inexpensive public **bus services**, and $1 will get you anywhere within each city. However, neither service the airport, which is the preserve of **taxi** drivers. Average taxi rates for each island are noted in the relevant sections of the chapter, but are on the high side – a taxi, for example, from the Potter's Cay ferry dock in downtown Nassau to the airport costs about $28.

Almost all the major **car-rental** agencies are found on New Providence and Grand Bahama, including Alamo, Avis, Budget, Dollar and Hertz. The international rental agencies don't operate in the Out Islands, but there are generally several private operators on any given island with at least a few vehicles available for rent, as listed in each section below. An economy-sized car costs approximately $60–80 a day or $350–450 a week. Cars drive on the left side of the road in the Bahamas, although many vehicles are right-hand drive, which keeps things interesting, especially after dark when the headlights from on coming cars can be blinding.

Bicycling can be a pleasant and inexpensive way to explore some islands, with **motor scooters** and **motorcycles** a possibility for longer trips. These are generally available from resorts or rental agencies in tourist centres. Large resorts also often rent guests golf carts to drive around the grounds, and on Harbour Island, Treasure Cay and Hope Town on Abaco, **golf carts** are the vehicle of choice. It is, however, generally easy enough to get to most places you want to go **on foot**.

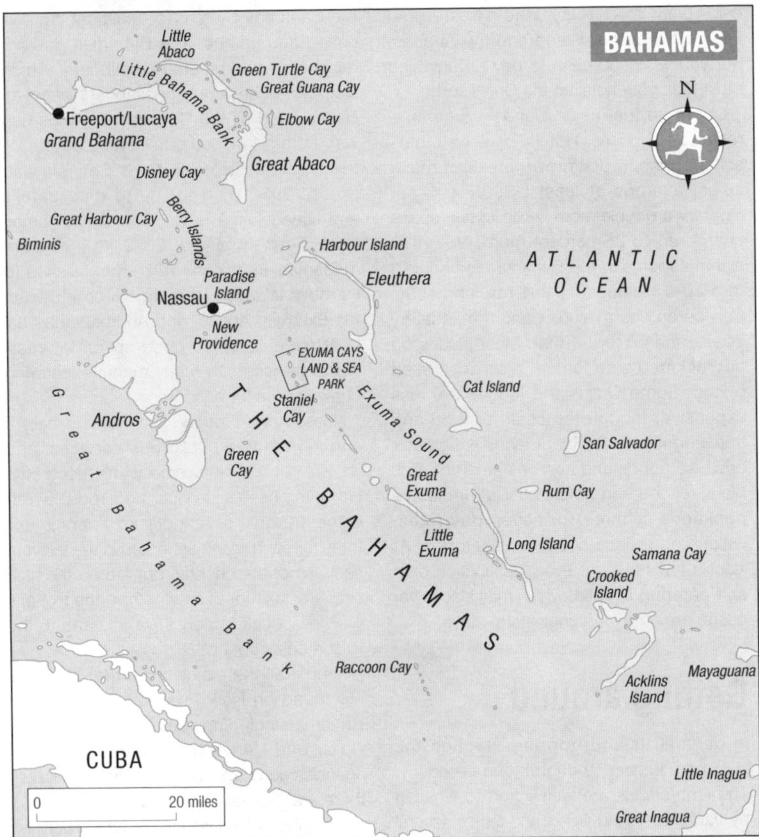

Accommodation

Although the Bahamas have relatively few inexpensive places to stay, the islands do offer many **accommodation** choices. Honeymooners and large families will find plenty of options among the large and small hotels, resorts, bed-and-breakfasts, inns and lodges. Popular among snowbirds and spring-breakers are the **all-inclusive resorts** that line the beaches in New Providence and Grand Bahama, while families and groups of friends may care to vacation at rental villas, vacation homes and long-term condos, most of which offer self-catering, some privacy and reduced rates for longer stays.

Scattered throughout the islands are traditional **Bahamian guesthouses**, anything from converted two-storey homes to small efficiency units surrounding a pool. Some guesthouses can be pretty basic, especially in the more southerly islands, while others are luxurious and spacious. There are lodges catering exclusively to **divers** and **anglers**, many of which are located at Out Island destinations. **Yachters** on the other hand may simply remain on board ship at one of the many marinas around the islands. The only place where unguided (ie only accessible by boat and no facilities at the sites) **camping** is permitted in the Bahamas is in the Exuma Land and Sea Park (see p.113).

Food and drink

Traditional **Bahamian meals** may include seafood like grouper, conch and snapper (usually grilled or baked in a tomato sauce), along with tropical fruits like guava and papaya. As a former British colony, the Bahamas have many traditional English dishes, or they have been adapted to suit local tastes. These include macaroni cheese, peas and rice, boiled potatoes and other vegetable dishes. A Bahamian **breakfast** may consist of anything from fried eggs, bacon, toast, tomato and coffee to more Caribbean-influenced dishes like johnny cakes, a heavy cornmeal bread jazzed up with coconut. **Lunch** tends towards seafood stews and soups or large conch salads.

Every town or settlement in the Bahamas has its share of **take-away restaurants**, featuring traditional offerings like fried chicken, french fries and deep-fried seafood. Most Out Island restaurants serve fairly simple and uniform fare, usually fish, conch or fried chicken, with fresh Bahamian lobster a rare treat. Island desserts are often delightful, especially the coconut concoctions, rice pudding, gingerbread and fruit cocktails.

The generally devout Bahamians are not much for **drinking** wine or liquor, although the national beer, Kalik, is a fine elixir enjoyed throughout the islands. Most bars serve up colourful tropical cocktails with little umbrellas, like the sweet and delicious Goombay Smash (coconut rum, pineapple and orange juices, with a squeeze of fresh lime juice) or a rosy Bahama Mama (rum, bitters, crème de cassis, grenadine, nutmeg and citrus juice). Fruit juice and soft drinks are popular, and major brands like Coke and Pepsi are predictably ubiquitous. Fast-food chains have also invaded the Bahamas, although the Out Islands have yet to see such development. To Bahamians, fast food means a conch burger, pig's feet or sheep's tongue souse.

Mail and Communications

Batelco is the national telephone company, and it maintains excellent phone service for all but the most isolated islands. **Public phones** are available in all tourist areas, though some Out Islands phones may be out of service for long periods of time. **Long-distance calls** may be made from public phones by using phonecards purchased from Batelco or through the local long-distance operator. Beware the non-Batelco operated public phones that take credit cards where the costs for making a long-distance call can be breathtakingly high – $35 for five minutes to Canada, for example.

Postal service to and from the Bahamas is fairly reliable.

Internet connections and **email** are a still-developing feature of most Bahamian telephone networks, although **wireless connections** are rapidly becoming available on most islands and in most hotels. If getting online is a necessity for you, it's advisable to check in advance with your hotel or resort.

The **country code** for the Bahamas is ⓣ242.

Opening hours, festivals and holidays

Shops are typically **open** Monday to Saturday 9am–5pm. **Banks** generally operate Monday to Thursday 9am–3pm and Friday 9am–5pm, although Out Island banks may have very limited opening hours or open only one or two days per week. On the whole, things shut up pretty tight on Sundays, although many establishments are now opening half days on **Sunday**.

Visiting the islands during one of the many **festivals** held throughout the year is a good way to experience Bahamian culture. Thousands of costumed revellers, drummers and dancers fill Bay Street in Nassau for the all-night Junkanoo rush-outs on December 26 and New Year's Eve. Junkanoo parades and parties are also held in villages on Eleuthera, Green Turtle Cay in the Abacos and on Grand Bahama.

Many Out Island settlements hold **Homecomings** during July or August, when Out Islanders who have left to seek their fortunes in Nassau or elsewhere come home for a week of community parties, music, games and often a sailing regatta. During spring and summer countless **fishing tournaments** and **regattas** take place, including the famous Bahamas Family Island Regatta at George Town in the Exumas during the last week of April. Long Island and Abaco also host popular regattas. Other fun times include the Eleuthera Pineapple Festival in early June in Gregory Town and the Cat Island Music Festival, also in June.

Bahamians, especially those in Fox Hill in Nassau, celebrate **Emancipation Day** on the first Monday in August, marking the abolition of slavery with parades and food, as well as cultural events. Fireworks and parades highlight **Independence Week**, which culminates on July 10. Bahamian tourist centres provide lists of the many festivals, holidays and craft shows that occur year-round.

Sports and outdoor activities

Sunny weather, sandy beaches, exquisite reefs, shallow water, steady winds and proximity to the Gulf Stream make the Bahamas an ideal choice for all manner of **sports** and **outdoor activities**. Islands like Bimini are rightfully regarded as great spots for **fishing** (especially for wahoo, tuna, barracuda, shark, grouper and snapper), while many Out Islands like Andros, Long Island, Cat and Abaco are famous for their **bonefishing** – so named after the silvery catch. Likewise, the islands' shallow, calm waters have made **sailing** a popular activity, especially around the Exumas, Abaco and Eleuthera.

Nearly every resort, hotel and lodge offers a range of **aquatic sports**, including diving, snorkelling, boating, windsurfing, parasailing and swimming. **Golf** and **tennis** are provided at resorts and hotels on the major islands, with golf courses located in Lucaya on Grand Bahama, at Cable Beach in Nassau, on Paradise Island and on Great Exuma. **Biking, hiking and sea kayaking** are growing in popularity as well, and a number of operators specialize in trips to isolated spots throughout the islands. **Birdwatching** is a major draw, especially for seabird species like the rare Bahamian parrot on Abaco, and flamingos on Inagua. There's also **horseriding** at stables on New Providence and Grand Bahama.

History

The name Bahamas probably comes from the Spanish "Baja Mar", meaning "shallow seas", an apt description of the area attributed to Columbus. After the European discovery of the islands in 1492, and the subsequent rapid annihilation of the aboriginal Lucayans, the islands remained a backwater until a few English settlers from Bermuda arrived on Eleuthera in 1647. Soon after, farmers colonized New Providence and established Charles Town, the name of which was changed in 1690 to Nassau in honour of England's new ruler, William, Prince of Orange and Nassau.

With the islands ruled by a series of incompetent royal governors, Nassau gradually slipped into chaos and piracy, becoming home to such notorious figures as the pirate **Blackbeard** and his ilk, who preyed on Spanish and French ships as they passed through the islands loaded with gold and other riches from the Spanish mainland and the reverse Caribbean route to Europe. Not until the arrival of Royal Governor Woodes-Rogers in 1717 was piracy finally curtailed.

During the American Revolution, several thousand **Loyalists** came to the Bahamas from the North American colonies, settling in Abaco, Eleuthera, the Exumas and Long Island and creating an economy and society based on plantations run by slave labour. However, their cotton, tobacco and fruit crops failed due to crop diseases and soil exhaustion. After the **abolition of slavery** here in 1834, island residents turned to salvaging from shipwrecks, sponge harvesting, fishing and subsistence farming to make a living.

During the American Civil War, Nassau and West End on Grand Bahama became boom towns built on **blockade running**, later turning to rum-running during America's Prohibition of the 1920s and early 1930s. **Tourism**, popular since the mid-nineteenth century, gained a firmer foothold after World War II with the advent of modern air travel, seven-storey cruise ships and air conditioning. On July 10, 1973, after 325 years of British rule, the Bahamas became an **independent**, democratic state supported by tourism, banking and fishing.

The last decade has seen a dramatic expansion in the **tourism** industry, with the opening of the massive **Atlantis Resort** on Paradise Island, which is the largest employer in the Bahamas. Similarly, the economy of Grand Bahama and the Out Islands are getting a boost with the ongoing construction of large resorts.

1.1 New Providence

NEW PROVIDENCE is the thumping heart and epicentre of the Bahamian archipelago with more than two-thirds of the country's population calling it home. Steeped in nearly 230 years of swashbuckling history, this tiny 21-mile-long and 7-mile wide island plays host to around two million visitors each year. On the north-eastern side of the island is **Nassau,** the bustling capital with roughly 100,000 residents and hub for international business, banking and tourism. Most of the tourist action is focused around **Prince George Wharf** and **Bay Street**, a block inland from the water and regularly teaming with shoppers fresh off cruise ships. Two long toll bridges east of downtown Nassau connect the city centre to **Paradise Island,** where you find the massive mega-resort *Atlantis* and many other hotels alongside an assortment of shops, restaurants and private vacation homes. Short on seclusion, you might find a peaceful plot of sand on the north coast on **Cabbage Beach** or **Paradise Beach**.

Much of eastern New Providence is populated and dense with island traffic and getting to the high-rise lined, four-mile stretch of powdery white sand at **Cable Beach** could take forty minutes from downtown.

Continuing westward past Cable Beach, you will come across more sheltered strands of sand, including **Orange Hill Beach** and **Love Beach** near Gambier Village, which features the new *Marley Resort & Spa*. Beyond the western tip of the island is **Lyford Cay**, an exclusive gated community sprinkled with celebrities. New Providence's **south shore** has few notable beaches and a few hotels. Diving and snorkelling draw many enthusiasts to the south shore's outer reef and reef walls.

Although the **central interior** of New Providence is mainly marshy scrub, local **eco-tourism** operators offer canoeing on **Lake Killarney** as well as combination biking-kayaking tours.

Arrival and information

Nassau International Airport (Arrivals ⓣ242/377-6806 and Departures ⓣ242/377-6782), the hub of Bahamian air transport, is located on the west-central part of New Providence, a fifteen-minute taxi ride from downtown Nassau and only ten minutes from Cable Beach. While there are no buses from the airport, there are plenty of **taxis**; the fare for two people to Cable Beach is US$17, downtown Nassau US$25 and Paradise Island US$30. Current taxi rates are posted on a billboard at the taxi stand at the airport.

The Ministry of Tourism operates an **information booth** at the airport, while in downtown Nassau there are two information booths that provide useful maps and brochures. The smaller one can be found near the Straw Market on Bay St (Mon–Fri 9am–5pm; ⓣ242/322-7680), while the larger office is located in Rawson Square, about two blocks east of the market (Mon–Fri 8.30am–5pm, Sat 8.30am–4pm, Sun 8.30am–2pm; ⓣ242/326-9781).

Getting around

Getting around New Providence and Paradise Island is easy, as both islands are fairly compact and many destinations are never more than fifteen or twenty minutes apart. **Taxis** are ubiquitous, and almost all hotels and resorts have taxi stands (otherwise, dispatchers can be reached at ⓣ242/323-5111 and 323-5818). If you're travelling early in the morning, make a **taxi reservation** the night before.

Nassau's **buses**, known as **jitneys,** are frequent and convenient, serving all parts of Nassau, Cable Beach and surrounding areas for US$1; be sure to have exact change as drivers are required by law to keep the change. The #10 jitney runs along West Bay Street to Cable Beach, Sandy Point, Orange Hill and Gambier Village. You can pick it up at bus stops along the route; in downtown Nassau, it leaves from the main stop at Frederick and Bay streets, or from a stop outside the *McDonald's* across from the *British Colonial Hilton Hotel*. Eastbound lines go from downtown to the Paradise Island Bridge and can be accessed on Bay Street east of the Straw Market. The easiest way to reach Paradise Island, however, is by **ferry**, which runs every few minutes from Prince George Wharf to Paradise Island across the harbour (daily 9am–6pm; US$3 one-way).

To explore the rest of the island, you will probably want to **rent a car**. Avis has four locations on New Providence: downtown Nassau on Cumberland Street, across from the *British Colonial Hilton* (ⓣ242/326-6380); on Paradise Island at the Paradise Shopping Centre (ⓣ242/363-2061); in Cable Beach (ⓣ242/322-2889) and at the airport (ⓣ242/377-7121). Other rental agencies include Budget (Paradise Island ⓣ242/363-3095, airport ⓣ242/377-7405), Hertz (airport ⓣ242/377-6321), Dollar (downtown ⓣ242/325-3716, airport ⓣ242/377-8300) and Orange Creek Car Rentals (ⓣ242/323-4967), on West Bay Street in Cable Beach. Rates range from US$49–119 for 24 hours. If you are travelling in high season (Dec 15–April), it is advisable to book a car in advance. You can rent **motor scooters** and **bicycles** at local outlets as well.

Another option for **touring** New Providence is through Majestic Tours (ⓣ242/322-2606), which acts as agent for a variety of operators offering bus tours as well as historical, snorkelling and boating expeditions. It has booths in many of the major hotels in Nassau, as well as Cable Beach and Paradise Island. Other tours are advertised in the tourist magazine *What's On*, available almost everywhere in Nassau.

Nassau

Originally known as Charles Town, **NASSAU** is the modern-day face of the Bahamas. Though dingy in parts, enough historical flavour has been preserved to make a stop worthwhile. Much of this atmosphere comes from its development during the so-called Loyalist period from 1787 to 1834, when many of the city's finest colonial buildings were built. Before this build-up, Nassau had largely been a rustic haven for pirates, privateers and wreckers.

After alternating periods of decline and prosperity in the nineteenth and early twentieth centuries, the spike in trade and construction that followed World War II led directly to Nassau's emergence as a global centre for **tourism** and **finance**. By the mid-1950s, with the dredging of the harbour and the construction of the international airport, Nassau began to host more than a million visitors a year. A decade later, after the construction of the **Paradise Island Bridge** and the development of **Cable Beach**, the city was receiving twice as many.

Getting around

The historic centre of Nassau occupies about six square blocks, and can be easily explored on foot. **Taxis** are also readily available throughout the city, with Bahamas Transport and the Taxi Cab Union (ⓣ242/323-5111or 323-5818) as the most reliable companies. Any driver can be enlisted to give informal **tours** of the city or the whole island, with the cost usually running to about US$60 for three people and two hours

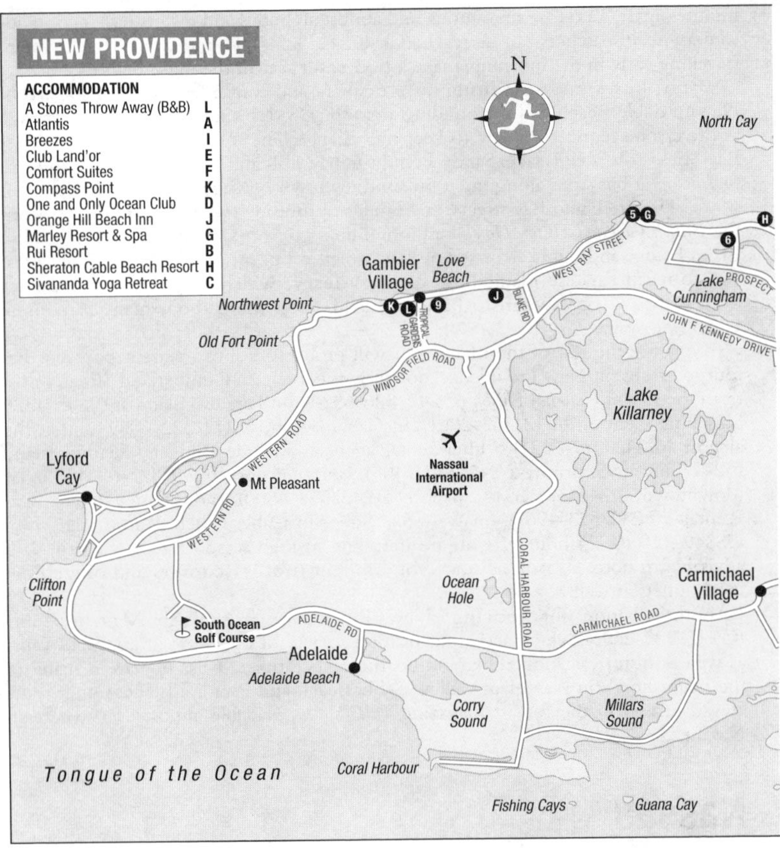

of sightseeing. Most hotels offer **bike rentals**, though you can also rent a **scooter** at Knowles Scooter and Bike Rental, located at Prince George Wharf (ⓣ242/322-3415). You can also tour Historical Nassau by **horse-drawn surrey** (US$10 per person for about 25 minutes, departing from Prince George's Wharf area), although the quality of these tours depends on how knowledgeable your guide is (it varies).

Accommodation

Accommodation in Nassau can be quite pricey, depending on the time of year. During the winter **high season** hotels are often fully booked, whereas the **summer season** brings lower prices and greater availability. The downtown area offers some decent budget options as well as a swanky old colonial hotel. Cable Beach boasts several chain hotels and a couple of exclusive resorts, while a few miles further west are a range of more secluded options.

Nassau

British Colonial Hilton Nassau 1 Bay St ⓣ242/322-3301 or 1-800/455-8667, ⓦwww.hiltoncaribbean.com/nassau. Built in 1922 and once the epitome of elegance in colonial Nassau, the *Hilton* still offers plush, upscale accommodation, particularly after a $70 million refurbishment in 2004. It is, however, sandwiched between the harbour and the busy main street in downtown Nassau, and its landscaping leans

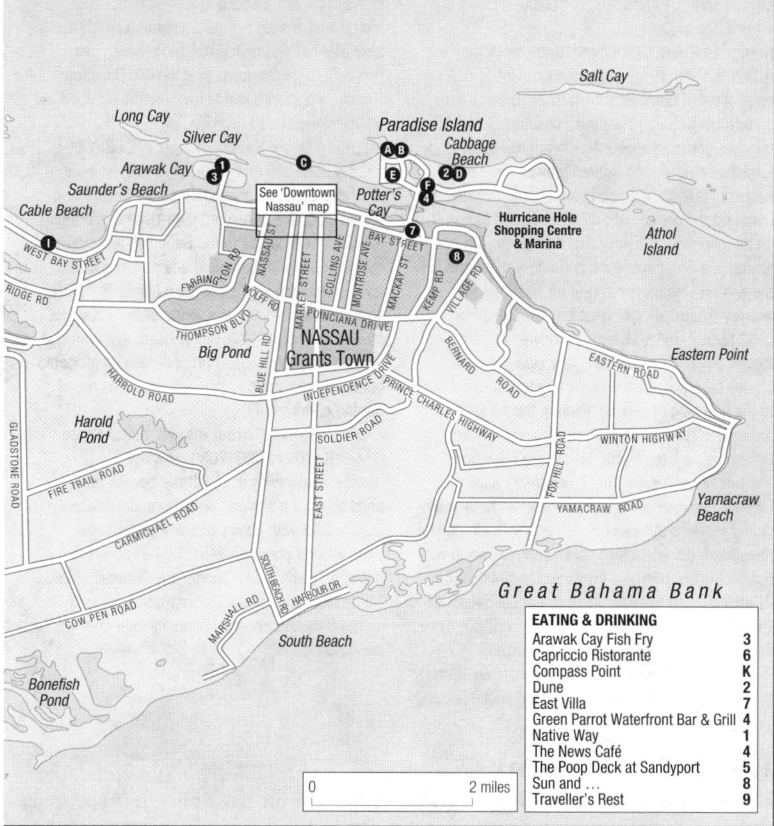

more towards brick and cement than greenery. The 291 rooms have opulent gold and claret decor, Internet access, CD players and TVs with pay-per-view movies, but no balconies. There is a formal dining room, a small swath of beach and a pool bar with a view of the cruise ship dock and Paradise Island. 8–9

Graycliff West Hill St ⓣ242/302-9150, ⓦwww.graycliff.com. Perched on a hill above Nassau, a glamorous British Colonial pile with secluded rooms opening onto a garden and private cottages where Churchill and the Beatles have slept, decorated in rich woods and luxurious fabrics and set in lush grounds. The hotel has one of the city's top restaurants. 9

El Greco Hotel West Bay and August streets ⓣ242/325-1121, ⓦwww.elgrecohotelbahamas.com. Centrally located across from the beach and near downtown on the main road, with 26 basic rooms positioned around a pool and courtyard. 6

Mignon Guest House 12 Market St ⓣ242/322-4771. Clean, bright six-room budget choice with simple, no-frills rooms, a/c, shared baths and a fridge and microwave for guest use. 3

Nassau Palm Hotel West Bay St ⓣ877/229-6322 , ⓦwww.nassau-hotel.com. Offering standard hotel rooms and a kids' suite on the pool level, and located right on the main thoroughfare, with no grounds or greenery, three blocks from downtown Nassau. There is a public beach across the road, a heated pool in a cement courtyard with a view of the street, and several restaurants nearby. 8

Cable Beach and around

Breezes West Bay St, Cable Beach ⓣ242/327-5356, ⓦwww.superclubs.com. A huge super-inclusive package hotel (part of the *Superclubs* chain) with standard hotel rooms, and serving up countless activities, including a full range of aquatic sports, to busloads of holiday-makers ages 14 and older. 9

Compass Point West Bay St, Gambier Village ☎242/327-4500, Ⓦwww.islandoutpost.com. A few miles west of Cable Beach on the #10 bus route, an upscale but unpretentious collection of eighteen rainbow-coloured, delightfully and luxuriously furnished cottages and guest rooms, some with kitchens. Built on a small patch of land between the road and the ocean but artfully designed to create an atmosphere of privacy and relaxation. The open-air bar is a great spot for lunch and a drink and there is an elegant restaurant for dinner. 9

Marley Resort & Spa West Bay St, Cable Beach ☎3242/327-1662, Ⓦwww.marleyresort.com. The former governor's mansion, now owned by the Marley family, is a pricey luxury resort-cum-tribute to the late king of reggae. Each of the 16 suites are named for a famous Marley tune and have Bose music systems and flat-screen televisions. The honeymoon suite, One Love, offers a Jacuzzi for two. Personal concierge, spa and 24 hr in-room dining services available. Simmer Down, the on site restaurant, dishes classic Caribbean fare along with some of Bob's personal favourites and Marley family recipes. Live entertainment in the courtyard. 9

Orange Hill Beach Inn West Bay St, at Blake, Love Beach ☎242/327-7157, Ⓦwww.orangehill.com. Four miles west of Cable Beach, away from the hustle and glitz, a laid-back, small motel popular with divers, with large, bright and comfortable rooms built around a small swimming pool. There's a relaxed bar and restaurant and a beach just two minutes' walk down over the hill. Downtown Nassau is a short bus ride away, and the airport is a five-minute, US$9 cab ride. 6

Sheridan Cable Beach Resort West Bay St ☎242/327-5968 or 1-866/716-8106, Ⓦwww.sheraton.com/cablebeach. Recently bought and remodelled, this 694-room high-rise hotel brings a touch of Las Vegas to the Bahamas and draws many guests with gambling and golf, but also boasts eighteen tennis courts, a health club, three pools and abundant watersports and a 1000 foot stretch of beach. Plush, nicely decorated common areas, lushly landscaped grounds and comfortable guest rooms with the standard amenities round out the offerings. 7

A Stones Throw Away Tropical Garden Rd ☎242-327-7030, Ⓦwww.astonesthrowaway.com. Off the beaten path, perched on a hill overlooking Gambier Village, a quite B&B with luxury finishes and a large wrap around porch. Built in 2004 to accommodate 20 guests with 8 rooms and 2 suites, this island treasure echoes the intimate setting of an old Bahamian home. Rates include gourmet breakfast. 8–9

Historic Nassau

The heart of **historic Nassau** is **Rawson Square** on Bay Street, just up from Prince George Wharf, where the major cruise lines dock. The square is the authentic crossroads of old Nassau, where tourists, government workers, hawkers and musicians congregate – especially during Christmas **Junkanoo festivities** when up to 30,000 onlookers jam the square and surrounding streets and balconies to watch the all-night parade.

Just west and north of the square, the **Hairbraider's Centre** features Bahamian women braiding hair for about US$2 a strand. Across Bay Street, south of Rawson Square, **Parliament Square** is the centre of Bahamian government whose grand colonial edifices were constructed in the early 1800s. These include the Opposition Building and the House of Assembly and Senate where a statue of **Queen Victoria** looks down sternly from the steps. Behind the Senate is the **Supreme Court** building, and its lovely **Garden of Remembrance** honouring Bahamian casualties of two world wars.

Back on Bay Street, a few blocks west of Prince George Wharf, is Nassau's famous **Straw Market** (open daily 9am–6pm). Filling much of a square block, the covered market squeezes in 150 vendors peddling everything from beads, tote bags and T-shirts to shark-tooth necklaces and expensive hand-carved wooden turtles. Just behind the market, the waterfront area is bounded by **Woodes-Rogers Walk**, named after the British colonial governor credited with ridding Nassau of pirates. It's worth a quick stroll for the view of the teeming harbour, usually brimming with multi-storey cruise ships.

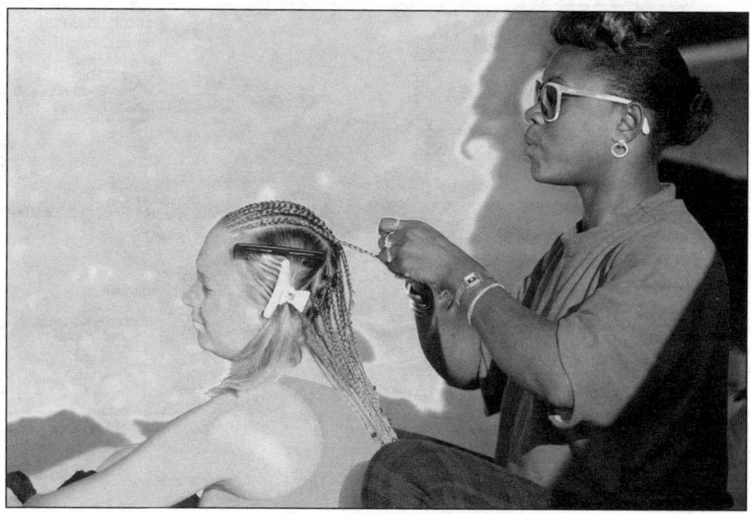

▲ Hairbraiding Centre

Just west of the Straw Market, the **Pompey Museum**, on the corner of Bay and George streets (Mon–Wed & Fri–Sat 9.30am–4.30pm, Sun 9–12.30, closed Thur, 2 day Sun; US$3; ⓣ242/356-0495), is located in Vendue House, on the site of the eighteenth-century slave auction, subsequently renamed to honour the slave who led a rebellion on Exuma in the 1830s. One of the city's oldest buildings, though gutted by a fire in 2001, it houses a collection of artefacts and documents tracing the history of Bahamian slavery.

A couple of blocks away, on the corner of George and King streets, kids especially will have great fun going through the small but well-done **Pirates of Nassau Museum**, complete with a replica of Nassau's seedy eighteenth-century waterfront, with creepy sounds and interactive displays (Mon–Sat 9am–6pm, Sun 9am–12pm, ⓣ242/356-3759, ⓦwww.pirates-of-nassau.com). Nearby, the fully restored eighteenth-century **Balcony House**, at 52 Market St near Bay, is believed to be the oldest wooden house in Nassau (Mon–Fri 9am–4.30pm, & Sat 10am–1pm; donations welcome; ⓣ242/302-2621).

Hillside area and west

South of Rawson Square, roughly bounded by Elizabeth Avenue to the east and Cumberland Street on the west, the **Hillside area** has a historical flavour enlivened by small **cafés** and some architecturally interesting pastel-coloured colonial buildings.

A block south of Parliament Square on Shirley Street is the **Nassau Public Library and Museum**, an octagonal building that was the first site of the Bahamian Parliament and later the city jail (Mon–Thurs 10am–8pm, Fri 10am–5pm & Sat 10am–4pm; free; ⓣ242/322-4907). The cluttered rooms house a remarkable collection of maps, photographs and engravings. Across from the library on the south side of Shirley Street is the restful **Royal Victoria Garden**, where you're free to wander among three hundred species of tropical plants on the former grounds of its namesake hotel, now a crumbling ruin. Following East Road, which runs along the eastern edge of the grounds, the road forks at East Hill Road. A right turn here will take you along a stretch containing much of Nassau's historic **architecture**, most prominently **Jacaranda House**, a two-storey private residence with peaked roofs and carved mansards.

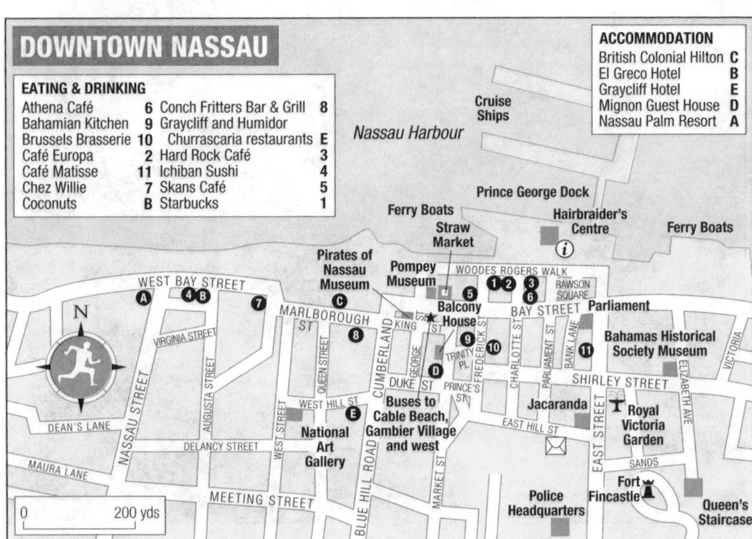

Moving west, East Hill Road turns into West Hill Road, where you'll find both the **Dunmore House**, built in the 1790s by governor Lord Dunmore and now a private home, and **Graycliff**, an imposing Georgian residence from the 1720s and now an exclusive hotel (see "Accommodation", p.73). The Bahamas **National Art Gallery** is located on the corner of West Hill Road and West Street Tues–Sat 11am–4pm, ⓣ242/328-5800 or 5801); showcasing a collection of Bahamian painting, sculpture, textiles and photographs. Alternatively, stay on East Road past the Royal Victoria Gardens and take a left turn on Sand Road, which links up with Elizabeth Avenue, where the road slopes up toward the highest points in Nassau: the 1793 **Fort Fincastle** and the **Water Tower** (currently closed at press time), providing fabulous views of the harbour. Just east of the Water Tower, the unique **Queen's Staircase** is a deep limestone gorge into which stairs were carved for the convenience of Nassau's elite.

The areas west of downtown are best visited by hopping on the #10 jitney from in front of the *British Colonial Hilton Hotel*. A mile or so from downtown is **Fort Charlotte**, on a magnificent overlook between Nassau Street and Chippingham Road (daily 9am–4.30pm; free). Built in 1787 by Lord Dunmore, the fort offers daily tours by guides occasionally sporting period costumes. Opposite Fort Charlotte is **Arawak Cay**, a man-made island and popular local hangout featuring food shacks and patio restaurants where Bahamian cooks serve up conch salad, cracked and fried conch and other local delicacies. Weekends are a good time to visit, when there is occasionally live music.

Cable Beach

Five miles west of downtown Nassau, and named after the first underwater phone cable that reached here in 1892, **CABLE BEACH** is home to numerous hotels, restaurants and sports facilities, along with a major golf course and tennis courts. Along the beach, whispering **casuarina trees** line the sands, and offshore lie **North Cay** and **Long Cay**, which make nice day-trips for snorkellers and picnickers. At the end of Cable Beach is **Delaporte Point Beach**, a chic assortment of brightly coloured town homes, fancy shops and restaurants.

Eating and drinking

Thanks in part to its international influx of tourists, Nassau's **restaurants** feature a wide variety of cuisines, highlighted by Bahamian seafood prepared by local chefs using fresh ingredients. Every large hotel also has its own restaurants, some of them world-class. The free and widely available *Dining and Entertainment Guide* contains a complete listing of restaurants, diners and take-aways.

Nassau

Athena Café Bay St, at Charlotte ☎ 242/326-1296. Attracts large numbers of hungry cruise ship day-trippers with tasty (though overpriced) Greek food, served on a pleasant second-storey veranda with a lively atmosphere. Entrance is located in the shop below.

Bahamian Kitchen Trinity Plaza, at Market St ☎ 242/325-0702. Authentic Bahamian home-cooking – wonderful grouper, snapper and conch dishes for US$10 – served in spartan surroundings.

Brussels Brasserie Fredrick St, Downtown Nassau. ☎ 242/326-4523 Belgian-French with a cosy, very European feel. Hot spot for local professionals. Speciality is the Coq au vin, good enough to bring you back again.

Café Europa Charlotte St, between Bay and Woodes Rogers Walk. A small Euro stainless-steel and black-leather coffee bar, serving Italian coffee, tasty deli sandwiches and pastries.

Café Matisse on Bank Lane behind Parliament Square ☎ 242/356-7012. One of the nicest places to dine in Nassau, a sophisticated but relaxed bistro with great service and a menu including seafood and fresh pasta, highlighted by duck-filled ravioli and seafood pizza. Occasional Thurs or Sun night jazz. Proper dress required and reservations recommended.

Chez Willie West Bay St ☎ 242/322-5364 or 5366. Just west of the *British Colonial Hilton*, this expensive though cordial French restaurant serves delicious mussels and steak tenderloin.

CoCo-Nuts Bay St in the *El Greco Hotel*. ☎ 242/322-6330, specializing in authentic downhome Bahamian food.

Conch Fritters Bar and Grill Bay St, across from the *British Colonial Hilton* ☎ 242/323-8778 or 8801. Convenient, pleasant location and tasty, inexpensive food, namely burgers, conch done several ways, buffalo wings and jerk chicken.

East Villa East Bay St, 3/4 mile past the Paradise Island Bridge ☎ 242/393-3377. Chinese and Continental cuisine in an elegant formal dining room; considered the best restaurant on the island by some residents. Reservations recommended.

Graycliff West Hill St ☎ 242/322-2796. Located in the eponymous hotel, with four elegant candlelit dining rooms in a restored colonial mansion and a 300,000-bottle wine cellar. The lengthy menu features French cuisine and Bahamian seafood dishes, as well as charcoal-grilled Ecuadorian white jumbo shrimp, Canadian sea scallops and meat dishes garnished with peppercorns brought in from Madagascar. The Humidor Churrascaria dining room specializes in Brazilian barbecued steak.

Ichiban Sushi West Bay St. ☎ 242/326-7224. Asian Fusion with the best of the east and west. Fresh sushi, seafood dishes with seating indoor or outdoor in a swanky setting overlooking Nassau Harbour. (Closed Mon)

Skan's Café on Bay St ☎ 242/322-2486. You'll find locals mixing it up with tourists in true Bahamian style. Diner style decor. The delicious food is very inexpensive with good size portions. Serving breakfast and lunch with daily specials that sell out so arrive early.

Sun and... Lakeview Rd, off Shirley St ☎ 242/393-1205. Considered one of Nassau's culinary highlights. Elegant, outdoor semiformal dining with a menu of imaginative, beautifully presented French cuisine. Jackets required for men and reservations recommended. Dinner only.

Cable Beach and around

Capriccio Ristorante West Bay St, across from *Sandals*, Cable Beach ☎ 242/327-8547. Nice little Italian eatery, with four tables inside and a few more on a covered terrace.

Compass Point West Bay St, Gambier Village ☎ 242/327-4500. Casual though expensive open-air dining by the ocean, with a typical seafood-focused menu.

Native Way on Arawak Cay. Casual, inexpensive yet delightful in its authentic Bahamian menu. Known for its friendly service, tasty conch fritters and owner Jason, who is usually found behind the bar.

The Poop Deck West West Bay St, on Sandy Point Beach ☎ 242/393-8175. Moderately priced waterfront eatery popular with residents and tourists for seafood and sunsets. Closed Mon.

Nassau tours and activities

Tours

Horse-drawn surrey rides US$10 per person for about 25 minutes, leaving from Prince George's Wharf and taking you past the Bahamian Parliament and other major sights of old Nassau.

Majestic Tours ⓣ242/322-2606, ⓦwww.majesticholidays.com. Has agents in most hotels and handles bookings for an extensive menu of Nassau–Paradise Island tour operators, including bus tours of Nassau, boat excursions to the Out Islands and nearby cays, snorkelling expeditions, canoe trips, booze cruises, cycling day-trips, tours of the rum distillery and a variety of other activities.

Nassau Walking Tours ⓣ242/323-3182 or 323-3183. Offers an approximately 60min walking tour of historic Nassau, departing twice daily (except Sunday) at 10am & 3.45pm from Festival Place on Prince George Dock. US$10 paid in cash directly to the tour guide. Reservations needed.

Boat excursions

Bahamas Fast Ferries ⓣ242/323-2166, ⓦwww.bahamasferries.com. Puts on day-trips to historic Dunmore Town on Harbour Island, off Eleuthera, including golf cart transportation, tour, lunch and cabana facilities on lovely Pink Sand Beach. US$179 adult, $99 child. Boat leaves on time or sooner if all ticket holders are present.

Barefoot Sailing Adventures ⓣ242/393-0820 or 393-5817. A real sailing excursion (ie no engine noise) limited to a small group to Rose Island and nearby cays, for snorkelling and a barbecue on the beach. Half-day outings US$65, full day with picnic $99, sunset champagne cruise $55.

Flying Cloud Catamaran Cruises ⓣ242/363-4430, ⓦwww.flyingcloud.info. Half-day sailing and snorkelling excursions to Rose Island on a catamaran (daily 9.30am & 2pm Mon-Sat; US$60), as well as evening cruises (Mon, Wed & Fri 6pm; US$60) and a five-hour Sunday outing to Rose Island with snorkelling and a barbecue lunch on the beach (10am; US$75). Children pay half price. All trips leave from the Paradise Island Ferry Terminal, but transportation to and from your hotel is included. Cruise times are subject to change according to season.

Powerboat Adventures ⓣ242/363-1466, ⓦwww.powerboatadventures.com. Runs an exhilarating day-trip to the Exuma Cays by high-speed powerboat, followed by snorkelling, a visit to the resident giant iguanas, an elaborate picnic lunch on the beach, shark and sting ray feeding demonstration, a nature walk and time for relaxation. US$190 adults and $120 children all inclusive, 9am-6pm daily, weather permitting.

Sail Nassau ⓣ242/363-1552, ⓦwww.sailnassau.com. The closest thing to an America's Cup race experience for a novice or seasoned sailor. You'll race for 2 hours in an America's Cup yacht. Be a part of the crew or simply sit back and watch, no experience necessary. Tenders leave from the Paradise Island Ferry Terminal where they will take you to one of 2 yachts. US$125 and $95 for children 7 to 12 years. Reservations required.

Diving and snorkelling

Long, deep reefs and drop-off walls line the south shore of New Providence, and shallow reefs fringe the western side. The main diving centre is **Coral Harbour** along

Traveller's Rest West Bay St, near Gambier Village ⓣ242/327-7633. Great casual lunch-time escape from the city, with shaded patio seating overlooking the beach at Orange Hill, offering great banana daquiris. Service can be comically slow, so be prepared to relax with a drink.

the south shore where several dive operators maintain shops and boats, although all operators provide complimentary transportation to and from your hotel. Most operations also offer snorkelling and swimming trips and combination snorkel-picnic packages, as do most hotels and resorts. All have similar rates, with a day of snorkelling for US$45, two-tank dives for around $85 and $250 for open-water PADI certification. Among the most popular and well-established operations are:

Bahama Divers ⓣ242/393-5644 or 1-800/398-3483 in the US and Canada, ⓦwww.bahamadivers.com. Local office is located at the Paradise Island Bridge on Paradise Island.

Custom Aquatics ⓣ242/362-1492, ⓦwww.divecustomaquatics.com. Offering dive charters and custom trips around New Providence and Northern Exuma Cays. Located in Coral Harbour on Baily Dr just south of the airport.

Stuart's Cove Dive Bahamas ⓣ242/362-4171 or 1-800/879-9832 in the US, ⓦwww.stuartcove.com. This large operation, with a well-stocked dive shop, is based at South Ocean Beach on the south side of the island. In addition to an extensive menu of snorkelling and diving excursions and certification courses, they offer underwater "field trips" in one-person submarines that look like a cross between a motor scooter and a space suit (US$110).

Fishing

The waters around New Providence are renowned for their deep-sea **sport fishing**, especially for grouper, snapper, deepwater amberjack, black fin tuna, bonito and blue marlin. Charter services include Born Free Charters (ⓣ242/393-4144, ⓦwww.bornfreefishing.com), Chubasco Fishing Charters (ⓣ242/324-3474, ⓦwww.chubascocharters.com), Hunter's Charters (ⓣ242/364-1546, ⓦwww.huntercharters.com) and Captain Michael Brown with Brown's Charters (ⓣ242/324-2061, ⓦwww.brownscharter.com).

Other outdoor activities

Bahamas Outdoors ⓣ242/362-1574, ⓦwww.bahamasoutdoors.com. Runs cycling, birdwatching and canoe day-trips in New Providence's little-visited interior, with groups limited to six people. Half-day outings US$59 per person, full-day excursions $99.

Dolphin Encounters ⓣ242/363-1003, ⓦwww.dolphinswims.com. Trips to visit and swim with the dolphins at Blue Lagoon Island, leaving four times a day from the Paradise Island ferry terminal. Observation/close encounter (petting)/swim with dolphins US$20/$85/$165 respectively.

Sailing is the Nassau pastime, and sailing boats are available for rent at most marinas and yacht harbours. Rates vary widely depending on the size and type of vessel and whether or not it's crewed; you'll need to reserve in advance and provide proof of experience if you are renting a boat without a crew. Marinas to try include Brown's Boat Basin (ⓣ242/393-3331), East Bay Yacht Basin (ⓣ242/394-1816), Lyford Cay (ⓣ242/362-7499), Nassau Harbour Club (ⓣ242/393-0771), Nassau Yacht Haven (ⓣ242/393-8173) and Atlantis (ⓣ242/363-6068).

Nightlife and performing arts

Generally, **nightlife** in Nassau and on Cable Beach is to be found in the major resort hotels and at a variety of bars and clubs. **Bambu**, a late night venue in downtown Nassau heats up the crowd on its open air, second floor with dancing and ear-piercing house music. There is no phone simply because the music is too loud to hear it ring (Open Tue-Wed & Fri-Sat 12am-5am). On Mackey Street, the **Dundas Centre for the Performing Arts** (☎242/393-3728) provides a year-round schedule of music, theatre and dance, featuring both local and foreign artists. The monthly free tabloid *What's On*, available at all hotels and at many shops and restaurants around town, contains a section on the latest nightlife offerings.

Paradise Island

Across the short span of the Paradise Island Bridge from Nassau's harbour, **PARADISE ISLAND** consists of 686 acres of hard-pack coral and wind-blown oolitic limestone sand. Until the mid-1960s this was Nassau's boat-building centre and supported a population of wild hogs and domesticated pigs. This former "**Hog Island**" also acted as a get-away for rich tourists with places like the posh *Ocean Club*, a 106-room Georgian charmer with a central courtyard garden and tennis courts. Whether or not you will enjoy your visit depends on your definition of "getting away from it all". If your tropical daydreams are full of lounging by the pool, people-watching, gambling the night away in the casino, enjoying some fine dining and escapist activities like waterslides and paragliding, you will have a good time here. If, however, your idea of getting away from it all means getting away from your fellow human beings, you'll find the Paradise Island carnival overwhelming. Still, the island has some quiet backwaters, namely a marvellous **north coast** where pink sands meet the soft turquoise of the Atlantic Ocean.

The island

Most visitors to Paradise Island arrive through **Nassau International Airport** and, as there is no public bus service from the airport, travel by taxi to their Paradise Island hotel (US$30). From downtown Nassau, the island is easily accessible by **water taxi** or **ferry**, which leave frequently from Prince George's Wharf and from the Paradise Island Ferry Dock on the other side (9am–6pm; US$3 each way).

Only four miles long and half a mile wide, Paradise Island tapers to a point on its western end, capped by a small **lighthouse**. The best **beaches** are on the north side facing the Atlantic Ocean, while the south side is dotted with marinas, docks and wharves. At the foot of the Paradise Island Bridge, drivers encounter a huge roundabout, the northern axis of which leads to the **Atlantis** hotel and its casino. North of the hotel is **Cabbage Beach**, two miles of fabulous blush-coloured sand, and further east, separated by a small anvil-shaped headland, is **Snorkeller's Cove Beach**, a striking and often deserted stretch where one can snorkel in peace.

Two main east–west roads cross the island: the first, **Paradise Island Drive**, heads east from the roundabout, passing the *One and Only Ocean Club* and other resorts and restaurants, and leading to the island's eastern end, home to private residences, a few exclusive hotels, the airport and a golf course. The only sights in the vicinity are the **Versailles Gardens** and **The Cloister**, built to resemble medieval ruins by the developers of the *One and Only Ocean Club*. The other street, **Paradise Beach Drive**, running west from the roundabout, heads out to the now-defunct *Club Med* and provides access to **Pirate's Cove Beach**, a secluded, windswept stretch, and **Paradise Beach**, two miles of sand that live up to the name.

Getting around Paradise Island is quite easy and many people simply walk. The **Casino Express**, a shuttle bus making the rounds of the major hotels for US$1, is based at the *Atlantis* hotel. For longer trips or when it is hot out, **taxis** circulate on the main roads and carry passengers across the Paradise Island Bridge for shopping in Nassau.

Accommodation

The sprawling, pricey *Atlantis* resort dominates Paradise Island and continues to gobble up any remaining real estate on the island. Still, there are plenty of other **accommodations** available, ranging from secluded, exclusive luxury resorts to relatively inexpensive, charming guesthouses and comfortable, standard hotel rooms near the beach.

Atlantis Casino Drive ⓣ242/363-3000 or 1-800/321-3000, ⓦwww.atlantis.com. A huge, package-tourist hotel with 3600 rooms including suites, 23 eateries, 22 bars, 20 swimming areas and 3 spectacular aquariums housing 250 species of marine life and 50,000 fish (tours available for outside guests; US$32), with every kind of recreation on offer – a casino, watersports, a putting course and a golf course, fitness centre, tennis courts, library, children's day camp, concerts by big-name performers, a comedy club, a shopping arcade stocked with designer gear and trinkets, and a movie theatre. The whole complex has been developed on the theme of the mythical civilization of Atlantis, and there is little here to suggest that you are in the Bahamas. If you just want to relax by the pool with a cool drink and are in the mood for glitz, decadence and lots of company, you will love it. If not, you might go mad here. ⑨

Chaplin House ⓣ242/363-2918. Located on the peaceful, secluded western tip of Paradise Island (call from the Paradise Island ferry dock for pick-up by water taxi), it is hard to imagine a greater contrast with *Atlantis*. Three homey, casually elegant, sun-bleached white clapboard cottages are set in a green, tree-shaded garden, each with a deep wooden veranda appointed with white wicker chairs for relaxation. Some rooms are directly on the beach, the others within steps of it, and all have a view of the water, including a private stretch of beach. There's no TV or telephones in the rooms (though phone and Internet are available on request in the main house). There are four studio units with kitchenettes ④, a one-bedroom cottage that sleeps four with full kitchen ④ and one oceanfront double room with full galley kitchen ⑤.

Club Land'or Paradise Beach Drive ⓦwww.clublandor.com, ⓣ1-800/552-2839. Overlooking the marina, 72 attractive one-bedroom suites with kitchens and balconies in a three-storey building surrounding a quiet, green courtyard where breakfast and lunch are served by the pool. Guests have access to *Atlantis'* beach, a 5min walk away. A formal dining room and laundry are onsite and a shuttle bus to the grocery store every Fri and Sat. ⑨

Comfort Suites Casino Drive ⓣ242/363-3680 or 1-877/424-6423, ⓦwww.comfortsuites.com. A three-storey pink hotel with 228 junior suites, nicely furnished rooms with a king-size bed, sofa, cable TV and bathroom. There is a pool and spa and Cabbage Beach is nearby. ⑦–⑧

One and Only Ocean Club Paradise Island Drive ⓣ242/363-2501 or 1-888/528-7157, ⓦwww.oneandonlyresorts.com. Once a private estate, now a chic hotel with a casual sophistication, set alongside a gorgeous beach and exquisite gardens, with a great restaurant and jaw-dropping prices. ⑨

Riu Resort Casino Drive ⓣ242/363-3500, ⓦwww.riu.com. Ornate, very grand beachfront hotel with a European feel. A 14-storey building with 379 nicely furnished pink and floral rooms, all with balconies (the best views are on the ocean side on the seventh storey and higher), an assortment of restaurants, including the blue and white-tiled breakfast room, a Japanese glass pagoda on the beach and white linen and silver service in a formal dining room. All-inclusive. ⑨

Sivananda Yoga Retreat West Island ⓣ242/363-2902, ⓦwww.my-yoga.net. Lovely, peaceful retreat for yoga practice and training, with accommodation in basic, comfortable cabins or camping. Located on the secluded western tip of the island on four acres of private beach, shaded by palms and accessible only by water taxi. Daily yoga classes and vegetarian meals included. ③

Eating, drinking and nightlife

Only a handful of **restaurants** on Paradise Island are unconnected to hotels or resorts, and if you stray from your hotel's offering, dining can be a rather expensive endeavour. *Atlantis* seems to have places to eat around every corner: *Atlas Bar and Grill* for hamburgers and ribs, the *Bahamian Club* for steaks and grilled seafood, and a multitude of other options. *Fathoms Seafood Restaurant* at *Atlantis* has glass walls affording diners a blue-lit view of the exotic creatures in the aquarium. All are uniformly expensive (US$15 for a hamburger). With the exception of the *Riu* all-inclusive resort, all hotel restaurants are open to guests staying elsewhere but most require reservations for dinner.

Drinking and **nightlife** hereabouts is largely confined to hotel bars and lounges. Most of these are found at *Atlantis*, which features Las Vegas-style entertainment with a dozen watering holes and a casino.

Dune at the *One and Only Ocean Club* ☎ 242 363 2501. The *place du jour* for expensive gourmet cuisine in a spare, glass-walled dining room with wraparound views of the ocean. The menu is a melange of French and Asian cooking infused with Bahamian seafood. Try the local grouper served in a tomato sauce accompanied by smooth coconut soup and shitake mushroom cakes.

Green Parrot Waterfront Bar and Grill at the Hurricane Hole Marina ☎ 242/363-3663. A pleasant open-air retreat away from the hustle and bustle of Paradise Island holiday-makers, serving drinks and light snacks, including a conch fritters for under US$7.

Johnny Rocket's in Marina Village, ☎ 242/363-3000. A family-friendly 1950s style hamburger joint serving burgers, hot dogs, shakes and salads.

The News Café at the Hurricane Hole Shopping Plaza. Serves inexpensive breakfasts, sandwiches and salads on an outside patio with a view of the road.

Outdoor activities

Paradise Island **beaches** are famous for their swimming and sunbathing. At the far western edge of the island, **Paradise Beach** is nicely secluded, though lined with resort properties that charge swimmers a small fee. More spectacular is three-mile-long **Cabbage Beach**, one of the longest in the Bahamas, a sunny pink stretch that links the inlet at the *Atlantis* to Snorkeller's Cove. Because of the trade winds along the beach, **parasailing** has become very popular here, often resulting in a brilliant display of sails outlined on the glowing horizon. There are all kinds of day-trips and activities on offer, and all operators offer free transportation from your hotel, whether you are staying on Paradise Island or elsewhere. See the boxed list of activities and outfitters on pp.78–79. A visit to the magical **aquarium** at *Atlantis* is not to be missed, although breathtakingly expensive (tours several times daily and the price of admission does not entitle you to access the resort's beachside eateries afterwards).

1.2

Grand Bahama

Fifty-five miles east of Miami, **GRAND BAHAMA** was developed in the 1950s, and sprung up largely as a big playground for North Americans, effectively built from the ground up on a hundred-mile-long flat slab of bleached limestone bristling with towering, thin pine trees and edged by a ribbon of silky white sand and shifting multihued bands of indigo and jade waters. The majority of life happens three miles inland in the town of **Freeport** and her seaside sister suburb of **Lucaya.** Nearly all of the 47,000 inhabitants reside in these two towns, where they are joined each year by almost a half-million visitors.

Having seen the ebb and flow of tourism yet positioned with easy access from Florida and North American cities, Grand Bahama receives a flow of guests ready to enjoy the island's new luxury resorts. With golf courses, a casino, shops and restaurants, Grand Bahama has much to attract those looking for an active outdoor adventure as well as offering a relaxed beach experience with the mile-long **Lucayan** strand and the less built-up **Taino**, **Churchill**, and **Fortune beaches**. To the east of Freeport/Lucaya are the unspoiled and unembellished expanses of **Barbary**, **High Rock** and **Gold Rock** beaches, as well as the **Lucayan National Park**, which includes walking trails, limestone caves and mangrove creeks that can be explored by kayak. An hour east of Freeport are two quiet fishing villages at **McLean's Town** and **Sweeting's Cay**, offering a glimpse of life in the Bahamas before the invention of the super resort. For the curious, **Paradise Cove at Deadman's Reef** west of Freeport is the site of Lucayan archeological excavations as well as great snorkelling right off the beach.

Some history

After the eradication of the native Lucayans at the hands of **Spanish conquistadors**, Grand Bahama remained virtually uninhabited for several hundred years. Bands of **pirates** and **privateers** often lurked at the west end to ambush ships sailing through the Florida Channel and heading to Europe loaded with gold and other treasures, and many Spanish galleons and British men-of-war wrecked on the reefs encircling the island. During the American Civil War, the island experienced a sudden growth spurt when the village of West End briefly became a staging ground for Confederate **blockade-runners** smuggling guns and supplies into the southern states, just as it later became a base for **rum-runners** during Prohibition in the 1920s.

When American businessman **Wallace Groves** acquired the rights to harvest timber on Grand Bahama in 1946, the island was still largely empty and undeveloped. Seemingly overnight the tycoon created a **winter playground** for the rich and famous. By the 1970s and 1980s, however, the novelty and glamour of the once-burgeoning casinos and hotels began to fade, and Freeport and Lucaya were left mainly to waves of college students on spring break and to cruise-ship day-trippers. After some years of decline, Grand Bahama has enjoyed a dramatic **economic rejuvenation** in the last five years, fuelled by a number of giant, five-star resort complexes, helping the island shake off its image as Nassau's poorer, more unsophisticated cousin. Whether this latest tourism boom can translate into long-term stability and prosperity, however, remains to be seen.

Arrival and information

Coming in by plane, you'll land at **Grand Bahama International Airport** (Ⓣ242/352-6020), located on the northern outskirts of Freeport. Although many hotel packages include **free transfers** to and from the airport, you may have to take a **taxi** or **rent a car**. Taxi ranks and car-rental agencies are at the front entrance to the terminal (see "Getting around", overleaf, for more), and the usual taxi fare to Freeport hotels is around US$15, and to Lucaya US$19.

If you arrive by cruise ship, ferry from Florida or on the mailboat from Nassau, you will come ashore at **Freeport Harbour**, five miles west of Freeport proper. Several **cruise ships** call here every week, including the Discovery Cruise Line (Ⓣ1-800-259-1579, Ⓦwww.discoverycruiseline.com). The ticketing office in Freeport is located at the Tanja Maritime Centre (Ⓣ242/352-2328, Ⓦwww.tanjaship.com), on Queen's Highway near the Port Facility.

Freeport/Lucaya has a number of full-service **marinas,** three of which are official ports of entry to the Bahamas. Dockage rates range from 75 cents to US$1.50 per foot/per day, prices may vary. All have electricity and freshwater hookups, as well as showers, bathrooms and laundry facilities (Ⓦwww.boating.bahamas.com).

GRAND BAHAMA

Little Bahama Bank
Memory Rock
Mangrove Cay
Cross Cays
Mud Cut
Water Cay
Wood Cay
Sandy Cay
Indian Cay
North Riding Point
Inn at Old Bahama Bay
West End Airport
West End
Bootle Bay
Buccaneer's Club
Paradise Cove
Deadman's Reef
Holmes Rock
Eight Mile Rock
Florida Channel
QUEEN'S HIGHWAY
Freeport Airport (International)
Freeport
International Bazaar
Hawksbill Creek/Harbour
Lucaya
Old Free Town
Gold Rock Town
LUCA YAN NATIONAL PARK
Gold Rock
PETERSON CAY NATIONAL PARK
Grand Lucaya Waterway
North Riding Pt. Club
Beven's Town
McLean's Town
Deep Water Cay Airport (Private)
Deep Water Cay
Sweetings Cay
Lightbourne Cay
Red Shank Cay
North West Providence Channel
N
0 10 miles

The Grand Bahama Island Tourism Board (PO Box F 40251, Freeport, Grand Bahama Island, Bahamas; ⓦwww.grand-bahama.com) has **information booths** at the airport, the cruise-ship dock and in the Port Lucaya Marketplace, as well as a main office in Freeport's International Bazaar. Copious maps, brochures and activity guides are available in most hotel lobbies, shops and restaurants around town, with free **maps** of Grand Bahama, Freeport and Lucaya available almost everywhere. Finally, the *Grand Bahama Island Snorkelling Map* is on sale at the UNEXSO shop in Lucaya, located next to the *Pelican Bay Hotel* on the harbourfront.

Getting around

Most visitors rarely venture beyond the resorts of Freeport/Lucaya, where the major attractions can easily be reached by foot, bicycle, motor scooter, public bus or organized bus tours. Complimentary **shuttle buses** to beaches, restaurants and the town centres of Freeport and Lucaya are offered by most hotels, and dinner shuttles are also available from some of the restaurants on the outskirts of town.

For those who want to roam further, a variety of transport options are available. **Car rentals** start from around US$80 a day. Options include Avis at the airport (ⓣ242/352-7666), Brad's (ⓣ242/352 7930), Dollar (ⓣ242/352-9325), Hertz (ⓣ242/352-9250) and Thrifty (ⓣ242/352- 9308).

Bahama Buggies (ⓣ242/352-8750, ⓔbuggies@batelnet.bs) rents bright-pink **dune buggies** for US$50 a day plus optional US$15 insurance, while **motorbikes** can be rented at Econo Car & Motorbike Rental on Queen's Highway (ⓣ242/351-6700). Most hotels have bicycles for rent for about US$20 per day with a $50 deposit.

Taxi companies include Freeport Taxi (ⓣ242/352-6666) and the Grand Bahama Taxi Union (ⓣ242/352-7101); any hotel can also call one for you. A **passenger ferry** makes a ten-minute trip on the inland waterway between Port Lucaya and the *Flamingo Bay Hotel* at the *Ritz Bay Resort* on Taino Beach (hourly 8am–11pm; US$3 one-way, $5 round-trip), leaving from the dock behind the *Flamingo Bay Hotel* at Taino Beach and the dock at Port Lucaya next to the *Ferry House Restaurant*.The ferry is not licensed to carry luggage, so only day-packs and handbags are permitted.

Freeport/Lucaya and other nearby communities are well connected by a fleet of privately owned minivan **buses**. To travel between Freeport and Lucaya, catch the bus in front of Freeport's International Bazaar or on the corner of Seahorse Road and Royal Palm Way in Lucaya. Bus stops throughout the city are marked by pink and white shelters. On busy routes, the buses run from early morning until around 7pm and a ride costs a mere dollar anywhere within the city limits, exact change is required. Buses to settlements east and west of Freeport/Lucaya leave regularly from the **main bus stand** in the car park of Winn Dixie Plaza in downtown Freeport.

Freeport and Lucaya

A no-frills town with no true centre or street life – everyone lives in the suburbs – **FREEPORT** is not an especially pleasant place for strolling or sightseeing, though it's easy enough to navigate on foot for visiting shops and restaurants. Freeport's main commercial district is centred on **The Mall**, located between **Ranfurly Circus** – named after the British royal governor who supported the city's development in the 1950s – and **Churchill Square**, about ten blocks north. Surrounding the city centre, The Mall is bound on one side by West Mall Drive, and on the other by **East Mall Drive**, where most of the hotels and restaurants are located. Tourist activity is focused on the south end of **East Mall Drive**, around Ranfurly Circus and the **International Bazaar**, a faded warren of simple shops and cafés marked by red Japanese-style Torii gates. In addition to several serviceable but uninspired restaurants, a straw market and assorted souvenir stands, there are duty-free shops selling jewellery, perfume, Cuban cigars, rum, resort wear and crystal.

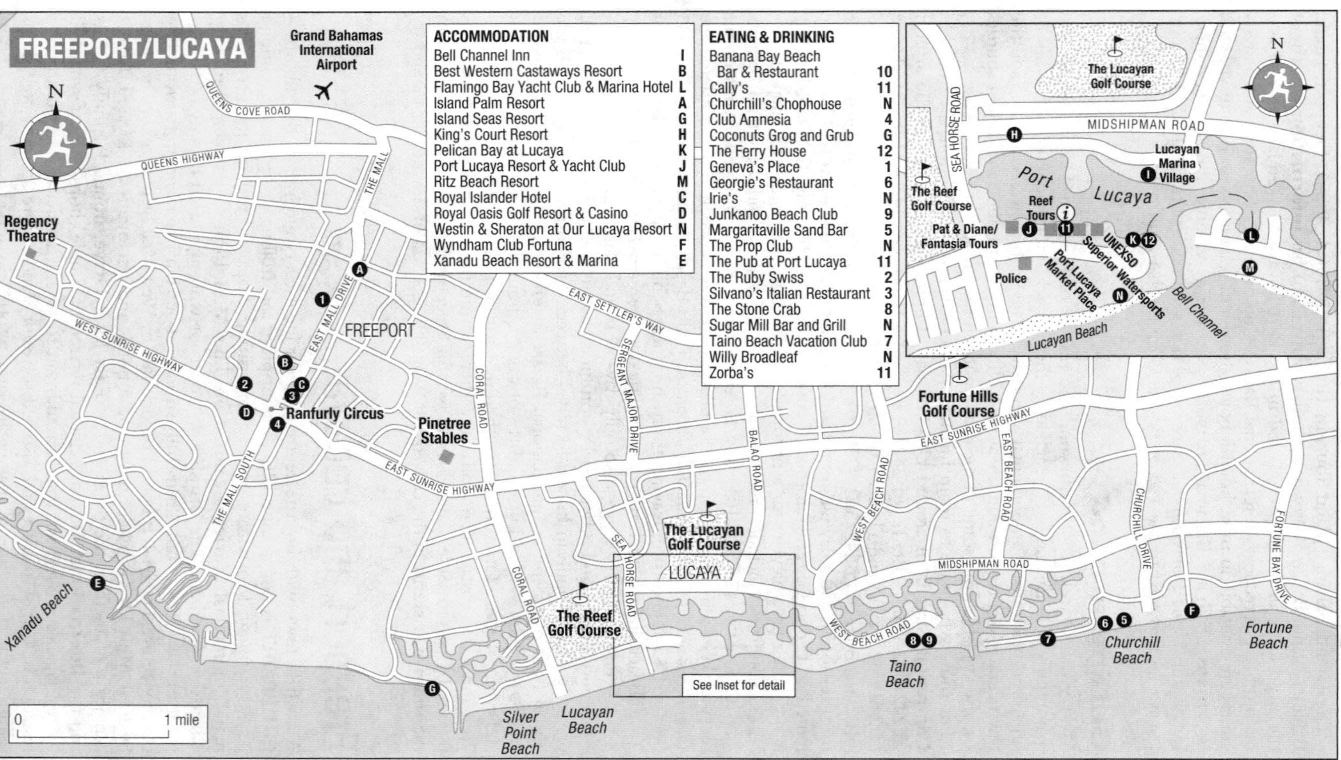
FREEPORT/LUCAYA
ACCOMMODATION
Bell Channel Inn I
Best Western Castaways Resort B
Flamingo Bay Yacht Club & Marina Hotel L
Island Palm Resort A
Island Seas Resort G
King's Court Resort H
Pelican Bay at Lucaya K
Port Lucaya Resort & Yacht Club J
Ritz Beach Resort M
Royal Islander Hotel C
Royal Oasis Golf Resort & Casino D
Westin & Sheraton at Our Lucaya Resort N
Wyndham Club Fortuna F
Xanadu Beach Resort & Marina E
EATING & DRINKING
Banana Bay Beach Bar & Restaurant 10
Cally's 11
Churchill's Chophouse N
Club Amnesia 4
Coconuts Grog and Grub G
The Ferry House 12
Geneva's Place 1
Georgie's Restaurant 6
Irie's N
Junkanoo Beach Club 9
Margaritaville Sand Bar 5
The Prop Club N
The Pub at Port Lucaya 11
The Ruby Swiss 2
Silvano's Italian Restaurant 3
The Stone Crab 8
Sugar Mill Bar and Grill N
Taino Beach Vacation Club 7
Willy Broadleaf N
Zorba's 11
Grand Bahamas International Airport
Queens Cove Road
Queens Highway
The Mall
Regency Theatre
Deadman's Reef & West End
West Sunrise Highway
East Mall Drive
FREEPORT
Ranfurly Circus
The Mall South
Pinetree Stables
East Sunrise Highway
Coral Road
East Settler's Way
Sergeant Major Drive
Balao Road
West Beach Road
East Beach Road
Churchill Drive
Fortune Bay Drive
Midshipman Road
Sea Horse Road
Fortune Hills Golf Course
The Lucayan Golf Course
LUCAYA
The Reef Golf Course
See Inset for detail
Xanadu Beach
Silver Point Beach
Lucayan Beach
Taino Beach
Churchill Beach
Fortune Beach
0 1 mile
N
Port Lucaya
Lucayan Marina Village
Reef Tours
Pat & Diane/ Fantasia Tours
Police
Port Lucaya Market Place
UNEXSO
Superior Watersports
Bell Channel
Lucayan Beach

East from Ranfurly Circus on Sunrise Highway, and south on Seahorse Road, **Port Lucaya** and the beachfront hotels of **LUCAYA** comprise a resort area with a more cheerful atmosphere than Freeport's, with carefully tended lawns and shrubbery, and tidy, candy-coloured shops and houses. A seaside suburb first developed in the 1960s, Lucaya is dominated by the massive *Westin & Sheridan at Our Lucaya Beach and Golf Resort*, fronting **Lucayan Beach**, with two golf courses. Across the street from this resort is **Port Lucaya Marketplace**, a busy, colourful tourist market overlooking the boats at **Port Lucaya Marina**, with shops selling the standard duty-free assortment of goods, open-air stalls displaying straw work and other souvenirs, and several lively restaurants and bars packed with vacationers.

Accommodation

When choosing **accommodation**, keep in mind that Freeport lies several miles inland, and although there are a number of nice hotels in town, it is not an especially attractive place. If you do stay here, you can take one of the complimentary **shuttle buses** to the beach at Xanadu or Lucaya (five and ten minutes away by car, respectively). The main advantage of staying in Freeport is generally lower prices than those found in Lucaya. Note also that Freeport and Lucaya are besieged with college spring-breakers in February and March, and if you don't want to party with them, either choose another time to travel or stay away from the resort strip.

Freeport and beyond

Best Western Castaways Resort East Mall Drive ⓣ242/352-6682 or 1-800/700-ISLANDS, ⓦwww.castaways-resort.com. Centrally located, the 118 attractive rooms and suites overlooking the pool or street offer an excellent budget option and are within a few minutes' walk of several restaurants and the town's main sights, such as they are. A pool, bar and restaurant are onsite, with complimentary beach shuttle service. ❺

Island Palm Resort East Mall Drive ⓣ242/352-6648, ⓦwww.islandpalm.com. A decent budget choice, with bright and cheerful rooms surrounding a courtyard and a small pool. Offers an outdoor bar, a restaurant that becomes a disco at night, motor scooter rentals and complimentary shuttle bus to the beach at Lucaya's *Island Seas Resort*. ❺

Old Bahama Bay at Gin sur Mer ⓣ800/572-5711 or 242/350-6500, ⓦwww.oldbahamabay.com. A secluded luxury resort offering privacy, beautifully appointed rooms, three restaurants, walking and snorkelling trails, tennis, a swimming pool and a sheltered curve of white sandy beach. ❾

Royal Islander Hotel East Mall Drive ⓣ242/351-6000, ⓦwww.royalislanderhotel.com. A small gem with a palm-shaded courtyard, restaurant, Jacuzzi, pool and poolside bar serving light meals. Rooms are nicely appointed, and free transportation to Xanadu Beach is provided. ❻

Xanadu Beach Resort and Marina Sunken Treasure Drive ⓣ242/352-6783, ⓦwww.xanadubeachhotel.com. Overpriced, disorganized monument to 1980s kitsch on a litter-strewn patch of beach. Only worth visiting as a last resort (or if you're a Howard Hughes fan; this was his final residence before moving to Las Vegas, where he died shortly thereafter). ❻

Lucaya and around

Bell Channel Inn Hotel Across the street from Port Lucaya ⓣ242/373-1053, ⓦwww.bellchannellinn.com. Offers pleasant, yet cheap rooms, free beach shuttles and a dive centre. Weekly dive schedules daily at 8am,10am and 1pm. Dive instructions and packages ⓣ242/373-9111. ❹

Flamingo Bay Yacht Club and Marina Hotel Taino Beach ⓣ242/373-5640 or 1-800/824 6623, ⓦwww.flamingobayhotel.com. Part of three Taino Beach Resort & Clubs properties which also includes the *Ritz Beach* and *Taino Beach* time-share condominium complexes and the Pirates of the Bahamas Theme Park. The three-storey, 68-unit *Flamingo Bay Hotel* sits on the edge of the waterway which connects Taino Beach to Port Lucaya, and is three minutes' walk across the parking lot and grounds to a fine white-sand beach. The pastel and white rooms are pleasant enough but a bit worse for wear. There are tennis courts, watersports, minigolf and ping pong to amuse, and the small, palm-shaded pool's waterfall and underwater

grotto bar are a delightful flight of fancy; however, the whole place suffers from poor management and badly trained staff. You could wait hours to be served in the bare-bones dining room or the otherwise inviting beachside patio café. ⑥

Island Seas Resort Silver Point Drive ⓣ242/373-1271, ⓦwww.islandseas.com. Small, isolated beachfront hotel with a pleasant, relaxed atmosphere, featuring one- and two-bedroom suites with kitchens and living quarters, a large swimming pool with rock garden and waterfall, swim-up bar and open-air restaurant. Offers watersports, bicycle rentals and free shuttle bus to the International Bazaar. ⑥

King's Court Resort 4 Kings Rd ⓣ242/373-7133, ⓦwww.kingscourtbahamas.com. Modest but comfortable efficiency units in this family-owned, homey and clean place with a loyal clientele. Kitchenettes, TV, laundry facilities and a small wading pool. ④

Westin & Sheraton at Our Lucaya Beach and Golf Resort Seahorse Rd ⓣ242/373-1333, or in North America 1-877/OURLUCAYA, ⓦwww.westin.com/ourlucaya and ⓦwww.sheraton.com/ourlucaya. Five-star resort to be compared favourably with anything on offer in Nassau or Paradise Island. *Our Lucaya* has 1350 beautifully appointed rooms in three seafront complexes. The *Westin* soars ten storeys in the middle of the resort, offering floor-to-ceiling views of the ocean – ask for an ocean view room. The low-slung *Sheraton* complex caters primarily to families, though the atmosphere can get frantic and very noisy during college spring break (Feb–Mar). The resort's beautifully landscaped grounds include two golf courses, seven acres of white sandy beach, nine swimming pools, four tennis courts, fourteen restaurants and bars, a fitness centre, spa and casino. ⑥–⑦

Pelican Bay at Lucaya Seahorse Rd ⓣ242/373-9550 or 1-800/852-3702, ⓦwww.pelicanbayhotel.com. Small, lovely hotel built around a quiet courtyard with a swimming pool, Jacuzzi and open-air bar serving light meals. Elegant rooms have tile floors, refrigerators and balconies furnished with Adirondack chairs, while the 96 luxury suites have kitchens as well. All guests have access to the beach at *Our Lucaya* resort across the street. ⑦–⑨

Port Lucaya Resort and Yacht Club Seahorse Rd ⓣ242/373-6618 or 1-800/LUCAYA-1, ⓦwww.portlucayaresort.com. Situated across from Lucaya Beach, this place features boat slips outside each of the hotel's 160 rooms, plus balconies overlooking the swimming pool or marina. Also with Jacuzzi and onsite restaurant. Very good value for the money, but occasionally noisy. ④–⑦

Wyndham Club Fortuna Fortune Beach ⓣ242/373-4000 or 877/999-3223, ⓦwww.wyndham.com and www.vivaresorts.com. Done up in bright yellows and greens, with a constantly jammed lobby and music blaring out of every corner, this all-inclusive summer camp for adults and families receives mixed reviews from guests. Some complain of erratic plumbing and tatty rooms, others report having the time of their lives – though the staff get high marks all around for friendly service. Found a couple of miles east of Lucaya on a stretch of powdery white sand at Fortune Beach, the resort has 276 rooms, two restaurants, two discos, tennis courts, a gym, sauna and children's day camp in a complex of twenty-odd buildings spread over 26 acres of nicely landscaped grounds, with a large swimming pool next to the beach. Organized activities include diving, snorkelling and other watersports, day-trips around the island, dance classes, theme parties and live entertainment nightly. You've got to like company to enjoy it here. ⑥–⑦

Eating and drinking

In general, hotel **restaurants** have most of the area's best food options. **Port Lucaya Marketplace** has a dozen or more moderately priced places to eat, most with pleasant outdoor seating and a view of the marina, people passing by and the occasional outdoor entertainment in Count Basie Square in the centre of the Marketplace. There are a few popular local **cafés**, but most residents prefer take-away – traditional dishes or fast food – to dining out. Also worth noting are the **beach bars** and restaurants along Taino Beach and Churchill Beach. Dining in Freeport/Lucaya is predictably expensive, though there are a few cheap eateries around.

On the beaches just east of Freeport/Lucaya are some cheerful and relaxed beach bars and restaurants that make a good change of pace. Note that the restaurants on **Taino Beach** listed below are not within walking distance of the ferry dock – you will need to drive to reach all of them; some establishments offer complimentary transportation.

Freeport/Lucaya resorts

Cally's Port Lucaya Marketplace ☎242/373-8657. Serving tasty and affordable Greek and Bahamian dishes, including Greek salad and savoury grilled vegetable wraps. Cheerful and relaxed atmosphere with indoor and outdoor seating on the wooden veranda.
Churchill's Chophouse *Our Lucaya* resort., ☎242/373-1333 An elegant glass-and-mahogany dining room open for dinner only, serving steak, lobster and other seafood dishes with a fine selection of vintage wines. Closed Sun and Mon.
The Ferry House on the waterfront at Port Lucaya ☎242/373-1595. Featuring an imaginative menu with dishes like grouper braised in Nassau Royale sauce and shrimp with a ginger glaze, as well as staples like chicken and pasta. Elegant dining room is sunny and inviting at breakfast, and candlelit with harbour views at dinner.
Geneva's Place East Mall Drive, at Kipling ☎242/352-5085. Popular and lively local eatery serving Bahamian and American food at reasonable prices.
Irie's behind the *Westin, Our Lucaya* resort ☎242/373-1333. A cosy replica of a colonial-Caribbean house featuring Cuban, Jamaican, Puerto Rican and Haitian cuisine, with traditional (though pricey) stews and seafood dishes like snapper steamed in banana leaf and served with plantains and voodoo fritters. Closed Wed.
The Prop Club on the beach at the *Sheraton, Our Lucaya* resort. A casual restaurant and sports bar decked out like an aircraft hanger. Inexpensive menu features pizza margherita, chicken, ribs and tropical drinks. Pool table and nightly music and dancing.
The Pub at Port Lucaya outside at Count Basie Square ☎242/373-8450. A busy, outdoor patio restaurant serving a moderately priced international menu.
Silvano's Italian Restaurant Ranfurly Circle, ☎242/352-5111. Inexpensive Mediterranean-based menu and decor, with a rough stone floor and sunny yellow walls, plus three additional tables on an terrazzo outside, though traffic somewhat spoils the ambience. Be sure to save some room for ice cream from **Silvano's Ice Cream Parlour** next door, which also serves breakfast, pastries and sandwiches.
Willy Broadleaf on the ground floor of the *Westin, Our Lucaya* resort. ☎242/373-1333. A series of themed dining rooms offering breakfast, lunch and dinner buffets, with eclectic Middle Eastern and Indian dishes, Mexican favourites, fresh pasta, crepes and sweets like baklava and Bahamian guava duff, a traditional island dessert.
Zorba's Port Lucaya Marketplace ☎242/373-6137. Tasty and inexpensive Greek favourites like souvlaki, pitta wraps and salads, with a no-frills seating area.

Taino, Churchill and Fortune beaches

Banana Bay Beach Bar and Restaurant on Fortune Beach. A delightful, moderately priced spot for breakfast or lunch, in a whimsically painted turquoise, pink and blue café with palm tree cut-outs, tropical fish tank and wall murals – or even better, on the broad wooden deck overlooking a lovely beach. Imaginatively presented lunch plates include conch burgers, cheese quesadillas, crab cakes, sandwiches and mouth watering desserts. Caters primarily to day-trippers off cruise ships, but worth the short drive out from Freeport.
Junkanoo Beach Club (formerly *Tranquillity Shores*) on Taino Beach ☎242/373-3133. A huge, two-storey, buoy-strung timber restaurant and beach bar, great for a day or night out. Also has hammocks, beach loungers and a full range of watersports.
Margaritaville Sand Bar on Churchill Beach, off Midshipman Rd ☎242/373-4525. The interior of this small, candy-striped bar is cool and dark, with a sand floor and coloured lights. You can have burgers, sandwiches, conch fritters and occasionally wild boar at picnic tables under a thatch roof overlooking the beach, and play some volleyball. The bar hosts a bonfire on the beach every Tuesday night, with a steak or fish dinner, dancing contests and a DJ. Transportation from Freeport/Lucaya available daily for diners.
The Stoned Crab on Taino Beach next to *Junkanoo Beach Club* ☎242/373-1442. An upscale seafood restaurant with a relaxed, tastefully designed dining room overlooking the beach; you'll know you've found it by its distinctive double pyramid roof. Serving seafood platters, steak, chicken and pasta dishes. Dinner only (US$22-$45).

Nightlife and entertainment

Freeport/Lucaya has no shortage of things to do **after dark**. A popular way to spend the evening is on one of the numerous **sunset dinner** or **booze cruises** leaving nightly from Port Lucaya. Otherwise, you can usually find a beachside **bonfire** and **fish fry** almost any night of the week at one of the major hotels or restaurants.

Hit the jackpot at Isle of Capri Casino at Our Lucaya (Ⓦwww.isleofcapricasino.com) or quench your thirst at one of several lively **bars** in the Port Lucaya Marketplace, patronized mainly by beach bums and yacht cruisers. In Freeport, locals and visitors mix on the dance floor at *Club 2000* (Thurs–Sun 10pm–3am; Ⓣ242/352-8866) and at *Amnesia* (Ⓣ242/351-CLUB), both on East Mall Drive near the International Bazaar. For a change, there are two **cinemas** on East Mall Drive with several daily showings: Columbus Theatres (Ⓣ242/352-7478) and RND Cinemas (Ⓣ242/394-FILM). Two local **amateur drama** societies put on plays throughout the year, the Freeport Player's Guild and the Regency Theatre (both at Ⓣ242/352-5533), located in the same theatre on Regency Boulevard, just west of the Ruby Golf Course.

The rest of the island

The two main attractions outside Freeport – Lucayan National Park and Paradise Cove – lie on opposites sides of the town. Straddling the Queen's Highway 25 miles to the east, **Lucayan National Park** (daily 9am–4pm; US$3; Ⓣ242/352-5438) encompasses forty acres of mixed forest, limestone caverns and sinkholes, mangrove creeks, a spectacular beach and several nature trails all less than a mile long. A trail from the car park on the north side of the highway leads to a six-mile-long **underwater cave system**, one of the world's longest. One of them, Ben's Cave, is named after Grand Bahamian Ben Rose, the first diver to explore the entire cave system. Others have died trying to repeat this feat, but certified divers may explore the underwater stalactites and stalagmites of the tunnels with a permit obtainable from the Bahamas National Trust (Ⓣ242/359-1821, Ⓔexumapark@aol.com); UNEXSO also offers guided expeditions (see box opposite). The opening of Ben's Cave, accessible by a steep staircase, is home to a large colony of bats and is closed to visitors in the summer months when they nurse their young. Nearby, in

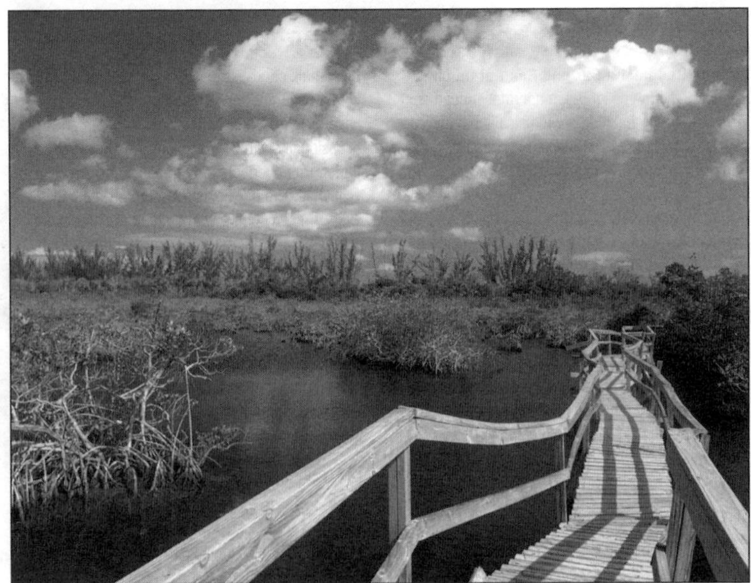

▲ Lucayan National Park

Grand Bahama tours and outdoor activities

Boat excursions

Pat and Diane/Fantasia Tours booth at *Port Lucaya* resort (Ⓣ242/373-8681, Ⓦwww.snorkelingbahamas.com) organizes an array of daily boat cruises and aquatic fun for all ages and all price ranges. **Reef Tours** at Port Lucaya Marketplace (Ⓣ242/373-5880, Ⓦwww.bahamasvacationguide.com/reeftours) offers several daily tours aboard a glass-bottomed boat, lasting about an hour and costing US$35, kids $20.

Smiling Pat's Adventures (Ⓣ242/533-2946, Ⓦwww.smilingpat.com) provides different outings every day, from all-day boat excursions to Abaco and Peterson Cay National Park to beach-hopping trips and spear-fishing expeditions. Prices starting at US$25.

Diving and snorkelling

East End Adventures Ⓣ242/373-6662, Ⓔeastendsafari@hotmail.com. A quality outfitter offering a seven-hour "Blue Hole Snorkelling Safari", which explores the marine life of blue holes off the eastern end of Grand Bahama, followed by a barbecue lunch on a deserted cay. Group size is limited to eight. Adults US$85, kids $35.

Paradise Cove at Deadman's Reef Ⓣ242/349-2677, Ⓦwww.deadmansreef.com. Twenty minutes' drive west of Freeport on a secluded beach, a place to snorkel over lush reefs, float in a glass-bottomed kayak or relax on the sand. A snack bar and grill serves tasty beach food as well. Includes transport to and from your hotel, lunch and equipment usage. US$35, kids $23.

Superior Watersports Pork Lucaya Marketplace Ⓣ242/373-7863, Ⓦwww.superiorwatersports.com. Uses a large motorized catamaran for hour-long snorkelling trips along Treasure Reef, departing four times daily. Another catamaran departs daily at 11am for a five-hour "Robinson Crusoe Beach Party", including 90 minutes of snorkelling followed by a full buffet lunch and volleyball on a deserted beach. US$59, kids $39.

Underwater Explorer's Society (UNEXSO) based at Port Lucaya Ⓣ242/373-1244 or 1-800/992-DIVE in the US, Ⓦwww.unexso.com. Well-established operation with equipment rental, courses and day or night snorkelling and diving trips, including swimming with dolphins and sharks, as well as visits to wrecks, reefs and blue holes. One/two-tank dives US$49/$89; night dive $70; dive with sharks $89; dive with dolphins $169.

Other outdoor activities

The Dolphin Experience ticket booth at UNEXSO Ⓣ242/373-1244 or 1-800-992-DIVE, Ⓦwww.dolphinexperience.com. Departing from the UNEXSO dock, a twenty-minute boat ride leads to Sanctuary Bay, where the dolphins live in a quiet cove. Three experiences are offered: petting dolphins, swimming with them and spending the day assisting their keepers. One of the most popular tourist activities on Grand Bahamas. Swim with dolphins US$169; dolphin encounter (pet a dolphin) $75 adult, $50 for children.

East End Adventures Ⓣ242/373-6662. Offers excellent all-day excursions to the unspoiled eastern tip of the island, visiting fishing villages, bumping along bush trails and sampling wild fruit before arriving at Sweeting's Cay for a conch-cracking demonstration. Final destination is the pristine beaches of Lightbourne Cay for picnic lunch, sunbathing and snorkelling.

Kayak Nature Tours Ⓣ242/373-2485 or 1-800/440-4542, Ⓦwww.grandbahamanaturetours.com. Runs enjoyable paddling excursions, including day-trips in Lucayan National Park, kayaking/snorkelling tours to Peterson Cay National Park (US$79). Tour group sizes are limited and tours include transport and picnic lunches.

Pinetree Stables Ⓣ242/373-3600, Ⓦwww.pinetree-stables.com. Offers a pleasant, two-hour guided trail ride through a pine forest and along the beach. Twice daily rides, no experience necessary. US$85, reservations required, minimum age 8 years old.

Burial Mound Cave, another limestone sinkhole, divers discovered the skeletons of four indigenous Lucayans.

Heading west from Freeport along Queen's Highway, a sign on the left marks the turn-off to **Paradise Cove** at **Deadman's Reef** (Ⓣ242/349-2677, Ⓦwww.deadmansreef.com), and a beautiful stretch of white sandy beach backed by tall grass and bush, with great snorkelling around the teeming reef just offshore. Deadman's Reef is the site of an important archeological find – the remains of a Lucayan settlement from the twelfth or thirteenth century that was discovered in 1996. Open daily 10am–Sunset.

1.3

The Abacos

The northernmost and most affluent of the Out Islands are **The Abacos.** Stretching for 130 miles, though the islands themselves are rarely more than four miles wide at any point, this shining-necklace islands chain is barely 100 miles north of Nassau and 175 miles east of Miami, making its fresh Colonial beach town experience within convenient reach. Resettled Americans and Canadians make up a significant proportion of the 13,000 residents and with visitors during the high season, Bahamians appear outnumbered.

Surrounded by charming cays and joined by a causeway, **Little Abaco** and **Great Abaco** serve as the main hub and are a top boating and sailing destination. The nexus of activity in the archipelago is **Marsh Harbour** (population 4000), located halfway down the Atlantic coast of Great Abaco. Running parallel to this landmass is a chain of approximately 25 cays that constitute a 200-mile-long barrier and reef system enticing boaters, divers and other holiday-makers to the many hidden coves and beaches. Four settled cays of particular importance to vacationers are **Elbow Cay**, **Green Turtle Cay**, **Guana Cay** and **Man O' War Cay**, which are easily accessed by short ferry ride. **Hope Town** on Elbow Cay and **New Plymouth** on Green Turtle Cay are lovingly preserved historic settlements with tidy, freshly painted eighteenth- and nineteenth-century wooden cottages lining their narrow lanes, most of which are now vacation rentals. The smaller fishing villages and long stretches of beach on **Man O' War Cay** and **Guana Cay** also make enjoyable destinations. South of Marsh Harbour on Great Abaco, the spectacular unbroken sandy coastline from **Cherokee Sound** to **Casaurina Point** offers pleasing vistas, solitude and a couple of spots for beachfront refreshment. At the southern tip of Abaco, **Sandy Point** is the jump-off point for serious bonefishers. North of Marsh Harbour, the isolated but bustling resort community at **Treasure Cay** boasts a long stretch of pale sandy beach.

The pine-covered Abacos have a temperate-to-subtropical **climate**, with cool winters and mild, windy summers, and an average yearly rainfall of 50–60 inches. In addition to threading their way through the cays, sailors may find ideal **yachting** in the shallows of the western coast, a fascinating landscape of mangrove islands, rocks and cays known collectively as **The Marls**. On the east side, **fringing reefs** and several **deep canyons** offer excellent **diving and snorkelling**.

Some history

The Spanish slave trade obliterated the original Lucayan population of the Abacos. After a few hundred years of solitude, the archipelago was first settled in 1783 when a few hundred **Loyalist emigrants** from New York, the Carolinas and Florida fled the fallout of the American Revolution. Some of these original settlers were black Americans who arrived near present-day Treasure Cay, founding the village of Carleton, named after the Governor of British North America, Guy Carleton.

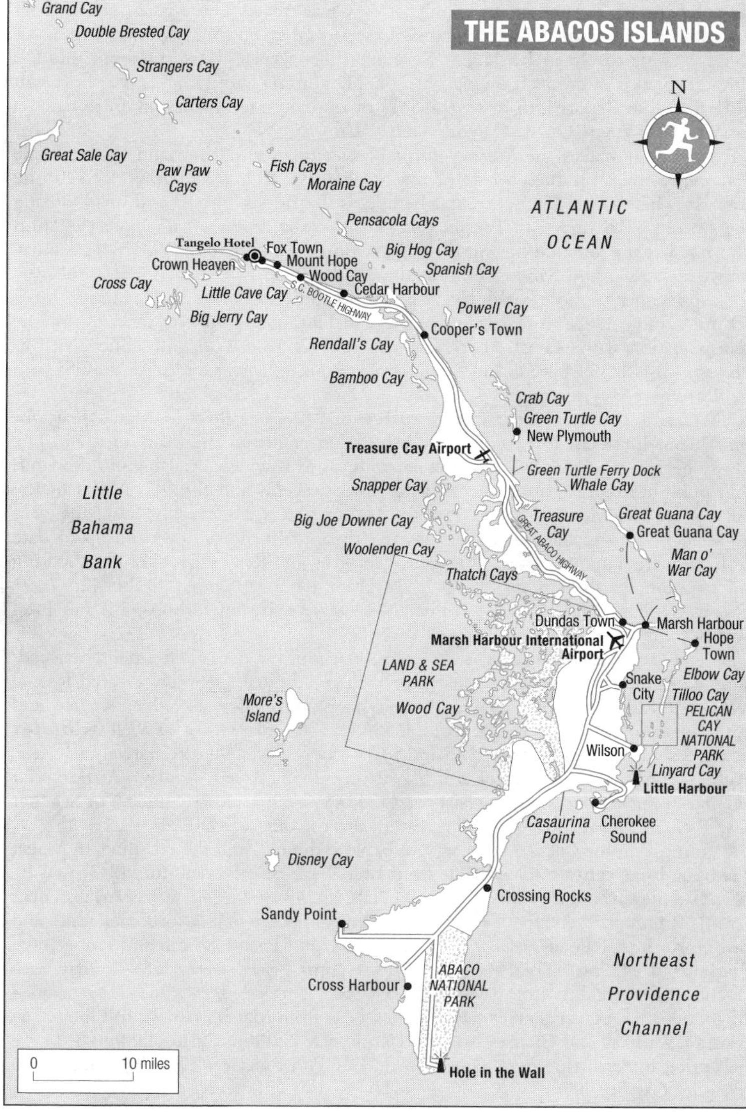

The Loyalists eventually colonized the areas around Marsh Harbour and the cays offshore, bringing with them their New England **architecture** of clapboard houses, steeply pitched roofs and tiny gardens surrounded by picket fences. This **Abaco style** survives today alongside the island's bright plantings of oleander, hibiscus and bougainvillea. A grand old tradition of boat building, carried on by the descendants of the original Loyalist settlers, is a further hallmark of the Abacos' unique heritage.

Arrival, information and getting around

The main entry point for most visitors to the Abacos is **Marsh Harbour International Airport**, located at the midpoint of Great Abaco. There is also an **airport** located near **Treasure Cay** that primarily serves guests staying at the cay's resort or those heading to Green Turtle Cay. Several airlines service Marsh Harbour, and the tiny terminal is often overflowing with people coming and going. It is a short **cab ride** from the airport into town (US$12) or on to the ferry dock ($15) to catch a ferry to Hopetown, Guana Cay or Man O'War Cay.

A **mailboat** makes the journey from Nassau to Great Abaco and Green Turtle Cay every week on Tuesdays, returning on Fridays (ⓣ242/393-1064, US$40 one way). It is best to call for a current schedule, as the ride is 7 hours and varies during the seasons. Bahamas Fast Ferries (ⓣ242/323-2166, ⓦwww.bahamasferries.com) also has a **ferry service** during the high season on Wednesday, Friday and Sunday between Nassau and Sandy Point, at the southern tip of Abaco (US$60 one-way for a passenger without a vehicle; 3 hours 45 minutes). Note that Sandy Point is 50 miles and a US$135 taxi ride from Marsh Harbour. Two **bus** services provide transportation daily: Great Abaco Express (ⓣ242/646-7072) and Enovah's Bus Service (ⓣ242/559-8465). They stop at a number of towns and it's only US$1 no matter where you're going.

There is a **tourist information office** (ⓣ242/367-3067) in Marsh Harbour on Queen Elizabeth Drive, in a small shopping centre in the heart of town. The glossy periodical *Abaco Life* (ⓦwww.abacolife.com) is widely available in the islands and publishes regular features on island history, events and the like. **Maps** of the Abacos are also widely available from tourism operators. The weekly newspaper, *The Abaconian* (ⓦwww.abaconian.com), is a good source for local news and up-to-date listings for restaurants, hotels, emergency services and ferry schedules. For yachting information, see the *Cruising Guide to the Abacos* by Steve Dodge (ⓣ386/423-7880, ⓦwww.wspress.com). Abaco Cruisers Net (ⓦwww.barometerbob.com) has local weather and yachting news.

Several **car rental agencies** are in Marsh Harbour but demand frequently exceeds supply and reservations should be made well in advance. Centrally located Rental Wheels (ⓣ242/367-4643, ⓦwww.rentalwheels.com) offers excellent service and well-maintained cars and vans from US$65/$300 a day/week as well as **motor scooters** and **bicycles** for US$45 and $10 a day, respectively. Alternatively, try A&P Auto Rentals (Don McKay Blvd; ⓣ242/367-2655, closed Sunday), Airport Car Rentals (opposite Treasure Cay Airport, ⓣ242/365-8961, closed Sunday) or Sea Star Car Rentals (ⓣ242/367-4887, ⓦwww.go-abacos.com/seastar).

Renting a motorboat is a great way to explore the cays and the coastline. In Marsh Harbour, **boat rentals** are available from Blue Wave Boat Rentals (ⓣ242/367-3910, ⓦwww.bluewaverentals.com), Rich's Rentals (ⓣ242/367-2742, ⓦwww.richsrentals.com), Rainbow Rentals (ⓣ242/367-2742, ⓔrainbowrentals@abacoinet.com) and Sea Horse Boat Rentals at Boat Harbour Marina in Marsh Harbour and Hope Town Harbour (ⓣ242/367-2513, ⓦwww.sea-horse.com). Prices start at US$45 a day, with discounts for rentals by the week. Albury's Ferry Service (ⓣ242/367-3147 or 367-0290) operates regular **ferries** several times a day from Marsh Harbour to Elbow Cay, Man O'War Cay and Guana Cay (US$15 one way, $20 round trip, children 6–11 are half price, under 6 ride free). Green Turtle Cay Ferry services New Plymouth from Treasure Cay (see p.98).

Marsh Harbour and around

Founded in 1784 by Loyalists, **MARSH HARBOUR** started life as a **logging**, **sponging** and "**wrecking**" town, with boat building as an auxiliary industry. These days, **tourism** is the town's major source of income, and its marinas are filled with yachts and surrounded by swanky holiday villas. Tidy and functional rather than picturesque, the town has a pleasant holiday atmosphere and offers most of the services you might require, including a post office, bookshop, grocery stores, gift and clothing shops, several marinas and tour operators for diving, fishing and kayaking. Several pleasant waterfront **bars** and **restaurants** offer live music a few nights a week. With the exception of the swath of beach in front of the *Abaco Beach Resort*, there is **no local beach**, but the town makes an ideal base from which to explore the surrounding cays and the rest of Abaco, where white sand and turquoise water are in abundant supply.

Accommodation

Abaco Beach Resort and Boat Harbour ⓣ1-800/468-4799 or 242/367-2158, ⓦwww.abacoresort.com. On a strip of beach a short walk from the town centre, this is a sprawling peach stucco complex with eighty comfortably appointed (though overpriced) oceanfront rooms, six two-bedroom cottages and a large marina, along with pool, swim-up bar, a casual restaurant, tennis courts, beach volleyball, kayaks and snorkelling and diving trips arranged. 9

Conch Inn Marina and Hotel ⓣ1-242/367-4000, ⓦwww.conchinn.com. Located on Bay St in the centre of town facing the harbour, nine rooms renovated and newly furnished following a thorough washdown from Hurricanes Jeanne and Frances in 2004. Each with room comes with fridge, coffee-maker, TV, a/c and use of the swimming pool. There is a small, plain restaurant and a pleasant outdoor bar serving light food and heavy drinks. Hotel marina has 75 slips and an excellent dive shop. 6

Lofty Fig Villas ⓣ242/367-2681, ⓣ800/688-452, ⓦwww.loftyfig.com. Centrally located on Bay St, across from the *Conch Inn*, six charming, tastefully decorated, quiet, private and very well-kept one-bedroom efficiency units grouped around a small kidney-shaped swimming pool. Set in grounds dotted with trees and flowers, each villa has its own screened-in porch, kitchen and television, with a barbecue out by the pool. 5

Pelican Beach Villas Pelican Shores Rd ⓣ1-877/362-3180 or 242/367-3600. On a secluded peninsula a couple of miles from the centre of town, six cute cotton candy-coloured two-bedroom cottages fronting a small scallop of beach facing the open sea. Each has a kitchen, TV and rattan furniture, with docking for boats, a small swimming pool, showers and laundry facilities. Can be windy, but serene. 5–8

Eating and drinking

Marsh Harbour **eateries** are for the most part casual and pleasant, but a bit pricey, catering primarily to tourists with menus heavy on seafood and tropical cocktails. Bahamian home-style cooking is served up at several reasonably priced restaurants that draw a local crowd. Most places are situated within easy walking distance of one another along Bay Street, the main road which runs along the waterfront. For **picnic provisions** and self-catering, head to *Da Best Bakery*, locally renowned for their oatmeal raisin cookies. Solomon's, in the big blue building in the centre of town, is a well-stocked **grocery store**, and Bahamas Family Markets, near the traffic light, offers fresh produce, baked goods, Internet access and local news.

The Conch Inn Bay St ⓣ242/367-4000. Popular for its fabulous breakfasts of jumbo French toast and great dinners of calypso grouper and stuffed jalapeños, plus fine gumbos and stews. Reservations recommended for dinner.

Hummingbird Restaurant and Bar in Memorial Plaza on Queen Elizabeth Drive. A dark and cool refuge from the heat, recommended for delicious, inexpensive Bahamian home-cooking and a grouper burger marinated in jalapeño pepper sauce and olive oil. Open only for breakfast and lunch during the week, with dinner served on weekends.

Jaime's Bay St. This popular, inexpensive local restaurant has home-cooked Bahamian favourites and good ice cream. The fried chicken is highly recommended.

Java Coffee Along the main road heading towards the ferry dock, this is a great place to start your day, with fresh coffee and pastries, comfy sofas and a patio where you can watch everyone else heading to work.

The Jib Room at the Marsh Harbour Marina, ⓣ242/367-2700, ⓦwww.jibroom.com. Come here for reasonably priced seafood, burgers, "drunken chicken" (chicken marinated in sherry) and salads at picnic tables indoors and outside facing the marina. Open Wed–Sat 11.30am–2.30pm and Wed & Sat evening for a BBQ dinner, with music and dancing on Sat night.

Mangoes on the waterfront in downtown Marsh Harbour ⓣ242/367-2957, ⓦwww.mangoesabaco.com. This white-linen service restaurant has a menu featuring pork tenderloin with mango sauce, grilled chicken with garlic and ginger, veal piccata, cracked conch and ribs, as well as home-made desserts such as coconut tart and pineapple sorbet. Live entertainment on weekends. Dinner only.

Sapodilly's Lookout and Bar on Bay St. ⓣ242/367-3498, A local hot spot, with tables on a rainbow-painted wooden deck, comfy wicker chairs and an open-air bar. The moderately priced menu features sandwiches and burgers served with Bahamian sides like rice and peas, coleslaw and plantains, as well as salads and seafood dishes. Live music Friday nights.

Wally's Bay St ⓣ242/367-2074. In a two-storey pink colonial house facing the water, elegant dining on a pleasant covered patio furnished with white wicker furniture and chintz tablecloths, with extra seating inside. The menu features burgers and conch salad for lunch, dinners with grilled lamb chops and cracked conch, and tropical libations. Open for lunch and dinner Tues–Sat, live music Wed and Sat evenings.

Outdoor activities

Dive Abaco, whose office is at the *Conch Inn* (ⓣ242/367-5871 or in the US 1-800/247-5338, ⓦwww.diveabaco.com) offers a full slate of **snorkelling** and **diving** trips at two dozen sites around Abaco. Lofty Fig can arrange dive or snorkel packages for you (ⓔloftyfig@diveabaco.com, ⓣ800/247-5338). Guided **fishing** can be arranged through J.R. Albury (on Abaco ⓣ242/366-3058 or in the US 1-800/800-3949, ⓦwww.bonefishabaco.com).

South of Marsh Harbour

The highway heading south from Marsh Harbour is a straight shot barrelling through a stretch of pine forest and scrub until you reach the turn-off to **Cherokee Sound** and **Little Harbour**, 13.5 miles south of Marsh Harbour. Follow the signs to *Pete's Pub* in Little Harbour, about eight miles in from the highway, or to the *Sand Bar* (erratic hours; call ⓣ242/366-2210 before you go) in Cherokee Sound a few miles further along the same road; both are fun and popular destinations for lunch or a sunset on the beach.

Back on the highway heading south, 17.5 miles south of Marsh Harbour is the turn-off to the settlement of **Casaurina Point**, where a few bungalows front an absolutely spectacular curve of white-sand beach and turquoise water that runs uninterrupted all the way back to Cherokee Sound. There are no accommodations or other services here, but it is nice for a swim and a picnic.

Continuing south on the highway, you pass **Abaco National Park**, a nature preserve crisscrossed by overgrown logging roads. Note that taking a rental car on these rough tracks is prohibited. Abaco Outback runs birdwatching and cycling tours in this area out of Marsh Harbour (see "Outdoor activities", above).

Fifty miles south of Marsh Harbour the highway and the island ends at **Sandy Point**, a quiet fishing settlement overlooking Disney Island, formerly Gorda Cay, where cruise ship passengers are let out to play. There is a marine mammal research centre here as well as some good bonefishing.

North of Marsh Harbour

The highway running north from Marsh Harbour passes a few small roadside settlements before reaching **Treasure Cay**, 24 miles north of Marsh Harbour. Not really a cay but rather a slender peninsula, Treasure Cay is an isolated and self-contained resort community, with its own shops, post office, bank, health clinic, restaurants and marina, plus a miles-long stretch of beach.

The centre of activity is the *Treasure Cay Beach Hotel Resort and Marina* (ⓣ242/365-8801 or 1-800/327-1584, ⓦwww.treasurecay.com; ❻), offering several hundred comfortable if uninspired and slightly shabby rooms, suites, condos and small, self-catering villas, with golf, tennis and dive packages. This is the area's centre of activity and the place is usually thronged with fun-seekers and spring-breakers – if you are looking for privacy, it is probably not for you. A more low-key local option is the *Bahama Beach Club* (ⓣ242/365-8501, 800/284-0382, ⓦwww.bahamabeachclub.com; ❾), which has condos with two or three bedrooms and ocean views.

Continuing northwards, the S.C. Bootle Highway cuts through **Little Abaco,** passing a number of quiet beaches while the coastline gradually grows rockier and the forest denser. By the time you pass **Cedar Harbour**, the shores are overtaken by rock-shallows and finally heavy mangroves. *Nettie's Snack Bar* at Cedar Harbour is a good spot for conch and fried fish.

The end of the line is tiny **Crown Haven**, a quiet tumbledown village with a wooden wharf and a struggling lobster business. A **ferry** to Grand Bahama leaves from here daily at 7am and 2.30pm (Abaco ⓣ242/365-2356; fare US$40 one-way, children $20), with a bus connection into Freeport, where you can rent a car.

Elbow Cay and Hope Town

Five-mile long **Elbow Cay** is home to six hundred residents, many of whom are descendants of Loyalist settlers. **HOPE TOWN**, the only village, is located at the cay's northern end, traversed by two narrow lanes known as **Back Street** and **Bay Street** – which locals call "Up Along" and "Down Along". The village is a compact and picturesque collection of a hundred tightly packed and brightly painted clapboard houses, many surrounded by white picket fences and flower gardens; most have been converted into holiday rentals.

Local attractions include the **Elbow Cay Lighthouse**, a candy-striped pole visible for miles (but unapproachable by foot from the centre of the village – you have to get the ferry to drop you here), and the **Wyannie Malone Museum** (Mon–Sat 10am–3pm; US$3 per person or $5 per family but hours are subject to volunteer availability, ⓦwww.hopetownmuseum.com), which houses an eclectic collection of island memorabilia. Hope Town also serves as a good base for visits to the natural sanctuaries of the **Pelican Cay Land and Sea Park** and **Sandy Cay National Sea Park** nearby. Island Marine Boat Rentals rents Boston Whaler powerboats (ⓣ242/366-0282, ⓦwww.islandmarine.com) for those wishing to explore the surrounding waters. Froggies Out Island Adventures (ⓣ242/366-0431, ⓦwww.froggiesabaco.com offers **scuba**, **snorkelling**, picnicking and **boating excursions**.

Practicalities

Many visitors **arrive** on Elbow Cay on their own sailboats. For others, there is regular **ferry** service from Marsh Harbour to Hope Town (Albury's Ferry ⓣ242/367-0290; US$20 round-trip). As there are few cars on the island, visitors and residents must walk or take **golf carts**; Island Cart Rentals (ⓣ242/366-0448, ⓦwww.islandcartrentals.com) rents them for US$45/$270a day/week.

Elbow Cay has several tropical **accommodation** options. Straddling both shores on a secluded spot south of Hope Town, the *Abaco Inn*, on Bay St (ⓣ242/366-0133,

Ⓦwww.abacoinn.com; ④–⑥), has fourteen rooms and eight one-bedroom villas with kitchenettes, as well as a pool, watersports and an elegant dining room. In the middle of the village, overlooking the harbour and the town, *Hope Town Harbour Lodge and Marina* (Ⓣ242/366-0095 or 1-866/611-9791; ⑥) offers twenty tightly set but cosy rooms, watersports, a pool with a popular outdoor bar and a nice restaurant. On the southern tip of the island, *Sea Spray Resort and Marina* (Ⓣ242/366-0065, Ⓦwww.seasprayrersort.com; ⑥–⑨) has brightly painted one-bedroom villas perched on a bluff overlooking the sea, each with kitchen, a/c, satellite television and broad wooden verandas complete with hammocks, as well as a good dockside restaurant, a seafront pool, the *Garbonzo Reef Bar* and access to watersports. *Hopetown Hideaways* (Ⓣ242/366-0224, Ⓦwww.hopetown.com; ⑥) offers dozens of lovely **cottage** and **beach house rentals** all over the island starting at US$1000 a week for a one-bedroom cottage.

All the resorts have decent **restaurants** and **pool bars**, but one of the most popular local eateries is *Cap'n Jack's* on the water near the harbour (Ⓣ242/366-0247). Serving three meals a day and open late for drinks, the restaurant is locally famous for its conch burger and macaroni cheese, with live music on Wednesday and Friday nights. *The Harbour's Edge*, is a popular spot for a drink and a bite (Ⓣ242/366-0087; closed Tues).

Green Turtle Cay

Eight miles north of Treasure Cay, **Green Turtle Cay** is the most popular and well visited of the Loyalist Cays, with a striking array of bays, inlets and sounds and one very well-preserved New England-style fishing village, **NEW PLYMOUTH**. While simply wandering the town's streets is enjoyable, you can also check out the **Albert Lowe Museum** (Ⓣ242/367-4094), housed in a 200-year-old colonial house displaying a fine collection of photographs, model ships and paintings. In the museum's basement, more art is on view at **Schooner's Gallery**. The cay is dotted with white-sand beaches rimmed with nearby reefs ideal for **snorkelling** and **diving**. Several operators offer **boat rentals** and **sport fishing** (one is Captain Rick Sawyer, Ⓣ242/365-4261, Ⓦwww.abacoflyfish.com), as well as **diving packages**, including Brendals Dive Centre on White Sound (Ⓣ242/365-4411, Ⓦwww.brendal.com).

Practicalities

To get here, take the **Green Turtle Ferry** (US$7 one-way; Ⓣ242/365-4166 or 4128), which departs from the Airport Ferry Dock near Treasure Cay on Abaco (with connections from Treasure Cay Airport) eight times a day from 8.30am to 5pm. It also departs from New Plymouth seven times daily from 8am to 4.30pm. There is also a **marina** at *Green Turtle Club and Marina* (Ⓣ242/365-4271 or 1-866/528-0439, Ⓦwww.greenturtleclub.com).

The most popular forms of transit on the cay are **golf carts**, **motor scooters** and **bicycles**, which can be rented at *Island Road Runners*(Ⓣ242/365-4610,Ⓦwww.islandroadrunner.com), *D&P Rentals* (Ⓣ242/365-4655) or almost any resort. There are two **taxi** services on the cay, Omri and McIntosh Taxis (Ⓣ242/365-4406 for both), although it is very easy to **walk** everywhere you might want to go.

The major **resorts** on Green Turtle Cay are located either around White Sound or in a cluster between New Plymouth and Gilliam Bay. Some isolated **cottages** are available in the far north of the island, or on the Atlantic shore closer to New Plymouth. Rental agencies include *Coco Bay Cottages* (Ⓣ800/752-0166 or 561/202-8149, Ⓦwww.cocobaycottages.com, 5 night minimum; ⑦–⑨) and *Bluff House Beach Hotel* (Ⓣ800/745-4911 or 242/365-4247, Ⓦwww.bluffhouse.com; ⑤–⑨) has a commanding view on a hilltop and offers hotel rooms, townhouse suites and large villas, as well as two miles of beach, tennis courts, boat rental and a marina. *Green Turtle Club and Marina* (Ⓣ242/365-4271 or 1-866/528-0539, Ⓦwww.greenturtleclub.com; ⑦–⑨), has 32 poolside rooms and eight villas, along with a full-service marina and a waterside restaurant and pub.

Guana Cay

Accessible by a short ferry ride from Marsh Harbour, **GUANA CAY** – sitting just north of Elbow Cay – is a popular destination for day-trippers. Inhabitants of the small **fishing settlement** have seen their community change dramatically with the influx of tourists in recent years, and plans for a new resort development on the cay have met with local resistance. The island is seven miles end to end, and the big draw is a five-mile stretch of powdery white sand beach, dotted with a couple of beach bars and small hotels, with great **snorkelling** and **diving** along the Great Abaco Barrier Reef, which sits fifty feet offshore.

Practicalities

From central Marsh Harbour, Albury's Ferry (Ⓣ242/367-0290; US$20 return) picks up passengers at the Union Jack Dock and the *Conch Inn* several times daily for the twenty-minute ferry run to Guana Cay. There are also several daily return trips to Marsh Harbour.

For **accommodation**, the delightful *Dolphin Beach Resort* (Ⓣ242/365-5137 or 1-800/222-2646, Ⓦwww.dolphinbeachresort.com; ⑥–⑨) has seven simple one-, two- and three-bedroom cottages plus four double rooms, each with kitchenette, screened-in porch, TV, video and CD player. There are hammocks strung in the trees, a small pool and a five-mile stretch of beach just steps away. There is a bar, and the casual *Docksiders Grill* is open for lunch and dinner by reservation (Thurs through Mon nights). *Ocean Frontier Hideaway* (Ⓣ1-888/541-1616 or 519/389-4846, Ⓦwww.oceanfrontier.com; ⑦–⑨) has a handful of log cabins closely grouped around a small pool, each equipped with a microwave, coffeemaker and a mini-fridge.

Most visitors to Guana Cay end up at *Nipper's* (Ⓣ242/365-5143, Ⓦwww.nippersbar.com), a colourful beach **bar** and **grill** on a broad wooden deck overlooking the ocean, offering tropical cocktails, cold beer and beach food as well as a regular Sunday Pig Roast and live music. *Dive Guana* (Ⓣ242/365-5178, Ⓦwww.diveguana.com) offers full and half-day **diving** and **snorkelling** excursions as well as open-water certification.

Man O' War Cay

Man O' War Cay has been a centre for **boatbuilding** for generations. The small harbour bristles with sailboat masts, and beyond it a sleepy, pleasantly calm settlement straddles a low hill. The small grid of tidy streets are lined by picket fences and cottages sporting window boxes full of flowers. The Atlantic shore has a long stretch of undeveloped beach to stroll. The island is easily explored on foot, and what little traffic you see is of the golf cart variety. A few dozen snowbirds have built vacation homes along the shore, and there are a few cottages to rent for those who want a quiet, sunny place to unwind.

Practicalities

There is regular **ferry** service from Albury's Ferry Dock in north Marsh Harbour to Man O' War Cay (Ⓣ242/367-0290; US$20 return; 20 mins). On Man O' War Cay, the *Hibiscus Café* (Ⓣ242/365-6380, Mon through Sat lunch and Tues through Sat dinner) serves simple, tasty **meals** such as coconut-fried fish burgers, conch cooked up several ways, lobster, salads and sandwiches. It is up the slope from the dock, to the left. Another option is the *Man O' War Cay Marina* (just to the left of the dock, facing the land), which offers deep-fried fare at its open-air, waterside snack bar. There are a couple of **shops** in the village where you can buy provisions and souvenirs. Jody Albury (☎242/367-5119, mobile ☎242/375-8068, call 5pm–10pm) will take you bonefishing, and if you want to explore the neighbouring cays, David Albury (☎242/365-6502 or 242/475-8768) has motorboats for rent for US$118 a day/$675 a week. There is **no hotel** on Man O' War. For condo and cottage rentals, try Samantha, associated with the Island Treasure Gift Shop (☎242/365-6143), which is also the number to call for Golf Carts R Us rentals.

1.4

Andros and North Bimini

Bahamians know the treasure trove of exotic land, air and water on Andros. Consider the thick bush that dominates the island, which in the north consists mainly of tropical and deciduous trees like **Andros pine** and **lignum vitae** – the latter virtually the national tree of the Bahamas – and in the south, a mix of mangroves, mud flats and tidal swamps. Not surprisingly, amid this rugged natural terrain, there are seemingly as many **birdwatchers** as there are birds, making the island an essential stop for avian enthusiasts. Lurking just a mile offshore, the massive 167-mile Androsian reef is what really makes Andros a natural aquatic wonder. This magnificent **barrier reef**, the third longest in the world after those in Australia and Central America, teems with all manner of mysterious underwater creatures. It is a truly spectacular place to explore, whether you **dive**, **snorkel** or **fish**, with an outer wall that plunges down dramatically through a myriad of canyons, caves, blue holes and sand chutes. In the shallower waters near shore, the sights are just as stunning, featuring a bright assortment of reef fish, starfish, sea cucumbers and southern manta rays, among countless others.

The island is divided into three zones: **North Andros**, home to most of the population; Central Andros, better known as **Mangrove Cay**; and **South Andros**, the most lightly populated and remote section. Aside from the north end, many parts of the rest of the island received electricity only in the last twenty-five years, and still have a rather poor, antiquated road system, giving the region a rather charming and rustic appeal.

Only fifty miles due east of Miami, the **Biminis** are the closest Bahamian islands to the US mainland. Composed of seventeen small, flat islands, the chain occupies a downwind position on the edge of the Great Bahama Bank, which helps explain why the entire eastern shore of the two largest islands, North and South Bimini, are one long white-sand beach. The local economy depends on fishing and most visitors are drawn here for some of the best sport fishing around. **Alice Town** on the very southern tip of **North Bimini** is the largest settlement in the Biminis, with a population of 600; it's also the hub of tourist services.

Arrival, information and getting around

Located 25 miles west of New Providence, Andros is easily reached **by air** from Nassau or mainland Florida. Bahamasair (ⓣ242/300-8359, or in the US ⓣ800/222-4262) is the main carrier between Nassau's International Airport and any of the four airports on Andros. The airline also has daily flights from Nassau to Bimini. Note that the airport for the Biminis is situated on South Bimini; if you are headed for North Bimini, a shuttle bus will transport you from the airport to the ferry dock where you can catch a water taxi to Alice Town (US$12 total).

Ferries and **mailboats** are a cheap and easy way to reach Andros and the Biminis from Nassau. Ferries can make the journey in just under three hours; mailboats take up to seven hours. Fares are US$35 one-way (ⓣ242/393-1064).

Tourist information offices are located throughout the island (ⓣ242/368-2286). There are only a few good options for **getting around** the island, mainly because there are so few roads, and major settlements are far apart. Renting a car can be a frustrating endeavour, and is typically best forsaken in lieu of **walking** and **bicycling**.

Taxis meet all incoming flights at the airport; cabs are mainly individual operators who can vary dramatically in service and price. With no official tour operators on the island, most taxi drivers also double as **tour guides**, and offer informal sightseeing jaunts, particularly on North Andros, for around US$300 per day for two people. Some hotels and resorts may also include a complimentary taxi service for guests.

North Andros

The most common pastime on **NORTH ANDROS**, and the major draw for many of the island's visitors, is the sport of **bonefishing**. Although many of the creeks, flats, bights and rivers here sport countless numbers of hungry bonefish, **North Bight** is the focus of the fishing scene, about thirty miles from Andros Town airport.

You can always find a great assortment of fishing boats parked at the wharf at nearby **Nicholl's Town**, a small burg of six hundred residents living in breeze-block and tin-roofed homes and scattered wooden shacks, lying near the island's north tip along a beach fringed by tall palm trees. To the east lies the pleasant fishing village of **Lowe Sound**, which has a guesthouse for visitors, several small bars and restaurants, and a few recommended bonefishing guides like Arthur Russell (ⓣ242/329-7372). Less appealing, the town of **San Andros**, further south along the east coast, consists of a few concrete houses surrounded by pine forest, with a nearby harbour at **Mastic Point**. Both settlements are tiny and virtually without services. On the island's rugged west coast, the tiny fishing village of **Red Bays** is the only real settlement, reachable by a bumpy, unpaved fifteen-mile road from San Andros.

South of San Andros airport, the delightful *Small Hope Bay Lodge* is the island's premier diving and fishing destination, while two miles south of Small Hope Bay is **Fresh Creek**, which actually encompasses two distinct settlements connected by a lovely single-lane bridge. The first, **Coakley Town**, is home to a few shops, restaurants and bars, as well as a large lighthouse on a cape. The town also has the only full-service marina around, the Andros Lighthouse Yacht Club and Marina (ⓣ242/368-2305, ⓦwww.androslighthouse.com), though the *Chickcharnie Hotel* (ⓣ242/368-2025) has slips as well. Across the bridge, **Andros Town** has a tourist office, a pleasant park with a few disused tennis courts, and the **Androsia Batik Factory** (ⓦwww.222.androsia.com, ⓣ242/368-2020), one of the few commercial enterprises on Andros. Operated by the Birch family, which also owns *Small Hope Bay Lodge*, the factory produces batik fabrics, using wax to create patterns on brightly coloured cloth. You can buy it by the bolt or done up in dresses, blouses, trousers, T-shirts, scarves and household linens that make popular keepsakes for visitors and are a decorating staple in hotel rooms throughout the Bahamas.

The rough road south from Fresh Creek to Cargill Creek runs through bush and pine scrub, and is devoid of settlements. Still, the towns of **Cargill Creek** and nearby **Behring Point** are in the midst of prime bonefishing country, and worth making the effort to visit if you don't mind the drive.

Practicalities

Most of the activities and tours of North Andros are based around bonefishing, and are often organized by the island's **lodges** and **resorts**. The *Andros Lighthouse Yacht Club and Marina* in Fresh Creek (Ⓣ242/368-2305, Ⓦwww.androslighthouse.com; ❺), is built around a central patio, with large, comfortable rooms with a/c, TV and fridges overlooking an eighteen-slip marina, and offers bonefishing and island tours. Further north, on an island off Staniard Creek, *Kamalame Cay* (Ⓣ242/368-6281 or 800/790-7971, Ⓦwww.kamalame.com; ❾) is a secluded luxury resort with stunning guest villas tucked into private corners of its 96 acres. At Cargill Creek, the best lodge is *Andros Island Bonefishing Club* (Ⓣ242/368-5167, Ⓦwww.androsbonefishing.com; US$3145 per person for a week of fishing, all-inclusive) with simple and neat guest rooms and a cheerful clubhouse.

The island's premier diving and snorkelling lodge is *Small Hope Bay Lodge* in Calabash Bay (Ⓣ242/368-2014 or 1-800/223-6961, Ⓦwww.smallhope.com; ❻ including meals). It's a lovely limestone and pine resort with guest cottages on the beach, a converted old boat for a bar and batik decor in the rooms. Diving and snorkelling trips are available, along with a beachside hot tub, kayaks, bonefishing, saltwater fly-fishing and reef fishing. **Dining** is excellent here, as it is at most of the lodges. Other good choices for meals include *Hank's Place* in Fish Creek, known for its great fried chicken (Ⓣ242/368-2447).

Mangrove Cay and South Andros

Most of the hotels and resorts in central and southern Andros are located directly on the beach, typically a rather narrow strip of soft, white sand. Offshore, the barrier reef is close enough for **snorkelling** and features stunning, close-up views of Caribbean spiny lobster, natural sponges, southern manta rays, parrotfish and iridescent displays of coral.

In central Andros, around **MANGROVE CAY**, the main settlement of **Little Harbour** is most interesting at its northern end, known as **Moxey Town**. With a tiny dock for harvesting fishing catches and bringing in ferries, Moxey Town has a few restaurants and bars, and good access to the offshore reef as well. The main diving centre on Mangrove Cay is the *Seascape Inn* (see below), with special snorkelling and diving packages, kayak dives and weekly night trips for advanced divers.

A few miles beyond Mangrove Cay, **SOUTH ANDROS** features thirty miles of coastal road edging white sands and coconut palms, and premier birdwatching and nature-hiking opportunities on its inland terrain. From **Drigg's Hill** to the north (where the ferry from Mangrove Cay disembarks), it's a slow and bumpy 25-mile trip to the road's southern end at Mars Bay. **Congo Town** is the site of the airport, offering a few places to eat, an ocean walk through coconut palms and, in the town centre, a **cemetery** where many of the island's founding families are buried. Everything west of here is mangrove and dense bush.

There are many attractive vistas on the road south and several worthwhile stops, namely **Long Bay**, departure point for long hikes into bromeliad- and orchid-covered hinterlands; **High Rock**, site of a magnificent blue hole perfect for diving and swimming; and little **Duncombe's Court**, a hole-in-the-wall village with a few restaurants. **Mars Bay**, at the road's southern terminus, is a pleasant little village with a quaint town square and a busy fishing dock, where loads of grouper and conch are stacked for cleaning and shipment.

Practicalities

As with North Andros, most of the **activities** and **accommodation** to the south are centred around hotels and resorts. Nestled in a palm grove on a white-sand beach, the refurbished *Seascape Inn* in Moxey Town (Ⓣ242/369-0342, Ⓦwww.seascapeinn.com; ⑤ including breakfast) has five simple but comfortable cabanas on the beach, excellent breakfasts and dinners, and a popular bar. In Kemp's Bay at New Bight near Drigg's Hill and Congo Town is the recently opened *Tiamo Resort* (Ⓣ242/471-8087, Ⓦwww.tiamoresorts.com; ⑨), a lovely small resort with eleven beachside timber cottages with spare, sophisticated decor, housing a maximum of 22 guests. Located between Drigg's Hill and Congo Town, *Emerald Palms Resort* (Ⓣ242/369-2713, Ⓦwww.emerald-palms.com; ⑥–⑨) gets rave reviews from contented guests. The resort resembles a relaxed seaside village with 22 pleasantly appointed cottages with kitchenettes, TV, a/c (but no phones), and more guest rooms in the main lodge. Bonefishing, hiking, blue-hole swimming and kayak **tours** are all available, along with **diving** equipment rental. The resort also offers a fine restaurant serving an eclectic blend of European and Bahamian cuisines, though the area has a few other good **dining** options as well. Congo Town's *Square Deal* (Ⓣ242/368-2593) is a solid choice, and in Drigg's Hill, the *Blue Bird Club* (Ⓣ242/369-4546) offers decent food. For dancing, give *Leadon's Creek Side Lounge & Disco Centre* (Ⓣ242/369-4167, Behring Point) a whirl.

North Bimini

The lightly settled Biminis are a fabled destination for fishers. South Bimini, where the international airport is located, has only a few residents and a smattering of retirement homes. Just 150 metres across a narrow channel is **Alice Town** on **North Bimini**, capital of the tiny Bimini island chain. Popularized by Ernest Hemingway, who described it as a hard-drinking fishing refuge, the town's numerous hotels and marinas continue to provide plenty of activity for anglers, divers and snorkellers, as well as a freewheeling, somewhat ribald atmosphere reminiscent of the town's glory days.

With more than two hundred hotel rooms in a six-block-square area, Alice Town has a number of notable **fishing clubs** and **resorts**. The original *Bimini Big Game Fishing Club and Hotel*, on King's Highway (Ⓣ242/347-3392 or 1-800/737-1007, Ⓦwww.biminibiggame.com; ④–⑨), has hotel rooms, two penthouse suites and twelve cottages around an attractive swimming pool and patio, and offers marina services along with excellent food and drink. Both the ★ *Bimini Bay Resort and Casino* (Ⓣ242/347-2312; ⑨) full service and child friendly, and the *Bimini Blue Water Resort* (Ⓣ242/347-3166; ⑤), where Hemingway wrote in a cottage called the Anchorage, offer comfortable surroundings and fine food.

King's Highway, the only paved road on the island, is lined with several **restaurants**, swinging **pubs** and garish souvenir stands. All of the hotels listed above have pleasant dining rooms and decent food. ★ *Captain Bob's* (Ⓣ242/247-3260), a popular spot for breakfast and lunch, is locally famous for its filling omelettes and French toast made with sweet Bimini bread. For a splash-out evening meal, The *Red Lion Pub* next to Brown's Food store (Ⓣ242/347-3259; Tuesday through Sunday dinner only) is the place to head for tasty barbecue ribs or seafood in a fun, relaxed atmosphere.

1.5

Eleuthera

The long, pencil-thin island of **ELEUTHERA** has 10,000 residents scattered in a dozen fishing villages spread up and down its long coastline and boasts miles of pristine pink, white and golden-brown sandy **beaches** with crashing surf backed by dunes on the Atlantic coast. Less than two miles wide for most of its 110-mile length, the landscape is rolling and green, farmed for citrus fruit, tomatoes and vegetables or clothed in tall grass punctuated by the occasional grove of pine or coconut trees.

Running north–south is Queen's Highway, the main artery, offering long views of the turquoise sea and occasionally of both coasts at once. The other three islands, tiny Harbour Island, Spanish Wells and its bedroom community of Russell Island, surround the northern tip of Eleuthera.

Along the Bight side, limpid sapphire shallows are fringed by soft sand and tall palms, shell-strewn strands or rocky cliffs. In the middle of the island, the genteel community of **Governor's Harbour** is the capital of Eleuthera and was one of the earliest (c 1648) settlements in the Bahamas. To the north is Gregory Town, built on a steep hillside surrounding a deep horseshoe-shaped harbour, and the self-proclaimed pineapple capital of the Bahamas. Further south, Tarpum Bay and Rock Sound are picturesque working fishing villages. Outside of a few comfortable small resorts, there is little in the way of organized activities for tourists.

By comparison only, pretty **Harbour Island** bustles with activity. The historic village of Dunmore Town boasts several upscale luxury resorts, fine restaurants and bars, and a couple of dive outfitters, as well as the three-mile-long **Pink Sand Beach**.

Arrival, information and getting around

Eleuthera has **airports** at Rock Sound at the southern end of Eleuthera, Governor's Harbour at the island's midpoint, and North Eleuthera at the north end of the island, with daily service from Nassau and Florida on Bahamasair, Continental and US Airways. Note that if your destination is Harbour Island or Spanish Wells, you should land at North Eleuthera Airport. For all other destinations on Eleuthera, you should land at Governor's Harbour or Rock Sound Airport.

Bahamas Fast Ferries (US$70 one-way, $115 round-trip; ⓣ242/333-3113, ⓦwww.bahamasferries.com) operates daily **ferry** services between Nassau, Harbour Island and Spanish Wells, and twice-weekly services to Governor's Harbour. Government **mailboats** call once a week at several points on the island.

The Ministry of Tourism has **information offices** in Governor's Harbour (ⓣ242/332-2142) and Dunmore Town on Harbour Island (ⓣ242/333-2621), theoretically open during regular business hours, but in practice more sporadically. Tarbox Publications offers an excellent, well-detailed four-sheet **map** of Eleuthera, Harbour Island and Spanish Wells, including their respective beaches and other local attractions (US$10), available at the *Rainbow Inn* and other local shops. There are also free maps available through the Ministry of Tourism.

There are no public buses on Eleuthera, and no organized tours. **Taxis** are readily available at the airports and ferry docks. If you are staying on Eleuthera and planning to do some exploring, you will need to **rent a car**. This is highly recommended, as one of the great pleasures of a stay on Eleuthera is meandering through its villages and seeking out its many lovely beaches. Johnson's Rentals on Harbour Island (☎242/333-2376) and Cooper's Automobile Rentals on Eleuthera (☎242/332-1726) have reasonable rates.

Accommodation

Cartwright's Oceanfront Cottages Tarpum Bay ☎242/334-4215. Offers three cosy two- and three-bedroom cottages on the waterfront at the western edge of town, with a homey and eclectic decor and a great view of the sea. 5

Cocodimama two miles south of Governor's Harbour airport on the Queen's Highway ☎242/332-3150, ⓦwww.cocodimama.com. A small beach resort with three two-storey cottages on the beach. Twelve spacious, pleasingly decorated rooms feature Balinese furniture, clay-tile floors and private balconies with hammocks, and a swath of white sandy beach and calm water. Windsurfing, kayaking and snorkelling gear available for guest use. Closed Sept–Nov. 6–7

The Cove Eleuthera two miles north of Gregory Town ☎242/335-5142 or 1-800/552-5960, ⓦwww.thecoveeleuthera.com. A small, casual resort, with a lovely sheltered cove for swimming and snorkelling, bicycle rentals, snorkelling gear, a swimming pool and patio with a spectacular view. There's a laid-back restaurant inside, and tennis courts and a dramatic coastline to explore by kayak. Features 24 comfortable rooms with ceramic-tiled floors, some with kitchenettes. 6–9

The Duck Inn on the Queen's Highway in Governor's Harbour ☎242/332-2608, ⓦwww.theduckinn.com. Located on the waterfront, with three charming wooden cottages built in the early 1800s and restored with lots of creature comforts and delightful touches. There's a lush enclosed garden, outdoor barbecue, kayaks for guest use and an orchid nursery. Cottages sleep two to eight. 5

Morgan's Bonefish Harbour Gregory Town ☎242/335-5077, ⓦwww.morgansbonefishharbour.com. Two cute rustic cottages for rent on a secluded bluff within walking distance of town, with kayaks and hammocks for guest use and guided fishing trips arranged. Studio sleeping two and a one-bedroom sleeping three. 3

Rainbow Inn ten miles north of Governor's Harbour airport on the Queen's Highway ☎242/335-0294, or in North America ☎1-800/688-0047, ⓦwww.rainbowinn.com. A relaxed resort with hexagonal wooden cottages (some with kitchens) built around a swimming pool overlooking the sea. Facilities include tennis courts, free bicycle use, kayaks, hobie cats, snorkelling gear and trips, hammocks and the best gourmet restaurant on the island. Closed Sept to mid-Nov. 5

Governor's Harbour

Governor's Harbour is a gracious seaside town and fishing community of a few hundred residents with a distinctly colonial feel and a tangible expatriate presence. Located at the midpoint of Eleuthera, with plentiful and charming accommodations and restaurants and several beautiful beaches close at hand, it makes a good spot to base yourself to explore the island. Daintily painted wooden cottages with gingerbread trim line the steep lanes which climb the hillside, surrounded by stone walls overflowing with hibiscus and oleander blooms. The harbour, dotted with fishing boats and pleasure craft, is enclosed by a curve of white sand joined to **Cupid's Cay** by a narrow causeway. Cupid's Cay, a small hunk of flat rock, was the site of the first settlement on Eleuthera, by the Company of Eleutheran Adventurers, exiles from Bermuda in 1648 (although a big sign proudly declares it to have been 1646). A church, a few cottages and the ruins of nineteenth-century wooden houses remain. The **mailboat** and passenger **ferries** dock at the north end of the cay.

On the south side of the harbour in front of the candy-pink **library** is **Arthur's Beach**, where a community fish fry is held every Friday and Saturday night. To reach the beach from the centre of Governor's Harbour, take Haynes Avenue up the hill from the Queen's Highway, past the *Cigatoo Resort* and down the other side, where you come to a T-junction. From here, take the wooded path just to the right of the junction, which arrives after 200 yards or so at the beach.

The rest of the island

North of Governor's Harbour the Queen's Highway passes through several small fishing villages as well as the larger hillside settlement of **Gregory Town**. Along the way, through rolling farmland and long stretches of dense bush, side roads off the highway lead to beautiful empty **beaches** on both the Caribbean and Atlantic coasts. After you pass through the **Glass Window** – a rocky, wave-doused moonscape where Eleuthera is barely a car-width wide – there's little to detain visitors (though you must come this way to catch a **ferry** to Harbour Island or Spanish Wells).

South of Governor's Harbour are two picturesque fishing villages worth a visit: sleepy **Tarpum Bay** and prettily painted **Rock Sound**, both of which offer refreshments and accommodations. The remaining highlights of southern Eleuthera are several stunning beaches, including **Ten Bay**, **North Side** and **Lighthouse**. There is not a lot to do down this way besides stroll along the shore and listen to the sound of the waves from the veranda of any number of beachfront rental cottages, but that is basically the point for many visitors.

Eating and drinking

Eating and **drinking** is a casual affair on Eleuthera. You can find some hearty Bahamian cooking and a local drinking hole in most settlements, and there are a few very nice restaurants for a memorable meal. Island **nightlife** is pretty subdued. Playing a game of pool and listening to the jukebox at *Mate and Jenny's* (☎242/332-1504, closed Tuesday) is a good option.

Charley's Bar & Grill Queen's Highway, Governor's Harbour, ☎242/332-3477. A popular local spot with fine, home-style Bahamian food like peas 'n rice and cracked conch, souse chicken and steamed fish.

Cocodimama two miles south of Governor's Harbour airport on the Queen's Highway ☎242/332-3150. Part of a small resort, with romantic seating on a wide terrace on the sands with a great sunset view. Nice choice for a special night out, serving Italian and Bahamian cuisine and featuring dishes such as gorgonzola cheese salad, grouper in a white wine sauce and crepes with Cointreau and ice cream. Breakfast, lunch and dinner service.

Nor'Side Rock Sound, ☎242/334-2573. Great Bahamian home-cooking and cool drinks in a lovely setting on a bluff overlooking the Atlantic. Closed Sun.

Water's Edge Café. Hatchet Bay down seaside, ☎242/335-0679. Newly opened, serving breakfasts and lunches at reasonable prices complete with Internet. Order a variety of sandwiches, coffee, tea and goodies.

Harbour Island

Sitting two miles off the northeast side of Eleuthera, **Harbour Island** is a different world altogether. Tourism is more prevalent on this tidy green island – just three miles end to end and less than half a mile across – focused on the spectacular **Pink Sand Beach**, which runs the length of the Atlantic side. There is not a high-rise or tour bus in sight, however. The island's only settlement is the picture-perfect village of **Dunmore Town**, which climbs a low hill overlooking the harbour. With neat narrow streets lined with freshly painted clapboard cottages, flower boxes and white picket fences, it evokes a New England seaside town. It was, in fact, built mainly by Loyalist exiles and their slaves from the American colonies at the end of the eighteenth century. These days, a clutch of intimate and exclusive beach **resorts** and heritage inns cater to a wealthy clientele.

Water taxis (US$4 each way) depart regularly from the wharf on Eleuthera to make the ten-minute trip to the dock in the centre of Dunmore Town, within walking distance of all hotels and restaurants and the famous Pink Sand Beach. If you're coming from **Nassau**, Bahamas Fast Ferries (ⓣ242/323-2166, ⓦwww.bahamasferries.com) has daily service to Harbour Island, and the government **mailboat** calls here weekly. Although the island is easy enough to navigate **on foot**, most locals buzz around on **golf carts**, which can be rented on the dock when you arrive or arranged through your hotel.

Accommodation

A well thought out site is ⓦwww.Eleuthera.com, which has an extensive listing of rentals for all manner of traveller.

Pink Sands Hotel ⓣ242/333-2030, ⓦwww.pinksandsresort.com. The most sophisticated yet relaxing resort on the island, situated on the beach and offering 25 cottages spread out on 20 acres, some with expansive ocean views and private decks. Full high-tech media room equipped with a row of Mac computers and flat screen TVs. 9

Ramora Bay Club ⓣ242/333-2325, or in North America ⓣ1-800/688-0425, ⓦwww.romorabay.com. This small hotel has an unpretentious and cosmopolitan sophistication. Cottages housing fifteen guest rooms and suites are staggered down a gentle green slope facing the harbour with a view of Eleuthera across the water. The decor is an eclectic and imaginative mix of Indian textiles, modern art and bold colour. Each room has a private patio and is furnished with fresh tropical flowers, CD player, TV, VCR and phone, with a selection of music, movies and books in the main house. Breakfast and lunch are served at wrought-iron café tables in a sunny alcove adjoining the terrace, and dinner is served by candlelight in an intimate dining area. There are tennis courts, a swimming pool with lounge chairs facing the harbour, an open-air bar and watersports arranged through Ocean Fox Dive shop. 8

Valentines Resort & Marina ⓣ242/333-2142, ⓦwww.valentinesresort.com. A one-stop shop for all your vacation needs. A mariner's dream with 50 slips able to accommodate up to 160ft yachts. Dive shop on site with dive packages as well as kayak and deep sea packages for nondiving adventures. 9

Tingum Village Hotel ⓣ242/333-2161. Several rustic, self-catering cottages and apartment units set in a quiet grove of coconut palms, with close beach access and the famous *Ma Ruby's* restaurant. 5

▲ Eleuthera's Glass Window

Eating

In addition to the **restaurants** listed below, along the waterfront on Bay Street are several **kiosks** selling fresh conch salad, hamburgers and chips, with wooden benches situated with a view of the harbour.

Angela's Starfish Restaurant ⓣ242/333-2253. A simple, inexpensive local restaurant perched on top of Barracks Hill that receives rave reviews for its seafood dinners. Its unfortunate proximity to the dump (out of sight over the hill) can occasionally be a problem when the wind blows the wrong way and you want to sit outside, but the dining room is scrupulously clean.

Blue Bar At the Pink Sands Resort ⓣ242/333-2030. An excellent way to experience the resort without having to shell out the money for a room. Caribbean fusion menu with an emphasis on fresh seafood. Dinner is served oceanside by candlelight.

Commander's Beach Bar at the *Coral Sands Hotel*. The patio bar has a sweeping view of the beach and a tasty lunch menu featuring a rock lobster salad sandwich, salads, burgers including a vegetarian burger, seafood nibbles and yummy frozen drinks.

Harbour Lounge on Bay St facing the government dock (ⓣ242/333-2031. With tables on a wide veranda, this popular people-watching spot has specialities including spicy tequila shrimp, a grouper sandwich and pumpkin soup. Closed Mon, dinner only Sun.

Romora Bay Club ⓣ242/333-2325. Casual yet upscale feeling with moderate prices. Fresh fish and cracked conch, friendly service with exceptional view of the ocean.

Sip Sip ⓣ242/333-3316. Lively atmosphere, expensive but delicious food with a breathtaking view of the ocean and pink sand beach. Serving lunch.

Sports and outdoor activities

There are no organized activities on Eleuthera, although several of the resorts offer bicycles, kayaks and snorkelling equipment for guest use, as noted above. On Harbour Island, Ocean Fox Dive Shop at the Harbour Island Marina (ⓣ242/333-2323, ⓦwww.oceanfox.com), offers **snorkelling** and **diving** excursions, **boat rentals** and **fishing** charters, as does Valentine's Dive Centre (ⓣ242/333-2080, ⓦwww.valentinesdive.com). Robert Davis presents ninety-minute **historical tours** of Dunmore Town (US$100; ⓣ242/333-2337) for up to three people, along with **horseriding** on the beach (US$20 for a half-hour, $30 for a full hour). It's best to call first for reservations.

1.6

The Exumas

With a name like an exhaled, contented sigh, **THE EXUMAS** are befittingly at ease. Over three hundred and sixty-five islands, cays and rock outcroppings of various sizes make up the Exuma chain, a narrow band that straddles the Tropic of Cancer and stretches over one hundred miles along the eastern edge of the Great Bahama Bank. The islands are mainly low-lying chunks of honeycombed limestone rimmed by powdery white sand and covered in dense vegetation. The landscape holds beautiful vistas of sand and brush, pristine expanses of soft white beach fringed in places with towering coconut palms and dunes covered with emerald green vines and exotic blooms. Most of the island chain's population of 3000 live at the southern end of the archipelago, in the small, lively capital of **George Town** and environs on **Great Exuma**, in neighbouring settlements on **Little Exuma**, or on **Staniel Cay**, **Little Farmer's Cay** and **Blackpoint** in the southern **Exuma Cays**. Those Exumians not engaged in fishing or farming cater to the small but growing tourist trade.

Boasting crystal clear tepid waters and an abundance of marine life, the islands are a choice destination for divers, snorkellers and sailors. The chain is edged by prime bonefishing and deep-sea fishing grounds and several fishing guides operate throughout the islands. Shallow protected waters and dozens of deserted sandy coves make the chain ideal for sea kayaking, and several outfitters run expeditions through the cays. The remote **Exuma Land and Sea Park** in the northern part of the chain is an area of extraordinary beauty, splendid in its isolation and desolation. If all that sounds like too much work, there is no shortage of beautiful, empty beaches to lounge on and gaze out at the gorgeous surrounds.

Arrival, information and getting around

Most visitors arrive in the Exumas at **George Town International Airport**, eight miles north of town on Great Exuma; two Bahamasair **flights** arrive daily from Nassau. American Eagle and Lynx Air fly to and from George Town daily from Miami and Fort Lauderdale, respectively.

Ferries and **mailboats** from Nassau arrive at the government dock in the centre of George Town, within walking distance of most hotels, restaurants and services. Try Bahamas Fast Ferries (ⓣ242/323-2166, ⓦwww.bahamasferries.com) but note that their schedules are subject to change without prior notice. The well-maintained *Grand Master* mailboat (US$45 one-way; ⓣ242/393-1064) departs Nassau for the 14-hour trip to George Town every Tuesday at 2pm, returning on Thursday at 10am.

Note that if your primary interest is visiting the **Exuma Land and Sea Park**, you would be better off landing at **Staniel Cay**, just outside the parks' southern boundary. The *Captain C* **mailboat** calls at Staniel Cay, Blackpoint, Farmer's Cay and the Ragged Islands, departing Nassau on Tuesdays for the twelve-hour trip (US$70 one-way; ⓣ242/393-1064). Alternatively, Flamingo Air (ⓣ242/377-0354; US$70 one-way) flies from Nassau to Staniel Cay daily except Saturdays. If your plan is to explore all of the Exumas and you don't own your own sailboat, it is difficult – though not impossible – to get to Staniel Cay from George Town. There are no commercial flights connecting the two, and it requires a combination of cars and boats or an airplane charter.

Located in the centre of George Town above Thompson's Car Rental, the **Bahamas Ministry of Tourism** provides information (Mon through Fri 9am–5pm; ⓣ242/336-2457) and a selection of **maps** and brochures.

There are no public buses on the Exumas and no shuttle services from the airport, but **taxis** meet every flight and any hotel will call one for you. The eight-mile trip to George Town costs around US$25 for two passengers. For reliable and courteous service, call Leslie Dames (ⓣ242/357-0015). **Hitchhiking** is easy on the Exumas, and many residents rely on it for travelling and commuting to work. Great and Little Exuma are easily explored by **rental car**. Three companies with reasonable vehicles are Airport Rent-a-Car (ⓣ242/345-0090, ⓦwww.exumacarrental.com), Thompson's Rentals, in the centre of George Town (ⓣ242/336-2442), and Don's Car Rental across from the baggage drop at the airport (ⓣ242/345-0112). All charge around US$70 a day, plus a $200 deposit.

Birdsong and picturesque rest stops make travelling by **motor scooter** or **bicycle** a fun way to get around, especially heading south from George Town. You can rent well-maintained 21-speed bikes at Starfish, The Exuma Adventure Centre (ⓣ242/336 3033), US$15 for a half-day and $100 per week. You can also rent a **motorboat**, **sailboat** or **kayak** to explore the coastline and the numerous cays offshore. Dive Exuma (Ⓣ242/357-0313, Ⓦwww.dive-exuma.com) offers a variety of dive and snorkel sites and options, while Minns Water Sports (Ⓣ242/336-3483, Ⓦwww.mwsboats.com) offers boating package deals, with discounts for rentals of three days or more.

Great Exuma and Little Exuma

Sitting head to toe at the southern end of the Exuma chain and joined by a narrow bridge, **GREAT EXUMA** and **LITTLE EXUMA** are the largest and most settled islands in the archipelago. The capital **George Town** is a bustling, slightly ramshackle little hub in the middle of 35-mile long Great Exuma. Here you will find a compact collection of pastel-coloured cement block buildings, plenty of small hotels, restaurants and nightly entertainment drawing the yachting and diving crowd. The town's most appealing sights lie offshore, however, in the azure and emerald depths of **Elizabeth Harbour** and the offshore cays. These include **Stocking Island**, with its long windswept beach (reached by ferry from the *Peace and Plenty Hotel*), and **Crab Cay**, site of the ruins of a Loyalist plantation. In late April, usually sleepy George Town springs into party mode for the **Out Island Regatta**, which draws crews from across the Bahamas to race their sloops and spectators from around the world. North and south of George Town are several modest settlements, including **Rolle Town** and **Williams Town** at the tip of six-mile-long Little Exuma, which make a pleasant day-trip by car or bicycle.

Accommodation

Accommodations on Great and Little Exuma range from a five-star resort to rustic cottage rentals. If you're planning to visit during the Out Island Regatta in late April, you must book months in advance. Most accommodation is found in George Town and environs, with a few other nice choices north and south of town.

George Town

Club Peace and Plenty in the centre of the village Ⓣ242/336-2551 or in the US Ⓣ1-800/525-2210, Ⓦwww.peaceandplenty.com. Comfortable rooms with wicker furniture, satellite TVs and balconies overlooking the pool or Elizabeth Harbour. ❻

Minns Cottages half a mile from the centre, on the Queen's Highway Ⓣ242/336-2127. Quiet cottages in a shady grove with screened-in porches, nice ocean views, tiled floors, fully equipped kitchens and satellite TV. One- and two-bedroom cottages. ❺

George Town outskirts

Coconut Cove Inn Queen's Highway Ⓣ242/336-2659, Ⓕ242/336-2658. A mile and a half north of town, a small beachfront hotel with twelve modern rooms featuring private balconies, most with ocean views. Also has a restaurant, palm-shaded terrace, beach bar and shuttle buses to and from George Town. ❺

Coral Gardens Bed and Breakfast Hooper's Bay five miles north of George Town Ⓣ242/336-2880, Ⓦwww.coralgardensbahamas.com. A pleasant B&B run by a friendly and knowledgeable English couple, perched on a breezy hilltop with views of both coasts. Three rooms with refrigerators and shared baths in the main house, a five-minute walk to a secluded beach, and two beachfront apartments sleeping two and four. A rental car is available for US$40 per day. ❹

Hotel Higgins Landing Stocking Island Ⓣ242/357-0008, Ⓦwww.higginslanding.com. Exquisite secluded resort with five timber guest cottages furnished with antiques, each with a private ocean view, includes dinner for two. ❾

Palm Bay Beach Club Ⓣ242/336-2192, Ⓦwww.palmbaybeachclub.com. Brightly painted Bahamian cottages dotting the beach's edge. Kayaks and sailboats available to guests without charge. ❻

South of George Town

Club Peace and Plenty Bonefish Lodge Queen's Highway at Hartswell ⓣ242/345-5555or in the US ⓣ1-800/525-2210, ⓦwww.ppbonefishlodge.com. Handsome timber and stone lodge with wraparound veranda overlooking Little Exuma, catering to serious fishers. Featuring eight rooms with tile floors, ceiling fans, deep balconies and ocean views, as well as a restaurant and bar. Fishing packages include lodging, meals, bonefishing guides and use of kayaks, bicycles and snorkelling equipment. Three nights and two days US$1284 per person, seven nights and six days $2568. 9

Master Harbour Villas ⓣ242/345-5076, ⓦwww.exumabahamas.com/masterharbour. Three miles south of George Town in a private grove of coconut palms, three white clapboard cottages set on a rocky shore overlooking Crab and Redshank cays, with high ceilings, overhead fans and motorboat rental for guests. One-bedroom villa 6, two-bedroom 8 and four-bedroom. 9

North of George Town

Four Seasons Resort at Emerald Bay ⓣ242/336-6800 or 1-800/819-5053, ⓦwww.fourseasons.com/greatexuma. A huge upscale resort on a secluded beach fifteen miles north of George Town, with an eighteen-hole golf course designed by Greg Norman, two restaurants offering formal and informal dining, and featuring local seafood and Italian cuisine, a full service spa, gym and three swimming pools set on lushly landscaped grounds. 9

Eating and drinking

George Town offers several pleasant **restaurants** to choose from, ranging from open-air pool **bars** to smart casual gourmet fare. South of George Town, *La Shanté Beach Club*, on the beach in Forbes Hill, makes a good spot for lunch, while in Williams Town, *Mom's Bakery*, *The Arawak Club* and *Santana's Grill* all serve tasty snacks and simple seafood meals. North of George Town, *Big D's Conch Spot*, on the beach at Steventon, is a local favourite, and the basic but friendly *Kermit's Hilltop Tavern* in Rolle Town and *The Fisherman's Inn* in Barreterre can fix you up if you are up that way.

The Chat and Chill ⓣ242/336-2700, ⓦwww.chatnchill.com. An open-air beach bar at Volleyball Beach on Stocking Island. A cheap and breezy place for burgers, seafood, cool drinks and a swim. Open daily 11am–7pm. Note that you can't get here by the ferry; you must take a water taxi or have your own boat.

Cheater's Restaurant and Bar ⓣ242/336-2535. Inexpensive no-frills roadhouse two miles south of George Town on the Queen's Highway, serving tasty home-style Bahamian food. Open for lunch and supper Mon 4pm–9.30pm, Tues–Sat 9.30am–10pm. Tuesday night fish fry with rake 'n' scrape music. Closed Sunday.

Club Peace and Plenty Restaurant ⓣ242/336-2551. Located off the hotel lobby and set in a glassed-in alcove with a nice view of Stocking Island, the upscale menu features fish, lobster and steak. Open for breakfast, lunch and dinner.

Coconut Cove Inn ⓣ242/336-2659. One of the best restaurants in the Exumas, with an extensive moderately priced menu, cosy atmosphere and attentive service. Offers delicious pizza, pasta and steak and seafood platters. The chef will prepare your day's catch, and the beachside *Sand Bar* serves sandwiches and snacks Fri 3–9pm. Breakfast daily 7.30–9.30am, dinner Tues–Sun 6–9pm; reservations recommended by 4pm.

Sam's Place ⓣ242/336-2579. Upstairs in a grey timber building overlooking the marina, the best place in George Town for breakfast, specializing in Bahamian boiled breakfasts and American-style bacon and eggs and pancakes. Also good lunchtime seafood, sandwiches and burgers, great oceanside views and quick and friendly service.

Two Turtles Inn ⓣ242/336-2545. An outdoor patio bar overlooking the wharf, and a great place for lunchtime sandwiches, salads, burgers and conch dishes. Friday nights, there is a barbecue with live entertainment 9pm–1am.

Outdoor activities

Several outfitters based in George Town offer an array of **outdoor activities**. Starfish, The Exuma Adventure Centre (ⓣ242/336-3033 or in North America ⓣ1-877/398-6222, ⓦwww.kayakbahamas.com) offers excellent guided **history** and **eco-tours** of Elizabeth Harbour, Crab Cay and Stocking Island by boat, along with **cycling trips** on quiet island byways and paddling excursions through the cays off George Town. Day-trips include beach picnics and snorkelling, and full-moon, sunset and sunrise **paddling excursions** are also available, as well as two- to six-day kayaking and camping trips (US$1195 for a week) and week-long **sailing excursions** through the Exuma Land and Sea Park (US$1995). Full-day kayaking or nature tours with some hiking and a boat excursion cost US$95; a half-day outing or three-hour full-moon paddle is US$70–$95. Kayaks can be rented from Starfish for US$50/$100/$275 for 2 hours/day/week.

The Exumas are one of the best places in the world to **snorkel** and **dive**. Dive Exuma (ⓣ242/336-2893, ⓦwww.dive-exuma.com) operates a half mile south of George Town out of *February Point Resort*.

The islands also offer superb **deep-sea fishing** and **bonefishing**, and a number of good fishing guides are based in George Town and the surrounding area: Cely's Fly Fishing (ⓣ242/345-2341), Fish Rowe Charters, Doug Rowe (ⓣ242/357-0870 or 242/336-3440) and Abby MacKenzie (ⓣ242/464-1973). Be patient and prepared to leave a voicemail when attempting to reach the charter companies as they are often out on a charter during the day.

The Exuma Cays

Off the northern tip of Great Exuma, the **Exuma Cays** is a forty-mile-long chain of a couple of hundred mainly uninhabited islands stretched along a northwest trajectory ending forty miles east of Nassau. These cays, of various shapes and sizes, share a similar topography of white sand, honeycombed black coral rock and hardy vegetation, surrounded by a rich marine environment.

The Southern Cays

The only permanent settlements in the cays are at the southern end of the chain, on sleepy **Little Farmer's Cay**; on Great Guana Cay in the scruffy village of **Blackpoint**; and on tidy, green and nicely painted **Staniel Cay.** Staniel Cay has a noticeably prosperous air, owing largely to its popularity with yacht cruisers and expatriate residents. Staniel Cay is also the gateway to the **Exuma Land and Sea Park**, with an airstrip, two marinas, volunteer-run clinic, and several restaurants and shops.

Sea kayaking in the Exumas

One of the best ways of exploring the Exumas is by **sea kayak**, and several outfitters offering guided expeditions through the cays. Starfish, The Exuma Adventure Centre (see above) rents kayaking equipment and offers excellent paddling **day-trips**. North Carolina Outward Bound, (ⓣ888/75-NCOBS, ⓦwww.ncobs.org), offers seven- and twelve-day **sea kayaking courses** in the southern cays (several times through the year, between Nov and June, US$1945 and $3295). Further north in the Exumas, Ibis Tours ⓣ914/409-5961 in the US, ⓦwww.ibistours.com) runs eight-day guided trips through the Exuma Land and Sea Park putting in at Staniel Cay, from March to May (US$1795 excluding air fare).

Arrival and getting around

Fishing expeditions and **day-trips** from Great Exuma to the southern cays can be arranged through Captain Martin (ⓣ242/358-4057) or Reverend A.A. MacKenzie (ⓣ242/355-5024) in Barreterre on Great Exuma. A good destination is **Leaf Cay**, home to a colony of giant iguanas. The *Captain C* **mailboat** (US$120 round-trip) serves the communities of the southern Exuma Cays – including Staniel Cay – from Nassau. It does not call at George Town and the schedule varies somewhat from week to week, so call ahead to the dockmaster at Potter's Cay (ⓣ242/393 1064). Flamingo Air (ⓣ242/377-0354) flies to Staniel Cay every day from Nassau (US$100 one way & $190 round-trip.

Accommodation

Happy People Marina ⓣ242/355-2008, ⓕ242/355-2025. Adequate motel-style rooms on the Staniel Cay waterfront and a nice two-bedroom apartment. ④ and ⑧ respectively.

Sampson Cay Club and Marina ⓣ242/355-2034, ⓦwww.sampsoncayclub.com. Just north of Staniel Cay on a small cay bordering the Exuma Land and Sea Park, with five cottages, a grocery store, restaurant and bar. Rent a 13ft Boston Whaler powerboat to explore the park for US$80 per day, kayaks and Internet are free. Call for cottage rental rates.

Staniel Cay Yacht Club and Marina ⓣ242/355-2024, ⓦwww.stanielcay.com. Five cute wooden cottages with coffeemakers, small refrigerators and verandas overlooking the water, with cottages sleeping four to seven people also available. ⑤–⑥

Eating

Club Thunderball on the north side of Staniel Cay overlooking Thunderball Grotto. (ⓦwww.clubthunderball.com). An eatery serving native dishes for lunch and dinner and offering a pool table and weekend dancing. Closed Mon.

Happy People Restaurant and Bar ⓣ242/355-2008. Next to the hotel and marina, a local hangout open for breakfast, lunch and dinner, serving Bahamian dishes, sandwiches and burgers. Call in advance.

Staniel Cay Yacht Club Restaurant and Bar ⓣ242/355-2024. Near the dock, a colourful and relaxed eatery with a nautical theme, offering American and Bahamian food and home-made desserts. Reserve by 5pm for dinner that night.

The Exuma Land and Sea Park

Beginning five miles north of Staniel Cay in the middle of the chain, the **Exuma Land and Sea Park** encompasses fifteen sizeable cays and many smaller outcroppings over 176 square miles – 22 miles long and eight miles wide. Bound on the east by the deep waters of Exuma Sound, and on the west by the shallow reefs and sandbars of Great Bahama Bank, the park was established in 1958 as a marine conservation area by the **Bahamian National Trust**, a non profit agency devoted to the preservation of the country's natural environment.

There are no commercial developments, resorts or restaurants within the park boundaries; the major events are spectacular sunrises and sunsets. The **park headquarters** is at the north end of **Warderick Wells Cay**, twenty miles north of Staniel Cay in the middle of the park (Mon through Sat 9am–noon and 3–5pm, Sun 9am–1pm; ⓣ242/359-1821, ⓦwww.bnt.bs/parks_exuma.php;ⓔexumapark@aol.com). Seven miles of well-marked **hiking** trails crisscross Warderick Wells Cay, leading through groves of thatch palm and silver buttonwood, past limestone sink holes and along a broad tidal creek-bed to lookout points and Loyalist plantation ruins. A dozen white **beaches** dot the secluded palm-fringed coves on the leeward side of the island. The other cays in the park offer similar delights.

Practicalities

Most visitors to the Exuma Land and Sea Park arrive on their own **sailboats** or with organized **kayaking** or **diving** expeditions. There are 22 moorings at the north anchorage of Warderick Wells by the park headquarters, and four more at the south anchorage. The mooring fee is US$15 a night. The park asks that you call them the morning before you intend to arrive so they can assign you a mooring. There are no hotels or resorts within the park boundaries, but there are dozens of soft sandy beaches on which you can pitch your tent. **Camping** fees are US$5 a night. The Bahamas National Trust functions entirely on private donations and relies on campers to drop their payment at the park headquarters or mail it in after they leave.

The park is most easily reached from Staniel Cay, where you will have to **rent** or **charter** a boat to take you into the park. The *Staniel Cay Yacht Club* (see "Accommodation", opposite) rents thirteen- and seventeen-foot Whalers for US$85 and $235 per day respectively, including fuel. You might also ask on the dock for a local fisherman who could take you into the park. Alternatively, Captain Bill Hirsch (Ⓣ305/944-3033, Ⓦwww.myknottymind.com) will run you up to Warderick Wells (a forty-minute boat ride) for US$100 if he's in the area; he also offers **guided tours** of the park aboard his yacht MY *Knotty Mind* for US$450 per day for up to four people, all-inclusive. From Nassau, Captain Paul Harding of Diving Safaris Ltd (Ⓣ242/393-2522 or 242/393-1179) can fly you directly to Warderick Wells or any other place in the park in his **floatplane**. The **sailboat** *Cat Ppalu* (toll-free in the US Ⓣ1-800/327-9600 or 305/888-1226, Ⓦwww.blackbeard-cruises.com/c-adven.html) makes **guided diving trips** through the park several times a year from Nassau, with plenty of time made for exploring the cays topside.

The Northern Exumas

Although the northern boundary of the Land and Sea Park lies at the Wax Cay Cut, the Exuma chain continues northwards for another ten miles. The **Northern Exumas**, however, are most easily reached from Nassau, forty miles to the west. Two companies offer **day-trips** to the cays, departing from the dock on Paradise Island: Island World Adventures (Ⓣ242/363-3333, Ⓦwww.islandworldadventures.com) makes a daily excursion to Saddleback Cay in a 45ft speedboat and Powerboat Adventures (Ⓣ242/327-5385, Ⓦwww.powerboatadventures.com) leads a full-day outing to the Sail Rocks and Allan's Cay, including snorkelling, a barbecue lunch on the beach and a visit with the island's resident giant iguanas.

1.7

Cat Island and San Salvador

A world away from the cruise ship crowds, casinos and duty-free shops of Nassau and Freeport, **CAT ISLAND** and **SAN SALVADOR** offer peace and a taste of Bahamian life before the advent of mass tourism. With economies traditionally based on farming and fishing, the islands have experienced economic difficulties in recent years and many of their young people have left for service jobs in New Providence and Grand Bahama. Nevertheless, both islands have considerable quiet charm to attract visitors, including long splendid stretches of powdery white and blush-coloured beaches, top-notch snorkelling and diving, and a few exquisite beach lodges far from the bustle of the outside world.

Cat Island

Lying 130 miles southeast of Nassau, **CAT ISLAND** is a relaxed and untainted150 square miles of sparkling beaches, small settlements and a few sizeable hills. The **southern end** of the island presents great opportunities for diving, with steep cliffs and offshore reefs, while the entire **east coast**, accessible only by dirt roads, offers a continuous strand of idyllic seaside, with hidden coves and rugged shores. The **west coast**, with its mud creeks and estuaries, is great for bonefishing. The major settlements are **Arthur's Town** in the north, the pre-Hollywood home of Sidney Poitier, and **New Bight** in the south, a sprawling town that runs for two miles along the road. Cat Island is served by a single good paved road, the **Queen's Highway**, which runs the length of the 48-mile island.

There are several choice beaches on the island. **Fernandez Bay**, just north of New Bight, is an exquisite curve of white sand and turquoise sea in a sheltered cove. The Atlantic beaches are wilder, harder to reach and home to big waves and high winds – a tempting challenge for windsurfers and swimmers. At the southern end of the island, **Greenwood Beach** is eight miles of blush-coloured sand and crashing surf. Towering over the island terrain near New Bight, **Mount Alvernia** stands a whopping 206ft above sea level – the highest point in the Bahamas – and offers a sweeping view of the island's rolling terrain and coastline.

Hiking and **birdwatching** are both excellent at the southern end of the island, where ponds and lakes abound. The island's major celebrations include the annual **Cat Island Regatta** in early August, which attracts hundreds of yachters, and the **Cat Island Music Festival** in early June.

Arrival and information

Bahamasair (US$82 one-way; ⓣ242/377-5505, ⓦwww.bahamasair.com) **flies** to Cat Island from Nassau several times a week, while Cat Island Air (US$75 one-way; ⓣ242/377-3318) has daily flights between Nassau and New Bight. Continental (US$333 round-trip; ⓣ1-800/231-0856), Air Sunshine (prices vary; ⓣ954/434-8900,ⓦwww.airsunshine.com) and Lynx Air (US$350 round-trip; ⓣ954/772-9808, ⓦwww.lynxair.com) all fly to New Bight from Fort Lauderdale. At the south end of the island, *Hawk's Nest Resort* (ⓣ242/342-7050 or 1-800/688-4752, ⓦwww.hawks-nest.com) has a private airstrip and a **marina**.

There are no formal **information** services on either Cat Island or San Salvador, but material is available through Nassau's Ministry of Tourism (ⓣ1-800/224-2627, ⓦwww.bahamas.com), or the Out Island Tourist Board (ⓣ305/931-6612 or 1-800/688-4752, ⓦwww.myoutislands.com).

Accommodation

Accommodation on Cat Island is in a clutch of small and secluded resorts, each with their own individual charm. There are a few bare-bones budget options, including the twelve room *Bridge Inn* (ⓣ242/342-3013; ❸), a decent motel-style place – it's devoid of charm but offers a free shuttle to the airport.

Fernandez Bay Village New Bight ⓣ242/342-3043 or 1-800/940-1905, ⓦwww.fernandezbayvillage.com. On an exquisite secluded curve of white sand backed by casuarinas and palm trees, this casually elegant beach lodge is one of the gems of the Bahamas. Eight pleasingly and thoughtfully appointed stone and timber guest rooms and cottages are tucked in along the shore, each with a private terrace, a/c, ceiling fans and outdoor shower rooms so you can bathe by starlight and fall asleep to the sound of the waves. Wonderful buffet meals are served in the airy main lodge and on the terrace with a sunset view, fresh flowers and candlelight. There are sea kayaks and snorkel gear for guest use, as well as a collection of board games, well-stocked bookshelves, a nice gift shop, a thatch-roofed honour bar, hammocks and lounge chairs shaded by umbrellas. A local musician entertains guests a few nights a week, and there is a nightly bonfire on the beach. ❽–❾

Greenwood Beach Resort 3.5 miles north of Port Howe, then 2 miles east on a coral road ⓣ242/342-3053, ⓦwww.greenwoodbeachresort.com. In an isolated spot on the Atlantic coast, this relaxed family-run resort is popular with divers, offering twenty cheerful, simple rooms a few steps from a gorgeous eight-mile strand of blush-coloured sand with crashing surf. There is a small swimming pool and hot tub, a colourful, airy restaurant and bar in the main lodge where guests eat together at a long table, a dive shop offering dives and certification courses and a meal plan available for US$54 a day for three meals. ❹

Hawk's Nest Resort and Marina Devil's Point ⓣ242/342-7050 or 1-800/688-4752, ⓦwww.hawks-nest.com. Set on four hundred acres of beachfront at the isolated southeast tip of the island, this laid-back small hotel caters to fishers, boaters and private pilots, with ten nicely decorated oceanview rooms done up in wicker and ceramic tile, situated about 100 yards from the water. There is also a large house for rent with two bedrooms. Meals are served in a small, simple dining room with a view of the pool, a few hundred yards from the beach (make reservations for dinner by 2pm). There is a 28-slip marina, an airstrip and three dive instructors on staff. ❺–❾

Sammy T's Resort Bennett's Harbour ⓣ242/354-6009, ⓦwww.sammytbahamas.com. This small seaside resort earns rave reviews from visitors, with a handful of tastefully appointed natural wood and stone cabins just steps from a long, lovely strand of white-sand beach. Each cabin is equipped with a kitchen, a/c, DVD player and movies, and a bedroom and sitting room. There is a game room, fitness centre, bar and restaurant in the main house, serving imaginatively prepared local seafood and other dishes. ❺–❼

Eating and drinking

Most resorts offer **dining** in casually elegant surroundings (outside guests call ahead for reservations). Dinner on the terrace overlooking the beach at *Fernandez Bay Village* resort (ⓣ242/342-3043, reservations required) is a memorable experience, with fine food, candlelight and a bonfire on the beach. Most of the major settlements also have a few road-side **eateries** and a **bar** where you can sample local fare. In New Bight, the *Blue Bird Restaurant and Bar* (ⓣ242/342-3095) is recommended for tasty fried chicken, seafood and Bahamian delicacies like pig's feet and sheep's tongue souse, and occasional rake 'n' scrape music and dancing, while in the far north at Smith's Bay, *Hazel's Seaside Bar* is a relaxed spot for a quiet drink at sunset.

San Salvador

Two hundred miles east of Nassau, small **SAN SALVADOR** is the easternmost island in the Bahamas. Only twelve miles long and five wide, this low-lying island features saline lakes and brine ponds surrounded by palmetto brush, a beautiful shore of uninterrupted white sands and a **western reef** that offers marvellous diving and snorkelling. Although it was the first place where Columbus first encountered the New World, San Salvador remained a backwater until diver Bill McGehee promoted the beauty and diversity of its western reef in the 1970s. Later *Club Med* added its own endorsement, building a resort north of **Cockburn Town** (pronounced "Coburn") in 1992. Though it's the main settlement on the island there's little to keep you in Cockburn, other than a few accommodation options.

Typical **island tours** take in the lovely **East Beach**, **Dixon Hill Lighthouse**, and the **Bahamian Field Station** (for prime birdwatching and hiking), each taking about four hours and available through the two major resorts (see below). Likewise, either resort can arrange **sport fishing** and **underwater photography**.

Practicalities

Bahamasair offers twice-weekly **flights** from Miami and Nassau to Cockburn Town, while Florida-based Spirit Airlines (Ⓣ242/377-0152, Ⓦwww.spiritair.com) flies once a week to Cockburn Town out of Fort Lauderdale, New York and Orlando. *Riding Rock Inn* provides charter air service for its guests.

There are only a few choices for **accommodation** on San Salvador, most clustered around Cockburn Town. *Riding Rock Inn*, southwest of the airport (Ⓣ242/331-2641 or 1-800/272-1492; ⑤), offers diving packages, as well as cottages and furnished rooms with patios. Cockburn Town has a number of grocery stores, **restaurants** and **bars**, though most visitors predictably dine at their hotel.

1.8

Long Island and the Southern Bahamas

South of Cat Island, **Long Island** is pretty, peaceful and virtually untouched by tourism. Its roughly 3200 residents live in a dozen or so small fishing settlements dotted along its seventy-mile-long coastline. For visitors, Long Island has the double virtue of unspoiled natural beauty and a handful of lovely small resorts offering appealing accommodation, fine dining and a full range of activities, including excellent **diving** and **snorkelling**. Long Island also boasts superb **fishing** year round, and there are numerous beautiful beaches to explore.

Lastly, the most remote islands of the Bahamian archipelago, the Southern Bahamas lie about 250 miles southeast of Nassau. Consisting of Long Island, Crooked and Acklins

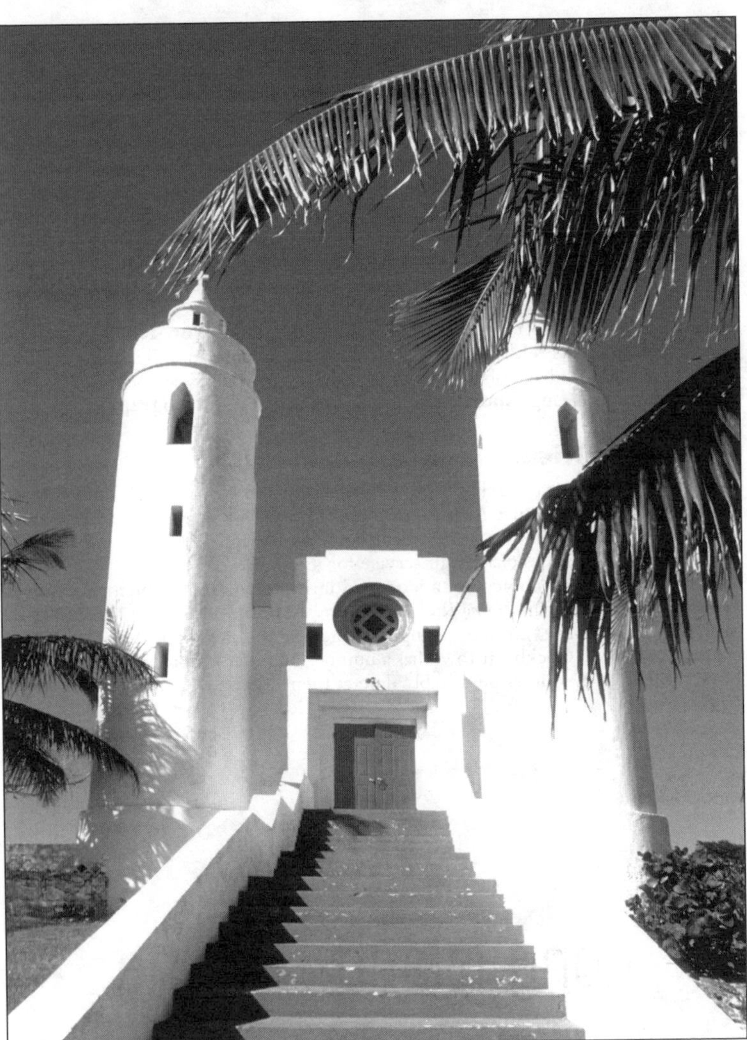

▲ St Peter Catholic Church, Long Island

islands, Great Inagua and Mayaguana, the south islands are comparatively free of tourist development and offer a taste of the slowly vanishing traditional Out Island life.

Long Island

Most locals on **LONG ISLAND** earn their living from the sea, as they have for generations. The island has a long tradition of boat building, and the **Long Island Sailing Regatta**, held at **Salt Pond** in mid-May for the past 35 years, is one of the premier social events in the Out Islands. The rest of the year, life in the tidy little villages is pretty quiet, with many of the young people off seeking their fortunes in Nassau or elsewhere. Long Islanders are a devout lot and on Sunday mornings the numerous **picturesque whitewashed churches** up and down the island fling open their doors and the air is filled with hymns and birdsong.

For sunseekers, at the north end of the island there's a pristine expanse of powdery white sand and turquoise water that stretches for three miles along **Cape Santa Maria**. There's also a soft golden curve of sand facing **Guana Cay** in the middle of the island, where there is good snorkelling from shore, and secluded **Lowes Beach**, stretching for several miles along the Atlantic side to the south. Long Island's rolling and varied landscape of steep rocky cliffs, sheltered white-sand coves, green velvety pastures specked with grazing goats and quaint seaside villages such as **Seymours**, **Simms**, **Millers** and **Clarence Town**, with its photogenic historic churches, make for pleasant sightseeing by car or bicycle.

At **Hamilton's Cave** near the village of **Cartwrights** are several underground chambers filled with colourful stalactites, stalagmites and pictographs; the site of a rich find of Lucayan artefacts in recent years. Another worthwhile expedition by car or bicycle is to the **Columbus Monument**, which tops a rocky bluff at the northern tip of the island, with a fantastic panoramic view of sapphire and jade bonefish flats and the white-sand-rimmed clots of land that Columbus surveyed on his two-week tour through the Bahamas in 1492.

Arrival and getting around

There are two **airports** on Long Island, one at Deadman's Cay in the centre of the island and the other at Stella Maris at its northern end. Bahamasair (ⓣ242/352-8341) operates one flight a day from Nassau to Long Island, stopping first at Stella Maris and then Deadman's Cay before heading back to Nassau. If you are staying at the *Stella Maris Resort* (ⓣ242/338-2051, ⓦwww.stellamarisresort.com), their plane flies several times a week to George Town on Great Exuma and to Nassau (US$88 and $124 one-way, respectively).

Two government **mailboats** serve Long Island. The *Mia Dean* departs Potter's Cay in Nassau on Tuesday at noon, reaching Clarence Town at the southern end of Long Island seventeen hours later (US$60 one-way). The *Captin Emmett* departs Nassau Tuesdays at 2pm, calling at Deadman's Cay, Salt Pond, Simms and Seymours in north Long Island after an eight-hour crossing (US$50 one-way). Call the dockmaster's office on Potter's Cay for information (ⓣ242/393 1064).

There are two full-service **marinas** on the island. The Stella Maris Marina (ⓣ242/338 2055), with fifteen boat slips, is located near the *Stella Maris Resort* at the north end of the island, while the Flying Fish Marina, in Clarence Town (ⓣ242/337-3430, ⓔflyfishmarina@batelnet.bs), also has fifteen slips and one nicely appointed double guest room (❹).

There is **no public bus service** on Long Island. Both airports are a couple of miles from the nearest hotel or guesthouse, but **taxis** meet every flight. If you plan to do some exploring on your own, you will need to **rent a car** or **motor scooter**, which can be arranged through your hotel. At the northern end of Long Island, Joe Williams (ⓣ242/338-5002) in Glinton's rents cars for US$65 a day.

With varied scenery and little traffic, Long Island is a wonderful destination for **cyclists**. The two biggest resorts on the island – *Cape Santa Maria Beach Resort* and *Stella Maris Resort* – have serviceable touring bikes for guest use, but if you are planning to put in a lot of miles, bring your own bike. It is reasonably safe to **hitchhike**, but not many people do it.

Accommodation

Cape Santa Maria Beach Resort in North America ⓣ1-800/926-9704 or at resort ⓣ242/338-5273, ⓦwww.capesantamaria.com. A small cottage resort situated on a pristine strand of powdery white beach on a flat, sandy peninsula at the northern tip of Long Island. Twenty double rooms in ten beachfront cottages are decked out with colourful tropical fabrics, clay tile floors and rattan furniture, each with a screened-in porch. There is an attractive dining room and bar and a fitness centre, and the resort offers a full range of watersports as well as fishing trips. Meal plans and all-inclusive packages available. Closed Sept & Oct. 7–9

Chez Pierre ⓣ242/338-8809, ⓦwww.chezpierrebahamas.com. Located on a serene stretch of beach at Miller's Bay (halfway between Deadman's Cay and Stella Maris), *Chez Pierre* has earned rave reviews from guests for the beautiful simplicity of its six elevated timber cottages and for the gourmet cuisine served in the casually elegant lodge. There are kayaks and snorkel gear for guest use, and fishing, car rental and other activities can be arranged. 5 including breakfast and dinner.

Greenwich Creek Lodge Cartwright's ⓣ423/432-0665, ⓦwww.greenwichcreeklodge.com. Situated on the mangrove-edged shore and catering to serious bonefishers, this well-maintained two-storey timber lodge with wraparound verandas houses eight nicely furnished doubles (containing two beds) and four king rooms, some with TV. There is a small dipping pool and a common room where meals are served. Based on double occupancy, a week of bonefishing including accommodation, meals and a guide costs US$2100. They also offer deep-sea and reef fishing charters. 8 All Inclusive.

Lochobar Beach Lodge ⓣ242/337-3123 or c/o Mrs Judy Knowles at *Earlie's Tavern* (ⓣ242/337-1628) in Mangrove Bush, ⓦwww.bahamasvacationguide.com/lochabarbeachlodge. A secluded idyll for those who really want to get away from it all, on an exquisite curve of white-sand beach at Lochobar Bay south of Clarence Town. The two-storey timber and stucco lodge houses two beautifully rustic studio apartments and a one-bedroom apartment sleeping up to five, with French doors that open onto a balcony or patio steps from the beach. 5

Stella Maris Resort in North America ⓣ1-800/426-0466 or at resort ⓣ242/338-2051, ⓦwww.stellamarisresort.com. Sitting atop a green hill with views of both coasts, this is a friendly, unpretentious resort with two dozen bright, comfortable guest rooms housed in a couple of one- and two-storey buildings tucked into a gentle slope, each with a private veranda. There are also several cottages scattered along the rocky oceanfront, three swimming pools, a Jacuzzi, tennis courts and a tennis pro on staff. The main lodge is a cosy place to gather in the evening, with a pleasant bar, a lounge with satellite TV, books and games and an airy appealing dining room. A scenic oceanfront drive leads to several secluded beaches within walking distance, and there is free transportation to other nearby beaches. Snorkelling, diving and fishing trips are offered daily. Meal plans and all-inclusive packages available. 6

Eating and drinking

Cape Santa Maria Resort North Long Island, ⓣ242/338 5273. Has a beautifully atmospheric dining room in a glass-walled two-storey timber beach-house facing the white sand at Cape Santa Maria. The menu features gourmet seafood dishes and imaginative American cuisine. Reservations required.

Harbour Restaurant Clarence Town, ⓣ242/337-3247. A clean and pleasant lunch room with windows overlooking the harbour, near the government dock. The menu has tasty versions of your basic seafood, deep-fried food and sandwiches.

Max Conch Bar and Grill Deadman's Cay ⓣ242/337-0056. A colourful local favourite serving conch cracked, frittered and marinated, as well as fried chicken, burgers and fries at an outdoor kiosk with bar stools and tables.

Oasis Bakery and Restaurant one mile north of Clarence Town on the Queen's Highway, ⓣ242/337-3003. A lovely spot for breakfast or lunch with tables set on a deep wooden veranda overlooking a small pond. Fresh-baked bread, pastries and cookies to eat in or take home, plus inexpensive sandwiches, pizza, burgers and conch done several ways for lunch. Closed Sun.

Stella Maris Resort ⓣ242/338-2050. A pleasant bar and a bright airy hilltop dining room with a sunny, sophisticated decor of potted greenery, honey-coloured rattan, linen tablecloths and huge windows on three sides with pleasing views of flowering trees and the ocean beyond. The delicious breakfast buffet is especially recommended. Reservations advisable.

The Southern Bahamas

The **southernmost islands** of the Bahamas have few inhabitants and receive few visitors. Those who do venture down this way are drawn primarily by the abundant wildlife – the rich fishing grounds that surround the islands and the flamingos, sea turtles and rare birds which inhabit the densely overgrown interior.

While there were around fifty Loyalist cotton plantations on **Crooked** and **Acklins islands** two hundred years ago, today just four hundred people live on each in a smattering of small coastal villages, most without electricity or running water. What the islands may lack in sightseeing destinations, they make up for it with some of the finest tarpon and bonefishing around. For non-fishers, there are several nice stretches of beach to explore. The nicest place to stay on Crooked Island is *Pittstown Point Landings* (ⓣ1-800/752-2322 or 242/344-2507, ⓦwww.pittstownpointlandings.com; ⑦) on a white-sand beach at Landrail Point. On Acklins, the tidy, nicely appointed cottages at *Acklins Lodge* (ⓣ242/344-3500, ⓦwww.acklinsislandlodge.com; ⑨ see site for list of booking agents) are recommended by fishermen.

Great Inagua lies 321 miles southeast of Nassau at the southern tip of the Bahamian archipelago. The shallow waters of Lake Windsor cover one quarter of Inagua's interior, and much of the remaining area is low, flat bush and swamp. The island sits squarely in the path of the relentless trade winds, which combined with a strong, hot sun provide ideal conditions for solar salt production. There is only one settlement on Inagua – **Matthew Town**, at the southwest corner of the island – with a population of about 1200, most of whom are employed at the **Morton Salt Works**, which you can tour by arrangement (ⓣ242/339-1847) The nineteenth-century **Great Inagua Light House**, still operational on a point of land a mile south of Matthew Town, makes a great destination for a short hike.

The bulk of the island – 127 square miles – has been set aside as **Inagua National Park**, a protected conservation area for a large colony of West Indian **flamingos** who nest on the shores of Lake Windsor. Within the National Park is the **Union Creek Turtle Reserve**, a protected habitat and research station devoted to giant sea turtles. The park entrance is twenty miles east of Matthew Town, and to visit you must first make arrangements with the park warden, Henry Nixon, who also takes bookings for the rustic bunkhouse in the park (US$50 per person; ⓣ242/339-1616, ⓕ242/339-1850).

In Matthew Town, you have a choice of simple but clean **guest rooms** with private bath, a/c and TV at the *Morton Salt Company Main House* (ⓣ242/339-1267; ③) or *Walkine's Guest House* (ⓣ242/339-1612; ③), half a mile south of Matthew Town across the road from the beach.

Mayaguana is about as far off the beaten track as you can get in the Bahamas. It receives few visitors apart from the occasional passing yacht cruisers, sport fishermen and scientists who come to study the unique bird and lizard life on the island. Electricity and telephone service arrived only in 1997. The island has about 320 residents in three small settlements tucked in along the shore on the western side of the island. *Baycaneer's Resort* in Pirate's Well (ⓣ & ⓕ242/339-3726, ⓦwww.baycanerbeach.com; ④) has sixteen **rooms** and a restaurant on an empty white-sand beach which runs for several miles in both directions. Local **fishing guide** Leroy Joseph (ⓣ242/339-3065) can take you out for a day of fishing, snorkelling or sightseeing by boat.

Bahamasair (ⓦwww.bahamasair.com) has **air service** to each of the southern islands two or three times a week. The government **mailboats** call at each island once a week; ring the dockmaster at Potter's Cay, Nassau (ⓣ242/393-1064) for departure times, which can vary from week to week. There is a government-operated **ferry** (US$5) from Cove Point, Crooked Island and Lovely Bay on Acklins.

Turks and Caicos

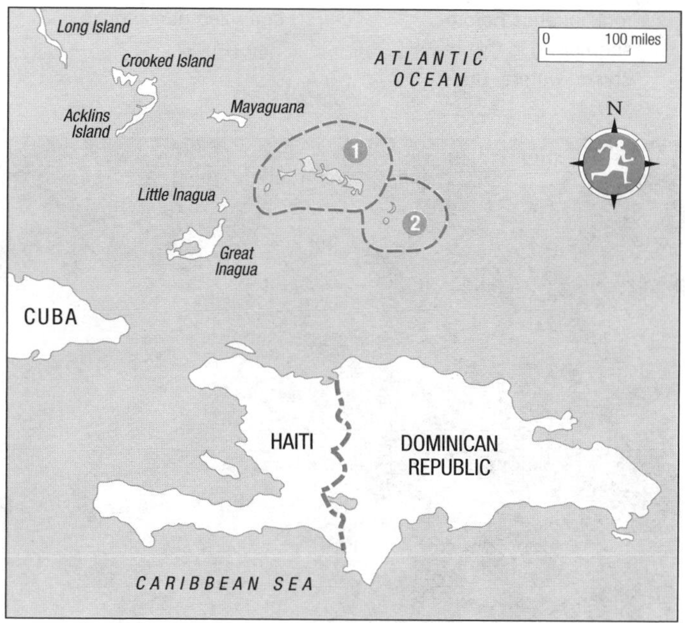

Turks and Caicos highlights

* **Grace Bay beach** Starting to get crowded but still fabulous for walking or swimming, this long white crescent is truly one of the world's great beaches. See p.129

* **Little Water Cay** Mingle with some prehistoric rock iguanas before snorkelling in this cay's crystal waters. See p.132

* **Grand Turk** The quaint colonial streets of this languid island are lined with fine examples of local architecture. See p.139

* **Salt Cay** Spend a day off the beaten track by staying the night in a charming guesthouse. See p.142

▲ Grace Beach

Introduction and basics

The tiny but gorgeous islands of the Turks and Caicos are scattered over a long swath of sea to the south of the Bahamas. Even though an orgy of condo developments has hit Providenciales making it seem like one big building site, the fantastic beaches and great diving on all of the islands keeps the country in the upper echelon of West Indian destinations.

The country comprises two groups of islands – eight inhabited and around forty uninhabited – separated by the Columbus Passage, a deep-water channel up to 6000 feet deep. To the east, the **Turks Islands** include Grand Turk and Salt Cay, the former the long-time home to government, the latter a tiny island named after the salt industry that once dominated the country. To the west, the **Caicos** chain includes South, Middle and North Caicos and the island of Providenciales, known as Provo and home to the great majority of the nation's tourist development.

The major attractions on all of the islands are the coasts: truly sensational white-sand beaches that stretch for miles offering world-class diving, snorkelling, deep-sea fishing and bonefishing. Inland there's not much to see other than low-lying scrubby vegetation and, particularly in the Turks Islands, large expanses of featureless *salinas* from which Bermudian settlers and traders harvested salt during the islands' early development.

Where to go

Most visitors head to **Provo**, which receives nearly all of the country's international flights and has the major hotels and restaurants. Even if you plan to stay on Provo you should consider excursions to one or more other islands, either as day-trips or to spend a night or two. Particularly recommended are **Grand Turk** which, despite its new cruise ship terminal, is a terminally calm, easy-going place just a thirty-minute flight away notable for its great colonial architecture, the National Museum and fantastic diving. Alternatively, join or charter a boat trip around the spectacular **Caicos Cays** to **Middle** or **North Caicos**, where you can check out some dramatic caves or the remains of an old plantation house.

When to go

The Islands are a year-round destination with the most popular periods being from mid-December to mid-April and during the school holidays in July and August. Rainfall is low year-round but, particularly from September to November, the weather can get a bit sticky as the trade winds die down. As elsewhere in the Caribbean, the hurricane season runs from July to November.

Getting there

All international **flights** arrive on the island of Providenciales. American Airlines flies daily from both Miami and New York. British Airways flies on Sundays from London,

Websites

Ⓦ **www.tcimall.tc** "Gateway to the island" with useful contact details and events listings.

Ⓦ **www.tcmuseum.org** Website of the superb national museum on Grand Turk, with lots of interesting features on the islands' history.

Ⓦ **www.tcifreepress.com** The island's principal newspaper, published fortnightly.

Ⓦ **www.turksandcaicostourism.com** The official website of the Turks and Caicos Tourist Board.

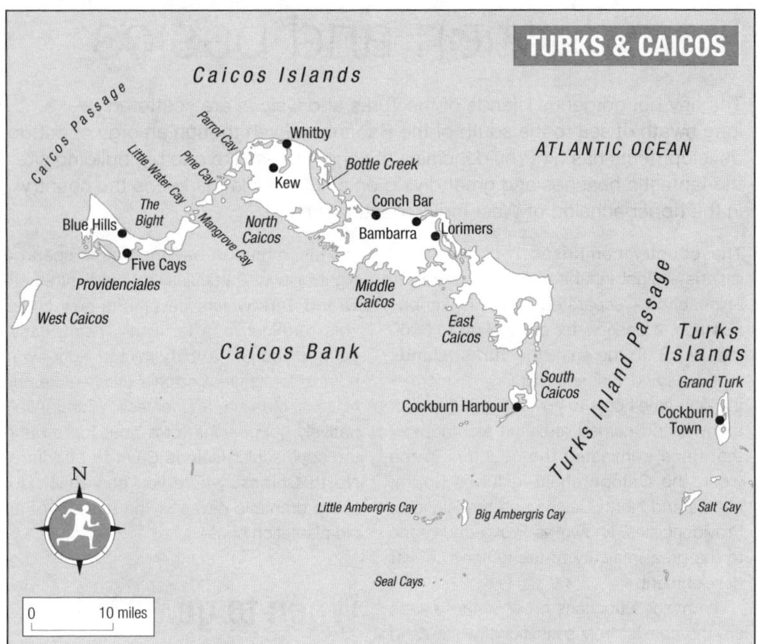

stopping in Nassau en route. Air Canada flies in from Toronto on Wednesdays and Saturdays and from Montreal on Thursdays. Bahamasair leaves Nassau on Tuesdays, Thursdays and Sundays.

Information

Before you leave home, brochures and **information** can be accessed from the Turks and Caicos Tourist Board's helpful website (see box). On the islands, visit the Tourist Board's offices on Front Street on Grand Turk or at the Regent Village in Grace Bay on Provo. See the box for several worthwhile Turks and Caicos **websites**.

The **country code** for Turks and Caicos is ⓣ649.

Money and costs

The official currency of the Turks and Caicos Islands is the **US dollar**. Costs are fairly high as most food, drink and other items are imported. There is a government room tax of 10 percent, and most hotels and restaurants automatically add a 10–15 percent **service charge** – so check your bill to ensure you're not paying twice. Unless a service charge is added, **tipping** is customary, with 15 percent being average. Most places take credit cards.

Providenciales and Grand Turk each have several banks with ATMs; the only one with international access is Scotiabank.

There is a $90 **departure tax**, incorporated into the cost of the airline ticket.

Getting around

Travelling between the main islands is relatively easy with two local **airlines** offering frequent connections: Air Turks and Caicos (ⓣ649/941-5481, ⓦwww.airturksandcaicos.com), and Skyking (ⓣ649/941-3136 ⓦwww.skyking.tc). Skyking has eight daily scheduled half-hour flights each way between Provo and Grand Turk, three stopping in South Caicos to pick up and drop off in both directions. Round-trip fares cost $150. Air Turks and Caicos has daily flights between Provo and North and Middle Caicos and Salt Cay (between $90 and $150 round-trip) and between Grand Turk and Salt Cay ($80).

Both Provo and Grand Turk have taxi services, and there will invariably be a **taxi** waiting for passengers at the airports. **Car and jeep rental** – about $70 a day – is easiest on Providenciales or Grand Turk. Elsewhere you may struggle to get a rental; it's worth asking at your hotel.

Accommodation

There are plenty of **places to stay** in the Turks and Caicos, though most options fall near the upper end of the price scale. Provo has by far the most choices while pickings are somewhat slim on the Turks Islands but you should still be able to find a suitable spot.

Food and drink

Visitors are spoilt for culinary choice on Providenciales, which has a fantastic range of restaurants catering to most budgets. Be warned, however, that since most of the **food** is imported there are few bargains. On the other islands the options are strictly limited, which is not surprising given the relatively low number of visitors. The islands' main speciality is the delicious conch – served raw in salads and cooked in fritters, chowder, or "cracked" (battered and fried) – and you'll find plenty of excellent fresh fish, particularly snapper and grouper.

Turks Head is the local beer but there is a wide variety of imported **beers** on offer and a surprisingly good selection of **wines** (at least on Provo).

Public holidays

Aside from the Caribbean-wide **holidays**, Turks and Caicos also celebrate the holidays listed below.

January 1	New Year's Day
March 10	Commonwealth Day
March/April	Good Friday
March/April	Easter Monday
May 26	National Heroes Day
June 16	Queen's Birthday
August 1	Emancipation Day
October 13	Columbus Day
October 24	International Human Rights Day
December 25	Christmas Day
December 26	Boxing Day

History

The first inhabitants of the Turks and Caicos Islands were **Amerindians** whose sites and relics have been found dotted across the islands; the more important recent finds include one at the Conch Bar Caves in Middle Caicos. The Amerindian period is well documented at the National Museum in Grand Turk.

A major debate endures regarding the first European visitor to the islands. While the island of San Salvador in the Bahamas has probably the strongest claim as the location where **Christopher Columbus** first set foot in the Americas in 1492, many argue that his ships actually first landed at Grand Turk.

With Spanish slaving ships raiding the islands for Amerindian labour for the gold mines of South America, by 1513 the population had been reduced to zero. Ownership of the islands passed between Spain, France and Britain but none was interested in setting up base. Between 1690 and 1720, **pirates** used Providenciales and the Caicos Cays as hiding places, and stories of buried gold and jewels still bring treasure hunters to the islands.

By the late seventeenth century a new treasure drew a new type of visitor to the islands: **salt-rakers** from Bermuda, who had discovered the ease with which salt could be produced from shallow saltwater ponds (or *salinas*) which were constructed across the islands. This was particularly true in Salt Cay, Grand Turk and South Caicos where large numbers of trees were felled to discourage rainfall (resulting in the largely bare landscape that endures today). "White gold", as the stuff came to be known, was a highly lucrative crop, much of it sent off to Newfoundland to preserve cod. The remaining grand houses on Salt Cay are testament to that profitable era. By 1781 the rakers had established a permanent settlement in Grand Turk.

Meanwhile the Caicos Islands were uninhabited until after the American War of Independence, when thousands of defeated **Loyalists** fled to the islands from the southern states such as Georgia and the Carolinas. Some were granted large tracts of land by the British government in recompense for what they had lost in North America. Around forty Loyalists arrived during the 1780s, bringing with them more than one thousand slaves, and began farming cotton.

Though immediately successful – **Caicos cotton** was said to be among the finest in the world – the cotton industry went into decline after only a generation with hurricanes and pests taking a heavy toll. While a few planters moved to the Turks Islands and went into salt production, almost all of the planters left the country by the mid-1820s, leaving their slaves behind to a subsistence existence of farming and fishing, similar to the lifestyle of the original Amerindians.

For the next century the economy was sustained by the remnants of the salt industry but there was little population growth. Things began to change with the arrival of a group of American investors in the 1960s who laid the foundations for **tourist development**, building a small airstrip on Provo and erecting the first hotel – *Third Turtle* – in Turtle Cove. A trickle of foreign visitors began to arrive, turning into a steady stream once *Club Med* insisted on a proper airport to service their Grace Bay resort in the mid-1980s, and became a small flood with the arrival of further resorts through the 1990s – including the ultra-trendy and prohibitively expensive *Parrot Cay* hotel and spa, home away from home to models, movie stars and fashion designers.

2.1

The Caicos Islands

The **CAICOS ISLANDS** form a rough semicircle, running clockwise from the lovely and uninhabited island of West Caicos, up through the major tourist centre of Providenciales and a chain of tiny islands – the Caicos Cays – to North Caicos, down through the largest island, Middle Caicos, by uninhabited East Caicos and ending with the once busy but now largely ignored island of South Caicos.

North and Middle have their individual charms and can be easily accessed from Providenciales by plane or via a fabulous boat trip from Leeward or Walkin Dock – a highlight of any stay in the islands.

Providenciales

PROVIDENCIALES, known as Provo, is the mainstay of the country's tourist industry. With little in the way of cultural life or historical interest, for decades only a handful of visitors made their way here, attracted particularly by the superb opportunities for diving and fishing in the offshore waters. Tourism began to heat up in the 1980s with the arrival of Club Med, and rocketed during the 1990s as investors spotted the great potential for resorts. The opening of *Beaches* (part of the enormously successful Sandals resort chain) in the late 1990s put Provo on the tourism map, and the island seems poised to buckle under the weight of the many condo developments underway. Despite the rapid development, the beach at Grace Bay remains world-class.

There's no town to speak of on the island. **Downtown**, as the business centre is known, is a rather ugly group of shops and offices that you'll pass through on your way from the airport. The three original settlements (which can loosely be described as villages) are little visited by tourists: **Blue Hills**, a pretty residential area that runs alongside the sea north of the airport; **Five Cays**, a drab collection of homes and shops on the south of the island; and a similar cluster around the *Beaches* resort known as **The Bight**.

For many visitors the only worthwhile land-based sightseeing is wandering along the twelve miles of magnificent beach on **Grace Bay**, running from Leeward in the far east of the island along to the Bight. It's a spectacular stroll beside a turquoise sea, with occasional shade offered by the casuarina trees.

More adventurous visitors will want to take advantage of the **boat trips** that run from Leeward or Walkin Dock to the Caicos Cays, where you can spot rock iguanas, hunt for sand dollars and make a picnic on a deserted island.

Arrival and getting around

Nearly all visitors arrive at **Providenciales International Airport** which sits roughly in the centre of the island. There's always a string of taxis waiting outside, and a ride to the hotels along Grace Bay costs $20–30. A couple of car rental desks can be found in the airport terminal.

A **bus service** operates along the island's main artery, Leeward Highway, but it does not stop at the airport nor does it have a set timetable. The Gecko shuttle

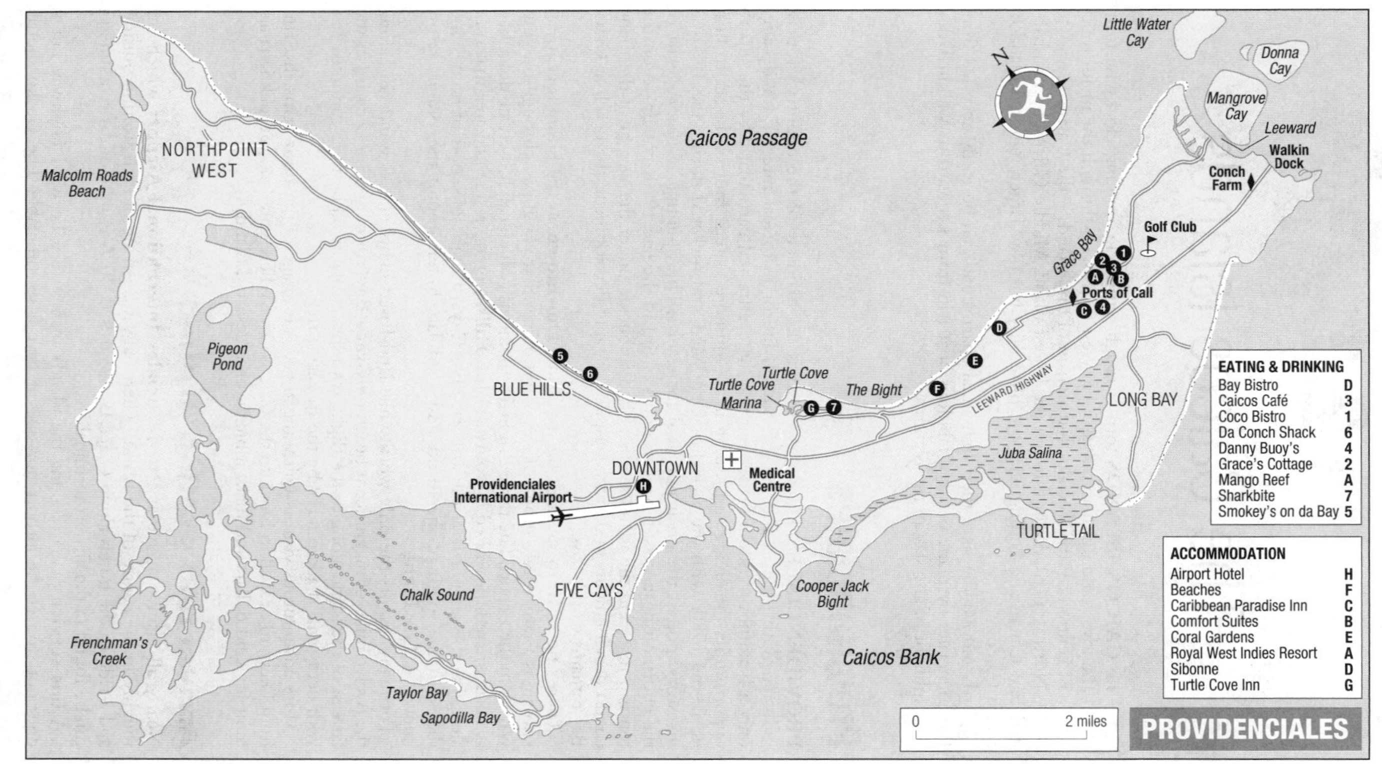
PROVIDENCIALES
Caicos Passage
Caicos Bank
Little Water Cay
Donna Cay
Mangrove Cay
Leeward
Walkin Dock
Conch Farm
Golf Club
Grace Bay
Ports of Call
LONG BAY
LEEWARD HIGHWAY
Juba Salina
TURTLE TAIL
The Bight
Turtle Cove
Turtle Cove Marina
Medical Centre
DOWNTOWN
Providenciales International Airport
BLUE HILLS
FIVE CAYS
Cooper Jack Bight
Chalk Sound
Taylor Bay
Sapodilla Bay
Frenchman's Creek
Pigeon Pond
NORTHPOINT WEST
Malcolm Roads Beach
0 2 miles
EATING & DRINKING
Bay Bistro D
Caicos Café 3
Coco Bistro 1
Da Conch Shack 6
Danny Buoy's 4
Grace's Cottage 2
Mango Reef A
Sharkbite 7
Smokey's on da Bay 5
ACCOMMODATION
Airport Hotel H
Beaches F
Caribbean Paradise Inn C
Comfort Suites B
Coral Gardens E
Royal West Indies Resort A
Sibonne D
Turtle Cove Inn G

service (☎649/232-7433, Ⓦwww.thegecko.tc) runs between the main hotels and restaurants on Grace Bay; one-stop tokens are $4, day passes are $11. If you want to explore the island for a day or two it's worth **renting a car** (or a jeep if you want to make a trip to Malcolm Roads); try Rent-a-Buggy (☎649/946-4158) or Grace Bay Car Rentals (☎649/941-8500). Expect to pay $40–70 a day, including insurance. **Scooters** can be rented from Scooter Bob's (☎649/946-4684) for $49/day.

For **taxis**, try Nell's (☎649/231-0051 or 941-3228) or Provo Taxi (☎649/946-5481).

Accommodation

Due to the resort boom of the past decade there are plenty of **hotels** on Provo, though most are at the top end in terms of price. By far the most popular are the **all-inclusives** like *Beaches* but several along the north coast offer excellent options.

If you're thinking of renting a **villa**, try Prestigious Properties (☎649/946-4379, Ⓦwww.prestigious properties.com), which has a superb range of places starting from around $3000/week.

Camping is permitted on the many cays ofTurks and Caicos as well as on Middle Caicos, though there are no official campsite, so you'll have to bring all your own gear. Campers are strongly encouraged to register with the Department of Environment and Coastal Resources (☎649/941-5122).

Airport

Turks and Caicos Airport Hotel Airport Rd ☎649/941-3514, Ⓦwww.airportinntci.com. Far from the beach (though they'll provide a free ride to get there), this is one of the cheapest options on Provo, with twenty-two clean and tidy rooms with a/c. All have cable TV, and there's a local restaurant and bar on site. ④

Turtle Cove

Turtle Cove Inn Turtle Cove ☎649/946-4203, Ⓦwww.turtlecoveinn.com. A ten-minute walk from the nearest decent beach, this is a relaxed and reasonably priced little place near the marina and a couple of good restaurants. There's a small, shaded pool, and the friendly *Tiki* Bar is right next door at the marina. ④

Grace Bay

Beaches Grace Bay ☎649/946-8000, Ⓦwww.beaches.com. This all-inclusive resort – part of the impressive Sandals chain – is aimed at families, with top-class facilities for entertaining children, including a pirate island, an arcade centre and their own restaurant and disco. Rooms are spacious and colourful, all within a short walk of the glorious beach and a number of pools. Watersports facilities are top-notch, while the eleven restaurants offer excellent options ranging from Italian and French to Caribbean and Japanese, some catering to adults only. ⑧

Caribbean Paradise Inn Grace Bay ☎649/946-5020, Ⓦwww.caribbean-paradise-inn.com. One of the cheapest options in the Grace Bay area and not a bad spot, the hotel is a five-minute walk from the beach and near the Ports of Call shopping area and restaurants. There are seventeen rooms, all with king or two double beds, cable TV, a fridge, telephone and a/c. ⑤–⑥

Comfort Suites Grace Bay ☎649/946-8888, Ⓦwww.comfortsuitestci.com. This chain hotel across the street from Grace Bay is a good value with 98 clean and serviceable rooms and, if you feel too lazy to walk across the street to the beach, a nice-sized pool. ⑤–⑥

Coral Gardens Grace Bay ☎649/343-0350, Ⓦwww.coralgardensongracebay.com. This small block of smart and good-value one-, two- and three-bedroom condominiums is popular with repeat visitors to the island. All condos are good-sized, with private balconies, sea views, fully equipped kitchens and daily maid service. Close to a good snorkelling site with an onsite dive shop. ⑥–⑦

Royal West Indies Resort Grace Bay ☎649/946-5004, Ⓦwww.royalwestindies.com. Attractive, comfortable and very popular condo-resort on a great stretch of beach, with well-kept gardens and a huge pool. The staff is particularly friendly and helpful. ⑧–⑨

Sibonné Grace Bay ☎649/946-5547, Ⓦwww.sibonne.com. One of the most charming and best-value options on the island, this small boutique hotel sits beside a magnificent stretch of white sand and houses the *Bay Bistro*, one of Provo's finest restaurants. The attractively landscaped two-storey hotel has a tiny pool and 27 medium-sized rooms, all with a/c. ⑤

The Caicos Cays

Strung out in a chain between Providenciales and North Caicos are the Caicos Cays, a dozen tiny islands, of which all but two are inhabited. The most likely way to set foot on any of the cays is by taking a boat trip from Leeward or Walkin Dock (see below). All beaches are open to the public and you're pretty much free to wander around at your leisure. Five minutes by boat from Provo, the nature reserve of Little Water Cay ($5 admission fee) is home to several thousand rock iguanas. These reptiles – unique to the region – were once found through the islands, but development has led to their virtual extinction elsewhere. Here, wooden boardwalks have been put up across the cay to allow you access to the heart of their protected habitat. You'll see dozens of iguanas – up to two feet long – sunning themselves on the beach or foraging around in the scrub. Northeast of the cay, Water Cay is fringed by small, sandy cliffs and fantastic white sand, while the adjoining Pine Cay has a small hotel and about 35 private homes dotted around its beaches and interior providing winter retreats for their wealthy and mostly US-based owners. The twelve-room Meridian Club hotel (ⓣ978/664-2587, in the US ⓣ1-866/746-3229, ⓦwww.meridianclub.com; ⑨) is one of the finest of its kind in the world, priding itself on being simple but classy ("barefoot informality" is the apposite slogan), with nature trails crossing the cay, and kayaks, snorkelling, fishing and diving all available for guests. Children under 12 are allowed only in June and July.

Beyond Pine Cay as you head east, Fort George Cay once housed a fort erected in the eighteenth century by the British to deter pirates from concealing themselves and plunder pinched from Spanish galleons sailing further south. The fort is long gone, though two of its iron cannons can be seen by snorkellers in shallow water just off the northwest shore.

Last in the chain and closest to North Caicos, Parrot Cay (formerly known as Pirate cay, and thought to have been a refuge for pirates such as Calico Jack, Anne Bonney and Mary Read) saw an ultramodern multimillion-dollar hotel (ⓣ649/946-7788, in the US ⓣ1-877/754-0726, ⓦwww.parrotcay.como.bz) open its doors in the late 1990s. With just fifty rooms and six villas, some with private swimming pools, and a fabulous spa, the place is altogether grander (and, most would say, rather snootier) than the Meridian Club on Pine Cay. Prices starting at $760 a room in high season ($3200 for a villa) mean that it's for the rich only, and in true copy-cat style a bunch of celebrities have beaten a steady trail to this island since the likes of Paul McCartney stayed.

Leeward and Walkin Dock

The eastern end of the island – near the new Leeward development of condos, shops and eateries – and overlooking the first of the Caicos Cays (see box above), is home to most of the chartered boat tour groups. You can just about make out the mangrove swamps of Mangrove Cay directly across the channel and, looking to your left, the sandy beaches of Little Water Cay where rock iguanas strut their stuff. If it's a calm day, it's worth renting a kayak from Big Blue ($20 per hour for a double, $15 for a single; ⓣ649/946-5034) for an hour or two of cruising across to the cay and stopping on a deserted sandbank or beach to look for shells.

If you're feeling less energetic, a number of professional operators are based here or at nearby Walkin Dock. The outfits run excellent **sailing boat or speedboat trips** to Little Water Cay to see the iguanas and to other nearby cays for shelling and picnics, normally stopping for some excellent snorkelling en route. Even more adventurous, and definitely worth trying, are the speedboat trips that race through the cays to Middle Caicos where you can visit the Conch Bar Caves. The journey takes about ninety minutes each way, with stops en route to see the iguanas and to do some snorkelling.

The main **speedboat operators** are Silver Deep (ⓣ649/946-5612) and J&B Tours (ⓣ649/946-5047). Both run similar trips for similar prices; expect to pay around $45 per person for the visit to Little Water Cay and $195 to Middle Caicos. Big Blue (☎649/946-5034) runs slightly pricier tours, with more emphasis on "eco-adventures".

Sailing, snorkelling and shelling trips are run by Sail Provo (☎649/946-4783) and Beluga (☎649/946-4396) on comfortable catamarans; both offer sunset cruises for around $60 per person.

The Caicos Conch Farm

Tucked away in the wilds of Leeward east of the marina, the **Caicos Conch Farm** on Leeward Highway (Mon–Fri 9am–4pm; $7, $3 for children) is the only one of its kind in the world. Started in 1984, the farm rears queen conch – a giant sea snail famous for its gorgeous pink shells and rare pearls – for export and for sale in the islands. Conch – pronounced *konk* – are subject to numerous predators in the sea, including sharks, stingrays, porcupine fish and octopus. At the farm they are protected, first in large hatcheries and then, as they grow towards adulthood at three to five years, in pens at sea. You can't see much of the shells in the sea, but frequently run, twenty-minute **tours** of the farm offer a chance to see thumb-sized baby conch, check out what they're fed, and see an impressive demonstration of this cehphalopod's arm strength as it tries to dig itself into the sand as a tour guide lifts it out.

Long Bay and the Hole

Just a short drive west of the Conch Farm, **Long Bay Hills** is a residential area on the south side of the island with an impressive stretch of sand. Unfortunately millions of conch shells wash up on the shore making swimming awkward, though you'll notice that some local house owners have tried to clear a path to the ocean. Follow signs to the hidden and rather dramatic **Hole** (always open; free), an eighty-foot drop down to a wide green pond. Brave souls have been known to scramble down for a swim in the icy water but there are no ropes or other protection, so be careful and make sure to keep small children well away.

▲ A queen conch peers out from its shell

Blue Hills and Malcolm Roads

West of Long Bay, Leeward Highway cuts straight across Provo to the island's tiny commercial centre, downtown. Just before you reach downtown, turn off to the right onto Blue Hills Road for what is perhaps the prettiest drive on the island. After about half a mile, take the right fork leading onto a coastal road that passes **Blue Hills**, the most attractive of Provo's original settlements. With an astounding variety of churches and a graveyard where all the graves face out to sea, the village has some great bars on the beach serving fish and conch snacks and lunches.

If you've got a jeep, you can turn around and take the left fork that you passed before and join the continuation of the road you avoided earlier by forking right, which continues west towards Malcolm Roads beach and Northwest Point. Where this road divides, take the left turn down a diabolical track for about four miles to Malcolm Roads. As you crawl along this rocky road look out for osprey nests – large bundles of twigs and sticks – and enjoy the great views over the bays as well as the virtually inaccessible inland ponds known for their spectacular birdlife.

The beach at **Malcolm Roads** is one of the most beautiful spots in the country, and well worth the tortuous passage. The surf crashes on the magnificent beach, which you can expect to have to yourself, though you may see dive boats moored offshore at some great dive sites. Bring water as there's no shelter and no facilities. You can also clamber around some rocky outcrops to find tiny coves for swimming.

Five Cays, Chalk Sound and the south

On the south side of the island lies one of Provo's original settlements at Five Cays (named after the small group of rocks just offshore) and the gorgeous Chalk Sound national park and semicircular Taylor Bay.

From downtown, turn south down the main road virtually opposite the airport road. A left turn at the gas station leads to **Five Cays** – an uninspiring and unkempt jumble of houses, schools and small businesses. Make sure, however, to stop at the excellent Liz's Bakery (6am–8pm; closed Sundays) on the main road for freshly baked breads, cakes and pastries.

Continuing south on the main road towards the island's main dock at South Dock, a turn to the right just before you reach the sea leads to the gloriously milky blue **Chalk Sound**, a stunning lagoon and national park; bear in mind that it's not a great place to swim because of the silty bottom. The Sound is protected from the sea by a narrow peninsula which is indented with a series of bays and sprinkled with grand and very expensive private homes. **Sapodilla Bay** is the first and largest of the bays, with a handful of yachts normally moored just offshore. At the eastern end of the bay are a number of inscriptions in the rock that were carved by shipwrecked sailors in the early nineteenth century.

Beyond Sapodilla Bay, **Taylor Bay** has a perfect crescent of sand. Like Chalk Sound and Sapodilla Bay, however, it's not a great place to swim.

Eating and drinking

Provo has a good range of places to **eat**, from fine French and Italian restaurants to local hostelries dishing up traditional island food. As you'd expect, seafood has pride of place on most menus, with conch taking centre stage. Vegetarians will struggle to find much in the way of variety.

Grace Bay

Bay Bistro *Sibonné*, Grace Bay ⓣ649/946-5396. Sip a cocktail at the bar and watch a fabulous sunset at this easy-going bistro. The fish and lobster are superb, and there's a smaller selection of fine cuts of beef or lamb. Finish with the *crème brûlée* – it's huge, but you'll manage it. Starters cost $8–12, mains $25–35. Lunch and dinner, brunch Sat–Sun.

Caicos Café Grace Bay main road ⓣ649/946-5278. Across the street from the beach, but with plenty of atmosphere on its wooden, Caribbean-style deck fairy lights in the tress. The menu is French-Caribbean with an emphasis on fresh seafood like tuna carpaccio for $21 and red snapper sautéed in olive oil for $29. Lunch and dinner, closed Sun.

Coco Bistro Grace Bay main road ⓣ649/946-5369. Nestled in one of the island's largest coconut groves, this charming spot features a good variety of meat and fish dishes like roast rack of Colorado lamb for $39 and soft-shell crab tempura for $36. Dinner only; reservations recommended.

Danny Buoy's Grace Bay main road ⓣ649/946-5921. The ubiquitous Irish-themed pub has now reached Provo, serving pints of Guinness as well as local Turks Head beer. Food is inexpensive and filling, with wraps, burgers and the like for around $10, and there are daily happy hours from 4–7pm. Lunch and dinner daily, breakfast Sat–Sun.

Grace's Cottage *Point Grace Hotel*, Grace Bay ⓣ649/946-5096. Gorgeous little cottage with outdoor seating serving wonderful food with an emphasis on the freshest catch. Expect to find dishes like sea bass with cassava purée and steamed grouper, and to pay around $50–60 for two courses. Dinner only; reservations required.

Mango Reef *Royal West Indies*, Grace Bay ⓣ649/946-8200. Even if you're not staying at the resort, it's well worth visiting this delicious spot. Prices are reasonable, with salads around $8 and mains around $20, and the menu features eclectic selections like Dominican paella with lobster and deep-fried spring rolls. Breakfast, lunch and dinner daily.

Other Areas

Da Conch Shack and Rum Bar Front Road, Blue Hills ⓣ649/946-8877. This waterside casual spot serves conch so fresh you can watch employees remove it from the shell. It comes cracked, stir-fried, sautéed and curried among other preparations. White picnic tables litter the sand and the rum punch is killer. Dishes run $8–15. Lunch and dinner daily, live music Thurs.

Smokey's On Da Bay Front Road, Blue Hills ⓣ649/941-7852. This is the place to come for traditional island fare like codfish, peas and rice and pig feet souse (a stew), if you dare. There's also a fish fry and live music on Wed. Lunch and dinner.

Sharkbite Turtle Cove ⓣ649/941-5090. This great spot overlooking the marina offers tasty meals from almond-crusted grouper in curry sauce ($25) to cracked conch ($13) and burgers ($10). Adjacent to the restaurant there's a long and busy bar, and underwater floodlights illuminate the sea life at night next to the outdoor deck. Lunch and dinner.

Nightlife and entertainment

Nightlife on Provo is fairly quiet. *Calico Jacks* (ⓣ649/946-5129), in the Ports of Call shopping centre, has live music every Friday and some Saturdays. *Jimmy's Dive Bar* (ⓣ649/946-5282), also in Ports of Call, is open till eleven and features $4 *mojitos* on Monday, and a regular happy hour. Local soca and reggae bands also play at a variety of venues around the island; ask at your hotel for what's on. If you want test your luck, head to the Casablanca Casino on Grace Bay Road or The Player's Club at Turtle Cove for blackjack and roulette, and finish off with a bop in the hotel's nightclub.

The biggest party of the year is the Turks and Caicos Music and Cultural Festival, which takes place in late July and early August and features a variety of musicians like India Arie and Alicia Keys as well as a beauty pageant.

Watersports and other activities

The **diving** around Provo is as good as you'll find anywhere in the Caribbean. Although the best wall diving is a lot further from shore than you'll find in Grand Turk, Provo has a great variety of excellent sites including those at Northwest Point and at West Caicos, between forty-five and fifty-five minutes by boat from Turtle Cove marina.

Reputable **operators** include the longstanding Provo Turtle Divers (ⓣ649/946-4232, ⓦwww.provoturtledivers.com), Dive Provo (ⓣ649/946-5029, ⓦwww.diveprovo.com), and Big Blue Unlimited (ⓣ649/946-5034, ⓦwww.bigblue.tc), which also run kayaking tours of the cays. Expect to pay around $100/200 for a two-tank/three-tank dive, $100 for a night dive or $250 for a resort course, which includes a two-tank dive. A four- or five-day open-water certification course, involving four or five two-tank dives, costs $500 with Provo Turtle Divers.

The best places to **snorkel** are near the *Coral Gardens* hotel and at Smith's Reef, just east of the entrance to the Turtle Cove marina on the north coast. At both places you'll find good reefs just offshore. Alternatively, take one of the island/snorkelling trips offered by the outfits at Leeward and Walkin Dock for around $75.

Other **watersports** abound, and the larger hotels all have good facilities for their guests. At Grace Bay, Windsurfing Provo (☎649/241-1687) offers rental and instruction on windsurfers, kitesurfers and small sailing boats.

Fishing charters offer superb deep-sea fishing for marlin, wahoo, tuna and shark, difficult but exhilarating bonefishing in the shallow flats around the islands and bottom-fishing for grouper, snapper and parrotfish. For deep-sea fishing, try Catch the Wave (☎649/941-3047) expect to pay $1600/850 for a full/half-day's fishing for up to six people or $250 on your own. For bonefishing or bottom-fishing, try Catch the Wave or Silver Deep (☎649/946-5612), both at Walkin Dock. In July there's a huge billfish tournament, with boats coming from around the world to hunt for the biggest blue marlin in the sea.

Provo Golf and Country Club (☎649/946-5991) offers a magnificent **golf** course rated by many as one of the finest in the region. You'll pay $160 for 18 holes and a cart or $90 for nine holes. Many of the hotels have private **tennis** courts.

Listings

Banks Scotiabank has branches at the IGA on Leeward Highway, Ports of Call shopping centre, and various other locations on Provo. Branch hours are Mon–Thurs 8.30am–2.30pm, Fri 8.30am–4.30pm.
Emergencies ☎911.
Internet access Try TCI Online at Ports of Call. Most hotels and some restaurants have wireless in their lobbies and/or bar areas.
Laundry Pioneer Cleaners, Butterfield Square, Downtown ☎649/941-4402.
Medical services Associated Medical Practices, Leeward Highway (☎649/946-4242, ⓦwww.doctor.tc); Grace Bay Medical Centre, Grace Bay (☎649/941-5252).
Police ☎649/946-4259.
Post office Airport Rd (Mon–Fri 8am–noon & 2–4pm).

North Caicos

NORTH CAICOS is the most lush and in many ways the most beautiful of the nation's islands. Receiving more rainfall than anywhere else, the vegetation is denser and taller here than on the other island, and many islanders keep vegetables patches and grow fruit trees, including tamarind, papaya and sapodilla. As you'd expect, the beaches are great too. Property speculators have pushed land prices to dramatic heights in the hope that North Caicos will become the "next big thing". Their optimism seems to be paying off, as tourist development is slowly beginning to increase, but for now the island remains delightfully quiet – almost like Provo a decade ago.

Arrival, information and getting around

There are no international flights to North Caicos and most people arrive by **plane** from Providenciales with Air Turks and Caicos. **Ferries** depart from Walkin Dock five times per day for $25 one-way or $40 return.

The island does not have a tourist office. Cars can be rented from Gardiners (☎649/946-7141), for around $75 per day, and there are **taxis** at the airport to meet incoming flights. Check ⓦwww.tcimall.com for more car rental agents.

Accommodation

Most of the **hotels** on North Caicos are scattered along the lovely sandy beaches of Whitby; the *Bottle Creek Lodge* is a delightful place on the other side of the island.

Bottle Creek Lodge Bottle Creek ⓣ649/946-7080, ⓦwww.bottlecreeklodge.com. Comfortable eco-friendly accommodation in two cottages and an apartment, overlooking the turquoise creek that divides North and Middle Caicos. Not ideal for the beach, but a very relaxed place offering free bicycles and kayaks. The owners will also arrange snorkelling and fishing expeditions. ⑥

Pelican Beach Hotel Whitby ⓣ649/946-7112, ⓦwww.pelicanbeach.tc. Laid-back and longstanding small hotel with excellent ocean views from the a/c upstairs rooms and unpretentious but comfortable furnishings and decoration. There's a cosy bar, and you can expect to find good local food at the roomy restaurant. ⑥

The island

At the west end of the island, **Sandy Point** is a small fishing community and your likely arrival point if you're coming by boat from Provo. Just offshore lie three prominent rocks known as **Three Mary Cays**; one of them has a huge osprey nest, whose occupant is often seen gazing imperiously over passing vessels. Back on land, and a short drive from Sandy Point, birdwatchers can douse themselves in bug spray and make for **Cottage Pond**, a small nature reserve with a deep sinkhole that's inhabited by ducks, grebes and other birds. A little further east, **Flamingo Pond** has a large expanse of brackish water where you can normally spy a flock of flamingos (though it's hard to get close – bring binoculars).

On the north side of Flamingo Pond, **Whitby** is home to North Caicos's main hotels and guesthouses and borders a number of excellent white-sand beaches with good snorkelling just offshore. On the village's western edge the powdery sands of Pumpkin Bluff Beach are especially magnificent while on the eastern side Pelican Point is a good place to snorkel.

South of Whitby, the road leads inland to the farming settlement at **Kew** – the only inland original settlement – named after the botanical gardens in London and home to many of the island's most productive fruit and vegetable growers. There is also a post office, church and general store.

A mile west of Kew are the extensive though unspectacular ruins of **Wades Green Plantation** where you're free to wander around the remains of the massive kitchen, overseer's house, stables and walled garden plots. Built in 1789 by Wade Stubbs, the plantation developed high-quality cotton and was a rare success story for the area; upon his death in 1822, Stubbs owned over 8000 acres on North and Middle Caicos and Providenciales as well as 384 slaves, many of whom took his surname. Consequently today Stubbs is one of the most common names on the islands.

On the eastern side of the island **Bottle Creek**, North Caicos's largest settlement, sits along the ridge overlooking the creek between North and Middle Caicos. It's a gorgeous spot, especially if you're passing through by boat, but there's little specific sightseeing. If you're driving, the Middle Caicos causeway links North and Middle Caicos at Bottle Creek, and deposits drivers at Conch Bar on the other side.

Eating and drinking

Away from the hotels, there's not much in the way of **restaurants** or bars, and **nightlife** tends to be quiet.

Club Titters Bottle Creek ⓣ649/946-7316. This local place dishes up tasty and inexpensive fare all day, including grouper with peas and rice and cracked conch, and there's occasional live entertainment at weekends.

Pelican Beach Hotel Whitby ⓣ649/946-7112. Good mixture of local and international food at this hotel's eatery, with plenty of fine grilled snapper and grouper, served up with fresh North Caicos vegetables. The place can lack atmosphere when it's quiet, but has a very easy-going vibe.

Middle Caicos

Home to just three hundred people, **MIDDLE CAICOS** is the country's largest island and one of its quietest. Despite the abundance of great beaches, especially at **Mudjin Harbour** near Conch Bar and further east at **Bambarra**, tourist development has been very slow and there are few facilities for visitors; you'll find just a handful of villas and a couple of taxi drivers. If you're after peace and quiet, you couldn't find many better refuges in the country, but don't expect the watersports or food choices of other islands.

Middle Caicos was settled by **Lucayan Indians** between the eighth century and around 1540, by which time Spanish slave traders had killed or shipped off the local population for servitude in South American mines. The island remained uninhabited until Loyalists and their slaves arrived from North America after the Revolution. As elsewhere in the islands, the settlers' attempts at growing cotton made little progress and, within a generation, they had departed, leaving their former slaves to run the three north coast settlements that survive today.

Arrival, information and getting around

Air Turks and Caicos operates daily **flights** to Middle Caicos from Providenciales, some of them stopping at North Caicos en route. The new causeway between Bottle Creek on North Caicos and Conch Bar on Middle Caicos also makes getting around convenient for drivers.

You won't find a tourist office on the island or a car rental outlet, but there are a couple of local **taxi** drivers who prowl around the airport and will be delighted to take you on a tour of the island – reckon on around $60 per hour. Try Cardinal Arthur (Ⓣ649/946-6107). They'll also be happy to organize fishing trips for you on the shallow waters south of the island.

Accommodation

With just one official **resort** and only a handful of rental villas, Middle Caicos is quiet indeed. Check Ⓦwww.tcimall.com for some suggestions.

Blue Horizon Resort Mudjin Harbour Ⓣ649/946-6141, Ⓦwww.bhresort.com. A handful of large and comfortable cottages perched on the hilltops above the harbour, with fine views over the coastline. It's a fabulously relaxed place, a short walk from a superb beach – sometimes pounded by waves, at other times blissfully calm – though don't come expecting much in the way of entertainment or nightlife. The staff will organize snorkelling or hiking expeditions on request. 6–7

Around the island

One of the main draws in Middle Caicos is a series of limestone **caves** at Conch Bar. Formed over millennia by water slowly carving into the soft rock, the extensive network was once home for the Lucayan Indians and various artefacts – including tools and pottery – are on display at the National Museum in Grand Turk. Tours of the caves need to be arranged in advance, either through a tour company in Provo or by booking a tour with one of the Middle Caicos taxi drivers (see above).

If you are here on a tour, you'll probably spend some time at **Mudjin Harbour**, a short drive east of the caves. It's a dramatic setting with tall cliffs dropping down to the sea, a rocky promontory just offshore and waves often crashing onto a yellow-sand beach. As you go down to the beach there's a short trail off to the left that leads to the top of the cliff where you'll have fantastic views down the coast and the island's scrubby, undeveloped interior.

East of here the road leads to the small settlement of **Bambarra**, which has a large and very quiet white-sand beach framed by casuarina trees; at low tide you can wade out along a sandbank for half a mile to the delightful beach at Pelican Cay. Continuing further east, **Lorimers** – named after a local plantation owner – is one of the most remote settlements in the country, though there's little here for visitors besides the Crossing Place Trail (see below).

The high point in the island's events calendar is **Middle Caicos Expo**, a great weekend party in August during which former residents return and others flood in to hear live bands and hang out at the beer tents set up on Bambarra beach.

Eating and drinking

Given the tiny population of the island (and the fact that most of it consists of either elderly people or children), there's nowhere much for **a night out**, other than a small bar in Conch Bar where local guys gather in the evening to drink beer and play dominoes. Plan quiet nights in your hotel, guesthouse or villa and lay in beer from the **grocery store** in Conch Bar.

Hiking and biking

The **Crossing Place Trail** makes Middle Caicos one of the best places in the country for hiking and biking. It's an ancient path that leads from Lorimers in the east around the north coast of Middle Caicos to Crossing Place (literally that) in the west, from where it's possible to cross to North Caicos at low tide. After years of being overgrown, the four and a half miles of track have been cleared and marked by the National Trust. Part of the path is on the beach and passes through Mudjin Harbour, which is a good starting point. You may want to arrange for a taxi to pick you up at the end of the route.

There is also a seven-mile **biking trail** on pretty easy terrain from Conch Bar to Bambarra beach, with good snorkelling spots along the way. Bikes can be rented from Sport Shack in Conch Bar for around $20 a day.

2.2

The Turks Islands

The small group of **TURKS ISLANDS** has just two inhabited islands: **Grand Turk**, the government's home, and tiny **Salt Cay**, with less than a hundred people. Despite the arrival in 2006 of a cruise ship terminal on Grand Turk, both places remain quiet and quaint, showcasing attractive remnants of the colonial era, with great beaches and diving to keep you entertained during the day but little in the way of nightlife.

Grand Turk

Major development has hit **GRAND TURK** in the form of a cruise ship terminal – bringing with it the attendant crowds – but luckily it hasn't changed the character of this small but delightful island. Those who make the effort to get here independently will find a still charming and unspoilt place.

A series of expansive, muddy-coloured **salinas** dominate the centre of the island, testament to the salt trade that first brought development to Grand Turk. In the island's capital, Cockburn Town, Front Street has much of the country's finest colonial-era **architecture** as well as the tiny but superb **National Museum**. The **diving** and **fishing** on Grand Turk are world-class and the **beaches** lovely. Consider renting a car or scooter for a day to tour the island, which will only take a few hours, or ask a taxi driver for a guided tour. Bicycling is an excellent alternative in the main tourist area; most hotels offer use free of charge.

Arrival and getting around

No international flights arrive into Grand Turk and you'll need to come in via Providenciales, from where there are eleven daily **flights** costing $160 return.

Car rental can be arranged from Tony's (Ⓣ649/946-1879) for around $70 a day; scooters for $60 a day. Taxis are found at the airport or can be reached by phone – try Val's (Ⓣ649/231-6442).

Accommodation

Though Grand Turk has none of the five-star hotels that you'll find on Provo, there's a good range of **places to stay**.

Bohio Dive Resort Pillory Beach Ⓣ649/946-2135, Ⓦwww.bohioresort.com. There are sixteen clean and breezy ocean view rooms at this laid-back dive resort right on the beach. There's an in-house dive operation, great snorkelling right offshore, a small pool, free bikes and three free yoga classes per week. The onsite restaurant serves breakfast, lunch and dinner. ⑥

Grand Turk Inn Front St Ⓣ649/946-2827, Ⓦwww.grandturkinn.com. This lovingly renovated B&B, housed in a 150-year-old refurbished Methodist manse, has five suites, all with full kitchens and private bathrooms. A top-floor sundeck lets guests gaze out at the sea. Rooms run $300/night in winter. ⑧

Manta House Front St Ⓣ649/9461111, Ⓦwww.grandturk-mantahouse.com. This funky B&B is the best option for budget travellers on the island, and popular with the diving crowd. There are three B&B rooms, all comfortable and clean, as well as two bungalows with living rooms and private bathrooms. ②–③

Osprey Beach Hotel Front St Ⓣ649/946-1453, Ⓦwww.ospreybeachhotel.com. Comfortable and tranquil little place on the beach with twenty-six tidy rooms, each with a patio or a balcony overlooking the sea, with an additional twelve across the road. There's a small restaurant a short walk from the main hotel, and a small pool around which the owners hold barbecues twice a week. ⑤

Turks Head Mansion Front St Ⓣ649/946-2066, Ⓦwww.turksheadmansion.com. One of Front Street's many charming colonial buildings, dating from 1830, the *Turks Head* pulls in tourists with its attractively furnished rooms and period charm, all just a short walk from the beach. There's also a good restaurant on site. ⑤–⑥

Cockburn Town

Although **Cockburn Town** is the country's capital, don't expect to find a bustling city. Comprising just a couple of streets of nineteenth-century homes and warehouses, it's rare to find much activity and the streets are often empty. A stroll down the main drags of **Duke Street** and **Front Street**, which run alongside the gorgeous blue ocean, will take you past many of the island's **architectural highlights**. At the southern end of Front Street, the *Salt Raker Inn* and *Turks Head Mansion*, two of Grand Turk's oldest hotels, are fine examples of the wooden houses built in the 1830s and 1840s by Bermudian shipwrights who came here to collect salt. Other colourful buildings like the General Post Office line this area of Front Street, many of them constructed with ballast and timbers taken from the trading ships of the time, and covered with purple and orange bougainvillea, as well as the occasional Turk's-head cactus, recognizable by its red fez-shaped flower.

The Turks and Caicos National Museum

Continuing up Front Street from the hotels, you'll come to the **Turks and Caicos National Museum** (Mon–Fri 9am–4pm, Sat 9am–1pm; $5; Ⓦwww.tcmuseum.org), chief among the island's highlights. Here you can examine the remains of the Molasses Reef wreck, the oldest recovered shipwreck in the Caribbean, dating from around 1515. After the wreck was discovered in the 1970s, some morons mistook it for a treasure ship and blew sections of it apart with dynamite looking for treasure. Key remains on display include the enormous main anchor, cannon and other weapons, hand- and foot-cuffs of prisoners and some tools.

The exhibits upstairs span the islands' history from pre-Columbian times to the present, and include a room given over to artefacts – notably pottery – from the Lucayan Indians and another explaining the islands' reefs and aquatic life. Also on display are items recording key visits to the island, from astronauts John Glenn and Scott Carpenter – who splashed down near here in 1962 and were brought to Grand Turk for debriefing – to present-day British monarch Queen Elizabeth II and members of her family who have visited periodically over the past forty years.

Governor's Beach and cruise ship terminal

Of the good **beaches** that line the west and east coasts, the pick of them is **Governor's Beach**, where the powdery sands dissolve into a turquoise sea. From Cockburn Town, head south ignoring the turn-off to the airport, and continuing towards the Governor's residence, known as **Waterloo**. Just before you reach the white walls, turn off to the right along a dirt track. At the end, take the path through the bush to a superb stretch of white sand, backed by casuarina trees and fronting onto a magnificent turquoise bay. Be sure to bring water, as there are no facilities on the beach. On days when cruises are in port, the ships will entirely monopolize the view. The ships are a surreal site as they dwarf the tiny island. The terminal (Ⓦwww.grandturkcc.com), on the south side of the island and only open when a ship is in port, is a gaggle of Disneyesque pastel-painted souvenir shops, as well as Jimmy Buffet's ubiquitous *Margaritaville* restaurant, complete with pool and swim-up bar.

Eating, drinking and nightlife

There's not much sophistication to **dining** out in Grand Turk, but there are plenty of decent options and prices are reasonable. Nightlife is quiet, though there's usually some late-night music and dancing at the *Osprey* on Sundays and Wednesdays and at the *Salt Raker* on Fridays.

Turks Head Mansion Front St Ⓣ649/946-2066. Serving what is likely the highest-end food on the island, the restaurant offers appetizers like goat cheese and mushroom parcels and mains ranging from grilled grouper to duck a l'orange.

Sandbar Duke Street Ⓣ649/946-1111. Across the street from the Manta House, and under the same convivial ownership, this open-air bar/restaurant serves great burgers as well as the more traditional items like cracked conch. Lunch from 12pm–3pm, dinner from 6pm–9pm.

Michael's Atrium Ⓣ649/946-2878. This casual restaurant across the street from the *Osprey* serves traditional dishes like stewed beef and curried mutton. The restaurant at the hotel is also a good choice, well-known for its poolside barbecue buffet on Sun and Wed nights.

Watersports and diving

Superb **diving** opportunities, many of them very close to shore, include fantastic deep and shallow dives at twenty sites along the five-mile wall that starts just off the west coast. You'll find both magnificent coral formations and abundant reef life.

The four independent **operators** are Blue Water Divers (Ⓣ649/946-2432, Ⓦwww.grandturkscuba.com), Oasis Divers (Ⓣ649/946-1128, Ⓦwww.oasisdivers.com), Sea Eye Diving (Ⓣ649/946-1407, Ⓦwww.seaeyediving.com) and Grand Turk Diving (Ⓣ649/242-1521, Ⓦwww.gtdiving.com). All offer one and two-tank dives (from $50 and $80, respectively), PADI certification courses, and are happy to take snorkellers along. **Snorkellers** are well catered for, with shops offering a variety of trips for around $30. Try to go to deserted Gibbs Cay, for around $60–the snorkelling is fantastic and you'll bump into some friendly southern stingrays. Sailors should head to Bohio resort where you can rent a sailboat for $25 or a kayak from $20. Hour-long lessons run for $20.

Listings

Banks Scotiabank has a branch on Front Street. Hours are Mon–Thurs 8.30am–2.30pm, Fri 8.30am–4.30pm. ATM open 24 hours a day.
Emergencies Ⓣ911.
Medical services Grand Turk Hospital Ⓣ646/946-2040.
Police Ⓣ649/946-2299.
Post office Front Street (Mon–Fri 8am–noon & 2–4pm).

Salt Cay

Tiny **SALT CAY** is one of the most appealing islands in the country, both for its natural beauty and its historical interest. Although measuring barely six and a half square miles and home to just eighty people, the island was once an important source for the Bermudian salt-rakers, whose relics still litter the place and provide much of the charm: fabulous old white-washed houses as well as the salt pans from which the "white gold" was laboriously scraped. Add to that some sugary white beaches (particularly along the north coast), great diving and snorkelling, and a small but fine range of accommodation, and you've got another great place to chill out.

Arrival, information and getting around

Flights with Air Turks and Caicos leave from Grand Turk three times daily and cost $80 return. There's also a **ferry** (Ⓣ649/946-6909; $12 for men and $8 for women) running between Grand Turk and Salt Cay, leaving Salt Cay at 7.30am and returning from Grand Turk at 2.30. There's no tourist office on the island and just a couple of taxis.

Accommodation

Salt Cay has a range of **accommodation** options to suit most budgets, ranging from simple guesthouses to private villas.

Mount Pleasant Guest House Ⓣ649/946-6927, Ⓦwww.mtpleasant.tc. This timber-beamed nineteenth-century salt trader's home on the great north coast beach caters mainly to divers. There's a comfortable lounge/library for guests, and rooms are colourful and quiet. ⑥

Pirate's Hideaway Ⓣ649/946-6909, Ⓦwww.pirateshideaway.com. Six comfortable suites and a friendly owner make this guesthouse a good option just across from the beach; there's also a lovely freshwater swimming pool. ⑥

Tradewinds Ⓣ649/946-6908, Ⓦwww.tradewinds.tc. This cheery and bright guesthouse on the beach has five one-bedroom suites, each with a/c and a full kitchen or kitchenette. The affable owners will stock your kitchen, or you can choose an all-inclusive meal and dive package with Salt Cay Divers. ⑤–⑥

▲ The salinas of Salt Cay

Around the island

Like Grand Turk, the centre of Salt Cay is dominated by the flat, shallow **salinas** that supplied the island's once-thriving salt industry. Recognizing the natural *salinas*' commercial potential, the salt traders built windmills and stone walls with sluice gates to create smaller ponds to speed evaporation. Scraping the salt into piles was fiercely hard manual work. Trading ships from Bermuda carrying limestone rocks as ballast (later used to build the traders' smart houses) loaded up with the rough salt and transported it along the eastern seaboard of the fledgling United States.

For centuries salt was the source of the island's wealth, but the industry was subject to stiff international competition and went into decline for decades before it finally ground to a halt in the 1960s. Nothing much has happened here since, and Salt Cay's population has slowly melted away, supplemented by a trickle of tourists.

On the west side of the island, **Balfour Town** is the principal settlement, home to government buildings, the local school and a couple of stores. It's also where you'll find the **White House**. The most spectacular of Salt Cay's two-storey jalousie-windowed limestone houses, it was built by local salt magnate Joshua Harriot after the great hurricane of 1812 had flattened his wooden home with a 15ft tidal wave. Elsewhere you'll see more recent and pastel-coloured wooden houses, with little courtyards and low stone walls to keep stray cattle at bay.

The island's best **beach** runs along the entire north coast, a magnificent swath of sand, with massive elkhorn coralheads in a couple of places just offshore perfect for snorkelling. The rocky east coast is dominated by sharp-edged ironshore limestone, and dotted by a series of small bays. It also has the island's highest point, Taylor's Hill – a whopping 60ft.

Off the west coast, a five minute boat ride will take **divers** to great spots with spotted eagle rays and a wealth of brightly coloured fish as well as deep-water gorgonians and black coral trees. Ten miles further south, the encrusted wreck of

HMS *Endymion*, an eighteenth-century British warship complete with cannon, lies in thirty feet of water. The island's principal **dive operator** is Salt Cay Divers (ⓣ649/946-6906, ⓦwww.saltcaydivers.tc), offering single dives for $45 and two-tank dives for $70. From January to March, humpback whales make their way to the nearby Mouchoir Banks to breed; for the best view, join one of the whale-watching tours organized by Salt Cay Divers (or their Grand Turk counterparts).

Eating and drinking

Though small, Salt Cay offers a few good options.

Green Flash Café ⓣ649/244-0836. You can sip a beer and munch on a hot dog or chicken wings while you watch the boats come in at this restaurant on the dock. The "Flash," as it's know, opens every day at three except Wed when it's closed.

Island Thyme Bistro ⓣ649/946-6977, ⓦwww.islandthyme.tc The menu at this brightly painted, cheerful spot runs the gamut from almond encrusted snapper to beef Wellington. Every day sees a new breakfast special (Tuesday's is coconut French toast), and there's also a long list of cocktails to whet your whistle. Free Wi-Fi available.

3

Cuba

0 200 km
UNITED STATES OF AMERICA
New Providence
Eleuthera
Cat Island
Andros
Great Guana Cay
The Exumas
Rum Cay
Long Island
Acklins Island
1
2
3
4
5
6
7
8
Isla de la Juventud
CUBA
Little Cayman
Cayman Brac
Grand Cayman
CARIBBEAN SEA
JAMAICA
HAITI

Cuba highlights

* **Habana Vieja** The old city, filled with elegant mansions, centuries-old churches and cobblestone plazas. See p.165

* **Cuban music in Havana** Check out at least one of the excellent *salsa*, jazz or *son* groups that regularly make the rounds of the best-known clubs. See p.174

* **Viñales valley** Bizarre limestone hillocks lend this valley a dreamlike air. See p.179

* **Baracoa** Isolated by verdant mountains, the quirky town of Baracoa has retained much of its charm and hospitality. See p.201

* **Castillo del Morro San Pedro de la Roca** This colossal fort makes for one of Santiago's most dramatic sights. See p.208

* **Trekking in Sierra Maestra** Head to Cuba's highest mountain range for its revolutionary landmarks and excellent hiking trails. See p.209

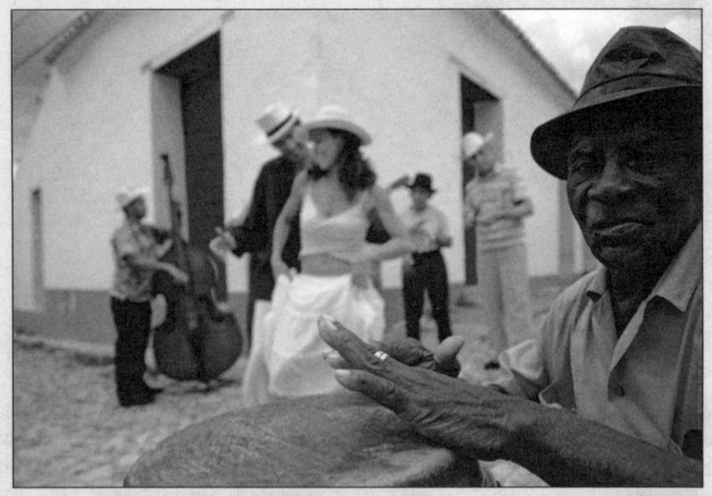

▲ Live music, Havana

Introduction and basics

Cuba's unique credentials as a Caribbean outpost of **communism**, where sun, sand, salsa and rum spike this land of socialist slogans, ration books and revolutionaries, are in the spotlight like never before. There may still be a Castro at the helm but it's **Raúl** not Fidel now steering the ship and both hopes and fears abound that Cuba is changing course. For some potential visitors this has increased the sense of urgency: go now before the island is lost to capitalism. For others the predicted changes are positive as they anticipate a more **liberal** Cuba, one which US citizens may be able to visit legally for the first time in decades.

In a country where politics infiltrates every aspect of society, the changes from the power swap have not been as radical as some forecasted. After all, Cuba has been in transition since the mid-1990s, shifting from socialist stronghold to one of the Caribbean's major **tourist destinations**, running on capitalist dollars. The ideological gamble seems to be paying off, and whilst tourist infrastructure slowly expands and improves so too does the construction of schools, housing and public transport that tourism funds. Cuba under Raúl represents a slight change in emphasis, such as a lifting of some of the restrictions on **private enterprise** and greater **social freedoms**, but a change in direction looks less likely and arguably less necessary.

Yet all the talk of a country in transition can seem strange for some visitors as it can feel like nothing has changed here for decades, even centuries: the classic American cars, moustachioed cigar-smoking farmers, horse-drawn carriages and colonial Spanish architecture endure. But **modernization** is happening, and the newly erected department stores and shopping malls, state-of-the-art hotels and resorts are the hallmarks of the new Cuba. This improbable combination of transformation and stasis is symbolic of a country riddled with contradictions and ironies. In a place where taxi drivers earn more than doctors, and where capitalist reforms are seen as the answer to preserving socialist ideals, understanding Cuba is a complex task.

Despite favouritism toward tourists and the crippling US trade embargo, there is surprisingly **little resentment** directed at foreign visitors. In most of the country it's easy to come into contact with the locals: the common practice of renting out rooms and opening restaurants in homes allows visitors strong impressions of Cuba and its people even in a short visit. It's a good thing, too, since Cubans are renowned for their love of a good time. Their energy and spirit are best expressed through **music** and **dance**, both vital facets of the island's culture. As originators of the most influential Latin music styles, such as *bolero*, *rumba* and *son*, which spawned the most famous of them all – **salsa** – people in Cuba seem always ready to party.

There are still occasional reminders that Cuba is a highly **bureaucratic** one-party state. Going to the police, finding your hotel room double-booked or simply needing to make an urgent phone call can prove to be frustratingly complicated. As such, having a certain determination and a laid-back attitude are essential requirements for a pleasant trip to Cuba, particularly when exploring less-visited parts of the country. Things are becoming easier all the time, though, with the introduction of a wider variety of more efficient services; whether these improvements also mark an irreversible move away from what makes Cuba unique remains to be seen.

Where to go

No trip to Cuba would be complete without a visit to the capital city, **Havana**, whose captivating diversity of distinct neighbourhoods range from its time-warped sixteenth-century colonial core, **Habana Vieja**, to its tree-lined, mansion-filled tribute to 1950s Miami,

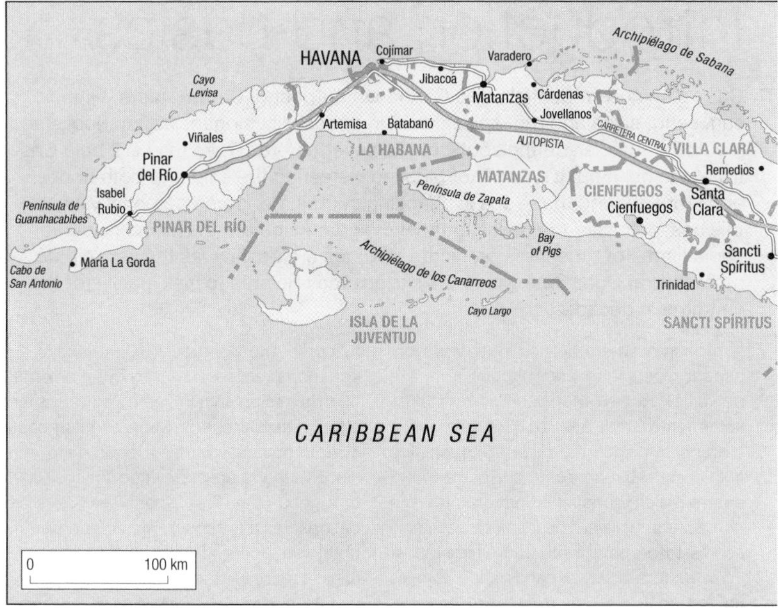

Miramar. More than anywhere else in the country Havana pulsates with life, generated by the shouts of street vendors, the tunes of café musicians, the sales patter of tourist-hungry hustlers and the drilling and banging emanating from countless construction sites as the never-ending job of resurrecting this historic city continues.

West of the capital and a world away from its frenzied busyness, rural **Pinar del Río** provides Cuba's most accessible nature resorts, ideal for mountain hiking, blessed with stunning scenery and characterized more than anything else by the peculiar *mogote* hills, which look more like gargantuan boulders than hills, of prehistoric **Viñales valley**.

The country's premier holiday destination and beach resort is **Varadero**, based along a breathtaking 25-kilometre highway of sand just two hours' drive east of Havana, one of Cuba's best-equipped bases for scuba diving and a mecca for sunbathers. On the opposite side of the same province, the **Península de Zapata** boasts a contrasting mix of beach holiday resorts, rough-and-ready wildlife excursions, neatly packaged day-trip destinations and an historic significance as the location of the 1961 Bay of Pigs invasion. Further east, **Trinidad**, a small colonial city, lures coach parties and backpackers in equal numbers with its impressively well-preserved colonial centre and its superb location between the beach and the mountains. The most popular destinations in central Cuba are the luxurious resorts of **Cayo Coco** and **Cayo Guillermo**, an isolated haven for sun-seeking tourists. Beach-goers also won't want to miss the ample opportunities for watersports at **Guardalavaca**, on the northern coast of Holguín province.

While **Guantánamo** province at the far eastern tip of the island is best known for its infamous US naval base, visitors will be enchanted by the jaunty seaside town of **Baracoa**. The vibrancy and energy of **Santiago de Cuba**, on the southeast coast, is second only to Havana, whilst its music scene is arguably the finest in the country. Trekkers and revolution enthusiasts will want to follow the Sierra Maestra as it snakes west of here into **Granma** province, offering various revolutionary landmarks and nature trails. Finally, lying off the southwest coast of Havana province, in splendid isolation, are the the deluxe package-holiday hotels of anodyne

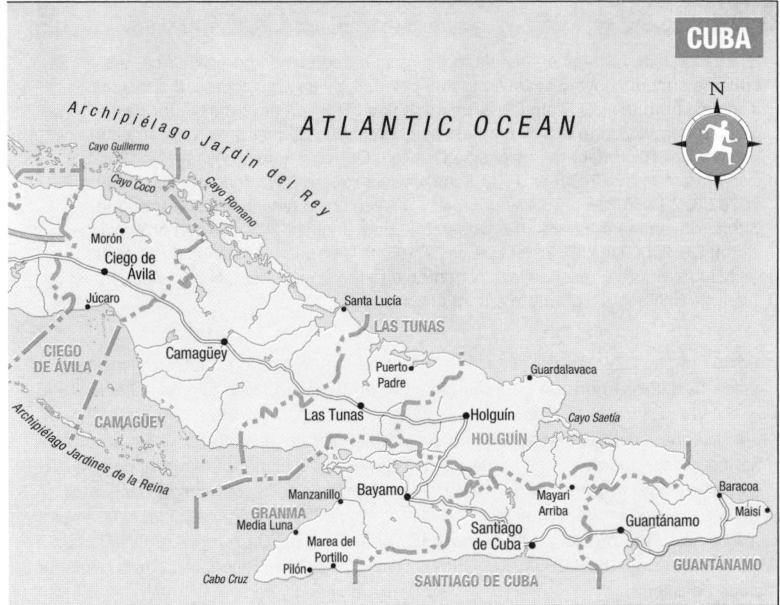

Cayo Largo, the only sizeable beach resort off the Caribbean coastline of Cuba.

When to go

Cuba generally has a **hot** and **sunny** tropical climate. While the average annual temperature is 24ºC (75ºF), temperatures can drop to 15º (59ºF) or lower in January and February, especially at night and in the mountains. The **dry season** runs roughly from November to April and the **wet season**, when you can expect it to rain at least a couple of days during a two-week holiday, lasts from May to October. Downpours don't usually last long, however, and are quickly followed by sunshine. September and October are the most threatening months of the annual **hurricane season** that runs from June to November.

The peak **tourist season** runs from about December to March and July to August (high summer). Prices and crowds are at their worst in summer when the holiday season for Cubans gets under way. The cities, particularly Havana and Santiago, are always buzzing and offer good value for money all year round.

Getting there

The majority of international flights arrive at Havana's **Jose Martí Airport**, although the international airports at Varadero, Holguín, Ciego de Avila, Santiago de Cuba, Cayo Coco, Cayo Largo, Santa Clara and Camagüey also receive (mainly charter) flights. There are no scheduled ferry services from neighbouring countries but a limited amount of European cruise ships dock at the **marinas** in Havana and Santiago de Cuba. It is, however, quite possible to sail by **private yacht** or cruiser to a number of spots on the island.

Entry requirements

Citizens of most Western countries must have a ten-year **passport**, valid for at least six months, a **tourist card** (*tarjeta de turista*) and an **onward ticket** to enter Cuba. Tourist cards are valid for thirty days and although you can buy one from Cuban consulates, you will get more efficient service if you buy it from your tour operator or travel agent. The charge in the UK is £15–20, in Australia

US citizens

Since the United States continues to maintain a trade embargo with Cuba, **US citizens** are not allowed to travel to the island freely and must instead apply for a licence from the US State Department. If you think you have a case for being granted permission to travel, perhaps as a journalist, student or as part of a humanitarian mission, contact the Licensing Division, Office of Foreign Assets Control, US Department of the Treasury, 1500 Pennsylvania Ave NW, Washington DC 20220 (Ⓣ202/622-2480, Ⓦwww.treas.gov/ofac). You can also get information from the Cuban government through the Cuban Interests Section, 2630 16th St NW, Washington DC 20009 (Ⓣ202/797-8609 or 797-8518). For most US nationals who want to visit Cuba for other reasons less acceptable to the government, like tourism, travel involves catching a flight from a third country.

Aus$35, in New Zealand NZ$44 and in Canada Can$24. **American citizens** (see box above) can travel to Cuba on tourist cards purchased in Canada, Mexico or other countries, and the Cuban authorities will on request stamp the card instead of your passport when you enter and leave Cuba to avoid the problems often caused when re-entering the US with a Cuba-stamped passport.

Note that you will pass through **customs** much more smoothly if you have entered the name of a state hotel on your tourist form as your destination, easily done since it is very rare that you will have to show proof of a reservation. If you don't have an address you may have to pay on the spot for three nights' accommodation in a hotel of the state's choosing.

Information

There is a shortage of printed travel literature in Cuba and getting hold of any kind of tourist **information**, particularly outside the major resorts, can be difficult. Before you leave home, therefore, it's worth contacting the nearest branch of the Cuban Tourist Board (Ⓦ www.cubagob.cu/des_eco/turismo.htm), which has information for visitors. On the island, the only tourist information network is **Infotur** (Ⓦwww.infotur.cu), which only has branches in Havana, but also has desks in many hotels and at the José Martí International Airport. Concentrating on booking organized excursions, hotel room reservations and car rental, Infotur has very little information on public transport other than the Víazul bus service (see "Getting around", p.152). Also, the staff, though generally helpful, do try to steer visitors towards the state-run tourist apparatus.

Finding a trustworthy **map** once in Cuba is also difficult. The exception is the invaluable *Guía de Carreteras* ($6), a national road map which has basic street maps for Havana and Varadero.

All areas of the **media** in Cuba are subject to tight censorship and are closely controlled by the state, much to the dismay of many Cubans. *Granma*, the principal national daily newspaper, openly declares itself the official mouthpiece of the Cuban Communist Party.

Money and costs

Cuba has two official currencies, the Cuban **peso** (CUP) and the **convertible peso** (CUC). The CUP, or *peso cubano*, is the national currency; the CUC, or *peso convertible*, was introduced to replace the US dollar, which is no longer accepted in the country. While Cuban salaries and other official transactions are paid in CUP, travellers and tourists will almost exclusively use the CUC. Both currencies are divided into 100 **centavos,** with CUC coins in denominations of 50c, 25c, 10c and 5c and a larger array of CUP coins which come in 1c, 2c, 5c, 20c, 40c, $1CUP and $3CUP denominations. Banknotes for both currencies are issued in denominations of 100, 50, 20, 10, 5, 3 and 1. At time of writing 1 convertible peso was worth 24 Cuban pesos. Exchanging US dollars for convertible pesos is costly, as this is subject to a **service charge** of ten percent. It therefore makes sense to arrive in Cuba with British pounds, Canadian dollars, euros or other internationally recognized currencies. Convertible pesos are useless outside Cuba so make sure you exchange any leftover notes before you leave the country.

You'll need to keep in mind that on the island Cuban pesos and convertible pesos are both represented by the **dollar sign** (**$**). To add to the confusion, though most goods and services must be paid for in one currency or the other, sometimes they are interchangeable, for example at some *paladares*. The most commonly used qualifier for Cuban pesos is *moneda nacional*; thus one Cuban peso is sometimes written $1MN and less frequently as $1CUP whilst you might see one convertible peso expressed as $1CUC. In this book we use the CUP and CUC qualifiers.

All official tourist-oriented facilities, including all state-run hotels, most state-run restaurants and pretty much all goods sold in shops, are **charged** in convertible pesos. You'll also be expected to pay in convertible pesos for rooms in people's homes, meals in *paladares* (small, privately run restaurants) and most private taxis, though there is some flexibility in these cases. Entrance to cinemas and sports arenas, local buses, snacks bought on the street and food from *agromercados* are all paid for with plain old Cuban pesos.

Hard currency is king in Cuba, so it's a good idea to **exchange** your money into convertible pesos as soon as you arrive. Although **traveller's cheques** are easily exchangeable in many banks, a significant number of shops and restaurants refuse to accept them. Travellers' cheques issued by a US bank are unusable in Cuba, though American Express cheques issued outside of the US are accepted. **Credit cards** – Visa and MasterCard in particular – are more widely accepted, but in most small- to medium-sized towns plastic is useless as a method of payment. Moreover, no card issued by a US bank (including American Express, regardless of country of issue) can be used in Cuba. Credit cards are more useful for obtaining cash advances, most efficiently through branches of the Banco Financiero Internacional. There are very few **ATMs** in Cuba and though their number is slowly increasing you shouldn't count on being able to find one outside of the major resorts. **Bank opening hours** are usually Monday to Friday 8am to 3pm; at weekends, when most banks are closed, it is virtually impossible to obtain money.

You should budget a bare minimum of $15CUC and more often $25CUC a night for accommodation, $8CUC and above for meals at restaurants and *paladares* and at least $10CUC per journey if you travel by

Websites

All Cuba-based websites are state-run and tend to be biased and endorse only official information; luckily, plenty of foreign-based sites fill in the gaps.

Ⓦ **www.afrocubaweb.com** Fantastically detailed site covering absolutely anything even remotely connected to Afro-Cuban issues, from history and politics to music and dance.

Ⓦ **www.cuba.com** This US-based site claims to be "The official web site to Cuba" and is designed for US citizens who want in-depth and impartial information in English about the island from a visitor's point of view.

Ⓦ **www.cubatravel.cu** The Cuban Ministry of Tourism site with practical information and advice on a wide range of issues from customs regulations to accommodation and transport.

Ⓦ **www.cubaupdate.org** An excellent source of information that details tours organized by the Center for Cuban Studies.

Ⓦ **www.cubaweb.cu** The Cuban government's official site includes news reports from the Cuban press, plus information on travel, investment and many other subjects.

tourist bus, the most efficient way to get around the country.

Getting around

Mastering Cuban **transport** can be a fascinating, if sometimes frustrating, experience; understanding its nuances can take years. However, with a public bus service aimed at tourists, a proliferation of car rental agencies and an abundance of reasonably priced state-run taxis, it's actually much easier for most foreign travellers to get around the country than it is for many Cubans, whose incomes keep them confined to the inferior peso-priced transport services.

Hitching a lift in Cuba, or *coger botella* as it is known locally (meaning literally "catching a bottle"), is as common as catching a bus. Crowds of people wait by bridges and junctions along the major roads waiting for vehicles to stop. Drivers often ask for a few pesos, and tourists, though they are likely to attract a few puzzled stares, are welcome to join in. The usual hitchhiking precautions apply.

By bus

Bus service, the most common method of transport for inter-provincial travel, is split between two very distinct companies, **Astro** and **Víazul**. Though technically available to anyone willing and able to pay the fares, Víazul (☎7/881-1413) is effectively a bus service for tourists. While limited to the larger towns, cities and resorts, it is by far the quickest and most reliable way to get around independently.

That said, most of the less-travelled bus routes are still the exclusive domain of Astro (☎7/870-3397), which is characterized, for Cubans at least, by long queues, overcrowding and a complicated system of timetables and tickets. Foreign passport holders are afforded the privilege of jumping queues should they choose to pay in convertible pesos rather than Cuban pesos though there are usually only two to four seats for this purpose on most Astro buses; to guarantee a seat you should arrive at the bus station at least an hour before departure.

By train

Cuba is the only country in the Caribbean with a functioning national **rail system** and, though slow, trains are a good way of getting a feel for the landscape. You'll need your passport to buy a ticket, which you must do directly from the train station at least an hour before departure. The main line, which links Havana with Santiago, also serves Matanzas, Santa Clara, Ciego de Ávila, Camagüey and Las Tunas. *Servicio Regular* trains, which are perfectly comfortable but lack air conditioning, leave once daily, stopping at all the main-line stations. **Fares** work out at around $4CUC per 100km, with Havana to Santiago, for example, costing $30CUC. *Servicio Especial* trains run every three days and are more expensive ($43CUC from Havana to Santiago), though they do have air conditioning and are significantly faster.

Cuban music

Music forms the pulsing backdrop to virtually all entertainment in Cuba, and if you're looking to hear traditional Cuban music, like that popularized by Buena Vista Social Club, you won't be disappointed. Along with Santiago and Varadero, Havana offers the best variety of places to soak up home-grown salsa, from lavish salsa palaces and open-air venues to hotel salons. Better still, you can also hear all the soulful *son* (which is the foundation, really, of most Cuban music), *boleros* (slow and romantic ballads) and *guajiras* (country music influenced by *son*), as well as *salsa* (itself an offspring of *son)*, in any **Casa de la Trova**. These atmospheric music halls specialize in traditional Cuban tunes, often have live groups and can be found throughout the country. For something a bit more riotous, Cuban street parties, held on holidays and at **carnival**, feature live bands, which expertly tease seductive moves from heaving crowds but you'll need to ask around to find out about them as advertising is almost always done by word of mouth.

By car

Given that so much of Cuba is not properly served by public transport, the most convenient (though substantially more expensive) way to get around the island is undoubtedly in a **rental car**. Traffic jams are almost unheard of and away from the cities many roads are nearly empty.

There is a confusing array of **car-rental agencies**, despite the fact that they are all state-run firms. Apart from **prices**, which are rarely less than $35CUC a day and more often between $50CUC and $70CUC, the essential difference between the agencies is the type and make of car they offer. Havanautos (ⓣ 7/203-9805 & 203-8925, ⓦ www.havanautos.cu) and Cubacar (ⓣ 7/835-0000 & 273-2277, ⓦ www.transtur.cu) have the most branches throughout the island and the widest range of vehicles. To get the cheapest model, it's essential to book at least a day in advance. All agencies require you to have held a driving licence from your home country or an international licence for at least a year, and that you are at least 21.

Driving in Cuba is on the right-hand side of the road. *El autopista* is the only motorway in the whole country, and runs roughly down the middle of three-quarters of the island from east to west, fluctuating between six and eight lanes. Road markings are almost nonexistent and the 100km/hr speed limit would undoubtedly lead to accidents were there more traffic. The main alternative route for most long-distance journeys is the two-lane Carretera Central, a more scenic though far more congested road with an 80km/hr speed limit.

By taxi

Taxis have become one of the most popular private enterprises in Cuba. The official metered state taxis are the easiest to spot as they are all newer, imported models and carry taxi signs on the roof and getting hold of one by telephone isn't usually a problem. Expect to pay between $0.30CUC and $0.90CUC per kilometre.

Privately owned cars, predominantly 1950s American classics or Russian Ladas, used as taxis are easy to find and though they are not necessarily any cheaper than state taxis, fares can be negotiated and the experience more of a novelty. The local name for these is *máquinas* or *taxis particulares*, but in this guide they are referred to as **private taxis**. Drivers charge in either convertible pesos or Cuban pesos depending on their licence, but most will try to charge tourists in convertible pesos. Intra-city journeys typically cost between $2CUC and $5CUC, but negotiation is part and parcel of the unofficial system. For longer trips, there is usually a specific area of a town, invariably next door to a bus station, where taxis wait for long-distance passengers. As a rough indicator, a driver will expect between $20CUC and $30CUC per 100km.

Peso taxis, known as *colectivos*, are a singular experience where drivers fit as many passengers as possible into the vehicle. More akin to a privately run bus service, *colectivos* are used almost exclusively by Cubans and are likely to ignore tourists – probably on the assumption that foreigners are unlikely either to understand the system or to be carrying pesos. There are no officially recognized indicators that a taxi is a *colectivo* but they tend to be large, battered American classics. A trip within Havana will cost $10CUP, with similar rates in other cities.

Accommodation

Accommodation in Cuba falls into two types: **state** and **private**. You'll find at least one state hotel in every large town, for which you should budget at least $30CUC per room per night. Private accommodation, in *casas particulares*, works out cheaper at between $15CUC and $30CUC – only in major tourist areas like Havana will you need to pay more. At the higher-end state hotels, expect to pay $120CUC or more a night. During low season, some hotels drop their rates by about ten percent.

State-owned **tourist hotels** are the most convenient type of accommodation – reservations are recommended but not absolutely necessary. Upon arrival, specify how many days you intend to stay to avoid having your room booked out from under you by someone else.

For many visitors, staying in *casas particulares* – "private houses" – is an ideal way to gain insight into the country and its people. Like a guesthouse, proprietors rent out rooms in their home. Most offer breakfast and an evening meal for an additional of $5CUC or so. Touts (called *jineteros* or *intermediarios*) wait to meet potential customers at buses; note that if you're brought to a *casa particular* by a tout you can expect to be charged an extra $5CUC per night. Many *casas particulares* operate illegally without paying taxes. They are usually no cheaper than their registered counterparts and, although you are not breaking the law by staying in one, if you encounter a problem you will get little sympathy from the authorities.

Campismos, quasi-campsites, are an excellent countryside option, and all provinces have at least one. Not campsites in the conventional sense, they offer basic accommodation in rudimentary concrete cabins that vary considerably in the facilities they provide though most come with bed linen, running water and a toilet and some have showers and kitchenettes. At as little as $5CUC a night per cabin they are extremely reasonable. For more details contact Cubamar, Ave. Paseo no.306 e/ 13 y 15, Vedado, Havana (Ⓣ7/66-2523, Ⓦwww.cubamarviajes.cu), which runs the best sites.

Food and drink

While you'll usually be able to **eat** decently in Cuba, mealtimes are not the gastronomic delight enjoyed on many other Caribbean islands. As with most everything in Cuba, restaurants are divided into state and private restaurants; the latter are small, privately run *paladares*. **State restaurants** differ greatly in quality – the best offer up tasty meals in congenial settings while the worst are simply atrocious. State restaurants that accept the Cuban peso, which you'll find away from the tourist areas, cater essentially to Cubans. The quality tends to be poor, though you can occasionally get a passable meal very cheaply. As a visitor you're more likely to eat in the state restaurants that take convertible pesos which, particularly in the large cities and tourist areas, have better-quality, more varied food, often including some international dishes, like Chinese and Italian. By way of contrast, state-run roadside cafés are unhygienic and poorly managed and should be avoided.

Paladares are a godsend. Usually run out of a spare room in someone's home, they offer visitors a chance to sample good Cuban home-cooking in an informal atmosphere. They are plentiful in Havana, and while most large towns have at least one, some smaller towns may not have any at all. Prices vary but don't expect to necessarily pay less than you would in an official state restaurant and you should budget for at least $8CUC per meal. Generally *paladares* can seat no more than twelve people and are subject to tight restrictions on what they can serve: beef and seafood are prohibited (though they may be offered anyway) and lamb and mutton are banned in some provinces. **Chicken** and **pork** are always on the menu and although there will be few, if any, **vegetarian** options, *paladares* are more accommodating than state restaurants in terms of off-menu ordering.

Also privately run, from front gardens and driveways, the peso **street stalls** dotted around cities and towns are invariably the cheapest places to eat and an excellent choice for home-made snacks and impromptu lunches.

One of the worst problems you will encounter when eating out is **overcharging**, which is so widespread that it's unlikely you will make it through your trip without being overcharged at all. Be suspicious of places where they claim there is no written or printed menu.

Breakfast in Cuba is commonly a bread roll eaten with eggs. The basis for a typical lunch or **dinner** is fried chicken or a pork chop or cutlet. Although there is not as much fish and seafood on offer as you might expect, what you can get is excellent, particularly the grilled lobster, prawns and tuna. Note that apart from garlic and onion, spices are not really used in Cuban cooking. Accompanying your meal will almost always be **rice and beans**, known as *congrí*, *moros y cristianos* or *arroz con frijoles* depending on preparation. Other traditional **vegetable side dishes** are fried plantain, cassava and salad. The best places to buy **fruit** are the *agromercados*, where you can load up cheaply with whatever is in season. Particularly good are the mangoes, juicy oranges and sweet pineapples.

For drinking **water**, it's best to stick with bottled, readily available from all convertible peso shops and hotels; otherwise tap water should be boiled. Take caution when buying drinks from streetside Cuban-peso food stalls as the water used to make them may not have been boiled.

If you like *ron* (rum) you'll have plenty of options on the island. Havana Club reigns supreme, but also look out for Caribbean Club and Siboney. Cuba is also famous for its cocktails, including the ubiquitous **Cuba Libre**. Made from white rum, Coca Cola and a twist of lime, it's second only in popularity to the **Mojito** – white rum, sugar, sparkling water and mint. Lager-type **beer** (*cerveza*) is plentiful and there are some excellent national brands, particularly Cristal and Bucanero. On average, cocktails cost $3–4CUC while a beer will run you $1–3CUC, though ritzier places will of course charge more.

Mail and communications

Although a more efficient digital **telephone** system has replaced much of the antiquated analogue system, using the phone in Cuba is still fairly complicated and frustratingly unreliable. **Payphones** are of three distinct types. The most common are coloured blue and are found in Telepuntos (the national chain of call centres), Minipuntos (a kind of large, walk-in phone booth), in hotels and an increasing number of public places. These phones, which don't accept coins, can only be used with Chip prepaid **phonecards** (as opposed to the Propia phonecards used by most Cubans), sold in convertible pesos in denominations of $5CUC, $10CUC and $20CUC. National **rates** are reasonable, starting at 5c per minute for calls within the same province. Blue payphones are the only ones that allow international calls; currently a payphone call to the US or Canada costs $2CUC per minute, or $4CUC per minute to Britain or Australia. Calling the US from Cuba is subject to a US-based **tax**, an extra cost of US 24.5¢/min and not included in the officially listed call rates. The older, least reliable payphones, generally coloured, grey. which only accept 5¢ Cuban peso coins, are still found in large numbers of Cuban towns and villages. New, reliable **Cuban peso payphones** are appearing around the country. They are grey with a digital display, and most are coin-operated, accepting 5 centavo, 20 centavo and 1 peso coins; some also accept peso phonecards (though these cards are available only to Cubans).

The simplest way to make a phone call is to use the Chip phones which have a simpler dialling procedure than home phones or Cuban peso phones. Using a Chip phone to **make a call** within the same province, simply dial ⓣ0 followed by the area code and number. For **interprovincial calls** you will need to dial first the appropriate prefix (usually ⓣ0 but there are a number of variations depending on where you are in the country) to get onto the national grid, then the area code, followed finally by the number. Some interprovincial calls are only possible through the operator. If you are consistently failing to get through on a direct line, dial ⓣ00 which will connect you with the operator. For **international calls** dial the international call prefix, which is ⓣ119, then the country code, the area code and the number. The **country code** for Cuba is ⓣ53.

Cuba's **postal service** has seen a slight improvement in recent times; it now takes weeks instead of months for airmail to leave the island. If you send anything other than a letter, within the island or to an overseas destination, there's a significant chance that it won't arrive at all, as pilfering is widespread within the postal system. You should also be aware that letters and packages coming into Cuba are sometimes opened as a matter of policy. Stamps are sold in both *convertibles pesos* and plain old Cuban pesos at post offices, from white and blue kiosks marked *Correos de Cuba* and in many hotels. All large towns and cities have a post office, normally open Monday to Saturday from 8am to 6pm. The full range of postal services, including DHL and EMS, is offered in some of the larger hotels, usually at the desk marked *Telecorreos*.

Getting online in Cuba is easier than ever, and all major cities have at least one cybercafé and many hotels feature email and Internet facilities, though their rates are sometimes exorbitant. In Havana hotels commonly charge between $7CUC and $10CUC an hour. The best places to get online are the Telepunto call centres. You will be required to show your passport for Internet access. Currently, Telepunto charges are 10¢/min with a minimum charge of $6CUC, giving you an hour online.

Always been keen to control the flow of information to the Cuban public, the government has, unsurprisingly, **restricted** its citizens' access to the Internet. Private home Internet connections are illegal but Cubans are allowed to have Cuba-based email accounts.

Opening hours, holidays and festivals

Cuban offices are normally **open** for business between 9am and 5pm Monday to Friday, with many closing for a one-hour break anywhere between noon and 2pm. Shops are generally open 9am to 6pm Monday to Saturday, sometimes closing for lunch, while the shopping malls and department stores in Havana stay open as late as 8pm. Sunday trading is increasingly common, with most places open until noon or 1pm, and longer in the major resorts. **Banks** operate Monday to Friday 8am to 3pm, but this varies.

Cultural **festivals**, like the International Theatre Festival and the International Festival of New Latin American Film have won Havana global acclaim. Lesser-known festivals celebrating dance, literature and other arts, as well as a whole host of smaller events in the outer provinces, are also worthwhile. Not to be missed if you're around in the beginning of July is Cuba's main carnival in Santiago; also well worth checking out are Havana's carnival celebrations held 3–4 weeks later.

Sports and outdoor activities

On the whole, participatory **sports** and **outdoor activities** in Cuba are still in the development stage. Watersports are the main exception, and with some of the richest and most unspoilt waters in the world, Cuba has great **scuba diving** and **snorkelling**. As well as reefs there are numerous underwater caves, tunnels and even shipwrecks to explore. Most of the major beach resorts, including Varadero, Santa Lucía and Guardalavaca, have well-equipped diving centres. Varadero, with its three marinas and two diving clubs, is one of the best places for novice divers.

Hiking is another good option and all three mountain ranges in Cuba have hiker-friendly resorts. Designated hikes tend to be quite short, rarely more than 5km, and trails are often unmarked and difficult to follow without a local guide. Furthermore, trail maps are all but nonexistent. This may be all part of the appeal for the more adventurous but it is generally recommended that you hire a guide.

The most popular spectator sport in Cuba is **baseball**, and it is a national obsession. Games in the national league, the Serie Nacional de Béisbol, take place between sixteen teams over a regular season which usually begins in October or November and runs through the playoffs in March or April, finishing with the finals a month later. Every provincial capital has a baseball stadium and, during the season, teams play five times a week; there's a good chance of catching a game if you're in the country during the winter months.

Entrance to sports stadiums and arenas in Cuba costs only a Cuban peso or two and tickets are always sold at the gate rather than in advance.

Crime and safety

Despite increasing worries about crime, Cuba is still one of the **safest destinations** in the Caribbean and the majority of visitors will experience a trouble-free stay. The worst

Public holidays and festivals

Public holidays

January 1 Liberation Day. Anniversary of the triumph of the revolution.
May 1 International Workers' Day.
July 25–27 Celebration of the day of national rebellion.
October 10 Anniversary of the start of the Wars of Independence.
December 25 Christmas.

Festivals

January

Cubadanza Gran Teatro, Habana Vieja ⓣ7/31-1357, ⓔparadis@turcult.get.cma.net. Cuban contemporary dance festival featuring performers from around the country.

Havana Jazz Festival Teatro Nacional, Havana ⓣ7/79-6011. See the best of Cuban jazz, including some legendary figures, play the town at different venues. International guest stars also feature.

July

Fiesta of Fire Festival Santiago de Cuba ⓣ22/62-3569, ⓔupec@mail.infocom.etecsa.cu. Santiago's week-long celebration of Caribbean music and dance culture takes place at the beginning of July.

Santiago Carnival ⓣ22/62-3302, ⓔburostgo@binanet.lib.cult.cu. Cuba's most exuberant carnival holds Santiago in its thrall during the first two weeks of July with costumed parades, congas, *salsa* bands and late-night parties.

Carnival de La Habana. Carnival festivities in Havana take place in late July/early August, with parades and street parties around the city centre for about three weeks.

August

Cubadanza Gran Teatro, Habana Vieja ⓣ7/31-1357, ⓔparadis@turcult.get.cma.net. The summer season of the Cuban contemporary dance festival which draws performers from all over the country to Havana.

September

Havana International Theatre Festival ⓣ7/31-1357, ⓔparadis@turcult.get.cma.net. Excellent ten-day theatre festival showcasing classics and contemporary Cuban works at various theatres around the city.

December

International Festival of New Latin American Film Havana ⓣ7/55-2854, ⓔrosalla@cimex.com.cu. One of Cuba's top events, this ten-day film festival combines the newest Cuban films with the finest classics, as well as providing a networking opportunity for leading independent film directors.

you're likely to experience is incessant and annoying attention from touts and hustlers, known as *jineteros*. **Women travellers**, however, particularly those travelling solo, should brace themselves for nonstop male attention. While violent sexual attacks are virtually unheard of, unaccompanied women are generally assumed to be on holiday because they're looking for sex. Fortunately, the persistent come-ons will be more irritating than threatening.

The most common assault upon tourists is **bag-snatching** or **pickpocketing**, so take the usual precautions and only carry the minimum amount of cash. Also avoid leaving personal possessions visible in a rental car. Put any valuables in the hotel security box, if there is one, or at least stash them out of sight. Registered *casas particulares* are, as a rule, safe. You should always carry your passport (or a photocopy) as the police sometimes ask to inspect them.

The **police** are generally indifferent to crimes against tourists – and they may even try to blame you for not being more vigilant. If you're the victim of theft, you may find it more useful to contact **Asistur** (☎7/866-8527 & 866-8920), a 24-hour assistance agency based in Havana and Santiago; they'll be able to arrange replacement travel documents, help with financial difficulties and recover lost luggage.

Drugs, specifically marijuana and cocaine, are increasingly common in Cuba. The authorities take a very dim view of drug abuse and prison sentences are frequently meted out, even for possession of small amounts.

The **emergency number** for the Cuban police differs from place to place. In Havana dial ☎106; in Varadero, Trinidad and Santiago dial ☎116.

Health

Providing you take common-sense precautions, visiting Cuba poses **no particular health risks**. It is essential, however, to bring your own medical kit, including painkillers and any other supplies you think you might need, as they are hard to come by on the island and the choice is extremely limited.

Cuba's famous free health service does not extend to foreign visitors so expect to pay if you get sick – the government uses its impressive medical advances to generate extra revenue. There are specific **hospitals** for foreign visitors, most of them run by Cubanacan (Ⓦwww.cubanacan.cu/espanol/turismo/salud) and its subsidiary Servimed (Ⓦwww.servimed.com), an institution set up in 1994 to deal exclusively with health tourism. If you wind up in hospital, one of the first things you should do is contact Asistur (see p.157), who usually deal with insurance claims. For minor complaints you shouldn't have to go further than the hotel doctor. If you're staying in a *casa particular*, your best bet if feeling ill is to inform your host, who should be able to arrange a house-call with the family doctor.

As with much else on the island there are two types of **pharmacies**: tourist pharmacies operating in *pesos convertibles* and Cuban-peso pharmacies for the population at large. Servimed runs the majority of the tourist pharmacies; ask a local for the nearest *clínica internacional* to find one.

History

Before Columbus's arrival, Cuba was inhabited for thousands of years by Amerindians who travelled up through the Antilles from the South American mainland. The last group, the Taíno, who arrived sometime around 1100 AD, were a mostly peaceful people, largely unprepared for the conflict they were to face with the arrival of the Spanish.

On October 27, 1492, **Columbus** landed on the northeastern coast of Cuba. On his second voyage in 1494, he erroneously concluded that Cuba was part of the mainland of Cathay, or China. Not convinced that Columbus had discovered a western route to Asia, Spain's King Ferdinand sent another expedition to the island, and in 1509 Diego Velázquez landed near Guantánamo Bay with three hundred men. The Indians who were not killed by the Spanish died later from European diseases or the harsh living and working conditions forced upon them.

As **Spain** consolidated its American empire, Cuba gained importance thanks to its location on the main route to Europe. The population grew slowly, with African **slaves** being imported as early as the 1520s to replace the dwindling indigenous population; by the end of the sixteenth century there was almost no trace of the **Taíno** natives.

Since the Europeans' arrival, the Cuban **economy** has been based heavily on agriculture. Cassava, fruits, coffee, tobacco and sugar were amongst the chief exports and the island slowly became a source of significant wealth. During the first half of the eighteenth century Cuban society become more sophisticated, with the emergence of its own identity, distinct from that of Spain. By the end of the century the colony had established its first newspaper, theatre and university.

Economic progress was **restricted** as the colony was forced to trade exclusively with Spain. This changed when the British seized Havana in 1762 and though the subsequent occupation only lasted a year it opened up new markets in North America and Europe.

The 1791 revolution in Haiti destroyed the sugar industry there and Cuba became the largest producer of **sugar** in the region. As the Cuban sugar economy boomed, the size of the slave population increased and the conditions of slavery worsened. Increasingly frequent **slave rebellions** divided Cuban society, pitting native *criollos* against Spanish-born *peninsulares*, black against white, and the less developed eastern half of the country against the more economically and politically powerful west.

In 1865 the **Reformist Party** was founded by a group of *criollo* planters, providing the most coherent expression yet of the desire for change. A revolution plotted by a group of landowners led by Carlos Manuel de Céspedes got no further than the planning stage when the colonial authorities sent troops to arrest the conspirators. Pre-empting his own arrest on October 10, 1868, Céspedes freed the slaves working at his sugar mill, effectively instigating the **Ten Years War**, the First Cuban War of Independence. The Pact of Zanjón (1878), a peace agreement signed by the Spanish and the Cuban rebels, ended most of the hostilities but failed to address the fundamental causes of conflict, including political representation for the *criollos* and the end of slavery, which was not **abolished until 1886**.

No one did more to stimulate the Cuban independence movement than **José Martí**. Born in Havana to Spanish parents, he eventually ended up in New York where he worked tirelessly to gain momentum for the idea of an independent Cuba. In 1892 he founded the **Cuban Revolutionary Party** (**PRC**), which began to coordinate with groups inside Cuba for a Second War of Independence. Martí was killed in his first battle, but the revolutionaries fought their way across the country, reaching Havana province, the stronghold of colonial power, on January 1, 1896.

Riots in Havana gave the US the excuse they had been waiting for to send in the warship *Maine*, ostensibly to protect US citizens. While anchored in Havana harbour on February 15, 1898, the *Maine* blew up, killing 258 people; the US accused the Spanish of sabotage and so began the **Spanish-American War**. To this day the Cuban government remains adamant that the US blew up its own ship to justify its intervention in the war, but evidence is inconclusive.

On December 10, 1898, the Spanish signed the **Treaty of Paris**, handing control of Cuba, as well as Puerto Rico and the Philippines, to the US. In 1901 Cuba adopted a new constitution, devised in Washington without any Cuban consultation, which included the **Platt Amendment**, declaring that the US had the right to intervene in Cuban affairs should the independence of the country come under threat. The intention to keep Cuba on a short leash was made even clearer with the establishment of a US **naval base** at Guantánamo Bay. On May 20, 1902, under these terms, Cuba was declared a republic and Tomás Estrada Palma was elected president, the first in a long line of US puppets.

With the **economy** in ruins following the war, US investors moved in. Havana and Varadero became flooded with casinos, strip-clubs, hotels and sports clubs, and the island gained a reputation as an anything-goes destination, a reputation enhanced during the years of Prohibition in the US. The global economic crisis spurred by the 1929 Wall Street Crash, caused widespread discontent, and opposition to the government became increasingly radical; the Cuban administartion, under President Gerardo Machado, ruthlessly repressed opposition groups. Amidst the chaos emerged a man who would profoundly shape Cuba's destiny.

A young sergeant, **Fulgencio Batista**, staged a coup within the army and replaced most of the officers with men loyal to him. He installed Ramón Grau San Martín as president, and then continued to prop up a series of Cuban presidents until 1940 when he was elected to office and a new constitution was drawn up.

He lost power in the 1944 elections to Grau San Martín and his Auténtico Party but Batista ran for President again in 1952. Two days before the election, fearing failure, he staged a **military coup** and seized control of the country. He abolished the constitution and established a dictatorship bearing little if any resemblance to his previous more socially progressive term as Cuban leader.

Amongst the candidates for congress in the 1952 election was **Fidel Castro**, a young lawyer who saw his political ambitions dashed when Batista seized power. Effectively frozen out of constitutional politics by Batista's intolerance of opposition, on July 26, 1953, Castro and about 125 others attacked an army barracks at Moncada in Santiago de Cuba. The attack failed and the rebels were either shot or caught. A trial followed in which Castro gave what has become one of his most famous speeches, uttering the immortal words, "Condemn me if you will. History will absolve me". He was sentenced to fifteen years' imprisonment but had served less than three when, under popular pressure, he was released and sent into exile.

Now based in Mexico, Castro set about organizing a **revolutionary force** to take back to Cuba; among his recruits was an Argentinian doctor named **Ernesto "Che" Guevara**. They called themselves the Movimiento 26 de Julio. After sneaking back into Cuba, the movement waged guerrilla warfare against Batista's forces, steadily building support amongst the general population and gaining the upper hand. Eventually the army surrendered to the rebels and Fidel Castro began a victory march across the country, arriving in Havana on January 8, 1959.

Though the revolutionary war had ended, this date marks only the beginning of what in Cuba is referred to as the **Revolution**. Amongst the first acts of the Revolutionary Government was to appropriate foreign-owned businesses, nationalize industries, and redistribute land, most of which had been in US hands. The US government retaliated by freezing purchases of Cuban sugar, restricting exports and backing counter-revolutionary forces within Cuba as well as supporting terrorist campaigns aimed at sabotaging the state apparatus. Finally, President Kennedy opted for all-out invasion and on April 17, 1961, a military force of Cuban exiles, trained and equipped in the US, landed at the **Bay of Pigs** in southern Matanzas. The revolutionaries, previously alerted to an invasion attempt, were ready and the whole operation ended within 72 hours.

In December of that year, in the face of economic and political isolation from the US, Castro declared himself a Marxist-Leninist. The benefits for Cuba were immediate as the **Soviet Union** agreed to buy Cuban sugar at artificially high prices whilst selling them petroleum at well below its market value. In 1962, at Castro's request, the Soviets stationed over forty **missiles** on the island. Kennedy declared an embargo on any military weapons entering Cuba. Krushchev ignored the embargo, and Soviet ships loaded with more weapons made their way across the Atlantic. Neither side would back down and nuclear weapons were prepared for launch in the US. A six-day stalemate followed, after which a deal was finally struck and the world breathed a collective sigh of relief – the **Cuban Missile Crisis** had passed.

The 1960s saw great progress in the education system and in public health but new economic policies aimed at reducing Cuba's dependence on sugar production were less successful, in part due to the mass exodus of professionals during the early years of the revolution and the crippling impact of the US embargo. As the decade wore on, the regime became more intolerant of dissenting voices, declaring all those who challenged government policy to be counter-revolutionaries.

During the politically repressive years of the 1970s and 80s the regime experimented with economic liberalization and diversification but ultimately Cuba managed to survive only with heavy Soviet support.

In 1989 the bubble burst. The **implosion of the Soviet Union** led to a loss of over eighty percent of Cuba's trade. In 1990, the government declared the beginning of the **Special Period**, a euphemism that essentially meant compromise and sacrifice for all Cubans. Public transport deteriorated dramatically as the country lost almost all of its fuel imports. Strict rationing of food was introduced and power shortages became frequent. In response to the crisis, economic reforms permitting limited private enterprise were introduced and the Cubans sought to rebuild the economy by appealing to the worldwide tourist trade.

Having survived the Special Period, Cuba is arguably now in a stronger position economically and politically than at any time since the fall of the Soviet Bloc. The country has gained a strong and wealthy ally in Venezuela, which has become a vital source of subsidized oil. Cuba's position and influence in the region looks set to gain strength.

Against this tumultuous history, the biggest recent change of all came with Fidel Castro's resignation as President in February 2008 after a half century in power – it seems that time finally accomplished what the US could not. Fidel enacted a seamless transition of power to his brother Raúl, and the changes so far have been slight at best – though speculation continues that Raúl will have a higher tolerance for political dissent and plans to further liberalize the economy. The more pertinent question, perhaps, is whether the US will shift its policy towards Cuba. Either way, the Cuban Revolution looks set to continue.

3.1

Havana and around

Havana is in a class of its own on the island, with five times as many inhabitants as the next largest Cuban city, Santiago de Cuba. Nowhere else are the contradictions which have come to characterize the country as pronounced as they are in the capital. There is a sense in some areas that Havana is on the move, with visitors pouring into **Habana Vieja**, the old city, where restoration projects have returned some of the most prestigious colonial architecture in the region to its original splendour, new museums and restaurants abound whilst Cubans themselves have benefited from new schools, renovated apartment buildings and cleaner streets. Yet even in this most touristy part of the city, whole neighbourhoods continue to be characterized by overcrowding and neglect, full of crumbling tenement blocks and broken sewage systems. Not everything on the island is defined by its relationship to tourism: Cuban **culture** is at its most exuberant in the capital, with an abundance of theatres, cinemas, concert venues and art galleries.

Any sightseeing you do will fan out from Habana Vieja, which once constituted the entire city, lining the western banks of a fabulous natural harbour and now a UNESCO-declared World Heritage Site. Most visitors spend their time either in the old city or in leafy **Vedado**, a laid-back district of the city occupying the western half of the seafront promenade, the Malecón, where many of the post-colonial mansions have been converted into ministry offices, embassies, music venues or museums. The best way to appreciate Vedado's compact, quiet suburban streets is on foot. Just a couple of kilometres south you'll find the famous **Plaza de la Revolución** the location for most of the major political rallies since 1959. Beyond Vedado to the west, on the other side of the Río Almendares, **Miramar** – modelled on mid-twentieth-century Miami – ushers in yet another change in the urban landscape. An upmarket part of town with a commercial district on its western fringes and a spread of large-scale, luxury hotels, you'll find some of Havana's most sophisticated restaurants scattered through the district's leafy streets.

East of the city are the region's best **beaches**, including the top-notch Playas del Este. To the south is the Museo Ernest Hemingway in the writer's long-time Cuban residence, while slightly further west, the impressive Jardín Botánico Nacional offers picturesque scenery.

Arrival and information

All major international flights land at **José Martí International Airport** (☎7/649-5777 & 266-4644), about 15km south of the city centre. At Terminal Three you'll find most of the airport services including a few shops, a restaurant and a bureau de change, though there are car rental desks in each of the three terminals. The only way to get to Havana from the airport is via taxi, and the half-hour journey should cost between $15–20CUC.

Arriving in the city by bus, you'll be dropped off at either the **Víazul terminal** (☎881-1413 or 7/881-5652), on Avenida 26 over the road from the city zoo, or the Astro-operated **Terminal de Omnibus** (☎879-2456), near the Plaza de la Revolución. Both bus stations are a $3–5CUC taxi ride from most centrally located hotels, and there's a car rental desk at the Víazul terminal. Trains arriving in the capital from the rest of Cuba pull in at Habana Vieja's **Estación Central**

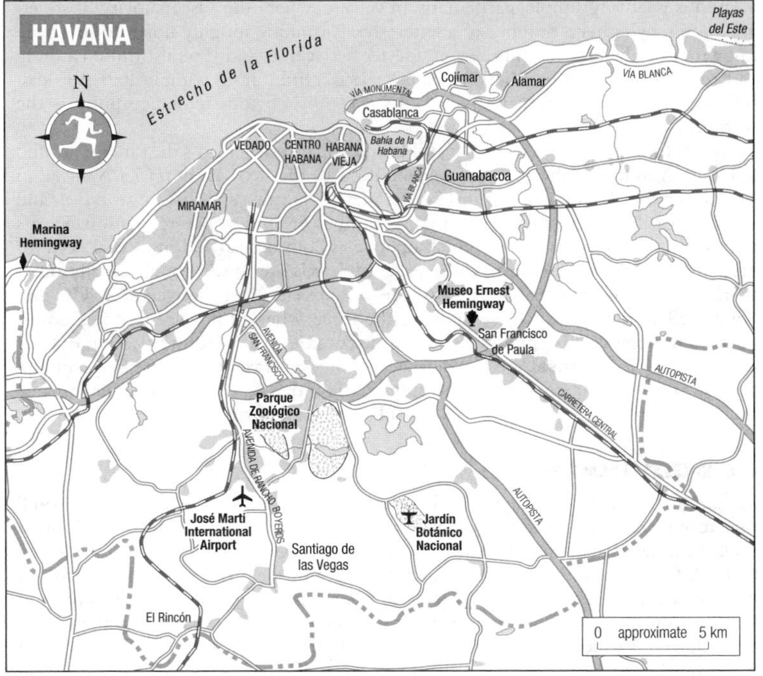

de Ferrocarriles (☎7/860-9448 & 862-1920), where you'll probably have to find yourself a private taxi or one of Havana's army of *bicitaxis* – three-wheeled, two-seater bicycle cabs – to get to your hotel. Cruise ships disembark at the splendid **Terminal Sierra Maestra** (☎7/866-6524 & 862-1925), which faces the Plaza de San Francisco in Habana Vieja.

The state-run Infotur chain operates several **information centres**, with the best-stocked found at Obispo no. 521 e/ Bernaza y Villegas in Habana Vieja (daily 9am–7pm; ☎7/866-3333 & 862-4586, ©obispodir@cubacel.net) and in Playa, in the western suburbs, at 5ta. Ave. y 112 (daily 9am–6pm; ☎7/204-7036, ©miramardir@cubacel.net). You can book rooms and excursions through these centres, though for a better choice of **maps and guides**, head for El Navegante at Mercaderes no. 115 e/ Obispo y Obrapía, Habana Vieja (Mon–Fri 8.30am–5pm, Sat 8.30am–noon; ☎57-1038).

The free monthly **listings guides**, *Bienvenidos* and *Cartelera*, both aimed at foreign visitors, are the most informative publications for up-to-date details on cultural events and activities but are only sporadically available. You may have to enquire in several of the four- and five-star hotels before you find one, though Infotur (see above) is also, in theory, a stockist. The tourist magazine *Prisma* ($1.95CUC), found in bookshops and hotel stores, is also worth seeking out, especially as it is published in parallel Spanish/English text.

Getting around

There's only one way to experience Habana Vieja – on foot – but **getting around** the rest of the city will almost inevitably involve taxis of some kind. Most of the central sections of Havana are laid out on a grid system and finding your way around is relatively simple, particularly in Vedado, where the vast majority of streets are known by either a number or a letter: streets running roughly north to south are known either by an even number or a letter between A and P, whilst those running east to west have odd numbers. Habana Vieja is a little more complicated, not least because of its narrower, densely packed streets; the obvious reference point is the seafront to the north.

Official tourist **taxis** are readily available and will take you across the city for around $5CUC. You'll find the highest concentration of the taxis at the *Hotel Nacional* in Vedado or the Parque Central in Habana Vieja. The most stylish way to travel, and not necessarily more expensive, is in any number of vintage pre-revolutionary cars found all over the city, most of which operate as both official and unofficial taxis. To take in the surroundings at a slower pace, **bicitaxis** are ideal though usually don't work out any cheaper than a car; a fifteen-minute ride costs between $2CUC and $3CUC. The most inexpensive taxis are the three-wheeled novelty motor scooters encased in large yellow spheres known as **cocotaxis**, usually found waiting outside the *Hotel Inglaterra*. **Buses** are far cheaper but they are overcrowded, infrequent and there is no route information at bus stops. If you decide to brave it, your journey will cost no more than 40 centavos in Cuban pesos (less than US3¢).

Accommodation

Accommodation in the capital is abundant and in most of the main areas you'll find rooms in *casas particulares* starting from $25CUC whilst in hotels the cheapest double rooms start at around $50CUC and are more commonly priced at upwards of $100CUC a night in high season. You'd do well to make a **reservation**, particularly in high season when the town is packed. Many visitors stay in the state hotels in **Habana Vieja**, handy for many of the key sights and well served by restaurants and bars. Quieter **Vedado** features some of the city's more spectacular *casas particulares,* but you'll need transport to make the trip to Habana Vieja.

Habana Vieja

Casa de Eugenio Barral García San Ignacio no. 656 e/ Jesús María y Merced ⓣ7/862-9877, ⓔfabio.quintana@infomed.sld.cu. Deep in southern Habana Vieja, this exceptional first-floor *casa particular* has a sensational garden roof terrace, very hospitable landlords and is spotlessly clean and beautifully furnished. The two double bedrooms both have a/c and a TV. ❷

Casa del Científico Paseo del Prado no. 212 esq. Trocadero ⓣ7/862-1604 & 862-1607, ⓔhcientif@ceniai.inf.cu. The least expensive hotel this close to the Parque Central. The aristocratic residence, unlike most of Havana's remodelled colonial buildings, has barely been touched, leaving much of the original opulent decoration. Rooms are comfortable but a little basic, some share bathrooms and there's a spacious rooftop terrace. ❷

Chez Nous Brasil no. 115 e/ Cuba y San Ignacio ⓣ7/862-6287, ⓔcheznous@ceniai.inf.cu. This majestic *casa particular* has two balconied first-floor rooms for rent, both with a/c, TV and minibar. From the airy, leafy central patio a spiral staircase leads up to the spacious roof terrace where there's another, more modern room with en-suite bathroom. The savvy owners speak English and French. Bookings essential. ❷

Florida Obispo no. 252 esq. Cuba ⓣ7/862-4127 & 861-5621, ⓔreservas@habaguanexhflorida.co.cu. A perfect blend of modern luxury and colonial elegance with marble floors, iron chandeliers, birds singing in the airy stone-columned central patio and potted plants throughout, this hotel is one of the outstanding success stories of the Habana Vieja restoration project. ❺

Hostal Conde de Villanueva (aka *Hostal del Habano*) Mercaderes esq. Lamparilla ⓣ7/862-9293, ⓦwww.hostalcondevillanueva.cu. Despite its relatively small size this place finds room for a fantastic cellar-style restaurant, a wonderful courtyard and a relaxing smokers' lounge and bar. The smartly furnished rooms come with satellite TV, minibar and most have a bath tub as well as a shower. ❺

Hostal Valencia Oficios no. 53 esq. Obrapía ⓣ7/867-1037, ⓔcomercial@habaguanexhvalencia. Plain but pleasant rooms in a beautiful building that feels more like a large house than a small hotel. Highlights include a cobbled-floor courtyard with hanging vines. ❹

Saratoga Paseo del Prado no. 603 esq. Dragones ⓣ7/868-1000, ⓦwww.hotel-saratoga.com. This impressively posh hotel is the latest Habana Vieja classic to be brought back from the dead, having gained fame in the 1930s. Dripping with lavishness and old-world style the interior feels like a Humphrey Bogart movie set with sleek bars and ritzy lounge areas whilst there is an impressive set of contrastingly modern facilities including a rooftop pool, a gym and solarium. Rooms feature pseudo-antique furnishings, DVD players and Internet connections. ⑥

Vedado

Casa de Idania Lazo Rodríguez Calle 25 no. 1061 e/ 4 y 6 ⓣ7/830-9760, ⓔdnsid@ccme.com.cu. Two bedrooms on a beautiful tree-lined street with a choice of twin beds or a double. Each has its own bathroom and there's an ample shared patio. ②

Casa de Mélida Jordán Calle 25 no. 1102 e/ 6 y 8 ⓣ7/833-5219, ⓔmelida@girazul.com. A big stylish house set back from the road and surrounded by a marble veranda overlooking an expansive garden. Two of the three rooms have their own bathrooms and all are beautifully furnished. The largest room has twin beds and the other two doubles, although extra beds can be added. The helpful and friendly owners speak English and there are various extra services available. ②

Habana Libre Calle 23 esq. L ⓣ7/55-4011 & 834-6100, ⓦwww.hotelhabanalibre.com. Large, slick, city hotel with lots of shops, a terrace pool, three restaurants, numerous bars and a cabaret, making it a solid, if somewhat anonymous, choice. ⑥

Hotel Nacional Calle O esq. 21 ⓣ7/836-3564, ⓦwww.hotelnacionaldecuba.com. The choice of visiting celebrities for decades, this handsome hotel looks like an Arabian palace and is deservedly recognized as one of Havana's best. Beautiful rooms, smooth service and excellent facilities. ⑤

Saint John's Calle O e/ 23 y 25 ⓣ7/833-3740, 834-4187, ⓔreserva@stjohns.gca.tur.cu. A plain but pleasant and well-located hotel. One of Vedado's least expensive, on a bustling street corner with a basement jazz club next door and within sight of the Malecón. Facilities include a 24-hr lobby bar and rooftop pool. ③

Habana Vieja

By far the most visited part of the city, bursting with centuries-old buildings and buzzing with a strong sense of the past, **Habana Vieja** – or Old Havana – is the richest sightseeing area in the city. Its narrow streets, refined colonial mansions, countless churches, cobblestone plazas and sixteenth-century fortresses make it one of the most rewarding colonial urban centres in the Americas. Yet there is much more to Habana Vieja than its physical make-up. Unlike many of the world's major cities, the tourist centre of Havana is also home to a large proportion of the city's residents, with some of its poorest families crammed into apartment buildings alongside the museums and hotels to which tourists flock in ever-increasing numbers.

The **Plaza de la Catedral** and the nearby **Plaza de Armas** are both good starting points for your visit. Heading up **Obispo**, Habana Vieja's main shopping street, to the **Parque Central** leads to other unmissable sights including El Capitolio and the Gran Teatro. Of Habana Vieja's many museums, some have rather half-hearted and incoherent collections but several museums are excellent, most notably the **Museo de la Revolución** and the **Museo Nacional de Bellas Artes**.

A word of warning: Habana Vieja is the **bag-snatching** centre of the city, with an increasing number of petty thieves working the streets, so use extra precaution. Even at night, however, there is very rarely any violent crime.

Plaza de la Catedral

The **Plaza de la Catedral**, in northeastern Habana Vieja, is one of the most architecturally uniform squares in the old city, enclosed on three sides by a set of symmetrical, eighteenth-century aristocratic residences. The striking **Catedral de la Habana** (Mon–Fri 10.30am–3pm, Sat 10.30am–2pm; free), hailed as the consummate example of the Cuban Baroque style, dominates the plaza with its swirling detail, curved edges and cluster of columns. While the less spectacular interior bears an endearing resemblance to an archetypal local church, don't miss the lavishly framed portraits by French painter Jean Baptiste Vermay and other artwork.

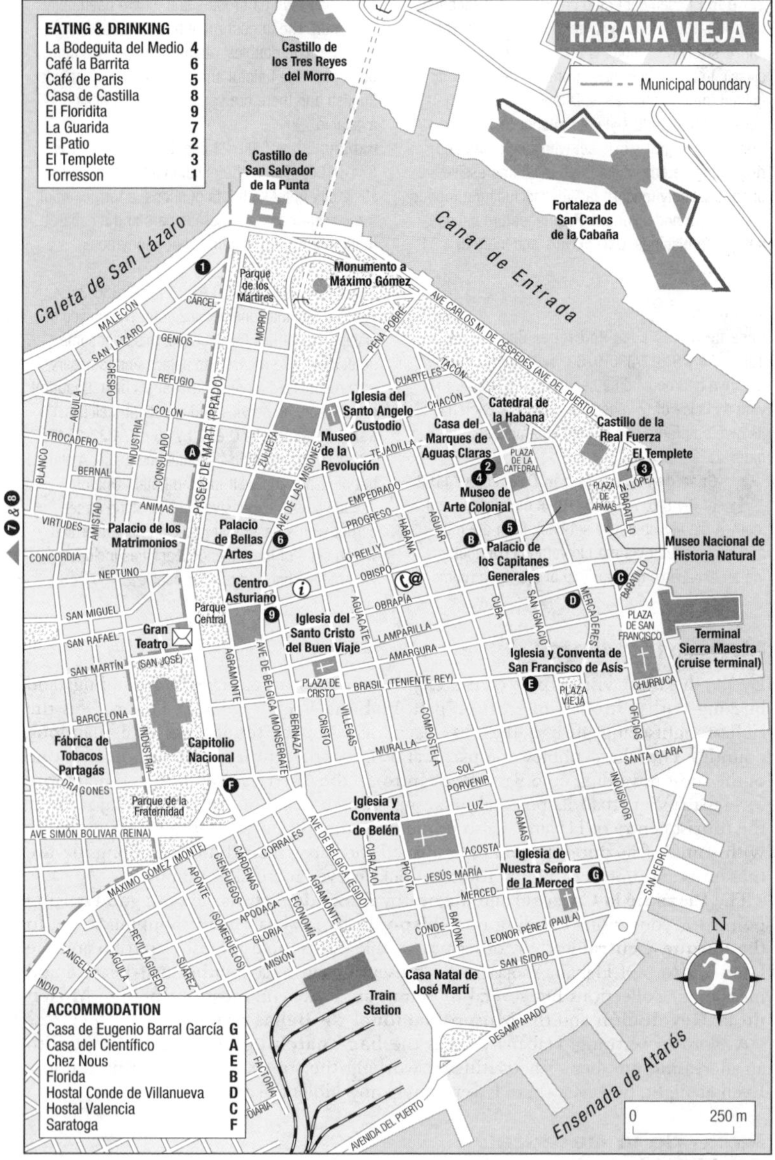

Opposite the cathedral, the Casa de los Condes de Casa Bayona, built in 1720, houses the **Museo de Arte Colonial** (daily 9am–7pm; $2CUC, guided tour $1CUC extra, $2CUC to take photos). Its comprehensive collection of well-preserved, mostly nineteenth-century furniture and ornaments offers a clear insight into aristocratic living during the later years of Spanish rule in Cuba. The predominantly European-made artefacts have been collected from colonial residences around the city and include mahogany dressers, gold and porcelain vases and a fantastic antique piano. The most elegant of the colonial mansions on the plaza is the **Casa del Marques de Aguas Claras**. Its serene fountain-centred courtyard encompassed by pillar-propped arches and simple stained-glass portals is actually part of the delightful *El Patio* restaurant, so you'll need to eat there to see it.

Plaza de Armas and the Castillo de la Real Fuerza

A couple of blocks southeast of the Plaza de la Catedral on San Ignacio and then on O'Reilly, the area around the **Plaza de Armas**, the oldest and most animated of Habana Vieja's squares, was where Havana was founded in the second half of the sixteenth century. Based around an attractive, leafy, landscaped core, the plaza seethes with tourists as live music wafts from restaurant *La Mina* and browsers crowd the stalls of the outdoor book market.

The refined **Palacio de los Capitanes Generales**, on the western side of the plaza, was the seat of the Spanish government from the time of its inauguration in 1791 to the end of the Spanish-American War in 1898. It's now home to one of Havana's best museums, the **Museo de la Ciudad** (daily 9am–6.30pm; $3CUC, $1 extra for guided tour), a fine representation of the city's colonial heritage. A number of the upstairs rooms have been precisely restored, amongst them the Salón del Trono (Throne Room) with dark-red, satin-lined walls, and the Salón Verde where the governor of the city used to receive his guests amidst golden furniture and precious porcelain.

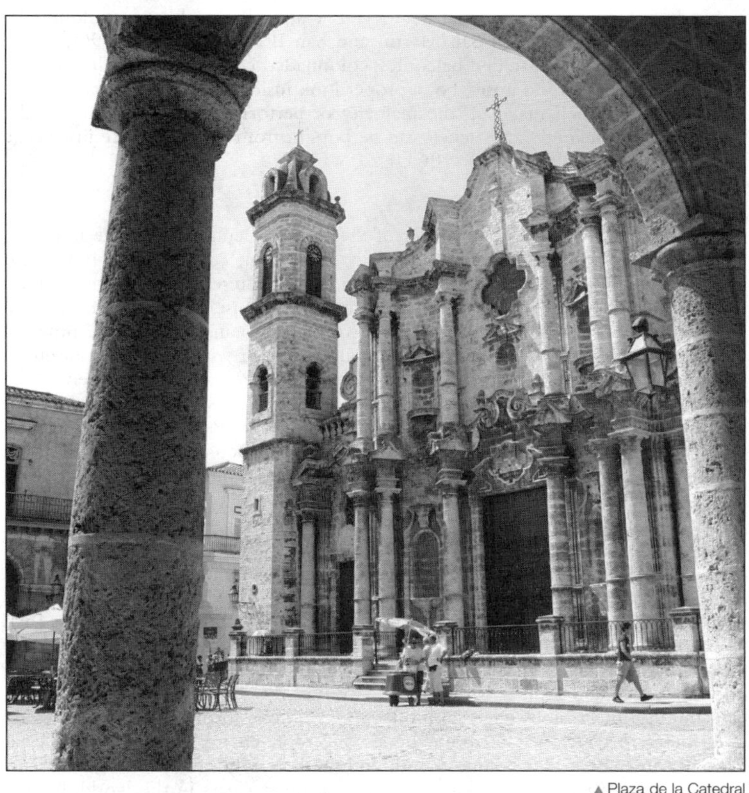

▲ Plaza de la Catedral

There's more to see around the rest of the square, including two more museums. The **Museo Nacional de Historia Natural**, on the corner of Oficios and Obispo (Tues–Sat 10am–4pm, Wed–Sun 10.30am–6pm; $3CUC, $4CUC with guide), with its rather uninspired stuffed-animal displays and primitive interactive exhibits, is nevertheless the country's most substantial museum of its kind and one of the few in Habana Vieja likely to appeal to children.

In the square's northeastern corner, the incongruous classical Greek architecture of **El Templete** church (daily 9am–6.30pm; $1CUC) marks the exact spot of the foundation of Havana and the city's first Mass in 1519. In the same corner, just beyond the northeastern border of the plaza, is the **Castillo de la Real Fuerza**, a solid sixteenth-century fortress surrounded by a moat. It is placed well back from the mouth of the bay, a location which allowed the English, in 1762, to take control of Havana without ever coming into the firing range of the fortress's cannon. Following lengthy interior repairs, the fort is currently awaiting the installation of a collection of exhibits from a former maritime museum.

Parque Central

From the Plaza de Armas, busy Obispo leads to the **Parque Central**, which straddles the border between Habana Vieja and Centro Habana and is within shouting distance of the Capitolio Nacional. Although the speeding traffic detracts somewhat from the whole, the grandeur of the surrounding buildings, characteristic of the celebratory early twentieth-century architecture in this section of town, lends the square a stateliness that's quite distinct from the residential feel pervading the rest of Habana Vieja. The attention-grabber is undoubtedly the **Gran Teatro** between San Martín and San Rafael (☎7/861-3096), which is an explosion of balustraded balconies, colonnaded cornices and sculpted stone figures striking Classical poses. For a proper look inside, you'll have to attend one of the ballets which make up the majority of performances here; these usually take place at weekends, and tickets can be bought from the box office just inside the main entrance for around $10CUC.

Capitolio Nacional

Just beyond the southwestern corner of the Parque Central looms the imposing dome of the **Capitolio Nacional** (daily 9am–7pm; $3CUC or $4CUC for guided tours). Opened in 1929 (and bearing a striking resemblance to the Capitol Building in Washington DC), it was the seat of the House of Representatives and the Senate prior to the Revolution. The two ornate main chambers are now the centrepiece of visitor tours, and the walk round, with or without a free tour guide, shouldn't take you longer than twenty minutes as only one floor is open to the public, much of it behind ropes. Nevertheless, the sheer size of the magnificent polished entrance hall known as the Salón de los Pasos Perdidos (The Room of Lost Steps) and the breathtaking gold and bronze Rococo-style decoration of the Hemiciclio Camilo Cienfuegos, a theatrical, echoing conference chamber, leave a lasting impression.

Fábrica de Tobacos Partagás

Behind the Capitolio stands one of the country's oldest and largest cigar factories, the **Fábrica de Tobacos Partagás** (tours every 30min Mon–Fri & alternate Sat 9am–2.30pm; $10CUC), which was founded in 1845 and still churns out such famous makes as Cohiba, Monte Cristo Bolívar and Partagás itself. Although very pricey compared to most museum entrance fees, the 45-minute tour is easily among the most fascinating things to do in the city, with English-speaking guides taking you through the various stages of production – drying, sorting, rolling and boxing – all performed in separate rooms under one roof. There's even a kind of cigar school from where, after a nine-month course, those who graduate move upstairs and join the 250 workers making some of the finest cigars in the world. Here, a sea of expert rollers – expected to produce on average over 100 cigars a day during their eight-hour shifts – are read to while they work, from a newspaper in the mornings and from a book in the afternoons. It's entirely uncontrived and there's a very genuine sense of observing an everyday operation, with most of the workers almost oblivious to the flashing cameras. There is also an excellent **cigar shop** just inside the entrance.

Museo Nacional de Bellas Artes

The **Museo Nacional de Bellas Artes** (Tues–Sat 10am–6pm, Sun 10am–2pm; $5CUC for one building, $8CUC for both, under 15s free) is the most spectacular of Havana's museums, containing by far the largest collection of art in the country. The museum is divided between two buildings: the Art Deco Palacio de Bellas Artes, opposite the Museo de la Revolución on Trocadero, showcases exclusively Cuban art, and the Centro Asturiano, across Agramonte from the Parque Central displays art from the rest of the world.

The best way to tackle the **Cuban collection** in the **Palacio de Bellas Artes** is to take the lifts in the entrance lobby up to the top floor and walk round clockwise, as the exhibits are laid out in chronological order. The most historic pieces are on the gantry that runs most of the length of the first two rooms, including a great lithograph of nineteenth-century Havana by Eduardo Laplante. The rest of the top floor leaps straight into the twentieth century, beginning with paintings by Victor Manuel García (1897–1969), including his portrait of a gypsy girl, *Gitana tropical*, considered a national treasure and one of the most widely reproduced Cuban paintings. Amongst the more modern stuff, the jumbled-looking *Esta es la Historia* (*This is history*) by Gilberto de la Nuez (1913–1993) is a large picture made up of numerous tiny scenes, all set against the same background but each portrays a separate and significant moment in Cuban history.

Down the road, the grandiose **Centro Asturiano** is divided up by country of origin, with collections from Britain, Italy, Spain and France, as well as Dutch, Flemish, Latin and North American rooms and a smaller Asian section. No single collection particularly stands out, as many of the artists are lesser-known painters with no classic or renowned works on display. However, there are several paintings by notable artists, including *Malvern Hall* by John Constable and *Kermesse* by Jan Brueghel (the younger), interesting as much for the fact that they somehow ended up in Cuba as for their artistic merit. Most of the fourth floor is dedicated to the ancient art of Rome, Egypt and Greece, with highlights of the Egyptian section including a 3000-year-old tomb.

Museo de la Revolución

From Parque Central it's a two-minute walk along Agramonte to Havana's most famous museum, the **Museo de la Revolución** (daily 10am–5pm; $5CUC, $2CUC extra for guided tour), defiantly housed in the sumptuous presidential palace of the 1950s dictator General Fulgencio Batista. The events of the 1959 revolution are covered in unparalleled detail but your attention span is unlikely to last the full three storeys. Visitors work their way down from the top floor, which is the most engaging part of the museum and where you should concentrate your efforts. The events of the revolutionary war and the urban insurgency movements during the 1950s were surprisingly well documented, with some fantastically dramatic pictures, like one of the police assault on the Socialist Party headquarters. Some of the classic images of the campaign waged in the Sierra Maestra by Castro and his band of followers will look familiar but no less captivating, but even serious students of Cuban history will struggle to keep track of the chronology amidst an onslaught of battle plans and miscellaneous firearms. Located outside, to the rear of the museum, is the **Granma Memorial**, which houses the boat that carried Castro and his men from Mexico to Cuba to begin the revolution.

Habana del Este

Many people miss the sights in **Habana del Este** across the bay from Habana Vieja, erroneously believing it's an inconvenient place to visit. Those who do make it across the bay will find it an easy and worthwhile excursion. Broadly speaking, Habana del Este comprises the area on the immediate east side of the bay, visible from the western side and flanked by the Via Monumental.

A visit to the castles and fortifications that collectively make up the **Parque Morro-Cabaña** on the east side of the harbour is really rewarding. Part of the Havana skyline, the structures dominate the view across the harbour and, along with the fortifications in Habana Vieja, comprise the city's oldest defence system. The **Castillo de los Tres Reyes Magos del Morro** (daily 8am–8.30pm; $3CUC, $2CUC extra for lighthouse) was built between 1589 and 1630 to complement the **Castillo de San Salvador de la Punta** on the opposite side of the bay. The dual fortifications proved inadequate, however, when the British invaded overland in 1762 and occupied the city for six months. From the high parade grounds, studded with rusted cannons and Moorish turrets, you could easily spend an hour or so surveying the bay. A highlight of the visit is watching the sun set over the sea from the summit of the **lighthouse** that was built on the cliff edge in 1844.

Roughly 250m further east, the **Fortaleza San Carlos de la Cabaña** (daily 10am–10pm; $4CUC before 6pm, $6CUC after 6pm, guide $1CUC extra) needs more time to do it justice. The most complex and expensive defence system in the Americas when it was designed in the 1760s, it took eleven years to complete, and you can see why with one look at the extensive grounds, whose cobbled streets lined with houses (where soldiers and officers were originally billeted) now shelter a miscellany of workshops, artisans' boutiques and restaurants.

The easiest way to get to Habana del Este is to take a metered or private taxi ($2CUC–$4CUC), or a bus (40¢) from the stop near the Monumento Máximo Gómez on the Malecón in Habana Vieja – get off at the first stop after the tunnel. From the fortifications it's a brisk half-hour walk to the seventeen-metre-high **Cristo de La Habana**, the gigantic hilltop Christ figure, or a pleasant ride on the foot-and-bicycle ferry ($1CUP) that leaves every thirty minutes from Avenida del Puerto e/ Sol y Luz, ten minutes' walk south from Plaza San Francisco and the main Sierra Maestra Terminal.

The Malecón

For many visitors, the crumbling buildings and bustling streets of **Centro Habana**, crammed between Habana Vieja and Vedado, are glimpsed only through a taxi window en route to the city's more tourist-friendly areas. Yet this no-frills quarter has a character all of its own, as illuminating and fascinating as anywhere in the capital, and its residential, late eighteenth- and nineteenth-century neighbourhoods throb with life.

The warts-and-all appeal also means that this part of town is for the most part not that attractive on the surface. Full of broken sewage systems, potholed roads and piles of rubbish, Centro Habana has not enjoyed the degree of investment and rejuvenation seen in Habana Vieja, save for the **Malecón**, where painfully slow restoration work is returning the famous seafront promenade to its former glory.

The most picturesque way to reach Vedado from Centro Habana or Habana Vieja is to stroll down the **Malecón**, Havana's famous seawall that snakes from La Punta westwards along the coastline for about 4km. Crowded with schoolchildren hurling themselves into the churning Atlantic, sun-worshippers and wrinkled anglers, it's the city's defining image, and ambling along its length, drinking in the panoramic views, is an essential part of the Havana experience. People head here for free entertainment, particularly at night when it fills up with guitar-strumming musicians, vendors offering cones of fresh-roasted warm nuts, and star-gazing couples, young and old alike.

Pot holed and sea-beaten, the Malecón looks much older than its hundred years. Construction began in 1901 after nearly a century of planning and it wasn't until 1950 that the walkway finally reached its destination, the Río Almendares, on the border between Vedado and Miramar. The Centro Habana stretch is referred to on signs as the "*Malecón tradicional*", marked at the eastern end by the Paseo del Prado and at the western end by the Parque Antonio Maceo. This is the postcard section of the Malecón, lined with a patchwork of mostly grand neo-colonial arch-fronted apartment buildings and dotted with cafeterias and one or two restaurants, newly installed as part of the tortoise-paced reconstruction project that began over a decade ago.

Vedado

The cultural heart of the city, graceful **Vedado** draws crowds with its palatial hotels – the backbone of so much of Havana's social scene – contemporary art galleries, concert venues, restaurants, bars and nightspots. Loosely defined as the area running west of Calzada de Infanta up to the Río Almendares, Vedado is less ramshackle than other parts of the city and is blessed with a relaxing sense of space and relative calm around its wide streets, detached houses and leafy little parks. Pock-marked with crowds, which lend a veneer of activity, there are a few bustling focal points, most notably around Havana's massive ice-cream parlour, *Coppelia*.

The most visited part is modern **La Rampa** (Calle 23), and the streets immediately to the north and south, throbbing with battered Chevrolets and Buicks and bordered by high-rise 1950s hotels and utilitarian buildings. It's a relatively small space but it dominates your immediate impression of Vedado, firstly because the peeling, 50-year-old, skyscrapers are such a rarity in Cuba and, secondly, because as a visitor you end up spending a fair amount of time here – confirming or booking flights, changing money in the hotels, souvenir-shopping in the street markets or eating at the restaurants. Although it's an area for doing rather than seeing, you will find some worthy museums, including the **Museo Napoleónico** on San Miguel (Mon–Sat 9am–4.30pm, Sun 9am–noon; $3CUC, guided tour $2CUC extra), a treasure trove of artefacts relating to the erstwhile French emperor. Nearby, the **Universidad de La Habana** comprises a series of beautiful buildings in verdant grounds, attended by well-behaved students who personify the virtues of post-revolutionary education.

Beyond here, to the south, the **Plaza de la Revolución** sports immense monuments to the two great heroes of Cuban independence, José Martí and Ernesto "Che" Guevara, as well as the exhaustive **Museo José Martí** (Tues–Sat 10am–6pm; $3CUC, $5CUC including lookout point), which charts Martí's luminary career. The uncompromising concrete sweep of the plaza itself forms a complete contrast to the area's other key attraction, the atmospheric **Necrópolis de Cólon** (daily 8am–5pm; $1CUC), one of the largest cemeteries in the Americas, with some of the most grandiose and stunning tombs in the country.

Further to the north west in a quieter part of Vedado, sandwiched between Calle 23 and the Malecón, where the backstreets narrow and avenues are overhung with leaves from pine, rubber and weeping fig trees, is the **Museo de los Artes Decorativos**, 502 Calle 17 (Tues–Sat 11am–7pm; $2CUC, $1CUC extra with guide, $3CUC extra to take a camera), a dizzying collection of fine furniture and *objets d'art*. Further afield, dotted around the broad avenues of Linea, Paseo and Avenida de los Presidentes, are several excellent galleries and cultural centres, notably the **Casa de las Américas** (Sala Contemporánea Mon–Fri 10am–5pm; free; Galería Latino-Americana Mon–Thurs 10am–5pm, Fri 10am–noon; $2CUC), set up to celebrate Pan-Americanism and displaying quality artworks from all over Latin America as well as hosting regular musical events.

Miramar and the western suburbs

Miramar and the western suburbs, an area collectively known as Playa, are Havana's alter ego: larger than life, with ice-white Miami-style residences surrounded by sweeping gardens, flashy business developments, spanking new hotels and wide tree-lined avenues. The area is divided into four main suburbs: oceanfront **Miramar**, reached from the Malecón through the tunnel under the Río Almendares; **La Sierra** to its immediate south; **Kohly** tucked further south; and **Almendares** to the west. Although the houses and embassies are good for a gawp, the area is short on tangible focal points and low on specific attractions and, given that it occupies a much larger space than Habana Vieja, Centro Habana or Vedado, an aimless wander here can turn into a tiresome trek. That said, as the most peaceful, uncluttered part of the city this neighbourhood offers a stark, and for some welcome, retreat from cacophonous Habana Vieja. Many visitors who venture over the river do so for the famous *Tropicana* cabaret in Marianao (see p.174), just south of Kohly, and some of the city's best **restaurants**, which provide a welcome respite from pork, rice and beans. Amongst the one or two other prominent visitor attractions are the **Acuario Nacional de Cuba** at Avenida 1ra and Calle 60 (Tues–Sun 10am–6pm, $5CUC adults, $4CUC children), featuring sea life indigenous to Cuban waters and shows laid on throughout the day, and the **Marina Hemingway** on the outskirts of Miramar which pulls in scores of yachties and divers.

Eating

Havana has the most varied culinary scene in Cuba, even if the setting of many establishments is more notable than the food. The best restaurants tend to be in Miramar and the western suburbs, while numerous *paladares* dish up good-value portions of local fare. A number of **ethnic** restaurants can be found Havana; the most common are Chinese, Italian and Spanish. **Vegetarians** will find decent though predictable choices (pizza and omelettes featuring heavily) at most places, although the city is now benefiting from several well-equipped vegetarian restaurants. Stick to the hotels for **breakfast**, most of which welcome non-hotel guests, as elsewhere the choice is a bit patchy; the *Habana Libre* does a particularly fine buffet for $13CUC. A good option for an inexpensive **lunch** is to grab a snack from one of the **street stalls** dotted around Centro Habana and Vedado, which sell tasty fritters and pizzas for just a few pesos each.

Habana Vieja and Centro Habana

La Bodeguita del Medio Empedrado e/ San Ignacio y Cuba, Habana Vieja ☎7/867-1374 & 866-8857. A renowned Hemingway haunt and home of the *mojito*, this classic Havana restaurant relies more on its fame than its standard Cuban pork, beef and seafood dishes all for between $9CUC and $16CUC . The mini-maze of little rooms and corners helps to create a great atmosphere. Book ahead.

Casa de Castilla Neptuno no. 519 e/ Camapanario y Lealtad, Centro Habana ☎7/862-5482. With its entrance set back from the street, this restaurant appears to be some kind of private club but it is in fact one of the cheapest places worth eating at in Centro Habana. Way off the tourist circuit in terms of both character and location, the fresh and well-prepared *comida criolla* main dishes starting at $1.70CUC are worth seeking out. Tues–Sun noon–10.30pm.

El Floridita Monserrate esq. Obispo, Habana Vieja ☎7/867-1300 & 867-1301. Expensive seafood dishes, such as thermidor lobster for $42CUC in one of the most exclusive restaurants in the old city. It's another Hemingway heritage site and a velvet-curtain doorway leads from the equally famous bar to an elegant circular dining area.

La Guarida Concordia no. 418 e/ Gervasio y Escobar, Centro Habana ☎7/862-4940. The meat and fish menu at this expensive but unbeatable *paladar* breaks with all the Cuban norms, dishes such as coconut-glazed tuna with sugar cane ($13CUC) food bursting with flavour and the whole place run with unusual professionalism. Set in the aged apartment building where the acclaimed *Fresa y Chocolate* was filmed, the decor is eye-catchingly eclectic. Reservations are essential and a meal here unmissable.

El Patio Plaza de la Catedral, Habana Vieja. The serenity of this leafy, eighteenth-century mansion courtyard goes a long way to justifying the above-average prices, with pepper steaks setting you back $20CUC, as does the excellent choice of main dishes, with an emphasis on seafood, set vegetarian meals and plenty of optional extras.

El Templete Ave. Carlos Manuel de Céspedes (Ave. del Puerto) no.12–14 esq. Narcisco López, Habana Vieja ⓣ7/860-8280. The gourmet seafood at this roadside, harbour front restaurant is the finest and tastiest in Habana Vieja, thanks in large part to the Basque head chef. From tasty starters like octopus *a la gallega*, to mouth-watering mains like red snapper in green sauce almost everything on the menu stands out and delivers. Main dishes start at $8CUC.

Torresson Malecón no. 27 e/ Prado y Cárcel, Centro Habana ⓣ7/861-7476. Chicken, pork and fish dishes for around the $8CUC mark in a basic balcony spot overlooking the seafront with a good view of El Morro.

Vedado

Carmelo Calzada e/ D y E ⓣ7/832-4495. You can choose from a range of well-prepared dishes at this excellent vegetarian restaurant, including steamed okra and fried aubergine for less than $2CUC. Brightly lit and very clean, the only drawback is the habitual overcharging but the vegetarian pros far outweigh the cons.

Coppelia Calle 23 esq. L. Havana's massive ice-cream emporium contains several peso cafés and a peso convertible open-air area, serving rich sundaes with tropical flavours like coconut and guava. Closed Mon.

Decameron Linea, no. 753 e/ Paseo y Calle 2 ⓣ7/832-2444. Inspired, low-key decor and ambience complement a mix of Italian, Cuban and European food at this cosmopolitan place where most main dishes cost between $7CUC and $15CUC. The giant pizzas are possibly the largest in town, the pasta is nicely *al dente* and there's a decent attempt at salade nicoise. Strong and sweet *mojitos*, plus attentive service, gild the lily.

Nacional Calle O esq. 21. This expensive but not unreasonably priced all-you-can-eat buffet restaurant in the hotel's basement provides one of Havana's best feeds, with an extensive range of fish and meat and a welcome array of green vegetables. Buffet breakfasts cost $13CUC whilst lunch and dinner are priced at $20CUC each.

Nerei Calle 19 esq. L ⓣ7/832-7860. Elegant and expensive *paladar* where you can dine alfresco on escalope of pork or fried chicken, all served with yucca, fried banana and salad. Expect a dinner for two to cost around $35CUC.

La Torre Calle 17 no. 55 Edificio Focsa piso 36 ⓣ7/55-3088 to 89. Mesmerizing views from the city's second tallest building are matched by the excellent French menu. Definitely worth splashing out $40CUC or so to dine on foie gras, fillet of beef with rosemary, shrimps caramelized in honey, and profiteroles.

Miramar and the western suburbs

El Aljibe Ave 7ma e/ 24 y 26 Miramar ⓣ7/204-1583. Similar to many of the Miramar restaurants, El Aljibe is a place to head for a touch of luxury. The food, including house specialties of beef kebabs, pulls no surprises but it is well prepared and tasty, and there's plenty of it. All this and an ambient open-air setting make it a must.

La Esperanza Calle no.105 e/ 1ra y 3ra ⓣ7/202-4361. The owner of this fabulous *paladar* has created a 1930s homage to the house's previous owner, the eponymous Esperanza. The creative menu is expertly prepared and offers dishes like chicken in soy and ginger sauce, fresh fish and smoothly prepared cocktails. Prices are around $30CUC a head. Open 7–11pm; closed Sun.

Drinking, nightlife and entertainment

Havana nightlife does not jump out at you but instead works its magic from isolated corners all over the city, in secluded clubs, hotel basements and rooftops, anonymous little bars and in hidden courtyards or concealed rooms in backstreet colonial buildings. Spontaneous nights out are difficult as there's no single area with much of a buzz but discovering world-class musicians performing in modest neighbourhood venues or sipping cocktails in clandestine bars buried in apartment buildings has its own enchanting appeal. There are, however, obvious places to go, with most of the biggest and brashest night spots found in the high-class hotels around Vedado. Whatever the venue, what the capital does best is **live music**, and you should definitely try to catch one of the excellent *salsa*, jazz or *son* groups guaranteed to be playing somewhere in the city every night.

Bar crawls involve a lot of walking, although Obispo in Habana Vieja can lay claim to the biggest concentration of drinking spots whilst the nearby Plaza de la Catedral district is also usually quite lively at night. However, for sheer *joie de vivre* you can't beat taking some beers or a bottle of rum down to the Malecón and mingling with the crowds beneath the stars.

Bars and cafés

La Bodeguita del Medio Empedrado e/ San -Ignacio y Mercaderes, Habana Vieja. Made famous by Hemingway, this is the consummate "been-there-got-the-T-shirt" location in Havana and is one of the few places where you'll have to fight to get to the bar. The overcrowding makes it lively and atmospheric but at $4CUC for a mediocre *mojito* and $5CUC for other cocktails this tiny bar is definitely a tourist trap.

Café La Barrita Edificio Bacardi, Ave. de las Misiones e/ San Juan de Dios y Empedrado, Habana Vieja. Hidden away on the mezzanine level behind the foyer of the Bacardi Building is this stylish Art Deco café, a comfortable and congenial little hide-out and a great spot to take a break. Good-value snacks too.

Café de Paris San Ignacio esq. Obispo, Habana Vieja. Popular with an even mix of tourists and locals, this simple little bar enjoys a party atmosphere stirred up by a nightly live band.

Gato Tuerto Calle 0 e/ 17 y 19, Vedado ⓣ7/55-2696. This pre-revolution, beatnik jazz bar has kept its cool edge despite a complete renovation. Excellent live Feelin' (*trova* jazz fusion) is played nightly from midnight to 4am, making it one of the best nights out in the area, though for a slightly older crowd. Entry is free but subject to a $5CUC consumption minimum. There's a stylish eating area upstairs.

Opus Bar Teatro Amadeo Roldan Calzada esq. D, Vedado. A good-looking, long bar with the air of a darkened departure lounge, with big squashy easy chairs and sultry lighting. While it gets busier between 8pm and 1am, it's not the place for a thumping night out but rather a sophisticated retreat for those in search of a laid-back drink. There's a good range of cocktails.

Cabarets, discos and live music

Cabaret Nacional San Rafael esq. Paseo del Prado, Habana Vieja. Below the Gran Teatro, this seedy basement cabaret and disco is more than just a pick-up joint, though it is certainly that, too. The show starts around 11pm and the disco usually gets going at about 1am. Entrance is between $5CUC and $10CUC depending on the night.

Casa de la Cultura Aguiar no. 509 e/ Amargura y Brasil, Habana Vieja ⓣ63-48-60. In the converted Convento de San Francisco, this centre for local talent runs a full programme of evening performances, ranging from folk music to rap. Entrance is usually between 2 and 5 national pesos.

Casa de la Música Ave. de Italia (Galiano), Centro Habana ⓣ7/862-41-65. This is the biggest, snazziest and one of the newest and hippest club and live music venues on this side of the city. All the hottest names in Cuban *salsa* play here, where you can enjoy the music from a table or on the sizeable dance floor. Afternoon performances start at 4pm and at night the club is open 10pm–4.30am. Entrance $10–25CUC, depending on who's playing.

Tropicana Calle 72 no. 504 Marianao. Possibly the oldest and most lavish cabaret in the world, Cuba's much-hyped and not to be missed open-air venue hosts a pricey extravaganza in which class acts such as Pablo Milanes, and a ceaseless flow of dancing girls, (under)clad in sequins, feathers and frills, regularly pull in a full house. Starts at 8.30pm with the show from 10 to 11pm. You can arrange all-inclusive bus trips from $65CUC from most hotels, otherwise entrance is $75–90CUC. Closed Mon.

Listings

Banks and exchange The *cambio* in the *Nacional* hotel in Vedado has the longest opening hours (daily 8am–noon & 1–11pm), while Banco Internacional de Comercio (Mon–Fri 8.30am–3pm) at Empedrado esq. Aguiar in Habana Vieja is the best bank in the old city for foreign currency transactions.

Car rental Micar offers the cheapest deals and has an office in the Galerias de Paseo shopping mall at Paseo esq. 1ra in Vedado and at other locations including Ave. 3ra esq. 70, Miramar (ⓣ7/204-8888). Alternatives include Havanautos at Calle 23 esq. M, Vedado (ⓣ7/833-3484) and Ave. 5ta esq. 112, Miramar (ⓣ7/204-3203); Cubacar in the Terminal Sierra Maestra opposite the Plaza de San Francisco, Habana Vieja and Miramar Trade Center, 5ta Ave. e/ 70 y 80, Miramar (ⓣ7/204-9081).

Embassies Embassies in Havana include the Canadian Embassy, Calle 30 no. 518, Miramar, Playa (ⓣ 7/204-2516, ⓕ 204-2044); the British Embassy, Calle 34 no. 702–704, Miramar, Playa (ⓣ7/204-1771, ⓕ204-8104); and the US Special Interests Section, Calle Calzada y L, Vedado, Havana (ⓣ7/ 833-3531, ⓕ833-3700). Australia and New Zealand do not have consulates or embassies; citizens are advised to go to either the Canadian or UK embassies.

Immigration and legal Asistur, Paseo del Prado no. 208-212 esq. Trocadero (ⓣ7/866-8920 &

866-83-39 & 7/866-8527, Ⓕ7/866-8087), deals with insurance claims and financial emergencies and is open 24hr. Otherwise, try the Consultoria Juridica Internacional in Miramar at Calle 16 no. 314 e/ 3ra y 5ta (Mon–Fri 8.30am–noon & 1.30–5.30pm; Ⓣ204-2490 & 7/204-2697).

Medical There is no single emergency number for ringing an ambulance but as good as any are Ⓣ7/55-1185 & 7/838-2185. You can also contact Asistur (see above) on their emergency number Ⓣ7/866-8339 for a tourist ambulance. The Clínica Internacional Cira García in Miramar at Calle 20 no. 4101 esq. Ave. 41 (Ⓣ7/204-2880 & 204-2811) is run predominantly for foreigners, while two floors are reserved for foreign patients at the Hospital Hermanos Ameijeras, San Lázaro no. 701 e/ Padre Varela y Marqués González, Centro Habana (switchboard Ⓣ7/876-1000).

Pharmacies Farmacia Internacional at Ave. 41 no. 1814, esq. 20, Miramar (Ⓣ7/204-4359), is one of the best-stocked in Havana.

Police Habana Vieja's police headquarters are in the mock-colonial fort at Tacón e/ San Ignacio y Cuba. The main station in Centro Habana is at Dragones e/ Lealtad y Escobar Ⓣ7/862-4412. In an emergency ring Ⓣ106.

Post offices The branch at Ave. Salvador Allende esq. Padre Varela, Centro Habana (Mon–Sat 8am–6pm), offers national peso services only. The branch in the Gran Teatro building, at Paseo del Prado esq. San Martín, offers fax and telegram services as well as poste restante facilities (daily 8am–7pm).

Taxis Habanataxi (Ⓣ7/53–9086); Panataxi (Ⓣ7/55-5555); Transtur (Ⓣ7/208-6666); Taxis OK (Ⓣ7/204-0000 & 877-6666); Transgaviota (Ⓣ7/267-1626).

Around Havana

East of the city, **Guanabacoa** is a quiet provincial town with numerous attractive churches and a fascinating religious history. The big attractions for most people, however, are the boisterous **Playas del Este**, the nearest beaches to Havana, with clean sands and a lively scene. South of Havana, the **Museo Ernest Hemingway**, a perfect preservation of the great writer's home, is the most neatly packaged day-trip destination. Not far away, the sprawling **Jardín Botánico Nacional** is the best bet for a relaxing escape from the city grime. Outside the city proper, public transport is scarce and unreliable, and you'll really need a car to see many of these sights, though Víazul buses depart Havana for Playas del Este three times daily from the station in Nuevo Vedado (see p.162 Arrival and information).

Playas del Este

Twenty kilometres east of the bay, on the outskirts of what is still technically the city though you'll travel through open countryside to get there, the Vía Blanca reaches Havana's nearest beaches – Playa Santa María del Mar, Playa Boca Ciega and Playa Guanabo – collectively known as the **Playas del Este**. Hugging the Atlantic coast, these three fine-sand beaches form a long, twisting, ochre ribbon, which vanishes in summer beneath the crush of weekending Habaneros and tourists. Not a whole lot differentiates the beaches, although as a general rule the sand is better towards the western end.

With an abundance of excellent self-catering and hotel **accommodation** around the beaches, staying here could provide an excellent mini-break if you're based in Havana for most of your holiday. Those craving creature comforts should head for the big hotels in Santa María such as the *Aparthotel Las Terrazas* (Ⓣ7/97-1344; ❸); budget travellers will find the best value in Guanabo's inexpensive hotels and *casas particulares*. As good as any is the *Casa de Mileydis y Julito* (Ⓣ7/96-0100; ❷), an apartment close to the beach with a pretty garden. Other than the rather anonymous, all-inclusive *Club Blau Arenal* (Ⓣ7/97-1272; ❺) there's nowhere to stay in Playa Boca Ciega. Although a number of **restaurants** serve cheap meals, these all tend to be rather alike, and your best bet is to eat at the *paladar* in Guanabo; or, see if a *casa particular* can recommend somewhere.

Museo Ernest Hemingway

Eleven kilometres southeast of Habana Vieja, in the suburb of San Francisco de Paula, is **La Vigía**, an attractive little estate centred on the whitewashed nineteenth-century villa where Ernest Hemingway lived for twenty years until 1960 and wrote a number of his most famous novels. Now known as the **Museo Ernest Hemingway** (Mon–Sat 9am–4.30pm, Sun 9am–noon; ☏7/91-0809; $3CUC), it makes a simple but enjoyable excursion from the city. To get there by car, take the Vía Blanca through the southern part of the city and turn off at the Carretera Central, which cuts through San Francisco de Paula. Alternatively try braving the M-7 *camello* bus, one of the converted juggernauts used for longer bus journeys in and around the city; catch it at the Parque de la Fraternidad and walk from the bus stop to the museum. A taxi to the museum from Habana Vieja or Vedado should cost about $10CUC.

On top of a hill with splendid views over Havana, the single-storey colonial residence has been preserved almost exactly as Hemingway left it – with drinks and magazines strewn about and the dining-room table set for guests. Frustratingly, entrance into the rooms is forbidden but by walking around the veranda you can get good views through the windows. In the well-kept gardens, Hemingway's fishing boat is suspended inside a wooden pavilion and you can also visit the graves of four of his dogs next to the swimming pool.

The museum closes when it rains to protect the interior from the damp and to preserve the well-groomed grounds, so time your visit to coincide with sunshine.

Jardín Botánico Nacional

About a 25-minute drive south of the city via the airport road (Avenida Rancho Boyeros) and then branching right onto Avenida San Francisco is the entrance to the **Jardín Botánico Nacional** (Wed–Sun 9am–4pm; ☏7/54-9170 & 54-7278; $1CUC, $3CUC for guided tour). The grounds are split into sections according to continent, with the different zones blending seamlessly into one another. Highlights include the collection of 162 species of palm from around the world, and the picture-perfect **Japanese Garden**, built around a beautiful little lake and donated by the Japanese government in 1989 on the thirtieth anniversary of the Revolution. The Japanese Garden is also the best place to stop for **lunch**, in *El Bambú* (☏7/54-7278; 1–3.30pm) where $10CUC lets you eat your fill from a tasty vegetarian buffet. Near the main entrance are the indoor **Pabellones de Exposiciones**, two large greenhouse-style buildings with raised viewing platforms and twisting pathways, one housing a fantastic collection of cacti, the other a jungle of tropical plants and flowers.

Although you can explore the botanical gardens by yourself, the lack of posted information means you'll learn far more by taking the one- to two-hour **guided tour**, whether in the trackless train or with a guide in your own car (at no extra cost). There's usually at least one English-speaking guide available. Tours leave every hour or so from just inside the main entrance, near the useful **information office**. There's also a small **shop** selling ornamental plants. At weekends, for those people that want to head straight for the main attraction, a park bus takes passengers from the entrance directly to the Japanese Garden (every 30min; $1CUC).

3.2

Pinar del Río

Despite its relative proximity to Havana, life in **Pinar del Río** is a far cry from the noise, pollution and hustle of the capital. The butt of national jokes, native Pinareños are caricatured as the island's most backward country folk, a stereotype that fits the slower, relaxed feel of the province. Most of the highlights are well away from the population centres, the majority situated in and around the green slopes of the **Cordillera de Guaniguanico**, the mountain range that runs down the length of this narrow province, invitingly visible from the *autopista* running alongside. Hidden within the relatively compact **Sierra del Rosario**, the eastern section of the *cordillera*, the peaceful mountain retreats of **Las Terrazas** and **Soroa** provide perfect opportunities to explore the tree-clad hillsides and valleys. Both are set up as centres for eco-tourism, though of the two, Las Terrazas offers the best the chance to get a little bit closer to the local community. Most visitors head straight for what is justifiably the most heralded location in Pinar del Río, the **Viñales valley**, whose unusual flat-topped mountains, or *mogotes*, form a prehistoric-looking landscape unique in Cuba and worth the trip alone.

Las Terrazas

Eight kilometres beyond the signposted turn-off at Km 51 of the *autopista* is **LAS TERRAZAS**, a harmonious tourist resort and small working community that forms the province's premier eco-tourism site. The motorway very quickly seems a long way behind as the road takes you into a thickly wooded landscape and up to a junction where, after a left turn, you'll reach a tollbooth ($4CUC per person; resort guests free), which marks the beginning of the main through road for Las Terrazas. It's here, just a few metres past the checkpoint, where you'll turn for the **Cafetal Buenavista**, a hilltop colonial coffee plantation accessible by car or as a hiking destination (see "Hiking trails at Las Terrazas" box on p.178). The plantation also has great views and a restaurant. About 2km beyond the tollbooth, a left-hand turn leads several hundred metres down to a complex of red-roofed bungalows and apartment buildings, beautifully set into the grassy slopes of a valley, at the foot of which is a lake. The cabins belong to the resident population, which numbers around a thousand. The community has lived here since 1971 as part of a government-funded conservation and reforestation project, covering some fifty square kilometres of the Sierra del Rosario. A large proportion of the locals work in tourism, either directly or indirectly, many as employees at *Hotel Moka* (Ⓣ82/57-8600 to 03, Ⓔreservas@commoka.get.tur.cu; ④), a resort hotel that blends perfectly with its natural surroundings.

A set of official **hiking and nature trails** wind around Las Terrazas, varying between 3km and 20km in length; the three best are covered in the box below. There is no better way to experience the diversity of Sierra del Rosario than along these routes, which collectively offer the most comprehensive insight available into the region's topography, history, flora and fauna. All hiking in this protected reserve must be done with a guide available for hire at the complex's visitor centre, **Rancho Curujey** (Ⓣ82/57-8555 & 57-8700, Ⓔreserva@terraz.co.cu), where you can also get a map of the area. Though the centre has no formal opening hours, it's generally a good idea to arrive around 8.30am before staff disappears on hikes and excursions. To get to the **restaurant** and the one or two other buildings that make up Rancho Curujey, take the signposted right-hand turn off the main through road just before the left turn that leads down to the village and hotel. **Guides** cost between $10CUC and $40CUC per person if you pre-book an excursion, depending on the size of the group and your specific requirements. It works out considerably cheaper if you're in a group of six or more; you may be able to join another visiting group if you call a day or so in advance, or if you arrive before 9am.

Soroa

The tiny village of **SOROA** nestles in a long, narrow valley sixteen kilometres southwest of Las Terrazas, with a single mountain road linking the two resorts, allowing you to travel between them without returning to the motorway. To get here, follow the main road through Las Terrazas until you reach a tollbooth, marking the western end of the resort, where you should turn left. If you do arrive direct from the *autopista* look for the turning marked by the first petrol station en route to Pinar del Río from Havana. Soroa's location is cosy and inviting, but as access into the hills is limited, with nothing comparable to the hiking opportunities at Las Terrazas and the list of attractions brief, this place is best for a short stint rather than a protracted visit.

All of the official attractions are based around the **Villa Soroa** (Ⓣ85/52-3534 & 52-3556, Ⓔrecepcion@hvs.co.cu; ❷), a well-kept hotel complex encircling a swimming pool. Most of what you'll want to see is within ten minutes' walk of the reception building, but if you've driven up from the *autopista* the first place you'll reach, 100m or so from the hotel, is the car park for **El Salto** (open during daylight hours; $3CUC), a twenty-metre **waterfall** and one of Soroa's best-known attractions.

Back at the car park, follow the sign pointing in the direction of the small bridge to **El Mirador**, one of the two easily accessible local viewpoints. A thirty-minute hike scales an increasingly steep dirt track, though it's mercifully shady and a set of steps has been installed for the final stretch. There are a number of possible wrong turns on the way up; follow the track with the horse dung. At the summit you'll find vultures circling the rocky, uneven platform. **El Castillo de las Nubes** is the more developed of Soroa's two hilltop viewpoints and the only one you can drive to. You'll have to follow the road up to the summit even if you're walking as there are no obvious trails through the woods. Soon after the turn-off for this road, which is between the car park for El Salto and the hotel, you can take a brief detour to the **Orquideario** (daily 9am–4pm; $3CUC), a well-maintained botanical garden where the guided tours take in some 700 species of orchids. Beyond the gardens, it shouldn't take you more than twenty minutes on foot to

Hiking trails at Las Terrazas

Cascada del San Claudio (20km) The longest hike available, lasting a whole day, or around eight to ten hours. A gruelling affair scaling the hills looming over to the north-west of the complex and down the other side to the San Claudio river.

El Contento (8km) This pleasant, easy-going hike descends into the valley between two of the local peaks and joins the Río San Juan. It passes the La Victoria ruins, one of the area's nineteenth-century coffee plantations, as well as fresh and sulphurous water springs, and reaches its limit at the Baños del San Juan, a beautiful little set of pools and cascades where you can bathe.

La Serafina (4km). This nature trail, through rich and varied forest, is the best route for birdwatching. Your guide will point out the red, white and blue tocororo, the endemic catacuba and the enchanting Cuban nightingale amongst the 73 species which inhabit the sierra.

▲ Viñales valley

reach the hilltop **restaurant**, housed in a building resembling a toy fortress with a single turret (the *castillo* – or castle – in question). It's worth stopping for a meal (daily 11.30am–4pm), as the views are fantastic.

Viñales

The jewel in Pinar del Río's crown, the **Viñales valley** is by far the most visited location in the province. Though only 25km from the provincial capital, also called Pinar del Río, the valley feels wonderfully remote and somewhat lost in time with its slightly surreal landscape characterized by the *mogotes*, 160-million-year-old boulder-like hills, which look like they've been dropped from the sky onto the valley floor.

Despite the influx of visitors, the region has remained largely unspoilt with the tourist centres and hotels kept in isolated pockets of the valley, often hidden away behind the *mogotes*. Most of the locals live in the small **village of Viñales**, a four-hour bus ride from Havana. If time is limited, concentrate your visit on the **San Vicente** region, a valley within the valley, much smaller and narrower than Viñales and home to the **Cueva del Indio** cave system. On the other side of the village, the **Mural de la Prehistoria** is by far the most contrived of the valley's attractions.

Accommodation

There's an even spread of good **places to stay** in Viñales, with costs relatively low. Both *Los Jazmines* and *La Ermita* offer comprehensive programmes of **activities** and **excursions**, including horseriding, trekking and birdwatching.

Campismo Dos Hermanas on the road to the Mural de la Prehistoria ⓣ8/79-3223. This *campismo*, hidden away within the *mogotes*, is better equipped than most, despite having no a/c or fans in its well-kept cabins. The cheapest of the official options, this is the place to come to share your stay with Cuban holiday-makers, but be prepared for the blaring music around the swimming pool in peak season. ❶

Casa de Doña Hilda casa no. 4, Km 25 Carretera a Pinar del Río ⓣ8/79-6053. Two rooms for rent – the biggest (with bath, fridge and colour TV) is in its own small bungalow, next door to the main house where the other smaller room is located. A large dirt courtyard joins it all together, and parking is available. ❶

La Ermita Carretera de Ermita Km 2 ⓣ8/79-6071 to 72, ⓔreserva@vinales.hor.tur.cu. Gorgeous, open-plan hotel in immaculate grounds high above the valley floor. With some of the best views in Viñales, this tidy complex features three apartment buildings, a central pool, tennis court and a wonderful balcony restaurant. Rooms are attractive and reasonably well equipped. ❷

Hostel Inesita Salvador Cisnero no. 40 ⓣ8/79-6012. Run by an elderly couple, the two rooms (one with a/c) in this *casa particular* on the principal street in the village are in a separate apartment taking up the entire top floor of the house. With a wide balcony running around it, this house stands out from the Viñales norm. ❶

Los Jazmines Carretera de Viñales Km 25 ⓣ8/79-6205 & 79-6210, ⓔreserva@vinales.hor.tur.cu. The first hotel along the road into Viñales has an unbeatable hillside location; almost all the rooms in the colonial-style main building have panoramic views, though some could do with sprucing up. Most rooms are in a separate, modern building, with a few housed in tile-roofed cabins. There's a pool, two bars, a small disco and car rental. Be warned that the food is below average. ❸

Mogote Dos Hermanas and the Mural de la Prehistoria

Less than a kilometre west of the village, the flat surface of the valley floor is interrupted by the hulking mass of the **Mogote Dos Hermanas**, a pair of archetypal *mogotes* and the face of Viñales as seen on the front of most tourist brochures. It plays host to the misleadingly named **Mural de la Prehistoria** (daily 8am–7pm; $2CUC), hidden away from the main road down a dust track. Rather than the prehistoric cave paintings you might expect, the huge painted mural, measuring 120m by 180m, desecrating the face of one side of the *mogotes*, is in fact a modern depiction of evolution on the island, from mollusc to man. While impressive for its scale, its size also makes it an eyesore. The bar, restaurant and souvenir shop just off to the side of the mural do nothing to alleviate the contrived nature of the place, although it's not an unpleasant spot to have a drink and a bite to eat. The **restaurant**'s speciality is "Viñales-style" pork – roasted and charcoal-smoked – the highlight of an otherwise limited menu.

The Cueva del Indio

By taking the left-hand fork at the petrol station at the northeastern end of the village, you can head out of Viñales through heavily cultivated landscape to the narrower **San Vicente** valley, about 2km away. Past the lackluster Cueva de San Miguel, it's a two-minute drive or a twenty-minute walk north to San Vicente's most captivating attraction, the **Cueva del Indio**, 6km north of the village (daily 9am–5pm; $5CUC). Rediscovered in 1920, this entire network of caves is believed to have been used by the Guanahatabey Amerindians, both as a refuge from the Spanish colonists and, judging by the human remains found here, as a burial site. The walls are marked with natural wave patterns, testimony to the flooding which took place during the caves' formation millions of years ago. Only the first 300m of the tunnel's damp interior can be explored on foot, before a slippery set of steps leads down to a subterranean river, where a tour guide in a boat steers you for ten minutes through the remaining 400m of accessible cave. The boat drops you off out in the open, next to souvenir stalls and a car park, around the corner from where you started.

3.3

Varadero and the Península de Zapata

Varadero is Cuban tourism at its most developed: a world apart from much of Cuba, but for its thousands of foreign visitors, the familiar face of the Caribbean. The Península de Hicacos, the slender finger of land protruding from the mainland on which Varadero makes its home, reaches out from the northern coastline of the western **province of Matanzas** into the warm currents of this part of the Atlantic as the ocean merges with the Gulf of Mexico. Its 25-kilometre stretch of fine white-sand beaches and turquoise waters are enough to fulfil even the most jaded sun-worshipper's expectations. On the opposite side of the province, the **Península de Zapata**'s sweeping tracts of unspoilt coastal marshland and wooded interior are easy to explore, thanks to an efficiently run tourist infrastructure. It's perfectly suited to a multitude of activities, including walking through the forests, birdwatching on the rivers, scuba diving in crystalline waters and, to a lesser extent, sunbathing on admittedly less-than-perfect beaches. The peninsula also boasts a recent history featuring an event as renowned as any other in the entire revolution: the invasion at the **Bay of Pigs**.

Varadero

Cuba's answer to the Costa del Sol in Spain or Cancún in Mexico, **VARADERO** is dominated by tourism and almost nowhere on this slender peninsula are you out of sight of a hotel. However, anyone hoping for a polished, Disney-style resort will be disappointed. With hotels, shops and nightclubs spread thinly across the peninsula, there are areas where activity is more concentrated but it's not as slick as major holiday resorts on many Caribbean islands. This does not detract from what most people come here for, namely the **beach**: a seemingly endless runway of blinding white sand. This is also the best place in Cuba for a wide variety of **watersports** concentrated in one place, including scuba diving and fishing and boat trips, with three marinas and two diving clubs offering a broad range of activities.

Varadero is divided into three distinct sections, though all are united by the same stretch of beach. The bridge from the mainland takes you into the **main town** area, where all the Cubans live and where nightlife, eating and entertainment are most densely concentrated. The streets here are in blocks, with calles numbering 1 to 65 running the width of the peninsula; dissecting them is **Avenida Primera**, the only street running the five-kilometre length of the whole town. The two-kilometre section of the peninsula west of the town, separated from the mainland by the Laguna de Paso Malo, is the **Reparto Kawama**, largely the exclusive domain of hotel guests. The majority of the all-inclusive luxury hotels lie **east of the town** on a part of the peninsula wholly dedicated to package tourism.

Arrival, information and getting around

All international and most national flights arrive at the **Juan Gualberto Gómez Airport**, 25km west of Varadero (☎45/24-7015 & 25-3614). The airport has an

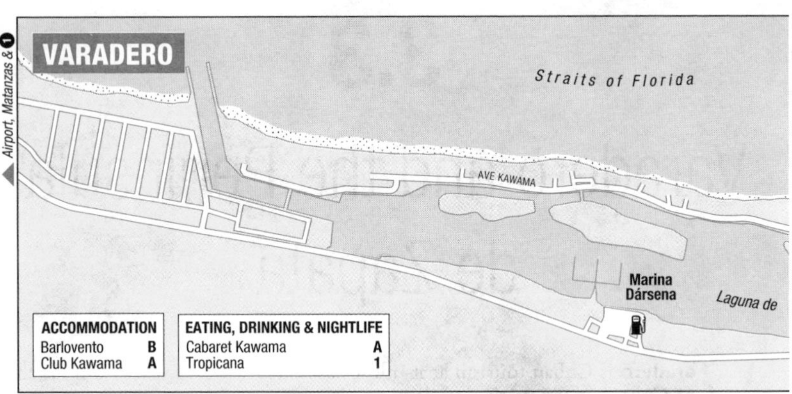

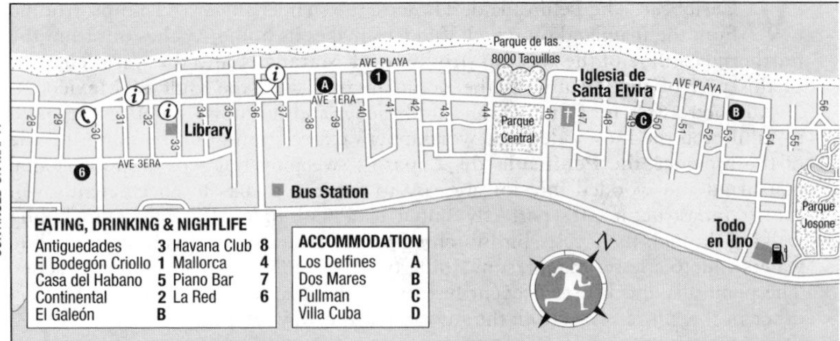

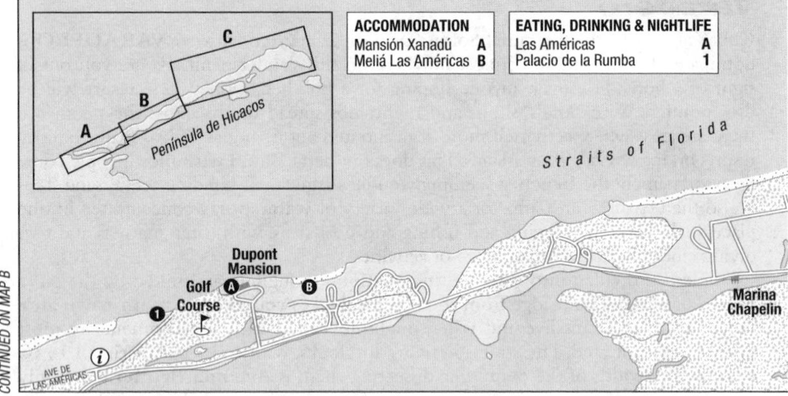

information centre and several car rental agencies, and although there's no public bus service many hotels send buses to pick up guests with reservations. It's worth talking to the driver or tour guide to see if there are any spare seats. Alternatively, there are plenty of taxis which will take you to the centre of Varadero for $25CUC. Inter-provincial **buses**, whether Víazul (ⓣ45/61-4886) or Astro (ⓣ45/61-2626), arrive at the small **Terminal de Omnibus** on Calle 36 and Autopista Sur. The daily services from Havana take two and three-quarter hours, or nearly six hours

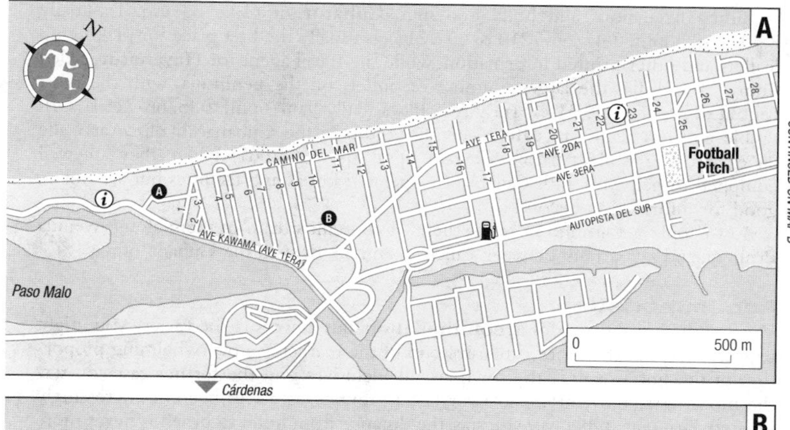

CONTINUED ON MAP B

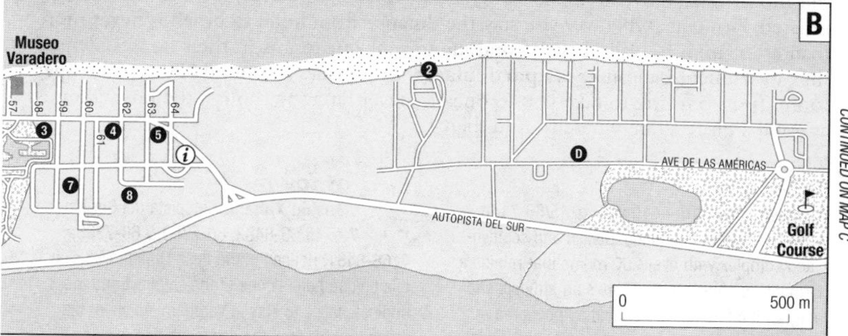

CONTINUED ON MAP C

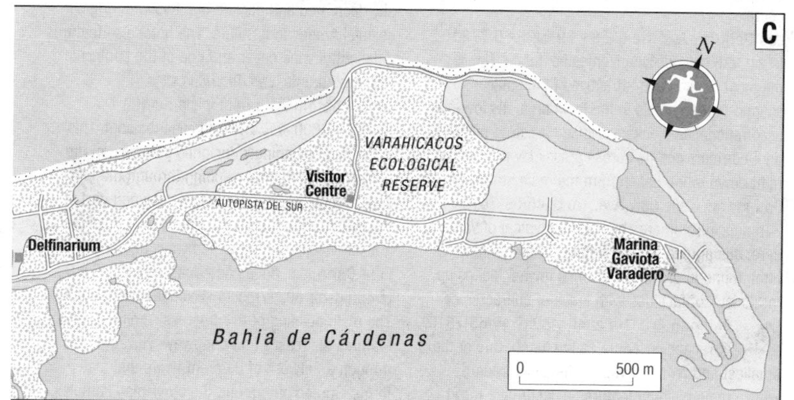

from Trinidad. There are five hotels within ten blocks of the terminal, some less than five minutes away on foot, and there are often two or three **taxis** waiting out front. If not, call Taxi OK on ⓣ45/61-4444 or 61-1616. At least half of central Varadero's hotels are within a $5CUC ride of the bus terminal.

The three most prominent national tourist travel agencies, all accustomed to doubling up as **information** centres, are represented in most hotel lobbies, whilst they each also have their own offices in the town. All offer very similar services, including excursions and hotel bookings. **Cubatur**, at Calle 33 esq. 1ra (daily 8.30am–8.30pm; ⓣ45/66-7216 & 66-7217), is usually the best place for picking up leaflets and other printed information, while the travel agent for **Havanatur**, called Tour y Travel, has the largest number of outlets on the peninsula, with the most central office at Calle 31 e/ 1ra y Ave. Playa (daily 9am–6pm; ⓣ45/66-7154). Less visible and less accustomed to receiving visitors is the Cubanacán office at Calle 24 e/ Ave. 1ra y playa (Mon–Sat 9am–6pm; ⓣ45/66-7061) where they are well equipped to help you with Cubanacán-operated hotels and facilities but are not so good for information beyond this.

Most people get around in **taxis**; there's a constant stream of them along Avenida Primera, and a taxi rank between calles 54 and 55, next to the Cubana office.

Accommodation

Varadero has no shortage of **accommodation**, but there isn't the variety you might expect, except at the more expensive end of the market. An overwhelming proportion of the hotels east of the town are all-inclusives, and the further east you stay the more restricted you are to your hotel grounds, as places become increasingly isolated. However, wherever you stay, the distance from hotel to beach is never more than a ten-minute walk. Locals continue to rent out rooms in their houses, despite the government ban on **casas particulares**, with prices at around $20–30CUC per room. Touts offering to take you to one are never far away, though the bus station is as good a place as anywhere to find them.

The town

Barlovento Ave. 1ra e/ 10 y 12 ⓣ45/66-7140, ⓔreserva@ibero.gca.tur.cu. Stylish and sophisticated complex with over 200 rooms that retains a harmonious atmosphere. There's an atmospheric lobby with a fountain, a captivating pool area enveloped by palm trees, plus tennis and basketball courts. ⑥

Los Delfines Ave. 1ra e/ 38 y 39 ⓣ45/66-7720 to 21, ⓔh.delfines@horizontes.hor.tur.cu. This is the most tasteful and attractive of the smaller landscaped-garden hotels in the town area. Its low-rise accommodation blocks are linked together by outdoor corridors cutting across grassy lawns leading right down to the beach from the main street. ④

Dos Mares Calle 53 y Ave. 1ra ⓣ45/66-7510, ⓔrecepcion@dmares.hor.tur.cu. Atypical of Varadero, this agreeable little hotel is of the kind more often found in provincial colonial towns. Makes up for its lack of facilities with loads of character. ②

Pullman Ave. 1ra e/ 49 y 50 ⓣ45/66-7510, ⓔrecepcion@dmares.hor.tur.cu. One of the smallest and most adorable hotels in Varadero, whose main building features a castle-like turret. Very relaxing atmosphere and ideal if you want to avoid the hullabaloo laid on as entertainment at most of the other hotels on the peninsula. ②

East of town

Mansión Xanadú Autopista del Sur km 7 ⓣ45/66-8482, 66-7750 & 66-7388, ⓕ66-8481. Housed in the flush Dupont Mansion, this unique hotel is one of the smallest and most original places to stay in Varadero. All six of the refined rooms face the sea, each one individually decorated and decked out, two with original colonial American furniture. The hotel also features a delightful wine cellar and one of the peninsula's best restaurants, *Las Américas*. ⑥

Meliá Las Américas Autopista Sur Km 7 ⓣ45/66-7600, ⓦwww.solmeliacuba.com. This is the most stunningly designed complex on the peninsula, with paths wending through the intricately landscaped grounds to a secluded part of the beach. Even the pool drops down a level while it twists itself around the pathways and pond. ⑨

Villa Cuba Ave. de las Américas, Km 3 e/ C y D ⓣ45/66-82-80, ⓔreserva@vcuba.gca.cma.net. The main building of this impressive all-inclusive features staircases and gangways zigzagging through a network of different floors and platforms. Spread out around the open-plan complex, which stretches down to the beach, there are various smaller residences, some with their own swimming pool. ⑥

The town and the beach

Varadero is low on sites of cultural or historic interest, and those that do exist are quickly exhausted. **Central Varadero**, specifically the area between calles 56 and 64, has the highest proportion of things to see, as well as the greatest concentration of shops and restaurants. At the beach end of Calle 57, the **Museo Varadero** (daily 10am–7pm; $1CUC) contains exhibits of varying degrees of local historical, cultural and zoological interest, including some memorable photographs of pre-revolutionary Varadero in its aristocratic heyday, such as a portrait of the straight-faced local sailing club. Over the road from the grounds of the Museo Varadero is the entrance to **Parque Josone** (daily noon–midnight; free). Sometimes referred to as Retiro Josone, the park is the most tranquil and picturesque spot in central Varadero. Its simple design, with no intricately designed gardens, includes well-kept lawns dotted with trees and a small lake with its own palm-tree-studded island. Four restaurants and an often-closed cafeteria help prolong what would otherwise be a short visit.

Of course it's the **beach** that attracts the most attention with its golden carpet of fine sand stretching from one end of Varadero to the other bathed by placid, emerald-green waters. Along the entire length of the town the beach is accessible to anyone, but east of the Dupont Mansion (see below) the only beach access is via the exclusive hotel complexes. There is actually very little to differentiate any one section of this ten-kilometre highway of sand from another. In general if you want peace and quiet stay away from the beachfront hotels and restaurants, most of which blast music out across the sand.

Eastern Varadero

To the east of town, about 2km from central Varadero and next door to the *Meliá Las Américas* hotel, is the **Dupont Mansion** (daily noon–midnight), also referred to as the Mansión Xanadú. Built in 1926 by the American millionaire Irenée Dupont at a cost of over US$600,000, it has hardly changed since Dupont and his family fled the island in 1959, and stands as a testament to the wealth and decadence of the pre-revolutionary years in Varadero. It was once open to the public as a museum, but these days to appreciate the splendidly furnished rooms you have to eat at the restaurant or sip a cocktail in the dignified bar, from where there are fine views of the coastline.

At the eastern extreme of the peninsula, three square kilometres of land have avoided development and been declared the **Varahicacos Ecological Reserve**. Billed by its founders as "the other Varadero", it's the only part of the peninsula where you can experience relatively unspoilt landscapes, albeit on a very small scale, with a chance of viewing the flora and fauna up close, focusing predominantly on the local birdlife and including an impressively large 500-year-old cactus. The reserve's **visitor centre** (daily 8am–5pm) is by the side of the road, about a kilometre past the Marina Chapelin. For individuals, the charge for being guided around any of the three set routes is $2.50–3.50CUC, but you can also arrange tailor-made excursions.

Eating

For an international holiday resort the quality and variety of food in Varadero's **restaurants** is remarkably mediocre, though the choice is wider than anywhere

Watersports and activities

Most **watersports and activites** in Varadero are organized through one of the three following marinas: **Marina Dársena**, Vía Blanca, 1km from the Varadero bridge (☎45/66-8060), which does good-value fishing trips around northern Varadero, lasting four, six or eight hours (daily; $240–300CUC); **Marina Chapelin**, Autopista Sur Km 12 (☎45/66-7550 & 66-7565), which does a two-hour "Boat Adventure" on two-person ski-bikes (hourly 9am–4pm; $39CUC); and **Marina Gaviota Varadero**, at the end of Autopista Sur, Punta Hicacos (☎45/66-7755 or 56), which runs fishing trips with an open bar on board a motorized yacht (9am–3pm; $270 for up to four people, plus $25CUC per extra person).

else outside Havana. It's well worth trying some of the restaurants in the deluxe hotels, where the quality of food is often higher, thanks to their more direct access to foreign markets; even the all-inclusives usually open their doors to non-guests. Like *casas particulares*, *paladares* are forbidden by law in Varadero and though there are sometimes touts wandering around offering home-cooked meals to tourists the punishments for getting caught are severe enough to make this a rarity.

The town

Antiguedades Ave. 1ra e/ 58 y 59. A small selection of exquisite seafood dishes at around $15CUC each, served with decent-quality side orders so often lacking elsewhere. From pictures of jazz greats and bygone Hollywood stars to a wall of old clocks and even a rocking chair hanging from the ceiling, somehow nothing in this atmospheric Aladdin's cave of a restaurant looks out of place.

El Bodegón Criollo Ave. Playa esq. 40. Varadero's version of Havana's famous *Bodeguita del Medio* has a similarly bohemian look and vibe, its walls covered in handwriting and signatures; it's also one of the best-known purveyors of Cuban cooking in the area and most main dishes are priced around $10CUC or less.

Mallorca Ave. 1ra y 62. One of the few Spanish restaurants in Varadero, specializing in paella and $7CUC-set meals. The five varieties of paella start at $3.50CUC but it's worth paying extra for the house special as the cheaper versions are a little one-dimensional. Eat in the sombre and smart interior or out on the terrace.

East of town

Las Américas Dupont Mansion, Autopista Sur Km 7 ⓣ45/66-7750. One of the classiest and most expensive restaurants on the peninsula, with seating in the library, out on the terrace or down in the wine cellar. The international menu won't win any awards but is a cut above average; more outstanding is the selection of cocktails and wines. Expect to pay at least $30CUC per person for a full meal.

Drinking, nightlife and entertainment

Nightlife is almost entirely restricted to the hotels, most of which offer something more akin to a school disco, with music to match, than a fully equipped nightclub. The majority are open to non-guests, although some of the all-inclusives may restrict entrance to their own clientele. The most popular alternative to a night on the dance floor is an evening at the **cabaret**, almost all of which are, again, run by the hotels. Wherever you go the shows themselves are basically the same displays of kitschy glamour, overly sentimental crooners and semi-naked dancers – the only considerable difference is ambience. Surprisingly few places offer **live music** in Varadero, the only venue established solely for that purpose being the relatively new **Casa de la Música** at Ave. Playa e/ 42 y 43 where most nights of the week there are top *salsa*, *son* and jazz artists playing.

Bars and cafés

Casa del Habano Ave. 1ra e/ 63 y 64. Upstairs at this excellent cigar shop is a dinky, stylish, balconied bar which makes a good place for a quiet drink. Closes by 10pm.

El Galeón in the *Hotel Dos Mares*, Calle 53 esq. Ave. 1ra. One of the most colourful bars in town, set just below street level and with a slight Mediterranean feel. A perfect place to come if you're fed up with hotel bars – this is just a straight-up, laid-back place to get a drink.

Piano Bar Centro Cultural Artex, Calle 60 e/ Ave. 2da y Ave. 3ra. A sleek little bar, suited to something more refined than the karaoke that it hosts most nights of the week. Avoid the "singing" by leaving before 11pm.

Clubs and discos

Havana Club Calle 62 y Ave. 2da. The biggest nightclub in town and a popular pick-up joint. Often the last place to close at night. Cover $10CUC. Daily 10.30pm–3am.

Palacio de la Rumba at the end of Ave. de las Américas just beyond the *Bella Costa*. Often referred to simply as *La Rumba* and as lively a nightclub as anywhere in Varadero. It's $10CUC to get in but there's an open bar that guarantees night of lost inhibitions. Daily 10pm–5am.

La Red Ave. 3ra e/ 29 y 30. You'll find a good mix of Cubans and foreigners at this popular and friendly club, which gets packed at weekends. Cover $3CUC. Daily 10pm–4am.

Cabarets and live shows

Cabaret Kawama in the *Hotel Kawama*, Calle 0 y Ave. Kawama. One of the more stylish cabarets, set in a cosy underground jazz-style nightclub. Cover $5CUC for non-guests. Mon–Sat 11pm–late.

Continental in the *Hotel Internacional*, Ave. de las Américas ⓣ45/66-70-38. It costs $40CUC to see Varadero's best and most famous cabaret but it's worth it. Exceeded in reputation only by the *Tropicana* in Havana, the exaggerated costumes and heartfelt renditions of cheesy love songs make this a classic show with a disco afterwards. Tues–Sun 8pm–3.30am.

Tropicana 50m off the Vía Blanca (the road to Havana) at the Río Canímar bridge, 30km from Varadero ⓣ45/26-5380, reservations ⓣ26-5555. The Matanzas version of Havana's world-famous cabaret nightclub is set in a huge outdoor auditorium and is no less spectacular than the original, with a full cast of over one hundred singers and dancers and lasers shot into the night sky. Ticket prices start at $40CUC and can go as high as $70CUC if you opt for all the extras which include a meal, transfers to and from your hotel and a stage-side table. Show nights are Thurs–Sat 8.30pm–2.30am, showtime from 10pm. After the show there is a disco.

Península de Zapata

Forming the whole of the southern section of Matanzas province is the **Península de Zapata**, a large nature reserve covered by vast tracts of wild and unspoilt swampland and dense forests. It's equally appealing as a more orthodox holiday destination, situated on the Caribbean side of the island, with over 30km of accessible coastline and crystal-clear waters. As one of the most popular day-trips from Havana and Varadero, the peninsula has built up a set of relatively slick and conveniently packaged diversions. **Boca de Guamá** draws the largest number of bus parties with its **crocodile farm**; it's also the point of departure for the boat trip to **Guamá**, a convincingly reconstructed lakeside Taíno Indian village. The beaches at the **Playa Girón** and **Playa Larga** resorts, where the famous **Bay of Pigs** invasion took place in 1961, are not a patch on those of Varadero and their appeal is as part of the package of attractions on the peninsula, not as attractions in their own right. There's a greater emphasis on scuba diving than sun-bathing here, most of which takes place relatively close to the shore.

The travel agent and tour operator **Cubanacán** runs most of the facilities and organizes all excursions on the peninsula; the best place to go for **information** is the Cubanacán-run **La Finquita** (ⓣ45/91-3224), a snack bar-cum-information centre by the side of the *autopista* at the junction with the main road into Zapata. Cubanacán also runs buros dE Turismo in the lobbies of the *Hotel Playa Larga* (ⓣ45/98-7294) and the *Hotel Playa Girón* (ⓣ45/98-4110). **Public transport** in this area is virtually non-existent and unless you're content to stick around one of the beach resorts you're best off **renting a car** or scooter. Both Havanautos (ⓣ45/98-4123) and Transautos (ⓣ45/98-4126) rent out cars from Playa Girón, while scooters are available from either of the two beachfront hotels. That said, the hotels all run various excursions of their own and if you take advantage, having your own transport becomes less of an issue.

Boca de Guamá and Guamá

Eighteen kilometres from the *autopista*, down the Carretera de la Ciénaga, **Boca de Guamá** is a heavily visited roadside stop. Boca, as it's referred to locally, is famous for the **Criadero de Cocodrilos** (daily 9am–5pm; $5CUC), a crocodile-breeding farm. The stars of the show are left more or less to themselves and you may have trouble spotting even one on the short circuit around the small swamp where they are kept. For a more dramatic encounter, it's best to visit at one of the twice-weekly feeding times, though unfortunately there is no regular timetable. For more details ring **La Finquita** (ⓣ45/91-3224) at the entrance to the reserve (see above).

Boca also serves as the departure point for boats travelling to **Guamá**. Located on the far side of the open expanse of the **Laguna de Tesoro**, the largest natural lake in Cuba, Guamá is a Taíno-themed hotel resort featuring wooden buildings on stilts suspended above the water, a small museum and life-sized statues of Taínos, the last of the Amerindian groups to settle in Cuba around a thousand years ago.

Passenger **boats** seating 35 people leave Boca for the village at 10am and noon every day; alternatively you can cross in a five- or six-seat **motorboat** any time between 9am and 6.30pm. In either case, an English-speaking guide is available and the round-trip costs $10CUC per person.

Playa Girón

Following the road down to and then along the coast, it's a drive of around 35km from Boca de Guamá to **Playa Girón**, where the course of Cuba's destiny was played out over 72 hours in April 1961 during the **Bay of Pigs** invasion. Aside from the hotel and beach, the main reason for stopping here is the **Museo Girón** (daily 9am–noon & 1–5pm; $2CUC), a two-room museum documenting the events prior to and during the US-backed invasion. Outside the building is one of the fighter planes used in the defence of the island; inside, the most arresting displays are the dramatic photographs of the sabotage and terrorism committed by Cuban counter-revolutionaries, some of them backed by the US, that preceded the attack and some incredible photography taken in the heat of the battle itself.

The **Hotel Playa Girón** (Ⓣ45/98-4110 & 98-4118, Ⓔrecepcion@hpgiron.co.cu; ❸), a stone's throw from the museum, is the largest of all the tourist complexes on the peninsula, with most of its family-sized, fully furnished bungalows facing the sea. There's a diving centre, pool, tennis court, car rental and all the usual services. The beach is more exposed than that at Playa Larga, to the northwest, and though it's blessed with the same transparent green waters, there is an unsightly three-hundred-metre-long concrete wave-breaker which creates a huge pool of calm seawater but ruins the view.

3.4

Trinidad and around

While **Trinidad** attracts more tourists than many of Cuba's larger cities, its status as a UNESCO-declared **World Heritage Site** has ensured that, as in Habana Vieja, its marvellous architecture is perfectly preserved. Plenty of other Cuban towns evoke a similar sense of the past but there is a harmony about Trinidad's traffic-free centre, its jumble of colonial mansions and its red-tiled rooftops that sets it apart. Wandering the cobbled streets of the colonial district in particular evokes a quaint village feel – albeit a large and prosperous village – where horses are as common a sight as cars and, lately, where tourists are as common as locals. From Trinidad most of the province's highlights are within easy reach. In fact, the city's proximity to the Caribbean beaches at **Península de Ancón** and the lush mountain slopes around the **Topes de Collantes** hiking resort, make central Cuba's most visited town one of the best bases on the island for discovering the diversity of the island's landscape.

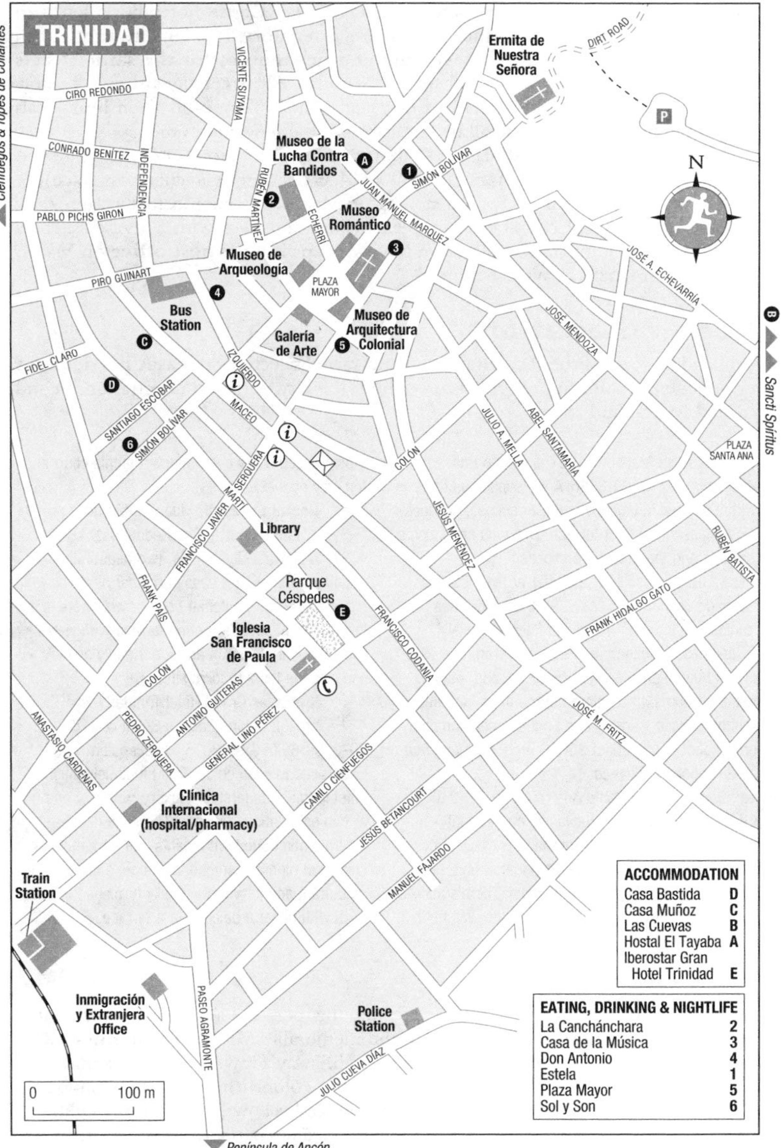

Arrival and information

Inter-provincial buses use the **bus terminal** (☎41/99-4448) at Piro Guinart e/ Maceo e Izquierdo, just inside the colonial centre and within easy walking distance of a number of *casas particulares*. Arriving on the coastal road by **car** from the west will bring you into town on Piro Guinart, which leads directly up to the two main roads cutting through the centre of the city, Martí and Maceo. From Sancti Spíritus and the east, the Circuito Sur takes cars closer to *Las Cuevas* hotel, but a left turn at Lino Pérez will take you into *casa particular* territory. Incidentally, the Cuban phenomenon of towns and cities with **old and new names for the same streets** is particularly prevalent and confusing in Trinidad. All street signs show the new names, as used in the addresses listed here and although you will often hear locals using the old names they will all be familiar with the new names too.

For **information**, the best place is **Cubatur** either at Maceo no.129 esq. Francisco Javier Serquera (daily 9am–7pm; ⓣ41/99-6314, ⓔoperaciones@cubaturss.co.cu), or their other office at Simón Bolívar no.352 e/ Maceo y Izquierdo (daily 9am–7pm; ⓣ41/99-6368). They can also arrange excursions and help with activities such as diving or horseriding. Your best bet for buying **maps** is at the **post office** on Maceo e/ Colón y Francisco Javier Zerquera.

Accommodation

Trinidad has one of the most impressive and varied selections of **casas particulares** in the country and they're spread throughout the city, with a concentration on and around Maceo and Martí.

Casa Bastida Maceo no. 587 e/ Simón Bolívar y Piro Guinart ⓣ41/99-3186. A very spacious triple with a streetside balcony and roof access, overlooking a pleasant outdoor terrace. This was once also a *paladar*, and the meals are excellent. ❶

Casa Muñoz José Martí no. 401 e/ Fidel Claro y Santiago Escobar ⓣ41/99-3673, ⓦwww.casa.trinidadphoto.com. One of the finest colonial residences in Trinidad, this house is crammed with original nineteenth-century furniture, and features two bathrooms, three large bedrooms, a fantastic rooftop terrace, parking and English-speaking owners. Expect to pay about $5CUC more than average prices; book in advance. ❷

Las Cuevas Finca Santa Ana ⓣ41/99-6133 & 99-6434, ⓔreservas@cuevas.co.cu. A twenty- to thirty-minute walk east from the Plaza Mayor, this large cabin complex is superbly located on a hillside overlooking the town and coast. There's access to the cave network over which the site was built, a music-based show every night, a tennis court and the only pool in town. ❸

Hostal El Tayaba Juan M. Márquez no.70 e/ Piro Guinart y Ciro Redondo ⓣ41/99-4197, ⓔeltayaba@yahoo.es. Two beautifully appointed rooms in a *casa particular par excellence*, dotted with colonial *objets d'art*. There is a lovely central patio, a rooftop terrace with views over the nearby church and the friendly owners can arrange tours to local sites. ❶

Iberostar Grand Hotel Trinidad Martí no.262 e/ Lino Pérez y Colón ⓣ41/99-6073, 99-6074 & 99-6075, ⓔrecepcion@iberostar.trinidad.co.cu. This fabulously plush hotel is full of understated luxury, with just one or two ostentatious touches. There's a delightful central patio dotted with plants and a fountain, a cushy yet dignified smoker's lounge, a large buffet restaurant and forty fantastically furnished rooms, each with either a balcony or a terrace. ❼

The Town

Trinidad boasts the highest number of museums per capita in the country, three on the central **Plaza Mayor**, including the memorable **Museo Romántico**, with another two no more than a few minutes' walk away. However, simply wandering around the narrow streets in the shadows of the colonial houses, whose shuttered porticoes form a patchwork of blues, greens, reds and yellows, is one of the highlights of any stay and it's worth conserving enough time and energy to do just that, even if it means missing out some of the museums. If you're prepared to walk a little further, north of the Plaza Mayor are wide-reaching views from the hillside that overlooks Trinidad, marked by the ruined **Ermita de Nuestra Señora** church.

Plaza Mayor

At the heart of the colonial section of Trinidad is the beautiful **Plaza Mayor**. Comprising four simple fenced-in gardens, each with a palm tree or two shooting out from one of the corners, and dotted with various ornamental touches, this is the

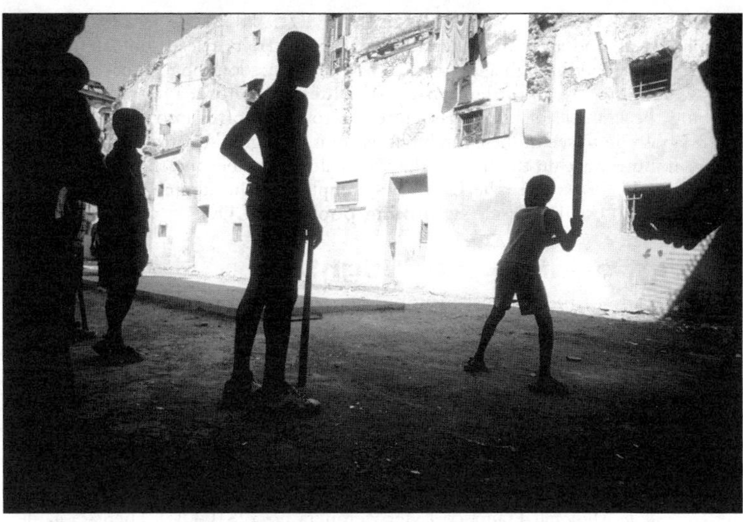

▲ Street baseball

focal point of the old town, surrounded by colourfully painted colonial mansions adorned with arches, balconies and terraces.

Overlooking the plaza on the corner of Echerrí and Simón Bolívar is the **Museo Romántico** (Tues–Sun 9am–5pm; $2CUC), which contains one of the country's most valuable collections of antique furniture, all packed into its fourteen rooms. Dating from 1808, the house itself is a magnificent example of elegant, yet restrained, nineteenth-century domestic Cuban architecture, built for the Brunet family, one of the wealthiest in Trinidad during the sugar-boom years. The contents have been gathered from various buildings all over town, with highlights including the exquisite dining room, with its Italian marble floor, and the master bedroom featuring a four-poster bed and French wardrobe, ingeniously constructed without nails or screws.

Working your way clockwise around the square from Echerrí, you'll find the **Museo de Arquitectura Colonial** (Sat–Thurs 9am–5pm; $1CUC), a sky-blue and white building with a plant-bedecked courtyard, whose central theme is the development of domestic architecture in Trinidad during the eighteenth and nineteenth centuries. Its samples of rooftops, doorways and walls needn't delay you for long before stepping into the **Galería de Arte** (daily 9am–5pm; free), at the bottom end of the square, from where – through the open shutters upstairs – there is a perfectly framed view of the plaza.

Museo de la Lucha Contra Bandidos

A block north of Plaza Mayor, where Echerrí meets Piro Guinart, the **Museo de la Lucha Contra Bandidos** (Tues–Sun 9am–5pm; $1CUC) can be easily picked out by the dome-topped, yellow- and white-trimmed bell tower that's become Trinidad's trademark image. Displays concentrate on the counter-revolutionary groups – the *bandidos*, or bandits – that formed during the years immediately following Castro's seizure of power in 1959. The most striking exhibits are in the central courtyard where a military truck and a motorboat mounted with machine guns stand as examples of the hardware employed by and against the *bandidos* in their struggle to overthrow the revolutionary government. But even if the museum's contents don't appeal, it's well worth paying the entrance fee to climb the tower for the panoramic view over the city and across to the hills and coastline.

Ermita de Nuestra Señora and the hillside walk

As it heads up and away from Plaza Mayor, Simón Bolívar leads out of Trinidad's historic centre and through a less pristine part of town; soon the road becomes a dirt track leading steeply up to the **Ermita de Nuestra Señora**, a dilapidated church marking the last line of buildings before the town dissolves into the countryside. There's nothing to see of the church but its ruins, though it's worth making the easy fifteen-minute walk up the hill for the views alone. Just beyond the ruined church you can easily cut across to the *Las Cuevas* complex, on the adjoining hillside, where non-guests can use the hillside **swimming pool** for $5CUC.

Eating, drinking and nightlife

With so many of the colonial mansions converted into **restaurants**, eating out is one of the easiest ways to soak up Trinidad's gracefully ageing home interiors. Although the choice of food is almost exclusively restricted to *comida criolla*, the quality is, as a rule, far higher than in most of Cuba's larger cities.

For **drinking**, you're best off in the restaurants listed below, many of which have separate bars. One of the few places operating principally as a bar is *La Canchánchara* at Rubén Martínez Villena e/ Piro Guinart y Ciro Redondo, where you can enjoy the house special, a honey and lemon based rum cocktail, in the shady courtyard.

Nightlife in Trinidad is decidedly subdued. The headline spot for **live music** is the *Casa de la Música* at Francisco Javier Zerquera no.3 ($1CUC). There's a garden and a large terrace where traditional Cuban bands as well as modern *salsa* outfits play most nights. As lively as anywhere at weekends is **Parque Céspedes**, where an open-air disco is held most Fridays and Saturdays, the modern *salsa* and pop music geared very much to the large crowd of young locals.

Restaurants

Don Antonio Izquierdo no.112 e/ Simón Bolívar y Piro Guinart. Open for lunch only, there's a fair selection from meat dishes to salmon or lighter meals such as tuna salad or vegetable omelette. The canopied courtyard and comfortable interior are equally appealing.

Estela Simón Bolívar no. 557 e/ Juan Manuel Marquez y José Mendoza. Although there are only three (meat-based) main courses on offer at this peaceful, backyard *paladar*, a feast of extras is laid on and the two-tier patio within high walls and under tree-tops makes this one of the most relaxing spots in town.

Plaza Mayor Rubén Martínez Villena no.15 esq. Francisco Javier Zerquera. Large, slickly restored colonial mansion invaded every day by tour groups. The best offer here is the $8CUC-lunchtime buffet (daily noon–3pm) which offers some rarely seen though unremarkable alternatives – such as pastas and decent salads – to the usual Cuban cuisine found in Trinidad.

Sol y Son Simón Bolívar no.283 e/ Frank País y José Martí. Choose from a number of spaghetti dishes, an array of fish, or plenty of chicken and pork plates. Everything is carefully prepared and full of flavour, served in a romantically lit courtyard.

Around Trinidad

From Trinidad some of the province's foremost attractions lie within easy reach. The most laid-back option is the twenty-minute drive to the **Península de Ancón**, one of the biggest beach resorts on the south coast, though still tiny by international standards. For something a little more energizing, head west out of the city for **Topes de Collantes**, a rather run-down mountain resort that nevertheless offers excellent hikes around the peaks and valleys of the **Sierra del Escambray**.

Península de Ancón

The **Península de Ancón** – a five-kilometre finger of land curling into the placid waters of the Caribbean and backed by rugged green mountains – enjoys a truly marvellous setting. Covered predominantly in scrub, the peninsula itself is not terribly impressive but boasts at least 1.5km of sandy **beach** and an idyllic stretch of largely undisturbed coastline. Shrubs and trees creep down to the shore and there is more than enough fine-grained sand, the best of it around the hotels, to keep a small army of holiday-makers happy. On the beach, the **International Diving Centre** (daily 9am–5pm) rents out pedal boats, kayaks, surfboards and the like. Opposite the *Hotel Ancón* (see below), on the other side of the peninsula, **Marina Trinidad** (Ⓣ41/99-6205, Ⓔmarinastdad@ip.etecsa.cu) offers a selection of boat trips, including diving and fishing trips, from around $30CUC per person.

To **get here** from Trinidad, follow Paseo Agramonte out of town and head due south for 4km to the village of Casilda. Continue for another 4km west along the northern edge of the Ensenada de Casilda, the bay clasped between the mainland and the peninsula, and you will hit the only road leading into Ancón. The taxi fare is around $6CUC one-way and there is no public bus service linking the beaches to the town. Of the **places to stay**, *Brisas Trinidad del Mar* (Ⓣ41/99-6500 to 07, Ⓔreservas@brisastdad.co.cu; ⑤) is the newest, flashiest hotel on the peninsula and by far the most comfortable and luxurious place to stay. *Hotel Ancón* (Ⓣ41/99-6120 to 26, Ⓔreservas@ancon.co.cu; ④), right on the best bit of beach, is an older, family-oriented all-inclusive where most activity on the peninsula is focused; facilities include a number of bars and places to eat, plus a pool, two tennis courts, a basketball hoop, a volleyball net and pool tables.

Topes de Collantes

Rising to the northwest of Trinidad are the often misty, pine-covered slopes of the Guamuhaya mountain range, more popularly known as the **Sierra del Escambray**. Three kilometres from central Trinidad along the Trinidad–Cienfuegos coast road, a right turn takes you the 15km or so to the resort of **Topes de Collantes**. Don't expect too much in the way of eating, entertainment or nightlife, but as a base for **hiking** this is the obvious starting-point for visiting the much larger area encompassed by the 175-square-kilometre Topes de Collantes national park, characterized by steep slopes densely covered in pines and firs, pock-marked with waterfalls and abundant in birdlife.

If you want to go hiking around Topes de Collantes the best way to do it is to book an organized excursion in Trinidad, which you can do at Cubatur (see p.201). If you arrive independently, the place to head first is the Centro de Información (daily 8am–6pm; Ⓣ42/54-0219, Ⓕ54-0117, Ⓔcomercial@topescom.co.cu), the park's **information centre**, right at the heart of the resort. If you want to follow any of the official trails, which are the only permitted hiking routes through this protected area, you'll need to pay for them here. Charges are between $3CUC and $6.50CUC per person, depending on the length of the trail. The English-speaking guides at the centre can advise you on the various trails and make recommendations but if you want a guide, you will need to join an organized excursion.

Practicalities

Although the rather worn-out resort is unlikely to lure you into staying the night, it might prove necessary if you want to stick about long enough to enjoy more than one of the trails. The resort has four **hotels**, all within easy walking distance of one another and three of which are permitted to rent rooms to non-Cubans. Best is *Villa Caburní* (Ⓣ42/54-0330; ②) – the majority of the villa's modestly-furnished brightly coloured bungalows have kitchenettes whilst they all feature wonderful views of the mountains. Offering the best and one of the only alternatives to the distinctly uninspired food at the hotels is *Restaurante Mi Retiro*, 3km along the road back to Trinidad, where meat-based dishes are served on a veranda on top of a small hill in a scenic valley enclosed by two big hills shaped like camels' humps.

3.5

Cayo Coco and Cayo Guillermo

Spanning the trunk of the island 450km east of Havana, the provinces of Ciego de Ávila and Camagüey form the farming heart of Cuba, their handsome lowland plains given over to sugar cane, fruit trees and cattle pasture. Though the eponymous capitals of both provinces are well worth visiting, the main draws are the paradisiacal **Cayo Coco** and **Cayo Guillermo**. These cays lie north of Ciego de Ávila and offer the twin pleasures of superb beaches and virgin countryside. With one of the longest offshore reefs in the world, the cays offer excellent **diving**, and they are also home to a variety of wildlife, prompting the government to designate them an ecologically protected zone.

There's a ban on locals visiting the resorts, the Government having deemed that this should be the exclusive preserve of affluent foreigners rather than peso-earning nationals, so getting to the cays without the umbrella of a tour guide, state taxi or rental car can be a bit of a mission. Don't try to go in a private taxi, as your driver will have monumental hassle with the authorities before being routed back home, leaving you dumped at the barrier. All **road traffic** enters the cays along the causeway – where passports are checked and rental cars looked over to make sure they're not harbouring nationals – and then takes the fork for either Coco or Guillermo. **Flights** from Havana arrive three times weekly at the Jardínes del Rey airport (Ⓣ33/30-8228) on the east of Cayo Coco, from where hotel representatives whisk passengers off to their accommodations. **Tour buses** drop you off at the hotels.

Once on the cays, the best way to **get around** is by moped. All the hotels rent mopeds, jeeps and sand buggies and can supply **maps** of the cays though these are usually distinctly lacking in specifics. There's no tourist office, but each hotel has a public relations officer who can provide general **information**.

Cayo Coco

With 22km of creamy white sands and cerulean waters, **Cayo Coco** easily fulfils its hyperbolic tourist-brochure claims. The islet is 32km long from east to west, with a high round hill rising from the middle. The best beaches are clustered on the north coast, dominated by the all-inclusive hotels, whose tendrils are gradually spreading along the rest of the northern coastline.

The big three **beaches** take up most of the narrow easternmost peninsula, which juts out of the cay's north coast. Spanning the tip, and home to the *Sol*

Club Cayo Coco hotel, **Playa Las Coloradas** is exceptionally picturesque, with fine sand and calm, shallow waters. It's a good place for watersports and is busy with cruising **catamarans and pedalos** – a $50CUC all-inclusive day pass, which includes all meals and drinks, lets you join in. The fee is waived for hotel guests. Three kilometres west, **Playa Larga** and **Playa Las Conchas**, divided by name only, form a continuous strip of silvery sand. They are arguably the best beaches on the island, although very crowded during the organized activities laid on by the *Hotel and Club Tryp Cayo Coco*. Non-guests are welcome to use the beaches during the day – accessed through the hotel – but are required to pay $40CUC for an all-inclusive day pass; access is restricted at night.

For solitude, head west along the main dirt road to **Playa Los Flamencos**, demarcated by a stout stucco flamingo, which boasts 3km of golden sands and clear waters where tangerine-coloured starfish float through the shallows – this is a good place for **snorkelling**. The beach gets busy in the daytime but wandering away from the lively, expensive bar should guarantee some privacy.

Away from the beach strip, dirt roads – perfect for rented mopeds – allow easy access into the lush wooded **interior**, where hidden delights include sightings of hummingbirds and pelicans, some gorgeous lagoons and **Sitio La Güira**, a re-creation of an early twentieth-century Cuban peasant village. Although it's something of a novelty theme park, a number of interesting exhibits rescue it from tackiness; entrance is free, there is an on-site restaurant (see below), and walking and horseback riding tours are offered ($5CUC an hour for the horse; rates for a guide are negotiable).

At the western tip of the island is **El Bagá Nature Reserve** (Mon–Sat 8.30am–5pm; free), well situated in radiant countryside. The park is speckled with lakes and crisscrossed by several trails, enlivened by various well-tended animal enclosures where iguanas, crocodiles and *jutías* (indigenous rodents similar to large guinea pigs) are all on display. The easiest – albeit most pedestrian – way to see the park is on one of the **guided walks** leaving from the Visitors' Centre at the reserve's entrance on the hour from 9am to noon and then at half past the hour from 1.30pm to 3.30pm.

Accommodation

With no towns or villages to offer *casas particulares*, **accommodation** on Cayo Coco is almost totally limited to a few plush **all-inclusives**, grouped together on the main beach strips. The only alternative is at the other end of the scale (and quite isolated – you would need your own transport): *Sitio la Güira* (see above) has two very basic rooms in a reproduction of a nineteenth-century *campesino* cottage.

All-inclusive hotels

Blau Colonial Playa Larga ⓣ33/30-1311, ⓔreservas@blaucolonial.co.cu. This luxury hotel built in the style of a colonial village with red-tiled roofs, wooden balconies and cobbled pathways has a friendly and warm atmosphere. The pool is expansive while the six restaurants on site provide endless choices. ⑦

Hotel Oasis Playa Coco Carretera a Cayo Guillermo ⓣ33/30-2250, ⓦwww.hotelesoasis.com. A good-looking hotel with a couple of features to set it apart from the herd, including a shallow stretch of sea, a long adults' pool, a separate kids' pool and, adding an unusually cosmopolitan touch, a Japanese restaurant. ⑦

Meliá Cayo Coco Playa Las Coloradas ⓣ33/30-1180, ⓔjefe.reservas.mcc@solmeliacuba.com. This opulent hotel is aimed squarely at the couples market, with deluxe chalet-style accommodation set around a natural lagoon, a large pool and a full range of activities, including sauna, gym and watersports. The lack of a disco makes it peaceful and quiet, there are special deals for honeymooners and you can even get married here if you want to. ⑨

Sol Club Cayo Coco Playa Las -Coloradas ⓣ33/30-1280, ⓔjefe.reservas.scc@solmeliacuba.com. Painted in bright tropical colours, this popular family-oriented hotel has a mini-club for kids, free non-motorized watersports, a buffet, snack bar and beach grill and a lively atmosphere with excited children running around causing mayhem. ⑧

Tryp Cayo Coco Playa Larga ⓣ33/30-1300, ⓔtryp.cayo.coco@solmeliacuba.com. The strip's oldest hotel is actually two hotels combined: one part has modern, ochre-coloured buildings and the other is in a more charming colonial village-style. Although reminiscent of a theme park, and impressively well equipped with seven restaurants as well as a fitness centre, theatre and disco, it actually feels more Cuban than the other all-inclusives because the buildings have a passing resemblance to authentic Cuban architecture. 8

Eating, drinking and nightlife

With all **food** and **drinks** included in your hotel bill you probably won't need to look elsewhere for meals, although there are a few places that cater for day-trippers. If you've paid for a day pass at one of the hotels, you can dine there and go on to the hotel disco afterwards. *Sol Club Cayo Coco* has a disco with **live salsa** and tacky floorshows, but the one at *Tryp Cayo Coco* is better, with a raucous palm-wood bar overlooking the sea at the end of a pier, and a house DJ alternating *salsa* with Europop.

Cueva del Jabalí This natural cave 5km inland from the hotel strip takes its name from the one-time resident wild boar evicted to make way for this cabaret venue where discos follow the glittery nightly shows. Closed Sun & Mon.

Playa Los Flamencos Bar A friendly, though pricey, beach bar at the western end of this beach with trestle tables under a palm wattle roof, serving Cuban cuisine, and occasionally lobster, to the strains of a mariachi band.

Playa Prohibida Bar A tiny beach bar serving tasty barbecued chicken and fish.

Sitio La Güira A ranch restaurant in the midst of the theme park due south of Playa Larga, serving moderately priced spaghetti and steaks and expensive seafood, and holding a *Guateque*, "a farm party with animation activities and lessons on typical dances". Closes at 10pm.

Cayo Guillermo

Bordered by pearl-white sand melting into opal waters, **Cayo Guillermo** is a quieter, more serene retreat than its neighbour. It is here that the cays' colony of twelve thousand **flamingos** (celebrated in all Cuban tourist literature) gathers and, although they are wary of the noise of passing traffic, while crossing the causeway that links the cay with Cayo Coco you can glimpse them swaying in the shallows and feeding on the sandbanks. As the presence of the birds testifies, there is a wealth of fish, notably marlin, in the waters and the cay's marina offers a range of deep-sea fishing expeditions. At only thirteen square kilometres the cay is tiny, but its 4km of stunning beaches seem expansive. It's quite a trek from the mainland if you are not staying overnight, but arriving early and spending a day lounging on the sands and exploring the offshore **coral reef** definitely merits the effort.

All the hotels and beaches are strung along the north coast, apart from gorgeous **Playa Pilar** on the western tip of the cay. This was Ernest Hemingway's favourite hideaway in Cuba and is named after his yacht, *The Pilar*. With its limpid waters and squeaky-clean beaches, Playa Pilar is the top beach choice on Guillermo, if not the entire cays, though there are no facilities other than a small beach bar. The two other beaches on Guillermo are **Playa El Medio** and **Playa El Paso** on the north coast. Popular with package-tour holiday-makers, both have shallow swimming areas and lengthy beaches, though El Medio also has towering sand dunes, celebrated as the highest in the Caribbean.

Practicalities

Accommodation on Cayo Guillermo has been steadily growing. The **hotels** are fairly close together on Playa El Medio and Playa El Paso while the rest of the cay's stunning beaches remain largely untouched. *Villa Cojímar* on Playa El Paso (Ⓣ33/30-1712, Ⓔalojamiento@cojimar.gca.tur.cu; 5) is a quiet and calm hotel, set apart from the others, with snazzy rooms, a large pool, four restaurants and ample sports facilities. On Playa El Medio, *Sol Club Cayo Guillermo* (Ⓣ33/30-1760, Ⓔventas1.scg@solmeliacuba.com; 6) has similar facilities with pleasant, spacious rooms – some with a sea view. At Playa El Paso, *Meliá Cayo Guillermo* (Ⓣ33/30-1680, Ⓔjefe.rrpp.mcg@solmeliacuba.com; ⑨) is a swish luxury hotel that's stylishly and imaginatively decorated in cool aquamarines, and is popular with divers on account of its in-house diving centre. *Iberostar Daquiri*, Playa El Paso (Ⓣ33/30-1650, Ⓔcomercial@ibsdaiq.gca.tur.cu; ⑦) offers colonial-style bungalows and a private beach, along with the usual amenities. **Day-passes** for all the hotels (inclusive of meals and drinks) will set you back $40-50CUC, but there are plenty of other places to access the beach if that's all you want. Outside the hotel **restaurants**, eating options are limited to a few basic beach bars and a simple wooden lean-to on Playa Pilar where you can eat excellent but pricey barbecued fish and lobster. Opening times fluctuate, but service around lunchtime is usually guaranteed.

Dive trips are organized by Cuba Divers, at the entrance to the cay near the *Villa Cojímar* (Ⓣ33/30-1704, Ⓦwww.cuba-divers.com). For deep-sea **fishing** excursions and yacht "seafaris", with time set aside for offshore swimming and snorkelling, head to the Marina Puerto Sol (Ⓣ33/30-1637, Ⓦwww.cayoguillermofishingclub.com) on Playa El Paso, home to the Cayo Guillermo Fishing Club.

3.6

Northern Oriente

Traditionally, the whole of the country east of Camagüey is known simply as the "Oriente". Running the length of the north coast, the three provinces that make up the **northern Oriente** – Las Tunas, Holguín and Guantánamo – form a mountainous landscape fringed by flatlands, with some of the country's most breathtaking peaks and stunning white-sand beaches.

Possibly the quietest and least dynamic province in Cuba, Las Tunas is justifiably overlooked by visitors pushed for time. By contrast, larger Holguín province has a variety of attractions, not least the **Guardalavaca** resort, whose beaches and lively atmosphere draw scores of holiday-makers. Of the three provinces it is undoubtedly Guantánamo, with the notorious US naval base at **Caimanera**, that is best known. Many Cubans living in this region are of Haitian and Jamaican origin – the result of late nineteenth- and early twentieth-century immigration. This is the only place in Cuba where vestiges of pre-Columbian peoples still exist.

The provincial capital of Guantánamo, small and quiet **Guantánamo town**, is a very ordinary place, though it forms a useful jumping-off point for the seaside settlement of **Baracoa**, one of Cuba's most enjoyable destinations. Sealed off from the rest of the island by a truly awe-inspiring range of rainforested mountains, fantastic for trekking, Baracoa's small-town charm is immensely welcoming and a visit here is the highlight of many trips.

Guardalavaca and around

Despite being the province's main tourist resort, **GUARDALAVACA**, on the north coast 72km northeast from Holguín, retains a charmingly homespun air. Surrounded by hilly countryside and shining sugar cane fields, it combines small-scale intimacy with a vibrancy lent by its joyful visitors. The lively **Playa Guardalavaca** and **Playa Las Brisas** have one plush hotel complex each, while the two exclusive satellite resorts to the west, **Playa Esmeralda** and **Playa Pesquero**, which incorporates the nearby Playa Turquesa, are popular with those seeking luxury and solitude. **Guardalavaca town**, which backs onto the resort, is little more than a clutch of houses, though the surrounding area has enough sights to keep you busy for a couple of days should you tire of sunning yourself on the beaches.

Arrival and information

Flights for visitors on package holidays land at Holguín's Aeropuerto Frank País and visitors are ferried to the resort by special buses. There's no public transport from Holguín to Guardalavaca, but a metered **taxi** will take you there for $25CUC and bring you back for the same amount. Each hotel has its own excursions officer who arranges trips to the local sights and can supply some information in the absence of formal tourist offices.

Accommodation

As a prime resort, Guardalavaca's **accommodation** consists of all-inclusive hotels at the top end of the price range, and while most deliver the standards you would expect, a couple fall short. As the region has grown up with the tourist industry, there are no peso hotels nor any registered *casas particulares*.

Some of the hotels, for example *Las Brisas*, offer day passes to non-guests for between $25 and $40CUC which cover meals and use of all facilities, whilst they all offer organized excursions into the surrounding countryside.

Playa Guardalavaca and Playa Las Brisas

Las Brisas ⓣ24/30-218, ⓦwww.brisasguardalavaca.com. The plusher of the two hotels, *Las Brisas* boasts four restaurants, two snack bars, a beauty salon, massage parlour, kids' camp and watersports, as well as mercifully restrained variety show-style entertainment. There's a choice between rooms and suites within the hotel block or more privacy in newer bungalow-style rooms, although all are equally luxurious (suites have hot tubs). ⑥

Club Amigo Atlántico Guardalavaca ⓣ24/30-180, ⓔbooking@clubamigo.gvc.cyt.cu. A friendly and unpretentious resort that feels more Cuban than the others and attracts a varied clientele. Compiled from three previously independent hotels, with blocks of guest rooms, pools, bars and restaurants dotted around in a seemingly random layout and connected by meandering pathways. There's a variety of accommodation options varying in cost and quality: the "Villa" section is easily the most appealing with airy, balconied houses and simple but attractive furnishings while the best-avoided "Bungalow" section seems stuck in a 1970s time warp. ⑤

Playa Esmeralda

Paradisus Río de Oro ⓣ24/30-090, ⓔjefe.reservas.pro@solmeliacuba.com. Undoubtedly one of the best in Cuba, this hotel is aimed at those seeking Caribbean-style five-star luxury. The accommodation blocks, attractive two-storey villas in muted yellow, orange and rose, are set amongst gorgeous gardens brimming with fragrant tropical plant life. The hotel boasts four excellent à la carte restaurants including, unusually, a Japanese one, as well as an airy buffet restaurant. ⑨

Sol Club Río de Luna y Mares ⓣ24/30-030 or 60. Comprising two previously separate hotels, the "Luna" section is more attractive and offers spacious, light-filled accommodation in three-storey blocks arranged around a central pool while the rooms in the "Mares" section are grouped in a single block. Facilities include six restaurants, tennis courts, sauna and gym. ⑥

Playa Pesquero and Playa Turquesa

Grand Playa Turquesa ⓣ24/30-540, Ejef_reservas@occidentaltuequesa.cu. The only hotel situated on the exquisite Playa Turquesa features extensive gardens in which the original forest habitat has been preserved and indigenous tree species flourish. Attractions include elegant rooms, a range of restaurants, and circular swimming pools arranged in a descending series and fed by a cascade of water. ⑨

Playa Pesquero ⓣ24/30-530, ⓔjefe.ventas@ppesquero.tur.cu. This huge complex offering the ultimate in get-away-from-it-all luxury is the biggest hotel in Cuba. With a large selection of restaurants, including one specializing in vegetarian fare, a vast swimming pool, its own mini shopping mall, sports facilities and activities for babies, children and teenagers, this is a good option for families. The cool, stylish rooms, furnished with natural materials, are set in two-storey blocks painted in white and pretty pastels; each has its own balcony with flower-filled window boxes and wicker furniture. ⑦

The beaches and local excursions

A 1500-metre-long stretch of sugar-white sand dappled with light streaming through abundant foliage, **Playa Guardalavaca** is a delight. One of its most refreshing aspects is that, unlike many resort beaches, it's open to Cubans as well as tourists, which gives it a certain vitality. A shady boulevard of palms, tamarind and sea grape trees runs along the centre of the beach, the branches strung with hammocks and T-shirt vendors. If you want quiet, head to the eastern end where the beach breaks out of its leafy cover and is usually fairly deserted. Midway along, a restaurant serves simple snacks and drinks, and there are stands renting out **snorkelling equipment** to explore the coral reef offshore.

The beaches at **Playa Las Brisas**, divided from Playa Guardalavaca at its eastern end by a chain of boulders, and **Playa Esmeralda**, a five-kilometre trip west from Guardalavaca, are owned by the hotels and are only accessible to guests or day pass holders (see above). At the latter is the Rancho Naranjo **horseriding centre**, opposite the *Sol Club Río de Luna y Mares* hotel, with negotiable rates for treks into the countryside. The hotel's **dive centre**, Delphis, offers dives for $35CUC and courses for between $350CUC and $800CUC.

Fifteen kilometres west of Playa Guardalavaca, the resorts at **Playa Pesquero** and exquisite **Playa Turquesa** are the most recent developments along this stretch of coastline. Playa Pesquero, lined with gnarled and twisted sea grape trees is a 1.2-kilometre-long horseshoe-shaped bay of sparkling sand. The quieter Playa Turquesa is one of the most beautiful in the region. The shallow bay, bordered by mangrove forest at its eastern boundary, boasts its own small coral reef a short swim offshore, while a strip of dense forest between *Grand Playa Turquesa* and the beach makes it feel like an undiscovered paradise. Both beaches can be accessed from the road but those wishing to use any of the hotels' facilities will have to purchase day passes (see above). There are no facilities outside the hotels.

All the hotels arrange excursions to the fascinating **Museo de Chorro de Maita** (daily 9am–5pm; $2CUC), on the site of a Taíno burial ground, 6km east of the Playa Guardalavaca hotel strip in a somewhat isolated spot in the Maniabon hills. Just across the road is the **Aldea Taína** (daily 9am–5pm; $3CUC), an excellent and evocative reconstruction of a Taíno village that really brings the lost culture to life. Close to Playa Esmeralda, at the Bahía de Naranjo, an offshore **aquarium,** the **Acuario Cayo Naranjo** (daily 7am–4pm, marine show noon–1pm; ⓣ24/30-132), offers an entertaining day out. Visits can be arranged with the hotels. Alternatively, one of the most rewarding pastimes is to rent a bicycle or moped and head off into the countryside to enjoy stunning views over the hills and sea.

Guantánamo town and around

GUANTÁNAMO town is only on the tourist map because of the proximity of the **US Guantánamo naval station**, 22km southeast, but the base plays a very small part in the everyday life of the town itself. For the most part, this is a slow-paced provincial capital, marked by a few ornate buildings, attractive but largely featureless streets and an easy-going populace. Many visitors come to see the US base and although you can get to the two lookout points, **Mirador Malones** and **Caimanera**, there really isn't a lot to see as you cannot enter the base itself.

Buses from Santiago, Baracoa, Havana and Holguín arrive at the **Astro Terminal de Omnibus**, Carretera Santiago, 2.5km out of town. Daily trains from Santiago, Havana and Las Tunas pull in at the central **train station**, housed in a squat Art

Deco folly on Pedro A. Pérez. The main **hotel**, *Guantánamo*, 5km from the centre at Ahogados esq. 13 Norte, Reparto Caribe (☎21/38-1015; ❷), is a typical, hulking, old-style Cuban hotel. Much nicer are some of the *casas particulares* clustered near the centre. Friendly *Casa de Elsy Castillo Osoria*, Calixto García no.766 e/ Prado y Jesús del Sol (☎21/32-3787; ❶) boasts a sunny courtyard, and, nearby, *Casa de Campos y Tatika,* Calixto Garcia, no.718 e/ Jesús del Sol y N López (no phone; ❶) is attractive and welcoming.

There are several **restaurants** in the centre, though few are well stocked with food. *La Cubanita*, a *paladar* on Martí esq. Crombet, serves enormous portions of pork or chicken with rice and beans for around $6CUC, while the *Guantánamo* hotel restaurant, *Guaso*, boasts a more interesting menu than most, with a house speciality of chicken "Gordon Blue" – stuffed with ham. The tastiest food, including fritters, milkshakes and hot rolls, comes from the **street stands** clustered at the south end of Pedro A. Pérez, while *Coppelia*, at Pedro A. Pérez esq. Varona, does bargain bowls of ice cream for a couple of pesos.

Mirador Malones

The more easily accessible of the two naval base lookouts, **Mirador Malones** is 38km from town, on the east of the bay, near Boquerón. At the top of a steep hill of dusty cacti and grey scrubs, a purpose-built platform is equipped with a restaurant and high-powered binoculars. From a distance of 6km, and at 320m above sea level, the view of the base is rather indistinct, but you can make out a few buildings and see the odd car whizzing past. The real wonder is the view of the whole bay area: dramatically barren countryside, luminous sea and unforgiving desert frequented by hovering vultures. You can arrange authorization for the trip here through the *Guantánamo* hotel in town (see above; $5CUC per person plus around $30CUC for an unmetered taxi and an extra $10CUC if you choose to take a guide).

Caimanera

Bordered by salt flats that score the ground with deep cracks, **CAIMANERA**, 23km south of Guantánamo, is the last point in Cuba before you reach the US naval base. The village is a restricted area, with the ground between here and the base one of the most heavily mined areas in the world, although this hasn't stopped many disaffected Cubans from braving it in the hope of escaping to the US. The village is entered via a **checkpoint** at which guards scrutinize your passport before waving you through. The lookout is within the grounds of the prosaic but functional **Hotel Caimanera** (☎21/9-1414; ❶), which has a view over the bay and mountains to the base – though even with binoculars ($1CUC), you only see a sliver of it. At the time of writing, only groups of seven or more people were being admitted, both as guests of the hotel or visitors to the viewpoint, but this may change in the future. A taxi from town costs $25CUC, and you will need a guide, which you can arrange through the *Guantánamo* hotel (see above).

Guantanamera: the song

Synonymous with the beleaguered history of the US naval base, Guantánamo is an enduring legacy of the struggle between the US and Cuba. In name at least, it's one of the best-known places in Cuba, thanks to the immortal song **Guantanamera** – written by Joseito Fernández in the 1940s as a tribute to the women of Guantánamo. Made internationally famous by North American folk singer Pete Seeger during the 1970s, it has become something of a Cuban anthem and a firm – if somewhat hackneyed – favourite of tourist bar troubadours the world over, a sad fate for the song which includes words from José Martí's most famous work, *Versos Sencillos*.

Baracoa

In the eyes of many who visit, **BARACOA** is quite simply the most beautiful place in Cuba. Set on the island's southeastern tip and protected by a deep curve of mountains, its isolation has so far managed to protect it from some of the more pernicious effects of tourism creeping into other areas of the island. Surrounded by awe-inspiring countryside – whose abundance of cacao trees makes it the nation's **chocolate** manufacturer – Baracoa is fast becoming an absolute must on the travellers' circuit.

On a spot christened Porto Santo by Christopher Columbus, who arrived here in 1492 and, as legend has it, planted a cross in the soil, Baracoa was the first town to be established in Cuba, founded by Diego de Velázquez in 1511. The early conquistadors never quite succeeded in exterminating the indigenous population and direct descendants of the **Taíno** population are alive today, with Baracoa the only place in Cuba where they survive. Their legacy is also present in several myths and legends that are habitually told to visitors, including the notion that anyone who takes a dip in the Rio de Miel, to the west of town, will return to Baracoa a second time.

Half the fun of a visit to Baracoa is **getting there**. Before the revolution, the town was only accessible by sea, but the opening of **La Farola**, a road through the mountains that provides a direct link with Guantánamo, 120km away, changed all that, and a flood of cars poured into town. Considered to be one of the triumphs of the revolution, the road was actually started during Batista's regime but was temporarily abandoned when he refused to pay a fair wage to the workers, and work was only resumed in the 1960s. Today, it makes for an amazing trip through the knife-sharp peaks of the Cuchillas de Baracoa mountains.

Arrival, information and getting around

The airport, **Aeropuerto Gustavo Rizo** (☎64/5375), is near the *Porto Santo* hotel, on the west side of the bay, 4km from the centre; taxis wait to take you into town for $2–3CUC. Buses pull up at the **Astro bus terminal** (☎64/3880), west on the Malecón; it's a short walk down Maceo to the centre, or you can take a *bicitaxi* for ten pesos.

There's no official **information** bureau in town, but the staff at the Cubatur office at Martí no.181 (☎64/5306), are extremely helpful and can book bus and plane tickets as well as **organized excursions** to the surrounding countryside. The best way to **get around** is on foot, as most of the places you'll want to see are within easy reach of the centre. To travel further afield, catch a *bicitaxi* or unmetered **taxi** from outside the tobacco factory at Calle Martí no. 214. There's little point relying on public transport – buses are scarce and always jam-packed.

Accommodation

In *El Castillo* and *La Habanera*, Baracoa has two of the most delightful **hotels** in Cuba, though the sheer volume of visitors means that these and the two other hotels in town are often full. You'll find, however, a number of superb **casas particulares**, all within a few streets of one another.

Casa de Dulce Maria Máximo Gómez no. 140 e/ Pelayo Cuervo y Ciro Frias ☎64/2214. The charming little room here comes with a double and a single bed, as well as a private bathroom and a kitchen with fridge. Good for a longer stay. ❶

Casa de Isabel Artola Rosell Rubert López no. 39 e/ Ciro Frías y Céspedes ☎64/5236, ©olambert@infomed.sld.cu. A very hospitable, pretty little house with two rooms near the town centre. One bedroom has twin beds making it a good choice for friends sharing. The owners also provide meals and laundry service. ❶

Casa de Ykira Mahiquez Maceo 168A e/ Céspedes y Ciro Frías; ☎64/2466. Excellent accommodation on a friendly street one block from the main square. The owner knows almost everyone in town with a room to let, so if her place is full she'll point you elsewhere. ❶

El Castillo Calixto García ☎64/5165. Perched high on a hill overlooking the town, this former military post, one of a trio of forts built to protect Baracoa between 1739 and 1742, is now an intimate, comfortable and very welcoming hotel. Glossy tiles and wood finishes give the rooms a unique appeal, while the handsome pool patio ($2CUC for non-guests) is the best place in town to sip *mojitos*. Very popular and often fully booked; reservations essential. ❷

Hostal La Habanera Maceo 68 esq. Frank País ☎64/5273 and 5274. Baracoa's newest hotel, and its pretty pink exterior and airy reception filled with comfy sofas is a treat. The 10 rooms, arranged around a courtyard, are clean and comfortable with TV, a/c and private bathrooms. ❷

The Town

Although many will be happy simply to wander through the town, enjoying its easy charm, there are several tangible attractions. Baracoa's most notable exhibit is **La Cruz de la Parra**, the celebrated cross reputed to have been erected by Christopher Columbus himself. It is housed in the picturesque **Catedral de Nuestra Señora de la Asunción**, on the edge of leafy **Parque Independencia**, a local gathering point. On the east side of town you'll find the **Fuerte Matachín**, one of a trio of forts built to protect colonial Baracoa, and now the site of the town museum (daily 8am–noon & 2pm–6pm; $1CUC). A steep climb up the thickly forested Loma Paraíso brings you to Las Cuevas del Paraíso, a series of caves once used by the Taíno for ceremonies and funeral chambers that are now home to Baracoa's fascinating new **archeological museum** (daily 8am–6pm; $2CUC), a treasure trove of pre-Columbian artefacts. At the eastern end of the Malecón is the main beach, **Playa Boca de Miel**, shingled in jade, grey and crimson stones, and a lively summertime hangout. Converted from the second of the town's fortifications perched on the northern hills, the **El Castillo** hotel is a peaceful retreat, while on the western side of town, the third fort, **Fuerte La Punta**, is now a restaurant and overlooks the **Playa La Punta** – the best beach for solitude seekers.

Eating

After the monotonous cuisine found in much of the rest of Cuba, **food** in Baracoa is ambrosial, drawing on a rich local heritage and the region's plentiful supply of coconuts. Tuna, red snapper and swordfish fried in coconut oil are favourite dishes. Look out for *cucurucho*, a deceptively filling concoction of coconut, orange, guava and lots of sugar, sold in a palm-leaf wrap. Other treats for the sweet-toothed include the locally produced Peter's chocolate and the soft drink *Prú*, widely available from *oferta* stands, a fermented blend of sugar and secret spices that's something of an acquired taste.

Casa Tropical Martí no. 175 e/ Céspedes y Ciro Frias. A central *casa particular* with a cool interior and a friendly atmosphere that offers food to non-guests. Excellent swordfish and generous helpings of shellfish, when available, are served in a courtyard beside an ailing papaya tree.

El Castillo Calixto García ☎64/2125. The Saturday night buffet at this hotel restaurant offers possibly the best meal you will have in town: a feast of Baracoan dishes featuring coconut, maize, local vegetables and herbs, all for $10CUC.

La Colonial Martí no. 123 e/ Maraví y Frank País ☎64/5391. A homey place offering standard, though well-prepared, Cuban dishes for $6–8CUC per person. It gets very busy, so reservations are recommended, as is early arrival.

La Punta Ave. de los Martires, at the west end of the Malecón. An elegant restaurant in the grounds of La Punta fort, serving traditional Cuban and Baracoan food, some spaghetti dishes and the house speciality, *bacan*, a delicious baked dish with meat, green bananas and coconut milk. There's a cabaret show 9pm to midnight, Thurs to Sun so arrive early if you want a peaceful meal.

Nightlife and entertainment

Baracoa has quite an active **nightlife**, perhaps surprisingly so for such a small town, though it's essentially centred on two small but boisterous venues near Parque Independencia. The most sophisticated option is twilight cocktails at the *Hotel El*

Castillo rooftop bar. Baracoa's small **cinema**, Cine-Teatro Encanto, Maceo no. 148, screens Cuban and North American films every evening.

Casa de la Cultura Maceo e/ Frank País y Maraví ⓣ64/2364. A worn-out but charming haven for live music and dancing that takes place on the patio nightly. Tends to get going around 9pm.

Casa de la Trova Victorino Rodríguez no. 149B e/ Ciro Frias y Pelillo Cuevo. Concerts take place in a tiny room opposite Parque Independencia, after which the chairs are pushed back to the wall and exuberant dancers spill onto the pavement. Mon–Fri 9pm–midnight, Sat 9pm–1am.

La Terraza Maceo no.120. A rooftop terrace venue whose varied repertoire includes magic shows and comedians, as well as dancing to western disco music with a smattering of *salsa*. Popular with Cuban couples and visitors. Cover $1CUC. Open daily 8pm–2am.

3.7

Santiago de Cuba and Granma

The southern part of Oriente – the island's easternmost third – is defined by the **Sierra Maestra**, Cuba's largest mountain range, which binds together the provinces of Santiago de Cuba and Granma. Rising directly from the shores of the Caribbean, the mountains make much of the region largely inaccessible, a quality appreciated by the rebels who spent years waging war here.

At the eastern end of the *sierra*, the romantic provincial capital city of **Santiago de Cuba** draws visitors mainly for its music, at its best in July when **carnival** drenches the town in *rumba* beats, fabulous costumes, excitement and song. This talent for making merry has placed Cuba's second city firmly on the tourist map, but there's much more to the place than carnival. Briefly the island's first capital, Santiago has a rich colonial heritage. The city also played an equally distinguished role in more recent history as the place where Fidel Castro and his small band of rebels fired the opening shots of the revolution. Further west, bordering Granma province, the heights of the Sierra Maestra vanish into awe-inspiring cloud forests, and although access to the **Parque Nacional Turquino** – around Pico Turquino, Cuba's highest peak – is often restricted, you can still admire it from afar. Unlike Santiago de Cuba, which is centred around its main city, the province of Granma has no definite focus. The small black-sand beach resort at **Marea del Portillo** gives Granma some sort of tourist centre, but the highlight of the province, missed by many, is the **Parque Nacional Desembarco del Granma**, lying in wooded countryside at the foot of the Sierra Maestra and easily explored from the beach of **Las Coloradas**.

Santiago de Cuba city

Nowhere outside Havana is there a Cuban city with such distinct character or such determination to have a good time as **SANTIAGO DE CUBA**. Set on a deep-water bay and cradled by mountains, the city is credited with being the most Caribbean part of Cuba, a claim borne out by the laid-back lifestyle and rich mix of inhabitants. It was here that the first slaves arrived from West Africa, and today Santiago boasts a larger percentage of black people than anywhere else in Cuba. **Afro-Cuban culture**, with its music, myths and rituals, formed its roots here, with later layers added by French coffee-planters fleeing revolution in Haiti in the eighteenth century.

Music is a vital element of *Santiaguero* life, oozing from the most famous *Casa de la Trova* in the country, not to mention numerous impromptu gatherings. Although music and the July carnival are good enough reasons to visit, the city offers a host of other attractions too. Diego Velázquez's sixteenth-century merchant house and the elegant governor's residence, both around **Parque Céspedes**, and the commanding **El Morro** castle at the entrance to the bay, reflect the city's prominent role in Cuban history. Added to this, the part played by townspeople in the **revolutionary struggle**, detailed in several fascinating museums, makes Santiago an important stop on the revolution trail.

Arrival, information and getting around

Flights arrive at the **Aeropuerto Internacional Antonio Maceo** near the southern coast 8km from the city (☎22/69-1052). Metered and unmetered **taxis** wait outside and charge around \$15–18CUC to take you to the centre, while there is sometimes a bus that meets flights from Havana, charging around \$5CUP for the same journey. You can arrange car rental at the Havanautos desk (☎22/68-6161) at the airport or at agencies in town, including Micar at Heredia no.701 esq. San Pedro (☎22/62-9194).

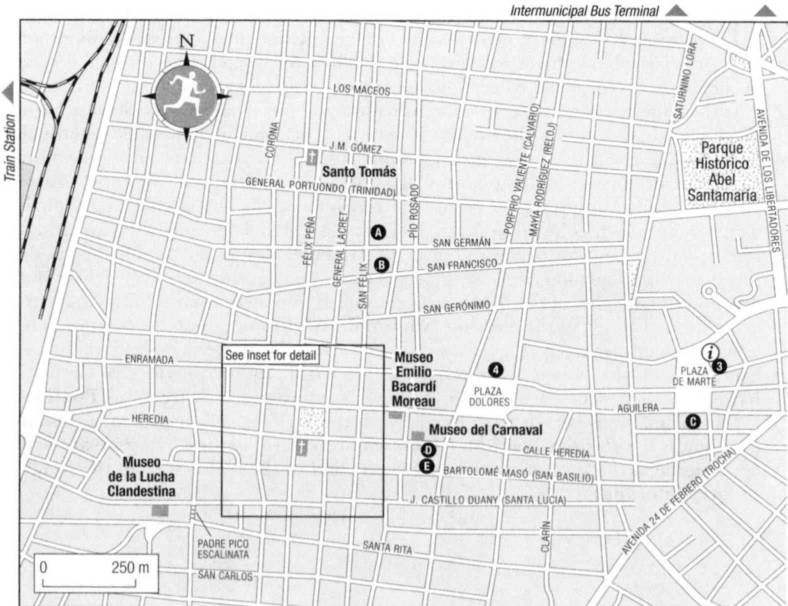

Inter-provincial buses pull in at the **Astro bus terminal** on Avenida de los Libertadores, 2km from the town centre (☎22/62-3050). Next door, tourist buses arrive at the **Víazul bus depot** (☎22/62-8484); there are daily services to and from Havana (15hr 30min). A taxi to the centre from either terminal takes about ten minutes and costs $5–6CUC. Provincial buses use the **Terminal de Omnibus Intermunicipal**, on Paseo de Martí, a five-minute cab ride north of Parque Céspedes (☎22/62-4325).

Arriving by **train** (10 weekly services from Havana; 14hr) you'll alight at the station near the port, on Paseo de Martí esq. Jesús Menéndez (☎22/62-2836), from where horse-drawn buggies and *bicitaxis* can take you to the centre for around $3CUC, while a taxi will cost around $5CUC.

Information

Santiago does not have an official tourist **information** bureau but the staff at the two Cubatur offices – one on Parque Céspedes at Heredia 701 esq. San Pedro, the other, shared with a couple of other tour companies, at the *Hotel Santiago de Cuba* – can help with general enquiries as well as book you onto **city tours** and **excursions** around the province. You can buy **maps** in the Librería Internacional on Parque Céspedes under the cathedral and at the shop in the *Hotel Casa Granda's* basement. Santiago's weekly newspaper, the *Sierra Maestra* (20¢), is available from street vendors and occasionally from the bigger hotels, and has a brief **listings** section detailing cinema, theatre and other cultural activities.

Getting around

Although a large city, Santiago is easy to negotiate, as much of what you'll want to see is contained within the historic core around Parque Céspedes. Even the furthest sights are no more than around 4km from Parque Céspedes, making it an excellent city for **exploring on foot**. However, taxis are the best way to reach outlying sights, as the buses are overcrowded and irregular.

Metered taxis wait on the cathedral side of Parque Céspedes or around Plaza de Marte and charge between forty and eighty centavos per kilometre, with a $1CUC surcharge; negotiate a rate for the whole journey with **unmetered taxis**, parked on San Pedro – expect to pay about $3–4CUC to cross town.

Accommodation

Accommodation in Santiago is plentiful and varied. Except during carnival in July, when rooms are snapped up well in advance, you can usually turn up on spec, though making a reservation will save you the possibility of having to trudge around the city looking for a place.

Hotels

Casa Granda Heredia no. 201 e/ San Pedro y San Félix ⓣ22/68-6600, ⓔcomercial@casagran.gca.tur.cu. A tourist attraction in itself on account of its beauty, the regal *Casa Granda* is a lovingly restored 1920s hotel overlooking Parque Céspedes. From the elegant, airy lobby to its two atmospheric bars, it has a stately, colonial air matched in its tasteful rooms. ❹

San Basilio Bartolomé Masó (San Basilio) no.403 e/ Calvario y Carnicería ⓣ22/65-1702, ⓕ68-7069. This gorgeous little hotel, with a blue-and-white exterior that makes it look like a frosted cake, offers excellent value for money. Its eight tastefully furnished rooms, arranged around a bright, plant-filled patio, come with cable TV, fridge and a/c. ❷

Casas particulares

Casa de Arlex Rojas Cruz San Francisco no. 303 e/ San Félix y San Bartolome ⓣ22/62-2517. Although there isn't much natural light in either of the two a/c rooms, this colonial house is still a good option. It boasts a tranquil patio furnished with rocking chairs, is home to two docile dogs and run by entertaining owners. ❶

Casa Colonial Maruchi San Félix no. 357 e/ San Germán y Trinidad ⓣ22/62-0767, ⓦwww.casasantiagodecubacolonial.sitio.net. Two rooms are available in this magnificent colonial house. Vintage brass beds, exposed brickwork and wooden beams add romance. Breakfast is included in the price. An excellent place to stay. ❶

Casa de Leonard y Rosa Clarín no. 9 e/ Aguilera y Heredia ⓣ22/62-3574. Two-room mini-apartment with two beds, a bathroom, a fridge and a small patio in a wonderful eighteenth-century house featuring period ironwork, wooden walls, high ceilings and red-and-blue stained-glass windows. ❶

Casa de Raimundo Ocaña y Bertha Peña Heredia no. 308 e/ Carnicería y Calvario ⓣ22/62-4097, ⓔco8kz@yahoo.es. A charming, very central house with an attractive, sunny patio; unfortunately bedevilled by noisy passing traffic. Two rooms, both with a/c, and private bathrooms with hot water. ❶

The historic centre and around

While many of the sights are clustered around the **colonial quarter** in the western part of town – and you will need at least a day to do this area justice – you'll also want to take some time to explore the newer suburbs out to the east and north. The other sights of interest are dotted randomly on the outskirts and can be squeezed into the tail end of a visit to other areas.

The colonial district's must-sees are focused around the picturesque **Parque Céspedes**, the spiritual centre of Santiago. Originally the Plaza de Armas built by the conquistadors, it is more of a plaza than a park, and is usually bustling with activity. A known pick-up spot, it also draws everyone from brass bands to old folks to tourists, and is great for people-watching. On its south side stands the handsome **Catedral de Nuestra Señora de la Asunción** (Tues–Fri 8am–noon & 5–6.30pm, Sat 8am–noon & 4–5pm; Mass Tues–Fri at 6.30pm, plus Sat at 5pm and Sun at 9am & 6.30pm). The first cathedral in Cuba was built on this site in 1522, but repeated effects wrought by earthquakes and pirates made their mark, and *Santiagueros* had to rebuild several times. The present cathedral was completed in 1818. A Baroque-style edifice, its twin towers gleam in the sunshine and its doorway is topped by an imposing herald angel, statues and four Neoclassical columns. Cherubs and angels are something of a theme in the interior, and you'll find them strewn across the ceiling and up the walls. The cathedral's prize piece, though almost hidden on the left-hand side, is the tremendous **organ**, now disused but still replete with tall gilded pipes. Lining the wall is a noteworthy frieze detailing the history of St James, patron saint of Santiago. In a small upstairs room round the cathedral's east side, the **Museo Arquidiocesano** (Mon–Sat 9.30am–5.30pm; $1CUC) has a small collection of calligraphic correspondence between various cardinals and bishops, portraits of all the past bishops of the cathedral and numerous other religious artefacts gathered from the city's churches and the cathedral itself.

On the north side of the square is the brilliant-white **Ayuntamiento**, or town hall, dating from the sixteenth century. During colonial times, the building on this site was the Casa del Gobierno, the governor's house, though the first two structures were reduced to rubble by earthquakes; the present building, erected in the 1940s, is a copy of a copy. It's not open to the public but you can admire the front cloister covered in shiny red tiles and fronted by crisply precise arches. The balcony overlooking the park was the site of Fidel Castro's triumphant speech on New Year's Day 1959.

The magnificent stone structure on the west side of the park, built in 1515 for Diego Velázquez, one of the first conquistadors of Cuba, is the oldest residential building in Cuba. It now houses the **Museo de Ambiente Cubano**, Parque Céspedes esq. Félix Pena (Sept–April daily 9am–4.45pm; May–Aug Mon–Fri 9am–5.45pm, Sat 9am–5pm, Sun 9am–12.45pm; $2CUC), a wonderful collection of early and late colonial furniture, curios, weapons and ornaments which offers one of the country's best insights into colonial lifestyles, and is so large that it spills over into the house next door. Much of what's on display is imported from Europe and shows off the good life enjoyed by the bourgeoisie, but the most interesting items are native to Cuba, like the *pajilla* chair with latticework back and seat, invented in Cuba to combat the heat, and the reclining *pajilla* smoking chair with an ornate ashtray attached to the arm, made for the proper enjoyment of a fine cigar.

A couple of blocks southwest of Parque Céspedes, in the **El Tivolí** district, the **Museo de la Lucha Clandestina**, perched on the Loma del Intendente (Tues–Sat 9am–7pm, Sun 9am–5pm; $1CUC), is a tribute to the pre-revolutionary struggle. Spread over two floors of a reproduction of a historically important eighteenth-century house, the museum comprises a photographic and journalistic history of the final years of the Batista regime and is a must for anyone who desires to understand the intricacies of the events leading up to the revolution. The best exhibits are those that give an idea of the turbulent climate of fear, unrest and excitement that existed in the 1950s in the lead-up to the revolution. Adjoining the museum is the celebrated **Padre Pico escalinata**, a towering staircase of over five hundred steps, built to accommodate the almost sheer hill that rises from the lower end of Calle Padre Pico.

Heading east from Parque Céspedes lands you on the liveliest section of **Calle Heredia** with its craft stalls, music venues and museums, amongst them the quirky **Museo de Carnaval** at no. 301 Heredia (Tues–Sat 9am–8pm, Sun 9am–5pm; $1CUC). Be sure to stop here if you can't make it for the real thing in July. Thoughtfully laid out on the ground floor of a dimly lit colonial house, the museum is a bright and colourful collection of psychedelic costumes, atmospheric photographs and carnival memorabilia. When the museum closes, the flamboyant carnival atmosphere continues with a free, hour-long **dance recital**, the Tardes de Folklórico (folklore afternoon; Mon–Sat 4–5pm), which is given outside on a patio to the back of the museum.

In the street parallel to Heredia, on the corner of Aguilera and Pío Rosado, the superb **Museo Emilio Bacardí Moreau** (Mon 2–8.15pm, Tues–Sat 9.15am–8.15pm, Sun 9am–12.15pm; $2CUC) is the one Santiago museum you should definitely visit if your time is limited. Styled along the lines of a traditional European city museum, it was founded in 1899 by Emilio Bacardí Moreau, then mayor of Santiago and patriarch of the Bacardi rum dynasty. Its colonial antiquities, excellent collection of Cuban fine art and archeological curios – including an Egyptian mummy – make it one of the most comprehensive hoards in the country.

East of the historic centre, just off the Avenida de los Libertadores, the town's main artery, are the **Moncada barracks** where Santiago's much-touted **Museo Histórico 26 de Julio** (Tues–Sat 9am–7.30pm, Sun 9am–1pm; $2CUC) fills you in on Fidel Castro's celebrated – though futile – attack on the barracks on July 26, 1953. With a commanding view of the surrounding mountains, the building, peppered with bullet holes, is a must-see, if only for the place it has in Cuban history.

Out of the city

Presiding over the bay eight kilometres outside the city is Santiago's most magnificent sight, the **Castillo del Morro San Pedro de la Roca**, or "El Morro" (daily 8am–7pm; $4CUC), a statuesque fortress built by the Spanish between 1633 and 1639 to ward off pirates. Despite its indomitable appearance – including a heavy drawbridge spanning a deep moat, thick stone walls and, inside, expansive parade grounds stippled with cannons – it fell to the English pirate Christopher Myngs in 1622 (who, much to his surprise, found the fort unguarded). Ramps and steps cut precise angles through the heart of the fortress, which is spread over three levels, and it's only as you wander deeper into the labyrinth of rooms that you get a sense of how awesomely huge it is.

Eating, drinking and nightlife

As in most of the country, the majority of Santiago's **restaurants** fall back on the old favourites of pork or chicken accompanied by rice and beans, although many state restaurants, especially the ones at the top end, usually have a tasty seafood dish or two as well. Fortunately you won't be at a loss for places to try, with plenty of restaurants and cafés around the centre all serving decent meals at affordable prices. Away from the state arena, choice is very limited as high taxes and tight controls on what food can be served have pushed out most of the **paladares**; some *casas particulares* make meals for their guests.

As for **bars**, since much of the action in Santiago revolves around music there are few places that cater specifically for drinkers, although the *Hotel Casa Granda* has two excellent bars. **Musical** entertainment in Santiago is hard to beat, and you'll find several excellent live *trova* (traditional Cuban music) venues – all a giddy whirl of soulful *boleros* and *son*. Keep an eye out for the superb Estudiantina Invasora *trova* group, who often play at the *Casa de la Trova* (see opposite). And you won't have to exert too much effort to find the best music; it often spills onto the streets at weekends. The best nights are often the cheapest and it's rare to find a venue charging more than $5CUC. Around **carnival** in July, bands – including some of the biggest names in Cuban *salsa* – set up just about everywhere, with temporary stages in many of the open spaces, notably at the Guillermón Moncada Baseball Stadium on the Avenida de las Américas and parks around the centre.

Discos tend to draw a young, boisterous crowd, including plenty of *jineteros;* expect to pay between $1CUC and $5CUC entrance.

Restaurants and paladares

Don Antonio Plaza Dolores. The smartest establishment on this restaurant-lined square has a classic *comida criolla* menu which includes good but expensive lobster.

Las Gallegas **Bartolomé Masó** (San Basilio) no.305 e/ General Lacret y Hartmann. Excellent *paladar* close to the centre with a range of typical, well-prepared Cuban food. There's a tiny balcony that's perfect for a pre-dinner drink.

La Maison Ave. Manduley no.52 esq. 1ra, Reparto Vista Alegre ⓣ22/64-1117. A swanky restaurant in the La Maison fashion-house complex serving good steaks, red snapper and seafood specialities including paella and "surf 'n' turf" grill. Prices start at $8CUC.

Salón Tropical Fernando Markane Rpto Sta Barbara e/ 9 y 11 ⓣ22/64-1161. A brisk *paladar* with a pleasant terrace for pre-dinner drinks. Tasty though salty chicken fricassee and grilled fish served with *tamales* are good choices. Round the meal off with crème caramel and coffee. As this is really on the outskirts of town, you'll want to arrange a taxi to and fro. Reservations advised.

Bars and live music venues

Bar Claqueta Santo Tomás e/ San Basilio y Heredia. A small, welcoming open-air club with excellent, energetic live music from the two resident bands, Los Amantes del Son and Sonora Huracán.

Casa de la Trova Heredia no. 208 e/ San Pedro y San Félix. A visit to the famous, pocket-sized *Casa de la Trova* is the highlight of a trip to Santiago, with musicians playing day and night to an audience packed into the single tiny room or hanging in through the window. Although this venue attracts much tourist attention, it is still the top choice in town for hearing excellent music. Entrance costs $2–5CUC depending on who's playing.

Los Dos Abuelos Pérez Carbo no.5, Plaza Marte. A variety of local groups play *son* and *guaracha* on this bar's pretty patio, shaded by fruit trees, at 10pm every night. An extensive range of rums and snacks are available.

Pista Bailable Teatro Heredia, Ave. de las Américas s/n ☎22/64-3190. Pumped-up *salsa, son, bolero* and *merengue* tunes all get the crowd dancing at this unpretentious local club, with live music some nights.

Granma and the Sierra Maestra

Protruding west from the main body of Cuba, cupping the Bahía de Guacanayabo, **Granma** is a tranquil, slow-paced province, bypassed with impunity by those pressed for time. A visit to the small, simple rural town of **Pilón**, however, gives a worthy insight into life beyond the tourist trail. On the southwestern tip of Granma's coastline, **Las Coloradas**, where Fidel Castro and his revolutionaries came ashore on the boat *Granma*, is the highlight of any revolution pilgrimage, while nearby the **Parque Nacional Desembarco del Granma** has several excellent guided nature trails.

The **Sierra Maestra**, Cuba's highest and most extensive mountain range, stretches along the southern coast of the island, running the length of both Santiago and Granma provinces. The unruly beauty of the landscape – a vision of undulating green-gold mountains and remote sugar fields – will take your breath away. Once you've admired the countryside there's not an awful lot else you can do: national park status notwithstanding, much of the Sierra Maestra is periodically declared out of bounds by the authorities, who sometimes give the reason of an epidemic in the coffee crops but more often give no reason at all; the area is possibly still used for military operations. Should the park be open, don't bypass the opportunity to trek on the area's excellent trails, including those leading through the stunning cloud forest of the **Parque Nacional Turquino** to the island's highest point, **Pico Turquino** (1974m). Your best bet for getting information in advance on access to the Sierra Maestra is the Agencia de Reservaciones de Campísmo in Bayamo (☎23/42-4200).

Parque Nacional Desembarco del Granma

The province's southwestern tip is commanded by the **Parque Nacional Desembarco del Granma**, which starts at the tranquil holiday haven of **Campismo Las Coloradas**, 47km from Pilón, and stretches some 20km west to the tiny fishing village of Cabo Cruz. The forested interior of the park is littered with trails, but the most famous feature is the **Playa Las Coloradas**, on the western coastline, where the *Granma* yacht deposited Fidel Castro and his 81 comrades on December 2, 1956, on their clandestine return from exile in Mexico.

Named after the red colour that the mangrove jungle gives to the water, the beach is completely hidden and you can't see or even hear the sea from the start of the path that leads down to the **Monumento Portada de la Libertad** (Tues–Sat 8am–6pm, Sun 8am–noon; $1CUC, including guide), which marks the spot of the landing. Flanked on either side by mangrove forest hedged with jagged saw grass, the kilometre-long path presents a pleasant walk even for those indifferent to the Revolution, and the guide's enthusiasm for his subject is infectious as he compellingly narrates (in Spanish) the rebel's journey.

The tour also takes in a life-size replica of the **yacht**, which the guide can sometimes be persuaded to let you clamber aboard, and a rather spartan **museum** with photographs, maps and an emotive quotation from Castro on the eve of the crossing that neatly sums up his determination to succeed: "*Si salimos, llegamos. Si llegamos, entramos, y si entramos triumfamos*" ("If we leave, we'll get there. If we get there we'll get in, and if we get in we will win.").

The park's interior is made up of idyllic woodland that skirts the western verge of the Sierra Maestra. From Las Coloradas you can walk to the start of **El Guafe** (Mon–Fri 8.30am–5pm, Sat & Sun 8am–2pm; $3CUC entrance plus $5CUC for a guide), one of the four trails in the park, and celebrated for the intriguing stone petroglyphs found in the vicinity. It's an easy and reasonably well-signposted walk – roughly a three-kilometre circuit – which you can do on your own or with a guide.

The only **place to stay** in the park, *Campismo Las Coloradas*, has excellently simple and clean chalets with air conditioning and hot water, along with a **restaurant** and **bar**. Bookings should be made via **Cubamar** in Havana (Ⓣ7/831-2891; ❶) and are essential at weekends, when things fill up with Cubans.

3.8

Cayo Largo

South of the mainland, the little-visited Isla de la Juventud (Island of Youth) is the largest of over three hundred scattered emerald islets that make up the **Archipiélago de los Canarreos**. Most visitors to the archipelago, however, are destined for its comparatively tiny neighbour **CAYO LARGO**, arguably Cuba's most exclusive holiday resort.

Some 140km east of the Isla de la Juventud, the cay is a narrow, low-lying spit of land fringed with powdery beaches, and is entirely geared to those on package holidays. The tiny islet, measuring just 20km from tip to beachy tip, caters to the quickening flow of European and Canadian tourists who swarm here to enjoy the excellent watersports, diving and Club Med-style hotels. In November of 2001, **Hurricane Michelle** wrought havoc on the cay; large-scale evacuations took place and some of the hotels were heavily damaged. Now, though, all the damage has been repaired and plans are under way for even more hotels.

Arrival, information and getting around

The only way to reach **Cayo Largo** is by **plane**, and its airport sees numerous international arrivals, as well as domestic flights with Aero Caribbean on rickety Russian twenty-seaters from Havana (2 daily; 40min); you'll be required to book accommodation along with your flight. The tiny Vilo Acuña airport is 1km from the main belt of hotels and courtesy hotel buses meet every flight.

Though there is no main **tourist office** on the cay, the representatives of various tour companies who share a desk (daily 9.30–11am & 6–7pm) at the *Sol Cayo Largo* offer general information and organize excursions. You can buy **maps** at all the hotel shops or from the post office (daily 8am–7pm) in front of the *Isla del Sur* hotel and there's a **bank** (Mon–Fri 8.30am–noon & 2–3.30pm, Sat & Sun 9am–noon) on the corner of the village plaza.

The island is small enough to negotiate easily and courtesy **buses** regularly do the circuit of the hotels, running from early morning to midnight. A **ferry** ($4CUC per person) leaves from the marina to Playa Sirena and Playa Paraíso twice daily at 9.30am and 11am, returning at 3pm and 5pm.

Accommodation

Hotel standards are high and rooms are not cheap as they tend to be block-booked by overseas package-tour operators at a specially discounted rate. All the hotels are all-inclusive – the price codes below represent what you'll pay if you book through a Cuban tour operator.

Sol Cayo Largo ⓣ45/24-8260, ⓔjefe.reservas.scl@solmeliacuba.com. An appealing, Caribbean-themed hotel with airy rooms in smart blocks set around palm trees and rather parched lawns. With an all-inclusive buffet, beach grill and à la carte restaurants, two swimming pools, free non-motorized water sports, a health centre, tennis courts and a football field, this is the biggest and plushest place on the cay, with a clientele of twenty-something couples, families and retirees all mingling happily and providng the place with an atmospheric buzz. 8

Sol Pelícano ⓣ45/24-8333, ⓔjefe.reservas.spl@solmeliacuba.com. A family-friendly luxury hotel with dedicated play area and children's entertainment, four all-inclusive restaurants, two swimming pools and bold blue-and-yellow two- and three-storey villas with cheerful sun-and-sea inspired decor. 7

Villa Coral ⓣ 45/24-8111, Ereserva@isla.cls.tur.cu. This family-oriented hotel offers rather gaudy pink and green blocks with red-tiled roofs, divided by neat beds of sea shrubs and palms to ensure a sense of privacy. Rooms have spacious balconies and smart sun terraces, with shaded seating surrounding a sparkling circular pool. 5

Exploring Cayo Largo

Life on the cay began in 1977 when the state, capitalizing on the extensive white sands and offshore coral reefs, built the first of eight hotels that now line the western and southern shores. There is still ample room for development, however, and while plans are under way for more hotels, the cay has a long way to go before it is spoilt; indeed there is arguably not yet enough development, with infrastructure away from the hotels so sparse that the cay offers little to discover or explore beyond the boundaries of the accommodation complexes. The artificiality which works well in the hotels fails somewhat in the **Isla del Sol village** on the west of the island, which has a distinctly spurious air: it's just a sparse collection of a shop, restaurants, a small museum and a bank gathered around a tiny square, the Plaza del Pirata and, just off the square, an uninspiring **Turtle Farm** (daily 7am–noon & 1–6pm; $1CUC) housing restless turtles in small pens.

There's more activity around the beaches to the south and along the hotel strip, where warm shallow waters lap the narrow ribbon of pale downy sand. Protected from harsh winds and rough waves by the offshore coral reef, and with over 2km of white sands, **Playa Sirena** enjoys a deserved reputation as the most beautiful of all the beaches and is consequently the busiest. There's a road to the beach from the *Sol Pelícano* but, as it's frequently covered by drifts of sand, you're better off catching one of the ferries or speedboats from the marina (see above). There's a **café** on the beach serving drinks, sandwiches and snacks. Further south along the same strand, **Playa Paraíso** is almost as attractive and popular as Sirena, with the added advantage that the shallow waters are ideal for children. Heading east, **Playa Lindamar** is a serviceable 5km curve of sand in front of several hotels and is the only one where you can play volleyball and windsurf.

With over thirty dive sites in the clear and shallow waters around the cay, Cayo Largo is also known as one of Cuba's best **diving areas**. Particularly outstanding are the coral gardens to be found in the shallow waters around the islet, while other highlights of the region include underwater encounters with hawksbill and sea green turtles, as well as trips to the tiny **Cayo Iguana** where the eponymous reptiles are tame enough to be fed by hand. The cay's dive centre (Ⓣ45/24-8214) at the Marina Puerto Sol offers dives for $50CUC, including all equipment and transfer to the dive site; prices per dive decrease with subsequent dives. The marina also runs a variety of day-long snorkelling expeditions which usually include a visit to the coral gardens, Cayo Iguana and a "natural swimming pool" where the water is only 1m deep, along with a lobster lunch and an open bar for $69–73CUC.

Eating, drinking and entertainment

Although all the hotels' packages include free meals, guests can choose to pay for meals in other hotels. Within the packages, menus are fairly standard, with all the buffets offering a range of international dishes. The à la carte options tend to be of a higher standard and it's worth remembering that all the hotels will provide a free picnic lunch for those who wish to spend the day at the beach. The *Villa Coral's* à la carte restaurant, *La Piazzoletta*, serves authentic Italian food; of the buffet **restaurants**, the *Sol Pelícano* has the largest selection and the cheeriest atmosphere.

Down in the quiet of the village, the thatched *Taberna del Pirata* **bar**, on the plaza overlooking the picturesque harbour, is a great spot to enjoy the cooling sea breezes as you watch the sun go down. Next door, the *El Criolla* restaurant has a distinctive Wild West flavour with a wooden ceiling, cow-hide-covered chairs and some ornamental saddles. It serves classic Cuban chicken and pork dishes as well as lobster and shrimp cooked in a variety of ways. Other than the *Taberna del Pirata* bar, there is no **nightlife** on the island outside of the hotels. The *Sol Cayo Largo* is probably the liveliest spot at night, with a friendly lobby bar and a larger one by the pool that's mercifully set back from the stage where an entertainment team puts on nightly cabaret shows with forced hilarity. Should you feel like providing the entertainment yourself, there's also a karaoke bar. For a cover charge of $15CUC, guests from other hotels can join in the festivities and drink at the open bars.

4

The Cayman Islands

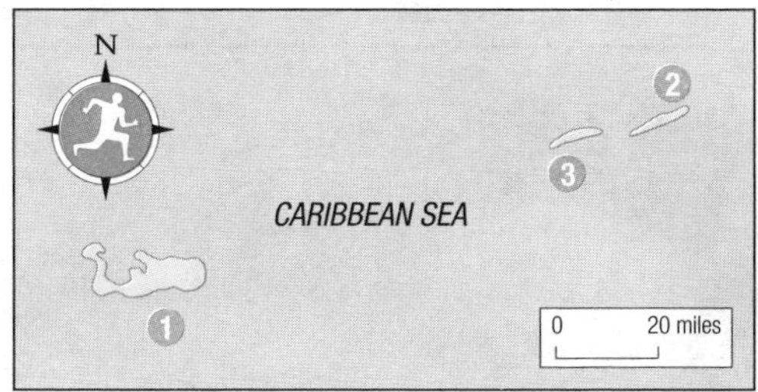

The Cayman Islands highlights

* **Seven Mile Beach** Miles of soft white sand and sparklingly blue, gentle surf draw visitors to this popular and easily accessible stretch. See p.221

* **Stingray City** Superb spot where you can get friendly with the local stingray population. See p.222

* **Botanic Garden** Meander through a living rainbow: 2.5 acres of colour-coordinated flora, and then stop to visit the blue iguanas See p.226

* **Bloody Bay Wall** Swim amongst luminescent corals and colourful fish at Little Cayman's premier wall dive. See p.232

▲ Stingray

Introduction and basics

Just northwest of Jamaica, the Cayman Islands have truly grown up during the past forty years, driven by tourism and banking. Today they boast one of the highest per capita incomes in the world and are a global provider of specialized financial services. On the tourism side of development, they attract more than two million visitors a year (most by cruise ship) and have been a scuba-diving paradise since the 1960s.

Of the 52,000 people who live in Cayman (rather than "The Caymans", "Cayman" is the accepted abbreviated name), 49 percent were born elsewhere. While expatriates move here from all over the world, the majority come from Jamaica and the United States, with smaller numbers from the United Kingdom and Canada. The islands are just a 90-minute flight from Miami, Florida, and being a British overseas territory, English is the official language – making for a quick, convenient and easy getaway for North Americans. Since the fast-food chains along with many hotels and products also hail from the US, it's sometimes easy to forget you're in the Caribbean.

That being said, Cayman does have its unique draws, the chief one being superb **scuba diving**. Like many islands, the Cayman Islands are essentially the peaks of underwater mountains, and the submerged terrain here is especially dramatic: the spectacular underwater walls and caverns are some of the world's best. With its crystal clear water and sandy **beaches** (Grand Cayman's Seven Mile Beach is among the finest in the Caribbean), Cayman is also an ideal destination for those who enjoy other watersports or simple sunbathing. A variety of tropical birds flock to the islands, making **birdwatching** popular. Life in Cayman is laid-back; if rousing casinos and wild nightlife are what you seek, these are not the islands for you. Families will be pleased to find that many larger resorts have daily kids' camps, restaurants often have a children's menu and most attractions have discounted rates for young ones.

Grand Cayman is the most developed of the three islands and where you will find the largest selection of accommodation, restaurants and attractions. The Sister Islands **Cayman Brac** (pronounced "brack") and **Little Cayman** have far fewer options, and most travellers to these islands choose all-inclusive packages. Compared to Grand Cayman, the pace is far mellower on the Sister Islands. They've yet to put up stoplights on either island, and on Little Cayman bikes are the transportation of choice.

The islands are all sparsely populated and much of each is uninhabited swampland or rough ironshore; other than in the busier west end of Grand Cayman, homes are lightly dotted along the coastlines. All three islands are low-lying and arid; a ridge on Cayman Brac that rises to 140 feet above sea level is the country's highest point. The **vegetation** throughout is predominately scrub brush and mangrove but there are also colourful flowering **plants** and **trees** such as the brilliant poinciana tree that grows as high as 40 feet and develops a blossoming orange canopy that spreads across the roadways.

Where to go

To soak up the sun on a gorgeous stretch of sand within reach of assorted restaurants and bars, head to **Seven Mile Beach**, just north of George Town on Grand Cayman. For a total escape, spend some reflective time **hiking** or **birdwatching** on quiet Cayman Brac, or quieter Little Cayman.

The main reason to come to Cayman, though, is the premier diving attractions on all three islands: frolic with the friendly rays at **Stingray City** off Grand Cayman, shore-dive just a few yards off Cayman Brac, or head to **Bloody Bay Wall** just off Little Cayman for superb underwater adventure; snorkellers can explore the wall in about 20 feet of water while a short distance away divers can slip into a 6000-foot abyss.

When to go

The **average temperature** hovers around 24°C (75°F) in winter and 29°C (85°F) in the summer. If travelling during the holiday season (late Nov to early Jan), be sure to reserve hotels and vehicles a few months in advance. Off season (April to mid-Nov) lodging rates can drop twenty percent or more and the islands are less crowded.

There are **two seasons**: "rainy", lasting from mid-May to October, followed by the "dry" season, November to April. Don't let the term "rainy season" deter you from visiting; in general you'll encounter brief afternoon showers followed by sun and higher humidity than in the drier months. **Hurricane** season, though, is from June 1 to November 30 (at its worst in Sept), and while chances of your holiday coinciding with a major storm are slim, Cayman is by no means immune. Note that most resorts on Little Cayman close for the month of September.

Getting there

Virtually all flights touch down first at **Owen Roberts International Airport** (Ⓣ345/949-7811) on Grand Cayman, with connecting flights to Cayman Brac and Little Cayman usually departing the same day. Year-round, up to seven cruise **cruise ships** dock daily at the **Port of George Town**.

Information

Once you arrive on Grand Cayman, you'll find an array of brochures and maps at the **information booth** at Owen Roberts International Airport and at the North and South Terminal cruise ship docks and Royal Watler Cruise terminal in central George Town. The Department of Tourism (Ⓣ345/949-0623, Ⓦwww.caymanislands.ky) is located in the Windward Three building of the Regatta Office Park on West Bay Rd, opposite the Westin Casuarina resort. Cayman Brac's airport also some brochures; Department of Tourism (Ⓣ345/948-1849) has its Brac office in the West End Community Park.

Money and costs

The official currency is the **Cayman Islands dollar (CI$)**, which comes in $1, $5, $10, $25, $50 and $100 notes; the coins are 1, 5, 10 and 25 cents. The exchange rate is fixed at 80 Cayman cents to one US dollar. Both Cayman and US dollars can be used everywhere on the islands, although change will generally be given in CI$. All other currencies will need to be exchanged at either a bank or your hotel, but travellers' cheques and all major credit cards are widely accepted.

Although Grand Cayman has almost 300 licensed **banks**, only a handful provide customer banking services as most visitors know it; try Scotiabank, Bank of Butterfield, Royal Bank of Canada, Cayman National Bank and First Caribbean Bank. **ATMs** accepting Visa and MasterCard linked to the Cirrus and Plus systems are located along West Bay Road as well as at Owen Roberts International Airport on Grand Cayman. **Bank hours** are generally Mon–Fri 9am–4pm. There is one bank on each of the Sister Islands, both of which keep limited hours; Cayman Brac has an ATM but not Little Cayman.

The Cayman Islands are far from a bargain hunters' paradise; **prices are fixed** and haggling is not the norm. High-season prices kick in from late November and begin to drop in April.

Websites

Ⓦ**www.caymanislands.ky** The official website of the Cayman Islands Department of Tourism, where you can read up on Cayman and plan your vacation.

Ⓦ**www.caycompass.com** Online version of the national newspaper.

Ⓦ**www.itsyourstoexplore.com** Information to help you plan your visit to Cayman Brac and Little Cayman.

Getting around

Cayman Airways Express (Ⓣ345/949-2311 or 1-800/GCAYMAN) offers at least four trips daily between all three islands. The flight between Grand Cayman and either of the Sister Islands takes about 40 minutes and costs just over US$100 return. Although the Sister Islands are only about five miles apart, no ferries run between them.

Car Rentals are available on all three islands but they are not the norm on Little Cayman where the transportation of choice is a bicycle. To drive a car on any of the islands a visitor's licence is required and available for US$7.50 at rental agencies and at the central police station in George Town on Grand Cayman. Roads are in excellent condition on Grand Cayman and Cayman Brac, but a bit rough on Little Cayman. Petrol costs about US$5 per gallon. Remember to drive on the left and wear a seatbelt.

The **bus** system on Grand Cayman is efficient, but there are no buses on either of the Sister Islands. **Taxis** are available on Grand Cayman and Cayman Brac, but not on Little Cayman.

Accommodation

Cayman is **expensive** by any standards; expect to pay at least US$125 per night for even the most modest accommodation. **Packages** (diving, fishing, golfing) can be a way to save and are offered throughout the year; other specials are sometimes advertised on the Department of Tourism website (Ⓦwww.caymanislands.ky). If you're serious about diving, you might consider staying on a live-aboard dive boat.

Renting a **villa** on any of the three islands is another popular option; there are more than a hundred available and you may even find yourself with a private stretch of beach (many have a pool and maid service). You can try Cayman Villas (Ⓣ345/945-4144 or 1-800/235-5888, Ⓦwww.caymanvillas.com) or the Department of Tourism website which lists all available properties.

A 10 percent **government tax** is added to all bills, and most properties also tack on a **service charge** of 10–15 percent. When making reservations, be sure to ask if the quoted rate includes these additional charges.

Food and drink

Thanks to Cayman's historical connection to Jamaica, it's no surprise to find **jerked meats** – heavily spiced meats smoked over hardwoods in enclosed barbecue grills – as one of the island specialities. **Turtle**, though not as popular as it once was, is part of traditional Cayman cuisine and usually prepared in stews. Also prevalent is **conch**, popularly served as fritters but traditionally prepared in stews or as steak.

Cayman-style **fish** can really be any fish pulled fresh from the sea and sautéed with pepper, onions and green peppers. Typical sides are plantains, yams, rice and peas cooked in coconut milk. **Heavy cake** is a real treat; it's made with grated cassava root, white yam or papaya, sweetened with sugar and has the consistency of a thick bread pudding – you can find in small grocers and at some petrol stations.

You'll find **locally grown produce** such as mango, grapefruit, ackee, coconut, breadfruit, plantain and cassava along with home-made goodies at most supermarkets on the islands. Though restaurants tend to specialize in Continental or international fare, traditional Cayman cuisine occasionally appears on menus.

The local brew in Cayman is **Caybrew**, a fairly nondescript lager that tourists tend to enjoy more than locals. **Rum Punch**, made with orange and pineapple juices, rum, and grenadine, is as popular here as elsewhere in the Caribbean. More unique to Cayman is the **Cayman Lemonade** made with sweet and sour mix, peach schnapps, cranberry juice, vodka and rum. There's no distillery in Cayman, but **Tortuga Rum Company** makes its own Cayman blend of Jamaican and Barbados rums.

The **tap water** in restaurants and hotels on all three islands is desalinated seawater and fine for drinking.

Mail and communications

When making a **phone call**, watch out for hotel surcharges: they can be double the already expensive per-minute rate. A less expensive option is to purchase a phone card, available in most stores, and make your call on a public phone.

The main **post office** branch is in downtown George Town at Edward St and Cardinal Ave (Mon–Fri 8.15am–5pm Sat 9am–12.30pm; ⓣ345/949-2474); branch locations can be found throughout the island. The main post office on Cayman Brac is in West End, and Little Cayman's one post office is at 898 Guy Banks Rd.

Grand Cayman has all the latest high-tech communications infrastructure and devices. There are an ever-increasing number of **Internet** cafés, including *The Thai Restaurant* in downtown Georgetown (CI$6/hour) and *Café del Sol* in the Marquee Shopping Centre off West Bay Rd (CI$4/hour), and most hotels have free wireless access in their lobbies. Several hotels on Cayman Brac and Little Cayman offer access as well, some of them with available wireless connections. There is no public access on Little Cayman, but the West End post office on Cayman Brac has one computer available (CI$6/hour).

The **country code** for the Cayman Islands is ⓣ345.

As Cayman is a British Territory, you won't find any embassies on the islands; the closest embassy is in Jamaica. For assistance, call the Department of Tourism main office at ⓣ345/949-0623 or the Government Administration Building at ⓣ345/949-7900.

Public holidays and festivals

The main event on Grand Cayman is the annual **Pirates' Week** (ⓣ345/949-5078, ⓦwww.piratesweekfestival.com), a ten-day celebration held in mid-November. George Town is centre stage for the major activities at the weekends, but special events take place all over the island and include street dances into the wee hours, sports contests, a mock pirate invasion, glittering parades and treasure hunts. It's a popular event with islanders and tourists, so book hotel accommodations well in advance.

Spring brings **Batabano** (ⓣ345/949-7121, ⓦwww.caymancarnival.com), Cayman's annual **Carnival** which takes place at various venues around the island over four days in early May, featuring parades and live soca and calypso bands, along with street stalls offering tasty Cayman and Caribbean delicacies. April, meanwhile, sees the Cayman Islands International **Fishing Tournament** (ⓣ345/945-3131, ⓦwww.fishcayman.com), where international anglers compete to catch blue marlin, yellowfin tuna, wahoo and the like for hefty cash prizes.

Little Cayman also has its share of events, the most popular being the **Annual Mardi Gras Festival** (ⓣ345/948-1010). This is small-town parade atmosphere at its best; many people visit during this time just to take part and there are always more participants than spectators.

Public holidays

January 1 New Year's Day
Fourth Monday in January National Heroes' Day
February Ash Wednesday
March/April Good Friday, Easter Monday
Third Monday in May Discovery Day
First Monday after second Saturday in June Queen's Birthday
First Monday in July Constitution Day
First Monday after November 11 Remembrance Day
December 25 Christmas Day
December 26 Boxing Day

Sports and outdoor activities

Given the clear, warm sea it's no surprise that **watersports** predominate, the greatest variety being available on Grand Cayman.

Scuba diving

Excellent conditions and unique terrain have made the seas around the Cayman Islands the domain of **scuba divers.** The underwater landscape is dominated by the massive Cayman Trench, which plunges down some 25,000 feet to the deepest point in the Caribbean Sea. The drop-off is dramatic with 6000ft cliffs in some places no more than a few hundred yards offshore. To scuba divers, diving these walls is akin to exploring the Grand Canyon; sea fans, barrel sponges and sea whips abound, as does a plethora of marine creatures that crawl, hover and dart around the reefs. Given the popularity of the sport, dive operators and packages are abundant. Returning divers may prefer to go to the Sister Islands as they attract fewer divers and conditions are more pristine. Every hotel on Little Cayman has an affiliated dive operation, as does the resort on Cayman Brac. Grand Cayman has a wide variety of **dive shops**; the following are just a few of the best.

Grand Cayman dive shops

Divetech Lighthouse Point in West Bay and Cobalt Coast resort ⓣ345/946-5658

Don Foster's George Town and Seven Mile Beach ⓣ345/949-5679 or 1-800/83-DIVER.

Eden Rock South Church St ⓣ345/949-7243.

Red Sail Sports Seven Mile Beach and Rum Point ⓣ345/945-5965 or 1-877/RED-SAIL.

Scuba diving and **snorkelling** are by far the most popular; visibility can exceed 100 feet (see box above). For those who prefer to stay dry, a glass-bottom boat or an air-conditioned submarine will shuttle sightseers down to the underwater world.

There is as much to do on top of the water: deep-sea fishing, bonefishing on the flats around Little Cayman, windsurfing (especially good on the breezy East End of Grand Cayman), jet skiing, parasailing, sailing and simply swimming or floating around on the salty sea.

Grand Cayman has well-maintained and challenging **golf** courses. At the *Grand Cayman Beach Suite's* Britannia Golf Club, the Jack Nicklaus signature course (greens fees US$100–150) is actually two courses in one: a par 58 executive-style, or short, course, and a par 70 championship course. The *Ritz Carlton Grand Cayman* has a Greg Norman-designed nine-hole course and the North Sound Club at Safehaven is an eighteen-hole, par 71 championship course.

The Sister Islands offer some distinct nature-based sports. Cayman Brac sets itself apart from the other islands with various **hiking trails** that criss cross the island. Be sure to wear sturdy shoes as some of the trails are over sharp ironshore coral, and bring water as it's easy to get dehydrated in the heat. On the less strenuous side, there's excellent **birdwatching** on Little Cayman, where the centre of the island is dominated by a mangrove swamp – the red-footed booby, black frigate and snowy egret are commonly seen here.

History

Christopher Columbus is the first European credited with discovering the islands in 1503, though not surprisingly he stumbled upon them. While en route between Panama and Hispaniola he was blown west off course and recorded seeing two small islands (Little Cayman and Cayman Brac) "full of tortoise". He dubbed them "Las Tortugas", Spanish for turtle, but the name didn't stick. In 1586 British explorer Sir Francis Drake passed through, recording that the islands were flush with "great serpents… like large lizards". These were caimans – marine reptiles related to crocodiles, after which the islands were renamed.

Except for the animals and marine creatures, it's generally assumed the islands were uninhabited until seafarers began using them as **replenishment centres** in the sixteenth century. English, Dutch, French and Spanish explorers all stopped here. Historians dispute whether any of these explorers were pirates, but legend has it that in the eighteenth century **Blackbeard** stashed his treasures in Cayman caves.

The **Spanish** and **British** were the two main colonial powers battling for control of the islands in this region. The Cayman Islands became part of the British Empire in 1670 under the Treaty of Madrid, which also bestowed nearby Jamaica and other islands onto the British. Most of the original settlers to Cayman were English, Welsh and Scottish who came from Jamaica, some of whom brought their **African slaves** with them to work on cotton plantations, cut mahogany and farm the rocky land for produce. Under this arrangement, for the next two hundred years or so the Cayman Islands were governed as a dependency of Jamaica.

By the 1950s, with a population of just a few thousand, life in Cayman was quiet and uncomplicated, with boatbuilding, thatch rope making and turtle fishing the mainstays of the economy. But a post-World War II economic boom opened possibilities for the island. Propelled by a reputation for **political stability** and a relatively crime-free atmosphere, Cayman followed the example of Bermuda and the Bahamas in creating an **offshore finance** industry and developing a high-end **tourism** sector. Crucial factors encouraging visitors were the opening of Owen Roberts International Airport in 1954 and the work of the Mosquito Control and Research Unit to eradicate the pesky and widely spread mosquito in the 1960s (which didn't altogether succeed). Financial investors were drawn by **bank secrecy laws** (now relaxed since their strictest form in 1976), an efficient tele communications system and no direct taxation. In 1962 when Jamaica gained independence, the Cayman Islands preferred to remain under the British Crown, in part with the aim of securing continued foreign investment.

The industries grew rapidly, and by 1998, more than 40,000 companies were registered in Cayman, banking assets exceeded US$500 billion and yearly tourist arrivals at almost two million (mainly by cruise ship). Today, finance and tourism are the mainstays of the Cayman economy.

In recent years, Cayman's prosperity suffered a setback when Hurricane Ivan slammed into the island in September 2004. Despite the storm, the financial sector hardly had a pause in business and has continued to grow, and tourists have returned to find newly refurbished accommodations and restaurants, along with the same alluring beaches and azure waters. Barring any additional storms of Ivan's magnitude in the near term, Cayman's financial future continues to look bright.

4.1

Grand Cayman

With a total landmass of 78 square miles, **GRAND CAYMAN** has the most surface area, population and development of the three Cayman Islands. As such it receives the greatest number of visitors and certainly feels the most like a traditional Caribbean vacation spot, with a small colonial capital, a beautiful stretch of beach and lots of big resorts that will arrange your whole holiday for you.

The island is carved into five districts, of which only two see much traffic – George Town and West Bay, which comprise the entire western portion. The capital city of George Town is on the western coast in the district, which bears its name. Each week nearly 35,000 cruise ship passengers shoulder their way along the narrow sidewalks of the harbour town's main streets, where duty-free shops hawk everything from Cuban cigars to fine emeralds. The crowds are never overwhelming but do lend an air of activity to an otherwise quiet place. Once you've covered downtown, you'll likely head to the fine powder and calm waters at **Seven Mile Beach**, just a ten-minute drive away and arguably one of the finest stretches of sand in the Caribbean.

It's easy to explore the rest of the island in a day or two, and while the eastern districts each have individual charm and a far mellower pace than George Town, there are few stops of much interest. **East End** has prime places for diving, and the beach at **Rum Point** makes a nice escape from the bustle of the west. No place on the island is much more than an hour from any other, so you can base yourself anywhere and come and go as you please.

Getting around

The main roads around Grand Cayman are in good condition. You might find it easiest to **rent a car** to get around but the public bus service is efficient, and taxis are relatively comfortable, with fixed rates that aren't too astronomical.

Many agencies provide complimentary pick-up/drop-off, but you'll find all the American big boys – Avis, Budget and Dollar – along with some island-based ones like Coconut Car Rentals (☎345/949-7703), which offers various discount specials, right across the street from the airport. Economy-size car rentals start at US$60 per day in high season.

The **bus terminal** is adjacent to the public library on Edward Street in downtown George Town and serves as the dispatch point for all buses. The fleet of minibuses is distinguished by blue license plates with white numbering, and each bus displays its route on large, round colour-coded stickers. All districts are served by bus, though you may have to transfer, and fares range from CI$2.00 to $3.50. Daily bus service is reliable, beginning at 6am and running until 11pm for the West End, and until 9pm for the East End (with extended service on Fridays and Saturdays).

Taxis are available from the airport, all resorts and from the taxi stand at the cruise ship dock in George Town. While you won't often see them cruising for fares, you can also call for one – try Ace Cayman Nice Taxi & Tours (☎345/777-777) or Charlie's Super Cab and Tours (☎345/949-4748). Rates are fixed and posted at the downtown dock and at the dispatch stand at the airport; cabbies rarely try to rip off visitors. Rates from the airport to the Seven Mile Beach resorts run about US$25 one-way.

Stingray City and Stingray Sandbar

Heralded as the "world's best twelve-foot dive", **Stingray City** in Grand Cayman's North Sound has become a definitive goal for divers in the Caribbean. Plunging in these shallow depths about a mile from shore can be an astounding experience, offering the chance to mingle up close with Atlantic southern stingrays in the wild. The rays were first attracted to these waters by the scraps left by fishermen, who used the area to clean their fish. Local dive operators recognized the economic possibilities and began offering trips to Stingray City, with the opportunity to touch the elegant creatures who have wingspans of up to five feet and skin like wet velvet. Snorkelling is a good alternative if you don't dive – you'll still be able to get up close to the rays.

A few miles east and just as good is **Stingray Sandbar**. The water is only waist-deep (despite being miles from shore) and perfect for splashing about even without a mask. Rays frequent this spot and haven't been scared off by locals who set up volleyball nets, perhaps thinking more snacks would be involved.

Check out any number of boat operators throughout the island – excursions start at about US$35 per person with gear rental.

Accommodation

Most **hotels** are along Seven Mile Beach proper, which is located within the George Town district. As would be expected, hotels along this main drag, especially those with beachfront, are pricier than those located elsewhere; they also tend to be chain resorts. For a touch more personality, seek out spots scattered throughout the other districts. Virtually every hotel offers wireless Internet, even the smaller guesthouses.

George Town and Seven Mile Beach

Comfort Suites Seven Mile Beach ⓣ345/945-7300 or 1-800/517-4000, ⓦwww.caymancomfort.com. This all-suites hotel is popular for its reasonable prices and location within walking distance of restaurants, shops, the beach and the cinema. There's also a pool, beauty salon, dive shop and bar on site. Deluxe continental breakfast included in the rates. ❻

Grand Cayman Beach Suites Seven Mile Beach ⓣ345/ 949-1234; ⓦwww.grand-cayman-beach-suites.com. This British colonial-style resort has 53 one- and two-bedroom suites with kitchenettes on the beach. Amenities include a Jack Nicklaus-designed golf course, top-notch sushi restaurant, and full-service spa. ❾

Marriott Grand Cayman Seven Mile Beach ⓣ345/949-0088; from the US 1-800/399-7641, ⓦwww.marriotgrand cayman.com. Situated on a serene stretch of beach, and with large rooms, extra-comfortable beds and an onsite branch of the popular Red Sail Sports, this hotel is a solid choice. ❽–❾

Ritz-Carlton West Bay Rd ⓣ345-943-9000 or 1-800/241-3333, ⓦwww.ritzcarlton.com. Stretching 144 acres from Seven Mile Beach to North Sound, the Ritz-Carlton is the ultimate in luxury, with twice-daily maid service and large marble bathrooms. Sensational restaurants, a tennis centre, private nine-hole golf course and La Prairie Spa ensure guests feel fully pampered. ❾

Sunset House South Church St ⓣ345/949-7111 or 1-800/854-4767, ⓦwww.sunsethouse.com. This popular full-service dive resort – the only Caymanian-owned hotel in Grand Cayman – includes an underwater photo centre (courses available), oceanside pool and plenty of offshore diving along the ironshore. Hungry divers can refuel at the onsite restaurant, and George Town is a fifteen-minute walk away. ❻

Sunshine Suites West Bay Rd ⓣ345/949-3000, 1-877/786-1110, ⓦwww.sunshinesuites.com. Don't let the location behind a strip mall put you off from this pretty yellow all-suites hotel, with rooms split into sleeping and eating areas, including well-equipped kitchens. There's a pool and open-air bar and grill on site. A dive centre, restaurants and the beach are all within walking distance. Rates include full breakfast. Wireless access costs an extra US$10 per day. ❻

Westin Casuarina Seven Mile Beach ⓣ345/945-3800 or 1-800/WESTIN-1, ⓦwww.westin.com/casuarina. Marble baths and

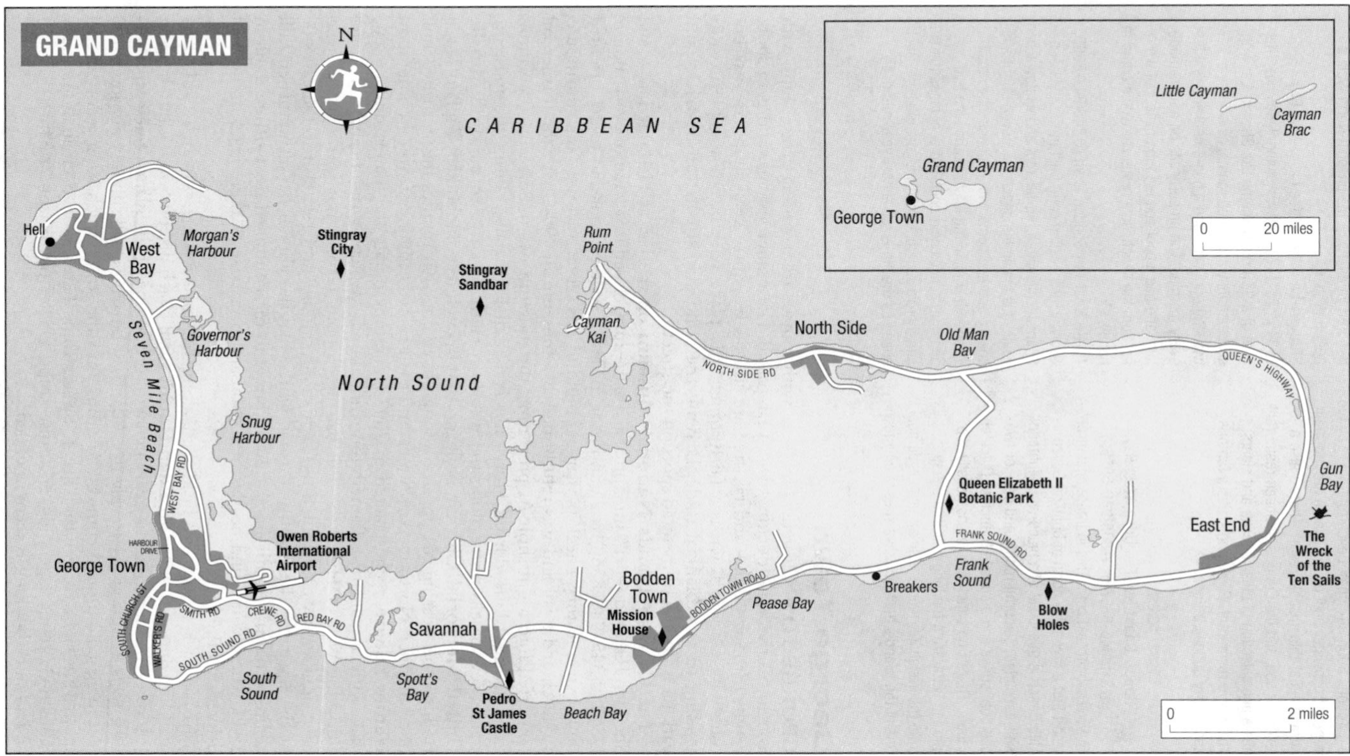
GRAND CAYMAN
N
CARIBBEAN SEA
Little Cayman
Cayman Brac
Grand Cayman
George Town
0 20 miles
Hell
West Bay
Morgan's Harbour
Stingray City
Stingray Sandbar
Rum Point
Cayman Kai
North Side
Old Man Bay
QUEEN'S HIGHWAY
NORTH SIDE RD
Seven Mile Beach
Governor's Harbour
North Sound
Snug Harbour
WEST BAY RD
HARBOUR DRIVE
George Town
Owen Roberts International Airport
SOUTH CHURCH ST
WALKER'S RD
SMITH RD
CREWE RD
RED BAY RD
SOUTH SOUND RD
South Sound
Spott's Bay
Savannah
Pedro St James Castle
Beach Bay
Bodden Town
Mission House
BODDEN TOWN ROAD
Pease Bay
Breakers
Frank Sound
FRANK SOUND RD
Queen Elizabeth II Botanic Park
Blow Holes
East End
Gun Bay
The Wreck of the Ten Sails
0 2 miles

a gorgeous 800ft stretch of beachfront (lined by the largest freshwater pool on the island) are the main attractions at this upscale resort. There's also a luxurious spa, and the Cuban-Caribbean restaurant has a fine selection of cuisine, wine and cigars. The onsite restaurant, *Ferdinand's*, has a famous and hearty Sunday brunch. 9

Outer Districts

Cobalt Coast Sea Fan Drive, West Bay ℡345/946-5656 or 1-888/946-5656, www.cobaltcoast.com. This intimate oceanfront resort just a few miles north of bustling Seven Mile Beach is this jewel of a place with eighteen well-appointed, colourful rooms and one- or two-bedroom suites and an onsite branch of Divetech scuba. There's no beach but you can easily slip into the water from the long pier that extends from the ironshore; there's also an oceanside pool. One of the island's best wall dive sites is only few hundred yards away: the unspoilt North Wall, a 6000ft drop. 6

Shangri-La Sticky Toffee Lane, West Bay ℡345/526-1170, www.shangrilabb.com. This gem of a B&B really seems like Shangri-La, with six beautifully appointed rooms, as well as a two-bedroom suite and a home-cooked breakfast every morning. The property sits on a man-made lake and has a pool and hot tub onsite, but it's far from the beach, so a rental car would come in handy. 5

Turtle Nest Inn Bodden Town ℡345/947-8665, www.turtlenestinn.com. Built in the style of a Spanish villa with a red-tile roof and whitewashed walls, this inn on the beach has seven bright and cheery one-bedrooms with kitchens, one small village-view room (no kitchen) and nine two-bedroom condos next door. The pool faces the sea and there's superb snorkelling just offshore. Book ahead as the inn is full almost year-round. 6

George Town

GEORGE TOWN is generally dense with tourists from visiting cruise ships, with as many as five ships docking daily year-round. The numerous cigar and gem shops – which though duty- and tax-free are still no bargain – keep shoppers busy but otherwise George Town is a fairly quiet little place with businesspeople in suits tending to the financial trade. Driving the congested streets can be tricky and parking is limited to metered spots on the street.

The **Cayman Islands National Museum** on the bay at Harbour Drive and Shedden Rd (Mon–Fri 9am–5pm, Sat 10am–2pm, closed first Mon of every month; US$5; ℡345/949-8368) is a good spot to start a walking tour and to get oriented on Cayman history. The 170-year-old building has served variously as a courthouse, a church and a jail and was refurbished as a museum in 1990, with the former jail converted into a gift shop. At press time, the museum was undergoing renovations from damage done during Hurricane Ivan; call for details. From the museum, walk a few blocks north along the water on Harbour Drive to the small **Elmslie United Memorial Church**, built in 1920 by architect-shipbuilder Captain Rayal Bodden and bearing his signature design: a ceiling that mimics the upturned hull of a schooner. North to Fort Street, and then right heading east, you'll come upon **Heroes Square**, reconstructed in 2003 to commemorate the islands' quincentennial, with a palm-tree framed fountain, murals depicting significant milestones along the Wall of History, and a Wall of Honour recognizing 500 islanders who have significantly contributed to Cayman's development. Cross over to the east side of the square to the **public library**, which like the church has an upturned hull ceiling. Continue south along Edward Street to the columned **post office**, built in 1939, where you'll find nearly three thousand post boxes – there is no home mail delivery on the islands.

To get back to the bay, head west along Cardinal Avenue, which is flanked by sparkling duty-free shops. At **Eden Rock's** small beach just off South Church Street you can rent snorkel/scuba gear and swim out to one of the island's finest **snorkelling** reefs. If you prefer to stay dry, Atlantis submarines will shuttle you down 100 feet in air-conditioned comfort. You can't miss the store, which has a yellow model submarine right on South Church Street. Tours last a little over an hour (daily 8.30am–3.30pm, depending on cruise ships; US$89 per person, ℡345/949-7700) and advance booking is recommended.

Seven Mile Beach and West Bay

Actually only five and a half miles long, **Seven Mile Beach** is a wide, powder-soft stretch of white sand that curls around the west side of the island. The waters are generally calm, warm and crystal-clear owing to a lack of northwest winds. The slope heading out to sea is an easy and gradual one, ideal for swimming or just wading. It's by far the most popular beach around; even so, it never gets towel-to-towel. If you want to slip away from the crowds, walk north to where there are fewer hotels.

Near the beach and worth a visit is the **Butterfly Farm** on Lawrence Boulevard, (daily 8.30am–4.30pm; $US15; ⓣ345/946-3411; ⓦwww.thebutterflyfarm.com) which offers great guided tours of the butterfly habitat, home to colourful, exotic species from around the world. Come early in the morning to see the butterflies emerge from their equally spectacular chrysalises and bring your camera for some great photo ops.

The community of **WEST BAY** begins at the northern edge of Seven Mile Beach and is the second most populated area on the island. Though mostly residential, the **Boatswain's Beach Marine Park** (pronounced Bosun's) on West Bay Rd (daily 8.30am–4.30pm; ⓣ345/949-3894; ⓦwww.boatswainsbeach.ky) is a 23-acre property where guests can see thousands of breeding green sea turtles and pose for a photo with baby turtles. A small percentage of the turtles are raised to meet the local demand for turtle meat but most are bred for research – conservation-minded visitors can sponsor a turtle for release into the wild for a hefty fee. Other than the thrill of seeing so many endangered turtles in one place, the other activities – a salt water snorkelling lagoon, an aviary and a reconstruction of an historic Caymanian street – don't really justify the high entrance fees, US$18 for the turtle farm or US$55 for the whole park. Also in West Bay is the town of **Hell**, named for a jagged patch of uninhabitable ironshore. While scarcely worth the visit, it's popular for the opportunity of sending postcards stamped by the local post office.

The rest of the island

Travelling on from the west end of the island, you'll encounter the districts of Bodden Town, East End and North Side which reveal a fuller picture of life on Grand Cayman.

The first stop of note, eight miles on from George Town in the town of Savannah, is **Pedro St James Castle** (daily 9am–5pm; US$10; ⓣ345/947-3329), not so much a castle but rather a traditional plantation house. The island's oldest stone building (built in 1780), Pedro St James is known as the birthplace of democracy in the Cayman Islands: it was while meeting here in 1831 that Cayman residents decided to hold their first election. In the 1990s the site was painstakingly restored to traditional splendour, including the sprawling grounds, which are full of tropical fruits and native flora. The **visitor centre** was built with a state-of-the-art multimedia theatre, where the story of the castle unfolds in a twenty-five video.

East of the castle is **Bodden Town**, Grand Cayman's original capital (which moved to George Town in the late nineteenth century for its protected harbour). At kitschy **Pirates Cave** (daily 9am–5pm; adults US$8, kids US$5; ⓣ345/947-3122) the property's owners have placed fake treasure and pirate-bedecked mannequins throughout the cavern. Though plans are in the works to fully renovate the exhibit, its current incarnation will probably only entertain the kids in the group. Adding to the atmosphere is the island's oldest **cemetery** just across the road where pirates are rumoured to be buried. Also in Bodden Town is the Mission House (Tues–Sat 9am–5.30pm; CI$5, ⓣ345/947-5805; ⓦwww.nationaltrust.org.ky), a replica of one of Cayman's oldest buildings and home to Presbyterian missionaries in the 1800s. The engaging guided tour takes you through three of the home's rooms and explains many of its odd artefacts.

Next along the south shore road is the tiny community of **Breakers** where a white lighthouse has been transformed into a restaurant, making a lovely stop on the seaside. Just after the lighthouse, the road becomes **Queen's Highway**, off which you can watch plenty of spray from crashing waves and blowholes worn into the ironshore. As the road progresses towards **East End**, look out to sea at the island's easternmost point and you'll see remnants of the **Wreck of the Ten Sails** where ten ships successively crashed into the reef one fateful day in 1794.

The highway loops around East End until heading back west along the northern coast of the island through **North Side**. It dead-ends at **Rum Point**, a favourite stretch of white-sand beach second only to Seven Mile, where you are welcome to use the facilities and snorkel about in the shallow waters. Along with chairs and hammocks, there's a reasonably priced beach bar good for burgers and salads, and Red Sail Sports has watersports equipment for rent.

The return trip to George Town from Rum Point requires backtracking through North Side again but heading south on Frank Sound Road shortcuts the journey. Along the way is a turn-off for the 65-acre **Queen Elizabeth II Botanic Park** (daily April–Sept 9am–6.30pm, Oct–March 9am–5.30pm; last admission one hour before closing; US$10; ☎345/947-9462). Much of the park is a woodland nature preserve where more than half of Cayman's native plants grow naturally, including orchids, palms, mahogany and cacti. Near the entrance to a mile-long walking trail through the preserve you'll pass an enclosure where you can catch a glimpse of the endangered native **blue iguana**, raised at a breeding facility in the grounds. The informative tours of the Blue Iguana Recovery Program, available at 10.30am and 2.30pm Monday through Saturday, are well worthwhile and give patrons a good idea of what the facility is doing to preserve the species. The 30-minute tour costs CI$16 and includes entry to the botanic park. Also in the park is a 3-acre lake, a good place to spot rare aquatic birds like the West Indian whistling duck, and nearby is a 2.5-acre **colour garden**, a series of gardens arranged by colour, and designed to bloom year-long. There's also a traditional Cayman sand garden of medicinal plants and fruit trees on display.

Another great option for nature lovers is the **Mastic Trail**, a wilderness trail winding through the centre of the island that snakes through the largest remaining contiguous area of untouched, old growth dry forest on the island. The two-mile former footpath passes through a variety of habitats, and is administered by the National Trust, which offers a two and a half hour guided walk every Wednesday for CI$20.

Eating and drinking

Of the three Cayman Islands, Grand Cayman has by far the most dining choices with **gourmet options** galore and **international tastes** like Thai, Chinese, Italian and Indian easily found. Most restaurants are on West Bay Road along the Seven Mile Beach corridor. **Local food**, such as rice and peas, jerked meats and fried plantain, is most common on menus in the outer districts.

The island has many well-stocked and conveniently located **supermarkets**, including Foster Food Fair, which carries gourmet and vegetarian products. The self-serve lunch buffet at the **Fort Street Market**, a grocery store in downtown George Town on the corner of Fort and Panton streets (weekdays 7am–6pm), has a fine selection of island dishes prepared in-house; you can have a meal here for under US$10.

Café Mediterraneo Galleria Plaza on West Bay Rd ☎345/949-8669. Portions are large and the wine selection ample at this Italian restaurant, known around town as *Café Med*; the best seats are inside in the plush semi-private booths. Thurs nights are packed for *salsa*, and there is a free lesson at 9pm.

Calypso Grill Morgan's Harbour, West Bay ☎345/949-3948. The waterside setting, lights strung in the trees and brightly coloured interior create a whimsical, charming atmosphere at this fantastic long-time favourite of visitors to the island. The menu favours seafood, with specials like wahoo escovitche (US$10) and ginger tuna US$27) Try one of the bartender's excellent mojitos, and don't miss the sticky toffee pudding for dessert.

Champion House Two 43 Eastern Ave, George Town ☎345/949-7882. Of the two restaurants at this address, be sure to go to *Champion House*

Two at the back (*Champion House One* is a little seedy). *Two* serves fabulous island fare in a comfortable, air-conditioned setting. The inexpensive menu features items like curried goat (US$8), codfish and ackee (US$8.50) (a fruit resembling scrambled egg when prepared).

Coconut Joe's West Bay Rd ☎345/943-5637. An eclectic menu with everything from Tortuga Rum BBQ ribs (US$20) to Japanese rice bowls (US$8). Breakfast is tasty, too, and Starbucks coffee addicts can get their fix here. Come evening, *Coconut Joe's* is hopping, with an outdoor projection-screen TV showing sports nightly, a festive deck and drink specials like the massive Beergarita (a Corona tipped into a 48oz margarita).

Grand Old House South Church St ☎345/949-9333. Outdoor oceanside gazebos provide an elegant backdrop for romantic dinners. The gourmet cuisine is international with a local flair, specializing in seafood. Meals are complemented by a fantastic wine selection and a pianist plays at sundown. Reservations are essential. Mon–Fri 11.45am–2pm, daily 6–10pm.

Heritage Kitchen Boggy Sands Rd, West Bay. This little place offers great local food and a relaxed outdoor setting. Indulge in fish tea (basically a fish soup touted as an aphrodisiac) or one of the freshly fried fish options (CI$12). If you're brave, try one of the home-made hot sauces, made from some of the world's hottest peppers – the habanero and the scotch bonnet. Open Wed, Fri & Sat 5pm–late.

Kaibo 585 Water Cay Rd, Cayman Kai ☎345/947-9975. There's a full-service marina here but don't be put off – no membership is needed at this relaxing beach bar and grill serving burgers, salads and sandwiches at reasonable prices (around US$10); don't miss the signature battered fries. Above the beach bar is The Upstairs, a posher restaurant serving dishes ranging from coconut crusted sea scallops (US$30) to filet mignon ($US38).

Luca Seven Mile Beach ☎345/623-4550. The chic urban interior makes diners feel like they're in a city but the menu keeps the emphasis on fresh, local ingredients, serving plenty of seafood and Italian dishes like pumpkin ravioli with shaved parmigiano ($US19) and spinach gnocchi (US$18).

The Reef Grill at Royal Palms Seven Mile Beach ☎345/945-6358. Especially at weekends the beach bar is a popular spot. For a more formal affair, head to the adjacent restaurant where the best tables are in the outdoor garden setting. Seafood reigns supreme, and the house speciality is coconut-crusted grouper with pineapple salsa and lobster mashed potatoes (US$25).

The Wharf Restaurant and Bar West Bay Rd ☎345/949-2231. Reservations are a must to sit waterside, where you can watch a tarpon feeding nightly at 9pm. Grilled Caribbean spiny lobster in a lemon butter sauce (market) along with basil and pistachio-crusted Chilean sea bass ($US30) are excellent.

Nightlife

It may seem like things are quiet in the evenings on Grand Cayman but that's mainly because venues are spread out – there's no main strip for nightlife. That doesn't mean you won't find a number of fun **outdoor bars** and **dance clubs** if you know where to look, mostly in the Seven Mile Beach area. Friday is the biggest night out – on Saturday, everywhere closes by midnight by law.

Calico Jack's Public Beach, West Bay Rd ☎345/945-7850. The perfect island beach bar, just steps away from the water on a gorgeous stretch of sand with hardly a condo in sight. Live music and dancing on Friday and Saturday nights; also plays host to a rocking full-moon party every month. Come for the sunsets and happy hour from 5–7pm. No cover. Mon–Sat 9am–midnight, Sun 11am–10pm.

The Next Level West Bay Rd ☎345/946-6398. Nightly DJs playing reggae, calypso, hip-hop and house draw locals, expats and tourists alike. A Fri and Sat night dress code means no hats or beach attire. Cover charge from CI$5–20 most nights, sometimes all-you-can-drink. Mon–Fri 10pm–3am, Sat 9pm–midnight.

OBar Queen's Court West Bay Rd ☎345/949-6227. A hot spot for a predominately twenty-something ex pat and tourist crowd, with a plush red interior and a generally packed dance floor – DJs spin music from hip-hop to Top 40 remixes and house. Mon–Fri 10pm–3am.

The Office 99 Shedden Rd, George Town ☎345/945-5212. At this office, ties are left at the bar and games are on TV. The restaurant next door caters free appetizers on Fri evenings, usually gone by about 6.30pm. Live jazz Weds nights from 9pm–12am, karaoke Sat nights. Mon–Fri 10am–1am, Sat 10am–midnight, Sun noon–midnight.

4.2

Cayman Brac

About ninety miles northeast of Grand Cayman, and accessible by a half-hour plane hop, lies tiny **CAYMAN BRAC**, only fourteen square miles and home to around 1800 people. With none of the fast-food outlets or tourist bustle of the larger island, the Brac (as it's colloquially known) offers the chance for an isolated Caribbean vacation; this is where residents of Grand Cayman come to get away from it all.

There's no main town, nor any major developments, but all modern amenities are available, including a few grocery stores, post offices, a bank and a handful of restaurants. Those looking to keep busy come for the supreme **diving**, although growing numbers are also being drawn by land activities like **caving** and **hiking**, enough to keep you occupied for a day or two, and popular here because of the Brac's unique

▲ The endangered Cayman Brac parrot

Hiking the Brac

The **hiking trails** on Cayman Brac are fairly easy to navigate on your own – and the longest is only about three hours round-trip – but for a unique experience and a chance to really learn about the island from an expert, contact District Administration (☎345/948-2222 ext. 4420) to arrange a guide. You'll **need a car** to drive you and your guide around the island, but otherwise – remarkably – there's no cost (tipping is at your discretion), and you'll get taken caving, birdwatching or hiking by a native-Bracker who knows every inch of the island. If that doesn't appeal, you can also get hiking maps from District Administration, the DOT, or from your hotel. Sturdy shoes are essential as many trails weave through sections of sharp ironshore; carry some water and consider a light long-sleeve shirt to reduce scratches from twigs.

There are hundreds of **caves** within the bluff (about 200 people sheltered in them during Ivan), and although many are hidden or difficult to reach, five have been marked by the District Administration agency as having easy accessible entryways and are worth exploring. There will likely be bats dangling from the ceiling; bring a small pen-light if you want a better glimpse. Also gaining popularity here is **rock climbing** on the bluff, but you must be an advanced climber and bring your own equipment, as there are no guides and climbs are rated between 5.8 and 5.12 – if you're not familiar with this scale, don't even consider a climb.

landscape among the three islands. The island is named after the striking limestone bluff ("brac" means "bluff" in Gaelic) which runs along its spine, culminating with great ocean views at its peak of 140 feet on the eastern coast – a perfect place to catch the sunrise. Much of the bluff surface is covered by woodland making it a **birdwatching** haven.

Around the island

The best way to explore the Brac is to hike along one of its numerous **trails**, accessible off the main road and marked by large white and blue Heritage Site signs that designate the name of the trail (see box above). Don't miss the one along Bight Road, which cuts across the bluff from east to west within the **Brac Parrot Reserve**, threading its way through a tropical woodland brimming with native trees, including candlewood and wild fig, plus varieties of cacti and orchids. The path has a few entrance points, one of which leads along a 600ft stretch of wooden boardwalk, a perfect place to watch for the rare, emerald-green Cayman Brac **parrot** which has its nesting colonies here.

Cayman Brac is not known for miles-long strips of sand: the coastline is chiefly ironshore, and the few small beaches, most located on hotel property, have a fair amount of seagrass in their waters. The **public beach** is the best stretch around, and has picnic tables and showers on offer – it's on the same south side as most hotels and just a ten-minute bicycle ride away.

The ironshore does, however, make for superb **snorkelling and diving**. Along with natural formations like Handcuff Reef on the north shore and Radar Reed in Stake Bay, perhaps the most popular site is the wreck of the *Captain Keith Tibbetts*, a Russian destroyer sunk on purpose in 1996 just yards off the northwest coast. The Department of Tourism (☎345/948-1649; Mon–Fri 8.30am–5pm) can suggest additional places to go and give specific directions. The Brac's dive sites are not much more than a ten-minute boat ride away and offer abundant marine life, including eels, lobster, turtles and the occasional octopus, along with walls encrusted with purple sea fans and massive barrel sponges. Note that Bloody Bay Wall off Little Cayman can also be visited from Cayman Brac.

The **Cayman Brac Museum** in Stake Bay (Mon–Fri 9am–noon & 1–4.30pm, Sat 9am–12pm; donation suggested; ☎345/948-2222) was the first museum to

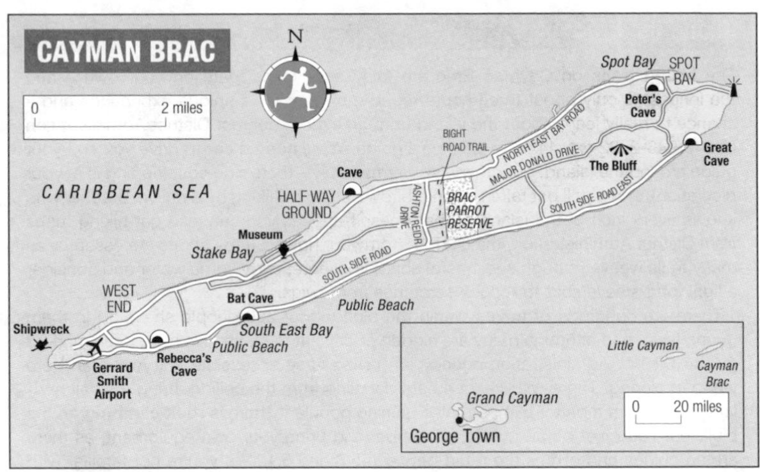

open in the Cayman Islands, in December 1983. Upstairs is an exhibit on the 1932 hurricane that killed more than 100 people on Cayman Brac, with pictures of the event and write-ups by Caymanians who experienced the storm. Also of note is a display on the Caymanian catboat, developed in 1904 on Cayman Brac and used for turtling through the mid-twentieth century.

Practicalities

Flights arrive at **Gerrard Smith International Airport** (☎345/948-1222) on the western tip of the island. You'll probably want to have a **car** to get around, both for exploring the island and for accessing various shore dive and snorkelling spots; the handful of agencies can arrange for complimentary drop-off and pick-up at your hotel or the airport. Rentals start at US$30 a day for an economy car. At US$12.50, **bicycle** rentals are a pleasant alternative.

The Brac doesn't have many restaurants, and you'll probably do the majority of your noshing at your hotel on a meal plan; some accommodation options have use of a kitchen. *Biggie's* (☎345/948-2449) serves salads, pastas and an island buffet lunch; *Aunt Sha's* (☎345/948-1581), just down the road, also focuses on island food like jerked meats and fish. **Dive packages** are the norm (and diving is "valet-style": drop off your gear when you arrive, and it will be cleaned and carried for you throughout your stay), but be sure to ask exactly what's included.

Brac Caribbean & Carib Sands South Side ☎345/948-1121, or 1-866/843-2722, Ⓦwww.866thebrac.com. Two condo complexes on the beach, offering spacious one- to four-bedroom units, a small shared fitness room, a pool on each property and one of the island's few restaurants, *Captain's Table*. Diving is arranged with nearby Reef Divers at *Brac Reef Beach Resort*. 7–8

Brac Reef Beach Resort South Side ☎345/948-1323, Ⓦwww.bracreef.com. Divers love this property for its reasonable rates and knowledgeable dive staff. The poolside bar is popular with locals, and the illuminated dock off the beach attracts sea creatures at night, like tarpon, stingrays and the occasional octopus. A tennis court and the island's only spa (with room for one) are also onsite. The three-night-minimum dive package includes three dives per day, all meals, government tax and service charge at US$638 per night based on double occupancy. 9

La Esperanza Stake Bay ☎345/948-0591, Ⓦwww.laesperanza.net. Located on the island's north side, this property has a handful of small and rustic but clean two- and three- bedroom apartments. There's a grocery, restaurant and bar across the road, but you'll need a car to reach the beach and dive shops. 4

Walton's Mango Manor Stake Bay ⓣ345/948-0518, ⓦwww.waltonsmangomanor.com. A well-run B&B set in landscaped gardens stretching from the bluff to the ocean, where there's a private swimming beach. Nestled among the fruit trees is an intimate synagogue (one of only a handful in the Caribbean), open to all. All five rooms come with private bath; also available is a pretty two-storey beach villa perched right along the sea. Rooms ④, Villa ⑥

4.3

Little Cayman

On string-bean-shaped **LITTLE CAYMAN**, road signs read "iguanas have the right of way", which is fitting for an undeveloped island on which the two thousand or so of these primordial-looking creatures greatly outnumber the people. Although just a few square miles smaller than the Brac, this least developed of the Cayman Islands has barely 125 full-time residents, of whom just one was actually born and raised here, and only a handful are Caymanian. Even more so than Cayman Brac, Little Cayman attracts visitors looking for untrammelled seclusion (Brackers come here on vacation). The island only has one small general store and one à la carte restaurant, and its homes are few and far between.

Those who come tend to either love it or hate it. This is not a lush tropical paradise: the landscape is flat with mostly low-lying shrubs, mangroves and seagrape trees. In the winter, the pond beds of the **marshy interior** dry up and, depending on the prevailing winds, a sulphurous odour sometimes wafts over parts of the island. Most visitors are scuba or wildlife enthusiasts eager to take advantage of a top dive site and an inland nature sanctuary. Since prices here are the highest of the three islands, you may prefer Cayman Brac for a secluded escape. It's less than a ten-minute hop between the two, so if you're intrigued you can easily spend just a day here; **flights** cost about US$50 return. From Grand Cayman, it's a pricier journey at around US$130, but still just forty minutes away. If you'd like a guide, MAM's Island Tours (ⓣ345/926-0104, ⓦwww.mamstour.ky) will pick you up at the airport and take you on a day's tour of the island for around US$50 per person. If you see a handful of people anywhere, consider it crowded.

Around the island

The mangrove-filled wetlands in the centre of the island are home to as many as 200 species of birds, including West Indian whistling-ducks, egrets, frigates and herons. Just a few steps east of the airport is a 1.2 mile-long nature reserve known as **Booby Pond** 20,000 red-footed boobies have a nesting colony – the largest in the Western Hemisphere and a Ramsar site (designating it a wetland of international importance). The **National Trust Visitors Centre** (Mon–Fri 9am–12pm and 2pm–6pm; ⓣ345/948-1107) at the reserve's western tip has a balcony offering panoramic views of the marshy reserve, along with telescopes for close-ups of the birds, which are fairly easy to spot. The little café onsite serves up delicious home-made ice cream.

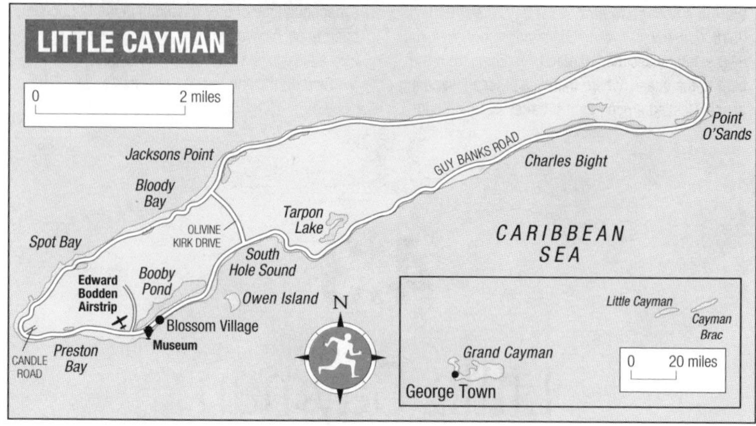

To get up close and personal with animals that won't fly off, head to Candle Road on the southwestern end of the island, a favoured hangout for **West Indian iguanas**, which can grow to be as long as four feet. They tend to roam about in the afternoons and are used to being fed (preferably fruit), but take care as they are wild and can be aggressive; attempts at handfeeding are very unwise – it's best to leave the fruit on the road for the iguana to eat whenever it chooses.

Most resorts in Little Cayman are along the southern shore, which is also where the best **beaches** are found (although they're somewhat narrower and rockier since Hurricane Ivan; the southside took the brunt of the storm). In most spots, even by the resorts, the water isn't especially inviting – it's shallow and the bottom is covered with turtle grass. For the best swimming and snorkelling, visit **Point O' Sands** on the southeastern tip; just stay to the west of the point, as the current is strong at the reef mouth on the eastern side. Or try kayaking (most resorts provide them free of charge for guests) out to what's likely to be your own private island: **Owen Island** off South Hole Sound, a great picnic spot.

Diving and fishing

For divers, Little Cayman is a true gem. Aside from having obvious assets like phenomenal water clarity and abundant marine life, it doesn't get as crowded as the other islands (in part because of stringent marine park restrictions), making dives here all the more special. The famed **Bloody Bay Wall**, a mere ten- to fifteen-minute boat ride from most hotel docks, is hailed as one of the **world's best dive sites**. Like North Wall on Grand Cayman, Bloody Bay features a sheer drop-off plunging 6000ft down into the depths; here, though, conditions are at their most pristine. Groupers as well as seahorses, sharks, eagle rays and elegant arrow crabs are common sights. Interested divers can also tour the Central Caribbean Marine Institute (Ⓣ345/948-1094; Ⓦwww.reefresearch.org; call to arrange) to learn more about the state of the Caribbean's coral reefs and sea life, or participate in the Dive with a Researcher (DWAR) program, which runs six times per year and includes five days of diving with a resident scientist.

Anglers can partake in deep-sea **fishing**, bonefishing on the flats and tarpon fishing at the fifteen-acre **Tarpon Lake** on the south shore. Hotels can arrange for gear and guides through the *Southern Cross Club* (Ⓣ345/948-1099) and *McCoy's Diving and Fishing Lodge* (Ⓣ345/948-0111).

Practicalities

On the southwest end of the island, **Edward Bodden Airstrip** handles incoming flights. The island does not have public transport. There's little need for a **vehicle** but if you're on a day-trip it will make things easier. A short walk from the airport, McLaughlin Rentals (Ⓣ345/948-1000) rents Ford Explorers and the like starting at US$100 per day – you can easily drive around the island in an hour. Scooters are also available from either McLaughlin or Scooten Scooters (half-day US$32, full day US$45; Ⓣ345/916-4971). **Bicycles**, available at most properties, are the best (and most environmentally friendly) way to get around.

Every **hotel** on Little Cayman has a **meal plan**, but cottages and condos with kitchens are available as well. Non-diver options are always available, but since dive packages are the norm, rates listed here – all based on double occupancy – include dives as specified; multi-night packages are usually cheaper. Unlike most all-inclusives, many places here have fewer than twenty rooms, and can feel quite cosy.

Little Cayman Beach Resort Blossom Village Ⓣ345/948-1033 or 1-800/327-3835, Ⓦwww.littlecayman.com. The island's largest hotel, with forty rooms, spa, dive and photo shop, tennis court and fitness room. Nearby sister properties *Conch Club Condos* and *The Club* have rather luxurious one-, two- and three-bedroom condos available, most right on the beach. The three-night-minimum dive package includes five dives, all meals, government tax and service charge at US$650 per night; condos start at US$235. 6–9

Paradise Villas Blossom Village Ⓣ345/948-0001 or 1-877/322-9626, Ⓦwww.paradisevillas.com. Perhaps the best buy on the island for non-divers: twelve simple ocean-front one-bedroom villas, each with patio, kitchenette, a/c and cable TV. There's a pool on site, along with the island's only à la carte restaurant, The Hungry Iguana, should you prefer not to cook. Dives available with Conch Club Divers at Little Cayman Beach Resort. 6

Pirates Point Resort Preston Bay Ⓣ345/948-1010, Ⓦwww.piratespointresort.com. The island's finest chef keeps the repeat guest rate high at this well-run and informal resort, with touches like guests' inventive artwork made from materials found on the beach during their stay, and the island's biggest pool. Ten bungalow rooms are clustered around the property; those seaside are the most appealing. Rates, including two-tank computer dives daily, all meals and alcoholic beverages, start at US$580. 9

Southern Cross Club Blossom Village Ⓣ345/948-1099 or 1-800/899-2582, Ⓦwww.southerncrossclub.com. A small, charming full-service diving and fishing resort comprising eight pretty, pastel cinderblock cottages dotted along a beautiful 900ft stretch of beach; there's also a small pool, alfresco bar and intimate dining room. Two-night minimum stay for divers at US$915 per night includes three-tank dives daily, service charge, government tax and all meals. 9

5

Jamaica

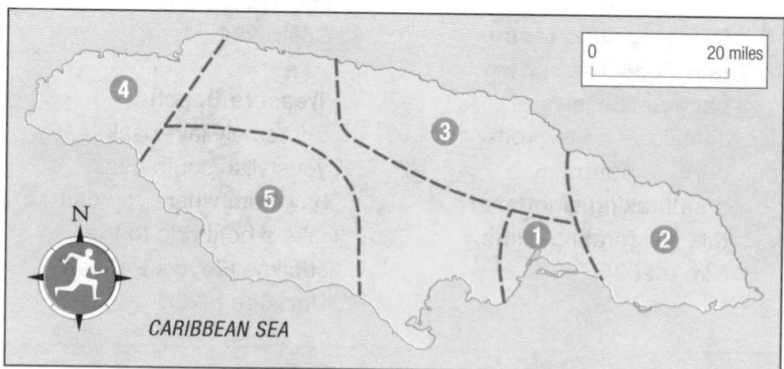

Jamaica highlights

* **Jamaican nightlife** Whether it's reggae icons singing under the stars or a steamy nightclub session, Jamaican nightlife is unmissable. See p.253

* **Hellshire beach on Sundays** Best visited on Sunday when the beach comes alive with booming sound systems, crowds of swimmers and sizzling grills. See p.257

* **Climbing Blue Mountain Peak** The superb panoramic views of Jamaica's coast from north to south are a breathtaking sight after this invigorating climb. See p.262

* **Frenchman's Cove and Blue Lagoon, Portland** Take in the cove's soft white sand, warm waters and fabulous reef or dip into the nearby lagoon. See p.268

* **West End sunset, Negril** With a string of excellent bars to choose from, Jamaica's western tip is the best place to watch the sun go down with a cocktail in hand. See p.294

* **Treasure Beach** Supremely laid-back yet stylish south coast bay, from where you can take a boat ride to the sublime **Floyd's Pelican Bar**. See p.298

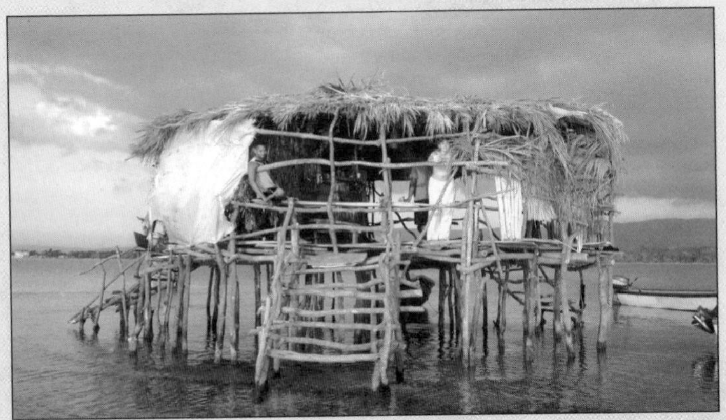

▲ Floyd's Pelican Bar

Introduction and basics

Rightly famous for its beaches and music, beautiful, brash Jamaica is much more besides. The island has plenty of white sand, turquoise sea and swaying palm trees but there are also spectacular mountains and rivers, tumbling waterfalls and cactus-strewn savanna plains. Far more than just a resort, the island also boasts captivating towns and cities such as sprawling Kingston, which inspired the music of Bob Marley and countless other reggae stars.

Jamaica is a country with a swagger in its step – proud of its history, sporting success and musical genius – but also with a weight upon its shoulders. The island faces the familiar problems of a developing country, including dramatic inequality of wealth and social tensions that occasionally spill over into localized violence and worldwide headlines. As a result Jamaicans are as renowned for being sharp, sassy and straight-talking as they are for being laid-back and hip. People don't beat around the bush here, sometimes making them appear rude or uncompromising. Particularly around the big resorts, this directness sometimes is taken to extremes, with solicitations from vendors and hustlers frequent.

But there's no reason to be put off. As a foreign visitor, the chances of encountering trouble are minuscule, and the Jamaican authorities have spent millions making sure the island treats its tourists right. As the birthplace of the "all-inclusive" hotel, Jamaica is well suited to those travellers who want to head straight from plane to beach, never leaving their hotel compound. But to get any sense of the country at all, you'll need to do some exploring. It's undoubtedly worthwhile, as this is an island packed with first-class attractions, oozing with character and rich with a musical and cultural heritage; if you're a reggae fan, you're in heaven.

Where to go

Most of Jamaica's tourist business is concentrated in the resorts of **Montego Bay**, **Ocho Rios** and **Negril**, which together attract hundreds of thousands of visitors every year. Montego Bay (or MoBay, as it's known) is a busy, commercial city with hotels lined up along its lively main strip, a stone's throw from a couple of great beaches. There's a large entertainment scene, especially during the annual August **Reggae Sumfest** festival. To the west is Negril, its low-rise hotels slung along seven miles of fantastic white sand and two miles of dramatic cliffs. It's younger, more laid-back and has a long-standing reputation for hedonism that still carries a hint of the truth. East of MoBay, and the least remarkable of the big three, Ocho Rios embodies high-impact tourism – purpose-built in the 1960s to provide the ultimate package of sun, sand and sea. It's not an overly attractive place, and the beaches don't compare favourably with Negril and MoBay, but its tourist infrastructure is undeniably strong, and nearby are some of Jamaica's leading attractions, including the famous **Dunn's River waterfall**.

Jamaica's quieter east and south coasts offer a far less packaged experience. In the east, lush, sleepy **Port Antonio** and its increasingly popular neighbour, **Long Bay**, provide gateways to some of Jamaica's greatest natural attractions like the cascading waterfall at Reach. The south coast offers different pleasures, from gentle beach action at easy-going **Treasure Beach** – the perfect base from which to explore area delights such as the YS waterfalls – to boat safaris in search of local wildlife on the Black River.

Last, but in no way least, **Kingston** is the true heart of Jamaica, a thrilling place, pulsating with energy and spirit, that is home to more than a third of the island's 2.5 million people. This is not just the nation's political capital but the focus of its art, theatre and music scenes, with top-class hotels, restaurants and shopping, a clubbing scene that is second to none and legendary fried fish on offer at the fabulous **Hellshire beach**. A stunning backdrop to the city, the cool, coffee tree-smothered **Blue Mountains** offer

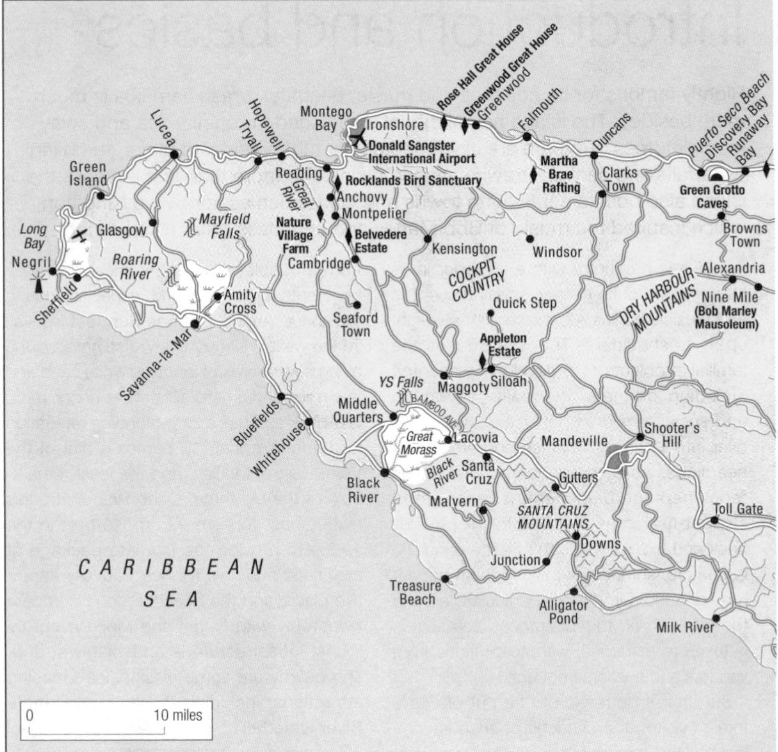

plenty of hiking possibilities, while the nearby fishing village of **Port Royal**, once a pirate refuge, provides historic diversion.

When to go

Jamaica's tropical climate is at its best during the peak **mid-December to mid-April** tourist season, when rainfall is lowest and the heat is tempered by cooling trade winds; it can also get quite chilly at night at this time, so pack a sweater or light jacket. Things get noticeably hotter during the **summer**, and particularly in September and October the humidity can become oppressive. September is also the most threatening month of the annual **hurricane season**, which runs officially from June 1 to October 31; however, on average, the big blows only hit about once a decade.

Prices and **crowds** at the attractions and beaches peak during high season. Outside this period it's quieter everywhere, and though the main resorts throb with life pretty much year-round, quieter areas like Port Antonio and Treasure Beach can feel a little lifeless. The good news is that in the off-season hotel prices fall by up to 25 percent and bargains are available in every field of activity.

Getting there

Most airlines fly into Donald Sangster Airport in **Montego Bay**. Many also land at Norman Manley in **Kingston**, which is more convenient if you're heading for Port Antonio, Ocho Rios or the Blue Mountains. For information on transportation to and from each airport, see p.282 and p.247, respectively.

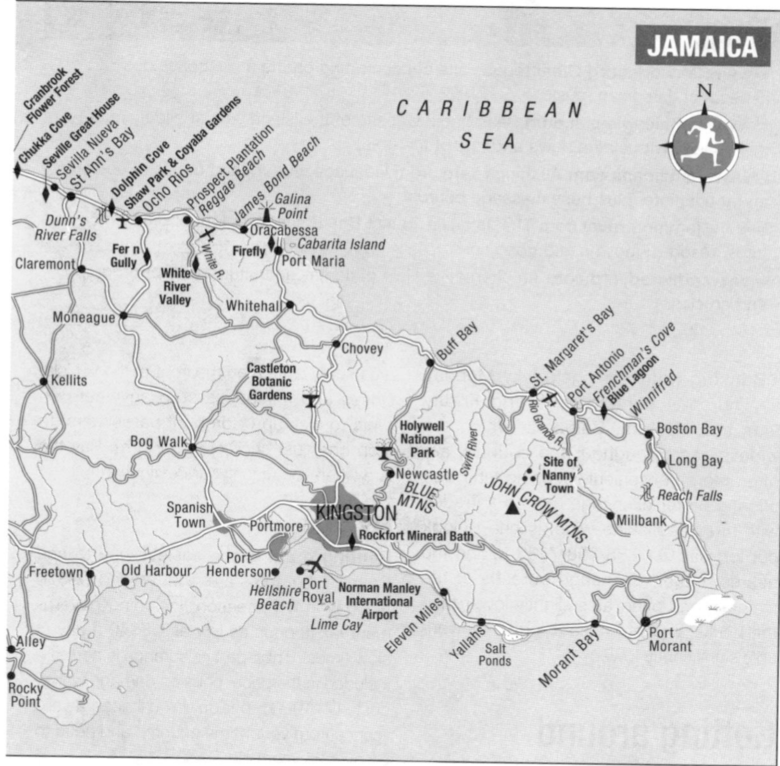

Information

Before you leave home, check out the website of the **Jamaica Tourist Board** (JTB), which has information on the main tourist attractions, schedules of events and accommodation listings. Once in Jamaica, you can pick up glossy brochures and a useful **map** of the island from JTB desks at the Kingston and Montego Bay airports, as well as JTB offices in those cities. You can also pick up also visitor-oriented publications such as *Discover Jamaica* and the *Jamaica Tourist* free newspaper at hotels and attractions. Special events are advertised on the radio (particularly Irie FM on 105.5 and 107.7 FM).

Money and costs

Jamaica's unit of currency is the **Jamaican dollar** (J$), divided into 100 cents. It comes in bills of J$1000, J$500, J$100, J$50 and J$20, and coins of J$20, J$10 and J$5. It's worth keeping a sharp eye on J$100 and J$1000 bills, which look alarmingly similar. At the time of writing the **rate of exchange** is roughly J$72 to US$1. Prices for tourist-oriented goods and services are often quoted in US$.

Accommodation is likely to be your major expense on the island, although extremely basic rooms can be found for as little as US$30. Expect to pay US$70–100 for a room with air-conditioning and cable TV. Accommodation aside, if you travel around by bus or shared taxi and get your food from markets and the cheaper cafés and roadside stalls, you can just about survive on a daily budget of around US$40 per day. Upgrading to one decent meal out, the occasional taxi and a bit of evening entertainment, expect to spend a more realistic US$50–70; after that, the sky's the limit.

Websites

ⓦ **www.jahworks.org** Great reggae site concentrating on the more conscious aspects of Jamaican music.

ⓦ **www.jamaicagleaner.com** Searchable website of the island's most widely read daily paper, with all the news and lots of features.

ⓦ **www.jamaicans.com** All things Yard, from language, culture and music to cookery and tourist info, plus busy message boards.

ⓦ **www.jamaicatravel.com** The Jamaica Tourist Board site, with lots of pretty pictures, resort rundowns and good links.

ⓦ **www.afflictedyard.com** An alternative view of Jamaican culture, with photography and articles.

Banking hours are generally Monday to Thursday 9am to 2pm and Friday 9am to 3 or 4pm. Cambios, which are widespread throughout the country, are often more convenient, opening later and offering better exchange rates. FX Trader, with branches island-wide, is one to look out for; call ⓣ1-888/398-7233 to find the nearest outlet. Exchange bureaus at the main airports offer rates slightly lower than the banks, and at hotels the rate is invariably significantly lower.

Getting around

Buses and minibuses are inexpensive if uncomfortable. Renting a car offers maximum independence but will eat heavily into your budget; if you just want to make the odd excursion or short trip, it's cheaper to take a taxi or hire a private driver.

By bus

Jamaica's **buses** (privately owned minibuses and, in Kingston and Montego Bay, government-owned single-decker buses) can be a little disquieting: timetables are nonexistent outside Kingston, drivers can show little interest in the rules of the road and passengers are often squeezed in with scant regard for comfort.

On the other hand, public transport is a great way to meet people, and it's also absurdly **cheap** – about J$100 per 50 miles for a bus and J$250 per fifty miles for minibuses. Each town has a bus terminal of sorts, often near the market; destinations are usually written on the front of the vehicle. Buses and minibuses stop anywhere en route to pick up or drop off passengers; to stop one, just stick out your arm. Pay the fare when you reach your destination.

By car

Renting a car is the easiest way to see Jamaica, but rates are high, around US$70 per day in high season, including government tax (though as low as US$40 a day at slow times). Third-party insurance is normally included in the price; collision damage waiver costs US$12–15 per day. You'll need a valid licence from your home country, and need to be over 25 years old.

There are **rental companies** all over the island. Further details are within the chapter but Kingston, Montego Bay and Ocho Rios have the best selection. Reliable operators include Island (ⓣ929 5875, ⓦwww.islandcarrentals.com), Budget (ⓣ868/952-3838, ⓦwww.budgetjamaica.com), and Thrifty (ⓣ868/952-5825, ⓦwww.thrifty.com).

Driving in Jamaica is on the left and (unless otherwise specified, as on the new highway along the south coast from Kingston) speed limits are set at 30mph/50kph in towns and minor roads and 50mph/80kph on highways. Roadside speeding checks by way of radar gun are increasingly frequent, and speeding tickets extortionate; the safest bet is to always stick to 30mph/50kph unless you seen a sign indicating otherwise. Wearing front seatbelts is mandatory, and police frequently levy fines on those who don't wear them.

By taxi

Taxis in Jamaica carry red number-plates with "PP" or "PPV"; make sure to use only official cars. The Jamaican Union of Travellers Association (JUTA; ⓣ868/927-4534, 926-1537 or 952-0623) are a local taxi association which has drivers island-wide.

On the whole, **fares** are hefty – around US$25 for ten miles, and you'll always pay a little more if you take a taxi affiliated with a hotel. Always establish the fare before you get in (or over the phone if you call for one), and don't be afraid to negotiate.

Shared or "route" taxis are usually crammed with as many passengers as the driver/owner can fit in, and operate on short set routes around the main towns, picking up and dropping off people anywhere along the way. Prices are a little more than bus fares.

By motorbike

Renting a **motorbike** or **scooter** can be an exhilarating way to tour the island. Outlets abound in the main resorts, and at US$35–50 per day, prices are very reasonable. Though in theory you'll need to show a regular driving licence, these are rarely asked for. Under Jamaican law, all motorcycle riders must wear helmets.

Accommodation

Even though Jamaica has a staggering amount of **accommodation** options, it's rare to find anywhere to stay for less than US$30 per night in the large resort areas, and you usually need to pay more than twice that for a place with reasonable security and comfort. The island has some of the world's finest luxury hotels, and there are plenty of options in the middle.

It is always worth **haggling** over the price of a room. Even in high season, a lot of hotels have surplus capacity, and in low season you have even more leverage. Prices in the resort areas tend to be more seasonal than elsewhere; in this chapter rates are for the low season (mid-April to mid-Dec) or most of the year.

Throughout Jamaica, hundreds of **villas** are available for rent, ranging from small beachside chalets to grand mansions. JAVA, the Jamaica Association of Villas and Apartments (ⓣ868/974-2508, ⓦwww.villasinjamaica.com), represents scores of villas island-wide.

Food and drink

From fiery jerk meat to inventive seafood dishes and ubiquitous rice and peas, Jamaican cuisine is deliciously varied, and the Rasta preference for natural cooking means you can get good vegetarian food fairly easily. Snacking is excellent, too, with beef, vegetable or chicken patties the staple fare, and you'll find a vast selection of fresh fruit and vegetables.

The classic – and addictive – Jamaican **breakfast** is ackee and saltfish. The soft yellow flesh of the ackee fruit is fried with onions, sweet and hot peppers, fresh tomatoes and boiled, flaked salted cod. It's served with the delicious spinach-like callaloo, boiled green bananas and fried or boiled dumplings.

At most of Jamaica's cheaper restaurants and hotels, chicken and fish are the mainstays of **lunch** and **dinner**. Chicken is typically fried in a seasoned batter, jerked or curried, while fish can be grilled, steamed with okra and pimento pods, brown-stewed in a tasty sauce or "escovitched" – fried and served in a spicy sauce of onions, hot peppers and vinegar. "**Jerking**" is the island's most distinctive cooking style. Meat – usually chicken or pork, but occasionally sausage, fish and lobster – is seasoned with pimento, hot peppers, cinnamon and nutmeg, and then grilled slowly, often for hours, over a fire of pimento wood and under a cover of wooden slats or corrugated zinc sheets in a customized oil drum. The result is smoky and utterly delicious

Rice (cooked with coconut, spices and red kidney beans) and peas is the accompaniment to most meals, though you'll sometimes get bammy (a substantial bread made from cassava flour), festival (a light, sweet, fried dumpling), sweet or regular potatoes (the latter known as Irish potatoes), yam, dasheen (like yam, but chewier), or dumplings (fried or boiled).

Jamaica's **water** is safe to drink, and locally bottled spring water is widely available. For a tasty nonalcoholic drink, look no further than the roadside piles of coconuts in every town and village, often advertised with a sign saying "ice-cold jelly"– local vendors will open and serve your coconut to you. **Soft drinks** include Ting (a refreshing sparkling grapefruit drink), Malta (a fortifying malt drink), throat-tingling ginger beers and fresh limeade. Fresh natural **juices** – tamarind, June plum, guava, soursop and cucumber – are always delicious, if occasionally over-sweet. Jamaican Blue Mountain **coffee** is among the best and most expensive in the world, though the other local brews, such as High Mountain, Low Mountain or Mountain Blend, are also good.

The national **beer** is the excellent Red Stripe. Wray and Nephew make the classic white overproof **rum** – it's cheap, extremely potent, available everywhere and best knocked back mixed with Ting. If you're after taste rather than effect, try gold rums such as Appleton Special or Myers, and the older, aged varieties such as Appleton Estate twelve-year-old.

Mail and communications

Though fairly efficient, Jamaica's **telephone system** is expensive for overseas calls; local calls are far cheaper, but watch out for the shocking surcharges imposed by most hotels. You can bypass the high charges by using a locally available international calling card. The **mail** service is less dependable. **Internet** access is available in all of the major resorts for anything from US$2 to US$6 for half an hour.

Phone booths accept phonecards only, available from hotels, post offices and gift shops, where you can also buy Worldtalk calling card to make cheap international calls from any land line (including hotel phones). Most European **mobile phones** will work in Jamaica,, but unless they're tri-band, US phones won't. Local Digicel SIM cards are widely available; you add credit by way of the pay-as-you-go "Flex" system.

The **country code** for Jamaica is ⓣ876. For domestic and international **directory assistance**, phone ⓣ114.

Opening hours, festivals and holidays

Business hours for shops, banks and post offices are normally 8.30am to 4.30/5pm Monday to Saturday, although some shops and offices close at noon on Saturdays. Museums normally close for one day a week, either Sunday or Monday.

Most special events are timed to coincide with the winter tourist season. The main exceptions are Montego Bay's **Reggae Sumfest** in August and spring break – roughly in March and April – when young American students take over the big resorts for a fortnight of raucous, beer-fuelled cavorting. April is **Carnival** time and, though not on the same scale as Trinidad's, it is an increasingly popular event. **Emancipation Day** and **Independence Day** celebrations – concerts, dance and theatre performances and parades – are held in late July to early August; contact the Jamaica Tourist Board for details. The JTB's annual **calendar of events** is posted on the website (see p.240).

Sports and outdoor activities

Sport is a Jamaican obsession – hardly surprising in a country that has produced so many world-class athletes. Cricket is the national game, and bringing it up in conversation is a sure-fire icebreaker. The atmosphere at matches is very Jamaican – thumping reggae between overs and vendors hawking jerk chicken and Red Stripe. You'll come upon cricket pitches throughout the island, and you should try to attend a match; visit ⓦwww.windiescricket.com for schedules.

Scuba diving and **snorkelling** are concentrated on the north coast between Negril and Ocho Rios. The state of the reefs varies but there are some gorgeous sites very close to shore. The resort areas are packed with operators offering dive and snorkelling excursions (details within the chapter).

Jamaica boasts no fewer than thirteen **golf** courses, from the magnificent championship Tryall course near Montego Bay to less challenging nine-hole links in Mandeville. All are open to the public, except during tournaments, and green fees vary from US$10 to US$100 in winter, less in summer. Visit Ⓦwww.jamaicagolfassiciation.com for details.

Crime and safety

While Jamaica's murder rate is undeniably high – the average is about a thousand per year – the JTB is keen to stress that you are more likely to be mugged in New York than Montego Bay. Nonetheless, robberies, assaults and other **crimes** against tourists occasionally occur, and it's wise to apply the precautions you'd take in any foreign city.

Hustling can be irritating. Especially in Montego Bay and Negril, young hopefuls aggressively (or humorously) accost foreigners in the street with offers of transport, ganja, aloe massages, hair-braiding and crafts. While an inevitable few street touts see tourists as easy prey for exploitation, most are just trying to make a living in an economically deprived country. Best advice is to keep things in perspective, employ a dash of humour and keep your valuables out of sight.

Though tourism officials are loath to acknowledge it, many people come to Jamaica in search of what aficionados agree is some of the finest **marijuana** in the world, so expect to be offered ganja in the tourist areas; if you're not interested, calmly and firmly refuse. Bear in mind that the possession, use, export or attempted smuggling of any quantity of ganja is against the law in Jamaica and carries stiff penalties.

The **emergency number** for the Jamaican police is Ⓣ119.

History

Jamaica's first inhabitants were Taíno (also called Arawak) Indians, who arrived from South America around 900 AD and led a simple life of farming and fishing until the arrival in 1494 of Columbus, who claimed the island for Spain. Spanish settlement began in 1510, first at Sevilla Nueva on the north coast and then at the site of today's Spanish Town, just northwest of Kingston.

Spanish Town was completely sacked by the **British** in 1596, and again in 1643. In 1655, fifteen British ships, having failed in their assault on the island of Hispaniola, captured Spanish Town but didn't successfully defeat the Spanish until five years later. Before fleeing for Cuba, the Spanish freed and armed their slaves, most of whom escaped to the mountainous interior. The **Maroons**, as they were called, later waged a successful guerrilla war against the British.

Under British rule, new settlers were gifted land and established vast **sugar cane** plantations; in the eighteenth century, the island was the world's biggest producer of sugar. The planters amassed extraordinary fortunes, but their wealth was predicated upon the appalling inhumanity of **slavery**.

Despite heavy opposition from a West Indian lobby desperate to protect its riches, pressure from the Church of England finally brought about the **abolition of slavery** in 1834. Across the country, missionaries set up "free villages", buying land, subdividing it and either selling or donating it to former slaves. Meanwhile, planters found another source of cheap labour by importing 35,000 indentured labourers from India in the 1830s.

Despite an economic downturn in the nineteenth century in the aftermath of abolition and the introduction of free trade in sugar, the early twentieth century saw considerable economic prosperity. Inevitably, though, most of the new wealth bypassed the black masses, and serious poverty remained throughout the island.

By the 1930s, as the **Great Depression** took hold worldwide, unemployment spiralled and riots and strikes became commonplace. **Alexander Bustamante** founded the first trade union in the Caribbean in 1938 – the Bustamante Industrial Trade Union (BITU). An associated political party was born too, with the foundation of the **People's National Party** (PNP) by the lawyer Norman Manley. Both events boosted Jamaican nationalism, already stirred by the campaigning of black-consciousness leader **Marcus Garvey** during the 1920s and early 1930s.

After serving as a major Allied base during World War II, Jamaica experienced new-found prosperity in the late 1940s, thanks to early **tourism** and the first **bauxite** exports. In 1944, a new constitution introduced universal adult suffrage, and first elections for a government that would work in conjunction with the British-appointed governor were held. Bustamante's newly formed **Jamaica Labour Party** (JLP) won, and gradually the island's two political parties drifted in the different ideological directions which they loosely pursue to this day, with the JLP adopting a basic liberal capitalist philosophy, and the PNP leaning towards democratic socialism.

On August 6, 1962, Jamaica became an **independent state** within the British Commonwealth, with Bustamante as its first prime minister presiding over a newly prosperous Jamaica. Ten years later, the JLP were ousted by the PNP under the charismatic leadership of **Michael Manley**, who set out to improve the conditions of the black majority via reforms such as a minimum wage and increased funding for education and health care sectors.

The bauxite companies whose taxes were funding the social programmes promptly scaled down their Jamaican operations, and economic decline ensued, compounded by the 1973–1974 **oil crisis**. Manley sought to promote a greater degree of self-sufficiency, rejecting closer ties with the US in favour of an alignment with communist Cuba. US reaction was furious; economic sanctions were applied and it became increasingly difficult for Jamaica to attract foreign investment.

Politics became ever-more polarized during the Manley years, and the 1976 election – won by the PNP again – saw a disturbing increase in **political violence**, particularly in the ghettos of Kingston. Violence flared again during the 1980 election campaign, with hundreds of people killed in shoot-outs and open gang warfare. Amid the carnage, Jamaican voters turned to the JLP. In turn, the JLP turned to the US, realigning the island with the US by way of signing up for American economic initiatives; nonetheless, they were still obliged to continue the cutback of government services begun under the PNP. The JLP's honeymoon with the Jamaican people proved short-lived; in 1989, Michael Manley and the PNP were returned to office. Ill health forced Manley's resignation in 1992; his successor, **P.J. Patterson**, became the first black man to become Jamaica's prime minister. After wins in the 1993, 1997 and 2003 polls, Patterson retired in 2006, with Portia Simpson Miller becoming Jamaica's first female Prime Minister; she was ousted by the JLP's Bruce Golding in 2007.

Tourism, bauxite and agriculture remain the mainstays of the Jamaican economy but the island carries a huge burden of **debt** to foreign banks, and much of the foreign currency earned is required to repay interest and capital on that debt. Consequently, education, roads and public transport have suffered, and the lot of the average Jamaican remains hard. **Crime** is the key concern. Kingston's garrison communities are ruled by the whims of drug dons rather than by political allegiances, and gun battles occur far too frequently. Despite these problems, there remains much **positive** energy. Whatever the challenges, it seems hard to quench the island's spirit, and Jamaica's future, on balance, seems fairly bright.

Music

Close your eyes practically anywhere in Jamaica and you'll hear music. Radios blare on the street, buses pump out nonstop dancehall and every Saturday night the bass of countless sound-system parties wafts through the air. Music is a serious business here, generating an average of a hundred record releases per week and influencing every aspect of Jamaican culture from dress to speech to attitude. Reggae and DJ-based dancehall dominate, but Jamaicans are catholic in their musical tastes: R&B, hip-hop, jazz, rock 'n' roll, gospel and the ubiquitous country and western are popular.

Jamaica's music scene first came to international attention in the late 1950s with **ska**, the staccato, guitar-and-trumpet-led sound heard in Millie Small's smash hit *My Boy Lollipop* and Desmond Dekker and the Aces' *007 (Shanty Town)*. By the mid-1960s, ska had given way to the slowed-down and more melodic **rocksteady** sound. Rocksteady didn't carry the swing for very long, and by the late 1960s it was superseded by the tighter guitars, heavier bass and sinuous rhythm of **reggae**. Bob Marley's lyrics, drawn from the tenets of Rastafari, emphasized repatriation, black history, black pride and self-determination. Reggae became full-fledged protest music – anathema to the establishment, which banned it wherever possible.

The 1970s stand out as the classic period of **roots reggae**. But while Burning Spear was singing *Marcus Garvey* and *Slavery Days*, the era also offered a sweeter side: the angelic crooning of more mainstream artists like Dennis Brown or Gregory Isaacs found an eager audience, their style becoming known as **lovers' rock**. As the 1970s wore on, studio technology became more sophisticated and producers began manipulating their equipment to produce **dub** – some of the most arresting and penetrating music ever to emerge from Jamaica. With a remarkable level of inventiveness and often limited means, dub pioneers King Tubby, Prince Jammy and Scientist brought reggae back to basics, stripping down songs so that only bass, drums and inflections of tone remained. Snippets of the original vocals were then mixed in alongside sound effects (dog barks, gunshots). Before long, scores of DJs clamoured to produce dub voice-overs. The craft was mastered by U-Roy, who released talk-based singles to great success throughout the 1970s.

As the violent elections of 1976 and 1980 saw the pressure in Kingston building up, the sound systems multiplied and the DJs "chatted" on the mike about the times, analysing the position of the ghetto youth in Jamaica. But reggae struggled to find direction and purpose after the 1981 death of **Bob Marley**; his legacy of cultural consciousness began to seem less relevant to the ghetto world of cocaine-running and political warfare.

Meanwhile the lewd approach and overtly sexual lyrics – or "slackness" – of DJs such as Yellowman became hugely popular, leading to the rise of **dancehall**, a two-chord barrage of raw drum and bass and shouted patois lyrics. Dancehall is now the most popular musical form in Jamaica; big names include Beenie Man, Bounty Killer, Lady Saw, Elephant Man and Movado, while acts like Sean Paul have made it to the international stage.

Dancehall, though, isn't to everyone's taste, and the battle between cultural and slackness artists continues. The culturally conscious lyrics and staunch Rastafarian stance of the late Garnet Silk, who burst on the scene in the mid-1990s, led the way for artists such as Capleton, Sizzla and Luciano, while singers such as Beres Hammond and Ritchie Spice continue to release wonderful reggae tunes.

5.1

Kingston and around

Fast, furious and fascinating, **KINGSTON** is unlike anywhere else in the Caribbean. With a population fast approaching one million, the city seethes with life, noise and activity; it's a side of Jamaica that couldn't be more different from the resorts. In addition to being the seat of government and the island's administrative centre, Kingston is Jamaica's **cultural heart**, the city that spawned Bob Marley, Buju Banton, Beenie Man and countless other reggae stars.

Practically all of the Kingston's violent **crime** is confined to the ghettos, which are not places for casual sightseeing and by avoiding them, you're no more at risk in Kingston than in any other big city. Take the usual precautions – take cabs after dark, keep jewellery and valuables out of sight – and you're unlikely to run into any problems. You'll find that not only is it easy to steer clear of the troubled areas, but that there's little of the persistent **harassment** that bedevils parts of the north coast.

The city's handful of interesting museums, galleries and the botanical gardens can easily fill a couple of days of sightseeing; the island's best clubs, theatres and some great restaurants will take care of the evenings. In addition to the lovely Blue Mountains, the surrounding area is littered with historic sites, such as the forts of the English buccaneers in atmospheric **Port Royal**, while white-sand **Hellshire** and **Lime Cay beaches** are the perfect places for a dip in the ocean.

Some history

Kingston saw little development until 1692 when thousands fled a violent **earthquake** that devastated Port Royal. Kingston's population was further expanded in 1703, when more Port Royalists decamped to the other side of the harbour after a devastating **fire**. In 1872, when Kingston replaced Spanish Town as Jamaica's capital, many wealthy families were already moving beyond the original town boundaries to the areas that today comprise **uptown** Kingston. Meanwhile the less affluent, including a growing tide of former slaves, huddled downtown and in the **shanty towns** that began to spring up on the outskirts of old Kingston, particularly west of the city.

Jamaica's turn-of-the-twentieth-century boom, engineered by tourism and agriculture, largely bypassed Kingston's poor. The **downtown** area was neglected by the government and continued to deteriorate; the effects of a catastrophic earthquake in 1907 were felt most fiercely by the island's poor. Those who could afford to continued to move out, leaving behind an increasingly destitute population that proved fertile recruitment ground for the **Rastafari** movement during the 1920s and 1930s. Since then the faith, with its message of love, peace and rebellion against the "Babylon system" of the establishment, has attracted a significant following in Jamaica and the wider Caribbean, and its tenets have formed the basis of many a classic reggae tune.

In the 1960s, efforts were made to give the old downtown area a face-lift. Redevelopment of the waterfront resulted in a much-needed expansion of the city's **port facility** and a smartening up of the harbour area, sparking a mini **tourist boom**. But the redevelopment of downtown was only cosmetic. Crime soon proliferated, and tourists headed for the new beach resorts on the island's north coast as the city sank into a quagmire of unemployment, poverty and crime. Today there are hints that the capital's fortunes may be turning, with some serious attempts to tackle crime and improve economic fortunes but Kingston remains a divided city.

Arrival and information

All of Kingston's international and some domestic flights land at **Norman Manley International Airport** (Ⓣ876/924-8546 or 8452, Ⓦwww.manley-airport.com.jm) on the Palisadoes – the strip of land that frames Kingston Harbour southeast of the city. A number of **car rental** firms have desks in the arrivals area; others will meet you there on request.

City **bus** #98 runs from just outside the arrivals area to downtown roughly every half-hour (around J$50). Downtown, however, is not a good place for a suitcase-toting tourist, and you're far better off opting for a **cab** – the fare for the thirty-minute journey to New Kingston is US$20–25, and there are plenty of JUTA drivers around. You can **change money** in the arrivals lounge.

The main office of the **Jamaica Tourist Board** is slap in the middle of New Kingston at 64 Knutsford Blvd (Mon–Fri 9am–4.30pm; Ⓣ876/929-9200); staff can answer basic queries and dole out JTB pamphlets, but it's not really geared to assist visitors. There's a smaller, more tourist-oriented booth at the airport (Ⓣ876/924-8024).

Getting around

Finding your way around Kingston is pretty straightforward. Downtown uses a grid system, while uptown is defined by a handful of major roads; the mountains to the northeast serve as a good compass. The heat and the distances between places mean you're not going to want to do a lot of **walking**, though the downtown sights are easily navigable on foot. It's not advisable to walk the streets at night in any part of the city; Kingstonians certainly don't.

Taxis are the best way of getting around the city and are reasonably cheap; a ride from New Kingston to downtown costs around J$400. There are bustling taxi ranks downtown at Parade, and along Knutsford Boulevard. Reputable firms include Miracle (Ⓣ876/757-4227) and Prime Time (Ⓣ876/948-6833). If you want to take a **tour** of the city, see p.255 for details of reliable firms.

The introduction of a fleet of new, larger buses makes **city buses** a viable option. Fares are absurdly cheap – no more than J$50 for any journey around the city – and all services radiate from the brand-new terminal at Half Way Tree as well as the less salubrious one at Parade.

Accommodation

Most of Kingston's **hotels** are scattered around the uptown district of **New Kingston**, a convenient base for sightseeing and close to many restaurants, theatres, cinemas and clubs. Prices are not as seasonal as in the resort areas, and there are few discounts available during the summer. Although it is wise to reserve in advance, finding a room is rarely a problem.

Altamont Court 1 Altamont Terrace Ⓣ876/929-4497, Ⓦwww.cariboutpost.com/altamont. The best mid-range option in New Kingston, in the heart of the action but tucked away from the noisy main drag, with a swimming pool, Jacuzzi, restaurant and bar. The comfortable rooms have a/c, cable TV, phone, hairdryers and wireless Internet access, and rates include breakfast. ④

Christar Villas 99 Hope Rd Ⓣ876/978 3933, Ⓦwww.christarvillashotel.com. Appealing studios and suites with kitchen, a/c, phone and cable TV; the more luxurious units have private Jacuzzi and gym equipment. Business centre, wireless Internet, gym, pool, Jacuzzi, sun deck, restaurant and popular bar on site, a great location near the Bob Marley Museum and free airport transfers (Mon–Sat 8am–5pm). Studios ④

Courtleigh 85 Knutsford Blvd Ⓣ876/929-9000, Ⓦwww.courtleigh.com. Easily the most appealing of the New Kingston high-rise hotels, with a tasteful lobby decked out in Asian style, a business centre, good restaurant, popular bar/nightclub, a pool, gym and luxurious rooms with a balcony and lots of welcome extras, from hairdryer to Internet jack. 6

The Gardens 23 Liguanea Ave ⓣ876/927-5957, ⓦwww.forrespark.com. With a central location and a relaxing ambience, this delightful complex is one of Kingston's best choices. Set in landscaped grounds with a pool, the expansive two-bedroom townhouses have full kitchen and living room; you can rent just a room as well as a whole unit. Rooms 3, townhouses 5

Hilton Kingston 77 Knutsford Blvd ⓣ876/926-5430, ⓦwww.hiltoncaribbean.com/kingston. Lively, glitzy complex dominating New Kingston, with a huge pool, nightclubs, restaurant and bar. Rooms afford good views and have all the facilities you'd expect from the Hilton chain. 6

Indies 5 Holborn Rd ⓣ876/926-2952, ⓦwww.indieshotel.com. Compact, clean and appealing little hotel next to *Holborn Manor*, set on two levels around a garden courtyard and small restaurant. Rooms have a/c and phone – you pay a little more for a TV. 3

Knutsford Court 16 Chelsea Ave ⓣ876/929-1000, ⓦwww.knutsfordcourt.com. Newly refurbished, with lots of greenery outside and redecorated rooms with all mod cons. Business centre, coin-op laundry, pool and restaurant on site; rates include Continental breakfast. 4

Mikuzi 5 Upper Montrose Rd ⓣ876/978 4859 or 813 0098, ⓦwww.mikuzijamaica.com. Wonderful and unique guesthouse set in a colonial-era house in residential New Kingston. The eclectic en-suite rooms have stylish, funky decor, fans and kitchenettes; some have a/c and cable TV; there are also a couple of budget cottages in the pretty flower-filled gardens. Very friendly staff. 2

Sandhurst 70 Sandhurst Crescent ⓣ876/927-8244, ⓕ876/927-7239. Excellent value in a peaceful spot near King's House and behind the Bob Marley Museum, with a nice pool and a terrace restaurant overlooking the mountains. Rooms range from simple fan-only to units with a/c, cable TV and veranda. 2

Sunset Inn 1A Altamont Crescent ⓣ876/929-7283, ⓔsunsetinn@mindspring.com. Rather cramped but functional, in a great New Kingston location, with a range of clean, pleasant en-suite rooms with fridge, a/c and cable TV; some have a kitchenette. 3

The City

Kingston's main sights are divided between Downtown, which stretches north from the waterfront to the busy traffic junction of Cross Roads, and Uptown, spreading up into the ritzy suburbs at the base of the mountains. **Downtown** is the industrial centre, its factories and all-important port providing most of Kingston's blue-collar employment. On the other end of the scale, **Uptown** is attractive and has an easy-going feel. Most of Kingston's hotels, restaurants, clubs and shopping centres are here, and it's where you'll spend most of your time. Some of the residential districts are simply beautiful, while the central high-rises suggest a modern city anywhere in North America.

Downtown

Flattened by an earthquake in 1907, **downtown Kingston** has lost most of its grand eighteenth-century architecture, though a handful of historic buildings can still be found along Rum Lane, Water Lane and King Street. Much of Kingston's economic strength comes from its impressively huge natural **harbour**, one of the world's best, but it is grimly polluted these days. Once buzzing with trading ships, the wind-whipped waterfront is a good spot to start exploring. The chief beneficiary of the city council's 1960s effort to beautify downtown, the waterfront saw its historic buildings swept away and replaced by spanking new high-rises, which today define the eastern end of the waterfront's main strip, Ocean Boulevard. Housed in an unprepossessing iron building at the western end of Ocean Boulevard, the **Craft Market** (closed Sun) is the least expensive place on the island to buy souvenirs, and shopping here is usually a hassle-free experience.

The National Gallery

Just up from the waterfront, the **National Gallery**, at 12 Ocean Blvd on the corner of Orange St (Tues–Thurs 10am–4.30pm, Fri 10am–4pm, Sat 10am–3pm; J$100,

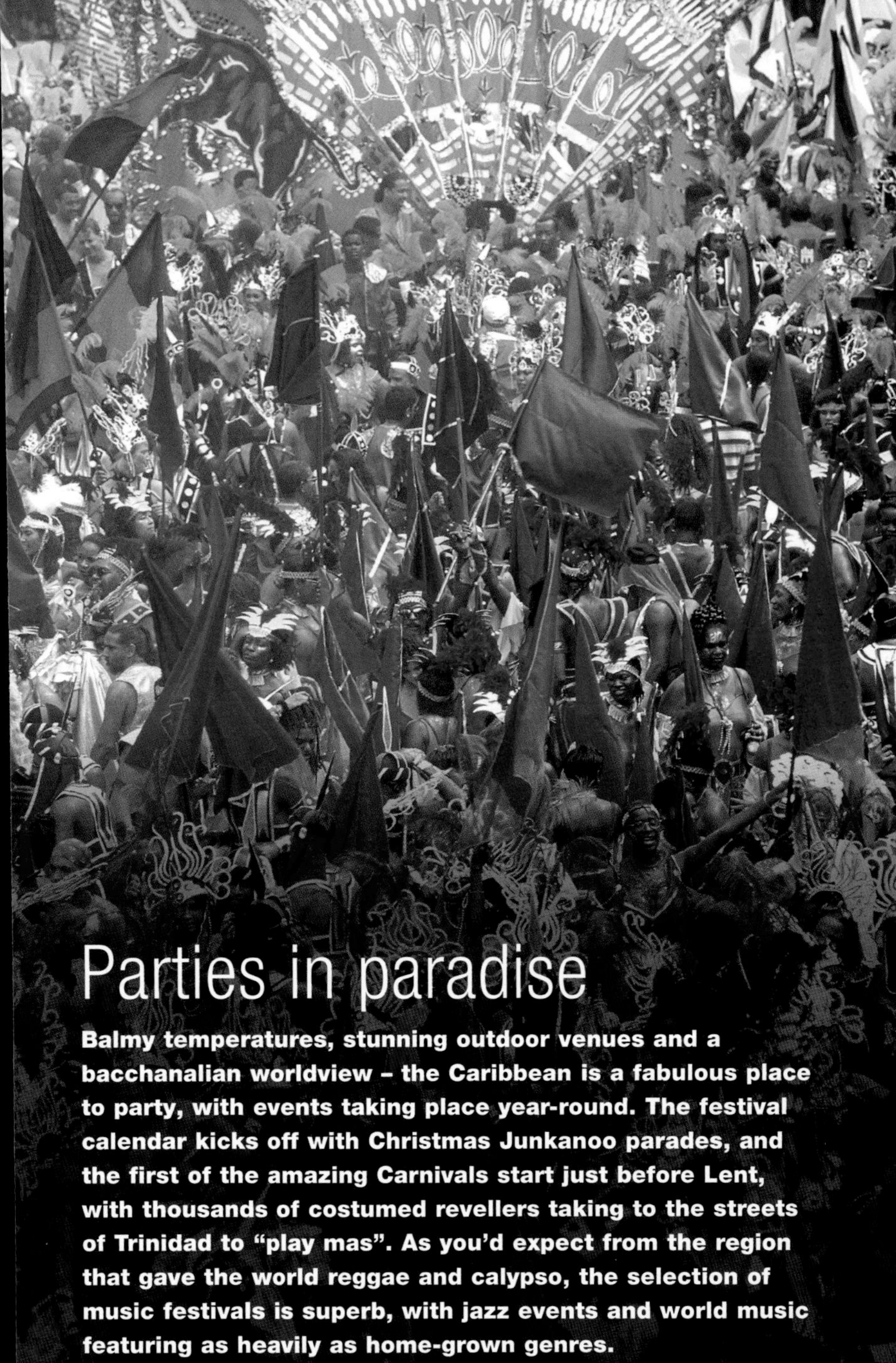

Parties in paradise

Balmy temperatures, stunning outdoor venues and a bacchanalian worldview – the Caribbean is a fabulous place to party, with events taking place year-round. The festival calendar kicks off with Christmas Junkanoo parades, and the first of the amazing Carnivals start just before Lent, with thousands of costumed revellers taking to the streets of Trinidad to "play mas". As you'd expect from the region that gave the world reggae and calypso, the selection of music festivals is superb, with jazz events and world music featuring as heavily as home-grown genres.

Carnivals

Bursting with pure, unbridled energy, **Carnival** is the ultimate Caribbean party, a joyful celebration of life with an infectious appeal that hooks in even the most circumspect vistiors. Carnival culture runs pretty much year-round, with substantial events in January (Aruba), March (Jamaica), April (St Maarten, St Thomas, Cayman Islands), May (Bermuda), July (St Lucia, St Vincent, Cuba), August (Barbados, Grenada, Antigua and Barbuda) and December (St Kitts, Montserrat, St Croix), as well as the pre-Lenten events in Trinidad and Dominica.

Carnival is all about joining in: for the price of a costume (anything from US$100 to US$800), you can become a member of a **mas band** and dance through the streets to pounding soca booming from speaker-laden trucks. Bands range from the huge 3000-strong Tribe and Island People in Trinidad to more intimate collectives on smaller islands, and some include food and drink in the costume price. Whatever band you choose, being a part of the parade is infinitely more fun than watching it from the sidelines. The precursor of the feathers and sequins of the daytime parades is the distinctly unglamorous **Jouvert**, a no-holds-barred event that involves getting coated in mud, paint or oil and dancing to the raw beats of rhythm sections into the wee hours.

If all that sounds a bit too wild, Carnival's other elements offer more sedate appeal. All the carnivals stage **competitions** to crown the best steel band and soca and calypso singers, with judging based on entertaining live shows. The huge King and Queen costumes of each band – depicting anything from a butterfly to

Steel pan music ▲

Blue devil, a traditional Carnival masquerader ▲

Jouvert revellers ▼

a coral reef – are visual feasts that tower up to five metres over the wearer and are smothered in intricate decorations to catch the judges' eyes.

Music festivals

Music is one of the Caribbean's strongest suits, and the array of festivals staged across the islands testifies to the locals' love of a good tune. **Jazz** has long been popular, with St Lucia's festival in May leading the way for a host of others, most notably the Air Jamaica Jazz and Blues Fest in January (Jamaica), Barbados' Paint It (January), Tobago's Heritage and Jazz (April), Puerto Rico's Jazz Festival (May) and the Dominican Republic's event (November), all of which feature acts from the Caribbean alongside the best international artists. Other major happenings with a uniquely Caribbean flavour include Jamaica's **Reggae Sumfest** (August), held next to the sea and under the stars – the ultimate way to enjoy the cream of reggae performers on their home turf. And of the roster of annual stageshows in Jamaica, **Rebel Salute** in January is one not to miss, a Rastafarian-oriented event where patrons spread out their blankets on a grassy cricket field and watch performances that carry on till sunrise. The region's other main genres, soca and calypso, get a bit of a short shrift when it comes to festivals, though Dominica's **World Creole Music Festival** (October) gives lesser-known styles such as bouyon and cadence an airing – both genres are similar to the fast, danceable beats of Trinidadian soca. For more intimate events, Anguilla hosts the **Moonsplash Festival** each March, featuring reggae, jazz and world music acts performing to an audience of just 500.

▲ Queen of Carnival

▼ Reggae star Elephant Man

Antigua Sailing Week ▲

Junkanoo costume, Bahamas ▼

Top 10 festivals

The following (in no particular order) comprise the best of the Caribbean's annual celebrations.

▸▸ **Carnival, Trinidad** The mother of Caribbean Carnivals. Starts after Christmas, building to an electrifying crescendo just before Lent, typically in February or March. See p.754.

▸▸ **St Lucia Jazz, May** Perhaps the best of the region's many jazz fests, featuring an enviable lineup of local and international artists. See p.629.

▸▸ **World Creole Music Festival, Dominica, October** Excellent celebration of Creole music, with outdoor concerts in the capital Roseau. See p.609.

▸▸ **Antigua Sailing Week, early April or late May** The largest Caribbean regatta, with seriously huge parties at the Yacht Club in Falmouth. See p.541.

▸▸ **Reggae Sumfest, July or August** Three nights featuring Jamaica's best performers, from reggae crooners to the best of the dancehall acts as well as big international stars. See p.242.

▸▸ **Crop Over, Barbados, August** The best Carnival after Trinidad's, with all the usual trappings as well as a parade route that culminates alongside a beautiful beach. See p.666.

▸▸ **Junkanoo, Bahamas** Raucous event celebrating the new year with parades of dancers grooving to goombay music, cowbells and toots on a conch shell. See p.67.

▸▸ **Festival of the Bulls, Dominican Republic** Held in Higuey on August 14, this rustic, colourful fiesta patronal features processions of cowboys and large herds of cattle. See p.313.

▸▸ **Fiesta del Fuego, Cuba, July** Santiago de Cuba celebrates the African side of Cuban culture, from dance to music and religion. See p.157.

▸▸ **Jump-ups** Throughout the Caribbean, these informal outdoor parties offer music, sizzling grills and an all-round good time. See pp.429, 493, 546, 640.

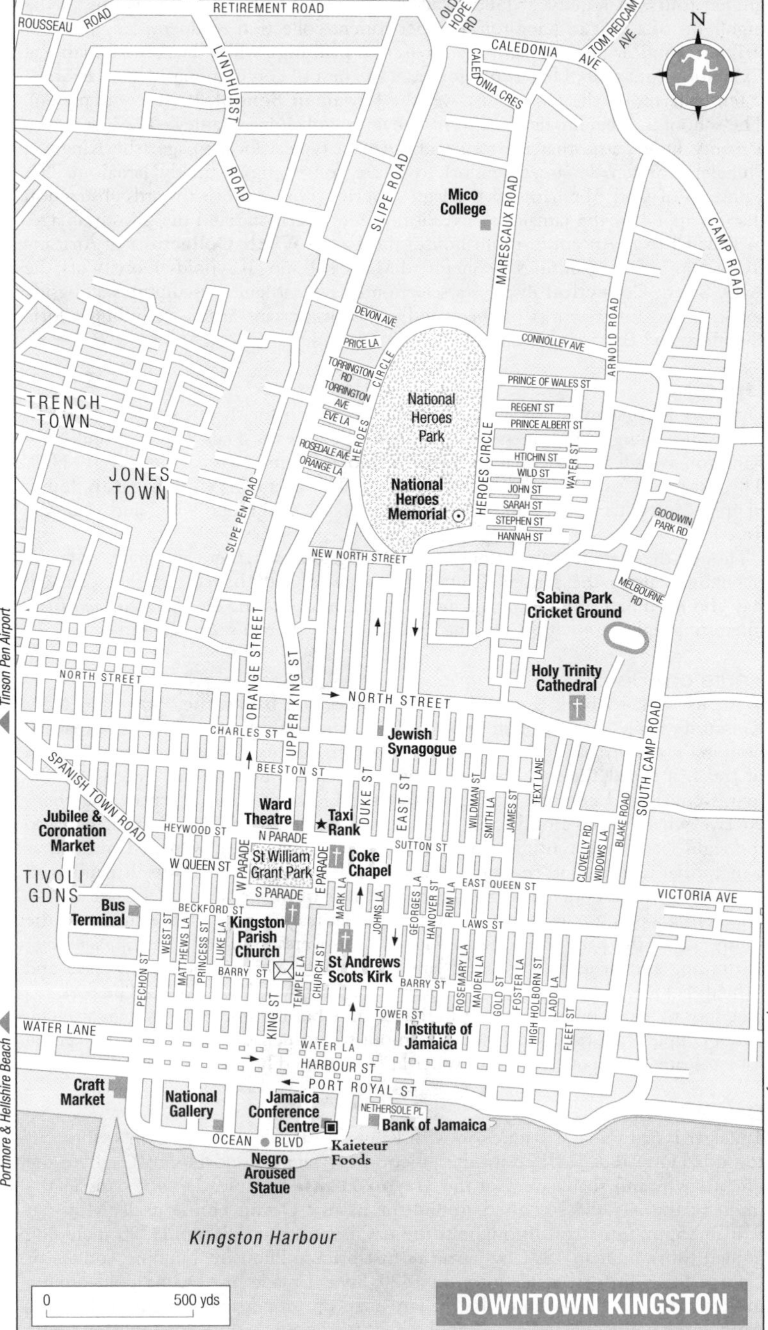
DOWNTOWN KINGSTON
Cross Roads & Uptown
Tinson Pen Airport
Portmore & Hellshire Beach
Airport & Port Royal
Mico College
National Heroes Park
National Heroes Memorial
Sabina Park Cricket Ground
Holy Trinity Cathedral
Jewish Synagogue
Ward Theatre
Taxi Rank
St William Grant Park
Coke Chapel
Jubilee & Coronation Market
Bus Terminal
Kingston Parish Church
St Andrews Scots Kirk
Institute of Jamaica
Craft Market
National Gallery
Jamaica Conference Centre
Bank of Jamaica
Kaieteur Foods
Negro Aroused Statue
Kingston Harbour
TRENCH TOWN
JONES TOWN
TIVOLI GDNS
0
500 yds

guided tours on request at J$800, call ☎876/922-1561 to arrange), is one of the highlights of a visit to Kingston. The permanent collection is superb, ranging from striking woodcarvings to flamboyant religious paintings, while the Annual National Exhibition (normally Dec–Feb) showcases the best of contemporary Jamaican art.

Ten galleries on the first floor cover the **Jamaican School**, 1922 to the present. The school is generally deemed to have begun with Edna Manley's 1922 *Beadseller*, a dainty little statue that married Cubism to a typical local image (the Kingston "higgler", or female street vendor) to create something distinctly Jamaican. The paintings of Carl Abrahams in the later galleries show a move towards abstraction that is capped by the Jamaican surrealism of Colin Garland and the ghostly images of David Boxer. An entire room houses the **Larry Wirth Collection** of African-style sculpture and paintings by Shepherd Mallica "Kapo" Reynolds. Downstairs, the **A.D. Scott Collection** displays a selection of Edna Manley's sculptures alongside some of the finest works of the island's most important artists, including Gloria Escoffery and Barrington Watson.

Uptown

Uptown Kingston is used as a catch-all description for the areas north of Cross Roads, including the business and commercial centres of Half Way Tree and New Kingston as well as residential areas such as Hope Pastures, Mona and Beverly Hills. The heart of Uptown is the high-rise financial district of **New Kingston**, found in an eccentric triangle bounded by Trafalgar Road, Old Hope Road and Half Way Tree Road.

Though there are few attractions in New Kingston itself, there are plenty of facilities ranged along the central Knutsford Boulevard, and chances are that you will stay and do much of your eating and drinking in or around this area. Some of the interesting sights are within walking distance; the rest are a short taxi ride away.

Knutsford Boulevard

With its back-to-back restaurants, bars, offices and banks, the "Strip", as New Kingston's main street is often known, is a permanently busy stretch of tarmac, all honking taxi horns and scurrying office workers. Past its first straight stretch south of Trafalgar Road, the street bends and widens, flanked by high-rise hotels. Past the tennis courts and colonial architecture of the Liguanea Club, a private member's enclave where James Bond took cocktails on the terrace in *Dr No*, a turn-off to the right leads to **Emancipation Park** (no set hours; free). Opened in 2002 as a memorial to the 1838 cessation of slavery, it is a manicured and well-maintained space, with more concrete than grass, piped jazz from speakers ensconced in fake boulders, a jogging track and a concert stage that features regular free shows. At the south end of the park stands Laura Facey's controversial sculpture *Redemption Song*, a stunning and majestic study of a Jamaican couple whose prominent breasts and genitals led to calls for its immediate removal after it was first installed. The park is a nice spot to take a breezy breather in the daytime but it comes into its own at night, when couples canoodle and families turn out to promenade and gaze at the central "sky cascade" fountain, the jets of water lit by coloured lights to delightful effect.

Devon House

Trafalgar Road forms a T-junction with Knutsford Boulevard, and then swings east towards Hope Road. Opposite the junction of Trafalgar and Hope Road are the green lawns and shady trees of the **Devon House** complex, a cool oasis in the midst of the city that's centred around the palatial Devon House itself (Mon–Sat 9.30am–5pm, tours run throughout the day, last tour at 4.30pm; J$250 including guided tour), built in 1881 by Jamaica's first black millionaire, building contractor George Stiebel. Born in Kingston in 1820, Stiebel made his fortune gold-mining in Venezuela, returning home in 1873 to snap up properties throughout Jamaica. Among these was Devon Pen, where he built the house that was his Kingston home

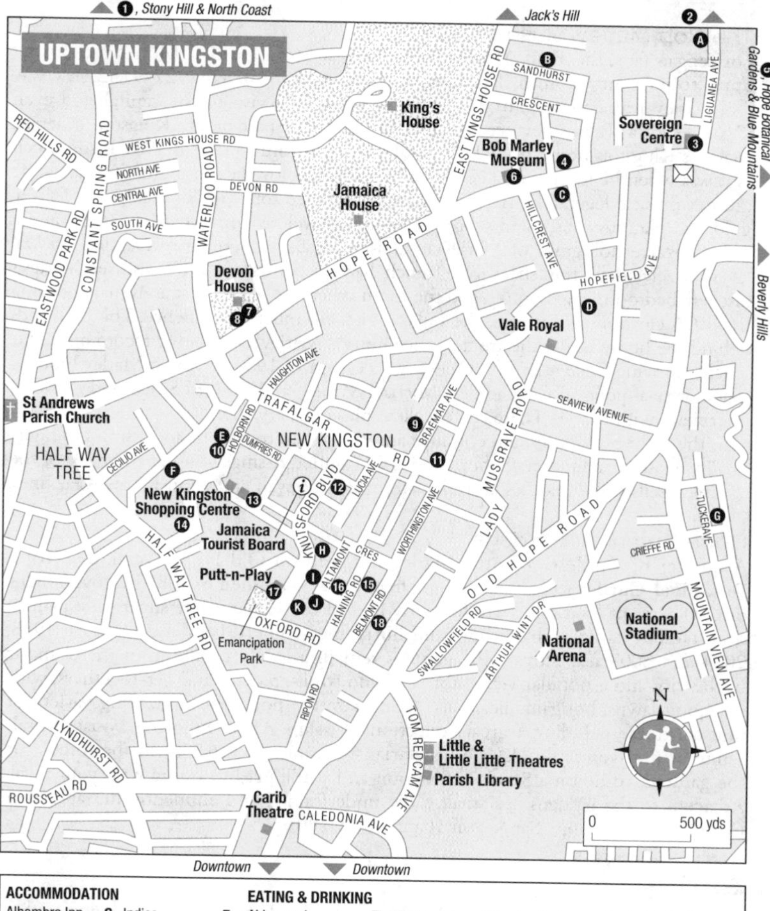

ACCOMMODATION

Alhambra Inn	G	Indies	E
Altamont Court	I	Knutsford Court	F
Christar Villas	C	Mikuzi	D
Courtleigh	K	Sandhurst	B
The Gardens	A	Sunset Inn	J
Hilton Kingston	H		

EATING & DRINKING

Akbar and Thai Gardens	10	The Deck	11	JamRock	12	So-So Seafood	14
Ashanti	5	Deli Works	3	Norma's on the Terrace	7	Starapple	4
Bob's Café	6	The Grog Shoppe	8	Prendy's	17	Village Café	2
Carlos Café	18	Heather's Garden Restaurant	15	Red Bones Blues Café	9	Weekendz	1
Cuddy'z	13	Hot Pot	16				

until he died in 1896. Bought by the Jamaican government in 1967, it has gradually been furnished with West Indian and European antiques as well as more modern Jamaican reproductions.

The landscaped grounds make a fine place for a leisurely stroll, but most people head straight for the former stables in the middle of the lawns where the central courtyard, with its benches, trellises and flowerbeds, is surrounded by a number of **shops** and **cafés**. You can pick up good-quality (if expensive) souvenirs from the gift shops, a heavenly home-made Devon House "I Scream" (try the soursop or Guinness flavours), a smoothie or blended juice from the *Jamaica Juice* bar, or an excellent patty or gooey cake from the *Brick Oven* bakery. *Café What's On*, with tables outside and in the air-conditioned interior, has good sandwiches, bagels, rotis, cappuccinos and Internet access.

The Bob Marley Museum

For reggae fans, the **Bob Marley Museum**, at 56 Hope Rd (Mon–Sat 9.30am–5pm, tours every 20min, last tour at 4pm; US$10; ⓣ876/927-9152, ⓦwww.bobmarley-foundation.com), is the whole point of a visit to the capital, and even if you're not a serious devotee, a visit is an obligatory part of any Kingston itinerary. Marley's Kingston home from 1975 until his death from cancer in 1981 is still much as it was when he lived here, a gentle and surprisingly low-key monument to Jamaica's greatest musical legend. During the hour-long guided tour you'll see legions of silver, gold and platinum discs and scores of awards as well as concert memorabilia and a rather bizarre hologram of Marley in action. Upstairs, there's a re-creation of Wail 'n' Soul – Marley's tiny, shack-like Trench Town record shop. You'll also see Marley's kitchen, bedroom, stage outfits, and the room where he was almost assassinated during the 1976 election campaign – the bullet holes still much in evidence. The tour ends behind the house in the theatre that once housed Marley's Tuff Gong recording studio. There's moving footage of the "One Love" concert of 1980, at which Marley brought together rival political party leaders Michael Manley and Edward Seaga, and a film of interviews with Marley. There's an excellent photo gallery, too.

To the right of the museum entrance are a juice bar/restaurant and a series of high-quality, Rasta-oriented craft shops and a CD outlet. A small shop at the back of the complex sells stylish clothes and shoes from the Cooyah and Zion Roots Wear lines.

Hope Botanical Gardens

A quarter of a mile east of the Marley museum on Old Hope Road, the **Hope Botanical Gardens** (daily 6am–7pm; free) were established in 1881 by government on 200 acres of land that were formerly part of the Hope Estate sugar cane plantation. Despite taking a battering from hurricanes Gilbert, Ivan and Dean, in 1988, 2004 and 2007 respectively, the gardens remain a lovely escape from the clamour of the city and a popular venue for weekend strolls, picnics and get-togethers, with sweeping lawns, bougainvillea walks, a lily-covered pond and a dizzying variety of unusual trees, including a great collection of palms. After exploring, you can grab a bite at the wonderful *Ashanti* vegetarian restaurant (see p.253) in the middle of the gardens; come on a Sunday afternoon and you'll get live music with your meal. Adjacent to the gardens is a small, sadly underfunded and eminently missable **zoo** (Mon–Fri 10am–5pm, Sat & Sun 10am–6pm; J$80).

Eating

After the sun goes down, Uptown Kingston is hard to beat for open-air dining, with a wider choice of **restaurants** than anywhere else in Jamaica and an excellent standard of food. Most places offer variations on traditional Jamaican fare, but you'll also find sushi, Chinese, Indian and Italian cuisine. If you want a meal with a view, head to Port Royal for the waterside restaurant at *Morgan's Harbour* hotel, or any of the fish places dotted around the village. For informal lunches, visit the **food courts** at Sovereign Centre in Hope Road; though it's a bit out of the way, the huge Marketplace complex in the Constant Spring Arcade has some excellent options, including sushi at *East*, the *Roma* pizzeria and deli, and lovely pastries and cakes at *Nicole's*. For **patties**, *Tastee's* has a convenient branch on Knutsford Boulevard, while the *Juicy Beef* outlet on Hope Road, just up from Sovereign Centre, also does great breakfast – try the porridge. If you're after truly authentic **jerk chicken**, try any of the smoking oil-drum barbecues set up on street corners; one of the best is outside the open-air Dragon Plaza shopping mall, just up from the Sovereign Centre on Hope Road.

Akbar and Thai Gardens 11 Holborn Rd ⓣ876/922-3247. The best Indian food in town, with all the regular dishes (including plenty of vegetarian options) served up in a tastefully decorated a/c indoor dining room. In the *Akbar* restaurant's shady backyard, *Thai Gardens* offers decent Thai food, with a full range of starters – fish cakes, spring rolls – as well as red and green curries and noodle dishes.

Ashanti Hope Gardens. Relaxing, inexpensive open-air restaurant in the centre of the gardens, offering a daily-changing lunch/early dinner vegetarian menu that always includes a delicious thick soup (split peas, red peas, pumpkin) and main dishes such as soya and vegetable balls served with rice, salad and ratatouille. Veggie burgers with chutney, natural juices and soya ice cream also available.

Bob's Café Marley Museum, 56 Hope Rd. Open-air café within the hallowed grounds of the museum, with an eclectic menu that runs from cheese and callaloo spring rolls to kebabs, tempura fish fingers, Ital stew and veg and meat rotis with proper dhalpuri skins. Nice spot for a natural juice, too.

Cuddy'z 25 Dominica Drive ⓣ876/920 8019. New venture operated by ex-Windies cricket superstar Courtney Walsh, this slick, modern a/c restaurant offers a wide-ranging, mid-priced international-style menu of build-your-own salads, steaks, ribs, pasta and local favourites, from stewed chicken to steamed fish.

Deli Works Sovereign Centre, Hope Rd. Reliable a/c canteen-style diner that's a great lunch spot, with local fare alongside veggie or meat lasagne, macaroni cheese and lots of salads. Good breakfasts, too, and a reasonably priced Sunday brunch (9am–4pm; J$510, or J$590 with Jamaican-style ham).

The Grog Shoppe Devon House ⓣ876/926-3512. A shady spot on the Devon House grounds serving standard Jamaican meals at lunchtime and more European fare (and prices) in the evening. Features regular theme nights such as all-you-can-eat crab night; call ahead to check. Closed Sun.

Heather's Garden Restaurant 9 Haining Rd. With tables ranged around a pretty garden, with both covered and open-air sections, the setting here is perhaps more of a draw than the solid, if uninspired, Middle Eastern and Jamaican menu.

Hot Pot 2 Altamont Terrace. Popular spot for typical Jamaican meals in the heart of New Kingston, with excellent breakfasts, including cornmeal and banana porridge and saltfish combinations, and lunches of fish and bammy (cassava bread), curry goat, stewed beef and the usual Jamaican staples.

JamRock 69 Knutsford Blvd. A perfect and popular combination of bar, hangout, restaurant and patisserie; favourite among Jamaican dishes is the sumptuous jerk chicken sandwich, and you can also get salads, soups, burgers, sandwiches, excellent patties, pastries and espresso or cappuccino.

Kaieteure Foods Jamaica Conference Centre, 14 Duke St. This first-floor dining area is the best place in downtown Kingston for lunch, with sea breezes fanning over tables in an open-sided dining area. The excellent food is served canteen-style, and there's a wide choice of quality salads and daily specials, from fish and chicken to Jamaican staples such as oxtail.

Norma's on the Terrace Devon House ⓣ876/968-5488. Upscale eatery, situated on the terrace of the old Devon House stables and serving gourmet Jamaican food with an international twist. Menus might include peppered beef salad, smoked marlin and seafood chowder; afternoon teas feature delectable pastries. It's also good for a late-night espresso accompanied by one of the superb desserts.

Prendy's Putt 'n' Play, 75 Knutsford Blvd ⓣ881 9689. Three nights a week (Wed, Fri & Sat), Hellshire's premier fish restaurant opens up in the heart of New Kingston. Wednesday is crab night, with a divine curry and garlic crab, while the last Fri of each month sees early opening (from noon), and a set menu of fish, lobster, festival, bammy and soup. Otherwise, there's delicious Hellshire-style fried fish and lobster, a fabulous fish tea and an unmissable steamed fish served in a thick pumpkin broth.

Red Bones Blues Café 21 Braemar Ave ⓣ876/978-8262, ⓦwww.redbonesbluescafe.com. Stylish, upmarket restaurant-cum-music venue with a distinguished but laid-back atmosphere, serving imaginative Jamaican-style food on the outdoor covered terrace or at the indoor dining room. Good wine list.

So-So Seafood 4 Chelsea Ave. Busy place with an appealing outdoor setting and a decently priced seafood-based menu, from garlic, curry and coconut stir-fried shrimp and lobster to fish priced by the pound, as well as Jamaican daily blackboard specials and an excellent conch soup on Thurs and Fri. DJs play oldies and 1970s soul at the weekends.

Starapple 94 Hope Road ⓣ876/927 9019. Set in a lovely old house, all creaky polished floors and gingerbread tracery, and offering a solid, mid-priced Jamaican menu, from yam and saltfish, oxtail and beans, steamed fish and all the usual variations. Interesting veggie options include callaloo quiche, vegetable rundown (veg cooked in coconut) and aloo and channa curry.

Drinking and nightlife

Kingston has legions of great places to get a **drink**, and many of them also double up as restaurants; *Red Bones* and the *Grog Shoppe* (see above) are both worth a try. Many of the bars also have poetry, open-mic and film nights, which offer interesting insight into the Kingston scene – expect a cover charge of around J$400. You'll find scores of **clubs** around town, ranging from state-of-the-art places featuring big-name DJs to sedate in-hotel affairs and dancehall dives. Anticipate a cover of around J$500. It's also worth keeping a lookout for posters and press advertisements for one-off nights at places such as Mas Camp Village or all-inclusive parties staged at outdoor venues in and around the city; these are usually well attended by a friendly uptown crowd, and invariably lots of fun. For more on what's on, visit Ⓦwww.whaddat.com.

Live music in the capital is less predictable; some of the best shows are during the annual Heineken Startime concerts, featuring the best of Jamaica's stalwart reggae artists. Big shows are promoted in the press, on the radio and by way of posters and banners slapped up around town. Annual celebrations include **Carnival**, with numerous events held around Lent. It's similar to Trinidad's Carnival but on a far smaller scale and with more organized parties than street parades. For more on Carnival, visit Ⓦwww.jamaicacarnival.com or Ⓦwww.bacchanaljamaica.com.

Bars

Carlos Café 22 Belmont Rd Ⓣ876/926-4186. Outdoor bar with an uptownish feel, which stages various themed nights, from Martini Mondays to Latin on Thurs.

Cuddy'z 25 Dominica Drive Ⓣ876/920 8019. Operated by cricketing legend Courtney Walsh, who often passes through to the delight of patrons, this newly opened sports bar is a lively place for a drink or to catch a baseball, cricket or football game shown on numerous TVs, the big screen at the back of the mini basketball court or one of the monitors in the "Superbooths", which also have Internet access and instant messaging that enables you to send messages to other patrons or pics to your mates back home.

The Deck 14 Trafalgar Rd. Easy-going and central outdoor bar under a cavernous thatched roof, popular with a friendly, older set. Different snacks on offer each night, and low-key music from a DJ; women get half-price drinks each Thurs between 5pm and 8pm.

Peppers 31 Upper Waterloo Rd. Late-opening and permanently popular outdoor bar that pulls in post-work drinkers and then younger clubbers, who come for a snack or to dance to sound-system DJs.

Village Café Orchid Village Plaza, Barbican Rd. Open-air, split-level venue at the top of this small plaza that stages a range of popular and ever-changing events such as Thursday's Fashion Night and open mic on Tues.

Weekendz 80 Constant Spring Rd. Outdoor club-bar, set back from the road in gardens and attracting a mixed-age, friendly crowd. Weekends tend to be busy, with a music policy ranging from dancehall and reggae to R&B, hip-hop and house, and Thurs see the hugely popular Bembe Thursdays, with DJs including Tony Matterhorn, and Razz and Biggy.

Clubs

Asylum 69 Knutsford Blvd Ⓣ876/929-4386. Kingston's clubland stalwart, pumping out reggae and dancehall for a lively, loyal crowd. There's a different music policy each night, but Wednesday nights, when more conscious reggae is played, are typically the best introduction; Thursday's dancehall night is more hardcore, with Stone Love sound system on the decks.

Quad 20–22 Trinidad Terrace, off Knutsford Blvd Ⓣ754-7823. Kingston's newest club, this upmarket indoor venue has *Christopher's Jazz Café* on the ground floor, a comfortable a/c lounge with a weekday happy hour (5–8pm). Above, *Oxygen 2* is a flashy North American-style nightclub, playing commercial dance music for a youngish crowd. The top-floor *Voodoo Lounge* is aimed at the slightly more mature, with music from the 1960s to the 1990s and a small outdoor deck. Cover charges vary from J$200 to J$600.

Waterfalls 9 Mona Plaza, Liguanea Ⓣ876/977-0652. Indoor club that's best on a Fri when Winston "Merritone" Black spins an excellent oldies selection.

Theatre and cinema

Kingston's **theatre** scene is limited but buoyant, with a small core of first-rate writers, directors and actors producing work of a generally high standard. Most of the plays are sprinkled with Jamaican patois, but you'll still get the gist. **Comedies** (particularly sexual romps and political satire) are popular, and the normally excellent annual **pantomime** – a musical with a message, totally different from the English variety – is a major event, running from December to April at the **Ward Theatre** (Ⓣ876/922-0453) and, later, the **Little Theatre** (Ⓣ876/925-6129).

Kingston's **cinemas** invariably screen recent mainstream offerings from the States. Tickets are around J$300, and there's usually a snack interval in the middle of the show. Most of the cinemas are uptown and include the **Palace Cineplex** (Ⓣ876/978-3522) at the Sovereign Centre, the **Island Cinemax** (Ⓣ876/920-7964) at the Island Life Centre on St Lucia Avenue and the plush **Carib Cinema** at Cross Roads (Ⓣ876/926-6106).

Shopping and galleries

A multitude of American-style malls means that **shopping** in Kingston is nothing if not convenient. The major players are the New Kingston Shopping Centre on Dominica Drive, the Sovereign Centre on Hope Road and the multitude of malls on Constant Spring Road.

For **books**, the bookshop at the University of the West Indies in Mona is far and away the superior choice for both novels and books on Jamaica; the reliable Sangster's has branches on Knutsford Boulevard and in the Sovereign Centre.

Music fans are in shopping heaven in Kingston where there are **record shops** in most of the shopping malls, and downtown's Orange Street has several places stocking everything from dancehall to rocksteady and reggae classics.

Souvenirs hunters should try the Crafts Market downtown or the malls on Constant Spring Road, which hold excellent, reasonably priced craft shops such as Craft Cottage, in the Village Plaza mall, 24 Constant Spring Rd.

East of Kingston

The main route east out of Kingston, Windward Road, follows the coastline, winding through an industrial zone of oil tanks and a cement works that towers over the ruined defensive bastion of Fort Rock. A mile or so further on, turning right at the roundabout takes you on to the **Palisadoes** and, ultimately, Port Royal.

Port Royal

PORT ROYAL captures the early colonial spirit better than any other place in Jamaica. Originally a tiny island, this little fishing village is now joined to the mainland by the **Palisadoes**, a series of small cays that silted together over hundreds

Tours from Kingston

All of the places around Kingston can be explored on an **organized tour** from the city. Although you shouldn't need a tour to see Port Royal, which is easy to reach on the ferry and small, safe and relaxed enough to wander around alone, tours are a good option for Spanish Town, which is a bit awkward to get to and – as a major industrial city – can feel rather unwelcoming. You'll get a fuller perspective on all the sights by engaging the services of a tour company, many of which offer individualized, small-scale jaunts. **Our Story Tours** (Ⓣ876/1-377 5693 or 876/1-699 4513, Ⓔcrompton@hotmail.com) is brilliant for historical perspectives, offering custom-designed tours of Kingston, Spanish Town, Port Royal and horse racing at Caymanas Park; tours start at US$120 per day, with reductions for groups. **Sun Venture** (Ⓣ876/960 6685 or 469-4444, Ⓦwww.sunventuretours.com) is your best choice if heading into the Blue Mountains; trips include the so-called High Blue, with some light hiking, a waterfall swim and a trip to Cinchona botanical gardens, as well as the trek to Blue Mountain Peak. Again, prices vary according to group size; Blue Mountain Peak is US$105 per person for groups of 4–6.

of years and, with a bit of human assistance, now form a narrow, ten-mile long roadway and a natural breakwater for Kingston's harbour, and which affords fantastic views of the city.

After wresting Jamaica from Spain in 1655, the British turned Port Royal into a **battle station**, with five separate forts and a palisade at the north to defend against attackers coming over the cays. As added protection, they encouraged the buccaneers who had for decades been pillaging the area to sign up as **privateers** in the service of the king. Merchants took advantage of the city's great location to buy and sell slaves, export sugar and logwood, and import bricks and supplies for the growing population. The privateers wreaked havoc on the ships of Spain, and the fabulous profits of trade and plunder brought others to service the town's needs: brothels, taverns and gambling houses proliferated, and by the late seventeenth century, the population had swollen to six thousand.

A huge **earthquake** on June 7, 1692 caused sixty percent of Port Royal to sink into the sea, and led to the deaths of three thousand people. Most of the remaining population fled for Kingston; almost all who remained later died or deserted when a massive fire swept the island in 1703.

Despite the destruction, Port Royal continued to serve as the country's **naval headquarters** until the advent of steamships saw the Royal Navy close its dockyard in 1905. Though Port Royal retains its naval traditions as home to the JDF naval wing and the Jamaican coastguard, it's a far less exotic place today. Visitors find a compact and atmospheric fishing village, proud of its very low crime rate and happy to serve up some of the tastiest fresh **fish** you'll find anywhere in Jamaica.

Getting there

Driving from Kingston, you simply follow signs southeast to the airport, and keep going past the turn-off; a **taxi** will cost around US$25. Local **buses** run several times a day to Port Royal Square, but you'll have to board and disembark downtown, at the often dodgy Parade bus stand.

The Town

Look out to sea from anywhere in Port Royal and you'll get not only a great view of the harbour, but a clear idea of the area's strategic military importance and a glimpse of its former limits.

What remains of Port Royal is easily navigable on foot. Five minutes' walk from the ferry terminal, behind the old garrison wall, are the decaying red bricks of the **Old Naval Hospital**, the oldest prefabricated structure in the New World. The ramshackle structure now holds the offices of the National Heritage Trust.

Ten minutes' walk south and on the main Church Street, **St Peter's Church** (irregular opening hours) was built in 1726 and, apart from the roof, has survived largely intact. It's unremarkable apart from an intricately carved mahogany and cedar organ. More interesting are the ancient tombs in the small and rambling graveyard. A left turn out of the church leads down the main road to fascinating **Fort Charles** (daily 9am–5pm; J$200). Originally known as Fort Cromwell, Charles was the first of the five forts to be built here, though none saw any action. In the courtyard, a **museum** provides a lucid history of Port Royal and its maritime history, and displays items – bottles, coins, cannonballs, shipwrights' tools, a rather nasty-looking urethral syringe and a set of ankle shackles used to restrain slaves – dredged up from the underwater city.

The raised platform on the other side of the small parade ground is known as **Nelson's Quarterdeck**; the great commander (still under 21 when he was stationed here) used to pace up and down here spoiling for a fight with the French. From the quarterdeck you can see how the land has built up around the fort as the sea has continued to deposit silt – over a foot per year – against the former island. The two structures that now stand between the fort and the water both date from the 1880s. The squat, rectangular **Giddy House** was an ammunition store, while the circular bunker beside it was the **Victoria and Albert Battery** – an emplacement for a nineteenth-century supergun that was fired only once, at a British soldier attempting to desert.

There are a couple of **beaches** around Port Royal, but both sea and sand are pretty dirty; if you want to **swim**, you're better off taking a boat out to Lime Cay (see below).

Lime Cay

Just fifteen minutes by boat from Port Royal, **Lime Cay** is a tiny undeveloped island with fine white sand, clear and clean turquoise waters and easily accessible snorkelling, perfect for a day on the beach. It was here that Ivanhoe ("Rhygin") Martin – the cop-killing gangster and folk-hero immortalized in the classic Jamaican movie *The Harder They Come* – met his demise in 1948, but this gorgeous swath of sand is better known today as the beach of choice for well-to-do Kingstonians. At the weekend, there's a sound system and food and drinks on sale; at other times, take your own picnic. Boats to Lime Key run regularly from Port Royal for around J$400 per person return at the weekends (J$500 at during the week); boats leave from *Y-Knot*, or *Morgan's Harbour Hotel* (see below).

Practicalities

The grandest place to **stay** in Port Royal (and a five-minute drive from the airport) is the elegant and atmospheric *Morgan's Harbour Hotel* (ⓣ876/967-8030 or 8040, ⓦwww.morgansharbour.com; ⑥), all dark wood and seafaring charm with a open-air bar and a nice pool by the sea's edge; rooms have all mod cons. The only other option is the charming *Admiral's Inn* (ⓣ876/353-4202 or 365-6839, ⓕ876/750-0391; ②), in the housing scheme to the left by *Kevin's* restaurant as you enter Port Royal (head for the street closest to the sea, and it's in the middle on the left – if you can't find it, ask anyone for the owner, Ena Powell). The spick-and-span en-suite rooms have king, twin or double beds, air-conditioning, fridge and microwave, and there's a pretty garden out back for relaxing. The owners offer Lime Key trips, boat tours and airport transfer with advance notice.

Morgan's Harbour Hotel has two restaurants: the relatively informal *Red Jack*, with tables overlooking the harbour and a menu of sandwiches, salads, seafood and Jamaican dishes, and the more upscale, air-conditioned *Quartermain*, serving up lovely plates of seafood. Several cheaper **eateries** near the ferry pier serve Port Royal's best fish; the most popular is *Gloria's Rendezvous* at 5 Queen St, where you can enjoy a tasty plate of fish and bammy and watch the pelicans and frigate birds fishing just offshore. The best time to go out to eat in Port Royal is Friday evening when a sound system sets up in the main square and locals have stalls selling fried fish, bammy and other seafood delicacies; the curried crab and conch soup sold at the *Martin's Sweetness* cart is particularly delicious, and usually runs out by 7pm. For a drink, a meal or a dance on the deck at the weekend and during the week, head to *Y-Knot*, a lovely bar right by the sea's edge adjacent to *Morgan's Harbour*; you can also get a good seafood meal here.

Hellshire and around

Southwest of Kingston via the spanking new bridge and toll road (JS$60 for cars) is the bland but booming city of **Portmore**, in the neighbouring parish of St Catherine. Portmore lies at the eastern fringe of the **Hellshire Hills**, an arid and scrubby expanse of "makko" thorn bushes and towering cacti that shelters the closest beaches to the capital. Virtually the only inhabitants are the migrant birds, a few conies and a handful of Jamaican **iguanas**, once thought to be extinct. From the small fishing community of Port Henderson, the signposted road to the Hellshire beaches runs under the flanks of the hills. Follow the road to **Hellshire beach** (no set hours; free), separated from the less enjoyable Fort Clarence beach (Mon–Fri

10am–5pm, Sat & Sun 8am–6pm; J$150) by a barrier reef that makes the Hellshire water a lot calmer. Hellshire buzzes at the weekends, with booming sound systems and a party atmosphere. Most Jamaicans come here for the **fish restaurants** as much as the sea and sand, and Hellshire fried fish or lobster, best eaten with vinegary home-made escovitch pepper sauce and festival sweetbread, beats anything you'll find in town. Cookshops are lined along the top of the beach, and you'll be approached by operators as you drive in. The best option is *Prendy's on the Beach*, directly opposite as you drive in; as well as fried fish, they do a fabulous steamed fish in pumpkin broth. Other operators worth a try are *Flo's* and *Seline's*, the latter has wonderful wall art. At weekends, **watersports operators** offer jet-ski rental and snorkelling equipment, and there are horse rides for children, while you can get an excellent therapeutic massage or a spot of reflexology from the highly professional Tommy (aka Nathan Griffiths; ⓣ876/872 1839), who's usually to be found around *Prendy's*.

Following the main road past Hellshire takes you to **Two Sister's Cave** (Wed–Fri 9.30am–5pm, Sat & Sun 10am–6pm; JS$200), a series of deep caverns in the limestone rock surrounded by landscaped grounds that show off the cacti and other plants that make up Hellshire's dry scrub forest. Accessed by way of wooden walkways and stairs, the caves are part-filled with brackish water and inhabited by bats, crabs and fish, and one has an Amerindian petroglyph on its wall.

5.2

The Blue Mountains and Portland

Towering behind Kingston, the **Blue Mountains**, named after the mists that colour them from a distance, are an unbroken, undulating spine across Jamaica's easternmost parishes. At 28 miles, they form one of the longest continuous ranges in the Caribbean, and their cool, fragrant woodlands dotted with coffee plantations, offer some of the best **hiking** on the island. The most popular hike is to **Blue Mountain Peak** – 7402ft, the highest point in Jamaica – but there are dozens of other trekking possibilities, such as the marked trails within the gorgeous Holywell Recreational Park. Otherwise, **coffee** is the chief interest is here, and you can visit several of the estates producing some of the most expensive – and delicious – beans on earth.

On the other side of the Blue Mountains (here officially known as the **John Crow** range), the northeastern parish of **Portland** is justifiably touted as one of the most beautiful parts of Jamaica, with jungle-smothered hillsides cascading down to a postcard-perfect Caribbean shoreline. If you stay in the parish capital of **Port Antonio**, you'll be close to the lovely **Reach waterfalls** and fabulous swimming at the magical **Blue Lagoon**. Inland, you can hike in pristine tropical **rainforest** or take a gentle rafting trip on the **Rio Grande**.

▲ Coffee plantation, Blue Mountains

Papine to Section

At Papine in northeast Kingston, the city slams to an abrupt halt as it meets the southern edge of the Mona Valley. From here, Gordon Town Road (B1) winds slowly upwards into the riverine hills. The road forks at the tiny village of **The Cooperage**; turning left here, the road winds for three miles to the friendly settlement of **IRISH TOWN**. Just over 3000 feet above sea level, it's a small farming community dominated by one magnificent **hotel**, *Strawberry Hill* (Ⓣ876/944-8400, Ⓦwww.islandoutpost.com; ⑨ including food and drink). This is among the most attractive places to stay in all of Jamaica, with beautifully landscaped gardens, a glorious decked pool providing panoramic city vistas, a sauna and an Aveda spa. It's fashionable amongst a well-heeled Kingston set, and is a favourite venue for society weddings and photo shoots. Bob Marley was also brought here to convalesce after being shot in 1976. Perched on the hillsides, the twelve individually designed luxury cottages – from studios to two-bedroom villas with full kitchens – offer fabulous views.

Even if you don't stay here, **eating** at *Strawberry Hill* is a must. The setting on the Great House balcony overlooking Kingston is exceptional, and the menu offers an eminently delicious combination of fresh local ingredients and sophisticated international-style cooking. The Sunday brunch (11.30am–3pm; book ahead) is an immensely popular local institution and very reasonably priced (around US$40). If you're after a less formal meal in Irish Town, the *Crystal Cove* at the roadside just south of the village offers excellent Jamaican cooking (including jerk chicken at the weekends) and lots of good-natured chat. Next door, *Café Blue* offers Blue Mountain coffees and delicious cakes.

From Craighton, the road continues through the tiny village of **Redlight**, named after the former brothels that kept the Irish coopers entertained. There are a few basic bars and a couple of hole-in-the-wall stores where you can buy provisions. Four thousand feet up and multiple switchback turns from here is **NEWCASTLE**, an old British military base still used by the JDF as a training facility. The main road cuts across the **parade ground**, emblazoned with insignia of the various regiments

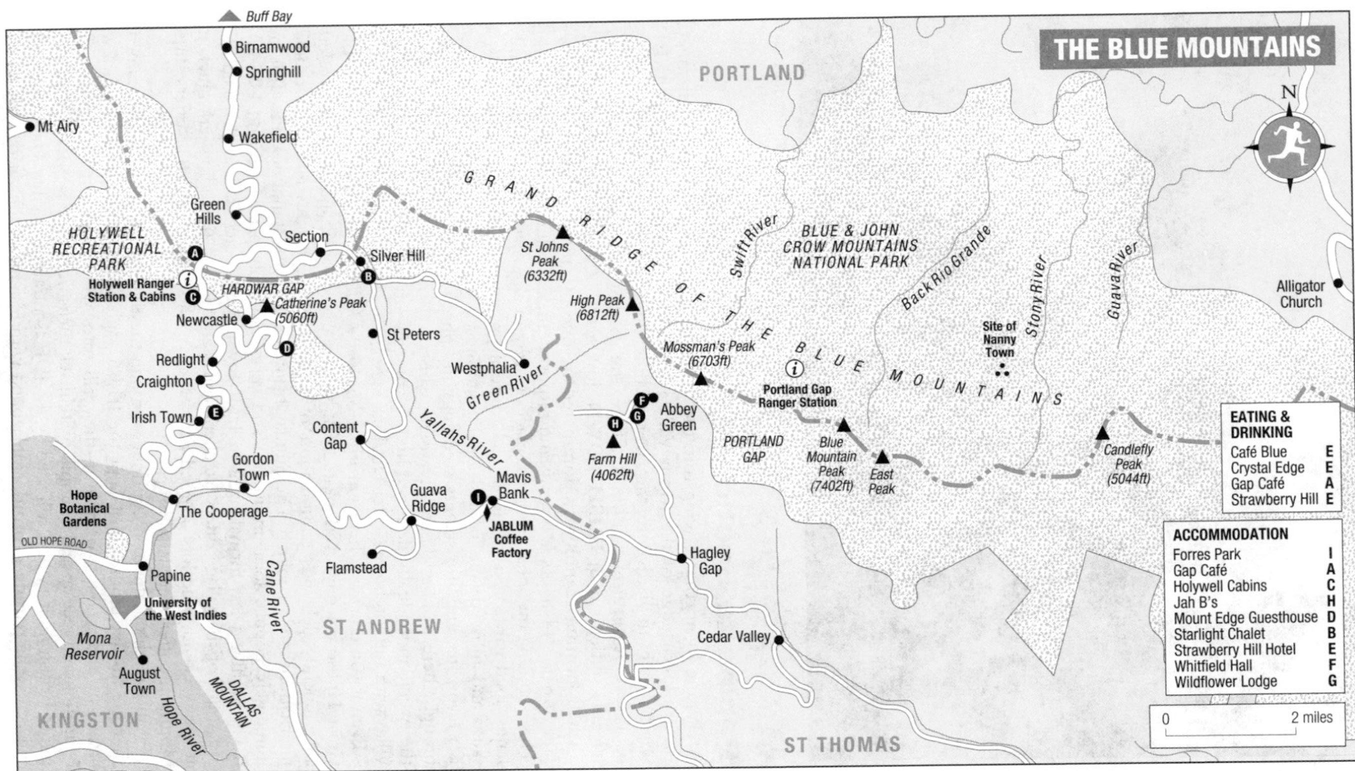
THE BLUE MOUNTAINS
N
PORTLAND
Buff Bay
Birnamwood
Springhill
Mt Airy
Wakefield
Green Hills
Section
Silver Hill
HOLYWELL RECREATIONAL PARK
Holywell Ranger Station & Cabins
HARDWAR GAP
Catherine's Peak (5060ft)
Newcastle
St Peters
Redlight
Craighton
Irish Town
Westphalia
Green River
Content Gap
Yallahs River
Gordon Town
The Cooperage
Hope Botanical Gardens
OLD HOPE ROAD
Papine
University of the West Indies
Mona Reservoir
August Town
KINGSTON
Hope River
DALLAS MOUNTAIN
Cane River
ST ANDREW
Flamstead
Guava Ridge
Mavis Bank
JABLUM Coffee Factory
GRAND RIDGE OF THE BLUE MOUNTAINS
St Johns Peak (6332ft)
High Peak (6812ft)
Mossman's Peak (6703ft)
Farm Hill (4062ft)
Abbey Green
Hagley Gap
Cedar Valley
ST THOMAS
Swift River
BLUE & JOHN CROW MOUNTAINS NATIONAL PARK
Portland Gap Ranger Station
PORTLAND GAP
Blue Mountain Peak (7402ft)
East Peak
Back Rio Grande
Stony River
Site of Nanny Town
Guava River
Candlefly Peak (5044ft)
Alligator Church
EATING & DRINKING
Café Blue E
Crystal Edge E
Gap Café A
Strawberry Hill E
ACCOMMODATION
Forres Park I
Gap Café A
Holywell Cabins C
Jah B's H
Mount Edge Guesthouse D
Starlight Chalet B
Strawberry Hill Hotel E
Whitfield Hall F
Wildflower Lodge G
0
2 miles

stationed here during the past century or so. The views across the mountains and down to Kingston are dazzling, while behind you, immediately above Newcastle, **Catherine's Peak** (5060ft) marks the highest point in the parish of St Andrew.

For **accommodation**, just below Newcastle and clinging to the side of the valley, *Mount Edge* (Ⓣ876/944-8151, Ⓦwww.jamaicaeu.com; ❷) is a laid-back counterculture-ish guesthouse-cum-restaurant. The simple rooms inside the main house and separate but small units just outside are perfect for backpackers, while the bar is a great place to chill out. Meals (cooked to order; call ahead for dinner) are also available, ranging from crab in coconut milk to crayfish. Otherwise, you can press on to the *Gap Café* (Mon–Thurs 10am–5pm, Fri–Sun 10am–6pm; Ⓣ876/997-3032) at **Hardwar Gap**, 4200ft above sea level and some two miles up past Newcastle. Constructed in the 1930s, it's a pretty, flower-wreathed place offering yet more fabulous views. It serves American and Continental breakfasts, and excellent if expensive lunches and dinners. There's also a small room for rent (❹ including breakfast); it's nicely decorated and offers TV and a compact kitchen; breakfast is included in the rates.

Just beyond the café is the entrance to the 300-acre **Holywell Recreational Park**, affording a spectacular view over Kingston, Port Royal and Portmore when not bathed in mist. Easily accessible from the city, this "park within a park" is the busiest part of the mountains, latticed with enjoyable, well-maintained hiking trails. Just past the entrance is the ranger station, the signposted Oatley Mountain jaunt (2 miles; 40min), an easy, varied circular hike through the tunnel-like jungle. If you want to **stay**, there are three basic cabins; they were out of action at the time of writing due to storm damage, but contact the Jamaica Conservation and Development Trust (se p.262) for an update.

Section

Past Holywell, the scenery becomes more beguiling as you wind your way higher, with fantastic views over mountain gaps planted with neat rows of coffee trees. The next break in the trees comes at **SECTION**, a friendly little settlement that's home

Getting around the mountains

You'll need a **car** to get the most out of the mountains. The principal access road, B1, cuts straight through the slopes; a right fork at the small village of **The Cooperage** leads to Mavis Bank, the main access point for Blue Mountain Peak, a left fork to Newcastle and Holywell. You'll need to be extra-attentive when behind the wheel here. Landslides are inevitable in the wet season and you can expect bumpy roads throughout the year. Though the roads appear wide enough only for a single vehicle, delivery trucks loaded with precariously balanced crates frequently barrel up the slopes, sounding their presence with blasts on the horn. It's wise to turn off the radio here and listen for oncoming traffic, and also toot your horn at every corner.

Public transport will only take you as far as the main settlements – from Papine in northeast Kingston, **buses** (roughly J$100) go to Newcastle via Irish Town (with the occasional minibus managing to get up as far as Holywell) and to Mavis Bank via Gordon Town. Ask around in Papine Square the day before you plan to travel for an idea of when servics are running, and avoid starting out on a Sunday when services are greatly reduced. **Cycling** is an attractive option if you've got your own mountain bike (finding one to rent can be difficult). Several hotels run day-long biking expeditions, among them the *Mount Edge Guesthouse* (Ⓣ876/944-8151, Ⓦwww.jamaicaeu.com; US$40; see above). Blue Mountain Tours (Ⓣ876/974-7075, Ⓦwww.bmtoursja.com; US$93 including transfer, lunch and refreshments) will pick you up from Ocho Rios and Runaway Bay, drive you up into the mountains and let you freewheel sixteen miles or so down to Fishdone waterfall near Buff Bay.

to several small-scale coffee farmers – it's a great place to both enquire about a local hiking guide and buy some coffee. Taking the right fork in the road here brings you eastwards via several switchback turns towards **Silver Hill Gap**, a stunning spot some 5000ft above sea level offering more awesome views across coffee-planted peaks. The *Starlight Chalet and Health Spa* (ⓣ876/969-3116 or 985-9380, ⓦwww.starlightchalet.com; ③) is an isolated and extremely appealing **hotel** on a gorgeous flower-filled bluff. The rooms are modern and comfortable, with balconies and private bathrooms, and there's a sauna and steam room. Try the good, inexpensive Jamaican meals served up in the **restaurant**, which, like the attached bar, is open to non-guests; call ahead if you plan to eat. There are a couple of bicycles available for guests to use, and several short trails surround the property, one leading down the valley to a swimmable river; guides are available. Staff also offer guided **hikes** to nearby destinations such as Cinchona botanical gardens and Clydesdale.

Mavis Bank and Blue Mountain Peak

Back down the hill at The Cooperage, the right-hand fork of the Gordon Town Road passes through the comparatively lively village of Gordon Town. Turn right at the bridge over the Gordon Town River, and a bumpy half-hour drive takes you to neatly arranged **MAVIS BANK**. Nestled in the Yallahs River valley, it's the last full-scale settlement on the route to Blue Mountain Peak. There's little to the tiny village itself; the main attraction is the government-owned **JABLUM coffee factory** (Mon–Fri 8am–2pm; US$8; tours by appointment on ⓣ876/977-8015) on the west side. The factory is Jamaica's main Blue Mountain coffee-processing plant, and an engaging tour takes you through the whole process.

The main reason to visit Mavis Bank, however, is hiking up to **Blue Mountain Peak**. As only the sturdiest of Land Rovers can take the abominable road up to Penlyne Castle, where the peak trail starts, it's best to make arrangements in advance; contact Sun Venture (see box p.255), which will take care of everything, or call one of the lodges at the base of the trail (see below) and arrange for a pick-up, which

Hiking in the Blue Mountains

There's no charge to enter most parts of the Blue Mountains; however, visitors pay US$5 to enter the managed Holywell Recreational Park area and another $5 to walk its trails (however, you'll often find there's no one around to pay your fee to). Park information is available from each of the Blue and John Crow national parks' three **ranger stations**, located at **Holywell**, **Portland Gap** and **Millbank**. Theoretically always open (though Holywell is the liveliest and by far the most accessible), but not always manned, these stations can provide advice on weather conditions and trail access, and ordnance survey maps are on display. None of the ranger stations has a phone, but you can make prior contact through the Jamaica Conservation and Development Trust in Kingston (ⓣ876/920 8278–9, ⓦwww.greenjamaica.org.jm).

No matter where you're walking in the Blue Mountains, it's almost always advisable to use a **guide**; given the changeable weather conditions and poor hiking maps (in a terrain with few obvious landmarks), it's very easy to get lost. Security can also be a problem for unaccompanied hikers, particularly on the Kingston side of the mountains. A guide will ensure your safety, clear overgrown paths and provide an informed commentary. You can arrange a guide through any of the accommodation options listed in this section, but if you just want a day tour or guided hike, contact Sun Venture (see p.255), which offers trips to the gorgeous Cinchona gardens, as well as various day-long mountain walks and the hike to the peak. You can also arrange guided hikes through the *Mount Edge* and *Forres Park* guesthouses (see p.261 & p.263); the latter can take you up to the Peak, to a coffee plantation on the Peak's foothills, and on birding tours.

costs J$2500 one-way per vehicle, or $4000 round-trip. You can **stay** at *Forres Park* (ⓣ876/927-8275 or 5957, ⓦwww.forrespark.com; ❸), a delightful collection of self-contained wood cabins set around a large house that holds appealing, comfortable rooms with private bathrooms; there's also one fantastic luxury room with huge windows overlooking the mountains (❺). **Meals** are available on request (non-guests are also welcome), as are guides for the peak trail, hikes in the Mavis Bank area and birding trips.

From Mavis Bank, it's a fabulous drive up to Abbey Green, just over five miles northeast. On the way up, you'll turn left through **HAGLEY GAP** – a one-street village where you can buy provisions and get a hot meal – after which you'll traverse one of the least road-like roads in Jamaica, with huge gullies carved through the clay by coursing water and a constant scree of small boulders in your path. At some 4500 feet above sea level, **ABBEY GREEN** is a completely different world, where wind whistles through eucalyptus trees and mists billow over the mountainside only to evaporate in the sun. You're unlikely to meet anyone save the odd coffee-grower or scallion farmer. The only building of note is the atmospheric hiking lodge, *Whitfield Hall* (ⓣ876/926-6612 or 927-0986; bunks ❶, cabin ❷), set in an old stone planters' house, with a grand piano, a log fire, low ceilings and an old-fashioned kitchen. You sleep in bunks or in a self-contained cottage, and meals are available. Another option, on the hillside just below *Whitfield*, is the simple, friendly guesthouse run by local Rasta Jah B (ⓣ876/377-5206, ⓔfarmhillcofee@yahoo.com; ❶); meals are available. Whichever lodge you choose, it's a good idea to arrange to have a **hot meal** ready for when you return from the hike. Any of the lodges will be able to provide a peak guide for around US$30.

The highest point on the island, **Blue Mountain Peak** (7402ft) seems daunting but it isn't the fearful climb you might imagine – though it's hardly a casual stroll, either. It is magnificent by day, when you can marvel at the opulence of the canopy, the thousands of orchids, mosses, bromeliads and lichens, the mighty shadows cast by the peak, and the coils of smoke from invisible dwellings below. It's also thrilling by night, when after a magical moonlit ascent, Kingston's lights occasionally twinkling in the distance, you find yourself at Jamaica's zenith as a new day dawns – a completely heart-stopping experience.From Penlyne Castle, the climb to the peak is around eight miles and can take anything from three to six hours depending on your fitness level. Most people start at around 1am to catch sunrise at the peak. If you synchronize your walk with a full moon, you'll get beautiful natural floodlighting – but take a flashlight anyway. Regular signposts make the route easy to follow without the aid of a guide, but in this remote area it's sensible to go with someone who knows their way. Don't stray onto any of the tempting "short cuts" – it's illegal, you'll damage the sensitive environment and you'll almost certainly get lost.

The Portland Gap ranger station, about a third of the way up, offers the opportunity to refill your water bottle. From here it's another three and a half miles to the peak. At around 7000ft, the plateau at **Lazy Man's Peak** is where many hikers call it a day, but it's worth struggling on for another twenty minutes, as a far more spectacular panorama awaits you at the peak. As the sun burns off the mist, you can make out Cinchona and, on a good day, Buff Bay and Port Antonio's Navy Island to the north, and Kingston, Portmore and coastal St Thomas to the south.

Portland

North of the Blue Mountains, **Portland** is rightfully touted as the most beautiful of Jamaica's parishes – a rain-drenched land of luscious foliage, sparkling rivers and pounding waterfalls. Small-scale **Port Antonio** is the largest settlement, a relaxed country town with some inexpensive accommodation options. To the east lie a string of fabulous **beaches** and swimming spots, including the lovely Blue Lagoon, while if you head into the interior, you can be poled down the **Rio Grande** on a bamboo raft or hike through the rainforest along the centuries-old trails of the Windward Maroons. An increasing number of visitors are venturing further east along the coast for the even more laid-back pleasures of **Long Bay** – with a growing young travellers' scene and the best surf in Jamaica – while the roadside vendors in **Boston Bay** offer some of Jamaica's best jerk pork and chicken in a lovely oceanside setting.

Some history

Portland's early economy depended on sugar, and large estates were scattered throughout the parish. As the industry declined in the nineteenth century, the parish's fertile soil proved ideally suited for **bananas**. Port Antonio boomed as the country's major banana port, ushering in an era of prosperity for the town and the region. Cabin space on the banana boats was sold to curious tourists, and the place became a favourite of glitterati such as William Randolph Hearst, J.P. Morgan, Bette Davis and Errol Flynn.

Celebrities still sequester themselves in Portland, and there's a burgeoning backpacker scene at Long Bay, but despite the revitalizing of areas such as Port Antonio's harbourfront, with its spanking new marina and waterside promenade, the area can't yet compete for the mainstream vacationer, losing out to the more accessible and better-marketed resorts of Montego Bay, Negril and Ocho Rios. Agriculture is still important, but the area is still a long way from the prosperity of its heyday – something which many find its greatest charm.

Port Antonio

A magnet for foreign visitors during the 1950s and 1960s, the quiet town of **PORT ANTONIO** feels more like an isolated backwater these days. But that may change following the redevelopment of the harbour; across the bay, the hotel and beaches at Navy Island (currently closed, but call the tourist board on ⓣ876/929-9200 for an update) are slated to receive some much-needed attention, too. Though Port Antonio has no dedicated attractions save the new waterside promenade, it's a friendly and beguiling place with a bustling central market and a couple of lively clubs.

Arrival, information and getting around

Buses and **minibuses** from Kingston (3hr 30min) and Montego Bay (5hr) pull in at the main terminus by the seafront on Gideon Avenue, or by the town's central square on West Street (which also serves as the main **taxi rank**). If you're **driving**, the A4 highway runs straight into and through the town.

To get your bearings, head up to the *Bonnie View Hotel* (signposted off Harbour Street at Port Antonio's eastern outskirts), overlooking the entire town and providing great views of the twin harbours, Navy Island and the shimmering reefs. You can **walk** between the handful of sights in Port Antonio, while most places of interest outside town (and all of the beaches) can be reached by **public transport**. Shared taxis run along the main road as far as Long Bay. Reliable taxi drivers include the cheerful Mr Palmer (ⓣ876/993-3468 or 707-4276), the Port Antonio taxi cooperative (ⓣ876/993-2684) or JUTA (ⓣ876/993-2684).

Accommodation

Port Antonio has plenty of good **accommodation** with the lowest prices on the island.

De Montevin Lodge 21 Fort George St, Titchfield ⓣ876/993-2604, ⓔde_montevin@cwjamaica.com. Good value in a lovely old gingerbread house, a relic from colonial days. Clean, cool and simple rooms with cable TV, balconies and shared or private bathrooms, and great food from the restaurant downstairs. ❷, en-suite ❸

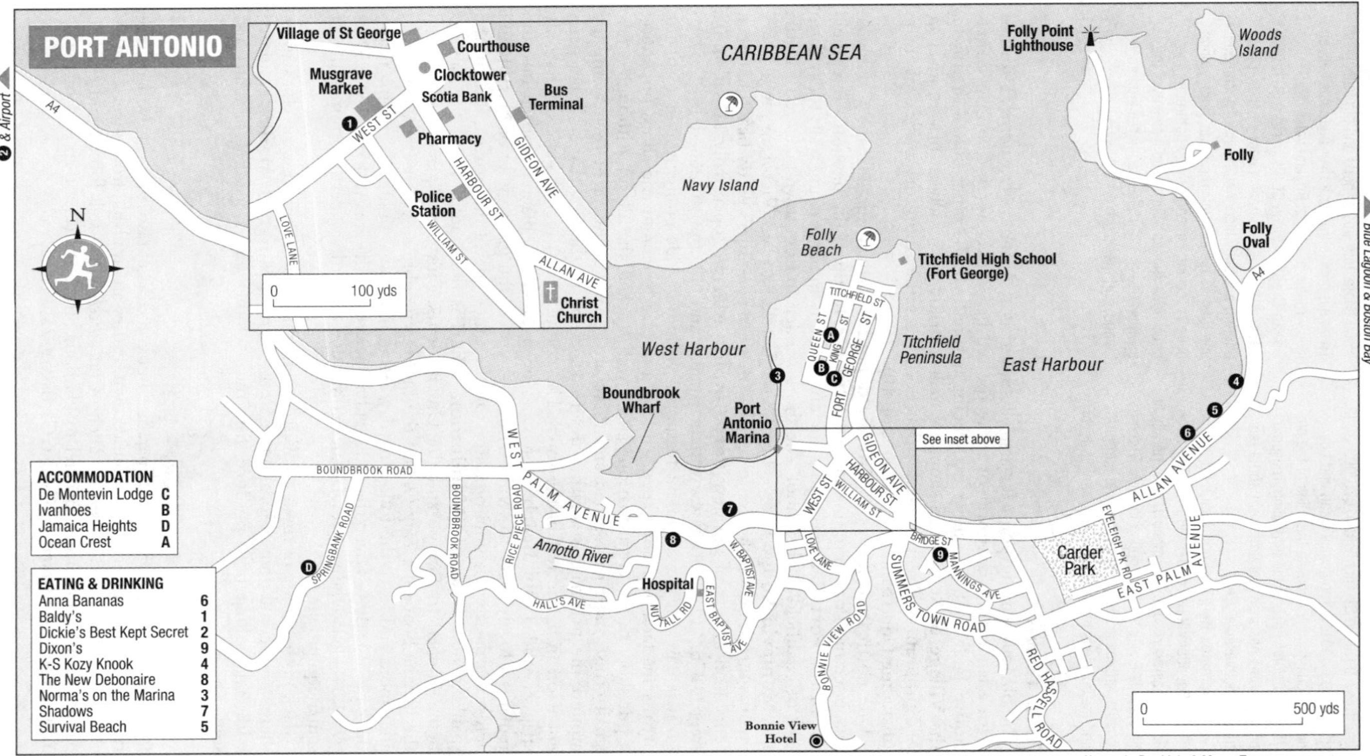

PORT ANTONIO
CARIBBEAN SEA
Village of St George
Courthouse
Musgrave Market
Clocktower
Scotia Bank
Bus Terminal
Pharmacy
Police Station
WEST ST
HARBOUR ST
GIDEON AVE
WILLIAM ST
LOVE LANE
ALLAN AVE
Christ Church
0 100 yds
Navy Island
Folly Beach
Titchfield High School (Fort George)
Titchfield Peninsula
West Harbour
East Harbour
Boundbrook Wharf
Port Antonio Marina
See inset above
Folly Point Lighthouse
Woods Island
Folly
Folly Oval
A4
Blue Lagoon & Boston Bay
2 & Airport
Nonsuch, Berridale & Moore Town
TITCHFIELD ST
QUEEN ST
KING ST
FORT GEORGE ST
WEST PALM AVENUE
BOUNDBROOK ROAD
RICE PIECE ROAD
SPRINGBANK ROAD
Annotto River
HALL'S AVE
NUTTALL RD
Hospital
EAST BAPTIST AVE
W. BAPTIST AVE
BONNIE VIEW ROAD
Bonnie View Hotel
BRIDGE ST
MANNINGS AVE
SUMMERS TOWN ROAD
RED HASSELL ROAD
EAST PALM AVENUE
EVELEIGH PK RD
Carder Park
ALLAN AVENUE
0 500 yds
N
ACCOMMODATION
De Montevin Lodge C
Ivanhoes B
Jamaica Heights D
Ocean Crest A
EATING & DRINKING
Anna Bananas 6
Baldy's 1
Dickie's Best Kept Secret 2
Dixon's 9
K-S Kozy Knook 4
The New Debonaire 8
Norma's on the Marina 3
Shadows 7
Survival Beach 5

Ivanhoes 9 Queen St, Titchfield ⓣ876/993-3043, ⓕ876/993-4931. Scrupulously clean and tidy, no-frills guesthouse opposite the ruins of the old *Titchfield Hotel*. Each of the appealing, reasonably priced rooms has a private bathroom and a fan; meals are available. ②

Jamaica Heights Spring Bank Rd (off Boundbrook Rd) ⓣ876/993-3305 or 2156, ⓦwww.jasresort.com. This mellow, very friendly little place is easily the best option in town. The lofty location affords grand views of the twin harbours, and the spacious rooms have clean, simple decor, wood floors, four-poster beds and big balconies. There's a pool, a trail to a river and waterfall, and lovely meals available. Brilliant value. ③

Ocean Crest 7 Queen St, Titchfield ⓣ876/993-4024, ⓔlydia.j@cwjamaica.com. Friendly place offering a slightly higher standard of accommodation than its neighbours. The clean, homey units have TV, ceiling fan and private bathroom; the three newest ones afford good views over the town and have a/c. There's a shared kitchen and lounge, and meals are available. ②

The Town

The obvious starting-point for a stroll around Port Antonio is its **central square**, with a landmark clocktower opposite the red-brick, two-storey Georgian **courthouse**, built in 1895 and currently being restored. On the other side of the road is the **Village of St George** shopping mall, a striking if somewhat bizarre melange of European architectural styles that houses a rather desultory parade of stores (including Don J's Internet café at shop 10).

Due north from here, the **Titchfield peninsula** juts out into the Caribbean Sea, bisecting Port Antonio's **twin harbours**. The tip of the peninsula once held the British **Fort George**, whose ancient cannons and crumbling walls today form part of Titchfield High School. The short wander up from town takes you past the **De Montevin Lodge** hotel – besides the hotel's excellent Victorian gingerbread architecture, there's little else to see now that the peninsula's pretty beach has been fenced-off as part of the new **Port Antonio Marina** (open daily, no set hours; free; ⓣ876/715-6044, ⓦwww.themarinaportantonio.com). Opened in 2002 to great fanfare, the development features a wide waterside promenade, state-of-the art marina facilities, landscaped gardens, a pool, a restaurant and shops (including a gift shop, an ice-cream parlour and a well-stocked chandlery). Although a few small cruise ships have called and there are usually a few yacht-owners milling around, the marina has a rather deserted air due to the fact that its huge gates cut it off from the rest of the town. The complex also includes the town's only strip of sand, **Folly Beach**, which has been tidied up, planted with palms and remains a lovely place to swim, with clear waters and great views of Navy Island across the narrow channel of water. On the other side of the marina, next to the spanking new boatyard, **Boundbrook Wharf** is the loading point for bananas being shipped to Europe and the United States. This is the place that inspired the banana boat song *Day O*, and the hulking freighters, which arrive on Friday afternoons and leave the following day, are an impressive sight. The marina is also the base of Lady G'Diver, the only scuba operator in the area (ⓣ876/715-5957 or 995-0246, ⓔladygdiver@cwjamaica.com); they offer dives, certification, and rent scuba equipment.

Back in the centre of town on West Street, which shoots off from the clocktower, there's a welcome dose of local bustle in the form of **Musgrave Market**, crammed with stalls selling fresh produce, fish, meat, clothes and a handful of crafts and souvenirs.

Eating

Port Antonio isn't a gourmand's paradise, but you can get tasty, inexpensive Jamaican **meals** at a handful of places around town. Patties are available from several outlets along West Street, and there's a branch of *Juicy Beef*, which sells lobster and chicken patties, on William Street (parallel to Harbour Street at the eastern end of town). You can get great baked goods at *CC's Bakery*, 25 West St.

Anna Bananas Allan Ave. A seaside restaurant overlooking the bay, this is one of the better choices in the area. Popular with tourists and locals alike, the food is reliable Jamaican, from curry lobster to brown-stew chicken; breakfast, lunch and dinner are served daily.
Dickie's Best Kept Secret On the A4 just west of town ⓣ876/1-809-6276 (mobile). On a knoll as you round the far bend of Port Antonio's west harbour, this simple wooden house scaled down the cliffside is easily missed, but is one of the most unique choices around. The moderately priced four-course dinners are fabulous (order the morning before you want to eat); choices include ackee on toast, garlic lobster and steamed fish. You can also drop by for breakfast, lunch or afternoon tea.
Dixon's Bridge St. Take-away lunch joint offering delicious vegetarian food (salads, curried tofu stew, stir-fried vegetables, etc) at rock-bottom prices. There's an airy upstairs room if you want to eat in.
The New Debonaire 22 West St. Hole-in-the wall eatery serving inexpensive local fare daily from 7am to midnight. Jamaican breakfasts, and lunches and dinners such as roast pork and beef, curry goat and chicken, and escovitched, steamed or sweet-and-sour fish.
Norma's at the Marina Port Antonio Marina. Run by one of Jamaica's most celebrated chefs, offering casual dining (lunch and dinner) at tables overlooking the water. The mid-priced menu includes starters such as crab-backs or tomato mozzarella salad, while the sophisticated main courses range from teriyaki ribeye steak to grilled chicken glazed with local apple preserve.
Shadows 40 West St. Excellent omelettes for breakfast and good Jamaican and Chinese meals, served at the pleasant outdoor gazebo or in the smarter, less atmospheric a/c restaurant.
Survival Beach Allan Ave. Inexpensive vegetarian lunches and dinners and fresh seafood in a friendly, easy-going setting with outdoor tables on a little strip of sand by the water.

Drinking and nightlife

The few places to head for a **drink** in town are often very quiet. The best and busiest option is *Baldy's*, a breezy rooftop bar above the Town Talk Plaza, opposite the courthouse, which usually has music pouring from the speakers and plenty of friendly chat – it's an excellent spot for watching the shenanigans at the market below. Just east of town, there are a couple of low-key rum bars right by the sea on Allan Avenue – try the friendly *K-S Kozy Knook*, with a large circular bar and plenty of dominoes action.

The fluorescent-streamer-bedecked UV palace of the *Roof Club* at 11 West St (nightly; J$150) is a Portland **clubbing** institution and one of the best, most laid-back and friendly places in Jamaica for a night on the tiles. It's busiest for Ladies' Night on Thursdays when women get in free; DJs play the latest dancehall, R&B and hip-hop alongside a dollop of more conscious tunes. Just down the street by the square, the *Roof* has some competition in the shape of the *La Best* club, with a ladies' night on Wednesdays, a Friday after-work jam and a Sunday oldies night.

East of Port Antonio

The coastline east of Port Antonio is a tropical fairytale landscape of jungle-smothered hills rolling down to fantastic beaches, from upmarket **Frenchman's Cove** and **Dragon Bay** to laid-back **Winnifred** and **Long Bay**. It also boasts the sublime **Blue Lagoon**, made famous by the eponymous 1980 movie starring Brooke Shields and Christopher Atkins. Further east, the smoking, sizzling jerk stands at Boston Bay are an essential stopoff en route to **Reach Falls**, a lavish natural cataract in the hills pounding down into a deep pool. A series of smart hotels vie for business with a handful of less expensive guesthouses, the latter mostly slung along the palm-fringed, wind-whipped beach at funky, laid-back Long Bay.

East to Winnifred

Just past Port Antonio's eastern outskirts, Allan Avenue swings past the fantastical **Trident Castle**. Built by European baroness Zigi Fami, owner of the *Jamaica Palace* hotel, the turreted white edifice is now the property of the *Trident Hotel* and is occasionally rented out for private functions.

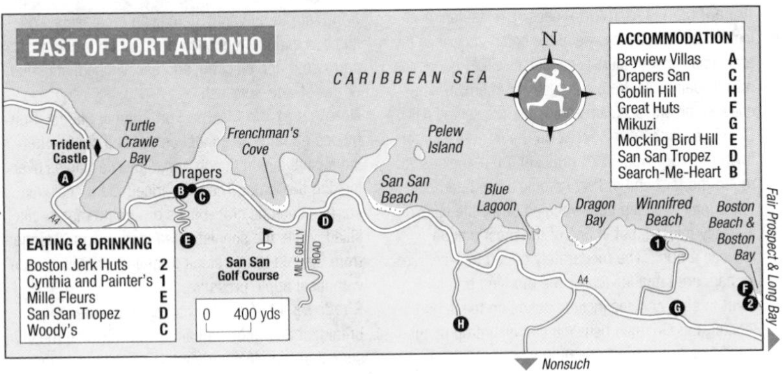

Three miles east of Port Antonio is **Frenchman's Cove**. The formerly sumptuous hotel villas have deteriorated, but the grounds are still beautifully maintained, and the **beach** (daily 9am–5pm; J$300), though small, is splendid. The curve of fine sand is enclosed by verdant hills, and a freshwater river, its bottom lined with white sand, empties into the sea. Food and drink are usually available from a tent set up on the sand (Tues–Sun), and you can rent loungers or take a boat tour to nearby beaches or the Blue Lagoon (US$10 per person). Just opposite the gates to the beach, local man Delroy keeps a couple of lovely horses and offers rides (US$25 per hour) along local beaches and into the interior. To find him, ask at the gates or call ⓣ876/383 1588. The signposted entrance to Frenchman's Cove is opposite the turn-off to the San San Golf Course, closed at the time of writing.

The next option for a swim is privately owned San San beach, open to tourists for around US$5 and somewhat neglected; you're far better off pressing on to the **Blue Lagoon**. Enclosed by greenery-smothered cliffs, the remarkably turquoise lagoon is a result of several underwater streams which run down from the mountains and bubble up here. The whole effect is incredibly picturesque, and it's a peaceful place to swim, made more unusual by the sensation of chilly spring water at the surface mixing with warm seawater below. You can swim for free from a pebbly "beach" or from the fenced-off restaurant complex, which usually charges a fee but was closed at the time of writing.

There's more marvellous swimming four miles east at supremely laid-back **Winnifred Beach**. One of the biggest and most appealing beaches on this side of the island, its wide, golden crescent of sand is justly popular with locals; at the time of writing, however, plans were afoot to fence off and "upgrade" what was one of Jamaica's last undeveloped swathes of sand, and impose an entry fee. Protests by local people outraged at the thought of losing one of the few places they can swim for free have been vociferous, but whatever the outcome, Winnifred remains a fabulous place for a day by the sea. The small reef is perfect for snorkelling (bring your own gear) and protects the bay from the waves; at the eastern end a small mineral spring offers a freshwater rinse. Winnifred has good, unobtrusive food and drink facilities; the best is *Painter and Cynthia's*, tucked into the western corner and serving up delicious platefuls of ackee and saltfish, chicken and fresh fish.

The coast road swings away from the sea parallel to Winnifred; to get to the beach, take the road opposite the *Jamaica Crest Resort* and follow it for half a mile or so. You can park and walk down to the sand where the tarmac ends; if it hasn't been raining recently, you should be able to drive right down onto the beach.

Practicalities

There are several upmarket **accommodation** options on the coast east of Port Antonio. Just east of town past Trident Castle is *Bayview Villas* (ⓣ993 3118,

ⓦwww.bayviewvillas-ja.com; ❹), a small hillside hotel with attractive wood-panelled rooms with fans, air-conditioning and cable TV. A pool with great views and a lovely flower garden are onsite, breakfast is included in the rates and meals are available. A little further east, green-conscious *Mocking Bird Hill* (ⓣ876/993-7267, ⓦwww.hotelmockingbirdhill.com; ❹–❻) boasts a lovely airy setting on a peaceful bluff above San San, with great Blue Mountain views, too. The comfortable rooms have balconies, and there's a pool and a good restaurant. Italian-style *San San Tropez* (ⓣ876/993-7213, ⓦwww.sansantropez.com; ❻) is another possibility. Its large rooms have air-conditioning and cable TV, and a pool and renowned restaurant are onsite; rates include breakfast. A less expensive option is *Drapers San*, right on the road at Drapers (ⓣ876/993-7118, ⓦwww.go-jam.com; ❷). It's a funky, friendly, Italian-run guesthouse with an eclectic collection of rooms, some with kitchen, some with shared bathroom; all have fans and mosquito nets. Breakfast is included, and the owner is a great source of local information. Next door, *Search-Me-Heart* (ⓣ876/353-9217, ⓦwww.searchmeheart.com; ❷ including breakfast) is a pretty Italian-Jamaican guesthouse offering three airy en-suite bedrooms with fan; guests can use the kitchen and laundry room, and there's a large veranda and well-kept garden. Just opposite the turn-off to the Blue Lagoon, a steep road leads inland to *Goblin Hill* (ⓣ876/993-7443, ⓦwww.goblinhill.com; ❺), a genteel complex of villas with a classy whiff of old Jamaica. With lovely contemporary decor, each villa is staffed with its own cook-housekeeper, and there's a pool, bar and tennis courts on site, as well as extensive grounds that offer lovely views of San San. Passes to Frenchman's Cove are included in the rates. Within walking distance of the beach (also accessible from the main road just past the Winnifred turn-off – keep an eye out for the sign on the left), *Mikuzi* (ⓣ876/978-4859 or 329-8589, ⓦwww.mikuzijamaica.com; rooms ❶, cottage ❷), set in pretty gardens and painted in fetching shades of orange and purple, consists of a couple of compact, nicely decorated rooms with fan and kitchenette, and a self-contained cottage (sleeping up to four) with screened windows, kitchen, living room and a veranda.

Rafting and hiking in the Rio Grande valley

Portland's interior – the **Rio Grande valley** – is a fantastically lush and partially impenetrable hinterland of tropical rainforest, rivers and waterfalls. The **Rio Grande** – Jamaica's largest source of freshwater – pours down from the John Crow Mountains through the deep and beautiful valley of virgin forest, with none of the soil erosion and deforestation found on the south side of the Blue Mountains. The paucity of good roads means it's not a heavily visited area, but it does offer some marvellous **hiking**, as well as the chance to slide down the waters of the Rio Grande aboard a bamboo raft. Once just an easy way to transport bananas to the loading wharf in Port Antonio, **rafting** has been Portland's most popular attraction ever since Errol Flynn began organizing rafting races here for his friends in the 1950s. From the put-in point at **Berridale**, six miles southwest of Port Antonio, rafts meander down the river on a three-hour journey through some outstanding scenery before terminating at the Rafters' Rest complex at St Margaret's Bay. The raft captain stands at the front and poles the craft downstream, stopping periodically to let you swim or buy snacks from vendors positioned along the route. Unfortunately, legal wrangles have closed the building at Rafter's Rest, just by the bridge in St Margaret's Bay, but raft captains still hang out here touting for business; trips cost US$52. Because it's a one-way trip, you'll need to first take a taxi up to Berridale; from town, rafting and a taxi should cost about US$70.

If you fancy some hiking in the valley, contact Attractions Link, based at Travel Express in the City Centre Plaza on Harbour Street (ⓣ993 2102 or 4828, ⓔattractionslink@cwjamaica.com), who also do general area tours.

There are a few **places to eat** this side of Port Antonio. For a formal meal, head to *Mille Fleurs* at *Mocking Bird Hill Hotel*, where the terrace restaurant offers a daily-changing menu of imaginative but expensive dishes based on Jamaican staples including lobster poached in coconut milk with sesame and chilli or jerk-spiced snapper with wafer potato scales. Breakfasts are also excellent, from great omelettes to corn pancakes with goats' cheese, or avocado and herb cream cheese. The Italian chefs at *San San Tropez* serve up bruschetta, smoked marlin salad, fresh pasta, fantastic thin-crust pizzas and fish and meat dishes, as well as lovely home-made ice cream. As you'd expect, there's a good wine list. A less expensive option is *Woody's*, a friendly family-run café on the coast road at Drapers offering great burgers (including veggie burgers); the lovely Jamaican staples such as fish with pumpkin rice, pepperpot soup, jerk pork or chicken and curries have to be ordered a day in advance. Another excellent option is to head to Boston for some jerk.

Boston to Long Bay

Though blessed with a perfectly good public beach, **BOSTON BAY**, further east along the A4, is better known for its collection of **jerk stands**. Jerking of meat originated in this part of the country, and the pork and chicken sold here is still reckoned to be the best in Jamaica. You'll pay around J$300 for a half-pound of chicken, and J$400 for half a pound of pork; both are best eaten with a dollop of ketchup and jerk sauce and accompanied by roast yam, breadfruit or a hunk of fresh bread and, of course, an ice-cold Red Stripe.

Still owned by the widow of Errol Flynn, the rolling pasturelands past Boston Bay give way to **LONG BAY**, home to a relaxed tourist scene. The area took a battering from Hurricane Dean in 2007, and at the time of writing, many places to stay and eat have closed for business; given that the town recovered fairly swiftly from the depredations of Ivan in 2004, most places are likely to have reopened by the time you read this. With its wide swath of surf-pounded honey sand, Long Bay tends to attract European backpacker types, some of whom have settled here and opened guesthouses. Pre Dean, two simple, friendly beach bars, *Yahimba* and *Chill Out*, catered to the demand for entertainment. It's a far cry from the developed resorts on the north coast: tourists are outnumbered on the beach by local people, and there's a

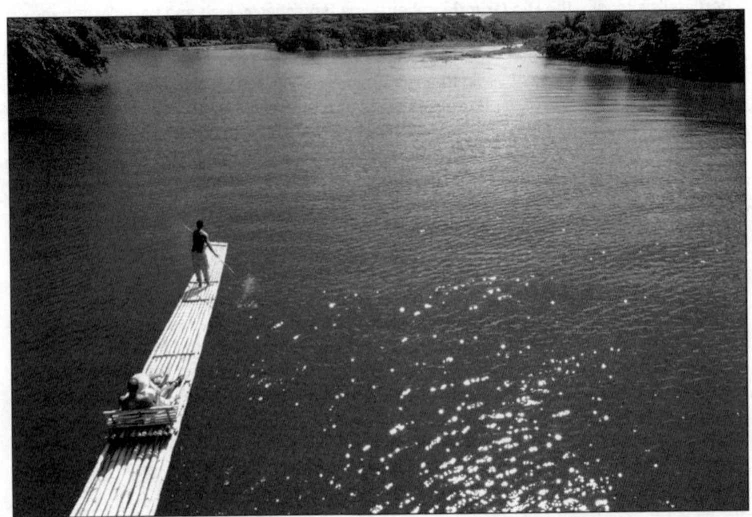

▲ Rafting down the Río Grande

lot of ganja-wreathed hanging out. There isn't much to the village, which has grown up piecemeal on either side of the main road. The north end of the beach is best for **surfing**; the locals should be able to help you find a board, and they'll also know who can take you out **fishing**. **Swimming** is excellent here, too, but watch out for a dangerous undertow and rip tides; never swim out further than you can stand.

When you're able to drag yourself away from the beach, head a few miles further east to a signposted turn-off that swings inland from the coast road to spectacular **Reach Falls** (Wed–Sun 8.30am–4.30pm; US$10), where the Drivers River cascades thirty feet into a wide, green pool. You can stand right underneath the falls for an invigorating water massage. From the base of the falls, there's a lovely walk upriver through the rainforest. At the time of writing, Reach Falls were being redeveloped, with lots of concrete being added à la Dunn's River. If you'd rather a more natural experience, visit on closed days and take a guided tour with Renee and Nya, who have a shack on the approach road and charge J$500 for a guided walk up the higher reaches.

Practicalities

There's plenty of budget **accommodation** in Long Bay, though much of it was closed for repairs at the time of writing. On the inland side of the road, and undamaged by the winds, try *Likkle Paradise* (Ⓣ876/913-7702; ❷), which has spotless rooms with fans and private bathrooms; guests can use the kitchen. *Fishermen's Park* (Ⓣ876/913-7482; ❶–❷) is a rambling family home offering atmospheric but basic local-style rooms with cold-water bathrooms, fans and mosquito nets. Over on the beach adjacent to the *Cool Runnings* bar, the two African-style huts of *Yahimba* (Ⓣ876/913-7067, Ⓦwww.yahimba.com; ❸) suffered lot of damage but were being rebuilt with mosquito nets, verandas overlooking the water and private bathrooms with hot water. Twenty minutes' drive east of town, past the small fishing community of Manchioneal, there's another lovely and unique accommodation option. Run by knowledgeable and chilled-out Dutch emigrée Free-I, *Zion Country Beach Cabins* (Ⓣ876/993-0435, Ⓦwww.zioncountry.com; ❷ including breakfast) are ranged up a landscaped hillside and offer simple accommodation with gorgeous views over the bay. There's a private beach, and Free-I offers great tours in Portland and the rest of the island.

For **food** and **drink**, the appealing *Yahimba* usually offers tasty meals (fish in coconut, chicken in satay sauce, calamari fritters, pizza). There's good **music**, too, and occasionally parties (including a monthly full-moon beach party with a bonfire and conscious reggae) or sound-system jams. Just east with a slightly roomier thatch-roofed patio, *Chill Out* offers good meals (burgers, pizzas and salads as well as good Jamaican food, including curry goat at weekends). Either of these is a great place for a drink, and there are also several friendly **rum bars** on the main road. Otherwise, the classiest place to eat locally is *Jamaican Colors* (Ⓣ913 7014 or 893 5185, Ⓦwww.hoteljamaicancolors.com; ❷), south of the village, whose French owner cooks very reasonably priced lobster and calamari, and has a bar serving great cocktails. They also have some really nice rooms for rent, and a pool.

5.3

Ocho Rios and around

With its high-rise blocks, buzzing jet skis and duty-free stores, the classic resort town of **Ocho Rios** typifies the commercial feel of Jamaica's north coast. Home to a wealth of slick attractions – from the famous **Dunn's River Falls** to **Dolphin Cove**, as well as a couple of lovely **botanical gardens** – the town is geared to the needs of cruise shippers and beach vacationers. East of town, the quiet coastal villages of **Oracabessa** and **Port Maria** boast a funky beach club and Noel Coward's former home, while west of town hotels line the shore at the resort-oriented coastal sprawls of **Runaway Bay** and **Discovery Bay**. The lush St Ann hills hold one of Jamaica's major draws, the **Bob Marley Mausoleum** at the singer's birthplace, Nine Mile.

Ocho Rios

The first town in Jamaica to be developed specifically as a resort, **OCHO RIOS** (usually just called "Ochi") abounds with neon-fronted duty-free stores, fast-food chains, bars, clubs and visitor-oriented restaurants. Local culture takes a back seat to the tourist trappings, so this isn't the place to get an authentic flavour of Jamaica. It's not the best choice amongst the island's "big three" resorts for the classic Caribbean beach holiday either – the town's strip of hotel-lined sand just can't compete with the beaches of Negril and Montego Bay, and the club and bar scenes are less vibrant. Nonetheless, the nightlife is improving, and Ochi compensates for its deficiencies with a certain neon energy.

Arrival and information

All **buses** pull in at the terminus behind Main Street. It's within walking distance of most hotels, but taxi drivers usually hang around plying for fares. If you're **driving** in from Montego Bay, the coast road forks as you enter town; left takes you onto the one-way section of Main Street where the majority of hotels are located, while right takes you along DaCosta Drive, which connects with the bypass (the route to hotels east of town) and with Milford Road, which leads to Fern Gully and, eventually, Kingston. If you drive in from the east, you'll enter town via the bypass; there are numerous signposted exits onto Main Street.

Organized tours and activities

In terms of quality and choice, the Ocho Rios roster of **organized tours** is second only to Montego Bay – you'll see advertisement fliers at practically every tourist-oriented spot in town. The tours market has been pretty much sewn up by the highly professional Chukka Cove Adventure Tours (Ⓣ876/972-2506, Ⓦwww.chukkacaribbean.com; tours US$65–100); choices range from a brilliant **canopy tour**, swinging along nine traverses at Cranbrook Flower Forest, to **tubing** along the White River and an unusual encounter with the island's dog sled team, with includes a sled ride. Hooves (Ⓣ876/972-0905, Ⓦwww.hoovesjamaica.com; rides US$55–65) offers **horseback trail rides** around the Seville Great House at St Ann's Bay that include swimming your horse and an inland "Bush Doctor".

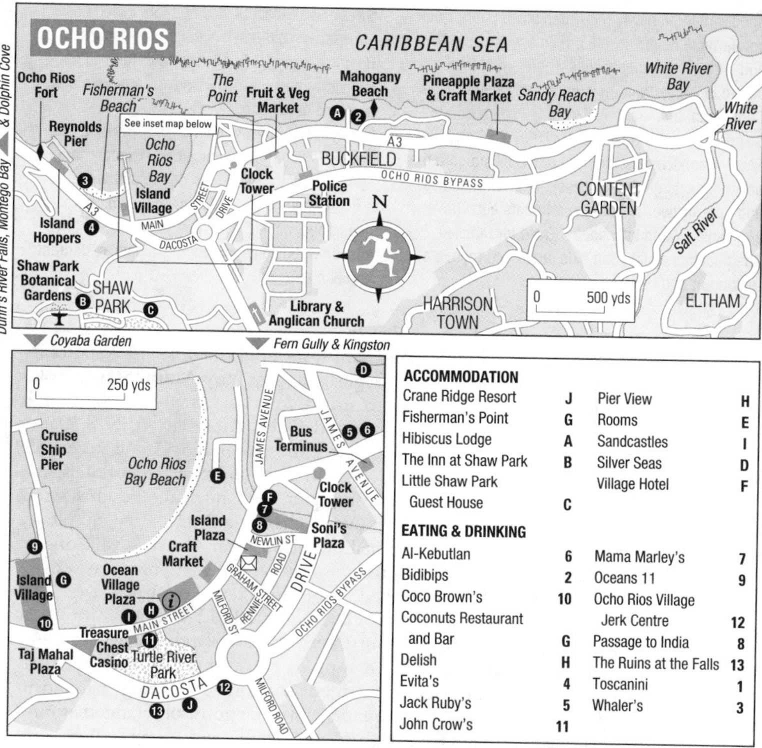

Accommodation

There are abundant **accommodation options** in Ochi, including many all-inclusive resorts and villas to rent; the latter can work out to be surprisingly inexpensive if you're travelling in a group. See p.241 for villa contacts.

Hibiscus Lodge 83-87 Main St ⓣ876/974-2676, ⓦwww.hibiscusjamaica.com. Set back from the road in beautiful gardens, this is the most attractive hotel in the town centre. The clean, pleasant cliff-side rooms all have balconies and wireless Internet, and there's a pool, hot tub, tennis court, sun deck, sea access, excellent restaurant and a bar. Rates include breakfast. 5

Fishermen's Point off Main St ⓣ876/974 5317, ⓦwww.fishermanspoint.net. Centrally located high-rise on the road to the cruise ship pier, offering clean and comfortable apartments with private balconies, a/c, cable TV and kitchenettes, plus a pass to the UDC beach. Friendly staff, Jamaican restaurant and a small pool. 3

The Inn at Shaw Park Shaw Park Botanical Gardens ⓣ976/974-2723, ⓦwww.shawparkgardens.com. Gorgeous rooms at the entrance to the gardens, offering spectacular views over town, and feature handsome decor, private balcony, a/c, cable TV, fridge and kettle. A real retreat. 4

Little Shaw Park Guest House 21 Shaw Park Rd ⓣ876/974-2177, ⓦwww.littleshawparkguesthouse.com. Easy-going, family-owned place overlooking town, set in gardens. The homey rooms have cable TV and fan; some share bathrooms, others have kitchen facilities and a/c. Meals are available. 2

Pier View 19 Main St ⓣ876/974-2607, ⓕ974-1384. Busy, friendly and laid-back apartment development, next to UDC beach and popular with younger travellers. Standard rooms have fan, fridge and cable TV; you pay more for a/c and kitchen, and there are some suites, too. All have access to the pool and sun deck. Rates include breakfast. 2–5

Rooms Main St ⓣ876/974-6632, ⓦwww.roomsresorts.com. Overlooking the beach, this middle-market, newly renovated place offers clean, comfortable resort-style a/c rooms with cable TV and wireless Internet access. There's a fitness centre, pool, bar and restaurant, and rates include Continental breakfast. ④

Sandcastles 120 Main St ⓣ876/974-5626, ⓦwww.sandcastlesochorios.com. Backing onto the beach (guests get free access), these airy studios and one- or two-bedroom apartments each have a/c, cable TV and kitchenette. Good for families (the pool has a slide and kids' area) and there's a restaurant and bar. ⑤

Silver Seas Main St ⓣ974 2755. Faded but atmospheric old hotel, popular with backpackers. Rooms are simple but comfortable, and all have sea views and private verandas. Large garden, pool and bar onsite. ③–④

Village Hotel 54-56 Main St ⓣ876/974-3193, ⓦwww.villagehoteljamaica.com. Friendly, family-run property slap in the centre of town and a five-minute walk to the beach. Rooms have queen bed, cable TV, a/c and phone (some have kitchen or balcony) and there's a pool, restaurant and bar. ④

The Town

Home to most of the town's hotels, bars, banks, shopping plazas and restaurants, as well as the bustling craft market, Ochi's permanently busy **Main Street** holds little interest for sightseeing. You're likely to spend your days lazing on the **beach** – variously known as UDC, Mallards, Turtle and Ocho Rios Bay (daily 8.30am–6pm, last entry at 4.30pm; J$200). Tucked under the tower blocks and accessible from the western end of Main Street near the *Pier View* and *Sandcastles* hotels, and from Island Village via the back of the cruise ship pier, the white-sand beach is wide, fairly attractive and well maintained, with showers, changing rooms, bars and plenty of activity. Patches of sea grass and occasional pollution mean that this isn't one of the north coast's most appealing places to swim, however, particularly when it's overshadowed by the massive bulk of docked cruise ships across the bay.

These days, the main centre of activity in Ochi is the **Island Village** complex at the far west end of Main Street (no set hours; free; ⓦwww.islandvillageja.com). An unashamed and not unattractive attempt to capture cruise-shippers' dollars, this is a shopping complex-cum-theme park of wooden, fretworked buildings painted in faded rainbow colours housing shops, restaurants and attractions, all arranged around a grassy central plaza with fountains, a Bob Marley statue and a stage where free entertainment – dance, poetry, drumming and the like – are put on at various points throughout the day. The entrance hall contains the **Cove Cinema** (ⓣ876/875-8353), screening the latest US releases, and the brilliant **Reggae Explosion** (daily 9am–5pm; US$15), an expertly executed exhibition dedicated to Jamaican music and culture. It's an illuminating collection of photographs, music and video clips of all of the island's musical heroes, from Prince Buster to Bounty Killer. Presented

Watersports

Although there isn't that much to see underwater at Ocho Rios's main beach – you'll find much richer pickings east of the harbour or at the reef at the bottom of Dunn's River (see below), the sand is lined with **watersports concessions**. Prices are set and displayed on boards at the main entrance, and offerings range from jet skiing to banana boat rides, water-skiing and parasailing. You can also take a glass-bottom boat ride; many go along the coast towards Dunn's River Falls. For **scuba diving**, try Resort Divers at 2 Island Plaza (ⓣ876/974-5338, ⓦwww.resortdivers.com), which also offers all the watersports and deep-sea fishing from US$450 per half-day.

Many private boats offer **pleasure cruises**. Day-trips go to Dunn's River for snorkelling and climbing the falls, with an open bar and lunch or snacks; sunset cruises include drinks only. Most operators offer dinner cruises, too. One of the better operators is Red Stripe (ⓣ876/974-2446), which runs a day-cruise to Dunn's River (daily except Sun 12.30–3.30pm; US$69, including an open bar and entry into the falls) and a sunset dinner cruise (Thurs–Sat 5–8pm; US$59) with drinks and Jamaican cuisine.

▲ Dunn's River Falls

chronologically, the displays cover mento, ska, roots reggae, dub and dancehall – the latter section has a dance floor on which you can follow footprints of various popular dance styles, from bogle to dutty wine. Understandably, the section devoted to Bob Marley is the largest, with plenty of rare photos and a re-creation of Lee Perry's infamous Black Ark studios. Island Village's other main attraction is its pretty stretch of **beach** (US$3), a heavily manicured curve of white sand with showers and changing rooms, where you can indulge in all manner of watersports or get a massage, hair braid or fancy nail job as well as take a swim.

The only other stretch of sand in Ochi that's not the private domain of an all-inclusive hotel is **Mahogany Beach**, set at the eastern stretch of Main Street as it climbs uphill (turn off just past the *Hibiscus Lodge* hotel). This compact wedge of beach with calm, clean waters and good snorkelling is a low-key place for a swim, with loungers for rent and watersports available. Management of the bar changes frequently; entry was free at the time of writing, but a small charge is sometimes levied.

Dolphin Cove and Dunn's River Falls

Heading west of town along Main Street, a boardwalk allows easy pedestrian access to Ochi's two biggest, and best, organized attractions. The first, some ten minutes' walk from the centre, is **Dolphin Cove** (daily 8.30am–5.30pm; ⓣ876/974-5335, ⓦwww.dolphincovejamaica.com). The main draw at the landscaped, theme-park-style complex is the chance to interact with the trained bottlenose dolphins kept in a fenced-off section of the bay. There are three choices of "interactive programme": the "Touch Encounter" (US$67), in which you stand in knee-high water and get to stroke a dolphin and have your photo taken; the "Encounter Swim" (US$129), which gets you into the water to kiss and play with the animals; and the "Swim with Dolphins" (US$195), in which you spend a bit more time in the water, and get a dorsal pull and a foot push. While it's all very organized, nothing much can take away from the delight of being so close to the dolphins. Elsewhere in the complex, there's a pool containing sharks and rays, with trainers doing daily displays; you can also pet the rays and swim with the sharks (US$119). The entrance fee of US$45 allows you to stay all day and includes a nature trail with stops for petting macaws, iguanas and snakes; a small beach from where you can snorkel or go glass-bottom kayaking; and a boat ride. Buffet lunch costs US$12. Dolphin, shark and stingray programmes take place at regular intervals throughout the day; it's advisable to book ahead, and you must arrive half an hour before the programme starts. There are changing facilities and lockers on site, but most people arrive in their bathing suits.

A couple of minutes' walk further west, **Dunn's River Falls** (daily 8am–5pm, last ticket 4pm; US$20, plus a tip for the guide) is Jamaica's best-loved waterfall and a staple of tour brochures. Masked from the road by restaurants, craft shops and car parks, the wide and magnificent 600ft waterfall cascades over rocks down to a pretty tree-fringed, white-sand beach that's far cleaner than the one in town. There's a lively reef within swimming distance, and snorkel gear is available to rent. With water running so fast you can hear it from the road below, the falls more than live up to their reputation, despite the concrete and commerciality. The main activity is climbing up the cascade, a wet but exhilarating and easily navigable hour-long clamber (last climb starts at 4pm). The step-like rocks are regularly scraped to remove slippery algae, and visitors form a hand-holding chain led by one of the very experienced guides. Wear a **bathing suit** – you're showered with cool, clear water all the way up. Most people also rent "sticky feet" shoes to help grip on the stones. There's a restaurant and bar, craft and hair-braiding shacks and full changing facilities at the beach and at the top of the falls.

Shaw Park and Coyaba

From the main roundabout at Ochi's western outskirts, a twenty-minute walk starting along Milford Road takes you to two of Ochi's better-known pastoral attractions, both on the ill-maintained Shaw Park Road (turn right from Milford Road 100ft from the junction at the Shaw Park signpost). Some 550ft above sea level, **Shaw Park Botanical Gardens** (daily 8am–5pm; US$10) afford stunning aerial views of town and do a cracking trade with cruise ship passengers. The former grounds of a long-gone hotel, the 25-acre gardens are resplendent with unusual flowers, plants and trees – including a huge banyan – set amidst grassy lawns; there's even a near-perpendicular (but non-swimmable) waterfall. You can walk unaccompanied, but the knowledgeable gardeners-cum-guides will introduce you to the wonders of tropical horticulture. There's an onsite bar, and crafts and jewellery on sale at the gift shop.

About five minutes further up Shaw Park Road, **Coyaba River Garden and Museum** (daily 8am–5pm; US$10), a meditative and restful miniature hothouse of lush, well-watered flowerbeds, is another favourite tour bus stop off. Wooden walkways allow easy viewing of the tropical foliage, and the flowerbeds are bisected by streams teeming with fish and turtles, with glass panels providing views of the underwater goings-on. Housed in an elegant cut-stone building, the museum has a limited but thoughtful collection of exhibits spanning Jamaican history; special weight is given to St Ann's own Marcus Garvey and Bob Marley. There's also a gorgeous **waterfall** which you can splash about in and climb à la Dunn's River.

Surrounded by foliage, its steep, fast cascade has been made accessible via wooden steps and platforms, and there are lookout points over Ocho Rios.

Prospect Plantation, Reggae Beach and White River Valley

A ten-minute drive east of town, **Prospect Plantation** (ⓣ876/974-2058, ⓦwww.prospectplantationtours.com) is a slick attraction designed to introduce the more sedentary visitor to the delights of tropical farming. You can sit atop an open trailer and trundle through sugar cane patches and groves of coconut palm, pimento, lime, ackee, breadfruit, mahoe and soursop trees, or tour the complex on the back of a camel or horse. There are also ostriches to feed, and a butterfly aviary. Tours cost US$44–89; book in advance.

A few minutes' drive east of Prospect along the A3 is **Reggae Beach** (Mon–Fri 9am–5pm, Sat & Sun 9am–6pm; JS$200). A pretty curve of coarse yellow sand, it's cleaner than the strip in town, though there's also some sea grass. Pluses include brightly painted showers and changing rooms, rope swings from the trees, plenty of shade and a good snack shop – and, as it's a little way out of town, it's usually very quiet.

Eating

Ochi's **restaurants** aim to please the foreign palate, and Italian, Indian, Chinese and American fare are available in addition to the Jamaican staples, including a couple of excellent vegetarian options. You'll find several patty shops around town, including a branch of *Juicy Beef* by the clocktower and *Tastees* a little further up Main Street, as well as numerous **fast-food** joints. For Jamaican food on the go, head to one of the smoking jerk stands that set up around the clocktower in the evenings.

Al-Kebutlan 1 James Ave. Rasta-oriented indoor diner offering good Ital-style breakfasts (including plantain, cornmeal and oat porridges) and various vegetarian delights for lunch and dinner, as well as a full array of natural juices.

Bibibips 93 Main St. Set back from the road with tables overlooking the sea, this place serves reliable and moderately priced fish dishes as well as coconut curry chicken, veggie wrap, Red Stripe or tequila shrimp and all the usual Jamaican favourites.

Coco Brown's Island Village &t876/675-8991. Appealing place with tables on a veranda overlooking a pond, and offering tasty food, from substantial sandwiches (tuna, roast beef, tofu melt) to burgers and full meals such as jerk chicken, lasagna or steamed fish. Good veggie options, and wireless Internet throughout.

Coconuts on the Bay Off Main St. On the road to the cruise ship pier, this open-air restaurant offers an appealing, mid-priced and wide-ranging menu from spring rolls and stuffed jalapeño peppers to salads, wraps, fajitas and Jamaican staples. Good service.

Delish 16 Main St. Café with a good onsite bakery, serving natural juices and tasty, good-value Chinese and Jamaican lunches.

Evita's Eden Bower Rd ⓣ876/974-2333. The best-advertised pasta on the north coast, served on a pretty veranda overlooking the bay. Huge choice of starters, salads and soups; main courses include pasta – even "Lasagna Rastafari" with ackee, callaloo and tomatoes – and seafood. Expensive, but worth the splurge.

Jack Ruby's 1 James Ave (behind *Ben R's Bar*). Friendly diner serving all the Jamaican staples, especially fresh fish (US$4–5), plus delicious lobster for as little as US$10.

John Crow's 10 Main St ⓣ876/974-5895. Just back from the road, with tables by a bar or in the open air, this is a relaxed spot for a meal, with Jamaican staples from curry goat and oxtail with beans to pizzas, pasta with calamari or salads.

Mama Marley's Main St. Bob-themed bar, restaurant and gift shop owned by the Marley family. The food and atmosphere is far from the clean-living, vegetarian lifestyle Bob espoused; nevertheless the lobster curry and ackee and saltfish are nice enough and prices reasonable.

Ocho Rios Village Jerk Centre just before the roundabout on DaCosta Drive. Renowned for the consistently good and sensibly priced jerk pork, chicken, fish and barbecued spare ribs as well as the piped dancehall, which draws in an evening crowd of drinkers.

Passage to India Soni's Plaza, 50 Main St ⓣ876/795-3182. Rooftop restaurant serving excellent Indian cuisine. The menu is pretty comprehensive; breads are particularly good, as are the lassi yogurt drinks and desserts.

The Ruins 17 DaCosta Drive. The main restaurant, built around a waterfall, is a pretty, upmarket spot for a Chinese meal in the evenings; next door, an annexe serves inexpensive lunches.

Toscanini Harmony Hall ⓣ876/975-4785. A ten-minute drive east of the centre under the eaves of pretty Harmony Hall, and easily Ochi's best restaurant. Service is great, and the justifiably expensive menu features all the Italian classics. Vegetarians are well served, and the puddings are sublime. Closed Mon.

Whalers Fishing Beach ⓣ479 6103. Overlooking the water on the fishing beach (turn off the road just before the Main Street turnoff), this two-storey wooden-built restaurant is one of the best of the collection of places here selling inexpensive fresh seafood. As well as a gorgeous conch soup and seafood served every which way, they have hearty local breakfast from 8.30am.

Nightlife and entertainment

Given Ocho Rios's dedication to the cruise ship trade, its nightlife can seem a bit limited, mostly revolving around whatever's going on at *Margaritaville* in Island Village – though the *Treasure Chest* **casino** on Main Street is usually lively and good for an inexpensive drink even if you don't want to hit the slot machines; it's open 24 hours a day. If you want to get away from the all-pervasive Americana, the pretty outdoor bar at *Toscanini* restaurant (see "Eating," above) offers a more sophisticated ambience, with some great wines available and a Friday happy hour (6.30–8.30pm). At the other end of the scale, there are rum bars and a couple of decidedly locals' clubs along James Avenue – it's best to go with a Jamaican companion, as the area can be a bit risky after dark.

Amnesia Disco above the Mutual Security building, 70 Main St ⓦwww.theamnesia.com. The nightclub of choice for most locals, with an indoor, air-conditioned dance floor and an outdoor bar area. Wed is a fairly quiet, with free entry; Thurs is the busy Ladies' Night, when women get in free; Fri sees an after-work jam with drinks promotions; on Sat there's a party night, with dancehall, R&B, hip-hop and dance; and there's an old hits party on Sundays.

Coconuts on the Bay off Main St. On the road to the cruise ship pier, the gazebo bar of this friendly restaurant is a great, hassle-free spot for a drink, with great cocktails and welcome sea breezes.

Margaritaville Island Village, Main St ⓦwww.margaritavillecaribbean.com. This neon-bedecked US-style place is Ochi's busiest nightspot, right on the beach and offering plenty of wet-and-wild action on the waterslide and in the pool, as well as good cocktails and dancing. The roster of theme nights, some all-inclusive, changes regularly (pick up flyers around town), and big-name DJs usually play at weekends.

Oceans 11 off Main St. Overlooking the Island Village beach on the road to the cruise ship pier, this professional and slick spot is a nice place for a drink, with karaoke on Tues and Latin night on Thurs.

Shopping

Shopping is big business in Ocho Rios. The town's three **craft markets** (daily 7am–7pm) have enticed many a hapless soul to leave Jamaica laden with "Yeh mon it irie" T-shirts and the like. Among the dross you'll find really nice T-shirts and sculptures. The main market is to the right of Ocean Village Plaza. **Island Village** has the usual roster of T-shirt and craft emporia as well as the self-explanatory Hemp Heaven, and an outlet selling the wonderfully aromatic Starfish aromatherapy products. Don't miss the gorgeous **art gallery** and shop at Harmony Hall (Tues–Sun 10am–6pm), ten minutes' drive out of Ochi on the way to Tower Isle. Set in a beautifully restored great house, it features works by renowned contemporary Jamaican artists and a variety of crafts and books.

East of Ocho Rios

As the clamour of Ocho Rios recedes, the A3 coast road switchbacks through the countryside towards the quiet, close-knit communities of **Oracabessa** and **Port**

Maria, where tourism is only just starting to take hold; the area has long been a favourite haunt of the rich and famous. Noel Coward and Ian Fleming (creator of James Bond) both lived here in the fifties and sixties, and their old homes, **Firefly** and **Goldeneye**, are still standing, with Firefly now a prime tourist site and Goldeneye the centrepiece of a luxury villa complex.

Oracabessa

Lit in the afternoons by an apricot light that must have inspired its Spanish name *Orocabeza*, or "Golden Head", **ORACABESSA**, some sixteen miles east of Ocho Rios, is a friendly one-street town with a covered produce market (main days Thurs & Fri) and a few shops and bars. A centre for the export of **bananas** until the early 1900s, Oracabessa became something of a ghost town when the wharves around the small natural harbour closed in 1969, taking with them the rum bars, gambling houses and most of the workers. The town snoozed quietly until the mid-1990s when the **Island Outpost** corporation (owned by Chris Blackwell, the former boss of Island Records and the producer of Bob Marley's most well-known albums) bought 100 acres of prime coastal land and opened up the village's main draw, the **James Bond Beach Club** (Tues–Sun 9am–6pm; US$5), signposted just off Main Street along Old Wharf Road. Jamaica's most stylish beach, the pretty but tiny strip of white sand offers brightly painted changing rooms, a watersports centre, and a bar/restaurant with a good selection of wines and meals such as curry or garlic shrimp, jerk chicken and burgers. The expansive lawns are a regular venue for large-scale **concerts**.

East of the turn-off for James Bond Beach, Oracabessa merges into the residential community of **Race Course**. This is the site of **Goldeneye** (Ⓣ876/975-3354, Ⓦwww.islandoutpost.com; ⑨) the unassuming white-walled bungalow in which Ian Fleming wrote almost all of the James Bond novels. Now an exclusive hotel with a selection of gorgeous villas that include the former home of Ian Fleming himself, it's off-limits to all but the very well-heeled.

Port Maria and Firefly

The diminutive capital of St Mary, **PORT MARIA**, nestled around a crescent bay some five miles east of Oracabessa, is a delightfully picturesque town – but once you've taken in the bay view and strolled the few shopping streets, there's little to keep you here. Most people turn off the main road before getting into town and travel the precipitous route up the hill to **Firefly** (daily 9am–5pm; US$10), the Jamaican home of Noel Coward and his partner Graham Payn from 1956 to Coward's death in 1973. The house remains much as Coward left it, with the table laid as it was on the day the Queen Mother came to lunch in 1965. Coward died here and is buried on the property. It's worth going to Firefly for the view alone. The panorama takes in Port Maria bay and Cabarita Island to the east, with the peaks of the Blue Mountains poking through the clouds, while to the west lies **Galina Point**, where a **lighthouse** overlooks the northernmost tip of Jamaica – you may even see Cuba on a clear day.

West of Ocho Rios

The coast road west of Ocho Rios swings past a couple of engaging attractions. Some eight miles west of town is the former site of **Seville**, Jamaica's first Spanish settlement, now an overgrown wasteland dotted with the crumbling remains of once-impressive buildings. The best way to see it is on horseback; see box p.272 for details of the rides offered here by Hooves. Across the road is **Seville Great House and Heritage Park** (daily 9am–5pm; U$5; Ⓣ876/650-1500), one of the few sites on the island focusing on the lives, customs and culture of Taínos and Africans (as well as the Spanish and British), with a great collection of artefacts arranged in chronological order, and intelligent interpretive information; 45min tours are included in the entrance fee.

Carrying on along the main road, you pass **Chukka Cove**, the most prestigious equestrian facility and polo ground in Jamaica and home to Chukka Adventures tours (see p.272). Just beyond, a tiny paved road cuts inland towards the signposted **Cranbrook Flower Forest** (daily 9am–5pm; US$10; ⓣ876/770-8071, ⓦwww.cranbrookff.com), an exquisitely landscaped, 130-acre nature park with several grassy lawns, a fishing pond where you can catch your lunch and have it cooked for you, and a swift-running river with plenty of swimming spots; it's also the home of the pulleys and ropes of Chukka Adventures' fabulous new Canopy Tour (see p.272). It's the perfect place for a **picnic**: bring your own or buy it onsite.

Runaway Bay and Discovery Bay

Halfway between Ocho Rios and Falmouth, the neighbouring mini-resorts of **RUNAWAY BAY** and **DISCOVERY BAY** bask in isolated indolence. Dominated by lavish all-inclusives, neither demands much of your time unless you've checked into one of the hotels. Runaway is the more developed of the two, though beyond the hotel fences and Italianate marble lobbies, life jogs along at a slow pace. For swimming, sugary-sanded **Cardiff Hall public beach**, opposite the Texaco petrol

Bob Marley – king of reggae

Born February 6, 1945, **Robert Nesta Marley** was the progeny of an affair between seventeen-year-old Cedella Malcolm and 51-year-old Anglo-Jamaican soldier Captain Norval Marley, who was stationed in the Dry Harbour mountains. Marley's early years in the country surrounded by a doting extended family and by the rituals and traditions of rural life had a profound effect on his development. He clung to the African side of his heritage and revelled in the rich cultural life of downtown Kingston, where he spent most of his later life.

Fusing African drumming traditions with Jamaican rhythms and American rock guitar, Marley's music became a symbol of unity and social change worldwide. Between 1961 and 1981, his output was prolific. Following their first recording *Judge Not* on Leslie Kong's Beverley's label, his band, The Wailers (Marley, Bunny Livingstone and Peter Tosh), went on to record for some of the best producers in the business. In 1963, the huge hit *Simmer Down* meshed perfectly with the post-independence frustration felt by young Jamaicans, and the momentum of success began in earnest. International recognition came when the Wailers signed to the Island label – owned by Anglo-Jamaican entrepreneur Chris Blackwell. The first Island release was *Catch a Fire* in early 1973, and the eleven albums that followed all became instant classics. After the departure of Peter and Bunny from the group in 1974, Marley continued to tour the world with a new band under the name of Bob Marley and the Wailers.

After being injured in a 1976 **assassination** attempt, Marley left Jamaica to recover and record in Britain and the States. Two years later, he returned to perform at the historic **One Love Peace Concert**. Marley ended his performance by enticing political arch-enemies Michael Manley and Edward Seaga on stage to join hands in a show of unity. But Marley's call for unity and freedom was not restricted to Jamaica; one of his greatest triumphs was performing the protest anthem *Zimbabwe* at the independence celebrations of the former Rhodesia.

In the midst of a rigorous 1980 tour, Marley was diagnosed as suffering from cancer; he died a year later in Miami, honoured by his country with the Order of Merit. The Bob Marley Foundation, administered by his wife, Rita, continues to sponsor the development of new Jamaican artists, and many of the Marley children have forged their own musical careers, most notably Damian "**Junior Gong**" and Steven Marley, the latter having also found success as a producer. In the hearts of Jamaicans, though, the master's voice can never be equalled.

station, is popular with locals. Midway between the two bays are the **Green Grotto Caves** (daily 9am–5pm; US$20), a system of expansive limestone caves that's been made accessible to the public. The guides inject plenty of humour into their tours, but nothing really justifies the high entrance fee.

Even more pacific than its neighbour, with fewer hotels, Discovery Bay is mostly a coastal clutch of shops, snack bars and houses. But it does have the fantastic **Puerto Seco beach** (daily 9am–5pm; J$250), which, despite gleaming sand and crystal-clear water, is relatively deserted on weekdays.

Marley's mausoleum and the St Ann interior

Both the B3 from Runaway Bay and the inland road from Discovery Bay lead towards **Alexandria**, a tiny hamlet where you turn left for the only tourist attraction in the St Ann interior, Bob Marley's Mausoleum at his former home of **Nine Mile**. Though the red-earthed pastures and sweeping hills and gullies of the Dry Harbour mountains are stunning, there are few specific points of interest. You'll need to have your own transport or charter a taxi to get here; a round-trip in a taxi from Runaway or Discovery bays should cost US$80–90, and from Ochi around US$100. From Alexandria, the narrow road off the B3 to the **Bob Marley Centre and Mausoleum** (daily 9am–6.30pm; US$15 ⓣ876/995-1763, ⓦwww.bobmarleyfoundation.com) winds through the hills past **Alva** and **Ballintoy**. You know you're in Nine Mile when you see red-gold-and-green flags flying high above a bamboo-fenced compound to the side of the main road. If driving, you'll be directed into the compound car park. There's also a vegetarian restaurant and a small gift shop selling CDs and high-quality Marley memorabilia. Led by a Rasta guide, the tour includes the wooden shack that Marley lived in between the ages of six and thirteen, an outdoor barbecue where Marley cooked up vegetarian feasts, and the Rasta-coloured "meditation stone", immortalized in the song *Talkin' Blues*. The **mausoleum**, a concrete building painted in Rasta colours with depictions of black angels, encases the marble slab that holds Marley's remains. If you don't fancy making your way to Nine Mile independently, you can join one of the jeep **tours** run by Chukka Adventures (see p.272).

If you want to linger in Nine Mile, you can stay in the relatively basic **hotel** opposite the complex, run by extended members of the Marley family; rooms cost around US$50 a night and you can have meals cooked for you or use the kitchen yourself. There's also more luxurious accommodation in the complex itself. The place comes alive every **February 6**, when Marley's birthday is celebrated with a sound-system jam and live show.

5.4

Western Jamaica

Home to two of the island's busiest resorts, western Jamaica is firmly on the tourist track. **Montego Bay**, once Jamaica's tourist capital, is losing out a bit to the hedonistic pleasures of **Negril** at the extreme western tip. In many ways, though, MoBay, as it's usually called, still delivers. Sitting pretty in a sweeping natural harbour and hemmed in by a labyrinth of protected offshore reefs, it remains the *grande dame* of Jamaican resorts and is particularly lively during its world-renowned summer **reggae festival**. Sybaritic Negril, boasting the longest continuous stretch of white sand in Jamaica and a front-row sunset seat, has a geographical remoteness that lends it a uniquely insouciant ambience. First visited by wealthy hippies in the 1970s, it is still immensely popular with those who favour easy living and corporeal indulgence, and is the best place outside Kingston for **live reggae** and **nightclubs**. Negril offers plenty of natural attractions around too, including the pleasant river walk at **Mayfield Falls** and the blue hole at **Roaring River**.

Montego Bay

Jamaica's second largest city, **MONTEGO BAY**, nestles between the gently sloping Bogue, Kempshot and Salem hills, and extends some ten miles from the haunts of the suburban rich in Reading at its western edge to the plush villa developments and resort hotels of Ironshore and Rose Hall to the east. It's made up of two distinct parts: the main tourist strip **Gloucester Avenue** (rechristened by the marketing people as the "Hip Strip"), and the city proper, universally referred to as "**downtown**" – a split so sharp that most tourists never venture further than the dividing roundabout.

The "Hip Strip" wouldn't exist were it not for Montego Bay's prize asset: a dazzling bay with miles of **coral reef** (now designated a marine park) and some beautiful **beaches**. Much of the coastline has been snapped up by the hotels but there are three main public beaches along the length of Gloucester Avenue, all with showers, changing rooms, snack outlets and watersports concessions and a minimal entrance fee.

Arrival, information and getting around

Upwards of eighty percent of visitors to Jamaica arrive at **Donald Sangster International Airport** (Ⓦwww.sangster-airport.com.jm), three miles east of the town centre and a mile from Gloucester Avenue. It has a 24-hour **cambio** and a branch of the NCB bank, a tourist-board desk (daily 9am–10pm) and numerous hotel, ground-transport and car rental booths. **Luggage trolleys** aren't permitted past immigration, but the official red-capped porters will carry your bags for a small charge. Larger hotels provide free airport transfers but you can charter a **taxi** from any of the omnipresent JUTA drivers – the trip to Gloucester Avenue, Queens Drive or downtown should cost no more than US$10. If travelling *very* light you can take one of the local **shared taxis** that leave from the petrol station past the airport's car par. There is no public bus service from the airport.

▲ Damian Marley

The main **Jamaica Tourist Board** office (Mon–Fri 8.30am–4pm, Sat 9am–1pm; ⓣ876/952-4425) is at the end of the access road to Cornwall Beach, just off Gloucester Avenue. For online information on Montego Bay check out ⓦwww.montego-bay-jamaica.com.

Unfortunately there is no public transport serving downtown Montego Bay or the strip, and consequently any tourist walking the streets will be assailed with offers from passing **taxis**. Be prepared to haggle and always settle the price before you get in. However, if you're spending most of your time on the strip, you can easily get around on foot.

Accommodation

The range of **accommodation** in Montego Bay is huge. This is prime **all-inclusive** territory, with the swankiest enclaves out at suburban Ironshore just east of town. Most people stay along the busy, buzzing Gloucester Avenue **strip**, and the best options are listed below. Many hotels include free airport transfers, and more distant properties throw in a free beach shuttle. Unless otherwise stated, rooms have air conditioning, cable or satellite TV and phone.

Altamont West 33 Gloucester Ave ⓣ952 9087, ⓦwww.altamontcourt.com. With all the panache of its sister property in Kingston (see p.247), this is an excellent new addition to the MoBay hotel scene, in a great location close to all the action and opposite Walter Fletcher Beach. The modern rooms have all mod cons and lots of useful amenities, from hairdryers to CD players, and there's a pool and a grassy sun deck on site, as well as wireless Internet throughout. Breakfast is included. ④

Bayshore Inn 27 Gloucester Ave ⓣ876/952-1046, ⓕ979-5087. Cheerful, brightly decorated en-suite rooms at the less frantic end of the strip, adjacent to the *Port Pit* restaurant. Reduced-rate weekly rentals available. 2

Beach View Apartments Gloucester Ave ⓣ876/971 3859, ⓦwww.marzouca.com. Appealing and inexpensive self-contained apartments in a great location. All have tiled floors, big bathrooms and a separate living area with kitchenette; one can sleep six, the others four. Rates include airport pickup and a daily pass to Aquasol beach. 2–3

Caribic House 69 Gloucester Ave ⓣ876/979-9387, ⓦwww.caribicvacations.com. Small hotel popular with European backpackers, in a great location opposite Doctor's Cave Beach. Adequate rooms with fridges; some have ocean views. 2–3

Coral Cliff Gloucester Ave ⓣ876/952-4130, ⓦwww.coralcliffjamaica.com. Tucked behind the Disney-esque gaming lounge and restaurant, the rooms here are functional and comfortable with all mod cons and balconies; there's a pool onsite. 4–5

Doctor's Cave Beach Hotel Gloucester Ave ⓣ876/952-4355 or 4359, ⓦwww.doctorscave.com. One of the better Strip hotels, across from Doctor's Cave Beach, with stylish decor, gorgeous tropical garden, pool, hot tub, restaurant, bar, games area and small gym. Rooms are pretty uniform, but the friendly atmosphere wins a lot of points. 4

El Greco Queen's Drive ⓣ876/940-6116, ⓦwww.elgrecojamaica.com. Sprawling complex of self-contained apartments perched high above the strip (access is via the lift of the adjacent *Montego Bay Club* resort). The modern suites have kitchens and balconies; tennis courts, pool and restaurant/bar are on site. Rates include breakfast and a pass to Doctor's Cave Beach. 5

Hotel Gloriana 1–2 Sunset Blvd ⓣ876/979-0669, ⓦwww.hotelgloriana.com. Cheap and cheerful place, popular with Jamaicans as well as tourists. Rooms are basic but nice (go for those in the new block, with tiled rather than carpeted floors), and have fridges and balconies; units with kitchens are available. There's a pool, whirlpool, restaurant and bar. 2–3

Ridgeway Guesthouse 34 Queen's Drive ⓣ952 2709, ⓦwww.ridgewayguesthouse.com. Homely and very friendly eight-room place within walking distance of the airport (turn left at the roundabout). The lovely tile-floor rooms, either fan-only or a/c, have wooden furniture and handsome marble bathrooms; those at the top afford sea views, and some have a fridge and kettle. Pluses include a rooftop sun terrace and free beach shuttle. 2–3

The Wexford Gloucester Ave ⓣ876/952-2854, ⓦwww.thewexfordhotel.com. Overlooking the only green space on the Strip, this reliable MoBay old-timer has clean, bright rooms with tiled floors, tropical-style decor and king beds; some have sweeping ocean views. There's a pool, bar and restaurant onsite. 5

Organized tours

Hundreds of **tour companies** operate out of Montego Bay; most have booths at the airport as well as offices along Gloucester Avenue and offer similarly priced trips to independent plantations and great houses. The **best operators** are slightly more adventurous: Barrett Adventures, Rose Hall (ⓣ876/995-2796, ⓦwww.barrettadventures.com), puts together customized packages to off-the-beaten-track waterfalls, farms and beaches from US$100 per person per day. Alternatively, hire a **local driver** and do some independent sightseeing. Reliable and friendly Dale Porter, aka "Shaka" (ⓣ876/316-2184 or 845 6635), offers all-day tours for around US$150; Danny of Danny's Tour's (ⓣ876/707-4767 or 979-4318) charges similar rates and has a minibus. Both can usually be found outside Doctor's Cave Beach.

Chukka Blue Adventure Tours (ⓣ876/979-6599, ⓦwww.chukkacaribbean.com) offers a number of very slick tour options in the area, from tubing along the Great River to an exhilarating **canopy tour** in which you skim through the tree tops on zipwires. Prices start at US$57.

If you want to go **horseriding**, by far the best option is the immaculate Half Moon Equestrian Centre (daily 9am–5pm; ⓣ953-2286, ⓦwww.horsebackridingjamaica.com) at the *Half Moon* hotel, who offer lessons (30min; (US$50) and a lovely beach ride in which you swim your horse in the sea (1hr; US$70).

River rafting (ⓦwww.jamaicarafting.com) is a more sedate pleasure, best done along the Martha Brae River, 45 minutes' drive east of MoBay near Falmouth. You can either turn up at the Rafter's Village departure point (signposted from Falmouth's main square) and pay US$55 for a 1hr 15min trip on a two-person raft; you can also opt to be transported there and back. To book, call ⓣ876/952-0889.

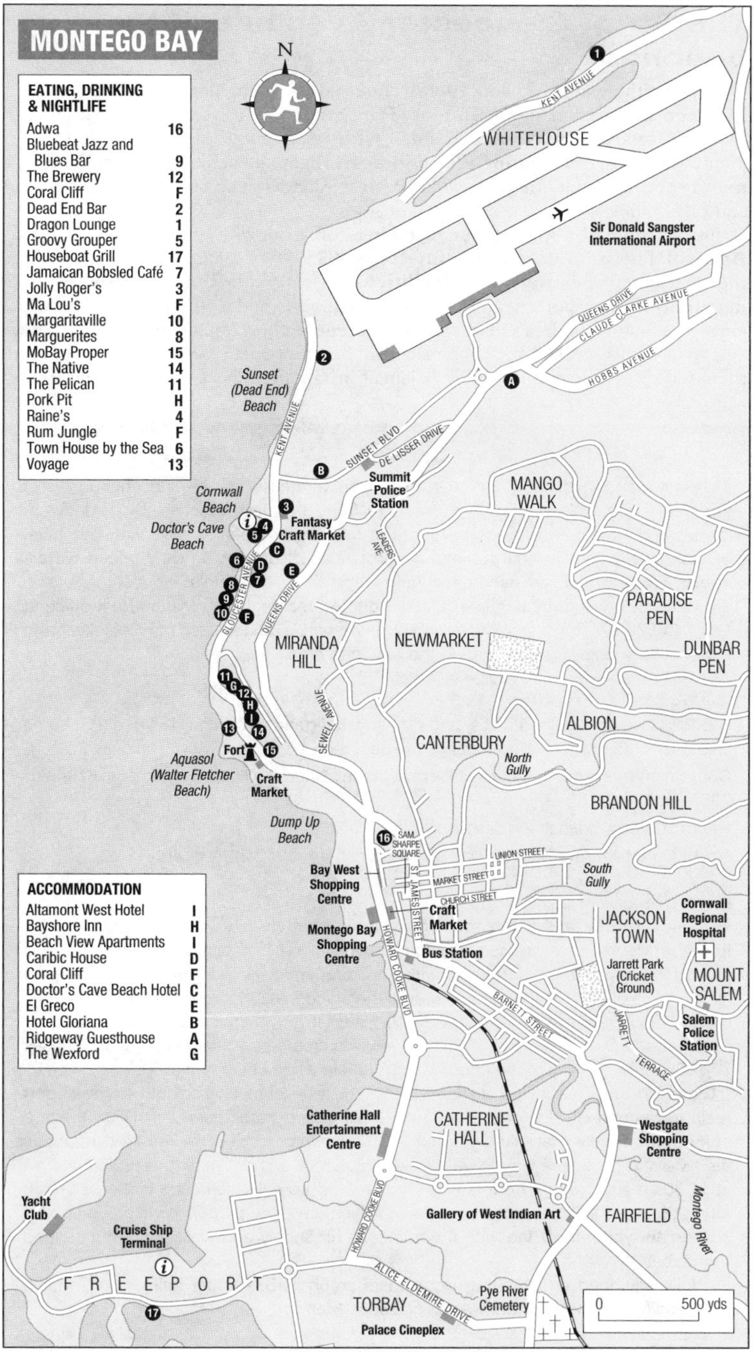

MONTEGO BAY

EATING, DRINKING & NIGHTLIFE

Adwa	16
Bluebeat Jazz and Blues Bar	9
The Brewery	12
Coral Cliff	F
Dead End Bar	2
Dragon Lounge	1
Groovy Grouper	5
Houseboat Grill	17
Jamaican Bobsled Café	7
Jolly Roger's	3
Ma Lou's	F
Margaritaville	10
Marguerites	8
MoBay Proper	15
The Native	14
The Pelican	11
Pork Pit	H
Raine's	4
Rum Jungle	F
Town House by the Sea	6
Voyage	13

ACCOMMODATION

Altamont West Hotel	I
Bayshore Inn	H
Beach View Apartments	I
Caribic House	D
Coral Cliff	F
Doctor's Cave Beach Hotel	C
El Greco	E
Hotel Gloriana	B
Ridgeway Guesthouse	A
The Wexford	G

N

WHITEHOUSE

KENT AVENUE

Sir Donald Sangster International Airport

QUEENS DRIVE

CLAUDE CLARKE AVENUE

HOBBS AVENUE

Sunset (Dead End) Beach

SUNSET BLVD

DE LISSER DRIVE

Summit Police Station

Cornwall Beach

Doctor's Cave Beach

Fantasy Craft Market

LEADERS AVE

MANGO WALK

GLOUCESTER AVENUE

QUEENS DRIVE

PARADISE PEN

DUNBAR PEN

MIRANDA HILL

NEWMARKET

SEWELL AVENUE

ALBION

CANTERBURY

North Gully

Fort

Aquasol (Walter Fletcher Beach)

Craft Market

BRANDON HILL

Dump Up Beach

SAM SHARPE SQUARE

UNION STREET

Bay West Shopping Centre

MARKET STREET

South Gully

ST JAMES STREET

CHURCH STREET

Craft Market

JACKSON TOWN

Cornwall Regional Hospital

Montego Bay Shopping Centre

HOWARD COOKE BLVD

Bus Station

Jarrett Park (Cricket Ground)

MOUNT SALEM

BARNETT STREET

JARRETT TERRACE

Salem Police Station

Catherine Hall Entertainment Centre

CATHERINE HALL

Westgate Shopping Centre

Montego River

Yacht Club

Cruise Ship Terminal

HOWARD COOKE BLVD

Gallery of West Indian Art

FAIRFIELD

FREEPORT

ALICE ELDEMIRE DRIVE

TORBAY

Pye River Cemetery

Palace Cineplex

0 500 yds

Rose Hall & Greenwood Great House

Rocklands, Nature Village Farm & Negril

The Strip: Gloucester Avenue and the beaches

Occupying the whole of Gloucester Avenue and stretching north into Kent Avenue, Montego Bay's glittering oceanfront "**Hip Strip**" builds to a bottleneck around Doctor's Cave Beach, the tarmac lined with restaurants, bars and gift shops, and plenty of taxi drivers touting for business. At night the action moves to MoBay's most happening joint, *Margaritaville*, and street vendors stake out jerk chicken stands and carts selling snacks.

Just up from the roundabout that filters off from Howard Cooke Boulevard, **Aquasol Theme Park** (daily 10am–10pm; U$5; Ⓦwww.aquasoljamaica.com) has the most comprehensive **sports facilities** of MoBay's three main beaches, with a multitude of watersports, tennis and basketball courts, and a go-kart track. The wide expanse of sand, children's playground, a decent seafood restaurant, a fish-fry kiosk and an attractive decked bar have made the beach popular with young tourists and the attendant hangers-on as well as Jamaican families. The water is usually lovely,

Watersports

Montego Bay is justifiably famed for its deep turquoise waters and abundant reef systems – some close enough to swim to from the main beaches. Discarded rum bottles and tyres can be disconcerting, but the deeper reefs are alive with fish, rays, urchins and the occasional turtle and nurse shark. Hosts of similarly priced **watersports operators** are on each beach and within the larger hotels; the most reputable are listed below. Information is available from the Montego Bay Marine Park office at *Pier 1* (Ⓣ876/971-8082, Ⓦwww.mbmp.org); the park's rangers also offer excellent and informative snorkelling trips around the bay for a small fee.

Diving and snorkelling

The following offer guided dives, and rent **snorkel gear** for around US$15 a day; some also offer guided snorkelling tours of the best reef.

Captain's Watersports and Dive Centre at the *Round Hill Hotel*, Hopewell Ⓣ876/956-7050 ext 378.

Resort Divers, *Holiday Inn*, Ironshore Ⓣ953 9699.

North Coast Marine Sports, *Half Moon*, Ironshore Ⓣ953 2211 or 406 9252.

Boat trips

With an open bar and sometimes lunch, **boat trips** are always popular and usually fun. Most depart from the *Pier 1* complex downtown or Doctor's Cave Beach, and sail around the bay to the airport reefs, with a stop for snorkelling. MoBay Undersea Tours (Ⓣ940 4465 or 952 5860) run trips aboard the wooden sailing boat *Calico* (3hr daytime cruise US$60; 2hr evening cruise US$40). Alternatively, there's *Tropical Dreamer, Bay Dreamer* and *Day Dreamer* (Ⓣ979 0102, Ⓦwww.dreamercatamarans.com; 3hr cruises US$60), three well-equipped and beautifully maintained catamarans.

Glass-bottom boats operate from all the main beaches and sail out to the airport reefs for around US$25 for half an hour. MoBay Undersea Tours (2hr; US$40) has a **semi-submersible** that takes you ten feet underwater to view the reef; a diver feeds the fish, and it's a nice way to get close to the coral without getting wet. Tours leave at 11.30am and 1.30pm from *Pier 1*. One step up from the semi-sub is the **Sea-Trek** tour (25min; US$67) operated by Chukka Adventures (see p.284), in which you don a spaceman-type helmet fed with a continuous air supply and walk along the seabed to the reef.

A fully equipped **sportfishing boat** costs around US$400 per half-day; try Marlin Madness (Ⓣ896 7279) or Salty Angler (Ⓣ863 1599).

but beware after a bout of wet weather when the town's gullies discharge into the sea across the bay.

Though Gloucester Avenue runs parallel to the water, the sea is mainly obscured by the buildings. The only place to fully appreciate the sweep of the bay is from the strip's only **green space**, opposite the restaurants and bars at Miranda Ridge; there are a couple of benches from which you can watch the sunset. The bucolic illusion is rudely shattered just past the park at **Margaritaville** (daily 10am–3am; Ⓦwww.margaritavillecaribbean.com), a mini-watersports park-cum-restaurant-cum-bar that proudly displays the second-tackiest facade along the strip, including a smoking volcano with vomit-like lava tumbling down the walls. As well as its bar and restaurant, there's a 110ft waterslide which sluices down into the sea, and inflatables in the water for bouncing and relaxing. Directly opposite, topped by a thatched African-style roof and with its faux waterfall and tableaux of life-size jungle animals spilling over onto the pavement, is the **Coral Cliff** complex, where the numerous arcade games, slot machines and ice-cold air-conditioning might tempt you to take a break from the heat.

The next point of interest is the magnificent **Doctor's Cave Beach** (daily 8.30am–sunset; J$350; Ⓦwww.doctorscavebathingclub.com), Montego Bay's premium portion of gleaming white sand and translucent water. The rapidly deepening waters really are the best in town, and facilities are excellent, including spotless showers and changing cubicles, a restaurant and bar and snack counters. On the downside, there's little shade (umbrella rentals are available but extortionate) and it can get very crowded.

Past Doctor's Cave is the diminutive **Fantasy Craft Market**, tucked behind a row of duty-free stores and offering some bargains. Opposite the market, and with its own driveway off Gloucester Avenue, **Cornwall Beach** is a lovely strip of sand, but was closed at the time of writing for an upgrade. An entrance fee usually applies; ask at the tourist board to see if it's opened up to visitors again.

The hotels peter out as Gloucester becomes **Kent Avenue** (known locally as Dead End Road) at the junction with Sunset Boulevard and continues to hug the coast before ending abruptly at the wall marking the distant section of the airport runway. The adjacent **Sunset/Dead End Beach** (or **Buccaneer Beach**) is a thin but attractive strip of public sand; it's popular with Jamaicans, despite the racket of aircraft landings and take-offs. The water is shallow and there are no facilities, but snorkelling is good and the view over the bay is fabulous, providing the best free sunset seat in town.

Downtown: Sam Sharpe Square and the craft market

Downtown MoBay announces itself with its very own stretch of undeveloped shoreline opposite the dividing roundabout. **Dump-Up Beach** looks pretty enough, particularly from a distance, but this is one of the dirtiest parts of the bay. Shooting off from the roundabout, the main route into the centre of town is **Fort Street**, a clamorous thoroughfare with dancehall flooding from storefronts and all manner of pushcarts and vehicles jostling for space with the thick human traffic. Past here, over the bridge across North Gully, you enter town proper. The lively covered fruit and vegetable market to the left is popularly known as the **Gully** (the correct name, William Street Market, is seldom used).

St James Street comes to an abrupt end at **Sam Sharpe Square**, the heart of downtown, with a central fountain and a seemingly permanent stream of traffic. The square is bordered by a jumble of old and new architecture, including **The Cage**, built in 1806 as a lock-up for disorderly seamen and runaway slaves. Just outside is a **bronze statue** of national hero Sam Sharpe by Jamaican sculptor Kay Sullivan.

Market Street weaves towards the sea from Sam Sharpe Square, passing the brand-new Georgian-style **Town Hall**, home to a basic but interesting **museum** of local history (Tues–Fri 9am–5pm, Sat 10.30am–3.30pm; J$150); occasional art exhibitions are held here, too. Past the Town Hall, pedestrianized Market Street leads to MoBay's main **craft market**. With 200-odd brightly painted stalls selling a colossal variety of craft items, it's a great place to pick up some souvenirs and is surprisingly hassle-free. Otherwise, there's little to see downtown, and given the prevalence of pickpockets, it's not a great area for a stroll.

Day-trips from MoBay

Tourist town that it is, Montego Bay is within easy distance of many managed attractions. Most are on the roster of tour companies, but all can also be seen independently. Most popular is **ROSE HALL**, six miles east from Mobay and site of the infamous **Rose Hall Great House** (daily 9am–6pm; US$20). Built between 1770 and 1780 by planter and parish custos (mayor) John Palmer, the dazzling white-stone structure is set back from the A1 and surrounded by gardens, woods and a swan-filled pond. The rather mechanical 45-minute tours that run every fifteen minutes make much of the vastly embellished legend of Annie Palmer, the "White Witch of Rose Hall", a planter's wife who supposedly dabbled in the occult and who's said to have dispatched numerous husbands by shady means. As the house was unoccupied and widely looted during the nineteenth century, almost all of its current contents have been transported from other great houses or from overseas.

Five miles east from Rose Hall, the A1 opens up to a magnificent sea view at diminutive **GREENWOOD**. Perched on a hill overlooking the sea, the off-white stone of **Greenwood Great House** (daily 9am–6pm; US$14) dominates the few houses and bars below. Surrounded by luscious flowering gardens, the house has managed to retain most of its original content. Built in 1790, Greenwood contains its owners original library and a wonderfully eclectic collection of objects. The tour, which ends in a bar set up in the original kitchen area, is much more enjoyable than the breakneck run round Rose Hall.

West of MoBay

On the west side of Montego Bay at the small community of Reading, the B8 winds inland off from the smooth tarmac of the new highway to a brace of well-signposted natural attractions. Look out for the signpost on the right for the turn-off to **Nature Village Farm** (Mon–Fri 10am–6pm, Sat & Sun 11am–7pm; free; mobile ⓣ912 0172), several miles along an appallingly potholed road. A sweeping collection of basketball, volleyball and netball courts, soccer pitches and a go-kart track, it's a very scenic spot on the Great River with manicured lawns, bamboo groves and an open-air restaurant on a deck overlooking the water. The cook-to-order Jamaican menu, from curried shrimp to sandwiches and salads, omelettes and fries, is excellent and inexpensive, and this is a marvellous spot to get away from it all. You can swim in the river and kick back afterwards with a game of pool.

Back on the B8, turn off to the left from the B8 at the small village of Anchovy for the **Rocklands Feeding Station** (daily 2–5pm; US$10; ⓣ876/952-2009), regularly visited by more than a hundred species of birds, including orange quits, vervains and the long-tailed doctor bird, Jamaica's national bird; hummingbirds will even perch on your outstretched finger to drink sugar water. Feeding peaks at around 4.30pm, when the air thrums with tiny wings.

Eating

Montego Bay has its fair share of swanky **restaurants** alongside the more usual Jamaican eateries. Pricier tourist restaurants almost always offer special deals; look out for flyers around town. There's a *KFC* and a *Pizza Hut* just beyond the downtown end of Gloucester Avenue, and a *Burger King* opposite *Margaritaville*.

Adwa City Centre Mall, Fort St. Great a/c vegetarian diner on the mall's top floor, offering breakfast (ackee, porridge), wholewheat ackee, vegetable or soya patties, salads and lunches/dinners of ackee and tofu stew, curried tofu and all manner of pulse and vegetable combinations. Smoothies, natural juices and power drinks also available.

The Brewery Miranda Ridge, Gloucester Ave. Late-opening bar and restaurant above the strip. Extremely varied menu with daily specials, a big burger selection, lots of salads and excellent fajitas. Good value and pretty views over the bay.

Dragon Lounge Kent Ave, Whitehouse. Lovely spot just past *Evelyn's* and great for lunch or dinner, with a nice open-air dining area shaded by trees. All meals come with a cup of soup, and the Jamaican meat and fish staples are tasty and good value.

Groovy Grouper Doctor's Cave Beach, ⓦwww.groovygrouper.com. On a raised deck overlooking the sand, this mid-priced seafood restaurant comes into its own at night, when lights twinkle in the greenery and the bay views are fabulous, but it's good for a local-style meal anytime – pepper shrimp, crab cakes, jerk calamari as well as fish, lobster and chicken. Best value is the all-you-can-eat Fri night seafood buffet for US$20.

Houseboat Grill Freeport Rd ⓣ876/979-8845. Fantastic, unique setting in a beautifully converted houseboat moored on Bogue Lagoon; you board by way of a rope-pulled launch, and a window in the floor allows perusal of the marine life gliding underneath (including choose-your-own live lobster). The menu is superlative and sophisticated, mixing Jamaican cooking with international dishes; the pepper shrimp with scotch bonnet beurre blanc is unmissable, and the desserts are pure indulgence. One of the best in town.

Jamaican Bobsled Café Gloucester Ave ⓣ876/940-7009. Gorgeous New York-style pizzas, with dough made in-house daily and a variety of succulent toppings, plus burgers, seafood and salads. Local deliveries available.

Jolly Roger's Shop 1, Fantasy Plaza, Gloucester Ave ⓣ971 0058. Pirate-themed indoor a/c restaurant serving good Jamaican food (ackee and saltfish, steamed fish etc) alongside mains such as curried duck, roast pork and burgers.

Ma Lou's at the *Coral Cliff* 165 Gloucester Ave ⓣ876/952-4130, ⓦwww.coralcliffjamaica.com. Upscale, indoor a/c restaurant serving Caribbean-wide specialities; stick to the Jamaica specials and you can't go far wrong.

Margaritaville Gloucester Ave. The loudest place on the strip, offering an international menu with a Mexican flavour, and saccharine-drenched American-style service with the emphasis on fun.

Marguerites Gloucester Ave ⓣ876/952-4777. Right on the seafront next to *Margaritaville*, this is perfect for a romantic meal, with elegant decor, faultless formal service, upscale atmosphere and a delicious Continental menu specializing in seafood; the *crème brûlée* is wonderful.

MoBay Proper Fort St. Brilliant, inexpensive little place on the approach to the strip that's popular with locals and offers a welcome remedy to the all-encompassing Americana. Reliable Jamaican lunches and dinners, from red pea soup and stewed chicken to steamed or brown-stewed fish, and there's a fish fry on Fri nights.

The Native 29 Gloucester Ave ⓣ876/979-2769. The best place on the strip for a sit-down Jamaican meal – take advantage of reduced-rate buffets and lunch specials. Try the "Boonoonoo's Platter" of ackee, curry goat, jerk chicken and escovitched fish, rice and peas and plantain.

The Pelican Gloucester Ave ⓣ876/952-3171. Long-established restaurant popular with locals and tourists. Highlights include American/Jamaican breakfast, the daily lunch specials, and the rum pudding and coconut or banana cream pie for dessert.

Pork Pit Gloucester Ave. The Strip's obligatory jerk spot, and very good it is too, with tables in a shaded dining area overlooking the Strip and well-seasoned chicken, pork, shrimp, ribs and fish grilled over a proper pimento-wood fire. There's yam, festival or hard-dough to help soak up the pepper, and a tasty, hearty pumpkin or chicken soup, too. Great for an inexpensive lunch or dinner.

Raine's St James Place, Gloucester Ave. Popular kiosk café between Doctor's Cave and Cornwall beaches with all-day local and international breakfasts, plus burgers and home-made cakes.

Drinking, nightlife and entertainment

Aside from the shenanigans at the permanently packed *Margaritaville* and *Coral Cliff*, Montego Bay is not particularly lively at **night**. Nonetheless, there are several places to enjoy a few beers or pickle yourself in rum punch (the *Groovy Grouper* on Doctor's Cave Beach and *Voyage* at Aquasol beach are good for a drink by the sea), and there are regular concerts and sound-system dances in and around town. The *Groovy Grouper* also holds regular full-moon parties.

The Palace Multiplex off Alice Eldemire Drive (☎876/979-8359) shows all the latest US **movie** releases.

Bars and clubs

Bluebeat Jazz and Blues Bar Gloucester Ave. Upmarket, icily air-conditioned little bar with high-tech jazz-themed decor, offering expensive cocktails and great live jazz or blues nightly.

The Brewery Miranda Ridge, Gloucester Ave ☎876/940-2433. Friendly place for a drink and/or a dance, with a cosy indoor bar and great bay views from the veranda. Usually packed with young Jamaicans and large groups of American tourists. Tues and Fri are karaoke nights, and there's a daily happy hour (4–6pm). Look out for Sat night promotions featuring well-known Jamaican DJs.

Coral Cliff 165 Gloucester Ave ☎876/952-4130, Ⓦwww.coralcliffjamaica.com. Temple to American-style entertainment and decor, centred around the 170 ringing, buzzing slot machines of the gaming lounge. Open 24 hrs, the *Rum Jungle* bar attracts a mixed crowd of tourists, well-to-do locals and flashily dressed gigolos, and offers a huge range of cocktails as well as nightly live entertainment, including the Viva Xaymaca cabaret-style performance on Tuesdays.

Dead End Bar Kent Ave. Laid-back spot perfect for sunset- and plane-watching. Thurs night is given over to a beach party, with a comprehensive mix of reggae, soca and hip-hop. Sun features classic reggae and rocksteady.

Jamaican Bobsled Café Gloucester Ave. Right in the heart of the Strip and bedecked with memorabilia from the infamous Jamaican bobsled team – you can even have your picture taken in one of their sleds. Reasonably priced drinks and a friendly atmosphere; happy hour Mon–Thurs 7–8pm.

Margaritaville Gloucester Ave ☎876/953-4777, Ⓦwww.margaritaville.com. Hugely popular bar, club and restaurant that usually draws the biggest evening crowd – if you're looking for guaranteed action, this is the place, though it can be something of a pick-up joint.

MoBay Proper Fort St. The best place on the strip to get a flavour of downtime Jamaican-style, with karaoke on Thurs, old hits night on Fri and jazz on Sun; Wed see the "Fort Street Jam", which spills out onto the street with crafts stalls, local snacks such as roast yam and saltfish or pan chicken, and live reggae. At other times, borrow one of the board games from behind the bar or test your skills at the pool table.

Pier 1 Howard Cook Blvd ☎876/952 2452, Ⓦwww.pieronejamaica.com. A lovely setting for a dance, extending along a pier into the harbour, with a regularly changing roster of club nights. Best on a Fri for the packed dancehall night.

Voyage Aquasol beach, Gloucester Ave. The beach bar offers lovely views across the bay, excellent margaritas, sea breezes and a pool table, and there are also regular sound-system parties, including a good oldies jam on a Sun.

Shopping

The best **craft market** is the huge Harbour Street complex (daily 7am–7pm), packed with straw and wickerwork, belts, clothes, jewellery, T-shirts and woodcarvings. The Fort and Fantasy craft markets along the strip (daily 8am–7pm) are worth a look but tend to be a little more expensive and have less variety. The **Gallery of West Indian Art**, 11 Fairfield Rd, Catherine Hall (Ⓦwww.galleryofwestindianart.com) has a huge range of works and is renowned for its hand-carved and painted wooden animals. Downtown, **record stores** offer custom-made reggae tapes (around US$3) as well as CDs and vinyl; one of the better ones is El Paso, at 3 South Lane, overlooking Sam Sharpe Square.

Negril

Jamaica's shrine to permissive indulgence, **NEGRIL** metamorphosed from deserted fishing beach to full-blown resort town in little over two decades. American hippies first started visiting what was then a virgin paradise in the 1970s, setting the tone for today's free-spirited attitude, but these days, the presence of deliberately risqué resorts like the infamous **Hedonism II** has ensured that Negril is widely perceived as a place where inhibitions are lost and pleasures of the flesh rule. The traditional menu of ganja and reggae draws a young crowd, but the north-coast resort ethic has muscled in too. All-inclusives of every ilk pepper the coast and hotels line every inch of the beach, while hustling has increased to an irritating degree.

Negril, however, shrugs off such minor issues and remains supremely chilled-out. Pristine miles of sand, comprehensive watersports facilities, open-air dancing to first-rate live music, a wide range of eating and drinking joints, gregarious company and the best sunsets on the island are all on offer. Many foreigners have stayed on permanently, blurring the distinction between tourists and locals and making for a relaxed, natural interaction that's a refreshing change from other resorts.

Arrival, information and getting around

Buses from MoBay and the north coast drop off passengers on the A1 (Norman Manley Boulevard) just before Negril's central roundabout; if you're staying on the

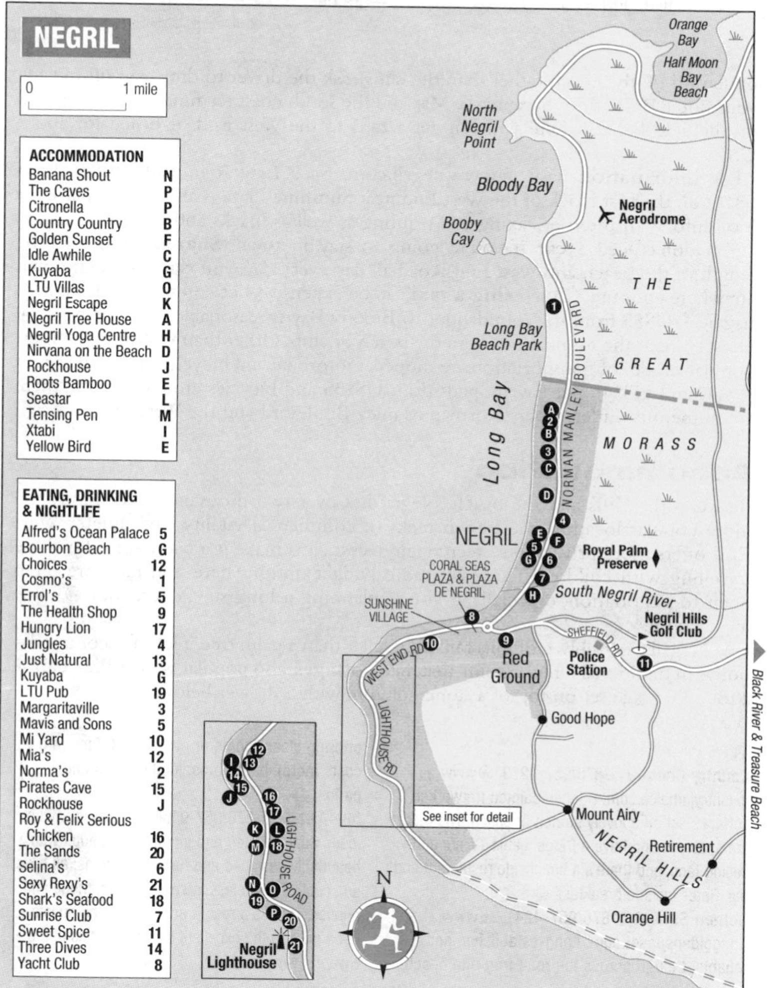

"Rent-a-dread"

Jamaica is a carnal kind of country, and while there's no sex tourism industry as such, monetary-based holiday liaisons are a well-established convention. Middle-aged women strolling hand in hand with handsome young studs has become so normal that pejorative epithets – "**Rent-a-dread**" or "**Rastitute**" – for the young men who make a career out of these cynical liaisons have entered the lexicon.

Negril is a centre for this kind of trade-off, and many women regularly return specifically to partake of an injection of "Jamaican steel". As a result, single women are almost unanimously assumed to be out for one thing only – prepare yourself for a barrage of propositions.

Male tourists are less involved in the holiday romance scenario, but **female prostitutes** are common and men should expect to be frequently propositioned. If you do choose to indulge, make sure that you practise safer sex; one in five prostitutes are HIV-positive, and STDs – including syphilis – are rife.

boulevard (ie the beach rather than the cliffs), ask the driver to drop you off outside your hotel. Buses from Savanna-la-Mar and the south coast terminate at the top end of Sheffield Road, where you can get a **taxi** to the West End or beach for about US$5.

For **information**, visit Ⓦwww.negril.com. *Sue's Easy Rock Café* (Ⓣ876/957-0816) on the first block of the West End near Sunshine Plaza is also a good place for local info, with Internet, faxing and printing as well as snacks and drinks.

You don't need a **car** if you're going to stay in town. **Shared taxis** run the length of the beach and West End Road all day, every day; you can flag them down anywhere en route. **Chartering a taxi** can be expensive, but competition is high, so haggle – US$5 from the roundabout to Bloody Bay is reasonable. There is no local bus service to the roundabout from the beach or cliffs. Other than **walking**, the most popular modes of transportation are moped, motorbike and bicycle. Motorbikes rent for around US$45 per day, mopeds from US$35 and bicycles around US$15; there are numerous outlets along Norman Manley Boulevard and the West End.

Accommodation

Between the cliffs and the beach, Negril has over two thousand **beds**. Easily the more popular location, the **beach** reeks of commercial vitality. The quieter **West End** offers more privacy, but steep open-access cliffs make it a bad choice for those travelling with children. There are more budget options here and rates are often open to negotiation, especially if you're planning a long stay; check out Ⓦwww.negril.com.

As Negril ostensibly prohibits buildings taller than a palm tree, a lot of accommodation is in traditional circular palm-thatched **cottages**; also popular is the **pillar cabin**, a round cottage set on top of a stone column, with a shower below.

The beach

Country Country Ⓣ876/957-4273, Ⓦwww.countryjamaica.com. Brightly painted fretworked cottages set on a lovely stretch of beach. The rooms are spacious and have a fridge, cable TV, a/c and ceiling fans, and there's a beachside restaurant and bar. Rates include breakfast. ❺

Golden Sunset Ⓣ876/957-4241, Ⓦwww.thegoldensunset.com. Long-established and reliable, though across the road from the beach, offering clean rooms or cabins with fans (a/c costs more), bathrooms, kitchenettes and patios. ❷–❸

Idle Awhile Ⓣ876/957-9566, Ⓦwww.idleawhile.com. Sophisticated and intimate little hotel with beautifully designed and furnished rooms; all have a/c, cable TV, wireless Internet access, fridge and phones. There's a restaurant on site, and guests get a pass to the excellent sports facilities of the *Swept Away* resort. ❻

Kuyaba ⓣ876/957-4318, ⓦwww.kuyaba.com. "Rustic cottages" set along a pretty landscaped track leading to the beach, with porches, a/c and fans; some have kitchenettes. There are more - luxurious (and expensive) options in the main block. Good restaurant on site, and rates are sensible. Cottages ❷, rooms ❸

Negril Tree House ⓣ876/957-4287, ⓦwww.negril-treehouse.com. An appealing complex of clean, comfortable rooms and villas with a/c, phone and cable TV, all set just back from the beach. Two bars, a restaurant, a pool and watersports are on site, and rates include buffet breakfast. ❺

Negril Yoga Centre ⓣ876/957-4397, ⓦwww.negrilyoga.com. Yoga centre and guesthouse overlooking the Great Morass. Attractive cottages of varying degrees of luxury surrounded by greenery; all beds have great Sealy mattresses. Whole food cooking and yoga classes available, and there's a communal kitchen. ❷–❸

Nirvana on the Beach ⓣ876/957-4314, in the US ⓣ716/789-5955, ⓦwww.nirvananegril.com. Attractive, fully screened a/c wooden cottages with kitchens, two bedrooms and kooky decorative touches, set in an unusually beautiful sand garden shaded by tall trees and dotted with sculptures and hammocks. Friendly atmosphere. ❻

Roots Bamboo ⓣ876/957-4479. Friendly, efficient place that's one of Negril's most popular budget options. Cottages are small and rather faded but cosy; some have private bathrooms, and there's also a communal row and a campsite ($20 per tent) with 24hr security. ❷

Yellow Bird ⓣ876/957-4252, ⓦwww.theyellowbird.com. Set around a sweep of lawn and right on the beach, this is a great option, with a range of rooms from basic "sleeping" options with fridge and fan to more luxurious a/c units. Great rates. And a restaurant onsite. ❷–❸

West End

All properties are on West End Road or its continuation, Lighthouse Road.

Banana Shout ⓣ876/957-0384, ⓦwww.bananashoutresort.com. Simple and attractive cottages right on the cliffs. Each has kitchenette, ceiling fan and hammocks on the veranda. There's a diving platform, sun deck, private cave and exceptional sunset views. ❹

The Caves ⓣ876/957-0269, ⓦwww.islandoutpost.com. Utterly gorgeous, very secluded and supremely romantic place that offers the very best of Negril, from candlelit dinners in a cave to a private hot tub with a sunset view. Aveda spa treatments, sauna, watersports equipment and a saltwater pool are onsite, and the stylish, individually decorated rooms are faultless, with batik bathrobes and CD players. Rates include wonderful meals and drinks. ❾

Citronella PO Box 2662, West End Rd ⓣ957 0379, ⓦwww.citronellajamaica.com. A private and tranquil resort next to the LTU Pub, this is a classic West End hangout with none of the irritating resort schmaltz of today's Negril. The five self-catering cottages (some sleeping as many as seven) are set in sprawling cliffside gardens, and there's access to the sea. ❺

LTU Villas ⓣ876/957-0382, ⓦwww.theltu.com. A great-value option offering spacious rooms in quiet gardens opposite one of Negril's best bars, the *LTU Pub*. Each room has a lounge, fridge and balcony; some have TV, and those with a/c cost a little more. ❷

Negril Escape ⓣ876/957-4220, ⓦwww.negrilescape.com. Formerly the *Mariner's Inn*, but redeveloped with a boutique flavour. All the rooms are themed, from India to Morocco, and have a/c, TV, wireless Internet and access to a balcony. There's access to the water, a restaurant and a boat-shaped bar, and spa treatments are available; there's a dive shop, too. Rates include breakfast. ❺

Rockhouse ⓣ876/957-4373, ⓦwww.rockhousehotel.com. Enviable location, Mediterranean styling, magnificent thatched bar/restaurant, spa and saltwater pool are highlights. The thatched studios and villas (some of which sleep four at no extra charge) have glass-doored patios overlooking the ocean, outdoor showers, fans and four-poster beds, and there's an innovative and excellent restaurant. ❺–❼

Seastar ⓣ876/957-0553, ⓦwww.seastarinn.com. Excellent option, set back from the cliffs but with swimming access at other West End properties and a beach shuttle. Rooms are spacious and neat; all have a/c and fridge, some a kitchenette, and there's a pool, and a restaurant and bar that gets busy on a Sat night with non-guests. ❷–❸

Tensing Pen ⓣ876/957-0387, ⓦwww.tensingpen.com. Stylish and exclusive retreat in pretty clifftop gardens with imaginatively decorated bamboo and wood cottages, a yoga room, saltwater pool and a lovely restaurant and bar. Some of the cliffs are linked by a tiny suspension bridge. Breakfast included in the rates. Bungalows ❻, cottages from ❼

Xtabi ⓣ876/957-0121, ⓦwww.xtabi-negril.com. Lovely West End veteran with flowering gardens and a network of caves. Accommodations in wooden cabins with private sun decks and sea access or two-storey concrete cottages with kitchens. Also pool, open-air restaurant and bar, and countless swimming platforms. Rooms ❷–❸, seafront cottages ❻

The Town

Negril doesn't really have a centre – just a roundabout feeding its three main roads – and most people leave the beach or cliffs only to change money, buy petrol or find a ride out of the area. However, **Sheffield Road** is the least tourist-oriented part of town and the closest approximation of a real heart, with the police station, market stalls, petrol station, restaurants and constant crowds dodging beeping mopeds. To the right of the roundabout are two **shopping plazas** – Coral Seas Plaza and Plaza de Negril; the car park in front is known as **Negril Square**, a base for taxi drivers, black-market currency touts and would-be guides. Nestled behind is **Red Ground**, a residential area that houses most of Negril's permanent population.

The beach

Parallel to Norman Manley Boulevard and with a strip of hotels and restaurants hiding the road from the sand, **Negril beach** is a near-perfect Caribbean seashore. The seven-mile stretch of whiter-than-white sand is overhung by palms and sea grapes, the water is warm, translucent and still, and the busy reefs are ornately encrusted. It's also packed with tourists, holidaying Jamaicans and locals selling everything from aloe massages to orange juice, perhaps even ganja or romance, and while it's great for lively socializing, the beach scene can be a bit wearing if you're after some time to yourself.

Though hotels guard "their" portion of beach with security men and strings of floating buoys, by law the sand is public up to the shoreline. The beach is roughly divided by the bank of all-inclusives at the outcrop splitting Long Bay and Bloody Bay. Beginning at the roundabout, **Long Bay** is the most heavily developed, by day a rash of bronzing bodies and flashing jet skis, by night a chain of disco-bars dedicated to reggae, rum punch and skinny-dipping. At the far end, the hotels give way to the grassy stretch of **Long Bay Beach Park**, with picnic tables, changing rooms, a snack bar and considerably fewer people.

On the inland side of the road, the **Great Morass** comprises six thousand acres of rivers, peat bogs and grasses. Fed by rivers flowing down from the Orange and Fish River hills, the morass is crucial to the area's supply of fresh water. Acting as a giant natural filter, the wetlands also protect the reefs from being smothered by silt and earth runoffs, and are a sanctuary for insects, shrimp, rare plants and birds – commonly seen species include Jamaican euphonias, parakeets and woodpeckers. This rare habitat has long been threatened by pesticide and sewage pollution and proposals to remove peat fuel, but received protected status in the 1980s with the creation of the 289-acre **Royal Palm Reserve** (daily 8am–6pm; US$10; ⓣ957 3736 or 364 7407, ⓦwww.preservenegril.net). The royal palm cluster here is one of the largest single collections of the tree in the world, and it is magnificent. Tall and graceful but devoid of coconuts, the palms have a stately presence that lends the reserve a patently tropical air. Wreathed in creepers and vines springing up from the nutrient-rich bog below, the trees are thick enough in places to block out views of the hills behind. Peat channels are now fish ponds, and there's a rickety birdwatching tower; a system of boardwalks allows you to go deep into the morass without getting wet. To access the reserve, you drive out of town along Sheffield Road, pass the golf club, and take the signposted turn to the left a little way beyond.

Jutting into the Morass on Norman Manley Boulevard itself, the **Kool Runnings Water Park** (Tues–Sun 11am–7pm; US$28, children US$19, ⓣ876/957-5400, ⓦwww.koolrunnings.com) has ten waterslides, including ones suitable for small children and a 40-foot monster, as well as kids' rides, a lazy river, bungees, trampolines and restaurants.

The West End

The **West End** begins at the town roundabout and meanders along the cliffs for some three miles, becoming Lighthouse Road at Negril Lighthouse and winding inland to Orange Hill and ultimately Sheffield Road. The first stretch is the liveliest, with jerk shacks, bars, juice stalls and craft shops lining the inland side and restaurants hanging over the sea's edge. Along a couple of ramshackle **beaches** fishermen moor their canoes but the murky water makes swimming inadvisable. The road opens up a little once you get to the Sunshine Village shopping mall but the true West End begins over the next blind bend; the road narrows, the water clears and the hotels that carve up the rest of the cliffs begin in earnest.

As this is Jamaica's extreme westerly point, the **sunset view** is the island's best. Sunset-watching is a West End institution; most bars and restaurants offer sunset happy hours and the half-hour or so before dusk is the closest the cliffs get to hectic. Coach parties descend in droves upon undeservedly popular **Rick's Café**, where you pay for your drinks with plastic tokens, cameras click and local lads dive off the cliffs; see below for some less commercialized spots to watch sunset.

After *Rick's* the road becomes a country lane and the hotels are interspersed with near-wild coastline. A main point of interest is **Negril Point Lighthouse**, standing 100 feet above sea level at Jamaica's westernmost tip. Built in 1894, the 66-foot tower now flashes a solar-powered beam ten miles out to sea. Workers who live onsite are usually willing to take you up all 103 leg-quivering steps to the top.

Around Negril

As most visitors to Negril are after a beach holiday rather than sightseeing, there aren't many managed attractions in the area. But if you fancy getting out of town, there are a few good options nearby. For some peaceful beachlife, head east out of town along Norman Manley Boulevard. Just outside Green Island, the nearest village to Negril, the unspoilt **Half Moon Bay Beach** (daily 8am–10pm; J$100 entrance, redeemable at the bar when you buy a drink) is full of the paradisiacal charm that originally brought tourists to Negril. The wide curve of white sand has no braiding booths, jet skis or hassle, just a little sea grass and some small islets; nude bathing is perfectly acceptable and snorkel equipment cheap. The **restaurant** serves excellent chicken, fish and sandwiches. On the way to Half Moon is **Rhodes Hall Plantation** (Ⓣ876/957-6333, Ⓦwww.rhodesresort.com), a 550-acre coconut, banana, plantain and pear farm with two private beaches – one a shallow, sea-grassy reef beach with a freshwater mineral spring bubbling under the brine, the other a more conventional sugar-sanded curve. Volleyball, football and basketball pitches and a restaurant/bar are adjacent but the main draw is **horseriding**. The well-kept mounts trot into the hills and along the beach (around US$50, depending on length of ride).

Mayfield Falls

One of the most popular excursions from Negril heads into the low-lying **Dolphin Head Mountains** to the 22 mini-cascades and numerous swimming spots at **Mayfield Falls** (daily 9am–5pm). The falls are very hard to find independently, and most people visit as part of an organized tour run by one of two operators, Original Mayfield Falls (Ⓣ876/957-4864, Ⓦwww.mayfieldfalls.com) and Riverwalk at Mayfield Falls (Ⓣ876/974-8000, Ⓦwww.riverwalkatmayfield.com). Both offer tranquil guided walks through bamboo-shaded cool water with swimming holes every twenty yards. Tours (around US$65 per person, plus tip) include transport from Montego Bay or Negril and lunch; you pay a lot less if you get there under your own steam. Wear a swimsuit and bring water shoes, as the stones are tough on bare, water-softened feet. Mosquitoes can also be a problem, so bring repellent as well.

Roaring River Park

An easy escape about five miles north of Savanna-la-Mar is gorgeous **Roaring River Park** (daily except Sat 9am–5pm) near the small community of **Petersfield**, approached on a rutted road that you'll probably need directions to find,

The West End's top spots

Many **hotels** will let you swim from their cliff area for the price of a drink, and though they all look pretty similar, some stand out. *Rockhouse* boasts a stylish saltwater swimming pool, a bar, excellent sea access and complete seclusion. The limestone cliffs are riddled with **caverns**, with a popular network below *Xtabi* hotel. The lovely *Pirate's Cave* watering hole is in prime position for the exploration of **Joseph's Cave**, one of the largest along the West End, made famous in the movies *Dr No*, *Papillon* and *20,000 Leagues Under the Sea*; there's a staircase from the bar which leads down into the cave. The cliffs are at their highest around *Rick's Café*, the venue of daily **cliff-diving** demonstrations; a less prominent and infinitely nicer place to have a go yourself is the *LTU Pub* next door, while the most stylish spot from which to take the plunge is *The Sands*, affiliated to the exclusive *Caves* hotel. Past the lighthouse, the cliffs peter out, coastal winds whip the sea into a frenzy and swimming becomes a little risky, but there is a sheltered spot just past the point where Lighthouse Road turns inland – turn straight onto the piece of undeveloped land and climb down the rocks.

though there are plenty of signposts from town. Set in a former plantation and still surrounded by cane fields, the first point of interest is an extensive system of **caves** (US$15) that have been developed with tourists in mind. A guide takes you through the caverns where steps, concrete walkways and lighting let you appreciate their full magnitude. Bats flit about, and there are two mineral pools for a disquieting swim in pitch-blackness. The guide then takes you through the surrounding gardens (US$6), where a dazzling swimmable **mineral pool** is overhung by trees and flowers.

Eating

Negril caters to a cosmopolitan crowd and some of the classiest, albeit somewhat pricey, dining is found in **hotel restaurants**; the best of these are included in the listings below. Thanks to Negril's hippie associations, there are plenty of **vegetarian** options, and you'll also find a lot of **pasta**, as the area attracts a huge number of young Italians. Vendors based at the first stretch of West End Road sell roast or fried fish, jerk chicken and soup.

Sheffield Road

Sweet Spice The best place on Sheffield Road for cheap, delicious Jamaican food to take away or eat in.

The beach

Cosmo's ☎876/957-4330. One of the best, busiest spots on the beach, equally popular with Jamaicans and tourists. Excellent, moderately priced seafood – conch soup is a speciality – and the usual selection of chicken variations.

Kuyaba ☎876/957-4318. Upscale thatch-roofed, open-sided restaurant with good food and regular crowds. The menu includes lobster and shrimp, crab and pumpkin cakes, vegetarian dishes and pasta. Good cocktails, too.

Margaritaville ☎876/957-4467. Negril branch of the islandwide chain, offering an American-oriented menu of burgers, salads, sandwiches and the odd Mexican dish thrown in for good measure.

Mavis & Sons on the beach. Now run by Mavis's grandchildren, this basic Jamaican shack has seen Negril through all the changes of recent decades, and still serves some of the best steamed fish, conch and lobster in town at knockdown prices.

Norma's *Sea Splash* hotel ☎876/957-4041. Upscale spot on the sand for dinner, from imaginative takes on seafood staples to peppered steak, pastas and lamb chops, as well as great breakfasts (try the Caribbean benedict, with smoked marlin and callaloo) and burgers, salads and sandwiches for lunch.

Selina's Excellent breakfast joint with friendly service, moderate prices and an extensive menu: eggs, filled bagels, banana pancakes and the like, as well as Blue Mountain coffee.

Sunrise Club Norman Manley Blvd. This smart Italian-run restaurant and bar on the morass side of the road specializes in fine yet mid-priced Italian food. The wood-fired brick oven turns out the best pizza in town, and honours are also due for the coffee – Blue Mountain beans roasted Italian style is unbeatable. In addition the menu includes unusual but tasty pink gnocchi and a range of lobster dishes.

West End

Choices Brilliant, inexpensive little place serving breakfast, lunch and dinner on an open-sided veranda. The Jamaican cooking is excellent, and all dinners come with complimentary soup and salad.

Hungry Lion ⓣ876/957-4486. The best vegetarian food in town, with seafood as well and gorgeous local art on the walls. A walled courtyard affords privacy, and the fairly priced food is always good – try the dill fishcakes or veggie kebabs.

Just Natural Fresh and cheap Jamaican food, callaloo omelettes, pasta, burritos and vegetarian options are served in a beautiful shady garden.

LTU Pub Laid-back venue with cliffside dining. Eclectic menu offers seafood, stuffed jalapeños, chicken filled with callaloo and cheese, and some German dishes.

Pirate's Cave Popular and efficient bar and grill, with stylish decor, moderate prices and excellent grilled chicken and ribs. The Sunday roast suckling pig, served with salad and bread (around US$12) is usually pretty popular.

Rockhouse ⓣ876/957-4373. Romantically set on a boardwalk right over the sea, with excellent service and an upscale menu that includes crab quesadillas with black beans and papaya salsa or blackened snapper salad for lunch, and dinner mains such as seafood rundown or shrimp linguine for dinner.

Roy and Felix Serious Chicken As well as the excellent chicken dishes, this semi open-air place serves excellent seafood and vegetarian dishes, as well as lovely natural juices.

Shark's Seafood A few tables in the open air on the covered veranda, with great, inexpensive Jamaican seafood (try the octopus), this is a good place to soak up some old-style West End atmosphere. Breakfasts and natural juices also available.

Three Dives Expansive jerk restaurant on the cliffs, with a nightly bonfire and tasty chicken, pork, lobster and fish.

Drinking and entertainment

Most **bars** want you to spend the **sunset** with them, and provide drink promotions or happy hours as an incentive. As the cliffs give the best view, bars along the West End tend to be livelier at dusk, with the action moving to the beach after dark. The larger places are distinctly tourist-oriented; if you want some local flavour, try the **rum bars** and **beer shacks** along Sheffield Road or West End Road near the roundabout.

Jungles (see below) is the only proper **club** in town, but there's also weeknight dancing at the **beach bars**, which use their portions of sand as dance floors. DJs play dancehall or Euro-disco, and the **live music** usually consists of a no-name reggae band singing Bob Marley covers. Ask around to see what's on each night.

Large **stage shows** featuring well-known reggae artists are advertised on roadside billboards and through a car-with-megaphone system. Main **venues** for large shows are *Bourbon Beach* (formerly *DeBuss*), *Alfred's* or *Risky Business* on the beach and *Samsara* or *Kaiser's* on the West End. Stage shows rarely begin before 11pm and often go on until 3 or 4am; cover charge is usually about US$10.

Norman Manley Boulevard

Alfred's Ocean Palace Busiest bar on the beach with thrice-weekly live reggae and crowds of happy holiday-makers dancing on the sand. Great fun, but watch out for the hustlers, particularly on gig nights.

Bourbon Beach Piped or live music every night in a covered area and a section of the beach. The jerk chicken is famously good.

Errol's Norman Manley Blvd. Small 24-hr beach bar with reggae videos, an overdose of fairy lights and hard-core drinking by guests who rent basic but adequate rooms in the yard behind the bar.

Jungles ⓣ876/957-4005. Negril's only true club is a fairly lavish place with a smoky, packed indoor dance floor downstairs and a breezy upper deck with pool, table tennis and a restaurant. Each night has a different theme and music. Cover charge US$10. Closed Mon and Tues.

Margaritaville The Negril incarnation is as busy as the others on the island, with a nightly bonfire, beach volleyball, two-for-one drink offers and big TV screens for sports fans. Hugely popular with American students, with various themed nights (some all-inclusive) throughout the week.

West End Road

LTU Pub Very cool bar, vastly superior to next-door *Rick's*, offers cliffside drinking, diving, snorkelling and food to boot. Ask the barman to make you a Bob Marley – and then try to finish it.

Mi Yard High-rise bar that's tourist-friendly but positively Jamaican. Open 24 hours a day for music, dominoes, drinking and jerk; always packed after 2am.

Mia's Wine Bar Busy sport for a cocktail or a glass of wine, with John Smith's beer on tap and terminals for Internet access.

Pirate's Cave Popular sunset spot, with a long cocktail list, a friendly, convivial atmosphere, and sunset cliff-diving.

Rick's Café Overpriced tourist trap puts on the West End's main sunset event. An appallingly tuneless band plays reggae while local boys dive from the high cliffs.

The Sands Part of the stylish *Caves* hotel, and displaying the same funky and chic decor, this is a wonderful sunset spot, with beach chairs to take in the show, a diving platform, a covered lounge with sofas and good barbecue.

Sexy Rexy's This small shack makes a surprising amount of noise around sunset, with reggae blaring from the speakers and plenty of smiles from the entertaining owner.

5.5

The south coast

If you want to catch a glimpse of Jamaica as it was before the tourist boom, head **south**. Mass tourism has yet to reach the southern parishes – only one all-inclusive has so far opened, and the beaches aren't packed with sun-ripened bodies – but there are some fantastic places to stay, and great off-the-beaten-track places to visit. It takes a bit of extra effort to get here, but it's definitely worth it. The parishes that make up south-central Jamaica are immensely varied; the landscape includes mountains, cactus-strewn desert, lush jungle and rolling fields. To the west, in beautiful St Elizabeth, **Treasure Beach** is an extremely laid-back place with decent beaches, lovely accommodation options and is the area's main draw. If you want to do some sightseeing, you can visit the **rum factory** at Appleton, the fabulous **YS waterfall** or drive around the tiny villages of the attractive **Santa Cruz Mountains**. **Black River** is the main town – an important nineteenth-century port that today offers popular **river safaris** and a handful of attractive colonial-era buildings. New roads have opened up large parts of the south coast in the last few years and it's now possible to drive along large stretches without losing sight of the sea. The scenery is often wild and unspoilt but you'll **need a car** to see most of it; buses and minibuses tend to stick to the main, inland roads, infrequently making side-trips down to coastal villages.

Treasure Beach

The easy-going, snoozy little community of **TREASURE BEACH** has become the main tourist centre on the south coast, particularly popular with a laid-back bohemian crowd. It has a wide range of **accommodation** options, including a delightfully eclectic collection of villas and beach cottages to rent. There are also some great places to **eat** and a couple of diverting attractions, while the bays boast some pretty **beaches**. The **Santa Cruz Mountains** rise up from the sea just east of

Treasure Beach and run northwest, providing a scenic backdrop for the village and protecting the area from rain clouds coming from the north. As a result, Treasure Beach has one of the **driest** climates on the island, with a scrubby, desert-like landscape. This is farming country nonetheless, and you'll see plantations scattered around the area.

Treasure Beach itself is made up of a string of loosely connected fishing settlements. Chances are you'll stay on the long sandy sweep of **Frenchman's Bay** where tourism has displaced fishing as the main industry, or smaller **Calabash Bay**, where brightly coloured fishing boats are pulled up on the beach below the newly constructed hotels and guesthouses. To the east, **Great Bay** remains a fishing village with a smattering of guesthouses and some lovely beaches, while west of Frenchman's Bay the road runs past **Billy's Bay**, home to several of the classiest villas in Treasure Beach, some shacks and a lot of goats.

Arrival, information and getting around

Public transport links with Treasure Beach are not great, although several **minibuses** and **shared taxis** run daily from Black River; a regular taxi costs around US$30 each way. Treasure Tours (see box below) can organize reasonably priced pick ups from anywhere in the island. If you're **driving**, there are two approaches to the village. Most traffic arrives via the road from Pedro Cross, passing the police station and post office north of the village. A turn-off to the left here leads to Great Bay, while the main road continues towards Calabash Bay where most of the recent tourist development has taken place. From Black River, follow the signs for *Jack Sprat* restaurant.

Treasure Beach has a comprehensive **website**, Ⓦwww.treasurebeach.net, which covers everything from community news to information on accommodation and tours.

If you're staying in or around Calabash Bay, you'll find that you can get everywhere on foot; if you're over in Great Bay, you might want to rent a bicycle, the locals' transport of choice hereabouts; you can rent one from *Q-En's*.

Accommodation

Treasure Beach is becoming ever more popular, and new places are appearing all the time; the most popular spot remains *Jake's*, however. Seemingly every other house is a rentable **villa**; these vary from simple beach cottages to luxurious homes; call Treasure Tours on Ⓣ876/965-0126 for details of places to suit all budgets. Most of the places below are listed on, and bookable via, Ⓦwww.treasurebeach.net.

Organized tours and activities

If you're interested in seeing the YS Falls, Gut River or other parts of the south from Treasure Beach, Treasure Tours (Ⓣ876/965-0126, Ⓦtreasuretours.info offers intelligent, reasonably priced **tours** (from US$90 for groups of 1–3 people). Dennis Abrahams (Ⓣ876/965-3084; US$40 per person for parties of two, less for bigger groups) runs excellent **boat tours** to Black River, Sunny Island sandbar and Alligator Pond; he owns the most powerful boat in town, and it's also well equipped with comfy seats. One of best tours offered by Dennis (and every other boatman in town) is to **Floyd's Pelican Bar**, a fantastic wooden platform sitting on stilts atop a sandbar in the middle of the sea; he also does a lovely sunset cruise along the coast; prices depend on number of people). **Fishing trips** with local fishermen can usually be arranged for around US$100 per day – ask the people at your hotel to put the word out that you're interested, or call *Sunset Resort Hotel*. If you need to unwind, Shirley's **herbal steams** and **massages** (from US$80) are excellent. Call Ⓣ876/965-3820 or 366 1726 to make an appointment. Practising from the therapy room at *Jake's*, Joshua Lee Stein (Ⓣ876/965-0583 or 389-3698; 1hr around US$75) blends massage with movement and healing energy work and is great for deep-tissue massages.

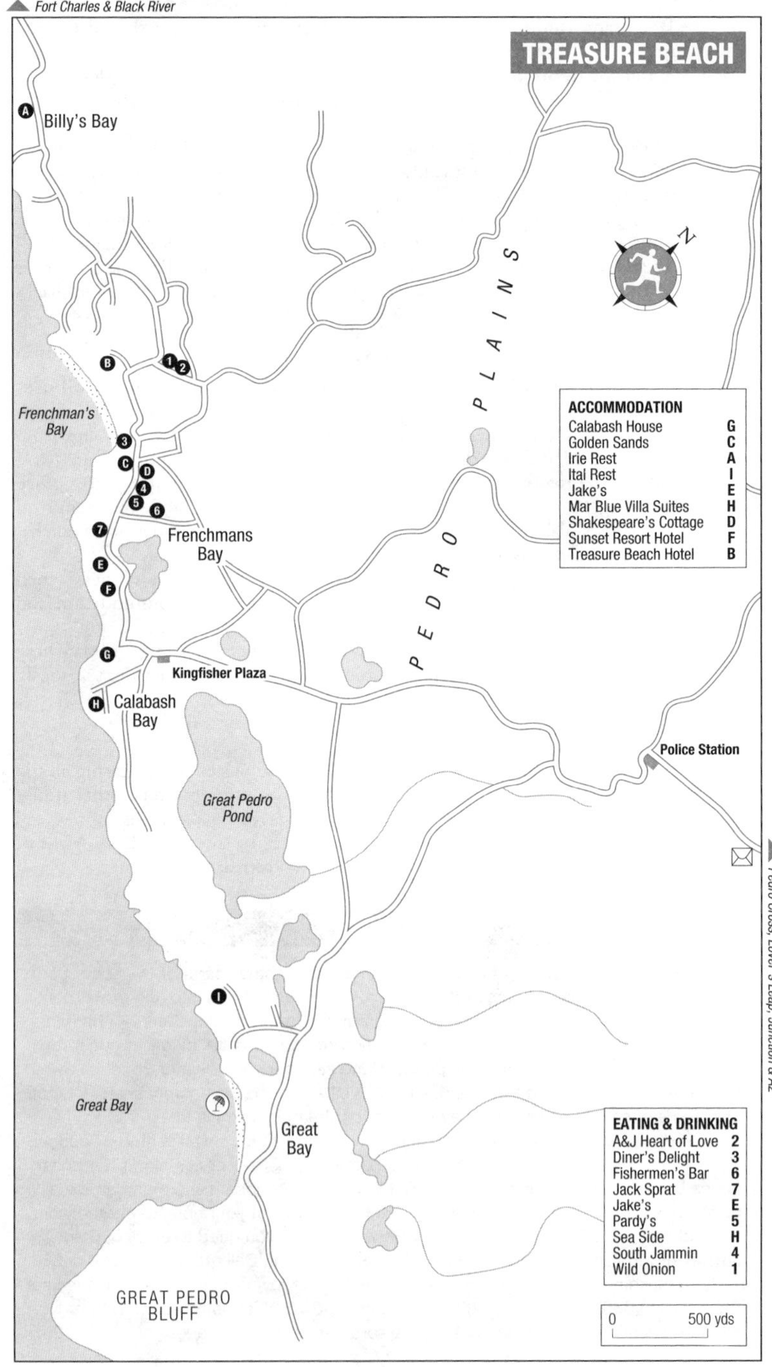

Fort Charles & Black River
TREASURE BEACH
Billy's Bay
Frenchman's Bay
Frenchmans Bay
PEDRO PLAINS
Kingfisher Plaza
Calabash Bay
Police Station
Great Pedro Pond
Great Bay
Great Bay
GREAT PEDRO BLUFF
Pedro Cross, Lover's Leap, Junction & A2
ACCOMMODATION
Calabash House G
Golden Sands C
Irie Rest A
Ital Rest I
Jake's E
Mar Blue Villa Suites H
Shakespeare's Cottage D
Sunset Resort Hotel F
Treasure Beach Hotel B
EATING & DRINKING
A&J Heart of Love 2
Diner's Delight 3
Fishermen's Bar 6
Jack Sprat 7
Jake's E
Pardy's 5
Sea Side H
South Jammin 4
Wild Onion 1
0 500 yds

Calabash House Calabash Bay ⓣ965-0126, ⓦwww.calabashhouse.com. Right on the sea, this is a cute, clean three-bedroom cottage with a kitchen, a/c rooms, a nice veranda and excellent rates. You can have the whole place for US$275, or rent a room only. Meals are available. ③

Golden Sands Beach Resort Frenchman's Bay ⓣ876/965-0167, ⓔgoldensandguesthouse@yahoo.com. Long-standing and deservedly popular place in a prime position on Frenchman's beach. The simple tile-floor rooms have a fan, screened windows, a bathroom and share a communal kitchen. One self-contained a/c cottage is also available (⑤), and there's a bar and restaurant. ②

Irie Rest Billy's Bay ⓣ876/965-0034, ⓦwww.geocities.com/irierestguesthouse. Extremely friendly place set back from, but within walking distance of, the beach. Rooms are simple and inviting, with a/c, screened windows and en-suite bathrooms; some have huge screened verandas. There's a bar-cum-restaurant and a cool communal area with a stereo and satellite TV. Brilliant value. ②

Ital Rest Great Bay ⓣ876/965-3231. Two cottages only at this gentle and beautifully landscaped place near the beach, each with separate rooms upstairs and down (ask for upstairs for the views and the breeze), and with kitchen and verandas facing the sea. Small bar and restaurant. Turn right just before the *Seacrab* restaurant and then take the first right. ②

Jake's Calabash Bay ⓣ876/965-0635, ⓦwww.islandoutpost.com. With an easy-going but cultured atmosphere, this delightful venue on its own tiny beach is the nicest and liveliest place to stay hereabouts. The gorgeous and unique rooms and cottages are decorated in funky colours and have CD players and coffee-makers. There's a pool and restaurant, and the bar draws a genial local crowd. ④–⑨

Mar Blue Villa Suites Old Wharf, Calabash Bay ⓣ876/965-3408, ⓦwww.marblue.com. German-run place right on the beach, with fabulous attention to detail. Spotless and fresh, rooms have a/c, balconies overlooking the sea, CD and DVD players, bathrobes, hairdryers and irons with boards; some suites have their own plunge pool. There's a bar and an excellent restaurant, two pools and delicious breakfast is included in the rates. ⑤–⑥

Shakespeare's Cottage Frenchman's Bay ⓣ876/965-0120. Excellent budget option, offering four basic but clean rooms with fans and shared bathrooms, and a kitchen for guests' use. The newer rooms have their own kitchen. ①–②

Sunset Resort Hotel Calabash Bay ⓣ876/965-0143, ⓦwww.sunsetresort.com. Extremely friendly, efficient resort in a lovely seaside setting, with a fabulously kitsch astroturfed central area. Huge, comfortable rooms have a/c, fans, cable TV and coffee-maker; self-catering cottages are also available, and there's a pool and restaurant/bar. ④–⑧

Treasure Beach Hotel Frenchman's Bay ⓣ876/965-0110, ⓦwww.treasurebeachjamaica.com. Big, attractive resort on one of the best stretches of beach, with two pools, a restaurant and bar. Modern suites with oceanfront views all have a/c, ceiling fan and cable TV. ④–⑤

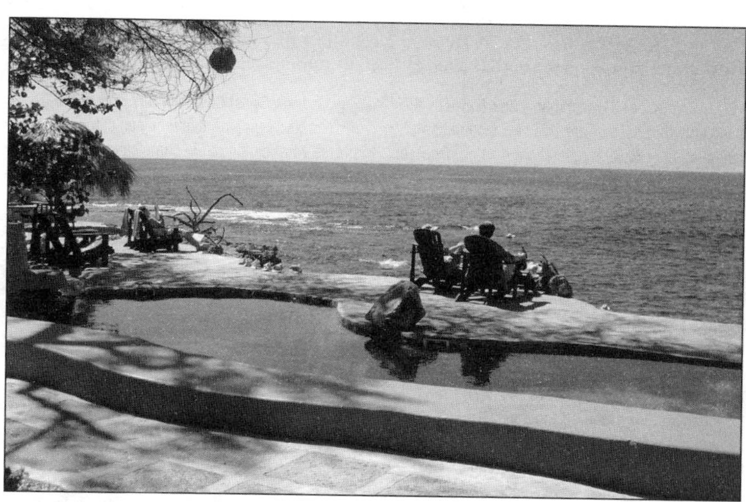

▲ Jake's boutique resort

BREDS

A nonprofit association established in 1998 to promote awareness of Jamaican cultural heritage, the environment, sports development, entrepreneurship and healthcare for the residents of Treasure Beach, **BREDS** (☎965-3000, ⓦwww.breds.org) has had a tangibly positive impact on quality of life in Treasure Beach. The brainchild of, among others, Jason Henzell of *Jake's* fame, BREDS (short for "bredrin", Jamaican slang for friend) embodies the strength of this close-knit community, very much a place where people look out for one another. By way of grants and endowments, as well as the profits from annual events such as the triathlon and fishing tournament and sale of T-shirts and postcards, BREDS has constructed some thirty homes for less-well-off locals, provided computers and office equipment for the local school, added a marine light to Frenchman's Beach to ensure safe navigation through the reef and conducted regular beach and town clean-ups. In late 2002, BREDS established the **Treasure Beach Response Unit**, training 27 local volunteers in various basic medical techniques to become "first responders" in the event of emergencies; now at least four volunteers are on call 24 hours a day to respond to emergencies. The unit also has an ambulance – an essential service in a town with no hospital (the nearest is in Black River) and where the majority of residents (and visitors) don't have access to a car.

The organization is always on the lookout for visitors who can contribute to the cause, whether materially or in terms of skills-sharing, and BREDS merchandise is on sale at *Jake's*. For more on upcoming projects, visit the website above or drop in at their main office, The Breds Store (also an Internet café), at Kingfisher Plaza.

The beach

The area just outside Treasure Beach has several sights worth checking out (see p.299) – otherwise it's just you and the **beach**. The swimming is excellent, though the undertow can get strong at times – ask at your hotel about current conditions. Although rocky headlands create occasional obstacles, you can stroll for miles on certain parts of the beach, particularly west of the *Treasure Beach Hotel*. If you want to explore by **bicycle**, rent a mountain bike from *Pardy's* (see opposite) for US$10 per day.

Eating and nightlife

Evenings are pretty low-key in Treasure Beach but there are a few good options for **food** and a couple of **bars** that keep late hours and get very full at the weekends.

A&J Heart of Love Frenchman's Bay. Formerly the renowned *Trans-Love Café*, this new incarnation maintains the excellent reputation of its predecessor. The laid-back thatched patio is the essential stop for breakfast or brunch, with fresh bread, cakes, fruit salads, muesli, French toast, home-made fruit jam, marvellous Spanish omelettes, baguette pizzas, sandwiches and salads. Open till 5pm.

Diner's Delight Frenchman's Bay, opposite Swaby's Plaza. Simple local place serving Jamaican food at excellent prices: callaloo with saltfish, liver, steamed fish with okra, etc.

Fishermen's Bar Frenchman's Bay. Easy-going local hangout up a lane off the main road with a small disco and a pool table out back. Very popular at the weekends with both locals and tourists, particularly Sun nights. It stays open after every place else has closed.

Jack Sprat Calabash Bay. Part of the *Jake's* empire, this fabulous café demonstrates what eating out in Jamaica should be like. With tables under the sea-grape trees, a sandy path down to the beach and a stylish veranda dining area, this is the perfect place for a relaxed, inexpensive meal. Fish, shrimp or lobster cooked any style and served with bammy or rice, as well as conch soup and excellent pizzas. Pastries, cakes and Devon House ice cream satisfy the sweet tooth.

Jake's Calabash Bay ☎876/965-0365. Open-air restaurant within the hotel, this is usually one of the busiest places in town, serving moderately priced Jamaican fare with a sophisticated twist. The breakfast, lunch and dinner blackboard menus change daily; highlights include breakfast banana porridge, pumpkin soup, curried shrimp and lobster cooked in various ingenious ways. Tables are under shade trees, and there's a good wine list.

Sea-Side *Mar Blue* hotel, Old Wharf, Calabash Bay ⓣ965 3408. Stylish, award-winning restaurant serving sophisticated, imaginative and invariably delicious dishes concocted by the German owner/chef. The menu changes daily but staples include pumpkin bisque with Appleton rum, Thai-style curry goat and snapper fillet with pastis shrimp. The new steakhouse section offers such delights as filet mignon with green peppercorn sauce, "Cowboy" steak rubbed with Scotch Bonnet pepper, and grilled duck with orange compote.

South Jammin Frenchman's Bay. Unpretentious and popular bar serves up burgers, pizza and seafood. There's a pool table and a cute pocket-sized garden.

Pardy's Frenchman's Bay ⓣ876/326-9008. Solid local fare; try the conch soup or the fish, lobster or crab mains. The excellent ackee and saltfish is far less oily than the usual.

Wild Onion Frenchman's Bay. A vibesy, down-to-earth Jamaican one-stop bar/lounge/disco with a cool alfresco dance floor, pool tables, and restaurant serving light meals. On weekends there's a great mix of locals dancing and visitors checking out the scene.

Black River

Although it's St Elizabeth's largest town, **BLACK RIVER**, 18 miles west of Treasure Beach along the main A2 coast road, is a relatively quiet spot, with just one central shopping street, and most travellers only drop in briefly to take a boat trip on the river. It wasn't always this way: in the mid-nineteenth century the town derived substantial wealth from exporting **logwood**, used to produce black and dark-blue dyes for the textiles industry. For a brief period the town was one of the most influential in Jamaica. The introduction of synthetic dyes signalled the end for the logwood trade, and today the only signs of those illustrious days are some wonderful but decrepit gingerbread houses. **Buses** and **minibuses** stop behind the market, just off High Street.

The nicest thing to do in Black River is to stroll along the **waterfront** and check out the old wooden buildings, many with gorgeous colonnaded verandas and gingerbread trim and most in a perilous state of collapse. The **Waterloo Guesthouse**, built in 1819, is reputed to have been the first place in Jamaica to get electricity – installed to provide air-conditioning for racehorses kept in the old stables – and to have boasted the island's first telephone. Nearby, the gleaming white **Invercauld Hotel**, built in 1889, reflects the prosperity of the town during its heyday.

The main reason most people come to the town, however, is to take a **boat safari** on the **Black River**, which, at 44 miles, is Jamaica's longest. So named because the peat moss lining the river bottom makes the crystal-clear water appear inky black, the Black River is the main source for the **Great Morass** – a 125-square-mile area of wetland that spreads north and west of the river and provides a swampy home for most of Jamaica's surviving crocodiles as well as some diverse and spectacular birdlife. The boat tour is a very pretty trip into the Great Morass, although the term "safari" promises rather more excitement than it delivers. You are almost sure to see crocodiles (albeit fairly tame ones), and there are some marvellous **mangrove swamps** where you can usually spot flocks of roosting egrets as well as whistling ducks, herons and jacanas. To go on the ninety-minute tour (five daily; US$16 per person), turn up at the dock by the bridge or contact St Elizabeth River Safari (ⓣ876/965-2374) or Black River Safari Boat Tours (ⓣ876/965-2513).

If you're in the mood for **lunch** or **dinner** whilst here, head over the bridge just west of town to *Cloggy's on the Beach*, in a lovely setting by the sea, with tables inside by the bar or under thatched gazebos on the sand. Great conch soup, curry conch or lobster, or a plate of fish (steamed with okra and pimento is delicious), served with rice, bammy and festival.

Middle Quarters and YS Falls

As you drive northeast from Black River, you'll reach an intersection directing you north for Montego Bay or east towards Santa Cruz and Mandeville. Head east and you'll soon pass **Middle Quarters**, a small crossroads where groups of women sell spicy, salty and delicious **pepper shrimp** from the Black River – perfect to add to your picnic if you're heading to the YS waterfall. Feel free to sample from the proffered bags before you buy, and reckon on around J$200 for a small bag (you're likely to get fresher fare from the roadside *Grassy's* bar on the left, just beyond the crossroads). Shortly after Middle Quarters, a left turn takes you two and a half miles north to **YS**, an area dominated by the **YS farm**, home of the magnificent YS Falls. The name is thought to derive from the farm's original owners in 1684, John Yates and Richard Scott, whose initials were stamped on their cattle and the hogsheads of sugar that they exported. Today the 2300-acre farm grows papaya for export and raises pedigree red poll cattle – a Jamaican breed that you'll see all over the country.

The **YS Falls**, a series of ten greater and lesser waterfalls, are great fun (Tues–Sun 9.50am–3.30pm; US$12). A jitney transports you across the farm's land and alongside the YS river to a grassy area at the base of the falls, where there's a changing room. You can climb up the lower falls or take the wooden stairway that leads to a platform beside the uppermost and most spectacular waterfall. Each fall has a pool for bathing and aspiring Tarzans can swing on the ropes. If water levels are low, you can also swim under the main falls and climb up into a hidden cave. Depending on river conditions, tubing is also available on the lower part of the river – a gentle to moderately speedy 25-minute trip that includes five mini-rapids – for US$6. Alternatively, there is a natural swimming pool with inner tubes and a sun deck for the less adventurous near the snack shop. Early morning is a good time to go, before the afternoon clouds draw in; take a picnic and a book and you can comfortably spend a few hours loafing around the gardens. Cold beers, soft drinks and food are sold in the gazebo at the base of the falls. Chukka Adventures (see pp.272 & 284) run a Canopy Tour here; a go on the three traverses costs US$30.

A **car** is extremely handy if you're heading for the falls, as they're a little off the beaten track. If you're relying on public transport, **buses** run along the main A2 highway south of YS between Black River and Santa Cruz. Ask the driver to drop you at the junction, and you can usually find **taxis** waiting to run passengers up to the YS farm – make sure you negotiate a price before you get in.

The Appleton Rum Estate

Some six miles east of YS Falls, the **Wray and Nephew Rum Estate** at **APPLETON** (Mon–Sat 9am–3.30pm; US$15; ⓣ876/963-9215, ⓦwww.appletonrum.com) has a great setting in the Black River valley among thousands of acres of sugar cane fields. At 250 years old, this is the oldest rum producer in the English-speaking Caribbean and the best-known of Jamaica's several brands.

You'll need a car to get here, or you can take a taxi from the nearby village of Maggotty. It's a good idea to call ahead to arrange a visit, if only to avoid arriving at the same time as a big tour party. The 45-min **tour** starts with a complimentary drink, followed by a whirlwind trip through the factory and warehouses and then outside to an old press, where donkeys used to walk in circles to turn a grinder that crushed juice out of the sugar cane. You finish at a "saloon", where you can sample all seventeen kinds of rum and various rum-based liquors.

6

Dominican Republic

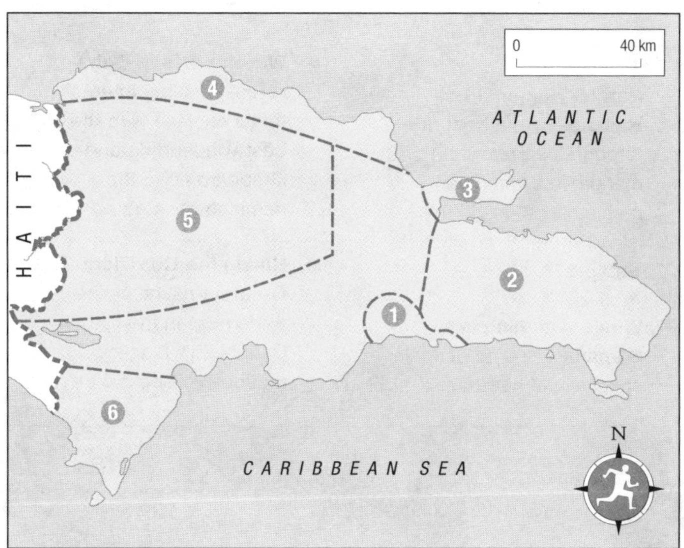

Dominican Republic highlights

* **Colonial Santo Domingo** Chock-full of 500-year-old architecture – including the hemisphere's first cathedral, university, hospital and more. See p.318

* **Old-style Cuban son at the Mauna Loa** Don't miss a Cuban son show in a plush Santo Domingo ballroom. See p.323

* **Parque Nacional Los Haitises** Take a boat ride through a surreal snarl of mangrove swamps and prehistoric caves in the island's remote southeast. See p.329

* **Whale-watching in Samaná** The unforgettable spectacle of humpback whale migration; catch it from December to February. See p.332

* **Playa Cosón** The best beach on the island bar none, with gentle turquoise currents, swaying palms and soft white sand stretching for miles – and no crowds. See p.336

* **Watersports in Cabarete** A bustling international enclave with the best windsurfing and kiteboarding in the hemisphere. See p.342

* **Hiking the Cordillera Central** Pristine alpine wilderness in the Caribbean's highest mountains. See p.348

▲ Kiteboarding

Introduction and basics

Occupying the eastern half of the island of Hispaniola, the Dominican Republic (or the DR, as it's often known) is a hugely popular destination, thanks to its parts that most resemble the image of a Caribbean playland: crystal-clear waters and sandy beaches lined with palm trees, of which the DR has plenty. This vision of leisurely days spent by the sea and romantic nights filled with *merengue* and dark rum is supported by what turns out to be the largest all-inclusive resort industry in the world.

Set on the most **geographically diverse** Caribbean island, the DR boasts virgin alpine wilderness, tropical rainforests, mangrove swamps, cultivated savannas, wide expanses of desert and everything in between. Within its relatively small confines – slightly smaller than the US states of New Hampshire and Vermont combined – the country provides staggering opportunities for eco-tourism and adventure travelling.

The DR also lays claim to some of the more intriguing culture and history in the area, dating back to its early cave-dwelling groups, the **Taínos**, who recorded much of their activities in the form of rock art – it's quite likely you'll find yourself clambering down a dark cave to view some of these preserved paintings during your stay. In addition, as Dominicans are often quick to point out, their land was the setting for Christopher Columbus's first colony, La Isabela, and Spain's first New World city, Santo Domingo, at the end of the fifteenth century. Though the island quickly lost this foothold, the events that took place during its brief heyday did much to define the Americas as we know them.

Where to go

The southeastern part of the country probably has the loveliest all-inclusive resort zones, **Bávaro** and **Punta Cana**, both with pristine coastline stretching for kilometres on end. These are slightly overshadowed, if not in attractiveness then in sheer magnitude, by the complex at **Playa Dorada** along the north coast. Fortunately, this is close by **Puerto Plata**, an historic city worth examining for its wealth of Victorian architecture and proximity to developed stations like windsurfing capital **Cabarete**, to the east. More great beaches are scattered about the **Samaná Peninsula**, poking out at the country's extreme northeast, from where you can also check out migrating humpback whales. In the mountainous interior a few **national parks** make for good hiking, and midway along the southern coast, **Santo Domingo** is an obvious draw for its history and big urban feel.

When to go

The northern hemisphere's winter is **high tourist season** in the Dominican Republic; this is when the Dominican climate is at its optimum, having cooled down just a bit. You'll therefore save a bit of money – and have an easier time booking a hotel room – if you arrive during the **spring** or the **autumn**, which is just fine, as the temperature doesn't really vary all that much from season to season. Keep in mind, though, that the Dominican Republic is right in the centre of the Caribbean hurricane belt, and gets hit with a major one every decade or so; August and September are prime **hurricane season**, though smaller ones can occur in the months preceding and following.

Getting there

The cheapest and most frequent **flights** depart from gateway cities such as **Miami** and **New York**. Flights from the latter average about US$450–550, though if you fly late-night on JetBlue you can get there for as little as US$100 one-way. As there are no nonstop scheduled flights to the Dominican Republic from the UK, many **British** and **Irish** visitors to the Dominican

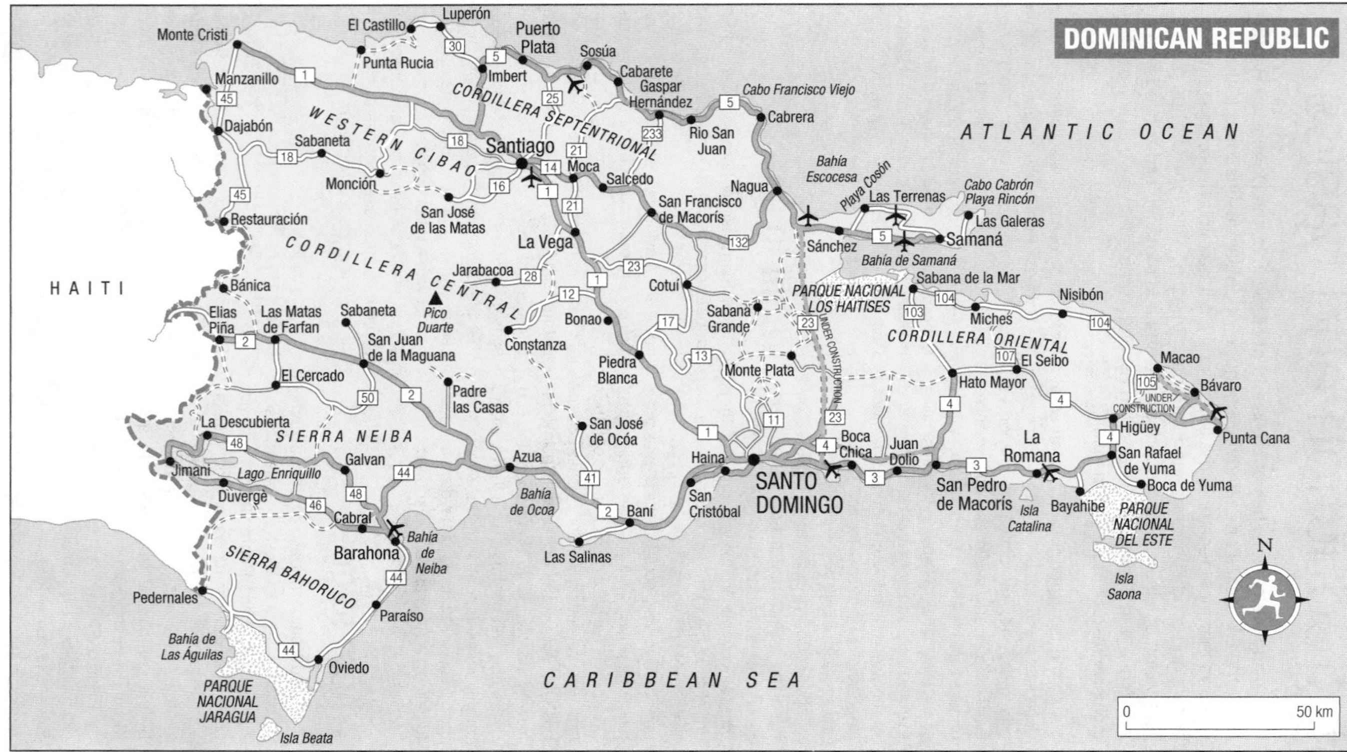

DOMINICAN REPUBLIC
ATLANTIC OCEAN
CARIBBEAN SEA
HAITI
Monte Cristi
El Castillo
Luperón
Puerto Plata
Sosúa
Punta Rucia
Imbert
Cabarete
Gaspar Hernández
Cabo Francisco Viejo
Cabrera
Manzanillo
CORDILLERA SEPTENTRIONAL
Dajabón
WESTERN CIBAO
Sabaneta
Santiago
Rio San Juan
Moca
Salcedo
Moncíon
Bahía Escocesa
Playa Cosón
Nagua
Las Terrenas
Cabo Cabrón
Playa Rincón
Las Galeras
San José de las Matas
San Francisco de Macorís
Restauración
La Vega
Sánchez
Samaná
Bahía de Samaná
CORDILLERA CENTRAL
Jarabacoa
Cotuí
Sabana de la Mar
Bánica
PARQUE NACIONAL LOS HAITISES
Nisibón
Elias Piña
Las Matas de Farfan
Sabaneta
Pico Duarte
Bonao
Sabana Grande
Miches
San Juan de la Maguana
Constanza
UNDER CONSTRUCTION
CORDILLERA ORIENTAL
Piedra Blanca
Monte Plata
El Seibo
Macao
El Cercado
Padre las Casas
Hato Mayor
Bávaro
La Descubierta
SIERRA NEIBA
San José de Ocóa
Higüey
Boca Chica
Juan Dolio
La Romana
Punta Cana
Galvan
Azua
Haina
San Rafael de Yuma
Jimaní
Lago Enriquillo
SANTO DOMINGO
San Pedro de Macorís
Boca de Yuma
Duvergé
Bahía de Ocoa
Baní
San Cristóbal
Isla Catalina
Bayahibe
PARQUE NACIONAL DEL ESTE
Cabral
Bahía de Neiba
Barahona
Las Salinas
SIERRA BAHORUCO
Isla Saona
Pedernales
Paraíso
Bahía de Las Águilas
Oviedo
PARQUE NACIONAL JARAGUA
Isla Beata
N
0
50 km

Republic arrive on a charter flight as part of a package holiday, though you can also fly via the States or various stops in Europe; try Iberia Airlines for the least expensive deals. Visitors from **Australia** and **New Zealand** will need to travel first to the US or Europe to pick up onward connections. Most flights fly into Santo Domingo, though some land at Puerto Plata. Those who arrive via cruise ship will likely dock at either Samaná in the northeast or Santo Domingo in the south.

Information

The glossy promotional material handed out by Dominican Consuls and tourist agencies are pretty to look at but seriously lacking in hard facts. With the emphasis on the package vacations that have earned the country so much money, they hold little value for independent travellers. Their **maps** are likewise relatively useless, though there are several excellent ones of the country available, including the 1:600,000 Dominican Republic map published by Berndtson & Berndtson. Better places to go for answers to specific questions are the websites listed below.

Money and costs

The official Dominican currency is the **peso** (RD$), which comes in notes of 5, 10, 20, 50, 100, 500, 1000 and 5000; there are also 10, 25, 50 centavo (100 centavos = 1 peso) and 1 peso coins. The **exchange rate** typically hovers at around 35 pesos to the US dollar. It's impossible to find Dominican pesos outside the country, and visitors are well advised to come armed with a substantial amount of US dollars, as these are the most readily accepted (and exchangeable) foreign currency in the land. The best places to change money are the banks, which offer good exchange rates; **keep your receipts** when exchanging money, as this allows you to exchange the pesos back into hard currency (dollars or euros) on departure; otherwise you're stuck with the pesos. At a pinch, smaller *casas de cambio* are fine, though you should avoid the street money-changers.

The Dominican Republic is one of the last true **budget destinations** in the Caribbean. Package deals are relatively low-priced, and in many parts of the country shoestring travellers can spend as little as US$60/£30 per day. You can obviously cut costs significantly by sticking with public transport; riding from town to town via public transport can cost as little as US$0.40¢/20p.

Getting around

The Dominican Republic's **bus** companies provide an excellent, inexpensive service covering much of the country. Lines at the stations move quickly, there's plenty of room

Websites

The Dominican Republic maintains a large presence on the **Web**, though, as ever, ferreting out a specific piece of information can take some time. The following are a few tried-and-true sites.

Ⓦ**www.activecabarete.com** Terrific website devoted to Cabarete, with a detailed interactive map and a complete listing of hotels, restaurants, bars, current wind conditions, a calendar of events and other local services.

Ⓦ**www.debbiesdominicantravel.com** A dizzying array of links to hundreds of Dominican-related sites and a deep archive of travellers' personal accounts of all-inclusive vacations.

Ⓦ**www.dr1.com** The most heavily trafficked Dominican message board, and the best place to get DR info on the Web. Also has a good daily news bulletin that you can sign up to receive.

Ⓦ**www.superpagesdr.com** Home page of the Dominican Republic's premier phone company, with a comprehensive yellow pages covering the entire country.

for luggage on the vehicles and trips are relatively pleasant. Even more extensive and cheaper is the informal network of **guaguas** *(pronounced gwa-gwa)* – ranging from fairly decent minibuses to battered, overcrowded vans – that cover every inch of the DR; in most cases, you should be prepared for some discomfort, and you'll have a hard time fitting in much luggage. **Taxis** are another option for getting around the cities, and by foreign standards they are relatively cheap; reputable operators are listed throughout the chapter.

Car rental is common as well, but the cost is generally high. **Domestic airlines**, on the other hand, are reasonably economical, and can be a sensible option if you're not exploring much beyond the main centres. Finally, a number of tour operators in Santo Domingo, Puerto Plata and the all-inclusive resorts organize individual itineraries and packages with transport included.

By bus

Caribe Tours (in Santo Domingo ⓣ809/221-4422, ⓦwww.caribetours.com.do) boasts by far the most extensive bus network, while **Metro** (in Santo Domingo ⓣ809/566-7126) can get you from the capital to the Cibao, Puerto Plata and the Samaná Peninsula. Both have comprehensive brochures available in their stations, listing destinations and departure times. In addition, you'll find several regional bus companies, though vehicles and drivers tend to vary more in quality. Unless it's a public holiday, you won't need advance reservations, but you should arrive at least an hour before the bus leaves to be sure of getting a seat. As the bus companies strive to stay in competition with *guaguas*, rates are extremely cheap. Even a cross-country trip from Santo Domingo to Samaná or Monte Cristi will set you back no more than RD$350, while shorter trips range around RD$150.

By guaguas, públicos and motoconchos

The informal system of **guaguas**, an unregulated network of private operators, is a distinctive Dominican experience that you should try at least once. Aside from the local colour, they're worth using because they're incredibly cheap and cover far more of the country than the bus companies. To catch a *guagua*, either ask for the location of the local station or simply stand by the side of the road and wave your arms at the first one that passes; they're typically battered minivans with a man drumming up business by hanging out of the side door and shouting at the top of his lungs. For longer trips, you'll often have to transfer *guaguas* at major towns, but even the longest leg of the trip will cost no more than RD$100; more often, you'll pay only RD$20; pay when you enter the vehicle to avoid an attempted inflation of the price later.

Santo Domingo to the southeast and the Barahona region are often served by far more comfortable, air-conditioned **minibuses**; along the Silver Coast, the vans are augmented by private cars called **públicos**, which charge RD$5 and only go to the next nearest town and wait to fill up before heading off. *Públicos* also make up part of the city transport system in Santo Domingo, and dominate it in Santiago. City routes rarely cost more than RD$10. In Puerto Plata and other smaller towns, city transit is instead in the form of **motoconchos**, inexpensive, small-engined motorbikes that ferry you from place to place; they're faster than the *públicos* but can be dangerous.

By car

Car rental is straightforward in the DR, as rental agencies are present at all of the major airports as well as major cities and tourist destinations. You can cut your costs a bit – and avoid a lot of hassle – by booking in advance with an international operator. Rates start around US$50–60 per day, with unlimited mileage but no discount for longer rental periods; you should also get full collision insurance, an extra US$10–12 per day. Even with collision, though, you're contractually responsible for any damage up to RD$25,000, but it's still worth taking out in case of catastrophic damage to the car. You should therefore take special care to note *all* dents, scratches and missing parts before signing off. Dominicans drive on the right-hand side of the road, often at a breakneck pace. You'll have to keep a careful eye out along the highways, as large commercial buses and cargo trucks constantly veer into the opposite lane to pass slower vehicles.

Accommodation

The Dominican Republic has become the most visited destination in the Caribbean thanks to its preponderance of **all-inclusive hotels**, which make package vacations here far cheaper than elsewhere in the region; look to spend around US$40–80 per person per night. The all-inclusives do, though, have their downside: the food is usually not that great, and you'll be stuck in a walled-off complex for the whole of your trip, which can get a bit claustrophobic. There are, however, plenty of other options for travellers wanting to get out and see the country: luxury high-rise resorts along the capital's Malecón, independently operated beach hotels, rooms for rent in Dominican family homes and an assortment of bearable budget hotels, many with private bath, hot water and air-conditioning. Away from the main tourist spots expect to pay around US$30–50 for the night; in resort towns prices rise to US$75–140. Reservations are essential for the all-inclusives, where you'll get up to 75 percent off the price by booking with a travel agent before you arrive.

The DR doesn't have any youth hostels or campsite but a good alternative are the traditional *pensiones* still found in many towns, though they are slowly dying out.

Food and drink

If you take all your **meals** at an all-inclusive hotel, you'll get little sense of how Dominicans eat and drink; the "international" buffet fare on offer at these resorts can't compete with the delicious, no-nonsense cooking at the many mom-and-pop restaurants just outside their walls. Dominicans call their cuisine "*comida criolla*", and it's a delicious – if often a bit greasy – blend of Spanish, African and Taíno elements, with interesting regional variants across the island. Dishes usually include rice and beans – referred to locally as *la bandera dominicana* (the Dominican flag) – using either *habichuelas* (red beans) or the tiny black peas known as *morros*. Most often the rice is supplemented with chicken, either fried, grilled or served *asopao* (in a rich, soupy sauce). Invariably main courses come with *plátanos* (deep-fried green plantains, which locals often inundate with ketchup), and a small coleslaw salad. Outside of the major cities, **vegetarians** will often have to stick to rice and beans.

Local **breakfasts** are traditionally starchy and huge, and typically include *huevos revueltos* (scrambled eggs), sometimes *con jamón* (with bits of ham); *mangú*, mashed plantains mixed with oil and bits of fried onion; and *queso frito*, a deep-fried cheese. Dominican **lunches** are the day's main meal. Aside from the omnipresent chicken, popular main courses include *mondongo*, a tripe stew strictly for the strong of stomach; *mofongo*, a tasty blend of plantains, pork rinds and garlic; and *bistec encebollado*, grilled steak topped with onions and peppers. Special occasions, particularly in rural areas, call for either *chivo* (roasted goat) with *cassava*, a crispy, flat bread inherited from the Taínos; or *sancocho*, a hearty stew with five different kinds of meat. For the very best in Dominican eating, go for the **seafood**, which is traditionally prepared one of five ways: *criolla*, in a flavourful, slightly spicy tomato sauce; *al ajillo*, doused in a rich garlic sauce; *al horno*, roasted with lemon; *al orégano*, in a tangy sauce with fresh oregano and heavy cream; and *con coco*, in a tomato, garlic and coconut milk blend especially prevalent on the Samaná Peninsula. The best local fish are the *mero* (sea bass), *chillo* (red snapper) and *carite* (kingfish). Other popular seafoods include *langosta* (clawless lobster), *lambí* (conch), *camarones* (shrimp), *pulpo* (octopus) and *cangrejo* (crab).

As far as **drinks** go, Dominican **coffee** is among the best in the world. Most Dominicans take it *solo*, with a great deal of sugar added, which is the way it's sold for RD$1 by morning street vendors, and handed out for free in the petrol stations. Dominican *café con leche* is made with steamed milk and is extremely good. *Jugo de naranja*, fresh orange juice squeezed as you order it, is another omnipresent Dominican morning drink; be sure to ask for it *sin azúcar* (without sugar). Later in the day you should sample the fresh coconut milk or the many Dominican *batidas*, popular fruit shakes made with ice, milk and either papaya, mango, pineapple or banana sold by street vendors.

There are several Dominican **beer** brands, but by far the best and most popular is Presidente, served in both normal-sized and surreally large bottles, and comparing favourably with beers from across the world. Also popular are the very good, inexpensive local **rums**, Brugal, Barceló and Bermúdez.

Mail and communications

It's not hard to keep in touch with home by phone while you're in the DR. Phone rates are typically expensive from your hotel room, but there are phone centres in every town that will allow you to call home at more reasonable rates. Mobile phones are cheap enough that buying one makes the best sense if your home phone doesn't get coverage in the country. You can purchase a phone for around RD$2000 and buy sim cards for it from RD$100 and up. Orange is by far the best value vendor with the most national coverage, and offices across the country. Their phonecards are sold in stores as well as by street vendors at major intersections of the cities and major highways. All of the DR has the same **area code**, ⓣ809. If at all possible avoid calling collect, as prices are exorbitant. The **country code** is 809.

Dominican *correos*, or **post offices**, are notoriously slow; even if you use special delivery (highly recommended) you'll still have to allow at least three weeks for your postcard or letter to reach North America, and at least a month for it to reach Europe or Australasia. Postage costs RD$3 to North America, RD$4 elsewhere.

Email is steadily growing in importance, with many phone centres in the larger cities offering **Internet** and email access, and a few private cybercafés cropping up in the resort areas. Internet rates typically run RD$1/minute, phone calls are RD$6/minute to North America and RD$15/minute to Europe.

Opening hours, festivals and holidays

Business hours in the Dominican Republic are normally 8.30am–6pm Monday to Friday, and 8.30am–12.30pm on Saturday. About half of the stores still close for the midday siesta. Banks are generally open Monday to Friday 8.30am–noon and 2–5pm, with a few open on Saturday. Pretty much everything is shut on Sundays, with the exception of some restaurants and most bars.

The Dominican Republic has a bewildering barrage of **festivals**. On every day of the year, there seems to be some kind of celebration somewhere, the majority of which are regional *fiestas patronales*, held in honour of the city's or town's patron saint. These traditional fiestas are one of the great pleasures of a trip to the DR; the box opposite covers only a few of the top events.

Outdoor activities

Opportunities for **watersports** are naturally tremendous, ranging from swimming, snorkelling and scuba diving, surfing and windsurfing, to deep-sea fishing and whale-watching. Though many beaches are protected from powerful ocean currents by natural barriers, others have dangerous riptides and should be avoided.

The vast majority of Dominican **reefs** have been damaged beyond repair by careless local fishing practices, notably the daily dropping of anchors by thousands of small vessels. The only place you'll still find a large system of intact reefs is the stretch west of Puerto Plata, between La Isabela and Monte Cristi. By no coincidence, this is also by far the most remote coastal region in the country, and devilishly difficult to access for scuba diving and snorkelling. A number of tour operators and most all-inclusive hotels in the resort towns can take you to the more modest reefs around the island.

The north coast resort of Cabarete is known internationally as the **windsurfing** and **kiteboarding** capital of the Americas. Learning here is a challenge due to the strength of the waves and wind, though a

Major holidays and festivals

January

Virgen de Altagracia, January 21, honours the country's patron saint and is therefore the most important religious day in the Dominican calendar, including a multi-day pilgrimage to Higuey.

Duarte Day Holiday in honour of the Father of the Country, with public fiestas in all major towns on January 26.

February

Carnival The pre-eminent celebration of the year, held on every Sunday in February and culminating on February 27. The biggest festival is in La Vega, with Santo Domingo a close second.

Independence Day Celebration of independence from Haiti and the culmination of the Dominican Carnival (Feb 27). The place to be is Santo Domingo.

April

Semana Santa The Christian Holy Week (variable, usually early to mid-April) is also the most important week of Haitian and Dominican vodú. Festivals take place in the Haitian *bateyes* (sugar plantations) and in Haina.

May

Espiritu Santo Huge celebrations in the capital's barrio Villa Mella, pueblo Santa María near San Cristóbal and the El Pomier caves, and San Juan de la Maguana; held seven weeks after Semana Santa.

June

San Pedro Apostol A colourful mummer festival in San Pedro de Macorís on June 29, with roving bands of masked singers and dancers performing dance dramas on the street.

August

Festival of the Bulls Higuey's fiesta patronal (Aug 14), with processions coming into the city from all sides – some from as far as 30km – with cowboys on horseback and large herds of cattle.

December

Christmas Guloya festivals in San Pedro de Macorís, Haitian Voodoo celebrations in the Haitian *bateyes* and rural groups of Caribbean-style Navidad carollers in the campos (Dec 25).

Festival of the Bulls Traditional cattle festival in Bayaguana (Dec 28).

dozen different clubs offer equipment rental and tutoring. Surfing is less organized and done mostly by locals. Popular venues include Playa Encuentra near Cabarete, Playas Grande and Preciosa just east of Río San Juan and Playa Boba north of Nagua.

The country's five separate mountain ranges provide several options for **mountain sports**; most popular are mountain biking, horseriding and several-day mountain treks. Cabarete's Iguana Mama is the one major mountain-bike tour outfit in the country, offering challenging day-trips into the Cordillera Septentrional and week-long mountain-bike and camping excursions from one side of the country to the other. The best hiking can be found along the trails leading from disparate parts of the Cordillera Central to Pico Duarte, the highest peak in the Caribbean. Horseriding excursions are also quite popular. In addition to the plethora of outfits that offer day-rides along the country's many beaches, you'll find quality mountain-riding operators in Cabarete, Punta Cana, Las Terrenas and Jarabacoa. Also in the mountains, Jarabacoa is the centre for white-water rafting and kayaking.

Several **golf courses** are spread across the island but three stand head and shoulders above the pack: the Pete Dye-designed Teeth of the Dog course at *Casa de Campo* in La Romana; the excellent Robert Trent Jones courses at Playa Dorada; and Playa Grande on the Silver Coast. All three are set on spectacular open oceanfront and are occasionally used as tournament venues.

History

Before Columbus, the island of Hispaniola was inhabited by the Taínos, an Arawak group that had migrated up from the Amazon basin and maintained an advanced culture on the island for centuries. This all came to an end in 1492 when Christopher Columbus "discovered" the New World. After stopping off at the Bahamian island of San Salvador, Columbus landed in what is today the Dominican Republic, where he encountered the Taínos. Attempting to circle around the island, his ship the *Santa Maria* grounded against a coral reef on December 25, 1492, forcing Columbus to set up a small fort, which he named La Navidad, leaving 25 men before heading back with his remaining ships.

Upon returning in late 1493, Columbus found his fort burned and the settlers killed. He established his first small colony further east at La Isabela, today the village of **El Castillo**; he set up a settlement to trade cheap European goods in return for large quantities of gold. La Isabela soon fell apart. Settlers died in the hundreds from malaria and yellow fever, and one disgruntled colonist hijacked a ship and headed back to Spain to complain. Columbus followed him back in 1496, and during his absence the colony was abandoned, with most Spaniards resettling at **Santo Domingo** along the mouth of the Ozama River. When Columbus returned in 1498, the colonists refused to obey his orders, and in 1500 he was sent back to Spain in chains.

Spain's King Ferdinand replaced Columbus with **Nicolás de Ovando**, with instructions to impose order on the unruly outpost. Ovando began building much of what still stands in today's Zona Colonial and engaged in the systematic destruction of Taíno society, apportioning all Taínos to Spanish settlers as slaves and forcing their conversion to Christianity. Lacking resistance to Old World diseases and subjected to countless acts of random violence, the Taínos were quickly exterminated.

To make up for the steep decline of forced labour, the Spaniards began embarking on **slaving expeditions** throughout the Caribbean and Central America in 1505, laying the foundation for future Spanish colonies; by 1515 the Spaniards had expanded and were importing slaves from Africa. Santo Domingo's power slowly eroded as Spain branched out across the Americas, and by the end of the sixteenth century was little more than a colonial backwater that continued to be ruled by the Spaniards until the nineteenth century. Meanwhile, the French began encroaching in 1629, settling the island of Tortuga and branching out onto the western side of Hispaniola. When the French colony's slaves revolted in the early nineteenth century, they had little trouble invading and occupying Spanish Hispaniola, ruling it for 21 years. Only in 1843 was a revolution by the Spanish colonists able to oust the invaders, and for the first time establish the Dominican Republic as an independent country.

Unfortunately, independence did not lead to internal stability. A series of Dominican warlords known as *caudillos* tore the country apart in their quest for money and power, and in 1861 strongman Pedro Santana sold the island back to Spain. Almost immediately a new revolutionary movement was formed, and the Spanish occupiers were forced to withdraw in 1865. A renewed period of extended **civil warfare** between *caudillos* ensued until the United States intervened in 1914. The Americans stayed for over eight years, successfully reorganizing the nation's financing but instituting a repressive national police. When the US left, this new police force took control, and its leader, **Rafael Leonidas Trujillo**, maintained totalitarian control over the Dominican Republic for three decades. In the late 1950s Cuba's **Fidel Castro** took an interest in overthrowing the dictator, and concerns about a possible communist takeover prompted the CIA to train a group of Dominican dissidents, who assassinated Trujillo in a dramatic car chase on May 30, 1961.

Upon Trujillo's death, Vice President **Joaquín Balaguer** rose to power, and continued the totalitarian practices. Balaguer was deposed in a popular 1965 uprising, but the US military again intervened and soon placed him back in control. Only in 1978 was he forced to hold free and fair elections – and was promptly thrown out of office. After an extended economic crisis, Balaguer was re-elected in 1986, and again managed to edge out his rivals again in 1990. In 1994 Balaguer dropped out of the election when it was obvious that he would not beat **Leonel Fernández** who ran a slick, centrist American-style campaign and edged the competition out by a few thousand votes. 1998 saw the first back-to-back free and fair elections in the Dominican Republic's history, as Fernández gave way to political opponent **Hipolito Mejia**. Hipolito made a mess of the Dominican economy, and is now known locally as "Huracán Hipolito" for his disastrous fiscal policies. As a result, Fernández returned to power in late 2004 and he's already making headway on the host of economic problems inherited from his predecessor. His most visible current project is a new subway system now under construction in the capital.

6.1

Santo Domingo and around

Santo Domingo isn't the tropical paradise most travellers come to the Caribbean in search of, but at the core of the rather bewildering sprawl the old Spanish colonial capital – the very first European city of the New World – lies magically intact along the western bank of the Río Ozama. This was the domain of **Christopher Columbus**: founded by his brother Bartolomé, ruled by him for a time and claimed a decade later by his son Diego. After five centuries, the Columbus palace can still be found alongside the cobblestone streets and monumental architecture of the walled, limestone city the family built.

Far more than just history makes Santo Domingo an integral part of any trip to the Dominican Republic; it is, after all, the modern face of the country, and has a nonstop liveliness not seen in many other places. The vitality extends, though in a slightly more disappointing manner, to the nearby beaches east of the city, at **Boca Chica** and **Juan Dolio**, both fairly built-up resorts.

Santo Domingo

Most visitors to **SANTO DOMINGO** understandably make a beeline for the **Zona Colonial**, Santo Domingo's large, substantially intact colonial district, home to dozens of wonderful old buildings in a dramatic setting right on the river. Many never bother to venture outside of this expansive, historic neighbourhood, and while it deserves the most attention you should also make the effort to check out at least a few other diversions throughout the city, especially around the barrios of the **Gazcue** and **Malecón**.

Arrival and getting around

The majority of visitors arrive at **Aeropuerto Internacional Las Américas** (☎809/549-0081), the country's largest, located 13km east of the city proper. The airport is far enough away from the city centre to make a **taxi** the most efficient way into town if you're not renting a car; you shouldn't pay more than RD$500.

If arriving by **bus**, you'll have no trouble finding a taxi or public transport from your terminal, including Caribe Tours (Av 27 de Febrero and Navarro, ☎809/221-4422), Metro (Máximo Gómez 61 and Av 27 de Febrero, ☎809/566-7126) and Terrabus (Guarocuya 4, ☎809/531-0383).

There is no official **public transit** system in Santo Domingo, but the informal network of *públicos* and *guaguas*, covering nearly every inch of the city, can get you pretty much anywhere for under RD$20. Just stand on the corner of a major street and wave your arms at the first car with a taxi sign. More comfortable are private **taxis**; the most reputable operator is Apolo (☎809/537-0000).

Accommodation

The city has a wide variety of **accommodation** but budget rooms in decent neighbourhoods are hard to come by. Most expensive are the high-rises along the **Malecón**, which have great rooms and service. If you've got this kind of money,

though, consider one of the smaller *pensiones* tucked away in the **Zona Colonial**, which are more intimate and welcoming than the large waterfront hotels. For peace and quiet at a more reasonable rate, head to one of the small hotels in residential **Gazcue**.

Zona Colonial

Aida El Conde 474 and Espaillat ☎809/685-7692. The only hotel with balcony rooms on El Conde and a good bargain for clean, simple accommodation. ②

Conde de Penalba El Conde 111 and Meriño ☎809/688-7121, Ⓦwww.condepenalba.com. A fair compromise between comfort and colonial character, this small hotel on the second floor of a century-old building on Parque Duarte boasts good service, comfortable rooms (a/c, cable TV, phone) and excellent showers. You pay for the location, though. ③

Nicolás Nader Luperón 151 and Duarte, ☎809/687-6674, Ⓦwww.naderenterprises.com/hostal. A well-regarded, small luxury hotel with spacious, tastefully decorated rooms in a colonial-era mansion. ③

Palacio Duarte 106 and Ureña ☎809/682-4730, Ⓦwww.hotel-palacio.com. Perhaps the best place in the old city for the money, featuring large rooms, attentive service and all the amenities in a 1628 mansion. ③

Malecón and around

El Embajador Sarasota 65 ☎221-2131, Ⓕ532-5306, Ⓦwww.occidental-hoteles.com. Far and away the best of the upscale hotels in the capital, but far from the action – stay here only if you have your own rental car. The gorgeous grounds include gardens, tennis courts and a great swimming pool. Breakfast included. ⑤

Maison Gatreaux Llúberes 8 ☎809/687-4856. Large, great-value rooms with a/c, comfortable beds and especially strong, hot showers. US$2 extra for cable TV. ③

Gazcue

Felicidad Aristides Cabrar 58 ☎809/221-6615. Clean rooms in a small *pensión* with hot water. Not particularly attractive but the neighbourhood is quiet and pretty. ①

La Grand Mansión Danae 26 ☎809/689-8758. Unpretentious and functional on a quiet residential street, with private hot-water bath and nice rooms. ①

Quisqueya Cayetano Rodriguez 201 ☎687-6037. Unremarkable, mid-range private rooms and a dormitory with RD$140 beds – one of the best deals in town for budget travellers and in a safe location – though it's a good long walk to the colonial district. Very big with Peace Corps volunteers, so it's a good place to meet people who know a bit about the country. ①

The Zona Colonial

Though the **Zona Colonial** – straddling the western mouth of the Río Ozama – is crammed with monumental architecture, it's very much a living neighbourhood thanks to the many cafés and clapboard row-houses where thousands of people live and work. The most important monuments can be seen in a single day; thorough exploration requires two or three.

The town gates east to Parque Colón

A good place to begin is the massive **Puerta de la Misericordia** (Gate of Mercy) on Hincado and the Malecón, a sixteenth-century fortified city entrance. On February 27, 1844, Ramón Mella fired off the first shot of the revolution against Haiti here. Follow Mella's torchlit route up Hincado to Calle El Conde and the **Puerta El Conde**, an imposing stone structure where Mella first raised the new national flag. The gate leads into beautiful **Parque Independencia**, a popular meeting-place encircled by a traffic-choked ring road.

Stretching east from Parque Independencia is **Calle El Conde**, once Santo Domingo's main thoroughfare but closed off to motorized traffic in the 1970s and now a broad promenade lined with cafés, restaurants and stores. Follow it eight blocks to **Parque Colón**, a pleasant open space surrounded by beautiful colonial and Victorian buildings. At the west end of the park is the nineteenth-century town hall, while to the north you'll find a series of cigar and souvenir shops.

The cathedral and around

Most imposing of the buildings along Parque Colón is the **Catedral Santa María de la Encarnación** (daily 8am–6pm). Built between 1521 and 1540, the cathedral's **western facade** is a prime example of Plateresque architecture, which features an overabundance of fanciful ornamentation. The gold Habsburg seal and statuary that once surrounded the main portals were stolen by Sir Francis Drake – the current ones are modest reproductions. Inside, under a Gothic-styled ribbed vault, and just to the right of the pulpit, **Santa Ana Chapel** bears the tomb of colonial administrator Rodrigo de Bastidas and the only surviving original stained-glass window, depicting an angel hovering over Virgin and Child. Beside it, the **Chapel of Life and Death** has a Rincón Mora window – reminiscent of Chagall – showing a decidedly deranged John the Baptist baptizing a clean-shaven Christ.

Pass through the cathedral's southern door and you'll enter the enclosed **Plaza of the Priests**, once the city cemetery. Across the plaza, the **Alley of the Priests**, an attractive walkway lined with bougainvillea, leads past the old priests' quarters. Exiting onto the street from here, it's a block north to **Iglesia Santa Clara**, the New World's first nunnery. Built in 1552, it was severely damaged by Drake and renovated by a blustery local businessman named Rodrigo Pimentel.

From the entrance to the Alley of the Priests you can also walk a half-block west to **Plaza Padre Billini**, at Billini and Meriño, a small public plaza backed by a row of expensive antique, jewellery and clothing shops. If you're in no mood to shop, cross to **Casa Tostado**, on the plaza's southeast corner, built in 1503. Inside you'll find the **Museum of the Nineteenth-Century Dominican Family** (Mon–Sat 9am–4pm, ⓣ689-5000; RD$50), featuring a number of antique furnishings.

Calle de las Damas

Calle de las Damas (Street of the Ladies), the first road laid out by Nicólas de Ovando when he moved the town to the river's west side, received its name in 1509 thanks to a retinue of women who accompanied Diego Columbus' wife María de Toledo down the street to church. On the street's southern end, **Fortaleza Ozama** (Mon–Sat 9.30am–6pm, Sun 10am–3pm; RD$20) was long Santo Domingo's most strategic site. Built in 1502 and enlarged over the centuries, it was the departure point for the Spanish conquests across the Americas. The largest structure is the medieval **Tower of Homage**, the most impenetrable part of the fortress and long used as a prison.

Across the street you'll pass two more restored colonial buildings before arriving at **Casa Francia**, originally the home of conquistador Hernán Cortes. It was here that he plotted his conquest of Mexico; you'll find his family's coat of arms in the second gallery. Across the street, **Hostal Nicólas de Ovando** incorporates the homes of the Ovando and Davila families, both prominent in the early colony. Attached to the hotel's north wall is **Capilla de los Remedios**, the Davilas' private chapel, with an especially pretty triple-arched belfry.

Casa Davila looks directly across at **Plaza María Toledo**, a broad walkway with a sixteenth-century fountain, and the **Panteón Nacional** (Tue–Sun 9am–7pm, Mon 2–6pm; free), built from 1714 to 1745 as a Jesuit convent. In 1955 Trujillo renovated it and reinterred most of the major military and political figures from Dominican history. The building's Neoclassical, martial facade seems particularly suited for its sober task, topped with a prominent cupola flanked by statues of Loyola and Jesus. The interior has been completely redone, with Italian marble floors and an enormous central chandelier. Beside the Panteón is **Casa de las Gárgolas**, named after the prominent row of five grimacing gargoyles above the door.

Plaza España

Calle de las Damas ends at **Plaza España**, an attractive, tiled open space surrounded on all sides by monuments and with terrific views across the river – hence the outdoor cafés that proliferate. An intact section of the old town wall skirts the eastern plaza, extending to **Puerta San Diego**, the colonial-era entrance from the port.

At the southern end of the plaza, **Museo de las Casas Reales** (Tues–Sun 9am–5pm, ⓣ682-4202; RD$50), built between 1503 and 1520, was the administrative centre of the West Indies, housing the Royal Court, Treasury and Office of the Governor. The museum features a rather hodgepodge collection, including Taíno and Spanish artefacts. Opposite the Casas Reales is the **Alcazar de Colón** (Mon-Sat 9am–5pm, Sun 9am–4pm; RD$50), the fortified palace of the Columbus family, built by Diego from 1511 to 1515. This building is the finest local example of the late Gothic style called **Isabelline**, characterized by plain, linear surfaces adorned only with Islamic portals and delicate vine ornaments. The museum itself holds an array of sixteenth-century ornaments, including religious tapestries, a display case of period silverware and a sixteenth-century harp and clavichord.

Bordering the Alcazar to the north is a winding row of colonial storefronts known as **Las Atarazanas**. Follow it to the end where the Reales Atarazanas, once the colonial port authority, contains the **Museo de las Atarazanas**, Colón 4 (daily 9am–5pm, ⓣ682-5834; RD$50), which has the recovered booty from the wreck of the sixteenth-century Spanish galleon *Concepción*, sunk during a hurricane in the Bahía de Samaná.

El Convento de los Dominicos and around

Back to the south of El Conde, towards the Malecón, stand three ancient churches worth a detour. The oldest, the 1510 **Convento de los Dominicos**, Billini and Hostos (Mon–Fri 7–9am & 5.30–7pm, Sun 7.30am–noon & 7–8pm), held the New World's first university, San Tomé de Aquino. Its striking stone facade is framed by decorative two-dimensional pillars; blue *Mudéjar* tiling runs along the top of the portal, and a profusion of red Isabelline vine ornamentation surrounds the circular window in the centre. A block east on Billini/José Reyes is nunnery **Regina Angelorum**, with huge external buttressing, decaying gargoyles and a sombre stone facade. Knock on the caretaker's door in the back to have a peek inside. Smaller but prettier is **Iglesia del Carmen**, erected at Arz Nouel and San Tomé in 1590.

The Malecón

The **Malecón**, the capital's oceanfront boardwalk, commences within the Zona Colonial. An intact section of the old city wall follows it for 100m to **Fort San José**, built on a strategic oceanfront promontory after an attempted invasion by the British in 1655. The cannons that remain appear to point across the street at a fifty-metre high statue of **Fray Montesino**, a sixteenth-century priest who preached against the Taíno genocide. Further on you'll find **La Obelisca**, placed by Trujillo in 1941 to honour repayment of a long-outstanding debt to the US. A kilometre west is another obelisk, **El Obelisco**, built in 1936 to commemorate Santo Domingo's temporary re-christening as Ciudad Trujillo. Informal **party zones** abound along the capital's boardwalk, with especially lively scenes occurring nightly at the municipal port at Calle del Puerto, La Parillada along the San Jose fort and at the intersection with Av Máximo Gómez.

Gazcue

West of the Zona Colonial and north of the Malecón is rambling, tree-shaded **Gazcue**, a middle-class neighbourhood highlighted by the **Plaza de la Cultura**, Máximo Gómez and Ureña, a complex of museums alongside the National Theatre.

The first stop should be the magnificent **Museo de Arte Moderno** (Tues–Sun 10am–6pm; RD$50; ⓣ685-2153, ⓦwww.museodeartemoderno.org.do), four storeys dedicated to twentieth-century Dominican art, with a superb permanent collection. Look out in particular for the paintings of **Candido Bidó**, whose stylized idealizations of *campesino* life have won international acclaim.

The plaza's other main attraction is the **Museo del Hombre Dominicano** (Tues–Sun 10am–5pm; RD$50, RD$50 extra for English language guide; ⓣ687-3623,

Ⓦwww.museodelhombredominicano.org.do), which holds an extraordinary collection of Taíno artefacts and has a good anthropological exhibit on Dominican *fiestas patronales*. Less enticing is the **Museo de Historia y Geografía** (Tues–Sun 9.30am–4pm; free; Ⓣ686-6668), which takes you through an uneven collection of historical memorabilia.

East of the Ozama

Though most attractions lie west of the Río Ozama, a few scattered points of interest are along the eastern bank and beyond. The best-known is the **Columbus Lighthouse** (Tues–Sun 9.30am–5.30pm; RD$100; Ⓣ591-1492), known locally as **El Faro** ("the lighthouse"), a monument completed in 1992 on the 500th anniversary of Columbus' "discovery". Within this mammoth, cross-shaped concrete edifice stands the Baroque **mausoleum of Christopher Columbus**, which supposedly holds the body of Columbus (a church in Seville makes the same claim) with dozens of flowery angels hovering above the marble casket alongside a 24-hour honour guard.

El Faro towers over the western end of **Parque Mirador del Este**, a pleasant stretch of manicured woodlands spanning the length of the barrios east of the Ozama. At the park's far eastern tip are a series of large caves dotted with freshwater lagoons. Known as **Los Tres Ojos** (daily 9am–5pm; RD$10), the Taínos used them for religious ceremonies; more recently they've been the setting for some half-dozen Tarzan movies. The atmosphere is quite peaceful and gives off a true jungle feel, despite being located inside Santo Domingo city limits.

Eating

Dining options range from the omnipresent *comedores* and *pica pollos* to gourmet restaurants with speciality cuisines from around the world. At the more expensive restaurants, expect to spend RD$300–400 per person for a meal with a drink.

Zona Colonial

La Briciola Arz Meriño 152 Ⓣ688-5055. Impeccable service and elegant, candlelit ambience in a restored colonial palace that features a menu of fresh home-made pastas and seafood. There's also a very elegant bar called *Doubles* where you can order the same great food in a more casual environment. Prices are fairly expensive at around RD$300 per meal.

La Cafetería El Conde 253. Best of the cafés along El Conde and a hangout for local artists. Delicious breakfasts with fresh orange juice and *café con leche*.

Dominican syncretism

The syncretic religion **vodú dominicana** – the mixing of European and African religions in South America and the Caribbean – is very much a part of Dominican culture, though Eurocentrism and official disfavour make it an object of shame. Cousin to Haitian Voodoo, it came about during the colonial era, when European Christianity was imposed on African slaves from the Congo and West Africa. The Africans mixed Catholicism with their own belief system, and over time various Christian saints came to be linked to deities imported from Africa.

Vodú involves ceremonies using altars covered with depictions of saints, offertory candles, plastic cups of rum and crosses honouring the **Guedes**, bawdy cemetery spirits known to spout lascivious songs when they possess humans. **Possession** is an integral part of *vodú* ceremonies, both by saints and the spirits of dead Taíno warriors. You'll see *vodú* paraphernalia, including love potions, spray cans that impart good luck in the lottery and Catholic icons at the many *botánicas* in towns throughout the country.

Meson de Bari Hostos 302 and Ureña. This local tavern serves great food at affordable prices, particularly the *filet encebollado* – perhaps the best steak in the country. The exceptionally fresh seafood includes *cangrejos guisados*, a house speciality that features local soft-shell crabs in a garlic sauce. Swift service and great pub atmosphere.

Malecón

D'Luis Parrillada Plaza Montesino, Malecón and Fiallo. The capital's most popular late-night spot, with outdoor seating along the ocean, cheap food and a hyped-up *merengue* atmosphere. The speciality is Argentine-style grilled meat dishes, and the quality of the cooking makes the long waits for service more than worth it. Open 24 hours.

Vesuvio Malecón 521. Most renowned restaurant in the city, deservedly so for its vast array of delicious, if expensive, pastas. Next door they have a more downscale dining room for pizza, sandwiches and crepes.

Gazcue

El Conuco Casimiro de Moya 152 ⓣ686-0129. Dominican cuisine glorifying life in the *campos* – you'll be attended to by singing, dancing waiters. The daily RD$75 buffet is a bargain, and the menu features *sancocho*, *chivo orégano* and *guinea aisá*. Set in an oversized *bohío* – a traditional *campesino* common area inherited from the Taíno.

Don Pepe Pasteur 41 and Santiago ⓣ809/689-7612. This is the place to go if you've budgeted for one big splurge, with by far the freshest and most well-prepared seafood in the city.

El Provocón 4to Santiago and José Pérez, with other locations throughout the city. Outdoor patio offering heaping portions of grilled chicken, rice and beans and salad. Open 24 hrs.

Outer districts

Meson de la Cava J Contreras 237, Mirador del Sur at eastern end of park ⓣ533-2818. Funky restaurant set in a large Taíno cave, with lobster, shrimp *ajillo* and rib-eye steaks. The food is decent enough, but it's more notable for the unique atmosphere.

Tacos del Sol Av Lincoln 609 and Locutores. Popular outdoor Mexican joint with tacos, burritos and fajitas, though the frozen daiquiris and pleasant outdoor plaza are the draw.

Drinking, nightlife and entertainment

The Malecón is the traditional focus of **nightlife**; along with some of the city's finest dance halls, the boardwalk is crowded with outdoor restaurants that start getting packed around 10pm and stay open into the early morning. There are also clubs across the city that specialize in **Cuban son**. Weekends see plenty of activity, but the busiest night for local clubs is Monday, when most are booked with big-name acts.

The Zona Colonial is a great place to go **bar-hopping**. At night the ruins are especially atmospheric, a variety of neighbourhood joints, jazz bars and slick New York City-style clubs are dotted about. The other major centre is the Plaza Central, where most wealthy young Dominicans hang out. The Malecón also has a number of informal setups with a liquor shack surrounded by tables and chairs; most popular of these is *Plaza D'Frank*, two blocks west of the *Centenario Hotel*.

Bars

Ocho Puertas José Reyes 107, Zona Colonial. Trendy techno bar set in a gorgeously restored colonial warehouse, with lounge rooms and a young, wealthy crowd.

La Parada Cerveza Plaza D'Frank, just west of the *Hotel Inter-Continental*, Malecón. The most popular of the outdoor beer joints dotting the boardwalk and a favourite hangout of Sammy Sosa. They've recently added a roof and a large neon sign, and are reputed to have the coldest beer in town.

S Bar Billini and Sánchez. Managing to be stylish without putting on airs, this venerable hipster bar is the best place in the neighborhood for a late-night hangout, and to meet locals.

Discos and live music

La Guácara Taina Av Mirador del Sur, Gazcue, ⓣ809/530-0671. Probably the most famous club in the city, set in a huge, multi-level natural cave, that now focuses almost exclusively on electronica and is a popular spot for ravers, who call it simply "The Cave".

Jaragua Malecón 367, in the *Renaissance Jaragua Hotel*, Malecón ⓣ809/688-8026. Luxurious hotel disco featuring great sound and light systems, though serving expensive drinks.

Jet Set Independencia 2253, Malecón ⓣ809/535-4145. Very nice seventh-floor disco with great views of the city.

Baseball in Santo Domingo

Baseball is the most exciting spectator sport in Santo Domingo due to the high level of play and the passions of the fanatical crowds; two separate professional teams, Licey and Escogido, play in the winter professional league from mid-November to early February; games are at Estadio Quisqueya, Máximo Gómez and Kennedy, tickets RD$300-800; ⓣ540-5772.

Mauna Loa Calle Héroes de Luperón at Malecón, Centro de los Héroes ⓣ809/533-2151. Super-suave nightclub and casino with tables looking out onto a big-band stage. If you love *Buena Vista Social Club*, this place is a must. RD$25 cover.
Monumento del Son Av Charles de Gaulle and Los Restauradores, barrio Sabana Perdida. Famous outdoor *son* hall 5km north of the Las Américas highway.
Murano Mercedes and Duarte. Set in a renovated colonial courtyard, this great techno/house club is partially outdoors and stays open until 3am. RD$100 cover.
Rumbatón Av Máximo Gómez, barrio Villa Mella. Great outdoor *son* hall best on Thurs and Sun nights, when they hold old-style dance contests.

Listings

Airlines Air Canada, Churchill 63 (ⓣ809/541-5151); American, Churchill 2 (ⓣ809/542-5151); JetBlue, Aeropuerto Las Américas (ⓣ809/621-8870).
Banks Banco Popular (24hr ATMs), Calle Isabela la Católica and Tajeras; Calle Duarte and Mella. Scotiabank (24hr ATMs), Av Duarte and Mella; Calle Isabela la Católica and Mercedes.
Embassies Canada, Marchena 39 (ⓣ809/685-1136); UK, 27 de Febrero 233 (ⓣ809/472-7111); US, Calle Nicolás Pensión (ⓣ809/731-4294).
Hospitals Centro Médico Semma, Perdomo and Joaquín Peres (ⓣ809/686-1705); Clínica Abreu, Beller 42 (ⓣ809/688-4411).
Internet Café Internet, Ovando 100. Rates run about RD$1 per minute.
Pharmacies Carol, Ricart 24 (ⓣ809/562-6767); San Judas Tadeo, Independencia 33 (ⓣ809/685-8165).
Police Dial ⓣ911 from any phone.
Post office Av Héroes de Luperón just off the Malecón (ⓣ809/534-5838).
Telephone Verizon, El Conde 137; Tricom, Hermanas Mirabal 127.
Wiring money Western Union, El Conde and Espaillat (Mon–Sat 9.30am–noon & 2–5pm).

Around Santo Domingo

Boca Chica

Once one of the island's prime swimming spots, **BOCA CHICA** curves along a small protected bay, with transparent Caribbean water paralleling a long line of beach shacks. Sadly, the town has become so overwhelmed with tourism – and an accompanying plethora of shysters and informal "guides" – that it's no longer the best coastal spot, and a major draw these days is prostitution. Sitting on the **beach** and swimming is the main daytime activity. Expect a big crowd at weekends.

Accommodation

There are plenty of **hotels** in Boca Chica, including three **all-inclusives** (only two are on the beach) and a sprinkling of small **hostels** all across town.

Dominican Bay Vicini and 20 de Diciembre ⓣ809/412-2001, ⓕ523-6310. Best local all-inclusive resort, with beautiful grounds, modern rooms and good food. ❸
Europa Calle Dominguez and Duarte ⓣ809/523-5721, ⓔhtleuropa@verizon.net.do. Highly recommended hotel right on the beach with sociable and efficient proprietors who keep the place up

to the highest standards and make everybody feel at home. ❷

 **Zapata** Abraham Núnez 27 ⓣ523-4777, ⓕ523-5534, ⓔg.zapata@verizon.net.do. This hotel has some serious draws for independent travellers, including a huge, secluded beachfront bar, doorman, strong showers and free breakfast if you're staying two nights or more. ❷

Eating and drinking

The very best places to **eat** are the beachside food shacks serving fresh seafood. The **bars** are all along the main strip, Calle Duarte.

Boca Marina Prolongación Duarte 12 ⓣ809/523-6702. Fantastic seafood that's relatively pricey but well worth it. The waterfront setting is ideal; if you bring your bathing suit, you can jump off the edge of the restaurant for a swim between courses.

D'Nancy Duarte 1. Best pizzas in town and surprisingly good pasta in this unpretentiously elegant terrace restaurant that looks out onto the main strip. Try the *margherite* pizza, pasta *arrabiata* with shrimp or the mixed seafood with rice, including chunks of lobster, shrimp and calamari.

Terraza Quebec Vicini 45. Good French-Canadian restaurant with *filet de poisson*, a good house lasagne and fresh seafood.

Juan Dolio

Just east of Boca Chica begins a 25-kilometre-long line of rocky coast dotted with all-inclusive resorts, collectively known as **JUAN DOLIO**. This resort area has never quite matched Boca Chica, its northern rival, but a couple of its new resorts are the equal of any all-inclusives in the country – if it weren't for the beach. Though the sand is perfectly acceptable, dead coral under the water makes swimming and walking in the water uncomfortable, and the beaches are no match for what you'll find at Punta Cana. Nonetheless, you can have a good time, primarily because of a couple of great independent hotels and the plethora of local nightlife.

Accommodation

Barceló Talanquera Carretera Las Américas Km 13 ⓣ809/526-1510. The tops of the Juan Dolio resorts, with palatial grounds, great rooms and suites, plus shopping gallery, three swimming pools and sports facilities. ❸

Fior di Loto Calle Central 517 ⓣ809/526-1146, ⓔhfdiloto@verizon.net.do. Highly recommended independent hotel decorated in the style of a Rajasthan palace in India, with twenty well-appointed rooms. The restaurant is outstanding, and it's a great place to meet other travellers. ❷

Eating, drinking and nightlife

For **dining**, stick to the two excellent Italian restaurants along Juan Dolio's main strip. The best place for **nightlife** depends on which night of the week it is. The entire Juan Dolio crowd heads to the pleasant indoor bar *Café Giulia* (Vila del Mar 288) on Mondays, the outdoor *Chocolate Bar* (Calle Central 127) on Fridays and the full-out dance hall *El Batey* (Calle Central 84) on Saturdays.

Fior di Loto Calle Central 517. Tremendous pastas, traditional Dominican seafood dishes and some really excellent Indian curries set amid a pleasantly off beat dining room with Far Eastern artefacts and private couches shielded by billowing curtains.

Restaurante El Sueño Calle Central 330. Formal Italian fare in a relatively swank outdoor patio and with outstanding service. In addition to the excellent pastas, try the chicken scallopini in white wine sauce or bass fillet in mushroom sauce.

6.2

The southeast

The Santo Domingo valley stretches east along the coast from the capital, encompassing vast tracts of sugar cane. North of these fields roll the verdant hills of the Cordillera Oriental, which terminate at the bowl-shaped swamp basin of Parque Nacional Los Haitises. This is the Dominican Republic's **southeast**, known primarily for its popular resort zones **Bávaro** and **Punta Cana**, bookends of a forty-kilometre strip of uninterrupted sand lined with all-inclusive hotels.

Past these attractions, the southeast is fairly poor, rural and bereft of must-see sights – with the exception of two national parks. **Parque Nacional del Este**, poking into the Caribbean at the southeastern tip of the Dominican Republic, continues the theme of great beachfront, especially along **Isla Saona**, while the mangrove swamps of **Parque Nacional Los Haitises** hide several Taíno caves you can visit by boat.

San Pedro de Macorís

Crowded **SAN PEDRO DE MACORÍS**, seventy kilometres east of Santo Domingo, owes its uneven development to the boom-and-bust fortunes of the sugar industry. Victorian civic monuments built during the crop's glory years stand along the eastern bank of the Higuamo River, a far cry from the squalor of the surrounding neighbourhoods. Many of the 190,000 people of San Pedro are descendants of *Cocolos* – "The English", as many of them prefer to be called – imported during the early twentieth century as seasonal field labour. This heritage is celebrated during the **Cocolo festivals** held at Christmas and the Feast of San Pedro (June 24–30) when competing troupes of masked dancers known as **mummers** wander along the major thoroughfares in elaborate costumes and perform dance dramas depicting folktales and biblical stories.

The bulk of San Pedro is a pretty miserable place, and the first view of its smoke-stacks and sprawling slums is a bit off-putting. What redeems it is its **Malecón**, a bustling seaside boardwalk with public beaches at either end. Head north from the Malecón onto Avenida Charro at the *Hotel Macorix* to get a quick glimpse of the Victorian architecture built during the city's heyday. Foremost is the 1911 **Iglesia San Pedro Apostol**, Av Charro and Independencia, a three-aisled whitewash church with a prominent bell tower. Time has been less kind to the old **town hall** a block south of the church, partially in ruins and occupied by a metalwork factory.

San Pedro is famous for its baseball players, including Pedro Guerrero, George Bell and Sammy Sosa – and a pilgrimage to **Estadio Tetelo Vargas**, Av Circunvalación and Carretera Mella (Ⓣ809/246-4077, Ⓦwww.estrellaorientales.com), a spacious, tattered concrete temple to the sport, is compelling for serious fans. Look in Santo Domingo newspapers for schedules; tickets to watch the home team, the perennially underachieving Estrellas Orientales, during the winter baseball season are available on the night of the game for RD$200–600.

5km east of San Pedro on the highway to La Romana, you'll find prominent national park signs marking the entrance to the **Cueva de las Maravillas** (Tues–Sun 10am–6pm; adults RD$200, children under 12 RD$100). This is a truly first-rate attraction, with scores of Taíno petroglyphs, beautifully odd geologic formations and walkways that make the caverns easy to explore during the one-hour guided tours. Only a few of the guides speak English, but those that do are well versed in the cave's history and the significance of the various petroglyphs.

Practicalities

Though San Pedro is fairly large, there's not much in the way of **accommodation**; the top hotel is the rather ordinary mid-range *Hotel Macoríx*, Malecón/Deligne (ⓣ809/529-2100, ⓦwww.hotelmacorix.com; ③), which has 179 well-equipped rooms, all with balconies. Its swimming pool area thrums with live *merengue* at weekends. For **food** head straight to *Robby Mar*, on Av Charro, 100m north of Iglesia San Pedro, a romantic and very reasonably priced little riverside restaurant hidden behind the clapboard stalls where local fishermen sell the day's catch. San Pedro's **nightlife** is clustered along the boardwalk; the current hot spot is the *Justin disco*, and there are outdoor beer halls with ocean views and dancing all along the Malecón.

La Romana and Casa de Campo

LA ROMANA, 37km east of San Pedro, has been a one-company town since the South Porto Rico Sugar Company built the mammoth Central Romana mill in 1917. The mill was sold to Gulf & Western in 1967, who used the profits to construct the lavish *Casa de Campo* resort. The town itself is not especially interesting, though **nightlife** is good and a walk along the rambling barrio that borders the river's western bank makes for a pleasant hour. Also worth a visit in winter is **Michelin baseball stadium**, on Abreu and Luperón at the city's west end (ⓣ809/556-6188, ⓦwww.lostorosdeleste.com), home of Los Toros del Este (check Santo Domingo newspapers for schedules; RD$150–600 for tickets) – perhaps not as exciting as the games in San Pedro, but good play nevertheless.

Just east of La Romana, the **Casa de Campo** resort, accessible via a marked Highway 4 turn-off, is a massive complex. It costs a fair bit more than the all-inclusives along Bávaro Beach, but you'll be spared the security paranoia and compulsory plastic wristbands of most large resorts. The crowning pleasure of the resort is **Playa Minitas**, a gorgeous strand of beach protected by a shallow coral reef – nice enough that some spend their whole vacation on it.

Flanking the resort to the east is another Gulf & Western brainchild, **Altos de Chavón**, a high-concept shopping mall perched atop a cliff overlooking the Chavón River. Constructed to the specifications of a sixteenth-century Italian village with artificially aged limestone, it exudes dreary kitsch, its cobblestone streets littered with double-parked tour buses and its "Tuscan" villas crammed to the gills with dime-store souvenirs.

Practicalities

Accommodation at *Casa de Campo* (ⓣ809/523-3333, ⓦwww.casadcampo.com; ⑦) won't disappoint, as rooms are large, well appointed and include all the amenities one would expect for the price. Encompassing seven thousand seaside, manicured acres, the resort boasts three golf courses, a 24-hour tennis centre, fourteen swimming pools, equestrian stables, a sports shooting centre and more. In addition to the spacious, comfortable rooms, there are 150 luxury private villas with butler, private chef and maid. Within town, the solid but somewhat drab *Olimpo*, Abreu and Llúberes (ⓣ809/550-7646, ⓕ550-7647; ②), qualifies as the best overnight option, with good service, air-conditioning, telephone and cable TV.

Casa de Campo's **food** is a cut above what you'll find at other Dominican all-inclusives. The best option is their beachfront seafood restaurant, *El Pescador*, which does good lobster and blackened grouper fillets. Altos de Chavón has several restaurants, the best of which are the pizzeria *Café del Sol* and the Mexican *Sombrero*, both of which are mid-priced options. The best restaurants in La Romana are around the town's *parque central*, including *Shish Kebab*, on Calle Reales a block south of the park, a decent (and decently priced) little Lebanese joint, and the more formal, and expensive, *La Casita*, Richiez 57 and Doucuday (Ⓣ809/349-6155), whose Italian menu includes seafood pastas and lobster in cognac. La Romana's **nightlife** nets few tourists but can be a lot of fun. Try *Ricamo* disco just off the park or *Club Onno's* in *Altos de Chavón*.

Bayahibe and Parque Nacional del Este

The former fishing village of **BAYAHIBE** was once the most beautiful and remote spot along the entire coast. While the town itself still retains some of its low-key charm, the surrounding area is now thick with all-inclusives, with more going up all the time. The town serves primarily as a convenient base camp from which to visit **Parque Nacional del Este**, just east of Bayahibe. The national park maintains a maze of forests, mangroves, trails, caves and cliffs, home to an impressive array of birdlife and signs of early Taíno activity. Not much of the park, however, is conveniently accessible; no roads lead directly into its interior, and the best method of approach is to hire boats from Bayahibe to hit specific destinations.

The most popular part of the park – and rightfully so – is **Isla Saona**, an island off the southern coast lined with alternating stretches of idyllic, coconut tree-lined beachfront and mangrove swamp, unpopulated except for two tiny fishing villages. Larger ships stop off at **Mano Juan**, a strip of pastel shacks with a hiking trail that leads inland, an expensive restaurant and a couple of modest beachfront eateries, or **Piscina Natural**, a sand bar with a clear lagoon and good snorkelling.

Another option is to **hike** into the park to the **Cueva del Puente**, 3km south of the entrance, a system of caverns filled with stalactites and stalagmites, bats and sparkling seams of bright, crystallized minerals. You can also hire a boat to reach another set of caves, **Peñon Gordo**, the interior of which is decorated with Taíno rock art.

Practicalities

The road that leads into town ends at a crowded car park where resort patrons are shuttled to the nearby docks. If you're on your own, you can sign on for a trip to Saona at **Scubafun** (Ⓣ809/833-0003, Ⓦwww.scubafun.info; US$59), a local tour operator located right in the village centre.

Budget **accommodation** in Bayahibe is plentiful. Some of the best options include the German-owned *Villa Iguana* (Ⓣ809/833-0203, Ⓦwww.villaiguana.de; ❶), a couple of blocks from the beach, which offers a mixture of small, modest rooms and spacious apartments; and the recently refurbished *Hotel Bayahibe* on Calle Principal (Ⓣ809/833-0203, Ⓔhotelbayahibe@hotmail.com; ❷), with nice bright rooms and a decent restaurant. Of the **all-inclusives**, *Sunscape Casa del Mar*, just west of town (Ⓣ809/221-8880, Ⓦwww.sunscapecasadelmar.com; ❺), is very well equipped with half a dozen restaurants, an activity centre offering free scuba lessons, a large pool and spa; while the *Viva Wyndham Dominicus Beach*, close to the border of Parque Nacional del Este (Ⓣ809/686-5658, Ⓦwww.vivaresorts.com; ❺–❻), has 500 rooms set in lavish grounds, decent food (by all-inclusive standards) and a great stretch of beach where numerous watersports are offered.

For **lunch** try *Restaurante Leidy* on the beach just west of the port, or *Punta* on the central promontory, both of which serve good fresh fish dishes daily – mains from RD$280 at both. At night head to *Marie Nostrum*, on the seafront at the end of Calle Principal (Ⓣ809/833-0055), the town's most elegant dining space where an excellent array of Italian-inspired pasta and risotto dishes are offered from RD$300–550.

Boca de Yuma

On the northeastern tip of Parque Nacional del Este sits *pueblo* **BOCA DE YUMA**, for the most part passed over by tourism because of its lack of easily accessible beaches, though its setting along squat, ocean-pounded bluffs is undeniably impressive. There's just one hotel, *El Viejo Pirata*, on the main road into town (ⓣ809/804-31151, ⓦwww.elviejopirata.com; ②), which is a rather refined affair with nicely decorated rooms and a decent seafood restaurant. However, if this is booked up, Boca is still a nice enough spot to spend a day, with a decent little beach across the river which you can reach via a RD$30 ferry.

The other major nearby attraction is the fortified **Casa Ponce de León**, located northwest of town in *pueblo* San Rafael de Yuma (Mon–Sat 9am–5pm; RD$50). Conquistador Ponce de León settled here and established an extremely profitable farm that provided Santo Domingo and the gold mines of San Cristóbal with cassava bread and salt pork. It's now maintained by the parks department, who have renovated the two-storey house into a museum meant to evoke de León's life and times. If you don't have a car use one of the hourly *guaguas* that ply the route between Boca and San Rafael.

Punta Cana and Bávaro

Higüey is an unpleasant, completely concrete town 50km or so north of Boca de Yuma, and known throughout the country as a holy city because it holds a basilica that honours the nation's patron saint, the Virgin of Altagracia. Out of Higüey, a paved road winds 35km east to the tropical playgrounds of **PUNTA CANA** and **BÁVARO**. Formerly two separate towns at either end of a long curve of coconut tree-lined beach, an extraordinary spate of construction over the past decade and a half has rather blurred the boundaries between them. These days "Punta Cana" describes everywhere from the original village all the way up to Uvero Alto, some 45km north. It's a big area and its development is still far from complete. New hotels are going up along the coast, malls are being erected inland and to the south the vast **Cap Cana** mega-resort is being constructed, which will boast the largest marina in the Caribbean, as well as numerous luxury hotels, condominiums and golf courses. It's still possible to find glorious stretches of uninterrupted sand but if you want to explore the country, go elsewhere – the resorts are cities unto themselves, encompassing vast swathes of beachside territory.

Practicalities

If you're not flying to the resorts via charter at **Aeropuerto Punta Cana** (ⓣ809/688-4749), from where you'll be ferried to your hotel by bus, you'll have to get here by private car or *guagua* from Higüey. **Taxis** are usually waiting at the airport and the entrance to the resorts; otherwise, call ⓣ809/552-0617 for pick-up.

Most people staying in the **all-inclusives** are on package tours, and you'll get much better deals case if you book at home through a travel agent. In the unlikely event you stray from your resort to **eat**, go to *Capitan Cook* in the town of Cortecito, with a beachfront patio where you can feast on grilled seafood from around RD$300, served up from a mammoth barbecue pit.

Resorts and inns

Bávaro Beach Resort ⓣ809/686-5797, ⓦwww.barcelo.com. Lovely grounds, spacious rooms and a whole heap of activities (golf, watersports, tennis etc), though the food is lacklustre. Guests can use the facilities of the adjacent Bávaro Caribe, Golf and Casino hotels, but not the five-star Barcelo Palace. ⑤

Cortecito Inn Calle Playa Cortecito ⓣ809/552-0639, ⓕ552-0641. This is the place if you don't want to go all-inclusive. It's on the main street, around 30m from the beach, some rooms have private balconies, and there's a swimming pool and restaurant too. Breakfast included. ②

Paradisus Palma Real ⓣ809/688-5000, ⓦwww.solmelia.com. The top Bávaro resort, slightly more expensive but well worth it, with sculpted tropical gardens, luxury suites (with whirlpool baths, plasma TVs, balconies and free minibars) and a choice of Chinese, Japanese and Mediterranean restaurants. ⑦

La Posada de Piedra Calle Playa Cortecito ⓣ809/221-0754, ⓦwww.laposadadepiedra.com.

One of the few budget options, with a half-dozen water view rooms located in the large beachfront home of a local family; not exactly luxurious, but meticulously clean and fairly quiet. ❷

Riu Resort ⓣ809/687-4242, ⓦwww.riu.com. The five hotels that make up this mega-complex offer a wealth of facilities with dozens of pools, restaurants and sporting activities to choose from. The Palace has the best architecture and rooms – some with hot tubs – but all the hotels are of a high standard. ❺

Sivory Punta Cana ⓣ809/552-0500, ⓦwww.sivorypuntacana.com. As the resort zone's northernmost hotel, with miles of pristine empty beach, this is top choice if you want to get away from it all, although you'll have to pay for the privilege as its standard package is not all-inclusive. The rooms are beautifully appointed and the restaurants are a distinct cut above. ❼

Cortecito and Cap Cana

If you're not staying at one of the resorts, head to the public-access beach at **Cortecito**, a kilometre north of the first Bávaro turn-off from the highway, the only village left along the entire stretch. It's a small, agreeably laid-back hangout populated by backpackers, independent European vacationers and a slew of Dominican vendors.

At the other extreme, the southern end of the resort zone is now occupied by the brooding presence of **Cap Cana** (ⓣ809/955-9501, ⓦwww.capcana.com), the would-be resort to end all resorts, filled with mega-hotels, multi-million dollar condiminiums and Jack-Nicklaus-designed golf courses. The development is aimed squarely at the luxury end of the market, although whether the Dominican Republic can attract the jet set remains to be seen. Currently this resort city is still relatively village sized, comprising part of the marina, a hotel, the Altabella Sanctuary (ⓣ809/688-5000, ⓦwww.solmelia.com; ❽), and just one of the proposed three golf courses – but it's a twenty-year project, and there's still plenty of building to be done. Access to the resort is restricted to guests of the hotel or would-be investors.

Sabana de la Mar

Sabana de la Mar, at the end of Highway 103, is a dusty little port unremarkable but for its use as a setting-off point for the highly recommended boat tours of Parque Nacional los Haitises (see below) or to catch a ferry to the Samaná Peninsula; passenger ferries depart four times a day from the wharf at the northern end of town (9am, 11am, 3pm & 5pm; RD$140). You won't really want to use Sabana de la Mar as a base for anything but just east of the town (and close to the entrance of Los Haitises) is *Paraiso Caño Hondo* (ⓣ809/556-7483, ⓦwww.paraisocanohondo.com; ❷), which has a small restaurant and a very nice set of rooms, plus a natural pool with cascades.

Parque Nacional Los Haitises

Parque Nacional Los Haitises, a massive expanse of mangrove swamp that protects several Taíno caves, 92 plant species, 112 bird species and a wide variety of marine life, spreads west of Sabana de la Mar around the coastal curve of Bahía de Samaná. Though twelve hundred square kilometres in total, only a small portion is open to the public, accessible by organized tours.

The **Ruta Litoral** – the standard 2.5-hour boat tour – hits three main areas of interest within the park. First up is **Cueva Arena**, a large grotto that has numerous Taíno drawings. You can stop for a half-hour at the beach cove from where you get a good look at **Cayo Willy Simons** – once a hideout for the infamous pirate – recognizable by the dozens of birds circling around: pelicans, herons, terns, frigates, even an occasional falcon. The next stop is grottoes **San Gabriel** and **Remington**, both with Taíno faces carved into their walls. From here you'll pass the ruins of a 100-year-old banana wharf to reach **Cueva de la Linea**, which was once intended to hold a railroad station for the area's sugar cane.

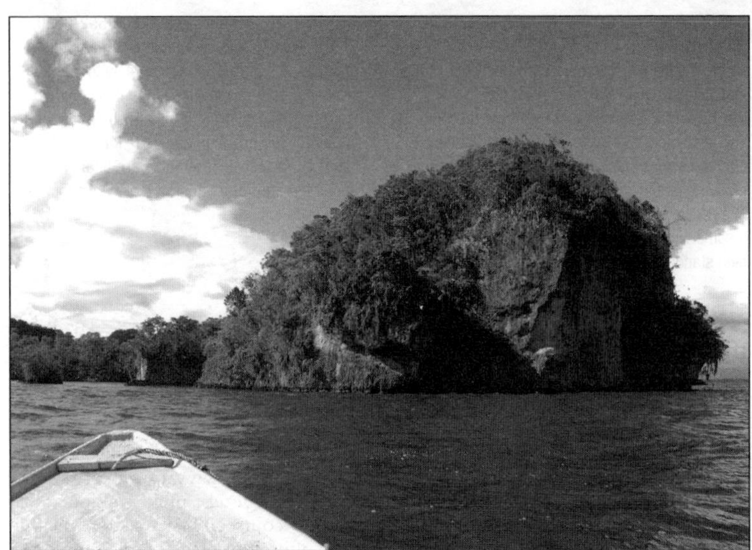

▲ Parque Nacional Los Haitises

Practicalities

The *Paraiso Caño Hondo* hotel in Sabana de la Mar near the entrance to the park offers tours for US$45, including guide, lunch and entrance fee (RD$100). Otherwise, you'll need to hire a **guide** from Sabana de la Mar's national park office at the town pier, which should run to around RD$1000 for up to four people. The port of entry to the park is a tiny pier called **Caña Hondo**, entered via a signposted turn-off on the road to Hato Mayor at the village's southern end. From there you'll travel 12km along a bumpy dirt road to the pier before you set off along a mangrove-lined canal and into the bay.

6.3

The Samaná Peninsula

It's not hard to appreciate the beauty of the **Samaná Peninsula**, a thin strip of land poking from the Dominican Republic's northeast. Perhaps the most appealing part of the whole country, the region boasts a coast lined with beaches that conform strictly to the Caribbean archetype of powdery white sand and transparent green-blue sea.

Besides bumming on the beach, visitors come to see the thousands of **humpback whales** that migrate to the Bahía de Samaná during the winter. Whale-watching has become a thriving local industry, peaking between mid-January and mid-March. Most whaleboats depart from **Santa Bárbara de Samaná** (generally shortened to Samaná), the largest town on the peninsula and a welcome break from the more typical beach-oriented tourist resorts. To the east, **Las Galeras** is a pristine horseshoe of sand that, despite considerable development in recent years, still maintains an air of tranquillity. Along the peninsula's north coast you'll find the beautiful beaches of the remote expat colony of **Las Terrenas**, an ever-growing hangout for independent travellers.

The **Carretera 5 (C-5)** that skirts the Dominican north coast leads all the way from Puerto Plata to Santa Bárbara de Samaná. To get to Las Terrenas you can catch the half-hourly pick-up trucks from the Texaco station on the C5 in Sánchez, which follow a good, but narrow and winding, road up over the mountains, or you can take the flatter, longer route via Samaná. A paved (if not entirely pristine) roads also links Samaná with Las Galeras.

Samaná

Protected on its southern side by an elongated strip of land that breaks apart into a series of small islands, **SANTA BÁRBARA DE SAMANÁ** is a very pretty harbour town that in the winter months is the embarkation point for **whale-watching** tours. Previously given over almost exclusively to independent tourism, it now boasts its own all-inclusive hotel operated by the Bahía Principe group, who also maintain a number of other all-inclusives in the area.

Arrival, orientation and accommodation

Driving into town, the C-5 leads directly onto the Malecón, a wide concrete boardwalk that divides the shops and restaurants from the ocean. The C-5

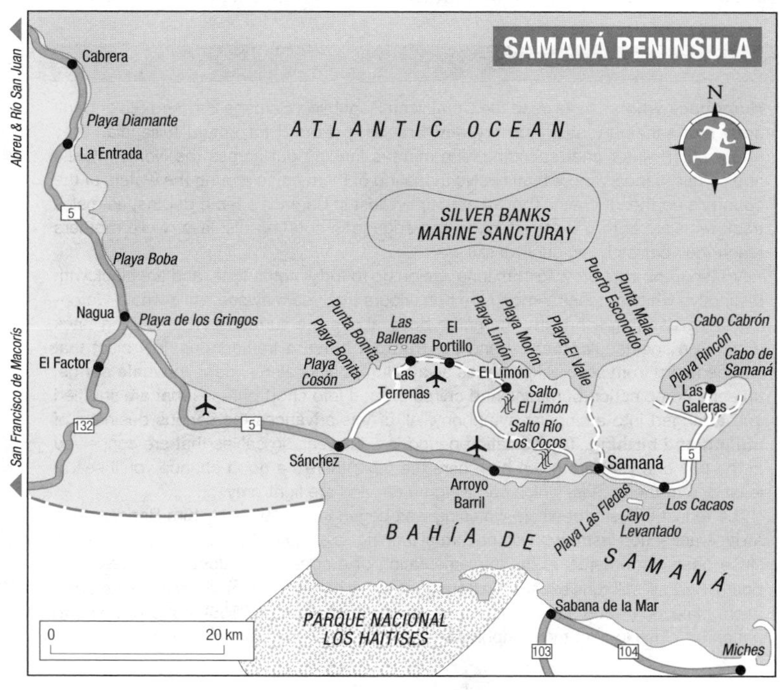

(known locally as Avenida Rosario Sánchez) and the Malecón are the only major thoroughfares in the city. Incoming **buses** stop in the centre of the Malecón, within easy walking distance of most hotels, while *guaguas* stop and set off from the large city market (El Mercado), right on the C-5 and close to a few budget accommodations but a half-kilometre north of the seafront. Samaná has an array of **accommodations**, from luxury resorts to dirt-cheap options, but the latter are not quite as comfortable as those you'll find in Las Terrenas to the north.

Bahia View Av Circunvalación ⓣ809/538-2186, ⓔasavachao@aol.com. The Pueblo Principe complex now rather obscures the eponymous views, but this is still the town's best option for budget travellers, with a friendly proprietor, better-than-average rooms and private showers. ❷

Casa de Huespedes Mildania Calle Fco. Del Rosario Sánchez 41 ⓣ809/538-2151. Clean and tidy rooms with private showers, TVs and a/c in an immaculate house. ❷

Gran Bahía Principe Cayacoa Lorna Puerto Escondido, ⓣ809/538-3131, ⓦwww.bahia-principe.com. Perched overlooking the town, the remodelled *Cayacoa* is a stylish all-inclusive with large rooms, a top-floor restaurant and a small stretch of beach. Entertainment is provided at the Pueblo Principe entertainment complex in Samaná town. ❺

Gran Bahía Principe Samaná Carretera 5 6km east of town ⓣ809/538-3434, ⓦwww.bahia-principe.com. Thoroughly revamped, this is a class act with a majestic oceanfront setting east of town, immaculate grounds and well-maintained rooms. ❹

Hotel Docia Duarte 1 ⓣ809/538-2041. Wildly popular small hotel off the Malecón, though it's hard to see why. Clean, basic and well placed, but nothing special. ❶

The Town

Samaná is undeniably charming, with pretty, spacious neighbourhoods, winding streets that amble up the hills and a warm sense of community. The centre of activity is the city's **Malecón**, a broad, concrete boardwalk, at the centre of which is **Samaná Port**, the departure point for ferries to Cayo Levantado, Sabana de la Mar

Whale-watching

Humpback whales have used the Dominican Republic's Samaná Bay and Silver Bank coral reef sanctuary as a **nursery and breeding ground** for untold millennia. They return each winter after spending nine months fanning out across the North Atlantic and by mid-January more than twelve thousand of them move around the waters of the country's northeast coast. They're at their liveliest in Samaná's tepid depths, as males track females, compete for attention and engage in courting displays, while mothers teach their calves basic survival skills.

Adult humpbacks grow to 15m long, weigh up to forty metric tons, and are black with distinctive white patches. Among the behaviours that you may see while whale-watching are **breaching** – hurtling the entire body above the surface before landing back down in a spectacular crash – and the **trumpet blow**, a tremendous, low blast that can be heard from several kilometres away. Humpbacks also engage in **whale songs**, an eerie combination of moans and chirps formed into short phrases that are shuffled and arranged into a singular symphony. All of this advances the serious business of **mating and birthing**. The gestation period is a full year, so calves that are conceived in the bay one year are given birth here the next; there's a good chance you'll see at least one of the babies, which can weigh a ton and are light grey.

The tourist industry of whale-watching was begun in the 1980s by Kim Beddall, then an itinerant scuba instructor with no formal training as a marine biologist – although she's since been instrumental in the implementation of a code of conduct for whale-watch boats. Beddall still runs excellent **whale boat tours** through her Victoria Marine operation, Malecón (ⓣ809/538-2494, ⓦwww.whalesamana.com; US$55) that allows you to get an up-close look at the humpbacks; sightings are almost guaranteed in season.

and the whale-watching boats. Come night-time, the Malecón's restaurants and bars buzz with activity and music, with a fairly mixed scene of Dominicans, expats and foreign visitors.

You can learn a little more about the town's annual visitors at the small **Whale Museum** (Ⓣ809/538-2042, Ⓦwww.samana.org; RD$100), just west of the Malecón, which has recordings of whale songs and a 12m-long whale skeleton. A few blocks from the waterfront, the old First African Wesleyan Methodist Church of Samaná, popularly known as **La Churcha**, on Santa Bárbara and Duarte (daily 9am–6pm), maintains what African-American culture is left in Samaná. The prefabricated, tin-roofed structure was originally shipped over from England by the English Methodist Church in 1823.

Eating and drinking

Samaná's best **restaurants** are concentrated on the four blocks of the Malecón around the port, with waterside expat joints serving great French and Italian and several good spots for Dominican food. West of here lies Pueblo Principe, an incongruous looking "entertainment complex" of pastel-coloured clapboard shops, restaurants and bars built by the Bahia-Principe group to service the clients of its three local hotels.

Le France Malecón Ⓣ809/538-2257. Reasonably priced gourmet Dominican dishes with some French fare as well, in a relaxed open-air patio. The *gambas* (small bay shrimp) are wonderful and it's the best people-watching spot on the waterfront. Main courses RD$300–450.

L'Hacienda E De León 6 Ⓣ809/538-2383. Below *Naomi* disco, affordable French food (main courses start around ED$250) and the best steaks in town.

La Mata Rosada Malecón Ⓣ809/538-2494. Excellent high-end Italian cuisine that can be enjoyed either in an indoor dining room or an outdoor patio. Try the *filete pesca de criolla* (RD$340).

Nightlife

Samaná has great **nightlife** during the busier times of the year, with most of the action centred, inevitably, on the Malecón. The prime spot is *Naomi* (cover RD$40), a slick, dark, bustling meat market with a sound system playing a mix of *merengue* and European dance.

Around Samaná

Samaná's best attribute is its convenience as an inexpensive base from which to explore some of the peninsula's more compelling sights. Ferries leave three times daily to nearby **Cayo Levantado**, the original Bacardi Island photographed in the 1970s rum campaign. Although it's undisputedly beautiful, the huge tourist infrastructure somewhat destroys its desert island charm; and unless you're visiting as part of a whale-watching tour, or staying at the refurbished *Gran Bahia Principe Levantado* (Ⓣ809/538-2042, Ⓦwww.samana.org; ❺–❻), a luxury all-inclusive hotel on the island's more secluded half, there are better places on the peninsula to spend a day on the beach. Along the eastern tip of the peninsula, and easily reachable by *guagua*, a series of attractive beaches lead toward **Las Galeras**, as pretty a spot as any along the coast, and the even better beach at **Playa Rincón**.

Las Galeras

Set in a horseshoe-shaped cove at the far eastern end of the peninsula, **LAS GALERAS** is gradually becoming mainstream. The road from Samaná has been improved (at least in part) and the number of hotels continues to rise steadily. Despite this growth, the small village maintains a peaceful, timeless ambience. The solitude that Las Galeras was once famous for has now gone but it's been replaced with some tasteful amenities that should make most visitors' stays more comfortable. The beaches, however, are as stunning as ever.

Accommodation

Las Galeras's **hotels** are mostly found along the main road or spread out to the east and west behind the beach.

La Isleta Beach Road West ⓣ809/538-0016, ⓦwww.la-isleta.com. A stone's throw from the beach, set amid charming tropical gardens, these cheerfully decorated "creole-style" apartments come equipped with kitchens and sleep up to four, making them something of a bargain. ❷

Plaza Lusitania ⓣ809/538-0093, ⓦwww.plazalusitania.com. Selection of large, clean rooms with balconies and a/c (some with kitchens) above shops and restaurants in the heart of the village. Not super cheap, but very pleasant. ❷

Paradiso Bungalows Calle Las Galeras ⓣ809/967-7295. The best of several bungalow complexes, on the main crossroads, just back from the beach with a cosy, tropical garden and a good restaurant. ❷

Todo Blanco Beach Road South ⓣ809/538-0201, ⓦwww.hoteltodoblanco.com. Tasteful to the extreme and a genuine haven of tranquillity, with huge rooms, a pretty garden and a superb authentic Italian restaurant. ❸

Villa Serena Beach Road North ⓣ809/538-0000, ⓦwww.villaserena.com. Housed in a beautiful faux-Victorian mansion with a large, manicured tropical garden on the beach. Perfect for honeymooners. The restaurant is one of the best in town, with traditional French cooking fused with tropical fruits and spices. ❹

Eating

Plenty of **eating** options are scattered along the main road on the way into town and there is also a good selection of restaurants in the main hotels.

Chez Denise Calle Las Galeras. Traditional French food and creperie on a terrace near the beach. Crepes start at around RD$200.

Dominican Kitchen Calle Las Galeras at the beach entrance. Not so much a restaurant as a collection of shacks serving excellent seafood dishes. Expect to pay RD$400 for a large sharing platter of seafood.

Pescador Calle Las Galeras. The best fish in town served at the town's most stylish eaterie, 500m from the beach. Extremely friendly proprietor. Mid-priced.

Playa Rincón

Hidden from the rest of the peninsula by the upper prong at its easternmost end, **Playa Rincón** boasts the top Samaná beach bar none. From the Samaná–Las Galeras road, follow the signposted paved road north for approximately 8km and then turn right onto a rocky dirt road that leads to the beach (4WD recommended). Alternatively take a boat from Las Galeras – several make the trip daily, including one departing at 9am from the *Casa Marina Bay Resort* (US$12). Of all the warm, clear waters on the island, Rincón has the very finest, combined with a three-kilometre stretch of whiter-than-white sand and a sprawling coconut forest behind it. For now the only buildings are a couple of Dominican fish shacks serving fresh seafood at both ends of the beach; check prices before ordering but expect to pay around RD$300 per person. This is an eminently more enjoyable day out than Cayo Levantado.

Las Terrenas and around

Set midway along the peninsula's remote northern coast, the former fishing village of **LAS TERRENAS** has gone from a backwater to an expat-dominated resort town renowned for its buoyant nightlife. Though development has seen it linked via new highways to surrounding towns, much of the town centre, which is packed with restaurants, bars and shops, remains unpaved and extremely bumpy, and the inland barrio is much the same as it was two decades ago.

Las Terrenas makes for a pleasant base camp from which to explore the northern part of the Samaná Peninsula; on either side are less developed beaches such as **Playa Bonita**, and a day-trip to the **El Limón waterfall** is also highly recommended.

Arrival and getting around

These days many visitors to the town's larger hotels arrive either at the new international airport at El Catey, just west of the peninsula, which welcomes **flights** mainly from Europe and Canada, or at the small domestic airport in El Portillo to the east of town. Two airlines offer daily scheduled flights to Aeropuerto El Portillo: Take Off (Ⓣ809/552-1333, Ⓦwww.takeoffweb.com) and Aero Domca (Ⓣ809/412-5888, Ⓦwww.aerodomca.com).

If **driving**, you have the choice of two routes. From Sánchez the highway winds its way up over the Cordillera Samaná to Las Terrenas and is one of the most scenic roads in the entire country. It's also extremely narrow and twisty and can be a bit hairy for the uninitiated. The alternative route takes you via Samaná and El Limón and will add an extra 45 minutes (at least) to your journey, but it is considerably flatter.

The best way to get to Las Terrenas if you don't have your own car is via *guagua*, which leave every half hour from the Texaco garage in Sánchez, and every hour from the Samaná Malecón (RD$140).

Once you arrive, you probably won't have too much trouble just **walking** where you want to go as Las Terrenas' layout is exceedingly straightforward. Note that the beachfront roads in the town's western half are unpaved and largely unlit. If you need a lift anywhere, *motoconcho* rides within town are RD$30 during the day, double that at night. You could also look into hiring a quad bike (also known as an ATV), which are available from at least half a dozen agencies in town for around US$55 a day.

Accommodation

Development in Las Terrenas has meant the loss of most of its rock-bottom **accommodation** options. What remains are pricier inns and *cabañas*, plus a few hotels aimed squarely at the luxury end of the market. Note that nearby Playa Bonita (see p.336) also has a collection of more secluded hotels.

Fata Morgana on Playa Bonita road, Ⓣ809/836-5541, Ⓔeditdejong@hotmail.com. Very basic and cheap cabins with a communal kitchen, set in gardens. ❶

Palapa Av 27 Febrero Ⓣ809/240-6797, Ⓦwww.palapabeach.com. At the eastern end of town where kite-surfing rules the waves (a couple of schools are on site), this French-owned place has tastefully minimal bungalows, elegant gardens, a pool, and a lively bar that sees a lot of weekend action. Good breakfast included in the price. ❷

Las Palmas as Mar Av 27 Febrero Ⓣ809/240-6292, Ⓦwww.laspalmasalmar.com. A good choice for an extended stay, for which it offers significant reductions. Just across from the beach, its villas are large – some sleeping up to six – if a little bland, but well equipped with satellite TV, DVD players, safes and internet connections, and there's a swimming pool. ❹

Playa Colibri Ⓣ809/240-6434, Ⓦwww.playacolibri.com. Spacious family-friendly self-catering apartments in a series of three-storey blocks laid out around a central pool and tropical garden. Large rooms with full kitchens, cable TV and private balconies. Guarded parking at rear. ❷

Villas Eva Luna Calle Playa Las Ballenas Ⓣ809/978-5611, Ⓦwww.villa-evaluna.com. Highly recommended small hotel with five great villas that sleep up to four, with private terraces, kitchen and king-size bed, set around a tropical garden and swimming pool 300 metres off the western beach. The friendly owner can provide meals on request and has plans to open a health spa here in the near future. Minimum 3 night stay. ❹

The Town

Aside from spectacular day-trips to the surrounding countryside, the **beach** is the focus of daytime entertainment. The stretch to the east of the main intersection is the older, more established core of the resort, lined with hotels, low-end *cabañas* and restaurants. The waters here have become increasingly populated by kitesurfers and windsurfers.

The western beach, which stretches a full 2km to **Playa Las Ballenas** – named for three oblong islands just offshore that resemble breaching humpback whales – is the more up and coming area, with a livelier, funkier feel. Several old fishing shacks have been renovated to house a cluster of restaurants and bars, but they stand far enough away to leave the sand undisturbed. The ocean is calm and good for swimming, protected by a coral reef 100m out that provides decent snorkelling.

Eating and drinking

In keeping with its expat-dominated culture, Las Terrenas' **restaurants** have a fully international flavour with Italian, Spanish, French, Mexican and even Indian options available. Most of the hotels along the beach have their own restaurants and **bars**, which tend to cater as much for passing trade as they do for residents. The thriving social scene, too, tends to be based around the beachfront joints, with most of the action close to the main road.

Barrio Latino Calle de la Playa ⓣ809/240-6367. Simple, ever-bustling, and relatively bargain-priced café with a huge menu including breakfasts, sandwiches, burgers and pizzas. Good for people-watching.

Casa Coco Calle El Portillo ⓣ809/240-6095. Reasonably priced pizzeria (margherita RD$170, *frutas del mar* RD$300) with a candlelit outdoor seating area.

Comedor Jahaira The only place to go for *comida criolla* in Las Terrenas, and incredibly inexpensive. From the town centre, head up the Carretera Las Terrenas and take the second dirt track on the right after the Centro Commercial.

Cuca Marina Fisherman's Village, Calle de la Playa ⓣ809/240-6351. A range of fiery, highly seasoned dishes (try the aptly named *pollo al Diablo* for RD$280) served in a charming wooden dining room overlooking the water.

El Mambu Social Club Av 27 Febrero ⓣ809/877-8374. Exquisite fine dining presided over by a former Michelin starred chef (try the creole crab in coconut milk for RD$380), as well as a stylish lively bar.

Nuevo Mundo Carretera Las Terrenas. This insanely popular disco a couple of hundred metres south of the main crossroads is the place to party.

La Terrasse Fisherman's Vilalge, Calle de la Playa ⓣ809/240-6351. A handsome dining space – linen table clothes, heliconias in vases – and top-notch, albeit rather pricey, cooking. Fisherman's Village's most upscale offering; advance booking recommended.

West of Las Terrenas: Playa Bonita and Playa Cosón

Playa Bonita, 13km of uninterrupted beach that begins just west of Playa Las Ballenas, boasts the kind of powdery white sand you might expect to see only in tourist brochures. There's been a fair bit of development in recent years – particularly inland where a new golf course, the Las Terrenas Country Club, is due to open soon – but this has been done carefully and the **hotels** do little to detract from the beauty and serenity of the heavenly beaches. If you're looking for natural beauty, peace and quiet, you're far better off staying here than in Las Terrenas.

The best of Playa Bonita's hotels is the *Atlantis Hotel & Restaurant* (ⓣ809/240-6111, ⓦwww.atlantis-hotel.com.do; ❷), whose rooms are palatial and pretty; try to book either the Jamaica or the El Paso room, both with panoramic views of the beach. Also nice is the *Hotel Costa Las Ballenas* (ⓣ809/240-5153, ⓦwww.costa-las-ballenas.com; ❷), with beautifully decorated *cabañas* and an apartment block set in a lovely garden. It's also home to one of the area's top dive schools, Las Terrenas Divers. *Casa Grande* (ⓣ809/240-6349, ⓦwww.casagrandebeachhotel.com; ❷) has five good-sized rooms in a large house, and by far the best food on the beach, with gourmet French meals available nightly – try the *crevettes au miel* (shrimps in honey) for RD$550.

From Playa Bonita's entrance, a sand road provides access for four-wheel-drives and quad bikes past the front of the hotels and along an increasingly empty beach to **Playa Cosón**, a small fishing village 6km along the coast. Less developed than Playa Bonita, it boasts just a couple of hotels, plus a handful of gourmet beach shacks with tables and chairs on the sand, serving grilled, fresh-caught fish for a few pesos.

East of Las Terrenas: El Limón

Eleven kilometres east of town, and little more than a intersection with a few shacks attached, dusty **El Limón** seems unpromising at first, but makes an ideal base for excursions to the magnificent El Limón waterfall to the south. Upon arrival you'll be beset by several local *buscones* trying to steer you to one of the excursion outfits; the best is the combined ranch-restaurant *Rancho Santi-Casa Berca* (Ⓣ809/343-0776, Ⓔlimonsanti@terra.es) just south of the intersection on the road to Samaná. The **waterfall** is accessible by horse from the town and takes 2.5 hours round-trip, well worth it to see the 50m of torrential white water dropping from a cliff in the middle of the wilderness. Expect to pay around RD$700 for the round-trip with a good lunch included.

From Las Terrenas, a **motoconcho** costs RD$100, and during the day *guaguas* ply the El Limón route once an hour for RD$30. Getting back is more of a problem if you're depending on public transport. Every hour or so, a *guagua* will pass by.

6.4

The Silver Coast

The Dominican Republic's **Silver Coast**, 300km of prime waterfront property on the country's northern edge, is the most popular tourist destination in the Caribbean. With a seemingly unending supply of great beaches around the booming towns of **Puerto Plata** and **Cabarete**, such a designation is no surprise. The Carretera 5 skirts the coast all the way east from Samaná to just past Puerto Plata, making **getting around** a breeze. The country's major bus company, Caribe Tours, traverses the highway, along with *guaguas* and plentiful *público* taxis. Heading west of Puerto Plata is more of a challenge (but not impossible) if you don't have a four-wheel-drive vehicle.

Puerto Plata and Playa Dorada

PUERTO PLATA and **Playa Dorada** comprise the mass tourism capital of the Caribbean. The city of Puerto Plata is a vibrant Dominican town of 200,000 that's well worth exploring for its historic architecture and nightlife. Its core, the **Old City**, borders the port to the east, a narrow grid of streets that was once the swankiest neighbourhood in the country. Around the original town sprawls a patchwork maze of industrial zones and concrete barrios known as the **New City**, formed over the past century with the growth of the town's industry. Most visitors, though, are here for package tours to the Playa Dorada complex – located a kilometre east of the city limits – a walled-off vacation factory that pulls in over a half-million tourists each year.

Arrival and getting around

Six kilometres east of town, **Aeropuerto Internacional Gregorio Luperón** (Ⓣ809/586-0408), usually referred to as Puerto Plata Airport, is the main northern entry point into the country. There is a Banco de Reservas **ATM** and **currency**

exchange (Mon–Fri 8.30am–6.30pm) within the strip of shops lining the front of the airport, alongside a number of **car-rental** offices. While most of the more expensive hotels have shuttle buses, any of the *motoconchos* can take you into town for RD$30, and there are plenty of taxis to take you to points further out. Arriving by **bus** is another option; the city is a major junction point for Caribe Tours (Ⓣ809/586-4544, Ⓦwww.caribetours.com.do) and Metro (Ⓣ809/586-6062, Ⓦwww.metroservicioturistocos.com), whose vehicles arrive here from the south (via Santo Domingo and Santiago) and from Samaná in the east (Caribe Tours only).

Central Puerto Plata is compact enough to make **walking** your best option for getting around, although be aware that once you hit town you will probably be pounced on by a local "guide". Despite their insistent entreaties, it is not recommended that you use them to orientate yourself or find accommodation. If you want to go to Playa Dorada or Costambar, you may want to take one of the ubiquitous *motoconchos*, which should cost RD$30 (RD$20 within town). Cheaper but far slower are the **public buses** shuttling between Playa Dorada and the Parque Central. The price is RD$10 but it can take up to 45 minutes to get from one side of town to the other. **Taxis** are relatively expensive (RD$300 to Playa Dorada), but are the fastest mode of transport and far safer than *motoconchos*.

Accommodation

The best luxury **hotels** are east of town within Playa Dorada but as they are **all-inclusives**, your freedom is somewhat limited. If you want to explore the city itself, a few budget options are in and around the old town and on the Malecón.

Puerto Plata

Lomar Malecón Ⓣ809/320-8555, Ⓕ586-5050. One of the better options offering a reasonable degree of basic comfort. Rooms are clean and come with TVs, a/c, mini-fridges and plenty of hot water. ❶

Montesilva La Estancia Ⓣ809/320-0205, Ⓕ320-0105. Clean, simple and safe on a quiet backstreet, the Montesilva is one of Puerto Plata's cheerier budget offerings with 12 rooms, all with cable TV and a/c, and a small swimming pool. ❶

Puerto Plata Beach Malecón just west of Av Hermanas Mirabal Ⓣ809/586-4243. A rather forlorn option, good as a short-notice standby as its full service apartments are rarely fully booked. ❷

Victoriano San Felipe 33 Ⓣ809/586-9752. Clean but depressingly plain rooms with cable TV and a/c, but little hot water. Can be very noisy at night. ❶

Playa Dorada

Bluebay Villas Doradas Ⓣ809/320-3000, Ⓦwww.hotetur.com. Right on the beach and offering a higher standard of accommodation than the Playa Dorada norm, this has good sized, nicely decorated rooms, three pools, tennis courts and a decent French restaurant. A good choice for couples. ❹

Gran Ventana Ⓣ809/320-2111, Ⓦwww.granventanahotel.com. Right in the centre of Playa Dorada's stretch of sand and aimed squarely at families, this is not the quietest hotel, but its rooms are large and it boasts good sports facilities, as well as offering a range of tours. ❻

Viva Wyndham Playa Dorada Ⓣ809/291-0001, Ⓦwww.vivaresorts.com. Tastefully transformed in the past couple of years and now offering a superior standard of mid-priced family friendly accommodation. The rooms are large, with all mod cons, the food reasonable and the beach nicely maintained. ❻

Puerto Plata: The Old City

The once-exclusive **Old City**, a compact area bounded by Avenida Colón, the Malecón and Calle López, is long past its heyday. Time has not been kind to many of its grand Victorian buildings, once populated by wealthy landowners, dock workers and European merchants. A good place to begin wandering is the colonial-era **San Felipe** fort (9am–noon & 2–5pm; closed Wed; RD$20), a limestone edifice perched atop a rocky point at the seaside Malecón off Avenida Colón. The Spaniards constructed it in 1540 as a defence against corsairs and a prison for smugglers.

The heart of the Victorian city is the **Parque Central**, at the corner of Separación and Beller, which is bordered to the south by **Catedral San Felipe**. Both are currently closed for restoration. The remaining three sides of the park are still accessible

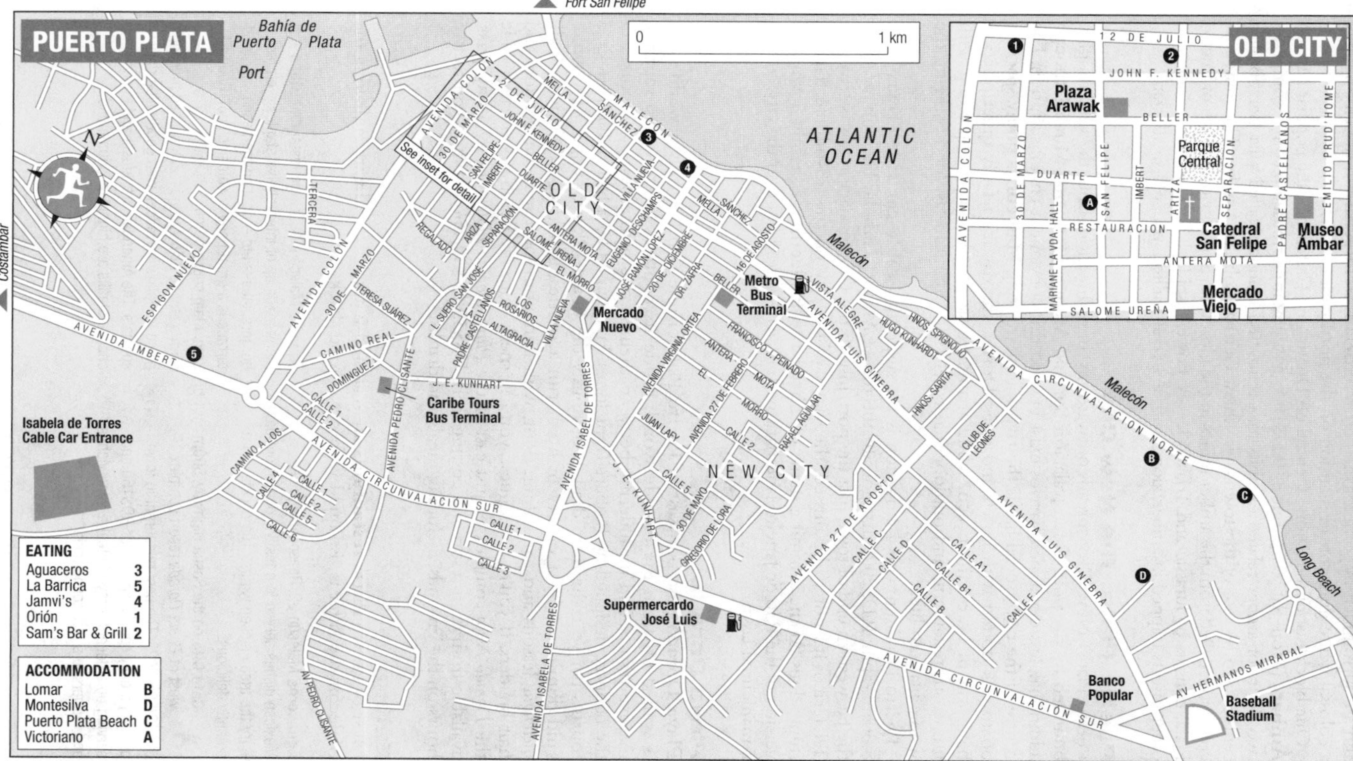
PUERTO PLATA
OLD CITY
Fort San Felipe
Costambar
Airport, Sosúa & Playa Dorado
Bahía de Puerto Plata
Port
ATLANTIC OCEAN
Malecón
Long Beach
OLD CITY
NEW CITY
See inset for detail
0
1 km
Metro Bus Terminal
Mercado Nuevo
Caribe Tours Bus Terminal
Isabela de Torres Cable Car Entrance
Supermercardo José Luis
Banco Popular
Baseball Stadium
Plaza Arawak
Parque Central
Catedral San Felipe
Museo Ámbar
Mercado Viejo
AVENIDA COLÓN
12 DE JULIO
JOHN F. KENNEDY
BELLER
DUARTE
30 DE MARZO
SAN FELIPE
IMBERT
ARIZA
SEPARACIÓN
RESTAURACION
ANTERA MOTA
SALOME UREÑA
MARIANE LA VDA. HALL
PADRE CASTELLANOS
EMILIO PRUD'HOME
MALECÓN
SÁNCHEZ
MELLA
VILLA NUEVA
EUGENIO DESCHAMPS
JOSÉ RAMÓN LOPEZ
20 DE DICIEMBRE
DR. ZAFRA
16 DE AGOSTO
VISTA ALEGRE
AVENIDA LUIS GINEBRA
AVENIDA CIRCUNVALACION NORTE
AVENIDA CIRCUNVALACIÓN SUR
HNOS. SPIGNOLIO
HUGO KUNHARDT
HNOS. SARITA
CLUB DE LEONES
FRANCISCO J. PEINADO
AVENIDA VIRGINIA ORTEA
AVENIDA 27 DE FEBRERO
EL MORRO
RAFAEL AGUILAR
CALLE 2
JUAN LAFY
CALLE 5
30 DE MAYO
GREGORIO DE LORA
J. E. KUNHART
AVENIDA ISABEL DE TORRES
AVENIDA ISABELA DE TORRES
AVENIDA 27 DE AGOSTO
CALLE C
CALLE D
CALLE A1
CALLE B1
CALLE B
CALLE F
AV HERMANOS MIRABAL
AVENIDA PEDRO CLISANTE
AV PEDRO CLISANTE
LOS ROSARIOS
ALTAGRACIA
PADRE CASTELLANOS
L. SUERO SAN JOSÉ
REGALADO
TERESA SUÁREZ
CAMINO REAL
DOMINGUEZ
CALLE 1
CALLE 3
CALLE 4
CALLE 6
CAMINO A LOS
AVENIDA IMBERT
ESPIGON NUEVO
TERCERA
30 DE MARZO
EATING
Aguaceros 3
La Barrica 5
Jamvi's 4
Orión 1
Sam's Bar & Grill 2
ACCOMMODATION
Lomar B
Montesilva D
Puerto Plata Beach C
Victoriano A

and are surrounded by some of the best **Victorian architecture** in the city, notably a colossal white gingerbread mansion on the northwest corner.

One block east of the Parque Central on Duarte and Castellanos, the popular **Museo Ámbar** (Mon–Sat 9am–6pm; RD$100, Ⓦwww.ambermuseum.com) comprises two floors of amber-related exhibits in a renovated mansion called Villa Berz, built a century ago by one of the town's wealthiest German tobacco families. The museum's collection, culled from the amber mines in the Cordillera Septentrional south of Puerto Plata, consists of Jurassic and Triassic leaves, flowers, spiders, termites, wasps, ants and other insects trapped in amber, along with a several-million-year-old small lizard.

Puerto Plata: The New City

Puerto Plata's **New City** spreads outwards in three directions from the Old, roughly bounded by the port, Circunvalación Sur and Avenida Hermanas Mirabal, though additional, less developed barrios exist beyond this convenient circumscription. The centre of the city's social life is the two-kilometre-long **Malecón**, a sunny, spacious boardwalk dotted with hotels and cafés. During the day it's a fairly quiet place to hang out or lie on the beach, while at night a strip of bars open up along with numerous restaurants and outdoor shacks selling Dominican fast food bringing the whole place to life.

Puerto Plata's crowning attraction is the suspended **cable car ride** (Thurs–Tues 8.30am–5pm; RD$200) that goes to the top of **Mount Isabela**. The entrance is at the far western end of town past the port, just off the Circunvalación Sur on Avenida Teleférico. It's not to be missed; the views of the city on this 25-minute trip are stupendous. At the summit a statue of **Christ the Redeemer**, a slightly downsized version of the Rio de Janeiro landmark with its arms spread out over the city, crowns a manicured lawn.

Playa Dorada

Playa Dorada, just 1km east of Puerto Plata on the C-5 but truly a world away, is walled off from the outside world; inside its confines are fourteen separate massive resorts, and meandering between them is one of the best golf courses in the country, designed by Robert Trent Jones. Frequented by a half-million package tourists per year, the main draw is obviously the **beach**, 2km of impeccably white sand dominated by a variety of hotel-run activities, including beach volleyball, *merengue* lessons and parasailing, along with numerous local souvenir vendors and hair braiders. If you're not a guest, you can sneak onto the beach via entries beside the *Dorado Naco* complex or just east of the *Playa Dorada Hotel*, or buy a **day pass**, available from each resort and costing from US$35 to $50, and entitling you to five hours on the grounds, including meals and drinks.

Eating

Most of Puerto Plata's **restaurants** are scattered within the Old City and along the Malecón; the latter is also lined with cheap food shacks.

Aguaceros Malecón 32. Reasonably priced Mexican dishes served in a festive, oceanfront barn – try the fried chicken wings. The cocktails are potently delicious.

Cafe Cito on the Sosúa Highway, 500m west of *Costa Dorada* resort complex Ⓣ809/586-7923. The best restaurant in town offering a daily special combo for RD$160 and serving up a decent array of steaks, sandwiches and burgers to a jazz soundtrack.

Jamvi's Malecón 18. Large restaurant with a menu made up of international staples – pizzas, burgers, steaks etc – right on the beach. Its raised terrace is a great people-watching spot. Open till 3am. Main courses from RD$250.

Sam's Bar & Grill Ariza 34. Established meeting place for fellow travellers, with good-value daily specials. The American breakfasts and Philly cheese steaks are highly recommended.

Drinking and nightlife

Fed by a metropolis full of dance-crazy Dominicans and vacationing foreign hordes, Puerto Plata's **nightlife** establishments are crammed with dancers until dawn. While Playa Dorada resorts and their restaurants are off limits to non-guests (except for day passes), the discos are open to all.

La Barrica Circunvalación Sur and Av Colón, Puerto Plata. Hip, strictly Dominican music disco catering mostly to city-dwellers cutting vicious moves. There are no lights in the entire club – the waiters use flashlights. No cover.

Hemingway's Cafe in *Playa Dorada Plaza*, Playa Dorada. Haven for crazed drunken tourists intent on having a good time. Mon and Thurs play host to ear-splitting karaoke, Wed to live rock, Fri are a "rave party", while Sat are "Latin nights". No cover.

Orión 30 de Marzo and 12 de Julio, Puerto Plata. Rough-and-tumble local nightclub, but once of the most popular dance spots in town, featuring strictly *merengue* and *bachata*. RD$40 cover.

East of Puerto Plata

The resort development that began around Puerto Plata has gobbled up most of the prime beachfront east of the city. As such, you'll have to keep going east for approximately 70km to the small, friendly fishing village of Río San Juan to find anything approaching unspoilt coastline. Even closer, though, and easier for those with limited time, is the bustling resort town of **Cabarete**, a kiteboarding and windsurfing enclave that's quickly being swallowed by tourism construction.

Cabarete

Stretched along the C-5 between the beach and lagoon that bears its name, **CABARETE** is a crowded international enclave that owes its existence almost entirely to **windsurfing**. The main beach, Playa Cabarete, has ideal conditions for the sport, and the multicultural cross-section of its aficionados attracts a growing community from around the globe.

Arrival and accommodation

Virtually all of Cabarete is on the **Carretera 5**. Buses, *guaguas* and *motoconchos* will drop you off along the main strip, a crowded patchwork of restaurants and bars, tour operators and souvenir shops.

Agualina Carretera 5 ⓣ809/571-0805, ⓦwww.agualina.com. Nice full-service apartments right on Kite Beach, with an in-house kiteboarding school. Unlike most similar places, these rooms are not only spacious and comfortable, they're also stylishly done. Highly recommended if you're going to spend most of your time on Kite Beach. ❸

Casa Blanca Carretera 5 ⓣ809/571-0934, ⓦwww.casablancacabarete.com. Solid mid-range budget option with eight sparse but spacious rooms plus seven studios with kitchenettes. Free gear storage and a pleasant pool area where breakfast is served. ❷

El Magnifico Carretera 5 ⓣ809/571-0868, ⓦwww.hotelmagnifico.com. Well-designed condos spread over six buildings, linked together by paths running through lovely tropical gardens. Far enough from the action to feel remote, but just a couple of minutes' walk along the beach to the downtown restaurants. Tranquil central pool area. ❸

Villa Taina Carretera 5 ⓣ809/571-0722, ⓦwww.villataina.com. The best hotel in town with top-notch service, a good restaurant and a selection of large, clean and tidy rooms spread over a number of beachfront buildings, some with sea views. ❹

Viva Wyndham Tangerine Carretera 5 ⓣ809/571-0402, ⓦwww.vivaresorts.com. One of Cabarete's growing band of all-inclusives, this is a stylish affair with 221 large rooms (with minibars and terraces), three restaurants and easy beach access. ❹

Exploring Cabarete

What there is of a town consists of the hectic strip of restaurants, hotels, souvenir shops and tour operators spread right along the C-5. The real action takes place on

Cabarete adventure sports outfitters

Carib BIC Center ⓣ809/571-0640, ⓦwww.caribwind.com. Slick windsurfing/kiteboarding outfit with almost two decades of experience. Great equipment shop and a well-trained, friendly staff always willing to give you pointers. At the Board Test Center, you can try out boards from different manufacturers. US$220 for ten hours of use on the water; US$200 for six 1hr classes; US$45 equipment insurance.

Iguana Mama ⓣ809/571-0908, ⓦwww.iguanamama.com. Offers US$30 mountain-bike day-trips and week-long bike tours of the island, as well as hikes up Mount Isabela (see p.340) and several-day treks through the Cordillera Central to Pico Duarte (see p.348). They also do whale-watching in Samaná Bay for US$139/day, horseriding for US$55/half-day and a whole stack of cultural tours. Excellent option.

Vela/Spinout/Dare2Fly ⓣ809/571-0805, ⓦwww.velacabarete.com. The best-stocked of Cabarete's windsurf centres with free daily clinics and a lively social scene at the adjoining bar. US$290 for a week's windsurfing equipment rental. Their Dare2Fly station on Kite Beach offers equipment rental and kiteboarding lessons daily. US$390 for a three-day introductory course with equipment.

the **beach**, which is full of windsurfers during the day – calm morning conditions make it perfect for beginners, but as the day wears on, and the trade winds kick in with full force, the experts take over. Further out from the centre, both east and west, you can have the beach to yourself. At night, the bars and restaurants spill out onto the sand, helping create a hedonistic atmosphere.

Two kilometres further west, on a white-sand beach hidden behind Punta Goleta, is Kite Beach, which over the past half decade has become a major centre of **kiteboarding**. In many ways similar to windsurfing, a kiteboarder needs less wind to really get moving and the best riders perform huge jumps and tricks. See the box above for details about how you can get in on the action.

Eating and drinking

Cabarete has an array of good **dining** options, most of them opened by European expats, and hence serving some unusual cuisines for this part of the country. The entire town is packed with **bars**, but a select few garner the majority of the business.

Café Pittu Carretera 5. A relaxed, friendly beach café during the day – they do a mean chicken enchilada for RD$299 – which lays on themed night-time entertainment. Wi-Fi hotspot.

Casa del Pescador Carretera 5. The best seafood in town. Pick the lobster of your choice from the pool out front, and then enjoy your meal on the sand overlooking the water. Mains around RD$400.

Casanova Carretera 5. High quality international menu in a charming dining room that leads from the road to the beach where flaming torches illuminate the tables. Mains RD$300–400.

Lax Carretera 5. With couches looking out over the sea, this is the most popular place to come both during happy hour (4pm–6pm) and in the early hours when everything is winding down. Occasional live music.

Miro Carretera 5. The best and most expensive food on Cabarete Beach. Superior sushi in an elegant dining space. The beef filet in shitake sauce is out of this world (RD$545).

Onno's Carretera 5. Lively bar/restaurant which really gets going in the small hours – plays mainly European and American hits.

Panadería Dick Carretera 5. Various gourmet breads for a few pesos, great Danishes and croissants. Excellent breakfasts with fresh-squeezed orange juice and cappuccino.

West of Puerto Plata

The contrast between east and **west of Puerto Plata** couldn't be more striking. In place of the paved highways and resort complexes you'll find vast stretches of untrammelled wilderness along rough dirt tracks, though some are slowly being converted into freeways. One thing that doesn't change, however, is the proliferation of lovely **beaches**.

El Castillo and La Isabela

From Puerto Plata, the C-30, or Carretera de las Américas, branches off from the C-5 and heads 50km west to **EL CASTILLO**, a seaside village located on the site of Columbus's first permanent settlement. It's easy to see why he picked it, given the setting of a splendid bay of tranquil, blue water with a solid wall of imposing, Olympian peaks.

Just off the main highway, before you make town, is the entrance to **Parque Nacional La Isabela** (9am–5.30pm, closed Sun; RD$50), which preserves the ruins of La Isabela, the first European town in the New World. Centred around the private home of Columbus himself, which is perched atop a prominent ocean bluff, the park also encompasses the excavated stone foundations of the town and a small museum with Columbus-era relics.

A few kilometres further on, you enter the village, draped over a steep hillside above Playa Isabela, which attracts few beach-goers and is instead marked mainly by small wooden boats. A kilometre offshore the healthy, multicoloured **coral reef** is home to thousands of tropical fish and sea creatures.

If you're looking to **spend the night**, the Belgian-owned *Miamar*, Calle Vista Mar (ⓣ809/471-9157, ⓕ471-8052; ❷ breakfast included), is a modern hotel with a swimming pool and enormous rooms with lovely ocean views. For good Dominican cuisine try *Milagro*, near the entrance to *Rancho del Sol*, a small and friendly *comedor* with a good selection of local dishes.

Monte Cristi

West of El Castillo the roads gradually deteriorate. Past the beautiful beach of **Punta Rucia**, from where you can take a trip to the coral-fringed desert island of **Cayo Paraíso** with El Paraíso Tours (ⓣ809/612-8499, ⓦwww.cayoparaiso.com), the only sensible way to travel is to turn south back onto the C-1 at **Villa Elisa**. The further west you go, the more the landscape transforms itself – gone are the swaying palms and grassy pastures, replaced by scrubby cactus plants and dusty dry soil inhabited mainly by goats. The *carretera* terminates at the westernmost outpost of the Silver Coast, **MONTE CRISTI**, founded in 1501 and at one point one of the country's most important ports. These days it resembles a dusty frontier town bearing only the occasional tarnished remnant of its opulent past along wide, American-style boulevards. Most visitors use the town as a base from which to explore the local **beaches** and the **Parque Nacional Monte Cristi**, an expanse that protects a towering mesa named El Morro and an enormous mangrove-filled river delta, which can be reach to the north of **Playa Juan de Bolaños**, the area's most popular beach.

The park's eastern section is often referred to as **Parque El Morro**, after the flat-topped mesa that takes up a good chunk of it. Climbing the mesa is a lot easier these days as the park office has built a set of steps up from the road's highest point (RD$50 entrance fee). At the foot of El Morro's eastern slope is a lovely and unpopulated **beach** accessible by parking at the end of the road and continuing down on foot. The western half of the national park encompasses a dense mangrove coast dotted with small lagoons; informal tours are led from the *Los Jardines* hotel (from US$20 per person; see below), on which you'll see several river deltas thick with mangroves and perhaps even a couple of crocodiles.

Practicalities

The best **accommodation** option in Monte Cristi is *Cayo Arena*, Playa Juan de Bolaños, 250m west of the beach entrance (ⓣ809/579-3145, ⓦwww.cayoarena.com; ❷), a set of large, full-service apartments right on the beach with ocean view balconies, air-conditioning, kitchenettes, swimming pool, bar and 24-hour security.

Also on the beach, a little more basic but definitely better value is *Los Jardines,* Playa Juan de Bolaños (Ⓣ809/579-2091, Ⓦwww.elbistrot.com; ❷), which has simple rooms with cold-water showers. Note that these hotels get busy over the weekend and the rates go up accordingly. *Los Jardines* also operates the best **restaurant** in town, *Bistrot*, Calle Bolaños (Ⓣ809/579-2091), which serves great moderately priced seafood dishes in an atmospheric courtyard.

6.5 The Cibao

Cibao (rocky land) is the word Taínos used to describe the **Cordillera Central** mountain range that takes up much of the Dominican Republic's central interior. These mountains are the highest peaks in the Caribbean, including Pico Duarte, the Caribbean's tallest at 3087m. The heart of the range is protected as **Parques Nacionales Bermúdez and Ramírez**.

Today, though, Dominicans use the term Cibao more to describe the fertile Cibao Valley, a triangle of alluvial plain that contains some of the deepest topsoil in the world. In the valley sits vibrant **Santiago**, the country's second largest city after Santo Domingo, well positioned for short excursions into the neighbouring farmland.

The **C-1**, also known as the Autopista Duarte, snakes throughout the region, linking the northwest with the southeast, via Santiago and Santo Domingo. With most interest focused on the northern reaches, many visitors also take advantage of the good roads that hurdle the Cordillera Septentrional from the north. Once in the mountains, the best progress is made by following the biggest and best roads between towns, even when the distance travelled is far greater, which is often the case. Buses link most of the towns and *guaguas* make up for any shortfall.

Santiago

Founded in 1504 as a mining town and demolished by an earthquake in 1562, **SANTIAGO** has been associated with tobacco since 1697, when local farmers began producing it for the French colony on the west side of the island. The city is also the home of *merengue périco ripao* – the classic Dominican music using accordion, *tambora* and *güira*. Today the Domincan Republic's second city is a growing metropolis that seems less and less provincial, though its economy is still based on its status as an agricultural depot and centre for the cigar industry. There's a good club scene based mostly around the indigenous music, so you won't lack for fun at nights. During the day, **downtown Santiago** supplies enough cultural diversions to merit a full day or two of ambling about.

Arrival and getting around

All three highway entrances to town – the Autopista Duarte, the Carretera Duarte and the Carretera Turística – lead directly to the city centre. If you're arriving by **bus**, your station will likely be on the north or east side of town, from where you can get a RD$100 taxi closer to the heart of downtown. If you arrive by *guagua*, you'll end up at one of the city's **guagua stations**, one on the corner of 30 de Marzo and Cucurullo (from Mao, Monciòn and Santo Domingo) and on Calle Valerio a block west of Parque Valerio (from San José de las Matas and Puerto Plata). Another arrival point is the **Cibao International Airport** (ⓣ809/582-4894), a twenty-minute drive (or a RD$300 taxi ride) from the centre.

A complex system of battered public taxis – referred to locally as **conchos** or **carro públicos** – should cover most **city transport** needs; a one-way ride costs RD$20. **Private taxis** wait at the city parks, though you can call directly for pick-up; try Camino (ⓣ809/971-7788). As always, you're best off sticking with an established international firm for **car rental**, including Adventure, airport (ⓣ809/612-5494); Budget, 27 de Febrero (ⓣ809/724-7868); and Nelly, Av Salvador E. Sadhalá 204 (ⓣ809/583-6695).

Accommodation

Santiago is pretty well set up for **accommodation**, from budget options up to the *Gran Almirante*, the one five-star hotel in town.

Aloha Sol Del Sol 50 ⓣ809/583-0090, ⓦwww.alohasol.com. Modern hotel with a/c, TV and great hot showers right in the centre of the shopping district. ❷

Colonial Cucurullo and 30 de Marzo ⓣ809/247-3122, ⓕ582-0811. Great little budget hotel with excellent service, clean rooms, a/c and TV. ❶

Hodelpa Centro Plaza Mella 54 ⓣ809/581-7000, ⓦwww.hodelpa.com. Large western-style hotel with large comfortable rooms, a gym, a casino and a top floor restaurant offering great views of the city. ❷

Hodelpa Gran Almirante Estrella Sadhalá and Calle 10 ⓣ809/580-1992, ⓦwww.hodelpa.com. Luxury hotel in a wealthy northeastern suburb with all the amenities. ❹

The City

Most places of interest are **downtown** and within walking distance of one another. Many visitors spend their whole stay in the area bounded by the main city park and the recently revamped **Monumento a los Héroes de la Restauración** (Mon–Sat 9am–noon & 2–5pm; free), Santiago's distinctive symbol and most impressive sight. Built by Trujillo in honour of himself, it was quickly rededicated upon his death to the War of Independence with Spain. Climb the stairs up the monument – a statue of Victory personified as a woman tops its seventy-metre pillar – to take in the breathtaking panorama of Santiago. The surrounding square has been laid out into three small plazas dedicated to Santiago's traditions, writers and baseball team, each adorned with a smattering of representative bronze statues.

Calle del Sol, which borders the monument to the south, is the city's major shopping district and the heart of downtown activity, lined with department stores, banks and sidewalk stalls selling clothing, household wares and fast food. Follow Del Sol west to 30 de Marzo and the **Parque Duarte**, a bit overcrowded but covered by a tree canopy and lined with horse-and-carriage drivers. At the park's southern end stands the **Catedral Santiago** (1895), a concrete building with intricate carvings on its mahogany portals.

In the opposite direction, a few blocks northwest of the park, sits the fascinating **Museo Folklórico de Tomas Morel**, Restauración 174 (Mon–Fri 8.30am–1.30pm & 3.30–5.30pm; free). Inside is a remarkable collection of papier-mâché Carnival masks, alongside various Taíno artefacts and early Spanish household items. The masks, though, are the main focus, with an array of spectacularly Baroque and evil-looking demons.

The city's most compelling attraction, the **Centro León**, lies north at 27 de Febrero 146 (Tues–Sun 10am–7pm; RD$70, Tues free; ⓣ809/582-2315, ⓦwww.centroleon.org.do). This outstanding, multi-faceted cultural centre is divided into four large air-conditioned sections, including collections on local history and anthropology and Dominican Art. There's even a mock tobacco factory (a sure highlight) where you can observe cigars being made and sample a stogie afterwards.

Eating

You'll have no problem finding plenty to **eat** in Santiago, whether it's at fine dining establishments, low-key *comedores* (small Dominican kitchens) or American fast-food chains.

Camp David Carretera Turística Km 12 ⓣ809/223-0666, ⓦwww.campdavidranch.com. Former Trujillo mountain home, now converted into a gourmet restaurant and hostelry that offers a long list of choice seafood dishes and steaks. Look for the turn-off on the Carretera Turística, then drive up a winding road for 2km.

Pez Dorado Del Sol and Parque Altagracia. Venerable Santiago instituion offering high end *comida criolla* in a fairly formal environment.

Olé JP Duarte and Independencia. American-style pizzas plus a few Creole and Dominican standards in a sheltered terrace. Moderate prices.

Rancho Luna Carretera Turística km 7 ⓣ809/736-7176. Top-quality steakhouse and piano bar with excellent service, a huge wine list and great views over the city. Moderate–expensive.

Drinking and nightlife

Santiago **nightlife** is rowdy, diverse and seemingly nonstop; most clubs are completely empty until midnight and don't close until dawn.

Ahí Bar Restauración 71. This bar's tree shaded patio just west of the monument is the place to wind down at the end of the day. Also offers a decent bar menu.

Doce Lounge Plaza Sone Rosa, Calle Salle. Attracts a young hip crowd with a playlist that alternates American hits with more hard-core slices of *merengue*, *salsa* and *reggaeton*. Ladies drink free on Wed.

Francifol Del Sol at Parque Duarte. Classy pub with the coldest beer in town. A good place for drinks and conversation.

Kukara Macara Av Francia in front of the monument. A campy, wild west-themed bar, with giant cacti, waiters in full cowboy regalia and a replica stagecoach above the door. Offers great Dominican and Mexican food, plus cold Presidentes and frozen tropical drinks.

▲ Carnival masks

Jarabacoa tour operators

Rancho Baiguate on the road to Constanza, km 5 ⓣ809/574-6890, ⓦwww.ranchobaiguate.com.do. One of the island's biggest tour operators, with most of their clients coming on excursions from the all-inclusives on the north coast. They run a wide range of adventure trips including white-water rafting (US$50), canyoning (US$50) and three-day guided hikes to Pico Duarte (US$450).

Rancho Jarabacoa Hato Viejo 21 ⓣ809/248-7909. Less expensive option than Baiguate for horseback riding in pueblo Sabaneta. 2km north of Jarabacoa – just US$30 for a day-long excursion.

The Cordillera Central

The **Cordillera Central** contains the Caribbean's tallest, most beautiful mountains. For the most part, the roads are horrific, and getting from place to place often requires a convoluted route, leaving the mountains via one paved road and then re-entering them via another. To head deeper into the range you'll need a donkey; blazed trails lead to **Pico Duarte** from several points.

La Vega

LA VEGA, just 30km south of Santiago, started out as one of Columbus's gold-mining towns. Aside from the ruins of this old settlement, **La Vega Vieja**, there's little in today's noisy, concrete city to hold your attention. However, La Vega's **Carnival** celebrations in February are generally acknowledged to be among the most boisterous and authentic in the nation. A twenty-block promenade is set up between the two main parks, along which parade platoons of demons in impressively horrific masks, the making of which is somewhat of a local speciality craft.

There are no good in-town **hotels**; most lack even the most basic amenities like a toilet seat, mosquito net or hot water. *San Pedro*, Cáceres 87 (ⓣ809/573-2844; ❶), is the least seedy and cleanest, but is still not especially comfortable. You'll fare slightly better with local **restaurants**, notably the second-floor *Salón Dorado* above Engini Car Wash, Cáceres and Restauración, which has a hip decor, fun crowd and pool tables. The **bus** stations, Caribe Tours (ⓣ809/573-3488), Metro (ⓣ809/573-7099) and Vegano Express (ⓣ809/573-7079), are all on the Carretera La Vega, just off the Autopista Duarte. **Guaguas** to Jarabacoa set off from the corner of 27 de Febrero and Restauración.

Jarabacoa

JARABACOA, a sleepy mountain resort peppered with coffee plantations, is popular with wealthy Dominicans for its cool summers, and with foreign travellers for the nearby natural splendour and adventure sports opportunities. While there's little to do in the town itself, the pine-dominated mountains immediately surrounding the town hold three large waterfalls, several rugged trails fit for day-hikes, three rivers used for white-water rafting and the busiest starting-point for treks up Pico Duarte; see the box above for local outfitters.

Arrival and accommodation

Located some 30km southwest of La Vega, Jarabacoa is well served by **public transport**. *Guaguas* do the road from La Vega at hourly intervals and Caribe Tours, with a station at the main crossroads across from the Esso station, runs four buses daily from La Vega, Bonao and Santo Domingo. *Guaguas* pick up and drop off at Esso in the centre and by the Shell station on the Constanza road.

With the recent increase in visitors, Jarabacoa's **accommodation** options have improved radically. In addition to the possibilities listed below, you can **camp** around Manabao or at Balneario la Confluencia; if you want to get further away from civilization, most farmers will let you camp on their land, provided you ask first.

Pico Duarte and the Cordillera Central's national parks

Two national parks, **Bermúdez** and **Ramírez**, protect much of the mountains, cloud forests and pines in the Cordillera Central, each encompassing over seven hundred square kilometres. By far the best way to explore the region is on an organized trek up **Pico Duarte**, at 3087m the tallest mountain in the Caribbean, which is actually located between the two parks but generally approached via Bermúdez.

A number of strenuous treks lead up the peak, which towers over the centre of the range alongside its sister mountain La Pelona. The most popular one starts from the tiny *pueblo* of La Ciénega, 25km southwest of Jarabacoa, where you'll need to register for the 46km round-trip at the park's entrance office on the far side of the village. You'll have to pay the RD$200 **park entrance** and hire at least one **guide** for every five people (RD$500/day plus meals). It's also a good idea to rent at least one **mule** (RD$300/day) – chances are the guide will insist upon it – to carry water and food as well as to get you down safely if things go wrong.

The best bet is to arrive in the afternoon, sort out the formalities and then camp down in the village with a view to starting out early the next morning. The first leg is a comfortable 4km riverside stroll to a bridge across the river at **Los Tablones**. Once over the river, however, the climbing starts in earnest and you'll gain over 2000m in the next 14km, mostly on a badly eroded track that wends its way through some wonderfully wild woodland. Regular stops at official picnic sights allow you to catch your breath and to peep out through the canopy for a glimpse of the utterly pristine wilderness. You'll spend the night in a ramshackle cabin at **La Comparticíon** and then scramble up the last 5km at around 4.30am to be on the bare rocky summit for sunrise. It's quite a stirring sight to watch the sun creep over the horizon, casting a bright-red hue on the banks of clouds beneath your feet.

Treks can be made any time of the year, but should never be attempted without a waterproof coat, winter clothing, a sleeping bag and hiking boots. You'll also need to bring enough food for yourself and the guide (this is best bought in Jarabacoa). It's definitely worth considering using the two **tour operators** who operate trips up this trail: Iguana Mama, in Cabarete (see p.342); or Rancho Baiguate, in Jarabacoa (see box p.347), as they'll take care of all the logistics for you.

Brisas del Yaque Luperón ⓣ809/574 4490. Clean, modern hotel just off the town centre. Nothing special but perfectly comfortable. The rooms come with a/c, TV, hot water and a fridge. ❷

Gran Jimenoa Av La Confluencia, Los Corralitos ⓣ809/574-6304, ⓦwww.granjimenoa.com. Best hotel in town with large a/c rooms in a riverside building overlooking a pleasant pool area. Some rooms have river views. Price includes breakfast. ❷

Mi Vista C-28, 2km outside town 34 ⓣ809/574-6696, ⓦwww.mi-vista.com. Good value mountain resort with five large, elegant two-bedroom bungalows, all with glorious views. Swimming pool, open-air restaurant a whole raft of tours also offered. ❶

Pinar Dorado on the road to Constanza, km 1 ⓣ809/574-2820, ⓦwww.ranchobaiguate. Pleasant Swiss chalet-style architecture and amiable staff. The hotel has nice rooms (if a bit worn around the edges) with TV, a/c, hot water, private balconies, restaurant and bar. ❷

The Town

Most of the action in town centres on the major crossroads, a few blocks north of the small **parque central.** The point at which the Río Yaque del Norte and Río Jimenoa meet is a popular spot for swimming, a half-kilometre north of the main crossroads.

The most popular local attractions are the three **waterfalls** (*saltos*), which are all enough of a trek that you'll want either your own transport or a ride on a *motoconcho* (RD$50–100 one-way). Most popular is the crashing **Lower Salto Jimenoa**, or Salto Jimenoa Dos, 3km east of town off the Carretera Jarabacoa (daily 8.30am–7pm; RD$100), which boasts a deep pool good for swimming. **Salto Baiguate**, 1km south of town on the road to Constanza (daily 8.30am–7pm; free), is a bit taller, plus it has a large cave and a swimming hole. The steepest Jarabacoa waterfall is the **Higher Salto Jimenoa**, or Salto Jimenoa Uno, as it's often called. This isn't so easy to find but if you head out on the road to Constanza for 7km, you'll pass through a small *pueblo* before coming to a few shacks on the right. Almost directly opposite these is a jeep-size driveway that quickly deteriorates into a narrow and steep footpath. Continue down to the bottom and scramble over some huge slabs to the pool at the waterfall's base. It's a pretty awesome sight: the water drops 75m from a hidden lake above, and thunders into a huge pool at its base – it's easy to see why this was chosen as a setting for a scene in *Jurassic Park*.

Eating

Jarabacoa has a couple of quality restaurants catering to the Dominican families that weekend here. The moderately priced *D'Parke Galeria*, at the corner of Duarte and the *parque central*, is a decent pizzeria that's particularly popular with locals. At the main crossroads at the town entrance, *El Rancho* is an excellent high-end restaurant serving good pizza plus specialities like baked chicken stuffed with banana.

6.6

Barahona

Occupying the coast west of Santo Domingo and taking its name from the major city at its centre, the **Barahona Region** was once the focus of Trujillo's personal sugar empire; vast tracts of cane still take up much of the land north of **Barahona** city, but today this is one of the country's poorest regions. As a result, the stunning Barahona **coastline** is almost completely undeveloped, making it perfect for independent travellers willing to rough it a bit in exchange for unblemished natural beauty.

Barahona and around

BARAHONA city isn't an especially pleasant place. Founded in 1802, the city has fallen on hard times due to the closing of the local sugar mill. That said, the locals are friendly and it does have a couple of good hotels, making it a useful base to explore the undeveloped coastline that stretches west of the city. If sticking around, head either to the Malecón, which is quite beautiful, or the *parque central*, a major hangout at night.

Most visitors arrive **via guagua or car**; coastal Highway 44 connects the city with Azua, Baní and Santo Domingo to the east before continuing west all the way to the border. If spending the night, most **accommodations** are within a couple of blocks of the seaside Malecón. The best of the lot is a bit pricey, the *Costa Larimar*, Malecón 18 (Ⓣ809/524-3442, Ⓦwww.hotelcostalarimar.com; ❸), which has just about every amenity you can think of and a prime beachfront location to boot. The best of the rest is the *Gran Barahona*, Mota 5 (Ⓣ809/524-3442; ❷), with comfortable rooms that have air-conditioning, TV and hot water. There's **places to eat**; *Melo's*

Café, Anacaona 12 (ⓣ809/524-5437), is the best of the lot, an unpretentious diner with delicious American breakfasts and nightly dinner specials. Also well worth checking out is *Brisas del Caribe*, a seafood restaurant on the far eastern end of the Malecón; the creole shrimp and broiled kingfish are house specialities.

West of Barahona

The gorgeous coastline **west of Barahona** is the region's premier attraction, yet it remains virtually undiscovered by outsiders. The first major beach spot is Baoruco, 15km west of Barahona along Highway 44, a tiny fishing village with the best hotel in the Barahona region, *Casa Bonita* (ⓣ809/540-5908; ⓦwww.casabonitadr.com; ⑤), with great views, a swimming pool and an elegant restaurant.

Five kilometres beyond Baoruco, *pueblo* **San Rafael** holds an enticing beach, if one with a strong, crashing surf. Fortunately, a **waterfall** thrums down the nearby mountains and forms a natural swimming pool at the entrance. **Paraiso**, another 5km to the west, is the biggest town along this stretch, but still doesn't boast much in the way of facilities. It does have a long strand of superb sandy beach, along which stands *Hotel Paraiso* (ⓣ809/243-1080; ①), a decent place to stay for the night.

A better beach lies yet 5km further west, in **Los Patos**, where the ocean is joined by a river descending from the mountains to form a freshwater swimming pool. The beach, surrounded with dense mangroves, stays pretty active throughout the week, and beach vendors take care of most visitors' needs.

East of Barahona

Heading **east of Barahona** towards San Cristóbal and the capital stand a string of colonial-era towns that appear congested and unappealing at first sight, but hide beaches that make stopovers worthwhile. First up is **Azua**, 60km east of Barahona on Highway-2. Though there's nothing left of the original city, Azua is one of the oldest European cities in the New World, founded by future conqueror of Cuba, Diego Velázquez, in 1504. What is still here, though, is the five-kilometre-long **Playa Monte Río**, a short drive south of town, which offers beautiful views of the rolling El Número mountains. There's very little development around the beach; rather, the calm waters are lined with fishing boats and a few locally run outdoor restaurants.

Tucked away in the mountains along the Río Ocóa between the town of Azua and Baní is **San José de Ocóa**, 27km north of the Carretera Sánchez along Highway 41, attracting weekenders from across the country, most of whom are eager to beat the valley heat, visit the local river *balneario* (swimming hole) and take advantage of the lovely, sometimes rugged, mountain landscape. The town itself is an easy-going and fairly modest hamlet, unremarkable but for its majestic setting. Just south of town, though, is **El Manantiel**, another swimming spot a kilometre down a dirt road off the highway, where you'll find several good places to bathe among the boulders and ice-cold cascades. **Accommodation** options in town are plentiful but decidedly no-frills, intended as they are to serve families who don't mind shacking up several to a room. The best of the lot is the spartan *Sagrato de Jesús*, Cañada/San José (ⓣ809/558-2432; ①), not especially luxurious but acceptable with private cold-water bath. *Baco*, a half-block west of the *parque central*, serves quality **meals** like *chivo guisado* (goat stew) or chicken with rice, beans and plantains.

Another 40km east on the Carretera Sánchez, less than 20km east of the San José turn-off, coastal **Baní** has in recent years turned relatively prosperous, an upswing that has spurred much population growth, if not exactly prettified the place. The best of the nearby beaches is **Las Salinas**, with a small town consisting of little more than a few dozen houses scattered about a white-sand beach, 16km southwest at the end of the Carretera Las Calderas. Sand dunes, salt pans and rolling hills surround the village, which makes for a fine place to do some **windsurfing**; taking advantage of these conditions is the *Salinas High Wind Center*, Puerto Hermosa 7 (ⓣ809/470-6646; ④), a small but extremely nice resort catering mostly to wealthy Dominicans.

7

Puerto Rico

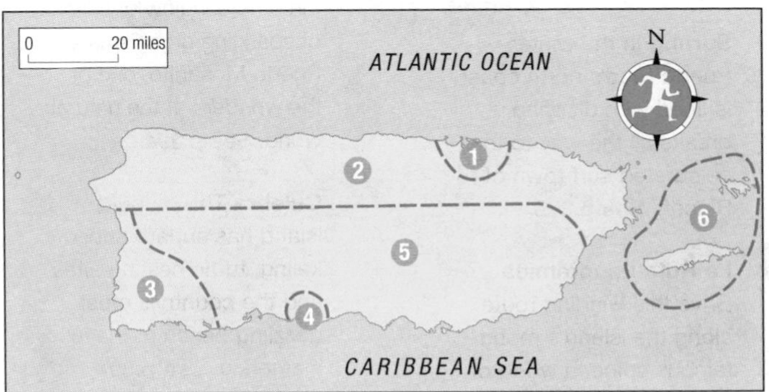

Puerto Rico highlights

* **Old San Juan** Explore one of the best-preserved colonial centres in the Americas, with some of the finest museums and restaurants on the island. See p.366

* **El Yunque National Forest** Hike or birdwatch in this enchanting tropical rainforest that smothers the island's eastern mountain range. See p.376

* **Surfing** In the winter, Puerto Rico's north coast is lined with dizzying breaks all the way to the celebrated surf town of Rincón. See p.379

* **La Ruta Panorámica** Drive this winding route along the island's mountainous spine, a world of misty peaks and forests, coffee farms and smoky roadside food stalls. See p.388

* **Beach-hopping on Vieques** With the US Navy long gone, tour the pristine beaches of Vieques, untouched slices of Caribbean wilderness. See p.393

* **Bioluminescent bay, Vieques** Be mesmerized by the ethereal glow of trillions of sparkling organisms at Puerto Mosquito, one of the wonders of the natural world. See p.394

* **Culebra** This languid island has superb snorkeling, turtle nesting sites and the country's most dazzling beach at Playa Flamenco. See p.394

▲ Surfing

Introduction and basics

Puerto Rico – or Boriquén, as the island's pre-Columbian inhabitants called it – commands a pivotal spot in the Caribbean, the last substantial island before the sprawling arm of the Antilles swoops south towards Venezuela and South America, fragmenting into the tiny Leeward and Windward chains. Puerto Rico's unique status as a commonwealth of the US, however, keeps it a world apart from its island neighbours – a difference that can be measured not just in kilometres, but in dollars. It's a place that combines island life with a level of infrastructure seldom seen in the region: excellent interstate highways allow travellers to zip from coral reef to five-star restaurant, and hikers can traipse through the spell-binding El Yunque rainforest on well-paved trails maintained by the US Forest Service. American influence is undeniably strong, but the island's core retains a distinctly Latin character. Beyond the glitzy resorts of the capital, Puerto Rico's rich stew of cultures – African, European and Taíno – survives in an exuberant array of festivals, tantalizing *criollo* food, handsome colonial towns, spectacular rum and a dynamic musical tradition that gave birth to *salsa*.

Despite the threat of overdevelopment, most of the 56-by-160-kilometre island has managed to elude despoilment. Even in the crowded capital, it's hard to find a sullied beach, and nature is largely untouched outside the major cities, especially in the jungly, mountainous interior and on the offshore islands. Puerto Rico's diversity makes it just as appealing to the eco-tourist as to the sun-worshipper. Quite apart from the plentiful picture-postcard beaches, there are excellent opportunities for **diving**, **snorkelling**, **sailing**, **fishing**, **surfing**, **caving**, **birding** and **hiking**.

Where to go

No matter where you are in Puerto Rico, you're never more than a couple of hours by car from **San Juan**, whose colonial architecture in its old town is a must-see. More historic vestiges can be found in the southern cities of **Ponce** and **San Germán**.

Numerous pretty and isolated beaches are within easy reach, some fringed with otherwordly pristine coral reefs. For diving and snorkelling, choose from **Desecheo** off the west coast, the beautiful offshore islets of **Vieques** and **Culebra** in the east, or **La Pared** ("the **Wall")** running just off the southwest coast. Vieques and Culebra have particularly stunning beaches, with the former also home to the mind-blowing **bioluminescent bay**. With advance planning you can also reach the uninhabited island of **Mona**, the so-called "Galápagos of the Caribbean", a wildlife reserve halfway to the Dominican Republic. Surfers should make for the northwest coast and the low-key resort town of **Rincón**.

Hikers won't want to miss **El Yunque**, the only tropical rainforest in the US park system, with exotic and rare flora and fauna. There are also good walks in the **Cordillera Central**, especially through the **Cañon de San Cristóbal** outside **Barranquitas**, accessible via **La Ruta Panorámica**. The subtropical dry forest of **Guánica** in the southwest is not only a UN Biosphere Reserve, but also has the added attraction of idyllic **Guilligan's Island** nearby.

And the spelunking is superb: the vast labyrinth of caves in the **northwestern karst country** is among the largest in the world, and set amid abruptly eroded limestone landscape around the **Río Camuy** which features giant sinkholes and peculiar haystack hills.

When to go

Puerto Rico's pleasant **tropical climate** is virtually seasonless, with an average

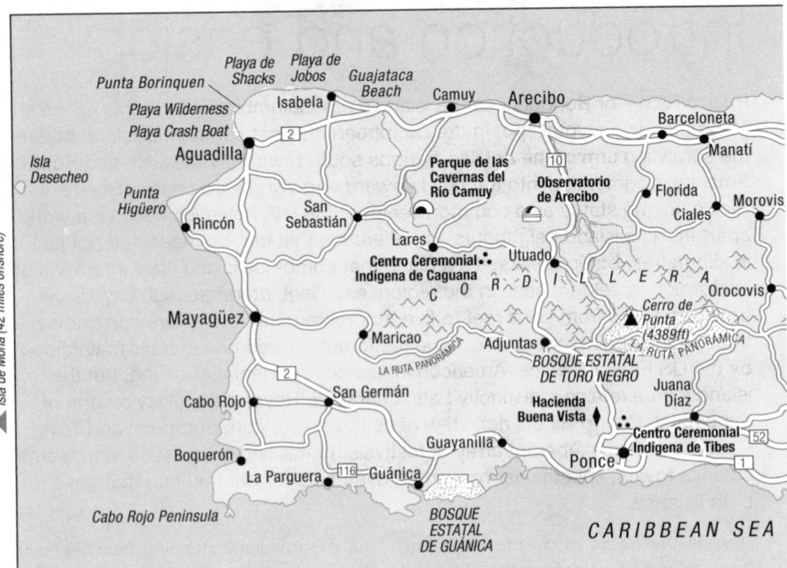

temperature of 80°F (26°C); note it can be considerably cooler in the mountains. **Rainfall** varies around the island – El Yunque receives up to 200 inches (5m) a year, while Guánica's dry forest in the southwest gets as little as 30 inches (76cm). **Hurricanes** are so common in Puerto Rico that they were named after the Taíno god of malevolence, Jurakán (pronounced hu-ra-kan). Hurricane season runs from June to November, when the weather is hottest and wettest: in 1998 the 115mph (185km/h) winds of Hurricane Georges did US$2bn of damage. Call the National Weather Service on ⓣ787/253-4586 for current information. The peak tourist season runs roughly from December to April and all of July and August. The island is also a popular spring break destination for US college students from February to March.

Getting there

San Juan is one of the world's top **cruise ship** destinations, with most of the pleasure boats docking at the **port** by the old town. But you are most likely to arrive at **Luis Muñoz Marín International Airport**, 14km east of Old San Juan and just behind the resort area of Isla Verde. Several airlines also fly direct between the US and smaller airports at Ponce and Aguadilla, particularly discount carrier JetBlue.

Information

The **Puerto Rican Tourism Company**, or PRTC (ⓦwww.gotopuertorico.com), has offices in San Juan at the international airport (ⓣ787/791-1014) and Old San Juan (ⓣ787/722-1709), in Ponce (ⓣ787/843-0465), Vieques (ⓣ787/741-0800) and Aguadilla (ⓣ787/890-3315). The helpful and multilingual staff are eager to suggest hotels and restaurants, and arrange activities. Be sure to grab a copy of their annual 70-page *Travel Planner* (ⓦwww.travelandsports.com), which has lists of accommodation and phone numbers for many transportation and recreation services. The PRTC's flagship publication is *¡Qué Pasa!* (ⓦwww.qpsm.com), a bimonthly glossy with a calendar of events, feature-length stories on various attractions and regions, and helpful listings. Another useful publication, *Places to Go* (ⓦwww.enjoypuertorico.com), is free at hotels and tourist offices.

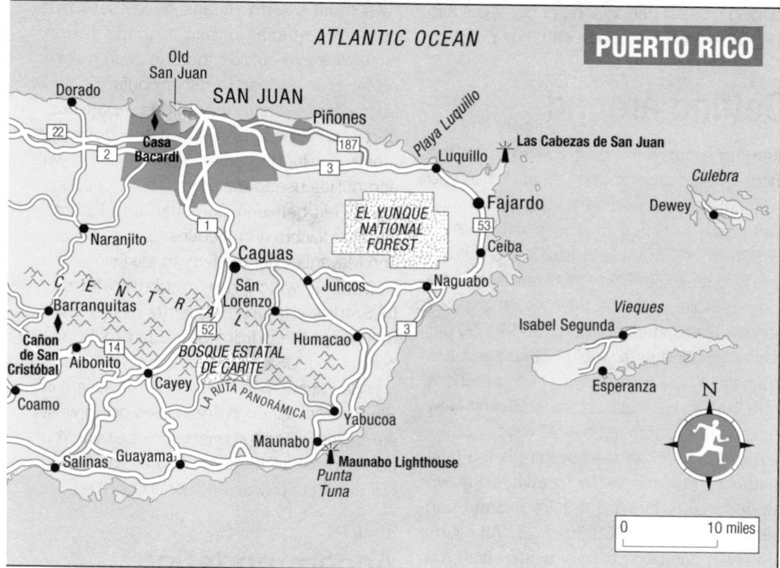

Basic **maps** of the island are available at PRTC offices or through Metro Data (ⓦwww.metropr.com), which produces a handy booklet of maps covering every municipality on the island (*Guía Metro*; US$15.95), usually available in San Jaun's pharmacies and bookstores.

The **country code** for Puerto Rico is ⓣ787. The **emergency number** is ⓣ911.

Money and costs

Puerto Rico uses **US currency**, which comes in bills of US$1, $5, $10, $20, $50 and $100; the dollar (sometimes referred to as a *peso*) is made up of 100 cents in coins of 1¢ (penny or *chavo*), 5¢ (nickel or *ficha*), 10¢ (dime) and 25¢ (quarter or *peseta*). Major credit cards are accepted almost everywhere.

Although Puerto Rico's GNP is lower than that of any of the fifty states, **prices** are not drastically cheaper than on the mainland, although it is less expensive than other parts of the Caribbean. On a strict budget (which would mean forgoing a car) you can get away with spending less than US$100 a day, while you can travel in style on over US$200 a day. In San Juan, the least you can expect to pay for accommodation with air-conditioning and your own bath is US$80 for a single/double room (all hotels in listings have air-conditioning and bath unless mentioned); an average lunch at a modest establishment runs US$7 to US$12, with comparable dinners from US$15 to US$30 and up. The standard tip is 15 percent.

ATMs – called ATHs (*a todas horas*, or "at all hours") – are abundant in cities; you'll find them in banks, supermarkets, casinos and most of the larger hotels. In smaller towns and rural areas, find the local Banco Popular or Westernbank. Official banking hours are 8.30am to 4pm from Monday to Friday, though some also open on Saturday mornings.

Puerto Rico has a 5.5 percent basic **sales tax** (payable on tours, food and drink, but not accommodation). Ponce, Río Grande (El Yunque) and Fajardo charge additional municipal taxes to give a total of 7 percent. San Juan levies 6.5 percent in total. Taxes on hotel occupancy are 11 percent for hotels with casinos, 9 percent for hotels without casinos, and 7 percent for small inns (*paradores*) and short-term rentals. Any charges in excess of this are levied by the hotel as a **service charge**. San Juan and Carolina (Isla Verde) also have a "head tax" ranging US$2-5 per person per night, but this may be rescinded – check with the PRTC.

Getting around

Renting a car is the best way to make the most of your time on the island. While you may get a cheaper deal from a local rental company, national chains such as Avis (☎800/874-3556), Hertz (☎800/654-3131) and Budget (☎787/791-0600) are likely to be more reliable, and offer 24-hour emergency service. Rates start at around US$40–50 per day or US$250 for a week, but can escalate dramatically during holidays. Driver's licences from the UK, US, Canada, Australia and New Zealand are valid for up to 120 days.

The Puerto Rican road system is the best in the Caribbean, with freeways known as *autopistas* fanning out from San Juan carrying tolls of US$0.50–1.25. All roads are given numbers, usually written with the prefix "PR", as in PR-2 - note that "INT" (for *intersección*) above a road number denotes a forthcoming turning *onto* that road. Distances are given in kilometres (1km=0.62 miles), gas is sold in litres and signage is in Spanish, but speed limits are in miles per hour. Road rules otherwise follow US norms and cars drive on the right. Your biggest headache is likely to be the sheer volume of traffic around San Juan and much of the densely populated coastline.

As most Puerto Ricans have their own cars, no official public transportation network exists outside the San Juan metropolitan area. Instead, a rather confusing and fragmented system of **públicos** – part-bus, part-taxi – runs throughout the country, mostly serving the areas around each town and of little use to travellers. The exceptions are routes between San Juan and Fajardo (for the Culebra and Vieques ferries), Ponce, and Mayagüez (for the ferry to the Dominican Republic), which run regularly Monday to Saturday (more frequently in the early morning). A trip from San Juan to Ponce costs about US$15 one-way.

In San Juan, many *público* terminals are in Río Piedras, although some lines going west are based in Santurce (see box below). You can also ask to be picked up at your hotel, but expect to pay an additional US$10–15.

Accommodation

Puerto Rico has a wide range of **accommodation**, from rustic mountain cottages to fancy beachfront high-rises, though there are no hostels and budget options are conspicuously lacking. For a room endorsed by the PRTC, with air–conditioning and TV, you can spend anything from US$70 to over US$500. Cheaper places are more numerous in the mountains or in Old San Juan but in the latter you'll have to settle for a fan and share

Major público services

The following transportation services all originate in San Juan:

Blue Line ☎787/250-0717, Plaza de Convalecencia, Río Piedras (to Aguadilla)

Chóferes Unidos de Ponce ☎787/764-0540, Calle 2, just off Avda Gandara near c/Saldana, Río Piedras (to Ponce)

Línea Caborrojeña ☎787/723-9155, Avda Las Palmas and c/Cerra, Santurce (to Cabo Rojo)

Línea San Germaña ☎787/722-3392, Avda Las Palmas and c/Cerra, Santurce (to San Germán)

Línea Sultana ☎787/765-9377, c/Esteban Gonzalez, near Avda Universidad, Río Piedras (to Mayagüez)

Terminal del Este ☎787/250-0717, c/Arzuaga near c/Vallejo, Río Piedras (to Fajardo)

Daily domestic flights depart from San Juan's international airport for Ponce, Mayagüez, Vieques and Culebra. Flights for the offshore islands also depart from Isla Grande Airport (☎787/729-8790), in Miramar (nearer Old San Juan), and from Fajardo. Vieques and Culebra can also be reached by regular daily ferries from Fajardo.

a shower in dingy surroundings. The finest hotels cost a minimum of US$200 a night; prices increase during the high seasons, mid-December to mid-April and July to August (when you should definitely book ahead, especially at weekends). Standards vary considerably depending on location and age of the property – price isn't always a good indication of quality so always check the room before agreeing to pay. **Renting apartments** and **villas** is an appealing alternative to staying in hotels; check PR West (ⓣ787/420-5227 or ⓣ787-826-6748, ⓦwww.prwest.com) to get started.

Note that the 21 hotels in the PRTC-sponsored **paradores** ("country inn") programme have nothing to do with the Spanish system of extremely upmarket historic properties. Though located in areas of historic or cultural importance, not all *paradores* are first-rate. For the official list see ⓦwww.gotoparadores.com.

The Compañia de Parques Nacionales (ⓣ787/622-5200, ⓦwww.parquesnacionalespr.com) operates six beach **campsite** around the island with showers, toilets and grills, from US$10 per night. It also runs a system of rustic *cabañas* known as Centro Vacacionales, geared towards Puerto Rican families. Rates range US$65–75 and you can make reservations by phone or on the website. Campsites within Puerto Rico's forest reserves are managed by the Departamento de Recursos Naturales y Ambientales (DRNA, ⓣ787/999-2200, ⓦwww.drna.gobierno.pr), but to stay at any of them you must apply for a **permit** in advance. You can apply by mail, fax, online or in person in San Juan (PR-8838 km 6.3, Sector El Cinco, Río Piedras). Rates are just US$4 per person per night.

Food and drink

Puerto Rico, and San Juan in particular, is well-established as the culinary hot spot of the Caribbean. World-renowned chefs at vanguard restaurants prepare dynamic **Nuevo Latino** cuisine – a twist on traditional *criollo* cooking, emphasizing fish, fruits, tubers and dark rum sauces or marinades with tropical ingredients. You'll also find every manner of ethnic food in the capital, including Indian, Thai, French and Chinese.

Criollo fare, however, is still the basis of the Puerto Rican diet. Staples are plantains (*plátanos*) a type of savoury banana, and rice and beans (*arroz con habichuelas*) richly stewed in pork and spices. Made from fried plantains mashed with garlic and olive oil, **mofongo** is the national dish and essential eating, at least once, while another favourite is *asopao*, a rice stew flavoured with *sofrito*, a sauce of cilantro, onions, garlic and peppers. *Sofrito* is used to season many dishes, as is *adobo,* a mixture of garlic, oregano, paprika, vinegar and oil. Puerto Ricans also love pork and chicken, and *arroz con pollo* (chicken and rice), *chuletas* (pork chops) and *churrasco* (skirt steak) appear on just about every menu. Fresh seafood and shellfish are widely available, especially crab, prawns, *chiollo* (red snapper) and *dorado* (mahi-mahi).

Budget travellers can fill up at roadside stalls known as *kioscos*, most famously in Luquillo or Piñones. The most common *kiosco* food is deep-fried fritters, especially *alcapurrias* (mashed plantain stuffed with ground meat) and *bacalaítos* (thin cod fritters), but you'll find plenty of other snacks on offer. In larger towns, the market (*mercado*) is the best place to seek out no-frills snack food as well as fresh fruit and coconut juices. If you get desperate, the major US fast-food chains can be found all over the island.

Thirty of the best Puerto Rican **restaurants** are members of the *mesones gastronómicos* programme, which was established by the PRTC. Most guarantee clean, well-crafted Puerto Rican food, but quality varies and most charge higher prices than normal restaurants. Note that in all but the best restaurants, fresh vegetables are hard to come by but supermarkets like Pueblo usually carry a good supply.

Meals invariably end with vanilla **flan** (a bit like a custard tart) and strong **coffee**, served black or with hot milk (*café con leche*). On the roads, look out for signs for refreshing *coco frío* – chilled coconuts punctured with drinking straws. While not as common, **fresh-fruit drinks** made from mangoes, papayas and oranges (known as *jugo de china*) are also available and *batidas* (fruitshakes) are also worth a try. Not surprisingly, **rum** (*ron*) is the national drink – *piña colada* being a favourite – as Puerto Rico is the world's largest producer of this sugarcane-based liquor; more than twenty brands are distilled here. The locally brewed **beer** is Medalla; Presidente, from the Dominican Republic, is also popular.

Tap water is generally safe to drink. It's wise to stick to bottled water after storms. If in doubt, ask the locals.

Mail and communications

Post offices, located in most major and small towns, are open from 8am to 5pm weekdays, and some have Saturday morning hours.

Outside Puerto Rico, dial ⓣ787/555-1212 for **directory information**. Attendants usually answer in Spanish but will switch to English at your request; within Puerto Rico, dial ⓣ411 (charges vary). All telephone numbers are seven digits long and preceded by ⓣ787 (or, increasingly, ⓣ939 for some mobile telephones), which must be used for both local and long-distance calls; for long-distance, dial a "1" first. US cell phones work in Puerto Rico, but coin-operated payphones are also easy enough to find in populated areas. Decent **Internet** service is available but not abundant; you will find it at larger hotels and the occasional cybercafé. Wi-Fi access is far more prevalent, available in many hotels and some cafés – *Starbucks* is the most convenient in San Juan.

Opening hours, holidays and festivals

In general, **business hours** in Puerto Rico are Monday to Friday 8.30am–5.30pm, with many businesses closing for lunch (noon–1pm).

On **public holidays** (see box), government offices, banks and schools are closed, and museum hours and transportation schedules may change.

The following **festivals** are the most popular organized events in Puerto Rico. In addition to these, each town celebrates its patron saint's day (*fiesta patronal*) and the ten days leading up to it. Check PRTC's website (ⓦwww.gotopuertorico.com) for details.

Festivals

January

Festival de la Calle San Sebastián Old San Jan. This street in the old town holds animated nightly celebrations that include music, parades, *criollo* food and handicraft exhibitions every third week of January.

February/March

Carnival Ponce. Boisterous celebration during the six days preceding Ash Wednesday, featuring parades of traditional *vejigantes*, or masked revellers.

Festival Casals San Juan. Two weeks of orchestral music with world-renowned musicians.

Public holidays

January 1 New Year's Day
January 6 Three Kings' Day
Second Monday in January Eugenio María de Hostos's Birthday
Third Monday in January Martin Luther King, Jr, Day
Third Monday in February Presidents' Day
March 22 Emancipation Day
March/April Palm Sunday, Good Friday, Easter Sunday
Third Monday in April José de Diego Day
Last Monday in May Memorial Day
July 4 Independence Day
Third Monday in July Luís Muñoz Rivera's Birthday
July 25 Constitution Day
July 27 José Celso Barbosa's Birthday
First Monday in September Labour Day
Second Monday in October Columbus Day
November 11 Veterans' Day
November 19 Discovery of Puerto Rico Day
Fourth Thursday in November Thanksgiving Day
December 25 Christmas Day

May/June

Heineken Jazzfest San Juan. Four days of Latin jazz, performed by Puerto Rican and international musicians, at the Sixto Escobar Park in Condado.

San Juan Bautista Day/Noche de San Juan (June 23-24) San Juan's *fiesta patronal.* Parties and festivities in Old San Juan culminate with crowds walking backwards into the sea three times, in honour of St John the Baptist.

July

Fiestas Tradicionales de Santiago Apóstol, Loíza (July 25). Festival of St James, but very African in flavour, with costumed parades and *bomba* drumming. Not to be missed.

November

Festival Nacional Indígena, Jayuya (third weekend in Nov). Celebrates the culture of the Taíno through music, traditional craft stalls, food and games.

December

Festival de las Mascaras (Mask Festival), Hatillo. On the 28th, watch children chased through the streets by costumed revellers commemorating King Herod's infamous "massacre of the innocents".

History

Some four thousand years ago, the Arcaicos were the first people to arrive in Puerto Rico, spreading through the Caribbean from the mainland. Later came the Igneri and Pre-Taíno cultures, finally emerging as the Taíno in around 1200 AD, who dubbed the island "Boriquén", or "Boriken" – "the land of the valiant and noble lord". This last group had a long-lasting effect on Puerto Rican culture and bloodlines; many Puerto Rican words come from the Arawak language they spoke, and it is estimated that sixty percent of Puerto Ricans today have some Taíno ancestry.

Christopher Columbus reached the island in 1493 on his second voyage to the Americas, naming it San Juan Bautista. The island was largely ignored by the Spanish until 1508 when **Juan Ponce de León** established the village of Caparra just inland from today's San Juan Bay, which he named "Puerto Rico" (or rich port).

Having convinced the Taíno they were supernatural beings, the Spanish wasted no time in setting the natives to work mining the little gold on the island, which had all but run out within a few decades. Disillusioned, in 1510 the Taíno decided to test Spanish immortality by drowning a soldier, and when he failed to come back to life realized they had been fooled. A violent **rebellion** ensued in 1511, resulting in total defeat for the Taíno. The remainder fled the island, took refuge in the mountainous interior or ended up as slaves. The church sanctioned intermarriage between Spanish men and Taíno women in 1514, and with the rapid decline of pure Taíno people, the Spanish began importing West African slaves to work plantations of sugar cane, fruits and ginger; by 1530 West Africans constituted almost two thirds of the island's population.

After much wrangling, **San Juan** (today's Old San Juan) was officially founded in 1521, across the bay from Caparra in a much healthier, more accessible location; how the original names for the city (Puerto Rico) and the island (San Juan) were switched remains a mystery, but by the seventeenth century the current conventions were well established. By 1539, *sanjuaneros* had recognized both the strategic value and vulnerability of their port – as had Spain's European rivals – and began constructing the formidable stone fortification known as El Morro to guard the harbour. After a first attempt by Sir Francis Drake in 1595 failed to take the city, the English succeeded in occupying the fort in 1598, but were soon defeated by dysentery. The Dutch attacked in 1625, burning the city but failed to capture El Morro and were eventually repulsed.

By the mid-seventeenth century Puerto Rico was little more than a strategic stronghold largely overlooked by Spain and began to languish. Impoverished islanders were not allowed to participate in government, trade with other nations, or move around the island. In rebellion, they began trading sugar and rum illegally, and the island soon became a hotbed of pirates and contraband. The English continued to attack Puerto Rico throughout the period, with Sir Ralph Abercromby's massive but ultimately doomed attack on San Juan in 1797 the last attempt.

Spain, in one of its last gasps, sent **General Alejandro O'Reilly** to establish order in the latter half of the eighteenth century. He built roads and schools and encouraged literate, conservative Spaniards to immigrate to the island, while dropping trade restrictions and lowering taxes. By the turn of the century, Puerto Rico was thriving. In the wake of the **Haitian Revolution** (1791–1804), many French plantation owners were driven to Puerto Rico, boosting sugar and rum production on the island, where slavery wouldn't be abolished until 1873.

Starting in 1810, a movement spearheaded by **Simón Bolívar**, the "Liberator", resulted in the independence of almost all Spain's colonies by the mid-1820s, except for Puerto Rico, Cuba and the Philippines. To keep the islanders happy and nurture their loyalty, the Spanish further lowered taxes and opened up more ports for trade. And to *guarantee* their loyalty, they established a repressive military government that lasted 42 years.

An independence movement grew in strength, staging the first serious uprising in 1868. The **Grito de Lares** ("Cry of Lares") was planned by exiles such as **Ramón Betances**, and rebels captured the mountain town of Lares, proclaiming the Republic of Puerto Rico. The Spaniards, however, quashed the revolution in a matter of days. In 1897 Puerto Rico was finally granted **autonomy** from Spain, just in time for the **Spanish-American War** the following year. American forces landed in Guánica Bay and took Puerto Rico for themselves – it wasn't until 1917 that its inhabitants became US citizens.

Puerto Rico's economy suffered terribly from the **Great Depression** in the 1930s, and revolutionary movements continued to simmer. This led to several bloody altercations between radicals and police, notably the 1937 **Ponce Massacre** in which seventeen civilians died. In 1948, **Luis Muñoz Marín**, head of the Popular Democratic Party, became the island's first elected governor (which he remained until 1964), and its first constitution was drafted in 1952. Under "Operation Bootstrap", tax breaks encouraged US manufacturing companies to set up on the island, thus kick-starting industrialization and making the island less dependent on its primary agricultural products, sugar, coffee and tobacco.

After World War II, huge numbers of Puerto Ricans in search of the American Dream emigrated to the US mainland, mostly New York. Here a new hybrid culture evolved whose people became known as **Nuyoricans** – famously depicted in Leonard Bernstein's 1957 musical *West Side Story*. Today, there are reckoned to be some eight million Puerto Ricans living outside the island, about half of them on the American mainland.

A botched assassination attempt on US President Truman in 1950 by Puerto Rican nationalists notwithstanding, the

US granted the island **commonwealth** status in 1952. Puerto Rico became the "Estado Libre Asociado" (free associated state) it remains today, which allows self-government in internal affairs as well as fiscal independence, although islanders cannot vote in presidential elections. Furthermore, the US Congress retains full authority to determine the status of the territory and apply federal.

In the first referendums addressing the issue of **sovereignty** in 1967, Puerto Ricans overwhelmingly voted to remain a commonwealth, rather than become a full US state or independent nation. Two much narrower referendums followed in 1993 and 1998, and although both were voted down in favour of the status quo, a much larger proportion favoured statehood.

The movement for **independence** won its most recent victory with the termination of the US Navy presence on Vieques in 2003, after years of bitter protest. But support for outright independence is very small, and considered something of a pipe dream. Puerto Ricans recognize the need for – and inevitability of – change, with supporters of an adjusted version of the status quo only slightly outweighing those in favour of becoming the 51st state. Many fear that statehood would result in a dilution of Hispanic culture, especially the language, but that independence would lead to economic catastrophe and political chaos. Conventional wisdom suggests that the current situation, whilst not ideal, delivers the most economic benefit to the island whilst retaining a degree of healthy separation from the Anglocentric mainland.

7.1

San Juan

Founded in 1521 and the capital of Puerto Rico, **San Juan** is a world apart from the rest of the island; with around 1.5 million people, Greater San Juan contains over a third of the island's population. The city is best known for its beautifully restored historic district, **Old San Juan**, situated on a rocky peninsula girded by twenty-feet thick walls. Unlike other such gems of Spanish colonial architecture, San Juan also offers miles of smooth, clean **beaches**, a wide range of accommodation, fabulous restaurants and a lively nightlife.

Resort-filled **Condado** is the second most popular neighbourhood for visitors thanks to its excellent beachfront and fine boutiques. But there's plenty more of the city to explore: further east is up-and-coming **Santurce** with its numerous art galleries and trendy nightclubs; and the coastal neighbourhoods of **Ocean Park** and **Isla Verde**, beyond which are the deserted palm-fringed beaches of **Piñones**; to the south lies **Río Piedras** with its easy-going college-town vibe.

Some of the island's top attractions make excellent day-trips from the capital: east to **El Yunque** rainforest and the inviting beach at **Luquillo**; or west to the **Parque de las Cavernas del Río Camuy** and the striking **Observatorio de Arecibo** in karst country.

Arrival and information

Old San Juan is fifteen to thirty minutes' drive west from the airport along PR-26. Major **car rental** agencies operate airport desks. **Taxi** fares to the main tourist areas are fixed according to a zone system: Isla Verde is US$10, Condado is US$15 and Old San Juan is US$19. **Public buses** are air-conditioned and cheap (75¢), but the trip can take a full hour. Bus number C45 from the airport only goes to Isla Verde, where you have to change to the A5 to get to the bus terminal in Old San Juan, located on the bay side near the **cruise ship** port. If you're going on to Condado, you'll have to change again to the B21 at the terminal. If you're getting off at the bus terminal, the main **taxi** rank in Old San Juan is a block away at the southwest corner of Plaza Colón.

The **Puerto Rican Tourism Company** (PRTC) runs an information centre (daily 9am–7pm; ⓣ787/791-1014) at the airport, just outside concourse C, on the lower level. The invariably friendly staff will help you arrange transportation and lodging, even going so far as to call around for the best deals. The **PRTC**'s other main office is on the south side of Old San Juan in Plaza de la Dársena near the cruise-ship piers in a pale yellow building known as **La Casita** (Mon–Fri 8.30am–8pm, Sat & Sun 9am–8pm; ⓣ787/722-1709).

Getting around

If you're staying in Old San Juan or Condado for just a few days, the most pleasant way to sightsee is **on foot**. Outside these areas, the cheapest way to get around is to use the **city buses**, which are easy to use and relatively convenient during the day. **Taxis** are expensive but a safer choice at night. **Renting a car** is essential if you intend to explore outside the city.

By car

If you rent a **car**, it's worth spending a little extra on insurance, as scrapes and knocks are common (especially in car parks). Note also that the main highways in and around San Juan are severely congested and traffic can be a pain – it's best to travel at off-peak times to avoid the worst of it. While drivers in Puerto Rico are no more aggressive than those in London or New York, speeding, jumping lanes and pulling out without warning is normal practice. Car jacking in San Juan isn't as big a problem as it once was but to be safe, avoid driving in urban areas after midnight and ignore anyone trying to wave you down.

Prepare yourself for many narrow **one-way streets**, which are sometimes signposted but not always; when in doubt, drive slowly and note the direction of parked cars.

Parking can be a nightmare. Although street parking is often free, it's nearly impossible to find a space. Certainly avoid driving into the old town – there are several car parks lots in the port area.

By taxi

Plenty of **taxis turísticos** cruise the streets during the day in Condado and Old San Juan; in other neighbourhoods, you may have to call first. Charges are set according to tariff zones: zones 1–3 cover trips from the airport (see p.362); trips within Old San Juan and Puerta de Tierra are US$7; runs between Old San Juan and Condado are US$12; and Old San Juan to Isla Verde is US$19. All other trips go by the meter: the initial charge is US$1.75, and then it's 10¢ per 1/19 of a mile thereafter. From 10pm to 6am there is a US$1 surcharge, and you'll pay an extra 50¢ for each piece of luggage. Try Atlantic City Taxi (ⓣ787/268-5050) or Metro Taxi (ⓣ787/725-2870). Taxis run much less frequently after 10pm; call in advance from a safe location as you may end up waiting as long as an hour for a cab to show up.

By bus

City buses, or *guaguas* (pronounced *wah-wahs*), are cheap, safe and usually air-conditioned. Bus stops are indicated by a "Parada" sign. The M1 and M2 buses cost 50¢; otherwise fares are a flat 75¢ throughout the city – pay as you get on the bus and make sure you have the correct change. M1 runs every few minutes but most services operate every 15 to 20 minutes on weekdays, less frequently at weekends (see box p.367 for useful routes). You can also check schedules at the bus terminal in Old San Juan, or at PRTC offices. *Sanjuaneros* use the numbered stops, or *paradas*, as reference points; if you ask for directions, you may get "*está cerca de parada 23*" (it's near stop 23) as an answer.

By train

The Caribbean's only metro system, San Juan's **Tren Urbano,** opened in December 2004 after years of delays. It's super clean, comfortable and very safe, but – until the lines are extended – the 17.2km system is not much use for tourists. All fares are US$1.50.

Accommodation

Most of San Juan's **accommodation** is concentrated in Old San Juan, Condado, Ocean Park and Isla Verde. Old San Juan boasts the city's most historic and atmospheric hotels, while popular Condado has a wider range of options with the added attraction of surf and sand on the doorstep. Ocean Park offers a quieter experience with a selection of affordable, unique guesthouses. Isla Verde is the most developed beach area, with fancy all-inclusive beachfront **resorts** and some much cheaper places along the freeway, still just a few blocks from the beach. For longer stays or larger groups, consider **rental apartments** via agents such as Caleta Realty (ⓦwww.caletarealty.com) or PR West (ⓦwww.prwest.com).

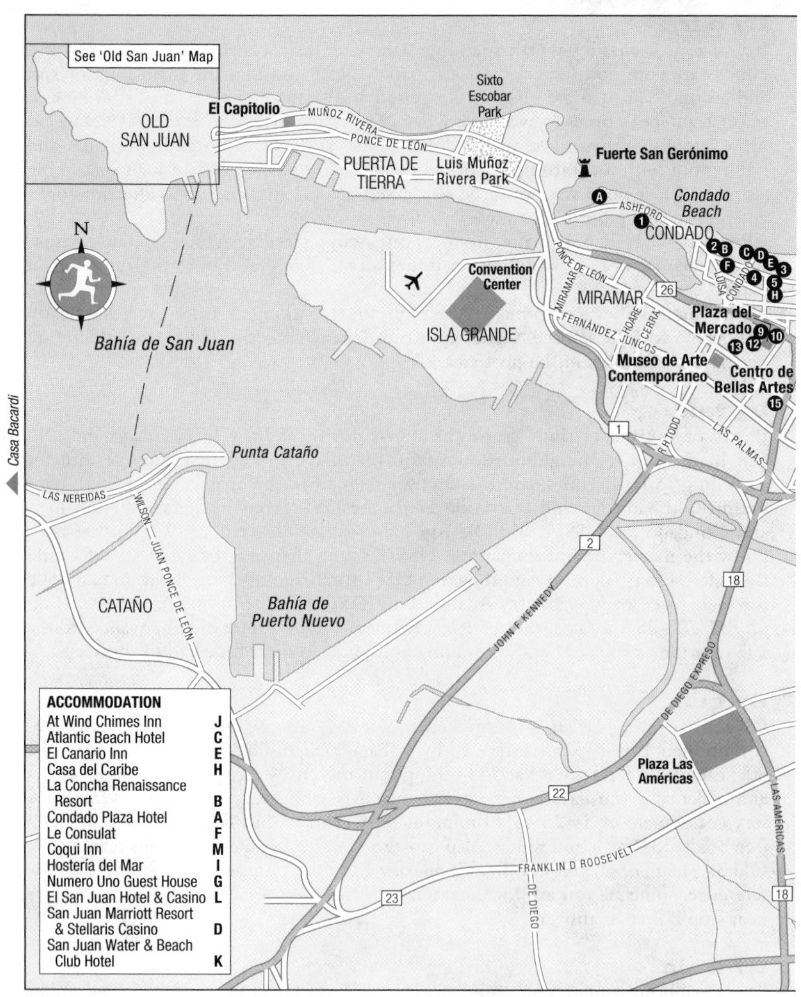

Old San Juan

Chateau Cervantes c/Recinto Sur 329 ⓣ 787/724-7722, ⓦwww.cervantespr.com. Plush boutique hotel with twelve exquisite (but pricey) suites designed in a contemporary Puerto Rican theme that uses plenty of wood and marble, embellished with LCD TVs, balconies, free Wi-Fi and modern art. ⑥

Da House Hotel c/San Francisco 312 ⓣ787/366-5074, ⓦwww.dahousehotelpr.com. Simple but stylish place, just above the *Nuyorican Café* (the entrance is on Callejón de la Capilla), rooms decorated with original Spanish tiled floors and large, dazzling paintings. Extras include free Wi-Fi, access to a local gym, and the roof-top sun deck. The streets outside can be noisy though, and there are no TVs. ③–④

Gallery Inn c/Norzagaray 204–206 ⓣ787/722-1808, ⓦwww.thegalleryinn.com. Enchanting, lovingly restored eighteenth-century house with hidden courtyards, fountains, luxuriant plants and friendly tropical birds. Some of the 24 luxury rooms, all unique, have balconies overlooking the Atlantic. Continental breakfast is served in an indoor garden. ⑥

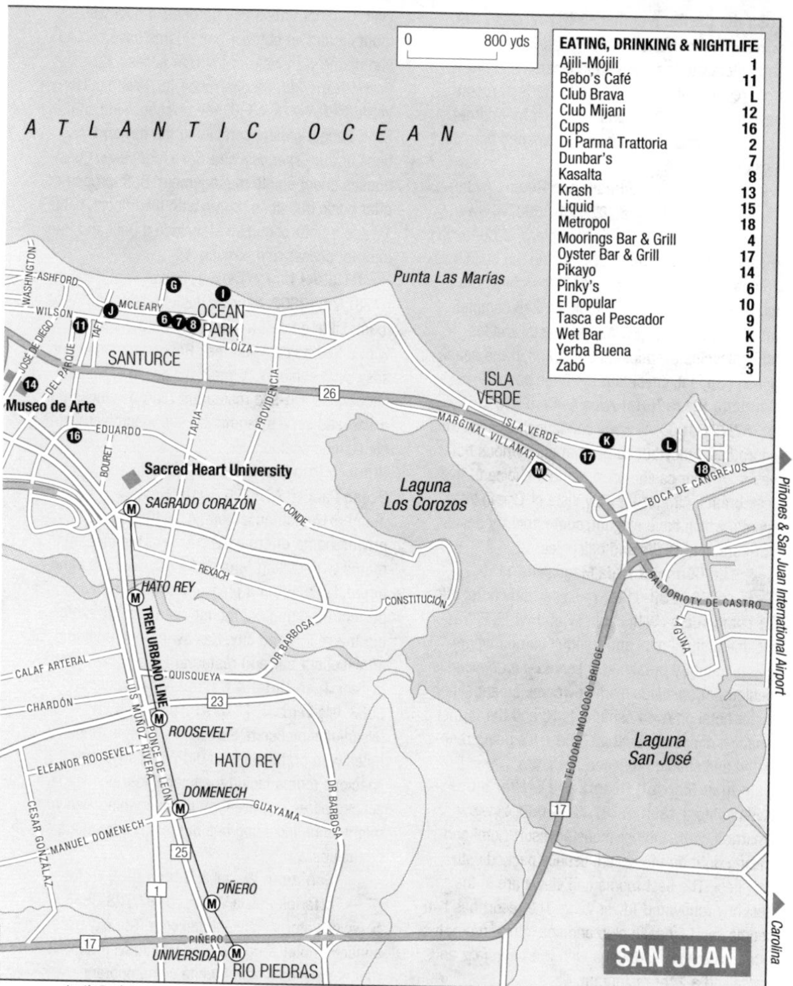

Hotel El Convento c/Cristo 100 ☎787/723-9020, ⓦwww.elconvento.com. Former seventeenth-century convent, now one of San Juan's smartest hotels; the rooms have vaulted ceilings, balconies overlooking a patio, cable TV, VCR, fridge, phones and bathrobes. Several on-site restaurants. ❼

San Juan Guest House c/Tanca 205 ☎787/722-5436. Something of a dive, but if you're on a shoestring budget, this is the one to go for – very run-down, but in an excellent, safe location, and has a jovial staff. Shared showers. More expensive rooms have a/c, the rest fans. The best double rooms are on the upper floor, facing the road. ❷

Condado

Atlantic Beach Hotel c/Vendig 1 ☎787/721-6900 ⓦwww.atlanticbeachhotel.net. This beach-front hotel has been a gay landmark for decades. The boisterous indoor/outdoor bar showcases live drag shows and DJs almost daily, and there's also a rooftop deck and Jacuzzi. Simple but clean rooms have TV and a room safe. ❹

El Canario Inn Avda Ashford 1317 ☎787/722-3861, ⓦwww.canariohotels.com. Small, basic, clean rooms with safes, cable TV and phones; Continental breakfast included. Access to patio and garden area. ❹

Casa del Caribe c/Caribe 57 ⓣ787/722-7139, ⓦwww.casadelcaribe.com. Walled-in escape with interior garden and patio located one block from restaurants and the beach. Thirteen rooms have safe, cable TV, phone with jack for Internet access and offstreet parking. Continental breakfast included. ③

La Concha Renaissance Resort Avda Ashford 1077 ⓣ787/721-8500, ⓦwww.laconcharesort.com. This centrepiece of Condado's regeneration opened in 2007, fusing the building's original "Tropical Modernist" 1958 architecture with a chic contemporary look. Its 248 completely refurbished rooms have bright, pastel shades and balconies overlooking the ocean. If the beach doesn't appeal, check out the huge pool. ⑦

Condado Plaza Hotel Avda Ashford 999 ⓣ787/721-1000, ⓦwww.condadoplaza.com. This enormous, fancy but somewhat anonymous hotel has a 24-hour casino on site and a choice of five restaurants. Aim for the City Vista or Ocean Vista rooms, which have elegant, contemporary design, flat-screen LCD TVs and balconies. ⑥

Le Consulat Avda Magdalena 1149, ⓣ787/289-9191. This cosy new hotel offers 21 comfy rooms with cable TV and Wi-Fi. Extras include a small pool and tranquil garden where complimentary breakfast is served. *Le Consulat* is behind *El Consulado* (same owners), an appealing sister hotel on Avda Ashford 1110 and the former Spanish consulate built in 1906 – it's being renovated and should reopened soon. ④

San Juan Marriott Resort and Stellaris Casino Avda Ashford 1309 ⓣ787/722-7000, ⓦwww.marriott.com. Another monster resort-hotel and casino right on the beach, usually packed with families. The best rooms and views are in the recently renovated Tower Wing. The resort has two tennis courts, health club and spa, game room, two oceanside pools, a lounge with live Latin jazz and *salsa* and a 24hr restaurant. ⑥

Ocean Park and Isla Verde

At Wind Chimes Inn Avda McLeary 1750, Ocean Park, ⓣ787/727-4153, ⓦwww.atwindchimesinn.com. This intimate, restored 1920s Spanish villa a few blocks from the beach has whitewashed stucco walls, interior patios and gardens, a pool with fountain and an outdoor bar. Rooms have cable TV and phone with jack for Internet access. ④

Coqui Inn c/Mar Mediterraneo 36, Villamar, Isla Verde ⓣ787/726-4330, ⓦwww.coqui-inn.com. Solid budget option, combining the former locations of the *Green Isle* and *Casa Mathiesen* guesthouses under single management. Both properties offer basic but clean rooms with tiled floors, cable TV and a bathroom. Extras include a pool and free Internet access and parking. ④

Hostería del Mar c/Tapia 1, Ocean Park ⓣ787/727-3302, ⓦwww.hosteriadelmarpr.com. Little gem of a hotel right on the beach, with a Southeast Asian feel. Rooms are small but cosy, with cable TV; some have ocean views and kitchenette. On-site restaurant *Uvva* overlooks the ocean and serves vegetarian and macrobiotic fare, steaks and seafood. ④

Numero Uno Guest House c/Santa Ana 1, Ocean Park ⓣ787/726-5010, ⓦwww.numero1guesthouse.com. A 1940s former private home offering 12 compact but elegant rooms with ceiling fans and a gay-friendly atmosphere. Located on a pleasant stretch of beach perfect for lounging, though not ideal for exploring the rest of the city. Has swimming pool and an excellent bar and restaurant (*Pamela's*). ⑤

El San Juan Hotel & Casino Avda Isla Verde 6063, Isla Verde ⓣ787/791-1000, ⓦwww.elsanjuanhotel.com. San Juan's most luxurious hotel, with pretensions to Old World style. Has spacious rooms facing the beach, fourteen landscaped acres and pretty much everything else you might want, including one of the city's trendiest nightclubs. ⑧

San Juan Water & Beach Club Hotel c/Tartak 2, Isla Verde, ⓣ787/728-3666, ⓦwww.waterbeachclubhotel.com. The city's top boutique hotel is right on the beach, with funky rooms dressed with all-white contemporary furnishings, cable TV, CD players and iPod docks. There's a tiny rooftop pool with mesmerizing sea views, a waterfall that trickles down the elevator shaft (behind glass) and some of the best bars and restaurants. ⑥

Old San Juan

As recently as the 1970s **OLD SAN JUAN** was a run-down colonial relic in little better shape than the collapsed empire it once served. Now, however, after extensive and careful restoration, it is one of the best-kept troves of Spanish colonial architecture in the Americas. Steep, narrow streets are distinctively cobbled with smooth, iridescent bricks known as *adoquines*, originally used as ballast in ships, and feature buildings – some of the oldest in the Western hemisphere – with bright pastel facades and wrought-iron balconies abloom with plants and flowers.

The old town occupies the headland of a 4km-long island (connected by bridge to the mainland) that shelters San Juan Bay, for centuries a key port. This is where the Spanish established their first permanent settlement on Puerto Rico, fighting off English, Dutch and French attacks from the great fortress, **El Morro** and **La Muralla**, a thick, imposing wall that originally surrounded the whole city.

While the bay was once a hub for exports of New World riches, including gold, silver, sugar, coffee, slaves, tobacco and rum, today San Juan receives nearly 1.4 million **cruise-ship** passengers annually, making it the third busiest cruise port in the world.

If you only have a day here, you're best off losing yourself among the streets or joining an organized walking tour (ask the PRTC). If the heat and steep, crowded streets get to be a bit much, you can ride the **free trolley** that leaves from the main bus terminal and stops near the PRTC office at La Casita (Mon–Fri 7am–7pm, Sat & Sun 9am–7pm, every 15–20min). You can get on or off anywhere along the route.

La Muralla

Begin your wanderings along the **Paseo de la Princesa**, a busy cobblestoned promenade, and head west along the southern city wall. The prim, grey and white Neoclassical building near the bronze statue and fountain at the end is known as **La Princesa** (Mon–Fri 8am–4.30pm; free). Built as a prison in 1837, it now houses the main PRTC offices, as well as a gallery showcasing the work of contemporary Puerto Rican artists.

La Muralla is an impressive sight, and until 1897 its two-and-a-half miles of sandstone encircled all of Old San Juan. Constructed in phases beginning in the seventeenth century, this vast barrier – which measures 20ft thick in places – was finally completed in 1782. Today **La Puerta de San Juan**, at the far end of Paseo de la Princesa, is the last remaining of six wooden city gates. Completed in 1635, and also known as the Water Gate, this sturdy red door was the check-in point for Spaniards delivering colonists and goods from the harbour. You can re-enter the old town here, or continue along the waterside via **Paseo del Morro** as far as the headland beneath the fortress – a much better (and cooler) option at sunset.

After going through the gate, turn left and you'll come to a tall sculpture known as **La Rogativa**. This striking, Giacometti-like bronze was created by Lindsay Daen to commemorate the defeat of the British fleet in 1797. Legend has it that the hapless Brits mistook a religious procession (*rogativa*) of women for Spanish reinforcements, and decided to retreat. A little further is **Casa Blanca** (Tues–Sat 9am–4pm; US$3) at c/ San Sebastián 1, the romantic hill top mansion that for 250 years served as the residence Juan Ponce de León's descendants, the first governor of Puerto

Useful San Juan bus routes

All of the following buses, with the exception of C45, start or finish at the Old San Juan bus terminal.

Bus	Route
M1	Río Piedras, Hato Rey, Sagrado Corazón (Tren Urbano), Santurce, Old San Juan
M1 Express	Río Piedras, Hato Rey, Sagrado Corazón (Tren Urbano), Old San Juan
A5	Old San Juan, Parada 18 (Stop 18), Isla Verde, Iturreguí
B21	Old San Juan, Condado, Parada 18, Sagrado Corazón (Tren Urbano), Plaza Las Américas
C45	Iturreguí, Airport, Isla Verde, Piñones, Loíza

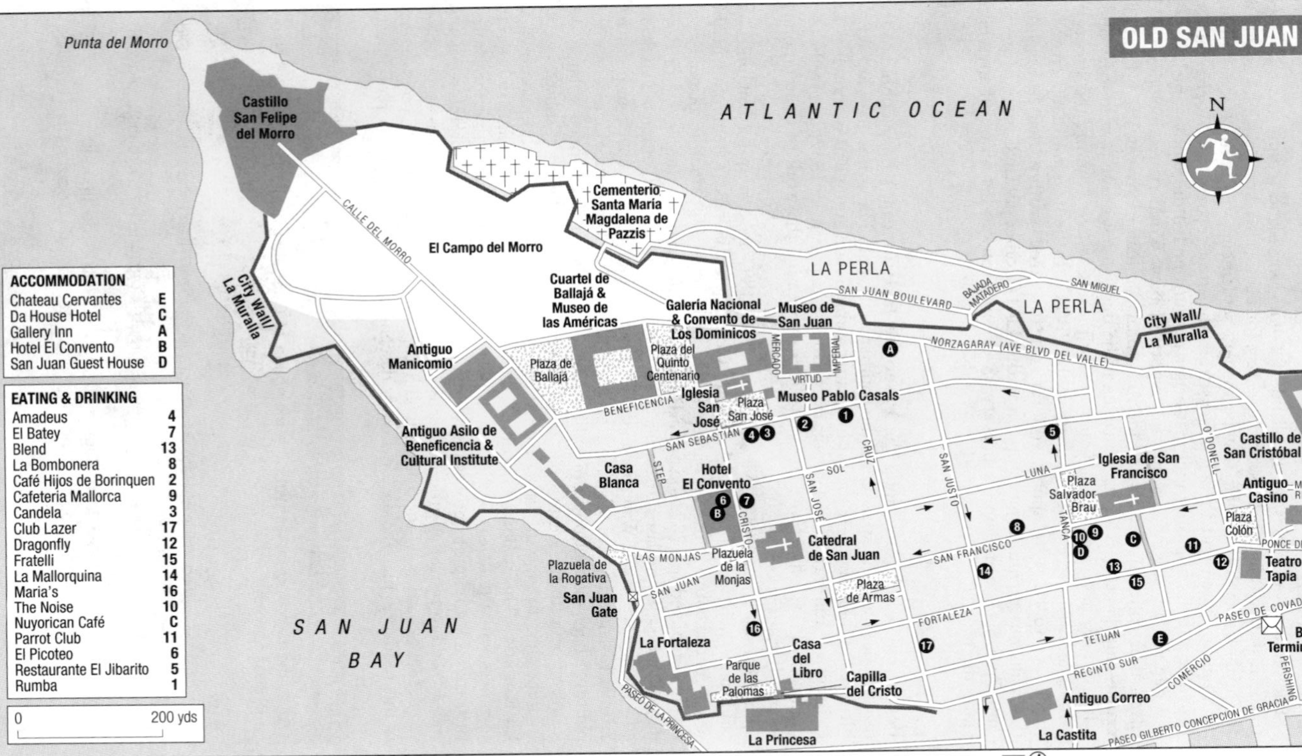
OLD SAN JUAN
ATLANTIC OCEAN
SAN JUAN BAY
N
Punta del Morro
Castillo San Felipe del Morro
City Wall/ La Muralla
El Campo del Morro
CALLE DEL MORRO
Cementerio Santa María Magdalena de Pazzis
Cuartel de Ballajá & Museo de las Américas
Plaza de Ballajá
Antiguo Manicomio
Antiguo Asilo de Beneficencia & Cultural Institute
Galería Nacional & Convento de Los Dominicos
Plaza del Quinto Centenario
Museo de San Juan
LA PERLA
SAN JUAN BOULEVARD
BAJADA MATADERO
SAN MIGUEL
NORZAGARAY (AVE BLVD DEL VALLE)
MERCADO
VIRTUD
IMPERIAL
Museo Pablo Casals
Iglesia San José
Plaza San José
BENEFICENCIA
SAN SEBASTIÁN
STEP
SOL
CRUZ
SAN JOSÉ
SAN JUSTO
LUNA
TANCA
O'DONELL
Casa Blanca
Hotel El Convento
CRISTO
Catedral de San Juan
Plazuela de la Monjas
LAS MONJAS
Plazuela de la Rogativa
San Juan Gate
SAN JUAN
Plaza de Armas
SAN FRANCISCO
FORTALEZA
TETUAN
RECINTO SUR
COMERCIO
PASEO GILBERTO CONCEPCIÓN DE GRACIA
PASEO DE COVADONGA
PASEO DE LA PRINCESA
La Fortaleza
Parque de las Palomas
Casa del Libro
Capilla del Cristo
La Princesa
Antiguo Correo
La Castita
Iglesia de San Francisco
Plaza Salvador Brau
Plaza Colón
Castillo de San Cristóbal
Antiguo Casino
MUÑOZ RIVERA
PONCE DE LEON
Teatro Tapia
Bus Terminal
PERSHING
HARDING
ACCOMMODATION
Chateau Cervantes E
Da House Hotel C
Gallery Inn A
Hotel El Convento B
San Juan Guest House D
EATING & DRINKING
Amadeus 4
El Batey 7
Blend 13
La Bombonera 8
Café Hijos de Borinquen 2
Cafeteria Mallorca 9
Candela 3
Club Lazer 17
Dragonfly 12
Fratelli 15
La Mallorquina 14
Maria's 16
The Noise 10
Nuyorican Café C
Parrot Club 11
El Picoteo 6
Restaurante El Jibarito 5
Rumba 1
0 200 yds

Rico, though he never lived here himself. The house has been carefully restored in sixteenth-century style, and is surrounded by charming palm-filled gardens.

Castillo San Felipe del Morro and around

Following c/ del Morro to the headland's northwest tip, eventually you reach the unmistakeable **Castillo San Felipe del Morro** (June–Nov daily 9am–5pm; Dec–May daily 9am–6pm; US$3 fee valid for 24hrs, free for kids under 15; US$5 with San Cristóbal, valid for 7 days), known simply as **El Morro**. This hulking fortress dominates the headland of San Juan Bay, rising 140ft above the Atlantic. Established as a small gun battery in the 1540s, the imposing defences were completed in 1787, thanks in large part to an enterprising Irishman in the pay of Spain, Thomas O'Daly. Today the thick walls are so old and weathered they have begun to look like outcroppings of bedrock, as though its six levels of towers, barracks, secret passageways, dungeons and ramps were carved from a natural cliff. Many of Puerto Rico's most illustrious citizens are buried nearby in the **Cementerio Santa María Magdalena de Pazzis** (daily 7am–3pm; free). It's one of the most picturesque sights in San Juan, with ornate, tightly packed marble tombs and monuments backed by an immense span of blue stretching far into the horizon. Beyond here is **La Perla,** a slum clinging outside the northern city wall between El Morro and San Cristóbal, a deceptively quaint-looking neighbourhood that is best avoided.

Heading back towards town across the windswept Campo – a famously good spot for flying kites – to c/ Norzagaray, you'll see the imposing Cuartel de Ballajá. Built in 1864, it served as a barracks for the Spanish army until their abrupt exit in 1898, and today houses the **Museo de las Américas** (Tues–Sun 10am–4pm; ⓦwww.museolasamericas.org). Entrance fees differ for each exhibition: El indio en América (US$2) is a poignant introduction to 22 indigenous American tribes, while rooms dedicated to the slave trade and North and South American folk art are free – don't miss the collection of *santos* (saints carved in wood).

Further along c/ Norzagaray in the old market place built in 1855, is the **Museo de San Juan** (Tues–Fri 9am–4pm, Sat & Sun 10am–4pm; free), offering a brief account of the city's history, with modest displays highlighting all the major political events as well as the earthquakes and hurricanes that periodically devastated the

▲ Cementerio Santa María Magdalena de Pazzis

city (Spanish labels only). Between the two museums is the **Plaza del Quinto Centenario**, dominated by a curious column studded with shards of nearby-excavated pottery, which was built to commemorate the five-hundredth anniversary Columbus' 1493 discovery of the island. On the plaza's east side, in the former Convento de los Dominicos, the **Galería Nacional** (Tues–Sat 9.30am–4.30pm, Sun 10.30am–5.30pm; US$3, free Tues) contains beautifully presented Puerto Rican art, from caste painting of the eighteenth century to abstract pieces from the 1960s, and including work from icons José Campeche and Francisco Oller. The convent adjoins the **Iglesia de San José** (under renovation, to reopen soon), the oldest original church on the island (construction began in 1523), featuring fairly typical Spanish colonial architecture, but with rare late-Gothic elements. Painter José Campeche is buried here. The church faces south onto **Plaza San José**, on the east side of which is the **Museo Pablo Casals** (Tues–Sat 9.30am–4.30pm; US$1), which displays manuscripts, photographs and instruments of the much-loved virtuoso Spanish cellist who lived in Puerto Rico from 1955 until his death in 1973.

Along calle del Cristo

Walk down c/ del Cristo from Plaza San José for two blocks and you'll reach shady Plazuela de la Monjas, the oldest square in the city which is dominated by the **Catedral de San Juan Bautista** (daily 8am–5pm; free). The first stone cathedral on the site was completed in 1549 but it's been reconstructed many times since and most of what you see today was part of a major restoration in 1917. Architecturally the cathedral is rather plain but the interior boasts a few interesting features, notably a marble monument on the left side containing the remains of Juan Ponce de León, reinterred here in 1908 (his body was brought back from Cuba in 1559, and originally laid to rest in the Iglesia de San José), and the relics of the early Christian martyr San Pío, transferred from Rome to satisfy the whims of a former bishop.

A block further on c/ del Cristo, turn right down c/ Fortaleza to **La Fortaleza** (Mon–Fri 9am–5pm, tours only; suggested donation US$3; ⓣ787/721-7000 ext 2211). Finished in 1540, it is touted as the oldest executive residence in the western hemisphere. The island's original fortress, it proved to be inadequately sited, and instead this palatial mansion has served as the governor's home since 1639. While there is no access to the government offices, visitors may take a free, guided tour through the inner patio, chapel, dungeon and lush Moorish gardens.

At the south end of the c/ del Cristo is the **Capilla del Santo Cristo de la Salud** (Tues 11am–3pm; free), a delicate stone chapel erected in 1753 at the edge of a precipice overlooking San Juan Bay. Inside you'll find a beautiful altar of silver repoussé work, laden with silver and gold *exvotos*, offerings to the saints.

To one side of the chapel is the **Casa del Libro** at c/ del Cristo 255 (Tues–Sat 11am–4.30pm; free; ⓦwww.lacasadellibro.org), a repository of over five thousand aged books, with around two hundred created before 1501, mostly in Spain. It has been closed for renovation since 2006 but will reopen soon. Opposite is the **Parque de las Palomas**, a pleasant garden overlooking the walls and bay, aptly named considering the great flocks of pigeons that congregate here (*paloma* means "dove" or "pigeon").

Castillo de San Cristóbal

Guarding the northeastern corner of Old San Juan at the east end of c/ Norzagaray is the sprawling **Castillo de San Cristóbal** (daily: June–Nov 9am–5pm, Dec–May 9am–6pm; US$3, valid for 24hrs; free for kids under 15; US$5 with El Morro, valid for 7 days), San Juan's second most important stronghold. Whereas El Morro defended against attacks by sea, San Cristóbal was intended to fight off land-based assaults. Built in stages between 1634 and 1790 on 27 acres, it was the largest Spanish military base in the Americas. Today, like El Morro, the US National Park Service maintains the labyrinthine fortress, and visitors can explore its secret tunnels, moats, dungeons and 150-foot high walls.

Condado

Three kilometres east of Old San Juan, the resort of **CONDADO** was the first part of the city to undergo tourist development in the 1950s. After a long period of stagnation, the area is experiencing a remarkable renaissance, and though it still feels shabby in places, the strip hums with the construction of vast, luxury resorts. Beyond the beach, Condado remains a relatively wealthy community of high-rise condos with little to see. Avenida Ashford is the main strip, running along the beachfront and lined with fast food outlets, shops and restaurants. **Playa Condado** proper starts at Plaza de la Gran Ventana al Mar, a new park opposite the junction with Avenida Magdalena. While the sand is thick and golden, it can get dirty and there's not much shade. Loungers can be hired for US$3 (daily). Condado also has a lively **nightlife**, and the area is very gay-friendly.

Ocean Park, Isla Verde and Piñones

Beyond Avenida José de Diego, the hustle and high-rises of Condado peter out into the tranquil, residential community of **OCEAN PARK**. The beach here is far more attractive than Condado's: it's wider, less busy and backed by a thin line of palm trees, the only downside is that it is slightly harder to reach by bus and has fewer amenities. At the end of the beach on the other side of the Punta Las Marías headland lies **Isla Verde**, a highly sanitized version of Puerto Rico composed of a brash resort of malls, self-contained hotels and international restaurants. It is, however, newer and more upmarket than Condado, and the palm-tree fringed beach, split in half by the rocky Punta El Media headland, is the best in the city. It's wide with fine sand and gentle waves, and the proximity of so many stylish hotels and beach bars creates a party atmosphere at the weekends, attracting a diverse crowd.

Just 2km beyond central Isla Verde, **PIÑONES** is an entirely different world, a languid, low-rent Afro-Caribbean community of shacks and houses scattered along the coast and PR-187. At the weekends the whole area comes alive with *salsa* and *sanjuaneros* drinking beer and enjoying deep-fried *kiosco* snacks. You can also **rent bikes** here (US$5/hr; photo ID required) and follow the well-marked **Paseo Piñones** bike trail along the coast to the Bosque Estatal de Piñones, a reserve of thick mangrove swamps around the Laguna de Piñones, rich in crab and birdlife, and finally to some pristine, palm-lined beaches, excellent for **surfing**, especially in winter.

Santurce

The working-class *barrio* of **SANTURCE** lies behind the main beaches, and is a gritty neighbourhood that offers a refreshing contrast to the coastal tourist zones. In recent years the area has been undergoing much needed regeneration, with a couple of excellent art museums, exuberant nightlife and plenty of cheap places to eat along central Avenida Ponce de León, though you still need to take care at night.

The **Museo de Arte Contemporáneo** (Tues–Sat 10am–4pm, Sun noon–4pm; free; ⓦwww.museocontemporaneopr.org) is housed in a tastefully restored building on the corner of Ponce de León and Avenida Roberto Todd. The gallery holds temporary exhibitions of often bold and experimental post-1940 art from Puerto Rico and elsewhere in the Caribbean, such as the photography of Néstor Millán Alvarez and abstract work from José Morales.

From the museum it's a short walk south along Ponce de León then left up c/ Dos Hermanos to the **Plaza del Mercado** where a vibrant indoor market (Mon–Sat 5am–5pm, Sun 5am–noon) is surrounded by a collection of fashionable places to eat and drink known as La Placita. The market contains mostly fruit and vegetable stores and retains a distinctively local character despite the growing number of tours that come through; try the *Cocos Bien Frios* stall for fried snacks and *batidas*.

Displaying the finest ensemble of Puerto Rican art on the island, the **Museo de Arte** (Tues & Thurs–Sun 10am–5pm, Wed 10am–8pm; US$6; ⓦwww.mapr.org) is a short walk east of the market, on Avenida José de Diego. Its permanent collection on the first floor is arranged thematically, in roughly chronological order from the seventeenth century to the present day, including vivid pieces from Francisco Oller, Myrna Báez and Rafael Tufiño. The second floor contains the museum's substantial collection of contemporary painting, sculpture and installation art.

From here it's another 2km south to **Hato Rey** and the tower-lined Milla de Oro ("Golden Mile"), the city's financial heart with little for the traveller to see.

Río Piedras

Founded in 1714 and incorporated into San Juan in 1951, **RIO PIEDRAS** is a low-rise residential district south of Hato Rey (12km from Old San Juan), home to the main campus of the **Universidad de Puerto Rico** (Ⓦwww.uprrp.edu) and the city's largest market. Thanks to the university, you'll also find a high concentration of Spanish bookstores along Avenida Ponce de León south of the campus, particularly La Tertulia at no. 1002 (Ⓣ787/765-1148).

The university is worth a visit for the engaging **Museo de Historia Antropología y Arte** (Mon, Tues & Fri 9am–4.30pm, Wed & Thurs 9am–8.30pm; free), just inside the campus's main entrance on Ponce de León (buses stop outside). Though it's small, the galleries contain a number of significant artefacts, including some enigmatic Taíno finds and Francisco Oller's masterpiece, *El Velorio*, a moving depiction of a wake in rural nineteenth-century Puerto Rico.

A ten-minute walk southeast of the university is the not-to-be-missed **Plaza del Mercado** (Mon–Fri 6am–5pm, Sat 6am–1pm), an indoor market of primarily fruit and vegetable stalls but also fascinating *botánicas* selling all sorts of herbal remedies and charms associated with *santería*. The real highlight, however, is the no-frills food court at the back, where almost every Puerto Rican dish is served up at bargain prices; try *El Tropical* for fruit shakes and *Doña Alice* for chicken and stews.

Eating

San Juan is garnering a reputation as the **culinary capital of the Caribbean** – a smorgasbord of both international cuisines and endless variations on Puerto Rican staples. The highest concentrations of enticing restaurants are in Old San Juan (particularly on c/ Fortaleza near Plaza Colón) and Condado (along Avenida Ashford), while cheaper, no-frills diners can be found in Santurce.

Old San Juan

Amadeus c/San Sebastián 106 Ⓣ787/722-8635. Excellent nouvelle Caribbean cuisine served until 2am to a hip crowd; try the dumplings with guava sauce and arrowroot fritters or the smoked salmon and caviar pizza; entrees run US$20–30.

Blend c/Fortaleza 309, Ⓣ787/977-7777. This bar, lounge and restaurant features an elegant interior of plush crimson seats and booths, and a blend of Mediterranean, Asian and Puerto Rican cuisines: sumptuous tuna tartare, lamb chops, lobster ravioli and sweet-soy steak. You'll spend at least US$30.

La Bombonera c/San Francisco 259 Ⓣ787/722-0658. Established in 1902, this atmospheric diner is packed at weekends, especially for breakfast, when scrambled eggs or *mallorcas* (toasted pastries filled with bacon, ham or cheese and dusted with icing sugar; US$2-5) are served with rich mountain-grown coffee. Closes 8pm.

Caféteria Mallorca c/San Francisco 300 Ⓣ787/724-4607. People line up at this eatery for its famous *mallorcas* and hot chocolate; also on offer: *café con leche*, fruit salads, pancakes and eggs for breakfast, and *criollo* staples for lunch and dinner. You can eat well for US$5–10. Closes at 6.30pm.

Dragonfly c/Fortaleza 364 Ⓣ787/977-3886. One of the most innovative restaurants in San Juan, fusing Caribbean classics with Asian flavours: Mongolian beef *ropa vieja*, Peking duck nachos with wasabi sour cream and marinated *churrasco* with "dragonflies" (shoestring potatoes). Entrees US$13–25.

Fratelli c/Fortaleza 310 ⓣ787/721-6265. This outstanding Italian restaurant is a stylish, romantic retreat, replete with Renaissance frescoes, giant mirrors on the walls and a lovely antique bar. Feast on *risotto di mare* with squid and the luscious pork fillet with gorgonzola and pears. Entrees US$15-25.

La Mallorquina c/San Justo 207 ⓣ787/722-3261. Founded in 1848, this is San Juan's oldest restaurant. It's pricey, but the refined colonial setting fits the bill. The soupy rice dish *Asopao* is the speciality, which is served with chicken or seafood in small "kettles" for US$14–18.

Parrot Club c/Fortaleza 363 ⓣ787/725-7370. This requisite San Juan experience is pure Nuevo Latino. Impeccable dishes are accompanied by mellow live Latin jazz on Tues, Thurs and Sat. The house specials include rare tuna broiled with dark rum and orange essence with yucca mash and *mojitos* (US$8). Entrees US$18-36.

El Picoteo *Hotel El Convento*, c/Cristo 100 ⓣ787/723-9202. Choose from over a hundred tasty but pricey *tapas* such as *jamón serrano* (US$14) and sardines (US$11), or more substantial, moderately priced Spanish dishes, and enjoy the cool breeze on the open terrace overlooking *El Convento*'s central courtyard.

Restaurante El Jibarito c/Sol 280 ⓣ787/725-8375. This re-creation of a rustic mountain diner offers a nostalgic slice of traditional Puerto Rico with daily specials and hearty *comida criolla* such as the oven-baked pork with sweet plantains and mouth-watering ribs. Most mains are under US$10.

Condado

Ajili-Mójili Avda Ashford 1006 ⓣ787/725-9195. Upmarket *criollo* cuisine prepared by chef Mariano Ortiz, set in an opulent Spanish Revival villa. The large, seasonal menu is heavy on seafood; try the *mofongo* specials, *asopaos* or more substantial *lechón asado* (roast pork). Entrees US$18–30.

Bebo's Café c/Loíza 1600 ⓣ787/726-1008. Neighbourhood institution, this Dominican-owned cafeteria sits back from the beaches on the edge of Ocean Park. The menu includes hearty portions of *comida criolla* classics such as *mofongo* for under US$10, but it's also a good place for cheap Mexican-style breakfasts.

Yerba Buena Avda Ashford 1350, ⓣ787/721-5700. Popular bistro knocking out Caribbean and Cuban classics such as *ropa vieja* (shredded beef) and yam fritters with creole hot sauce for under US$20 but best known for its authentic *mojitos* and live Cuban music Thurs–Sat.

Zabó c/Candina 14 ⓣ787/725-9494. Elegant setting in rustic wooden *criollo* house with a snappy menu of international dishes created by lauded chef Paul Carroll; masterpieces include the smoked fish blinis, mini beef Wellingtons and guava-glazed spare ribs. Entrees US$15–27.

Ocean Park and Isla Verde

Dunbars Avda McLeary 1954, Ocean Park ⓣ787/728-2920. A sprawling, collegiate dive with pool tables and upscale bar food that's always boisterous. Live music at weekends. Entrees US$14–25.

Kasalta Avda McLeary 1966, Ocean Park ⓣ787/727-7340. This venerable canteen and deli of cured meats and cheeses, breads, wines and fine imported goods is a requisite stop. The *café con leche* is superb. Eat for under US$5.

Metropol Avda Isla Verde, next to Club Gallistico ⓣ787/791-4046. Family favourite established in 1965 specializing in Cuban and Puerto Rican food. Try the guinea hen stuffed with *congri* or the Fiesta Cubana – one of several Cuban favourites (tamales, pork, cassava). Entrees for under US$20.

Oyster Bar & Grill Avda Isla Verde 6000 ⓣ787/726-2161. New Orleans-inspired cuisine, with substantial bowls of jambalaya (US$16) and decent burgers (US$7), as well as the signature oysters (flown in from the mainland) from US$12 per half dozen. Open till 7am weekends, when it transforms into a lively bar and *salsa club*.

Pinky's c/Maria Moczo 51, ⓣ787/727-3347. Perfect for a wholesome brunch before hitting the beach, this bright café is justly popular with expats and locals alike, addicted to the eclectic menu of comfort food: pork plantains, hummus, vegetarian specials and various wraps.

Santurce

Pikayo Museo de Arte, Avda José de Diego 299 ⓣ787/721-6194, ⓦwww.pikayo.com. The constantly changing menus by celebrated chef Wilo Benet and views over a sculpture garden have earned this ultra-chic spot inside the museum a deservedly revered status. Dishes such as conch spring rolls with orange *sofrito* sauce are extraordinary. Entrees US$28–52.

El Popular c/Capitol 205. One of the best cafés in La Placita, a Spanish-style dining room with slow service but the best *chicharrones de pollo* (fried chicken) and *olla Española* (Spanish beef stew) on the island, for around US$10.

Tasca el Pescador c/Dos Hermanos 178 ⓣ787/721-0995. Another excellent restaurant in La Placita, with an antique wooden bar and a menu of fresh fish (try the fabulous salmon in guava sauce; US$18), but this place is best for lunch or a very early dinner, as it closes at 6pm.

Drinking and nightlife

Going out in San Juan can be a raucous, all-night affair, with weekends especially crazy. The old town has the highest concentration of lively **bars** and **clubs**, quite apart from restaurants-cum-lounge bars like *Blend*, *Dragonfly*, *Fratelli* and *Amadeus* (see p.372). **Piña coladas** get served up everywhere, in posh glasses or plastic cups on the beach – San Juan claims to have invented the tropical cocktail in the 1950s. Puerto Rico is also the birthplace of **salsa** (see box opposite), and there's lots of it around, with Condado's smart hotels putting on some classy shows. C/ San Sebastián in Old San Juan and the Plaza del Mercado in Santurce (La Placita) both have a good choice of inviting small bars, some with live music, while on or near Avenida Ponce de León in Santurce are some of the city's most gay-friendly dance clubs. For hip-hop and the newest home-grown craze, **reggaetón**, try *Club Lazer* or *The Noise* at c/ Tanca 203 in Old San Juan.

Old San Juan

El Batey c/Cristo 101. This dark, grungy fixture, open until 6am, is usually mobbed. Has a very "local bar" feel, despite the number of outsiders.

Café Hijos de Borinquen c/San José 151. This classic old town bar opened in 1954, with plenty of faded memorabilia on the walls. Expect it to be empty till 10pm but overflowing 1–2am, with live music at the weekends.

Candela c/San Sebastián 110 ⓣ787/977-4305. This lounge bar is worth a peek for its cool retro theme alone. It gets busy late, with a resident DJ on Sat.

Club Lazer c/Cruz 251 ⓣ787/721-4479, ⓦwww.clublazer.com. Club on three packed floors with an outdoor rooftop area, and *reggaetón* dominating the DJ line-up on Fri and Sat; cover is usually US$15. Fri–Sun 10pm–4am.

Maria's c/Cristo 204. This small bar has been around for over forty years and is noted for its quality *piña coladas* and *margaritas* (US$6). Quite touristy these days, but serves decent Mexican food and a wickedly potent cocktail, *La Norta*.

Nuyorican Café c/San Francisco 312 (entrance on Callejón de la Capilla), ⓣ787/977-1276, ⓦwww.nuyoricancafepr.com.

Music in Puerto Rico

Puerto Rico is probably most famous as the cradle of **salsa**, in which a very diverse stew of musical influences have produced a distinctly Latin product. *Salsa* is a fusion of Caribbean folk music (mostly from Puerto Rico and Cuba) and North American jazz, set to complex African rhythms. First developed by migrant Puerto Ricans in New York nightclubs during the 1940s, and popularized by legendary figures such as Tito Puente and Héctor Lavoe, *El Cantante* himself, *salsa* is experiencing a resurgence of popularity on the island. In San Juan you can take lessons, dance at *salsa* clubs, attend live performances (mainly in the resort hotels) and even check out the annual **Salsa Congress** (ⓦwww.puertoricosalsacongress.com), held in July. *salsa* eventually spawned Latino pop, with acts such as boy-band Menudo and megastar **Ricky Martin**, but the latest trend is **reggaetón**, a blend of rap, reggae and *salsa* rhythms; some of the biggest stars are Daddy Yankee, Don Omar and Calle 13.

The musical dance tradition called **bomba** still has a presence in Puerto Rico. Much like Cuban *rumba*, it's based on intricate West African percussion. The drummer – traditionally using an old barrel with leather stretched over one end – provokes a response from a dancer, inciting a sort of rhythmic duel where honour can be at stake, as each attempts to outdo the other. The island's other important folk music is **plena**, said to have originated in Ponce in the early twentieth century. The sometimes moralistic lyrics of a lead singer are repeated by a choir, set to the music of a ten-string guitar, called a *cuatro*, and a hollowed gourd, like a maraca, called a *güiro*. Considered Puerto Rico's national dance and the most formal of its musical traditions, the **danza** derived from the Cuban *habanera* in the nineteenth century, a less rigid version of the waltz and classical music of Europe.

This alternative venue has live *salsa* (Wed, Fri & Sat), Latin dance (Sun) and a fusion of everything (Thurs), with the narrow alley outside packed with locals drinking at the kiosk opposite.

Rumba c/San Sebastián 152, ⓣ787/725-4407. With its young crowd, this is one of the liveliest bars and clubs on San Sebastián. DJs and live music, from *salsa* to Latin jazz, Tues–Sun 9pm–4am.

Condado

Di Parma Trattoria Avda Ashford 1901, at Plaza de la Gran Ventana al Mar, ⓣ787/289-7400. This Italian restaurant serves reasonable food, but is best as a fashionable spot to sip drinks on the terrace overlooking the park and beach.

Moorings Bar & Grill Avda Ashford 1214 (across from the Marriott), ⓣ787-725-2192. Sports-style bar with two levels and music ranging from hip-hop and disco to techno and pop; it becomes very club-like Thurs–Sat.

Santurce

Club Mijani c/Dos Hermanos 252. This club is tucked in amongst the action in La Placita, and packed from midnight on. Thurs is the main *salsa* night, while Fri feature a variety of Latin sounds.

Krash Avda Ponce de León 1257 ⓣ787/722-1131. Basically a gay club, but all persuasions come here on Sat. *Salsa* and New York-style house with dance, drag and strip acts. Wed–Sat 10pm–4am.

Liquid Avda Ponce de León 1420 ⓣ787/722-1130. Upbeat club with a hip crowd and a mix of house, hip-hop and Latino dance music, taking inspiration from South Beach, Miami. Open to 4am Thurs to Sat.

Isla Verde

Club Brava El San Juan Hotel, Avda Isla Verde 6063 ⓣ787/602-8222, ⓦwww.bravapr.com. Hard techno in the main room, a more relaxed "ultra lounge" and a steady stream of glamorous clients. You'll need ID to get in (over 21s on Fri, over 23s Sat), and don't even think about wearing jeans. Thurs–Sat 10pm–3am, cover US$8–15, free for hotel guests.

Wet Bar San Juan Water & Beach Club Hotel, c/Tartak 2, ⓣ787/728-3666. Seductive rooftop bar and lounge, with panoramic views of the city and beaches below – it's worth having at least one drink just to lounge on the white double beds, though it's US$8 for beers and US$10 for mixers.

7.2

Around San Juan

Most of the island is easily accessible from the capital, allowing for enticing day-trips. One of the simplest is the pilgrimage across San Juan Bay to the **Casa Bacardi Visitor Center**, a great shrine to rum-making, but save at least one day for the lush **El Yunque** rainforest, 43km southeast of the capital. Another tempting target that's nearby is **Luquillo**, a palm-lined *balneario* (public beach) on the northeast shore.

In the other direction from San Juan is the rugged landscape that characterizes the island's northwest – the so-called **karst country**, formed as rivers originating in the Cordillera Central carved their way to the ocean through porous limestone, creating vast networks of sinkholes and crumbling peaks. The area conceals several popular attractions: world-class spelunking in extensive underground network of caves, showcased at the **Parque de las Cavernas del Río Camuy**; the world's largest radio telescope, lodged in a sinkhole at the **Observatorio de Arecibo**; and the enigmatic Taíno petroglyphs and ball courts at the **Centro Ceremonial Indígena de Caguana**.

Casa Bacardí Visitor Center

The slick **Casa Bacardi Visitor Center** (Mon–Sat 9am–5.30pm, last tour 4.30pm; Sun 10–5pm, last tour 3.45pm; free; ⓣ787/788-8400, ⓦwww.casabacardi.org) inside the "cathedral of rum", the vast Bacardi distillery across San Juan Bay in Cataño is a series of fun and illuminating interactive exhibits that cover rum history, production and just about anything related to the Caribbean's favourite tipple. Established in Cuba in 1862 but exiled from the island since Castro's revolution, the Bacardi empire now dominates the global rum market, supplying 75 percent of rum sold in the US alone. Free guided tours (45min) depart every 15 to 30 minutes and end with two free drinks. To get to the distillery, take the ferry from Pier 2 in Old San Juan (50¢), then take a taxi or catch bus C37 to the main gate.

El Yunque National Forest

Sacred to the Taíno long before the Spanish conquest, the lush, jungle-drenched slopes of **El Yunque National Forest** (daily 7.30am–6pm; free; ⓣ787/888/1880, ⓦwww.fs.fed.us/r8/caribbean), dominate eastern Puerto Rico like a protective wall, an untouched wilderness crowned by 3500ft peaks. As part of the US National Forest system, it's the most accessible reserve in the Caribbean.

You can drive right into the heart of the forest on PR-191 but to really appreciate the area you need to get **hiking**. The Forest Service maintains thirteen easy-to-moderate trails, and even the trek up El Yunque itself (the name refers to the reserve and the mountain) is manageable for anyone in reasonable shape, and well worth the effort for the momentous views from the top. Less taxing highlights include a series of plunging waterfalls and natural swimming pools, and a smattering of whimsical structures created by the Civilian Conservation Corps in the 1930s.

Deluged with more than 100 billion gallons of rainfall a year, El Yunque is home to 240 tree species and a panoply of rare flora and fauna, most notably the endangered *cotorra puertorriqueña*, or Puerto Rican Green Parrot, of which there are only around 44 in the wild, all of them here. Seventy percent of the reserve is smothered in **tabonuco** forest, found on slopes below 2000ft, while some of the trees in the **palo colorado** zone, forest that grows above 2000ft, have stood for more than a thousand years. The region above 2500ft is dominated by **sierra palms**, ferns and mosses, while the highest peaks are crowned with **cloud forest**, also known as dwarf forest, where trees, stunted by strong trade winds, rarely grow higher than twelve feet tall – this is supposedly where Yokahú (or Yukiyú), the chief Taíno spirit, made his home.

If you only have one day for hiking, head straight to the trailheads around the tiny **Palo Colorado Information Center** (daily 9.30am–5pm) at Km 11.8. One of the most popular walks is **La Mina Trail** (1.2km), following the river downhill through a Jurassic-like landscape of giant palms, rustic barbecue pavilions and *palo colorado* forest to La Mina Falls, a modest waterfall surrounded by inviting pools of cool mountain water. The most rewarding hike is along the **El Yunque Trail** (4.4km) to the summit of El Yunque (3445ft), an exhilarating three-hour loop that can also take in Mount Britton (3087ft), topped with a mock medieval observation tower. Keen hikers take on the **Trade Winds Trail** (6.28km), which begins on PR-191, around 400m beyond the metal gate at Km 13, and climbs **El Toro**, the **highest peak** in the forest, at 3522ft. Wear good walking shoes and light, loose clothing, and be prepared for at least some rain.

Practicalities

El Yunque covers 28,000 acres but most visitors focus on the northern section of the reserve accessible from PR-191. While El Yunque is not served by public transport, organized tour buses do pick-ups at San Juan hotels most days. You can also join **walking tours** (daily 10.30am–3.30pm; 1hr; US$5 adults, US$3 children) run by the Forest Service from the Palo Colorado Information Center. By car from San Juan, head east on PR-3 towards Fajardo, turn right onto PR-955 and then left on PR-191 in the village of Mameyes, just off the highway. After 5km you'll reach the forest and **El Portal Rain Forest Center** (daily 9am–5pm; US$3) which provides the best introduction to the park. Visitor information, maps and brochures are also available.

To **camp** in the park you'll need to apply for a permit (free) by filling in a form available at El Portal or Palo Colorado, but there are also several **guesthouses** nearby. One of the best is the *Rainforest Inn* (Ⓣ800/672-4992, Ⓦwww.rainforestinn.com; ❺), off PR-186 on the west side of the forest, with two plush and unique suites in a gorgeous five-acre estate. Alternatively, try the beautifully situated *Casa Cubuy Ecolodge* (Ⓣ787/874-6221, Ⓦwww.casacubuy.com; ❹), a haven on the south side of the forest that is overlooked by the vast majority of the million people who come here each year. The hotel, which also organizes walks to nearby waterfalls, is reached by continuing on PR-3 and then PR-53 past Fajardo, turning right onto PR-31 and right again onto PR-191, which you follow to the end.

Luquillo

Many day-trippers from San Juan round out a morning trip to El Yunque with an afternoon lounging on the picture-perfect sands of the **Balneario de Luquillo** (daily 8.30am–5pm; parking US$3), formally known as the Balneario de Monserrate. Just 45 minutes from the capital on PR-3, with calm waters perfect for swimming, the beach – especially at weekends – can be jam-packed. Nearby, just off the highway, Luquillo's celebrated **kioscos** sell everything from *piña coladas* and beers to grilled meats and crispy seafood *empanadillas*. For starry nights rather than city lights, you can also **camp** here (Ⓣ787/889-5871; US$13 a night or US$17 with hook-up in campsite; US$10 in open areas).

Karst country

Squashed between the north coast and the peaks of the Central Cordillera, **karst country** is a region of narrow gorges, cavernous sinkholes and crumbling limestone

▲ Arecibo Observatory

hills smothered in jungle. Less than two hours' drive west of San Juan, the region harbours several absorbing attractions, a couple of which could make for a full day's sightseeing.

You don't need to have an interest in the night sky to visit the **Observatorio de Arecibo** (Aug 1–Dec 14 & Jan 16–May 31, Wed–Fri noon–4pm, Sat, Sun, holidays 9am–4pm; June 1–July 31 & Dec 15–Jan 15, daily 9am–4pm; US$5, kids US$3; Ⓦwww.naic.edu), the largest radio telescope in the world and one of the most unusual sights in Puerto Rico – its awe-inspiring 1000-foot-wide dish covers a gaping sinkhole. At the visitor centre, you'll find thought-provoking exhibits about astronomy and how the observatory, which helped discover the first extrasolar planets, studies radio emissions from galaxies, quasars and pulsars. To get here from San Juan, take PR-22, turn off onto PR-129 and follow the brown signs to the observatory at the end of PR-625.

Tapping into one of the largest cave systems in the world, the nearby **Parque de las Cavernas del Río Camuy** (Wed–Sun 8am–5pm, last entry 3.45pm; US$12, kids US$7; Ⓣ787898-3100) is clearly signposted at PR-129 Km 20, with plenty of parking (US$3 extra). Note, however. that in early 2008 the **park was closed** after a tourist was accidentally killed by falling rocks during a tour – it is expected to reopen in stages as new safety procedures are put in place, but check with the PRTC. Tours last around 1.5 hours, beginning with a walk through the largest cave, **Cueva Clara**. Inside there are enormous boulder-like stalagmites and bats flit about in caverns up to 170 feet high. In places, the raging Río Camuy is visible far below. The tour also includes a look at the Tres Pueblos sinkhole, a vast chasm that measures 650 feet wide and 400 feet deep – large enough to fit El Morro.

Thrill seekers should get in touch with Aventuras Tierra Adentro (Ⓣ787/766-0470; Ⓦwww.aventuraspr.com) which arranges **caving** trips to the Río Camuy every Saturday (US$160). Tours (5.45am–5pm) involve an exhilarating 76m rappel into **Angeles Cave**. These expeditions aren't cheap but the safety expertise and extensive knowledge of the guides make it worthwhile.

Further east, the **Centro Ceremonial Indígena de Caguana** (daily 8.30am–4pm, closed holidays; US$2; Ⓣ787/894-7325) is a precious remnant of Taíno civilization from around 1200 AD and one of the most important pre-Columbian sites in the Caribbean. From San Juan, take PR-22 then head south on PR-10, turning right after Utuado onto PR-111 – the park is at Km 12.3. Hidden within a tropical forest and backed by a majestic karst ridge, the site contains the stone foundations of a series of ball-courts known as *bateyes*, as well as some rare petroglyphs. While it seems to be a sort of Caribbean Olympia, built purely for ceremonial games rather than as a settlement, the true purpose of Caguana remains a mystery. The small museum at the entrance exhibits Taíno artefacts gathered from all over the island – very little has been found at Caguana itself.

7.3

Porta del Sol and the southwest

Western Puerto Rico holds some of the island's greatest natural treasures, not least the alluring, sun-bathed **beaches** which have earned the region the touristy designation of **Porta del Sol** (ⓦwww.gotoportadelsol.com), "gateway to the sun". Beach-lovers apart, many are drawn here for the world-class **diving** off **Mona** and **Desecheo islands**, as well as along **La Pared** near La Parguera. Just outside **Guánica** is the world's largest **subtropical dry forest**, and the remarkably well-preserved colonial town of **San Germán** offers a window into the seventeenth century.

If you need more, the natural beauty of the **southwest coast** is almost enough to warrant a visit alone, with Guánica, and nearby La Parguera making the best hubs for exploring the area. In the **northwest**, base yourself in **Rincón**, the **surfing** capital of the Caribbean, for short trips to Desecheo. Trips to **Mona**, which lies stranded halfway between Puerto Rico and the Dominican Republic, requires advance planning, but this "Galápagos of the Caribbean" is worth the effort (see box p.380).

Rincón and around

Surfers have been coming to **RINCÓN** in droves since the 1960s – some never left and the area has a substantial expat community. You can see why: the beaches around the small town are among the island's finest, and offer a good enough reason to come, even if you don't surf (the surf season is October to April).

Rincón is also known for its romantic sunsets, best seen at the island's most westerly point at the restored **Punta Higüero lighthouse**, north of town. The surrounding park overlooking the sea is also a pretty spot for **whale-watching** in the winter – February is the best month. Next door is the innocuous-looking dome of Latin America's first nuclear power station, no longer operational and soon expected to open as museum of local history and nuclear power. On either side of the cliffs below the lighthouse is a series of excellent **beaches** where the surfers congregate, although in calm weather there's also good snorkelling around Tres Palmas beach, where a protected reserve of elkhorn coral proliferates.

For more serious **snorkelling** or **diving**, you shouldn't leave Rincón without exploring the otherwordly, incredibly clear waters around the 360-acre protrusion of rock that is **Isla Desecheo**, just 19km offshore. Underwater ravines, pinnacles and grottoes teem with flying gurnards, peacock flounders, snappers, triggerfish, octopus and nurse sharks. Your best bet is Taíno Divers, PR-413, Black Eagle Marina (ⓣ787/823-7243, ⓦwww.tainodivers.com), whose professional staff run daily boat trips taking 45 minutes; US$75 for snorkelling or US$109 for two dives, includes kit.

Other beaches in the northwest

If you get bored of Rincón's beaches, plenty more are within easy reach. Half an hour's drive north is **Punta Borinquen**, once the site of a major US Air Force base and now the hub of series of wild beaches with some of the best surf breaks

Isla de Mona

One of the last genuinely wild islands in the Caribbean, the **Isla de Mona** is a blessedly isolated nature reserve, 74km off the west coast of Puerto Rico. Staying on the island requires advance planning, though it's much easier to arrange day-trips to dive or snorkel off its deep, unbelievably clear waters and richly-stocked barrier reef. The diving is unparalleled, with visibility averaging 150–200ft and 270 kinds of fish lurking in its waters. Depending on the time of year, you may see sailfish, dorado, tuna, marlin, sharks, rays, turtles, pods of dolphins and even pilot whales. In the winter months, migrating humpback whales often come close to shore. The island is completely uninhabited, with 200-foot high cliffs rimming the mostly flat, dry interior, and 8km of empty beaches, hiking trails and caves to explore, as well as diverse wildlife that includes giant iguanas (among them the endangered Mona Iguana), red-footed boobies and countless other sea birds.

The Mona Passage is notoriously rough and the journey can take from three to six hours. Several outfits arrange trips, but they tend to be expensive. Try Acampa (Ⓣ787/706-0695, Ⓦwww.acampapr.com), AdvenTours (Ⓣ787/831-6447, Ⓦwww.adventourspr.com) and Oceans Unlimited at the *Rincón Beach Resort* (Ⓣ787/823-2340 Ⓦwww.rinconbeach.com), which runs dive trips (minimum six people) and three-day excursions to the island (minimum eight people).

on the island. To find the waves, turn left off PR-107 on the unmarked narrow lane that cuts across the golf course, just before the turning to Aguadilla airport. As you near the sea you'll pass a small turn-off to **Playa Borinquen**, a soothing carpet of fine sand and ideal for swimming in the summer. The main road continues along the coast until it's replaced by an extremely battered dirt track laced with potholes, passing the ruins of an old Spanish lighthouse flattened by the earthquake of 1918, and ending up at **Playa Wilderness**, a pro surf beach where groundswells of 30ft are possible.

To the south, **Playa Crash Boat** is a wide, fine stretch of sand at the end of PR-458 (off PR-107), with a festive atmosphere at the weekends and the celebrated break known as **Gas Chambers**, home to Puerto Rico's best right tube.

Further north, on the eastern side of the old base, **Playa de Shacks** is perfect for snorkelling, with a wide reef riddled with tunnels and underwater caves just metres offshore. You'll find it at the end of a narrow road off PR-4466 at Km 1.9. Keep driving along PR-4466 for another 2km and you'll reach **Playa de Jobos**, a sumptuous crescent of sand facing a shallow bay perfect for swimming and easily the best surf beach for **beginners**.

Practicalities

Rincón has one of Puerto Rico's best selections of **accommodation**, ranging from charming rustic guesthouses to seriously exclusive hotels. The classiest hotel in Rincón, and perhaps all Puerto Rico, is the *Horned Dorset Primavera*, PR-429 Km 3 (Ⓣ787/823-4030, Ⓦwww.horneddorset.com; ➒). It has eight immaculate luxury suites in Spanish colonial-style villas above a secluded beach. At the other end of the scale is *Rincón Inn*, PR-115 Km 11.6 (Ⓣ787/823-7070, Ⓦwww.rinconinn.com; ➋), with good basic accommodation as well as a youth hostel-style dormitory, and free Internet (US$1/10min for non-guests). To the north of town, beyond the lighthouse, is a collection of relaxed **guesthouses**, including *Beside the Pointe Inn*, PR-413 Interior Km 4.4 (Ⓣ787/823-8550, Ⓦwww.besidethepointe.com; ➍), right on the beach with eight rooms, some with sea views and kitchens. It has a decent restaurant, *Tamboo Seaside Grill*, serving grilled food on a wooden deck overlooking the sea, and also *Tamboo Tavern*, one of the most happening bars in town. The *Lazy Parrot Inn*, PR-413 Km 4.1 (Ⓣ787/823-5654, Ⓦwww.lazyparrot.com; ➍) sits on top of a hill with beautiful views and a charmingly meandering outdoor area, including a pool. It also has an excellent restaurant.

Rincón's large youthful population, thanks to the hordes of surfers it attracts, means the **nightlife** can get quite animated at the many beach bars. *Calypso Café* on PR-4413, (T787/823-1626, W www.calypsopr.com) is a favourite surfer bar just off María's beach, while *The Spot*, by the Black Eagle Marina (T787/823-3510), is a funky waterside restaurant. South of town is the fashionable *Bohío Bar* on the beach at the *Villa Cofresí Hotel*, PR-115 Km 12 (T787/823-2450, W www.villacofresi.com); try their *pirata special*, a potent rum-based concoction served in a coconut.

San Germán

An hour's drive southeast of Rincón, **San Germán** is steeped in colonial history, its ravishing centre a proudly traditional zone of narrow streets and ornate mansions adorned with stained glass and elaborate stucco. The town has the island's oldest architecture outside Old San Juan but with a fraction of the visitors, its faded charm is wonderfully evocative of bygone days.

The humble **Museo Porta Coeli** on the Plazuela de Santo Domingo (Wed–Sun 8.30am–noon & 1–4.20pm; US$3) is Puerto Rico's oldest church outside San Juan. Once part of a larger Dominican convent, it was originally a chapel and today houses religious artwork and statuary from around the region. Maps with information of nearby historic buildings are available, and there are fine views of the surrounding countryside from the top of its steep front steps. The chapel was established in 1606 but what you see today dates mostly from the 1690s; the rest of the convent was demolished in 1874, with only the ruined front wall remaining.

The more elaborate **Iglesia Católica San Germán de Auxerre** dominates the Plaza Francisco Mariano Quiñones, a block west of Plazuela de Santo Domingo. The original was completed in 1573, with many subsequent enlargements, notably in 1842 when the current structure took shape, blending Spanish Baroque and Colonial styles, including a gleaming facade and decorative bell tower. It is notable for its Carrara marble altar and the trompe l'oeil fresco on the nave's ceiling, lit by a brilliant Spanish crystal chandelier. Doors open half an hour before Mass (Mon–Sat 7am & 7.30pm, Sun 7am, 8.30am, 10am & 7.30pm), or you can call T787/892-1027 to see if the priest will let you in.

There are no decent places to stay in San Germán, but *Casa Vieja* on c/ Estrella (T787/264-3954) facing Plaza Quiñones is easily the most appealing place to have dinner, offering quality Puerto Rican food in historic surroundings. For lunch try *Le Casa del Sandwich* at c/ Luna 79 (opposite Walgreens) or the restaurant at the hotel *Parador El Oasis* at c/ Luna 72 (T787/892-1175; 3).

La Parguera

Some 10km directly south of San Germán is the fishing village of **La Parguera**, surrounded by a maze of mangrove swamps, channels, coral reefs and cays. The diving is superb, and the village makes a pleasant hub from which to explore the surrounding region, with rustic diners, a lively bar culture and a decent selection of agreeable hotels. At the weekends the atmosphere is unusually young and upbeat for a place of its size and despite efforts by the local authorities to quiet things down by imposing curfews.

Divers are drawn to La Parguera's innumerable coral reefs offshore, many of them still unexplored. About 8km from the coast, **La Pared** ("the wall") runs for 35km from Guánica to Cabo Rojo at the island's southwest tip and drops to 2000ft, with visibility up to 120ft. Snorkelling, too, is excellent: barracudas, morays, manatees, nurse sharks and sea turtles abound. Try West Divers at PR-304 Km 3.1 (T787/899-3223, W www.westdiverspr.com), which also rents kayaks for US$10 per hour, or Paradise Scuba (PR-304 in town, T787/899-7611, W www.paradisescubasnorkelingpr.com). Dive trips cost US$70-80.

In a nearby mangrove swamp is the **Bahia de Fosforescente**, the island's most accessible bioluminescent bay but thanks to pollution, it's also the least impressive and can't compare to Puerto Mosquito on Vieques (p.394). Nevertheless, for US$6 you can take a nightly boat tour from the pier, while for US$25 Paradise Scuba will take you out for a swim. During the day, outfits such as Johnny's Boats (Ⓣ787/460-8922) run tours through the mangroves for around US$25 per boat (or US$5 per person), or will drop you at the island of your choice for US$30 – tiny **Cayo Caracoles** is the most inviting.

Practicalities

La Parguera has a number of reasonable **places to stay**. *Posada Porlamar*, PR-304 km 3.3 (Ⓣ787/899-4015, Ⓦwww.parguerapuertorico.com; ④) looks like an old wooden warehouse, with plain but adequate rooms right on the water, and an attractive deck jutting over the bay. A stone's throw away *Parador Villa Parguera* (Ⓣ787/899-7777, Ⓦwww.villaparguera.net; ④) has comfortable units with private balconies and lovely views, as well as a pool, a good restaurant and cabaret acts on Saturday. There is also a selection of cheap guesthouses, one of the best being *Gladys Guest House*, c/ 2 no. 42B (just off PR-304; Ⓣ787/899-4678; ③).

The cheapest **food** in the village is by the pier where vendors grill a variety of fresh fish for less than US$4; you'll find plenty of stalls here at weekends, but less choice during the week. On the main drag just above, in addition to the *parador* (see above) there is plenty of good, inexpensive grub. *El Karacol* is best known for its zesty *sangría marca coño* (US$5), but also offers a range of cheap fresh seafood and *mofongo*. For high-quality dining, try *Agua Azul* (opposite the main car park, Ⓣ787/899-7777), which knocks out contemporary *criollo* dishes and exceptional lobster (from US$25). Dinner only.

Guánica and around

Home to the **Bosque Estatal de Guánica**, the world's best example of subtropical dry forest, the diverse and wild landscape around **Guánica** is dotted with blanched trees curling like arthritic old bones and suggestively-shaped cacti called *dildos*. The reserve stretches to the water's edge, where you'll find some splendid beaches and mangrove swamps whose groping roots ensnare everything in their way. There's not much to the dusty town of Guánica itself, but nearby hotels are ideal for exploring the southwest, with lots to see within a thirty-minute drive.

Bosque Estatal de Guánica

Scientists surmise that a mere one percent of the world's subtropical dry forest remains; almost 10,000 acres of it survive in the **Bosque Estatal de Guánica**, or Guánica State Forest (daily 8am–5pm; free; Ⓣ787/724-3724), a UN Biosphere Reserve just east of town that accommodates some 700 plant species and over 100 types of bird. It has the best **birdwatching** in Puerto Rico and boasts several rare species, including the Puerto Rican emerald-breasted hummingbird, the yellow-shouldered blackbird and (rarest of all) the endangered **Puerto Rican nightjar**. Easier to see (or hear) are bullfinches, the Puerto Rican woodpecker, the lizard cuckoo and crested toads.

The reserve also includes a half-dozen beaches on the mainland and a number of offshore islets, including the gorgeous mangrove cay of **Guilligan's Island** (Tues–Sun; take the frequent ferry from the *San Jacinto Restaurant*, see below; US$6.42 with tax). You can **hike** through the forest on twelve unchallenging trails – some very short, although they can be hot and buggy, so bring plenty of water, sunscreen and insect repellent. The hikes mostly depart from the **ranger station** (daily 8.30am–4.30pm) at the end of PR-334, where you can get very basic trail maps. In a couple of hours you can walk down to the beautiful and isolated **Tamarindo beach** and back, most directly via the Ballena trail (2km) which passes a thousand-year-old lignum vitae

▲ Kayaking amongst the mangroves, Guilligan's Island

tree. You can also drive to Tamarindo and nearby **Balneario de Caña Gorda** on PR-333, and from the roadhead follow the coast along the Meseta trail (3.5km) into the driest part of the forest, studded with cacti.

Practicalities

Conveniently located approximately midway between Ponce and San Germán, Guánica has a better selection of **accommodation** than either of its neighbours. In fact, *Mary Lee's by the Sea*, PR-333 Km 6.7 (Ⓣ787/821-3600, Ⓦwww.maryleesbythesea.com; ⑤) is one of Puerto Rico's most enchanting places to stay. Overlooking the coast and mangroves, with kayaks and motorboats to take guests to beaches or nearby cays, it has ten cheerful, sprawling apartments with a whimsical, tropical feel, some with sea views. Nearby, the posh, all-inclusive *Copamarina Beach Resort*, PR-333 Km 6.5 (Ⓣ787/821-0505, Ⓦwww.copamarina.com; ⑥), has a narrow beach, two pools, beachside bar, tennis courts, spa, gym, Internet access and two excellent restaurants (see below) – they also run diving trips to La Pared.

For something **to eat**, try *San Jacinto Restaurant*, PR-333 Km 6.6 (Ⓣ787/821-4941), a lively locals' favourite by the Guilligan's Island ferry dock, serving *criollo* staples, many with fresh fish and seafood, for around US$12–25. For something a bit more upscale, *Alexandra* at the *Copamarina Beach Resort* is well worth the price for its grilled fish and meat dishes with inventive tropical marinades and sauces. *Copamarina*'s runs the casual *Las Palmas Café*, open 7am to 9.30pm, where *criollo* staples, burgers and sandwiches will cost you less than US$18.

7.4

Ponce

PONCE, Puerto Rico's second city, is best known for its art museum and handsome centre – a pristine example of nineteenth-century *criollo* architecture. The city is liveliest during **Carnaval** (February) when the streets fill with parades of musicians, floats, dancers and *vejigantes* – revellers in devilish-looking painted masks. Things also heat up in November during the **Fiesta Nacional de Bomba y Plena**, when drummers and dancers gather to compete. In between festivals, a number of interesting sights are on the outskirts of town, including the **Centro Ceremonial Indígena de Tibes** and **Hacienda Buena Vista**.

Ponce's heyday was in the late nineteenth century, underpinned by riches generated from its surrounding sugar and coffee plantations, but the good times did not last. Nowadays if you arrive from San Juan, you will need to downshift a gear or two to adjust to its sleepier pace of life. Note that on Mondays and Tuesdays many of Ponce's cultural and historical institutions are closed.

Some history

Known as La Perla del Sur ("the pearl of the south"), the settlement of Ponce was recognized by the Spanish in 1692, and named after **Ponce de León y Loíza**, the great-grandson of Juan Ponce de León. It developed into an important cultural and commercial centre. In 1831 it was designated an official trade port, but only for Spanish ships.

Contraband flourished for the better part of the nineteenth century, as did the **arts** under the auspices of the Serrallés family, the makers of Don Q rum. The family commissioned European architects to construct mansions downtown, and imported European paintings, music and books. The city became known as a haven for liberal ideas, safe from San Juan's allegiance to Spain, and eventually became a breeding ground for the **nationalist movement**. As a means of throwing off Spanish sovereignty, the city was glad to surrender to American troops in 1898, but soon regretted the choice after the island was handed to the US at the end of the Spanish-American War. Nationalism remained a potent force: in 1937, seventeen people were shot and killed by police at a demonstration, a tragic event known as the **Ponce Massacre** (see p.386). After World War II, Operation Bootstrap focused development on the north coast and the southern agrarian economy collapsed. Things have improved somewhat in recent years, and since 1992 the government has spent over US$400m for the restoration of the historic centre, leaving Ponce today fresh-faced and a pleasure to wander around.

Arrival, information and getting around

Ponce is a 90-minute drive from San Juan via PR-52. Alternatively, Cape Air makes four to five daily flights (25min) from San Juan into **Mercedita Airport** (☎787/842-6292), located 6km east of central Ponce on PR-5506, off PR-1. A taxi ride into the city centre costs US$13 from the airport. **Públicos** leave from and arrive at *la terminal* on c/ Unión, between c/Vives and c/Victoria, three blocks north of Plaza las Delicias in the historic part of town. See the list of *público* lines on p.356.

The **PRTC**'s main Ponce office (☎787/843-0465) is in the Paseo del Sur shopping centre on PR-1 but information is more conveniently available at the **Ponce**

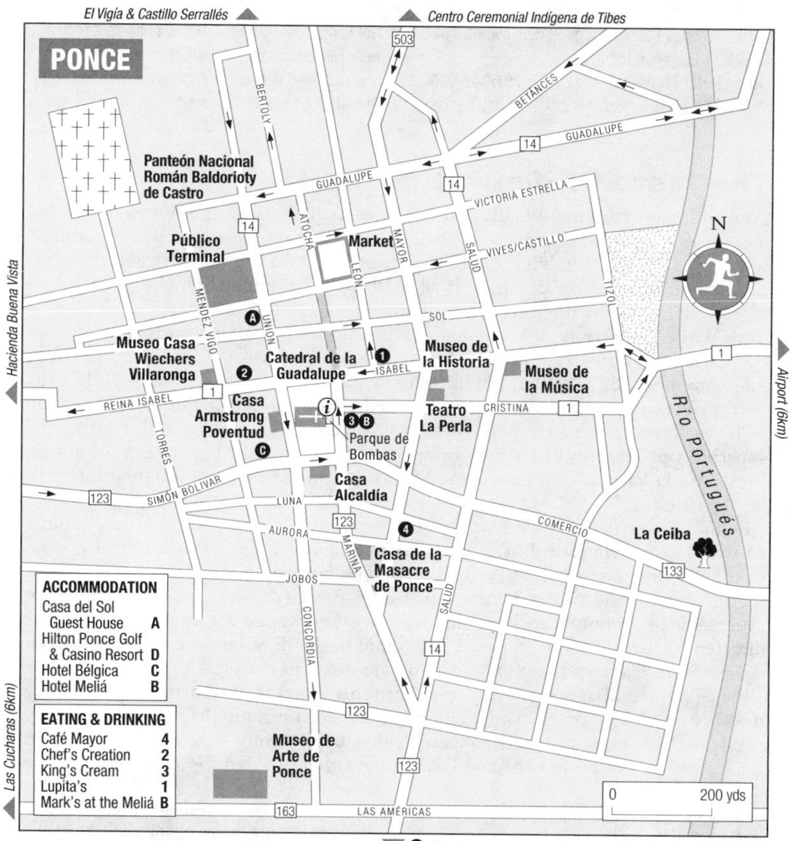

Municipal Tourist Office (daily 9am–5pm; ⓣ787/284-3338, ⓦwww.visitponce.com), located in the Parque de Bombas building on Plaza las Delicias. The office sells a tour package of the city for US$2, including a ride on a **trolley bus**, taking in all the main sights, and a guided walking tour which takes one hour.

Ponce has several **taxi** companies, the most reliable of which is Ponce Taxi (ⓣ787/842-3370). Otherwise, you can easily walk around the city.

Accommodation

The old **hotels** in downtown Ponce have more character than the chains on the outskirts, though as a base for exploring the southwest, you may want to consider staying in Guánica or La Parguera, both within half an hour's drive of Ponce.

Casa del Sol Guest House c/Unión 97 ⓣ787/812-2995, ⓦwww.casadelsolpr.com. This cosy hotel has nine very plain but comfortable rooms with bathroom and TV. Relax or read in the shady patio, or soak in the bubbling hot tub. ❷

Hilton Ponce Golf & Casino Resort Avda Caribe 1150 ⓣ787/259-7676, ⓦwww.hiltoncaribbean.com/ponce. Expensive, glittery compound outside of town, facing a small, rocky Caribbean beach, with two restaurants, three bars, a pool, tennis courts, golf course, fitness area, spa and full business centre. ❻

Hotel Bélgica c/Villa 122 ⓣ787/844-3255, ⓦwww.hotelbelgica.com. Established in 1872, this fusty gem occupies a restored Neoclassical building with heaps of charm, and though it's fairly basic, the price makes it a good deal overall. Ask for a high-ceilinged room. ②

Hotel Meliá c/Cristina 75 ⓣ787/842-0260, ⓦwww.hotelmeliapr.com. Best hotel in central Ponce, dating from 1915, with elegant rooms tastefully decorated with smart new bathrooms and equipped with cable TV, free Internet and Wi-Fi. Breakfast on the rooftop sundeck is included. ④

The historic district

Ponce is an enchanting old city, with much of its allure coming from its fine architecture; its traditional clapboard *criollo* houses, flamboyant Neoclassical mansions and several Art Deco gems offer a complete contrast to the eighteenth-century streets of Old San Juan. At the centre of it all is **Plaza las Delicias** which is punctuated with lively fountains (the illuminated Fountain of Lions came from the 1939 New York World's Fair) and 100-year-old Indian laurel topiary. The space is divided by the **Catedral Nuestra Señora de la Guadalupe** (Mon–Fri 6am–2pm, Sat & Sun 6am–noon & 3–8.30pm), which began life as a rustic chapel in 1670 but the current French-inspired Neoclassical cathedral was rebuilt in the 1920s after the 1918 earthquake. Nuestra Señora de la Guadalupe, the earliest and most sacred apparition of Mary in the New World, is the patron saint of Ponce, and the annual **Fiesta de la Virgen de Guadalupe** (Dec 12) is one of the most important festivals on the island.

Behind the cathedral is Ponce's signature red-and-black striped, Moorish-inspired **Museo Parque de Bombas**, a museum of antique fire fighting equipment housed in the old firehouse (daily 9am–5pm; free). The building is the real attraction, built for the 1882 trade fair and then donated to the city's very active fire company, eventually becoming a social gathering place and venue for the firemen's band, directed by Juan Morel Campos. A key figure in the development of Puerto Rican *danza* music, Campos is commemorated by a statue in the plaza.

Ponce's tranquil old cemetery, the **Panteón Nacional Román Baldorioty de Castro** (Tues–Sun 8.30am–5pm; free), has been beautifully restored, its neatly manicured gardens and ruins containing the stately tombs of abolitionist Román Baldorioty de Castro and Manuel Tavarez, the father of Puerto Rican *danza*, among

The Ponce Massacre

The early twentieth century was a rough time for Ponce. Profits stalled, hurricanes destroyed coffee production, the price of sugar bottomed out and the US favoured San Juan for development over its uppity nationalist rival to the south. By the time the Great Depression took hold, Ponce had had it. Revolution fomented more fervently than ever, leading to one of the US's most egregious injustices towards the territory of Puerto Rico: the **Ponce Massacre**.

Along with the influx of European art and culture in Ponce had come a substantial number of students and intellectuals. On March 21, 1937, a group of Puerto Rican nationalists gathered outside what is now the museum commemorating this event, to stage a march celebrating the abolition of slavery and protest against the imprisonment of their leader, **Pedro Albizu Campos**. They had permission, but their North American governor, General Blanton Winship, revoked it at the last minute. Nevertheless, about 100 unarmed men and women turned up and found themselves face to face with a multitude of heavily armed police officers. When the marchers began to sing the national anthem, *La Borinqueña*, a shot rang out, culminating in a blaze of gunfire that lasted fifteen minutes. Five nationalists, twelve bystanders and two policemen died; around 200 more civilians were wounded. The police blamed the protesters, who were tried – and found innocent. A subsequent investigation by eminent Puerto Ricans on behalf of the American Civil Liberties Union corroborated the protesters' innocence.

others.. The cemetery can be reached by a fifteen-minute walk northwest of the plaza at the top of c/ Torre.

The museums

Save some time for Ponce's excellent museums, all of which are housed in noteworthy buildings. Next to the hulking Neoclassical **Teatro La Perla** is the **Museo de la Historia** (Tues–Sun 9am–5pm; free; ⓣ787/844-7071), c/ Isabel 53, which provides a useful introduction to the city's 300-year history – ask for an English-speaking guide (free), as there are no English descriptions. A block further down c/ Isabel is the **Museo de la Música** (Wed–Sun 8.30am–4.30pm; free; ⓣ787/848-7016), in the elegant townhouse that once belonged to the Serallés family. It gives an interesting overview of Puerto Rican music and has a thorough display of the instruments used; *ponceños* are rightly proud of their musical tradition, and claim that *plena* (see box, p.374) was invented in the city. The **Casa de la Masacre de Ponce** (Wed–Sun 8am–4.30pm; free; ⓣ787/844-9722), at the corner of calles Marina and Aurora, commemorates this infamous episode (see box opposite), which took place right outside the museum, and also examines the history of the Puerto Rican independence movement.

Outside the historic district

A few sights outside Ponce's historic district warrant a visit – in particular, the **Museo de Arte**, just south of the centre at 2325 Avenida Las Américas (daily 10am–5pm; US$5, children US$2.50, students US$1.25; ⓣ787/848-0505, ⓦwww.museoarteponce.org), considered the best art museum in the Caribbean. With over three thousand works, the collection is strongest on the British Pre-Raphaelites, with important paintings by Frederic Leighton (don't miss *Flaming June*) and Burne-Jones. Look out for works by Van Dyck, El Greco, Velázquez, Rubens, Goya and Delacroix, as well as Puerto Rico's two most esteemed masters, José Campeche and Francisco Oller.

Just northwest of town, sharing a hill with the 100-foot-tall, 70-foot-wide cross of **El Vigía**, is the **Museo Castillo Serrallés** (Tues–Thurs 9am–5pm, Fri–Sun 9am–5.30pm; US$6, US$2 gardens only; ⓣ787/259-1774). This lavish 14,000-square-foot, Spanish Revival mansion was built in 1930, on the eve of the Great Depression. Home to the Serallés family, whose riches stemmed from their rum empire (and later, the Don Q brand), the mansion has a commanding view over Ponce and is now worth around US$35 million. It was passed from one family member to another until 1986 when it became too impractical to keep up and was sold to the city. Many of the family's eccentric period possessions lie around the house, including cutting-edge technology of the early twentieth century, bizarre grooming equipment and eerie-looking dolls. The house can only be visited on guided tours (1hr) that usually run every 30–45 minutes, but call in advance to confirm.

About 3km north of Ponce, at Km 2.2 on PR-503, the **Centro Ceremonial Indígena de Tibes** (Tues–Sun 9am–noon & 1–4pm; US$3; ⓣ787/840-2255) is an ancient burial ground discovered thanks to 1975's Hurricane Eloise. The storm exposed 187 graves, some dating from 300 AD, making it the oldest burial ground in the Caribbean. The centre also features Pre-Taíno *bateyes* (courts used for ceremonial ball games), a star-shaped stone formation indicating the precise location of sunrise and sunset during the solstice and equinox, and an enlightening museum. Note that on arrival you will be assigned an English-speaking guide. Tours are free and last up to 1hr.

At the painstakingly restored **Hacienda Buena Vista** (Wed–Sun by reservation only; US$7; ⓣ787/722-5882), about 16km north of town, at Km 16.8 on PR-123, you can get a glimpse of what life was like on a nineteenth-century coffee plantation. Slaves worked to grow coffee, cacao, plantains, pineapple, yams and corn, although the hacienda was one of the first on the island to use industrial machinery, such as the corn mill, cotton gin and coffee depulper.

Eating and drinking

Eating options in central Ponce are surprisingly poor, limited to local cafeterias, a handful of upmarket restaurants and fast food on the plaza. *Ponceños* spend more time zipping around the outskirts in search of good meals, particularly along the section of PR-2 known as **Las Cucharas**, 6.5km west of the city, or at **La Guancha**, the boardwalk near the port to the south. As for **drinking**, there's also a surprising shortage of enticing places; try c/ Isabel, or La Guancha at the weekends.

Café Mayor c/Aurora 2638 (on the corner of c/Mayor). This charming colonial house serves fresh juices indoors or in the leafy garden, as well as the best Puerto Rican coffee on the island, roasted on site. They also do sandwiches and local food (from US$4). Reverts to cosy bar at night.

Chef's Creation c/Reina 100. This crowd-pulling lunch-only cafeteria is the best place to gorge on cheap (US$5-6), no-frills local food; pick up a tray, select what you want and grab a table indoors or in the back patio.

King's Cream c/Marina 9223, on Plaza las Delicias. Delicious ice creams with unusual tropical flavours such as tamarind.

Lupita's c/Isabel 60 ⓣ787/848-8808. This former Mexican restaurant will start cooking again once they find a chef, but it's best for drinks anyway, with expertly mixed margaritas and genial bar staff.

Mark's at the Meliá *Hotel Meliá*, c/Cristina 75 ⓣ787/284-6275. Most upmarket restaurant downtown, with acclaimed chef Mark French preparing inventive variations on *criollo* staples, like creamy swordfish carbonara *or* corn-crusted red snapper with yucca purée. Entrees US$18–28.

7.5

La Ruta Panorámica

The often wild and sparsely populated interior of Puerto Rico is dominated by the Cordillera Central, which runs like a mountainous rudder, east to west, along the length of the island. The sights are best explored along the heartstopping **Ruta Panorámica**, a 266km assemblage of about forty roads, renowned for its dazzling natural beauty and for its unpredictable twists through mist-shrouded peaks, sheer canyons and impenetrable forests.

In the mountains, the temperature is much cooler, the air heavy and wet, and the vegetation lush and jungle-like. You'll hear roosters and thousands of chirping *coquís*; see houses built on stilts and towns wrapped in fog; and pass through coffee plantations clinging to abrupt hillsides, shaded with banana trees. At various points along the route, you'll catch glimpses of both the Atlantic and the Caribbean, with impressively open views of the island's coastline.

It matters little whether you start in the east at **Maunabo**, or in the west at **Mayagüez**. But to do the entire length – without stopping – would take a full and very exhausting day, so plan on at least two days and take your time on the sometimes hair-raising roads. Unless otherwise indicated, all the stops described below lie directly on the route; follow the brown "Ruta" signs carefully, and be aware that the road numbers change constantly.

Maunabo to Bosque Estatal de Carite

Going from east to west, the first major attraction is the 6600-acre **Bosque Estatal de Carite**, less than an hour south of San Juan, where you can hike, camp, fish, bird-watch, swim and escape the heat. The best spot is **Charco Azul** (daily 9am–5pm), a pretty pond and campsite surrounded by lush forest at the end of the Charco Azul Trail, 500m from the road and a short 1km detour south of the *ruta* at PR-184 Km 16.6. The tiny ranger station (maps available; Mon–Fri 7am–3.30pm; ⓣ787/747-4545) and second campsite are within the **Area Recreativa Guavate** (Mon–Fri 9am–4.30pm, Sat & Sun 8am–5pm) further along the route at PR-184 Km 27.3, a series of shady picnic areas ending abruptly at Guavate's celebrated *lechoneras*, just outside the forest. These roadside restaurants specialize in *lechón*, juicy roast suckling pig cooked on an outdoor spit. *Lechón* is charged by weight (about US$7–8 a pound) – the best place is *Lechonera El Rancho Original* (daily 9am–5pm). *Sanjuaneros* come in droves at the weekend, when boisterous *salsa* dancing fills the outdoor seating area.

Cañón de San Cristóbal and Barranquitas

From the forest the route continues west some 40km to the town of Aibonito and the **Cañón de San Cristóbal**, a stunning, 500-foot-deep volcanic gorge that stretches for 9km and is home to Puerto Rico's highest **waterfall** and the Río Usabón. The ravine offers some of the island's best **hiking** opportunities, although the path to it is not easy to find – ask locally for directions – and the slopes are extremely steep and can be dangerous in wet weather.

For those confident enough to go it alone, take the turn off at PR-725 km 5.1 (on the right side coming from Aibonito), downhill to the blue building on the corner; the trail leads down from here but before you start, ask the person that lives in the house if it's OK to leave your car (and trespass on his land). The path descends abruptly for some 15 minutes until you are confronted with the strikingly beautiful **Neblina waterfall**, whose pool makes for wonderful bathing. You can **hike** some way downstream; you will have to clamber down the left-hand side of a second smaller waterfall to reach the third, which is not passable. Allow about three hours there and back. Less experienced walkers can visit the **Vivero Árboles Más Árboles** (Mon–Fri 1–3.45pm; free; ⓣ787/857-3511) outside Barranquitas on PR-156 in the local Conservation Trust Office. From PR-156, heading towards Comerío, take a right turn at around Km 17.7 (c/ B), follow this street to the end, turn left along c/ A and keep going to where the road narrows (the office is on the right). You'll find plenty of information on the canyon, and staff can direct you to the best viewing point nearby. Alternatively, arrange a **guided tour** in advance with experienced local Samuel Ortiz (ⓣ787/857-2094, ⓦviajes.barranquitaspr.org). Prices range US$60-100.

Nearby on PR-162 and nestled into the hills is the charming little town of **Barranquitas**, best known as the 1859 birthplace of **Luis Muñoz Rivera**, champion of Puerto Rican independence before Spain ceded rule to the US. Rivera is remembered at the **Casa Natal Luis Muñoz Rivera**, c/ Luis Muñoz Rivera 10 (Tues–Sat 8.30–4.20pm; US$2; ⓣ787/857-0230), a museum in the very simple *criollo* home where Rivera was born. Meanwhile, the **Mausoleo Familia Muñoz Rivera**, c/ Padre Berríos 7 (same hours as Casa Natal; free), contains the remains of Rivera and his son, Luis Muñoz Marín, the first elected governor of Puerto Rico and founder of the Popular Democratic Party. Barranquitas makes a convenient place to break the journey for the night, especially if you're planning to see the canyon. Try *Hotel Hacienda Margarita* (ⓣ787/857-4949; ❸) to the north of town off PR-152, at Km 1.7, set in a commanding spot overlooking the valley.

Bosque Estatal de Toro Negro to Maricao

From Barranquitas, head south on PR-162 and west onto PR-143, an uphill drive which will take you into the 7000-acre **Bosque Estatal de Toro Negro**. Continuing for some 16km above 3000ft, this is the most remote and highest stretch of La

▲ Traditional lechón in Guavate

Ruta Panorámica. You'll find a **ranger station** (daily 7am–4pm) at PR-143 Km 32.4 in the Area Recreativa Doña Juana, where you can get sketchy maps indicating the 18km of **treks** available. The most impressive trail takes you on a two-hour circuit up to an observation tower with commanding views over the island. You can **camp** close to the ranger station at Los Viveros (☎787/844-4660; US$4), but you must apply for a permit in advance at the DRNA in San Juan (☎787/724-3724). Further west on PR-143, turn right off the *ruta* onto PR-149 for the Salto de Doña Juana, a pretty **waterfall** thundering down right beside the road.

Back on PR-143, the road passes the highest peak in Puerto Rico, **Cerro de Punta** (4389ft), crowned with a clutch of radio and television towers. To reach the very top, turn right 5km after the turning for PR-577 at a rough parking area, once PR-143 has begun to descend (at around Km 17), and then follow an almost impossibly steep metalled road up until you reach the *mirador* beside the giddying pylons. The views are stunning, with both coasts visible on a clear day.

From where La Ruta Panorámica crosses over fast PR-10, it is just a twenty-minute drive south to central Ponce, an easy option for spending the night.

Continuing west will bring you across some of the most poorly maintained, narrow and windy stretches of the route, although also some of the most beautiful. The final stop is **Maricao**, justly regarded as *La Ciudad del Café*, "coffee town", celebrated with a **coffee harvest festival** in mid-February, but worth a visit any time of year. The town has a compact centre of ramshackle wooden *criollo* houses, a smattering of cheap cafés and shops, and picturesque gorges and streams just on the outskirts. The **Vivero de Peces** (Thurs–Sun 8.30–11.30am & 1–3.30pm; free) is a tranquil fish hatchery, 2km south of town at the end of PR-410, while a wonderfully sequestered spot is Salto Pepe Curet, a small **waterfall** reached by taking PR-105 out of town; turn right onto PR-425, follow for 2km to the end, and the falls are five minutes further on foot.

7.6

Vieques and Culebra

Even if you're staying in Puerto Rico for just a week, it's worthwhile catching a ferry or hopping onto a puddle-jumper to **Vieques** or **Culebra**, the two little-developed islets lying off the eastern coast that are known as the Spanish Virgin Islands. The snorkelling, diving, fishing and swimming are about as good as it gets, while idyllic, often isolated, beaches abound on both islands.

Vieques

Just 12km off the eastern shore of Puerto Rico, 34km-long **Vieques** feels a world away. Despite the construction in 2000 of a five-star resort at Martineau Bay near the airport, the island remains stubbornly low-key and underdeveloped. Many locals still get around on horseback and chickens still stop cars in the road, which beyond the main town, are largely devoid of traffic.

The lack of widespread development on the island is partly due to the occupation of its western and eastern thirds by the US Navy, which used these portions for **bombing practice** from 1941 to 2003. For years this was undoubtedly the most substantive complaint about life under the US flag, provoking widespread protest on the Puerto Rican mainland and even from celebrities and politicians stateside. It took the killing of a local civilian by a stray bomb in 1999 to enact change, and President Bill Clinton started phasing out military training. You can now (safely) explore networks of empty bunkers dotted around the western end of the island. While the island's gorgeous public beaches are perfectly safe, much of the eastern half of Vieques remains off limits, contaminated by toxins and unexploded bombs. Critics assail the ongoing and highly controversial clean-up process, claiming that handing land to the US Fish & Wildlife Service was a ruse to allow superficial cleaning by the US Navy.

Arrival, information and getting around

Flights arrive at the tiny airport, 7.5km west of **Isabel Segunda** (Isabel II) the island's main town. *Públicos* operating like taxis usually meet flights, charging US$3

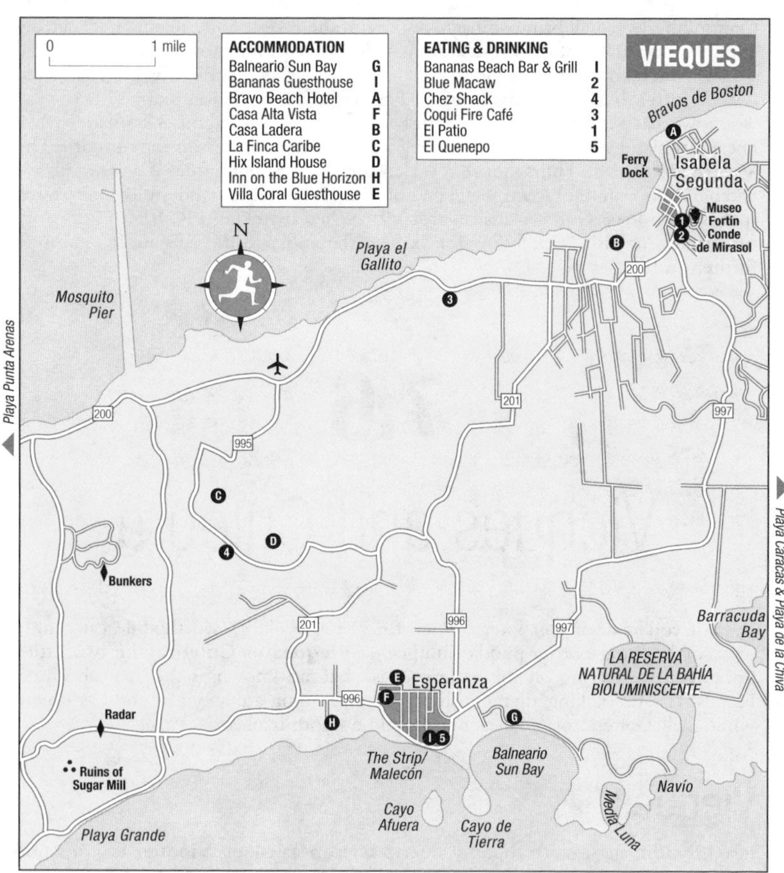

per person into town, or US$5 per person to Esperanza. In Isabel II you'll also find the ferry dock and the island's only **post office**, **ATM** and **tourist office** (daily 8am–4.30pm; ⓣ787/741-0800), on the main plaza.

Only Sun Bay (see opposite) is easily accessible by foot from Esperanza; for the remaining beaches you will need **transport**. *Públicos* generally run from 8am to 6pm, though Ana Luz Robles operates 24 hours (ⓣ787/313-0599). Otherwise, rent a car (try Acevedo's, PR-201 Km 1.3; ⓣ787/741-4380); scooters (Extreme Scooters; ⓣ787/741-8141) are a cheaper and more manoeuvrable alternative. Call La Dulce Vida (ⓣ787/435-3557, ⓦwww.bikevieques.com) for mountain bike rental and tours.

Accommodation

Balneario Sun Bay ⓣ787/741-8198. Fabulous (and legal) camping right on the beach, with outdoor showers, toilets and changing rooms. ❶

Bananas Guesthouse c/Flamboyán 142 ⓣ787/741-8700, ⓦwww.bananasguesthouse.com. Pioneer guesthouse established in the mid-1980s. Twelve rustic, airy rooms have refrigerators and are just off a breezeway that opens onto the jungle. The lively bar makes the front rooms nosier but safer. ❸

Bravo Beach Hotel North Shore Road 1, ⓣ787/741-1128, ⓦwww.bravobeachhotel.com. Smart contemporary styling makes this one of the island's hippest hotels. Overlooking the north coast with no beach but a gorgeous pool, the ten minimalist bleached-white rooms have mahogany beds, Playstations and iPod docks. 6

Casa Alta Vista c/Flamboyán 297 ⓣ787/741-3296, ⓦwww.casaaltavista.net. Homely and well-run, with ground-floor shop and scooters available for hire. Clean rooms have access to a roof terrace. 3

Casa Ladera Playa Monte Santo, PR- 200 ⓣ917/570-7558, ⓦwww.casa-ladera.com. This bright and comfy modern villa is a great deal, especially for families, with three two-bedroom units with kitchens, washing machines, large pool, DVD players and onsite car rental. Four night minimum. 6

La Finca Caribe PR-995 Km 2.2 ⓣ787/741-0495, ⓦwww.lafinca.com. Rustic, eco-sensitive lodging in a pretty hillside setting, offering run-down but charming and spacious cottages with hammocks everywhere, open-air showers and tropical vegetation. The main house, also for rent, sleeps 6–20. 3

Hix Island House PR-995 Km 1.6 ⓣ787/741-2302, ⓦwww.hixislandhouse.com. This is the most original hotel in Puerto Rico: 13 modernist, open-plan studios with one side completely open to the forest, replete with kitchenette, outdoor shower, and contemporary art. 6

Inn on the Blue Horizon PR-996 Km 4.2 ⓣ787/741-3318, ⓦwww.innonthebluehorizon.com. Vieques' most romantic hotel, an elegant Mediterranean-style mansion overlooking the sea. Colonial-style rooms embellished with four-poster beds, art and antiques. Very exclusive and extremely quiet, with no phones or TVs (and no a/c). 6

Villa Coral Guesthouse c/Gladiola 485 ⓣ787/741-1967, ⓦwww.villacoralguesthouse.com. One of the best bargains on the island, this new upmarket guesthouse has six compact but plush rooms equipped with mini-fridge, ceiling fans and stylish bathrooms. 3

Around the island

Isabel II is primarily a commercial centre, with a decent selection of hotels and restaurants but not much to see. The most engaging sight is the **Museo Fortín Conde de Mirasol** (Wed–Sun 8.30am–4.20pm; US$3), the old Spanish fortress and now an absorbing history museum with fine views across the town and ocean beyond.

Just a fifteen minutes' drive south from the capital, the village of **Esperanza** is far more inviting, and its cheerful *malecón* (c/ Flamboyán, or just "the strip") is a haven for independent travellers with a picturesque assemblage of restaurants and guesthouses. Without question, the beaches on this side of the island are superior (the Atlantic beaches tend to be rougher) and the landscape more attractive.

Heading east from town are Vieques' three most popular beaches. A ten-minute walk around the headland at the eastern end of the Esperanza beachfront will take you to the **Balneario Sun Bay** (daily 8.30am–5pm; parking US$3) a 3km crescent of bone-coloured sand lined with trees where wild horses graze. The beach can be busy at weekends, but on weekdays or in the off season, it's easy to feel as though you have it entirely to yourself.

East along the dirt road from Sun Bay is **Playa Media Luna**, a tidy, half-moon cove with powdery white sand. The beach is backed by sea grapes and almond trees, its waters incomparably calm and warm. Further on, **Playa Navío** is another attractive stretch, and the most popular with locals, enclosed by rock walls with stark white sands and impossibly translucent turquoise waters. The island has a number of other lovely beaches worth exploring – the more difficult it is to get to a beach, the more likely it will be quieter, if not empty. Many have English names based on colours, a legacy of when the navy used them for assault practice. On PR-977 halfway from Esperanza to Isabel II, turn right into the **Vieques National Wildlife Refuge** (daily 6am–6pm), through which you can access **Playa Caracas** (or Red Beach) and **Playa de la Chiva** (Blue Beach), among others; while on the far western tip of the island is **Playa Punta Arenas** (Green Beach), its offshore reef perfect for **snorkelling** and its narrow stretch of sand staring directly across the water to El Yunque.

The south side of **Cayo Afuera** offshore from the Esperanza beachfront also offers magical snorkelling and is easy to reach; Blue Caribe Kayaks (ⓣ787/741-2522), at c/ Flamboyán 149, rents kayaks for US$10/hr or US$55/day – perfect for exploring the coast.

La Reserva Natural de la Bahía Bioluminiscente

One of the highlights of any visit to Puerto Rico is a night-time trip to **La Reserva Natural de la Bahía Bioluminiscente** at Puerto Mosquito (or just "bio bay"), said to contain the highest degree of bioluminescence in the world. This shallow-water mangrove lagoon shelters trillions of microscopic dinoflagellates, which light up in self-defence when disturbed. A kayak trip is well worth it for a more immediate experience – use Blue Caribe Kayaks (see above). Otherwise, conservation-minded Island Adventures (Ⓣ787/741-0720, Ⓦwww.biobay.com; US$30) is the best tour operator, and has a useful **moon calendar** on its website – it's crucial to avoid full moon cycles, when it's impossible to appreciate the effect. Their electric boat glides across the bay leaving glittery contrails, with fish darting past like shooting stars, and stops mid-bay to let passengers take a dip. Wear a swimsuit under your clothes, and bring goggles.

Eating, drinking and nightlife

Bananas Beach Bar & Grill c/Flamboyán 142 Ⓣ787/741-8700. Tasty burgers, chicken wings and other bar grub are on offer at this lively, sometimes raucous, inexpensive open-air bar.

Blue Macaw c/Antonio G Mellado 358 Ⓣ787/741-1147. While this long-time favourite moved into Isabel II from the *Inn on the Blue Horizon* in 2007, owners Rick Gallup and Honor Stanley remain committed to the same high-quality Caribbean fusion cuisine. Entrees US$18–28.

Chez Shack PR-995 km 1.8 Ⓣ787/741-2175. The most alternative place to eat on Vieques, a ramshackle wooden house with an open terrace 10km northwest of Esperanza, surrounded by lush, tropical forest and featuring slabs for barbecued pork, ribs and signature crab cakes. Entrees from US$20.

Coqui Fire Café *Enchanted Garden Inn*, PR-200 km 2.6, Ⓣ787/435-1411. This homely restaurant is run by the makers of Coqui Fire Hot Sauce, offering Mexican breakfasts (Mon, Tues, Thurs & Fri) and sumptuous Mexican dinners on Tues and Thurs nights 5–9pm, from US$8.

El Patio c/Antonio G Mellado 340, Ⓣ787/741-6381. Cheap, no frills *criollo* food, cooked up in a busy diner with exposed brick walls, TV blaring all day and a small veranda. Local workers swarm here for breakfast (US$3-6) and lunch (US$5-20).

El Quenepo c/Flamboyán 148, Ⓣ787/741-1215. Most stylish bistro on the strip, with a tantalizing menu inspired by local, Caribbean and Asian cuisine: Thai-style snapper, pineapple-guava pork ribs and tuna with noodles in a shellfish broth. Mains from US$20.

Culebra

Effectively occupied by the US Navy until 1975, **CULEBRA** is an incredibly raw Caribbean island that, like Vieques, has resisted high-impact tourism and shrugged off attempts at large-scale development. There are no casinos, tour buses, mega resorts or traffic lights, crime is virtually unknown, and the **beaches** are simply staggering – Playa Flamenco is consistently voted one of the world's most entrancing stretches of sand, while the turtle-rich sapphire waters and shallow reefs offshore make **diving** and **snorkelling** a real treat.

Although Culebra's population is little more than two thousand, at times parts of the island can get uncomfortably busy, especially in July when an influx of Puerto Rican day-trippers arrive. For now it's still easy to avoid the crowds – but be sure to pack plenty of bug spray, as the flies and mosquitoes are voracious.

Arrival, information and getting around

Culebra is 14km northeast of Vieques, and 27km east of Fajardo. The main settlement is **Dewey**, known locally as *Pueblo*, a typically laid-back island village, the torpor punctured only by the arrival of the Fajardo **ferry** at one end of c/ Pedro Márquez, Dewey's main street. This is home to a post office, the **tourist information office** (Mon–Fri 7am–4.30pm; ⓣ787/742-3521) and Banco Popular, which has an ATM. Pick up a copy of the island newspaper, *Culebra Calendar* (ⓦwww.theculebracalendaronline.com), published monthly by Jim Petersen (who also rents kayaks). The minuscule **airport** is just north of Dewey, right by the main roads that run across the island.

Públicos will run you to beaches (US$2-5) and pick you up at a specified time – try Willy's (ⓣ787/742-3537). If need be, you can rent four-wheel-drive vehicles, but book ahead (U$45-60/day). Carlos Jeep Rental (ⓣ787/742-3514, ⓦwww.carlosjeeprental.com) has a desk at the airport. Otherwise, **bikes** may well be the way to go, available for US$20 a day from Culebra Bike Rental (ⓣ787/435-1779). To get to the outer cays, rent a **kayak** from your guesthouse, or get dropped off and collected later with Culebra Water Taxi (ⓣ787/360-9807, ⓔculebraoceanview@yahoo.com) or try the fun Tanamá Glass Bottom Boat (ⓣ787/501-0011) for around US$45.

Accommodation

Casa Robinson La Romana, off PR-250; ⓣ787/742-0497, ⓦwww.casarobinson.com. Modern, super comfortable three-storey house on a fabulous hill top perch. Immaculate rooms come with kitchenette and satellite TV. ④

Club Seabourne c/Fulladoza km 1.5 ⓣ787/742-3169, ⓦwww.clubseabourne.com. Culebra's first luxury hotel and the one with the most character. The Spanish plantation-style rooms overlook the bay and don't have phones or TVs; some rooms are showing their age. ⑤

Flamenco Beach Campsite ⓣ787/742-0700. Truly magical location right on the beach but avoid July, weekends and holidays, when the place gets mobbed and a party scene ensues. ①

Mamacita's c/Castelar 64-66, Dewey ⓣ787/742-0090. Handful of modest apartments and rooms above one of Dewey's most popular restaurants and bars, all with satellite TV. Try and get the top floor, which has the best view. ④

Palmetto Guesthouse c/Manuel Vasquez 128 (behind Carlos Jeep Rental), ⓣ787/742-0257, ⓦwww.palmettoculebra.com. This cosy inn has been fully renovated, and the compact but spotless rooms have fridge and brand new bathrooms. You get the use of two shared kitchens, free bikes, boogie boards, beach towels, chairs and coolers. ④

Villa Boheme c/Fulladoza 368 ⓣ787/742-3508, ⓦwww.villaboheme.com. Modern and cheery place on the waterfront, with eleven spacious, bright rooms; three have kitchens (others have access to a shared kitchen). The second-floor rooms have balconies, and the sun deck offers stellar views. ④

Villa Flamenco Beach ⓣ787/742-0023, ⓔesmer@coqui.net. These six units just off the beach, all with kitchenettes, are much nicer than nearby *Culebra Beach Villas*. The four studios upstairs accommodate two people each. Note the one-week minimum Dec 15–May 30 and closure Sept 3–Oct 31. ⑤

Around the island

For most visitors, **Playa Flamenco**, 3km north of Dewey, is the highlight of Culebra. The beach is a brilliant white crescent of sand as fine as baking flour, lapped by glittering turquoise and azure waters. Deserted during the week, it gets much busier at weekends thanks to the justly popular campsite and basic facilities (showers, snack stalls) on site.

A twenty-minute scenic hike over the hill from the entrance to Playa Flamenco (or a water taxi from Dewey) will take you to lovely **Playa Tamarindo** and **Playa Carlos Rosario**, which provide easy access to the **Reserva Natural Canal de Luis Peña**, a marine reserve of precious coral ideal for snorkelling.

Right at the end of bumpy PR-250, way over on the eastern side of the island, **Playa Soní** (or "Zoni") is another spectacular beach that stretches over 2km. It's a favourite nesting site for seven-foot-long leatherback turtles (which can weigh up to 1400 pounds), with nests roped off with yellow tape and the beach closed after dark

February to September. Between March and April, extra hands are needed to help out with **leatherback turtle breeding**, an extraordinary experience to behold. For more information or to sign up as a volunteer, call CORALations at ⓣ787/556-6234 (ⓦwww.coralations.org).

President Theodore Roosevelt created the first wildlife reserve on Culebra in 1909, but the modern **Culebra National Wildlife Refuge** was established in 1976. Covering 25 percent of the archipelago, its 1510 acres are overseen by the US Fish and Wildlife Service, the domain of endangered sea turtles and some 50,000 sea birds, including terns, boobies, white-tailed and red-billed tropic birds, and laughing gulls. Much of the reserve is off limits; find out which areas are open at the **visitor center** (Mon–Fri 7.30am–4.30pm; ⓣ787/742-0115), signposted off PR-250 at Km 4.2, on the north side of Ensenada Honda.

Of the offshore cays, **Isla Culebrita** is best-known for underwater wildlife, as well as its jaw-dropping beaches and ruined lighthouse, built in 1886 – take a water-taxi or kayak. Much of Culebra is fringed with pristine coral reef, where calm and clear waters provide excellent visibility for the barracuda, stingray, blue tang, brain corals, lavender sea fans, trumpet fish, parrot fish and hawksbill turtles that lurk around the island. Culebra Divers (ⓣ787/742-0803 ⓦwww.culebradivers.com), just across from the ferry terminal in Dewey, can take you for some of the best **diving** (US$65 one tank, $90 two tanks) and **snorkelling** (US$50) in the Caribbean. Try also Aquatic Adventures (ⓣ787/742-0605; ⓦwww.culebradiving.com).

Eating, drinking and nightlife

Club Seabourne c/Fulladoza Km 1.5 ⓣ787/742-3169, ⓦwww.clubseabourne.com. Caribbean gourmet cuisine keeps discerning *sanjuaneros* happy at this posh hotel restaurant overlooking the bay. Aim to spend at least US$50 per head.

El Batey PR-250 Km 1.1 (c/Escudero, towards the airport), ⓣ787/742-3828. Best burgers and cheeseburgers (US$3-5) on the island. In the evenings it becomes a friendly bar, especially worth visiting Sat night for *salsa* and serious local *Boricua* vibe.

Dinghy Dock c/Fulladoza, just across the drawbridge, ⓣ787/742-0233. Overlooking the bay, gourmet breakfasts – smoked salmon, eggs benedict, etc – and grilled foods for dinner, costing US$14–20. Lively bar.

Juanita Bananas Barrio Melones 1, ⓣ787/742-3171 ⓦwww.juanitabananas.com. Innovative island cuisine in lush gardens above Playa Melones, just outside town (follow the yellow arrows). Sensational dishes such as citrus-marinated salmon and citrus snapper cakes. Entrees $22-32.

Mamacita's Bar & Grill c/Castelar 66, Dewey ⓣ787/742-0090. Waterside dining under a tin-roof gazebo, where you can enjoy *criollo* food, burgers and burritos, accompanied by calypso and reggae music. The bar is justly acclaimed for its frozen cocktails and live conga drummers on Sat.

8

The Virgin Islands

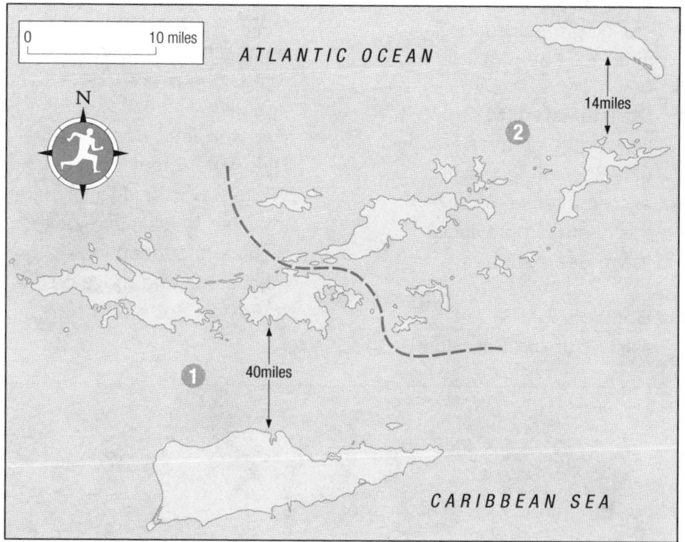

The Virgin Islands highlights

* **Magens Bay Beach, St Thomas** This half-mile-long stretch of powder on St Thomas is consistently voted one of the best beaches in the world. See p.412

* **Virgin Islands National Park, St John** Over 12,000 acres divided between pristine land for hiking and stunning beaches for sunning. See p.420

* **Christiansted, St Croix** Savour the great variety of history, shopping and excellent restaurants in this charming provincial town. See p.426

* **Bomba's Full-Moon Party, Tortola** Decadent bash presided over by the self-proclaimed King of Tortola. See p.441

* **Wreck of the RMS Rhone** View the haunting remains of the *Rhone* at the bottom of Sir Francis Drake Channel. See p.443

* **The Baths, Virgin Gorda** Scramble through the grottoes, caves and pools created by outsize volcanic rocks. See p.447

* **Bar Hopping, Jost Van Dyke** The *Soggy Dollar* in White Bay is said to have invented Painkillers – delicious rum concoctions – have one and move on to *Foxy's*. See p.451

▲ Wreck of the RMS Rhone

Introduction and basics

World-famous beaches or secret stretches of glowing sand, lush green mountain peaks or colonial port towns, a castaway's complete seclusion or the revelry of an all night party – whatever your fancy, the **Virgin Islands** have a bit of something to satisfy it. Made up of over one hundred islands, cays, islets, reefs and rocks, the islands attract in excess of two million visitors a year for the **fishing**, **sailing**, **snorkelling** and **diving**. No two islands are the same and their proximity to one another makes it easy to island hop. The colonial legacy, which has seen many flags flying over the islands in the past three hundred years (Dutch, French, Danish, British and Spanish to name a few), has left some charming historic architecture, particularly in the towns of the United States Virgin Islands, together with atmospheric ruins of sugar plantations and a culture that is something of a melting pot.

A territory of the USA, the **United States Virgin Islands (USVI)** can, with their international cuisine, mini-shopping malls and American-style amenities, initially seem too much like its big brother with the added advantage of duty-free shopping. But further exploration reveals the strong roots of West Indian culture, no more so than during Carnival when the streets of St Thomas are overtaken with colourful costume parades, bands and food stalls selling delicious Creole food. The **British Virgin Islands (BVI)** are less touched by tourism and the majority of visitors are yachters – the calm waters, gentle breezes, sheltered bays and short distances between anchorages have long made the BVI a **sailing** paradise.

The mainstay of the **economy** in the Virgin Islands is tourism, though the USVI have a lucrative sideline in the Hess Oil Refinery and a reasonable manufacturing industry; the BVI receive significant income from licence fees paid by foreign companies taking advantage of tax exemptions.

Where to go

Most visitors to the Virgin Islands head straight for St Thomas, though it can feel overcrowded and familiar; more serene surroundings await on St Croix and St John, especially the latter, which offers excellent **hiking**.

In the BVI, the main draws are the hopping **yacht harbours** and sandy **beaches**, along with a myriad of watersports and boating activities; **Brewer's Bay Beach** in particular has excellent snorkelling, while the well-preserved wreck of the **RMS Rhone** off Salt Island is the highlight of any visit. To the east, on peaceful Virgin Gorda are the unusual natural attraction known as **The Baths**, colossal boulders surrounded by pools teeming with marine life.

When to go

The Virgin Islands' **climate** is subtropical, with temperatures ranging from 26°C to 31°C (79–89°F) in summer to 22°C to 28°C (72–82°F) in winter. Easterly trade winds keep the humidity low, with May and June the stickiest months. Heavy rain is rare except during **hurricane season** (June–Nov) when most of the annual rainfall of 100mm arrives, though showers tend to be brief. The last major hurricanes to hit the Virgins, Hurricane Luis and Hurricane Marilyn, occurred within two weeks of each other in September 1995 and caused several billion dollars of damage. Unsurprisingly, good deals are readily available in hurricane season – November is the best because off season prices are still in effect, yet the weather is often just as good as in December. Some hotels and restaurants will close for the months of August and/or September.

Getting there

The main gateways to the Virgin Islands are the **Cyril E. King International Airport** on

St Thomas and **Henry E. Rohlsen Airport** on St Croix. No airlines fly directly to the BVI; you have to go via St Thomas or San Juan, Puerto Rico – American Eagle, LIAT, Air Sunshine and Cape Air all operate daily flights from San Juan to Tortola.

Cruise ships arrive in Charlotte Amalie, St Thomas, Road Town, Tortola, and are slated to return to Frederiksted, St Croix some time in 2009. If you are arriving on your own boat you must clear customs. See the end of the "Getting around" section for a list of customs points.

Information

All main towns in the Virgin Islands have **tourist offices**. The official agencies are the **US Virgin Islands Department of Tourism** (Ⓦwww.usvitourism.vi) and the **BVI Tourist Board** (Ⓦwww.bvitourism.com). Your lodgings may also be an excellent source of local information – resorts and large hotels in particular will often help guests (and sometimes non-guests) set up trips, car rental and activities, especially on the smaller islands without official tourist offices. The main USVI **publications** are *The V.I. Daily News* and *The Island Trader* – both on St Thomas, and *The St Croix Avis*. For **entertainment** listings, try the online papers the *St. Thomas Source* (Ⓦwww.sts.onepaper.com) and the *St. Croix Source* (Ⓦwww.stx.onepaper.com). In the BVI, news sources include the *BVI Beacon* (Thurs) and *The Island Sun* (Fri), plus the free weekly, *Limin' Times*, which carries **listings** of upcoming events.

Money and costs

The **currency** for the US and British Virgin Islands is the **US dollar**. Branches of major **banks**, most with **ATMs**, are located in most towns. Major **credit cards** are accepted widely on the islands at hotels, restaurants and car rental agencies. There's always a risk that some small out-of-the-way place won't take cards or their system might be down, so it pays to travel with some cash if you plan to go off the beaten track. **Traveller's cheques** are also widely accepted and most hotels allow guests to cash personal cheques. Be warned that there's a government **room tax** (8 percent in the USVI; 7 percent in the BVI) on all accommodation and an 8–15 percent service charge on everything else in hotels, so check bills before **tipping**. The standard tip for good service is 15 percent in restaurants and bars; around 10 percent for taxis.

Getting around

Hopping **from island to island** is easy either by air or, more popularly, using the network of inter-island ferries. Just remember to bring proof of citizenship when passing back and forth between the BVI and USVI. **On the islands** themselves you can do much of your exploring on foot using taxis, rental cars, bikes or boats for longer distances.

By air

Getting between the islands **by air** is relatively easy. Of the operators that fly between **St Thomas and St Croix** try American Eagle or Cape Aire (about US$175 round-trip) or Seaborne Airlines flies seaplanes (over one dozen daily flights; 15min; Ⓣ340/773-6442 or 1-888/359-8687, Ⓦwww.seaborneairlines.com; US$130-210), which are slightly cheaper if you book ahead, and more of a thrill. **St John** does not have an airport so you need to take a ferry either from Charlotte Amalie (nearest to the airport; US$10 one-way plus US$2 bag fee; 45min), or Red Hook (US$5 one-way; 20min). The car ferry from Red Hook costs US$42-50 round-trip.

To get **from the USVI to the BVI,** scheduled flights go from St Thomas to Tortola and Virgin Gorda daily with Air Sunshine. From St Croix flights are only on demand to Tortola and Virgin Gorda with Air Sunshine. Charter flights to Tortola, Virgin Gorda and Anegada are always available with Fly BVI.

By bus and car

On the main islands of the USVI **VITRAN** (Ⓣ340/774-5678) is the government-operated **bus** service, which makes designated stops (look for rainbow-coloured buses on signposts). While buses are cheap (generally US$.75 in Charlotte Amalie and US$1.00 outside the city), they are not very reliable, stops aren't always conveniently located and trips, especially in and around Charlotte Amalie, can be a slow process. Apart from the irregular shared taxi vans on Tortola there is no public transport on the BVI. In most cases you'll find it easier on both the USVI and BVI to get a taxi or, better still, rent a **car**, which is easily done on most of the major islands. Book your car in advance if you're coming during peak season and expect to pay upwards of US$65 per day (weekly rates are lower). Note that in the USVI and BVI cars **drive on the left** side of the road. **Taxis** in the Virgin Islands charge by the destination so it pays to pack in as many people as you can. Rates are set by the government and taxi drivers are required to carry a rate card; ask to see it if you're unsure of the fare and always agree on your price before you set off.

By sea

The islands have an excellent network of **inter-island ferries**, though it's advisable to call ahead for times as they often change. As a rough guide to prices, a return fare between Tortola and St John is US$40; between Tortola and Virgin Gorda US$25. Between St Thomas and St Croix there is ferry (90min; Fri–Mon, US$90 round-trip).

You may prefer to **charter a yacht**, either with a crew or by yourself (bareboat). Either way you're looking at upwards of US$2500 per week for a boat in high season, and if you're going **bareboat** you'll have to demonstrate that you have sufficient sailing experience. You'll also need accurate maps and charts to navigate the many reefs surrounding the islands. You must clear **customs** on entry to the USVI (unless you are coming from a US port) at Charlotte Amalie, Cruz Bay, Christiansted or Frederiksted. In the BVI, customs points are at Great Harbour, Jost Van Dyke, Spanish Town on Virgin Gorda, Road Town, Beef Island and Soper's Hole on Tortola.

Ferries between the BVI

Marina Cay Ferry ⓣ284/494-2174. Free ferry connecting Beef Island to Marina Cay.
New Horizon Ferry ⓣ284/495-9278. Between West End, Tortola and Jost Van Dyke.
North Sound Express ⓣ284/495-2138. Between Beef Island and Virgin Gorda.
Peter Island Ferry ⓣ284/495-2000. Between Tortola and Peter Island.
Saba Rock Ferry ⓣ284/495-7711. Between the North Sound and Saba Rock.
Smith's Ferry Services ⓣ284/495-4495. Between Tortola and Virgin Gorda, and Anegada.
Speedy's ⓣ284/495-5240. Between Road Town, Tortola and Virgin Gorda.

Ferries between the USVI and BVI

Inter-Island ⓣ340/776-6597 or 284/495-4166. Between Cruz Bay, St John, Tortola, Virgin Gorda and Jost Van Dyke.
Native Son ⓣ340/775-3111 or 284/495-4617, ⓦwww.nativesonferry.com. Between Tortola (Road Town and West End) and St Thomas (Charlotte Amalie & Red Hook).
Smith's Ferry Services ⓣ284/495-4495 or 340/775-7292. Between Tortola (Road Town and West End) and St Thomas (Charlotte Amalie and Red Hook)
Speedy's ⓣ284/495-5240, ⓦwww.speedysbvi.com Between Tortola, Virgin Gorda and St Thomas.
Road Town Fast Ferry ⓣ284/494-2323 or 340/777-2800, ⓦwww.roadtownfastferry.com. Between Charlotte Amalie, St Thomas and Road Town, Tortola.

Ferries between the USVI

Inter-Island ⓣ340/776-6597. Between Red Hook and St John.
Transportation Services ⓣ340/776-6282. Between Charlotte Amalie, Red Hook and St John (Cruz Bay).
V.I. Sea Trans ⓣ340/776-5494 or 340/775-7992. ⓦwww.goviseatrans.com. Run by Smith's Ferry Sevices, between Charlotte Amalie and St Croix Friday–Monday.

Accommodation

Accommodation in the Virgin Islands ranges from campsites with bare sites to super-luxury resorts on private islands. You won't find any any youth hostels in the Virgin Islands and budget accommodation is hard to come by. **Campsites** range US$20-30 for a bare site. The next rung up, **guesthouses**, vary widely in quality, price and size from basic rooms above a bar to cosy beachside inns, but you can expect to pay around US$100–150 for a double room per night. **Hotels** range from small places (mainly in towns and villages) with a pool and bar (for around US$120–200) to resorts with beachfront accommodation and all facilities (upwards of US$250). Bear in mind the **room tax** (see above). If you're planning on a lengthy stay it might be worth checking out renting a **private villa or home**.

Depending on the room you choose, it's generally 20–40 percent cheaper during low season (May 1 to Dec 14). If you are visiting in high season you should book a few months in advance.

Food and drink

Because the Virgin Islands have flown several flags during their history, a rich culinary heritage flourishes combining **Dutch, English, French, African, West Indian** and other influences. And while there's plenty of fine international cuisine to be had (albeit to a lesser extent on the smaller BVI such as Jost Van Dyke and Anegada), you should definitely try the many wonderful West Indian dishes showcasing the best of **Creole cuisine**. Generally speaking, you'll pay around US$10–20 for a meal at a café or standard restaurant; US$20–30 for an entree at more upmarket places. The USVI has the full range of international cuisine; eating on the BVI you're more likely to have to stick to West Indian food, with international dishes confined mainly to upmarket places or snack-style places serving sandwiches, burgers and pizzas.

Restaurants often close for several hours between meals, generally 3–5pm and many places close before 10.30pm. As always you should reserve in popular places and call ahead for those in out-of-the-way spots to make sure they're open. When it comes to dress, the BVI are a little more formal than most other islands. For some of the smarter restaurants men are advised to wear long trousers and a collared shirt.

West Indian fare is the food of choice for locals. An average dish consists of spiced meats, lots of starches and very few vegetables. **Conch**, a shellfish that has a similar texture and taste to squid, and **goat**, which is very similar to pork, are served almost any way you can imagine. A popular dish that often sells out quickly is conch in butter sauce. Common side dishes include fried **plantains**, fry bread called **johnny cakes,** and **fungi**, which is a sort of stuffing made from corn meal and okra. Many fish and chicken dishes are served with fruit salsa, or a coconut milk sauce. Spicy foods, such as foods rubbed with Caribbean curries or Jamaican jerk spices, are also popular. For a quick and inexpensive meal, locals grab a **roti** – meat, potatoes, carrots and onions simmered in a creamy curry sauce and folded between warm flatbread, occasionally with some chutney on the side. Be careful when you eat a chicken roti, because locals eat them with the bones. Similar is a **pate**, a deep-fried pasty with fillings such as beef, goat, chicken, conch or saltfish. **Kallaloo** (or callaloo) is a seasoned stew of assorted greens, meats and seafood.

Rum – in particular Cruzan rum made on St Croix – is definitely the spirit of choice and rum punch is the most popular rum drink. Locals drink a mixture of two shots of dark rum, a teaspoon of sugar and a splash of water.

Mail and communications

Local calls on public payphones, if you can find one that works, typically cost 50 cents for five minutes. For **international calls** use one of a number of prepaid phonecards which are available in US$10 increments

Emergency phone numbers

For **emergencies**, you can dial ☎911 in the USVI on any telephone for fire, police or medical assistance. In the BVI the number is ☎911 or 999. For **marine emergencies**, call Virgin Islands Search and Rescue (VISAR) by dialing the emergency numbers or via VHF Ch.16.

from shops, post offices and most hotels. If you carry a **mobile phone**, try dialling ☎6611 to enquire about use on the island, though it's best to enquire with your carrier well in advance of making your trip.

The **country code** for the BVI is ☎284; for the USVI it's ☎340

Post offices (open generally Mon–Fri 8am–4.30pm & Sat 8am–noon) can be found in most main towns. However, many hotels will sell you stamps and mail letters for you.

Many hotels offer free wireless **Internet access** to guests; otherwise you'll have to log on at one of the cybercafés – they're not widespread but most major towns will have one.

Opening hours, holidays and festivals

For the most part in the USVI and BVI **businesses** are open Monday to Saturday 8am–5pm, and **shops**, museums and historic sights Monday to Saturday 9am–5pm. On the USVI **bank opening hours** are Mon–Fri 9am–3pm, and some open Saturday morning; BVI banks close slightly earlier at around 2.30pm. Government buildings are open 9am–5pm weekdays. Always **call ahead** to make sure your destination is open, especially in the off season. Both the USVI and the BVI celebrate local **public holidays** as well as many of the holidays celebrated in their mother countries. The government and banks close for major holidays, but stores, restaurants and tourist attractions generally stay open. The main cultural event to look out for in the Virgin Islands is **Carnival** – a couple of weeks of costumed street parades including mocko jumbies (stilt walkers), calypso and steel pan bands, street stalls and all-night partying and dancing. St Thomas Carnival – the second largest in the Caribbean after Trinidad – takes place in April (see p.414). Some other Virgin Islands have mini-carnivals – Virgin Gorda's coincides with Easter and St John's the first few days of July – and if you happen to be in the BVI the last two weeks of July you'll be swept along in the nightly entertainment and music of the **BVI Summer Festival**.

Public holidays

USVI

January 1 New Year's Day
January 6 Three Kings' Day
January Martin Luther King Jr's Birthday (third Mon)
Third Monday in February Presidents' Day
March 31 Transfer Day
March/April Maundy Thursday, Good Friday, Easter Monday
Last Monday in May Memorial Day
July 3 Emancipation Day
July 4 Independence Day
July Supplication Day (date varies)
First Monday in September Labour Day
Second Monday in October Columbus Day
November 1 Liberty Day
November 11 Veteran's Day
Fourth Thursday in November Thanksgiving Day
December 25 Christmas Day
December 26 Boxing Day

BVI

January 1 New Year's Day
March 11 Commonwealth Day
March/April Good Friday, Easter Monday
May/June Whit Monday
June 11 Queen's Birthday
July 1 Territory Day
August BVI August Festival Days
October 22 St Ursula's Day
November 12 Birthday of Heir to the Throne
December 25 Christmas Day
December 26 Boxing Day

Sports and outdoor activities

The Virgin Islands are a paradise for almost any **watersports** you can imagine – diving, snorkelling, windsurfing, parasailing – as well as fishing, sailing and hiking. See the specific island sections for details of companies offering anything from snorkelling day-trips to weeklong sailing courses. **Fishing** is a popular pastime on the islands – wahoo are hot from August to February, marlin September to January, mahi mahi from February to May and tuna November to January. Note that the removal of any marine organism from BVI waters is illegal without a recreational **fishing permit**. Call the Fisheries Division at ☎284/494-3429 for information.

History

Some evidence suggests that the Virgin Islands were populated by Amerindian tribes as far back as 1500 BC but the earliest tribe known to have settled here was the Igneri, the first wave of **Arawaks**, who arrived from South America in huge canoes, landing on St Croix sometime between 50 and 650 AD. The next wave of Arawaks – the Taíno – arrived around 1300; skilled in agriculture they set about farming the islands of St Croix, St John and St Thomas only to be displaced in the early part of the fifteenth century by the aggressive warrior tribe known as the **Caribs**. By the time Columbus set foot on the islands in 1493 during his second voyage, the Caribs were well established and the indigenous Arawak tribes had dwindled to a fraction of their original number. Columbus named the islands **Las Virgenes**, "the virgins" – their sheer number and pristine condition reminding him of the legend of St Ursula, a feisty fourth-century European princess, and her "army" of 11,000 virgins, who were raped and killed by a Hun prince and his henchmen. After the Spaniards pretty much wiped out the entire population of native peoples, the islands were ripe for colonization and mass planting of sugar cane.

The first half of the seventeenth century witnessed a period of intense **colonial squabbling** with the British, Dutch, Spanish and French establishing proto-colonies on various islands until the **Danes** interceded in 1666 and began their period of domination over the islands west of St John, while the **English** gained control of the eastern section of islands. The Danes are credited with developing their islands into some of the busiest ports in the West Indies; the **slave trade** boomed, **pirates** were a common (and often welcome) sight, but more importantly, **sugar cane** flowered into a major cash crop. Owing to many factors, including natural disasters and the **emancipation of the islands' slaves** (1834 in the British West Indies, 1848 in the Danish West Indies), the economy of the islands soured in the early to mid-1800s.

The **US** didn't get their hands on the Danish West Indies until the twentieth century. Worried that the Germans would use the islands as submarine bases in **World War I**, the US government purchased them from the Danes in 1917 for US$25 million – to the approval of much of the population who anticipated American investment in education and health. Meanwhile in the BVI, a "crown colony" since the 1870s, rumblings of dissatisfaction were beginning over their negligent and distant ruling power. By the **Thirties** most citizens of the USVI were feeling similarly let down by the US: the expected improvements in living conditions hadn't materialized and the islands had become little more than a US naval base with the attendant problem of unruly sailors. A visit by President Roosevelt in 1934 revitalized the US attitude to the USVI and before long huge improvements to the islands' infrastructure were in full swing. But by the end of the **Forties** both territories were actively seeking more **independence** and the right to elect their own government – the BVI got theirs in 1967 when they were permitted a ministerial system of government headed by an elected Chief Minister. The following year, the USVI gained the right to elect its own governor. The highlights of the islands' history since have been the tragic devastation of **hurricanes**. The most potent were Hugo in 1989, which hit St Croix not once but twice on a sudden change of direction and Marilyn, which left St Thomas eighty percent devastated in 1995.

Today, the USVI are considered a territory of the United States and have one seat in Congress. Islanders are US citizens and pay taxes, but they cannot vote for the President of the United States. The BVI are a dependent territory of Britain and are overseen by a governor appointed by the British monarch, though they are more or less self-governing. The governor presides over the five-member Executive Council, while the Legislative Council consists of a twelve-member elected body with a ministerial system.

8.1

The United States Virgin Islands

Known as America's Caribbean, the **UNITED STATES VIRGIN ISLANDS,** with its sea-swept landscapes, historic towns, **duty-free shopping** and luxurious resorts, bask in a combination of familiar yet exotic that makes them one of the most popular cruise-ship destinations in the Caribbean. America aside, the Danes had the most influence on the look of the islands. Successful sugar cane exporters and slave dealers, they established most of the major towns, and there are plentiful reminders of their presence in the **colonial architecture** of the historic cities of Frederiksted and Christiansted, and in the ruins of sugar plantations scattered across the green mountainous slopes. But it's the slaves and their descendants that have defined the culture, creating their own forms of music and developing a rich cuisine.

Of the sixty islands, islets and cays (most of which are uninhabited) that make up the USVI, the biggest and busiest are St Thomas, St Croix and St John. Each has a distinctive mood and culture, and you haven't really seen the USVI until you've checked out all three. **St Thomas**, with its picturesque capital, Charlotte Amalie, is the most American – hip and stylish, with a history born of trade rather than sugar. **St John**, the greenest, is also the smallest, and its National Park, part on land, part underwater, is the major attraction. **St Croix** is the largest, the most distant and sees little of the hordes that flock to St Thomas and St John but its rich culture and the ports attract visitors with a mix of historic sights, shopping and good restaurants.

St Thomas

The most accessible and Americanized of the Virgins, **ST THOMAS** is high on the list of Caribbean destinations for cruise ships and honeymooners – some would say too high, with as many as eleven cruise ships docking at once. The port at **Charlotte Amalie** has been an important merchant centre since the 1700s, and today renovated old warehouses house a wealth of galleries, restaurants and shops. It can seem a bit too sanitized but if you look deeper, you'll find Caribbean culture alive and kicking. The small town of **Red Hook** offers all the amenities of Charlotte Amalie on a smaller scale, and its harbour hops with yachters and those seeking ferries for St John and beyond. The north and east of the island have the nicest **beaches**, including **Magens Bay**, consistently voted one of the world's best. Be aware that beaches, shops and the roads themselves can get congested depending on the number of cruise ships in port.

Arrival, information and getting around

St Thomas' **Cyril E. King Airport** is three miles west of Charlotte Amalie. VITRAN **buses** run from the airport to Charlotte Amalie (from 6am to 7pm). **Taxis** (for 2 persons) to Charlotte Amalie cost around US$6 per person; for resorts

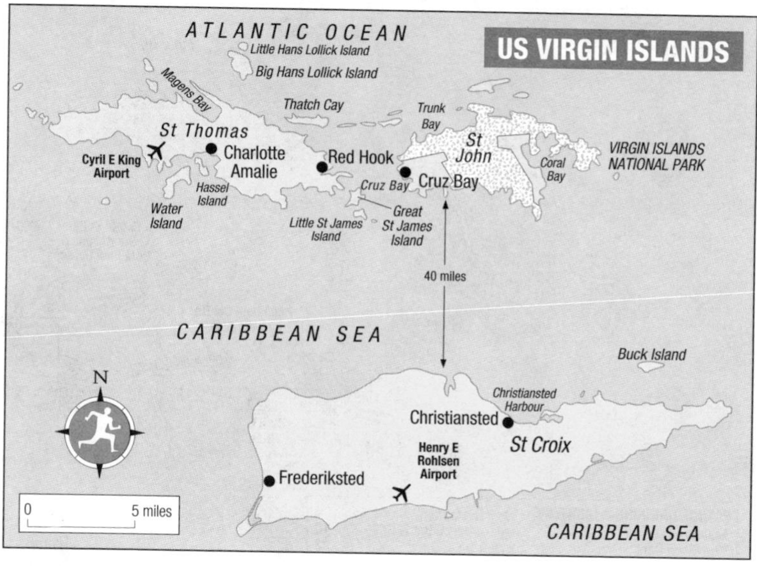

on the eastern end of the island it's around US$10–15, plus baggage charges. Most major **car rental** companies have offices at the airport and in Havensight Mall (see also below).

Information booths at the airport offer free brochures and maps, including helpful publications such as *St Thomas This Week* and *What to Do*. In downtown Charlotte Amalie, there is a USVI Division of Tourism office across from Nisky Center mall (☎340/774-8784). The National Park Service visitor centre sits across the street from Red Hook's ferry dock. **Post offices** are located in Emancipation Garden, Charlotte Amalie (☎340/774-3750); on Veteran's Drive, Charlotte Amalie (☎340/774-6980); and at the Havensight Mall (☎340/776-9897). You can't throw a conch fritter without hitting an establishment with wireless Internet access in Charlotte Amalie but there are also a few **Internet cafés**, including Beans, Bytes & Websites in the Royal Dane Mall (☎340/776-7265) and Barefoot Budda across from Havensight Mall (☎340/777-3668). **Getting around** the island, VITRAN **buses** (☎340/774-5678) operate services to Red Hook (every two hrs 5.30am–7pm) and to the west as well. **Taxis** come in all shapes and sizes – cars, vans and trucks; reputable operators include East End Taxi Service, Ferry Dock (☎340/775-6974) and Islander Taxi & Tour Services (☎340/774-4077). From town to the east of the island, including Red Hook, the fare for two people is US$10. General three-hour sightseeing tours go for about US$50 for one person, or US$25 per person for two or more. Dollar taxis, used mainly by locals, run the same routes as the public bus in the same open-air safari trucks as regular taxis. Just stand on the side of the road and flag down the truck, tell the driver where you want to get off, and pay your dollar (for short hops).

Although you don't need a **car** on St Thomas, it will give you a much better feel for the island and you can even take the car ferry (US$42–50 round-trip) over to St John for the day. Options include Budget (☎340/776-5774); Discount Car Rental (☎340/776-4858); and E-Z Car Rental (☎340/775-6255). You might opt for a **scooter** from Biz Rentals (☎340/774-5840) in Havensight or Zip Rentals (☎340/715-1501) in Red Hook.

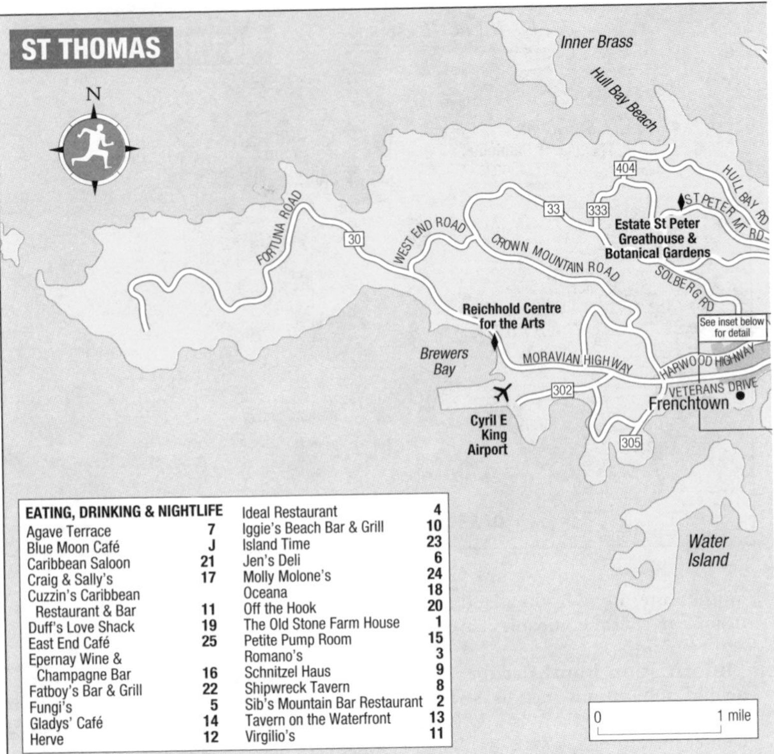

Charlotte Amalie and around

CHARLOTTE AMALIE sweeps around St Thomas Harbour in a striking combination of red-roofed whitewashed buildings backed by lush green villa-dotted hills. Up to eleven cruise ships can occupy the harbour on any given day – though usually there's only about five – and hundreds of ferries and yachts pass through each week, and at times the population of 20,000 doubles. Many bargain-hunting tourists head straight for the famous **shopping district** where renovated merchant warehouses contain shops selling everything from cut-rate diamonds, perfume and fine textiles to monstrous Cuban cigars. But there's much more to Charlotte Amalie than shopping – the town is full of historic sites like the **99 Steps**, **Fort Christian** and the **St Thomas Synagogue**. Named Charlotte Amalie in honour of the wife of Danish King Christian V, the Danish influence is strong – much of the historic **colonial architecture** is still standing and streets are commonly referred to by the Danish word *gades*, pronounced "gah-dahs". On the peninsula due west of Charlotte Amalie, the smaller, quieter neighbourhood of **FRENCHTOWN** has been home to most of St Thomas' French descendants for centuries. You will find some fantastic restaurants and bars here and the quaint yellow one-room cottage that houses the **French Heritage Museum** (☎340/714-2583, Mon–Fri 9am–6pm; closed 12pm–1pm for lunch, donations accepted).

Accommodation

Charlotte Amalie and Frenchtown contain the majority of the island's small **hotels**, **historic inns** and **cosy B&Bs**, all which generally have pools but not easy beach

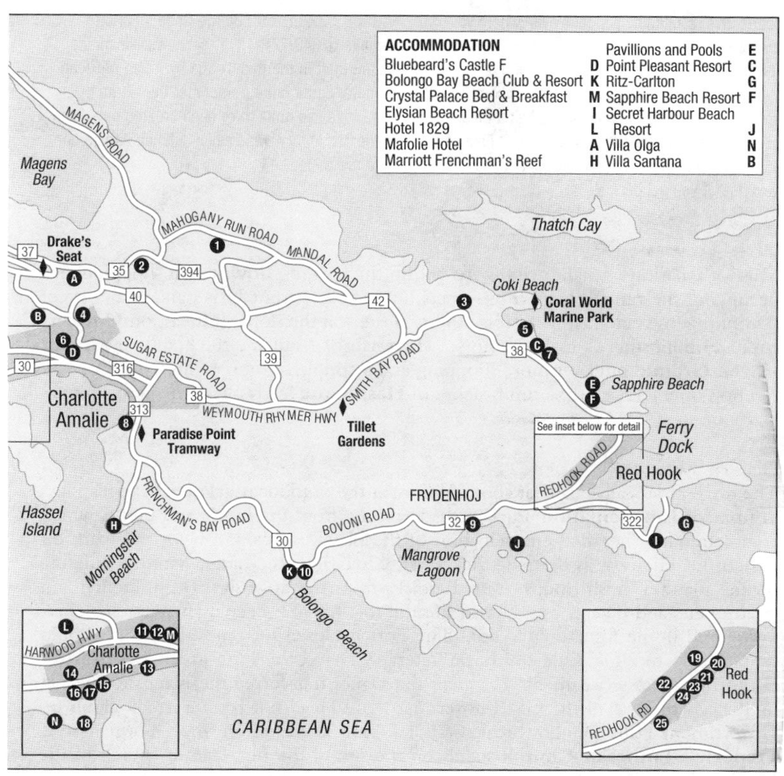

access – and this is reflected in the price. For groups, the many **villas and private homes** tucked in the hills are a better option; try Calypso Realty (Ⓣ340/774-1620 or 1-800/747-4858, Ⓦwww.calypsorealty.com); McLaughlin Anderson Luxury Villas (Ⓣ340/776-0635 or 1-800/537-6246, Ⓦwww.mclaughlinanderson.com); or *VIP* Villa Rentals (Ⓣ1-800/788-4847, Ⓦwww.viprentals.com). Unlike St John and St Croix, there is no camping on St Thomas.

Hotels and inns

Crystal Palace Bed and Breakfast Charlotte Amalie Ⓣ340/777-2277. This classy mansion is located in the heart of the historic district. Ask for a room overlooking the harbour. There are five rooms, two with private bath. Continental breakfast, free airport pick-up and wireless Internet access are included. 5

Hotel 1829 Government Hill, Charlotte Amalie Ⓣ340/776-1829 or 1-800/524-2002, Ⓦwww.hotel1829.com. This bright rust-coloured building with huge mahogany shutters is one of the most atmospheric small hotels on the island. The front porch is the perfect place to read a novel, and the rooms, though varying in size, are good value. 5

Mafolie Hotel 7091 Estate Mafolie, Charlotte Amalie Ⓣ340/774-2790 or 1-800/225-7035, Ⓦwww.mafolie.com. The rooms in this hillside retreat are clean, the view of the harbour is stunning and the free shuttles to Magen's Beach and one-way to downtown couldn't be more convenient. The hotel restaurant is a great place for a sunset meal or cocktail. 5–6

Marriott Frenchman's Reef 5 Estate Bakkeroe, South Shore Ⓣ340/776-8500 or 1-800/524-2000, Ⓦwww.marriott.com. After a 2007, US$25 million dollar renovation, the Marriot boasts everything you'd expect. The rooms all have sea views, and there are two private beaches, oceanfront tennis courts, five restaurants and bars everywhere you turn. 8

Villa Olga Frenchtown ⓣ340/715-0900 or 1-800/524-4746, ⓦwww.villa-olga-inn.com. The only lodging of note in Frenchtown, half a mile away from the hustle and bustle of town. Four of the twelve rooms have ocean views. *Oceana* is right next door if you get peckish. 5

Villa Santana 2602 Bierge Gade, Charlotte Amalie ⓣ340/776-1311, ⓦwww.villasantana.com. Built in the mid-1850s by exiled Mexican general Santa Anna (remember the Alamo?), this inn's five units have been created out of the general's library, wine cellar, kitchen and so on, and are a steal. 5

The Town

Most of Charlotte Amalie's sights are within the bustling **downtown** shopping area occupying the numerous narrow streets linking Waterfront Drive and Main Street (Dronningens Gade), while historic sights cluster on the slopes just east on **Government Hill**. Further east of downtown, **Havensight Mall** and the brand new **Yacht Haven Grande** offer yet more shopping and a couple of touristy diversions, or you can hop on a ferry to the calm beaches of **Hassel and Water Islands** in St Thomas Harbour.

Downtown

The town comes alive daily at about 5.30am at the outdoor **market** at Vendor's Plaza in front of **Emancipation Park**, a shady respite from the hustle and bustle, which commemorates the 1848 emancipation of the island's slaves. Just below the park on Waterfront Highway is the red-brick **Fort Christian,** the oldest standing building on the island. Danish troops resisted attacks from the Spanish, British, French and pirates here, and during its 300-year life the fort has also been a jail, church, courthouse and home for the governor. The Fort is closed for renovations but should reopen by late 2008. Due south, on Veteran's Drive, the lime-green **Legislature Building** (Mon–Fri 8am–5pm), where the Danes transferred the islands to the US in 1917, is the seat of the USVI governing body. Head north on a steady climb up Government Hill, taking a break first at Norre Gade, where the Georgian-style **Frederick Lutheran Church** stands on the site of the first Danish church in the Virgin Islands. The current structure, built by black parishioner Jean Reeneaus, dates to the early nineteenth century. Northeast of the church, on Kongens Gade, the imposing white mansion of **Government House** (Mon–Fri 8am–5pm; free), built in 1867, was originally a meeting place for the Danish Colonial Council. Now the administrative headquarters of the USVI, it also houses a museum showcasing work by famous local artists like Pepino Mangravatti. Just to the west is the start of the palm-lined **99 Steps** (actually 103), which lead north towards the top of Government Hill, affording exquisite views. Laid in the mid-1700s by Danes living in the hills, the steps were the original access to the waterfront and to **Blackbeard's**

The legend of Blackbeard

Blackbeard, made infamous in Robert Louis Stevenson's novel *Treasure Island*, is said to have walked the streets of Charlotte Amalie when the island was a legal refuge for pirates, who sold their contraband freely – wild days when anything and everything was legal and the town was affectionately known as Beer Hall. Born Edward Teach in Bristol, England, Blackbeard was the meanest man the seas have ever seen – a heavy drinker (rum mixed with gunpowder) and a notorious lady-killer (it is said he murdered all fourteen of his wives). Before boarding a target vessel he would light slow-burning fuse matches and tie them into his long hair and beard giving him a hellish appearance. When he was finally beheaded from behind while fighting the captain of a crippled vessel, his body was dumped into the sea where, legend has it that it swam three times round the ship before sinking.

▲ Blackbeard's castle

Castle, otherwise known as Fort Skytsborg, said to have been the tower the legendary pirate (see box opposite) used for an unobstructed view of the ocean.

On the way back to the main shopping area, stop off at Crystal Gade to see the charming **St Thomas Synagogue** (Mon–Thurs 9am–4pm, Fri 9am–3pm); its sand floor symbolizes the exodus from Egypt. The building dates to 1833 and is the western hemisphere's second oldest synagogue, not to mention the longest continually in service in America. Next door, the **Weibel Museum** (same hrs; free) is an interesting exhibition of the three hundred years of Jewish history in the islands. Just before you hit the shops check out the **Camille Pissarro Gallery**, 14 Main St, where the artist was born in 1830. One of the founders of the French Impressionist school, Pissarro's experiences growing up here would become the subjects of some of his later paintings.

Havensight and Yacht Haven Grande

At the eastern end of the bay, Havensight has a few malls, the cruise ship dock and a couple of interesting but expensive attractions. For US$89, **Atlantis Submarines**, Havensight Cruise Ship Dock (☎340/776-5650), has a two-hour tour that will take you out to Buck Island to board a sub that descends 90ft below the water's surface. You can peer through portholes at stingrays, sharks and whatever else happens to swim by. Going to the other extreme, **St Thomas Skyride**, 9617

Estate St, across the street from the Havensight Mall (☎340/774-9809; US$19), operates gondolas that whisk you 700ft above sea level up the side of Flag Hill for stunning views. Overpriced food and drinks await you at the top. Yacht Haven Grande, a new mall right next door to Havensight, contains mostly chain stores and a few good restaurants.

Despite the unfortunate location on the cruise ship dock near Havensight Mall, the **St Thomas Butterfly Farm** (☎340/775-1929, Ⓦwww.thebutterflyfarm.com; 8.30am–5pm last tour at 4pm; US$15) is a worthwhile place to wander among the lovely fluttering creatures. Come in the morning to see the butterflies at their most active.

Water and Hassel islands

Hop on a ferry from Crown Bay Marina just west of Charlotte Amalie's harbour (US$5 one-way, US$9 round-trip) for a relaxing day-trip across the harbour to **Water Island**. It's population is small but it is now considered the fourth USVI; bring a picnic and spend the day lazing on its glorious beaches or cycling around. **Water Island Adventures** (☎340/714-2186) does bike tours (US$65) and will pick up groups (eight minimum) from the cruise dock in Charlotte Amalie for a 20-minute narrated tour of the harbour as you make your way to the island for a bike ride and beach time. Ferries don't regularly go to **Hassel Island**, part of the Virgin Islands National Park system, but if you have a group of at least 15 people, you can hire a ferry for US$10 per person round-trip. It's a relaxing place for fun exploration but there's not much to see apart from the relics of an old British military garrison and the shell of a failed hotel (the hotel from Herman Wouk's novel *Don't Stop the Carnival*).

Around Charlotte Amalie

By car or by taxi it's worth seeking out some of the attractions just outside Charlotte Amalie. On Route 40 north of town, **Drake's Seat**, sometimes crowded with tour buses, is a popular lookout point where it is said Sir Francis Drake sat to watch for enemy ships. On the same road, roughly two miles west, the mountainside perch of **Estate St Peter Greathouse and Botanical Gardens** (daily 8am–4pm; ☎340/774-4999; US$12) offers breathtaking views. Grab a complimentary rum punch, shop for local art and take a tour of the luscious gardens. Come in the afternoon to avoid cruise-ship crowds.

Two and a half miles east of town on Route 38 at Tutu, **Tillet Gardens** (☎340/775-1929, Ⓦwww.tillettgardens.com) was once a Danish farm, and is now an artists' colony, where you'll find all sorts of artisans at work and a shop to buy their wares. Call ahead to time your visit with one of the occasional jazz and classical concerts.

Beaches

On the **north side** of the island, the mile-long sandy stretch of **Magens Bay Beach** (US$4) three miles north of Charlotte Amalie on Route 35 is the island's longest beach and is almost always included in lists of the world's best beaches. Protected by two dramatic peninsulas (the one to the east is the upmarket area of Peterborg where the elite keep their villas), it's the perfect beach for swimming and sunbathing, though the snorkelling isn't much to speak of. A grill serves sandwiches, pizza and burgers, and waitresses in bikinis walk the beach taking drink orders. On your way out, hit *Udder Delights* for one of their famous milkshakes. Round the peninsula to the west, **Hull Bay Beach**, also on Route 37, is a favourite with the locals, especially surfers. In the distance you can see Inner and Outer Brass, two USVI cays. *Hull Bay Hideaway* on the road in provides hot grub, drinks and the occasional live band.

Beaches on the **south side** of the island aren't as good but are easy to get to. **Brewers Bay Beach**, on Route 30, three miles west of town, is fairly unpopulated, except for students from the nearby university, and it has a few snack trucks, while **Morningstar Beach** at *Marriott Frenchman's Reef*, on Route 315 one mile south of Havensight, is the closest and easiest to access from Charlotte Amalie. On the waterfront at Charlotte Amalie, look for the small ferry called *The Reefer* which provides access throughout the day (last return trip to the *Marriott* at 5pm) for US$6 each way. Back on Route 30 and two miles east, **Bolongo Beach**, surrounded by the *Bolongo Bay Beach Club and Resort*, offers grill food and frozen drinks. The beach at **Secret Harbour** on the southeast of the island is perfect for sunsets. Snorkelling along the point to the right is popular to catch a glimpse of sea turtles. **Sapphire Bay Beach**, just north of Red Hook, is another fine place to don your mask and snorkel.

Eating and drinking

St Thomas' **restaurants** offer a complete range of menus, venues and prices. Throw a stone in **Frenchtown** and you'll hit any number of intimate places. While the finest spots abound with entrees approaching New York City prices, there are options for all budgets, from roadside stands to burger joints to ethnic cuisine.

Charlotte Amalie

Cuzzin's Caribbean Restaurant and Bar 7 Back St ⓣ340/777-4711. Located in an eighteenth-century stone building in the heart of the downtown shopping district, *Cuzzin's* serves up everything from stewed oxtail to burgers (around US$16). But it's the West Indian dishes like conch in butter sauce (US$19), sides like *fungi* and drinks like *maubi* (a root) that top the bill. Tues–Sat 11–9.30pm.

Gladys' Café Waterfront at Royal Dane Mall ⓣ340/774-6604. Bacon, eggs, French toast or fresh tropical fruit for breakfast, or well-priced West Indian fare for lunch, including the hard-to-find local favourite saltfish and dumplings US$15).

Herve Government Hill ⓣ340/777-9703. An eclectic fusion of contemporary American, French and Caribbean fare (lunch around US$15; dinner US$30) on a hilltop location next to *Hotel 1829*, just minutes from Main Street. The black sesame-crusted tuna with ginger-raspberry sauce is a dream.

Ideal Restaurant 2329 Comandante Gade ⓣ340/777-5321. Best roti in town with prices ranging from US$8 for the veggie version up to US$15 for conch or shrimp. Lunch only.

Jen's Deli Emancipation Park. A good place to pick up a sandwich or salad and the prices are decent (US$8–12).

Petite Pump Room Veteran's Drive ⓣ340/776-2976. You'll get fantastic food and a great view of seaplanes landing right outside the picture windows. The golden honey-dipped fried chicken (US$12) is delicious, as are local specialties like red pea soup and boiled pot fish (around US$18).

Shipwreck Tavern Al Cohen Plaza across from Havensight Mall ⓣ340/777-1293. If you just want a burger and a beer, this watering hole will set you up with three-quarters of a pound of beautiful beef (US$12). Steaks, chicken and ribs are also delicious.

Tavern on the Waterfront 30 Dronningens Gade ⓣ340/776-4328. Live jazz creates an inviting atmosphere but the menu's delicious appetizers and a nice variety of seafood and steak entrees are more than reason enough to stop by. Probably the only place in the Caribbean to get Polish pierogis and cabbage rolls. Entrees US$18–40.

Virgilio's 18 Dronningens Gade ⓣ340/776-4920. A cosy, elegant Italian restaurant but with casual dress. Pasta is the popular choice (US$25–40) but the veal is the signature dish.

Frenchtown

Craig and Sally's 22 Honduras ⓣ340/777-9949. Hands down the most intimate restaurant with the most delicious food on St Thomas. The menu is creative and ever-changing (though the eggplant cheesecake is a regular item and recommended; US$11) and there's a wine list with over 450 vintages. Lunch Wed–Fri and dinner Wed–Sun. Reservations highly recommended.

Epernay Wine and Champagne Bar 24A Honduras ⓣ340/774-5348. A small, hip, intimate bistro with an extensive menu serving everything from pizza (US$14–16) to sushi to shrimp over soft polenta (US$23), plus twenty wines by the glass; the bar is a great place for early evening cocktails.

Oceana Villa Olga ⓣ340/774-4262. Set on the terrace of an old stone house, this upscale restaurant serves innovative international cuisine with views of the Frenchtown peninsula. Try the oven-roasted sea bass with asparagus (US$36). Mon–Sat 5–10pm, open Sun during high season.

Nightlife and entertainment

Nightlife in Charlotte Amalie revolves around **bars**, particularly on Waterfront Drive, with live music and the occasional DJ. More cultured entertainment abounds, including art shows, community theatre and eclectic music ensembles; pick up a copy of *St Thomas This Week* for what's on when. The most anticipated (and drunken) event of the year is **Carnival** (Ⓣ340/776-3112, Ⓦwww.vicarnival.com) – St Thomas' is one of the oldest and largest celebrations in the Caribbean and really kicks into gear the last two weeks of April. The revels take place all around downtown Charlotte Amalie with elaborate costumed street parades, a dancing till dawn frenzy called J'ouvert, music competitions like the famous Panorama and a final blowout when fireworks light up the harbour. For a little primer, read Herman Wouk's novel *Don't Stop the Carnival.*

Bars and clubs

The Green House Bar and Restaurant Ⓣ340/774-7998. After the dinner crowd has left, the music starts pumping with DJs or live reggae and calypso bands on Tues and Fri.

Shipwreck Tavern (see p.413). Two-dollar domestics, big screen TVs and heavy-duty burgers make this place a favourite among sports fans.

Stereo Ⓣ340/775-6202 This late-night dance club is popular with the island's professional set. DJs spin disco, house, hip-hop, jazz and much more until the wee hours.

Tavern on the Waterfront (see p.413). The island's best spot for live jazz every Friday; check the schedule for a variety of great local performers.

Entertainment venues

Pistarckle Theatre Ⓣ340/775-7877, Ⓦwww.pistarckletheater.vi. Located at Tillett Gardens, this 200-seat air-conditioned venue is one of the island's main outlets for theatre and dance.

Reichhold Center for the Arts Ⓣ340/693-1559, Ⓦwww.reichholdcenter.com. Rte 30, west of the airport Ⓣ340/693-1559. Located at the University of the Virgin Islands, St Thomas' largest performance space showcases local and international music, theatre, dance and ballet.

Red Hook and around

Most of St Thomas' resorts are found on the east side of the island where the main settlement, **RED HOOK,** consists mostly of shops, restaurants and bars nestled around the bay. It caters mostly to the folks who come for the ferries to and from St John, Tortola and other Caribbean islands, and to the high-end resorts nearby, and is a fun little place to shop, eat or grab a drink. The late-night bars have a party atmosphere, and travellers linger longer than cruise ship patrons do in Charlotte Amalie. The main tourist attractions are the **beaches** and the **Coral World Marine Park**, on Route 38 at Coki Point (daily 9am–5pm; US$19, US$10 children; Ⓣ340/775-1555). This 4.5-acre park boasts an imaginative array of marine and non-marine attractions, some included in your admission fee, like an Undersea Observatory and Caribbean Reef Encounter; some cost extra like the Sea Trek (US$74/adults, US$65/children, including park admission) – an air helmet that enables you to walk along an underwater trail just off shore, and the new Sea Lion Splash, (US$100/adults, US$91/children, also including park admission) – an up close and personal encounter with two South American sea lions, where you'll be able to swim and cavort in the water with these affectionate giants. **Coki Beach** on Smith Bay right next to Coral World Marine Park is probably the best beach for **snorkelling** on the island, though it can get really crowded. Come early to avoid the throngs of cruise-ship snorkellers. There's a great natural reef, plus all the amenities you could want: snack trucks, drinks, rental equipment and much more.

Accommodation

On the east side of the island **accommodation** is limited to upmarket resorts, all of which have easy beach access.

Bolongo Bay Beach Club and Resort 50 Estate Bolongo, South Shore ⓣ340/775-1800 or 1-800/524-4746, ⓦwww.bolongobay.com. All of these recently updated rooms at this amiable resort have sea views. Social activities abound, with two pools, hopping nightlife, beach volleyball and a complimentary scuba lesson in the pool. High season rates *start* at US$660 per night. ⑨

Pavilions and Pools 6400 Estate Smith Bay, Eastside ⓣ340/775-6110 or 1-800/524-2001, ⓦwww.pavilionsandpools.com. Each of the 25 private, spacious villas has a bedroom (some have two), kitchen (maids do the dishes), living room, large bathroom, four-foot pool and patio, and though not on the waterfront, the complex is a short walk to Sapphire Bay Beach. Continental breakfast is included. ⑦–⑧

Point Pleasant Resort 6600 Estate Smith Bay, Eastside ⓣ340/775-7200 or 1-800/524-2300, ⓦwww.antillesresorts.com. The suites are pleasant at this mountainside resort, the pool is right on the ocean and there are two great restaurants (*Agave Terrace* and *Fungi's*) on the premises; 3 2-bedroom villas also available. There's beach access and equipment for snorkelling, windsurfing and kayaking. ⑧–⑨

Ritz-Carlton 6900 Great Bay Estate, Eastside ⓣ340/775-3333 or 1-800/241-3333, ⓦwww.ritzcarlton.com. Set on fifteen acres of beautifully landscaped beachfront land, with smallish rooms but friendly staff that cater to your every need. Resort staples like multiple restaurants, a spa, beach, watersports, tennis courts and fitness centre are on site. The resort has its own catamaran for sunset cruises. ⑨

Sapphire Beach Resort 6270 Great Bay Estate, Eastside ⓣ340/775-6100 or 1-800/524-2090, ⓦwww.antillesresorts.com. One of a number of managed condo hotels, families are well-catered for in spacious rooms and villas that accommodate up to six people. The excellent beach – both for its sand and snorkelling – can get quite crowded with cruise ship passengers. Dive shop on site as well as a beach party every Sun from 2.30–6.30pm. ⑨

Secret Harbour Beach Resort Ridge Rd, Red Hook ⓣ340/775-6550 or 1-800/524-2250, ⓦwww.secretharbourvi.com. Set in a peaceful corner of the island not far from town, *Secret Harbour* enjoys an envious location on a calm little cove. All rooms have sea views and are comfortable and clean with updates ongoing. Eight rooms have excellent handicap access as well as beach wheelchairs. The dive shop downstairs, Aqua Action, is the only one in the VI that specializes in scuba for people with disabilities. *Blue Moon Café* (see below) onsite. ⑨

Eating, drinking and nightlife

Delicious food from waterfront restaurants and a hopping **nightlife** make Red Hook a lively place; for a more local experience, head off to one of the several restaurants in the hills on the north side of the island. At the upmarket restaurants you'll need to dress smart casual. If you want to make up a beach picnic or stock up your kitchenette, head for Marina Market across from Ferry Dock.

Restaurants and cafés

Agave Terrace 4 Estate Smith Bay, *Point Pleasant Resort* ⓣ340/775-4142. One of the better resort restaurants and one of the better fine-dining choices on this side of the island, with spectacular views. The Alaskan king crab legs (US$46) are wonderful – the rest of the menu is mostly Caribbean – and the lobster bisque is recommended (US$9).

Blue Moon Café *Secret Harbour Beach Resort* ⓣ340/779-2262, ⓦwww.bluemooncafevi.com. Great food with a seaside view while you sip a glass from the award-winning wine list. Try the sautéed Caribbean dorado filet with lime (US$23). Live steel pan music on Tues and Fri and the bar is open until 11pm. Dinner entrees start at US$21.

East End Café American Yacht Harbour, Red Hook ⓣ340/715-1442. Reasonably priced Italian fare (US$25-35 for mains) make this café popular. Serves lunch and dinner. Next door, *The Cellar* serves a variety of hot and cold tapas for US$10–25.

Molly Molone's American Yacht Harbour, Red Hook ⓣ340/775-1270. This open-air, garden-setting Irish pub serves fairly authentic shepherd's pie (US$18) and corned beef and cabbage, plus an extensive breakfast menu. Perfect just for drinks or to watch sporting events on TV. Lunch, dinner and brunch on the weekends.

Off the Hook Red Hook ⓣ340/775-6350. Seafood is the speciality at this restaurant near the ferry dock, with an open-air deck. There's a delicious fish choice to suit every palate, from mesquite grilled swordfish to sesame seared tuna to jerk tuna steak (all US$27). Lunch and dinner.

The Old Stone Farm House Northside ⓣ340/777-6277. Set in a 200-year-old farmhouse and featuring a creative cuisine like apple-stuffed quail (US$34), this is a fantastic experience every time. Save room for one of the decadent home-made desserts.

Romano's 6697 Smith Bay, Smith Bay ⓣ340/775-0045. A swanky restaurant off the beaten path, Romano's is worth finding for the delicious northern Italian cuisine and excellent service. If you're adventurous, go for the veal tongue or the classic Osso Bucco (US$40). Always crowded but it's worth waiting at the bar. Closed Sun.

Schnitzel Haus Frydenhoj, Red Hook ⓣ340/776-7198. Authentic German restaurant specializing in veal – the wiener schnitzel (US$22) is recommended. Only open Mon–Fri 6–9pm.

Sib's Mountain Bar Restaurant 33-5 Estate Elizabeth, Northside ⓣ340/774-8967. Mostly locals come to the bar to catch up on gossip, play pool or watch football over beer and inexpensive burgers.

Bars and clubs

Caribbean Saloon American Yacht Harbour, Red Hook ⓣ340/775-7060. A DJ spins on Weds, Fri and Sat but the real draw is the kitchen, which can satisfy late-night munchies until 4am. It's on the second floor overlooking the harbour.

Duffy's Love Shack Red Hook Plaza, Red Hook ⓣ340/779-2080. During high season, the music is deafening and the crowds spread out into the parking lot. Shots and special potent cocktails are the favourites. Look for drink specials such as the Hour of Power starting at midnight on Fri & Sat when drinks are two for one.

Fungi's 4 Estate Smith Bay, *Point Pleasant Resort* ⓣ340/775-4142. Located on the beach below the resort (park above and walk down), this informal place to eat and drink is a great spot live music on Fri. Also has some excellent home-made BBQ sauce. US$13–25.

Iggie's Beach Bar and Grill 50 Bolongo Bay, Bolongo Bay Beach Resort ⓣ340/775-1800. Named for the ubiquitous iguanas on the property, there's frequent live music at this open-air beach bar, as well as theme nights such as Carnival night when the firewalkers and conga lines come out.

Island Time American Yacht Harbour, Red Hook ⓣ340/774-2929. This casual bar overlooking the harbour serves salads, subs, Mexican munchies and yummy pizzas, ranging in price from US$8-12. Good for take-away or when drinking is more important than eating.

Watersports and outdoor activities

The majority of the **dive sites** are around the small cays and the most popular, such as Buck Island, Cow and Calf Rocks, are to the southeast. The *W.I.T Shoal*, a 400-ft freighter in 90ft of water is the best of the wrecks. Most wrecks are visited from St Thomas rather than St John, the notable exception being *Major General Rogers*, a 120-ft Coast Guard vessel intentionally sunk off St Thomas in 1972 which rests at 40–60ft. Other diveable wrecks are to the west through Savana Passage and near Sail Rock and dive shops are mostly limited to Charlotte Amalie. Pillsbury Sound between St Thomas and St John is often protected from the weather and features shallow sites visited by operators from both islands. Divers should be aware that certain sites are visited by cruise ship passengers and multiple boats of 20 per boat is not uncommon. If that sort of thing bothers you, you might want to see where your operator is heading and how many cruise ships are in port.

Whether you are going **sportfishing** for the big boy-blue marlin or just looking to catch some tuna to throw on the grill, there are plenty of boats out of St Thomas including American Yacht Harbour (ⓣ340/775-6454) or Charter Boat Center (ⓣ340/775-7990), both in Red Hook. For **golf** lovers, the Mahogany Run Golf Course (Route 42 near Magens Bay, ⓣ340/777-6006, or 1-800/253-7103 ⓦwww.mahoganyrungolf.com), is St Thomas' only golf course – an eighteen-holer that skirts the coastline. You can rent clubs and shoes – greens fees for nine holes plus cart are around US$100, for 18 it's around US$165. Most resorts have **tennis** courts open to non-guests – try *Marriott Frenchman's Reef* (ⓣ340/776-8500; free); or *Wyndham Sugar Bay* (ⓣ340/777-7100; US$8/hour).

Watersports

Aqua Action *Secret Harbour Beach Resort* ⓣ340/775-6285 or 1-888/775-6285, ⓦwww.aadivers.com. Offers certification and Discover Scuba courses and caps dive groups at ten people. Master Instructor Carl Moore is specially certified as a divemaster for people with disabilities, and courses/dives are available for a broad spectrum of special needs clients including quadriplegics.

Caribbean Watersports and Tours Saga Haven ☎340/775-9360; Ⓦwww.viwatersports.com. Strap yourself in and be pulled high up in the air for US$75 for a ride of about ten minutes. This outfit will pick you up and drop you off at your resort.

Chris Sawyer Diving American Yacht Harbour, Red Hook ☎340/777-7804. This PADI five-star underwater centre can help you with all your diving needs. Their dive speciality is the wreck of the *Rhone* in the BVI (see p.443). Certification also available.

Coki Beach Dive Club *Coki Beach* ☎340/775-4220 or 1-800/474-2654, Ⓦwww.cokidive.com. Offers the standard training courses through dive-master. Two-tank boat dives for US$85 to sites like Dog Island and the wreck of the *General Rogers*.

Limnos Charters Compass Point Marina, ☎340/775-3203. Offers all kinds of package sails to the US and British Virgin Islands with extremely knowledgeable crews.

Nauti Nymph Powerboat Rental American Yacht Harbour, Red Hook ☎340/775-5066. Choose the way you want your boat outfitted (snorkelling, water-skiing) and set out on a bareboat adventure if you're an experienced sailor (US$365–560) or with a captain if you're not (US$675).

VI Snuba Excursions Coki Beach ☎340/693-8063, Ⓦwww.visnuba.com. If you aren't scuba certified and haven't the time for a course, then snuba – part snorkel, part scuba – is for you (US$68 including Coral World pass). After twenty minutes of instruction you dive a maximum depth of 20 feet at the end of a regulator attached to a scuba tank floating above you on a small raft.

Virgin Islands Eco-Tours 2 Estate Nadir, Red Hook ☎340/779-2155. Learn about Mangrove Lagoon while touring the Virgin Islands Marine Sanctuary by kayak and see quite a different snorkelling scene.

West Indies Windsurfing Vessup Beach ☎340/775-6530. If your resort doesn't offer windsurfing lessons, give these guys a call and they'll have you flying across the seas in no time.

Shopping

St Thomas, and Charlotte Amalie in particular, is the shopping capital of the USVI. As Charlotte Amalie is a **duty-free** port, there are big savings on jewellery, clothes, perfumes, cosmetics, alcohol and electronics. The heart of the **shopping district** is the six-block grid between Tolbod Gade to the east and Trom Peter Gade to the west. The Vendor's Plaza, a daily outdoor **market** (9am–5pm) just south of Emancipation Garden, offers better deals than the shops along Main Street, but also a lot more junk, so you'll have to search to find the deals. The following are a taster of some of the best places to bargain hunt around the island. All, with the exception of Elizabeth Jane's, are in Charlotte Amalie.

Club Cigar Main Street ☎340/774-8100. The best selection of cigars on the island for 10–20% less than you would pay in the US.

The Crystal Shoppe Main Street ☎340/777-9835. With three branches on Main St. and one at Havensight, this is the place to find a large selection of fine crystal from Waterford, Herend, Swarovski and Lladro among others.

Diamond's International Main Street ☎340/774-1516. If you're in the market for a pristine diamond, these guys have the largest selection of loose rocks in the Caribbean, though better deals can be found.

Elizabeth Jane's American Yacht Harbour, Red Hook ☎340/779-1595. A wide selection of sterling silver jewellery at the best prices.

K-Mart Tutu Park Mall ☎340/714-4902. Don't laugh, the popular US department store has a great selection of duty-free liquor at the cheapest prices in town.

Local Color Waterfront Drive ☎340/774-2280. This store is popular with tourists for its colourful sundresses, hats, T-shirts, and other gear emblazoned with the island's name.

Native Arts and Crafts Cooperative Tolbod Gade ☎340/777-1153. Every kind of art you could imagine made by local artists at rock-bottom prices.

Royal Caribbean Havensight Mall ☎340/776-8890. One of five locations of the largest camera store in St Thomas. Often carries underwater housings for digital cameras.

Tropicana Perfume Shop 2 Main Street ☎340/774-0010. Has the largest selection of perfumes in the Virgin Islands at prices 20% lower than US prices.

St John

Located just three miles east of St Thomas and only accessible by boat, **ST JOHN**, the smallest and most pristine of the USVI, is the perfect hideaway and a paradise for nature lovers. Twenty square miles of lush mountains rise from perfect white-sand beaches, and with two-thirds of the island designated a **National Park** – one of the largest areas of wilderness in the whole of the Caribbean – there's an abundance of flora and fauna, including wild cats and burros (be careful, they bite), hummingbirds and iguanas. You really need to come for longer than a day-trip to get the most out of the scenery, miles of hiking trails, numerous secluded beaches, and many reefs to snorkel. A hike into the mountains will take you past sugar plantation ruins dating from the eighteenth century when the island had a population of two hundred whites and one thousand slaves. The main town is **Cruz Bay**, home to half of the island's five thousand inhabitants, with the best of the island's shopping, eating and nightlife.

Arrival and information

You'll find maps and brochures on the **ferry dock** in Cruz Bay (next to the ticket booth); grab a free copy of the *St John Guidebook*, which has a great town map. The **tourist office** (☎340/776-6450) is located in town next to the post office. The **National Park Visitor Centre** (daily 8am–4.30pm; ☎340/776-6201), at the creek in Cruz Bay north of the town centre, has exhibits on what you can expect to encounter on your hike, provides park maps and helps plan your trip or arrange guided hikes. There is a post office in Cruz Bay (Mon–Fri 7.30am–4pm and Sat 7.30am–noon; ☎340/779-4227).

Connections (☎340/776-6922, Ⓦwww.connectionsstjohn.com), located in the heart of Cruz Bay, is known as "information central" for the island and beyond. The staff can recommend restaurants and accommodation, and schedule watersports activities. For boaters, they monitor and provide updates from VHF channel 72. You can check your email, as well as receive snail mail, get a document notarized and receive cash via Western Union. You can also access the **Internet** in Cruz Bay at *Quiet Mon Pub & Cyber Celtic Café* (☎340/779-4799) for US$10/hour.

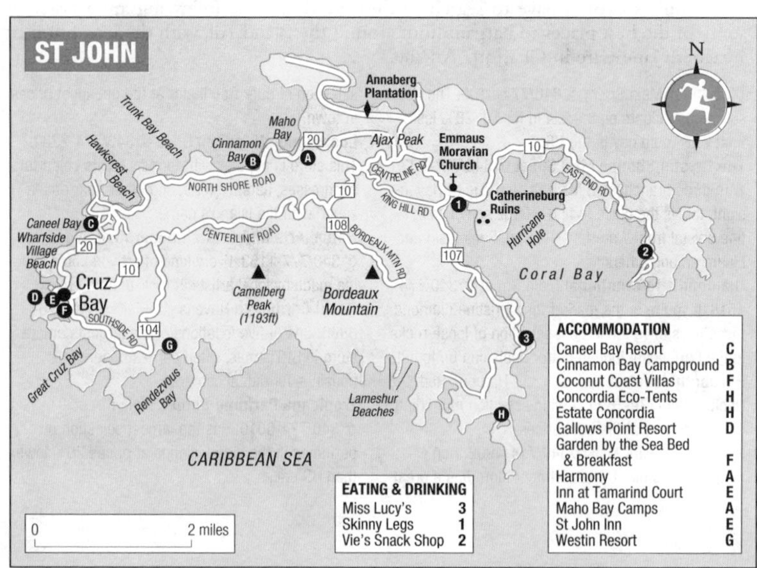

Getting around

VITRAN **buses** (US$1) are at the head of the ferry dock and are supposed to leave 15 minutes after each hour, making stops in the Park, Coral Bay and the East End. Schedules are erratic though, so this option is best if you're not in a hurry. **Taxis** – usually brightly painted pick-up trucks with open-air canopies – are plentiful in Cruz Bay and are also available for island tours (about US$25 per person for a one-and-half to two-hour tour). Don't be surprised if drivers try to pack in other people going your way. If you need to call ahead, try St John Taxi Services (ⓣ340/693-7530) or C&C Taxi Tours (ⓣ340/693-8164). Multiple **car rental** outfits are scattered throughout Cruz Bay and a quick walk around will present you with many options, most for US$80 per day. Note that most businesses only rent jeeps or 4x4 vehicles because of the hilly terrain. Try Best Car Rental (ⓣ340/693-8177); Conrad Sutton Car Rentals (ⓣ340/776-6479); Hospitality Jeep Rentals (ⓣ340/693-9160); or St John Car Rental (ⓣ340/776-6103).

Accommodation

The island holds all kinds of **accommodation options**, from beach camping, eco-cabins, and private boarding rooms to beachfront resorts and mountain villas, but given the small size of St John, the number of rooms is more limited and prices are generally higher. The smaller inns in **Cruz Bay** and the campsite outside of town, which also have eco-accommodations complete with air-conditioned and kitchenettes, are best for travellers on a budget. For groups, a villa may be the best option. A few great places to start your search include Caribbean Villas and Resorts (ⓣ340/776-6152 or 1-800/338-0987, ⓦwww.caribbeanvilla.com); Destination St John (ⓣ340/779-4647 or 1-800/562-1901, ⓦwww.destinationstjohn.com); and Private Homes for Private Vacations (ⓣ340/776-6876, ⓦwww.privatehomesvi.com).

Hotels and inns

Coconut Coast Villas 5000 A, Estate Enighed, Cruz Bay ⓣ340/693-9100, ⓦwww.coconutcoast.com. These breezy, bright and charming studio suites on Turner Bay, within a 10-minute walk to Cruz Bay, offer great value. Two 2-bedroom suites are also available. ⑦

Estate Concordia 16371 Estate Concordia, east of Cruz Bay ⓣ340/693-5855 or 1-800/392-9004, ⓦwww.maho.org. The nine units, located on the southeastern end of the island overlooking Salt Pond, are about 40 minutes from Cruz Bay. Most rooms are spacious and modern with terracotta floors, comfortable furniture and have balconies. ⑤–⑥

Garden by the Sea Bed and Breakfast Enighed, Cruz Bay ⓣ340/779-4731, ⓦwww.gardenbythesea.com. Just walking distance from town and surrounded by banana trees and coconut palms, this tranquil B&B offers colourful West Indian charm with a private snorkelling beach. Rooms have four-poster beds and lovely open-air showers. ⑦

Harmony Maho Bay, northeast of Cruz Bay ⓣ340/776-6226 or 1-800/392-9004, ⓦwww.maho.org. Located just above the *Maho Bay Camps*, these studios are a step above tent accommodation, offering creature comforts while adhering to *Maho's* eco-friendly environment. The electricity comes from the sun, rain is collected for the running water in your kitchenette and private bath, and wind scoops help pull breezes through lofted rooms. ⑥

Inn at Tamarind Court Cruz Bay ⓣ340/776-6378 or 1-800/221-1637, ⓦwww.tamarindcourt.com. This pink, twenty-room, B&B-style inn offers all the amenities and solitude you'll need while keeping you close to the action in Cruz Bay. Accommodation ranges from single rooms with shared baths to more spacious apartments with full kitchens and private baths. All have cable TV and a/c. The courtyard bar and restaurant are open for breakfast and dinner, and might be noisy for some guests. ③–⑥

St John Inn Cruz Bay ⓣ340/693-8688 or 1-800/666-7688, ⓦwww.stjohninn.com. On the outskirts of Cruz Bay, this little hideaway offers thirteen rooms, all of which are individually decorated, and have a fridge and microwave; some have kitchenettes and ocean views. ⑤–⑥

Resorts

Caneel Bay Resort Rte 20, north of Cruz Bay ⓣ340/776-6111 or 1-888/767-3966, ⓦwww.caneelbay.com. This eco-resort brainchild of Laurence Rockefeller opened in 1956 on a 170-acre peninsula. No phones, TVs or radios. Rooms are beautifully decorated and many offer views of one of the seven beaches. The garden rooms are the best deals and have large stone showers. Four restaurants and a wine bar are onsite. ⑨

Gallows Point Resort Gallows Point, just south of Cruz Bay ⓣ340/776-6434 or 1-800/323-7229, ⓦwww.gallowspointresort.com. The only resort within walking distance of Cruz Bay, set on a four-acre peninsula overlooking the Caribbean. The suites accommodate up to four people and all have fully equipped kitchens, spacious living rooms and water views. Beaches with snorkelling are a short walk away. *ZoZo's Restaurant* (see p.422) onsite. ⑨

Westin Resort Rte 104, southeast of Cruz Bay ⓣ340/693-8000 or 1-800/937-8461, ⓦwww.westinresortstjohn.com. The 175 guest rooms and 147 villas sit on a 47-acre compound overlooking Rendezvous Bay. The resort offers guests a little of everything – beach, restaurants, bars, shopping centre, deli, spa, tennis courts and gym. The one-bedroom villas at US$1089 and standard rooms at US$1079 per night are laughably expensive for what you (don't) get. ⑨

Campsite

Cinnamon Bay Campground Rte 20, northeast of Cruz Bay ⓣ340/776-6330 or 1-800/539-9998, ⓦwww.cinnamonbay.com. This site has a selection: forty smallish cottages (⑤) with patios, cooking equipment, utensils, charcoal grill, propane stoves and communal bathrooms; sixty canvas tents (③) with solid floors and lanterns but no electricity; or 26 bare campsites (②) with a picnic table and charcoal grill. Restaurant and weekly activities.

Concordia Eco-Tents Coral Bay ⓣ340/776-6240 or 1-800/392-9004, ⓦwww.maho.org. One of *Maho*'s sister eco-complexes on the eastern side of the island right next to *Concordia Estate*, these digs offer a few more modern amenities. The 24 tents offer wind and solar power, kitchenettes with running water, private toilets and solar-heated showers. A work exchange programme is available during the off season. Four of the seven newest units offer wheelchair access. ⑤–⑥

Maho Bay Camps Maho Bay, northeast of Cruz Bay ⓣ340/776-6240 or 1-800/392-9004, ⓦwww.maho.org. Stanley Selengut started these camps in 1976 before the term eco-tourism existed. Now *Maho* has 114 units tucked in the hills above Maho Bay connected by wooden walkways. The tent cottages have cots, linens, towels, propane stoves and cooking and eating utensils. The restaurant offers healthy fare and veggie options and the store sells foodstuffs and sundries. They also offer a four-hours-per-day work programme in exchange for lodging. ⑤

Cruz Bay and around

CRUZ BAY didn't become a port until the mid-1800s, when Danish soldiers from St Thomas used it as an outpost. Unlike towns on the other main USVI, there's not much in the way of architecture, but it's a great place to spend a leisurely day shopping, eating and drinking. As you get off the ferry, in front of you and beyond the collection of taxis is a municipal park and pavilion. With the water on your left, if you walk down Northshore Road you'll see on your right **Mongoose Junction**, an upmarket outdoor mall, which is worth a look. **Wharfside Village Beach**, to your right as you exit the ferry dock, is the only beach in Cruz Bay, and while technically you can swim, it's not recommended as this is a busy harbour. You're better off using the beach for powerboat rentals, sea-kayak tours and to book dive trips. Surrounding the beach is the outdoor mall, Wharfside Village. Apart from Cruz Bay, the only other commercial area on the island is **Coral Bay**, the site of St John's first Danish colony, which now hosts a growing number of restaurants and shops catering mostly to the boating crowd. It's also home to the **Emmaus Moravian Church**, the oldest church on St John from 1782.

The Virgin Islands National Park

This spectacular and varied **National Park** encompasses about 7200 acres above ground and 5600 acres of marine sanctuary. The land was donated – with the stipulation that it would be used for a national park – to the federal government in 1956 by Laurence Rockefeller, John D.'s son. Get park information from the **National Park Visitor Centre** at Cruz Bay (see p.418) and a copy of the Park Service's monthly schedule of ranger-led activities. For some easy self-guided **beach hikes** that leave from Cruz Bay, ask the park ranger about trailhead locations for Lind Point, Salomon and Honeymoon (the unofficial nude beach). You'll need to drive or get a taxi to the start of the self-guided trails to the Annaberg Sugar Mill Ruins

▲ Annaberg Sugar Mill Ruins

(see below), Cinnamon Bay Loop and the Francis Bay Trail. All of these trails are a half-mile over easy terrain. For the more adventurous, there's the **Reef Bay Trail**, on Centerline Road, accessible by bus. This three-mile (one-way) hike takes you downhill through moist tropical forest (look for the kapok trees, with their cloaked roots), cactus woodland, past petroglyphs and sugar mill ruins before bringing you out at a beach. If you chose to go on your own, you'll have to hike back out, or you can join one of the park service's organized hikes, where you'll get back to Cruz Bay via boat. Book far ahead, (☎340/776-6201 ext. 238; $21) as these hikes fill up weeks in advance. Note that you must book over the phone between 8.00am and 4.30pm, and confirm with a person – don't just leave a message.

The rest of the island and the beaches

Besides the obvious natural beauty, there are a few low-key attractions around the island. Four miles northeast of town, above Leinster Bay, a walk around the ruins of the well-preserved 1733 **Annaberg Plantation** offers the best impression of what a sugar plantation was like, plus some amazing views. If this whets your appetite for more ruins, visit the **Catherineberg Sugar Mill Ruins** (Rte 10), once a sugar plantation and rum factory, which, after the revolt of the 1730s served as the headquarters for the slave uprising. On the east side of the island the hills rise to a peak at **Bordeaux Mountain** (1277ft), the highest spot on St John. Stop for a scoop of ice cream or a snack on patios overlooking Coral Bay.

Beaches

St John has its fair share of white-sand **beaches** and stunning azure bays where you can sunbathe, nap in a hammock, float in tranquil waters and snorkel the reefs. Trunk and Cinnamon Bays offer dressing facilities, restrooms, food outlets and watersports rentals. Only **Trunk Bay** Beach charges admission (US$4), and by law all beaches (up to 15ft) are public, even those that skirt private resort property. For smaller, more out-of-the-way beaches, such as those on the eastern part of the island like Lameshur and Salt Pond, get a map from the National Park's Contact Station in Cruz Bay. Trunk Bay is St John's best and most popular beach. The **snorkel trail** here (marked by red, white and blue buoys) has underwater plaques to help you identify the coral and fish you see, but it won't knock your socks (or flippers) off. Better snorkelling is towards the west end of the beach. There are also food and facilities, and snorkel equipment for rent. VI Snuba Excursions (☎340/693-8063) offers **snuba**, but you'll need a reservation. Note that Wednesdays are very busy due to cruise ship day-trippers from St. Thomas.

Further east, at **Cinnamon Bay**, part of the National Park's campsite, you can rent kayaks, snorkel equipment, and even get a windsurfing lesson. This is also the best place for **surfers** to catch a northern swell in winter. For a break from the beach, head out on the Cinnamon Bay Nature Trail, which loops through ruins and returns you to the beach. **Hawksnest Beach**, on the other side of the peninsula from the *Caneel Bay Resort* (see p.419), is a favourite with locals because it's not tourist-heavy. There's snorkelling, changing facilities and picnic tables here. Advanced snorkellers might consider kayaking out of **Maho Bay** to Whistling Cay or Mary Point. **Salt Pond Bay** near Coral Bay has a rocky beach better for exploring than lounging on. Tide pools and some good snorkelling await.

Eating and drinking

St John has great **dining** options, whatever your taste. If you're self-catering, the island has several grocery stores, though don't be surprised by the prices and the limited supply. Although most **restaurants** and **bars** are located in Cruz Bay (or close by), some are springing up in Coral Bay.

Banana Deck Cruz Bay ☎340/693-5055. The ribeyes are a speciality (US$20–30) at this open terrace, which is the home to all things banana, from splits and banana caramel cheesecake to banana rum. The place is often packed so make a reservation.

J.J.'s Texas Coast On the municipal park, Cruz Bay ☎340/776-6908. Always a cheap, reliable option, *J.J.'s* serves tasty breakfast burritos as well as lunch or dinner outside or at tables around the indoor bar.

The Lime Inn Cruz Bay ☎340/776-6425. A mainstay since 1984, this open-air restaurant with full bar serves good seafood, steaks and an all-you-can-eat shrimp feast (US$22) on Wed night.

Paradiso Cruz Bay ☎340/693-8899. A standout, definitely stop at this comfortable Mongoose Junction restaurant. Ask for a table on the second-floor terrace and watch the world pass below. Entrees US$28–38.

Rhum Lines Cruz Bay ☎340/776-0303 Inventive pan-Asian cuisine reflects the chef's world travels in dishes such as a Mahi Mahi filet wrapped in a banana leaf (US$22) and a tasty Vietnamese chicken salad (US$9).

Sogo's Cruz Bay ☎340/779-4404 You'll have your pick of great island fare at this locally-owned establishment, with specialties like stewed curried goat (US$15) and steamed conch (US$22) taking top billing. Finish up with the fantastic coconut tart.

La Tapa Cruz Bay ☎340/693-7755. Serving phenomenal contemporary Mediterranean food in a setting reminiscent of a Parisian bistro, this should be one of your first dinner stops on the island. Try the mussels in white wine for an appetizer, followed by the to-die-for duck confit. Entrees US$35-40.

Uncle Joe's BBQ Cruz Bay ☎340/693-8806. Ask locals and their eyes will light up at the mere mention of this outdoor grill not far from the ferry landing. Hands down, this is the best barbecue on the island, so go early before the inexpensive food runs out, which it does.

Vie's Snack Shop Hansen Bay ☎340/693-5033. More like a snack shack, there's not much for your eyes to feast on. But some swear the conch fritters (US$12) are the best in the Caribbean. Other snacks include meat pies and johnny cakes.

ZoZo's Cruz Bay ☎340/693-9200. A favourite among locals who want to splurge on some killer Italian food like a handmade lobster fettuccini (US$16) that is out of this world and a sunset view to match.

Nightlife and entertainment

While the island doesn't have any discos, clubs or theatres, there are lots of great **bars** and festivals that give you a chance to tilt a few back and party.

The Beach Bar Wharfside Village ☎340/777-4220. The perfect spot for a burger and a beer after a tough day on the water. For appetizers, try the flying shrimp (US$13). Always hopping around happy hour from 3–7pm. Live music three or four times a week and a jazz jam on Sundays from 4–7.30pm.

Fred's Bar, Restaurant and Gaming Room Cruz Bay ⓣ340/776-6363. The food is missable but the live brass bands or calypso on Fri nights really hit the spot. Often a US$10 cover charge though some avoid it by listening from the street or a table at *The Lime Inn Restaurant*.

The Frontyard Cruz Bay ⓣ340/693-9275. At this pavilion-style bar that seems more of a backyard, Jagerbomb shots are the self-proclaimed house wine, live bands rock at the weekends and the hour happy hour runs from 3–6pm. Open until 4am.

Larry's Landing Cruz Bay ⓣ340/693-8802. Order a rum and Coke, and they'll give you the bottle, the can and a glass of ice at this pour-your-own bar across from Wharfside Village. There's pool, gambling games and TVs to watch the big game.

Miss Lucy's Restaurant and Bar Estate Friis past Coral Bay ⓣ340/693-5244. This beachside establishment serves West Indian fare for lunch and dinner, around US$15–20. There's also a Sunday jazz brunch and full-moon parties.

Skinny Legs Coral Bay ⓣ340/779-4982. Check out the Lost Soles shoe exhibit at this local shack bar. It's a fun drinking spot popular among the boating crowd and locals with occasional live music. Sandwiches and great burgers for US$10.

Woody's Seafood Saloon Cruz Bay ⓣ340/779-4625. The sight of people spilling onto the street means you've arrived at *Woody's* – a small joint serving fried seafood and a party. Open until 2am most nights. The crowd is perennially happy, and you can down shots like Surfer on Acid.

Watersports and outdoor activities

Arawak Expeditions (ⓣ340/693-8312) runs half- and full-day **mountain-bike tours** for US$50–90 per person. If you want to try **fishing**, Bite Me Charters (ⓣ340/693-5823, ⓦwww.bitemechartersvi.com) does full, three-quarter and half-day trips aboard *See Bee*, a 30ft Sea-Vee, for US$500–900 for four people, US$50 extra per person up to six. Dorado Sport Fishing (ⓣ340/693-5664) has a 32ft catamaran, which leaves from Coral Bay for fishing trips off the South Drop of St John. Fishing, drinks, bait and tackle are all included at a price of US$110 per hour or US$700 for 8 hours. For the ultimate fishing experience arrange a trip on *The Marlin Prince* (ⓣ340/693-5929, ⓦwww.marlinprince.com), a custom 45ft Viking with an air-conditioned gallery, deck shower, and even a washer/dryer. They provide all types of fishing, but their speciality is tournament fishing. Expect to pay US$1200 for a boat for six for a full day of marlin mania. You can go **horseriding** with Carolina Corral, Coral Bay (ⓣ340/693-5778) on a one and one-half hour-long ride that climbs the Johnny Horn Trail to the top of Hurricane Hole (US$75). There are public **tennis** courts on the outskirts of Cruz Bay (open till 10pm; free) or courts at *The Westin* (ⓣ340/693-8000; non-guests US$20 an hour).

Watersports

St John offers a little of everything for **watersports** enthusiasts. All kinds of chartered **sailing** excursions are available – most leave Cruz Bay at about 10am, returning at 4pm and include lunch. You can go through one of the services mentioned below, enquire inside Connections (see p.418) or just look at advertisements tacked on telephone posts. Snorkellers should stop in at the National Park Visitor Centre at Cruz Creek and pick up a pamphlet that gives good descriptions of the best sites. It's best to buy your own mask before you come or at a dive shop in Cruz Bay – rentals are often shabby and won't fit right. **Divers** will not find much on their own, but there's PADI training and excursions for certified divers can be booked to shipwrecks, larger reefs and underwater caves. Popular sites include Carvel Rock, Cow and Calf Rocks and wreck dives to the *Major General Rogers* (see p.416) and the RMS *Rhone*, just off the BVI's Salt Island (see p.443)

Activities Information Center Cruz Bay ⓣ340/715-4944, ⓦwww.bestofusvi.com. This catch-all booth at Mongoose Junction can help you book everything from sport fishing, sailing and powerboat charters to kayak rentals, scuba and snorkel trips and parasailing.

Arawak Expeditions ⓣ340/693-8312 or 1-800/238-8687, ⓦwww.arawakexp.com. Adventure outfitter that leads kayak expeditions (US$50 for half-day, US$90 for full-day) around St John and surrounding islands. Longer trips include camping on deserted beaches and inn-to-inn multi-island packages.

Cinnamon Bay Watersports Center ☎340/776-6330 or 1-800/539-9998. You can rent snorkel equipment, kayaks and small sailboats and surfboards at this campsite facility. They also offer windsurfing, sailing and surfing lessons and can help book other watersports activities.
Cruz Bay Watersports Lumberyard Complex and Westin, Cruz Bay ☎340/776-6234, Ⓦwww.divestjohn.com. This ultimate dive shop offers PADI and NAUI training and daily two-tank dives that leave at 8.15am and return by 12.30pm (US$95). Packages are available. Ask about the popular Jost Van Dyke trip, which is equal parts snorkelling and drinking.
Low Key Watersports Wharfside Village, Cruz Bay ☎340/693-8999 or 1-800/835-7718, Ⓦwww.divelowkey.com. There's a high-spirited crew at this PADI five-star training facility that offers great night dives and wreck dives. General two-tank dives go for US$90.
Maho Bay Water Sports Center *Maho Bay Camp.* Offers a wide variety of snorkel, sailboat, and windsurfing rentals, as well as a comprehensive scuba diving programme.
Noah's Little Arks Wharfside Village, Cruz Bay ☎340/693-9030. Rent one of the12ft or 14ft inflatable dinghies for the freedom to motor yourself around North shore of the island for exploring and snorkelling; each comes with a map of the reefs and a fish ID chart. Use that reef map – if you break the motor, you pay for it.
VI Snuba Excursions Trunk Bay ☎340/693-8063, Ⓦwww.visnuba.com. If you are interested in diving but find it a daunting prospect, try this snorkelling/diving hybrid called snuba. Basic instructions will you started and then you will swim along the bottom attached to an air tank that floats at the surface for US$65. Suitable for anyone at least eight years old.

St Croix

ST CROIX, the largest of the USVI, measuring twenty-eight miles by seven miles, is also the most remote, lying forty miles south of St Thomas. For many years this peaceful gem has been accessible only by air or cruise ship but now a fast ferry connects the island to St Thomas, and multiple daily seaplane flights connect Christiansted to Charlotte Amalie making it a must-see for all visitors to the USVI. The landscape is a mixture of gentle, rocky sierras, fertile coastal plain and rainforest and, of course, picturesque beaches. The towns contain more plentiful and beautiful examples of Danish colonial architecture than other islands and the landscape is dotted with the ruins of plantations and stone windmills from the island's days as king of the Caribbean sugar cane industry. St Croix is a fusion of cuisines, ideas and customs, and its employment opportunities (the Hess Oil refinery and tourism) and proximity to the US (and potential for US citizenship) attract people from all over the Caribbean.

St Croix's two major towns are historic **Christiansted** on the northeast coast and **Frederiksted** on the west coast. The latter had its heyday as a cruise ship port but has been very quiet since 2002 when cruise ships pulled up stakes. Christiansted is almost always lively, and often filled with Danes tracing their roots. Don't leave without a visit to the tiny but spectacular **Buck Island** off the northeast coast. The island has been administered by the National Park Service since 1948 and is a paradise of beaches, reefs and hiking and snorkelling trails.

Arrival and information

The **Henry E. Rohlsen Airport** is located on the southern side of the island. VITRAN **buses** (☎340/778-0898) are supposed to run between the airport and Christiansted every hour (ask at the airport for a route map and schedule) but are not very reliable; a **taxi** from the airport will cost about US$15 to Christiansted and US$16 to Frederiksted.

You can also take a **seaplane** to St Croix from St Thomas on Seaborne Airlines, which offers more than a dozen flights per day.

Tourist offices – at the airport, in Frederiksted (at the pier; ☎340/772-0357) and in downtown Christiansted (☎340/773-1404) – will load you up with maps,

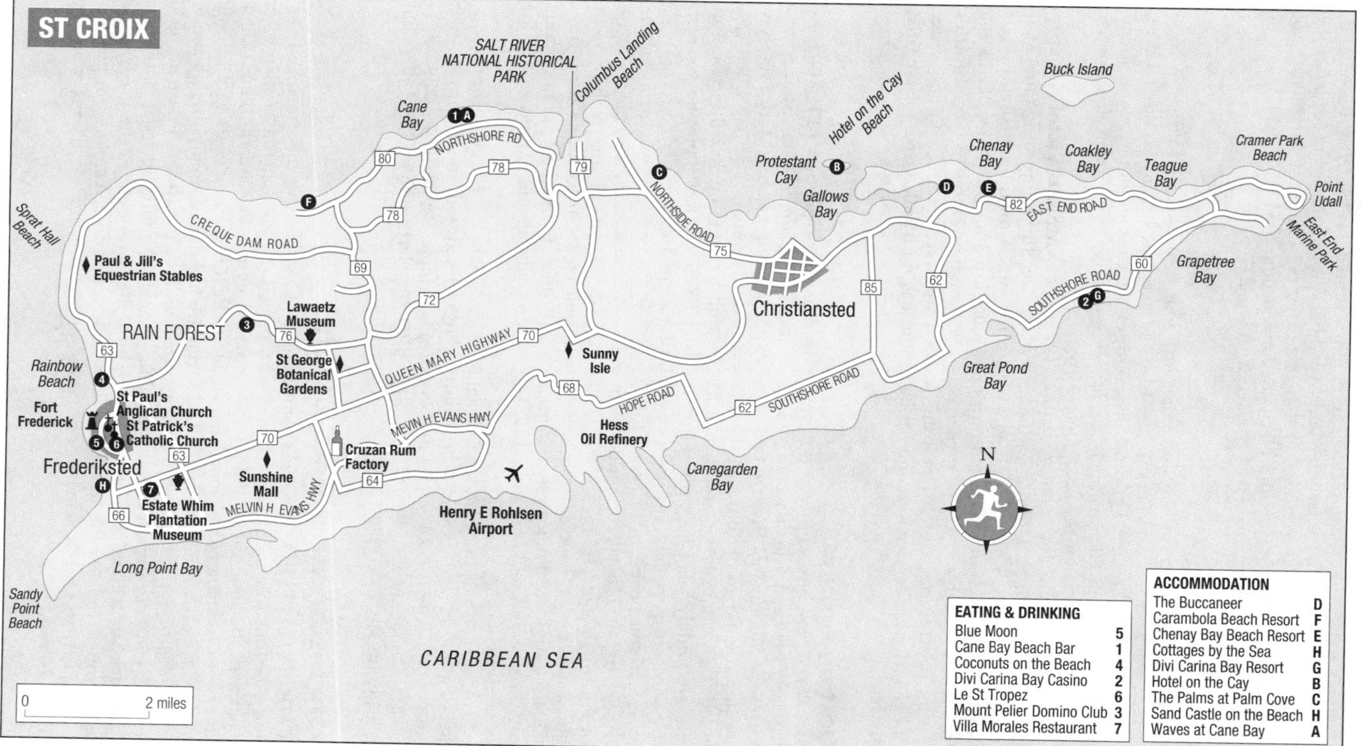
ST CROIX
SALT RIVER NATIONAL HISTORICAL PARK
Columbus Landing Beach
Buck Island
Cane Bay
Hotel on the Cay Beach
Protestant Cay
Gallows Bay
Chenay Bay
Coakley Bay
Teague Bay
Cramer Park Beach
Point Udall
East End Marine Park
Grapetree Bay
Sprat Hall Beach
NORTHSHORE RD
NORTHSIDE ROAD
EAST END ROAD
SOUTHSHORE ROAD
CREQUE DAM ROAD
Paul & Jill's Equestrian Stables
Lawaetz Museum
RAIN FOREST
Christiansted
St George Botanical Gardens
QUEEN MARY HIGHWAY
Sunny Isle
HOPE ROAD
Great Pond Bay
Rainbow Beach
St Paul's Anglican Church
St Patrick's Catholic Church
Fort Frederick
Frederiksted
MELVIN H EVANS HWY
Cruzan Rum Factory
Hess Oil Refinery
Sunshine Mall
Canegarden Bay
Estate Whim Plantation Museum
Henry E Rohlsen Airport
Long Point Bay
Sandy Point Beach
CARIBBEAN SEA
N
0 2 miles
EATING & DRINKING
Blue Moon 5
Cane Bay Beach Bar 1
Coconuts on the Beach 4
Divi Carina Bay Casino 2
Le St Tropez 6
Mount Pelier Domino Club 3
Villa Morales Restaurant 7
ACCOMMODATION
The Buccaneer D
Carambola Beach Resort F
Chenay Bay Beach Resort E
Cottages by the Sea H
Divi Carina Bay Resort G
Hotel on the Cay B
The Palms at Palm Cove C
Sand Castle on the Beach H
Waves at Cane Bay A

brochures and advice. **Post offices** are in Christiansted, Gallows Bay, Richmond, Sunny Isle, Kings Hill, Frederiksted and Mars Hill. You can access the **Internet** for about US$10/hr in Christiansted at A Better Copy (52 Company St, ⓣ340/692-5303) or for US$12 at Surf the Net (Pan Am Pavilion, ⓣ340/719-6245), and in Frederiksted at Rotsen Express (1 Market St, ⓣ340/277-6950).

Accommodation

Accommodation runs the gamut from small inns to bed-and-breakfasts to large all-inclusive resorts – and because the island is less visited than the other USVI, prices are usually cheaper. For those on a **budget**, the cheapest hotels can be found in Frederiksted and Christiansted. The luxury resorts on St Croix are less swanky than their St Thomas or St John counterparts.

If you're looking for a more natural experience, **Mount Victory Camp** (ⓣ340/772-1651 or 1-866/772-1651, ⓦwww.mtvictorycamp.com; rates start at US$600 per week) is the only **eco-camping** option on the island and offers rentals by the week only. Located north of Frederiksted on Mahogany Road, the grounds were built entirely by owner Bruce Wilson. Five canopied tent platforms feature beds, linens, coolers, propane stoves, cookware, utensils, running water and electricity. The clean communal bathroom has flush toilets and solar-heated showers.

Getting around

St Croix's few bus stops are not very conveniently located. **VITRAN** runs regularly between Christiansted and Frederiksted (5.30am–9.30pm from Mon–Sat every 30min) but **shared taxi vans** running along Queen Mary Highway are just as good an option. Flag them down as they approach and pay when you board. They stop on demand, which can be time-consuming, but they're cheap and are widely used by commuting locals (US$2.50 before 6pm; be warned, the vans are very few and far between after 6pm and the price is US$0.50 more). If you need to call ahead for one, try St Croix Taxi Association (at the airport, ⓣ340/778-1088); Antilles Taxi Service, Christiansted (ⓣ340/773-5020); or Rudy's Taxi and Tours (ⓣ340/773-6803 or 340/514-4600). Alternatively, most hotels and resorts have cut-rate shuttles that will take you back and forth from Christiansted and Frederiksted at prearranged times. From the East End, **taxis** to Christiansted will cost around US$40 for a round-trip and around US$50 for Frederiksted.

St Croix is a great island for driving around, and several **car-rental** firms have offices in and around Christiansted, Frederiksted and at the airport: Avis (ⓣ340/778-9395); Budget (ⓣ340/778-9636); Olympic Rent-a-Car (ⓣ340/773-8000); Centerline Car Rentals (ⓣ340/778-0450); Hertz (ⓣ340/778-1402); and Thrifty (ⓣ340/773-7200).

Christiansted and around

CHRISTIANSTED, St Croix's capital and its most historic and developed city, was established in 1735 by the Danes, who named the town after Christian VI of Denmark. Because of a building code installed by the forward-thinking Danes, much of Christiansted's original architecture still exists. In some cases, you can still see street signs written in Danish. The streets are laid out so simply that it's almost impossible to get lost, which makes it a great walking city. It has a pleasant, aged feel, its handful of historic sights mingling with small courtyard restaurants and a laid-back bar scene down on the Wharf, on the city centre's northern edge. And once you've tired of the town's low-key attractions, you can indulge in plentiful watersports and beach activities not far off, or go on nature excursions to nearby **Buck Island**.

Accommodation

Christiansted

Carringtons Inn Estate Hermon Hill ⓣ340/713-0508 or 1-877/658-0508, ⓦwww.carringtonsinn.com. A five-room bed-and-breakfast on a hill overlooking Christiansted. The owners are delightful and pay great attention to details, including fresh flower arrangements and excellent breakfasts. ⑤

Company House Hotel 2 Company St ⓣ340/773-1377. Recently purchased and refurbished by the owners of *King Christian Hotel*, this hotel offers good value. Rooms are basic but clean, and the small pool is a quiet oasis. ③–④

Hotel Caravelle 44A King Cross St ⓣ340/773-0687 or 1-800/524-0410, ⓦwww.hotelcaravelle.com. A 43-room, European-style hotel located just off the Wharf downtown, offering homey accommodation at a reasonable price. ⑤

Hotel on the Cay Protestant Cay ⓣ340/773-2035 or 1-800/524-2035, ⓦwww.hotelonthecay.com. This seven-acre island, located in Christiansted's harbour, is just a ninety-second ferry ride from the wharf. Rooms have kitchenettes and balconies, and though the place is showing wear and tear, the price is not bad and many watersports are available. Three night minimum during high season. ⑤

King Christian Hotel King's Wharf ⓣ340/773-6330 or 1-800/524-2012, ⓦwww.kingchristian.com. Clean bright rooms located right on the boardwalk, some of which were refurbished in 2007. Superior rooms have views of the sea and fort and the infinity pool is a nice place to while away an afternoon. ⑤

King's Alley Hotel King's Alley ⓣ340/773-0103 or 1-800/843-3574. Reopened in early 2008 after an extensive refurbishment, this wharf-front hotel offers the nicest digs in town for the price. Rooms have flat-screen TVs, plush bedding and lots of dark wood. ⑤

Pink Fancy 27 Prince St ⓣ340/773-8460 or 1-800/524-2045, ⓦwww.pinkfancy.com. An extremely cute and well-kept, gay-friendly historic inn (the oldest part of the four-building complex is a Danish townhouse from 1780) was a favourite hangout of stage stars like Noel Coward in the 1950s. Best value in town. Closed in Sept. ④–⑤

Around Christiansted

The Buccaneer 5007 Estate Shoys ⓣ340/712-2100 or 1-800/255-3881, ⓦwww.thebuccaneer.com. Situated on 340 pristine acres, with three beaches offering good snorkelling, an eighteen-hole golf course, eight tennis courts and huge rooms; the island's finest resort. ⑨

Carambola Beach Resort Estate Davis Bay ⓣ340/778-3800, ⓦwww.carambolabeach.com. Designed in the Tahitian Rockefeller style of *Caneel Bay*. The luxury suites recently got a $20 million dollar update, and now include flat-screen TVs and marble showers. Two restaurants, tennis courts, spa and a lovely stretch of beach. Good hiking in the hills along the coast and the golf course is the best on the island. ⑦

Chenay Bay Beach Resort Rte 82 ⓣ340/773-2918 or 1-866/226-8677, ⓦwww.chenaybay.com. Located on sedate Chenay Bay, east of Christiansted, this resort offers fifty, tightly situated West Indian-style cottages, all with kitchenettes, as well as a lovely infinity pool, located on a former sugar plantation. The restaurant is good, and Saturday features a pig roast and carnival-style entertainers. ⑤–⑥

Divi Carina Bay Resort 25 Estate Turner Hole ⓣ340/773-9700 or 1-800/823-9352, ⓦwww.divicarina.com. Though remote (a rental car is a must) this is not a sleepy resort. There's an 18-hole miniature golf course, PADI dive centre and casino across the street. All 180 rooms overlook the sea and have refrigerators, wet bars and microwaves. Wheelchair-accessible guest rooms available. ⑥

The Palms at Pelican Cove 4126 La Grande Princesse ⓣ340/718-8920 or 1-800/548-4460, ⓦwww.palmspelicancove.com. This resort is a peaceful delight situated on a white-sand peninsula surrounded by the ocean. Rooms feature private balconies and sea views. ⑦

Waves at Cane Bay Rte 80 ⓣ340/778-1805 or 1-800/545-0603, ⓦwww.canebaystcroix.com. Situated west of Christiansted on Cane Bay, this is the place to stay if you want to literally roll out of bed, don your scuba gear and hit the water. Shore dives to the wall are possible and guests are provided with snorkelling gear, maps and instructions. ⑤

The Town

Christiansted is the best-preserved colonial city in all the Virgin Islands and has a number of historic public buildings and churches. The best place to start a tour is the **Scale House** at the top of King Street by the Wharf (daily 8am–4.45pm; ⓣ340/773-1460), which was built in 1856 as the weigh house for all the goods that passed through the harbour and nowadays houses a small bookshop. Nearby are the **Customs House** (Mon–Fri 8am–5pm) and **Fort Christianvaern**, off

Hospital Street (daily 8am–4.45pm; US$3), constructed in 1749, and current home of the visitor's centre. St Croix's finest example of Danish military architecture, you can take a guided or self-guided tour through the dungeon's torture chambers, and visit the officers' kitchen and the barrack rooms. The same ticket grants admission to the **Steeple Building** across the road (daily 8am–4.30pm), the island's first Danish Lutheran church, built in 1753 and now housing the national park museum, which offers exhibits on the history of the church, St Croix's indigenous tribes, sugar plantations, rum factories and slavery. The **West Indies Guinea Warehouse**, serving as the headquarters for the National Park Service (Mon–Fri 8am–5pm) is on the same street and used to house the trading company that basically built the town of Christiansted. A short walk north, **Government House**, on King Street, was originally the mansion of a Danish merchant, built in 1747, but today this pretty, long, bright-yellow building houses the local government. If it's open, slip into the courtyard, where you'll be met by a flowing fountain and lush greenery. Afterwards, take in the **Lutheran Church of Lord God of Sabaoth**, further down King Street, built by the original Danish settlers in 1734, but later renamed the Dutch Reformed Church. It houses the original altar from the Steeple Building. Nearby, Company Street is the home of a regular Wednesday and Saturday **market** at which local farmers, fishermen and local craftsmen sell their goods on the site of the original 1735 slave market.

Around town

Around three miles west of Christiansted, the **Salt River National Historical Park and Ecological Preserve** is nowadays a freshwater channel by which lavish yachts enter the marina, but historically was the place where Columbus first sent sailors ashore in 1493. This is also the site of many successful excavations which have rendered artefacts from some of the indigenous peoples, and guided hikes are available. In the opposite direction from Christiansted, **Point Udall** is the easternmost point of the United States, and one of the most peaceful spots on the island. It's a windblown spot, but ideal for escaping the crowds. You can also hike down one of many trails to the beaches at the **East End Marine Park** (Ⓣ340/773-3367, Ⓦwww.stxeastendmarinepark.org) where the protected waters of **Jack's Bay** and **Isaac's Bay** butt up against lush, rolling hills. The snorkelling is excellent, and the park runs a variety of both land- and sea-based free interpretive tours; check the website for details. A mile out to sea to the north, **Buck Island Reef National Monument** is St Croix's crown jewel, with picture-perfect deserted beaches, great hiking and an underwater trail for snorkellers. It was proclaimed a National Monument in 1962 by President John F. Kennedy, and consists of 700 acres of Caribbean reef and sea and 180 acres of land. The underwater snorkel trail weaves through Elkhorn coral forests, unfortunately severely damaged by Hurricane Hugo in 1989, continuing overuse and global warming. The island itself is worth a day-trip – try Caribbean Sea Adventures (see p.432) for a variety of tours and charters. Best check with the National Park Service (Ⓣ340/773-1460) regarding rules for visiting on your own boat.

Beaches

The beach at the *Hotel on the Cay*, across the harbour from Christiansted, is the closest **beach** to town. It's accessible only by the regular US$3 ferry, and offers watersports rentals, a restaurant and bar. Further away, the beach at **Cane Bay**, six miles or so west of Christiansted off Route 80, has great snorkelling, plus a dive shop that offers trips, a beach bar and restaurant. Closer to town, **Columbus Landing Beach** is the beach off the Salt River where Columbus's men first came ashore.

Eating and drinking

Despite being the least touristed of the USVI, St Croix's cuisine varies from burgers to high-end Asian. While there are a few great **places to eat** in Frederiksted, Christiansted is the culinary capital of St Croix, and it's a mostly casual experience with no need to dress up.

Bacchus 52 Queen Cross St ☎340/692-9922. The food here lives up to its creative names – try the "Is there a fungus among us" stuffed Portabella mushroom (US$20) and be sure to save room for dessert – "5 reasons not to eat too much bread". Request a table overlooking the street and choose something special from the largest wine list on the island. Open Tues–Sun 6–10pm.

Fort Christian Brew Pub 55 King's Alley ☎340/713-9820. Hot sandwiches, pastas, gumbos and other Cajun favourites costing around US$10-15. The locally brewed beer is a must. Located on the boardwalk overlooking the water.

Full Moon Beach Bar Rte 80 ☎340/778-5669. Burgers and beer on the beach at Cane Bay, west of town. Cash only, US$10–18.

Harvey's Restaurant and Bar 11B Company St ☎340/773-3433. Reasonably priced fare (US$6–12), specializing in Creole dishes and barbecue. Lunch only Mon–Sat from 11.30 to when the food runs out. You don't want to be late for the seafood kallaloo on Fri. Also a good place to sample local drinks made from tamarind, soursop or *maubi* (a root).

Kim's 45 King St ☎340/773-3377. Dine among locals at this good-value West Indian eatery. The conch in butter sauce melts in your mouth (US$12). Mon–Sat 11am–9pm.

Luncheria 6 Company St ☎340/773-4247. Cheap and savoury Tex-Mex food with killer margaritas for just US$1.50. Open Mon–Sat 11am–9pm.

Rum Runners Christiansted boardwalk ☎340/773-6585. The steaks and lobster are particularly popular and the Eggs Benedict is a must for breakfast (US$9). Or just stop by for great happy-hour drinks and a half-pound of peel and eat shrimp with a tequila lime cocktail sauce for just under US$11.

Savant's Hospital Street ☎340/713-8666. Upscale restaurant serving a fusion of Thai, Mexican and Caribbean cuisine in a stylish atmosphere on the eastern edge of town. Mon–Sat 6–10pm. This place is small, the service is great, and reservations are a must. Dinner US$14–38.

Singh's Fast Food 23B King Street ☎340/773-7357. Serving up local food for over 30 years, this deli-style outfit has great roti and a variety of stews including curried goat (US$11). At US$2, a "Double" (spicy chick pea and potato sandwich) is a great snack option.

Twin City Coffee House and Gallery 1022 King St ☎340/773-9400. This charming coffeeshop and art gallery on Market Square serves a great cup of java as well as fresh-fruit smoothies, sandwiches and salads, featuring locally grown, organic produce. Lunch sandwiches and salads US$8–13.

Tutto Bene 2006 Eastern Suburb ☎340/773-5229. A favourite since 1991, serving northern Italian fare with a Caribbean twist. A "taste of Tutto Bene" is a delicious assortment of antipasti for US$17. Reservations suggested. Daily 6–10pm.

Nightlife and entertainment

St Croix isn't known for crazy **nightlife**, and Christiansted is your best bet for action after dark. During high season, take a moonlit stroll along the waterfront and you're bound to find a party of clinking beer mugs and live music. Cover charges almost don't exist on the island, so you can poke into any place and have a drink while you check out the scene. Most restaurants have bars, which offer live music (mostly on weekend nights). If you want to get a great taste of Caribbean **steel panning**, find out where local Bill Bass (Ⓦwww.billbasssteelpans.com) is playing. **Hermit crab races** are held at around 5pm at *Fort Christian Brew Pub* (Mon), *Divi Resort* (Wed) and *Deep End Bar* (Fri). Sponsor a crab for a couple of dollars and if he emerges first from a giant circle, you win a prize. Look for **full-moon parties** at Cane Bay. The social scene changes often, especially with high and low season; check local newspapers for listings.

Watch for the **Jump-Up** (Ⓦwww.gotostcroix.com/jumpup), a Carnival-like street party that takes place in downtown Christiansted regularly during tourist season between 6pm and 10pm. Expect live music, dancing, mocko jumbies (stilt walkers), crafts and lots of food. The **Whim Plantation** (☎340/772-0598) hosts a Candlelight Concert series throughout the year and the 1100-seat **Island Center for the Performing Arts** (☎340/778-5272) is the place to look for plays and concerts.

Bars, clubs and nightlife

Cheeseburgers in Paradise East End Rd ☎340/773-1119. This small, informal eatery offers live music ranging from acoustic guitar and calypso to rocking blues bands Thurs to Sun nights, generally beginning at about 6.30pm.

Club 54 54B Company St ☎340/773-8002. Check out this indoor/outdoor space, with multilevel decks and a tropical setting, for regular DJs and live performers. Open Wed–Sat until 9pm–4am.

Divi Carina Bay Casino 54 Estate Turner Hole ☎340/773-7529. Located on the southeast end of the island, this is currently the island's only casino, a modest collection of slots and table games. Open Mon–Thur 12pm–4am; Fri 12pm–Mon 6am. Often has live music.

Full Moon Beach Bar (see opposite). Often has live reggae or steel pan bands and music during Sunday brunch 9am–1.30pm. Watch for pig roasts and full-moon parties.

Off the Wall Bar and Grill Cane Bay ☎340/778-4771. Anything from jazz to steel pan Wed–Sat 6–9pm during high season. No shirt, no shoes, no problem. US$10–20 for various calzones, sandwiches and pizzas.

Frederiksted and around

FREDERIKSTED, seventeen miles away on the west coast of the island, is smaller than Christiansted, though it is closer to the airport. Its harbour has been somewhat deserted since 2002 when cruise ships stopped docking here but at least 40 ships are slated to pull in during 2009 and the town should liven up considerably. Frederiksted doesn't have many old buildings – at the local post office, a mural of **The Fireburn** captures the spirit and anger of the rioters that burnt much of the town in 1878 in protest against harsh economic conditions.The main strip of Strand Street, which skirts the renovated palm-lined waterfront, offers shopping, restaurants and the **Caribbean Museum Center for the Arts**, but overall Frederiksted is a fairly sleepy place. In town, be sure to visit **Fort Frederik**, a large red-coloured building and ramparts next to the pier that was built in 1760, and was the site of the 1848 slave emancipation. Inside, there's an art gallery and museum (Mon–Fri 8.30am–4pm; US$3). Other architectural highlights include **St Paul's Anglican Church**, built in 1812, and **St Patrick's Catholic Church**, built in the 1840s, both on Prince Street. Frederiksted is a bit dodgier at night and anywhere off the main strip should be treated with caution.

Around town

Outside Frederiksted are a few places to take in on a leisurely day-trip. North of town is the **Spratt Hall Plantation**, (☎340/772-0305), which dates from 1650. You can take an hour to hour-and-a-half tour of the great house and sugar mill ruins; call for pricing. The **St George Village Botanical Garden** is perhaps the highlight, a few miles inland (127 Estate St in Kingshill; daily 9am–4.30pm; US$8; ☎340/692-2874), with beautiful botanical gardens flourishing amid the ruined buildings of an old sugar plantation. Just south, across the Queen Mary Highway, the **Cruzan Rum Factory** offers tours and liberal samples (Mon–Fri 9–11.30am & 1–4.15pm; US$4; ☎340/692-2280), and the **Estate Whim Plantation Museum**, back towards Frederiksted on Route 76 (Mon–Sat 10am–4pm; grounds only US$5, house and tour US$10; ☎340/772-0598), has been restored as it was during Danish times, with a period museum of agricultural tools and other exhibits. If you like this, try the **Karl and Marie Lawaetz Museum** (☎340/772-1539, $US6, call for hours) on Route 76, which also devotes itself to mid-eighteenth century life on the farm; don't miss the nearby **St Croix Leap** (☎340/772-0421) on Mahogany Road, a woodworking studio that sells furniture and other work by local craftspeople.

For a unique experience, you must make a happy-hour trip to the **Mount Pellier Domino Club**, east of town on Route 76 (☎340/713-9052). Go for the beer-drinking pigs – yes, you hand them a can of non-alcoholic beer, they crush it between their jaws, drink it dry and then spit out the can – and stay for the ambience or a Mamawana, the house rum, flavored with local roots and spices, and not for the faint of heart. If jazz is more your thing, watch for **Sunset Jazz** when a large local crowd brings beach blankets, lawn chairs and picnics to the beach near Fort Frederiksted the third Friday of every month.

A fun and leisurely way to see some of the island is to take an open-vehicle safari tour with Sweeny's St. Croix Safari Tours, (☎340/773-6700, US$45 including admission fees), which will run you to the botanical garden, the Cruzan rum factory and the Whim Plantation, among other attractions. Note that although tours focus mostly on the western side of the island, pick up and drop off is in Christiansted. If you want to get off the beaten track, try Tan Tan Tours, (Ⓣ340/773-7041, Ⓦwww.stxtantantours.com; US$120 for full day including lunch, US$60-80 for half day), open-air jeep tours that will take you up and down tracks that only slightly resemble roads, to scenic overlooks, tide pools and ruins.

Beaches and activities

Several **beaches** are around Frederiksted, offering great amenities. **Rainbow Beach**, half a mile north on Route 63, has good snorkelling and several beach bars and restaurants, such as *Coconuts on the Beach* (Ⓣ340/719-6060), which offers so-so Tex-Mex and barbecue. At **Sprat Hall Beach**, a mile north on Route 63, there is the *Sunset Grill* (Ⓣ340/772-5855), which serves grilled food and drinks. Go **horse-riding** next door at Paul and Jill's Equestrian Stables (Ⓣ340/772-2880, Ⓦwww.paulandjills.com) where one- and one-half-hour ride into the nearby rainforest costs US$75. The largest beach in the entire Virgin Islands is **Sandy Point**, part of a nature preserve (only open Sat–Sun 10am–4pm) directly south of Frederiksted, which can be reached by following Melvin Evans Highway (Route 66). The final scene of the movie *The Shawshank Redemption* was shot here, but be aware the sand comes and goes with currents and seasonal storms, sometimes leaving large bare rocks at the water's edge. Closed April–August for turtle nesting season.

Accommodation

Cottages by the Sea 127A Est. Smithfield Ⓣ340/772-0495 or 1-800/323-7252, Ⓦwww.caribbeancottages.com. These breezy cottages are being remodelled one by one, with 11 done, and 11 to go. Quiet, at the edge of Frederiksted and on a lovely stretch of beach. ❹–❻

Frederiksted Hotel 442 Strand St Ⓣ340/772 0500, Ⓦwww.frederikstedhotel.com. This is a decent but not fancy, modern option if you want to stay in town, with a pool, bar and restaurant. ❹–❺

Sand Castle on the Beach 127 Est. Smithfield Ⓣ340/772-1205, Ⓦwww.sandcastleonthebeach.com. Located on a beautiful stretch of white sand, this is the nicest hotel on the west end with rooms of various size and price aimed mainly at the gay and lesbian community. The hotel's *Beachside Cafe* serves the best lunch in town. ❻

Eating and drinking

Though most of the high-end dining is in or around Christiansted, there are several great places to eat in Frederiksted.

Armstrong's Ⓣ340/772-1919. Just east of Frederiksted on Centerline Road, this is the place to try all sorts of home-made tropical fruit-flavoured ice cream (US$3).

Beachside Cafe *Sand Castle on the Beach* Ⓣ340/772-1266. Choose from a wide variety of fresh seafood as well as duck, chicken, pork, vegetarian dishes and more. This is the best place for lunch according to many – try a Caesar wrap with chicken/shrimp for US$12–14. US$20–35 for dinner entrees.

Blue Moon Victorian House, Strand St Ⓣ340/772-2222. Arguably the best eats in town, this intimate bistro serves Cajun and Caribbean fare and huge salads. It is also the place to catch some live jazz on Wed, Fri and for Sun brunch. Entrees US$24–30.

Pier 69 69 King St Ⓣ340/772-0069. Good for late night drinks, the biggest burger on the island and, talk is, the best steak (US$24). Chef Herbie promises you'll never find a hair in the food (he's bald and quite a character).

Le St Tropez 227 King St Ⓣ340/772-3000. A Mediterranean French restaurant in a charming courtyard serving lunch (Mon–Fri) and dinner (Mon–Sat) with entrees ranging US$17–36.

Turtles Deli Prince Passage Ⓣ340/772-3676. Mon–Sat 8.30am–5.30pm. Good-sized gourmet sandwiches (US$8–9) on a variety of fresh-made breads. Nice seaside patio.

Villa Morales Restaurant 82-C Est. Whim Ⓣ340/772-0556. Only open Thurs–Sat but if you want local and Puerto Rican fare, this is the place. The conch in butter sauce is excellent (US$15) and some former patrons have had the pâté frozen and shipped to them thousands of miles away.

Watersports and outdoor activities

There are two types of **fishing** offered on the island – fishing the flats or deep-sea fishing along the edge of the island. Catch-22 (☎340/778-6987) does full and half days on a Bertram 38 and Carl Holley (☎340/277-4042, Ⓦwww.fishwithcarl.com) captains *The Mocko Jumbie*, a 36-ft Hatteras with room for up to six anglers for half- and full-day trips (US$600/800). For **golfers**, Carambola Golf Club, ☎340/778-5638) a par-72 course at *Carambola Beach Resort* (see p.427), is the best on the island and has a four-star rating by *Golf Digest*. A round of eighteen holes with a cart will generally cost you US$100-120. St Croix offers great **hiking**: Ay-Ay, Kingshill (☎340/772-4079), runs personalized eco-hiking and tours at any price range by herbalist, naturalist and son of a long line of bush women, Ras Lumumba Corriette. For a special treat, ask him to show you where he lives. **Annaly Bay** is a somewhat serious hike from Carambola Resort with views of the sea-swept northern coast and some gorgeous tide pools to soak in at the end. There are also a number of hikes in the **East End Marine Park** (see p.428) around Jack's Bay and Isaac's Bay. **St Croix Environmental Association** (5032 Anchor Way, Christiansted; ☎340/773-1989, Ⓦwww.stxenvironmental.org) periodically schedules activities such as hikes, birding tours and lectures. Check the website for details.

Like all Caribbean islands, St Croix is **watersports** crazy. While most activities and trips can be booked along the waterfront in Christiansted, remember that many outfits offer hotel pick-ups and can help booking entire vacations. Also, most hotels and public beaches offer kayak, jet ski and snorkel rentals.

Watersports

The Beach Shack *Hotel on the Cay* ☎340/773-7060. This is the place to go to rent wave-runners, windsurfers, kayaks and snorkelling gear.

Big Beard's Adventure Tours Pan Am Pavillion, Christiansted ☎340/773-4482, Ⓦwww.bigbeards.com. This outfit specializes in snorkelling trips to Buck Island on one of two catamarans. They also do beach barbecues and sunset trips.

Bilinda Charters Green Cay Marina ☎340/773-1641, Ⓦwww.sailbilinda.com. Offers private sails for up to six people aboard Zulu, a 36ft sloop. Choose from half-day sails to multiple destinations, sunset sails and Discover Sailing. Custom trips are also available.

Buck Island Charters ☎340/773-3161. Full- and half-day sails on a trimaran leaving from Green Cay Marina. A five- to six-hour trip runs US$60 per person.

Caribbean Adventure Tours ☎340/778-1522 or 1-800/532-3483, Ⓦwww.stcroixkayak.com. In the same office as Anchor Dive (see below) this kayaking outfit offers island sightseeing excursions, sunset and moonlight trips, and photo tours.

Caribbean Sea Adventures ☎340/773-2628, Ⓦwww.caribbeanseaadventures.com. Located on the Christiansted waterfront, these guys offer everything from sailing charters to powerboat rentals to glass-bottom boat tours, and they are the only company authorized to take dive trips to Buck Island (by reservation only, minimum six divers).

Llewellyn's Charter, Inc St Croix Yacht Club/ Teague Bay ☎340/773-9027. One of the most respected sailing charters, which has been in service for over twenty years.

Virgin Kayak Co. Cane Bay ☎340/778-0071. Rents kayaks US$25 per day (reserve the night before) as well as running tours customized to taste and ability, including Salt River Bay tours for US$45 for a half-day.

Scuba diving and snorkelling

St Croix has plenty to see beneath the waves and its larger territory and smaller tourist crowds can make for a more relaxed experience. Great snorkelling and shore dives await you in **Cane Bay** where the seven-mile long **drop-off wall** that hugs the northern coastline is just 100 feet out. The island also has nine popular wreck dives, six of which are in **Butler Bay** (another good snorkelling spot) on the west end and can be accessed from shore. Other dive highlights are the **underwater canyon at Salt River** and west end reefs such as **The Swirling Reef of Death**, a photographer's dream. The **Frederiksted Pier** is a great place to see seahorses whether you dive or snorkel. **Buck Island** has an underwater snorkel trail, but beware that most of the coral on the tour is dead. If you have a boat and can go on your own, some spots on the northwest side are also quite nice; keep vigilant about the currents. **East End Marine Park's Isaac's Bay** has a nice barrier reef just off shore where at times coral sticks right up out of the water. Many of the beaches on the island are turtle nesting grounds and the creatures are common sights on dives. The three beaches at **The Buccaneer** resort offer excellent snorkelling but are generally for guests only; just tell the guard at the entrance you are going to the beachside restaurant. Grassy areas around *The Buccaneer* resort and Chenay Bay are frequented by spotted eagle rays. All dive shops give discounts on multiple dives and they often hook up with hotels to offer excellent packages.

Anchor Dive Center Salt River National Park ⓣ340/778-1522 or 1-800/532-3483, ⓦwww.anchordivestcroix.com. This five-star PADI shop is just a five-minute boat ride from the best of the wall dives and surface interval is done on shore which is nice when the seas are a bit rough. Has shops at Carambola and Buccaneer resorts.

Cane Bay Dive Shop Pan Am Pavilion in Christiansted ⓣ340/773-4663; ⓦwww.canebayscuba.com. This shop has four locations: in Cane Bay, Christansted and at the *Divi* and *Carambola* resorts. They offer all levels of instruction, rentals and sales and will even customize dive packages. How about a midnight, full-moon dive?

Dive Experience 1111 Strand St, Christiansted ⓣ340/773-3307 or 1-800/235-9047, ⓦwww.divexp.com. Friendly and knowledgeable, owner Michelle Pugh has been diving St Croix since the 1970s and runs dives to a wide range of sites, not just the wall. Dive the fish feed at the sunken Chez Barge.

N2 the Blue Diving Adventures ⓣ340/713-1475 or 1-866-712-2583, ⓦwww.n2blue.com. This beachfront shop just north of Fort Frederiksted rents equipment and does shore dives. It runs a small boat from the pier in Frederiksted and takes out a maximum of six divers.

St Croix Ultimate Bluewater Adventures ⓣ340/773-5994, ⓦwww.stcroixscuba.com. Located in the Caravelle Arcade in downtown Christiansted, this dive shop offers everything from wreck dives to rental and sales to introductory dives for kids aged 10 and above.

ScubaWest Strand St, Frederiksted ⓣ340/772-3701 or 1-800/352-0107, ⓦwww.divescubawest.com. Specializes in diving from the pier (a shore dive) and runs boats to other west end sites.

8.2

The British Virgin Islands

Forming roughly two chains separated by the Sir Francis Drake Channel, the **BRITISH VIRGIN ISLANDS** are a haven for snorkelling and fishing enthusiasts. The BVI also offers some of the best **sailing** in the world, and the towns and bays bustle with the constant comings and goings of yachts and cruise ships. Caribbean influences dominate the food, music and culture – the British connection is only really evident in the language. What the BVI lack in glitz and historical sites they make up for in unspoilt beauty – stunning tree-covered peaks, steep green hills, secluded coves, long palm-fringed sandy **beaches** and spectacular **reefs** whose breathtaking marine life and numerous shipwrecks make for some of the best diving and snorkelling in the Caribbean.

One of the islands, **Tortola**, houses the vast majority of the 25,000 residents. The largest and most developed, it's the main resort centre and home to the capital, Road Town. Quieter **Virgin Gorda** offers largely upmarket accommodation centred on its own mini-archipelago and watersports playground, the North Sound. Yachters flock to little **Jost Van Dyke** to clear customs and hit its infamous bars, while **Anegada**, the non-hilly Virgin, is a coral atoll teeming with wildlife whose endless beaches, maze of reefs and bonefishing pull in day-trippers. The **outlying islands**, several of which are privately owned, see transient populations of guests at exclusive resorts or yachters who swim ashore.

Tortola

TORTOLA ("land of turtle doves" in Spanish), with a population of around 21,000, is the commercial and cosmopolitan centre of the BVI. Also the largest of the BVI, Tortola's twenty square miles of stunning mountain scenery rise to a peak of 1780ft, the highest in the BVI, at **Sage Mountain** on the west of the island. **Road Town**, roughly halfway along the more developed southern coast of the island, is home to the governor's residence, and most of Tortola's historic sights. The **west of the island,** especially the **north coast**, has some of the **best beaches** and resorts and the liveliest nightlife – the **eastern end** is less well established on the tourist track but has some fine, often deserted beaches, including the island's best beach for surfing.

The island is best explored by car; **Ridge Road**, running east-west along the mountains' backbone, offers stunning views across the Francis Drake Channel. It gives access to the Belle View Overlook, **Mount Healthy National Park**, the touristy restaurant/bar *Skyworld*, which offers the island's only 360-degree view, and Sage Mountain National Park (just off Ridge Road).

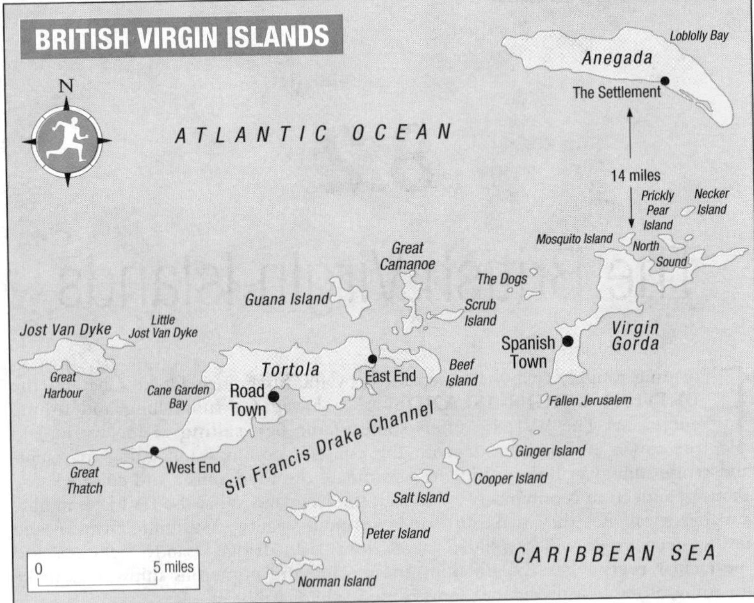

▲ Sage Mountain National Park

Arrival, information and getting around

From **Terrence B. Lettsome Airport** it's a short hop across the Queen Elizabeth II Bridge to East End on Tortola. Taxis cost US$24 for the six miles to Road Town; US$50 for destinations in West End. Hertz has an office at the airport and some other agencies offer a free pick-up and drop-off service (see below). The inter-island **ferries** dock at West End, Road Town or Trellis Bay.

Banks, **information** and post offices are all found in Road Town, though you will be able to get maps at the airport and most hotels. Some hotels and resorts offer free wireless **Internet** access to guests; otherwise, the best deals are at Serendipity Internet Bookshop and Café (Main St, Road Town; ☎284/494-5865; US$5 for 30min) and Trellis Bay Cyber Café (☎284/495-2447). Both cafés also offer free wireless to those with their own laptops.

Public **transport** is limited to a fleet of shared taxi-vans that run on no particular schedule with no particular stops – just flag them down as they approach and ask the price before getting in; should be about US$2–5. **Taxis** (often also vans) are easy to come by unless there are several cruise ships in town. Stands are at the ferry docks in Road Town and West End (look out for the brightly coloured stands with men chatting and playing draughts). If you need to arrange for one ahead of time, try BVI Taxi Association, Road Town (☎284/494-2322); West End Taxi Association (☎284/495-4934); and Beef Island Taxi Association (☎284/495-1982). **Car-rental**

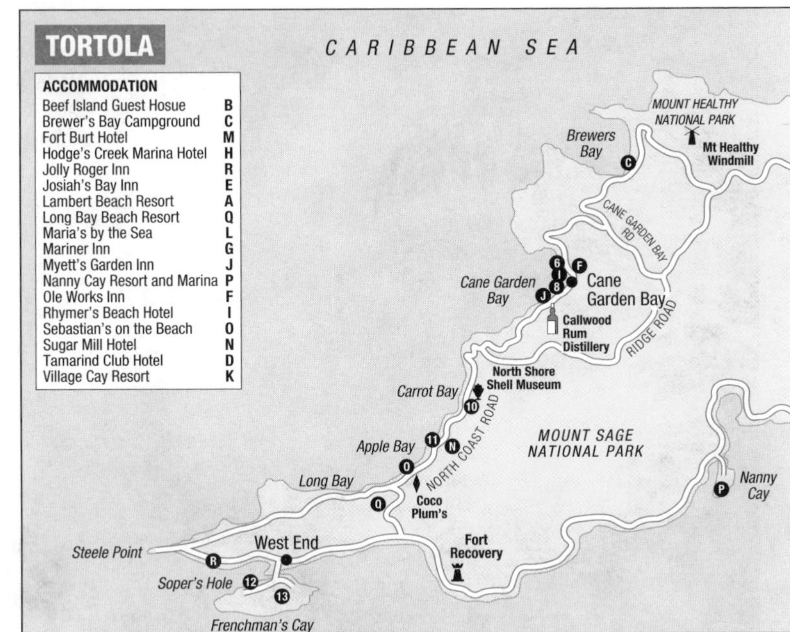

companies on the island include D&D Car Rentals (Road Town and West End; ⓣ284/495-7676); Dollar Rent-a-Car (East End and Long Bay Beach; ⓣ284/494-6093); Hertz (West End, Road Town and airport; ⓣ284/495-4405); and ITGO Car Rental (Wickham's Cay I; ⓣ284/494-2639; ⓦwww.itgobvi.com). If you'd rather be out on the water, you can hire a small **dinghy** or even a large **powerboat** to get around – (see p.444 for companies).

Road Town

Three-quarters of the island's inhabitants live in **ROAD TOWN**, either downtown, along its outskirts or in the hills above. The **harbour**, which over the centuries has provided shelter for fleets of Dutch, French, Spanish and English ships, fills with cruise ships, yachts and ferries unloading their cargo of tourists into the town's bustling and traffic-packed maze of streets. Road Town's sights are all low-key and fairly close together; most sights of interest, including the **Folk Museum** and **Botanic Garden**, together with the majority of shops and restaurants can be found on the two principal thoroughfares: historic **Main Street** and the more-touristy **Waterfront Drive**; both run parallel to the water.

Maps and brochures are available at the **BVI Tourist Board office** on the second floor of the AKARA Building (Wickhams Cay I; Mon–Fri 8.30am–4.30pm; ⓣ284/494-3134; ⓦwww.bvitourism.com) at the ferry terminal, at the airport and in most hotels.

Accommodation

There is no beachfront **accommodation** in Road Town but the hotels perched on the surrounding hills offer spectacular views, while those around marinas will have you falling asleep to the tinkling sound of halyards in the wind. If you'd prefer to rent a **villa** or private house try *Areana Villas* (ⓣ284/494-5864,

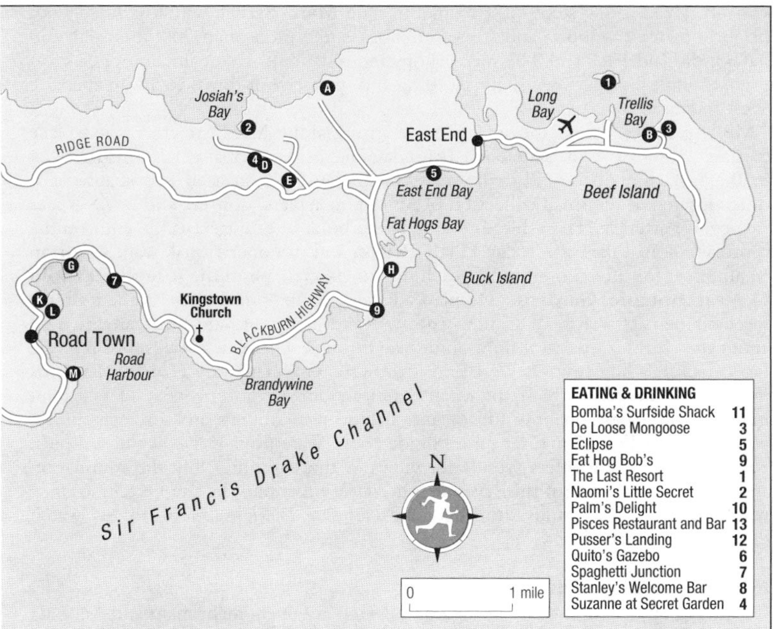

Ⓦ www.areanavillas.com); or *Purple Pineapple Villa Rentals* (Ⓣ 284/495-3100, Ⓦ www.purplepineapple.com). For accommodation just a few steps from the beach, head for the west of the island to Long Bay, Carrot Bay and Cane Garden Bay.

Fort Burt Hotel Waterfront Drive Ⓣ 284/494-2587 or 1-888/873-5226. The commanding harbour views from this hillside retreat built on the remains of a seventeenth-century fort make it a good option in town; the outdoor patio is perfect for a drink at sunset. Rooms, though in need of a coat of paint and new bed linens, are large, and there are also several multi-bedroom suites with private pools. All have balconies and a/c. 5

Maria's by the Sea Waterfront Drive Ⓣ 284/494-2595, Ⓦ www.mariasbythesea.com. Probably your best bet in town, rooms are bright and clean at this friendly, well-managed choice located along the waterfront. The decor is typical Caribbean with floral fabrics and wicker furniture, and each room has a balcony. Special deals are available for stays of seven days or longer. 5–6

Mariner Inn Waterfront Drive, Wickhams Cay II Ⓣ 284/494-2333 or 1-800/535-7289. Next to the docks, the hotel is convenient for the yachting crowd passing through. Rooms are standard. There's also a good-sized pool and restaurant on the dock. 5–6

Nanny Cay Resort and Marina Nanny Cay Ⓣ 284/494-4895 or 1-866/284-4683, Ⓦ www.nannycay.com. Almost a little city in itself, this resort overlooking a quaint marina has all you could need – restaurants, swimming pool, dive centre, tennis, volleyball, spa, small supermarket and charter services. All the rooms were refurbished in mid-2008. 6

Village Cay Resort and Marina Wickhams Cay I Ⓣ 284/494-2771, Ⓦ www.igy-villagecay.com. More a lush, small hideaway than a resort, with 19 large, well-appointed rooms, some of which have views. A great place to embark on watersports adventures. Relax in the waterside restaurant or poolside bar. Two-bedroom condos are also available next door for US$405 nightly. 6

The Town

Up to three cruise ships can pull in at once and **Waterfront Drive**, with its bars, restaurants, shops and markets, can become a sudden traffic jam. Don't let that put you off. Head a few steps west to picturesque **Main Street** which is lined with brightly painted wooden and stone buildings, some more than 200 years old, and has a more laid-back feel. The many shops and restaurants are quaint, and it's a great place to look for crafts, jewellery, clothing and spices, or sit down to an inexpensive West Indian meal.

Most of Road Town's tourist sights are strung along Main Street. A good place to start is the **VI Folk Museum** (Monday and Friday 8.30am–4.30pm, Tues–Sat 8:30–3pm), though the old traditional West Indian building itself is probably of as much interest as the small collection of Amerindian, plantation-era and RMS *Rhone* (see p.443) artefacts. The white building at the heart of the street is the eighteenth-century colonial prison – today **HMS Prison** and still operational. Walk north on Main Street for fifteen minutes to reach the three-acre oasis of the **Joseph Reynold O'Neal Botanic Gardens** (Monday–Saturday, 8am–4pm; US$3), named after a local dignitary. Its jasmine-scented pathways are a delight, and you can learn all about the wealth of tropical flora on display through self-guided walks. Just past the ferry dock heading towards West End is the **Old Government House Museum** (Mon–Sat 9am–2pm; US$3), the recently restored former governors' residence, built in 1880 and 1926 and now full of antique furniture, murals and artefacts. Finish with a visit to **Fort Burt**, set on a hillside above Waterfront Drive at the southern end of town, which offers wonderful views of the harbour. Only the foundation and mezzanine remain of this seventeenth-century fort built by the Dutch, so once you've glanced at the ruins, drop in at the *Fort Burt Hotel*, grab a drink and watch the sun set over the bay.

Eating and drinking

Conjuring up delicious dishes with seafood such as conch, mahi mahi and Anegada spiny lobsters, **Tortolan cuisine** is something to be savoured. Meats are often grilled and Tortolans are famed for their barbecue. In Road Town, you'll find superb local cuisine at bargain prices, including a wide selection of well-priced **West Indian and barbecue restaurants**, grilled seafood, simple sandwiches and plenty of vegetarian options. If you're self-catering or just putting together a beach **picnic**, Bobby's Market and Dockmaster's, a gourmet deli, are next to the Village Cay Marina and good places to hit.

C&F Restaurant Purcell Estate ⓣ284/494-4941. Located just east of town, this lively local favourite is difficult to find so call ahead for directions or take a taxi. It's worth it, though; the best barbecue ribs on the island and the barbecued fish are not to be missed. Dinner only. Main courses cost upwards of US$20–25.

Capriccio di Mare 196 Waterfront Drive ⓣ284/494-5369. An Italian restaurant whose outdoor patio is a great place to sip espresso or enjoy a light meal, including an array of pizzas, sandwiches and pastas for under US$15. The mango bellini is also a highlight. Open from breakfast to dinner but most popular for lunch. Closed Sun.

Crandall's Pastry Plus Fishers Estate south of town ⓣ284/494-5156. This bakery does the best patties on the island (US$5), though the coffee leaves something to be desired. Also sells West Indian food to go. Open Mon–Fri till 5.30pm.

The Dove 67 Main St ⓣ284/494-0313, ⓦwww.dovebvi.com. A charming West Indian cottage for a romantic dinner. The menu changes each evening but the Boston seafood flown in daily is a constant. The steak with chocolate and coffee sauce (US$35) raises some eyebrows but will make a believer out of you. Closed Mon.

Le Cabanon Main Street ⓣ284/494-8660. An airy and relaxed French bistro good for lunch (US$12–15) – try the warm goat cheese salad – or dinner (US$20–35). The bar is a popular after-hours hangout after the kitchen shuts down at 10.30.

The Pub Waterfront Drive, near Fort Burt ⓣ284/494-2608. Long-time Road Town favourite doles out everything from burgers to steaks to fresh fish (US$9–15), with nightly specials, such as prime rib. Has a great waterfront location to enjoy the happy hour and live music on Thurs and Fri.

Pusser's Pub in Road Town Waterfront Drive ⓣ284/494-3897. If you're hankering for some English fare, you can sup a pint and order up a plate of fish and chips (US$15), or go Carib-Italian and try the jerk pizza (US$22). Wash down your meal with a Pusser's Painkiller.

Road Town Bakery Main Street ☎284/494-0222. Offering the most scrumptious cookies, luscious cakes and tempting pastries in town, most under US$5, this place is hopping with locals and tourists alike from 7.30am on. All the bakery items are prepared by students from the local community college.

Spaghetti Junction Baugher's Bay ☎284/494-4880. An assortment of pasta dishes, some standard, some inventive (try the jambalaya pasta). Open Tues–Sat for dinner from 6–10pm, but serving lunch as *The Bat Cave* Tues–Sat. Entrees go for US$12–30. They also serve a lot of local food such as boiled fish, stewed conch, and whelk (Fri only). Wed night features live jazz.

Nightlife and entertainment

Road Town has a few night spots, just don't expect to party all night long – there's plenty of **nightlife** to keep you busy if you're content with **live music** (check the *Limin' Times* for what's on), or **drinking** and **dancing**.

The Bat Cave *Spaghetti Junction Restaurant* ☎284/494-4880. The closest thing to a disco on the island. When the pasta runs out, DJs get things hopping on Fri and Sat. There's an outdoor deck and happy hour specials 5–7pm. Sat night features live cabaret-style entertainment, and with four TVs, the bar is also a good spot to catch the big game you're missing.

Le Cabanon (see also above). Becomes perhaps the most international bar on the island when the restaurant shuts down at 10.30 each night. Hours are "flexible" and a mostly expat crowd ends the night here.

Pusser's Pub (see also p.441). This hopping Road Town institution is popular with locals, tourists and yachters and is the self-proclaimed home of the Painkiller – a potent concoction made with Pusser's own rum.

West End and around

The west side of the island, with its main area of settlement, **WEST END**, is home to Tortola's resort scene, more relaxed than Road Town and with an abundance of excellent **beaches**, seafront accommodation and nightlife. Popular with yachters and landlubbers alike, the anchorage of **Soper's Hole**, a quaint collection of shops and restaurants, is located just across the bay from the West End ferry docks. However, most of the resorts, hotels and small inns are clustered either around **Steele Point**, at the very western tip of the island, or along the stunning beaches and in the hills above **Long Bay**, **Apple Bay**, **Carrot Bay** and especially **Cane Garden Bay**. The western end is also the party side of Tortola; aside from the entertainment laid on by hotels, there are local favourites ranging from *Bomba's* wild full-moon parties to BVI reggae great Quito Rhymer. Tourist sights are few and far between but the **Callwood Rum Distillery** (Mon–Fri 8am–5pm; US$1 for a short tour) at the west end of Cane Garden Bay provides an interesting behind-the-scenes look at one of the BVI's most popular products. Their rum is still made in copper vats the same way islanders did centuries ago and at the end of the tour you can sample a bit and buy some to take home.

Accommodation

Almost all of the **accommodation** – from resorts to cosy inns – on the western end of the island have ocean views. Don't automatically expect air-conditioning; many rooms are simply cooled by overhead fans or the sea breezes. This side of the island is also home to Tortola's only **campsite**, at Brewer's Bay, while the hills are clustered with **villas** and **private homes** (see the *BVI Welcome Tourist Guide* for a detailed list). The following companies offer some of the best places: Villas of Fort Recovery (☎284/495-4467 or 1-800/367-8455, Ⓦwww.fortrecovery.com); Icis Villas (☎284/494-6979, Ⓦwww.icisvillas.com); Grape Tree Vacation Rentals (☎284/495-4229); and Purple Pineapple Rental Management (☎284/495-4848, Ⓦwww.purplepineapple.com).

Hotels and resorts

Jolly Roger Inn West End ⓣ284/495-4559, ⓦwww.jollyrogerbvi.com. At the entrance of Soper's Hole, just down the shore from the West End ferry dock, this five-room inn is definitely for the rough-and-ready traveller. Rooms are basic, only some have baths, and you can expect to pay about US$30 extra for a/c. ❸–❹

Long Bay Beach Resort Long Bay ⓣ954/481-8787 or 1-800/345-0356, ⓦwww.eliteislands.com. Located on a 52-acre estate, this is the largest and most well-rounded resort on Tortola, offering rooms, beachfront cabanas and family villas. The deluxe beachfront rooms are the way to go here though they can be pricey (US$355–605), depending on the season. *1748 at Long Bay*, an old stone plantation renovated into a restaurant and bar, offers tasty, well-prepared meals. Other amenities include watersports, tennis courts, a swim-up poolside bar and fitness centre. All-inclusive rates available. ❼–❾

Myett's Garden Inn Cane Garden Bay ⓣ284/495-9649, ⓦwww.myettent.com. Charming beachfront rooms with nice sunsets, quite close to all the action in the bay, which might not be ideal for those seeking solitude. Prices are good in high season (❻) but become magnificent from mid-April to Dec 14 (❹).

Ole Works Inn Cane Garden Bay ⓣ284/495-4837, ⓕ495-9618. Built on the remains of a 300-year-old sugar plantation, this eighteen-room inn is owned by renowned reggae performer Quito Rhymer, whose band plays across the street at *Quito's Gazebo* (see opposite). Rooms are basic but have a/c, and there's a pool. ❹–❻

Rhymer's Beach Hotel Cane Garden Bay ⓣ284/495-4639. This brightly coloured hotel is right on the beach and offers very simple motel-like rooms, all with a/c, kitchenettes, as well as a shared balcony offering views of the beach. ❹

Sebastian's on the Beach Little Apple Bay ⓣ284/495-4212 or 1-800/336-4870, ⓦwww.sebastiansbvi.com. A wide variety of standard tropical-decor rooms are available at this comfortable hotel, ranging from beachfront to ones across the street. There are also some lovely villas further up the hill with sweeping views. ❹–❽

Sugar Mill Hotel Little Apple Bay ⓣ284/495-4355 or 1-800/462-8834, ⓦwww.sugarmillhotel.com. Located in the ruins of a seventeenth-century sugar mill, this elegant, well-managed boutique hotel has 23 guest cottages, all tastefully decorated in colourful West Indian style; the round pool is located where oxen used to pull the grinding wheel to crush sugar cane. The onsite restaurant is the best on the island (see opposite). ❾

Camping

Brewer's Bay Campground Brewer's Bay ⓣ284/494-3463. Something akin to an upscale refugee camp, this campsite features US$40 prepared sites that include worn canvas tents, beds, linens, propane lamps and stoves, plus other cooking and eating utensils. The tents are rather crowded together but they sit on a great beach. You might prefer a bare site (you provide tent and so on) for US$20 for one or two people. Community bathrooms have showers and flush toilets. You'll need a ride to the nearest town to get cooking supplies, as the restaurant is open only sporadically. ❷

Beaches

Cane Garden Bay, a mile-long stretch of sand backed by lush green hills, is the most popular and most accessible of Tortola's beaches – a drawback when the cruise ships are in town as the crowds can be unbearable. It's also Tortola's party beach, attracting a mix of locals, tourists and yachters who come in for a day of sun or a night of fun. You can hire all kinds of **watersports** gear here, and there are plenty of restaurants, bars and hotels. The surf may not be nearly as good as at Josiah's Bay Beach (see p.442), but **Apple Bay**, south along the coast from Cane Garden Bay, still pulls the surfers in (especially during Jan and Feb). Restaurants, bars and several hotels line the beach, with more alongside the road skirting the western side of the island. North along the coast from Cane Garden Bay, palm-fringed **Brewer's Bay Beach** is the most secluded beach on the western side of the island; you won't find any crowds even during the height of the season. The abundant coral also makes it the best beach in the area for **snorkelling**. The island's only **campsite** (see above) is located here, along with a few beach bars and grills.

Eating and drinking

Some of the best **food** can be found on this side of the island. Many of the places listed below have **outdoor decks**, perfect for sipping a cocktail while the sun sets before tucking into a delightful spread of huge Anegada lobster. Always call to check if places are open as schedules can vary, especially in the off-season.

Coco Plums Little Apple Bay ☎284/495-4627. Although not on the water, this cute restaurant with a big outdoor deck is worth the trip for well-prepared local favourites like curry goat (US$19) and voodoo ribs (US$16). Lunch and dinner.
Myett's Garden Grill Cane Garden Bay ☎284/495-9649. This Caribbean-fare restaurant offers tasty conch chowder, and no matter what meal you order (mains US$18–35), be sure to ask for a side of the locally renowned peas and rice.
Palm's Delight Carrot Bay ☎284/495-4863. On the water's edge in Carrot Bay, this family-style restaurant serves up great West Indian food like *fungi* and patties and roti for US$10–25.
Pisces Restaurant and Bar Soper's Hole ☎284/495-3154. Serves up home-style West Indian breakfasts, lunches and dinners. Prices US$12–25. Open daily 7am–10pm.
Pusser's Landing Soper's Hole ☎284/495-4554. At this dockside bar with both informal outdoor eating and formal indoor dining, the menu ranges from English pub food to seafood cooked in various styles (char-grilled, Creole blackened or herb braised). US$25–35 for entrees.
Quito's Gazebo Cane Garden Bay ☎284/495-4837. The restaurant in the back half of this oceanfront spot offers basic meat, fish and pasta dishes (US$15–35), while the front half has a bar, dance floor and stage where owner and local favourite Quito Rhymer plays his killer reggae.
Sebastian's Seaside Grill Little Apple Bay ☎284/495-4212. Though service can be slow and a little surly, the food is good (US$8-22 – breakfast (banana pancakes), lunch (roti) or dinner (fresh fish). No matter what time of day, try one of Sebastian's superb rum coffees or pies.
Stanley's Welcome Bar Cane Garden Bay ☎284/495-9424. Find yourself a hammock on the beach and have a beer to whet your appetite for a decent cheeseburger (US$12). A good perch for watching the sunset.
Sugar Mill Restaurant Little Apple Bay ☎284/495-4355. This hotel restaurant, by far one of the best dining experiences on the island, is located in an old stone rum distillery and has a changing menu that's consistently good, including lobster bisque (US$13), scallops in puff pastry (US$35) and almond-crusted lamb loin.

Nightlife and entertainment

The centrepiece of the entertainment scene on the western side of the island is the monthly **full-moon party** at *Bomba's Surfside Shack* but there is also a fair share of **live reggae and calypso music** and dancing. If you are looking to keep things mellow, you won't have to look too hard to find relaxing steel pan or acoustic guitar playing.

Bomba's Surfside Shack Cappoon's Bay ☎284/495-4148. Bomba and his driftwood shack decorated with the left clothing of previous partiers are legendary in the BVI for the monthly full-moon parties, when hundreds of people pack the streets in a bacchanalian frenzy of dancing and drinking. Mushroom tea is served while Bomba presides over the party from a huge throne as the self-proclaimed King of Tortola. On a more mundane note, Wed and Sun nights feature live reggae or calypso and the occasional wet T-shirt contest.
Elm Beach Bar Cane Garden Bay ☎284/494-2888. Live music on Fri and Sun nights along with a wonderful barbecue causes this place to really fill up.
Jolly Roger West End ☎284/495-4559. Local bands attract a mixed crowd every Fri and Sat night, with dancing on the cramped outdoor patio overlooking Soper's Hole. Near the West End ferry dock.
Myett's Cane Garden Bay ☎284/495-9543. A daily sunset happy hour with free munchies 4–6pm, usually followed by live music. Bar closes when the last customer leaves.
Pusser's Landing Soper's Hole ☎284/495-4554. They do a little bit of everything here: happy hour deals (5–7pm), live music on weekend evenings and steel drums during Sunday brunch. Call ahead for details on upcoming events. There is an ATM here.
Quito's Gazebo Cane Garden Bay ☎284/495-4837. Reggae performer Quito Rhymer plays at his own restaurant and bar, singing Marley-esque songs with his band, The Edge, on Fri and Sat nights. One of the few places on the island where everyone from yachters and tourists to locals and the hardcore reggae crowd get together and pack the dance floor. Arrive early (before 9pm) to bag a spot and avoid the cover charge, usually US$5–10.

East End and around

The development on the **eastern side** of the island isn't excessive but there is definitely a fair share of attractions and activities on offer. You'll find several good bars and restaurants on Beef Island's **Trellis Bay**, which has become a very laid-back beach hangout with a decent beach whose breezes make it an ideal place to learn to windsurf. *Trellis Bay Cybercafe* (ⓣ284/495-2447) is the best source for local information, Internet access, or the self-described "awesome" sandwich, with a variety of fillings. Don't miss its **full-moon party** when large metal sculptures are filled with wood and set ablaze. The restaurants and marina at **Fat Hog's Bay**, to the south of East End, are worth looking into as well. The **beaches** on the east of the island are among its most secluded and peaceful. **Josiah's Bay Beach** is the surfer's favourite but even if you don't hang ten, it's worth a day-trip. Start early with a great beachside breakfast at *Naomi's* (see opposite), before exploring the dramatic beach and body-surfing the killer waves. On your way back, stop at **Josiah's Bay Plantation** to walk through the ruins and check out the artwork in the gallery.

Accommodation

The east of the island hasn't got the **accommodation** clout of the west or Road Town, but a few places deserve consideration, especially if you want to avoid the crowds, be near the airport or close to ferries to nearby islands.

Beef Island Guest House Trellis Bay ⓣ284/495-2303, ⓕ495-1611. This B&B has a nice location just down the beach from Trellis Bay and close to the airport and the North Sound Express ferry docks. The four beachfront rooms are simple and fairly well maintained, but only have fans. Each room has its own bathroom, and there's also a common room. Continental breakfast is included. ⑤

Hodge's Creek Marina Hotel Hodges Creek ⓣ284/494-5000. The 29 rooms (five with kitchenettes) of this hotel and anchorage are brightly though blandly decorated; pool and great restaurant on site (see below). Ask for a room with a balcony. ⑥

Surfsong Villa Resort Beef Island ⓣ284/495-1864, ⓦwww.surfsong.net. Though pricey, the four villas on this gorgeous property on Beef Island will certainly fulfill all your dreams of a secluded Caribbean vacation. They also offer yoga, massages, and free bicycles and snorkel gear for guests. ⑨

Tamarind Club Hotel Josiah's Bay ⓣ284/495-2477, ⓦwww.tamarindclub.com. Located on the northeast side of the island and not on the beach, this intimate hotel is off the beaten track. What it lacks in location it makes up for with charm, good prices, and peace and quiet. Each of the nine rooms is individually decorated and all have basic amenities, including a/c and a mini-fridge. The onsite restaurant is very good and the pool and bar area are idyllic (see below). ④–⑤

Eating and drinking

Restaurants on this side of the island are not only varied, but plentiful. On the other hand, **nightlife** is almost nonexistent with the exception of the **Trellis Bay full-moon party** and an occasional live performer in a bar or restaurant.

Brandywine Restaurant Brandywine Bay ⓣ284/495-2301. The gourmet menu at this small estate features an array of duck, lamb and seafood dishes in Florentine style (mains US$28–38). The finest dining on the island and a good place to go if you want to dress up a bit, which is enforced with a dress code. Extensive wine list.

De Loose Mongoose Trellis Bay ⓣ284/495-2303. Located on the water's edge next to the *Beef Island Guest House*, this bar and restaurant serves breakfast, lunch and dinner. The menu is light bar fare at good prices. The hamburger (US$12) and brownie sundae are noteworthy. There's live music every Sun night for a beach barbecue.

Eclipse Fat Hog's Bay ⓣ284/495-1646. Dishes at this small, homey spot, overlooking Penn's Landing Marina, range from Thai red curry to venison. Mexican food and cheese fondue available in the lounge. Open daily for dinner and Mon-Fri for lunch, with entrees running US$25–35, lunch pizzas around US$15.

Fat Hog Bob's Fat Hog's Bay ⓣ284/495-1010. This large, fun-loving place has a spirited ambience that's part Tahitian club room and part

American bar and grill. Eat on the patio overlooking the bay or drink at the bar or in the large cocktail lounge. There's a big-screen TV for the major sports events plus live music at the weekends. Open for breakfast, lunch and dinner.

The Last Resort Trellis Bay ☎284/495-2520. Located on an islet in the middle of Trellis Bay (call for the free two-minute ferry at the dockside phone). The casual and quirky atmosphere should be enough reason to stay, but the food is also quite spectacular. The chef emphasizes fresh Mediterranean ingredients in dishes like Moroccan lamb with couscous (US$37) and an excellent butternut squash risotto (US$22). Closed mid-Aug to mid-Oct.

Naomi's Little Secret Josiah's Bay ☎284/495-2818. This little beachside deck offers great West Indian breakfast, lunch and dinner at dirt-cheap prices, with hearty portions. Perfect for beach-goers and Naomi also loans boogie boards and rents surfboards. Accepts credit cards (when the system is working).

Suzanne at Secret Garden Josiah's Bay ☎284/495-1834. Part of the Josiah's Bay Plantation, this outdoor café set among the plantation ruins is about as peaceful as you can imagine. The menu includes delectable entrees such as herb-crusted rack of lamb with black cherry pepper sauce (mains from US$30).

Tamarind Club (see p.442). If you're staying at this cosy hotel, its restaurant is worth a visit. The tables are elegantly set near the pool. The menu changes often but typically features a couple of fresh fish dishes, steak and the chef's special chicken recipes (US$23–35). Open for breakfast, lunch and dinner. Sunday brunch is 11am–3.30pm.

Watersports and outdoor activities

Tortola has the full range of watersports and boating activities – **snorkelling**, **diving**, **windsurfing**, **powerboating**, **fishing** and **sailing** (from scenic day charters to full-moon booze cruises). Dolphin Discovery (☎284/494-7675, www.dolphindiscovery.com) at Prospect Reef offers various **swim-with-a-dolphin** programmes ranging US$79–139. The only place to play **tennis** is at resorts and hotels with courts. Your best bets are at *Long Bay Beach Resort* (US$20 per hr; see p.440) and at *Nanny Cay* (US$5 per hour) and **horse-riding** is a great way to explore the mountains in the **national park**. Shadow's Stables, on Ridge Road (US$100 per hr; ☎284/494-2262), offers rides through Sage Mountain National Park. The owner, Elton "Shadow" Parsons, is descended from a long line of local farmers who tilled the land where the stables now stand; his knowledge of local history and funny stories makes him the perfect guide. If you prefer to use your own legs, there are seven excellent **hiking trails** through the park; pick up a map at the tourist board.

Snorkelling, diving, surfing and windsurfing

If you are going **diving**, sinkholes, ledges, caves and canyons await you around the Sir Francis Drake Channel islands. Coral spawning takes place one week after the first full moon in August; check with shops about packages. North Tortola sites are less frequented and best visited from Jost Van Dyke. Among offshore locales especially worth seeking out: The Dogs are uninhabited little islands surrounded by excellent

The wreck of the RMS Rhone

The wreck of the **RMS Rhone** has been voted the Caribbean's number one **wreck dive** by several diving magazines. The 310-foot British mail steamer and passenger ship was torn in two during a devastating hurricane in 1867 and sank to the bottom of Sir Francis Drake Channel, near Salt Island, together with her cargo of cotton and copper and 124 passengers. The bow sits about 80 feet underwater and the stern in about 15 to 50 foot of water. The dive makes for an eerie experience as both parts are very well preserved – the crow's nest is fully intact, not to mention the engine room and the battered propeller. Colourful coral, large schools of fish and other marine creatures live on and around the ship. Most of the dive shops run trips to the wreck – see listings below.

reefs and include swim-throughs, a chimney and caves, while Painted Walls is a fine sponge-encrusted scene, as is *Alice in Wonderland*, so named for the mushroom-shaped coral formations. Of the several wrecks, the RMS *Rhone* (see box, above) is considered the signature dive, though the *Chikuzen*, a 246ft Japanese refrigeration ship resting in 75ft of water is perhaps equally impressive. Though technically a Tortola site, it is best reached from Virgin Gorda on a 45-minute boat ride. Seas are not always suitable to get to this dive site, but it is worth the wait. The **surfing** season runs Nov–March and the swells roll into Apple, Cane Garden and Josiah's bays.

Aquaventure Road Town ⓣ284/494-4320, ⓦwww.aquaventurebvi.com. Rents gear, does air fills and provides rendezvous diving. Two tanks for US$120.

Blue Waters Divers Nanny Cay ⓣ284/494-2847, ⓦwww.bluewaterdiversbvi.com. Offers PADI courses up to divemaster level. Two-tank dives are US$100. They will also rendezvous with your charter boat if you are moored at Norman, Peter, Salt or Cooper Island.

Boardsailing BVI Trellis Bay ⓣ284/495-2447, ⓦwww.windsurfing.vi. One of the best options for windsurfing, whatever your level. Also does kayaking lessons, tours, rentals and sales, as well as surfing, kiteboarding, and dive gliding.

Dive Tortola ⓣ284/494-9200 or 1-800/353-3419, ⓦwww.divetortola.com. Rents all equipment and sets up rendezvous dives with your charter boat. Two-tank dives are US$110.

Naomi's Little Secret Josiah's Bay ⓣ284/495-2818. This little beach restaurant rents surfboards and has free loaner boogie boards.

Sail Caribbean Divers Hodge's Creek Marina ⓣ284/495-1675, ⓦwww.sailcaribbeandivers.com. This 5-star PADI facility offers two-tank dives for US$105 as well as afternoon and night dives. You can be picked up from Norman and Cooper Islands as well as Marina Cay. Dive instruction runs the gamut from Discover Scuba to Dive Instructor and other high-level certifications. A second shop runs out of Cooper Island.

UBS Dive Center Fat Hog's Bay ⓣ284/494-0024, ⓦwww.scubabvi.com. Specializes in private, personalized diving. Get your own personal boat and divemaster for the day (9.30am–3.30pm) for US$350 per boat; includes all equipment, drinks and snacks.

We Be Divin Road Town/Cane Garden Bay ⓣ284/494-8261, ⓦwww.webedivinbvi.com. Rents gear, does air fills and provides rendezvous diving. Two tanks for US$85. This PADI shop is the only dive shop on the north shore.

Sailing, powerboating and fishing

BareCat Charters Sea Cow's Bay, Emanuel Reef Marina ⓣ284/495-1979 or ⓣ1-800/296-5287, ⓦwww.barecat.com. Offers great charter rates for catamarans. There are several sizes and price ranges for two to ten people.

King Charters Nanny Cay Marina ⓣ284/494-5820, ⓦwww.kingcharters.com. In operation since 1989, it can provide powerboat and motor yachts rentals (with or without captain).

The Moorings *Wickham's Cay II* ⓣ284/494-2331 or ⓣ1-888.952-8420, ⓦwww.moorings.com. Moorings is the largest charter boat company in the Caribbean. Whether you want to skipper your own boat or sail with a captain and crew they will help you plan your entire vacation.

Rob Swain Sailing School Nanny Cay ⓣ1-888/495-9376, ⓦwww.swainsailing.com. This experienced company offers basic learn-to-sail courses, including a live-aboard option, and seven-day fast-track to cruising courses. Prices start at US$695 for basic keelboat courses.

Sunsail Charters Wickham's Cay II ⓣ284/495-4740, ⓦwww.sunsail.com. Now owned by Moorings, Sunsail offers charter yachts from 32ft to 65ft.

White Squall II Village Cay Marina ⓣ284/494-2564, ⓦwww.whitesquall2.com. Take a day-trip to The Baths and Cooper Island or The Caves on Norman Island aboard an eighty-foot classic 1936 Schooner.

Caribbean Fly-Fishing Outfitters ⓣ284/494-4797. For a unique Caribbean fishing experience, go for tarpon, bonefish and permit on a fly rod.

Virgin Gorda

VIRGIN GORDA, twelve miles east of Tortola, might just be the perfect Virgin Island – peaceful, blessed with abundant natural assets and sometimes gloriously deserted. Ten miles long and two miles across at its widest, the island got its name – "fat virgin" – from Columbus in 1493. Most visitors stay at the luxury resorts (some accessible only by water) at **North Sound**. Skirted on one side by Virgin Gorda and on the other by several major reefs and a series of small islands – **Mosquito**, **Prickly Pear**, **Saba Rock**, **Eustacia** and **Necker** – the North Sound provides excellent watersports, hiking trails, deserted beaches and some of the best diving and snorkelling in the BVI.

The tourist dollar has yet to make much of an impact on **SPANISH TOWN**, Virgin Gorda's main settlement located at its southern end and home to most of the 3500-plus islanders. Unprepossessing and somewhat poor, it consists mainly of a jumble of run-down, windowless houses with chickens running around. **Virgin Gorda Yacht Harbour** is the island's main marina, where you'll find most of the handful of restaurants and shops, as well as a bank and tourist information centre. The North Sound Road leading from Spanish Town to the small village of **Gun Creek** is the starting point (well signposted or look for the stairs leading into the trees) for two short trails into the **Virgin Gorda Peak National Park**, a 260-acre area that rises to the island's highest point at 1359ft.

South of Spanish Town, **The Valley** is an area of even smaller settlements at whose southern tip lies Virgin Gorda's biggest and most photographed tourist attraction – **The Baths**. This bizarre landscape of volcanic, house-sized **boulders** stretches from the wooded slopes behind the beach and into the clear aquamarine sea, forming a natural seaside playground of grottoes, caves and pools. The **snorkelling** is excellent and, not surprisingly, it can get very crowded in high season, so come early or late. Lots of restaurants, bars and shops are both on the beach and in the hills above, connected via trails, and small coin-op storage lockers and facilities are available.

Arrival, information and getting around

Virgin Gorda's **airport** is east of Spanish Town, but most people fly to Tortola's Terrance B. Lettsome airport and take a ferry. **Taxis** meet flights or you can call Mahogany Rentals and Taxi Service (☎284/495-5469) or Speedy's Taxi Service (☎284/495-5240). A taxi for two from the airport to Gun Creek will cost about US$24, and from the airport to Spanish Town it's about US$6.

Maps and **brochures** are available from the BVI Tourist Board office (☎284/495-5181) at Virgin Gorda Yacht Harbour in Spanish Town. The post office is in Spanish Town, near the yacht harbour (☎284/495-5224). Get on the **Internet** at The Chandlery (☎284/495-5628) at Yacht Harbour or Java Connection (☎284/495-7421) in Leverick Bay. Many resorts and the Yacht Harbour itself have wireless access if you have a laptop.

Boat travel is easy via a good ferry network. The North Sound Express ferry makes stops at Trellis Bay on Tortola, and Yacht Harbour, *Leverick Bay* and *The Bitter End Yacht Club* on Virgin Gorda. For most other journeys you'll be able to hitch a ride on the **ferries** that most resorts provide for their employees, or catch one of the free ferries that runs between *The Bitter End* and Gun Creek and between *Saba Rock* and *The Sand Box* on Prickly Pear Island and anywhere in the North Sound. Call ahead to schedule a pick-up. Other options include **private water taxis** or renting your own powerboat, which can be pricey. When operating your own boat, make sure to enquire about a map of underwater reefs. If you find the need for a **car**, rental companies are Island Style Jeep & Car Rental (☎284/495-6300) and L&S Rentals (☎284/495-5297) or call 3P Scooter Rentals (☎284/495-6870) if a **scooter** is more suitable. The two main **taxi firms**, Mahogany and Speedy's, both provide special tours.

Accommodation

The best place to stay is **North Sound** but accommodation here doesn't come cheap. **Spanish Town** has a few inexpensive options but nothing as appealing as the North Sound resorts or rooms in **The Valley**, which are usually fairly simple

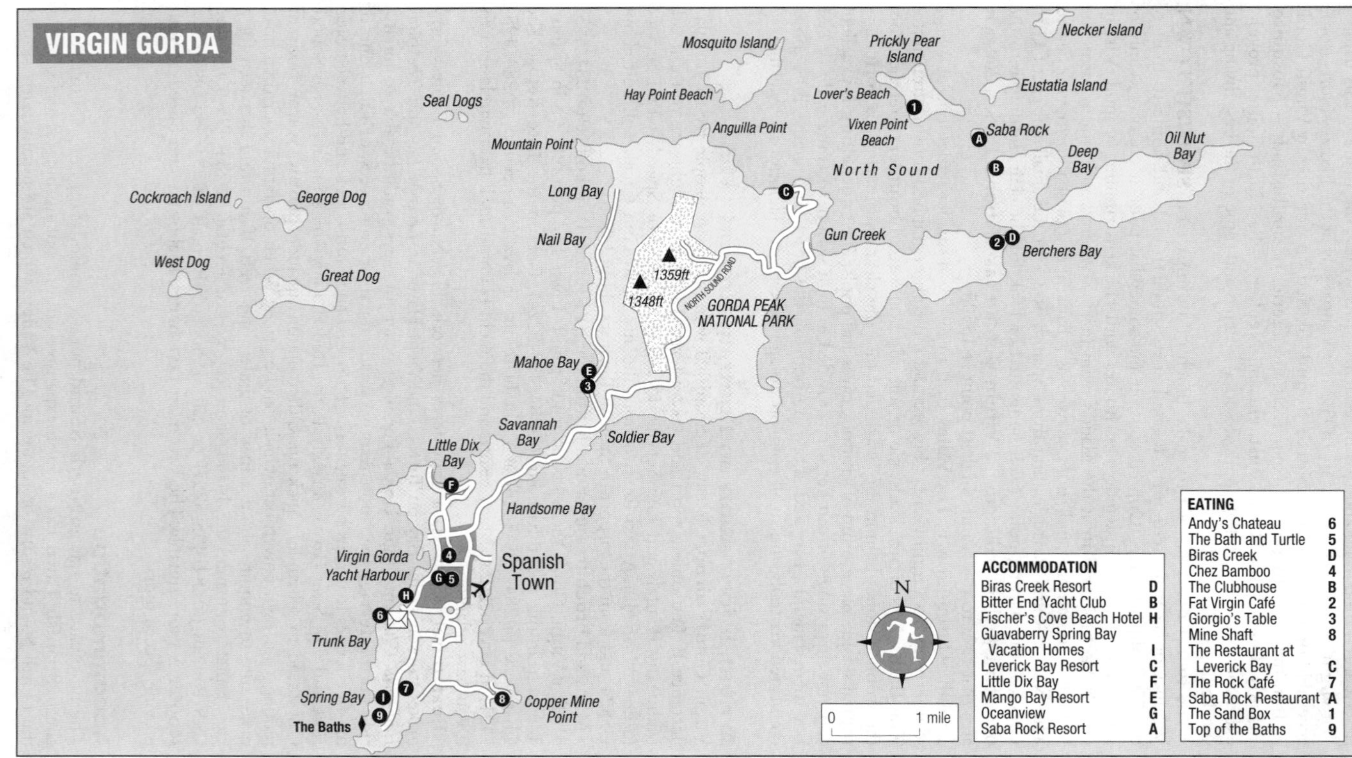
VIRGIN GORDA
Mosquito Island
Prickly Pear Island
Necker Island
Hay Point Beach
Lover's Beach
Eustatia Island
Seal Dogs
Anguilla Point
Vixen Point Beach
Saba Rock
Mountain Point
Deep Bay
Oil Nut Bay
North Sound
Cockroach Island
George Dog
Long Bay
Gun Creek
Nail Bay
Berchers Bay
West Dog
Great Dog
1359ft
1348ft
NORTH SOUND ROAD
GORDA PEAK NATIONAL PARK
Mahoe Bay
Savannah Bay
Soldier Bay
Little Dix Bay
Handsome Bay
Virgin Gorda Yacht Harbour
Spanish Town
Trunk Bay
Spring Bay
The Baths
Copper Mine Point
N
0 1 mile
ACCOMMODATION
Biras Creek Resort D
Bitter End Yacht Club B
Fischer's Cove Beach Hotel H
Guavaberry Spring Bay Vacation Homes I
Leverick Bay Resort C
Little Dix Bay F
Mango Bay Resort E
Oceanview G
Saba Rock Resort A
EATING
Andy's Chateau 6
The Bath and Turtle 5
Biras Creek D
Chez Bamboo 4
The Clubhouse B
Fat Virgin Café 2
Giorgio's Table 3
Mine Shaft 8
The Restaurant at Leverick Bay C
The Rock Café 7
Saba Rock Restaurant A
The Sand Box 1
Top of the Baths 9

but have great views and easy access to the beach. For a **private villa or home** try Virgin Gorda Villa Rentals (ⓣ1-800/848-7081, ⓦwww.virgingordabvi.com), Caribbean Villas (ⓣ1-888/776-1616, ⓦwww.cvoa.com) or Unusual Villa Rentals (ⓣ1-800/846-7280, ⓦwww.unusualvillarentals.com).

North Sound

Biras Creek Resort ⓣ284/494-3555 or 1-800/223-1108, ⓦwww.biras.com. Accessible only by water, this 140-acre, luxury resort offers a mixture of posh pampering and undisturbed freedom, natural beauty and cosmopolitan sophistication. There's a private beach, watersports centre, tennis courts and motorized dinghies and organized helicopter, scuba and sailing trips for an additional cost. But the *pièce de résistance* is the food (see p.448). All-inclusive rates start at US$950 in high season. 9

Bitter End Yacht Club ⓣ284/494-2746 or 1-800/872-2392, ⓦwww.beyc.com. This huge, lush waterfront resort (reachable only by water) has superb amenities including two restaurants, a great English pub, a decked-out commissary, several boutiques and even an outdoor movie theatre. Choose from beachfront villas or suites that sit in the steep hills like tree houses. The resort also offers many activities for the whole family. Rates start at US$860 per night, all-inclusive. 9

Leverick Bay Resort ⓣ284/495-7421 or 1-800/848-7081, ⓦwww.leverickbay.com. The rooms or one- and two-bedroom suites all offer great views, with a marina and a collection of shops nearby. Amenities include a laundry, grocery store, scuba shop, salon and spa, a restaurant and bar, a pool and tennis court. The North Sound Express ferry offers dockside access. Forty-three private villas are also available with a seven-night minimum stay in high season. 5–9

Saba Rock Resort ⓣ284/495-9966, ⓦwww.sabarock.com. This nine-unit collection of suites and villas, marina, restaurant and bar is perched on a huge rock just barely large enough to support it all in the middle of the North Sound. 5–9

Spanish Town and The Valley

Fischer's Cove Beach Hotel The Valley ⓣ284/495-5252, ⓦwww.fischerscove.com. This small beachside complex offers individual cottages and hotel rooms – some with views of Sir Francis Drake Channel. The Garden View rooms are plain, have patios and are the only ones with a/c. Special deals for stays of seven days or more. 5–6

Guavaberry Spring Bay Vacation Homes Spanish Town ⓣ284/495-5227, ⓦwww.guavaberryspringbay.com. A few minutes from the beach and just north of The Baths, these one-bedroom and two-bedroom houses are a steal, each with a kitchen, living room and a covered deck. There are also 18 privately owned villas available. Reserve well in advance as there is a high rate of return clients. No credit cards. 6–7

Little Dix Bay Little Dix Bay ⓣ284/495-5555, ⓦwww.littledixbay.com. A mile north of Spanish Town, this relaxed though very refined resort is set among rolling, flower-filled grounds near a crescent-shaped white-sand beach. The rooms are luxurious and there are hiking trails, a fitness centre, floodlit tennis courts and even a tennis pro on hand. Rates start at US$595. 9

Mango Bay Resort Mahoe Bay ⓣ284/495-5672, ⓦwww.mangobayresort.com. A small beachfront resort heavily influenced by Italian architecture and cuisine, and comprising nine duplex villas and five private homes. There are no tennis courts or gym, but the exquisite beach offers plenty of watersports. 8–9

Oceanview Spanish Town ⓣ284/495-5230. The ocean view isn't much to speak of, and the rooms are small and have musty carpeting. But if you're in a jam, the price is right. Think of it as camping with a/c and a TV. 3

Beaches

The Baths (US$3) are an absolute must-see but when the tours show up, they may be more like your local swimming pool on the hottest day of the year – cruise ships unload up to 300 people a day. Go early in the morning or late in the afternoon to avoid the crowds. Fortunately, Virgin Gorda has plenty of quiet **beaches**. The best spots to watch the sunset are accessible only by water so you'll need to hire a boat. **Prickly Pear Island** has a collection of secluded beaches including long, sandy Vixen Point, Sand Box Beach and idyllic Lover's Beach – as you'd expect, the smallest and most private of them all.

If you feel like having some facilities nearby, **Deep Bay Beach** is a good bet; it's the official beach for *Biras Creek Resort* but you don't have to be a guest to frolic in the ocean or plant yourself on a beach chair. You can reach Deep Bay by hiking from *The Bitter End* or by hiring a boat. The best beach for snorkelling, **Long Bay Beach**, just south of Mountain Point, can be reached by road or sea; if you're coming by car take Plum Tree Bay Road, a dirt road that winds due north away from North Sound Road about two miles out of Spanish Town. If you're staying in Spanish Town, **Savannah Bay Beach**, one mile of deserted beautiful white sand, is your closest option. When the beach at The Baths is too crowded, swim (or walk) north around the last outcropping of rocks to **Spring Bay Beach** and **The Crawl**, which offer more great boulders, snorkelling and sand without the crowds.

Eating

You can get anything from local food in the villages around Gun Creek to gourmet dining at lavish *Biras Creek Resort*. **Gun Creek** can be reached by ferry (the staff ferries from resorts to Gun Creek are free, but beware: they don't run late) or road. **Spanish Town** has plenty of moderately priced restaurants, most of which also double as bars and dance clubs (see opposite) later in the evening. If you want to make up a **picnic**, The Wine Cellar Bakery and Deli (☎284/495-5250; Virgin Gorda Yacht Harbour) is the best place for food to go.

North Sound

Biras Creek *Biras Creek Resort* ☎284/494-3555, VHF16. This elegant resort restaurant and bar on a hillside overlooking the North Sound welcomes non-guests for lunch or dinner by reservation only. Though pricey (US$85 per person), the food is delicious. Smart dress required.

The Clubhouse *Bitter End Yacht Club* ☎284/494-2746. The resort's main restaurant serves steaks, seafood, pasta and a selection of fusion foods in an open-air dining room, just steps from the beach. The buffets for lunch (US$28) and dinner (US$50) are popular. Reservations required.

Fat Virgin Café *Biras Creek Resort* ☎284/495-7052. A small, inexpensive, outdoor restaurant, located at the resort's Marina Village, on the dock just east of the main *Biras* landing, serving everything from baby back ribs (US$20) to flying fish sandwiches (US$15). Some say they have the best burgers (US$13) on the island. If you're staying at another North Sound resort, come by dinghy.

The Restaurant at Leverick Bay Leverick Bay ☎284/495-7154. Have breakfast, lunch or dinner in the shade next to the pool, take a pizza to go at the casual downstairs restaurant or indulge in the posher upstairs terrace. Friday night is a beach barbecue (US$25) with live music, mocko jumbies and a limbo contest. Free moorings, and ice with the purchase of four dinner entrees if you eat at the restaurant upstairs.

Saba Rock Restaurant North Sound ☎284/495-7711. A unique dining experience on a small rock between Virgin Gorda and Prickly Pear. The changing nightly buffet costs US$33 and an à la carte menu offers burgers and sandwiches. Open for lunch and dinner. Offers a free ferry for guests to and from any location in the North Sound.

Spanish Town

Andy's Chateau The Valley ☎284/495-5252. *Andy's* is a waterfront complex, holding the *Sea Dog Pub* and a dance club; live music most weekends. Its counterpart, *Mermaid's,* sits on the dock over the water and is a good place for sunset happy hour and grilled local seafood. Menu items run US$10–14.

The Bath and Turtle Lee Road, Virgin Gorda Yacht Harbour ☎284/495-5239. The reasonable menu has a variety of pasta dishes and sandwiches as well as pizzas. Highlights include the ginger chicken wings, West Indian chicken sandwiches and seared tuna. Open for breakfast, lunch and dinner. Live music Wed from 9pm.

Chez Bamboo Spanish Town ☎284/495-5752. Located on the town's main strip, this romantic spot serves great French-Caribbean food. Curried lobster is not to be missed and the desserts are excellent. Main courses run from US$30–45, and you can expect live calypso or reggae by local bands on Fri.

Giorgio's Table Mahoe Bay ☎284/495-5684, Sicilian cooking meets Caribbean seafood at *Giorgio's* where lobster ravioli and swordfish capriccio (US$22–36) are just a few of the spectacular entrees. Open for lunch and dinner. Reservations and smart dress required.

The Rock Café Tower Road ☎284/495-5472. This Italian restaurant, near The Baths, is a locals' favourite for dining, drinks and dancing. You can eat outside, at tables nestled between boulders similar to The Baths minus the sea, or inside. Nightly piano bar and an occasional live band.

Top of the Baths The Baths ☎284/495-5497. Located, as the name suggests, on the hills above

The Baths, this eatery serves breakfast and lunch, and is worth a visit for the views and sunsets. A piña colada completes the mood. The reasonably-priced food is delicious – try the fritters with the house sauce.

The Wheelhouse Spanish Town ☎284/495-6739. Good homestyle island cooking for about US$12 a plate at this open-air pavilion right across from the Virgin Gorda Yacht Harbour. Happy hour from 6–7pm features US$1 beers and quite honestly the best rum punch in the Virgin Islands.

Drinking and nightlife

Nightlife on Virgin Gorda takes the form of hopping from bar to bar by boat for a mellow drink and live music – many of the **bars** have their own ferries. **Gun Creek** is a good place to start. When you step off the ferry, grab a cold one at *The Last Stop Bar*, then, once up the hill, try the *Butterfly* for beer and dominoes. The party epicentre of the North Sound is *Saba Rock Resort*, with frequent **live music** and drink specials.

In Spanish Town a few of the restaurants (see above) liven up later in the evening. *The Bath and Turtle* has two happy hours daily (10.30–11.30am and 4–6pm) as well as live music every Wednesday night. *Chez Bamboo* hops on Friday nights when locals and tourists come to party. The *Mine Shaft* and *Andy's* host monthly **full-moon parties**, inspired by *Bomba's Shack* on Tortola (see p.441). *The Wheel House* brings in live bands, often calypso or *quelbe*.

Watersports and outdoor activities

Virgin Gorda isn't especially known for its **hiking**, but a few simple nature trails thread the hills connecting *Biras Creek* to *The Bitter End*; both resorts provide free maps to guests and non-guests alike. You can also hike to the top of **Virgin Gorda Peak National Park** (see p.445). Most of the resorts have **tennis** facilities, free to guests but also open to non-guests for around US$20 per hour. *Leverick Bay* and *Little Dix Bay* have the most courts.

The North Sound in particular offers excellent **watersports** opportunities – the companies below are recommended. Many outfits operating out of Tortola (see p.443) also provide watersports for travellers on Virgin Gorda, and more specific information on the **diving** can be found in the Tortola section on p.443.

Bitter End Yacht Club ☎284/494-2746. Offers equipment rentals, lessons and charters, including kayaks, kiteboards, and various boats. Sailing school onsite.

Dive BVI ☎284/495-5513 or 1-800/848-7078, ⓦwww.divebvi.com. This dive shop at Yacht Harbour (with a branch in *Leverick Bay*) has been in business since 1975 and offers rentals, sales, dive trips and five-star PADI training. Trips hit all the hot spots – a two-tanker is US$95. Snorkel trips every afternoon including the *Rhone* on Sat and Anegada on Tues and Fri. Very professional and accommodating. Also offers nitrox diving and instruction.

Double "D" Charters ☎284/495-6150, ⓦwww.doubledbvi.com. Snorkel, scuba, swim or just kick back on one of these day charters. Choose from a 50ft catamaran or one of two 42ft yachts.

Kilbrides Sunchaser Scuba ☎284/495-9638 or 1-800/932-4286. Located at the *Bitter End*, this legendary dive outfit is the most established in the BVI. Daily trips include The Dogs, Salt, Ginger and Cooper islands as private charters or groups. Lessons range from beginner to divemaster, and they can also videotape your dive.

Leverick Bay Watersports ☎284/495-7376, ⓦwww.watersportsbvi.com. From snorkel gear and sea kayaks to powerboats and dinghies, you can rent just about anything here. Also good for activities such as water-skiing and parasailing. Accessible by road, a claim the other watersports companies in the North Sound can't make.

Jost Van Dyke

JOST VAN DYKE, named after the seventeenth-century Dutch pirate who made it his hideaway, is a tiny, lightly developed, mountainous island three miles off the northwest coast of Tortola. Though its popularity is increasing, this idyll of wooded hills and secluded bays has changed little since a Quaker colony settled here in the 1700s to farm sugar cane – in fact most of the island's 160 inhabitants (all either Chinnerys or Callwoods) are descended from Quaker slaves. The island has had electricity for less than fifteen years and there's only one paved road. While the growing tourist scene owes much to the yachts that stop here to clear **customs** in Great Harbour, sailors and tourists alike flock here for the magical combination of friendly locals, unspoilt beauty and party atmosphere – two **bars** are infamous in the Virgin Islands and have helped earn Jost Van Dyke the title of party capital of BVI.

The three main areas are on the island's south side and accessible by car or boat. The focal point is the palm-fringed beach and settlement of **Great Harbour**. Along sandy laid-back Main Street, you'll find rooms for rent, bars, boutiques, a provision store and even an ice cream shop. *Foxy's* (see p.451), tucked in the corner, is the major draw. **White Bay**, half a mile west beyond Pull and Be Damm Point, has the island's best beach and is home to its other famous drinking hole, the *Soggy Dollar Bar* (see p.452), as well as a hotel, campsite and a few bars and shops. Just over a mile to the east of Great Harbour, **Little Harbour** is a good place to eat – the spiny lobster may well be the biggest you've seen in your life. On the **eastern side** of the island a short hike past mangroves and a salt pond leads to the **Bubbly Pool**, where a gap in the rocky coastline allows the foam of crashing waves to form a sort of natural Jacuzzi. To get on the **Internet** your best bet is Jost Van Dyke Scuba (US$5/fifteen minutes).

Getting around

Taxis in Great Harbour Bay will take you to White Bay for about US$5 and to Little Harbour for US$10 (call George's Land Taxi ⓣ284/543-5396 or White Stone Taxi Service ⓣ284/495-9487). Jost Van Dyke's only paved road is very steep and bumpy and curls around the hills offering views along the eastern and southern shore. Abe & Eunicy Rentals (ⓣ284/446-9329) in Little Harbour has **jeeps** for US$60–80 per day. Another fun way to get around is to take a ATV tour with Sea and Land Adventure Sports (see p.452).

Note that there are **no banks** on Jost Van Dyke. Some establishments accept **credit cards** but the connection is rather unreliable.

Accommodation

It might not last, but major development hasn't yet arrived on Jost Van Dyke. Still, you'll find of all levels of **accommodation** including private villas, a hotel, guesthouses and a **campsite**. *White Bay Campground* (ⓣ284/495-9358) offers bare sites for US$20 a night, sites equipped with tents for US$40, plus small and large screen-windowed cabins for US$65–75. Communal bathrooms have showers and flush toilets. Special barbecue, chicken, ribs and fish buffets are offered on Thursdays, but there's also a nice shared kitchen for cooking and storing refrigerated foods. Regardless of where you stay, it is a good idea to make reservations early. If you choose accommodation with a kitchen, bear in mind that the island has limited groceries; it is best to stock up on Tortola or wherever you are arriving from.

Perfect Pineapple Inn White Bay ⓣ284/496-8373, ⓦwww.perfectpineapple.com. Two villas with full kitchens and three studios with kitchenettes are perched halfway up the hill at the eastern end of the bay, with views of the entire inlet and its beautiful white beach. All are spacious with a/c and just a five-minute walk from the beach and its party. ❺–❾

Sandcastle White Bay ⓣ284/495-9888, ⓦwww.sandcastle-bvi.com. The best lodging on the island. Four large cottages (with outdoor showers) are cooled by fans, while the two newer cottages have a/c. There is also a restaurant, bar and beach to enjoy. Day sails, scuba diving and fishing can be arranged. ❻–❼

Sandy Ground Estates Little Harbour ⓣ284/494-3391, ⓦwww.sandyground.com. Seven secluded villas with a private beach and featuring stunning ocean views from tiled terraces. Most are two-bedroom and are available by the week only. It's out of the way so order groceries beforehand from Bobby's market here in Road Town. Reserve well in advance. Rates start at US$2000 per week. ⑨

Sea Crest Inn Great Harbour ⓣ340/495-9024, ⓦwww.bviwelcome.com/seacrestinn. These four beachfront units have private balconies, fully equipped kitchens, cable TV and a/c. Close to the local bar scene; good for stumbling in late at night, but possibly an occasional annoyance when trying to sleep. Three-night minimum stay. ⑤

White Bay Villas White Bay ⓣ1-800-778-8066 or 410/571-6692, ⓦwww.jostvandyke.com. Ten lovely villas perched above an idyllic bay and moments from the beach. The villas range in size from a huge plantation-style house to a one-bedroom unit. Stays are usually arranged by the week, but the owners try to be accommodating. US$1995–4095 for seven nights. ⑨

Eating and drinking

Jost Van Dyke is the party island of the BVI and has a vibrant **eating and drinking** scene. Most of the fun takes place during the day, particularly at weekends, in a variety of places in Great Harbour Bay, Little Bay and White Bay, some of which are no more than beachside shacks. Nature's Basket is a simple grocery in Great Harbour that has other odds and ends like sunscreen and film.

Abe's by the Sea Little Harbour ⓣ284/495-9329. A simple dockside joint with good seafood, ribs and chicken (US$20–22) for lunch or dinner. Happy hour 5–6pm.

Ali Baba's Bar and Restaurant Great Harbour ⓣ284/495-9280. BBQ, ribs, conch, lobster and catch of the day (around US$22). A pig roast with a live band every Mon.

Corsairs Great Harbour ⓣ284/495-9294. This beachside restaurant rivals *Foxy's Taboo* as the best food on the island. Serving mostly Italian and seafood dishes as well as some Mexican fare, its menu changes often (mains US$16–26). There's regular live music from local singer/guitarist Ruben Chinnery and the occasional limbo session.

Foxy's Great Harbour ⓣ284/495-9258. This is the bar that put Jost Van Dyke firmly on the yachters' map. When you think about waterfront bars, island music and beach barbecues, *Foxy's* is the standard by which everything else should be compared. Sit at picnic tables under the thatched roof or stretch out on the beach, drinking and eating. The legendary and larger-than-life Foxy Callwood occasionally entertains guests with stories and jokes. Barbecue buffet nights on Fri and Sat (US$28); live music Thurs–Sat.

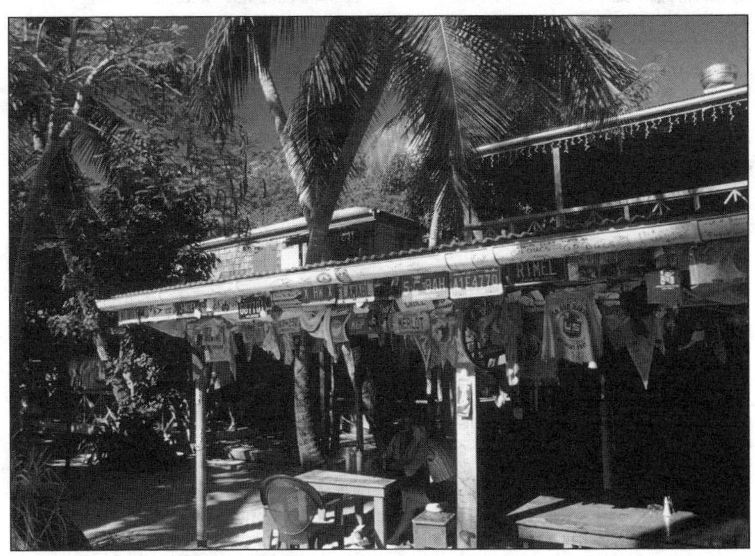

▲ Foxy's bar, Great Harbour

Foxy's Taboo Diamond Cay ☎284/446-9891. One of the island's best restaurants, with plenty of moorings and dock space. Lunch highlights include gourmet pizza, veggie pitas, and great burgers. Chicken, fish, steak, lamb and pasta dishes for dinner run around US$25; the eggplant cheesecake is a culinary event. The bar is open from 10.30am.

Ivan's Stress Free Bar White Bay Campground ☎284/495-9358. *Ivan's* has a barbecue (US$20) and live music Thurs nights. The bar operates on an honour system, so be sure to keep your own tab and pay when you leave.

One Love White Bay ☎284/495-9829. A thatch-roofed beach bar good for cheap drinks and if Seddy is in the mood, he'll show you a few sleight-of-hand tricks that get harder to follow with every rum punch.

Sandcastle Restaurant White Bay ☎284/495-9888. Non-guests can make reservations (and should, by 4pm) to eat alongside hotel guests. Jost Van Dyke's only fine-dining option, with a set menu of lamb, duck, crab cakes and the like for around US$39.

Sidney's Peace and Love Little Harbour ☎284/495-9271. T-shirts of the guests of parties past dangle from the ceiling at this Jost Van Dyke institution that's been serving up food and fun for over 35 years. Choose from steak, shrimp, ribs, chicken and conch stew, plus hearty helpings of rice and peas, coleslaw, potato salad, steamed vegetables for US$18–25. The highlight is lobster, bigger than anywhere else on the islands. Sidney still catches and cooks them himself, over an open fire the island way. Thursday night has all-you-can-eat lobster and live music for US$50. Self-service at the bar – mix 'em as you like 'em.

Soggy Dollar Bar *Sandcastle Hotel*, White Bay ☎284/495-9888. Named after the wet bills brought by patrons who swim to the bar, *The Soggy Dollar*, located right on the beach, is perhaps best known as the inventor of the Painkiller, a potent mix of dark rum, pineapple and orange juices, coco lopez and fresh nutmeg. Sat and Sun are especially fun but can get very crowded. Local musician, Ruben Chinnery, plays every Sun afternoon.

Watersports and other activities

Unless you go out with a tour, the best **snorkelling** is found on the eastern side around Diamond Cay and Little Jost Van Dyke. White Bay is where most gather for **beach activities**.

Ali Baba's Bar and Restaurant Stop in to inquire about half-day fishing trips for around US$500, all equipment included.

Jost Van Dyke Scuba ☎284/495-0271, Ⓦwww.jostvandykescuba.com. Just down the road from *Corsair's*, this well-run outfit pretty much has the lock on scuba diving (two tanks US$110). They operate by reservation only and will take you to any of 35 unmarked dive sites that only they know about. They also specialize in snorkel eco-tours and offer sportfishing, dinghy and kayak rentals as well as Internet service.

Sea and Land Adventure Sports White Bay ☎284/541-2369, Ⓦwww.bviadventure.com. Rent a variety of toys on the beach ranging from jet boats, kayaks and water trampolines to mountain bikes and ATVs. They also rent snorkels for US$25 per person per day, as well as fantastic self-drive ATV tours of the island at US$65 per hour.

Anegada

The name **ANEGADA** means the "drowned land," and with its highest point topping out at 28 feet it would seem this flat coral and limestone atoll just has its nose above the waves. Lying fourteen miles north of Virgin Gorda, the island is almost completely surrounded by the **Horseshoe Reef**, one of the world's largest and the doom of many a vessel – the plethora of wrecks only add to the already excellent **snorkelling** that draws day-trippers. Anegada's **lobsters** are huge and reputedly the best, its **beaches** are long and undeveloped, and the **bonefishing** is some of the world's best.

Anegada Harbour on the southwest coast is nothing much to speak of – just a long, thin dock with lobster traps tied to its side – but it's a good place to base yourself for exploring the island. The area, which includes Pomato Point and Setting Point, has plenty of lodging, restaurants, bars and gift shops. The little **Pomato**

Point Museum (☎284/495-8038) is worth a visit for its small but evocative display of items recovered from shipwrecks around the island, ranging from cannons to gin bottles. Around four miles east of here (southeast of the airport) is **The Settlement**, where most of the island's 195 inhabitants live. You'll find a bakery, a post office, a police station and a clinic with a nurse on duty – the doctor is on island only once a week.

The best of the beaches and snorkelling are on the north coast. At **LOBLOLLY BAY**, a picture-postcard Caribbean paradise with a bar and restaurant, the waters teem with schools of mojarra, needlefish and mantis shrimp as well as the occasional sea turtle or stingray. On the western side of the beach, the dark reef area in the middle of the lagoon contains three small caves and a wreck, among which you'll spot elkhorn and brain coral, angelfish, snapper and huge grouper. **Cow Wreck Beach**, six miles to the west, is another good snorkelling spot and with currents towards the shore it is great for kids; it has a changing room, plus food and drinks. **Jack's Bay** and **Keel Point** are also good places to put your face in the water. In the centre of the island is a salt pond and all of Anegada is a **wildlife sanctuary**, home to turtles, birdlife, including osprey and a flock of flamingos, and the endangered rock iguanas, which are bred and protected in its carefully monitored reserves.

Arrival and getting around

Every Monday, Wednesday and Friday, Smith's Ferry Services (☎284/494-4454) runs a fast ferry to Anegada from Road Town, Tortola (US$50 return), stopping at Virgin Gorda if you call ahead and make a reservation. This option might be best if you have time and a lot of luggage. Taxis run US$6-8 to most points on the island and some hotels might offer guests a free shuttle from the island's **airport**. Getting around the island is fairly easy – the main road loops round to most of the main places of interest. *The Anegada Reef Hotel* (see below), on the front of the harbour dock, can help you schedule car rental or a shuttle ride to beaches on the north side of the island (US$8). Scooter rentals are available at Lil Bit Cash & Carry (☎284/495-9932) for US$40. Alternatively, there will be taxis waiting at the ferry dock when you disembark, or rent a vehicle (around US$70 per day) through DW Jeep Rentals (☎284/495-9677). Most businesses monitor VHF channel 16 for boaters.

Accommodation

Most of the **accommodation** on Anegada is located on the **south shore** and is fairly basic, but varied; there is no camping on the island. For **villas** consider the six-person *Bonefish Villa* (☎284/495-8045) sitting nearly on top of a great place to seek its namesake, or the quite elegant *Lavenda Breeze* (☎1-888/868-0199, ⓦwww.lavendabreeze.com).

Anegada Beach Cottages Pomato Point ☎284/495-9234, ⓦwww.anegadabeachcottages.com. Four fully furnished seaside cottages with modern kitchen and bathroom set on a private beach (no a/c but plenty of cooling sea breezes). ⑤

Anegada Reef Hotel Setting Point, Anegada Harbour ☎284/495-8002, ⓦwww.anegadareef.com. This lovely hotel acts as a de facto tour operator arranging beach shuttles, rental cars and fishing trips. Stay in one of its sixteen rooms and eat a fantastic lobster meal in its restaurant. ⑤–⑥

Cow Wreck Villas ☎284/495-9932. Three simple beachside villas (1 and 2 bedrooms) with complete kitchens. The beach offers shallow snorkelling, great for kids and beginners, and fishing tours are available. ⑥

Neptune's Treasure Anegada Harbour ☎284/495-9439. Nine comfortable guesthouses, double and single rooms, all with private baths, a/c, and fridges. A nice restaurant and bar is onsite (see p.454). ⑤

Eating and drinking

Most **restaurants** catch their own **seafood** and will be happy to tell you where and how it was caught. The local speciality, the spindly but huge **Anegada lobster**, is delicious and worth ordering at least once. For dinner, it's advisable to call ahead for a reservation and to ensure lobster is available if you are interested.

Anegada Reef Hotel (see also p.453). Popular dining spot for cocktails and a candlelit dinner of grilled fish, chicken, steak and lobster (don't worry, you can still wear shorts). Main courses start at US$25.

The Big Bamboo The North Side ⓣ284/499-1680. This pavilion-style restaurant in Loblolly Bay caters to the beach crowd, with a good lunch and dinner menu – crab cakes (US$18), fish and shrimp and ribs (US$25-28). The lobster is quite good for such a simple place. All meals come with rice and a side dish, and try the rum-based Bamboo Teaser.

Cow Wreck Beach Bar and Grill ⓣ284/495-8047. Wash down conch fritters (US$11) or Belle's famous lobster with the bar's own rum-driven Wreck Punch. Serves lunch and dinner and sells food supplies for boaters. Call for a shuttle if you plan to dine.

Neptune's Treasure Anegada Harbour ⓣ284/495-9439. The owners catch, cook and serve their own grilled fish and lobster – main courses for around US$20. Try a Pink Whoopie, yet another rum and fruit juice concoction, at the bar.

Pomato Point Restaurant Anegada Harbour ⓣ284/495-9466. Located at Pomato Point, this pleasant airy spot serves dinner only. Chicken, ribs, fish and lobster are available (US$25–45). Check out the Pomato Point Museum (part of the same building) before dinner.

Watersports

Anegada doesn't have much in the way of organized **watersports** but the *Anegada Reef Hotel* (see above) can help you book fishing trips. Alternatively, both Virgin Gorda (see p.449) and Tortola (see p.444) have charter operators that run snorkelling and fishing trips to Anegada. If you want to try your hand at **bonefishing**, give Garfield Faulkner a call at ⓣ284/496-9699 or ask around The Settlement or at your hotel for a local reference. We Be Divin' (ⓣ284/499-2835 or 284/495-8002, ⓦwww.webedivinbvi.com) based at the *Anegada Reef Hotel* offers a variety **scuba diving** trips at US$125 for a two-tank dive.

Outlying islands

A few outlying islands accessible from Tortola are worth a visit. **PETER ISLAND**, three miles across the Francis Drake Channel from Tortola, is home to the luxurious *Peter Island Resort* (ⓣ284/495-2000 or 770/476-9988, ⓦwww.peterisland.com), which offers ocean-view rooms, an all-inclusive range of watersports, tennis, bikes, hiking and sailing activities, and extremely elegant dining at its *Tradewinds Restaurant* and wine room (also open to non-guests). If you're staying elsewhere, you can visit the island and use Little Deadman's Beach, the only one available for non-guests. The Peter Island Ferry (call the hotel for a day pass) connects the island with Road Town on Tortola (US$20 round-trip; free if you have a reservation at *Tradewinds*). There's more casual fare – wood-oven pizzas and salads – available at *Deadman's Beach Bar and Grill*. Rates start at US$950 per night including all food and watersports. Peaceful, unpretentious and good value, **COOPER ISLAND**, four miles east of Peter Island, has a lone hotel and a few vacation homes. *The Cooper Island Beach Club* (ⓣ284/495-9084 or 1-800/542-4624, ⓦwww.cooper-island.com; ❻–❼) offers eleven doubles without phones or TV set on beautiful **Manchioneel Bay**, which has a long beach and fantastic snorkelling – the thick sea grass attracts a dazzling assortment of green turtles, eagle rays and huge queen conch. There are no roads and no cars on the island and there's scheduled ferry service on Monday, Wednesday and Friday. Sail Caribbean Divers (ⓣ284/495-1675, see p.444) has a base on the island and runs a dive boat to Cooper daily from Hodges Creek on Tortola.

Eight-acre **MARINA CAY**, which offers great snorkelling, was made famous by author Robb White and his wife, Rodie, who moved here in 1936, built a home and lived without running water or electricity. His book about the experience, *Two on* *an Isle*, was made into a movie in the 1950s, starring Sidney Poitier. The only place to stay on the island is *Pusser's Marina Cay Resort* (Ⓣ284/494-2174, Ⓦwww.pussers.com; ❻–❾), connected to Trellis Bay by a short free ferry ride (seven daily), which has basic rooms or two-bedroom villas. The hotel can arrange everything from snorkelling and diving to surfing and powerboat rentals. The old White residence is now *The Robb White Bar*, which hosts barbecues and live music. A more extensive menu is available at the *Pusser's* beachside restaurant. Be sure not to miss Michael Bean's happy hour pirate show most days at 5pm at the upstairs bar.

Uninhabited and largely untamed **NORMAN ISLAND**, the westernmost BVI, is only accessible by hired boat and there are no places to stay, yet thousands of people in high season flock here every day to snorkel – and look for gold. Rumours are that there is hidden **treasure** all over the island – three chests of gold have reportedly been discovered since the mid-1700s, and some suggest that Norman Island was the model for Robert Louis Stevenson's *Treasure Island*.

Bar/restaurant *The Willy T* (Ⓣ284/494-0183, Ⓦwww.williamthornton.com) is a converted schooner permanently moored in the Bight, a large bay and a popular anchorage for yachters. It's one of the most raucous and unusual drinking spots in the BVI and the top deck often sees inebriated patrons removing their clothes and diving into the water. *Wet Willie* (Ⓣ284/496-6416), the bar's free ferry, departs at 5pm daily from Todman's across from Nanny Cay Marina and returns at an unpredictable hour around 10pm or later.

GUANA ISLAND is an 850-acre private island resort (Ⓣ914/967-6050 or 1-800/544-8262, Ⓦwww.guana.com) with its own nature preserve and wildlife sanctuary. Formerly a Quaker plantation, the resort offers secluded cottages decorated with simple elegance. With seven beaches and no non-guest access, this may be as secluded as it gets. Everything but alcohol and motorized watersports is included, as well as airport or ferry transfers with stays for four nights or longer and a golf cart to get around the island. Honeymoon rates available. Daily rates start at US$1495, or you can rent the entire island for a mere US$29,00 per day for up to thirty-two guests in high season.

Anguilla

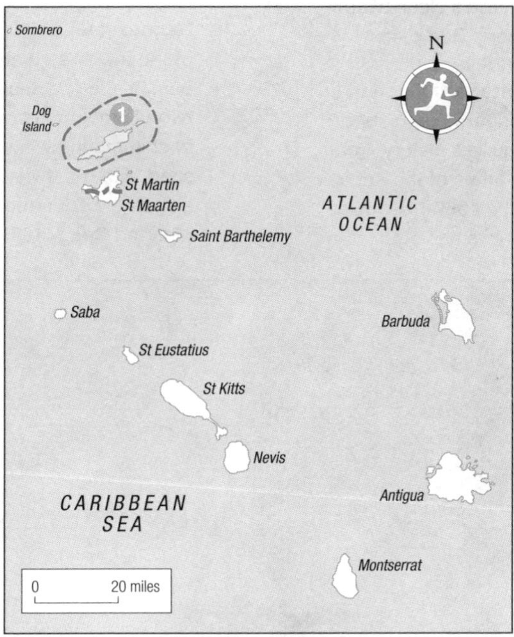
Sombrero
N
Dog Island
1
St Martin
St Maarten
ATLANTIC OCEAN
Saint Barthelemy
Saba
Barbuda
St Eustatius
St Kitts
Nevis
Antigua
CARIBBEAN SEA
Montserrat
0 20 miles

Anguilla highlights

* **Boat racing** Pick your vantage point to enjoy the excitement of Anguilla's boat racing during the summer carnival. See p.463

* **Wreck diving** Scuba dive the wrecks both ancient and modern around Anguilla's clear, warm waters. See p.463

* **Heritage Collection Museum** Learn about Anguilla's history, from the times of the Arawak to the 1967 "revolution", in this small but fascinating museum at East End Pond. See p.467

* **Fine dining** Take your pick from Anguilla's renowned fine-dining options – there's something to suit all palates. See p.469

* **Rendezvous Bay** One of the region's greatest beaches, a spectacular two-kilometre crescent of shimmering white sand with great views across the sound to Sint Maarten See p.469

▲ Summer Festival boat races

Introduction and basics

A favourite hide away for celebrities such as Janet Jackson, Robert de Niro and Denzel Washington, Anguilla is a superb place to relax. With its swaying palm trees and unpopulated powdery white beaches, the island is the ideal place to unwind by turquoise waters. Add world-class dining, unique luxury lodgings and a range of watersports, and Anguilla is easily the quintessential Caribbean holiday destination.

Barely 35 square miles in size, and only just over two hundred feet at its highest point, Anguilla has an **interior** that is dry, dusty and covered in scrubby vegetation. This, however, is largely ignored by an increasing stream of visitors who beat their way to melt into the glorious turquoise waters and explore the island's 33 beaches.

Going unnoticed by the Caribbean's early waves of **tourist development**, for many years tiny Anguilla's tourism focused on smaller upmarket development with relatively limited impact on the island's scarce resources. This has made it a top destination for stressed-out celebrities and the super-rich who want to get away from it all. Yet change is in the air; while exclusivity and luxury are still the bywords of current development, a series of major large resort and residence projects are underway along several of the top beaches, not to mention a second top-notch 18-hole golf course and a megayacht marina – all of which may make it harder in the future to escape the crowds as more of the beautiful coastline disappears under concrete, albeit stylishly designed.

Where to go

Anguilla's clean white-sand **beaches** provide the perfect spot to kick back and relax or pursue more active interests including scuba diving and windsurfing. Many are big enough for you to have your own secluded spot and are sprinkled with a selection of top-quality restaurants and the occasional beach bar. The swathes of powdery sand at **Rendezvous Bay** and **Shoal Bay East** rank among some of the world's finest while the more down-to-earth Crocus Bay in the early morning will give you a glimpse of island life, as locals take their daily exercise on the sands or in the water and fishermen prepare their nets.

When to go

Like other Caribbean islands, Anguilla is a year-round destination; however, the **best time to visit** is between mid-December and mid-April, when rainfall is low – although the annual average is only 35 inches – and the heat is tempered by cooling trade winds. At other times of year the weather is often very hot and humid, and storms are not unusual. From June to late October is **hurricane season**. And, even if a storm does not hit the island, Anguilla is still prone to flooding, due to its low-lying topography. Note that **prices** for accommodation and car rental in particular are higher between December and April, with some outrageous price hikes over Christmas and New Year.

Getting there

Visitors arriving by air will land at **Wallblake Airport** just south of The Valley. Taxis and rental cars are easily procured here. **Private vessels** arriving in Anguilla must go to a port of entry such as Blowing Point or Sandy Ground for immigration and customs clearance and will be required to obtain a permit to anchor in the marine park. For those visitors arriving for a day-trip from nearby St Martin, local taxis can operate as **tour guides** (US$25 per hr).

Information

At the airport a variety of useful publications are available, including excellent **maps** of

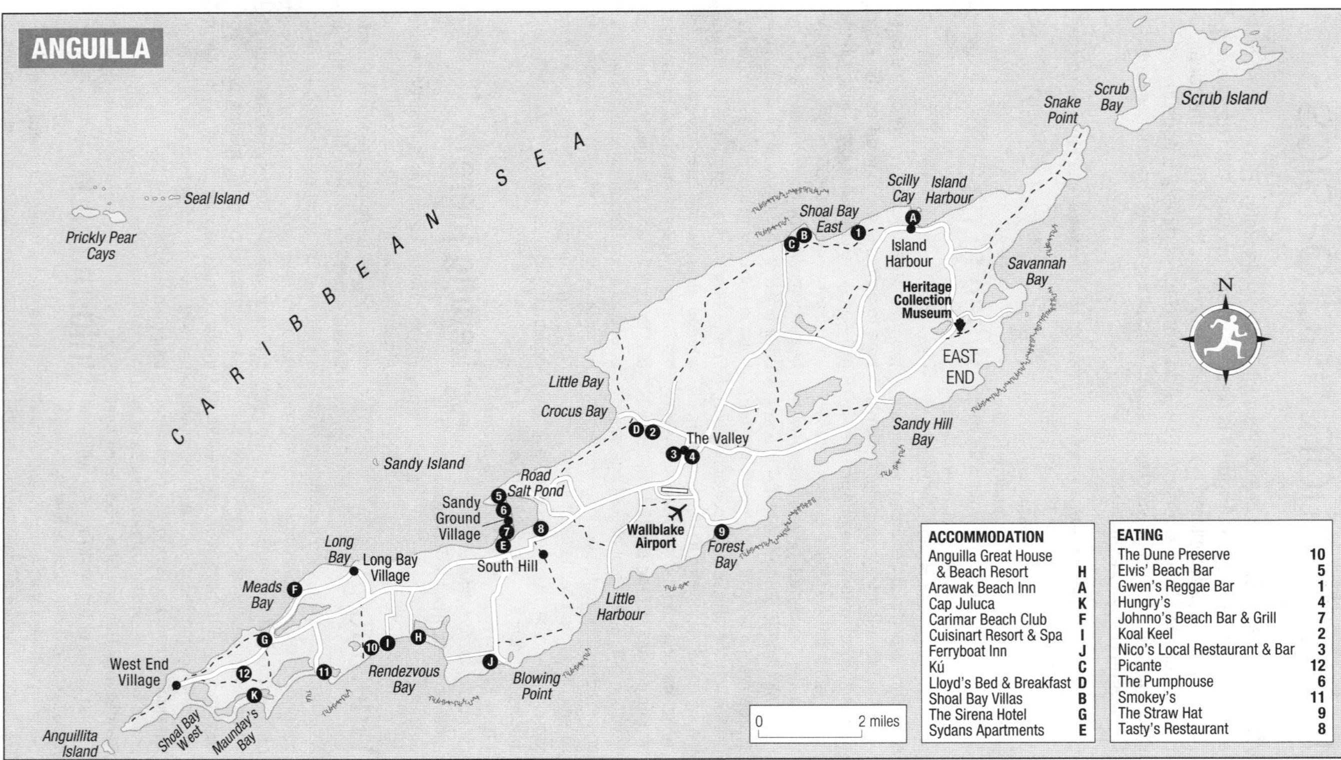
ANGUILLA
Dog Island & The Cays
CARIBBEAN SEA
Seal Island
Prickly Pear Cays
Sandy Island
Scrub Island
Scrub Bay
Snake Point
Scilly Cay
Island Harbour
Shoal Bay East
Island Harbour
Heritage Collection Museum
Savannah Bay
EAST END
Sandy Hill Bay
Little Bay
Crocus Bay
The Valley
Road Salt Pond
Sandy Ground Village
Wallblake Airport
Forest Bay
Long Bay
Long Bay Village
South Hill
Little Harbour
Meads Bay
West End Village
Rendezvous Bay
Blowing Point
Anguillita Island
Shoal Bay West
Maunday's Bay
N
0
2 miles
ACCOMMODATION
Anguilla Great House & Beach Resort H
Arawak Beach Inn A
Cap Juluca K
Carimar Beach Club F
Cuisinart Resort & Spa I
Ferryboat Inn J
Kú C
Lloyd's Bed & Breakfast D
Shoal Bay Villas B
The Sirena Hotel G
Sydans Apartments E
EATING
The Dune Preserve 10
Elvis' Beach Bar 5
Gwen's Reggae Bar 1
Hungry's 4
Johnno's Beach Bar & Grill 7
Koal Keel 2
Nico's Local Restaurant & Bar 3
Picante 12
The Pumphouse 6
Smokey's 11
The Straw Hat 9
Tasty's Restaurant 8

the island and current listings newspapers and brochures. These are also widely available in hotels, restaurants and shops as well as at the **Anguilla Tourist Board** office, located on Coronation Road in The Valley (Mon–Fri 8am–5pm; ⓣ497-2759, ⓦwww.anguilla-vacation.com).

Helpful publications include the tourist board office's annual *Anguilla Travel Planner,* which summarizes much of their website information with a calendar of events, restaurant and accommodation listings (including details of live music) and contact details for activities. *What We Do in Anguilla* is both a quarterly **magazine** and a monthly paper with some helpful info amidst the advertising. More useful is the annually produced gourmet guide since it also gives details on opening times and prices, as well as providing sample menus. The weekly national paper, *The Anguillian* comes out on a Friday, and is also available online (ⓦwww.anguillian.com). Bob Green's Anguilla News webblog (ⓦwww.news.ai) offers both practical advice and more informal insights into island issues.

Money and costs

The island's official unit of currency is the **Eastern Caribbean dollar (EC$)**, divided into 100 cents. Notes come in denominations of 5, 10, 20, 50 and 100 EC dollars; coins come in 1, 2, 5, 10 and 25 cents. However, since most visitors are from the US, prices are usually listed in US$, though both currencies are accepted almost universally. The **rate of exchange** is tied to the US dollar at around EC$2.70 for each US dollar. **Credit cards** are taken in most shops, restaurants and in hotels except for the smallest of transactions.

Most **banks** in Anguilla have offices in The Valley. Typically their opening hours are Mon–Thurs 8am–3pm and Fri 8am–5pm. **ATMs** are located at their branches and also at some supermarkets across the island. At most you can choose to receive your money in US or EC dollars.

There is a **departure tax** – payable in cash only – at the airport of US$20 (EC$53.00) for adults, less for children. Departure by ferry incurs a tax of US$5.

Anguilla has little in the way of natural resources for growing crops or rearing animals so most products apart from seafood are imported. This, along with the island's aim of attracting upscale tourists, means that **prices** tend to be higher than on neighbouring islands or in the US. Restaurant **meals** begin at around US$20 and can rise into the stratosphere, while most **rooms,** except the most basic, cost upwards of US$250 per night at peak times.

A **service charge** of fifteen percent is added to most restaurant bills – so further tipping is discretionary and not necessary unless service was outstanding. In hotels a ten percent service charge plus a ten percent government tax are added. These costs are rarely included in the advertised rates.

Getting around

Aside from the bumpy patchwork asphalt that paves The Valley, Anguilla's **roads** are among the best in the Caribbean. Signposting is good and petrol stations are sprinkled across the island. Stray goats are the island's main hazard as they occasionally bolt onto the road without warning.

The island does not have a **public transport** system, and the only way of getting around is by taxi or rented car. Driving is on the left but because most of the cars available from rental firms have the steering wheel on the left, driving can feel a little peculiar. Driving requires a local driving licence, which costs US$20 and is valid for three months. Licences can be purchased from all car rental agencies but payment for the licence is in cash only. Many hotels have their own fleets of rental cars on offer at competitive rates; others have deals with particular firms. Although there are no car rental firms at the airport, **airport delivery and pick-up** is easily arranged. There are numerous reliable operators including Apex/Avis (ⓣ497-2642, ⓔavisaxa@anguillanet.com); Connor's Car Rental (ⓣ497-6433, ⓔmaurice@caribserve.net); Island Car Rentals (ⓣ497-2723, ⓦwww.islandcar.ai); and the slightly cheaper Mitchel's Car Rental (ⓣ497-0712, ⓔanguillaandy2001@hotmail.com). It is worth shopping around and haggling to get the best **rates** for car rental.

Budget around US$40 to $55, plus optional insurance (US$5-10) per day depending on the type of vehicle. Check the tourist board website for further options.

For the purposes of determining taxi fares, the island is divided into ten zones. Taxi rates are fixed according to the number of zones crossed for up to two passengers and two pieces of luggage. Additional charges apply for extra passengers, luggage and for travel during antisocial hours; The tourist board website has a full listing of rates. If you're going to move about the island at all, hire a car for at least some of your stay.

The quality of the roads and the flattish terrain should make **cycling** relatively easy and enjoyable but the construction boom has increased the amount of traffic on the main roads. Still if you're still keen on cycling, check out Premier Bicycle Rentals (ⓣ235-8931), where you can rent a bike, lock and helmet for US$15 per day.

Accommodation

Most **accommodation** in Anguilla is at the expensive, luxurious end of the scale, and many hotels sit on superb stretches of sand (open to guests and non-guests alike – all of Anguilla's beaches are public). It's possible to find a few choice options in lower (but not cheap) price ranges but they are harder to find at peak times such as Christmas and Easter. Conversely, during the slow season, including most of the summer, prices at the top hotels can fall dramatically. Several hotels offer good **packages** if you pre-book activities such as spa treatments, scuba diving or a wedding. If you are in a large group, renting a private villa might be more cost-effective. The Anguilla tourist board website has a comprehensive accommodation rate guide with weblinks.

Food and drink

Anguilla's more than seventy **dining** options range from world-renowned gourmet restaurants to roadside barbecues, beachside bistros and grills. Many of these places focus on local **seafood** such as snapper, grouper, conch and lobster. **Island specialities** include pumpkin soup, conch salad and goat stew, though they are rarely featured at upmarket eateries. What you will not find are the major fast food chains, as these have been prohibited from the island. **Vegetarians** are well catered for with many restaurants offering some veggie options.

The upscale hotels all have terrific restaurants, which are open to non-residents. Dinner **reservations** are required for most of these, and in peak season, reservations are advisable in other popular places. Most **bars** serve imported beers, spirits and wines though you should not miss the opportunity to try out the lethal rum punch concoctions.

Mail and communications

Telephone kiosks in various states of repair are scattered around the island and most take coins and/or phonecards, sold at the many shops, hotels or at the Cable and Wireless office in The Valley (Mon–Fri 8am–5pm, Sat & holidays 9am–1pm; ⓣ497-3100). Mobile phones can be rented from Cable and Wireless for US$10 a day. While local calls are cheap and prices fixed regardless of length, hotels often add a hefty surcharge. The **country code** for Anguilla is 264.

The **post office** can be found on Carter Rey Boulevard in The Valley (Mon–Thur 8am–3.30pm, Fri 8am–4.45pm).

Most hotels now offer **internet** access; some are free though most charge (up to US$15 a day). Otherwise, internet access is available at the Anguilla National Library in The Valley (Mon–Fri 9am–6pm, Sat 9am–3pm, EC5 for 30mins) and at the post office (EC5 for 15mins); better still, if you have a wireless-enabled laptop go to the Cable and Wireless office, where you can get free Wi-Fi connection.

Opening hours, holidays and festivals

Shops and businesses are typically **open** Monday to Saturday 9am–5pm. Some eating

Public holidays and festivals

May 30 Anguilla Day commemorates the beginning of the 1967 Anguillian Revolution. The celebration includes a parade at Webster Park and a six-hour round-the-island boat race.

June Celebration of Her Majesty the Queen's Birthday on the second Monday of the month.

First week of August Anguilla Summer Festival includes a vibrant celebration of the Anguillian culture through dance, song, beauty pageants, colourful parades and boat racing. There are three public holidays during the festival: the first Monday in the month is Emancipation Day, followed by August Thursday the same week, and Constitution Day the Friday of the following week, when the street parades are held.

December 19 Separation Day – celebrating the separation from St Kitts and Nevis.

establishments are only open during peak season and many restaurants and hotels are closed in September and October.

Along with the public holidays of New Year, Easter and Christmas, Anguilla celebrates the **holidays** and **festivals** listed in the box above. Check the tourist board website for updates on additional events throughout the year.

Sports and outdoor activities

Anguilla offers a variety of **sporting** and **outdoor activities**. Many hotels have excellent facilities and there are some good independent providers as well. **Watersports** such as scuba diving, snorkelling, wind surfing and sailing are well catered for.

Diving & snorkelling

Diving on Anguilla focuses on a number of **wrecks** that were deliberately sunk and now have interesting coral formations that attract schools of colourful reef fish. Uniquely Anguilla has two **natural reefs** just a few hundred metres apart. The first is along the littoral of Anguilla and is composed of soft corals: sea fan, gorgonians and sponges. The second begins in Island Harbour in the east and continues all the way to Prickly Pear and Dog Island. This outside reef is made up from hard corals such as giant brain, pencil and giant plaque.

Anguilla's clear waters boast seven **marine parks**: Dog Island, Prickly Pear, Seal Island Reef System, Little Bay, Sandy Island, Shoal Bay Harbour Reef System and Stoney Bay Marine Park. All the dive sites are shallow – between 35 and 110ft – which along with the usually high levels of visibility make it a great place to learn to scuba dive. The best wreck dives include the MV *Oosterdiep* in Road Bay and the MV *Sarah*, off Prickly Pear. The highlight of the Stoney Ground Marine Park is the sunken remains of the Spanish galleon *El Buen Consejo,* which went down in 1772 and whose cannon and anchor are still visible, even to snorkellers, since the water is shallow.

The island has two recognized PADI resorts that can be used whichever hotel you choose to stay in: Shoal Bay Scuba (ⓣ235-1482, ⓦwww.shoalbayscuba.com) and Anguillian Divers (ⓣ497-4750, ⓦwww.anguilliandivers.com). Both offer a comprehensive range of dives and instruction with modern, well-equipped boats for more or less the same rates.

A **diving permit**, which the above operators can supply, is necessary to scuba dive. For single-tank dives budget around US$50–60, and US$85–90 for two-tank dives, excluding equipment rental. Discovery courses are on offer at US$85 while open water certification will set you back US$375. Both operators offer dive packages with various hotels.

Shoal Bay Scuba also organizes afternoon snorkelling outings to Prickly Pear cays on Wednesdays and Saturdays for US$60pp. Also based in the Shoal Bay area, Junior (ⓣ235-1008) offers the chance to catch sight of star fish, turtles, sting rays and schools of tropical fish amongst magical coral formations in his glass-bottomed-boat for US$25pp per hour; for US$40pp per hour he'll take you snorkelling and/or sightseeing further afield. *Johnno's* (see p.470) in Sandy Ground also runs picnic tours in his banana boat. Alternatively, you can probably negotiate a cheaper fee by dealing directly with a boat owner at Sandy Ground although you'll need to be clear on what the deal includes.

Other activities

Sailing trips from Sandy Ground to points around the island include those on the highly recommended *Chocolat* (Ⓣ497-3394, Ⓔruan@anguillanet.com). This 35ft catamaran offers a snorkelling day-excursion to the nearby cays (US$80pp including lunch) and romantic sunset cruises (US$60pp), both with complimentary drinks.

There are a variety of game **fish** to pursue around Anguilla, including tuna, wahoo, and marlin. Operators offering sport-fishing trips include Gotcha! Garfield's Sea Tours (Ⓣ497-2956, Ⓔgotcha@anguillanet.com). Budget around US$500 for a half-day trip, and US$900 for a whole day, including food, drinks and tackle, for a maximum of six.

Back on land, it is possible to ride **horseback** along beaches and through scenic trails. Both El Rancho del Blues at Blowing Point (Ⓣ497-6164) and Seaside Stables at The Cove (Ⓣ497-3667 Ⓦwww.seaside-stables.com) can put you on a horse for around US$60 per hour.

In 2006 the $250 million PGA-standard Temenos Golf Club (Ⓣ222-8200, Ⓦwww.temenosgolf.com) opened to give Anguilla its first golf course, complete with luxury clubhouse, residences and top-notch restaurant. If the US$400 green fees at Temenos are beyond your budget, you can amuse yourself with the aqua golf driving range at Cap Juluca's; open to non-residents, US$10 will buy you a bucket of balls.

While Anguilla's undistinguished dry scrubland vegetation is not as attractive as the lush tropical greenery carpeting many other Caribbean islands, it nevertheless boasts a rich bio diversity with over 300 native plant species and 135 recorded bird species; many of the birds are migratory and can therefore only be sighted at various times from early October through to March. The Anguilla National Trust (Ⓣ497-5297, Ⓦwww.axanationaltrust.org) organizes bird-watching tours to some of the salt ponds for US$25pp; it also has some excellent publications for nature enthusiasts, including *A Guide to the Birds of Anguilla* and *A Field Guide to Anguilla's Wetlands*. For a more personal experience contact Sir Emile Gumbs (former chief minister of the island), who is happy to share his extensive knowledge about birdwatching around Sandy Ground (Ⓣ497-2711).

History

Amerindians are thought to have settled in Anguilla around 1500 BC, living in small settlements dotted around the island. They named the island "Malliouhana", meaning arrowhead or sea serpent. Major remains have been found at more than forty sites including the Fountain, the island's only natural spring, near Shoal Bay.

Though **Columbus** missed the island on his trips to the New World in the 1490s, Spanish explorers who passed by shortly afterwards named the island Anguilla (Spanish for eel) for its long thin shape.

The first Europeans to establish a permanent base were the **British**, who arrived in 1650 and began growing tobacco and cotton, and raising livestock with a small number of imported slaves. Short on rainfall and without the size or the quality of soil to enable its plantations to compete with nearby islands, Anguilla never really flourished. Those who could afford to leave made off for more prosperous islands.

For centuries the islanders who remained managed on little more than subsistence **farming** and **fishing**. They developed a reputation for **boat building** and **seamanship**, running boats that exported salt and fish and carried local men off for seasonal work in the sugar fields of Santo Domingo (present-day Dominican Republic) and the oil refineries of Aruba and Curaçao.

After **World War II**, with its major Caribbean colonies pressing for independence, Britain showed little interest in continuing to maintain Anguilla. For convenience, it was decided in the 1960s that the island should be administered alongside nearby St Kitts and Nevis, and a union of the islands was put in place. Anguillians, who regarded the politicians on St Kitts as arrogant and bullying, were outraged and demonstrated against the union. They declared **independence**, sending home the policemen installed by St Kitts and calling in a Harvard law professor to draft a national constitution.

Showing a wholly disproportionate reaction, British troops decided to **invade** and crush "The Rebellion". In March 1969 a crack battalion of over three hundred stormed ashore, only to be met by local citizens waving flags and demanding to be put back directly under British rule. Not a shot was fired by the red-faced marines, and the event was dubbed Britain's Bay of Piglets.

Britain resumed **direct responsibility** for Anguilla, which it has maintained to this day. An elected government runs the island with a British-appointed governor handling defence and foreign policy. **Tourism** took off in the 1980s when day-trippers from nearby Saint Martin/Sint Maarten began to arrive in droves. Today the industry drives the local economy, leaving fewer and fewer of its nearly 14,000 inhabitants dependent on the trade in salt, lobster and fish that sustained previous generations.

9.1

Anguilla

ANGUILLA centres around its modest capital, **The Valley**, from which roads head both east and west to the island's fine beaches and natural attractions, chief among them shimmering **Shoal Bay East** and **Rendezvous Bay**. The island doesn't have any sizeable towns or villages but you'll find small clusters of houses in **Sandy Ground** and **Island Harbour**.

The island's small size means you are never far from the coast. The Caribbean side is particularly good for watersports such as **scuba diving** and **snorkelling**, while the Atlantic coast is a haven for **windsurfers** and **sailors**. Most of the island's income is derived from **tourism**, though there is a growing financial services industry. **Restaurants** with celebrity chefs and inspired menus along with a plethora of superior **hotels** ensure that Anguilla is firmly targeted at upscale visitors.

Accommodation

Anguilla Great House and Beach Resort Rendezvous Bay ⓣ497-6061, ⓦwww.anguillagreathouse.com. Attractive laid-back resort wonderfully situated on the beach. The 27 air-conditioned, comfortable – but not particularly special – rooms are located in a series of cottages in spacious grounds. Cheaper, self-catering villas are also for rent. Excellent beachside swimming pool and watersports equipment is available for a charge. 9

Arawak Beach Inn Island Harbour ⓣ497-4888, ⓦwww.arawakbeach.com. Warm and friendly British-owned inn at the water's edge overlooking the harbour though the rooms could do with some attention. A/c is extra and not available in all rooms. There's a freshwater pool and the restaurant serves up good food, especially pizzas, all day. You'll need transport to get to a decent beach though. 7

Cap Juluca Maunday's Bay ⓣ497-6666, ⓦwww.capjuluca.com. Fabulous resort with accommodation strung along one of the island's best beaches in tasteful and ultra-comfortable Moorish-styled villas, some with private solariums. Features three acclaimed restaurants and a large selection of spa treatments and complimentary sports activities, including tennis, water-skiing and sailing. 9

Carimar Beach Club Meads Bay ⓣ497-68881 ⓦwww.carimar.com. Set in lush tropical gardens on the beach, these attractive villa-style one and two-bedroom units are spacious and well appointed with fully equipped kitchens and private balconies affording sea views. Other pluses include tennis courts as well as loungers, towels and umbrellas for the beach. Cable TV is US$15 extra and there's no restaurant but plenty of dining options are within walking distance. Highly recommended. 9

CuisinArt Resort & Spa Rendezvous Bay ⓣ498-2000, ⓦwww.cuisinartresort.com. A series of cerulean blue-domed villas and an inventively shaped swimming pool leading down to the beach bar make this an architecturally unique resort. On the spectacular beach there are a number of activities including windsurfing. Several renowned restaurants, boutiques and the spa are also onsite. 9

Ferryboat Inn Blowing Point ⓣ497-6613 ⓦwww.ferryboatinn.ai. Relaxed Trinidadian-run family establishment with several well-equipped one-bedroom apartments set in pleasant gardens by a quiet beach. Splendid views of St Martin from the two-bedroom beach-house and the terrace deck of the onsite bar-restaurant, which has an unpretentious, reasonably priced lunch and dinner menu. Restaurant closed Mon. 7

Kú Shoal Bay East ⓣ497-2011 ⓦwww.ku-anguilla.com. Brilliant-white apartment blocks containing one or two bedroom suites tastefully decorated with small balconies overlooking the island's most fabulous beach. Lively beachside restaurant and the longest beach bar on the island. 9

Lloyd's Bed & Breakfast The Valley ⓣ497-2351 ⓦwww.lloyds.ai. The best value on the island. A guesthouse since 1959, this friendly family-run establishment offers a taste of bygone times in the original building at affordable rates. The communal dining arrangements, comfortable lounge and friendly staff all make for a convivial atmosphere. Rooms have fans, a/c and cable TV (though no phone) plus free Wi-Fi. ④ including breakfast.

Shoal Bay Villas Shoal Bay East ⓣ497-2051, ⓦwww.sbvillas.ai. Choice spot on the white sands at Shoal Bay East with thirteen comfortable one-and two-bedroom suites. All apartments have fans, their own kitchen and patio or balcony and there's a restaurant and pool. ⑨

The Sirena Hotel Meads Bay ⓣ497-6827 ⓦwww.sirenaresort.com. Excellent hotel with friendly staff a hundred metres off the beach set in extensive luscious tropical grounds with two pools and hammocks. The tastefully furnished rooms with a/c and private patio/balcony are good value. ⑧

Sydans Apartments Sandy Ground ⓣ235-7740 ⓦwww.inns.ai/sydans. Sparsely furnished and with some dilapidated fitments (but with cable TV), these apartments, run by the friendly and helpful owner Anne Edwards, nevertheless offer a more authentic slice of Anguillian life than most lodgings, and are a good option for backpackers. Handily situated for weekend nightlife, the flip side is that they can be noisy. Aim for the top-floor suites that are wonderfully light and afford great views of Road Salt Pond. ④

The interior

Flat, dry and dusty, **the interior** of the island is covered in sparse scrubby vegetation. Very little of interest can be found inland beyond the island's only town of any size, **The Valley**, which is a couple of minutes' drive from the airport, though it is not a place where many visitors will spend a great deal of time. It is a functional rather than inspiring place, home to government, banks and the main shops.

The main site of note in The Valley is **Wallblake House**, built in 1787 by a local sugar planter and one of the oldest buildings on Anguilla. The house and its outbuildings of stables and kitchens are not on the scale of plantation houses to be found elsewhere in the Caribbean – a sign that planters here were less successful – but the combination of thick-cut stone and intricately carved timber is of moderate interest. At the time of writing, the building had just been leased to the owner of the Art Café in Island Harbour (ⓣ497-8595), and you'll need to contact him for access.

In the village of **East End**, situated opposite **East End Pond**, is a small private museum, the **Heritage Collection Museum** (Mon–Sat 10am–5pm; ⓣ235-7440; US$5), which showcases the people and history of the island. After a brief overview by the curator, you'll be left to wander at your leisure through this modest but fascinating collection of artefacts, newspaper cuttings, and – best of all – photos. Don't miss the shots of the museum building submerged in water in the wake of Hurricane Lenny in 1999, or the rather gruesome photo of a human arm found inside a shark's belly. Best to phone in advance to ensure it's open.

The coasts

The island's prime attractions are clustered on the **coast**, specifically the magnificent, soft, dazzlingly white-sand **beach** areas. Anguilla has over thirty public beaches that cater to all types, whether you want to do some fun watersports or just relax with a book. Though development is moving apace, the beach areas have not yet been overdeveloped, with three or four hotels per beach being the norm – meaning a quiet spot is never far away. The pleasant ambience extends to waterside **restaurants** and beach **bars,** where you can enjoy a leisurely meal or sip cocktails.

Along the north coast

At over a mile long, **Meads Bay**, situated towards the western end of the island, is one of Anguilla's largest beaches, with the bluff at the east end providing a great vantage point from which to watch the annual round-the-island boat races (see p.463). The broad belt of soft sand is quiet and pristine and the bay's generally calm waters are excellent for swimming and snorkelling. The popular Dolphin Discovery has closed to make way for the Viceroy luxury resort development (due to open in

▲ Local musician and arts advocate, Bankie Banx

2008). The dolphin experience may relocate elsewhere on the island – check the tourist board office for developments.

A mile west of The Valley, friendly and relaxed **Sandy Ground** is the island's main low-budget hangout area, with a number of inexpensive places to stay and eat. It's also one of the island's main areas for nightlife. Here you'll find an attractive, long, curved beach lined with cliffs; the tiny village backs onto a large salt pond popular with local birdlife, such as egrets, stilts, herons and other wading birds. Offshore, visible from Sandy Ground, **Sandy Island** is a tiny deserted isle, with a bar-restaurant and a handful of palm trees, great for snorkelling and swimming. Boats leave from the pier between 9.30am and 4pm whenever there is demand, for a small fee.

Next up along the coast is the little-frequented but lovely **Crocus Bay**. Descending sharply from the highest point on the island, you'll find a delightful local beach, where, early in the morning or just before dusk, Anguillians exercise along the palm-fringed sands or in the cove's sheltered waters midst the diving pelicans and bobbing fishing boats. It is here also that you'll usually find Calvin (Ⓣ497-73939), who for US$12 return will take you in his small boat – leaving you as long as you want – to experience the truly exceptional snorkelling in nearby **Little Bay**. Surrounded by steep cliffs, **this** small, secluded beach has steeper drop-offs than other parts of the island; the views of the dramatic depths are extraordinary. The overland route to Little Bay is challenging and includes climbing a rope hanging from the cliff face.

On the island's north-eastern coast, **Shoal Bay East** is undoubtedly the most popular beach on the island, and is often voted one of the world's best. Backed by coconut palms and sea grape, the powdered white sand shelves gently down to translucent turquoise waters. Although sun-loungers and umbrellas often occupy the main areas near the hotels, bars and eateries, you can always find a patch of your own if you head down the beach. The nearby reef provides a protected swimming area and snorkelling opportunities. US$10 at Skyline Rental will get you snorkel equipment or a couple of lounge chairs with umbrella for the day. A number of the beach venues feature live music on Sunday lunchtimes.

At the west end of Shoal Bay East, a dirt track leads to **The Fountain**, a cave that is the island's most important archeological site, where many Amerindian petroglyphs were found in 1979. It is said to be the Eastern Caribbean's most intact ceremonial ground from this period. Unfortunately the Fountain is currently closed to the public, though it has been put forward for UNESCO World Heritage Site status, which would help garner funding to develop it into a tourist attraction.

Island Harbour, as the name suggests, is a working harbour – its fishing boats and rocky coastline evoke an authentic atmosphere in contrast to the powdery beaches elsewhere. In the harbour's centre lies Scilly Cay, a tiny islet with a popular rustic restaurant. Stand conspicuously around the jetty and someone will offer to ferry you across for no charge, which you'll make up for with the pricey though excellent seafood lunch.

Island Harbour is also the location of Anguilla's second most important Amerindian site, **"Big Spring"**, a ceremonial cave and water source. It's included on the Anguilla National Trust's heritage tours (see p.464; US$25), though the petroglyphs are badly faded and in need of restoration.

Along the south coast

The **south coast** offers Anguilla's more upmarket hotels and, in **Rendezvous Bay**, one of the island's most spectacular and pre-eminent beaches. The two-mile crescent of bright white sand is Anguilla's true natural wonder. The views of Saint Martin in the sunset can be enjoyed with a cocktail from a modest number of beachside bars and bistros. A variety of watersports are on offer from the hotels that dot the beach; reasonable snorkelling can be found at the rocky edges near the hotels, with sea fans and tropical fish rippling under the crystal blue surface.

Further west the secluded and intimate **Maunday's Bay** offers more shimmering sand but is still large enough to offer windsurfing, water-skiing and sailing. At the far west end of the island is **Shoal Bay West**, yet another beautiful beach. The public access point is hidden behind the West End Salt Pond, but is well worth seeking out. Of particular interest are the spectacular and distinctive sci-fi-like **villas** here – including the "castles in the sand", designed by award-winning New York architect Myron Goldfinger. The villas are interesting to look at but cost thousands of dollars to stay in.

Eating, drinking and nightlife

Restaurants are one of Anguilla's key attractions. After a day in the sun, the cuisine is tremendously rewarding if you can get a reservation. Plenty of options provide a variety to suit most palettes, and the restaurants are good places to spot Hollywood glitterati – but the island's etiquette is not to disturb them.

Anguilla has a small number of **nightlife** options and musical diversions, and many resorts and hotels offer their own nightly entertainment. The alternative is a number of local hot spots where you can dance barefoot in the sand to Caribbean tunes. Sandy Ground is usually the liveliest on Fridays and Saturdays, while on Sunday afternoons the place to be is Shoal Bay East. Check one of the **listings** publications for specifics.

The Dune Preserve Rendezvous Bay ⓣ729-4215, ⓦwww.bankiebanx.net. Multi-level beach bar-grill constructed of driftwood now serving upmarket gourmet beach food at upmarket prices. Owned by Anguilla's own reggae superstar Bankie Banx, who performs at weekends and DJs spin on other nights. This trendy funky venue is best known for Moonsplash, the annual three-day music-fest and non stop beach party held around March's full moon. Daily lunch & dinner.

Elvis' Beach Bar Sandy Ground ⓣ461-0101. At the far end of the beach this low-key hand-made boat bar is far less touristy than most of its neighbours. Elvis is a genial host offering well-priced beer and cocktails, as well as cheap and tasty fish or chicken burgers and sandwiches (US$6–8). Join locals and tourists alike dancing on the sand to the live music Fri–Sun nights. Daily from noon, in the season.

Gwen's Reggae Bar Shoal Bay East ⓣ497-2120. The food's nothing special but its location nestled under the coconut palms makes this a great place to chill with a drink while swinging in the hammock and listening to the Sunday string band.

Hungry's The Valley. Popular psychedelic lilac and lime green van parked up in the shade just up from the post office serving inexpensive local soups, quesadillas, pasta and salads (most under US$12). Mon–Sat from noon.

Johnno's Beach Bar & Grill Sandy Ground ⓣ497-2728. Relaxed timbered beach bar-restaurant by the jetty dishing up reasonably priced Caribbean seafood lunches (around US$13–22), with a more extensive menu for dinner (mains US$20–23). Live jazz Sunday lunchtime. Tue–Sun 10am–10pm.

Koal Keel The Valley ⓣ497-2930, ⓦwww.koalkeel.com. Originally constructed as a sugar and cotton plantation, this legendary restaurant is set in a lovingly reconstructed coral limestone and timbered building. It's worth risking the often desultory service to sample the gourmet menu of Eurasian-Caribbean flavours (mains US$24–32), plus an awe-inspiring dessert line-up. (If you fancy the desserts without the earlier courses, visit *Le Petit Patissier* (8am–2pm) upstairs.) Ask to be shown the wine cellar, which is packed with some 15,000 bottles that can be reserved for private parties. Live music on Fri & Sat. Mon–Sat from 6.30pm.

Nico's Local Restaurant & Bar The Valley ⓣ497-2844. Centrally located in the plaza opposite the GPO, this plant-filled patio eatery is a popular breakfast and lunchtime venue serving unpretentious Anguillan fare. You won't pay more than US$6–7 for breakfast, and US$8–14 for lunch; the lunch menu changes daily from steamed fish and mashed banana one day, to jerked chicken or stewed goat the next. Mon–Sat 8am–4pm.

The Pumphouse Sandy Ground ⓣ497-5154, ⓦwww.pumphouse-anguilla.com. A tourist's favourite, this historic salt factory turned barefoot bar and American grill boasts over 30 varieties of rum, with soca calypso (Thurs) and reggae (Sat) music on offer as well. Well-priced and tasty grilled half-chickens, burgers, steaks and pizzas as well as salads are served (from US$12). If you want a quiet dinner get there before 9pm when the live music starts. Mon–Sat 6.30pm until late.

Smokey's The Cove ⓣ497-6582. Tucked away at the end of dirt road with a fabulous view over charming Cove Bay, this friendly beachside eatery dishes up above-average grilled fish and chicken dishes alongside burgers, pizzas and pasta dishes for under US$20. Live music Sat lunchtimes. Open daily 11am–9pm.

The Straw Hat The Forest ⓣ 497-8300, ⓦwww.strawhat.com. Enjoy a delicious, gourmet and eclectic menu in a romantic setting over the water, looking across to the twinkling lights of St Martin. Try the likes of mango and papaya gazpacho (US$12) followed by sesame-crusted tuna tataki in noodles with ginger and soy dressing (US$30); alternatively, there's curried goat, which is in a different league from most on the island. Mon–Sat from 6.30pm.

Tasty's Restaurant South Hill ⓣ497-2737, ⓦwww.tastysrestaurant.com. This unmissable, brightly painted roadside restaurant is famed for its sumptuous Sunday breakfast buffet (8–11am, US$22) though on other days the Grand Marnier French toast will also hit the spot. Lunchtime sees inventive Caribbean-inspired dishes (US$12–20) such as conch and pineapple kebabs; at dinner try the coconut-crusted fish fillet with spicy banana rum sauce. Mains from US$18. The increased traffic on the road can make it noisy during the day on weekdays. Open Fri–Wed 8am until late.

Picante West End ⓣ498-1616. This friendly, efficient roadside *taqueria* serves excellent Mexican favourites such as burritos, enchiladas and tacos with deliciously fresh spicy fillings. The interesting array of tequilas – as well as beer or wine by the glass – wash it all down. From 6.30pm. Closed Tues.

10

St Martin/St Maarten

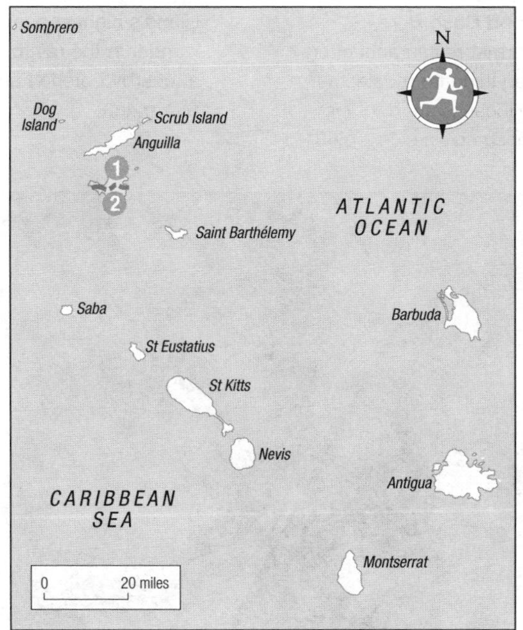

St Martin/St Maarten highlights

* **Day on the Water** Whether you want to paddle a kayak, sail an America's Cup-winning vessel or spend the day on board a party boat, St Martin caters for you. See p.478

* **Grand Case** Here, gourmet restaurants offer everything from delectable local seafood to fine French cuisine. See p.481

* **Orient Beach** Beautiful sands, warm sea and ample watersports. Avoid it, however, if you get claustrophobic. See p.482

* **Pic Paradis** Escape the crowds and hike to the island's highest point or wander in the rainforest at nearby Loterie Farm. See p.483

▲ St Maarten regatta

Introduction and basics

Shared by the French and the Dutch since the mid-seventeenth century, the tiny island of **Saint Martin/Sint Maarten** is one of the most developed in this part of the Caribbean, with lots of facilities and a huge duty-free shopping area. Opinions about the island are as divided as the island itself. Ask the streams of repeat visitors, cruise ship passengers and time-share owners and they will tell you that this tiny island is paradise on earth, with fabulous beaches and every type of tourist facility imaginable. Ask others and you may hear how rapid and barely controlled development has turned a once-beautiful place into "a graceless monument to vulgarian greed", as one disgruntled writer put it.

The truth lies somewhere in between. The island undeniably boasts some of the finest beaches in the Eastern Caribbean, particularly at **Orient Beach** on the French side, as well as some stunning scenery, most notably in the interior around **Pic Paradis**, and many excellent restaurants and hotels on both sides of the border. On the other hand, the hunt for the tourist dollar can feel unrelenting and, at times, it is hard to discern the real country under the veneer of concrete development, souvenir shops and the waves of tourists (all particularly acute on the Dutch side in the capital Philipsburg, where a huge new $100m port and cruise pier expansion, due to finish at the end of 2009, will accommodate even more cruise ship passengers). The island's traffic is also notorious.

If all you want to do is lie on the beach and play in the sea, both Saint Martin and Sint Maarten are not bad options. Travelling between the French and Dutch sides is hassle-free, since there are no border crossing formalities. Ultimately if the crowds get too much for you, bear in mind that it is a very short flight or ferry ride to nearby islands – some of which are the quietest, least developed and most rural in the entire Caribbean, including Saba, St Barts and Anguilla.

Where to go

The island offers plenty to see and do. It is suitable for all types of visitor, including party-goers looking for lively nights out, families with young children and upscale visitors mooring their luxury yachts in the marinas while enjoying the fine dining on land. **Philipsburg** and **Marigot** are the largest towns on the Dutch and French sides respectively, and they both offer plenty of opportunities to shop and eat. And you'll find a slew of well-maintained **beaches** on both sides of the island with plenty of sporting activities.

When to go

The **climate** is usually sunny and warm year-round, with some trade wind cooling particularly between early December and mid-April. Average temperature during this **winter** season is 80°F (27°C) and a few degrees warmer but much more humid in the **summer**. There are rain showers in summer and autumn, particularly in the late afternoon, while June to November is the official **hurricane** season. **Prices** for accommodation increase between December and April but good deals can be had at other times. Note that some hotels and restaurants close during September and early October.

Getting there

Visitors from Europe and the US pour onto the island from the **cruise ship harbour** in Philipsburg and from **Princes Juliana Airport**, both located on the Dutch side. It is not unusual to see lines of cruise ships waiting to moor on the island. On the French side **L'Espérance Airport** near Grand Case handles small planes for regional flights. **Taxis** and **rental cars** are easily procured at both airports and are the most effective form of transport to your hotel.

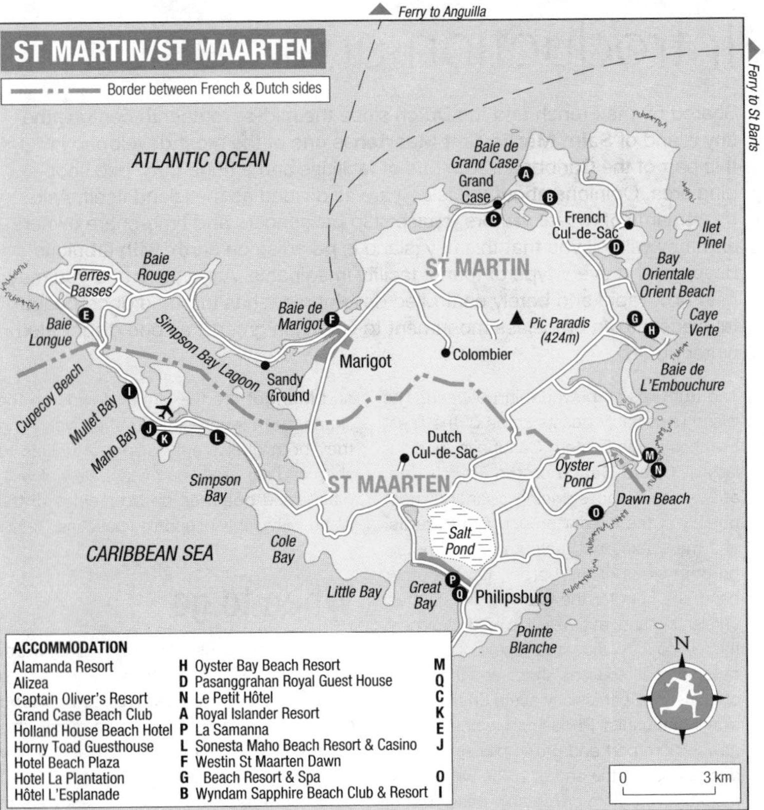

Cruise ship day-trippers can reach Philipsburg from the port on a ferry or by five minutes' walk. Taxi drivers will offer to take tourists to and from the port but this is a very expensive option if you're just going to Philipsburg. If you're heading to one of the other towns, the cheapest bet is a bus.

Information

At Princess Juliana Airport the brochures and leaflets near baggage reclaim, as well as an information desk near the check-in area with friendly, helpful staff are good starting places. In the town of Philipsburg, where the cruise ships arrive, there is another stand with friendly staff. The island has two **tourist offices:** on the Dutch side it is inconveniently located on Buncamper Road in Philipsburg (Ⓣ599/542-2337, Ⓦwww.st-maarten.com), although there's also a kiosk in Wathey Square; the office on the French side is in Marigot on Route de Sandy Ground (Ⓣ590/87 57 21, Ⓦwww.st-martin.org). For local **listings**, check out the *K-Pasa* weekly events guide and the Out 'N About section of Thursday's *Daily Herald*.

Money and costs

On the Dutch side, the currency is the **Netherlands Antilles Guilder** or **Florin** (**NAf**), although prices are nearly always quoted in US dollars. The rate of exchange fluctuates but it is usually at about US$1 to NAf1.78. On the French side, the **euro** is the local currency but most establishments will also accept US dollars.

Banks and a multitude of bureaux de change will **exchange** most major currencies but be aware that rates vary from place to place. **Banking hours** are Mon–Fri 8.30am–3.30pm. Some banks are also open on Saturday. Many **ATMs** can be found throughout the island (although note that there are none in Grand Case).

Credit and **debit** cards are accepted almost everywhere. **Traveller's cheques** are accepted too but visitors are advised to bring them in US$ denominations to avoid additional currency conversion fees.

A **departure tax** of $30 is required when leaving via Princess Juliana Airport but it's often already included in the price of your air ticket. If you arrive and leave within 24 hours you are exempt from paying. If you are heading on to another of the Netherlands Antilles (such as Saba) then the tax is only $10. For flights from L'Espérance Airport, the €3 departure tax is normally included in the ticket price. The tax is €4 by ferry to Anguilla from Marigot's pier.

Hotels on the French side of the island add a ten to fifteen percent service charge to bills, as well as a *taxe de séjour* (hotel tax) of around five percent. On the Dutch side, the service charge is also ten to fifteen percent, and there's an additional five percent government tax. Most restaurants add a **service charge** of between ten and 15 percent; as such, tipping in these establishments is discretionary. Elsewhere, **tipping** of ten to fifteen percent is the norm.

The overall **cost** of a holiday on the island depends on a number of factors. Tax-free shopping means that there are bargains to be had, particularly on jewellery, alcohol and tobacco. Prices in modest **hotels** during the off season can start at less than $100 per night, while in the peak season prices soar massively. There are accommodation options at all price points and if you choose to go all-inclusive you can keep the costs down further. Those looking for a true luxury experience, however, might want to go elsewhere: the island has few of the deluxe properties of the kind found on, say, St Barts.

Meal costs outside your hotel vary depending on the establishment. A burger, fries and soft drink from a fast food chain might cost around $5 but head up to Grand Case with its fine dining and expect to pay upwards of ten times that before you even add wine.

Getting around

While paved roads link the major tourist areas, bear in mind that in some areas they can become steep and narrow and sign posting is limited. The major problem, however, is the sheer volume of **traffic**. Even in off-peak hours traffic can slow to a crawl or a standstill – if you are holidaying to get away from the daily commute, forget it.

The local **bus service** is efficient and cheap. Buses run frequently from 7am to 11pm or midnight between Philipsburg, Mullet Bay, Simpson Bay, Marigot and usually continue up to Grand Case. The fare is around $2.50 depending on the zone, and drivers will accept dollars or euros (though not always florins if you're on the French side). **Minibuses** run all over the island, charging between $1.50 and $3 depending on the distance; the destination is indicated by a placard in the windscreen. Both buses and minibuses can be taken from **bus stops** in Philipsburg and Marigot; elsewhere, you can flag them down as they pass.

If you want to explore the island, consider **renting a car** for a few days. With lots of car-rental outlets, competition keeps prices reasonable. In addition to the agencies many hotels also offer rentals, although these tend to be the most expensive option. At the airport just past the arrivals area are a number of agencies which offer pretty competitive rates (anything from $25 per day), especially if you make it clear you are going to shop around. Good agencies include Avis (St Martin ⓣ590/875 060, St Maarten ⓣ599/545 2847, ⓦwww.avis-sxm.com), Paradise Car Rental (ⓣ599/545 3737) and Defis (ⓣ590/50 41 70, ⓦwww.defisagency.com). Driving on the island is on the right-hand side of the road. Roads are generally in good condition, except in areas undergoing major construction.

Finally, **taxis** are easy to come by in Philipsburg and Marigot, less so elsewhere (on the Dutch side, call ⓣ599/542 1680; on the French side, call ⓣ590/875 654). There are no meters: rates are fixed by the government, so check the price before you hop in (tourist information booths have a list). The rates can quickly mount up elsewhere and can soon make renting a car more economical. Taxis have a minimum charge and rates rise after 10pm and again after midnight.

Accommodation

Most visitors to the **French side** of the island stay either in the Orient Bay area on the northeast coast or in Grand Case on the west coast. On the whole, accommodation in Grand Case is low key, while Orient Bay has a broad range, from small boutiques to 400-room resorts. During the low season, **rates** can fall by as much as fifty percent.

In contrast to the French side, resorts on the **Dutch side** tend to be large and can feel somewhat impersonal. If you're here for the beach, there is no real reason to stay in Philipsburg; you will find a variety of beachfront places scattered along the south coast. Cupecoy in particular is undergoing some regeneration. Timeshares are also becoming increasingly popular on this side of the island.

Food and drink

The island has always boasted a wide **ethnic mix** within its population – not surprising given its Dutch/French colonial history, slave importation from Africa and immigration from the US, Europe, south Asia and the Indian subcontinent – and over the past decade the island has transformed itself into a cosmopolitan melting pot. All this is reflected in the **dining** choices, with over 350 restaurants providing mouth-watering fusion foods, Creole creations and exotic Asian dishes, along with more traditional gourmet French and Italian cuisine. **Grand Case** has long been the gastronomic capital of the Eastern Caribbean, with more than two dozen gourmet restaurants lining the town's narrow main strip.

Seafood is, of course, a speciality yet **vegetarians** will find many options. The local **drinks** not to be missed include guavaberry liqueur and home-made flavoured rums such as passionfruit, ginger and raspberry. In comparison to other Caribbean islands, **prices** often are good value because of the sheer amount of competition, although costs escalate quickly at upmarket venues. Keep in mind that reservations are required for the pricier restaurants.

As for **drinks**, most bars and restaurants serve imported beers, spirits and wines but because of the low duty levied, drinking will not burn a hole in your wallet unless you go for one of the vintage wines on offer.

Mail and communications

Telephone kiosks can be found all over the island. Most take prepaid phonecards which can be purchased from a variety of outlets such as post offices and hotels.

To **place a call** within the Dutch side of the island, simply dial the number without the area code. To place a call within the French side, dial 0590 then the six-digit number; for mobiles dial 0690 then the six-digit number. Calling one side of the island from the other is treated as an international call (and charged as such) – so when calling from the Dutch side to the French, dial ⓣ00 590 590 before the number for land lines, or ⓣ00 590 690 for mobile phones. When calling from the French side to the Dutch, dial ⓣ00 599 before the number whether it's a land line or a mobile.

The best option for **mobile phone users** is to register with East Caribbean Cellular (ⓦ www.EastCaribbeanCellular.com), which will allow you to roam on its network for $3 per day. Call charges are significantly cheaper than using hotel or public payphones, and service quality is much better. You can get set up before you go (instructions on the ECC website) or simply dial "0" on arrival and ask the operator to register your phone.

The **country code** for St Martin is ⓣ590; for St Maarten it is ⓣ599.

The main **post office** on the Dutch side is on E Camille Richardson Street in Philipsburg (Mon–Thur 7.30am–5pm, Fri 7.30am–4.30pm; ⓣ599/542 2947). On the French side the post office is on rue de la

Liberté in Marigot (Mon–Fri 7.30am–4.45pm, Sat 7.30–11.30am; ⓣ590/51 07 64).

Internet access is available at many hotels, sometimes for a fee. Internet cafés can easily be found in the major tourist areas, including Front Street in Philipsburg.

Opening hours, holidays and festivals

Typical **business hours** on the island are Mon–Sat 9am or 10am to 5pm or 6pm; some also open on Sundays. Restaurants and bars stay open later. On the French side, stores may close for lunch, generally between 1pm and 3pm, and stay open until 7pm. Clubs, meanwhile, open in the early evening and stay busy until dawn.

Sports and outdoor activities

The island has an amazing array of **sporting** and **outdoor activities**. As you might expect, watersports feature heavily, but the island also has plenty of areas to **hike** or to ride a **mountain bike**.

Watersports

Orient Beach in the northeast is the watersports centre of the island, with a host of outlets along the bay renting jet skis, windsurfers and snorkelling gear as well as parasailing and boat trips out to nearby Green Cay and Ilet Pinel. On the Dutch side of the island, Simpson Bay also has plenty of operators hiring out similar equipment.

Diving on the island is good (if not top-tier), with around 40 dive sites. PADI-certified dive operators run from both sides of the island and will bring you from your hotel to a harbour for a short boat trip to the dive spot. A recommended operator is Scuba Fun (ⓦwww.scubafun.com), which has dive centres at Great Bay Marina on the Dutch side of the island (ⓣ599/557-0505) and at Anse Marcel on the French side (ⓣ590/291164). A beginner's course is $75, with one-tank dives from $50 including gear. For something a bit different, Dive Safaris (ⓦwww.divestmaarten.com), which operates out of both Simpson Bay (ⓣ599/545-2401) and Philipsburg (ⓣ599/542-9001) on the Dutch side, runs a **shark awareness dive** twice a week where you will see sharks being fed ($70 and you must be a certified diver to take part). It also offers PADI courses (from $75) and a variety of dives every day (as well as a weekly night dive).

Public holidays and festivals

Both sides of the island have their own **carnival** each year. The French celebration takes place during Lent, while the Dutch set aside 17 days and nights in April with the main parade scheduled to coincide with the birthday of Her Majesty the Queen of the Netherlands, Beatrix, on the 30th of the month. Below is a list of other holidays on the island.

January 1 New Year's Day (Saint Martin/Sint Maarten)
Mar/Apr (date varies) Easter (Saint Martin/Sint Maarten)
May (date varies) Ascension Day (Saint Martin)
May 1 Labor Day (Saint Martin/Sint Maarten)
July 14 Bastille Day (Saint Martin)
July 21 Schoelcher Day (Saint Martin)
October 21 Antillean Day (Sint Maarten)
November 1 All Saints Day (Saint Martin)
November 11 Feast of Saint Martin and Sint Maarten Day
December 25 Christmas Day (Saint Martin/Sint Maarten)
December 26 Boxing Day (Saint Martin/Sint Maarten)

Messing about on the water

It's not every day you get the chance to step aboard – let alone help operate – an America's Cup-winning yacht. But that's exactly what the St Maarten 12-Metre Challenge (ⓣ599/542 0045, ⓦwww.12metre.com) offers. No previous sailing experience is necessary for the three-hour excursion, which costs $81 and runs up to four times a day from Bobby's Marina in Philipsburg. The fleet consists of five racing yachts built for the 1987 America's Cup (the last Cup regatta to use 12-metre yachts) and includes the winner of the race, the *Stars & Stripes '87*. Although you won't know which one you'll be sailing on until you board, whichever one it is, the thrill is incomparable. Highly recommended.

A top diving site is **Proselyte Reef** where the British Navy ship HMS *Proselyte* sank in 60ft of water in 1801. The reef surrounding the frigate rises to within 15ft of the surface, with plenty of fish and corals to see and on occasion turtles and rays. When Simpson Bay Bridge was replaced in the late 1980s the remains of the old bridge were submerged off Simpson Bay and now serve as an artificial reef. Another interesting spot is **Split Rock**, a large boulder that you can swim through. Nearby is **Cable Reef**, where large fish can often be seen.

Harking back to the era of Amerindians who used similar vessels to arrive and colonise, **sea kayaking** has become an increasingly popular way to explore the island's waters. Guided trips ($49) around the Simpson Bay Lagoon with TriSport (ⓣ599/545-4384, ⓦwww.trisportsxm.com) introduces you to the area's beaches, historical sites and mangrove eco system. The company also runs hiking and cycling tours, and does rentals.

Sailing and excursions

Sailing is particularly popular with visitors and residents, and the island is dotted with a dozen or so marinas, many offering the chance to rent and charter vessels. A reliable charter company is The Moorings (ⓣ590/87 35 26 or 1-888 952 8420, ⓦwww.moorings.com).

One particularly interesting way of getting yourself onto the water is an **excursion** with the tall ship *Lord Sheffield* which sails weekdays at 11am and 2pm on Sundays, and anchors at two spots for swimming and snorkeling (ⓣ599/552-0875, ⓦwww.stmaarten-shoretrips.com/lordsheffield). The cost is $69, including food, drink and snorkelling equipment. They also operate sunset cruises on most weekdays. The huge catamaran *Golden Eagle* (ⓣ599/542 3323, ⓦwww.sailingsxm.com) operates a variety of trips from Bobby's Marina in Philipsburg such as full-day sails around the island on Tuesdays and Fridays ($99), with snorkelling stops (including Tintamarre island) and a three-course lunch. If you'd rather not get your feet wet, Seaworld Explorer (ⓣ599/542-4078, ⓦwww.atlantisadventures.com) runs trips on a 34-passenger **semi-submarine**, which has an underwater observatory, giving non-divers a chance to see below the waves. The cost is around $30 per adult.

Other activities

Apart from Pic Paradis, more than 25 miles of **hiking** trails course through hills, valleys, clifftops and beaches. Hikes are rated from easy to strenuous and vary in length from 90 minutes to four hours; the two-mile Guana Bay hike is especially spectacular. Make sure to take plenty of water and protection from the sun. The Sint Maarten National Heritage Foundation (ⓣ599/542-4917) has information and maps.

Lastly, **horse**- and **pony riding** on the beach is a splendid experience. There are several stables willing to offer adults and children the opportunity to ride, whether novice or expert. Try Bayside Riding Club (ⓣ590/87 36 64, ⓦwww.baysideridingclub.com), which has one-hour rides through the island's nature marine reserve from $70.

History

Amerindian remains dating from as early as 2000 BC have been found near the village of Grand Case on the French side of the island. The vestiges indicate that these people settled in villages, cultivating crops and building boats. Because of the preponderance of salt ponds on the island, the Amerindians called it Soualiga, meaning "Land of Salt". On November 11, 1493 **Columbus** sailed past the island and named it for that day's saint, Martin of Tours, but the Genoan and subsequent navigators took little notice of it otherwise.

During the 1620s **French** and **Dutch colonists** began to settle, with the Dutch building the first fort at Philipsburg in 1631. The **Spanish**, however, were keen on the island for strategic reasons and claimed it, subsequently fighting off a lengthy siege by Dutch troops led by **Peter Stuyvesant**. By 1648 the Spanish had lost interest in the island, and the French and Dutch governments agreed to divide it in two. The settlers planted **sugar cane**, **cotton**, **tobacco** and **salt**, and imported **slaves** from Africa to work on the plantations. The soil was poor, however, and the island never prospered, largely sinking into great obscurity with each passing century.

Despite frequent **disagreements** between the French and the Dutch, including border skirmishes and wholesale invasions and deportations, the boundaries remain pretty much the same today as were agreed on in 1648. The Dutch side, is part of the **Netherlands Antilles**; the French side is part of France, with representation in the French parliament.

As throughout the region, **tourism** drives the modern economy, bringing floods of visitors and attendant social difficulties, particularly rising crime, in particular car break-ins. Although the island isn't necessarily more dangerous than others, you shouldn't keep valuables in your car, and should avoid unlit or isolated roads at night.

10.1

Saint Martin

Spread over 52 square kilometres, French Saint Martin is less commercialized than the Dutch side, despite its welcoming beaches, excellent restaurants and more attractive scenery. The pleasant capital, **Marigot**, is worth at least a day of your time, while the long stretch of white sand at **Orient Beach** is the pick of the beaches, with a great choice of watersports to keep you busy. The island's gourmet heart, **Grand Case**, boasts a string of excellent restaurants, while **Loterie Farm** offers great hiking away from the crowds into an unspoilt area of rainforest and up to **Pic Paradis**, the island's highest point.

Accommodation

Marigot

Hotel Beach Plaza Baie de Marigot ⓣ590/87 87 00, ⓦwww.hotelbeachplazasxm.com. A pleasant beachfront hotel situated within walking distance of downtown Marigot. Rooms all have private balconies, satellite TV, mini fridge and Wi-Fi. 6

Orient Bay and Cul-de-Sac

Alamanda Resort Orient Bay ⓣ590/52 87 40, ⓦwww.alamanda-resort.com. This 42-room resort is popular with repeat visitors for its friendly atmosphere and sizeable colonial-style rooms with views of the pool and beach. There's also easy access to activities, bars and eateries, including Kakao Beach (see p.484). Closed Sept–early Oct. 8

Alizea Cul-de-Sac ⓣ590/87 33 42, ⓦwww.alizeahotel.com. This fabulously landscaped hotel overlooks Orient Bay. The apartments sleep up to three people, the bungalows up to four, and all with kitchenette. 6

Hotel La Plantation C5 Parc de La Baie Orientale ⓣ590/29 58 00, ⓦwww.la-plantation.com. A sweet hilltop hideaway featuring 17 villas, each comprising a suite and two studios which can be rented together or separately. Orient Beach is about ten minutes' walk away. Closed Sept-mid Oct. 7

La Samanna Baie Longue ⓣ590/87 64 00, ⓦwww.lasamanna.com. A luxury resort that has much to recommend it: beautifully decorated rooms with lavish touches, a gorgeous infinity pool, a spa and an upmarket restaurant. Closed Sept & Oct. 9

Grand Case

Grand Case Beach Club ⓣ590/87 51 87 or 1-800 344 3016, ⓦwww.grandcasebeachclub.com. This friendly beachfront hotel features 71 spacious studios and apartments, all with kitchens. Popular with families, it also has tennis courts, watersports facilities, and the well-regarded *Sunset Café* (closed Sept–mid-Oct). 8

Hôtel L'Esplanade ⓣ590/87 06 55 or 1-866 596 8365, ⓦwww.lesplanade.com. This popular hotel on the hillside overlooking Grand Case is one of the nicest on the island. All rooms are chicly decorated and come with a kitchen. Closed Sept. 9

Le Petit Hôtel ⓣ590/29 09 65, ⓦwww.lepetithotel.com. One of the island's best hotels, this small Mediterranean-style property is right on the beach. Rooms feature modern decor and luxuries such as DVD and CD players and Wi-Fi. There's no pool but you can use the one at sister hotel *L'Esplanade*, a short walk away. Closed 2 weeks Aug. 9

Oyster Pond

Captain Oliver's Resort ⓣ590/87 40 26, ⓦwww.captainolivers.com. Attractive resort overlooking the lovely sheltered anchorage of Oyster Pond. There's a big pool, the 50 large rooms (ask for one with a sea view) are comfortably furnished, and at the restaurant you can watch turtles and nurse sharks swimming under the glass floor while you eat. Delightful Dawn Beach is a short drive away. 6

Marigot

Sporting a fusion of chic French and tropical Caribbean styles, **MARIGOT** is the main town on Saint Martin, and, although it can be cluttered with traffic, it is pleasant enough, especially if you want to shop, eat or just people-watch. The town extends along Marigot Bay with a selection of interesting restaurants, duty-free stores and a marina at its western end.

The main focus is the **harbour** at the bottom of Rue de la République, the booking and departure points for ferries to Anguilla and other islands; you'll normally see the ferries lined up alongside a fleet of fishing boats. Just west of here, beyond the taxi rank, lie a group of bars and "lolos", or food shacks, where you can get excellent and inexpensive island fare. Continuing west brings you to the island's largest **market**, a lively place with souvenir stands selling T-shirts, wooden carvings and the like. Vendors are here every day 6am–3pm, and on Wednesday and Saturday there is also a fresh fish and produce market.

Following the side streets away from the water brings you to **Rue de la Liberté** and **Rue du Général Charles de Gaulle**, home to restaurants and international designer boutiques. Further west still, the impressive development of the **Marina Royale** houses a number of classy shops selling designer clothes and jewellery, outlets offering boat and fishing trips and plenty of bars and restaurants overlooking the water.

Beyond the marina, make a point of stopping at the **archeological museum** (Mon–Sat 9am–1pm & 3–7pm; ⓣ590/29 48 36) for its detailed and highly informative exhibits on the Amerindians and more recent history, which provides a window into the island before tourism.

On the other side of the marina is **Le West Indies Shopping Mall**, with designer stores, a restaurant and a couple of cafés. A 15-minute climb from the harbour leads to **Fort Louis** (always open; free), the remains of a 1789 fort built to protect the town from the raids of British sailors; it offers fine views across the bay.

Sandy Ground and Baie Rouge

Less than a kilometre west of Marigot, the main road curves around to a long spit of land known as **Sandy Ground** which separates the huge Simpson Bay Lagoon from the sea at Nettle Bay. The isthmus is lined with hotels, restaurants and small shopping malls but if you're not staying here, the area holds little to detain you. The beaches are not particularly impressive and you are better off heading a couple of kilometres further west to the lovely and normally quiet white sandy stretch at **Baie Rouge** where you'll find a handful of traders selling food and drink on the beach; snorkelling gear is available to rent from local vendors.

If you are looking for even more privacy on the beach, continue past Baie Rouge and take the right-hand turn-off signposted for **Baie aux Prunes**, which is popular among surfers, or make your way round the headland to **Baie Longue**, where you'll find a vast expanse of white sand, perfect for strolling and shell collecting.

Grand Case

Grand Case has built itself a deserved reputation as one of the finest **dining centres** of the Caribbean and, as you walk down the town's main drag, it's easy to see why. A series of fairly expensive restaurants lines the otherwise unremarkable street, with daily specials chalked up outside and classy wine lists displayed in the windows (see p.484 for reviews).

Grand Case's sandy **beach** that lines the wide, sweeping bay is nice but modest compared to others on the coast – most people come here for the food anyway. Note that there are no ATMs in the village so bring cash as some places don't take credit cards.

▲ Grand Case

Anse Marcel, Cul-de-Sac and Ilet Pinel

If you drive east of Grand Case for 1.5km, past L'Espérance airport, the road forks, heading south towards fabulous Orient Bay or north for the tiny settlements of Anse Marcel and Cul-de-Sac. **Anse Marcel** is a mini-resort, with a few large hotels, a marina and a pleasant long sandy beach. **Cul-de-Sac** – home to Saint Martin's mayor and characterized by its cute little red-roofed houses – is even smaller, but popular largely as the departure point for trips to **Ilet Pinel**, a pristine and uninhabited island just offshore with excellent snorkelling (rent gear from the shack) and lovely, calm waters for swimming. Boats regularly make the two-minute trip from the pier in Cul-de-Sac, and there are umbrellas for rent on the island, along with drinks vendors and an excellent beach bar, *Karibuni*.

For a change of pace, take a trip to **Plantation Mont Vernon** (daily 9am–5pm; US$14, US$7 children; ⓣ590/29 50 62, ⓦwww.plantationmontvernon.com), between L'Espérance airport and Orient Bay. This former estate, dating from 1786, provides an overview of the island's agricultural history, with a sugar and rum museum and a coffee museum (complete with free sample).

Orient Beach

The area around **Orient Beach** (aka Baie Orientale, or Orient Bay) at the northeastern end of the island is a massive commercial development with hotels, villas and condominiums crowding a two-kilometre strip. The beach itself is an incredible hive of activity with restaurants, bars, watersports outlets and most of all hordes of people spread out along its length. Don't be put off by the crowds because this is one of the great beaches in the Eastern Caribbean, a fabulous swathe of white sand bordering an inviting turquoise sea.

The southern end of the beach, protected from the surf by nearby Green Cay, is the best area for watersports and where the main crowds congregate; beach chairs and umbrellas can be rented here. Note that the very southern end is largely given over to the "clothing optional" crowd.

Butterfly Farm

No prizes for guessing what's on display at the **Butterfly Farm** (US$12, US$6 children; ⓣ590/87 31 21, ⓦwww.thebutterflyfarm.com) just south of Orient Bay. The exhibition, with landscaped tropical gardens and pools, features numerous species of butterfly from Indonesia and South America fluttering around. It's colourful as well as informative, and a good distraction when you've had enough of the beach. **Tours** led by knowledgeable guides are offered daily every 15–20 minutes from 9am to 3pm. Butterflies are most active in the morning and you can witness the new ones emerging from a chrysalis – and even handle the caterpillars. The entry fee includes a free return pass valid on a different day, and there's also a lovely gift shop and café.

Oyster Pond

Divided in half by the border, **Oyster Pond** on the coast southeast of Orient Bay is an oyster-shaped anchorage popular with yachters. The marina and most of the hotel/condominium development is on the French side, although the best beach in the area is **Dawn Beach** on the Dutch side – the name says it all as this is a great place to watch the sun come up. There is good snorkelling offshore and, when the waves are rolling in, it's ideal for body surfing (though a little rough for small children). With lovely views across to St Barts and a few good restaurants, it's a delightful spot.

Loterie Farm and Pic Paradis

While most of Saint Martin's tourist development is along the coast, **the interior** remains charmingly unspoiled, its peaceful countryside makes an appealing day-trip if you have a car. Just north of Marigot, take a right turn onto a road signposted to **Colombier**, where a scattered settlement of old wooden houses, small farms and picturesque meadows strewn with munching cattle gives a picture of island life that has changed little over the last 50 years.

A little further north lies **LOTERIE FARM**, a nature-lover's delight and one of the highlights of a visit to Saint Martin. Once a sugar estate, it's now a 154-acre private nature reserve with trails (US$7 for a self-guided tour or call ahead for guided tours; ⓣ590/87 86 16). The trails head into a humid forest where you'll find giant silk cotton trees as well as groves of mango and palm fed by quiet streams. At the top, the Fly Zone features ziplining tours (US$50–80; come in the afternoon or at the weekend to avoid the cruise ship gang), while at the bottom the *Hidden Forest Café* (closed Sun dinner) provides much-needed refreshment; there's also the *Tree Lounge* for tapas (daily for lunch and dinner). Closed Sept (phone to check).

Those with the energy can make their way up to **PIC PARADIS**, the island's highest point at over 400 metres. It's a three-hour trek there and back; wear sturdy shoes as the trails can be rocky.

To get to the area, follow the main road from Marigot signposted to Pic Paradis. Five hundred metres up a steep hill, a right turn is signposted to Loterie Farm, taking you through fields of papayas, melons, bananas and vegetables. If you continue up the hill instead, it's another 2km to the **peak**, past some of the island's most expensive homes, many set back from the road with flamboyant vegetation to guard from prying eyes. Unless you've got a four-wheel-drive vehicle, you'll need to park at the top and walk for a further ten minutes to get fantastic views out over the island. Note: there have been occasional robberies near the peak in recent years, so always seek advice from your hotel before setting off.

Eating, drinking and nightlife

Dining on St Martin ranges from fast-food joints to lavish fine dining. As you might expect, plenty of French-accented cuisine is on offer but many other gastronomic styles are represented.

Although **nightlife** on the French side is more low-key than on the Dutch side, both have much to offer. Many hotels lay on their own entertainment during the evenings, while listings magazines (see p.474) are worth consulting for events elsewhere. In Grand Case, outside of restaurants there's little in the way of nightlife except on Tuesday evenings (6–11pm) between January and April or May when the **Harmony Nights festival** season begins and the main street is given over to pedestrians, bands and dancers.

Marigot and Sandy Ground

La Belle Epoque Marigot ⓣ590/87 87 70, ⓦwww.belle-epoque-sxm.com. This bustling French bistro in Marina Royale could have been lifted straight from the south of France. The long menu includes excellent pizzas (around US$16) and fish dishes (US$24), plus traditional Gallic touches such as profiteroles and citrons pressés. Mon–Sat 7.30am–11pm; Sun 5–11pm. Closed Sun Sept–early Dec.

Mario's Bistro Sandy Ground Bridge ⓣ590/87 06 36, ⓦwww.mariosbistro.com. The waterside location at *Mario's* makes it one of the island's most romantic restaurants. Delicious main courses include grilled rib-eye steak with tarragon shallot butter (US$47) and sautéed scallops with white truffle oil (US$37). Booking essential. Dinner only. Closed Sun & mid June–late Aug.

La Sucrière Marigot ⓣ590/51 13 30. Small but elegant French bakery, a pleasant spot to pick up breakfast to enjoy on the premises or take on a boat trip. Daily 6am–8pm.

Orient Bay

Kakao Beach ⓣ590/87 43 26, ⓦ www.kakaobeachsxm.com. This beach side, laid-back, open-air bar and restaurant serves up decent fish dishes, burgers (US$16) and ice cream. Water-sports equipment can be hired, and there's also a massage room and boutique. Daily 10am–6pm (last orders around 4.30pm).

Kontiki ⓣ590/87 43 27. A decent option, with a snack bar for burgers, pizzas and the like (from US$8), and a restaurant serving upmarket fare such as fresh fish and steak (up to around US$30). Live music and DJs play some Sun. Lunch daily; also dinner Sun. Closed Sept.

Grand Case

Lolos Around a courtyard, a range of shacks and barbecue pits serve cheap local cooking including fish, curried goat, barbecued chicken, ribs and lobster, together with side dishes such as potato salad, peas and rice, and macaroni cheese. There's also a location in Marigot.

Spiga ⓣ590/52 47 83, ⓦwww.spiga-sxm.com. An authentic Italian restaurant, showcasing such classics as pumpkin-filled ravioli (US$13) and osso buco for two (US$58). The extensive wine list is a further highlight. Dinner only. Closed Tue Apr–Nov.

Le Tastevin ⓣ590/87 55 45. Elegant French-owned place overlooking the water and offering a fine selection of French food, from foie gras and snails to fresh local seafood and steaks, all prepared with skill and imagination. This is one of the best places to eat in town, with prices to match. Daily for lunch and dinner.

10.2

Sint Maarten

Aside from the language and some of the names, there is little that could be described as characteristically Dutch about **SINT MAARTEN**. This side of the island, measuring a mere 37 square kilometres, has seen a huge tourist boom since the 1960s, making it one of the most heavily commercialized areas in the Caribbean – it can be hard to discern much individual identity.

The heavily developed town of **Philipsburg** is the main draw for shoppers and cruise ship passengers, with casinos, T-shirt and duty-free shops and fast-food joints. Situated right on Great Bay, the town has its own large beach.

Relatively few visitors stay in Philipsburg, however, and much of the recent development has been along the western end of the island, south of the giant **Simpson Bay Lagoon**, where a series of attractive bays indent the coast. Particularly alluring are **Cupecoy Beach** and **Mullet Beach** in the southwest. Despite the fact that this side of the island can feel crowded, there's plenty of fun to be had on the lovely beaches and at the multitude of lively bars and restaurants.

Accommodation

Holland House Beach Hotel Philipsburg ⓣ599/542-2572, ⓦwww.hhbh.com. Don't expect peace and tranquillity at this hotel, situated in the middle of the shopping area. The remodelled rooms match the trendy, buzzing bar and restaurant downstairs, and the beach is right on your doorstep. 6

Horny Toad Guesthouse Simpson Bay T599/545-4323 or 1-800 417 9361, ⓦwww.thtgh.com. One of the nicest places on the island, this friendly guesthouse is hugely popular. The eight rooms are large and full of character, with full kitchens and thoughtful extras, and the beach is gorgeous. Despite being near the airport, the location is pretty peaceful. 6

Oyster Bay Beach Resort Oyster Pond ⓣ599/543-6040 or 1-866-978-0212, ⓦwww.oysterbaybeachresort.com. Large, recently revamped resort spread over eight acres on the east coast of the island, a short distance from Dawn Beach. Rooms are spacious, and there are two restaurants, plus a gorgeous infinity pool. 6

Pasanggrahan Royal Guest House Philipsburg ⓣ599/542-3588, ⓦwww.pasanhotel.com. Once a guesthouse for royal visitors, this colonial-style hotel overlooks the sea on the south side of Front Street and makes a good base for exploring. Its former grandeur has faded but it's comfortable enough and there's a welcoming bar and a good restaurant. 5

Royal Islander Club La Terrasse Resort Maho Bay, ⓣ599/545-2115, ⓦwww.royalislander.com. Unpromising from the outside, on the inside the brightly decorated suites are large and fully equipped with kitchens, and a lovely pool and bar. There's a supermarket and spa in the same complex, and the airport is just minutes away. Closed 2 weeks Sept. 7

Sonesta Maho Beach Resort & Casino Maho Bay ⓣ599/545-2115, or 1-800 766 3782, ⓦwww.sonesta.com. This 537-room mega-resort has plenty of energy, including a wide choice of restaurants, an award-winning spa, a theatre, a club and a casino. Despite the scale, the beach is big enough that you can normally find a quiet spot of your own. 6

Westin St Maarten Dawn Beach Resort & Spa ⓣ599/543-6700, ⓦwww.starwoodhotels.com. Set on beautiful Dawn Beach, this swank resort boasts 317 luxurious rooms, plus a spa, casino and several restaurants. On the downside, service isn't always up to scratch. 9

Wyndham Sapphire Beach Club & Resort Cupecoy ⓣ599/545-2179, ⓦwww.sbcwi.com. This large resort's 180 well-equipped room recently underwent a face-lift. The many facilities include a freshwater pool, children's pool and Internet café. The nearest beach is a short walk away, but the ocean views are stunning. 7

Philipsburg and around

Overloaded with cruise ship visitors during the day, lively **PHILIPSBURG** makes an entertaining place to spend a couple of hours, even if shopping isn't high on your agenda. Founded in 1733 on a sand bar that separated the sea from a series of inland salt ponds, the town was named after Scotsman John Philips, one of the island's early pioneers. All four of its main roads run east–west along the thin strip of land that divides Great Bay from the Great Salt Pond, with busy **Voorstraat** and **Acherstraat** (often called Front Street and Back Street, respectively) facing south onto the blue expanse of the ocean and bursting with duty-free shops.

Although the town is unabashedly in search of the tourist dollar and most of the development is fairly modern, a handful of attractive eighteenth- and nineteenth-century buildings along the heaving main drag of **Front Street** and in the grid of quieter streets behind it keep things interesting, including some good places to get a bite to eat. In the evening the place takes on a different, slightly seedy feel, and can even seem a bit threatening if you move away from the main well-lit areas on Front Street or around Bobby's Marina in the east.

The recently redeveloped Front Street has a huge variety of **shops** selling everything from alcohol and cigars, jewellery, cosmetics, perfume, clothes, souvenirs and electronics. Front Street's pedestrian area is the heart of the main shopping area while Back Street is the focus of cheaper unbranded goods. Many **bars** and eateries of all varieties, including a few elegant **restaurants**, will tempt you as you shop. Many stores will deliver products back to the cruise ships or your hotel.

Towards the eastern end of Front Street, **Wathey Square** (pronounced "Watty") is effectively the town centre and the main focus for visitors, housing the **tourist information kiosk**, a couple of banks and a handful of bars and restaurants. The square is less than a minute's walk from the long, semicircular Great Bay Beach – not one of the most impressive but normally strewn with swimmers and sun-seekers.

On the north side of the square, check out the graceful architecture of the grand old **courthouse**, built in 1793 and serving in its time as a fire station and a jail. Just 200m west of the square, the quaint wooden **Methodist church** was built in 1851 and makes for a welcome sanctuary from the hustle and bustle outside.

At the eastern end of Front Street are the more attractive of Philipsburg's historic buildings, a group of elegant **colonial houses** distinctive for their downstairs store or warehouse with steps leading up from the street to a veranda for the living quarters above. Almost at the end of Front Street, the small **Sint Maarten Museum** (Mon–Fri 10am–4pm; donations appreciated; ⓣ599/542-4917) merits a look for its exhibits on island history from Amerindian times and articles salvaged from local shipwrecks. Just around the corner, heading south around the edge of the bay, there's always plenty of boating activity at Great Bay Marina and Bobby's Marina, as well as a couple of good places to eat.

Also on Front Street, look out for **Planet Paradise**, at No.19 (ⓣ599/542-4009, ⓦwww.thatyodaguy.com). Here, Nick Maley – also known as "the Yoda Guy", because he helped create the famous character – has opened an exhibition housing part of his private collection of movie relics and replicas. Inland from Front Street you will find a labyrinth of small streets and alleys leading back towards the huge **Great Salt Pond** where salt-rakers once scraped a living collecting the "white gold".

Sint Maarten Park Zoological and Botanical Gardens

The largest zoo in the Caribbean, **Sint Maarten Park** (daily 9am–5pm; US$10, children US$5; ⓣ599/543-2030), a few minutes north of Philipsburg on Acre Road, features 250 animals and nearly 80 unique species, including several endangered ones, such as golden lion tamarins. The zoo boasts two walk-through aviaries with a large collection of parrots, a petting zoo and a cave where Jamaican fruit bats wheel around as night falls. The grounds include beautifully coloured tropical plants including sea grape, cordia and yellow poui. A large playground, restaurant and gift shop round off the experience.

The southwest coast

The headland at the western end of **Great Bay** divides it from Little Bay and a series of smaller sandy bays that lead around the western coast to the great spread of Simpson Bay. For several kilometres, the road follows the narrow strip of land that divides the secluded beach at Simpson Bay from the vast **Simpson Bay Lagoon** that dominates this side of the island. Not exactly scenic but this area is home to an excellent guesthouse (see p.485) and some good restaurants; the lagoon is a popular spot for watersports.

Heading west beyond the airport brings you to further resort development and a series of good white-sand beaches at Maho Bay, Mullet Bay, Cupecoy Beach and Long Bay before you round the headland to Pointe du Plum. **Maho Beach** is often drowned out with noise as planes roar into the airport, and anything left on the beach under the flight path usually ends up being blown into sea by the aircraft engines. Nonetheless, the beach is popular and the *Sunset Beach Bar* (see below) is invariably packed when the sun goes down.

Mullet Bay tends to be the most crowded of the local beaches, with visitors pouring in for the gentle surf and white sugary sand as well as the ample shade provided by a lovely stretch of palm trees. The beach lacks sufficient facilities so bring a towel and some drinks. **Cupecoy** – the main beach in the area for nude bathing – is a dramatic place with sandstone cliffs and caves, though the once-beautiful beach has been spoiled in recent years by tide erosion. There are no facilities here either. Beyond Cupecoy, the turquoise waters of **Long Bay (Baie Longue)**, actually in Saint Martin, make it a delightful place to take long walks, and although it's good for snorkelling, the strong undertow means you should take care when swimming.

Eating, drinking and nightlife

Philipsburg is an excellent place for **eating out**, with everything from classy French and Indonesian to simple spots good for a snack. Consider making a trip in for lunch or breakfast at least once during your stay but bear in mind the traffic problems. The best **nightlife** in terms of bars and clubs is also on the Dutch side. If you like partying, there's something going on every night, from small Latin-themed bars to happy-hour two-for-one specials and clamorous, booty-shaking music in the nightclubs.

Bamboo Bernie's Simpson Bay, ⓣ599/545-3622, ⓦwww.bamboobernies.net. A little bit of everything (tiki bar, sushi bar, restaurant, live music venue), this place attracts a lively mix. Women get free drinks on Wed nights. Newer sister restaurant Tijuana Yacht Club, serving Mexican food and margaritas, is also in Simpson Bay.

Bliss Maho Beach ⓣ599/545-3996, ⓦwww.theblissexperience.com. A hip restaurant situated on the beachfront with a straightforward menu offering pastas, grills (US$45 for Dover sole) and salads (US$13). The place comes alive in the evening with international DJs making regular appearances. Tues is martini night, while Thurs is two-for-one drinks.

The Greenhouse Philipsburg ⓣ599/542-2941, ⓦwww.thegreenhouserestaurant.com. During the day, this is a great bar and restaurant to take a break from shopping for lunch. The food (salads around US$12, burgers and sandwiches from US$9) is good and happy hour lasts from 4.30pm to 7pm. Tues nights (two-for-one night) are especially popular. Don't leave without trying their rum-based special The Hurricane. Daily lunch and dinner.

Kangaroo Court Philipsburg ⓣ599/542-7557. "Doing justice to your appetite", this is a good stopping-off point when you're in town. As well as decent coffees and breakfast fare, there's a lunchtime menu of sandwiches, burgers and pizzas starting at less than US$10. Closed dinner.

L'Escargot Philipsburg ⓣ599/542-2483, ⓦwww.lescargotrestaurant.com. Colourfully tiled and brightly painted, *L'Escargot* is one of the town's longest-running restaurants. French specialities include frog's legs and various snail options, while the fresh Dover sole meunière (US$39) is not to be missed. Fri is cabaret night, which includes dinner and a show. Closed Sat & Sun lunch.

Mr Busby's Oyster Bay ⓣ599/543-6088, ⓦwww.dawnbeachsxm.com. Great spot by the marina, serving breakfast combos (from US$5.50), and salads, sandwiches (US$8) and fresh fish dishes such as mahi mahi and lobster at lunchtime. Closed dinner.

Saratoga Simpson Bay Yacht Club, ⓣ599/544-2421, ⓦwww.neostream.net/~sara. Superlative cuisine in a high-class yet relaxed waterside setting. Try starters such as spicy gazpacho with Saban lobster (US$12) and mains like fried whole sea bass with ginger sauce (US$30). Excellent wine list, too. Dinner only; closed Sun & Aug–mid-Oct.

Sunset Beach Bar Maho Bay ⓣ599/545-3998, ⓦwww.sunsetbeachbar.com. Lively bar on Maho Beach that's a great place to catch the sunset, with cheap beer and a barbecue menu (burgers from US$9). There's something happening every night of the week, including DJs, karaoke and drinks specials. On your way home it is something of a tradition to check in early and then watch the planes with a drink at this bar. Daily lunch and dinner.

Temptation Cupecoy ⓣ599/545-5714, ⓦwww.nouveaucaribbean.com. Set in the Atlantis Casino, this excellent restaurant serves such mouthwatering dishes as a starter of grilled peach salad with blue cheese, sugar-roasted pecans and hydroponic garden greens (US$12). The chef is also the brains behind *Rare* (also in the casino), a classic American steakhouse with a twist. Don't miss the "deconstructed" porterhouse for two: dry-aged Angus beef strip served with wet-aged filet mignon (US$79). Both restaurants are open for dinner only. *Temptation* closed Mon May–Nov. *Rare* closed Sun May–Nov.

11

Saba and St Eustatius

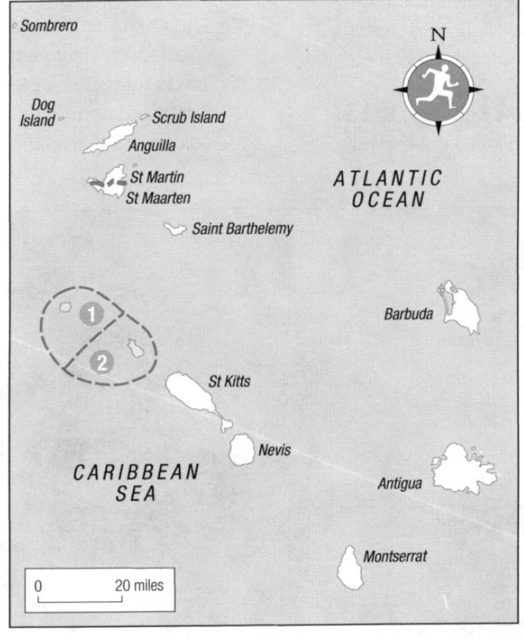

Saba and St Eustatius highlights

* **Rainforest Restaurant** Savour delicious, innovative home-grown food on Saba while marvelling at the sounds of the rainforest. See p.500

* **Saba's island fringes** Pristine reefs and multicoloured fish abound in the island's superb marine park. See p.500

* **Mount Scenery, Saba** The hike to the top may be hard work, but the magnificent island views repay the effort. See p.501

* **Oranjestad** Take in the Sint Eustatius' colonial past on a gentle wander through town. See p.503

* **The Quill** Explore the spectacular rainforest inside the crater of Sint Eustatius' dormant volcano. See p.506

▲ Oranjestad, St Eustatius

Introduction and basics

The pristine Caribbean endures in an overlooked corner occupied by the tiny Netherlands Antilles isles of **Saba** (known as the "unspoiled queen") and **Sint Eustatius**, which are set to become special municipalities of the Netherlands at the end of 2008. Sparsely populated and little known even to seasoned travellers to the area, Saba is a true pleasure to visit. Priding itself on showcasing the "Caribbean as it used to be", Saba's superb diving and great hiking more than compensate for the absence of a decent beach. Most refreshing of all – particularly after St Maarten, from where nearly all visitors connect – is the lack of tourist development and absence of cruise ships. Similarly, Sint Eustatius (or Statia, as it is known by locals), 27km to the northwest, moves at its own slow pace, with some wonderfully restored colonial buildings and other traces of its illustrious past, as well as good diving and hiking – the latter especially in the crater of the Quill, the island's dormant volcano.

Where to go

Saba and Sint Eustatius are attractive options for the eco-tourist with both offering some of the best **scuba diving** in the Caribbean along with plenty of fascinating **hiking**. Both have fairly small, low-key capitals and are excellent places to unwind.

When to go

The **climate** is usually sunny and warm year-round, with the cooling trade winds picking up between mid-December and mid-April, aka the peak **tourist season**. Diving visibility at this time of year is particularly good. On Statia there are light showers in April, June and September while on Saba you should be mindful that Windwardside is 1500 feet above sea-level and so can be relatively chilly once the sun has set. From June until the end of October is the **hurricane season**. Prices, however, between peak and off-peak season do not vary too much.

Getting there

The closest international airport to Saba and Sint Eustatius is **Juliana Airport** on Sint Maarten, and Winair (Ⓦwww.winair.com) makes the short connecting flight (five a day) to **Juancho E. Yrausquin Airport** in Saba, and then continues to Sint Eustatius, landing at **Franklin Delano Roosevelt Airport**. Taxis are available at both airports but in Saba it is advisable to arrange transport with your hotel beforehand.

Two **ferries** run from Sint Maarten to Fort Bay on Saba. Wednesday to Sunday you can take *The Edge* (book through Aquamania at Ⓦwww.stmaarten-activities.com), leaving from Simpson Bay at 9am, returning from Saba at 3.30pm (US$50 each way). Tue, Thur and Sat, *Dawn* II (Ⓣ416-3671, Ⓔsabactransport.com) leaves from Saba at 7am, returning from Dock Maarten, Phililipsburg at 5pm (US$50 one way, but US$75 for a day return). Note that the crossing, which can take 90 minutes plus depending on the seas, is often very rough. There are no ferry services operating on Statia.

Information

On **Saba** in Windwardside, the **tourist office** (Mon–Fri 8am–5pm; Ⓣ416-2231, Ⓦwww.sabatourism.com) has a large collection of books, brochures, maps and an extremely helpful staff. A short distance away at the path leading up Mt Scenery, you'll find the **Saba Trail Shop**, which also has a collection of maps and books. The Saba Conservation Foundation (Ⓣ416-3435, Ⓦwww.sabapark.org), the NGO which manages the Saba National Park and plays a significant role in preserving the Saba National Marine Park, has produced a series of exceptional visitor information guides and maps, which can be picked up in the above locations.

At **Statia's** airport is a small selection of information sheets plus maps. The same information along with a few other brochures can be found at the accommodating **tourism office** in Fort Oranje (Mon–Fri 8am–noon & 1–5pm; ⓣ318-2433, ⓦwww.statiatourism.com). These include a wonderful series of colourful maps and brochures detailing local history, flora and fauna, produced by the Sint Eustatius National Parks Foundation (STENAPA; ⓣ318-2884, ⓦwww.statiapark.org), the NGO responsible for the maintenance and management of both land and marine parks. These brochures, along with further information, are also available at the STENAPA visitor centre in Lower Town, Oranjestad.

Money and costs

The official **currency** on Saba and Sint Eustatius is the Netherlands Antilles guilder or florin (NAf), but the US$ is quoted and accepted everywhere. The guilder notes come in denominations of 5, 10, 25, 50, 100, 250 and 500 guilders; coins in 1, 2.5, 5, 10, 25 and 50 cents. The guilder is tied to the US$ at a rate of around US$1 to NAf1.80.

Saba has several banks in Windwardside, and in Oranjestad on Sint Eustatius. On both islands banking hours are weekdays from 8.30am–3.30pm. On Saba ATMs can be found in Windwardside, The Bottom and at the airport; on Statia, ATMs are in Oranjestad – on both islands you can choose to receive money in NAf or US$. **Credit cards** are accepted by most restaurants, dive operators and hotels.

Costs are comparatively high on Saba and Sint Eustatius as the great majority of food, drink and other items are imported. On **Saba** there is a government room tax of 5 percent, and most hotels and restaurants add a 10–15 percent service charge, often not included in the published rates. On **Sint Eustatius** a 7 percent tax is added along with a 10 percent service charge for hotels although some establishments include these taxes in their rates. There are no taxes for restaurant bills but a 15 percent service charge will often be added to your bill. Tipping taxi drivers and guides on both islands is discretionary and not expected.

Leaving from Saba, a cash-only **departure tax** of US$5 is charged if you're headed to other Netherlands Antilles islands such as Sint Maarten or Sint Eustatius, or US$20 for all other destinations. Leaving from Sint Eustatius, the departure tax is US$5.95 to Netherlands Antilles isles or US$12 for all other destinations.

Getting around

There is **no public transportation** on either Saba or Sint Eustatius; you'll need to either rent a car (or a scooter on Statia) or hire a taxi to get around, the latter of which is invariably cheaper, as not much driving is needed to cover the islands. **Taxis** will meet you at both airports. You can also get a taxi driver to squire you around on a **tour** of either island for US$40. Taxi rates are fixed on both islands. Most fares on Statia are US$5 or less with charges for extra luggage and pick-ups after 6pm. Saba's steep hills and windy roads mean higher prices: from the airport to Windwardside budget US$10, to The Bottom US$16 and to Fort Bay US$19.50. A ride from Windwardside to The Bottom will cost you US$8.

If you do decide to **rent a car** on Saba, ask your hotel to arrange it or call ahead to Caja's (ⓣ416-2388). On Statia, contact either Arc (ⓣ318-2595, ⓦwww.arcagency.com) or Rainbow (ⓣ318-2811) or one of the other firms on the tourist office list. There are no scooters or bikes for rent on Saba (the roads are way too steep) but scooters are fun and convenient on Statia **and** can be rented from LPN Scooter Rentals (ⓣ318-4152). Driving is on the right on both islands.

Hitchhiking is a common means of transport on Saba and locals are usually happy to give you a lift. The protocol in Windwardside is to wait by the wall by the Big Rock Market; in The Bottom stand by the Department of Public Works; and in Fort Bay, stand opposite Saba Deep.

Public holidays and festivals

April 30 Queen's Birthday (both islands).

May (40th day after Easter) Ascension Day (both islands)

Saba Summer Festival late July The week-long carnival includes a carnival king and queen, calypso competitions, a parade and fireworks display.

July (Sint Eustatius) Ten-day carnival with similar activities to Saba's Summer Festival, including an early-morning jump-up culminating later in the day with the effigy-burning of King Momo, the spirit of the carnival.

October 21 Antillean Day (both islands) celebrated with games and fetes.

November 16 Statia–America Day. Commemorates 1776 when Statia became the first foreign nation to recognize American Independence by firing its cannons in salute to a US Ship.

Saba Days Long weekend in the first week in December which sees sporting events such as an international triathlon and basketball, dancing, parades, barbecues and live music plus a host of other activities.

Accommodation

The **hotels** on Saba and Statia are generally fairly small, offering basic amenities, and **prices** reflect this. None of the giant, luxurious resorts you find on other Caribbean islands exist here. If you are visiting to **scuba dive** then it is worth comparing the many **packages** the hotels and dive operators put together; these often offer the best value. Several hotels have an annual closure in September.

Mail and communications

On both Saba and Statia a handful of **telephone kiosks** offer international calls via credit card or with prepaid cards that can be purchased at hotels or at the airport. The **country code** for both Saba and Statia is ⓣ599.

Saba's post office is in Windwardside while Statia's main post office is located on Fiscal Road in Oranjestad. For both islands, hours are Mon–Fri 8am–noon, 1.30–5pm, closing at 4.30pm on Friday.

A number of the hotels have free Wi-Fi access. **Internet access** is otherwise available on Saba from Island Communication Services in Windwardside at a rate of US$5 for 30 minutes. They also rent cellphones for US$10 a day, US$45 a week. On Statia Internet access is available in a couple of hotels. Additionally, you can get online in Oranjestad at the STENAPA visitor centre (US$3 per hour), at the public library, or at the Internet Café on Logeweg.

Opening hours

Although business hours are nominally Mon–Fri 8am–5pm, **opening hours** are pretty varied on both islands, and shops can easily be shut when they should be open if the proprietor has other business to attend to. A number of supermarkets stay open late on both islands, and are open on Sunday too. Some places close for lunch.

Outdoor activities

Diving and **hiking** are big draws on both Saba and Statia, with plenty of **reefs** and **trails** to explore. See pp.501 and 501 for details. Other activities include **ocean kayaking**. Dive Statia (ⓣ318-2435, ⓦwww.divestatia.com) rents out two-person kayaks for US$20 per hour, with reduced rates for longer excursions.

History

Though Saba and Sint Eustatius are outposts of the Kingdom of the Netherlands and shared some early settlement, the islands have had very different histories. Amerindians were the first visitors, coming to the islands in long dug-out canoes as they made their way from the river deltas of Venezuela up the chain of eastern Caribbean islands. During his 1493 voyage, Columbus and his crew were the first Europeans to pass the islands. While Saba became a hideout for pirates, Statia went on to become a regional trading superpower before its decline following US independence.

Saba

Geologically, **Saba** is the peak of a volcano that last erupted some five thousand years ago, leaving a steep-sided and now luxuriously vegetated island. The first Amerindian settlers probably arrived around 700 AD and lived in small communities based around fishing and simple farming. A handful of their artefacts are displayed in the museum in Windwardside.

Columbus did not stop in 1493, and the island was largely ignored by European travellers until 1632 when some English were shipwrecked on its shores. In 1635 the French claimed it for themselves but in 1640, the **Dutch** colonized the island, dispatching a team from nearby Sint Eustatius to take up residence near Fort Bay. Unlike many islands in the area, the steep terrain meant that large sugar, tobacco or cotton plantations were not feasible, and **development** remained limited to a handful of small farms. In the late seventeenth century Saba also became a hideout for **pirates,** who were largely British and Irish indentured servants whose work had been taken over by imported African slaves in other Caribbean islands. Many of today's population in Saba revel in their pirate ancestry.

Today the island remains part of the **Kingdom of the Netherlands**, one of five Dutch islands in the Caribbean with their central administration in Curaçao. This is set to change as Saba has voted (along with Statia and Bonaire) to become a special municipality within the Netherlands at the end of 2008.

The island's tiny population of 1500 is divided fairly equally between the descendants of the black slaves brought in to work the fields and the white farm-owners who ran them, although Sabans are often outnumbered by a combination of **medical school** students, expatriates and tourists.

Sint Eustatius

Sint Eustatius, or **Statia**, was settled by **Amerindians** from Venezuela and Guyana, with evidence of their occupation dating to at least 300 AD. They named the island Aloi, meaning "Cashew Island". Columbus' maps label the island "S Maria de Niebe," which was a name later given to Nevis. The island's next name was **Estasia** after a general in the Roman Army. It is likely that some Amerindians were still around when **Columbus** passed by in 1493 but there were none when the first European settlers arrived, beginning with the French in 1629, followed by the Dutch in 1636. The ruling command regularly swapped between European nations (22 times in all). Between 1665 and 1713 the island was occupied eight times by French and English. Between 1781 and 1816, there were five further foreign occupations. Through it all, **crops** including tobacco and sugar were planted, and the island flourished.

The **eighteenth century** was Statia's heyday, with an estimated twenty thousand inhabitants and more than 3500 ships visiting every year to trade both in local crops and in slaves. Janet Schaw, a Scot visiting the island in the

1770s, described the main town as "a place of vast traffic from every corner of the globe". The island prospered as a duty-free trading hub, particularly with the **colonies** that were later to become the USA, while other Caribbean islands were only allowed to trade with their mother country. It was during these glory days that the island gained the nickname "The Golden Rock".

At the time of Ms Schaw's visit, local entrepreneurs were also making great profits running arms and supplies to the troops of **George Washington**'s revolutionary army, and the island's most famous moment came in 1776 when Fort Oranje fired its cannons to salute an American ship. Needless to say the British, who largely controlled the eastern Caribbean, were not amused.

Ironically, after the US gained independence and established its own trade routes, the island's fortunes gradually declined. Following the **abolition of slavery** in the mid-nineteenth century (which was the death knell of the plantation system, prompting the relentless exodus of residents), the island returned largely to fishing and subsistence farming. Today Statia is home to around three thousand people largely reliant on **tourism** and **oil storage** for employment.

11.1

Saba

At the top of the Eastern Caribbean chain, and a mere thirteen square kilometres, **Saba** has plenty of small delights. The island's population of 1500, which includes 300 foreign medical students, live in quaint villages – neat and attractive places, where almost every building by law is painted white with red roof and green shutters. Even more appealing, the island's volcanic origins and limited development mean that spectacular **vegetation** and **scenery** is within easy reach of the main villages, as is an even more spectacular world of **coral** and fish just yards offshore.

Unless you are visiting St Martin, in which case you should at the very least make a day-trip here, the main drawback of visiting Saba is the difficulty and cost involved in **getting here**. If that doesn't put you off, and you aren't looking for an island with busy action and nightlife, Saba's a great choice to spend a few relaxing days.

Accommodation

Despite its small size, Saba has a good mix of elegant and simple **accommodation** to cater for most budgets. Places to stay are mostly concentrated in **Windwardside**, which makes the most convenient base for hikers and has the best dining options.

The Cottage Club Windwardside ⓣ416-2486, ⓦwww.cottage-club.com. Good-value low-key property with 10 Saban-style cottages plus a swimming pool with sun terrace. Each large one-room unit has a fully-equipped kitchen/dining area, cable TV, phone and private balcony. Views are best from cottages 1 & 2. ④

Ecolodge Rendez-Vous Windwardside ⓣ416-3888, ⓦwww.ecolodge-saba.com. A genuine ecolodge with a responsible approach towards the environment and energy resources, comprising twelve artistically decorated solar-powered wooden chalets (without phones or TV) situated a short way up the Mt Scenery trail in lush vegetation. Most chalets sleep four (some two) and all have private bathroom, balcony and hammock; some with their own hot tub or kitchenette. ③

The Gate House Hell's Gate ⓣ416-2416, ⓦwww.sabagatehouse.com. With five bright, spacious rooms (and a single villa and cottage) this intimate, though rather isolated, hotel offers spectacular views of the sea and nearby islands from the terrace. It also has a pleasant swimming pool and an excellent onsite restaurant, which possesses an award-winning wine cellar. ⑤ including full American breakfast.

Juliana's Windwardside ⓣ416-2269, ⓦwww.julianas-hotel.com. Bright and cheerful small hotel, comprising nine decent rooms with comfortable beds (as well as a separate apartment and two cottages), all with cable TV, private bathrooms and balconies. It's worth paying the extra US$10 for the much brighter ocean-view rooms. The hotel's common room has games, videos and internet access, plus there's a scenically located small pool and Jacuzzi across the road at the *Tropics Café* (see p.500). ④ inclusive of breakfast.

El Momo Cottages Windwardside ⓣ416-2265, ⓦwww.elmomo.com. A good budget option; small brightly painted basic rooms (bed only plus shelving though with Wi-Fi) with private bathrooms and patios – both offering splendid vistas – set amidst lush vegetation high on Booby Hill (and 70 plus steps up from the road!). There are hammocks, a small pool, and the best sunset views on the island from the breakfast terrace. Inexpensive healthy breakfasts too with home-made bread and banana jam. ③

Queen's Garden Resort The Bottom ⓣ416-3494, ⓦwww.queensaba.com. Elegant hotel with old-world charm in an isolated location halfway up Troy's Hill. One and two-bedroom suites are tastefully furnished with antique furniture, kitchens, TV and fans though you'll need to splash out on the superior suites for a decent view. Superb private

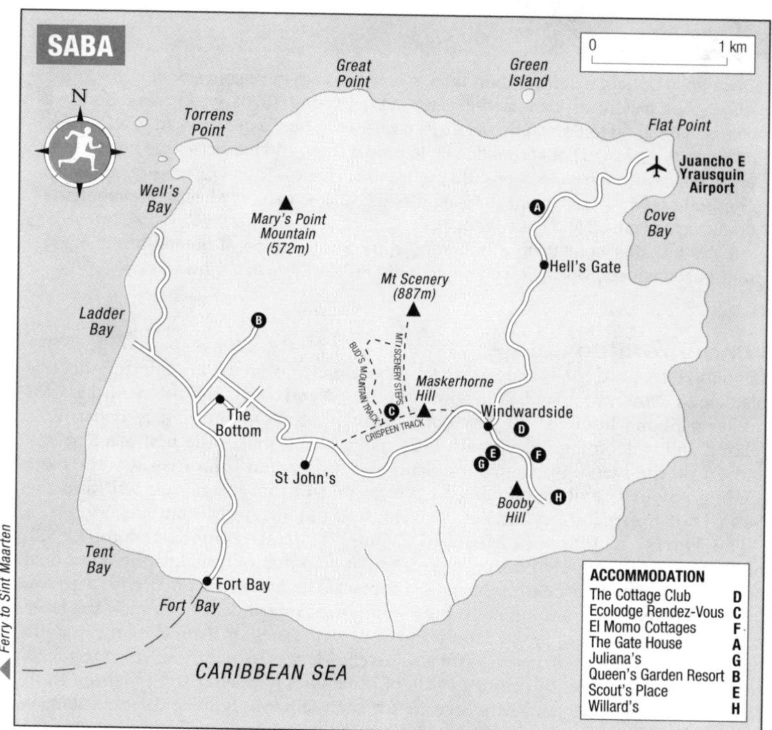

villa also available. Mellow Sunday alfresco tapas lounge every first and third Sunday of the month, 2–5pm. 7

Scout's Place Windwardside ⓣ416-2740, ⓦwww.sabadivers.com. The most centrally located of Saba's hotels with fourteen clean rooms, each fitted with fridge, cable TV, and with Wi-Fi access. Also a pool and vibrant bar-restaurant (see p.500). The place caters largely to the younger diving scene with good dive packages on offer. Prices include continental breakfast. 4

Willard's Windwardside ⓣ416-2498, ⓦwww.willardsofsaba.com. Perched high on Booby Hill, Saba's most luxurious hotel enjoys a truly spectacular cliff top location. The handful of rooms, all with private balconies, are spacious and attractively furnished affording magnificent panoramic views across to neighbouring islands and down to the crashing surf below. There is a large heated pool and Jacuzzi, also overlooking the ocean, plus a tennis court and a fancy restaurant (mains US$25–35). 9

The island

Saba's tiny airstrip is at the island's northern end. From here, the dramatic road – known simply as "the Road" – rises sharply towards the small village of Hell's Gate. Just outside the airport, a left turn off the Road takes you along Cove Bay Road towards a sign pointing to **Flat Point**, where you can see the remains of an abandoned boiling house, used during the eighteenth century to produce molasses from sugar cane grown on the island. Today Flat Point is a desolate place, with cacti and sea grape scattered around the coastal bluffs and plenty of good tidal pools for hunting crabs and sea urchins.

Back on the Road, after a dozen or more switchbacks you reach **Hell's Gate**. Landscape photo-taking apart, there's no great reason to stop here. The main landmark is the Holy Rosary Church, which was built in the 1960s.

Saban lace and spice

Once an important export, **Saban lace** is now the traditional souvenir of a trip to the island. The history of local lace-making started in the 1870s when Mary Gertrude Johnson returned to Saba from Venezuela, where she had learned the art in a Caracas convent. She passed her knowledge on to local women and the skills have been handed down through the generations. It's pretty stuff, if pricey. Saba Artisans Foundation in The Bottom (Mon–Fri 8.30am–4.30pm; ⓣ526-3491) has an outlet selling home-made crafts including lace and linen products.

If you are after something a bit stronger, try **Saban spice**, a potent locally made rum-based liqueur, which you can try out at the Trail Shop in Windwardside.

Windwardside

Beyond Hell's Gate, the Road cuts through rainforest-covered cliffs, offering spectacular views across the island as it winds towards **Windwardside**, the main base for hiking trips and home to the tiny but worthwhile Saba museum. It is a charming, relaxed and welcoming village with little traffic, and it makes the best place to stay and eat on the island. Bougainvillea plants and banana and palm trees line the road, lending colour to village gardens. At the far end of the village you will find the **Saba Trail Shop**; just beyond here you can start the hike to Mount Scenery.

The **Harry L Johnson Museum** (Mon–Fri 10am–noon & 1–4pm; US$2), housed in a 160-year-old cottage, re-creates with a touch of nostalgia the traditional home of a nineteenth-century Saban sea captain. The house is stuffed with artefacts from the island's past, among them pre-Columbian Amerindian finds such as a large cooking pot, polishing stones, tools and a cassava squeezer. Much of the island's history is told through magazine articles, as well as letters to and from Saban residents written in the eighteenth century. Pride of place goes to a letter from George Bush senior, thanking a Mr and Mrs Stewart for their support (gifts and letters sent to troops) during the first Gulf War. The bust in the pretty grounds is of revolutionary Simón Bolívar, a gift from the government of Venezuela. Should the museum not be open when advertised, it's worth asking the **tourist office** (also in Windwardside) to open up.

Also in the village you will find the **post office** and a couple of **banks**, along with most of the island's restaurants, grocery stores and a number of gift shops selling the distinctive Saban lace and spice.

The Bottom

Having crossed through Windwardside, the Road winds towards tiny **St John's** en route to Saba's main village, **THE BOTTOM**, the seat of government and the island's administrative centre. A viewpoint along the way offers fantastic panorama views and has a memorial plaque to Josephus Lambert Hassell, the Saban responsible for the Road. After taking a correspondence course in engineering, he defied experts by designing and overseeing the construction of "the road that couldn't be built", which twists and turns all the way from the airport in the north to Fort Bay in the south.

As you drop down the hill to The Bottom, the first buildings you'll see on the outskirts comprise the **Saba University School of Medicine**, whose 300 students are in evidence around the island. Further on is the department of public works in a white-stone old school building and, on your right, the oldest Anglican Church on the island, thought to date from the mid-1700s. Of greater interest, at the far end of the village, is the **Church of the Sacred Heart**, which contains a fabulous and unusual modern mural in the altar done by local artist Heleen Cornet. It took two years to complete and many of the young faces are based on children from the island.

Around the main square, a series of neat buildings house the fire and police stations and the courthouse, while a handful of **munching goats** and immaculately dressed schoolchildren are likely to be roaming the nearby streets. Out of school hours, if you're lucky, you might catch the local youth practising group drumming. At the western edge of the town, the grand **governor's house** (not open to the public) has particularly intricate wooden fretwork and splendid galleries.

Beyond The Bottom

West of The Bottom, a road ploughs through to Saba's only beach of note at **Well's Bay.** It is known to many as the wandering beach, as it is washed away for most of the year and then reappears in the spring for around four months. You may find a rather uninspiring patch of sand but it makes a good spot to snorkel (bring your own gear).

Heading south, the Road winds down through dry, cactus-strewn terrain to the scruffy-looking port at **Fort Bay**, home to the main dive operations and the arrival point for passengers coming to the island by boat. Prior to the Road's construction, all supplies and materials – including the organ and safe you can see in the museum – had to be lugged up the eight hundred stone steps, known as **The Ladder**, further round the coast in Ladder Bay.

Eating, drinking and nightlife

For a tiny island, Saba has a surprising variety of places to eat – most cater to tourists but prices are affordable. Most hotels have **restaurants** and there's a good series of other places in Windwardside. As you would expect, the local cuisine is heavily geared towards **seafood** and **goat** is also common though vegetarians have good choices too. Note that most places **close** for lunch by 3pm and for dinner by 9pm. Reservations are recommended in most places since tables are limited and on quiet nights the kitchen might close early.

Unless you arrive during one of the festivals, **nightlife** options and musical diversions are limited. Some hotels offer their own evening entertainment but most of the time you will have to entertain yourself.

▲ Lesser Antillean iguana

Brigadoon Windwardside ☎416-2380. Set in an attractive old Saban house on the edge of the village, this friendly place offers excellent, often imaginative, Creole fish dishes featuring grouper and snapper, as well as more typical chicken, steak and lobster options. Good veggie selections and the home-made desserts are mouth-watering. Shawarma wraps are on offer Wed and Fri, Thurs is rib dinner and Saturday sees a sushi hour (6.30–7.30pm). Closed Tues. Dinner only from 6.30pm.

Family Deli/Bakery The Bottom ☎416-3858. On the road to Fort Bay, this inexpensive family-run eatery is popular with locals and students, providing freshly baked bread, pastries and sandwiches, fresh fruit juices and tasty local dishes, including daily specials. Catch of the day US$15 and whole lobster only US$30. Daily 8am–9pm though often closed during the university vacations.

In Two Deep Fort Bay ☎416-3438. A good place to catch up on some lunch after a dive trip, offering inexpensive sandwiches and burgers, with fine views across the tiny harbour, though the noisy power station next door detracts from the ambience. Daily 8am–6pm.

Rainforest Restaurant Windwardside, (*Ecolodge Rendez-Vous*) ☎416-3348. Widely acclaimed as producing the best meals on the island, the kitchen serves up a variety of healthy options, predominantly from home-grown produce and fish caught locally. It's a relaxing place to have lunch after a hike while watching the humming-birds; dinner is accompanied by the sound of tree frogs. Open Tue–Sun, lunch & dinner.

Saban Groove The Bottom (turn right just as the Road drops down from the village to Fort Bay). Rare opportunity to mix with the locals at this casual weekend late afternoon/evening venue. Pleasantly situated, with picnic tables and benches, it offers good music, dominoes and barbecued fare – US$15–20 for chicken, ribs and plentiful sides, or curried conch and other local dishes if you prefer. Daily from 5pmish.

Saba's Treasure Windwardside ☎416-2819. Pleasant tavern surroundings, with decor describing famous maritime figures that have connections with the island. Tasty moderately priced deli-sandwiches, salads and burgers on the menu plus enormous and very good pizzas (US$8–12). Mon–Sat 11am–9pm.

Scout's Place Windwardside ☎416-2205. This pirate-themed bar-restaurant, draped in fishing nets and with faux cannons, offers a good, well-priced food and is one of the liveliest places on the island, popular with tourists, locals and students alike. The burgers, sandwiches and hot lunches are cheap (US$6–20), while the dinner menu boasts slightly fancier options but at reasonable rates. Specialities include Saban lobster and spit-roasted chicken. Karaoke on Fri nights. Daily 7am–11pm.

Swinging Doors Windwardside ☎416-2506. Lively American-style bar complete with saloon doors (hence the name) and wooden benches and tables on the covered outdoor terrace. Chicken and ribs with plentiful sides served on Tues and Fri barbecue nights (US$12). Sun is steak night. Open Mon–Fri 9.30am until late, from around 6pm at weekends.

Tropics Café Windwardside (at *Juliana's*) ☎416-2469. A friendly and inexpensive café with a fine array of breakfast options including muffins, croissants and chocolate-chip pancakes; adequate snacks, sandwiches and light lunches, including daily specials (US$10–15). Fri night (7pm) is movie night; US$10 entry also gets you a burger and fries at the island's only outdoor movie theatre, while Wednesday (from 6pm) is Caribbean evening. Breakfast daily 7–10am; lunch Tue–Sun 10am–5pm.

Diving

The volcanic activity that created Saba also created a spectacular underwater world, and superb diving lures many tourists to the island. A **marine park** was designated in 1987, and carefully controlled operation of the dive sites scattered throughout the park (which surrounds the entire island) has kept the reefs in pristine condition. Visibility is excellent and, as well as fine coral heads near the surface for snorkelling, there are sheer walls dropping hundreds of feet just offshore. Most of the best dive sites are on the calmer, western side of the island between Tent Bay in the south and Diamond Rock in the north and they require a very short boat ride.

The nearly 30 different **dive sites** around Saba include several pinnacle sites rising from the ocean floor up to depths of 90ft, covered in sponges and corals, which provide homes to groupers and turtles – sometimes even black-tip and grey reef sharks. The best of these is the **Eye-of-the-needle**. Other great spots include the **Tent Reef Wall** and the **Labyrinth**, a series of 50ft deep channels created by old lava flows, on which brain and star corals as well as brightly coloured tube sponges have formed.

There are three PADI-recognized **dive operators** on Saba, whose boats all leave from Fort Bay. Saba Divers (Ⓣ416-2740, Ⓦwww.sabadivers.com) operates out of Scout's Place; Sea Saba (Ⓣ416-2246, Ⓦwww.seasaba.com) also has its main office in Windwardside. Saba Deep is located (Ⓣ416-3347, Ⓦwww.sabadeep.com) at the harbour itself. Any of the three will arrange trips to collect you from your hotel in Saba, or wait until the ferry from Sint Maarten arrives, before heading out. A marine park **fee** of US$4 per dive is payable at your hotel or to the operator. Budget on around US$50–60 all in per dive initially, although multiple dive packages, with accommodation if you want, can bring the cost down dramatically.

Hiking

The most popular hike on the island is from Windwardside to **Mount Scenery**, up 1064 concrete steps. The path is easy to follow, starting just west of the trail shop, but it is a tough climb, taking an hour to ninety minutes to reach the top. Do not be put off; it is well worth the effort for the fantastic vistas and gorgeous tropical and quasi-alpine vegetation. Much of the hike goes through secondary rainforest, with elephant ear ferns and mountain palms among some of the dramatic plants. For variation, consider coming down Budd's Mountain Trail (branching off at the top shelter), which is easier on the knees.

An undisturbed and beautiful elfin forest of large mountain mahogany trees carpets the summit, their trunks and branches often covered in mosses, bromeliads and ferns. As for **wildlife**, you're sure to see colourful butterflies and birds including hummingbirds, bananaquits and tremblers if you are lucky; you may also spot a harmless racer snake or a large iguana slithering through the undergrowth.

There are several **shelters** en route to the summit, but there is nowhere to get refreshments, so bring water. If it has rained, the trail can be very slippery – wear appropriate footwear. Once at the top, do not miss the grand lookout over the neighbouring islands; to reach it head left of the communications tower and continue along the pathway. The other scenic views at the top require slithering along muddy tracks, clambering over boulders or hauling yourself up a rope.

For other **hiking options**, get hold of a copy of the *Saba Map* (US$10) available from the tourist office in Windwardside, the Trail Shop and most hotels. The Trail Shop (Mon–Fri 10am–4pm, weekends 10am–2pm) also collects the park fee (US$3), rents walking sticks (US$1) and offers the **guiding** services of James, the park manager (US$15–25 pp), who is very knowledgeable about the island's flora and fauna. Though the trails are well maintained by the Saba Conservation Foundation and a posse of Canadian volunteers, and generally well marked, you'll need a guide for the North Coast Trail.

11.2

Sint Eustatius

Once a proud and wealthy "entrepôt", or trading post between America and Europe, **Statia**, as everyone knows the little island of **Sint Eustatius**, has for some time been a tranquil tropical outpost of the Kingdom of the Netherlands (though it's set to become a fully integrated part of the "mother country").

As with Saba, the main drawback is the expense and awkwardness of getting here. But if you make the effort, you will find that you have left the tourists behind for a beguiling friendly spot, with fascinating traces of the island's **colonial glory** days and good **diving** and **hiking** opportunities.

Accommodation

You will almost certainly want to stay in the island's main town, **Oranjestad**, which has a few simple guesthouses and a couple of hotels.

Country Inn Concordia southeast of Zeelandia ⓣ318-2484. Six rather simple rooms at this longstanding and popular guesthouse just east of the airport, all with cable TV and a/c. The friendly owners attract repeat visitors and they're happy to cook meals on demand. Nice views of the bay. No credit cards accepted. ❷

Golden Era Hotel Oranjestad ⓣ318-2345 ⓔgoldenerahotel@gmail.com. Twenty clean and tidy rooms in this pleasant if slightly faded little hotel on the shoreline in Lower Town, just below Fort Oranje. All rooms have TV, a/c, fridges and private bathrooms. There's a small saltwater pool and a reasonable restaurant by the water. ❹

King's Well Resort Oranjestad ⓣ318-2538, ⓦwww.kingswellstatia.com Perched on a clifftop on the northwest edge of town, above Oranje Bay, *King's Well* affords some of the finest views on the island. Though the household great danes and splendid (free-flying) resident macaws mean the place may not be to everyone's taste, Win and Laura's warm hospitality and the spacious rooms, each with private bathroom, cable TV, fridge and ample shared balcony space, offer good value and there's also a pleasant pool. Ask for a seafront room. Savoury dining on the terrace 6–8pm. ❹ including full breakfast.

Old Gin House Oranjestad ⓣ318-2319, ⓦwww.oldginhouse.com. The most luxurious of the island's hotels, housed in a splendid old colonial-style brick building in Lower Town. The 14 fairly dark garden rooms are comfortable and nicely furnished with antique furniture (yet all with mod cons, including Wi-Fi). Their fairly ordinary aspect over the palm-shaded pool comes nowhere near the views from the lovely, luxurious oceanfront suites. There is a waterfront restaurant too. ❺ breakfast included.

The Statia Lodge White Wall ⓣ318-1900, ⓦwww.statialodge.com. Eight rustic but comfortable two-person chalets (plus two four-person family chalets) dotted around well-tended grounds on a bluff along the south-west coat. Each bungalow comes with private bathroom and patio with kitchenette and a sea view – some better than others – though the most splendid vistas to be had, across to St Kitts, are from the lovely lodge pool and adjoining bar area. Rates include scooter (or car for the larger units) hire, necessary since the place is a 40-minute hike from Oranjestad. ❹

The island

Virtually all visitors arriving in Statia land at the **Franklin Delano Roosevelt Airport**, which sits in the centre of the roughly pear-shaped island. A short drive to the southwest will get you to **Oranjestad**, the capital and only town, while the **Quill** – a dormant volcano that offers the most dramatic scenery and best hiking on the island – can be seen off to the southeast.

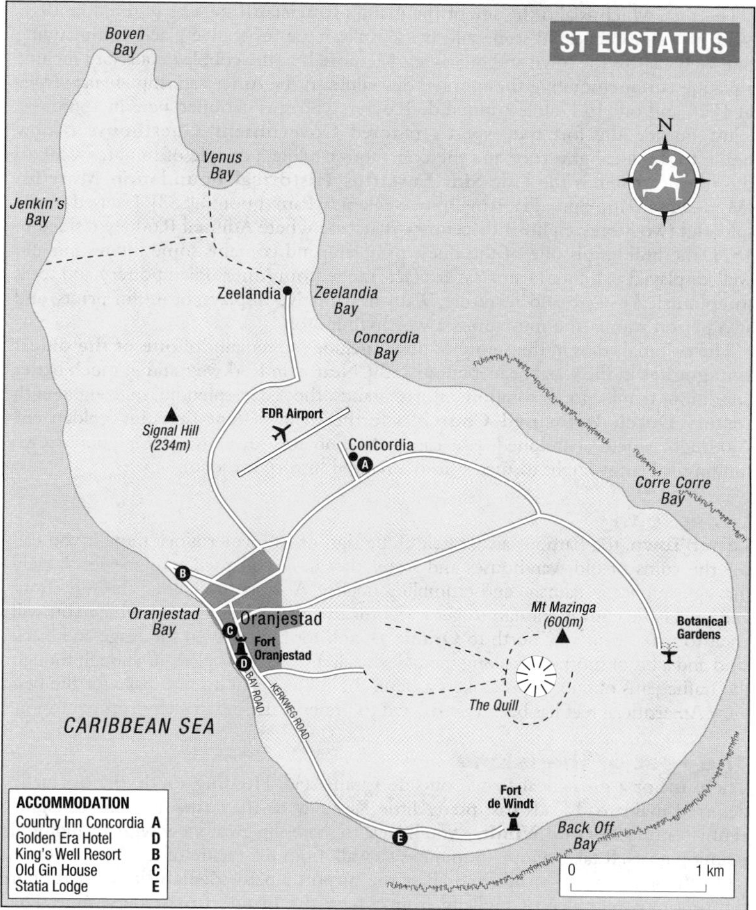

Oranjestad

You will almost certainly be staying in likeable, laid-back **Oranjestad** if you stop overnight on Statia. If you are just here on a day-trip, it's well worth spending at least a couple of hours to have a good look around, and there are several places where you can get a splendid lunch.

Upper Town is where most of the (leisurely) action is, and makes for a pleasant place to wander and visit the island's museum and main colonial buildings, some of which have been beautifully restored. Linked by a footpath to Upper Town, **Lower Town** is the area of the old port, now home to the best local beach and further ruins of the island's once-great past.

Upper Town

Fort Oranje (always open; free) is Oranjestad's dominant building, strategically situated on the cliffside overlooking Lower Town and Oranjestad Bay. The first fortifications were put up by French in 1629. After the French abandoned the island, the Dutch enlarged the fort in 1636 to its present size.

The fort, which is also the site of the island's **tourist office**, was restored in 1976. With its cannon and old stone and brick walls, it's an evocative place, commanding fine views across the town and out to sea. Memorials in the cobbled courtyard include a plaque commemorating the momentous salute to the American ship *Andrew Doria* in 1776 and one to Dutch Admiral de Ruyter, who was stationed here in 1665.

Just outside the fort the expertly restored **Government Guesthouse** is now home to the local governor and the courthouse, while a couple of minutes' walk to the northeast stands the little **Sint Eustatius Historical Foundation Museum** (Mon–Thur 9am–5pm, Fri 9am–3pm, weekends, 9am–noon; US$3). Housed in the splendid two-storey eighteenth-century structure where Admiral Rodney resided in 1871, the building is one of the finest of its era, and contains some interesting and well-displayed exhibits. Historical artefacts range from Amerindian pottery and tools to colonial glassware and furniture. With informative displays, beautiful prints, and two period rooms, the museum is a worthwhile stop.

The colonial ruins in the centre of town include the remains of **one of the oldest synagogues** in the Caribbean, built in 1739. Nearby in Kerkweg, and in much better condition thanks to restoration efforts, stands the once-splendid mid-eighteenth century **Dutch Reformed Church**, a further relic of Sint Eustatius' golden era. Although largely abandoned, you can still climb the tower (free) for good views; funding is being sought to turn it into a natural history museum.

Lower Town

Lower Town, the harbour area, carries little sign of its former glory, though you can see the ruins of old warehouses and stores that have collapsed into the sea, largely through hurricane damage and crumbling neglect. A short stroll along the waterfront and under the cliffs is enough to get a feel for the place's history, after which you will want to make your way north to **Oranje Beach** for a snooze on the beige and black sand and a bit of snorkelling along the old seawall. The beach is pleasant enough though the traffic jams of enormous tankers around the oil terminal do not make for the best view. An artificial reef has been constructed to preserve the beach after years of erosion.

The rest of the island

There is not a great deal to see outside Oranjestad. Heading south, the normally deserted main road leads past pretty little Key Bay to the sparse remains of eighteenth-century **Fort de Windt** – you'll have to share the great view with a handful of roaming goats. It takes about 45 minutes to walk from the centre of town to the fort.

North of town the road winds past the airport up to **Zeelandia**, named after the southern province of Holland from where the island's first settlers came. The decent two-mile-long dark-sand beach makes a good spot for beachcombing – to hunt for the famed blue-glass beads that were used for trading in the 1600s and are now collector's items – though not for swimming as the water is rough and known for dangerous undertows. West of the beach a dirt track leads north through the scrubland along which you can hike down to another beach at **Venus Bay** or into the **interior**. The nesting areas of four species of turtle can be found on the beach while the scrub-filled hinterland is a prime location for spotting some of the island's Lesser Antillean iguana population.

Finally there's the **Berkel Family Museum**, Lynch Bay (Ⓣ318-2338; free though donations are accepted) sometimes referred to as the Lynch Plantation Museum. You'll need to ring for an appointment and it's best if you can catch Ishmael Berkel to give you a tour of what is a family home stuffed full of artefacts and memorabilia of bygone times.

Eating, drinking and nightlife

Whether you're here for the day, or spending a few nights, there is enough variety of **restaurants** to keep you well fed throughout your stay. Seafood is the main staple though goat meat, saltfish and peas and rice feature at local eateries. Vegetarians have a limited choice of where and what to eat. Most places close for lunch by 3pm and for dinner by 9pm.

There is virtually no **nightlife** during the week and only marginally more at the weekend but look out for the occasional poster advertising a local band or DJ.

Blue Bead Bar and Restaurant Gallows Bay ☎318-2873. Considered by many to be the best culinary choice on the island, with a brightly painted veranda, just above the water in Lower Town. A good place for lunch, with tasty salads, sandwiches, fish and seafood options – saltfish fritters a speciality, as well as meat and chicken and pizzas – daily specials and a variety of tasty desserts. Mains from US$18. Lunch 11.30am–2pm, dinner 6.30–9pm. Closed Tue, Wed & Sept.

Cool Corner Oranjestad ☎318-2523. Across from the museum, this popular watering hole, otherwise known as Chucky's, attracts locals, ex pats and tourists in the evening, especially at weekends. Open from around 6pm.

Intermezzo Café Oranjestad ☎318-0075. Pleasant breezy café serving breakfast all day (US$6–12), including fresh fruit juice and excellent hot chocolate. Inexpensive hot and cold sandwiches (from US$3) for lunch. The comfy sofa and magazines make it a good place to chill especially on the 3rd Fri of the month (5–8pm) when there's live music and specials on drinks. Mon–Fri 7.30am–2pm, Sun and holidays 8am–1pm. Closed Sat and 3rd Sun of each month.

Ocean View Terrace Oranjestad ☎318-2934. Cosy inexpensive restaurant popular with locals and tourists alike, possessing a view overlooking the fort. The well-prepared simple home cooking includes various salads, chicken, pork steak and fish options (US$8–13) with lobster only US$25. More local dishes such as curried goat and oxtail are also on offer. Karaoke Fri evening. Mon–Sat 8am–2pm, 7–9pm.

Original Fruit Tree Oranjestad ☎526-8331. Former *Old Gin House* chef Aloysius serves delicious French international cuisine in a delightful tree-filled patio garden brimming with bougainvillea. The menu changes daily for lunch and dinner. Closed Sat.

Diving

Diving on Statia is excellent. It is one of the few locations in the world that offers **coral reefs**, **walls** and **archeological** and modern **wreck dives** in such close proximity. Over two hundred coral encrusted shipwrecks are thought to litter the water off the west coast of the island but only a handful are accessible to divers. Some of the top dive sites are just minutes from shore, and divers can expect to see turtles, stingrays, puffer fish and perhaps even the rare flying gurnard. Snorkelling is good, too, with many ruined buildings and some of the wrecks lying in shallow turquoise waters just offshore.

The western Caribbean shore is where the majority of Statia's thirty dive sites are located. A **marine park** that prevents any vessel from dropping anchor or any fishing extends all the way along the coastline except in the area where the tankers access the oil terminal. The sites range in depth from 20 to 220ft and visibility is often over 100ft.

Triple wreck, which used to be known as the Supermarket, curiously consists of two coral-encrusted shipwrecks lying just 150ft apart at a depth of 60ft. At the dive site known as the **Grand Canyon** – also sometimes known as Crack in the Wall – pinnacle coral reaches up from the ocean floor and you can see an abundance of life including large fish such as black-tip sharks or barracudas. Other popular dives include **Anchor Reef,** boasting an extensive variety of sponges, corals and sea fans, concealing in its crevices and shelves lobsters, sea turtles and countless species of fish. Resting on the seabed nearby at **Anchor Point** is a 14ft-long coral-covered anchor.

There are three PADI-recognized **dive centres** on Statia, all situated within walking distance of each other on the waterfront in Oranjestad: Dive Statia (☎318-2435, Ⓦwww.divestatia.com), Golden Rock Dive Center (☎318-2964, Ⓦwww.goldenrockdive.com) and Scubaqua Dive Center (☎318-5450, Ⓦwww.scubaqua.com). To protect the island's submerged history from souvenir hunters, only divers who are residents of Statia can dive without the accompaniment of a guide from one of the dive operators. Single tank dives cost between US$40–45, two-tank dives

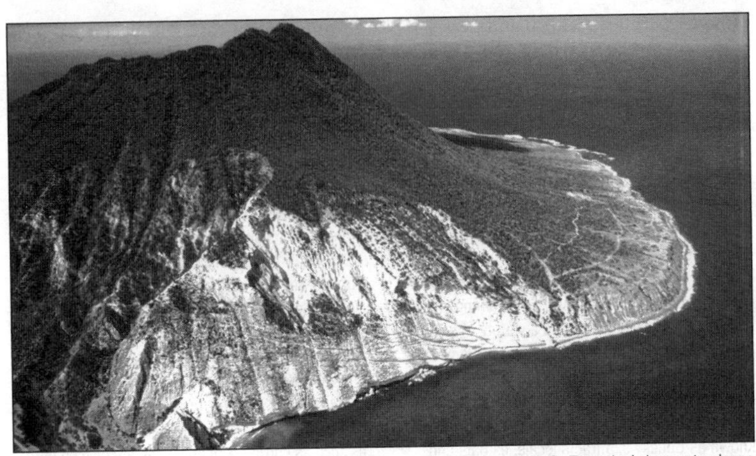

▲ The Quill, St Eustatius' dormant volcano

US$75–84, with multi-dive packages bringing the price down. Snorkelling for a couple of hours will set you back around US$30–40. You must pay US$4 park fee per dive (plus a US$1 government levy) or US$20 for an annual dive pass.

Hiking

By far the most popular hiking on Sint Eustatius is up the slopes and into the crater of **the Quill**, a dormant volcano that dominates the landscape of the southern end of the island, rising 2000ft to a crater that is itself nearly 1000ft across. You can follow good and well-signposted trails up and around the slopes of the volcano and into the crater itself, where a spectacular rainforest teems with wild orchids and anthuriums, hummingbirds and lizards.

To reach the Quill, take the road southeast out of Oranjestad and follow the signs leading to the trailhead (free **maps** and wildlife **guides** produced by STENAPA detailing the island's hikes, flora and fauna are available from the STENAPA and tourist offices). The footpath begins in low-level scrub, climbing through dry woodland and taller vegetation to the crater, a 45-minute walk away. On the way up, you're likely to trip over some of the thousands of hermit crabs that inhabit the Quill and spot a harmless racer snake sliding into the undergrowth.

From the crater rim, you can climb/slither down into the crater itself, though you'll need to take a little care as the path is not always easy to follow. Walking through the thick vegetation to the crater bottom, you may spot coffee, cocoa and cinnamon trees, remnants of once-cultivated crops, as well as masses of bananas. You can't miss the huge silk cotton or kapok trees, with giant buttress roots, that can grow up to 150ft tall.

Alternatively, turn right along the crater rim, following the often slippery **Mazinga track**, which offers fabulous views into the crater and across to neighbouring islands as you make your way through dense and humid rainforest with proliferations of elephant-ear ferns and bromeliads to the highest point on the island, often shrouded in clouds.

Another increasingly popular hike is to circumnavigate the Quill (at mid-height), dropping down into the **Miriam Schmidt Botanical Gardens** (open daily; free, but donations appreciated) on the southeast coast. Although in their very early stages of development (and underresourced and understaffed), the gardens offer a perfect picnic spot at the Lookout Garden, where shaded benches offer fine views across to St Kitts, and provide an excellent vantage point for spotting migrating humpback whales (Jan–April).

12

St Kitts and Nevis

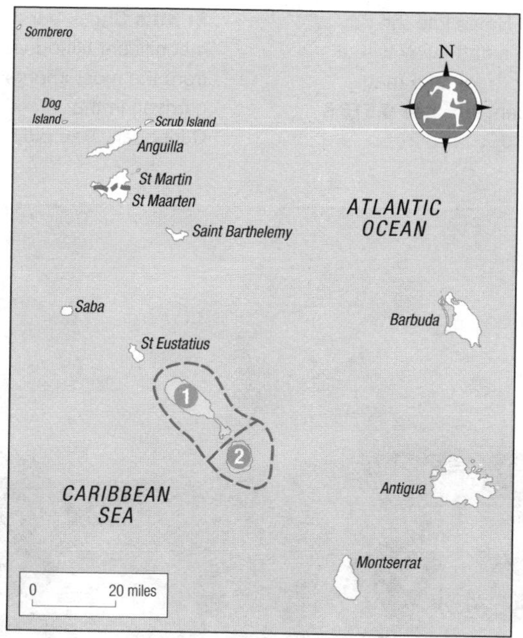

St Kitts and Nevis highlights

* **Windsurfing and mountain biking, Nevis** One of the West Indies premier destinations for outdoor activities, including triathlons. See p.512

* **Plantation inns, St Kitts and Nevis** Idle the day (and night) away with a good book at a magnificent inn. See p.515 & p.520

* **Monkeys, St Kitts** The chances of spotting green vervet monkeys are excellent on the southern peninsular. See p.517

* **Brimstone Hill Fortress, St Kitts** Check out the magnificent hilltop views from the most impressive garrison in the Caribbean. See p.518

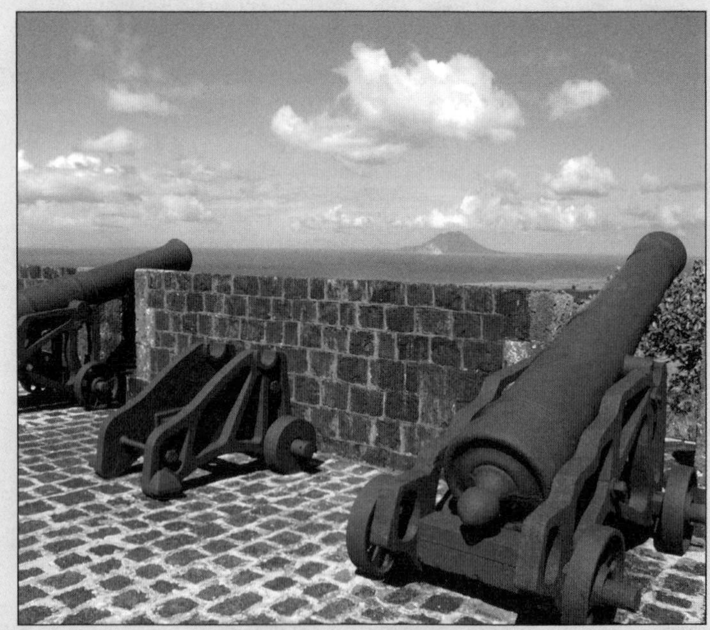

▲ Brimstone Hill Fortress

Introduction and basics

The islands of St Kitts (short for Saint Christopher's) and Nevis (from the Spanish *Nieves*, meaning 'snows' – see History, p.514), which together comprise the smallest nation in the Western Hemisphere, are unique in the Eastern Caribbean for their remarkable preservation of local culture. Nowhere else in the region will you find such pristine examples of British colonial architecture, gorgeous plantation inns and ramshackle sugar mills, together with genuine hospitality.

While there are ample opportunities for watersports, hiking, horseriding and mountain biking, just **kicking back** is the order of the day on both islands. And, for sheer atmosphere, St Kitts and Nevis' rambling **plantation inns** offer the islands' most captivating getaways; St Kitts' northern section or Nevis' Gingerland region have the largest concentration of inns.

With the exception of the sands at Nevis' Pinney's and Nisbet, the islands' **beaches** are nowhere near as grand as those in other parts of the Caribbean. Still, there are a good number to choose from, especially around St Kitts' **Frigate Bay area**. Nevis' options are less crowded, and ideal if privacy ranks high on your list.

Plentiful **marine life** and submerged **shipwrecks** provide interesting **diving** attractions, particularly on the Caribbean Sea side. Exhilarating **hiking** trails head into inland rainforests and up to the summits of Mount Nevis and St Kitts' Mount Liamuiga.

Last but not least, **Basseterre** and **Charlestown**, St Kitts' and Nevis' respective capitals, hold some interesting Caribbean heritage, including charming traditional skirt-and-blouse style houses.

Where to go

Being smaller and more intimate, Nevis has a slightly lower-key feel than its larger neighbour, though it outnumbers St Kitts in terms of luxury accommodation options. Nonetheless, the restored **plantation inns** on both islands make wonderful places to stay and eat. Both islands also have a smattering of budget-oriented apartments and guesthouses, and there's a campsite on St Kitts. If nightlife is important to you then look no further than the bright lights of **Frigate Bay** on St Kitts, which exceed anything its sister isle has to offer. An excellent **watersports** outfit on Nevis makes it the better destination for windsurfing; St Kitts has the more appealing **dive** sites.

When to go

The weather on St Kitts and Nevis is usually sunny and warm year-round with temperatures around 27 degrees celsius but the trade winds bring cool evenings from mid-December to mid-April; humidity and rainfall increase dramatically from September to November. Note that accommodation prices vary widely between the high season (Dec to mid-April) and the rest of the year.

Getting there

While modest in size, Nevis' **Newcastle Airport** is one of the newest and sleekest in the Caribbean, and recent refurbishments of St Kitts' larger **Robert Bradshaw Airport** just outside Basseterre have improved it as well. Both airports have plenty of **taxis** to hire and cars to rent while some hotels provide airport transfer.

On St Kitts, **cruise ships** dock at **Basseterre**'s deepwater **Port Zante**, capable of mooring ships up to 400ft in length. The port at **Charlestown** on Nevis is also able to receive liners, albeit smaller ones.

Regular **passenger ferries** run between the ports in Basseterre and Charlestown (☎ 869/466-4636 for information). Reservations are not required; passengers can simply show up for the 45-minute crossing and purchase tickets at the port – the last crossing is at 8pm. A small car ferry also operates from the end of the road on St Kitts

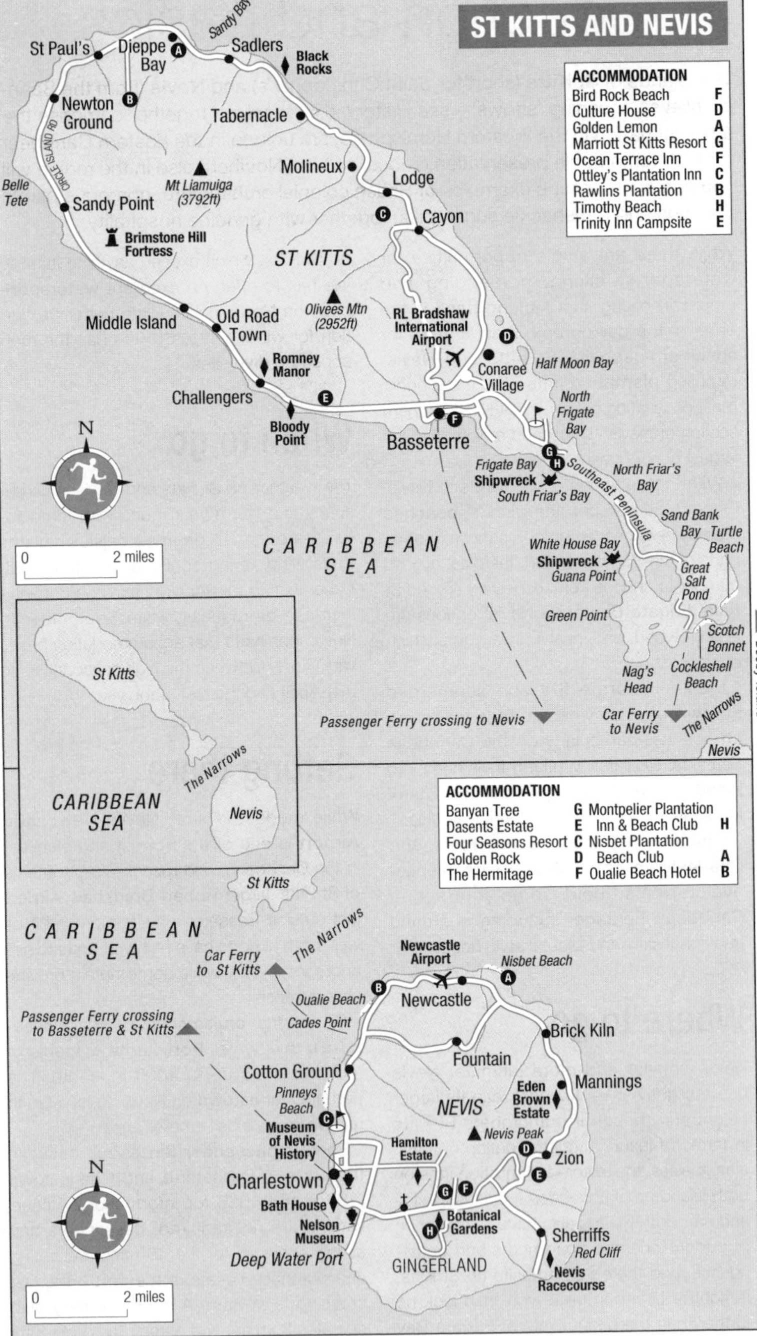

ST KITTS AND NEVIS
ACCOMMODATION
Bird Rock Beach F
Culture House D
Golden Lemon A
Marriott St Kitts Resort G
Ocean Terrace Inn F
Ottley's Plantation Inn C
Rawlins Plantation B
Timothy Beach H
Trinity Inn Campsite E
Sandy Bay
St Paul's
Dieppe Bay
Sadlers
Black Rocks
Newton Ground
Tabernacle
CIRCLE ISLAND RD
Molineux
Mt Liamuiga (3792ft)
Belle Tete
Lodge
Sandy Point
Cayon
Brimstone Hill Fortress
ST KITTS
Olivees Mtn (2952ft)
RL Bradshaw International Airport
Middle Island
Old Road Town
Romney Manor
Conaree Village
Half Moon Bay
Challengers
North Frigate Bay
Bloody Point
Basseterre
Frigate Bay
Shipwreck
South Friar's Bay
Southeast Peninsula
North Friar's Bay
Sand Bank Bay
Turtle Beach
CARIBBEAN SEA
White House Bay
Shipwreck
Guana Point
Great Salt Pond
Green Point
Scotch Bonnet
Booby Island
Nag's Head
Cockleshell Beach
Passenger Ferry crossing to Nevis
Car Ferry to Nevis
The Narrows
Nevis
N
0 2 miles
St Kitts
The Narrows
CARIBBEAN SEA
Nevis
ACCOMMODATION
Banyan Tree G
Dasents Estate E
Four Seasons Resort C
Golden Rock D
The Hermitage F
Montpelier Plantation Inn & Beach Club H
Nisbet Plantation Beach Club A
Oualie Beach Hotel B
St Kitts
CARIBBEAN SEA
The Narrows
Car Ferry to St Kitts
Newcastle Airport
Nisbet Beach
Oualie Beach
Newcastle
Passenger Ferry crossing to Basseterre & St Kitts
Cades Point
Brick Kiln
Fountain
Cotton Ground
Mannings
Pinneys Beach
Eden Brown Estate
NEVIS
Nevis Peak
Museum of Nevis History
Hamilton Estate
Zion
Charlestown
Bath House
Botanical Gardens
Nelson Museum
Sherriffs
Red Cliff
Deep Water Port
GINGERLAND
Nevis Racecourse
N
0 2 miles

Southeast Peninsular to near Cotton Ground on Nevis (ferry times are available by calling ⓣ869/662-7002).

Information

Each island has its own **tourism office** and official **website** with links to hotels and services that you can book yourself. The **St Kitts** tourism office is in Basseterre's Pelican Mall (Mon–Fri 8am–4.30pm; ⓣ869/465-4040, ⓦwww.stkittstourism.kn), while on **Nevis** it is located a two-minutes walk northeast of Charlestown's pier, on the east side of Main Street (Mon–Fri 8am–5pm, Sat 8am–noon; ⓣ869/469-7550, ⓦwww.nevisisland.com). Both are well staffed and can supply information and maps.

Other sources to try are the website of the St Kitts and Nevis Hotel and Tourism Association, ⓦwww.stkittsnevishta.org, which covers accommodation and tour operators, and, ⓦwww.stkittsnevis.co.uk, which provides useful lists of villas and apartments for rent.

Both islands' airports have staffed **information booths** with brochures, **maps**, transport details and dining guides.

Money and costs

The islands' currency is the **Eastern Caribbean dollar** (**EC$**), which comes in denominations of 5, 10, 20, 50 and 100 EC dollars, and coins in 1, 2, 5, 10 and 25 cents. Prices can be listed in either EC or US, but both currencies are accepted universally. The **rate of exchange** is fixed to the US dollar at EC$2.70 to US$1, although vendors normally convert at EC$2.5 to US$1, in their favour. Change will often be given in EC$, so try and carry bills in small denominations if you want to avoid this. **Credit cards** are taken in hotels and the more touristed shops and restaurants. **Traveller's cheques** are also accepted; visitors are advised to take cheques in US$ to avoid further conversions.

While both islands are **fairly expensive** even by Caribbean standards, you can get by on a budget with a little care, though some of the lesser guesthouses are hardly spectacular and most local-oriented eateries are only open at lunchtime. **Banks** have offices in each island capital; **opening hours** are Mon–Thurs 8am–2pm and Fri 8am–4pm, with some also open on Saturday morning. **ATMs** can be found at the banks, the airports and in some of the larger hotels such as the *Marriott*. Those at the *Marriott* and Royal Bank dispense US$ while all others issue EC$.

A **service charge** of around 10 percent is added to most restaurant and hotel bills, so tipping is not normally necessary. A **government tax** is added on all bills as well, 8 percent on Nevis and 9 percent on St Kitts. A cash-only **departure tax** is payable at the airports of US$22 or EC$54.

Getting around

The **roads** on both islands are mixed in quality. To drive on the islands, you'll need to purchase a temporary driver's licence for EC$62, valid for three months and available from car rental agencies. The many big chains and local car rental operators offer plenty of choice and competition but prices are generally high(US$60/day minimum for a basic vehicle). Note that if you intend to split your time between Nevis and St Kitts, some agencies arrange dual-island rental packages – and a car ferry also exists between the islands. Driving is on the **left-hand side**. **Rental firms** on St Kitts include Bullseye (ⓣ869/465-5656), Avis (ⓣ869/465-6507) and Thrifty/TDC (ⓣ869/465-2991); on Nevis there's also Thrifty/TDC (ⓣ869/469-1005) and Noel's (ⓣ869/469-5199). **Scooter** rental is not advised on St Kitts on account of heavy traffic, but are great for Nevis; rent from 3kB (ⓣ869/765-7701 or 469-5235; US$25/day).

Public **minibuses** serve north and west St Kitts and all of Nevis from 6am until around 7pm, Mon–Sat; service is sporadic on all evenings and on Sundays. The lively music-blaring minivans are easy to spot; you can catch them in the capitals or flag them down on the main roads outside of town; keep in mind that they do not follow any particular schedule. **Fares** are based on distance, with the most expensive trip on both islands costing EC$5; pay on alighting. When you board just call out your destination and the driver and other passengers will make sure you get off in the right place. **Note** that in

St Kitts, no buses serve the resort areas south of Basseterre, you'll have to drive yourself or take a taxi which will run about US$20.

Taxis congregate at both airports and by the piers downtown. There's no shortage of drivers and correct fares are generally kept to, (eg on St Kitts US$15 from the airport to downtown Basseterre; $20/40/60 from downtown to Ottley's/Brimstone Hill/Rawlins respectively. On Nevis, standard fares from Charlestown to Oualie Beach or Hermitage run at US$20) with surcharges of 50 percent between 10pm and 6am, for hefty luggage and for more than four passengers. To call for a taxi in St Kitts, dial ⓣ869/664-4592 or 465-8487 or 4253; in Nevis, call ⓣ869/469-9790 (airport taxi stand) or ⓣ869/469-1483 or 5631 (Charlestown). Several hotels and tour operators also offer private **shuttle services** between the airport and resorts and the beach.

Food and drink

In addition to the elaborate **dining** on offer in the plantation inns and upmarket hotels (which can cost US$70 for a three-course set-menu meal), there are a number of inexpensive spots to grab a bite, particularly on the beaches and in the capitals. The most luxurious offering is spiny lobster, though other seafood specialities include stewed saltfish, the national dish, and flying fish, served grilled and in sandwiches. The plantation inns have full West Indian/Euro-Asian **menus**, while Jamaican-inspired dishes such as **jerk chicken** and rotis are common at smaller restaurants and some beach grills, usually for less than US$8. **Vegetarians** are reasonably well catered for in most spots.

Most **bars** serve imported beers, spirits and wines though St Kitts does have its own Guinness brewery. One of the most popular **drinks** is a CSR (Cane Spirit Rothschild), a clear sugar-cane liqueur, mixed with Ting, a tangy, grapefruit soda.

Mails and communications

Smart Phone **kiosks** are scattered around the islands and take EC dollar coins and phonecards, sold at the many shops, hotels or at the Cable and Wireless offices on Canyon Street in Basseterre (ⓣ869/465-1000) and Main Street in Charlestown (ⓣ869/469-5000). These offices are open throughout the week and on Saturday morning. To **place a call** within St Kitts or Nevis, just dial the full seven-digit number.

The **post office** for Nevis is located on Main Street in Charlestown (Mon–Fri 8am–3.30pm; ⓣ869/469 5521), while the main post office for St Kitts is situated just off the Circus in Basseterre (Mon & Tues 8am–4pm, Wed–Fri 8am–3.30pm; ⓣ869/465 2521). **Internet access** is readily available at downtown locations all over Charlestown and Basseterre (normally EC$3 per half-hour).

The **country code** for both islands is ⓣ869.

Opening hours, holidays and festivals

Opening hours for most businesses are typically Mon–Fri 9am–4pm, though many retailers and restaurants are open much longer and at the weekend. St Kitts and Nevis celebrate the Queen's Birthday on the second Saturday in June, August Monday on the first Monday in August, which celebrates emancipation from slavery, and Independence Day on September 19. Some businesses on St Kitts also shut down during **festivals**, such as **Carnival**, which runs from just before Christmas until just after New Year's. Three-week long **Culturama** takes place on Nevis in late July through to the emancipation holiday, with music performances and beauty pageants celebrating local culture and island unity, while the **Nevis Triathlon** is fast becoming a major event in mid-March.

Sports and outdoor activities

As you would expect, St Kitts and Nevis have plenty of **watersports**, including scuba diving and snorkelling. On land the islands offer spectacular **golfing** facilities and you can go **horseriding, mountain biking** or **hiking**.

Diving and watersports

St Kitts has seen pirates carrying out assaults on treasure-laden ships, brutal naval battles, hurricanes, and – as the Leeward Islands' hub for the slave trade – plenty of merchant ships. The end result of all this sea faring traffic is thousands of **shipwrecks** in the waters around the island, with up to 300 in Basseterre Harbour alone. Despite this potential, St Kitts is not particularly well developed for **diving**, with only a handful of wrecks identified to date and just fifteen dive sites and three PADI-recognized resorts: St Kitts Scuba (Ⓣ869/466-8744, Ⓦwww.stkittsscuba.com), Kenneth's Dive Centre (Ⓣ869/465-2670, Ⓦwww.kennethsdivecenter.com) and Pro Divers (Ⓣ869/466-3483, Ⓦwww.prodiversstkitts.com).

That said, St Kitts' Caribbean side, where the majority of the sites are found, is well-sheltered and visibility underwater is typically in the 60–100ft range. Dive locations are easily reachable and accommodate all levels; the 144ft cargo ship **River Taw**, a very good wreck for novices to check out, was deliberately sunk in 1981 to create an artificial reef. Octopus, stingrays, lobster, nurse sharks, lizard fish and turtles can often be found, especially at **Monkey Shoals,** a square-mile coral atoll situated about three miles offshore, directly between St Kitts and Nevis.

For other **watersports** on St Kitts, visit *Mr X's Shiggidy Shack* in Frigate Bay, or *Reggae Beach Bar* at Cockleshell Beach (see St Kitts Restaurants).

On **Nevis,** just one dive operator is PADI-recognized: Scuba Safaris (Ⓣ869/469-9518, Ⓦwww.scubanevis.com) at Oualie Beach Resort offer a full range of dive packages and also operate tours for the *Four Seasons*, including a popular half-day snorkel tour with a marine biologist. Popular outfit **Windsurf Nevis** (Ⓣ869/469-9682, Ⓦwww.windsurfnevis.com) is also based at Oualie Beach, with a resident pro providing expert lessons.

Other activities

Unique for the Caribbean (except for Cuba), the **St Kitts Scenic Railway** is a double-decker air-conditioned train that takes you around the island past historic sites, villages and disused sugar plantations. Refreshments and musical entertainment are provided, as is a running commentary. The trip takes around four hours to complete; tickets can be purchased directly from the railway station near the airport (Ⓣ869/465-7263, Ⓦwww.stkittsscenicrailway.com). Many hotels also offer the trip at discounted rates.

With rainforest covering St Kitts' central mountain range thinning out to dense bushy cover, the island has interesting **hiking** opportunities; guides advised due to unclear trails. Greg's Safaris (Ⓣ869/465-4121, Ⓦwww.gregsafaris.com) offers half-day treks in the rainforest area, as well as more strenuous five-hour climbs up **Mt Liamuiga** and into its dormant volcanic crater. Other guides are available through the tourist office.

On Nevis there's a trail known as the **Upper Round Road** that connects the old plantations; this is excellent to **hike**, **mountain bike** or ride along on **horseback**. Wooded, rough and rocky in places, the higher the altitude you reach the better the views and the more rainforested the terrain becomes. The challenging hike up **Nevis Peak** itself is a six-hour trip; Top to Bottom (Ⓣ869/469-9080, Ⓦwww.walknevis.com) has numerous guided treks; local herbologist Michael Herbert (Ⓣ869/469-3512) also makes the ascent with interesting commentary. **Mountain Bike Nevis** offers tours and equipment at Oualie Beach (Ⓣ869/469-9682, Ⓦwww.mountainbikenevis.com) while Nevis Equestrian Centre (Ⓣ869/469-8118, Ⓦwww.ridenevis.com) features **horseriding** around the trails and beaches. Lastly, Nevis' (and possibly the Caribbean's) largest and grandest **spa** is located at the *Four Seasons* resort (Ⓣ869/469-1111), with hot and cold pools and a variety of body treatments and facials available. More reasonably priced massages are available at Carol's Beauty Haven at Cotton Ginnery Mall in Charlestown (Ⓣ869/668-5158).

History

The first settlements on St Kitts and Nevis existed around the coastal areas over 4000 years ago. The pre-ceramic Sibonay were followed by Arawak colonists from the area now known as Venezuela; the Caribs arrived later. St Kitts was known as Liamuiga (Fertile Land), while the Carib name for Nevis was Oualie (Land of Beautiful Water).

Christopher Columbus and his crew sighted the islands on their second New World voyage in 1493 and claimed them for Spain, naming them **San Jorge** and **Nuesta Señora de Las Nieves** ("our lady of the snows"), but otherwise left them to the Caribs. Contrary to popular belief, Columbus did not name St Kitts (a shortening of St Christopher's) after himself; rather, the moniker San Cristóbal came later on from inaccuracies in Spanish maps. This in turn was anglicized to "St Christopher's" after Englishman **Sir Thomas Warner** came ashore in 1623 and established Old Road Town. A small posse sailed for Nevis five years later and set up a camp called Jamestown near Cotton Ground that was destroyed by a tsunami in 1680. Local mythology has it that in certain conditions the submerged town can be seen.

Having been defeated by the Spanish, the first **French** colony in the Caribbean was formed on St Kitts in 1625, willingly accepted by Warner as increased opposition to the threat posed by the oppressed **Caribs**. Their combined European legions decimated the Caribs in a battle in 1626 at **Bloody Point**, where the river was said to have run red with the Caribs' blood for several days; women and children survivors were kept as concubines and slaves.

After the battle, the island was split between the two colonial superpowers, with the French lording over the northern and southern coasts and establishing the modern-day capital, **Basseterre**, and the British controlling the leftover areas in between. The Europeans turned on each other with great regularity, culminating in a one-month siege of the British fort **Brimstone Hill** in 1782. The **Treaty of Paris**, signed the following year, officially returned St Kitts to the British; the squabbles ended and many French settlers left for other islands.

Nevis, meanwhile, had no part in the struggle, and instead became the region's most profitable **sugar cane** producer and destination of choice for Britain's rich and famous thanks to its natural spas. In the last quarter of the seventeenth century the plantations made both of the islands amongst the richest in the Caribbean with labour supplied by African slaves and indentured Europeans. The islands became the depot for the **slave trade** in the Leeward Islands with up to 11,000 passing through annually until **emancipation** in 1838.

The two islands were joined as an **independent federated state** in 1983, though Nevis has made two failed attempts at seceding. Today the islands maintain their own traditions, as well as choosing to compete separately in **cricket**, the national sport. In 2005 the government closed the then heavily subsidised **sugar** industry, and consequently the island's economy has become almost entirely dependent on **tourism**. Although a range of current large-scale developments are impacting negatively on local environments, for the moment neither island has become overdeveloped.

12.1

St Kitts

Paddle-shaped **St Kitts** lies a few miles northwest of Nevis, just across The Narrows. Lush rainforest covers the central mountain range that forms the island's spine, while the surrounding lowlands are largely given over to disused sugar cane fields and small-scale agriculture. Most visitors tend to head directly to the resort area of **Frigate Bay**, focusing their time in the southern region where all of the island's beaches are found. The best beaches fringe the rapidly developing **Southeast Peninsula**, an undulating spit of land with the island's only white sand.

Nearer to St Kitts' centre, the capital, **Basseterre**, merits a visit for its concentration of traditional skirt-and-blouse-style houses, while traces of the island's imperial past lie closer to its north end, where the star attraction, **Brimstone Hill Fortress**, presides over the Caribbean. The **northern** and **Atlantic coasts** have their own quiet appeal, with fields of overgrown sugar cane sheltering gracious former plantation inns above dramatic coastal vistas.

Accommodation

The majority of St Kitts' **accommodation** is centred on resorts around **Frigate Bay**, though resorts and timeshares on the **Southeast Peninsula** are fast catching up. The north has a variety of **plantation inns** that offer smaller-scale exclusive lodging, while one or two **budget** options are dotted around north and west of Basseterre.

Bird Rock Beach Basseterre ⓣ869/465-8914, ⓦwww.birdrockbeach.com. With the only real beach around Basseterre, this hotel features 46 standard doubles and a swim-up pool bar, along with botanical gardens and tennis courts. Dive St Kitts is situated on the premises. Good value all-inclusive option available. ④

Culture House Conaree ⓣ869/466-1940, ⓦwww.stkittsculturehouse.com. Part guesthouse, part record label, part bar, the *Culture House* is the island's best budget option, with an inimitable and friendly owner. The large concrete structure lies just north of Basseterre and the airport (public bus possible during daytimes) close to windswept but attractive Conaree Bay. The five rooms are plain but comfortable with private bathrooms and cable TV; the onsite lounge/bar, though resembling a nightclub, won't disturb your sleep. Good, imaginative breakfast included. ②

Golden Lemon Dieppe Bay ⓣ869/465-7260, ⓦwww.goldenlemon.com. Picturesque and comfortable, this inn has a splendid location behind Dieppe Bay village, right on a black-sand beach with offshore reef. Eight spacious rooms in the seventeenth-century main house and eighteen luxurious villas with full kitchens and private plunge pools. ⑨

Ocean Terrace Inn Basseterre ⓣ869/465-2754, ⓦwww.oceanterraceinn.com. Basseterre's most luxurious hotel, with tropical gardens overlooking the bay, a "fantasy pool" with waterfalls and Jacuzzi, fitness centre, dive shop and the superb *Waterfalls* restaurant. Choices of accommodation include suites or apartments with kitchenettes. ⑥

Ottley's Plantation Inn ⓣ869/465-7234, ⓦwww.ottleys.com. Preserving a distinctly old-world ambience, this property has been painstakingly restored by its friendly New Jersey owners. The spacious supreme rooms or cottage suites, designed in colonial mahogany style and with private plunge pool, stand amongst the Caribbean's top accommodations and well worth the extra cost compared to the smaller standard rooms in the Great House. Other major selling points are the gourmet *Royal Palm* restaurant, the manicured grounds, onsite rainforest walk and helpful staff. Spa and tennis also on offer. ⑧

Rawlins Plantation ⓣ869/465-6221, ⓦwww.rawlinsplantation.com. Situated above extensive cane fields inland from the northern coastline, *Rawlins* is the island's most serene property, with a breathtaking view across the Caribbean to St Eustatius, and truly exquisite gardens. Bountiful fruit trees surround each antique-furnished stone cottage, and the library sitting room and restaurant terrace both have an authentic plantation feel; the new (owner-designed) prefab-style suites, whilst luxurious, may not be to everyone's taste. 8

Timothy Beach Frigate Bay ⓣ869/465-8597, ⓦwww.timothybeach.com. A laid-back hotel on the unexceptional South Frigate Bay beach. The sixty rooms, with king-size beds, a/c and wicker furniture, are not fancy but good value. Apartments with kitchens also available. 4

Trinity Inn Apartments Palmetto Point ⓣ869/465-3226, ⓦwww.trinityinnapartments.com. Slightly dilapidated property, but with comfortable rooms, with kitchenette, 2. The property is fifteen minutes drive west of Basseterre (bus available), with onsite pool and campsite, 1.

Basseterre

Settled by the French following the partition of St Kitts in 1628, the island capital, **Basseterre**, on the Caribbean coast, is French in name only today. Although boasting some Georgian architecture and a selection of reasonable quality **restaurants** and **bars**, it is not a particularly attractive town, of interest mainly for its hustle and bustle – made more frantic by street reggae and soca sound systems – and as the place to catch ferries, buses and taxis. You'll not need more than half a day to fully explore the town before heading on to more interesting island attractions.

With the recent growth in the number of **cruise ships** visiting the city, a new harbour facility, **Port Zante**, has been built for the purpose of retailing imported jewellery and overpriced souvenirs to shop-hungry tourists. Whilst lacking local soul, the development has brought much-needed employment to the city, as well as an expansion in facilities; alongside a couple of smart cafés, there's a new **tourist office**, Internet centre and post office in the adjoining **Pelican Mall** building. Upstairs in the neighbouring Old Treasury Building is the **St Christopher Heritage Society Museum**, which holds a decent collection of photographs, documents and colourful paintings from slavery days to independence and carnival (Mon–Sat 9am–4pm; ⓣ869/465-5584; EC$5).

The centre of Basseterre, **The Circus**, reflects the town's British dominion; the roundabout circling the green **Berkeley Memorial Clock** is allegedly modelled after London's Piccadilly, though the only obvious similarity is the traffic. Traces of British rule also appear in **Independence Square**, the historical town centre due east, where walkways imitating the spokes of a Union Jack are inlaid with red stones. A maiden-topped fountain at its nexus, a gift from Queen Elizabeth to commemorate St Kitts' independence in 1983, marks the spot that once hosted the Lesser Antilles' largest **slave market**; slaves were bathed at the small red fountain on the square's south side prior to mounting the stage. The square looks onto the staid 1927 **Immaculate Conception Cathedral**, its substantial twin-towered facade devoid of the drama associated with Anglican **St George's**, a few blocks northwest of the Circus. The latter church was built on the site of the former French parish, incinerated by the British in 1706.

Basseterre's most remarkable aspect, however, are its ingenious traditional **skirt-and-blouse homes** built with stone ground floors topped by wooden levels – the stone prevented flooding, the wood allowed a breeze – and trimmed with dainty gingerbread fretwork. On **Fort Street** in particular, old sentinel walls have been incorporated into their construction, whilst others were rebuilt using stones from Brimstone Hill Fortress (see p.518) following an 1867 fire that ravaged the town. (Note that if you want to take pictures of private homes, you should get the owner's permission first.)

Frigate Bay

St Kitts' only beach resort area, **FRIGATE BAY** lies three miles southeast of the capital on flatlands sandwiched by the Atlantic and Caribbean. On the Atlantic side is **North Frigate Bay Beach**, a deep golden band fronting unswimmable water except at the *Marriott* (Ⓣ869/466-1200, Ⓦwww.stkittsmarriott.com) hotel's section where an artificial reef has pacified the strong undertow. This 1000-room resort is one of the Caribbean's largest, with shopping, swimming pools, golf course and **entertainment** options such as a **casino**, bars and restaurants (open to non-guests except during peak times such as Christmas).

On the calmer Caribbean side, the narrow South Frigate Bay (also known as **Timothy Beach**) is the island's **nightlife** hot spot and has a couple of watersports outfits providing snorkelling gear, windsurfers and kayaks; snorkelling trips to nearby reefs and shipwrecks are readily available at negotiable prices.

Southeast Peninsula

The **Southeast Peninsula**, which extends towards Nevis from Frigate Bay, boasts grassy peaks and St Kitts' finest beaches, which only became publicly accessible when a road was built in 1990. Much of the peninsular has now been sold off to international hotel and timeshare interests, and construction beginning in 2008 will see the completion of a number of properties including a giant *Ritz Carlton* resort and, controversially, the conversion of much of the island's only **salt pond** into a new mooring facility for luxury yachts. Still, for the time being, much of the peninsula offers natural peacefulness – you're likely to spot one of the island's numerous green vervet monkeys as you head south towards the most happening pocket, **Cockleshell Beach**, home to a lively restaurant frequented by day-trippers. The shores around **Booby Island**, an islet facing the beach, abound with marine life and provide good snorkelling and diving.

Halfway down the western coast, **White House Bay** has some of the best snorkelling on the island thanks to a shallow-lying shipwreck, while **North Friar's Bay** and **South Friar's Bay** get more visitors due to their proximity to Frigate Bay – all have plentiful bars and shacks serving a variety of refreshments.

Along the Circle Island Road

The northern part of St Kitts, traversed by the **CIRCLE ISLAND ROAD**, is best seen on a full-day excursion – with a good part of it at Brimstone Hill Fortress. If you're not already staying at one of St Kitts' charming **plantation inns** that are concentrated in this part of the island, the drive could be broken up with lunch or dinner at *Rawlins* or *Ottley's* – the island's best West Indian restaurants. Abandoned sugar cane fields dominate the area's landscape, with windmills, ramshackle churches and sleepy villages sprinkled about.

Bloody Point to Middle Island

Passing the large American veterinary school that provides a good chunk of island income, the first stop of note on the Circle Island Road is four miles north of Basseterre – **Bloody Point**, a hillock on the outskirts of **Challengers** village that witnessed a brutal Carib massacre in 1626. A one-hour hike affords glimpses of cartoon-like petroglyphs engraved into the rocky hillside.

After the point, the road heads down to the seaside village of **Old Road Town**, the island's first settlement under Sir Thomas Warner's tenure; the only remnant is a derelict red-brick building that once served as Government House. Better maintained are the **petroglyphs** that predate Warner's arrival, etched on a boulder along the nearby road signposted to Romney Manor; the pregnant-looking character is a fertility idol. At the end of this signposted road you'll find the estate of **Romney Manor**, its smart yellow cottages now home to **Caribelle Batik** (Mon–Fri 8.30am–4pm; Ⓣ869/465-6253,

Ⓦwww.caribellebatikstkitts.com), a popular handicraft boutique. The grounds feature a botanical garden (free) with a 350-year-old saman tree as its centrepiece. The derelict ruins of a sugar plantation lie below, notable for the extensive aqueduct that's used today as the departure point for rainforest hikes.

Back on the main road, another mile north along the Caribbean coast lies **Middle Island** village, where an unkempt cemetery contains Sir Thomas Warner's extravagant marble tomb.

Brimstone Hill Fortress National Park

A few miles north of Middle Island, the tremendously impressive 800ft **Brimstone Hill** hulks over the flatlands, its name derived from the sulphuric odours exuding from nearby underwater vents. The British must not have minded the smell since they chose the site to support a **fortress** so grand it was nicknamed the "Gibraltar of the West Indies". Begun in 1690 and expanded over the following century with slave labour, the sprawling garrison ultimately proved insufficient defence – it was captured in 1782 after a month-long siege by 8000 French soldiers. A treaty forced its return a year later, but the fortress fell into disuse as the politics of sugar cane production stabilized and relations eased between the warring nations. Abandoned in 1853, an ambitious restoration project begun in 1965 has returned the fortress to its former splendour, and earned it UNESCO World Heritage Site recognition.

The prominent hilltop compound, the **Citadel** (daily 9.30am–5.30pm; Ⓣ869/465-2609, Ⓦwww.brimstonehillfortress.org; EC$20) provides spectacular views from its parapets, and the cannons and turrets impart rich historical atmosphere. The enclosing barracks house an engaging **museum** showcasing military paraphernalia, Carib and slavery artefacts and a rubbing of the petroglyphs at Old Road Town. On the grassy parade, stairs access the lower bastions on a promontory with a tiny **military cemetery** outside the rampart walls. Snacks and souvenirs are available. Note that the **bus** to Brimstone Hill drops you off on the main road, a steep 2km walk or hitchhike away.

Sandy Point to Black Rocks

Beyond the fortress the road passes the remains of **Fort Charles**, a 1672 military outpost used as a leper colony from 1890 to 1995, before reaching **SANDY POINT**, St Kitts' second largest town. The point itself is a rather grubby black-sand beach, while the town occupies the spot on which Thomas Warner and his crew came ashore in 1623. Sandy Point was the centre of the island's tobacco trade in the seventeenth century, and the most fascinating sight in the town is the tobacco warehouses that were constructed during this time.

Lying in the flatlands below the crater-capped **Mount Liamuiga**, the island's highest point at 3792ft, the northern coast retains windswept ocean vistas and the ruins of abandoned sugar plantations. *Rawlins Plantation Inn* makes for an excellent lunch or drink stop, and neighbouring art gallery Kate Design (Ⓦwww.katedesign.com) showcases some engaging island watercolours. The main settlement this far north, **Dieppe Bay**, is a former French village that marks the start of the Atlantic coast, while a couple of miles further is St Kitts' natural wonder, **BLACK ROCKS**, a jumble of solidified black pyroclastic lava formations that tumble into the sea; there's a viewing area signposted to the left of the main road.

Eating, drinking and nightlife

The best places **to eat** on St Kitts are in *Ottley's* and *Rawlins* **plantation inns** – even if you're not an overnight guest, you should make it a point to experience some of their old-world ambience. **Reservations** are required, particularly in peak season, and *Rawlins* often provides transport from Frigate Bay. Aside from extravagant dining, there are plenty of inexpensive spots in the **capital** and at **Frigate Bay** to grab a bite. Try the harbourfront in Basseterre for truly delicious fish on Friday and Saturday nights for a fraction of the price you would pay elsewhere.

As for **drinking** and **nightlife**, one of the Caribbean's most genuine and hippest spots is known simply as "The Strip" in **Frigate Bay**, where nights (especially **Fridays**) are spent at a series of open-air casual beach bars – which become more like nightclubs after midnight at the weekends. Each one has its own feel and music selection (*Ziggy's* has live music Sat), and are frequented by a refreshing mix of young locals, tourists, and American vet students from the large residences nearby. Aside from The Strip, most entertainment centres on the **hotels** and the *Mariott* casino, bars and nightclub. Look out also for occasional live shows in Basseterre.

Ballahoo Basseterre ☎869/465-4197. Perched on an airy verandah overlooking The Circus roundabout, this restaurant is popular with the cruise ship crowd and has a fine Caribbean and international seafood menu, including superb lobster thermidor (US$25–40). Closed Sun.

Circus Grill Bar and Restaurant Basseterre ☎869/465-0143. The large choice of items on the menu ranges from lobster to omelettes, with several vegetarian options. At the fully stocked bar you can try house cocktails or Planter's (rum) Punch.

Fisherman's Wharf Basseterre ☎869/465-2754. Moderately priced, tasty seafood served at picnic tables on a breezy pier; head to the buffet to pile on extra fixings like Creole rice and macaroni pie.

Marshall's Horizon Villa ☎869/466-8245. The most upscale option in Frigate Bay, this resort restaurant has a swanky poolside setting and opulent Euro/Caribbean seafood, steaks and poultry – try the Scallop and Coriander Wantons appetizer. Dinner only.

Mr X's Shiggidy Shack Bar and Grill Timothy Beach ☎869/663-3983. One of the strip's beachside shacks, offering grilled fish, lobster and chicken in traditional Kittitian style. Live music and a bonfire some mid-week nights.

Reggae Beach Bar Cockleshell Beach, Southeast Peninsular ☎869/762-5050. Having moved across from soon-to-be-built-on Turtle Beach, this relaxed spot is perfect for hanging out on an afternoon, enjoy a cocktail or barbequed lunch and have a swim or snorkel in the crystal-clear waters.

PJ's Pizza Bar and Restaurant Island Paradise Condos, Frigate Bay ☎869/465-8373. A good option, serving Italian cuisine and pizzas in an informal setting; gets lively Sun nights. They will even deliver to your hotel room, which can be much cheaper than room service. Closed Mon.

12.2

Nevis

Teeming with wild bougainvillaea and hibiscus, and sprinkled with vine-encrusted windmills, tiny **NEVIS**' rural beauty and backwater charm make it distinctive in the Caribbean, and are the keys to its appeal. Most sightseeing here consists of poking around the enchanting capital, **Charlestown**, where well-preserved skirt-and-blouse homes and a couple of excellent history museums provide an easy afternoon's distraction.

Outside the capital, you can wander about the odd country church, go horseback riding in the hinterlands, hike up Mount Nevis, snorkel off the coast or – as many visitors do – spend most of your time on one of the four white-sand **beaches**. The island is small enough that it can be experienced on a **day-trip** from St Kitts – though to get a good feel of the island you'll need a couple of days.

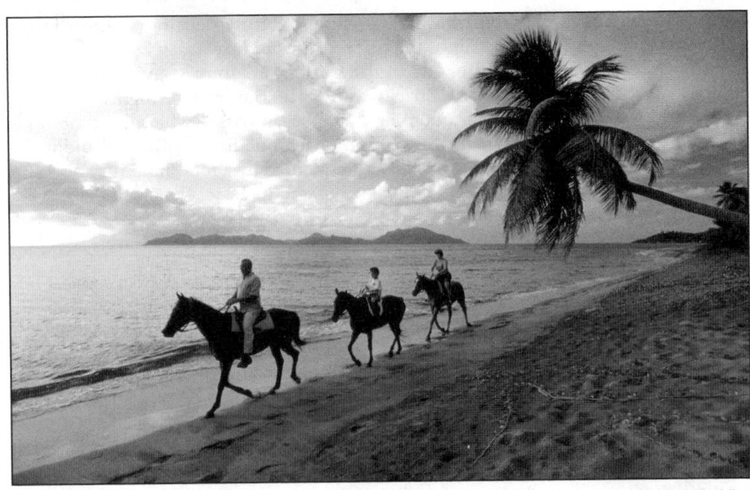
▲ Horse-back riding

Accommodation

Despite its small size, there are plenty of **accommodation** options on Nevis, ranging from luxury five-star resorts to villas and guesthouses. The five historic **plantation inns** on the island are all in Gingerland and eastwards, within a few miles of one another and accessed off the main road.

Banyan Tree Morning Star ⓣ869/469-3449, ⓦwww.banyantreebandb.com. Tucked away off the main road two miles east of Charlestown and with sweeping views of the ocean, this friendly American-owned guesthouse is set amongst banana and citrus groves on the slopes of Mount Nevis, perfect for hiking. The three smart and comfortable rooms have antique furniture, whilst Blackbelly sheep and other animals keep you company outside. Breakfast included. 4

Dasents Sugar Mill Estate Gingerland ⓣ869/469-2571 or 667-8768, ⓔrobliz69@yahoo.co.uk. Nevis' best-value property is in the southeast of the island, and set around the estate's old sugar mill. The one-bedroom cottage with kitchenette and two other self-contained apartments are all rustic but homely, and very private. Together with the property's gorgeous pool set amongst six acres of overgrown fruit trees and views across to Montserrat and Antigua make this is an extremely relaxing location. 2

Four Seasons Resort Pinney's Beach ⓣ869/469-6238, ⓦwww.fourseasons.com/nevis. Set on its own stretch of golden sand and attractively designed to blend in with its surroundings, this is one of the Caribbean's most exclusive resorts. Recent guests have apparently included Will Smith, George Bush and Bill Gates – and with ten tennis courts, an award-winning championship golf course and giant and luxurious spa, it's not hard to see why. 9

Golden Rock Gingerland ⓣ869/469-3346, ⓦwww.golden-rock.com. The relaxed *Golden Rock* has a number of homey rooms scattered about a newly restored 1815 plantation, with cosy communal areas, a tropical courtyard and a swimming pool perched 1000ft above sea level. 7

The Hermitage Gingerland ⓣ869/469-3477, ⓦwww.hermitagenevis.com. The island's oldest inn is its most attractive – a 1740 estate with antique-furnished colonial style cottages placed around the Great House. Also offers packages that include horseriding trips, hiking and jeep rental, weddings or scuba diving. 8

Montpelier Plantation Inn and Beach Club Charlestown ⓣ869/469-3462, ⓦwww.montpeliernevis.com. This exclusive and luxurious private hideaway spreads over sixty acres including beautifully landscaped gardens, with seventeen recently refurbished rooms. Once hosting the wedding of Admiral Lord Nelson, this is considered one of the best inns on the island, with facilities including a swimming pool, gourmet restaurant and private beach. 9

Nisbet Plantation Beach Club St James ☎869/469 9325, www.nisbetplantation.com. Occupying thirty acres backing a fine beach, with accommodation options ranging from small cottage rooms to one-bedroom suites. There are three good restaurants, including one overlooking the immaculate palm-lined lawn. 9

Oualie Beach Hotel Oualie Beach ☎869/469-9735, www.oualiebeach.com. Thirty-four casual, pretty gingerbread cottages right on the beach. Each has a mahogany four-poster bed, cable TV, screened-in verandah and free Wi-Fi. Very convenient for watersports including snorkelling, windsurfing and ocean kayaks, as well as mountain biking, all of which are organized through professional onsite outfits. 6

Charlestown and around

Nevis' small capital, captivating **Charlestown**, boasts an impeccable assemblage of skirt-and-blouse houses, in keeping with residents' often old-fashioned attitudes. A few scruffier, more modern buildings are around but overall the town is more attractive than its neighbour's capital, Basseterre.

Charlestown's traditional attitudes can be seen in the 1825 **courthouse** on a day when someone is being tried for swearing in public; admittedly now rare, you would see the defendant sitting in a draconian crib-like prisoner's box. Check out the upstairs **library** with its heavy-set ceiling braced by mahogany gunwales. **Hot outdoor springs** near the 1778 Bath House (closed since the 1950s but always rumoured to be reopening soon) at the south end of town are fed by volcanic sulphur, and remain as invigorating as when Lord Nelson's troops bathed in them; bring a towel and don your suit in advance, as there are no facilities. The water temperature is a constant 40°C and is not the place to cool off but the springs do have reputed therapeutic properties.

The best place to garner some island background is at the quaint **Museum of Nevis History** on Main St (Mon–Fri 8am–4pm, Sat 9am–noon; US$3). The informative collection of odds and ends occupies the main floor of a Georgian-style building on the grounds where Alexander Hamilton was born in 1757. Near the hot springs at the opposite end of town, the **Horatio Nelson Museum** on Building Hill Rd (Mon–Fri 8am–4pm, Sat 9am–noon; US$3) focuses on Lord Nelson, who came ashore in 1785 and wound up marrying the governor's niece, Fanny Nisbet. While the collection consists mainly of kitsch and some pilaster copies of Nelson's Column, it gives a captivating overview of Nelson's Caribbean adventures. Along Government Road lies a remnant of another chapter in Nevisian history, a **Jewish cemetery** whose oldest stone dates from 1684. It is thought that a nearby grey-stone building served as a **synagogue**.

Just a fifteen-minute walk from the Charlestown pier, you'll find by far the most popular beach on Nevis, **Pinney's Beach**. Some areas of sand are open to the public around *Sunshine* and *Chevy's* beach bars, though the best-manicured area belongs to the *Four Seasons* resort. At the northern end of the four-mile-long beach you'll find a smattering of rusty cannons and crumbling bastions belonging to **Fort Ashby**, one of eight fortifications that defended the coast in the 1700s.

Oualie and Nisbet beaches

Further up the west coast from Charlestown, **OUALIE BEACH** graces a calm cove with the island's most reputable watersports and outdoor activities outfits right on the sand. You can rent snorkelling gear and organize half-day outings from here. After Oualie, the island road wraps around the northern slopes of Mount Nevis and passes the airport before reaching attractive **NISBET BEACH**, although a substantial portion of it has been damaged by erosion. Its deep white sand, facing the Atlantic, is scattered with elegant coconut trees strung with hammocks.

Along the Atlantic coast to Gingerland

Nevis' **Atlantic coast**, a scenic haven of rustic settlements with evocative names like Brick Kiln, is completely devoid of resorts and beachfront but nonetheless worth the detour for its historic remnants and panoramic views. Centuries-old stone ovens line the road and some houses rest on piled rocks, holdouts from the days when landless squatters had to move from plantation to plantation.

Rambling **GINGERLAND** begins south of the crumbling ruins of the reputedly haunted Eden Brown Estate and stretches along the southern coast to the outskirts of Charlestown. All of the area's sugar plantations have been transformed into inviting inns, and the region's charm and lush vegetation create an idyllic atmosphere; the island's most picturesque and windswept **beach**, White Bay, is also here (continue past the racetrack at the base of Hanley's Road). Lord Nelson and Fanny Nisbet obviously thought so too – they opted to hold their nuptials in the picturesque **St John's Anglican Church**, built in 1680. The **botanical garden** near *Montpelier Inn* (Mon–Sat 10am–4pm; ☎869/469-3509), with its stepped terraces burgeoning with violet orchids and Spanish-moss-draped trees is also worth an hour or so of your time. Be sure to visit the rainforest conservatory showcasing Nevis' inland flora; the resident speaking parrots are a lark.

Eating, drinking and nightlife

The best **dining** on Nevis is at the plantation inns, of which the 1777 restaurant at *Montpelier* is probably the best; you'll dine on delicious West Indian curries and Nevisian seafood – **reservations** are nearly always required. On the beaches you will find less sophisticated surroundings but tasty options. If you're on a real budget (or just like to get off the beaten track), try two local options: the *Bush Bar* is located 10 mins walk inland from Newcastle Pottery and serves really tasty lunchtime lobster roti-wraps for EC$20; while Rastaman Legend has an ital (veggie) food shack at Stoney Grove in Charlestown, serving pumpkin rice, red bean stew and fresh fruit juices to the sounds of loud roots-reggae and TV football all day till 10pm.

Nevis has a small number of **nightlife** options and musical diversions on offer, with a different spot hosting the majority of local part-goers each night of the week.

Bananas Bistro Upper Hamilton Estate ☎869/469-1891. With a beautiful new location high above Charlestown (ask for directions), *Bananas* is a pleasantly relaxed bistro on a panoramic terrace with an imaginative mid-range menu including Thai curries, crab quesadillas, jerk pork and French onion soup. Lunch and dinner, closed Sun.

Café des Arts Charlestown ☎869/469-7098. A delightful place serving up sandwiches, quiche and strong coffee on the ground floor and gardens of Alexander Hamilton's estate house, across from the Museum of Nevis History. Breakfast and lunch only. Closed Sun.

Eddy's Bar and Restaurant Memorial Square, Charlestown ☎869/469-5958. *Eddy's* dishes up tasty fish 'n' chips for the ex pat crowd and local seafood dishes on this second-floor verandah on the main road. Wednesday's happy hour draws in the crowds.

Miss June's Cuisine Jones Bay ☎869/469-5330. One of Nevis' best restaurants, where thirty different Caribbean dishes are served family style, allowing you to meet fellow visitors and locals alike. Typically only one dinner per week, so call ahead to check. Drinks are included in the price.

Oualie Beach Oualie Beach ☎869/469-9735. Best of the hotel bars and as good for an evening drink as it is for its food. Right on the beach, it attracts locals as well as tourists. Fri night there's live entertainment and a good buffet feast.

Sunshine's and Chevy's Beach Bars Pinney's Beach ☎869/469-5817. Two bars at the same location – both have fun, lively atmospheres. *Sunshine's*, famous for its 'Killer Bee' rum cocktail, serves grilled seafood and lobster; *Chevy's* has a lively reggae party on Sun and karaoke on Mon.

Montserrat

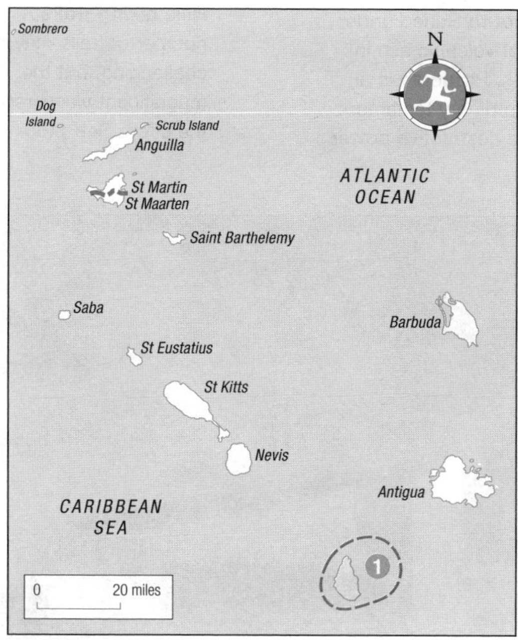
Sombrero
N
Dog Island
Scrub Island
Anguilla
St Martin
St Maarten
ATLANTIC OCEAN
Saint Barthelemy
Saba
Barbuda
St Eustatius
St Kitts
Nevis
Antigua
CARIBBEAN SEA
1
0
20 miles

Montserrat highlights

* **Montserrat Volcano Observatory** Visit the observatory for fantastic views of the astonishing natural wonder that is the volcano and meet scientists living and working in its shadow. See p.532

* **Plymouth** Buried under 40ft of volcanic ash in places, Plymouth is an extraordinary testament to the destructive power of the Soufrière Hills Volcano. See p.532

* **Coastal cliffs** Scuba diving under these cliffs reveals pristine reefs and abundant wildlife. See p.533

* **Centre Hills and Silver Hills hiking trails** A number of trails may be challenging, but the magnificent views repay the effort. See p.534

▲ Montserrat Volcano Observatory

Introduction and basics

Once famous for celebrity residents, in particular pop stars like Sting and Eric Clapton, **Montserrat** is now best known for its active volcano, **Soufrière Hills**, which has been erupting since 1995 and has buried much of the southern half of the tiny island, including the former capital of **Plymouth**. Though it's not currently possible to tour Plymouth, Montserrat remains one of the few places on the planet to witness first hand a volcano's unexpected impact on modern life. The island landmass is composed largely of three million years' of volcanic debris which has resulted in lush mountainous topography and black sand beaches. Montserrat suits a range of tastes, from those looking to laze about in a private villa to the more adventurous eco-tourist seeking an escape from crowded destinations.

Having seen the majority of its population depart after the destruction wrought by the eruptions of the 1990s, Montserrat has rebounded impressively, rebuilding infrastructure and developing tourist facilities oriented around points of ecological interest. These include the Montserrat **Volcano Observatory** (MVO) and maintaining healthy **coral reefs** and unusual rock formations to greet scuba divers underwater. The island also offers several **hiking** trails through rich and fertile landscape that hosts several rare species of birds. These natural attributes are Montserrat's signature attractions but the island's beaches – most black sand, beautiful and usually remarkably empty – are not to be missed. Lastly there's a relaxed yet very friendly attitude among Montserratians which, when considered in conjunction with the island's natural attributes, makes for a truly unforgettable visit.

Where to go

With its smoking plume visible from across the island, the **volcano** is the highlight of any trip to Montserrat. Even though the former capital, Plymouth, is inaccessible, there are several ways to glimpse the volcano and its effects on the island: from the MVO, the Jack Boy Hill Observation Area, and from Garibaldi Hill; only the latter requires a four-wheel drive vehicle. Aside from the volcano, the island has plenty of quiet **beaches** and good hiking trails. With no major towns or resorts, the island can feel a world away from its neighbours.

When to go

The **climate** on Montserrat is usually sunny and warm year-round, with some cooling between mid-December and mid-April, which is also the peak **tourist season**. Outside of this period, temperatures are only a few degrees higher but humidity increases dramatically and heavy afternoon downpours are customary. **Hurricane season** in the Caribbean stretches between June and November.

Getting there

All air arrivals come via Antigua and land at Montserrat's **new**, post-eruption **airport** at Gerald's. St Maarten-based Winair (Ⓦwww.fly-winair.com) has a monopoly on commercial air traffic in and out of Montserrat. Winair has a difficult website and requires passengers to complete and fax a credit card confirmation sheet after booking online. To avoid these annoyances, consider booking your air hop to Montserrat through a travel agent before you travel.

It is also possible to reach Montserrat by charter air service. Contact Norman Aviation (Ⓣ268/462-2445) or Carib Aviation (Ⓣ268/481-2401) for more information.

One way of seeing the island without touching down is via a 45-minute **helicopter tour**. Departing from Antigua, the trip includes dramatic flights over the volcano's boiling peak. The trips are organized by Caribbean Helicopters (Ⓣ268/460-5900, Ⓦwww.caribbeanhelicopters.com).

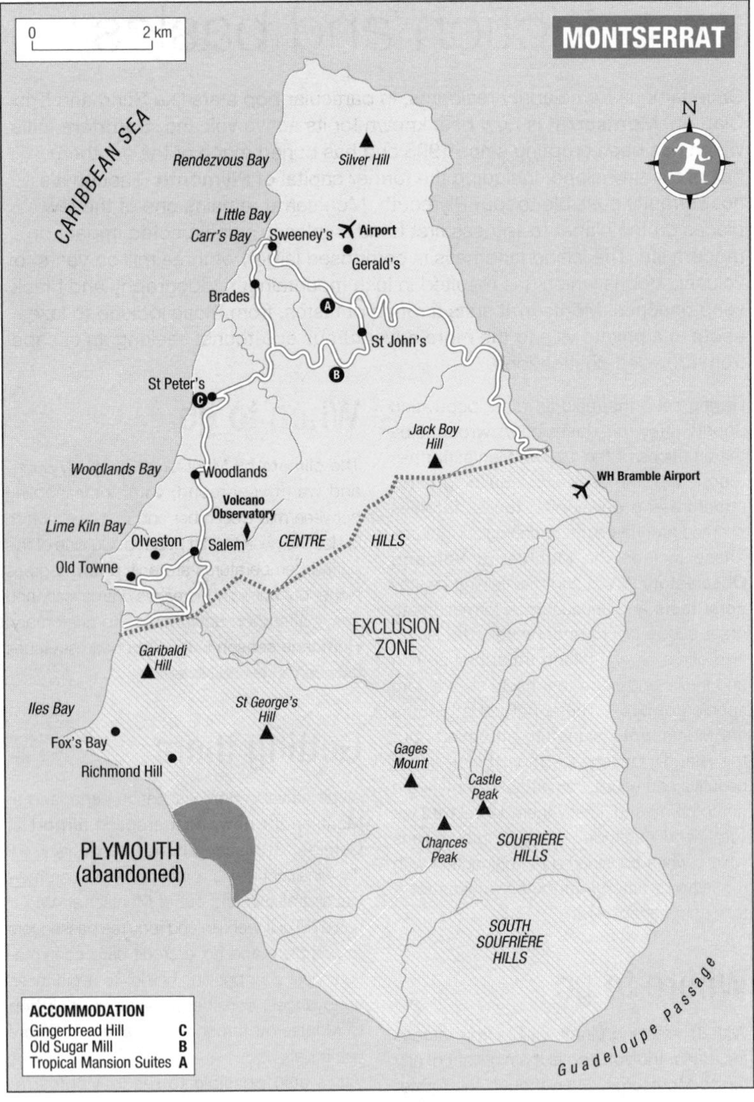

If you'd like to visit Montserrat on a day-trip, Antiguan **tour operators to Montserrat** include Carib World Travel (Ⓣ268/480-2999, Ⓔinfo@carib-world.com) and D&J Forwarders and Tours (Ⓣ268/773-9766).

Information

The **Montserrat Tourist Board** office is located in the Farara Plaza building on Brades Main Road (Mon–Fri 8am–4pm;

☎664/491-2230, ⓦwww.visitmontserrat.com). The office writes a comprehensive **tourist guide** with detailed listings of shops, accommodation and taxis available at the office, the airport and hotels. The tourist board also distributes a **map** outlining the major points of interest with detailed insets on the island's settled areas.

Money and costs

The island's unit of currency is the **Eastern Caribbean dollar** (**EC$**), which is divided into 100 cents. Notes come in denominations of 5, 10, 20, 50 and 100 EC dollars; coins in 1, 2, 5, 10 and 25 cents. Prices are often listed in both EC$ and US$ and both currencies are accepted universally. The rate of exchange is fixed to the US dollar at EC$2.65 for each US dollar, although vendors will vary conversion rates for cash payments between 2.60 and 2.70.

Credit cards are taken in some restaurants and in hotels. **Traveller's cheques** are accepted island-wide.

Montserrat's two **ATM**s are in Brades. One is operated by Royal Bank of Canada, the other by the Bank of Montserrat. Both banks are located on Brades Main Road and are open Mon–Thurs 8am–2pm; Friday 8am–3pm.

A **service charge** of 10 percent is added to most restaurant and all hotel bills; tipping is discretionary. A government tax of 10 percent is added to bills as well.

Costs on Montserrat are very reasonable in comparison to most other Caribbean islands. The island's modest hotels charge between US$50 and US$125 per night for double rooms. Meals will cost no more than US$25, usually much less.

Day-trips from Antigua, which typically include meals, transport and guides, cost between US$200 and US$300. The going rate for a helicopter tour is US$220 per person for a 45-minute tour.

The government levies a **departure and airport security tax**, payable in cash only, of US$13/EC$35 for CARICOM residents and US$21/EC$55 for everyone else; day-trippers only have to pay the security tax of US$4/EC$10. Children under 12 years of age are exempt.

Getting around

Unless you're on an organized tour, options are limited for getting around. **Taxis** are cheap and the drivers will take you on a personalized **sightseeing tour** of the island for about US$25 per person per hour. The tourist board publishes a list of almost 30 taxi drivers, among which Roy "Slym" Daley (☎664/491-4479), Eustace Dyer (☎664/491-2721) and Thomas Lee (☎664/491-2347) are highly recommended. Taxis are not metered, so agree on a currency and fare before setting off.

The cheapest and most efficient way of getting around the island during the day is by **minibus**, which can be waved down on most roads. The cost is set at EC$3 for daytime travel and EC$5 for night travel. There are no fixed schedules, stops or routes, but queuing locals will be happy to advise. At night it's best to arrange another form of transport, as minibus frequency tapers off after the sun goes down.

Cars and jeeps can be rented from Be-Beep's Car Rentals in Olveston (☎664/491-3787) or from Grant Enterprises & Trading in Brades (☎664/491-9654, ⓔgranten@candw.ms). Driving is on the left. The island has two **petrol stations**, A&F Service Centre in Sweeney's (Mon–Thurs 7am–8pm, Fri–Sat 7am–9pm, Sun 4pm–8pm; ☎664/491-6204) and Tower Hill Service Station in St Peter's (Mon–Sat 7am–9pm; ☎664/491-4070). To drive on the island, you'll need to purchase a temporary Montserrat **licence** for EC$50; it is valid for three months, and can be purchased from the police station in Brades.

Accommodation

Montserrat's orientation towards rental tourism and its active volcano mean that the big tourist hotel chains common in much of the Caribbean are not on offer here. Options include modestly sized **hotels**, **guesthouses** and a host of self-catered **rental properties** that often include private swimming pools. Rental properties are listed on the tourist board website. Tradewinds Real Estate (☎646/491-2004, ⓦwww.tradewindsmontserrat.com) manages almost 50 properties, the vast majority with swimming pools. They begin in high season at US$875 for one week in a one-bedroom house. Some of these properties represent very good value, especially for larger groups. **Rates** vary as expected between high and low season.

Food and drink

Dining in Montserrat is basic and unpretentious. The island has a few speciality dishes, including the national dish, goat water, which is a gravy-heavy goat stew. **Seafood** and local **fruits** are also widely available, though choices for **vegetarians** are pretty limited. Plenty of restaurants serve pizza and other fast food fare. Most bars serve imported **beers**, **spirits** and **wines**. **Cocktails** (of which there are a great many wicked local specialties) round out the liquor selection.

Mail and communications

Telephone kiosks are few and far between these days on Montserrat. Kiosks can be found only at the airport and near the Cable and Wireless office (Mon–Fri 8am–4pm, ⓣ664/491-2112) in Sweeney's; they only accept cards, which can be purchased at the Cable and Wireless office. Credit card calls can be made via the local operator.

To **place a call** within Montserrat, simply dial the seven-digit number; the 664 prefix is not required. Toll-free numbers use the 1800 prefix. The **country code** is ⓣ664.

The local network is not compatible with GSM telephones. To rent a **mobile phone** on Montserrat, try Hook Me Up Girlfriend (ⓣ664/491-2964) in St John's.

The main **post office** is in Brades (Mon–Fri 8.15am–4pm, ⓣ664/491-2457).

Internet access, in some cases wireless, is available at some hotels. *Tropical Mansion Suites*' Internet centre is free of charge to guests. Brades has two Internet cafés: Andy's Internet Café (ⓣ664/493-1421) and CompuGet Cyber Café (EC$16 per hr; ⓣ664/491-4633). Internet access at the public library in Brades (Mon–Fri 9am–4.30pm, Sat 10am–2pm) is free for use of up to an hour and runs EC$5 per hour thereafter.

Opening hours, holidays and festivals

Opening hours on the island are erratic – businesses normally open when the proprietor arrives in the morning or returns from lunch so it is worth checking with your hotel

Public holidays and events

Mid-March St Patrick's Week of Celebrations. St. Patrick's Day celebrations commemorate Ireland's patron saint and encompass a whole week of activities, which highlights Montserrat's Irish heritage and honours those who lost their lives in the 1768 slave rebellion. Activities include a "Slave Feast" and "Freedom Run", accompanied by calypso and soca band music.

May 5 Labour Day

July Look Out Day

August Cudjoe Head Day celebrates the abolition of slavery in 1834. Highlights include a bazaar that takes place at the village rectory.

August Roman Catholic Fete

October/November Police, Fire, Search & Rescue Community Week

December Tourism Week of Activities. Often features a street fair with arts, crafts and local produce, along with cultural shows.

December Christmas Festival Celebration. One of the year's highlights, this festival showcases the island's culture and performing talent. It's held during the last two weeks in December and climaxes on New Year's Day with a street parade.

Health and safety

In July, 1995, for the first time in recorded history, Montserrat's Soufriere Hills volcano stirred. In the **eruptions** that followed, the island's capital, Plymouth, was buried in mud flows. The city was quickly evacuated and its former residents dispersed – some, to northern parts of Montserrat; many others to the United Kingdom. Over the course of the next several years, subsequent eruptions were frequent. One of these, in June, 1997, took the lives of 19 farmers. There have been several subsequent phases of eruption. Currently, the volcano is undergoing a phase of **dome growth**, which means occasional extrusions, or emissions of magmatic material. After an ash-fall on the volcano or on windy days, the air may cause **breathing difficulties** for asthma- and bronchitis-sufferers. Those affected should bring appropriate medications and supplies, including masks. Wearers of contact lenses should also consider using spectacles during visits to the island to avoid irritation.

An island-wide **siren system** will sound to warn of volcanic activity. If the siren sounds, advice and safety-related messages can be heard on Radio Montserrat (ZJB), FM 88.3.

or with locals if you're interested in visiting an establishment at a specific time.

Montserrat observes the holidays and events in the box opposite.

Sports and outdoor activities

Scuba diving and **hiking** are Montserrat's two principal outdoor activities. Some locals will also run chartered **sailing** or **fishing** trips.

With its rugged terrain Montserrat is ideal for **mountain biking**. Imagine Peace Bicycle Shop in Brades rents bikes (Ⓣ664/491-8809, Ⓔghbikes@hotmail.com). *Gingerbread Hill* guests can also rent bikes from the hotel. Bike rentals go for US$25 per day.

The volcano's activity has produced some surprising benefits for scuba divers in the island's waters. While many believed that the **reefs** would be destroyed by ash and lava, the ash was swept away by tidal currents and the deposits that remained created interesting new dive sites. Instead of destruction, the pyroclastic flows brought massive new **boulders** into the sea, onto which new reefs are growing. What's more, the island's sparse population is too small to dangerously pollute the sea, which keeps the coral happily healthy.

Away from the violence of the volcano, Montserrat offers lush vegetation and tropical rainforests that exude peace and tranquillity. The Montserrat National Trust (Ⓣ664/491-3086, Ⓦwww.montserratnationaltrust.com) can help organize hikes to several **trails** on the island, from the mountainous volcanic spine of the island to fields of mango and banana or through picturesque colonial-style villages. Guides are quite reasonable, charging as little as US$15 per person for hikes of four people and more. Because maps of the trails are rare and signposting is inconsistent, a **guide** is highly recommended, especially on the more difficult trails.

History

Montserrat was first occupied by **Amerindians**, who colonized the chain of Lesser Antilles from the area now known as Venezuela. Arawak artefacts have been found in several sites around the island dating from 500 BC. When the **Caribs** arrived, they depopulated the island, though how or exactly when is not known. The Caribs named the island **Alliouagana**, which means "land of the prickly bush".

When **Columbus** arrived in the area in 1493, he named the island **Santa Maria de Montserrat**, as it reminded him of the location of the Montserrat abbey near Barcelona in Spain. Concerned that in the event of war the Irish might side with the Catholic French who shared St Kitts, the British authorities sent the Irish to form new colonies on Montserrat and Antigua. Although Montserrat was uninhabited when it was initially settled, the Caribs made their presence felt for five decades, launching regular raids on the island and the European colonists.

Even though the island has remained a **British territory**, it is unusual that the first European settlers were predominately Irish. Montserrat soon became known as an asylum for **Roman Catholics** in search of religious freedom, a unique motive for settlement in the Caribbean. Signs of the Irish influence are evident in the week-long annual celebration of **St Patrick's Day**, the faint Irish inflections that can be detected in many local voices, the heavy use of the shamrock emblem to illustrate the doctrine of the Holy Trinity and Montserrat's nickname, the **Emerald Isle**. Place names like Cork Hill and St Patrick's (not to mention Potato Hill) also bear witness to the Irish influence.

Between the mid-1600s and the mid-nineteenth century, thousands of enslaved Africans were transported to the West Indies to work on the booming sugar plantations. As with elsewhere in the Caribbean, **slaves** on Montserrat's sugar estates endured harsh conditions while making the oppressor country rich. Although slavery was **abolished** in 1834, it was many years before the island's population was able to shake off the legacy of poverty and the deprivation.

In the late twentieth century, **residential tourism** developed, and well-off people from all over the world built luxurious retreats on Montserrat. These included Beatles producer George Martin who established his famous Air Studio on the island, in which music has been recorded by Sting, Phil Collins, Elton John, the Rolling Stones and Stevie Wonder, among many others. The Air Studio, along with several other facilities, closed in 1989 when **Hurricane Hugo** devastated the island.

After recovering from Hugo, the island experienced a far more disruptive event, the **volcano eruption** in 1995. Nineteen people lost their lives, and, in the aftermath, locals left the island in droves, mostly for destinations in the United Kingdom; the population shrank from 11,000 to about 4000. Over the ensuing decade the population has slowly recovered, and by 2007 it had risen to almost 5000. With the passage of the British Overseas Territories Act in 2002, Montserrat-UK relations took an interesting turn. The Blair government-sponsored act reversed provisions of Margaret Thatcher's 1981 British Nationality Act that withdrew UK citizenship from the residents of British Overseas Territories. In so doing, British citizenship was extended to the citizens of Montserrat, among other British Overseas Territories.

13.1

Montserrat

Part of **Montserrat**'s attraction is its seclusion. Getting to this unique, pear-shaped island requires a little time and extra energy. This fact alone filters out the masses of tourists found throughout the Caribbean, and the island is never crowded.

Even with Winair's daily flights between Antigua and the airport at the town of Gerald's at Montserrat's northern end, tourist numbers have actually fallen; after the construction of the airport, ferry service was terminated and the number of day-trip visitors has dropped dramatically as a consequence. All-inclusive day-trips from Antigua are still possible through tour operators (see p.526).

Devastation caused by the island's **volcano** from 1995 onwards has earned Montserrat a lot of press. And while the **volcano** itself is certainly a draw for some, it's Montserrat's deserted **beaches**, green **hiking trails**, and pristine **waters** that drive most visits. The volcano's activity altered Montserrat dramatically. Its former capital, **Plymouth**, was buried in ash and abandoned, and the island's centre of gravity moved northward. In turn, **Brades**, in the northwest of the island, with its small collection of shops and government offices, became the island's makeshift capital.

Accommodation

Montserrat has very few **hotels** and no resorts. To augment the island's meagre options, a number of residents offer **apartments**, some located within owner-occupied private homes; the tourist board maintains a list of these. Villa rental (see p.527 in preceding section) is also big on Montserrat.

Gingerbread Hill St Peters ⓣ664/491-8767, ⓦwww.volcano-island.com. Possessing a friendly, relaxed, hippie vibe, *Gingerbread Hill* is set on three tropical hillside acres overlooking the sea. Accommodation options include a private villa, an apartment, and a newly built ultra-green eco-cottage. Rooms feature patios or balconies, fridges, microwaves, cable TV and free Wi-Fi. ②

Old Sugar Mill Baker Hill ⓣ664/492-1743. Run by the contagiously friendly Florence Griffiths, the Old Sugar Mill's nine cottages are set near a once-active sugar mill, around a pleasant pool with breathtaking views. Cottages are simple and more than adequate. Note that it's quite a hike up to the cottages, and a car (or a dedicated taxi hire) is essential. ④

Tropical Mansion Suites Sweeney's ⓣ664/491-8767, ⓦwww.tropicalmansion.com. Built in 1999, this was the first and still only hotel erected after the volcano eruption. Conveniently located near the airport, it has a restaurant and a small swimming pool. All rooms have balconies, and include a king-size or double bed in addition to cable TV and ceiling fans. Some suites have kitchenettes. ④

Brades

After the destruction of Plymouth, small, nondescript **BRADES**, near the island's northwest coast, became the temporary capital. The government relocated many of its operations here, and Brades also has the greatest concentration of shops and businesses. The commercial district is spread out at irregular intervals along the steep **Main Road**, and includes the tourist board office, the island's banks and a few restaurants. Besides these amenities, there's little to detain you in Brades, which feels less like a town than it does suburban retail sprawl.

The volcano and around

The Exclusion Zone which covers much of Montserrat keeps people away from the many unsafe parts of the island. Previously, a Daytime Entry Zone covered a piece of the island, from the northern edge of Plymouth to just north of Garibaldi Hill. This designation has been done away with, and the boundary of the Exclusion Zone begins north of the devastated former capital of Plymouth in the west and runs eastwards over **St George's Hill** to the site of the old airport.

Montserrat's former capital of **Plymouth**, which has been abandoned now for well over a decade, was covered in pyroclastic ash from the volcano's eruption. While the town is currently off limits to visitors due to safety precautions, decent vantage points near the southern end of the island's safe zone (listed below) allow you to gaze and wonder at the post-apocalyptic, eerie ruins. The ash has set as hard as concrete in places; in others, it is a fine dust. In some of Plymouth's ruined homes and businesses, you can see what was left behind in a rush during the evacuation including furniture, remarkably well preserved newspapers and random toiletries.

The town's natural inhabitants are regenerating amid the collapsed human infrastructure. Flourishing flowers and trees serve as a backdrop to the massive and obviously well-fed, feral cattle wandering around blissfully.

Hopefully tours into Plymouth will resume soon. In the meantime, visitors can see the volcano in its full glory at the **Montserrat Volcano Observatory** in Fleming's (Mon–Fri 8.30am–4.30pm; ⓣ664/491-5647, ⓦwww.mvo.ms; EC$10). The Observatory shows a **documentary** and maintains a wide range of informational **exhibits** for visitors.

A few good observation points can be found at **Richmond**, **Garibaldi** and **Jack Boy hills**. The first two provide good panoramic vistas of Plymouth, while the latter has excellent views over the damaged eastern side of the island, including the old WH Bramble Airport and the lava dome itself. If you're coming here on a day-trip and the volcano is your primary reason for visiting, you should choose a day when the **weather** will be fair, as low clouds can obscure the volcano's steaming peak.

The beaches

With a permanent population of only 5000, and fewer than 10,000 visitors a year, the deserted **beaches** on Montserrat are a welcome change from those ringing the island's more overcrowded and commercialized neighbours. All the beaches are on the western, Caribbean-facing side of the island. In the north is **Rendezvous Bay**, Montserrat's only white-sand beach. It boasts quality snorkelling and swimming and is perfect for a nice barefoot stroll. **Bunkum Bay**, **Woodlands Beach** and **Lime Kiln Bay** beaches – all with black volcanic sand – are worth visiting for their beauty and isolation. Woodlands and Lime Kiln Bay are near upmarket residential areas. Adjacent mud flows mean that, **Old Road Bay** is no longer a top bathing beach, though it does provide fantastic views of Soufrière Hills.

Eating, drinking and nightlife

Many **restaurants**, especially during the week, close before 9pm, so for dinner it's best to call ahead and make reservations. **Brades** has the most options. As for **nightlife**, various locations occasionally feature bands or disco music, particularly on Friday and Saturday nights. Ask at your hotel or guesthouse for information. The tourist board also publishes a list of nightlife venues and bars. You can visit the informal roadside bars known locally as rumshops on a Rumshop Tour (ⓣ664/491-5371 for more information).

Gourmet Gardens Olveston ⓣ664/491-7859. Slightly out of the way, this friendly garden café features surprises like bratwurst and fries (EC$22) and shepherd's pie (EC$20) for lunch and goulash (EC$35) and schnitzel (EC$55) for dinner. Don't miss the lethal house rum punch. Lunch daily

▲ Soufrière Hills volcano

noon–2pm. Dinner, 6pm–9pm; reservations recommended for dinner.

Jumping Jack's Bar and Restaurant Olveston ⓣ664/491-5645. Located on the proprietors' verandah in a leafy corner of the island, fresh fish is the ticket at this vibrant, open-air and friendly restaurant, with wahoo (EC$35) a staple. It's also possible to charter a four-man fishing boat with Danny "Jumpin' Jack" Sweeney and then return to have your catch prepared for your meal. Open Wed (lunch), Fri (lunch and dinner) and Sun (lunch); dinner by reservation only Wed and Sun.

Oriole Café Brades ⓣ664/491-7144. Next to the tourist board office, this restaurant serves up a small selection of good-quality Caribbean and local dishes. The sandwiches are very nice, though there's not much on offer for vegetarians.

Tina's Brades ⓣ664/491-3538. In an attractive wooden building, Florestina Farrell serves a variety of tasty Caribbean and international dishes. Standouts include affordable pizzas and grill items (starting at EC$25). Open for breakfast, lunch and dinner. Open late Fri & Sat, closed Sun.

Tropical Mansion Suites Sweeney's ⓣ664/491-8767. This hotel restaurant serves up a simple à la carte menu of reasonable quality, with a nightly selection of Caribbean and international dishes (chicken or beef) served with vegetables, rice and salad. The bar is well-stocked.

Diving

The most active dive sites on Montserrat are around the island's northern portion, mostly between **Old Road Bluff** and the **Northwest Bluff**. Some of the most impressive diving is under the **coastal cliffs**. In the shallowest areas neighbouring the cliffs, many scattered rocks and ledges can be found covered with sponges, sea plumes and sea fans with plenty of fish and the occasional octopus darting about. Divers can find schools of flying fish, barrel sponges and sea turtles. Some notable dive sites include **Little Redonda** in the far northwest and **Woodlands Beach**, which is great for night diving and for observing turtles heading ashore to lay eggs (from July through September).

Montserrat currently has just one **dive centre**, the Green Monkey Inn & Dive Shop (ⓣ664/491-2960 or ⓣ664/496-2960, ⓔtroy@divemontserrat.com, ⓦwww.divemontserrat.com), which offers professional training and equipment rental.

Dive sites can be reached by their boat or just by swimming out from many beaches.

Hiking

An easy hike can be had at **Runaway Ghaut**, a trail ideal for birdwatching and picnicking, with tables available en route and a drinking fountain that, if quaffed from, is said to bring visitors back to the island.

The **Centre Hills** trail leads visitors through the island's rainforest where the majority of the island's 33 local bird species can be found, including rare and threatened Montserrat orioles, mangrove cuckoos and bridled quail doves. Several varieties of reptile and amphibian can also be found. If you're very lucky, you'll sight the critically endangered Montserrat **galliwasp** lizard, which is the sort of creature that drives conservationists wild.

Another good hike is the trail to **"The Cot"**, a picturesque tramp that climbs 1000ft, leading hikers through abundant flora and affording views of ruined buildings in the Exclusion Zone.

In the northerly reaches, the **Silver Hills** trail winds through open fields and forest and up the flanks of a 1000ft defunct volcano. This trail is suited to bird-spotters, with a variety of land and sea birds making their homes along it, including a breeding colony of frigate birds. Lastly, the trail from **Little Bay to Rendezvous Bay**, along a steep mountain path, is one of the most challenging hikes, though it rewards at the end with a combination of black-and-white-sand beaches, allowing an opportunity to cool off with a spot of swimming or snorkelling.

To organize guided hikes, contact the tourist office in Brades or the Montserrat National Trust (Ⓣ664/491-3086, Ⓦwww.montserratnationaltrust.com).

14

Antigua & Barbuda

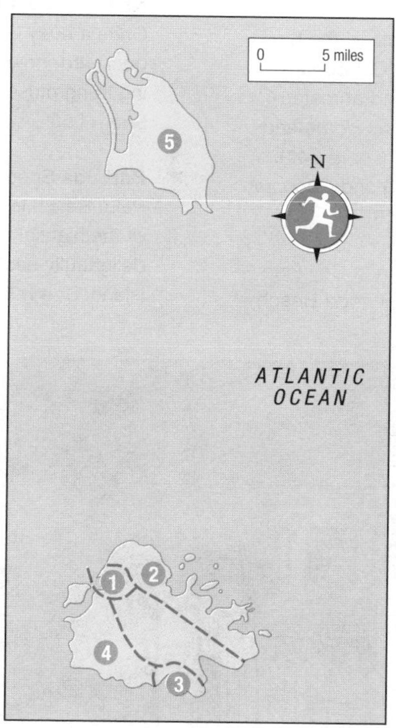

Antigua & Barbuda highlights

* **St John's** Antigua's charismatic capital is home to excellent restaurants and bars, as well as the fascinating National Museum. See p.544

* **Eating** Some of the best food in the Caribbean can be found at restaurants such as *Home* and *Papa Zouk* (see p.547), *East* (p.555) and *Coconut Grove* (p.550).

* **Beaches** Long Bay (see p.549), Darkwood Beach (p.557) and Half Moon Bay (p.550) are among the best of the island's beautiful stretches of inviting white sand.

* **Nelson's Dockyard** Once a busy Georgian dockyard, now an intriguing living museum. See p.553

* **Barbuda** Spectacular Palm Beach is just one of the highlights of this delightfully secluded island. See p.558

▲ Nelson's Dockyard

Introduction and basics

Famous around the world for its **cricket**, not to mention its **beaches** (the island is said to boast 365 – one for every day of the year), **Antigua** is one of the Caribbean's most popular destinations. The country (which includes the tiny neighbouring island of **Barbuda**) took full advantage of the publicity gained from its independence in 1981 – and the remarkable success of its cricketers since then – to push its name into the big league of West Indian tourism.

For centuries after the **British** settled the island in the 1600s, it was little more than a giant factory producing sugar and rum for export to the old world. The tall brick chimneys of a hundred deserted and decaying sugar mills scattered around Antigua bear witness to that long colonial era. Today, however, it is **tourism** that drives the country's economy. Dozens of hotels and restaurants have sprung up around the coastline, and a number of outfits run boat and catamaran cruises and scuba diving and snorkelling trips to the island's fabulous **coral reefs**. While some locals and frequent visitors may complain that Antigua has started to lose its identity – and it's true that there is a worrying amount of development on the island – Antigua manages to retain a feel of the "real Caribbean", unlike more overdeveloped islands. Go now before this changes.

A short flight away, Antigua's sister island Barbuda is much less visited but a delight in its own right.

Where to go

If all you want to do is crash on a **beach** for a week or two, you'll find Antigua hard to beat. The island is dotted with superb patches of sand – look out for **Dickenson Bay** in the northwest, **Half Moon Bay** in the east and **Rendezvous Beach** in the south – and while the nightlife isn't as raucous as on other islands, there are plenty of great places to eat and drink. But, however lazy and beach-bound you're feeling, it's worth making the effort to get out and see some of the country. The superbly restored naval dockyard at **English Harbour** is as impressive as any historic site in the West Indies, and there are lots of other little nuggets, including the capital, **St John's**, and the old sugar estate at **Betty's Hope**. If you're prepared to do a bit of walking, you'll find some great **hikes** that will take you out to completely deserted parts of the island.

Barbuda feels a world apart from its increasingly developed neighbour even though it's just fifteen minutes away by plane. Despite its spectacular beaches and coral reefs, the tourist industry is underdeveloped, although there are constant rumours of new resorts in the pipeline. Even if you can only manage a day-trip, you'll find Barbuda thoroughly worthwhile.

When to go

Antigua's tropical **climate** makes it a year-round destination. The weather is best during the high season, from mid-December to mid-April, when there is little rain and the high temperatures are cooled by the trade winds. As you'd expect, prices and crowds are at their peak during high season, particularly during Christmas and the New Year.

Things can get noticeably hotter during the summer and, particularly in September and October, the humidity can be oppressive. September is also the most threatening month for the annual **hurricane season**, which runs officially from June 1 to October 31.

Getting there

All flights to Antigua touch down at **V.C. Bird International Airport**, on the island's north coast. There is **no bus service** from the airport, although there are numerous **car rental** outlets. **Taxis** cost around US$12 to St John's, or US$30 to English Harbour.

If you arrive by cruise ship, you'll dock at **Redcliffe or Heritage quay**, in St John's.

From there, you can either take a taxi to anywhere on the island; take a bus to English Harbour, Parham or Willikies; or rent a car.

Information

The front desk of your hotel is generally the best source of information. In addition, the government **tourist office**, at the Government Complex on Queen Elizabeth Highway in St John's (☎268/462-0480), has a smattering of brochures and **maps**. There are also a few decent websites – see the box opposite.

Money and costs

The island's unit of currency is the **Eastern Caribbean dollar (EC$)**, divided into 100 cents. It comes in notes of $100, $50, $20, $10 and $5 and coins of $1, $0.50, $0.25, $0.10, $0.05 and $0.01. The rate of exchange is fixed at EC$2.70 to US$1.

In most tourist-related businesses – especially hotels, restaurants and car rentals – the **US dollar** is used as an unofficial parallel currency, and you'll often find prices quoted in US dollars (a policy we have adopted in this chapter). Bear in mind, though, that you can always insist on paying in EC$ (and the exchange rate usually works slightly in your favour). Changing money into EC$ is best left until you're in the country.

If you're using US dollars or travellers' cheques to pay a bill, your change will often be given in the local currency.

Banking hours are generally Monday to Thursday 8am–2pm and Friday 8am–4pm. Most of the banks are in St John's and include Antigua Commercial Bank, Barclays, ABIB and Bank of Antigua. The Bank of Antigua and ABIB in St John's are also open on Saturday morning, as is the Bank of Antigua in Nelson's Dockyard.

Most hotels and restaurants automatically add a **service charge** of 10 percent and government tax of 8.5 percent. It's always

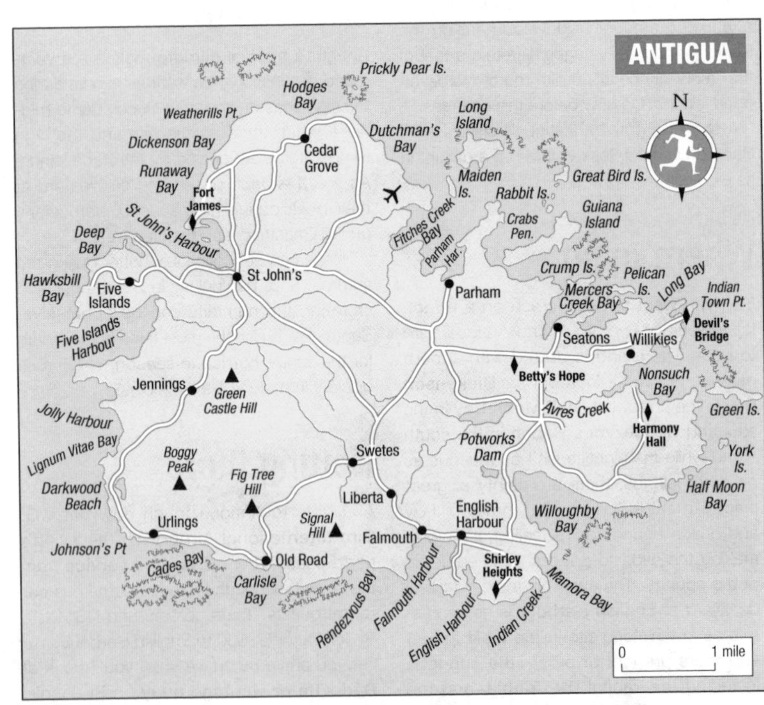

Websites

ⓦ**www.antigua-barbuda.com** Helpful tourism site, with information on events, weddings, places to stay, car rental outfits and more.

ⓦ**www.antiguanice.com** Masses of information, from hotels and restaurant reviews to the latest island news.

ⓦ**www.geographia.com/cgi-bin/antiguanews/discus.pl** Useful forum about Antigua and Barbuda.

worth asking if this charge is included in the quoted price or will be added on later.

Getting around

Antigua is not a big place, and it's easy to drive right round the island in less than a day. Buses are useful, but a car will get you off the beaten path.

See p.558 for how to get from Antigua to **Barbuda**.

By bus

Speedy and inexpensive, **buses and minibuses** run to certain parts of the island, particularly between St John's and English Harbour on the south coast and along the west coast between St John's and Old Road, although none go to the big tourist area of Dickenson Bay and Runaway Bay.

By car

If you want to tour around, you're invariably better off **renting a car** for a couple of days. Prices are fairly high, starting at around US$50 per day, or US$320 per week. It's worth taking out extra insurance if your credit card or travel insurance doesn't cover it, especially in light of the fact that Antigua's roads are generally in pretty poor condition. It's also worth renting a 4WD if your budget will allow it, as some of the trickier roads may otherwise be inaccessible. Don't forget to bring your driving licence from home; you'll also have to buy a **local licence** for US$20 (valid for three months and sold by all of the car rental firms). Reliable companies include Avis (ⓣ268/462-2840), Budget (ⓣ268/462-3009), Dollar (ⓣ268/462-0362), Hertz (ⓣ268/481-4400, airport number 481-4455), Oakland (ⓣ268/462-3021), Steads (ⓣ268/462-9970) and Thrifty (ⓣ268/462-9532). Bear in mind that driving on Antigua and Barbuda is on the left, and that driving at night presents its own challenges with poorly lit roads and people and livestock walking in the road. Maps provided by car rental companies are not always very accurate and there are very few road signs on Antigua. This shouldn't prove too problematic, however: if you get lost, just ask someone for directions – locals are usually very willing to help.

By taxi

If you just want to take a short trip, it can be cheaper to hire **taxis** which are easy to find at the main resorts, the airport, St John's and Nelson's Dockyard. Elsewhere you'll often need to call or ask your hotel to arrange for one. Try West Bus Station Taxis (ⓣ268/462-5190) or Antigua Reliable (ⓣ268/460-5353). Fares are regulated but there are no meters so be sure to agree on a price before you get into the car. Taxi drivers in Antigua are very friendly and helpful, and if you're unsure about how to get a taxi for the return part of your trip, many will be happy to come and collect you at an agreed time.

By bike and motorcycle

Since Antigua is so small, and there are few steep inclines, it is ideal cycling territory, and **bikes** can be rented for around US$18 per day, US$100 a week. A reliable bike hire outfit is Bike Plus on Independence Drive in St John's (ⓣ268/462-2453), which also sells bikes and accessories. Riding a scooter or **motorcycle** is fun but with the poorly maintained roads it can be dangerous and we don't recommend it.

Tours

If you don't fancy driving, there are a few local companies that feature islandwide **sightseeing tours**, offering set or customized itineraries. Remember to check whether the price includes entrance fees to the various attractions. Also note that many taxi drivers on the island double as guides, and can be hired for a set amount of time.

Tropical Adventures (Ⓣ268/480-1225, www.tropicalad.com) provides all manner of tours, from jeep tours through the rainforest, to "eco adventures" including kayaking and snorkelling, to catamaran trips to Barbuda (with a stop at the bird sanctuary). Prices start at US$90.

Mountain to Sea Bike Adventures (Ⓣ268/721-7350, Ⓦwww.mountaintoseabikeadventure.com) runs guided three-hour mountain bike tours from Shirley Heights down to Nelson's Dockyard, with an optional hike to Fort Berkeley.

For an extra thrill, book an aerial tour of Antigua or Montserrat (or customize your own) with Caribbean Helicopters (Ⓣ268/460-5900, Ⓦwww.caribbeanhelicopters.com). Prices start at US$85 for Antigua, and US$220 for Montserrat.

Accommodation

Most accommodation in Antigua is right on the coast. The west and northwest coasts have plenty of options, but there are a handful of good places on the much more isolated east coast and around Falmouth and English Harbour (where the beaches are less impressive). Accommodations on the quiet and undeveloped island of **Barbuda** range from the rustic to the luxurious. Always book in advance.

Although some rates can at first seem shockingly high, it's worth remembering that if you're travelling during the low season, prices can fall by as much as fifty percent (though this is rare at the cheapest places), and proprietors are far more amenable to bargaining. Many of the all-inclusive hotels have a minimum-stay requirement, and some of them allow you the option of booking on an all-inclusive or accommodation-only (European Plan, or EP) basis. Keep in mind that every place adds **government tax** of 8.5 percent to the bill and almost all add a **service charge** of 10 percent. Some places include those extras in the quoted price, some don't, so always ask.

Food and drink

There are plenty of good **eating** options on Antigua, with something for almost any budget. The majority of hotel and restaurant menus aimed at tourists tend to offer familiar variations on Euro-American-style food, shunning local specialities – a real shame, as the latter are invariably excellent. At the least, many menus offer one catch of the day dish which is usually worth trying.

Antiguan specialities include the fabulous ducana (a solid hunk of grated sweet potato mixed with coconut and spices and steamed in a banana leaf), pepperpot stew with salt beef, pumpkin and okra, often served with a cornmeal pudding known as *fungi*, various types of curry, salted codfish and souse (cuts of pork marinated in lime juice, onions, hot and sweet peppers and spices).

There are few **bars** aimed specifically at drinkers, and most drinking is done at restaurants or hotel bars. The local Wadadli beer is excellent, but there are always West Indian rums available if you need something stronger.

It's generally fine to drink tap water on Antigua but you should stick to bottled water on Barbuda.

During the winter high season (Dec–April) it's best to make **reservations** at many of the places recommended – and, if you've got your heart set on a special place, call a couple of days in advance. As for **prices**, some restaurants quote their prices in EC$, others in US$, and some in both. We've used US$ throughout. As with accommodation, a **government tax** of 8.5 percent is always added to the bill and, particularly at the pricier places, a 10 percent **service charge** is also automatic. As such, **tipping** is at your discretion.

On **Barbuda**, restaurants are low-key places with quiet trade. If you're coming on a day-trip package, your meal will normally be arranged for you but if you're traveling independently, make a reservation as soon as you can.

Mail and communications

Post offices are located in English Harbour, St John's (Long Street) and Woods Centre. Hours are 8am–4pm Mon–Fri.

Most hotels provide a **telephone** in each room and local calls are normally inexpensive. You'll also see phone booths all over the island, and these can be used for local and international calls. Most of the booths take phonecards only, available at hotels, post offices and some shops and supermarkets.

The **country code** for Antigua is ⓣ268. For fire, ambulance or police emergencies, dial ⓣ911 or 999.

Wi-Fi is now common at hotels (even the cheaper ones), and often it's included in the rate. There are a handful of **Internet cafés** across the island, including at English Harbour, Jolly Harbour and Falmouth Harbour.

Public holidays and festivals

The main events in Antigua are the summertime **Carnival** and the April **Sailing Week** but there are many more events, including international cricket and windsurfing tournaments. The tourist boards have more details.

Antigua celebrates **Caricom Day** in early July, **Carnival** on the first Monday and Tuesday of August, and **Independence Day** on November 1. See also the box on p.546.

Sports and outdoor activities

Antigua and, to a lesser extent, Barbuda, where facilities are not as built up, are great for **outdoor activities**. There's something for everyone, from diving and snorkelling to boat tours and cruises.

Festivals and events

January
Official start of West Indian cricket season ⓣ268/462-9090, ⓦwww.windiescricket.com.

January–March
Stanford 20/20 Cricket Tournament, ⓣ268/480-3551, ⓦwww.stanford2020.com.

March/April
Test cricket ⓣ268/462-9090, ⓦwww.windiescricket.com.

April/May
Antigua Classic Yacht Regatta ⓣ268/460-1799, ⓦwww.antiguaclassics.com.
Stanford Antigua Sailing Week ⓣ268/460-8872, ⓦwww.sailingweek.com.

May
Antigua Tennis Week, Curtain Bluff Hotel ⓣ268/462-8400, ⓦwww.curtainbluff.com.

July/August
Carnival ⓣ268/462-4707, ⓦwww.antiguacarnival.com.

November
Antigua & Barbuda International Literary Festival ⓣ268/480-2999, ⓦwww.caribbeanliteraryfestival.com.

December
Jolly Harbour Yacht Club Regatta ⓣ268/770-6172, ⓦwww.jhycantigua.com.

Watersports

Diving is excellent on the coral reefs around Antigua and Barbuda, with most of the good sites – such as Sunken Rock, Cades Reef and Cape Shirley – on the south side of the larger island and many of them very close to shore, rarely more than a fifteen-minute boat ride away. Expect to see a wealth of fabulously colourful reef fish including parrot fish, angelfish, wrasse and barracuda, as well as the occasional harmless nurse shark and, if you're lucky, dolphins and turtles. The reefs for the most part are still unspoiled, and even though most dives are fairly shallow, there are some good cliffs, canyons and a handful of wrecks.

Antigua has plenty of reputable **dive operators** conveniently scattered around the island so you should always be able to find a boat going out from near where you're staying. Rates are pretty uniform: reckon around US$100 for a two-tank dive with equipment. **Beginners** can get a feel for diving by taking a half-day resort course for around US$100. Full open-water certification ranges from US$400 to US$500. Call around for the best deal. Serious divers should consider a **package deal** – the prices can be excellent.

Barbuda's diving is at least as good as Antigua's, with countless wrecks dotted around the nearby reefs, but currently there is no established dive outfit on the island.

Snorkelling around the islands is excellent, and several of the dive operators take snorkellers on their dive trips. Reckon around US$20–25 for an outing, including equipment.

Dive operators

Dive Antigua *Rex Halcyon Cove Hotel*, Dickenson Bay ⓣ268/462-3483, ⓦwww.diveantigua.com. The oldest and best-known operation on the island, with knowledgeable staff and free drinks.

Dockyard Divers Nelson's Dockyard ⓣ268/460-1178, ⓦwww.divers-haven.com. Decent-sized dive shop providing diving and snorkelling trips around the south and west coasts.

Jolly Dive Jolly Harbour Marina ⓣ268/462-8305, ⓦwww.jollydive.com. Second-oldest dive shop in Antigua, and very popular with guests at the big local hotels. Numerous levels of training offered.

Boat tours

There is no shortage of **boat** and **catamaran trips** to take around Antigua, with the emphasis normally on a big crowd having a fun time together. Most of the cruises charge a single price, including a meal and drinks.

Boat operators

Adventure Antigua ⓣ268/726-6355, ⓦwww.adventureantigua.com. Owner Eli Fuller takes passengers by motorboat on a seven-hour eco-tour of the northeast coast of the island, taking in the mangrove swamps, offering several snorkelling opportunities and lunch on a deserted beach. Cost is US$100 per person, and the trip goes out between two and five times a week. Fans of *Miami Vice* might also like the high-speed Xtreme Circumnavigation tours which run five days a week for $170.

Wadadli Cats ⓣ268/462-4792, ⓦwww.wadadlicats.com. Offers circumnavigation cruises (Mon, Thurs & Sat; US$95), a Bird Island cruise (Fri; US$80) and a Cades Reef cruise (Wed; US$80).

History

Antigua's **first people** were the nomadic Ciboney, originally from present-day Venezuela, whose earliest traces on the island date from around 3100 BC. By the early years of the first millennium AD the Ciboney were replaced by Arawak-speaking **Amerindians** from the same region who called the island Wadadli ("our own").

The first European sighted Antigua in 1493 when **Columbus** sailed close by, naming the island Santa Maria la Antigua. The island remained uninhabited for over a century until 1624 when the first **British settlement** in the West Indies was established on the island of St Kitts, and the British laid claim to nearby Antigua and Barbuda. Within a decade, settlers at Falmouth on the south coast had experimented with a number of crops before deciding on **sugar cane**, which was to guarantee the island its future wealth. For the next two hundred years, sugar remained the country's dominant industry, bringing enormous wealth to the **planters**.

Unlike most of Britain's West Indian colonies, Antigua remained British throughout the colonial era. This was due, in large part, to the massive fortifications built around it, the major ones at places like Shirley Heights on the south coast.

As the centuries passed, conditions for the **slaves** who worked the plantations improved very slowly. Even after the abolition of slavery in 1834, many were obliged to continue to labour at the sugar estates for wages that were insufficient to provide even the miserly levels of food, housing and care formerly offered under slavery.

Gradually **free villages** emerged at places like Liberta, Jennings and Bendals, often based around Moravian or Methodist churches or on land reluctantly sold by the planters to groups of former slaves. Slowly a few Antiguans scratched together sufficient money to set up their own businesses – shops, taverns and tiny cottage industries. An embryonic black middle class was in the making. Nonetheless economic progress on the island was extremely slow. By World War II, life for the vast majority of Antiguans was still very tough, with widespread poverty across the island.

After the war, Antigua continued to be administered by Britain but gradually the island's politicians were given authority to run their country. The national economy began to take strides forward, assisted by the development of **tourism**. By the elections of 1980 all parties considered that, politically and economically, the country was sufficiently mature for full independence and the flag of an **independent Antigua and Barbuda** was finally raised in November 1981. Since then, politics has been completely dominated by the political dynasty of the Bird family – father V.C. and son Lester – but allegations of corruption took their toll and a new government of Baldwin Spencer's United Progressive Party swept into power in March 2004. The locals seem relatively happy with the current government, which has built better roads and improved the education system, among other things. While long-time tourists to Antigua might be worried by the amount of ongoing construction across the island, it has yet to reach levels anywhere near those on islands such as St Martin.

14.1

St John's and around

Bustling **ST JOHN'S** is Antigua's capital and only real city, with a population of around 40,000 – nearly half the island's total. It's not the prettiest city in the West Indies but it does have an authentic feel, a certain charm and plenty of attractive old wooden and stone buildings – some of them superbly renovated, others in a state of near-collapse. It'll only take you a couple of hours to see everything (allow extra time for the National Museum) but you'll want to come back for at least one evening to sample the excellent local **restaurants** and **bars**.

Arrival, getting around and accommodation

Flights touch down at **V.C. Bird International Airport** on the northeast coast. There is no bus service to and from the airport but you will find numerous **car rental outlets** as well as **taxis**. Expect to pay around US$12 to St John's and US$30 to English Harbour.

St John's offers little reason **to stay** the night; if you need to, try the friendly, centrally located *Joe Mike's Hotel* on Nevis Street (ⓣ268/462-1142; ❷).

The City

The main places of interest in St John's are close together, and the easiest way to see the city is **on foot**. You should certainly make your way to **Redcliffe Quay** – where the waterfront and its colonial buildings have been attractively restored – as well as to the tiny **National Museum**, which offers a well-presented rundown on the country's history and culture. Stroll through some of the city's old streets, and check out the twin-towered **cathedral** perched on top of Newgate Street. Redcliffe Quay and nearby **Heritage Quay** are the best places to eat, drink and shop for souvenirs, although you might want to avoid them when the cruise ships are in.

Around Redcliffe Quay

Spread over several acres by the waterside, **Redcliffe Quay** is a good starting point when visiting the city. Named in honour of the church of St Mary Redcliffe in the English port city of Bristol, this is one of the oldest parts of St John's and incorporates many former warehouses – now attractively restored as small boutiques, restaurants and bars – and a wooden boardwalk that runs alongside the water. There's not a huge amount to see, but it's a pleasant place to wander and soak up some of the city's history.

Many of the waterfront warehouses once housed supplies – sugar, rum, lumber, cotton and sheepskins – for the British navy and local merchant ships from the eighteenth century. Behind the quay around the western end of Nevis Street there once stood a number of *barracoons* which were compounds where slaves were held upon their arrival before they were sent to the plantations or shipped elsewhere.

Back at the front of the quay, a short stroll north takes you up to **Heritage Quay** at the foot of High Street. This modern concrete quay is given over to cruise ship arrivals and duty-free shops designed to catch tourist dollars. Take a quick look at the **monument to V.C. Bird**, first prime minister of the independent country, and the **Westerby Memorial**, which commemorates a nineteenth-century Moravian missionary who dedicated his life to helping Antiguans.

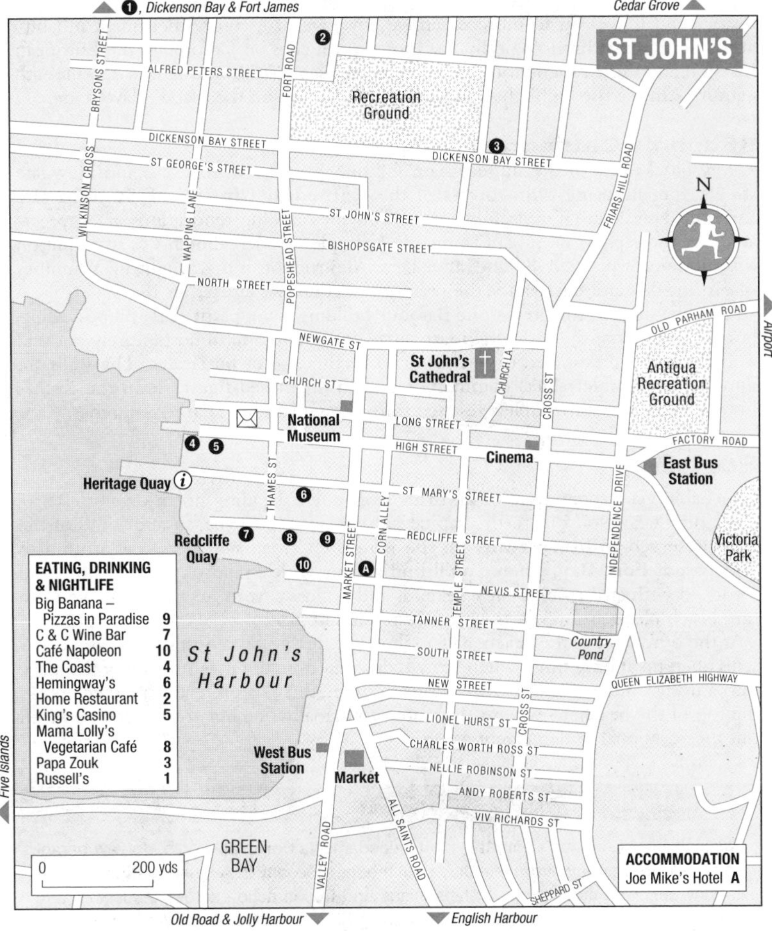

Long Street and around

From the water, Long Street runs east as far as the **Antigua Recreation Ground**, a major cricket venue and home to most of the action during the ten-day Carnival each July and August (see box p.546). The island's other main venues are the **Sir Vivian Richards Stadium** between St John's and the airport, built for the 2007 World Cup; and the **Stanford Cricket Ground** next to the airport. Many of St John's finest old buildings line this street, including a couple of fabulously colourful liquor stores, still in operation more than a century after first opening. Nearby, at the top of the High Street, is the **cenotaph**, a memorial to Antiguans who died during World War I. East of Independence Avenue is the revamped **Victoria Park**, a nice place for a stroll.

The National Museum

Housed in a 1747 Neoclassical courthouse on the corner of Long and Market streets, the **National Museum of Antigua and Barbuda** (Mon–Fri 8.30am–4pm, Sat 10am–2pm; US$3) occupies just one large room, but given the enthusiasm with which the collection has been assembled and displayed, it's indisputably worth thirty minutes of your time. The exhibits start by showing off the islands' early geological history and moves on to more extensive coverage of its first Amerindian inhabitants. Continuing chronologically, the museum touches on Columbus, the European invasion and sugar production – the country's *raison d'être* from the mid-seventeenth century. Among the highlights is an intriguing section on the island's slave trade.

St John's Cathedral

A few blocks east of the museum, on Church Lane between Long and Newgate streets, the imposing twin towers of the **Cathedral Church of St John the Divine** (daily 9am–5pm; free but donations for ongoing renovations are appreciated) are the capital's dominant landmark. A simple wooden church was first built on this hilltop site in 1683–84 and, after heavy destruction was wrought by a number of earthquakes and hurricanes, the present cathedral was erected in 1847.

From the outside, the grey-stone Baroque building is not particularly prepossessing, but the interior of the cathedral is attractive and interesting, almost entirely encased in dark pine and designed to withstand an earthquake or hurricane. The walls are dotted with marble tablets commemorating distinguished figures from the island's history, including some tablets rescued from the wreckage of earlier churches.

Fort Bay

Reachable via a short drive or taxi ride from town, heading north on Fort Road, a left turn takes you out to the capital city's most popular beach and some of the best-preserved **military ruins** on the island. The road winds its way around to the coast at **Fort Bay**, where you'll find a long, wide strand of grainy white sand – packed with city-dwellers at weekends and holidays. At its northern end, you can hire beach chairs from *Millers by the Sea* restaurant/bar.

At the other end of the beach, half a kilometre further on, a host of food and drink stalls open up at busy times when crowds descend from town, transforming the place into a lively outdoor venue. If you want to swim, there's a protected, marked area at the top of the beach; elsewhere, the water is normally fine but you'll need to watch out for occasional undercurrents.

Carnival

The highlight of Antigua's entertainment calendar is its **Carnival**, a colourful, exuberant party held for ten days from late July until the first Tuesday in August. Warm-ups start in early July with steel bands, calypsonians and DJs in action across the island, and Carnival proper gets cracking with the opening of Carnival City at the Antigua Recreation Ground in St John's. This is where most events are held, although you'll often find spontaneous outbreaks of partying across the city. A festival "village" is set up near the ground to provide space for the numerous food and drink vendors who emerge seemingly out of thin air each year.

The major Carnival events take place over the last weekend, during which you'll have to forgo sleep for a few days of frantic action. The **Panorama** steel band contest and the Monarch competition are both popular and well worth catching, while on the Monday morning – the day on which the islands celebrate slave emancipation in 1834 – **J'ouvert** (pronounced "jouvay", and meaning daybreak) is a huge jump-up party starting at 4am. The Judging of the Troupes and Groups competition in the afternoon sees ranks of brightly costumed marching bands and floats parading through the city streets, being judged for colour, sound and general party attitude.

Tuesday has a final costumed parade through the streets, finishing with the announcement of the winners and a 7pm–midnight "last lap" as the exhausted partygoers stream through St John's led by the steel bands. All in all, it's a great event – certainly one of the Caribbean's best summer carnivals – and a great chance to catch the Antiguans in a nonstop party mood.

Fort James

At the far southern end of Fort Bay stands eighteenth-century **Fort James**, built above the cliffs that overlook the entrance to St John's Harbour. You can walk or drive around to the south side of the fort where the main gate is still in place. Together with St John's Fort on Rat Island and Fort Barrington (see p.557), this fort was designed to deter ships from attacking the capital, which had been sacked by French raiders in 1668. Earthworks were first raised in the 1680s but the bulk of the fort was put up in 1739.

Today Fort James is pretty dilapidated and windswept but it offers plenty of atmosphere and great views. Rusting British cannons from the early 1800s point out to sea and down the channel, their threat long gone but still a dramatic symbol of their era. Elsewhere, the old powder magazine is still intact, albeit leaning precariously, and the stone buildings on the fort's upper level – the oldest part of the structure, dating from 1705 – include the master gunner's house, the canteen and the barracks. Russell's restaurant (see below) is also here.

Eating and drinking

St John's is well served for **restaurants**, with several good places down near the quay and a couple of top-notch options just north of town in the Gambles. For those on a budget, the capital is also home to cheaper eats such as *Roti King* on St Mary's Street.

Big Banana - Pizzas in Paradise Lower Redcliffe Street ⓣ268/480-6985, ⓦwww.bigbanana-antigua.com. Popular, long-established restaurant serving decent pizzas (from US$4 per slice), salads and sandwiches, as well as breakfasts and more typical Antiguan chicken and fish dishes (like lobster). Closed Sun lunch.

C & C Wine Bar Redcliffe Quay ⓣ268/460-7025. This wine bar with outside tables specializes in South African labels (prices from US$3 per glass), but also offers brandies and spirits, as well as snacks (closed Sun, and Mon lunch). The owners also run the nearby *Australian Homemade* café, which serves excellent coffee and ice cream.

Café Napoleon Redcliffe Quay ⓣ268/562-1820. French-owned café serving authentic Gallic fare such as filled baguettes (US$7), steak-frites (US$22) and salade niçoise (US$17) with popular English breakfasts (US$11). 8am–5pm (kitchen closes at 3.30pm). Closed Sun unless cruise ship in town.

Hemingway's St Mary's Street ⓣ268/462-2763. Atmospheric, early nineteenth-century wooden building with a balcony. The excellent, well-priced food ranges from lunchtime burgers, pastas and sandwiches (starting at less than US$10) to soups, gumbos and fish dishes for dinner. Closed Sun.

Home Restaurant Gambles Terrace, ⓣ268/461-7651. Attractive restaurant in a converted home just to the north of town, serving excellent, adventurous West Indian food. Look for starters like lobster bisque (US$13), main courses such as fillet of snapper stuffed with crab (US$29) and pork tenderloin with tamarind sauce (US$29). Dinner only; closed Sun.

Mama Lolly's Vegetarian Café Redcliffe Quay ⓣ268/562-1552. Small, friendly café open for breakfast and lunch daily, serving fresh-pressed juices and smoothies for around US$4–5. Large portions of curries, macaroni and cheese, salads and soups cost less than US$10. Daily 9am–9pm.

Papa Zouk Hilda Davis Drive, Gambles ⓣ268/464-6044. Imaginative Antiguan food served on a tiny patio festooned with flowers. The menu is small but interesting, with local produce showcased in dishes like Creole bouillabaisse (US$17) and fish platters (US$25). The range of rums covers more than 200 varieties. Dinner only, closed Sun.

Russell's Fort James, t268/462-5479. A breezy, colonial-style restaurant known for its excellent seafood, including shrimp, lobster, snapper, mahi-mahi and mussels. There's live jazz on Sun from 4–10pm. Daily 9am–10pm.

Entertainment and nightlife

The Coast Heritage Quay ⓣ268/562-6278, ⓦwww.coast.ag. This club/restaurant overlooking the quay has two dance floors (one open-air), and DJs spin everything from R&B to house. Free Wi-Fi. Lunch daily, dinner Wed–Mon. US$10 cover charge for men after 10pm Fri, Sat.

King's Casino Heritage Quay ⓣ268/462-1727. The city's main casino, with 300 slot machines and table games such as blackjack, roulette, Caribbean Stud and three-card poker tables for the more serious players. Live bands and karaoke give the place a bit of atmosphere after 10pm. The casino normally has a shuttle that will pick you up from anywhere on the island, but you'll have to get a taxi back. Open 10am–4pm; closed Sun unless a ship is in.

Listings

All services listed are in **St John's** unless otherwise stated.

Airlines American Airlines (☎268/462-0950); British Airways (☎268/462-0876); Carib Aviation (☎268/481-2403/4); LIAT (☎268/480-5600); Virgin (☎268/560-2079).
Bookshops Best of Books, Lower St Mary's Street (☎268/562-3198). The island's best bookstore, with a large fiction section.
Embassies British High Commission, Price Waterhouse Coopers Centre, 11 Old Parham Rd (☎268/462-0008/9); US Consular Agency, Suite 2, Jasmine Court, Friars Hill Road (☎268/463-6531).
Film Island Photo, Redcliffe and Market streets (☎268/462-1567), sells film and does one-hour photo development.
Pharmacies Full-service pharmacies include Benjies, at Redcliffe and Market streets in St John's (☎268/462-0733, open 8am–6pm Mon–Sat), and Woods, Woods Centre, Friars Hill Road (☎268/462-9287), open 9am–10pm Mon–Sat, 11am–6pm Sun.
Police The main police station is on Newgate Street ☎268/462-0125. Emergency ☎999 or 911.

14.2

From Runaway Bay to Half Moon Bay

North of St John's, **Runaway Bay** and adjoining **Dickenson Bay** constitute the island's main tourist strip, with a couple of excellent beaches and a host of good hotels and restaurants. Continuing clockwise around the island brings you to its Atlantic side, where the jagged coastline features plenty of inlets, bays and swamps but, with a couple of noteworthy exceptions, rather less impressive beaches. Tourist facilities on the Atlantic side of the island are much less developed but there are several places of interest. **Betty's Hope** is a restored sugar plantation; **Devil's Bridge** offers one of the most dramatic landscapes on the island; at **Harmony Hall** you can relax from your exertions with lunch and a boat ride to Green Island; and at picturesque **Half Moon Bay** you can scramble along a vertiginous clifftop path above the pounding Atlantic.

Accommodation

Antigua's **northwest coast** is the most popular destination for visitors, with a series of hotels dotted along the lovely beaches, and plenty of restaurants, watersports and beach life. The east coast is less visited but has two very good hotels.

Dickenson Bay Cottages Dickenson Bay ⓣ268/462-4940, ⓦwww.dickensonbaycottages.com. Twelve spacious, airy and excellently furnished cottages set around a well-landscaped garden and pool up on a hillside overlooking the bay. Just a short walk from the beach and the *Rex Halcyon Cove* hotel, where *Dickenson Bay* guests have subsidized use of the facilities, including tennis courts. 5

Harmony Hall Brown's Bay ⓣ268/460-4120, ⓦwww.harmonyhallantigua.com. A delightfully classy but laid-back place in the middle of nowhere. The 20 simple but stylish rooms have large bathrooms, comfortable beds and small patios. The beach is small but a free boat regularly ferries guests out to the clean, white sand at Green Island (see p.550). The splendid restaurant is normally busy. Closed mid-May–mid-Nov. 9

Long Bay Hotel Long Bay ⓣ268/463-2005, ⓦwww.longbayhotel.com. Small, friendly, secluded, all-inclusive choice located by a tiny turquoise bay, with 25 cosy rooms and cottages. Guests enjoy use of a few sailboats and windsurfers, and there's a good tennis court, a big library and a game room. Closed mid May-late Oct. 9

Sandals Grande Antigua Resort & Spa Dickenson Bay ⓣ268/462-0267, ⓦwww.sandals.com. Part of the popular, all-inclusive Caribbean chain, this huge resort boasts ten restaurants, six pools – one of which is the largest in the Eastern Caribbean, a top-notch spa and a wide range of entertainment and activities. 9

Siboney Beach Club Dickenson Bay, ⓣ268/462-0806. Owned by friendly Aussie Tony Johnson, this low-key hotel is set in jungle-like gardens on a gorgeous white-sand beach. The suites all come with kitchenettes and small lounges. The top-rate *Coconut Grove* restaurant (see p.550) is onsite. 6

Sunsail Club Colonna Hodges Bay ⓣ268/462-6263, ⓦwww.sunsail.com. This well-landscaped Mediterranean-style resort is handy for the airport; most guests are on all-inclusive packages. Lovely pool, and very child-friendly. 8

Trade Winds Hotel Dickenson Bay ⓣ268/462-1223, ⓦwww.twhantigua.com. Delightful place in the hills above the bay, with big, comfortable rooms. Guests can chill out by the freshwater pool overlooking the ocean or take the shuttle down to the beach. The hotel's restaurant (see p.550) has good-quality food and great views. 8

Runaway Bay and Dickenson Bay

A few miles north of St John's, a series of attractive white-sand beaches runs around the island's northwest coast. Most of the tourist development is concentrated along Runaway Bay and Dickenson Bay, where the gleaming beaches slope gently down into the turquoise sea, offering calm swimming and, at the northern end of Dickenson Bay, a host of watersports. **Runaway Bay** is the quieter of the two and, because there are fewer hotels to tidy up their "patch", is strewn with more seaweed and rocks. It's still a great place to wade in the gentle surf despite the northern end's erosion by heavy swells.

Trapped between two imposing sandstone bluffs not far to the north, **Dickenson Bay** is fringed by another wide, white-sand beach which stretches for almost a mile between Corbison Point and the more thickly vegetated woodland of Weatherill's Hill at its northern end. It's a lovely bay, shelving gently into the sea and with a protected swimming zone dividing swimmers from the jet skiers, windsurfers, water-skiers and parasailers. The northern half of the beach fronts some of Antigua's largest hotels thus the area can get pretty busy with a string of bars, hair braiders and T-shirt vendors.

Betty's Hope to Long Bay

Heading inland and southeast, the partly restored **Betty's Hope** (Tues–Sat 10am–4pm; US$2) was the island's very first sugar estate. Built in 1650, the place was owned by the Codrington family for nearly two centuries until the end of World War II. Its lack of profitability brought it to the edge of closure which followed soon after the war. Although most of the estate lies in ruins, one of the windmills has been restored to working condition, and a small and interesting museum at the visitor centre traces the history of sugar on Antigua as well as the development and restoration of the estate.

North of Betty's Hope, the village of Seatons is the starting point for a very enjoyable, informative and well-organized **eco-tour** attraction. Stingray City

Antigua (ⓣ268/562-7297, ⓦwww.stingraycityantigua.com) allows you to swim with stingrays in their "natural" environment, a large penned area of ocean not far offshore (US$50 per person, free for children under 4).

East of Betty's Hope and approaching Long Bay, a track signposted off to the right takes you out for half a mile to **Devil's Bridge** on a rocky outcrop edged by patches of grassy land, tall century plants and sunbathing cattle. Wander round the promontory to the "bridge", a narrow piece of rock whose underside has been washed away by thousands of years of relentless surf. The hot, windswept spot offers some of the most fetching views on the island. En route back to the main road, a dirt track on your right after 30 yards leads down to a tiny but gorgeous bay – the perfect place for a picnic.

Past the turn-off for Devil's Bridge, at the end of the main road, **Long Bay** is home to a couple of rather exclusive all-inclusives. The resorts don't prevent access to the great, wide bay that is enormously popular with local schoolkids. The lengthy spread of white sand is protected by an extensive reef a few hundred yards offshore (bring your snorkelling gear) and there's a laid-back beach bar for shelter and refreshment.

Harmony Hall to Half Moon Bay

Tucked away on the east coast overlooking Nonsuch Bay, the restored plantation house at **Harmony Hall** (closed mid-May–mid-Nov) is home to a chic hotel and restaurant (see p.549), as well as a free art gallery that showcases monthly exhibitions of local and Caribbean art.

From the jetty, boats regularly make the five-minute run out to deserted **Green Island**, where the beaches are powdery and the snorkelling excellent. If you're not a guest, there's a US$10 charge.

One of the prettiest spots on Antigua, **Half Moon Bay** has a half-mile semicircle of white-sand beach partially enclosing a deep-blue bay where the Atlantic surf normally offers top-class body-surfing opportunities. There's not much in the way of facilities aside from **Smiling Harry's Beach Bar** (open daily year-round), which serves up a great burger along with the requisite smile.

Eating and drinking

With a range of hotels scattered about the **north coast**, there is a steady stream of punters looking for good places to eat, and plenty of decent **restaurants** have popped up as a result, although there are few options in the low-budget range. **Dickenson Bay** has the widest selection. In the east, there's a decent beach bar handy for those loafing on Long Bay, and a good restaurant at Harmony Hall.

Bay House *Trade Winds Hotel*, Dickenson Bay ⓣ268/462-1223. Smart restaurant overlooking Dickenson Bay, and a romantic place for a drink at sunset. Starters include of seared scallops with sweet potato purée (US$15), while mains might be grilled swordfish with orzo and pumpkin gateau (US$31) or beef tenderloin with horseradish mash (US$37). Daily for lunch and dinner. No shorts or trainers.

The Beach Dickenson Bay ⓣ268/480-6940, ⓦwww.bigbanana-antigua.com. Brightly painted restaurant on the beach serving good food. Lunchtime dishes include sushi, fish and chips, burgers and salads for US$13–18; dinner specials might be sesame-crusted tuna, meaty pasta or seafood stew for US$15–30. Daily for lunch and dinner.

Le Bistro Hodges Bay ⓣ268/462-3881, ⓦwww.antigualebistro.com. This long-established, classy restaurant has a reputation for serving the best French food on the island. Expect classic dishes such as onion soup (US$9), sole meunière (market price) and duck à l'orange (US$28), along with more inventive combinations and a superior wine list. Reservations recommended. Dinner only. Closed Mon & most of Sept.

Coconut Grove *Siboney Beach Club*, Dickenson Bay ⓣ268/462-1538. Lunch at this delightful open-air beachside location is decidedly average; come instead for dinner and the mouthwatering starters such as calaloo soup (EC$27) and mains like pan-seared mahi mahi (EC$80) and Antiguan rock lobster (EC$95). Daily 7.30am–11pm.

Harmony Hall Browns Bay ⓣ268/460-4120, ⓦwww.harmonyhallantigua.com. This is one of the island's best restaurants. Built around an old sugar mill, the elegant but simple food is served on a terrace overlooking the bay. The menu includes fresh mozzarella salad (US$20) and steamed lobster (US$46). Daily for lunch, Fri & Sat also dinner. Closed mid-May–Oct.

14.3 Falmouth and English Harbour

An essential stop on any visit to Antigua, the picturesque area around **Falmouth** and **English Harbour** on the island's south coast not only holds some of the most important and interesting historical remains in the Caribbean, but is also now the region's leading yachting centre. The chief attraction is the eighteenth-century **Nelson's Dockyard**, which was the key facility for the British navy when they ruled the East Caribbean's waves. Today it's a living museum where visiting yachts are cleaned, supplied and chartered. Nearby are several ruined forts as well as an abundance of attractive colonial buildings on the waterfront, several of which have been converted into hotels and restaurants.

Across the harbour from the dockyard, there is further evidence of the area's colonial past at **Shirley Heights** where more ruined forts, gun batteries and an old cemetery hold a commanding position over the water.

The area also has a handful of worthwhile spots off the beaten path, including the massive military complex at **Great Fort George**, high in the hills above **Falmouth**.

A car is invaluable for touring around this part of the south coast. Frequent **buses** run between St John's and English Harbour, handy if you just want to explore Nelson's Dockyard, but to get up to Shirley Heights you'll need your own transport or a taxi.

Accommodation

With plenty of good restaurants and nightlife and its proximity to **Nelson's Dockyard**, this is an attractive area to stay in. If, however, you're after serious beaches you'll want to look elsewhere on the island.

Admiral's Inn Nelson's Dockyard, English Harbour ⓣ268/460-1027, ⓦwww.admiralsantigua.com. Built in 1788 as the dockyard's supply store and now attractively restored, this is one of the best accommodation options in Antigua, with a great colonial atmosphere, welcoming staff, a romantic setting by the harbour and sensible prices. An occasional free boat ferries guests to a nearby beach. 5

Catamaran Hotel Falmouth ⓣ268/460-1036, ⓦwww.catamaran-antigua.com. The beach isn't great for swimming and it's a bit of a hike to the action at the dockyard but this is a very friendly hotel with comfortable, well-equipped rooms (each balcony has a hammock) and a good value. There's also a bar, restaurant and small pool. ⑤

The Inn at English Harbour English Harbour ⓣ268/460-1014, ⓦwww.theinn.ag. This old hotel, popular with repeat guests, is spread over a large site beside the harbour next to a pleasant white-sand beach. Of the 34 rooms, the beachfront suites are by far the nicest, with minimalist decor and a modern feel. ⑨

Ocean Inn English Harbour ⓣ268/463-7950, ⓦwww.theoceaninn.com. Small, friendly inn perched on a hillside above English Harbour, with six doubles and four cottages – and stunning views. It's some distance from a good beach but there is a (small) pool and you're just five minutes' walk from Nelson's Dockyard. The excellent rates include continental breakfast. ④

Falmouth and around

The main road south from St John's, cutting through the very centre of Antigua, first hits the coast at **Falmouth Harbour**. This large and beautiful natural harbour has been used as a safe anchorage since the days of the earliest colonists, and the town that sprang up beside it was the first major settlement on the island. Today, although the harbour is often busy with yachts, the town of Falmouth itself is a quiet place as most of the activity has moved east to **English Harbour** and Nelson's Dockyard, which is divided from Falmouth Harbour by a small peninsula known as the **Middle Ground**.

Great Fort George

High above Falmouth offering terrific panoramic views of the harbour and surrounding countryside are the ruins of **Great Fort George** (also known as **Monk's Hill**). One of Antigua's oldest defences, the fort was built in the 1690s as a secure retreat for Antigua's tiny population.

These days the fort is in a very dilapidated state, but it's worth the effort to visit for the fabulous views and a quiet but evocative sense of the island's past. Much of the enormous stone perimeter wall is intact and just inside the main gate and to the right, the west gunpowder magazine (built in 1731) has been well restored.

To get to the fort you'll need a 4x4 vehicle or be up for a thirty-minute hike. A precipitous but passable track leads up from the village of Cobbs Cross, east of

▲ Fishing boats

Falmouth; alternatively, from Liberta (north of Falmouth) take the inland road to Table Hill Gordon, from where another track winds up to the fort.

English Harbour and around

The road east from Falmouth leads to the tiny village of Cobb's Cross, where a right turn takes you down to the small village of **ENGLISH HARBOUR**. Today the village consists of little more than a handful of homes, shops and restaurants. Another right turn leads down to **Nelson's Dockyard**, to the excellent **Pigeon Beach** and to the Middle Ground peninsula. Alternatively, head straight on for the road that climbs up into the hills to the military ruins at **Shirley Heights**.

Nelson's Dockyard

One of Antigua's definite highlights, the eighteenth-century **Nelson's Dockyard** (daily 8am–6pm; US$5, includes admission to Shirley Heights) is the only surviving Georgian-era dockyard in the world. Adjacent to a fine natural harbour, the place developed primarily as a careening station, a dock for refurbishing and repairing British ships. It also provided the military with a local base to repair, water and supply the British navy.

Construction began in 1743 but most of the present buildings date from 1785 and 1792. Many structures were built from the ballast of bricks and stones brought to the island by British trading ships which left their home ports with empty holds to load up with sugar and rum in the Caribbean.

During the nineteenth century, however, the advent of steam-powered ships (which needed less maintenance) coincided with a decline in British interest in the region, and the dockyard fell into disuse, finally closing in 1889. The 1950s saw a major restoration project, and in 1961 the dockyard was reopened as both a working harbour and a tourist attraction.

Entering the dockyard, the first building on your left is the **Admiral's Inn**, built in 1788 and originally used as a store for pitch, lead and turpentine, and is now a lovely hotel and restaurant. Adjoining the hotel, a dozen thick, capped **stone pillars** are all that is left of a large boathouse, where ships were once pulled in along a narrow channel to have their sails repaired in the sail loft on the upper floor.

From the hotel, a lane leads down to the harbour itself, passing various restored colonial buildings including the remains of a guardhouse, a blacksmith's workshop and an old canvas and clothing store. Just beyond is the Admiral's House (which never housed an admiral) that was built in 1855 and today serves as the dockyard's **museum** (daily 8am–6pm; free), which has a small but fascinating collection focusing on the dockyard's history and the island's shipping tradition.

Fort Berkeley

The narrow path that starts near the museum (behind the adjacent *Copper and Lumber Store Hotel*) and leads to **Fort Berkeley** is easily missed, but a stroll around these dramatic military ruins is rewarding. Perched above the crashing surf on a narrow spit of land that overlooks the entrance to English Harbour, the fort was the harbour's earliest defensive point and retains essentially the same long, thin shape today that it had in 1745.

Pigeon Beach

There's not much in the way of beach around Nelson's Dockyard but a good place to head after sightseeing is **Pigeon Beach**, five minutes' drive or twenty minutes' walk west of the dockyard. You'll find a wide expanse of white sand and a beach bar, **Bumpkins** (closed on Mondays in summer).

Shirley Heights

Spread over the hills east of English Harbour, numerous military ruins offer further evidence of the strategic importance of this part of southern Antigua. Collectively known as **Shirley Heights** (although technically this is only the name for the area around Fort Shirley), it's an interesting area to explore, with a couple of hiking opportunities (daily; from 9am to 5pm there's an EC$13 entry charge, which includes admission to Nelson's Dockyard).

Follow the road uphill from the tiny village of English Harbour and you'll pass the late eighteenth-century **Clarence House**, an attractive Georgian home built in 1787 for Prince William, Duke of Clarence (later King William IV), who was then serving in the Royal Navy. (At publication time, the house was undergoing renovation.) Past the house a right-hand turn-off leads down to the *Inn at English Harbour* (see p.552) and the attractive crescent of Galleon Beach.

Ignoring the turn-off and carrying straight on you'll pass the free **Dow's Hill Interpretation Centre** which has a fine collection of shells but, frankly, virtually nothing to do with the area's history and is pretty missable. Beyond the centre, the road runs along the top of a ridge before forking where a large cannon has been upended in the centre of the road. The left fork leads to the cliff known as **Cape Shirley** where you'll find a cluster of ruined stone buildings known as the **Blockhouse**. On the eastern side a wide gun platform looks downhill to a narrow inlet at **Indian Creek**, out to **Standfast Point** peninsula and beyond to the vast sweep of Willoughby Bay.

If you take the right-hand fork, the road will lead to the ruins of **Fort Shirley**. To the left, across a bare patch of ground, are the remains of the military hospital and, in a small valley just below the surgeon's quarters, the **military cemetery** with its barely legible tombstones dating mostly from the 1850s and reflecting the prevalence of disease, particularly yellow fever.

The road ends at the fort itself, where a restored guardhouse now serves as an excellent little bar and restaurant, *The Lookout* (see opposite). The courtyard – where a battery of cannons once pointed out across the sea – now sees a battery of cameras snapping up the fabulous views over English Harbour, particularly on Sundays when the tourists descend in droves for the reggae and steel bands.

Eating, drinking and nightlife

Most of the good south coast **restaurants** are concentrated around Nelson's Dockyard and nearby Falmouth Harbour. It's also worth driving up to *The Lookout* at Shirley Heights.

Abracadabra English Harbour ⓣ268/460-2701, ⓦwww.theabracadabra.com. This popular spot serves Italian food in the evening; from 11pm Mon to Sat it turns into a disco bar, with DJs, live music and monthly costume parties in season (for which a US$10 cover charge applies, although it's waived if you're in costume). On the same site is *Cloggy's Café*, offering Mediterranean food at lunchtime (closed July).

Caribbean Taste English Harbour ⓣ268/562-3049. Authentic Antiguan eats in this small restaurant tucked away among local residences just behind Dockyard Drive. Servings include large portions of ducana and salt cod, *fungi* and conch stew or curried goat, all for around US$10–15. Closed Sun.

Kesari Falmouth Harbour ⓣ268/460-1361, ⓦwww.kesarigourmet.com. If you fancy a change from local fare, try this Asian-influenced tapas bar. The lounge-style space complements the huge cocktail list and tempting menu of sushi and sashimi, small dishes such as salt and pepper squid, and larger curries (all for around US$10). Dinner only; closed Mon & Tues.

The Last Lemming Falmouth Harbour ⓣ268/460-6910. Tasty food and waterside views are the draws at this frequently crowded spot. The daily changing menu includes curries, steaks and a catch of the day, and the Sunday "Lounging at the Lemming" brunch, complete with DJ playing chill-out music, is a local tradition. Tuesday nights, featuring live music, are also popular (no cover charge).

Life English Harbour ⓣ268/562-2353. In the evenings this bar and restaurant often boasts a vibrant party scene, playing everything from 60s classics to the latest hits. Pub grub is served at both lunch and dinnertime, with curries, pies, fish and steaks for around US$11–13. Closed Mon & Sept–Oct. No cover charge.

The Lookout Shirley Heights ⓣ268/728-0636, ⓦwww.shirleyheightslookout.com. The only place for a refreshment break while you're up on the Heights, offering up lunch and dinner on a large patio with superb views. The Sun barbecues have a great party atmosphere (4pm–10pm, US$10). There's a lower-key vibe for the Thurs barbecues, when a steel band plays from 4pm–8pm (free). Fri nights showcase tapas-sized dishes and cocktails. Closed Mon dinner.

Trappas English Harbour ⓣ268/562-3534. Lively laid-back eaterie serving excellent curries, fish, steaks and chicken dishes for US$9 (starters) and US$15–20 (mains). Good wine list, too. Extremely popular, so book ahead. Dinner only; closed Sun & Mon except during big events.

14.4

The west coast

Tourism has made a firm impression on Antigua's **west coast**, with hotels dotted at regular intervals between the little fishing village of **Old Road** in the south and St John's. Two geographic features dominate this area: a series of lovely beaches – with **Darkwood** probably the pick of the bunch for swimming, snorkelling and beachcombing – and a glowering range of hills known as the **Shekerley Mountains** in the southwest, offering the chance for a climb and panoramic views. The lush and thickly wooded **Fig Tree Hill** on the edge of the range is as scenic a spot as you'll find, and you can take a variety of **hikes** inland to see a side of Antigua overlooked by the vast majority of tourists. Due west of St John's, the **Five Islands** peninsula is home to several hotels, some good beaches and the substantial ruins of the eighteenth-century **Fort Barrington**.

Accommodation

Antigua's **west coast** has more rooms than any other part of the island. The Five Islands peninsula has a handful of good hotels, although they feel a little more isolated than the rest of the coast's offerings.

Carlisle Bay Old Road ⓣ268/484-0000, ⓦwww.carlisle-bay.com. Highly exclusive (and highly priced) beachside resort and spa that's in a class of its own. Couples and families are generally well separated, although there's only one pool (albeit a stunner). The rooms are modern and beautiful, and the kids' club and variety of activities are excellent. The onsite *East* restaurant is one of the island's best. 9

Curtain Bluff Old Road, ⓣ268/462-8400, ⓦwww.curtainbluff.com. This all-inclusive may be pricier than others, but the list of complimentary services, including windsurfing, water-skiing and scuba diving, is impressive. Further attractions include a gorgeous spa, and breathtaking views of the windswept ocean. Service is very friendly. Usually closed late Aug–late Oct. 9

Galley Bay Five Islands ⓣ268/462-0302, ⓦwww.antigua-resorts.com. This secluded all-inclusive resort set on a gorgeous stretch of sand next to a lagoon features 98 luxurious rooms and cottages (the latter with splash pools). Children are only allowed during the Christmas/New Year period. 9

Hawksbill by Rex Resorts Five Islands ⓣ268/462-0301, ⓦwww.rexresorts.com.

Sprawling but quiet resort overlooking the bay. The main draws are the four beaches (one of them clothing-optional), dramatic views and landscaped gardens; the rooms themselves are nothing special. 9

Hermitage Bay Hermitage Bay ⓣ268/562-5500, ⓦwww.hermitagebay.com. One-of-a-kind all-inclusive resort boasting 25 luxuriously kitted-out hillside and beachfront properties, some with private plunge pools. Service is friendly, the beach beautiful and the food better than other all-inclusives. Rates drop by more than half outside of peak season. 9

Jolly Harbour Villas Jolly Harbour ⓣ268/462-6166, ⓦwww.hbkvillas.com. Fifty two-bedroom waterfront villas, each with a full kitchen and a balcony. Plenty of restaurants, shops (including a large supermarket) and sports facilities such as a golf course and large swimming pool are nearby, but the place feels somewhat bland and unimaginative. 5

Rex Blue Heron Johnson's Point ⓣ268/462-8564, ⓦwww.rexresorts.com. Medium-sized hotel on one of the best west coast beaches. The pool is small and the 64 rooms vary in quality – the beachfront ones are the nicest – but the service is friendly and you can often get excellent rates (all-inclusive is also available, but doesn't include watersports). Children under 16 not allowed. 5

Fig Tree Drive

This scenic road runs west from the town of Swetes through the most densely forested part of the island, **Fig Tree Hill**. You won't actually see any fig trees – the road is lined with banana (known locally as figs) and mango trees as it carves its way through some gorgeous scenery down to the south coast at Old Road. About halfway along the drive, you can stop at a small roadside shack ("culture shop"), which sells drinks and fruit and jams from local farms.

A dirt track leads uphill from the shack to a **reservoir** – the island's first – where you'll find picnic tables set up around the edge of the water. Those interested in a more serious hike can take the **Rendezvous Trail**, which starts on your left just before you reach the steps of the reservoir and crosses the **Wallings Woodlands** to the nearly-always empty beach at Rendezvous Bay – a two-hour walk. Even a short stroll down this trail repays the effort; the woodlands are the best remaining example of the evergreen secondary forest that covered the island before the British settlers arrived, and are home to more than thirty species of shrubs and trees, including giant mahogany trees, and masses of noisy birdlife. Bear in mind that, although it's pretty hard to get lost, the main path is little used and in places can quickly become overgrown and difficult to make out.

Nearby Antigua Rainforest Canopy Tours (ⓣ268/562-6363, ⓦwww.antiguarainforest.com) offers exhilarating ziplining tours of the rainforest every day in season, from 9am (from US$50 per person, book in advance).

Boggy Peak

The run-down village of Old Road contrasts with the opulence of two luxury hotels nearby – *Carlisle Bay* (see p.555) and *Curtain Bluff* (see p.555). Between the two is a gorgeous stretch of public beach. West of Old Road, the road follows the coast past a series of banana groves and pineapple plantations, and around **Cades Bay**, with delightful views out to sea over Cades Reef. On the right, half a mile from Old Road, a track leads up into the Shekerley Mountains to **Boggy Peak**, at 1312m the highest point on the island. The panoramic view from the top – on clear days you can even make out St Kitts, Guadeloupe and Montserrat – repays the effort of making the steep drive or the one-hour climb. Unfortunately the peak is somewhat marred by a communications station, safely tucked away behind a high-security fence. For a guided walk of the peak or Wallings Woodlands (see above), call the highly knowledgeable Winston Hazzard (ⓣ268/461-8195 or 770 2898; US$30 per person, minimum of four people). He also runs fishing and snorkelling trips to Cades Reef.

Darkwood Beach and around

Continuing west along the coast through the village of **Urlings**, the road runs alongside a number of excellent beaches. First up is **Turner's Beach** and **Johnson's Point**, where the sand shelves down to the sea beside a couple of good beach bars, including *Turner's* (see p.557), which rents snorkelling gear. The snorkelling is better just north of here at **Darkwood Beach**, a wide stretch of beach running right alongside the main road and a great spot for a swim. Look out for small underwater canyons just offshore, and schools of squid and colourful reef fish. Beachcombers will find this one of the best places on the island to look for shells and driftwood.

Just north of Darkwood Beach lies **Jolly Harbour**, where a marina complex includes rental apartments, a golf course, restaurants and shops. It's a world apart from the "real Antigua", but the supermarket is handy and the rental villas (see p.556) are a good value.

Further north, the road passes some spectacular scenery; turning left down a badly made up road before the village of Jennings brings you to **Hermitage Bay**, a gorgeous beach that's the location of one of Antigua's best resorts.

Five Islands

To the west of St John's the highway leads out through a narrow isthmus onto the large **Five Islands** peninsula, named after five small rocks just offshore. There are several hotels here, although the peninsula's interior is largely barren and scrubby and there's not a huge amount to see. To reach the excellent beaches at **Hawksbill Bay** (named for the hawksbill turtle-shaped rock just offshore), follow the main road straight through the peninsula.

On Goat Hill, at the northern point of the peninsula close to the *Royal Antiguan* hotel, the circular stone ruins of **Fort Barrington** overlook gorgeous Deep Bay. The British first built a simple fort here in the 1650s to protect the southern entrance to St John's Harbour but it was captured by the French when they took the city in 1666. Take the twenty-minute walk around the beach to the fort for a dramatic sense of isolation and excellent views.

Eating, drinking and nightlife

A series of eateries are lined up along the marina at Jolly Harbour, as well as the romantic Sheer further north and a couple of delightful little beach bars, including one at Darkwood Beach.

Dogwatch Tavern Jolly Harbour ⓣ268/462-6550. English-style pub right beside the marina, with pool tables, dartboards and a wide selection of beers. Adjoining it is *The Deck* restaurant, serving seafood and excellent burgers. Tavern open 4pm till late Mon–Fri, 5pm till late Sat & Sun; Restaurant open 6pm–11pm daily.

Rush North end of Runaway Bay ⓣ268/562-7874, ⓦwww.rushantigua.com. This entertainment complex includes a casino, piano bar, restaurant and sports bar. The highlight, however, is the nightclub, open on a Fri and Sat. Cover charges vary, but are never over US$12.

Sheer *CocoBay Resort* ⓣ268/562-2400 or 562-4510 direct line (3–11pm), ⓦwww.cocobayresort.com. Both the beautiful cliffside setting and Nigel Martin's imaginative cooking are the talking points here. Starters include the likes of smoked scallops with green apple sorbet (US$23), while mains might be baked sea bass with pumpkin seed crust (US$32), or tournedos of beef tenderloin with honey truffled beets (US$36). It's expensive, so save it for a romantic splurge. Book in advance. Lunch and dinner; closed Sun & Mon, and late July–mid-Oct.

Turner's Beach Bar and Grill Johnson's Point ⓣ268/462-9133. Unpretentious place on one of the best west coast beaches. It's as low-key as they come, with plastic furniture right on the sand, but the food isn't bad. The menu includes chicken or goat curry (US$13/16), barbecued chicken (US$12), fish cakes (US$9) and lobster (US$44). The owners also rent out beach chairs and snorkelling gear, and can arrange windsurfing lessons. Lunch and dinner daily.

14.5

Barbuda

If you have time, it's well worth the effort of taking a day-trip to the nation's other inhabited island, **Barbuda**, which lies 42km north of Antigua. With its magnificent and often deserted beaches, spectacular coral reefs and rare colony of frigate birds, the island is a definite highlight. Don't expect the same facilities as on Antigua; **accommodation** options are limited, and you'll need to bring your own snorkelling or diving gear. You'll also find that schedules – whether for taxis, boats or meals – are as laid-back as the locals.

Half the size of its better-known neighbour, **Barbuda** developed quite separately from Antigua and was only reluctantly coerced into joining the nation during the run-up to independence in 1981. The island is very much the poor neighbour in terms of financial resources, and its development has been slow. Tourism's impact has been minimal, and fishing and farming remain the principal occupations of the tiny population of 1500, most of whom live in the small capital, **Codrington**.

Away from the beaches, the island is less fetching – mostly low-level scrub of cacti, bush, small trees and the distinctive century plants and most of the year it is extremely arid and unwelcoming. There are a couple of exceptions: in the **southwest** the island suddenly bursts to life, with a fabulous grove of coconut palms springing out of the sandy soil and in parts of the interior, government projects are reclaiming land from the bush to grow peanuts and sweet potatoes for export. Overall the island is left to the scrub, the elusive wild boar, deer and hundreds of species of birds.

Getting there

The only scheduled **flights** to Barbuda are from Antigua to Codrington on Carib Aviation (Ⓣ268/481-2403, Ⓦwww.carib-aviation.com). They offer two flights a day from the main airport in Antigua (leaving at 8am and 6pm, returning thirty minutes later in each case). The flight takes 15 minutes, and the cost is around US$70 for a round-trip. The company also runs charter flights between the two islands. Several taxi companies operate on Barbuda. Reputable names include Byron Askie (Ⓣ268/460-0164, 783-7243 or 773-6082) and Lynton Thomas (Ⓣ268/773-9957); they both charge around US$50 per day and also offer tours of the island for a higher fee. Byron also has some watersports equipment. Other tour operators include MacArthur Nedd (Ⓣ268/460-0059 or 724-7490), who runs tours across the island and sea taxis to the Bird Sanctuary, and eXtra Taxi Service (Ⓣ268/460-0408 or 772-0917), which also offers boat trips to the sanctuary. Call for prices.

You can also make the journey by **catamaran** with Barbuda Express (Ⓣ268/560-7989, Ⓦwww.antiguaferries.com). The trip takes 95 minutes and costs US$148 including a lobster lunch and a visit to the bird sanctuary, the Highlands, Two Foot Cay and a quick stop at Pink Sands Beach. Departures are daily (except Mon) from Jolly Harbour at 8.15am, St John's at 9am and 3.30pm from Barbuda.

Tropical Adventures (see p.540) also offers trips to Barbuda (including a stop at the bird sanctuary), while Adventure Antigua (see p.542) runs private charters.

Codrington

CODRINGTON, the island's capital and only settlement, holds almost the entire population within its grid of narrow streets. It's a well spread-out place, with plenty of brightly painted single-storey clapboard and concrete buildings. A couple of guesthouses, a handful of restaurants, bars and supermarkets line the streets but for the most part people keep to themselves, and there is little sign of life apart from a few curious schoolchildren, dogs and the occasional goat. On Sundays the capital livens up with a cricket match at the Holy Trinity School.

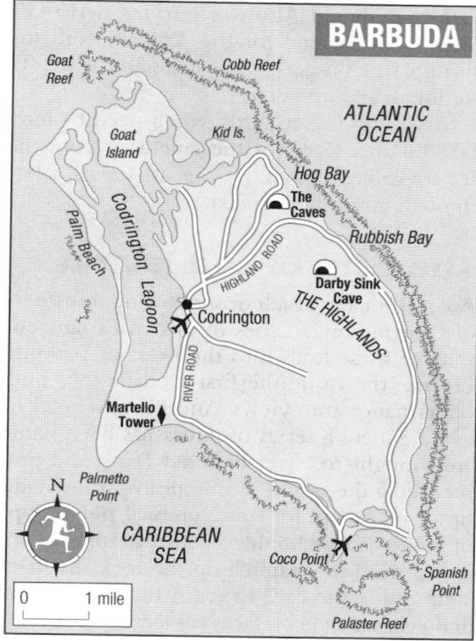

Codrington Lagoon

To the west of town, **Codrington Lagoon** is an expansive area of green, brackish water, fringed by mangroves. The lagoon is completely enclosed on its western side by the slender but magnificent strip of **Palm Beach** (only really accessible by boat), but there is a narrow cut to the north where fishing boats can get out to the ocean. Lobsters breed in the lagoon and you'll probably see them at the pier being loaded for export to Antigua – an important contribution to the local economy. The beach is a great place to snorkel and sunbathe, but there's not much shade, so ask your boatman to drop you by one of the groves of casuarina trees before arranging a time when he'll come back to collect you. Expect to pay around US$20 for a round-trip boat ride from Codrington Pier.

Equally significant in terms of tourism is a series of mangrove clumps to the northwest of the lagoon known as **Man of War Island**. The mangroves are the home and breeding ground for the largest group of **frigate birds** anywhere in the Caribbean. The sight as you approach them by boat (see p.540) is quite spectacular with multitudes of birds wheeling through the sky above and equal number watching imperiously from the nests. The display gets even more dramatic during the mating season from late August to December when hundreds of the males put on a grand show – puffing up their bright-red throat pouches as they soar through the air just a few yards above the females, who watch admiringly from the bushes.

Practicalities

If you want to **stay** in Codrington, there are a few budget choices. Of these, *Nedd's Guesthouse* (Ⓣ268/460-0059; ❷) is the epitome of "basic", offering four comfortable double rooms. There's a kitchen, plus a grocery store downstairs, and the owners will pick you up from the airport. Slightly more upmarket and in a busier part of town is the *Carriage House* (Ⓣ268/727-1761, Ⓔlnedd@hotmail.co.uk; ❸), which has two bedrooms (each with private bathroom), a kitchen and a common area. The whole house can be rented for a night or for an extended stay. Another option is the *Palm Tree Guest House* (Ⓣ268/ 784-4331 or 772-0166; ❷–❸), which has eight en-suite doubles, one of which has two bedrooms (all rooms have air-conditioning and satellite TV). At the restaurant (Ⓣ268 460-0517), conch, lobster, fish and chicken is served, plus fast food such as burgers. Main courses cost upwards of US$10. Open for lunch and dinner (closed Sun unless there are hotel guests).

Other **dining** options include the *Green Door Tavern* (Ⓣ268/562-3134), owned by Byron Askie (see p.558), which serves good-value island food. Open daily from

7am to midnight. Also worth trying is *Wa O'moni* (Ⓣ268/562-1933), run by Jackie Joseph, and named for the Arawak word for Barbuda. The menu covers lobster, shrimp, fish, burgers, sandwiches and salads (US$15–30), plus local juices. Mon–Sat for lunch and dinner.

To see the frigate birds, you'll need to hire one of the small **boats** (for around US$50) that leave for the sanctuary from the main pier just outside Codrington. It's advisable, though, to visit as part of a Barbuda tour or to make arrangements through your hotel or taxi.

The rest of the island

Apart from any beach or snorkelling stops, a tour of the island is a brief affair. North of Codrington, a series of dirt roads fans out across the upper part of the island. One of these leads into the heart of Barbuda to the scant remains of **Highlands House**, the castle the first Codringtons built in the seventeenth century, which offers panoramic views. Another dirt road heads to the northeastern side of the island, where a series of **caves** has been naturally carved into the low cliffs. These are thought to have sheltered Taíno and possibly Carib Indians in the centuries preceding the arrival of Europeans. Scant evidence of their presence has been found, however, except for some unusual **petroglyphs**. The entrance to the main cave is opposite a large boulder, with the ruins of an old **watchtower** built up alongside. You'll need to scramble up the rocks for five minutes then make a short, stooped walk inside the cave to reach the petroglyphs – a couple of barely distinguishable and very amateurish faces carved into the rockface.

River Fort

You can clamber around some more substantial remains at the **River Fort** in the southwest of the island, just beyond the coconut grove. The fort is a surprisingly large defensive structure for an island of Barbuda's size and importance. The island was attacked by Carib Indians in the 1680s and by the French navy in 1710 but with such a limited amount of valuable property, Barbuda hasn't tempted any further assailants. As a result the fort never saw any action, and its main role has been as a lookout and a landmark for ships approaching the island from the south.

The remains are dominated by a **Martello tower**, one of the many such small, round fortifications built throughout the British Empire during the Napoleonic Wars. Right below the tower, the **River Wharf** is the main point for access to Barbuda by boat and is always busy with trucks stockpiling and loading sand onto barges to be taken to replenish beaches in Antigua – a controversial but lucrative industry for the Barbudans.

Southwest of the tower, at the tip of the island, **Palmetto Point** features beautiful sun-drenched beaches.

Practicalities

One of Barbuda's most stunning resorts, the *Beach House*, at Palmetto Point, was closed as this guide went to press, but may reopen in future. *Coco Point* (Ⓣ268/462-3816, Ⓦwww.cocopoint.com; ⑨), on the gorgeous beach of the same name, is an exclusive resort. The nearby famed *K Club* closed a couple of years ago.

15

The French West Indies

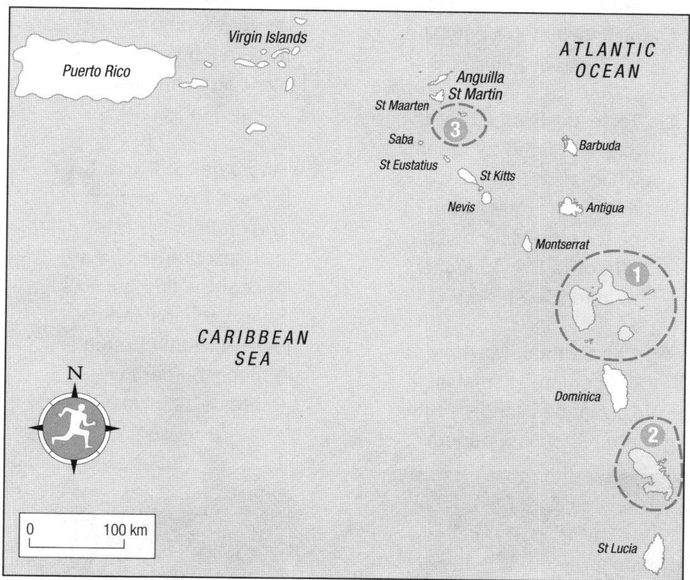

The French West Indies highlights

* **Markets** Haggle over spices and handicrafts at the animated outdoor markets of Pointe-à-Pitre and Fort-de-France. See pp.572 & 589

* **Parc National de Guadeloupe** Hike to thundering waterfalls, ascend cloud-capped mountain peaks, and explore lush rainforest at this outstanding reserve. See p.576

* **Terre-de-Haut, Guadeloupe** Fringed by dreamy white-sand beaches, the picturesque island of Terre-de-Haut boasts attractive Breton architecture. See p.580

* **Les Salines, Martinique** This stunning crystalline bay in the island's southern region is a perfect spot for watching the sunset. See p.593

* **St-Pierre, Martinique** The blackened, lava-ravaged ruins of the island's first capital make for a compelling visit. See p.593

* **Grand'Rivière, Martinique** Follow a thrillingly steep, winding road to the French West Indies' most authentic fishing village. See p.595

* **Gustavia, St Barts** Take a break from shopping and sunbathing with a cheeseburger and a beer at the laid-back *Le Select*, the inspiration behind Jimmy Buffett's "Cheeseburger in Paradise". See p.598

▲ Grand'Rivière, Martinique

Introduction and basics

Beaten by the Atlantic on one side and caressed by the Caribbean on the other, the four volcanic islands that comprise the **French West Indies** boast some of the Caribbean's most varied scenery. Extending almost 650km across the Eastern Caribbean, the islands of **Guadeloupe, Martinique, St Barthélemy (St Barts)** and French **St Martin** (covered in its own chapter, p.471), are an exotic blend of long sandy beaches, lush rainforests, craggy mountain peaks, dazzling turquoise waters and dramatic limestone coasts.

The larger islands are crowned by dormant volcanoes, including the Eastern Caribbean's highest summit, Guadeloupe's **La Soufrière**, and its most renowned, Martinique's historic **Mont-Pelée**. The crashing waterfalls that course their flanks feed dense interior rainforests before flowing out to sea where gorgeous **beaches** in hues ranging from white to gold and midnight-black drop off to a brilliant technicolour world of fish and coral that delights divers and snorkellers alike. The smallest island, St Barts, lacks the lush greenery of its southern siblings but compensates with spectacular secluded beaches and an unparalleled ambience of luxury and exclusivity.

Despite their setting amidst predominantly English islands, the French West Indies have remained remarkably French. While St Barts feels like a misplaced Mediterranean outpost, Guadeloupe and Martinique have merged the hallmarks of **French** culture – vices like wine, fine cuisine, coffee and cigarettes – with the best Creole traditions, from spicy food to atmospheric architecture and languid attitudes. The two meet head-on most noticeably in the major cities, like Guadeloupe's **Pointe-à-Pitre** and Martinique's **Fort-de-France**, where Caribbean marketplaces coexist with cafés, narrow streets jammed with honking cars, and fading wooden colonial houses.

Where to go

Guadeloupe has the most to offer one-stop island visitors, from a massive Parc National with impressive rainforest flora, hiking trails and ample beaches to a phenomenal dive site and four remarkable offshore islands, including the charming Terre-de-Haut.

In contrast, **Martinique** is geared more towards package-oriented travellers, with resort towns like busy Pointe-du-Bout. Still, visitors who search out less developed areas, like Presqu'île de la Caravelle will be rewarded with thrilling scenery and quiet, pristine beaches. Visitors can also visit authentically Martinican pockets like the ruins at St-Pierre and the superb Habitation Clément rum distillery, or escape the sun-worshipping throngs by hiking on Mont-Pelée.

For those who can afford it, tiny **St-Barthélemy** (St Barts) is the ultimate getaway – a decadent, beach-trimmed isle with a luxurious, self-pampering mindset, and little to do but shop and lie on the sand by day and eat sumptuously at night. While you may go home broke, you'll be completely rejuvenated.

When to go

Most of the year, puffy white clouds parade through clear blue skies and warm balmy breezes gently ruffle hair and sway palm fronds; T-shirt, shorts and sandals kind of weather, interrupted now and then by a tropical shower.

From July to November, this idyllic scene is slightly perturbed by the **hurricane season**, the wettest time of the year and also the most humid. The best time to visit (but also the most expensive) is between mid-December and mid-April, when the weather is dry and the heat is tempered by cooling trade winds.

Getting there

Whichever island you happen to be visiting, you will most likely fly through Guadeloupe's

Pôle-Caraïbes airport, which serves as a transport hub for this part of the Caribbean. From there, both ferries and flights are available to Martinique and St Barts.

Information

Each island has its own **tourism office** and **official website** with links to information and hotels and services that you can book yourself (see pp.55 and 56).

Money and costs

The islands of the French West Indies are overseas territories and collectivities of France, and prices for food and lodging are considerably more expensive than in much of the Caribbean. Thanks to its celeb status, St Barts is in a class all its own when it comes to budgetary considerations.

The **euro (€) is the official currency** on all three islands. Euro notes are issued in denominations of 5, 10, 20, 50, 100, 200 and 500 euros and coin denominations of 1, 2, 5, 10, 20 and 50 cents and 1 and 2 euros. The **US dollar** is also widely used on St Barts.

You'll find major **banks** on all island capitals and at resort areas, usually equipped with ATMs. Tellers exchange **traveller's cheques** and cash Monday to Friday 8am–noon and 2.30–5pm. Moneychangers don't charge commission; they can be found near the main island tourist offices.

Even with two people sharing a room, it will be a challenge to get by on less than $100/day, particularly on St Barts. The simplest double room costs around $65; the same room near a beach costs $100–115. Rates include all tax and service charges, and many also include breakfast. **Camping, hostelling and gîtes** are the cheapest options, with opportunities for the former two few and far between. As a general rule, the more built-up the resort, the more expensive the accommodations. Consider visiting the region in **low season** (May to Nov), when rates go down by almost half.

The best restaurant deals are the three-course **prix-fixe menus** offered in most establishments. On Guadeloupe and Martinique meals are commonly priced around US$35–45 for dinner, while St Barts charges closer to US$50–60 a head; they're usually modestly cheaper at lunchtime. The best lunch bargains are hefty ham and cheese baguettes and sodas from the beachside trucks that cost about US$7. Wine can actually be less expensive than soda, at about US$3 a glass in some bars.

Getting around

You'll be hard-pressed to make it to all French islands in one trip, as travelling between them is far from straightforward. Certainly checking out two islands per visit is feasible – Guadeloupe and Martinique both have regular ferry crossings between them, as do St Martin and St Barts.

The best way to get around each island is on your own wheels; what **public transportation** exists in Martinique and Guadeloupe is far from efficient, while St Barts – which happens to have the worst roads of the lot – has none whatsoever.

By bus

Getting around Martinique and Guadeloupe by bus is the most reasonably priced mode of transportation (€2–4 for short to medium-length journeys), but the service is not for those in a hurry. Known as *taxis collectifs* (or "TC"), the buses are actually cramped minivans that generally run from 6am to 6pm weekdays, with scant service after 2pm on Saturdays and none on Sundays. There's no real schedule to speak of – they leave from the capitals when they're full. To board one outside the capitals, simply flag it down along the road; keep in mind, however, that TCs are often packed in the hinterlands. Tell the driver where you're going when you board and pay him when you get off.

By taxi

Taxis in the French West Indies are expensive, charging a minimum of €5 even if you're just going down the street, and doubling their rates Monday to Friday 8pm–6am and all day Sundays and holidays. Fortunately, the only time you're really likely to need one is to get yourself to and from your hotel and the respective islands' ferry docks or airport.

By car and hitching

Driving requires a good dose of fearlessness. The locals are very aggressive on the roads – especially in Martinique, where drivers will pass each other even on winding turns. Guadeloupe is slightly less harried, but it's still important to be alert at all times, especially when driving in the heavy traffic of Pointe-à-Pitre. St Barts has grown increasingly dangerous in recent years as the cars plying its narrow, mottled-cement roads have become both bigger and faster. Most car rentals start around $50/day; see individual islands for details.

Hitchhiking is a way of life on Martinique and Guadeloupe due to the irregular bus service (the usual precautions apply), though you won't see many hitchhikers on St Barts, since just about everyone seems to drive.

By boat

The most common **passenger boats** are twin-hulled catamarans with a covered upper deck and an enclosed, air-conditioned lower one. Note that the trip from Guadeloupe to Martinique as well as between Guadeloupe and its outer islands can be choppy. Unlike the buses, ferries attempt to follow a schedule of sorts, especially those making the 40min–1hr 30min crossings to Guadeloupe's offshore islands (see p.581). The boats making the 1.5–3hr trips between Guadeloupe, Dominica and Martinique (see "Ferries", p.35), however, rarely leave on time as passengers must acquire a boarding pass and go through customs beforehand – despite this, it's a good idea to arrive at least 45 minutes before departure.

By plane

There are several **flights** daily between the three islands, but service is often erratic. Much of the air traffic consists of twenty-passenger aircraft that rarely leave on time and have low cargo weight restrictions. The fifteen-minute island hops between mainland Guadeloupe and its offshore isles are done by nine-seater planes with similar weight restrictions; they are often cancelled if they're under booked.

Accommodation

While Guadeloupe and St Barts have a wide range of **independent hotel** options, Martinique is heavily geared to **package-tour travellers**, with the result that most hotels are chains. To get the best rates, you should consult a travel agent.

Bungalow-style lodging is extremely popular on Guadeloupe and Martinique – basically a fully equipped studio or one-bedroom apartment with a kitchen. If you're concerned about costs, it's an effective way to save money since you're not paying for hotel services, and you can make your own meals. A growing **bed-and-breakfast industry** is also starting to make a dent in the hotel scene thanks to lower prices and familial service; the best are part of the Gîtes de France network (ⓣ01 49 70 75 75, ⓦwww.gites-de-france.fr). There are no B&Bs on St Barts, though there are plenty of luxurious villas to rent if you have the cash.

Camping is forbidden on St Barts, and there are few opportunities to camp on Guadeloupe. On Martinique, visitors are allowed to pitch their tents for free on a limited number of the island's beaches during French school holidays (July & August and the March break).

Food and drink

As St Barts has grown ever more popular among an international crowd of jet-setters, the island's dining scene has become just as cosmopolitan. **French-Creole** cuisine still rules, but you'll also find great Italian, sushi, and other global fare. Guadeloupe and Martinique's restaurants are less flashy and tend to stick to more traditional Creole seafood plates. The French influence shows most with breakfast, which usually consists of a small espresso, croissant and fruit juice, and beach fare, mostly filling sandwiches, crepes and pastries.

Lunch is the meal of the day – things pretty much shut down all over the islands noon–2pm, even in the touristy shopping districts of St Barts. Prix-fixe menus are the best deal, typically including at least a starter

Emergency numbers

Guadeloupe ⓣ15 (medical); ⓣ17 (police).
Martinique ⓣ15 (medical); ⓣ17 (police).
St Barts ⓣ18 or ⓣ0590/27 60 35 (medical); ⓣ0590/27 66 66 (police).

and a main course, plus a good selection of French wines to wash down the spicy Creole food. Dishes like *crabes farçi* (stuffed land crabs), *boudin* (blood pudding), *accras* (cod fritters) and the various *colombos*, a curry using *cabri* (goat), *poulet* (chicken), *lambi* (conch) and *ouassous* (crayfish), are the spiciest of all, though some resort areas tone them down. Most main courses come with rice or beans.

The most expensive item on any menu is *langoustine*, a lobster-like delicacy served grilled, fricasseed or in pasta. Other dishes, like *féroce d'avocat* (a zesty avocado and cod purée), *calalou* (a spinach-like soup), and grilled fish like *vivanneau* (red snapper), marlin and *requin* (shark) are less pricey and often equally tasty.

Individual islands have their specialities too. Guadeloupe's offshore Marie-Galante is known for a hearty **bébélé**, a thick "everything in the pot" soup of African origin made only on Saturdays, while Martinican chefs make **coq colombo**, a rich rooster curry.

French wine availability notwithstanding, the most popular drink on Martinique and Guadeloupe is **rum** – no surprise, since the rum-making industry thrives on both islands. **Ti-punch**, a potent rum, sugar and lime concoction, is popular as an apéritif; a diluted version, **Planter's Punch**, mixes the booze with fruit juice. It's common on Guadeloupe and Martinique for waitstaff to allow restaurant and bar guests to mix their own Ti-punch. Both islands also produce their own **local beers**: Guadeloupe's Corsair and Martinique's Lorraine are light brews that goes down nicely with rich Creole fare. On St Barts, most meals finish with a few sips of vanilla rum, a smooth, mellow digestif sold in souvenir bottles all over the island.

The **tap water** on Martinique and Guadeloupe is safe to drink; St Barts is more touch-and-go, as the island lacks a fresh-water source. The finer hotels all provide potable water. Budget inns may get theirs from unreliable rain-catchment systems; if you're staying at the latter, you're better off buying bottled water, which is widely available on all islands.

Mail and communications

Public telephones are on almost every square and many street corners, all of which accept only plastic *télécartes* (phonecards), available in units of 50 (about €7) and 100 (about €14) from any post office and most *tabacs* (tobacco shops). International phonecards are also available (€3–10) and offer good rates, particularly after 7pm. Many payphones list a 1-800 AT&T phone number to dial for collect calls.

Telephone numbers on all three islands are ten digits long, starting with 0. To make local calls on any of the islands, dial the ten-digit number. International calls to Martinique and Guadeloupe do not require the 0 – simply dial the international access code of the country you're calling from, followed by the digits after the 0. To make an international call to St Barts, however, dial the international access code, followed by the island's **country code** ⓣ590, then the ten-digit number. The country code for

Public holidays

January 1 New Year's Day
March/April Easter Sunday, Easter Monday
May 1 Labour Day
Fortieth day after Easter Ascension Thursday
Seventh Monday after Easter Pentecost Monday
July 14 Bastille Day
August 15 Assumption
November 1 All Saints Day
November 2 All Souls Day
November 11 Armistice Day
December 25 Christmas Day

Guadeloupe is ⓣ590 and on Martinique it is ⓣ596.

Sending letters home using the French **postal system** is straightforward – postcards and airmail letters cost €0.95 to North America, Europe, Australia and New Zealand.

The **Internet** is surprisingly less than ubiquitous in the French West Indies, and it's most common in cities and resorts. Consequently, checking email can be difficult and expensive. Until the islands catch up, the **fax** remains the preferred mode of written communication.

Opening hours, holidays and festivals

As a general rule, **opening hours** run 8am–noon and 2–7pm during the week and 8am–noon on Saturdays. On Sundays little is open, and some shops take Wednesday afternoons off, too. In addition to closures on national holidays (see box opposite) the islands also shut down to celebrate local holidays, the most notable being the abolition of slavery, celebrated on May 22 (Martinique) and May 27 (Guadeloupe); the man responsible for this feat, Victor Schoelcher, is honoured on July 21.

Holidays aside, some big **festivals** add spice to the region, the largest of all being **Carnival**, which runs yearly from January to Ash Wednesday in both Guadeloupe and Martinique, with dancing and music performances culminating in the election of the year's beauty queen. The **Christmas season** dovetails with the biannual International Guitar and Jazz Fest in Martinique, a weeklong music festival in Fort-de-France. The only other notable event is a spiritual one, **La Toussaint** (All Souls Day) on November 1, when red votive candles are lit in cemeteries.

The major annual event in St Barts is its own celebration on **August 24**, complete with watersports and music. Earlier in the year, the Cinéma Caraïbes **film festival** in late April showcases Caribbean films over five days, and a two-week international **music festival** takes place in January, which includes ballet and other dance performances.

Crime and safety

St Barts has so little **crime** that people leave their car doors unlocked. The same isn't true of Martinique, where break-ins at the parking lot near Mont-Pelée's hiking trails have been reported. Even so, the most common crime in Martinique and Guadeloupe is **pick-pocketing**. As long as you don't flash your money around, you're unlikely to have problems. The major cities feel sketchy at night, with **prostitutes** and **drug dealers** hanging out in squares. Many **women travellers** also experience catcalling and verbal harassment. Most of this activity is truly harmless, though the worst offenders have been known to grope publicy. You can avoid harassment by covering up off the beach and avoiding eye contact.

History

Though the islands of Guadeloupe, Martinique and St Barts were each discovered by **Columbus** on his voyages to the New World in the late 15th and early 16th centuries, it is the **French** who have had the most influence, having ruled over the islands as protected departments for the better part of 400 years. Peace has, for the most part, been the rule, and the islands have benefited from French trade and support; in recent years, though, the desire for a greater sense of **independence and autonomy** among the citizens of all three islands has emerged as a pressing issue.

Guadeloupe

Unlike the other islands under the French crown, the **Spanish** actually attempted to colonize Guadeloupe – twice – in the 1500s, after Columbus discovered its fertile soil during his second New World voyage. They were assailed both times by Caribs, and it took the **French**, who arrived in 1635, to establish the French West Indies' first capital a few years later, at **Basse-Terre**. Their successful implementation of slavery by the 1670s caught British attention, who strove to take over the island several times in the mid-1700s, and succeeded in occupying it from 1759 to 1763, when they built up the harbour at Pointe-à-Pitre and expanded sugar cane trade markets to North America. The 1763 **Paris Treaty** returned Guadeloupe to France but the British invaded again in 1794. The French responded by sending in troops led by black nationalist **Victor Hugues**, who launched a reign of terror by freeing and arming local slaves, killing hundreds of royalists and attacking American ships; not surprisingly, the US declared war on France.

Napoleon reinstituted order by appointing a governing general who restored slavery in 1802. Peace was not to endure for long, however, as the British were still keen on controlling the fiefdom, and they continued to manage parts of the island between 1810 and 1816, when the **Vienna Treaty** ended their attempts for good.

Slavery wasn't actually abolished in the French West Indies until 1848, after a dogged anti-slavery campaign mounted by French cabinet minister **Victor Schoelcher**. Since then, the only real issue has been Guadeloupe's status within the French government. The promise of political decentralization in the late 1900s gave birth to **pro-independence** uprisings. As recently as 1999, Guadeloupe, Martinique and French Guiana (in South America) joined forces to sign the **Basse-Terre Declaration**, which sought greater autonomy from the French government. Of late, the independence movement has lost some momentum; in late 2003, after two years of severe drought, residents of Guadeloupe voted to uphold the status quo, rejecting a referendum for increased autonomy. Also in 2003, St Barts and St Martin both voted to secede from Guadeloupe, to which they had previously been tied. The French Parliament took a few years to grant both islands a new status; in February 2007, both became "Overseas Collectivities" and ended their direct political association with Guadeloupe.

Martinique

Though discovered by Columbus on his last New World voyage in 1502, the Lesser Antilles' third largest island wound up being settled in 1635 by French colonizers. Starting from a small encampment on the northwest side that would later become **St-Pierre**, the French made their way to **Fort-de-France** and completed their island take over eight years later by massacring the remaining Caribs.

By this time, the French had begun importing slaves and sugar cane, and their efforts drew British interest near the end of the 1700s. An almost two-century power struggle ensued, with the French losing Martinique to the British over a century later, then getting it back as part of the **Paris Treaty** in 1763, only to lose it again 1794. The tug-of-war ended for good in 1815, when the British returned the island on **Vienna Treaty** orders.

Martinique's return to the motherland was bittersweet, as France continued to endorse slavery well after neighbouring British islands had abolished the practice in 1833. It didn't help matters that Emperor Napoleon had married the daughter of a local plantation-owner, **Joséphine Beauharnais** – it's said he continued to endorse slavery as a favour to his in-laws. As on Guadeloupe, the determined efforts of French cabinet minister **Victor Schoelcher** led to the abolition of slavery in 1848.

The twentieth century began tragically on the island; on May 8, 1902, a sudden eruption of **Mont-Pelée**, the volcano at its northern reaches, destroyed the bustling town of St-Pierre and all its inhabitants. The latter part of the century was marked by sometimes violent social unrest caused by pro-independence factions seeking **sovereignty** from France. In an effort to quell the movement, the French government granted Martinique greater overseas department status and powers in 1982–83. In recent years, the island has struggled with record unemployment rates, resulting in demand for greater trade with France and neighbouring islands, plus growing support for the Martinique Independence Movement (MIM).

St Barts

St Barthélemy was spotted by **Columbus** in 1493 and named after his younger brother, Bartolomeo. The first **French** delegation to settle the island, in 1648, came from nearby St Kitts. Their effort was disastrous, however, as native **Caribs** massacred the lot in 1665. Nearly ten years passed before another attempt was made, this time by Norman and Breton Huguenots. Under their reign, Gustavia's hurricane-proof harbour became a popular mooring port for **buccaneers**, who carried plunder from Spanish galleons in their holds; one legendary pirate, Montbars the Exterminator, even set up headquarters here.

Over a century later, in 1784, France's Marie-Antoinette ceded ownership to Sweden's King Gustaf II in exchange for free-port rights in Gothenburg. But after serving as an American-friendly port during the Revolution and, later, the War of 1812, Gustavia suffered a devastating fire in 1852 that proved too costly for the Swedes. They sold the island back to France in 1878, with the condition that it remain a duty-free port. The island's administrative status changed in 1974, when it came under neighbouring Guadeloupe's jurisdiction. In 2003, however, the residents of St Barts voted overwhelmingly to separate from Guadeloupe and become their own **overseas collectivity (COM)**, to give the island greater autonomy in its economic, political and social programmes. This new status came into effect in 2007, with noticeable changes to the island already, such as a law forbidding smoking in enclosed public spaces (in line with French law), which was introduced in January 2008.

15.1

Guadeloupe

The largest French West Indian island, **GUADELOUPE** encompasses a massive 1704 square kilometres, the majority of which is taken up by its two adjoining mainland islands, Basse-Terre and Grande-Terre, whose outline resembles a greenbacked butterfly in flight. Its two "wings" have entirely different personalities, and don't be fooled by their misrepresentative names: Basse-Terre ("low-land") is anything but and Grande-Terre ("large-land") is actually smaller than its sister to the west. **Basse-Terre**'s central core is dominated by mountain ranges, including the Lesser Antilles' highest peak, **La Soufrière**. These surround the island's bountiful **rainforest** and descend to meet twinkling, if often jam-packed, black-sand beaches like **Plage Malendure** that extend to protected underwater **dive** sites.

The eastern "wing", the furled **Grande-Terre**, is utterly flat by contrast, and predominantly rural. Most of the tourist action happens along its southern coast where one white-sand beach after another seems to merge endlessly along the coast, with the stunning **Plage Caravelle** forming the centrepiece. Its outer reaches are pounded by the savage **Atlantic Ocean** to produce jagged limestone outcroppings like the windswept **Pointe-des-Châteaux**, and **Lagon de la Porte d'Enfer**, an exquisite natural swimming pool.

Guadeloupe's offshore islands are equally varied. **Marie-Galante**, with its rural landscape of sugar cane, hearkens back to a Guadeloupe of thirty years ago, while **La Désirade**, the most desolate of the lot, remains happily undeveloped. The most visited offshore isle, tiny **Terre-de-Haut**, is the quaintest of them all, with tiny wooden buildings and fabulous bays and beaches.

Arrival, information and getting around

Guadeloupe is served by numerous airlines, including Air Antilles Express (Ⓣ0590/21 14 47), Air Canada, Air Caraïbes (Ⓣ0590/82 47 47), Air France, American Airlines, Corsair (Ⓣ0820/04 20 42) and LIAT (Ⓣ0590/21 11 40). Ferries also link the island with Dominica and St Lucia. For information about travelling by boat between Guadeloupe and Martinique see "Ferries", p.35.

Passengers arriving by **plane** land at one of mainland Guadeloupe's two airports: modern **Pôle-Caraïbes** or, less frequently, **Le Raizet**, a nearby terminal used by **charter** flights. Both lie about 6km outside of Pointe-à-Pitre and are well served by metered **taxis** that cost between €35 and €80 to southern points (SOS Ⓣ0590/83 63 94; Taxigua Ⓣ0590/83 90 00).

If you're planning to explore the island, renting a **car** at the airport is the best way to do it, since **minibuses**, the only other form of transport, are irregular and patience-wearing. Both terminals have numerous rental agencies, including Europcar (Ⓣ0590/21 13 52, Ⓦwww.europcar-gpe.com); Avis (Ⓣ0590/85 30 60, Ⓦwww.avis.fr); Budget (Ⓣ0590/21 13 48, Ⓦwww.budget-gp.com); Hertz (Ⓣ0590/84 20 23, Ⓦwww.hertzantilles.com); and Jumbo Car (Ⓣ0590/91 55 66, Ⓦwww.jumbocar.com).

Passengers arriving by **ferry** disembark at the westernmost of Pointe-à-Pitre's quays, the **Gare Maritime** (or Quai Gatine), just west of the city centre. From here, you can catch a taxi to Le Gosier (€20) or St-François (€50); while there are no car rental agencies near the docks, there are plenty at the bigger resort towns.

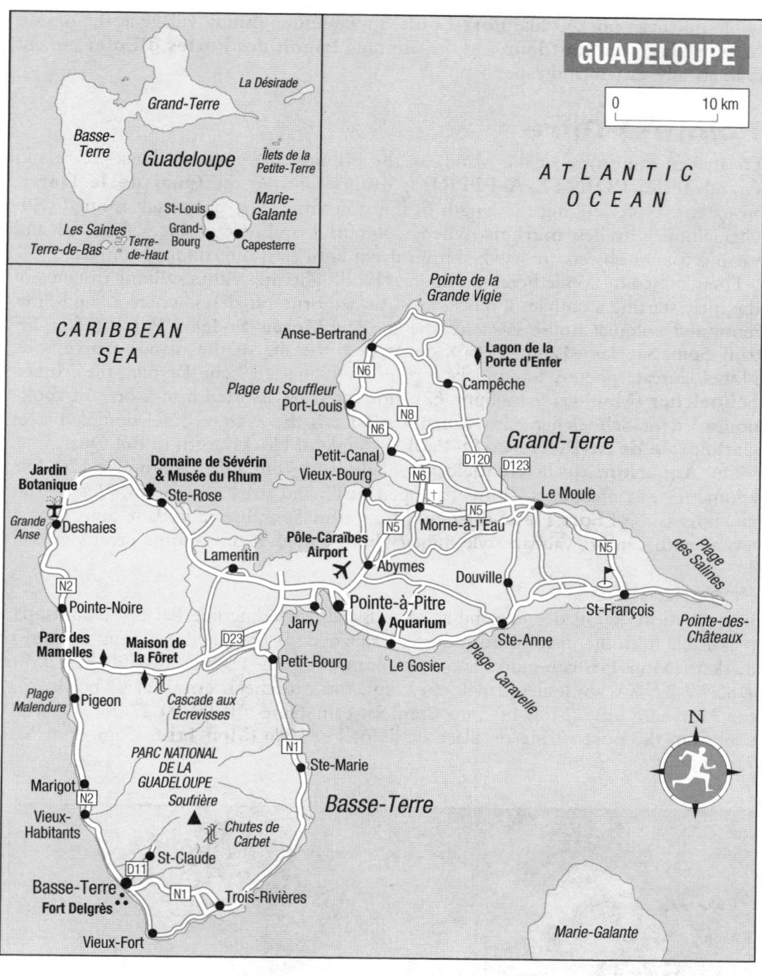

The airport has a tourism **information** booth near customs with flexible hours. Should it be closed, the main office in downtown Pointe-à-Pitre keeps regular hours (see opposite).

Grande-Terre

Remarkably flat **Grande-Terre** is skirted by beaches and studded with resort towns so glossy that the highway connecting them bears the nickname "Riviera Road". The busiest enclave, **Le Gosier**, has the most amenities and nightlife of the lot, making it the definitive one-stop destination for those seeking nothing but sun and resort fun. The crowds thin out a little bit further east, around boisterous **Ste-Anne** and yachty **St-François**, and are almost nonexistent along the magnificent **Pointe-des-Châteaux**, the sliver of land at the island's easternmost point. No visit would be complete without stopping at the colourful commercial hub of **Pointe-à-Pitre**, while northern pockets like **Port-Louis**, a picturesque fishing village at the mouth of calm **Plage du Souffleur**, and the stunning **Lagon des Portes d'Enfer** present dramatically varied landscapes.

Pointe-à-Pitre

Located in the centre of the island, on the isthmus that connects Basse-Terre and Grand-Terre, **POINTE-À-PITRE** is liveliest around the **Quai de la Darse**, an extensive pier edging the length of the waterfront. The quay itself is lined with Guadeloupe's liveliest **markets**, where a colourful jamboree of spices, fruit, fish and various tourist objects are hawked from dawn until early afternoon (Mon–Sat).

There's not a lot to see here, and the few local sights are within walking distance of the quay, starting a couple of blocks west, at no. 9 rue Nozières, where a handsome, renovated colonial house contains the modest **Musée St-Jean Perse** (Mon–Fri 9am–5pm, Sat 9am–12pm; €2.50), devoted to the life of the island's native-born Nobel laureate poet. A few blocks further west, at no. 24 rue Peynier, the **Musée Schoelcher** (Mon–Fri 9am–5pm; €2) showcases the assorted bric-a-brac of abolitionist Victor Schoelcher. Also worth a gander is the Gustav Eiffel-designed steel **Cathédrale de St-Pierre-et-St-Paul**, a couple of blocks north of the Quai.

The **Aquarium de la Guadeloupe** (daily 9am–7pm; €8.50, €5 under-12s), five kilometres east of Pointe-à-Pitre, has open turtle and shark aquariums. Nearby, not much remains of **Fort Fleur-d'Épée** (Mon 10am-5pm, Tues-Sun 9am–5pm; free), a seventeenth-century Vauban-style military base, though it offers some great views.

Practicalities

Information on Guadeloupe and its outer islands, including free, detailed road **maps**, is available from the main tourism office, 5 square de la Banque, across from la Darse's markets (Mon–Fri 8am–noon and 1pm–5pm, Sat 8am–1.30pm; Ⓣ0590/82 09 30, Ⓕ83 89 22, Ⓦwww.lesilesguadeloupe.com). You can check **email** at Cyber ka, 20 rue Alexandre Isaac (Mon-Fri 7am–8pm, Sat 8am–6pm; Ⓣ0590/90 27 06) and send mail from the **post office** on place de l'Hôtel de Ville (Mon–Fri 6.45am–6pm, Sat 7am–noon).

▲ Colonial houses, Pointe-à-Pitre

While there is little reason to **stay** in Pointe-à-Pitre overnight, the small, appealing rooms at the portside *Hôtel Saint-John*, Quai des Croisières (Ⓣ0590/82 51 57, Ⓕ82 52 61, Ⓦwww.saint-john-perse.com; ⑤ including breakfast) are ideal for those arriving late or departing early by sea.

The city has a smattering of good **restaurant**s. Friendly *Le Petit Palais*, 4 place de l'Église (Mon–Fri 8am–3pm; Ⓣ0590/89 47 39), has sandwiches from €1.70 and crepes starting at €3; *Maharaja Monty*, 47 rue Achille René-Boisneuf, serves up reasonably priced Indian curries (Mon–Sat noon–3pm and 7–11pm). The real standout is *Le Part des Anges*, 12 rue Alexander Isaac (Ⓣ0690/48 43 71) which offers excellent Creole fare, including some surprising Dominican items (plat du jour from €12).

Le Gosier

Guadeloupe's premier resort area, **LE GOSIER**, 7km east of Pointe-à-Pitre, is a small town with a dual personality. One side of town is the area known as **Pointe de la Verdure**, a secluded, gated complex, packed with car parks and unimaginative condominium-style buildings. Further east along the main road, **boulevard Général-de-Gaulle**, you'll find a Caribbean village of colonial houses, apartment buildings, and narrow streets perched above a small public **beach**.

Le Gosier's best beach is the lovely **Îlet du Gosier**, a minuscule, undeveloped isle located 100m offshore. Good **snorkelling** is right off the beach thanks to a capsized tug near the landing dock and a coral reef full of underwater life – bring a mask and flippers with you. Local fishermen ferry sunbathers back and forth daily from 8.30am–5pm in small motorboats from the pier at the east end of the town beach, closest to the islet. Bring a picnic lunch, or grab a bite from the dockside **snack** shacks.

Accommodation

Auberge de la Vieille Tour 5 Montauban Ⓣ0590/84 23 23, Ⓦwww.sofitel.com. This posh Sofitel property has English-speaking staff, two tennis courts, and 180 spacious, stylish rooms with minibar and satellite TV. ⑨

Canella Beach Hotel Pointe de la Verdure Ⓣ0590/90 44 00, Ⓦwww.canellabeach.com. At the end of the Pointe, with clean, comfortable a/c rooms with balconies and kitchenettes. ⑤

Créole Beach Pointe de la Verdure Ⓣ0590/90 46 46, Ⓕ90 46 66, Ⓦwww.leader-hotels.gp. Le Gosier's swankiest resort hotel definitely feels a cut above its peers. It has over 150 comfortable, well-equipped doubles with sea or garden views, a private beach and a beautiful swimming pool that glows at night. ⑦

Formule Économique 112-120 Lot Gisors Ⓣ0590/84 54 91, Ⓔlaformule.economique@wanadoo.fr. Friendly, bargain-basement lodging down a residential street north of the town beach. Nice bar, plus Wi-Fi and Internet station. ③

La Maison Créole Montauban Ⓣ0590/84 36 43, Ⓕ84 55 16, Ⓦwww.lamaisoncreole.com, Ⓔinfo@lamaisoncreole.com. *La Maison Créole* benefits from its distance from the Pointe de la Verdure tourist cul-de-sac. Motel-class rooms are augmented by a decent restaurant and a big pool. ⑤ including breakfast.

Eating, drinking and nightlife

L'Affirmatif 17 blvd Général-de-Gaulle Ⓣ0590/88 66 03. A cosy locals' hangout serving reasonably priced wood-oven pizzas (€7–11) along with the odd Creole dish in the centre of town. Daily lunch and dinner.

L'Agouba Plus rue Montauban Ⓣ0590/21 85 88. Locals throng to this casual dining spot on rue Montauban. Gigot, fish, and brochettes from €9–15. Mon–Sat 6pm–late.

Casino du Gosier 43 Pointe de la Verdure Ⓣ0590/84 99 50. Flashy neon nightspot draws tourists and locals alike with jazz concerts, movies (€8) and slot machines.

Le Napoli Rue Montauban Ⓣ0590/84 30 53. Cosy, open-air Italian place with filling Niçoise salads, pastas, and thin, crispy three-cheese pizzas (menu €18). Open daily for dinner only.

Le Tam-Tam rue Montauban Ⓣ0590/84 07 08. Popular with locals, this restaurant serves up *boudin créole*, fricassee, and ribs *frites* (€11–20) along with ti-punch and *planteur* (a punch made with rum and tropical fruit juice) in a garden setting. Lunch and dinner daily.

Plage Caravelle and Ste-Anne

As pleasant as they are, Le Gosier's beaches are nothing compared to **PLAGE CARAVELLE**, a sensational, palm-dotted swath of sand 13km eastwards, whose picture-postcard turquoise bay has been colonized by Club Med. If you're not a paying guest, you can still hit the beach by following the signs to *Le Rotabas* hotel (see below), where a dirt path ends at a turnstile. For **watersports**, head to casual **STE-ANNE**, a small village another kilometre eastwards, with its own adequate stretch of sand. A beachfront **watersports** centre here rents kayaks, body-boards, windsurfers and canoes.

Practicalities

Aside from Club Med there are only a few places to **stay** in the immediate vicinity. The closest to Plage Caravelle, *Le Rotabas* (ⓣ0590/88 25 60, ⓦwww.lerotobas.com; ❺ including breakfast) offers cute, though cramped, garden-view bungalows (most with TV and fridge) just a short stroll from the sand. Don't miss *Ils Café* right at the Club Med turnstile, with its funky sand floor and cheap crepes (from €2) and panini (from €4). In Ste-Anne, *Auberge le Grand Large* (ⓣ0590/85 48 28, ⓦwww.aubergelegrandlarge.com; ❹) has several small bungalows and doubles with air-conditioning 50m from the beach. Nearby, swank and very pricey *Le Diwali* (ⓣ0590/85 39 70, ⓦwww.lediwali.fr; ❾) has stylishly spa-like, well-appointed rooms, some with sea views, plus direct access to the beach. A handful of open-air **restaurants** line Ste-Anne's beach; try *Kontiki*, which serves omelettes, sandwiches and salads in a tiki-themed garden. Beach trucks along the beach also dish out *merguez*-stuffed **baguettes**, burgers and fries. Next to an open-air market off the beach, *L'Americano Café* (ⓣ0590/88 38 99) a Western-style **bar** popular with locals and tourists alike, pulls pints of beer and features weekend concerts. Note that Ste-Anne beach can be extremely crowded in high season.

St-François

Posh **ST-FRANÇOIS**, a harbour town another 20km due east of Ste-Anne, doesn't have much beachfront but makes up for it with its mast-filled **marina**, where a boardwalk lined with chic boutiques, cafés and restaurants draws an affluent crowd. It's more reminiscent of southern California than the Caribbean, however, and is not for everyone. The port is a convenient departure point for **ferries** to Guadeloupe's offshore islands (see p.581), as well as for **dive boats** carting scuba and snorkelling enthusiasts to explore nearby waters. Next door to the marina is Guadeloupe's only eighteen-hole **golf course**. The closest **beaches** are a few kilometres east of town, along the Pointe-des-Châteaux (see opposite).

The town centre has none of the marina's sterile polish, and is good for a wander. Radiating from the **Place du Marché**, a roundabout circled by an active covered **market**, the tapered one-way streets are disjointed and it's easy to get lost. You'll find some atmospheric, albeit downtrodden, **wooden colonial houses**. Pick up a **map** at the Office du Tourisme (Mon, Tue, Thurs & Fri 8am–noon & 2–5pm, Wed 8am–12.30pm, Sat 8am–noon; ⓣ0590/68 96 81) on the right-hand side of avenue de l'Europe as you head towards the marina.

Practicalities

In St-François, try the prim, simple *Amaudo* (ⓣ0590/88 87 00, ⓕ85 04 63; ❻) on Anse à la Barque. Another option, *Hotel Golf Marine*, sits across from the golf course on Av. de l'Europe (ⓣ0590/88 60 60; ⓔgolfmarine@golfmarine.com; ❺).

Most of St-François' **dining** options frame the marina: *L'Arganier* is a Moroccan restaurant and patisserie, closed Monday, with mains from €17. A much more casual vibe can be found at *Quai 17*, popular with tourists for its pizzas, pastas, and fish (mains €8-20). In town, local favourite *Jerco Chez Nise*, on rue Paul-Thilby, serves up a nine-course menu that makes a great island sampler, with dishes like *lambi au jus* (marinated conch) and *langouste grillée* (grilled spiny lobster). Toward Pointe-des-Châteaux in La Coulée (across from Anse du Mancenillier) is the excellent *Restaurant Le Colombo* (☎0590/88 41 29) for grilled fish (€20).

Towards Pointe-des-Châteaux

Guadeloupe's outermost tip culminates 11km east of St-François in the majestic **POINTE-DES-CHÂTEAUX**, where several barren limestone rock formations leap from the ocean, the tallest crowned by a wooden **cross**. As in several other tourist spots in Guadeloupe, home-made sorbet stands and foot trucks predominate in the car park; the hand-cranked sorbet is worth a few licks. If you fancy a dip, the nearby **Plage des Salines**, with its natural breakwater, is a fine spot. Back towards St-François, the small cove of **Plage Anse Tarare** is Grand-Terre's only official nude beach.

Le Moule

Guadeloupe's original capital, **LE MOULE**, a short drive north of St-François on the N5, is pleasant, windswept town without much in the way of tourist attractions. Two beaches are of note: the sea-grape shaded **L'Autre Bord**, on your way in, and **Plage des Baies**, about 1km north of town, which fronts a shallow, sheltered bay ideal for young swimmers. In the centre of Le Moule is the massive stone Church Saint Jean Baptiste, a Neoclassical structure, dating from the 1840s. It's a grand and beautiful anchor to an otherwise unremarkable town. The only other attraction is the modest display of Amerindian archeology at the **Musée Edgar-Clerc** (Mon, Tues, Thurs 9am–5pm, Wed, Fri 9am–1pm; free; under renovation in 2008), located past Plage des Baies on the right of the D123 towards Gros-Cap.

North to Anse-Bertrand

From Le Moule to Campeche, the D120 passes beautiful green slopes of sugar cane and old sugar mills. Beyond, still on the D120, is Guadeloupe's most enchanting swimming hole, the ominously named **LAGON DE LA PORTE D'ENFER** (Lagoon of the Gates of Hell). Two salt-ravaged bluffs create a heavenly setting by funnelling the raging Atlantic into a calm pool. A great **restaurant**, *Chez Coco*, cooks up tasty barbecued fish and chicken dishes (€10–15) at the water's edge. A ten-minute hike from the road to the top of the eastern barrier cliff offers stupendous coastal **views**.

Another 2km further on, **POINTE-DE-LA-GRANDE-VIGIE** is Grande-Terre's northernmost point and a **lookout** onto nearby islands.

Port-Louis and south to Morne-à-l'Eau

PORT-LOUIS is a quiet backwater of a fishing hamlet with immaculate **wooden colonial houses** and atmospheric antique street lights. The ambience alone warrants a stop, though most people come for the magnificent beach, **Plage Du Souffleur**, a long, expansive golden band with a boardwalk filled with locals selling fresh-churned sorbet. Along the beach, *Siwo Evasion* (☎0690/258 83 35), rents **jet skis** (from €23) and arranges guided outings to hard-to-reach beaches (from €90 per person). A few blocks away on rue Charles Caignet, **Le Petit Musée des Poupées Renovées** is an eccentric little spot run out of a local's home that displays hundreds of dolls and sells "Creole dolls" made of sachets of spices (daily 2–6pm; €1).

Basse-Terre

Undulating with mountain ranges, gushing with waterfalls and packed with rainforests, **BASSE-TERRE** provides a rugged antidote to Grande-Terre's glossy resorts. Scenic **hikes** in **Parc National de la Guadeloupe** lead to the base of the **Chutes**

de Carbet waterfall and ascend the volcanic slopes of **La Soufrière**. Outlying **beaches** range from golden pockets like **Grande Anse** to sparkling black stretches like **Plage Malendure**.

Despite everything it has to offer, Basse-Terre isn't big on resorts; instead you'll find bungalows and small hotels. Even if Grande-Terre is your base, you should still make time for a day-trip here – you can easily explore some of the rainforest in the morning, hit Grande Anse for lunch and go diving in the afternoon.

Parc National de la Guadeloupe

The most accessible parts of the **PARC NATIONAL DE LA GUADELOUPE**, a tremendous 17,300ha rainforest that encompasses the volcanic La Soufrière (see p.579) and the thundering Chutes de Carbet (see p.579), branch off from the Route de la Traversée (D23), Basse-Terre's cross-island road. A UNESCO Biosphere Reserve, the park has numerous **hiking** trails, the easiest of which, the stroll to the **Cascade aux Écrevisses** and the meandering **Bras David**, can be done in a morning. The former is signposted to the left about 7km inland on the Route de la Traversée; it's a pleasant site with picnic tables and a straightforward 100m walk along a jungly pathway that culminates at the modest cascade. The latter begins another two kilometres westwards along the same route, behind the small information hut that is the **Maison de la Fôret** (Wed–Mon 9am–1.15pm & 2–4.30pm; closed Tues), which has free English trail **maps** for three nearby walks. The **Découverte de Bras David** is the shortest of these, consisting of a twenty-five minute loop through lush, moss-covered white gum trees. Be sure to wear sturdy shoes, as things can get muddy and slippery, especially during the rainy season. The park's fauna is showcased 3km further west, at the entertaining **Parc des Mamelles** (daily 9am–5pm; €12.50), where native endangered species including iguanas, green monkeys and raccoons are bred. Admission includes the thrilling Visite de la Canopie, a 25- to 40-minute trek along suspended walkways atop the rainforest canopy up to 30m above the ground. From the park, the Route de la Traversée makes a steep descent to end at the southern outskirts of Pointe-Noire and the coastal N2 (see below).

Practicalities

Across the road from the Parc des Mamelles is *Le Dynaste* restaurant and gîte. The restaurant only serves lunch, with menus from €18 (☎0590/80 45 62). Six simple bungalows (❸) are arranged along a hill in back of the restaurant. *Le Tapeur*, an eco-adventure park, is also part of the complex (admission €20; €16 for children).

Northern Basse-Terre

The N2 north of the Route de la Traversée makes a roller-coaster drive up the Caribbean coast with innumerable picture-perfect spots along the way. Though this coast is rocky in places, there are a couple of soft sand beaches, including Basse-Terre's finest, **Grande Anse**. The scenery changes dramatically the further northeast you go, as fields of sugar cane dominate the landscape around **Ste-Rose**. A couple of **rum distilleries** and a phenomenal **botanical garden** are the main draws this far north.

Pointe-Noire

The first settlement north of La Traversée, quiet **POINTE-NOIRE** owes its name to the dark volcanic highlands that encircle and shade its tangled streets. Some rays filter through to **Plage Caraïbe**, a laid-back beach of golden-brown sand just south of town where **dive** outfit Anse Caraïbe Plongée (Mon–Fri 9am–3.30pm, 4.30pm–6pm; ☎0590/99 90 95) rents snorkelling gear and organizes outings to the depths around Îlets Pigeon twice every weekday (see p.578). Grab a bite on the beach at *Délice Caraïbes*, which whips up €15 menus of *fricassee de lambis* and *colombo poulet* (closed Wed).

The area is renowned for its Arabica coffee beans, which perfume the grounds of the magnificently restored **Caféière Beauséjour** (Tues–Sun 10am–5pm, closed mid-Sept–mid-Oct; Ⓦwww.cafeierebeausejour.com; €6), a plantation house and café high on a hill with stunning views. Also in the area is the homespun **Maison du Cacao** (Mon–Sat 9.30am–5pm, Sun 9.30am–1pm; €5), an eco-museum that traces the path from cacao tree to chocolate. Admission includes a cup of hot chocolate made from pure cacao. Opposite is the hospitable *Kaz la Traversée* (Ⓣ0590/98 21 23, Ⓦwww.kazlatraversee.com; ❷), which has several fan-only bungalows with kitchenettes and access to a pebble beach. Ponti-Néris are adept carpenters; you can check out the tools of their trade and exquisite mahogany furnishings at the **Maison du Bois** (Tues–Sun 9.30am–5pm; closed Sept; €9).

Deshaies and Grande Anse

Quaint **DESHAIES**, Basse-Terre's most inviting village with wooden Creole houses clasped around a deep harbour, lies a few kilometres up the coast. The tempo is so relaxed that the toughest part of your day may well involve deciding where you want to watch the sunset after a day of lounging on **GRANDE ANSE**, Basse-Terre's longest beach, a peaceful 1.5km stretch of sand 2km north of town. To get to the beach, follow the signs to *Le Karacoli* (see below); do not take the road signposted to Grande Anse – it's rocky and unpaved.

Practicalities

You can **stay** up in the hills at *Le Rayon Vert* (Ⓣ0590/28 43 23, Ⓦhotel.lerayonvert.free.fr; ❻), which has 21 pleasant hillside tin-roofed rooms and a breathtaking infinity pool. Closer to the sand, *Fleurs des Îles* (Ⓣ0590/28 54 44, Ⓦwww.fleursdesiles.com; ❺) rents by the week, with comfortable poolside bungalows and direct access to the beach. Good budget accommodation can be found at inviting, low-key *Ti-Paradis* (Ⓣ0590/28 25 15, Ⓦwww.ti-paradis.com; ❹, just up from the beach on Allée du Coeur (turn at the Total petrol station). The seven bungalows are clean and comfortable, with kitchenette and air-conditioning; the site has a grill and small pool.

Beachside **restaurants** range from food trucks and shacks, to terraced affairs with three-course Creole menus. The best of the lot is *Le Karacoli*, an atmospheric lunch place serving spicy *crabe farçi* (stuffed land crabs) and delicious *conch fricassé* on an enchanting tree-shaded beach terrace (mains €12–25). Deshaies' rue Principale has several fine options for eating and sunset-watching, including the stylish Italian spot *Barbuto* (mains around €20) and traditional Creole joint *Le Kaz* (dinner only) just down the block in a beautiful wooden house.

North to Ste-Rose

The one can't-miss spot along Basse-Terre's north coast is the **Jardin Botanique de Deshaies** (daily 9am–4.30pm; €13.50; Ⓦwww.jardin-botanique.com), about 1km before Deshaies. A path leads through the expansive, immaculately tended gardens, which feature waterfalls, orchid-covered trellises and lily ponds and are home to pink flamingos, loriquets and parrots.

Past Deshaies, the N2 heads into a region dominated by sugar cane and bamboo with not much worth stopping for until you hit the east coast **STE-ROSE**, an important agricultural town near two inland **rum** establishments. Closest is the **Domaine de Sévérin** (Mon–Sat 8.30am–5.30pm; free; Ⓦwww.habitation-severin.com), Guadeloupe's last waterwheel-operated distillery; to see the 200-year-old wheel in motion, you'll have to get there before 12.30pm. A ride on the Domaine's "petit train" runs €9 (€5 for children).

Further inland, the multifaceted **Musée du Rhum** (Mon–Sat 9am–5pm; €6) counts an impressive scythe collection among its rum-related equipment, and a spectacular insect collection upstairs; another chamber houses forty-odd model ships.

Southern Basse-Terre

Southern Basse-Terre is significantly more developed than the north, with sizeable coastal towns merging into one another along the N2. Guadeloupe's capital, also named **Basse-Terre**, is the largest of these towns. Dominated by the island's highest point, the sulphuric **La Soufrière**, the region's other draws are the **Chutes de Carbet** waterfalls and the abundant underwater marine life around **Îlets Pigeon**.

Plage Malendure and Îlets Pigeon

The French West Indies' top dive site lies 4km south of La Traversée on the N2, off **Plage Malendure**, a sliver of dark volcanic sand that can get brutally crowded in high season as busloads arrive for thrice-daily **diving** outings. Dives take place around two uninhabited offshore islands, **Îlets Pigeon**, in a 400ha reserve brought to international acclaim in the 1960s when Jacques Cousteau declared it to be one of the best dive sites he'd ever visited. Since then, upwards of 60,000 dives take place here yearly. Despite the traffic, local marine life still thrives. Visit in the late morning, when the sun hits the water directly and the coral and multicoloured fish are most vibrant.

Practicalities

For **information**, hit the tourism bureau right in the middle of the beach action (Mon–Sat 9am–4pm, Sun 10am–2.30pm). Dive shops are plentiful. You can also explore the underwater action aboard *Nautilus*, a boat with a glass hull that makes hour-plus voyages with snorkelling pit stops (€20; eight departures in low season and four in low; ⓣ0590/98 89 08, ⓕ98 34 35, ⓦwww.nautilius97.com).

Despite its popularity, the area has few accommodation and restaurant options. The appealing *Rocher de la Malendure* (ⓣ0590/98 70 84, ⓕ98 89 92, ⓔrocher-malendure@wanadoo.fr; ④) is right on the water, and has air-conditioning bungalows with balconies and kitchenettes. The family behind *Rocher de la Malendure* also runs *Le Jardin Tropical* (ⓣ0590/98 77 23, ⓕ98 74 33, ⓦwww.au-jardin-tropical.com; ④) high in the hills above Pigeon. Ten bungalows hug a welcoming pool and an open-air bar; the views are awesome.

While beach trucks sell sandwiches and crepes by day, your best night-time **dining** options are *Rocher de la Malendure*, which serves up plates of locally caught seafood (€15–40), and *La Touna*, on the N2, with Creole and French lunch and dinner menus from €16 (closed Mon). Should you simply fancy a pint, casual *Le Ranch*, 2km south of Malendure beach, has a lively **bar** and pizzas, salads and fish (menu €13).

South to Basse-Terre

The N2 hugs the coastline as it makes its way south, passing a slew of charming fishing villages with deep bays. A couple coffee-related sites provide entertaining diversions before Basse-Terre: **La Maison du Café** (hour-long guided tours daily 10am–5pm; €6.10) is a majestic former coffee plantation up a winding road several kilometres from the N2 in Vieux-Habitants. Not as picturesque but much more accessible is the working coffee mill at the **Musée du Café** (daily 9am–5pm; €6) on the outskirts of Vieux-Habitants. The entrance fee includes a bracing cup of local coffee and the boutique sells coffee products and other souvenirs.

You'll know you've reached the outskirts of **BASSE-TERRE**, the French West Indies' first settlement, when traffic comes to a halt. There's not much pay-off once you reach the town's core, either, as Guadeloupe's capital is a bland administrative centre. The main public square, **Place du Champs d'Arbaud**, is a modern concrete creation; many of the surrounding buildings are reminiscent of a busy mainland French suburb.

Two sights on Basse-Terre's southern outskirts are worth checking out if you've come this far. **Notre-Dame-du-Mont-Carmel**, a church fronted by Art Nouveau lamps, is reputed to have curative powers – look for marble thank-you plaques along the apse from those who've been healed. For its commanding scale alone, the nearby ruins of the 1643 **Fort Delgrès** (daily 9am–4.30pm; free) are worth a visit.

La Soufrière

The easiest way to reach the Lesser Antilles' highest peak, the 1467-metre **LA SOUFRIÈRE**, is by heading north on Basse-Terre's main north–south artery, avenue du Général Félix-Éboué. North of town, it becomes the D11 and cuts a steep path to **St-Claude** – the last place en route for water and food supplies. An amusing stop in St-Claude is **La Boniferie** (Tues–Sun 10am–4pm), a restaurant and working coffee mill that also houses an orienteering maze and **Mangofil**, a self-guided adventure park (€20; 9am–5pm), where participants glide across fields on ziplines.

You'll need good walking shoes to make the 1.5hr ascent to La Soufrière's often cloud-covered summit, as the path that winds up its western flank gets rockier, tighter and more slippery as it nears the top. The trailhead starts about 8km past St-Claude, at **Savane à Mulets**, a car park at an elevation of 1142m. You'll pass deep gorges and panoramic vistas of the surrounding countryside before arriving on a moonscape plateau of boiling sulphuric cauldrons. Though you're officially not allowed to hike to the very top, most people ignore the sign and continue the ascent at their own risk. The intrepid can make the four-hour hike from Savane à Mulets to the Chutes du Carbet (see below).

Trois-Rivières

Lying at the confluence of three rivers a few kilometres east of the capital, **TROIS-RIVIÈRES** was a significant Amerindian settlement before French colonizers arrived and ousted the natives. What traces remain of its original tenants can be seen at the intriguing **Parc Archéologique des Roches Gravées** (currently closed; €2), a park scattered with blackened boulders engraved with cartoonish human **petroglyphs** dating from circa 300 AD.

Trois-Rivières also serves as a **ferry** departure point for Les Saintes (see p.580), which lie just 10km offshore (see box p.581 for times). The pier is at the end of a well-marked spur road 2km south of the town centre and has a couple of decent **cafés** alongside the nearby car park: *Les Etoiles des Mers* is a relaxed sit-down joint with ocean views and seafood specialities, while *Chez Ako* does chicken and sausage sandwiches on the cheap (€2.50).

Les Chutes de Carbet

Praised by Christopher Columbus in 1493 and marvelled at by thousands of tourists since, the magnificent **CHUTES DE CARBET** plummet down La Soufrière's flanks from 1300m above. The falls are 10km inland from the N1 north of Trois-Rivières. While Columbus only referred to one chute in his diary, there are in fact three **waterfalls**; the middle one, a mighty 110-metre cascade, gets the greatest attention as it's the most accessible. To reach it, follow the signs (and the crowds); a stairwell descends to a dirt path that reaches the fall's basin in twenty minutes.

The secondary trails for the **first** and **third falls** branch off from the same path – the former is the highest, at 115m, and reached by a 4.5hr round-trip hike along an occasionally muddy but otherwise decent trail. The third waterfall, a mere 20m high, is the least dramatic, and the hardest to reach; the 5.5hr circuit cuts through some narrow and slippery patches. An easier way to get to it is via Capesterre, a couple of kilometres north on the N1; a well-signposted turn-off in the centre of town ends at the start of a 2hr round-trip trail. Be warned that the paths are occasionally closed after heavy rains.

North to La Traversée and Pointe-à-Pitre

Little happens along the stretch of N1 that connects the falls with the Route de la Traversée and Pointe-à-Pitre. The only commendable stop is the **Domaine de Valombreuse** (daily 8am–5pm; ⓦwww.valombreuse.com; €8), a botanical garden and animal reserve in the hinterlands of Petit-Bourg. You'll see blooming red alpinia, porcelain roses and heliconia in the shade of papyrus and oleander trees, plus iguanas, raccoons and tropical birds. Another twenty minutes along the N1 lands you back in Pointe-à-Pitre (see p.572).

Offshore islands

Guadeloupe's **OFFSHORE ISLANDS** make for delightful day or overnight trips from the mainland. The popular and Mediterranean-like **Terre-de-Haut** and its quieter and drier sibling, **Terre-de-Bas** form **Les Saintes**. Further out lies **Marie-Galante**, a laid-back island with graceful beaches that are seldom crowded. In the far distance looms sparsely populated **La Désirade** and its tiny, uninhabited neighbour, **La Petite Terre**, each so undeveloped that visitors may feel blissfully lost to the world.

Terre-de-Haut

Excellent beaches and attractive architecture make tiny **TERRE-DE-HAUT** the most striking of Guadeloupe's outer islands. Its dry climate prevented the introduction of sugar cane, and as a result it was settled by white Breton and Poitevin fishermen whose descendants are today touted as the Antilles' best. Their unique fishing boats, light and rapid wooden outboards called **Saintoises**, are famous in the trade.

Measuring a mere 5km from end to end, the craggy spit is capped by the 309-metre **Chameau** and anchored by a darling village simply called **Le Bourg** – The Town – which borders the **Baie des Saintes**, a glorious harbour enclosed by hilly outcroppings. Though Terre-de-Haut is by no means a castaway's secret, it possesses just the right amount of run-down charm to prevent it from becoming irrecoverably twee.

Arrival and information

Ferries to Les Saintes depart from Pointe-à-Pitre, St-François, Marie-Galante and Trois-Rivières; you can also **fly** with Air Caraïbes (ⓣ0590/82 47 00, ⓕ82 47 48; 4 flights Mon–Fri; 2 flights Sat & Sun; €141). Most hotels will arrange to pick you up from the airport, ten minutes outside the town centre, or from the pier. You can easily get around on **foot**, though **scooters** are favoured for island-roaming and several pier-side outfits rent them for €25–30/day. The island does not have a bank but there are two **ATM**s, one at the pier and one beside the *mairie* (town hall). For island **information**, including **maps**, head to the helpful Office du Tourisme at 39 rue de la Grande Anse, behind the *mairie* (Mon–Fri 8am–noon & 2–4pm; occasionally open on weekends; ⓣ0590/99 58 60, ⓦwww.omtlessaints.fr).

The island

Most of the action happens around the **pier**, which drops arriving boat passengers off onto a miniature square where elderly women sell sets of fabulously yummy coconut and guava *tourment d'amour* (agony of love) cakes, a tradition started by the wives of fishermen mourning their husbands' absence at sea (€2.50).

East of the pier, atop a steep incline, you can get a bird's-eye **view** of Les Saintes from the 1867 **Fort Napoléon** (daily barring holidays 9am–12.00pm; €4), an outpost that got more use as a penitentiary than as a defensive camp. The restored barracks now host the small **Musée d'histoire et traditions populaires**, showcasing traditional *Saintoise* crafts and fishing boats. Outside, sections of the parapets have been transformed into an iguana-inhabited **cactus garden**.

Ferries to the offshore islands

Several **ferries** make crossings to Guadeloupe's outer islands from Pointe-à-Pitre, St-François and Trois-Rivières, and a couple of companies run passengers between the outer islands as well. As a general rule, the largest operators – Brudey Frères and Express des Îles – are more reliable than the smaller outfits. Schedules are subject to change, and boats often leave late. Crossings can be extremely rough. You have been forewarned.

Ferry operators

Brudey Frères (Guadeloupe ⓣ0590/90 04 48, Martinique ⓣ0596/70 08 50; ⓦwww.brudey-freres.fr)

Le Colibri-Sarl La Somade (Guadeloupe ⓣ0590/21 23 73, ⓔprintempshugues@wanadoo.fr)

Comatril (Guadeloupe ⓣ0590/22 26 31, ⓕ82 57 73)

CTM Deher (Guadeloupe ⓣ0590/99 50 68, ⓕ99 56 83, ⓦwww.ctmdeher.com)

Express des Îles (Martinique ⓣ0596/42 04 05, Guadeloupe ⓣ0590/91 69 68; ⓦwww.express-des-iles.com)

Societe Maritime des Îles du Sud (Guadeloupe ⓣ0590/98 30 30, ⓕ0590/99 84 56)

Viking Transport (Guadeloupe ⓣ0590/85 00 55, ⓕ82 57 73)

Routes

Pointe-à-Pitre to: **Grand-Bourg**, Marie-Galante (5-6 daily; 45min; €39 round-trip); **St-Louis**, Marie-Galante (1 daily; 45min; €39.30 round-trip); **Terre-de-Haut** (1–2 daily; 45min; €39.50 round-trip).

St-François to: **La Désirade** (4–5 daily; 45min; €22 round-trip); **St-Louis**, Marie-Galante (Tues, Thurs, Fri; 45min; €30 round-trip); **Terre-de-Haut** (Tues & Thurs; 1hr 40min; €30 round-trip).

Trois-Rivières to **Terre-de-Haut** (8 daily; 25min; €22 round-trip).

Basse-Terre to **Terre-de-Haut** (2 daily except Sun; 30min; €24 round-trip)

Terre-de-Haut to: **Basse-Terre** (2 daily except Sun; 30min; €24 round-trip); **Pointe-à-Pitre** (1–2 daily; 45min; €39.50 round-trip); **St-François** (Tues & Thurs; 1hr 40min; €30 round-trip); **St-Louis**, Marie-Galante (Tues, Thurs, Fri; 45min; €32 round-trip); **Terre-de-Bas** (8 daily; 15min; €6 round-trip); **Trois-Rivières** (8 daily; 25min; €22 round-trip)

Terre-de-Bas to **Terre-de-Haut** (8 daily; 15min; €6 round-trip).

St-Louis, Marie-Galante to: **Pointe-à-Pitre** (1 daily; 45min; €39.30 round-trip); **St-François** (Tues, Thurs, Fri; 45min; €30 round-trip); **Terre-de-Haut** (Tues, Thurs, Fri; 45min; €32 round-trip)

Grand-Bourg, Marie-Galante to: **Pointe-à-Pitre** (5–6 daily; 45min; €39 round-trip).

La Désirade to **St-François** (4–5 daily; 45min; €22 round-trip).

The island's best beach, windswept **Plage de Pompierre**, lies southeast of the fort, along an almost perfectly enclosed bay. Free-roaming goats and roosters lie right down beside you, and they usually want some of your **food**, which you can get from women selling baguettes and drinks near the entrance. To get to the beach, turn left when you reach the T-junction at the base of the hill from the fort, or take the road behind Le Bourg's church. Terre-de-Haut's other good beaches are on the southwest coast: the tiny and oft-crowded yet undeniably gorgeous **Pain du Sucre** – a modest nod to Rio's Sugar Loaf – leads to a deep cove; nearby **Anse Crawen** gets fewer visitors.

Hundreds of white sand crabs scuttle the headland of the island's longest beach, **Grande Anse**. Unfortunately its location on Terre-de-Haut's Atlantic coast makes swimming impossible due to strong currents. Still, it's the best spot for sunrise, and you can take a plunge a few minutes east, off narrow **Anse Rodriguez**.

Accommodation

Terre-de-Haut's **accommodations** are plentiful, from posh bungalows to budget options; many boast English-speaking staff.

Auberge des Petits Saints ⓣ0590/99 50 99, ⓦwww.petitssaints.com. This inn in the hills above Grande Anse has twelve tastefully decorated doubles have balconies with views of the pool and sea. ⑤ including breakfast.

Bois Jolie ⓣ0590/99 50 38, ⓦwww.hotelboisjoli.fr. The only hotel near Anse Crawen and Pain du Sucre; bungalow-style doubles have a/c, porches and private beach and pool access. ⑤ including breakfast.

Lo Bleu Hotel Rue B-Cassin ⓣ0590/99 50 41, ⓦwww.lobleuhotel.com. Charming hotel on Le Bourg's western outskirts; some rooms have harbour views. Run with a degree of stylish cool unduplicated on Terre-de-Haut. ⑤ including breakfast.

La Saintoise Rue B-Cassin ⓣ0590/99 52 50. Ten straightforward no frills budget doubles with private bath and a/c right in the centre of Le Bourg. ③

Eating and drinking

More than a dozen **restaurants** are scattered across the island, with several close to the ferry dock offering day-tripper-friendly menus of salad and pizza. Seafood is obviously a speciality, with many spots serving up delectable plates of *blaff de poisons*.

Auberge les Petits Saints The place to splurge; decadent dishes include seafood and a Basque plate that hearkens back to the proprietor's ethnic background, as well as duck and smoked fish. Dinner, served on an antique-strewn terrace, is really very special. Mains €18–25.

Coleurs du Monde Ferry dock. Wave goodbye to all the day-trippers from this dockside venue, with its mix of Creole, Continental, and Asian dishes. Mains €17–20.

Le Triangle Rue B-Cassin. Very popular, casual Creole beachside restaurant, down a little passageway near *Lo Bleu Hotel*, Superb seafood and lively crowd make for a charming lunch. Closed Sun.

Terre-de-Bas

Twenty minutes west of Terre-de-Haut by **ferry** (see p.581), **TERRE-DE-BAS** needn't rank high on your must-see list unless you're looking for isolation. There's only one easily accessible beach at **Grande Anse**, a small, languid community ten minutes' walk from the pier, and a handful of rugged, well-marked **hiking** circuits through the arid inland foothills. Few forge on to quaint **Petites-Anses**, the island's largest settlement. Those wanting to bask in the silence should contact *Restaurant Soleil La*, which operates a bungalow with pool (ⓣ0590/92 30 93, ⓕ81 58 74; ③).

Marie-Galante

Although Columbus baptized round **Marie-Galante** after his ship, Guadeloupe's largest offshore island is colloquially known nowadays as Grande-Galette, after its flat-stone shape. Overgrown with **sugar cane** and scattered with crumbling **windmills**, the 158-square-kilometre island 25km south of Pointe-à-Pitre remains a rural, unhurried place that produces Guadeloupe's best and strongest **rum** – a woozy 59 percent alcohol – by adhering to customs that have altogether disappeared elsewhere. You'll likely see sugar cane cut by **scythe** and hauled on oxen-pulled **cabrouets**, wooden chariots typically only found in museums nowadays. The island also has lovely **beaches**, which remain mostly empty even during high season.

Marie-Galante's 13,500 inhabitants are split between three towns: the capital of **Grand-Bourg** and smaller **St-Louis** and **Capesterre**. The island's flatness – its highest point is a mere 150m – makes it ideal **walking** and **biking** terrain. There's also some good **diving** off the southern coast.

Arrival, information and getting there

While you can **fly** to Marie-Galante with Air Caraïbes (Ⓣ0590/82 47 00, Ⓕ82 47 48; three flights daily; €148), most visitors arrive by boat (see p.581). Depending on where you've caught the **ferry** – Pointe-à-Pitre, St-François or Les Saintes – you'll arrive either at Grand-Bourg or St-Louis. The sea crossing can be quite turbulent; those prone to seasickness might want to consider flying. Both quays have nearby **car** rental booths with rates around €35/day. For **automatic** cars, try Hertz (Ⓣ& Ⓕ0590/97 59 80). Regardless of the company, booking ahead is always advisable. **Minibuses** and **taxis** also service the island and can be reserved or picked up anywhere on the island; a hop between towns will cost €15-17. Navette minibuses are much more reasonable, and charge €1.50–2 for journeys between the towns. **Bike** rental is available at either pier starting at €12 per day.

For **information**, the Office du Tourisme on rue du Fort in Grand-Bourg (Mon–Fri 9am–4pm; Ⓣ0590/97 56 51, Ⓦwww.ot-mariegalante.com), has a very useful guide to the island, activity brochures and an excellent **map**, plus a **trail guide** to the island's hiking paths.

Grand-Bourg

Largely destroyed by fire in the early 1900s and hit by a brutal hurricane in 1928, the island capital of **GRAND-BOURG** was rebuilt with a lot of two-storey cement structures, but has enough surviving wooden Creole houses to remind visitors of its roots. It's a compact place, with a few narrow streets heading north of the harbour, where the peeling, cavernous **Notre-Dame-de-Marie-Galante** church overlooks the town **market**, which brims with spices, fruit and produce (Mon–Sat 6am–noon). There's little to do here by day except wander about and peruse the market goods, and even less to do by night. The main attraction is the ruins of the island's one-time richest sugar plantation, **Habitation Murat** (Mon–Fri 9am–noon, 2.30–5.30pm; free), 1.5km east of town. At its acme, in 1839, over 300 slaves worked the surrounding fields. Today, it houses Marie-Galante's écomusée.

Practicalities

Hotels are scarce in Grand-Bourg, but there are plenty of *gites* to choose from like *Le Cerisier Créole* on Grande Savane (Ⓣ0590/97 93 54; ❸), which features two comfortable, clean apartments with high ceilings, air-conditioning, TV and kitchen-ette on a residential street. For **food**, there's *Le Soleil Levant*, a pleasant bakery selling sandwiches on Petite Place du Marché close to the church. More substantial fare can be had at *Calypso*, on rue Beaurenon, with moderately priced Creole options (from €13). For a light dinner, try *Le King Pizza*'s tasty pizza.

St-Louis

Marie-Galante's oldest hamlet, quiet **ST-LOUIS**, is mostly visited as a debarkation point from inter-island ferries (see p.581) and for its nearby **beaches**. Starting 3km north of town, the lovely sands of **Plage Moustique**, **Anse Canot** and **Anse de Vieux-Fort** are rarely crowded. All are idyllic, with Moustique particularly dreamy.

Getting drunk before noon

Marie-Galante's major sights are the **distilleries** that ferment some of the region's strongest rum, which you can taste liberally and free of charge most mornings before lunch. All three – Bellevue in Capesterre (daily 7am–1pm; closed Sept–Oct), Bielle (Mon–Sat 10am–12.30pm, Sun 10am–noon) and Poisson, (Père Labat) (Mon–Sat 7am–1pm), both in Grand Bourg – maintain morning hours only. If you have time to visit only one, make it Bielle – it's the most bustling of the three. Just be sure to eat breakfast first.

None has facilities, so be sure to bring **food and drink** with you from St-Louis. You can stock up on pastries and sandwiches at *Délice Saint Louisiennes* (daily 6am–7pm; holidays 6am–2pm), a corner bakery facing the pier. *Le Coin Tranquille* scores with lovingly made, fresh-from-the-pier seafood specials in a laid-back beach location (daily lunch and dinner; "formule" menu €18). *Le Refuge*, another restaurant 2km south of town via the N9, doubles as a *gite* with comfortable though somewhat worn air-conditioned **rooms** and individual apartments (ⓣ & ⓕ 0590/97 02 95, ⓦwww.refugehulman.com; ❸). Call ahead for dining reservations. The soon to open *Cohoba* (ⓣ0590/97 50 50, ⓦwww.cohobahotel.com; ❻) is a studiously eco-friendly resort (the island's only one), which uses solar power and local products. The resort's beach is a turtle nesting area and there are tennis courts and a swimming pool. North of Saint-Louis in Ménard is the lovely *Village de Ménard*, which has villas and bungalows (ⓣ0590/97 09 45, ⓦwww.villagedemenard.com; ❹). Just off the D205 several km east of St-Louis, the charming stone *Habitation Grand Bassin* (ⓣ&ⓕ0590/97 31 27; ❸) features mosquito-netted poster beds and kitchenette.

Capesterre

A popular spot for scuba diving, laid-back **CAPESTERRE** occupies scenic lowlands near the southern coast's best beach, **Plage de la Feuillère**. Dive enthusiasts can check out a couple of island outfits: Man'Balaou, 22, avenue des Caraïbes in St-Louis (ⓣ0590/97 75 24, ⓦwww.manbalaou.com), and Ti'bulles (ⓣ0590/97 54 98, ⓦwww.tibulles-plongee.com), on rue Beaurenon on the eastern outskirts of Grand Bourg; both offer daily dives in the €35–40 range.

Practicalities

Capesterre's **lodging** options include the relaxed, hacienda-styled *Hôtel Hajo* (ⓣ0590/97 32 76; ❷) between the two beaches on the N9; its rustic fan-only rooms have ocean views, and most have private bath. On a hillside overlooking town, *Le Soleil Levant* (ⓣ0590/97 31 55, ⓦwww.im-caraibes.com/soleil-lavant; ❷) has impeccable air-conditioned rooms, some of which open onto a communal terrace. Capesterre's **dining** scene is mostly limited to beach kiosks selling snackish fare; for a sit-down meal, *Hajo's* onsite restaurant serves up salads, grilled *langouste* and other traditional Creole fare by the beach (lunch and dinner €20–22).

La Désirade

Sighted by Columbus during his second New World voyage in 1493, **LA DÉSIRADE** appeared an oasis to his sailors, whose yearning for land earned the hump-backed isle its name – "the desired one". It ultimately proved anything but, as it's the most arid and rocky of Guadeloupe's outer islands. From the early 1700s to the late 1950s, it served as a leper colony. Today, ever-greater numbers of visitors and day-tripping crowds are drawn by its peaceful, off-the-beaten-track charm.

Lying 11km off Guadeloupe's Pointe-des-Châteaux (see p.575), and measuring 11km from end to end, the two-kilometre-wide island is cut by mountain peaks topped with wind turbines. While the north coast is marked by rough seas, the south side has some pleasant beaches within easy access of the ferry dock and the main settlement, **Beauséjour**, a wee village with a cute little wooden church, fading wooden houses and beautiful **Plage à Fifi**. Two smaller communities, **Le Souffleur** and **Baie-Mahault**, are a few kilometres eastwards along the only island road; the latter hosted the leprosarium, whose only vestiges, the chapel walls, lie in ruins on the outskirts of town. Both villages front the island's nicest beaches; the best of them is the coconut tree-shaded **Le Souffleur**.

Practicalities

The island's small size makes it an ideal day-trip. **Ferries** make the 45-minute crossing from St-François. There are currently no flights between Guadeloupe and

La Désirade. Regular **mini-buses** are a convenient and inexpensive way to get around; a few euros will get you from one end of the island to the other, and for €10 per person drivers will offer an entertaining, 90-minute historical tour. If you prefer your own wheels, you can rent **bikes** and **scooters** from a handful of outfits facing the pier for €10 (bikes) and €20 (scooters) per day. Cars rent for around €30. Note that, unlike the rest of Guadeloupe, La Désirade has two **high seasons**: one from December through April and the other from July to September, when the rain renders the countryside greener.

Accommodation options are plentiful, with a few hotels and around 20 *gîtes*. Stop in at the friendly tourist office at the ferry dock in Beauséjour (Tue–Fri 8am–noon & 2–5pm, Sat 8.30–11am & 3–5pm, Sun 8.30–11am; ⓣ0590/85 00 86, ⓔotladesirade@wanadoo.fr) for a list. It's also possible to obtain a camping permit for short-term (one- or two-night) tent-pitching stays at Plage à Fifi. Visit the Mairie in Beauséjour (Mon, Tues, Thurs, Fri 7.30am–noon & 2–5pm; Wed, Sat 7.30am–noon; ⓣ0590/20 03 82). *Oüaliri Beach* (ⓣ0590/20 20 08, ⓦwww.rendezvouskarukera.com; ❹) is a cheerful hotel with six small, pleasant rooms with TV, air-conditioning and fridge plus beach access close to the pier. *Club Caravelles* in the Quartier du Souffleur is the splashiest *gîtes*, with a pool and access to a sheltered beach (ⓣ0590/20 04 00; ❹). From a hillside perch near Soffleur, *gîtes Alizea* (ⓣ & ⓕ0590/20 06 14, ⓦgite-alizea.web.ool.fr; ❸), has stellar ocean views from four clean, cheerful bungalows. *Gite des Remparts* (ⓣ0590/20 08 01; ❸) is a cute, well-maintained property near Baie-Mahault. The few **restaurants** that serve the island are mostly concentrated near the pier; *La Payotte* whips up fabulous seafood plates on a terrace (menus €11–16.50). The island doesn't have a **bank** but there is an **ATM** at the post office in Beauséjour.

La Petite Terre

For true isolation, nothing compares to the gorgeous, uninhabited slivers of **LA PETITE TERRE**, two tiny islands that sit 12km south of La Désirade and 7.5km east of Pointe des Châteaux. The larger of the two, called **Terre-de-Bas** (not to be confused with Les Saintes' isle of the same name), is a draw for day-tripping cruises on the way to La Désirade. There's no pier or facilities to speak of; boats simply drop anchor offshore, and visitors wade through waist-high water to the **beach** to relax, sunbathe and **snorkel** at a small offshore reef. The rocky island was once inhabited by 28 people, including a lighthouse keeper who finally left in 1974. Today the old lighthouse is solar-powered, and the only inhabitants of note are the many iguanas. The aptly named Iguana Sun (ⓣ0590/22 26 31) runs day-trips from St-François starting at €42 (€26 for children).

15.2

Martinique

Columbus once lauded **MARTINIQUE** as the "most charming country there is in the world", and the 1100-square-kilometre island is indeed breathtaking, a tropical mix of lush forests, towering mountains, and some of the loveliest beaches in the region. Solitude can be hard to come by in the southern resort towns where artificial beaches and anonymous hotels predominate. That said, it's not difficult to travel independently or to organize day-trips to undeveloped beaches or pristine wilderness.

The second largest French Caribbean territory, Martinique's terrain is topped by a series of mountain peaks. The most imposing, the dormant **Mont-Pelée** volcano, utterly destroyed northern **St-Pierre** in 1902; though the city has done much to rebuild itself, it's still an eerie experience to walk through the charred ruins of the fabled city and visit its museum. **Botanical gardens** teeming with indigenous flora evoke Martinique's original designation as Madinina (island of flowers), while the stupendous **Habitation Clément** distillery hosts a fascinating anti-Columbus exhibit. In between these sights, villages like isolated **Grand'Rivière** and Atlantic-facing **Tartane** steadfastly retain traditional Caribbean fishing village customs; the latter, on the **Presqu'île de la Caravelle**, is also the island's most laid-back destination, a wonderfully underdeveloped stretch that boasts some of Martinique's finest beaches.

Most **package tours** head straight to the built-up arc of resort territory south of Fort-de-France. Further south, visitors will find a host of less developed hamlets like **Ste-Anne** and **Diamant**, as well as the spectacular **Les Salines** beach. The island's beaches get increasingly black as you head north, culminating in the breathtaking **Anse Couleuvre** at the island's furthest reaches – the place to go for total isolation.

Arrival, information and getting around

Airlines serving Martinique include Air Antilles Express (☎0596/42 16 71), Air Caraïbes (☎0820/83 58 35), Air France (☎0820/82 08 20), Air Transat, American Airlines, Corsair (☎0892/68 59 92) and LIAT (☎0596/42 16 11). Ferries link the island with Dominica and St Lucia. For information about travelling by boat between Martinique and Guadeloupe, see "Ferries", p.581.

Passengers arriving by **plane** land at Martinique's **Aéroport du Lamentin**, a snazzy terminal about 9km from Fort-de-France and 11km from the nearest southern resort town. Taxis from the airport charge €20 to the capital and €40 and up to the southern coast; there are no public buses from the airport. If you intend to do any additional island exploring, your best bet is to rent a **car** on the spot; several agencies (see below) are located to the left of the airport exit, with rates starting around €50/day. The airport's tourism counter dispenses **information**, and staff can make reservations; the main tourism office is in downtown Fort-de-France (see p.589). You can also check out Ⓦwww.martinique.org.

Passengers arriving by **ferry** disembark at the **ferry terminal** on the southern outskirts of Fort-de-France. The fastest way to reach resort areas south of the capital is by taking a **taxi** (Madinina Taxi ☎0596/70 40 10 or Martinique Taxi ☎0596/63 63 62) straight to the **débarcadère** in downtown Fort-de-France, and hopping aboard a cross-bay **vedette** (see p.589) to avoid the brutal traffic jams on the southern highways. You can rent a car in southern resorts, and most agencies will let

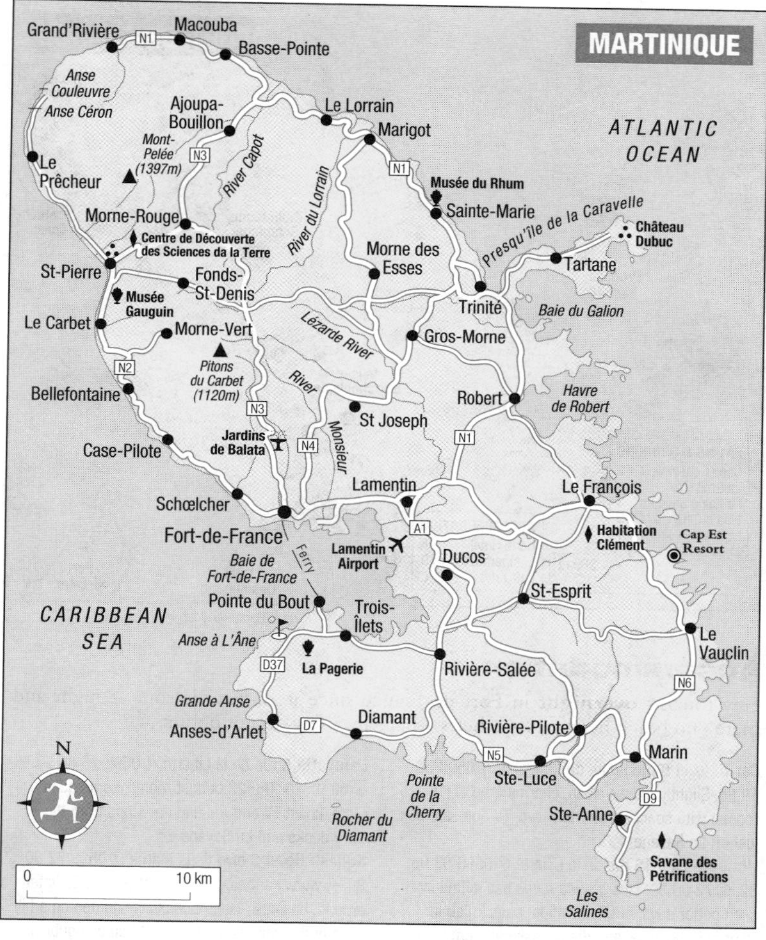

you drop your rental off at the airport when you leave. Agencies with outlets at the airport and most resort towns include Avis (ⓣ0596/42 11 00); Budget (ⓣ0596/42 16 79); Europcar (ⓣ0596/42 16 88, ⓦwww.europcar.com); Hertz (ⓣ0596/42 16 90, ⓦwww.hertzantilles.com); Jumbo Car (ⓣ0596/42 16 99, ⓦwww.jumbocar.com); and Rent-a-Car (ⓣ0596/42 16 15, ⓦwww.rentacar-caraibes.com).

Fort-de-France

Charming, scrappy and very French, **FORT-DE-FRANCE** is stunning to behold, particularly when arriving by sea, with its panorama of colonial houses and multiple church steeples wrapping around the **Baie des Flamands** and ascending into the surrounding mountainside. Traffic is often stifling but the city charms with high-fashion boutiques on **rue Victor Hugo** and the wide, bustling pedestrian walkway **rue de la République**. The best day to visit is Saturday before lunch when the streets buzz with people, and the sounds of tam tam and steel drums resonate throughout the main core.

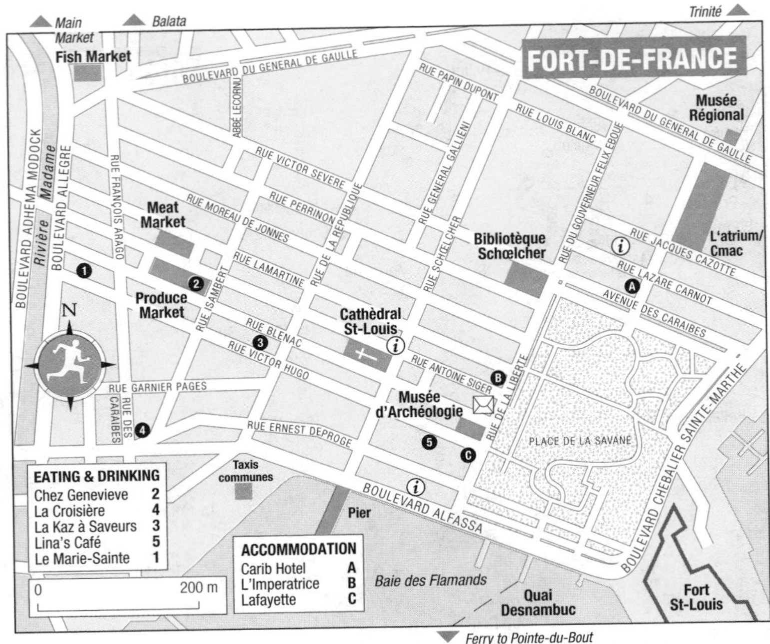

Accommodation

Few tourists **overnight** in Fort-de-France since it all but dies out at night and there's no beach nearby. Nonetheless, there are a few decent options.

Carib Hotel 9 rue Route du Matouba, ⓣ0596/60 19 85. Slightly musty, clean, charming hotel (16 rooms) with spacious quarters, a/c, TV and safe box, just off Le Savane. ❸

L'Impératrice 15 rue de la Liberté ⓣ0596/63 06 82, ⓕ72 06 30. This *grande dame* has definitely seen better days, but its location, smack dab in front of La Savane, and the occasional room with four-poster bed and balcony, make it a reasonable mid-range option. ❹

Lafayette 5 rue de la Liberté ⓣ0596/73 80 50, ⓕ60 97 75. The 22 budget rooms, some quite worn, boast TV and a/c and are steps from the ferry docks and La Savane. ❹

Squash Hotel 3 blvd de la Marne ⓣ0596/72 80 80, ⓦwww.karibea.com. The most upscale hotel around, business-class *Squash* is situated on a hill west of the city centre. It has 102 small doubles with a/c and TV, infinity pool, fitness centre and three squash courts. ❻

The Town

The city's most striking landmark, the unusual Byzantine and Beaux-Arts styled **Bibliothèque Schoelcher**, overlooks **La Savane** from the west, on rue de la Liberté (Mon 1–5.30pm, Tues–Thurs 8.30am–5.30pm, Fri 8.30am–5pm, Sat 8.30am–noon). Designed to house abolitionist Victor Schoelcher's personal book collection, the ornate library was shown at the Paris 1889 World's Fair before being dismantled and shipped piecemeal to Martinique's capital. Just down the street, at 9 rue de la Liberté, the engaging **Musée Départemental d'Archéologie et de Préhistoire** (Mon 1–5pm, Tue–Fri 8am–5pm, Sat 9am–noon, closed Sun; €3.05; ⓦwww.cg972.fr/mdap) has a two-storey exhibit devoted to Amerindian artefacts from Martinique and the surrounding islands dating from 100 BC to 1400–1600 AD. For a modernist architectural blast, look up along rue de la Liberté between rue Lamartine and rue Moreau de Jonnes, to see the splendidly restored **Crédit Martiniquais building**.

The **post office** is nearby on rue de la Liberté, across from La Savane (Mon–Tues, Thurs & Fri 7am–6pm, Wed 7am–5pm, Sat 7am–noon); for **Internet access** try CyberDeliss, which features terminals and Wi-Fi, as well as a kitchen, at 113 rue Ernest Deprogue (Mon–Sat 7am–10pm, 60 min/€5).

La Savane itself is worth a stroll, a park planted with royal palms and bamboo along the harbourfront. It faces **Fort St-Louis**, an imposing 1640 Vauban-style military base set on a promontory above the bay now closed to the public. North of La Savane is Martinique's cultural centre **CMAC/L'Atrium**, with its packed calendar of performances, concerts and films (Ⓣ0596/70 79 29, Ⓦwww.cmac.asso.fr). One block north, at 10 blvd Général-de-Gaulle, the **Musée Régional d'Histoire et d'Éthnographie** (Mon, Wed–Fri 8.30am–5pm, Tues 2–5pm, Sat 8.30am–noon; €3) occupies a Neoclassical 1887 villa. The main interest is upstairs, where four rooms are decorated with mahogany furniture, gold candelabra and fine latticework to evoke a late 1800s bourgeois home. Look for the display of dolls in ornate period dress, complete with lace and gold jewellery.

Another Fort-de-France landmark, the rust-coloured **Cathédrale St-Louis** on rue Schoelcher, boasts a 57-metre steeple and an apse inset with Martiniquan-themed stained-glass windows. The church is open to visitors before 11am; entrance is free. On the northwest outskirts, you can barter for meat, fish and produce at the busy **markets** (daily 6am–5pm) across the street from the run-down **Parc Floral**. Prime **shops** are on rue Victor Hugo, where duty-free boutiques offer great deals on perfume, jewellery and more.

Fort-de-France-specific **information** can be obtained at the small Office de Tourisme, near the cathedral on rue Schoelcher and rue Antoine Siger (Mon–Fri 9am–1pm, 2–5pm, Sat 9am–1pm; Ⓣ0596/70 23 36, Ⓦwww.ot-fortdefrance.fr), which has maps and brochures and organizes two-hour tours by foot (€12) and minibus (€20). Another office is located at 76 rue Lazare Carnot (Mon–Fri 8am–5pm).

Eating and drinking

Chez Genevieve Market, rue Blenac. Locals swear by this very casual lunch-only spot in the public market, which serves up authentic goods including *accras* and divine chicken and fish.

La Crosière 99 rue Ernest Deproge. Upstairs on rue Deproge, this inviting, nautically-themed restaurant boasts an extensive bar, a lively mood, and jazz on Fri and Sat nights. Mains €10–30.

La Kaz à Saveurs 84 rue Victor Hugo. Creole spot in the centre of the action. Mains begin at €14, and include a *magret de canard au miel* for €17.

Lina's Café 15 rue Victor Hugo. Gourmet café with delicious, fresh-made sandwiches (€3–8), quiches and the best coffee in town, in a hip, upscale atmosphere. Closed Sun and Mon evenings.

Le Marie-Sainte 160 rue Victor Hugo. The town's best Creole food, with spicy concoctions like *accras* (fritters of cod or vegetables) and rich *coq fricassé* (chicken fricassee). Menu €14; budget-friendly "formule" €12. Lunch only. Open Tues–Fri 9am–3pm, Sat 8am–3pm.

Moving on from Fort-de-France

From Fort-de-France, the fastest and easiest way to reach Martinique's southern beaches is by a vedette (ferry boat) run by Madinina (Ⓣ0596/63 06 46, Ⓦwww.vedettesmadinina.com). A regular ferry service connects the capital to Pointe-du-Bout with service on the half-hour (6.20am–8.45pm; €6.50 return). Ferries for Anse Mitan and Anse à l'Âne have a similar schedule between 6am and 6.30pm. From Anse à l'Âne and Anse Mitan to Fort-de-France, the last vedettes are at 5.50pm and 6pm, respectively; the final ferry from Pointe-du-Bout to Fort-de-France leaves at 9.30pm. For points elsewhere in Martinique, you can catch one of the minibuses that cover the island from Pointe-Simon, southwest of the tourism office.

Southern Martinique

Most sun-worshippers head directly to **SOUTHERN MARTINIQUE**, where the Caribbean is bordered by the island's only white-sand **beaches**, including the glorious **Les Salines** at the southernmost tip. Built up in recent years, many of the towns have lost much of their Martiniquan character; **Pointe-du-Bout** (with neighbouring **Anse Mitan** in its orbit) is the blandest and the busiest. Further south, **Diamant** and **Ste-Anne** are both more authentic and less crowded.

Trois-Îlets to Pointe-du-Bout

TROIS-ÎLETS, the first hamlet along the southern coast, is a cute town on a hill, with rustic wooden houses featuring gingerbread trim. It is visited mostly for its **tourism office**, which handles nearby Pointe-du-Bout. Find it on place de l'Église (Mon–Fri 8am–5pm, Sat 9am–1pm, Sun 9am–noon). On the town's outskirts, **Le Village de la Poterie** hosts potters, artists and other craftsmen selling their wares alongside cafés and a kayak rental shop. More pottery can be found nearby at the **Domaine Château Gaillard**, a complex that also hosts the charming **Musée Café & Cacao** (daily 9am–5.30pm; free) and, for the more adventurous, Héli Blue (ⓣ0596/66 10 80, ⓦwww.heliblue.com), which offers helicopter tours of the island by English-speaking guides (€34–175). Across the road is the outdoor adventure park Mangofil (daily 9am–5pm) where adrenaline junkies glide across high wires (€25; €17 for children). Further west is the engaging **Maison de la Canne** (Tues-Thu 8.30am–5.30pm, Fri 8.30am–5pm, Sat 8.30am–1pm, 2–5pm, Sun 9am–1pm, 2–5pm; €3), a sugar cane museum that presents the history of slavery on the island.

Past Trois-Îlets in the direction of Anse à l'Âne, the main road branches off to the right and left around Martinique's **golf course**. The right leads to Pointe-du-Bout (see below), the left to **La Pagerie**, Empress Joséphine's homestead until the age of 16. While the main house was destroyed by a hurricane in 1766, the stone kitchen now hosts an engaging **museum** (Tues–Fri 9am–5.30pm, Sat & Sun 9.30am–12.30pm & 3–5pm; €5) dedicated to the empress's torrid relationship with Napoleon. You'll find some intriguing pieces, like the doctored wedding certificate stating their mutual ages as 28, and a falsified coronation scene depicting Napoleon's mother among the guests – in fact, she didn't attend because she disliked Joséphine. Access to the very lovely park and pavilion is just €1.50.

Pointe-du-Bout

Anchored around an almost perfectly square harbour, **POINTE-DU-BOUT** gets most of its traffic from French tourists with money to spare – the costs of staying here are the highest on Martinique. While the town has a suburban, one-size-fits-all feel, there are some bargains, especially toward Anse Mitan, and the area makes a great base for exploring both southern Martinique and Fort-de-France. You can escape the scene with Anthinea (ⓣ0596/66 05 26; €50), a friendly **diving** outfit toward Anse Mitan that heads up to St-Pierre and hits the grottoes around the Rocher du Diamant (see opposite). Or rent a **boat** on the harbour's western side; Turquoise Yachting (ⓣ0596/66 10 74) offers small motorboats by the hour (€35) or the day (€150). A range of companies offer **boat tours** including Katamambo (ⓣ0596/66 11 83) and Schéhérazade (ⓣ0696/39 45 55). Check **email** at Jus't @ kôté in Anse-Mitan, across the road from *Au Poisson d'Or* (see below) (Mon–Sat 9am–5pm; ⓣ0596/71 87 93).

Accommodation

Pointe-du-Bout has at least a dozen places to **stay**. You can save money by checking into one of the hotels clustered to the west in Anse Mitan, the natural white-sand beach at the mouth of the Pointe.

Auberge de l'Anse Mitan ⓣ0596/66 01 12, ⓦwww.aubergeansemitan.com. In a quiet location at Anse Mitan's westernmost edge, this personable, family-run inn has twenty rooms with sea or garden views, and character to spare; neither luxurious nor packed with amenities, it's a great fit for budget travellers. ❹ with breakfast.

Hotel Bambou ⓣ0596/66 01 39, ⓕ66 05 05, ⓦwww.hotelbambou.fr. This cluster of colourful bungalows is packed with French package tourists. It's notable for its wheelchair-accessibility and easy access to the Fort-de-France *vedettes* pier. ❻, with partial board (breakfast and dinner).

Carayou Martinique ⓣ0596/66 04 04, ⓕ66 00 57, ⓦwww.hotel-carayou.com. Secluded Pointe-du-Bout option has a private beach, ample water toys and 201 comfortable rooms, many with sea views. ❾

La Pagerie ⓣ0596/66 05 30, ⓔhpagerie@cgit.com. Smack dab in the heart of the Pointe, this hotel features 98 spacious rooms with a/c, TV and phone. ❻, including breakfast.

Sofitel Bakoua ⓣ0596/66 02 02, ⓦwww.sofitel.com. The area's most exclusive hotel boasts 137 spacious, well-appointed rooms, an alluring bar and a terrific infinity pool with lovely views. ❾

Village Créole ⓣ0596/66 03 19, ⓦwww.villagecreole.com. Upscale studios and one- to two-bedroom apartments in the hub of Pointe-du-Bout with full kitchen, TV, a/c and parking (reception desk located in *La Pagerie*). ❺

Eating and drinking

Scads of **restaurants** on the Pointe serve international cuisine; authentic local restaurants can be found near Anse Mitan.

Au Poisson d'Or Anse Mitan. Generous portions of Creole fare are served up for lunch and dinner at this delightful spot on the coastal road (entrees €12–21). Order the insanely gorgeous fish in coconut milk. Closed Mon.

Manureva 25 rue des Anthuriums, Anse Mitan. Stylish, upscale Anse Mitan restaurant boasts specialties like house-made foie gras, filet mignon, and grilled *langouste* (mains €20 and up).

La Marine Pointe-du-Bout. In the hyperactive centre of the marina hubbub, with reasonable French, Creole and seafood options (entrees €12–25) and lunch formules for €13.50.

Paul Pointe du Bout Casino. This exquisite bakery, one of four in a local chain, is located on the ground floor of the Pointe du Bout casino. It features a full range of breads, pastries, sandwiches, salads and coffees. Open daily.

Anse à l'Âne

The crescent-shaped **ANSE À L'ÂNE** is cosier, friendlier and much less expensive than Pointe-du-Bout, 2km to the east. It has its own all-inclusive resort, the *Club des Trois-Îlets* (ⓣ0596/68 31 67, ⓦwww.hotel-club3ilets.com; ❽). Popular **dive** shop Corail Club Caraïbes is on the hotel premises (ⓣ0596/68 36 36, ⓦwww.corail.fr.st; single dive €45; three dives €120) and clients can use the hotel's pool. There are few places to **stay** otherwise; a good budget option is *Le Courbaril* (ⓣ0596/68 32 30, ⓦwww.courbarillocation.com; ❸), which offers 40 faded and rustic fan-only bungalows with kitchenettes and terraces right on the beach. To **eat**, there's the convivial *Le Nid Tropical*, a casual beachside lunch and dinner terrace (closed Mon) with tasty *salade Niçoise* (€7.50) and a "menu Créole" for €15. Le Nid also has a few cheap rooms (ⓣ0596/68 38 16; ❷).

South to Diamant

The D37 south of Anse à l'Âne skirts Grande Anse, a gorgeous harbour packed with colourful fishing boats, followed by Anse d'Arlet and Petite Anse, both quiet seaside villages with their own agreeable sandy stretches, before climbing 477-metre Morne Larcher, southern Martinique's highest point. The road here can get pretty tight, with a number of hairpin turns, but it's worth the grinding gear-shifting to reach the south side, where the road plunges down to the sea and **Rocher du Diamant**, a rocky outcropping, leaps majestically into view. This volcanic islet 3km off the coast of Martinique is popular with scuba divers, as its depths are loaded with violet coral, multicoloured sponges and finely carved grottoes.

The town of **DIAMANT** itself, which lies a few kilometres east of the eponymous Rocher, is a picturesque place, with pretty blue and coral houses overlooking a fine bay bounded to the east by the cloistered Pointe de la Chery. The four-kilometre beach is one of Martinique's nicest, but the swell can be rough; it's still worth checking out for the awesome vista of the Rocher huddled below Morne Larcher. **Diving** around the rock is stellar. Contact Aqua Sud Diamant (ⓣ0596/76 51 01). In Diamant, stop by the **Espace Museographique Bernard David** (39 rue Justin Roc; ⓣ0596/66 07 36) with its permanent Amerindian exhibit and live camera feeds of Rocher du Diamant.

Practicalities

Diamant's hotels are located outside of the town centre. About five kilometres west, *L'Anse Bleue* (ⓣ0596/76 21 91, ⓦwww.hotel-anse-bleue.com; ③) has attractive wooden cottages and a highly regarded restaurant, *La Paillotte Bleue* (ⓣ0596/58 33 21; closed Sun evening and Wed). There's also the *Mercure Diamant*, on Pointe de la Chery (ⓣ0596/76 46 00, ⓦwww.mercure.com; ⑥), which has 149 rooms with air-conditioning, satellite TV, fridge and phone – all with sea views.

Among Diamant's **restaurants**, *Snack 82* behind the town pharmacy sells cheap fast food. Down the street local favourite *Chez Lucie* (closed Tues and Sun) has a wide choice of Creole dishes on their prix-fixe menu, including *poulet boucané* (smoked chicken) and *colombo de crevettes* (shrimp curry).

Ste-Anne

Delightful **STE-ANNE**, Martinique's southernmost village, seems almost blissfully unaware of the *Club Med* and hopping beaches nearby. The town itself revolves around two miniature squares. Place Abbé Morland, at the north end, fronts a charming sandstone church with striking chandeliers, while place 22-Mé to the south hosts the bus depot. The two narrow roads that run between them are lined with lovely two-storey houses that overlook a deep emerald-blue bay.

The **tourism office** on the left side of the road as you head into town (Mon, Tues, Thus, Fri 8.30am–6pm, Wed 8:30am-4pm, Sat 8.30am–2pm, Sun 8.30am–noon) has information on what's going on in the area. Across the street, quality **dive** outfit Kalinago (ⓣ0596/76 92 98, ⓔkalinago@wanadoo.fr) offers trips to Rocher Diamant and night dives with English-speaking instructors (€42–50). You can also check out the underwater action on the glass-bottomed *Aquabulle*, which leaves the pier in nearby Marin three times daily; the last trip makes time for snorkelling (1.5–2hrs; €26).

Accommodation

Domaine de l'Anse Caritan Route des Caraïbes ⓣ0596/76 74 12, ⓦwww.anse-caritan.com. Ritzy hotel with an exceptional beachfront location and 240 well-appointed and spacious rooms; there's also a gorgeous pool and landscaped grounds. ⑦

Domaine de Belfond ⓣ0596/76 92 32, ⓕ0596/76 82 19, ⓦwww.hotel-de-belfond.com. Friendly, affordable medium-range hotel with acceptable rooms and three swimming pools on offer for guests. ④

La Dunette Rue JM Tjibaou ⓣ0596/76 73 90, ⓦwww.ladunette.com. A bit ratty but charming, *La Dunette* has a great location right on the main drag with eighteen straightforward a/c and TV-equipped rooms. Ask for one overlooking the water. ⑤ with breakfast.

Eating and drinking

Le Coco Nèg 4 rue Abbé Huard. A cosy restaurant run by a Martiniquan couple who emphasize simple but flavourful dishes like local crayfish and *columbo de cabri* (curried goat); most plates €15–25. Dinner only.

L'Épi Soleil Rue JM Tjibaou. Small counter with a few tables serves pastries, sandwiches (€3–4) and other picnic staples.

La Ronde des Yoles Pointe Marin. The best beachside restaurant along busy Pointe Marin, serving up top-notch local fare, including light-as-air codfish fritters and perfect conch.

Les Tamariniers Place de L'Église. A wonderful diner with delicious Creole dishes like red snapper, avocado and lobster, and grouper. Basic menu €17; Creole menu with *langouste* €35. Closed Wed.

Les Salines

The stupendous **GRANDE ANSE DES SALINES**, 5km south of Ste-Anne, is considered Martinique's best beach, and with good reason: its pristine white sands trim an azure bay framed by swaying palm trees. The one hazard is the toxic manchineel trees (see p.37), especially common at the southernmost end; they're marked with bands of red paint. Should you get bored with sun-worshipping, the sand is backed by a natural **salt pond**, after which the beach is named, and borders a desolate petrified forest, **La Savane des Petrifications** (also rife with manchineel trees); both make good side-explorations.

While the beach has countless **snack** trucks selling baguettes, crepes and drinks, **facilities** are minimal – if possible, don your suit in advance. **Camping** (free; see p.565) is permitted on the beach during school holidays. If you don't have your own wheels, you can catch a taxi to Les Salines from place 22-Mé, or call Ste-Anne Transport (☎0696/21 20 99). Return fare is €4; confirm return times upon arrival.

Northern Martinique

The blend of ruins, botanical gardens, rainforests and mountainous areas throughout **NORTHERN MARTINIQUE** offers a sharp counterpoint to its southern resort towns. The roller-coasteresque Route de la Trace cuts through the lush valleys of cloud-shrouded **Mont-Pelée** and **Morne-Rouge**, while the Caribbean-hugging N2 is lined by silver-tinted black sand beaches. A remarkable site is **St-Pierre**, the town destroyed by Mont-Pelée in 1902, while **Anse Couleuvre**, at the northernmost tip, is Martinique's most secluded beach.

Up the Caribbean coast

Once past the suburban communities on the outskirts of the capital, the N2 passes through a series of fishing villages before reaching **Le Carbet**, the spot where Columbus claimed the island for Spain in 1502. North of here, two roadside black-sand beaches blend into one another, the first of which, **Anse Turin**, appeared in some of Paul Gauguin's works. He and his friend Charles Laval stayed in a nearby slave cottage during a brief, unhappy stint in Martinique in 1887, when the two were recovering from malaria. While the shack is long gone, the eclectic **Musée Paul Gauguin** (daily 9.30am–4pm; €4), off to the right before the tunnel to St-Pierre, commemorates Gauguin's short residency with everything from reproductions of his works and assorted personal effects. (The museum will undergo a six-month renovation late in 2008.)

Immediately north on the N2 are the superb ruins and grounds of the pre-1643 **Habitation Anse Latouche** (daily 9.30am–5pm; €5.50), once the island's largest sugar plantation. The grounds and buildings were destroyed by Mont-Pelée's 1902 eruption, though vestiges of a 1716 aqueduct and dam are still visible – the only examples of their kind on Martinique. Also fascinating are the immaculately tended cactus gardens cultivated on the grounds.

St-Pierre

Little Pompeii, as Martinique's former capital **ST-PIERRE** is now known, begins due north of the Habitation Anse Latouche. On May 8, 1902, a sudden eruption of Mont-Pelée devastated the then 250-year-old town along with its nearly 28,000 inhabitants – all in a few seconds. The lone survivor, **Louis Cyparis**, was in prison and made it out alive only because his cell was sufficiently ballasted to withstand the heat. The grim effects of the lava's path are evident throughout the compact town, where blackened **ruins** can't be missed.

The best place to start your explorations is the **Musée Historique et Vulcanologique** on rue Victor Hugo (daily 9am–5pm; €2.50), a small museum that houses contorted glass and soot-streaked porcelain salvaged from the rubble; the centrepiece is a squashed church bell that once sounded Mass.

Facing the museum are St-Pierre's most impressive ruins, those belonging to the 1831–32 Bordeaux-inspired **theatre**. All that remain are the twin entrance staircases and the archway-encircled oval auditorium, but they evoke something of its former splendour. South towards the waterfront finds the **Quartier du Figuier**, the ruins of several eighteenth-century portside storehouses.

After exploring the ruins of St-Pierre, the **Centre de Découverte des Sciences de la Terre** on the northern outskirts of town (Tue–Sun 9am–4.30pm; €5) is a fascinating follow-up. Built on the green flanks of Mont-Pélee, the multi-level centre has hands-on exhibits that demonstrate the physics of soil and the history of natural tragedies. Made of neoprene and cement, the boxy, Niemeyeresque structure is an attraction in itself, designed to withstand level 5 hurricanes and earthquakes of up to 8.0 on the Richter scale. Also near St-Pierre is the gorgeous **Distillerie Depaz**, worth a visit for the views of the ocean and Mont-Pelée it affords alone (Ⓣ0596/78 13 14, Ⓦwww.depaz.fr).

Practicalities

While St-Pierre is easily walkable, the rubber-wheeled *Cyparis Express* train covers the town with a narrated one-hour tour starting opposite the Quartier du Figuier (Mon–Fri 11am & 2pm; €10). The adventurous should contact the Bureau de la Randonnée (Ⓣ0596/55 04 79), an outfit that arranges **canyoning** (combination white-water and rainforest expedition) trips and gives out **hiking** information. Tropicasub, on the southern outskirts (Ⓣ0696/24 24 30, Ⓦwww.multimania.com/tropicasub), takes **divers** out to explore shipwrecks.

There is currently just one place to **stay** in St-Pierre. Above town, *Le Fromager* (Ⓣ0596/78 19 07; ❷) has sea views from four terraced mountain-edge bungalows. **Dining** options include a handful of bakeries; *Bleu des Îles*, next to the theatre ruins on rue Victor Hugo, with a €15 menu with lots of *accras* and grilled fish; and *La Vague*, with a lovely beachside terrace and a lunch menu starting at €14, across from the beautifully restored **Exchange House**.

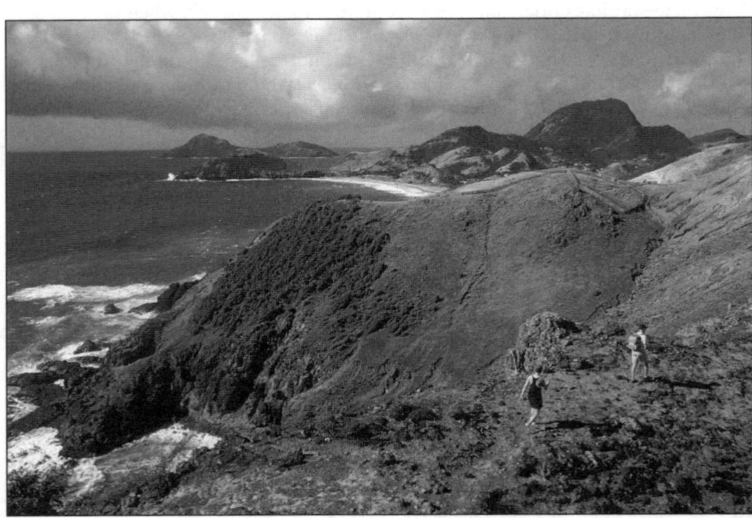

▲ Hiking on the island

Beyond St-Pierre

North of St-Pierre, the coastal road rims the Caribbean after passing the **Tombeau des Caraïbes**, the limestone cliff from which the last of the Carib chieftains committed suicide in 1658 rather than submitting to colonization. The villages along this quiet northern stretch, **Le Prêcheur** and **Anse Belleville**, are among the island's oldest, and their harbours are picturesque.

Beyond is **Anse Céron**, a relatively secluded black-sand beach and littoral forest, equipped with changing facilities and *La Marrynoise*, a snack bar. For total isolation, forge onwards on the N2 to **Anse Couleuvre**, a magnificent emerald bay with a volcanic sand beach. A path to the left of the car park hits the sand in short order; a longer one to the right passes the ruins of a chocolate plantation. The latter trail is also the start of a grinding eighteen-kilometre (6hr) walk to Grand'Rivière (see p.595).

Route de la Trace

Opened by the Jesuits in the early 1700s, the snaking **ROUTE DE LA TRACE**, or N3, rises into the foggy altitudes of **Mont-Pelée** and the **Pitons du Carbet** northwest of Fort-de-France before heading to the Atlantic coast.

At the start of the N3 just outside Fort-de-France, the Byzantine **Sacré-Coeur-de-Balata** overlooks the capital from a hillside plateau; built in 1928, the domed church is a miniature replica of Montmartre's Sacré-Coeur. Several kilometres further northwest is the route's major tourist stop, the botanical **Jardin de Balata** (daily 9am–5pm; €6.50; Ⓦwww.jardindebalata.com), where buses deposit cruise ship day-trippers to check out the flowers. The landscaped gardens are lush with lily ponds and hundreds of palms and fruit trees, and afford awesome vistas of the Pitons de Carbet.

Heading another 10km inland from the gardens, the N3 reaches the **Site de l'Alma**, a cascading river with shallow pools in a dark rainforest, then moves onward to Martinique's highest-altitude town, **Morne-Rouge**, located 450m above sea level. The town's proximity to **Mont-Pelée**, the 1397-metre-high volcano that dominates northern Martinique, is the main reason to stop here. For information about Mont-Pelée, visit the **Maison Régional des Volcans** (Mon 2–5pm, Tues–Fri 8.30am–5pm, Sat–Sun 8.30am–2pm; €3) or the local **Syndicat d'Initiative** on rue Emile Maurice (Mon–Fri 9am–1pm). Nearby (look for the green gate), the island's modest **youth hostel**, *Auberge de Jeunesse*, on rue Jean-Jaurès (Ⓣ0596/78 50 99, Ⓕ52 59 81, Ⓦwww.fuaj.org; ❶ with breakfast) has dormitory beds and private rooms.

A junction at the northern outskirts of Morne-Rouge marks the end of the Route de la Trace; the eastern N2 hits St-Pierre (see opposite) in 8km while the westward N3 carries on past the access road to Mont-Pelée, signposted to Aileron 2km after the turn-off. For **lunch**, it's worth driving up the Route de l'Aileron to *Auberge de la Montagne Pelée* (daily; lunch only; menu €13) for the curried mutton.

Onward to the Atlantic coast

The most notable stop along the stretch of N3 that heads towards the Atlantic is the **Gorges de la Falaise** (daily 8am–5pm, closed on rainy days; €7), on the southern outskirts of Ajoupa-Bouillon. With the help of a guide, visitors meander through the rainforest before descending into rushing cascades for an invigorating swim. While the one-hour hike is not difficult, the stone pathways can be slippery, so bring good shoes.

North to Grand'Rivière

Though it's a hike, **GRAND'RIVIÈRE**, a jewel of a fishing village huddled on lowlands framed dramatically by Mont-Pelée, is worth a visit. The thirty-minute drive from Basse-Pointe is the island's most thrilling, with tight hairpin turns, overgrown hillsides and bridges suspended over gorges. The roller coaster ends at the village's black-sand beach, and it's literally the end of the road. The only way to go further from here is by foot or boat. A **syndicat d'initiative** facing the town church (Mon–Fri 8am–5pm, Sat & Sun 9am–1pm; ⓣ0596/55 72 74) organizes outings. Grab a bite nearby at friendly Creole **restaurant** *Chez Tante Arlette*, 3 rue Lucy de Fossarieu (Tues–Sun noon–4pm), where Arlette herself cooks up generous three-course prix-fixe menus (€16). There's also a handful of **rooms** upstairs (ⓣ0596/55 75 75, ⓔcarinetantearlette@wanadoo.fr; ❸ breakfast included).

Central Martinique

CENTRAL MARTINIQUE extends south from the capital to Trois-Îlets and north to Ste-Marie. Though the region is mostly suburban, it boasts the show-stopping **Presqu'île de la Caravelle**, a verdant peninsula that juts into the mighty Atlantic. Also worth a side trip is **Habitation Clément**, a remote rum distillery that came to international fame when it hosted the 1991 Gulf War summit between French President François Mitterand and US President George H.W. Bush.

Presqu'île de la Caravelle and around

Despite flaunting some of Martinique's most beautiful beaches, the twelve-kilometre long **Presqu'île de la Caravelle** has remained delightfully underdeveloped. Sweeps of sugar cane fields and bamboo crush up against the access road before opening onto dramatic ocean vistas and arriving at the peninsula's solitary village, the quaint **Tartane**, where a glorious Atlantic-facing beach is busy with fishing boats.

Aside from Anse Tartane, five other Atlantic-facing **beaches** are nearby, the best of which, **Anse l'Étang**, is 1km east of town. Another kilometer along is **Anse Bonneville**, a haven for windsurfers. The protected **nature reserve** at the peninsula's tip has several **hiking** trails and contains what's left of the 1740 **Château Dubuc** (daily 8.30am–6pm; €3), a homestead with the ruins of several slave *cachots*, tiny solitary-confinement units.

A couple of sights within easy driving distance combine to make a good half-day outing. In the vicinity of Ste-Marie is the engaging **Musée du Rhum** (daily 9am–5pm; free entry and tasting), where a collection of rum-related paraphernalia is complemented by outdated advertising campaigns. The area's main attraction, however, is the stellar **Habitation Clément**, 10km south of the peninsula, at the western outskirts of Le François (daily 9am–5.30pm; closed Sept; €7, rum-tasting included; ⓦwww.habitation-clement.com). The graceful property sits on eighteen hectares of grounds.

Practicalities

The best **hotel** value near Anse l'Étang is the charming, family-run run *La Caravelle* (ⓣ0596/58 07 32, ⓦwww.hotel-la-caravelle-martinique.com; ❹), east of the beach on a commanding hillside perch on route du Chateau Dubuc. 15 quaint studios and apartments all have kitchenette, TV, air-conditioning and easy beach access. Cookie-cutter posh lodgings can be found at *Baie du Galion* (ⓣ0596/58 76 10, ⓦwww.karibea.com; ❻), with spacious balconied suites and kitchenettes.

For true luxury, head north or south. To the south is the decadent *Cap Est Lagoon Resort* on the coast between Le François and Le Vauclin (ⓣ0596/54 80 80, ⓦwww.capest.com; ❾); the 50 stylish, deluxe suites feature private terrace and loads of amenities. 5km north of La Trinité is the remarkable *Le Domaine Saint Aubin* (ⓣ0590/69 41 14, ⓦwww.ledomainesaintaubin.com; ❼). A meticulously restored estate house and several adjacent buildings make an inspired and very well-designed hotel.

Most of the **restaurants** in the area are casual spots near Anse Tartane, typically offering daily seafood specials and traditional Creole fare. The peninsula's standout dining destination is *La Table de Mamy Nounou* at La Caravelle (see above), which serves a *terroir*-based menu utilizing local products and French culinary traditions (mains €13–27). For something less fancy, the *Restaurant de la Plage* by Anse l'Étang serves pizzas and cocktails and offers Wi-Fi access alongside a mini-golf course.

15.3

St Barthélemy

The Caribbean playground of the rich and famous, **ST BARTHÉLEMY (usually St Barts, St Barths or St Barth)** is sleek, chic, but rarely snooty. The tiny boomerang-shaped island, just 21-square-kilometres in size, looks and feels like it's been plucked from the Côte d'Azur and dropped into the Antilles. The island is sprinkled with picturesque red-roofed **villas** and edged by some of the Caribbean's loveliest **bays** and **beaches**, some of which are only accessible by sea, giving a rare sense of **seclusion**. Even the most beautiful stretches of sand – **Anse de Grande Saline**, **Anse du Grand Colombier** and **Anse du Gouverneur** – never get crowded and, thanks to laws forbidding big resort developments, everything is small-scale, including the capital, **Gustavia**, whose tallest buildings are shorter than the highest palm trees.

St Barts' privacy doesn't come cheap, and you will pay dearly for your visit; if you come on a tight budget you will need to choose your accommodation and restaurants very wisely.

Arrival, information and island transport

Winair, Air Caraïbes, St Barth Commuter, Air Antilles Express and Tradwind Aviation all fly to St Barts. St Martin is a major hub, but some direct flights to/from other islands are now possible (Winair, for example, now flies directly between Antigua and St Barts.) Ferries run daily between St Barts and both St Martin and St Maarten (see "Ferries", p.35).

Most visitors arrive by (very) small **planes** on a miniature runway that ends at the water – making for a spectacular, if daunting, arrival. Banks and ATMs are found across the island; the latter include one opposite the airport at the La Savane Centre Commercial where you can also **change currency**. There's also Change Caraïbes on rue de la République in Gustavia (Ⓣ0590/27 57 57). The euro is the official currency, although the US dollar is widely accepted.

Many hotels meet flights or ferries on request. While there are two **taxi** stands – one at the airport, the other at Gustavia's Quai Général-de-Gaulle – there are no public **buses**. (Call ahead for a taxi on Ⓣ0590/27 66 31 in Gustavia, or 27 75 81 in St-Jean.) Most visitors rent a **car**; several agencies are located just to the right as you exit the airport. Your best bet is a jeep, as some of the island's roads are steep and get quite slick when it rains. Reservations are a must. There are many reliable companies, from well-known names such as Hertz (operating as Henry's; Ⓣ0590/27 71 14, Ⓔhertz

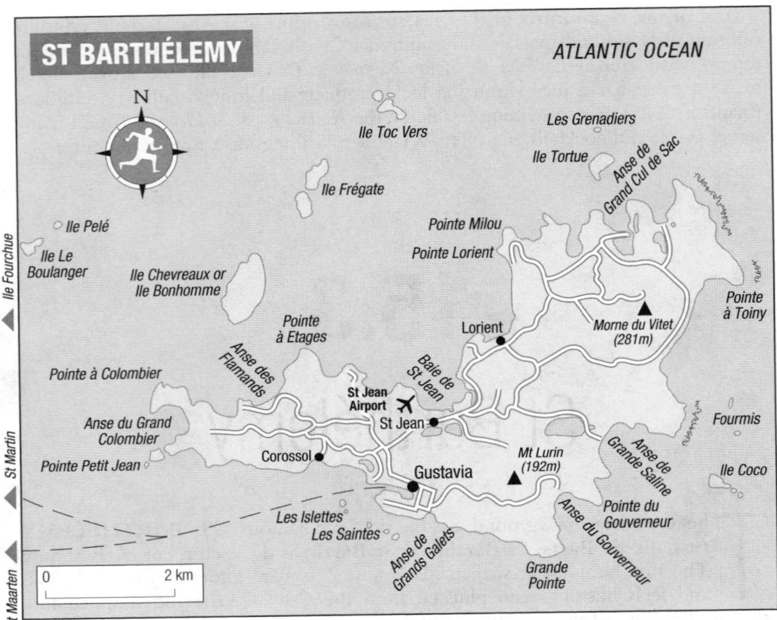

.stbarth@wanadoo.fr) and Avis (Ⓣ0590/27 71 43, Ⓦwww.avis-stbarth.com) to local outfits such as Island Car (Ⓣ0590/27 70 01, Ⓔislandcr@wanadoo.fr), Soleil Caraïbe (Ⓣ0590/27 67 18, Ⓔsoleil.caraibe@wanadoo), Top Loc (Ⓣ0590/29 02 02, Ⓦwww.top-loc.com) and Turbé (Ⓣ0590/27 71 42, Ⓔ turbe.car.rental@orange.fr). Driving is on the right, and there are only two petrol stations on the island – one across from the airport and one in Lorient; the airport one operates 24 hours a day via a credit-card system. If you don't rent a car, consider staying in St-Jean; it has the highest concentration of restaurants and shops outside the capital, plus two popular beaches.

For **information**, head to the helpful Office de Tourisme (Mon–Fri 8am–6pm; Sat 9am–noon; Ⓣ0590/27 87 27, Ⓔinfo.odtsb@wanadoo.fr) in Gustavia on Quai Général-de-Gaulle, on the north side of the marina. Before you arrive, check Ⓦwww.st-barths.com, which has useful links. The main **post office** is in Gustavia on rue du Centenaire (Mon, Tues, Thurs & Fri 7.30am–12.45pm low season/3pm high season, Wed & Sat 7.30am–noon). Many hotels and some restaurants have WiFi; high-speed access is also available at Centre Alizés on rue de la République (Mon–Wed 9am–6.30pm, 9am–1pm Sat, longer hours in season, Ⓣ0590/29 89 89), which has 30 computers and also rents cellphones and laptops.

Several of the island's biggest **watersports operators** are based on La Pointe, on the west side of Gustavia's port. The highly recommended **Marine Service** (Ⓣ0590/27 70 34, Ⓦwww.st-barths.com/marine.service) offers all manner of excursions, including sunset cruises, PADI dives and half- and full-day snorkelling trips ($88–176). Nearby Plongée Caraïbes (Ⓣ0590/27 55 94, Ⓦwww.plongee-caraibes.com) focuses on scuba diving and snorkelling, with highly qualified instructors leading excursions to coral reefs, shipwrecks and other prime dive spots (snorkelling $59, diving $88–162).

Gustavia

Quaint as a dollhouse, St Barts' capital, **GUSTAVIA**, is an appealing blend of red-roofed villas and heavy-set grey-stone buildings that hug a deep, U-shaped harbour where yacht-watching over a glass of wine at a waterfront **café** ranks as the unofficial town pastime. A close runner-up for that title is **shopping**, as dozens of duty-free boutiques line the main drag, **Rue de la République**.

The town's historical sights can all be seen in under an hour. The architectural highlight, on the west side of the harbour, is the circa-1800 Swedish **Wall House**, which is now a restaurant. Next door is **Place Vanadis**, named after the last Swedish military vessel to leave the island after the 1878 French repossession. The former storehouse now contains the **Musée Territorial** (Mon, Tues, Thurs, Fri 8.30am–1pm, 2.30–5.30pm; Wed, Sat 9am–1pm; $3), a modest collection of tools, maps and assorted oddities. On the south side of the port is the intimate 1855 **St Bartholomew Anglican church**, with sandstone facade, original marble floor and wood-shingled belfry; nearby is the church of **Notre-Dame de l'Assomption**, with its sober stone arches. Across the street from the Anglican church, a 10-ton **anchor** juts skyward; found in 1981 when a tugboat accidentally got stuck on it, the iron anchor is thought to have come from an 18th-century American warship. A short walk west from both churches along rue de l'Église is Gustavia's small quiet beach, the pinkish seashell-covered **Anse de Grands Galets** (aka **Shell Beach**). At the other end of town on a promontory offering magnificent **views** of Gustavia and the surrounding islands are a red-topped lighthouse and the crumbling remains of **Fort Gustave**.

Accommodation

While most of St Barts' **hotels** are located outside the capital, a couple of in-town options are the island's best **bargains**.

Carl Gustaf Rue des Normands ⓣ0590/29 79 00, ⓦwww.carlgustaf.com. A decadent hideout on a hill above the town with easy access to Shell Beach. Most of the 14 luxurious suites have a private plunge pool, while the revamped restaurant and bar offer gorgeous sunset views. Closed Sept–mid-Oct. ⑨

Presqu'île La Pointe ⓣ0590/27 64 60. These ten basic rooms on the west side of the port, among the cheapest lodgings on the island, have a/c, private bath and fridge. Request one with a balcony. ②

Sunset Rue de la République ⓣ0590/27 77 21, ⓔsunset-hotel@wanadoo.fr. Offering a great deal, this cosy waterfront hotel has ten comfortable rooms, plus a sunny veranda with a lovely view. ⑤

Eating and drinking

Gustavia's **dining** scene is as cosmopolitan as its clientele. The town doesn't have a huge **late-night scene**, although a couple small dance clubs keep things going till the wee hours.

Baz Bar Rue Samuel Fahlberg ⓣ0590/29 74 09, ⓦwww.bazbar.com. Hip, friendly hangout on the water with live music every night till midnight and excellent sushi (from $10). Closed June–early Oct.

Casa Nikki Rue Courbet ⓣ0590/27 63 77, ⓦwww.nikkibeach.com. DJs spin nightly from 11pm till 3am at this unpretentious spot, one of the only late-night hangouts. Next door is *The Strand* (open 7.30pm–midnight), a champagne bar/restaurant that's also part of the Nikki group. A shuttle bus service runs between *Casa Nikki* and *Nikki Beach* (see p.600).

La Crêperie Rue du Roi Oscar II ⓣ0590/27 84 07. Locals pack this cheerful cheap-eats nook for crepes ($13), salads, pastas, steaks, panini and ice cream. Closed Sun out of season.

Dõ Brazil Shell Beach ⓣ0590/29 06 66, ⓦwww.dobrazil.com. Stylish spot with a lovely terrace overlooking the beach (mains $29–37). For a more relaxed vibe (and cheaper sandwiches), check out the *Zen* snack bar downstairs, right on the sand. Lunch only on Tues.

Maya's Public Beach ⓣ0590/27 75 73. Popular and pricey, this beachfront restaurant has a daily menu of clean, simple plates like roast chicken with rosemary ($47) and sautéed wahoo in ginger sauce ($41). Dinner only; closed Sun. For a more casual take, try *Maya's To Go* café opposite the airport (closed Mon).

O'Corner Rue du Roi Oscar II ⓣ0590/51 00 05. With its live music and well-priced food, this relative newcomer already has a loyal, trendy following. Closed Sun night out of season.

La Saladerie 6 Quai du Yacht Club ⓣ0590/27 52 48. On the quiet western side of the marina, this low-key destination offers an extensive list of salads, pastas, burgers, pizzas and lobster from $20. Closed Wed, Sun lunch, 3 weeks May & late Aug–mid-Oct.

Le Sapotillier Rue du Centenaire ⓣ0590/27 60 28, ⓦwww.le-sapotillier.com. A superlative setting with an expensive but delicious menu, featuring snail fricassée ($26), veal chop with black truffle risotto ($50) and Dover sole meunière ($53). Dinner only; closed Mon in low season & Sept–Oct.

Le Select Rue de la France ⓣ0590/27 86 87. This quirky outdoor pub serves the best cheeseburger and fries on the island. It's often wrongly quoted as being the inspiration behind Jimmy Buffett's classic tune "Cheeseburger in Paradise", although he has performed here. Closed Sun & 1 week in Sept.

The Wall House Rue de la France ⓣ0590/27 71 83, ⓦwww.wallhouserestaurant.com. Excellent French restaurant, right on the waterfront, specializing in spit-roast dishes such as duck and monkfish. The pesto gnocchi ($21) are legendary. The prix-fixe dinner ($43) is a steal. Closed Sun lunch & June–Sept.

Le Yacht Club 6 rue Jeanne d'Arc ⓣ0690/49 23 33. Done up in white leather, this stylish *boîte* attracts a chic, moneyed crowd with thumping house music and posh cocktails. Nightly from 10.30pm till late; closed Sun in low season; open Thur–Sat only in Sept.

St-Jean

St Barts' other main village, the twin-beached **ST-JEAN**, lies so close to the airport that incoming planes practically land on the longer of the two white-sand crescents. This hasn't prevented the area from becoming the island's premier resort, though; its first hotel, the spectacular *Eden Rock*, was established here in the 1950s atop the quartzite promontory that divides the two stretches. St-Jean is a happening spot, with plenty of shops, restaurants and bars, both on and off the sand. The bay itself, protected by coral reefs, has good **windsurfing** conditions.

Accommodation

Several good **beachfront hotels** are in St-Jean; budget properties are few and far between, but *La Normandie* (see opposite) in nearby Lorient is a good bet.

Eden Rock ⓣ0590/29 79 99 or 1-877/563-7105, ⓦwww.edenrockhotel.com. Iconic luxury hotel with 34 deluxe cottages, cabins, suites and villas. There's no pool, but you won't even notice; the beach is stunning, the complimentary breakfast buffet excellent and the service superior. In-room treatments are available, plus yoga and Pilates. 9

Emeraude Plage ⓣ0590/27 64 78, ⓦwww.emeraudeplage.com. Thirty bright, whitewashed bungalows and cottages with terraces, kitchenettes and all mod cons, just steps from the beach, with private bar. 9

Tom Beach ⓣ0590/27 53 13, ⓦwww.tombeach.com. This trendy beachfront property boasts 12 lovely rooms with canopied beds and private patios. There's a small pool, but most of the action centres on *La Plage*, its hip beachfront eaterie. 9

Le Village St Jean ⓣ0590/27 61 39, ⓦwww.villagestjeanhotel.com. Recently revamped family-run hotel on a hill above St-Jean beach, with wonderful bay views. Most of the 29 stylish rooms, cottages and villas have kitchenettes, and there's also a pool and restaurant, *Le Cesar* (closed Sept). 7 with breakfast.

Eating and drinking

Most of the action in St-Jean takes place along the village's main drag, Route de Saline, which is dotted with upscale boutiques, **restaurants** and hotels.

The Hideaway ⓣ0590/27 63 62. The menu reads "Corked wine, warm beer and lousy food", but don't believe it – this casual joint packs 'em in for tasty, cheap pizzas (from $13), salads and pastas. Closed Sun lunch & Mon.

KiKi-é Mo Route de Saline ⓣ0690/58 78 71. Busy café dishing up reasonably priced panini, pizza and pasta, plus gourmet goodies like Champagne and antipasto. Closed Tue in summer.

Nikki Beach Plage de St-Jean ⓣ0590/27 64 64. Everyone's a supermodel or a wannabe at this breezy restaurant and lounge, where DJs pump out music and servers drop off platters of sushi and dishes such as beef tartare ($37). Beach

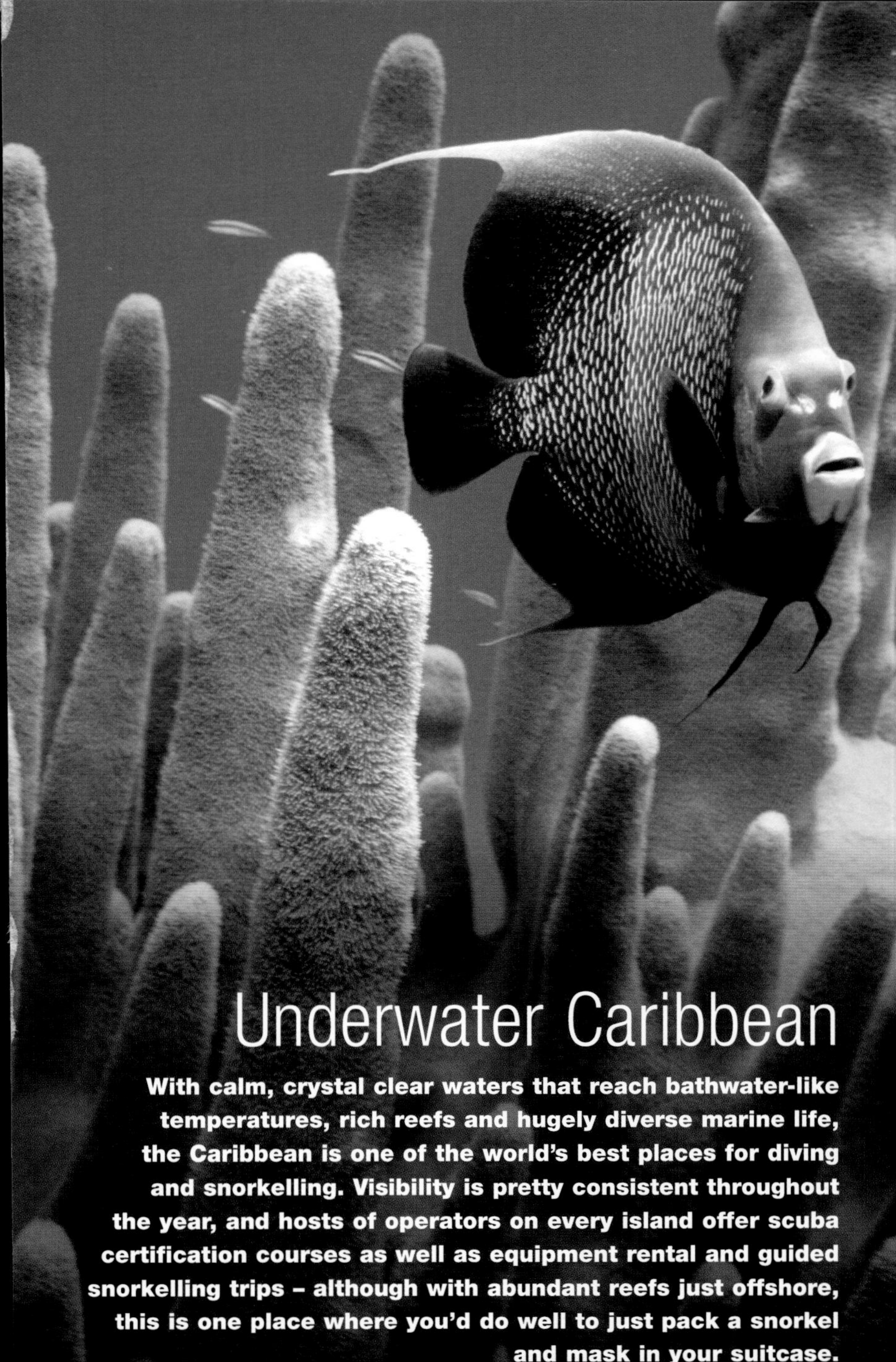

Underwater Caribbean

With calm, crystal clear waters that reach bathwater-like temperatures, rich reefs and hugely diverse marine life, the Caribbean is one of the world's best places for diving and snorkelling. Visibility is pretty consistent throughout the year, and hosts of operators on every island offer scuba certification courses as well as equipment rental and guided snorkelling trips – although with abundant reefs just offshore, this is one place where you'd do well to just pack a snorkel and mask in your suitcase.

Brain coral ▲

Feather star soft coral and sponge ▼

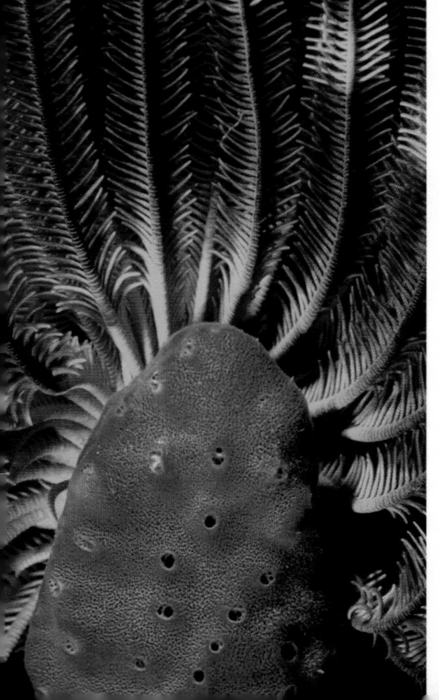

Coral reefs

As well as being one of the region's main tourist attractions, the Caribbean's **coral reefs** are vital to the ocean ecosystem, supporting some 25 percent of all marine life. The reefs provide spawning grounds and protection for fish and other creatures, and play a crucial role during hurricane season, acting as natural breakwaters during storm surges – often to their detriment, as half of the Caribbean's reefs have been badly damaged by pounding waves over the last few years.

Distantly related to jellyfish and anemones, corals are actually colonies of marine animals which feed by way of tiny tentacles that capture particles of plankton (and which deliver a stinging cut if touched); each coral **polyp** also holds millions of microscopic algae that feed their host by way of photosynthesis. Reefs themselves are formed from the skeletons of dead corals, which secrete calcium carbonate as they develop and provide a frame for new polyps to grow on.

Intricate formations comprised of many different varieties of hard and soft corals living side by side, reefs are the planet's largest living structures. The Caribbean's common **hard corals** include rotund brain coral, patterned with distinctive convex furrows, as well as the tree-like branches of elk and staghorns, pillar varieties (somewhat reminiscent of stalagmites), and green-tinged star and lettuce corals. **Soft corals** include gorgeous sea plumes, whips and fans of the gorgonian family, which undulate slowly in the currents while anemones and sponges provide vibrant colours. You'll also see fire coral, not technically a coral, but looking very like one and capable of delivering a nasty sting; as with all parts of the reef, avoid touching it.

Reef life

While the reefs are stunning in themselves, it's their inhabitants that make them so fascinating for snorkellers and divers. **Reef fish** are far too numerous to describe here, but some of the common species include shoals of tiny sergeant majors, yellow with black stripes, and the ubiquitous parrot fish, named both for the distinctive birdlike beaks which they use to graze on hard coral and for their rainbow colouring. The many varieties of angelfish are especially lovely, shaped like the classic fish of a childs' cartoon and with myriad takes on technicolour scales, from electric blue and green to deep purple. The largest of the reef fish are the groupers, big-lipped hunters that feed on smaller reef-dwellers, while the tube-like trumpetfish must count as one of the most unusual, a deep blue specimen with an elongated snout.

A close inspection of the reefs reveals the waving talons of **Caribbean spiny lobsters**, and gaping, rather threatening looking **moray eels** poking their heads out of crevices. Often covered with seagrass beds between the reefs, the sea floor is home to brightly coloured **sea stars**, spiny black **urchins** and **conch snails**, who cruise along enfolding blades of grass, and hunt encrusted organisms to eat.

Of the bigger creatures, **manta rays** are particularly beautiful, gliding effortlessly through the waters, while fish on the hunt include pointy-faced silvery **barracudas**. **Nurse sharks** bask on the sea bed by day, and you may also see **reef sharks**; neither are considered aggressive to humans. And if you're in the eastern Caribbean, you can even head away from the reefs to get a glimpse of the **humpback** and **sperm whales** that frequent the waters around St Lucia and Dominica – an unforgettable sight.

▲ Manta ray

▼ Moray eel

▼ Humpback whale

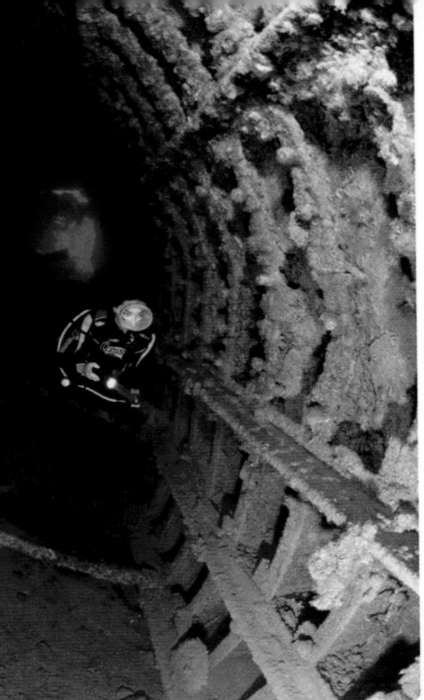

Wreck of the RMS Rhone, British Virgin Islands ▲

Underwater Sculpture Park, Grenada ▼

Where to go

The lists below comprise some of the best places for diving and snorkelling in the region.

Top 5 diving destinations

▶▶ **Cayman Islands** All-round, some of the most stunning diving in the Caribbean, including Little Cayman's world-renowned Bloody Bay Wall. See p.232.

▶▶ **Turks and Caicos Islands** Dramatic diving, including the richly encrusted West Caicos Wall, which drops off for some 7000ft. See p.135.

▶▶ **Bonaire** Protected as a marine park for the last 25 years, Bonaire's pristine reefs offer some of the world's best diving. See p.817.

▶▶ **Saba** Little-known and wonderfully unspoilt Saba offers fantastic diving around the peaks of submerged mountaintops. See p.500.

▶▶ **British Virgin Islands** A multitude of excellent sites, including the submerged bulk of the *RMS Rhone*, one of the top wreck dives in the Caribbean. See p.443.

Top 5 snorkelling spots

▶▶ **Speyside, Tobago** The offshore reef here is astonishingly rich, frequented by huge manta rays as well as the usual shoals of colourful fish. See p.783.

▶▶ **Stingray City, Grand Cayman** Transparent waters and the chance to swim with throngs of docile stingrays that congregate here. See p.222.

▶▶ **Champagne Beach, Dominica** Named after the hot-water bubbles caused by underwater volcanic vents, Champagne has gorgeous sponges, coral, and lots of marine life too. See p.612.

▶▶ **Underwater Sculpture Park, Grenada** The teeming Moliniere reef is delightful but the real thrill is in discovering 65 underwater sculptures, fast being overtaken by the reefs. See p.735.

▶▶ **Tobago Cays** This marine park of bluer-than-blue, crystalline water ticks all the Caribbean fantasy boxes, with lovely reefs to boot. See p.783.

barbecue every Thursday. Dinner only Thurs–Sat; closed Sept–early Nov.

On-the-Rocks At *Eden Rock* This lofty terrace bar/restaurant is a stunning setting for high-quality cuisine, with dishes such as lobster ravioli ($43) and filet mignon ($50). Downstairs, the *Sand Bar* attracts a chic crowd for lunch.

Le Piment Route de Saline, ⓣ0590/27 53 88. Casual, reasonably priced restaurant open for breakfast, lunch and dinner, serving burgers (from $18), salads ($22) and panini (from $12). Closed Tues in low season.

Lorient

From St-Jean the road makes a short climb before descending into quiet **LORIENT**, the site of the first French settlement in 1648. Today its smallish bay is popular with **windsurfing** aficionados. Otherwise the town's main appeal is its proximity to St-Jean. In terms of accommodation, there's the modern, minimalist *La Banane*, on the way into the village (ⓣ0590/52 03 00, ⓦwww.labanane.com; ❾ including breakfast), with two Zen-like swimming pools and nine ultra-stylish bungalows, or the newly revamped *La Normandie* (ⓣ0590/27 61 66, ⓦwww.normandiehotelstbarts.com; ❻ including breakfast), an excellent budget option with eight rooms and impressive facilities for the price bracket, including a garden, pool and free WiFi. Lorient's only upscale **restaurant**, *K'Fé Massaï* (ⓣ0590/29 76 78; dinner only; closed Tues), doesn't look like much from the outside but is very popular; its French-Creole set menus (€43–72) feature dishes such as sirloin with gorgonzola sauce and chicken curry. Nearby divey walk-up *Jojo Burger* keeps locals happy with a cheap-eats lunch menu of burgers and sandwiches (closed Sun). Pick up salads, sweets and more for the beach at the local branch of mini bakery chain *La Petite Colombe*, also on the main drag (open daily for breakfast and lunch).

Anse de Grande Saline and Anse du Gouverneur

Two of St Barts' best beaches are approached from well-marked secondary roads south of St-Jean and Lorient. The local favourite is the white-sanded **Grande Saline**, which is reached via a five-minute walk along a rocky (then sandy) path. The facility-less **Anse du Gouverneur** lies around another headland at the end of a steep descent that passes hidden villas and offers marvellous sea views. You can **eat** near Grande Saline at *Le Grain de Sel* (closed Mon in low season & some of Sept), a relaxing lunch spot with excellent goat-cheese burgers ($21) and house-made coconut tart (€10).

Pointe Milou to Grand Cul-de-Sac

A couple of kilometres past Lorient, the main road passes the island's swankiest neighbourhood, **POINTE MILOU**, a collection of stunning villas on a rocky cliff. The lone **hotel** here, *Le Christopher,* was closed for a total renovation as this guide went to press. The wild and sexy *Ti St-Barth* (ⓣ0590/27 97 71; dinner only, closed Sun in low season) scores with its hipster bar scene and barbecued dishes.

Grand Cul-de-Sac

From Pointe Milou, the road slopes down to reach the golden beach at **GRAND CUL-DE-SAC**, a tranquil, shallow lagoon ideal for families with small children. At the time of writing several of the existing hotels and restaurants had been knocked down and construction on new properties was underway.

Of the existing hotels, two of the most luxurious are near each other: *Le Sereno* (ⓣ0590/29 83 00, ⓦwww.lesereno.com; ❾; closed Sept–mid-Nov), a gorgeous hideaway with 37 minimalist rooms and villas, plus the open-front *Restaurant des Pêcheurs*, serving spectacularly fresh fish (don't miss the bouillabaisse on Fri).

The beach isn't the nicest, but there is a pool, and treatments using Ligne St Barth products are available. Close by, the *Guanahani* (ⓣ0590/27 66 60, ⓦwww.leguanahani.com; ⑨) is St Barts' largest hotel (69 rooms) and one of its poshest, with expansive grounds, two restaurants and a Clarins spa. For cheaper eats right on the beach, try *Kazz'n blues* (ⓣ0590/52 21 26; closed Sun night), a laid-back piano bar serving panini, salads and sandwiches (from $9) during the day, and tapas and sushi (from $16) at night.

West of Gustavia

Tiny **COROSSOL**, a charming fisherman's village 4km west of Gustavia, evokes an Antillian flavour altogether absent elsewhere on St Barts. The local women wear white, shoulder-length sunbonnets, and weave latanier leaves into baskets and hats, which they sell from their front porches. The main sight is the red-roofed, quaint **Inter Oceans Museum** (Tues–Sat 9am–12.30pm & 3–5pm; €4) along the waterfront, which showcases a fascinating collection of nearly 20,000 seashells from around the world.

On the opposite coast, **FLAMANDS** village alongside the golden sand at **Anse des Flamands**, a broad bay backed by *latanier* and banana trees. Close by is another secluded beach, **Anse du Grand Colombier** (also called **Anse à Colombier**), reached by a twenty-minute hike (wear sturdy shoes to navigate the narrow and rocky path) around a headland at the island's westernmost tip; if you're lucky, you'll have the gorgeous stretch of sand to yourself. This area has several appealing places to **stay**. At the start of the trail to Anse du Grand Colombier, the charming *Auberge de la Petite Anse* (ⓣ0590/27 64 89, ⓔ apa@wanadoo.fr; ⑤) offers 16 small, simple bungalows with kitchenettes and stellar ocean views. *Baie des Anges* (ⓣ0590/27 63 61, ⓦwww.hotelbaiedesanges.fr; ⑦) has ten spacious rooms with terrace-kitchenettes right on Anse des Flamands, plus the excellent pool-side **restaurant** *La Langouste*, which features fresh lobster, onion soup ($15) and escargots ($15). Nearby, the *Isle de France* (ⓣ0590/27 61 81 or 1-800/810-4691, ⓦwww.isle-de-france.com; ⑨ including breakfast) has 33 deluxe doubles, suites, bungalows and villas, two pools and a Molton Brown spa. For true seclusion, there's friendly *Le P'tit Morne* (ⓣ0590/52 95 50, ⓦwww.timorne.com; ⑦), one of the best deals on St Barts. Set on a hilltop in Colombier, the hotel's 14 apartments boast private terraces, kitchenettes, and gorgeous views of the rocky offshore islands. There's also a pool.

16

Dominica

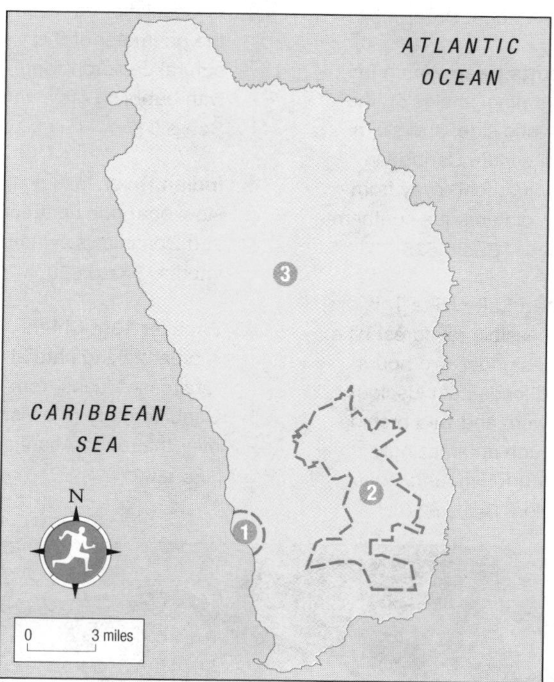

Dominica highlights

* **Eco-tourism** Dominica is one of the Caribbean's best destinations for tourism that has a low-impact on the environment and is good for the local economy – like the *Crescent Moon Eco-Lodge*. See p.608

* **Scotts Head** Watch for migrating whales on the Atlantic side, and swim in the calm Caribbean bay just feet away from this picturesque southern village. See p.615

* **Boeri Lake Hike** This accessible rainforest hike takes under two hours and leads past luscious flowers and wild orchids though an amazingly colourful, mountainous region. See p.616

* **Titou Gorge** Swim against the cold current to reach the warm waters of a hidden waterfall. See p.616

* **Boiling Lake** Hike inland through the eerie Valley of Desolation to reach the perimeter of this natural cauldron filled with bubbling grey water. See p.617

* **Indian River** Take a slow boat ride upstream into Dominica's swampy interior. See p.620

* **Escalier Tête Chien** A breathtaking natural "staircase" leads from Carib Territory to a vista over the rough Atlantic. See p.621

▲ Crescent Moon Eco-Lodge

Introduction and basics

No past trips to the Caribbean can prepare you for the view of **Dominica** (pronounced "doh-min-EE-ka") as you fly over it – instead of the bright green, gentle, rolling hills of other Caribbean islands, Dominica is an island of tall, sharp peaks, covered with the dark green of a lush rainforest and almost entirely comprised of volcanic rock. Unlike most Caribbean islands, which at best may have one active volcano, Dominica has nine, and their underground activities result in innumerable hot sulphur springs bubbling up to ground level, including one of the world's true natural wonders – a boiling lake. The steep-sided peaks rear up 4700 feet to meet cloud-capped summits that receive enough heavy rainfall to feed the innumerable of mountain streams that make for fantastic freshwater swimming, while these in turn nourish the majestic rainforest vegetation that covers over sixty percent of Dominica's centre. The island is so unspoiled that it provided the perfect location for the *Pirates of the Caribbean* movies; some 25 sites around Dominica were used in the second and third films.

Lying halfway between Guadeloupe and Martinique, Dominica's appeal has little to do with the traditional Caribbean attraction, beaches – what few exist have black rather than white sand. The waters may be clear and lovely for swimming but you're unlikely to spend many idle days under a palm tree. Rather the mountains and rainforests invite excellent **hiking** to deep emerald pools, waterfalls and bubbling lakes. Offshore, the superb drop-offs, volcanic arches and caves busy with stingrays, barracuda and parrotfish, as well as wonderfully healthy and colourful reefs, make for excellent **diving**, while **whales** and **dolphins** often play off the southern coast near Champagne, a unique effervescent bay.

Despite all that Dominica has to offer in terms of **eco-tourism**, it's still vastly under-visited, in no small part because it's not easy to reach. There are no direct flights from the US or Europe, and ferries from surrounding islands don't stop daily. In addition, the island lacks luxury resorts. A vacation here involves travelling all around to see the island; luckily Dominica is an unparalleled place to explore.

Where to go

Most hikers head directly to **Morne Trois Pitons National Park**, the expansive rainforest covering most of Dominica's southern reaches. Its centrepiece, Boiling Lake, requires a full-day trek, but getting to the park's numerous waterfalls, like Emerald Pool, means little more than a gentle walk. Divers, in contrast, head to the waterfront south of Roseau, where several outfits run trips to impressive underwater craters around **Scotts Head** and the northern **Cabrits National Park**'s drop-offs.

When to go

The **best time to visit** is between January or February and June, when the weather is at its driest; during August and October, the wettest months, rainfall ranges from thirty inches in Roseau to ten times that in the interior. As elsewhere in the Caribbean, **hurricane season** lasts from June 1 to November 30.

Getting there

The island has two small **airports**, Canefield and Melville Hall, neither with the capacity to accept an international jet. Canefield is close to Roseau on the Caribbean side of the island; Melville Hall, further afield on the north Atlantic side, is the larger airport where most flights arrive and depart.

Ferries arrive at the northern edge of Roseau, within walking distance of most guesthouses and hotels. If you're staying

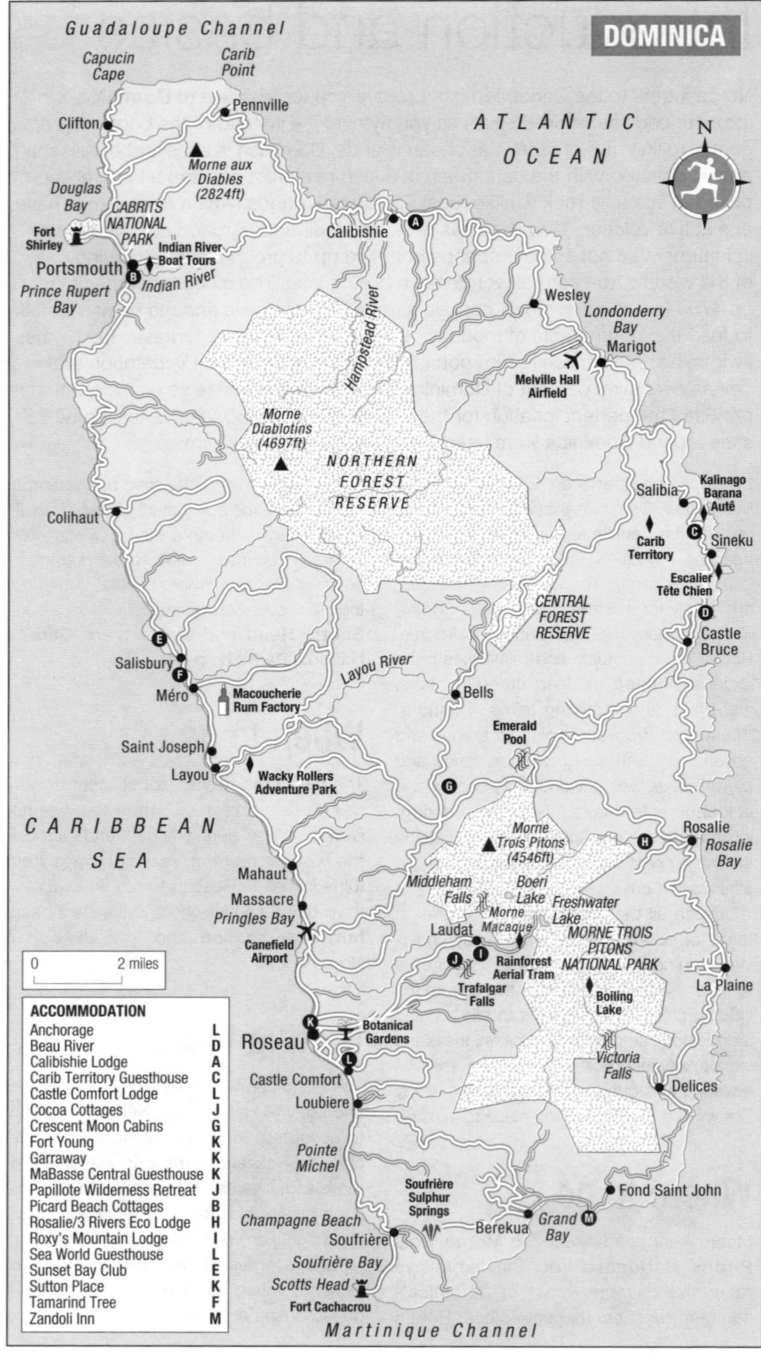
DOMINICA
Guadaloupe Channel
Capucin Cape
Carib Point
Pennville
Clifton
ATLANTIC OCEAN
N
Morne aux Diables (2824ft)
Douglas Bay
CABRITS NATIONAL PARK
Fort Shirley
Indian River Boat Tours
Portsmouth
Indian River
Prince Rupert Bay
Calibishie
Hampstead River
Wesley
Londonderry Bay
Marigot
Melville Hall Airfield
Morne Diablotins (4697ft)
NORTHERN FOREST RESERVE
Salibia
Kalinago Barana Autê
Carib Territory
Sineku
Escalier Tête Chien
Colihaut
CENTRAL FOREST RESERVE
Castle Bruce
Salisbury
Méro
Macoucherie Rum Factory
Layou River
Bells
Emerald Pool
Saint Joseph
Layou
Wacky Rollers Adventure Park
CARIBBEAN SEA
Morne Trois Pitons (4546ft)
Rosalie
Rosalie Bay
Mahaut
Middleham Falls
Boeri Lake
Freshwater Lake
Massacre
Pringles Bay
Morne Macaque
Laudat
MORNE TROIS PITONS NATIONAL PARK
Canefield Airport
Rainforest Aerial Tram
Trafalgar Falls
La Plaine
0 2 miles
Boiling Lake
Botanical Gardens
Roseau
Victoria Falls
Castle Comfort
Delices
Loubiere
Pointe Michel
Soufrière Sulphur Springs
Fond Saint John
Champagne Beach
Berekua
Grand Bay
Soufrière
Soufrière Bay
Scotts Head
Fort Cachacrou
Martinique Channel
ACCOMMODATION
Anchorage L
Beau River D
Calibishie Lodge A
Carib Territory Guesthouse C
Castle Comfort Lodge L
Cocoa Cottages J
Crescent Moon Cabins G
Fort Young K
Garraway K
MaBasse Central Guesthouse K
Papillote Wilderness Retreat J
Picard Beach Cottages B
Rosalie/3 Rivers Eco Lodge H
Roxy's Mountain Lodge I
Sea World Guesthouse L
Sunset Bay Club E
Sutton Place K
Tamarind Tree F
Zandoli Inn M

in the Castle Comfort area, a mile south of Roseau, grab a taxi or a bus (EC$1.50).

Information

In addition to information divisions within embassies and consulates abroad, Dominica has **information kiosks** at both airports and the ferry dock. The main island **tourist office** is in Roseau on the Bay Front (Mon–Fri 8am–4pm, Sat 9am–2pm; ⓣ767/448-2045). All locations have detailed island **maps**.

The island's **official website**, ⓦwww.discoverdominica.com, has links to hotels and services that you can book yourself; the corporate-sponsored ⓦwww.avirtualdominica.com is also useful, with a good "ask the experts" feature.

Money and costs

The official currency is the **Eastern Caribbean dollar** (EC$), although US dollars are widely accepted and used to quote hotel and service rates. The EC$ is divided into 100 cents. Notes come in denominations of 5, 10, 20, 50 and 100 EC dollars; coins in 1, 2, 5, 10 and 25 cents. At the time of writing, the **exchange rate** was roughly EC$2.65 to US$1.

Roseau's **banks** have ATMs dispensing local currency, and inside tellers will change money (Mon–Thurs 8am–3pm, Fri 8am–5pm). Hotels almost universally list their prices in American dollars, while food prices are listed in EC$.

Even though Dominica is relatively poor by Caribbean standards, it's not necessarily a cheap place to visit. Additional costs for guides and activities have a way of increasing your bill, as do incidentals like the EC$55 **departure tax** levied at the airport when you leave (which must be paid in local currency). A whale-watching outing costs US$55–60 for a four-hour trip; the rainforest tram (see p.617 also costs US$55; a guide to the Boiling Lake will charge around US$50, not including transportation to the trailhead; and diving prices are about US$50/single-tank dive.

At the bottom of the scale, you can probably manage on a **daily budget** of US$55 if you split the cost of a fan-only double in a Roseau guesthouse, travel by bus, hike without a guide, and skip diving and whale-watching altogether. A budget of US$100/day will allow you to stay in a rainforest guesthouse (sharing a double) and to hire a guide.

Getting around

The best and most economical way to **get around** is by car, which will take you where buses rarely or never go, and will be far cheaper than taxis or a guide. The coast roads are especially manageable, and for hikes to the furthest regions you'll usually be taking a guide along to direct you (guides will walk you to the Boiling Lake or Victoria Falls, but they won't drive you to the trailhead). You can arrange a guide either through your guesthouse or hotel; each hotel has its own guides whom they use consistently.

By bus

Dominica's **public buses** are 15-seat vans run by private individuals who drive the buses somewhat wildly and with various degrees of reliability. Buses are easy to find during the weekdays around Roseau – heading towards Scotts Head (see p.615), Trafalgar Falls (see p.617), or Castle Comfort (see p.611) for example. You can flag them down on the road or meet one in Roseau before it leaves from King George V Street, the main drag. Buses run from 6am to 6pm but are less reliable on Saturday (officially 6am–2pm) and nonexistent on Sundays. When cruise ships come into port there are also fewer buses because many of the buses become private taxis.

Buses cost EC$1.50–10; flag them down on the road, tell the driver your destination, and pay when you get off.

By car

Driving is on the left on narrow, sometimes potholed roads. In the mountains you'll be hard-pressed to exceed the 20mph speed limit as certain spots have no guardrails whatsoever, even on precarious switch-backs. Other routes are nothing more than mud-covered rock (be aware that local car insurance does not cover damage to tyres). The **coastal roads** are better, wide enough for two lanes at some points.

A **four-wheel-drive vehicle** is the better, albeit more costly, option (from US$45/day). Aside from Budget, Dominica's **car rental agencies** are based in Roseau, but all of them will meet you at the airport if you've made advance reservations. Companies include Budget, Canefield Airport (ⓣ767/449-2080, ⓔbudgetdominica@cwdom.dm); Best Deal, 15 Hanover St (ⓣ767/449-9204, ⓦwww.bestdealrentacar.com); and Courtesy, 10 Winston Lane (ⓣ767/448-7763, ⓔcourtesyrental@cwdom.dm). The tourist board website lists many more operators.

To drive on the island, you'll need to buy a one-month local driver's licence (EC$30) from the car rental provider. Renters must be over 25 and under 65, though the upper age limit is less strictly monitored than the lower one.

By taxi

A **taxi** is usually just a bus which agrees to only carry one passenger. If your driver picks up locals along the way, you should demand to pay the shuttle rate, not the taxi one. In theory, taxi rates are regulated by the government and are not supposed to vary based on the number of passengers but in practice prices vary wildly – try to negotiate before settling on a price. Prices are usually in US dollars – a ride from Roseau to Portsmouth will cost anywhere from US$45 to $75; the hourly rate is around US$20. While taxis congregate at the airport and at the cruise ship docks, you're not likely to see one otherwise unless you call. Try Choice Taxi (ⓣ767/235-2012); John Vee Tours (ⓣ767/235-2375), or On Time Tours and Taxi ⓣ767/225-5173.

Accommodation

Dominica's **accommodation** options are nowhere near as fancy as elsewhere in the Caribbean, but that's a large part of the island's appeal. Hikers will find a clutch of rainforest **guesthouses** nestled amidst the greenery offering terrific packages that include guides, hearty food and casual lodging in a convivial atmosphere. The disadvantages of these places are that they're often far from civilization and social opportunities of any sort. What modern **hotels** exist are mostly concentrated in Roseau and the Castle Comfort area, and cater predominantly to divers with packages and well-equipped, if impersonal, rooms. Note that most hotels apply a ten percent tax and five to ten percent service charge to the bill, so ask whether it's included when booking.

Eco-tourism in Dominica

Eco-tourism helps visitors have a lighter impact on the environment but the term can mean any number of things. Generally eco-friendly lodges use less **water** than the typical resort and may also have solar powered heat. The idea of "environmental impact", however, goes beyond tourism's impact on the earth and includes its impact on the local community. Eco-lodges aim to hire **locals** instead of importing staff from more affluent countries, they farm **food** without using pesticides and sometimes they build on land that was already in use to avoid having to clear a new area.

Dominica has been promoting itself for several years as the foremost eco-friendly location in the Caribbean, and recently more and more of the hotels on the island have become **Green Globe certified** or **benchmarked** (see ⓦwww.greenglobe21.com). Several accommodations on the island, however, go beyond the tasks of getting certified as environmentally friendly and really do an excellent job of having a philosophy and atmosphere that compliments the environment instead of dominating it; we especially recommend the *3 Rivers/Rosalie Eco Lodge*, *Crescent Moon Cabins*, and *Cocoa Cottages* (all p.618).

Food and drink

With a Creole flavour, Dominica's **cuisine** is simple and tasty. Your best bets will often be a chicken or goat curry – both locally raised animals – or a plate of local fish such as tuna or kingfish. Other island specialities include callaloo soup (similar to creamed spinach), and Caribbean staples like roti (curry-filled flat bread). Meals all come with rice and several sides, which could include fried plantains, mashed cooked green bananas or beans (usually referred to as peas). The food is hardly cheap, however. **Breakfast** usually starts around EC$20, **lunch** – the least expensive meal – ranges from EC$12–40 and a **dinner** entree in most restaurants will cost EC$50–90. Restaurants ("snackettes") that are not geared towards tourists are slightly less expensive, but very few are open regularly for dinner. Similarly, because most manufactured food is imported, groceries are not a bargain, but can be found at the Whitchurch IGA on Old Street in Roseau.

Currently, hunting the *crapaud* (toad) that supplies its legs to make the island's national dish, "mountain chicken", was banned due to its dwindling numbers.

Fresh fruit and juices are ubiquitous for breakfast, and mango and other fruit juices are mixed with one of the island's two local rums, Soca or Macoucherie to make rum punch. The island's best drink is its tasty, locally brewed lager, Kubuli, or a freshly cut water coconut.

Due to the countless water sources, the island's tap water is often superb. Your hotel should let you know if they have a good water source. Bottled water is also readily available.

Mail and communications

Public **telephones** are at every square and most street corners. Many phones take coins – those that don't will accept phonecards, which you can buy from the post office, Cable & Wireless outlets and some convenience stores. For the best rates, call after 7pm. Roseau has several places to check your **email** (see p.613), with surprisingly reasonable rates, and many hotels have a computer with Internet access – prices range from free to US$6/hr. The **country code** is ☎767.

The sluggish Dominican **postal service** is headquartered at the corner of Roseau's Hillsborough and Bay streets on the waterfront (Mon–Wed & Fri 8am–3pm, Thurs & Sat 8am–noon).

Public holidays

January 1 New Year's Day
First Monday in March Carnival Monday
March/April Good Friday, Easter Monday
May 1 May Day
Eighth Monday after Easter Whit Monday
First Monday in August August Monday
November 3 Independence Day
November 4 Community Service Day
December 25 Christmas Day
December 26 Boxing Day

Opening hours, holidays and festivals

Generally **opening hours** are Monday to Friday 8am–1pm and 2–4pm. Banks tend to keep shorter hours (Mon–Thurs 8am–3pm, Fri until 5pm). Shops and services close altogether on Sunday, when the only establishments open are hotel restaurants and the odd bar or restaurant in Roseau. In addition to closures on holidays (see box), Dominica often shuts down during its festivals, the biggest of which, **Carnival**, takes place during the last two weeks of Lent, with calypso performances, costumed street dancing to *lapo kabwit* (goat-skin drum) bands, beauty pageants and such. The first week of June is the **Dive Fest**, with waterfront parties and cruises, while October showcases the three-day **World Creole Music Festival**, a jamboree of local *cadence* and *bouyon* with Caribbean soca, African *soukous* and Louisiana *zydeco*. One of the biggest parties around happens the week prior to **Independence Day** (Nov 3), with colourful celebrations and traditional Creole food and music.

History

In a rare imaginative lapse, Columbus simply named **Dominica** after the day he discovered it in 1493: Sunday. He didn't stick around long and, for over two centuries, interest in Dominica was virtually nonexistent, so much so that a 1660 treaty between the British and French declared the island a neutral territory, leaving it to the resident **Caribs**. The French rescinded the deal when they colonized the island in the 1720s, starting a near-century-long tug-of-war with the British. Neither power was particularly interested in the island's resources but its strategic location between **Martinique** and **Guadeloupe**, both established French colonies, made it desirable to both nations. In 1763 the island went to the British in the treaty that ended the Seven Years War but in 1778 – with the British occupied by the revolution in the American Colonies – the French successfully invaded. A second Treaty of Paris returned the island to Britain, and two subsequent invasions by the French were unsuccessful.

After **slavery** ended in the British colonies in 1834, there was little reason for colonizers to remain on Dominica. The British ceded so much power, in fact, that Dominica was the only island to have a black-controlled legislature in the nineteenth century. However, by 1865 the British government had taken back control, and Dominica's history continued much like the other British Caribbean colonies until it achieved **independence** in 1978. Just six months later, in 1979, the island was ravaged by **Hurricane David**, which devastated the country's infrastructure and left its citizens on the verge of starvation. The political instability that began with the waves of that storm continues, arguably, to this day. The island's first prime minister, Patrick John, was forced to resign in 1979 after making a questionable land deal with US developers. Rebuilding after the hurricane was left to his successor, Eugenia Charles, the Caribbean's first female prime minister, who withstood two coups against her government. Subsequent leadership has been dogged by embezzlement and corruption charges, and though a beloved politician, Roosevelt "Rosie" Douglas, was elected prime minister in 2000, he died suddenly just eight months later. His successor, Pierre Charles, died, again suddenly, in 2004, and was replaced by the current prime minister, Roosevelt Skerrit, who was re-elected in 2005.

Dominica's history is perhaps most notable for the uninterrupted presence of the **Carib Indians** on its soil. Dominica's mountainous and challenging landscape made it more difficult for the British and the French to take control of every corner on the island. Thus the Caribs did not leave – by will or by force – with the colonizers' arrival but merely retreated to the Atlantic side of the island where their territory remains today (see p.621).

The island is also the birthplace of two important English-language authors: **Jean Rhys**, whose most famous novel, *Wide Sargasso Sea*, a reimagining of *Jane Eyre* from the point of view of the minor character Bertha, takes place largely on Dominica, and **Phyllis Shand Allfrey**, whose novel *The Orchid House* is well known in Britain. More recently, Antiguan-born Jamaica Kincaid's searing novel *The Autobiography of My Mother* takes place on Dominica and focuses on the life of a young woman of Carib, African and Scottish origin.

16.1

Roseau

One of the few traces of modernity in Dominica's capital, **ROSEAU** (pronounced "rose-oh"), is its lengthy, tidy waterfront promenade, **Bay Front**. Otherwise, the compact town is a colourful and picturesque assortment of ramshackle West Indian **colonial houses** with louvred windows, intricate fretwork, and sagging second-floor French-style balconies held up over narrow streets by stilts. It's a remarkably atmospheric place to explore: the roads get narrower as you head inland, passing covered **markets** and distinctively fretworked colonial-era buildings.

Accommodation

Aside from a couple of upmarket options near the Bay Front, most of Roseau's **accommodation** is in low-key guesthouses. The Castle Comfort area, a strip of road one mile south of town, has a handful of waterfront hotels that offer a less noisy night's sleep than what you're likely to find in Roseau.

Roseau

Fort Young Hotel Victoria Street ⓣ767/448-5000, ⓦwww.fortyounghotel.com. An attractive waterfront hotel incorporating the walls of an eighteenth-century fort, and offering standard doubles, spacious suites, a seaside pool, Jacuzzis, and an activities desk. It's about as close to a luxury resort as you'll come on the island. ❺

Garraway 1 Dame Eugenia Charles Blvd ⓣ767/449-8800, ⓦwww.garrawayhotel.com. A sterile but comfortable midrange option with 31 commodious doubles that have picture windows overlooking the sea or the town, but no balconies; the suites on the top floor are especially nice. Restaurant and bar onsite, and Internet access in the rooms. ❺–❻

Ma Bass Central Guesthouse 44 Fields Lane ⓣ767/448-2999. The most appealing of the inexpensive guesthouses in the centre of town, with eight spotless fan-only rooms, a comfortable common room, shared or private bath, and a shared balcony with pleasant views. ❷

Sutton Place 25 Old St ⓣ767/449-8700 or 4313, ⓦwww.suttonplacehoteldominica.com. The best place to stay in the centre of town, this is an atmospheric and beautiful eight-room boutique hotel with appealing touches like wrought-iron gates, antique-furnished rooms and suites trimmed with damask and animal-print flounces, and a courtyard restaurant. ❹

Castle Comfort

Anchorage ⓣ767/448-2638, ⓦwww.anchoragehotel.dm. A great deal – inexpensive waterfront rooms with pool, dive centre, and a waterfront bar next to an enormous whale skeleton. Motel-style rooms are clean with balconies, a/c, TV, and phone, most with water views. ❸

Castle Comfort Dive Lodge ⓣ767/448-2188, ⓦwww.castlecomfortdivelodge.com. The place to stay if you plan to spend most of your Dominican vacation underwater. The rooms aren't any nicer than its neighbour, *Anchorage*, and half have no water view, but most people stay here primarily for the dive lodge. Visits are priced by the number of dives per stay. The garden has a hot tub and a small pool; breakfast, dinner, unlimited shore dives, tax and airport transfer are included in rates. ❺ with breakfast and two daily dives.

Sea World Guesthouse ⓣ767/448-5068, ⓔseaworlddominica@yahoo.com. Eight bright, clean rooms with fan, TV and telephone in a cheery yellow building with a ground-floor grocery store. Rooms facing the water cost the same price as those facing the road. ❷

The Town

Roseau is small enough that it is easy to navigate on foot, and all of its sights can be explored in under an hour. The **Dominica Museum** on the Bay Front (Mon–Fri 9am–4pm, Sat 9am–noon; US$3) does a bare bones job of tracing the island's history and culture through artefacts and short historical explanations. Exhibits include Amerindian artefacts, replicas of Carib and colonial-era houses, and King George III's silver mace, given to Dominica in 1770. For further historical information, head south along the Bay Front, up a small hill past the *Fort Young Hotel* (see p.611) to peruse the books at the **Free Library**, built from funds donated by American philanthropist Andrew Carnegie in 1905 (Mon–Fri 9am–6pm, Sat 9am–noon; free). Across from the library sits the **New Parliament Building**, a pink two-storey mansion surrounded by landscaped grounds (closed to the public).

In the cobblestoned square behind the museum, and filling the alleyway alongside, is the **Old Market** (Mon–Sat); formerly the site of the island's slave market, it's now filled with vendors selling handicrafts. Fresh produce is sold at the **New Market** at the end of Mary E. Charles Boulevard past the ferry docks. It's open every day but most busy on Saturday when vendors and buyers flock here from all over the island.

Heading northeast on Church Street away from the Old Market and taking a left turn onto Virgin Lane leads to the colourful **Methodist Church** (closed to public except for services), and the staid Gothic **Roman Catholic Church**. The latter

Diving, snorkelling and whale-watching

The waters off Dominica are ideal for **diving**: the sites are plentiful and rarely crowded, and provide some of the best opportunities in the Caribbean to see seahorses. Most guides leave from around Roseau and head to the impressive sites off **Scotts Head**, where submerged volcanic craters are covered with seafans and busy with schools of fish and lobster. Easily accessible for snorkellers as well as divers are nearby **Soufrière Bay** and **Champagne Beach** – while the bubbles from the subaquatic hot spring that creates the champagne reef are fun to swim in, the reef around the point towards Soufrière holds more to see, including bright parrotfish and clownfish.

The best dive sites in the north on the Caribbean coast are around **Cabrits National Park** where reefs drop off to sandy bottoms over 100ft below the surface. Nearby **Douglas Point** has three sites worth exploring, including a coral-and-sponge-covered canyon and a 50ft wall teeming with lobster, barracuda and mackerels. For **wreck** diving, Pringles Bay near Canefield Airport holds the remains of a tug and barge. Dive outfits will rarely take tourists to the Atlantic side of the island but if you're very experienced and have a week-long dive itinearary, you might be able to arrange a trip.

In the south, Anchorage Dive Centre (ⓣ767/448-2638, ⓦwww.anchoragehotel.dm) and Castle Comfort Dive Lodge (ⓣ767/448-2188, ⓦwww.castlecomfortdivelodge.com) have the largest assortment of boats and equipment, though Nature Island Dive (ⓣ767/449-8181, ⓦwww.natureislanddive.com) is closer to most sights and will provide more personalized service; they also offer kayaking in Soufriére bay. In the north near **Portsmouth**, head to Cabrits Dive Centre (ⓣ767/445-3010, ⓦwww.cabritsdive.com); near the mid-way point on the Caribbean side is home to East Carib Dive (ⓣ767/449-6575, ⓦwww.east-carib-dive.com).

Dominica's waters are also one of the best places in the Caribbean for **whale-watching**. Some six families of sperm whales live permanently in the coastal waters surrounding the island, and between November and April, migrating sperm whales visit the area to mate. Whale-watching is best off the southwest coast, and trips are run by the Anchorage and Castle Comfort dive centres (see above); they last for about 3.5 hours, and cost US$55–60; you've a 95 percent chance of seeing a sperm or humpback whale, and even if you don't, you'll almost always see dolphins.

Hiking and Park Practicalities

Trail **maps** (EC$1) are available at the **Forestry Division** offices in Roseau's Botanical Gardens (☎767/448-2041, ext 417; see below). Of all the treks, only the seven-hour hike to the Boiling Lake absolutely requires a **guide**; the terrain is harsh and it's easy to get lost; conveniently, all of Dominica's guesthouses can arrange someone reputable. Otherwise, unaffiliated guides charge US$30–50 depending on the hike's length and difficulty; try Off the Beaten Trail (☎767/275-1317, ⓔadquatics@yahoo.com), or ask any of the guides who hang out at the trailheads where **park fees** must be paid (individual entry to sites US$2, day pass for all sites US$5, weekly pass US$12). All of the trails can be done in a day; the longest – the hike to the Boiling Lake (see p.617) – is a seven-hour round-trip affair. In general the trails are well kept, meaning that once you've found the trailhead, you're unlikely to lose your way. However, a guide will usually enhance the experience, pointing out plants, flowers and birds of interest, and giving you a little local history; also, if it's been raining, rivers crossing the trails can be high, and the absence of footbridges means that wading is sometimes necessary – you might feel more secure with someone along to show the way. In all cases, make sure you have sturdy shoes and rain gear; for longer hikes, bring plenty of water and food.

has a complex history – it was built between 1790 and 1916, and varied groups from French estate owners to Carib volunteers took part in its creation (open daily 8am–4pm).

Past the churches, a right turn on Queen Mary Street leads to the entrance to the fanciful forty-acre **Botanical Gardens** (daily 6am–10pm; free) below Morne Bruce hill, home to a variety of local flora and enormous trees, as well as an old yellow school bus crushed by a massive baobab commemorating Hurricane David's destructive powers. From just behind the research buildings of the Forestry Commission, a steep fifteen-minute trail ascends **Morne Bruce** for stellar summit views of the town and sea below.

Eating, drinking and nightlife

Dining out in Roseau ranges from casual diners to upmarket restaurants serving delicious Creole cuisine. The smaller snackettes are mostly open for lunch only. What **nightlife** exists revolves around the hotels and a couple of bars.

Bambuz Loubière, just beyond Castle Comfort ☎767/448-2899. Lovely waterside location, with tables on a deck overlooking the sea and an Asian-influenced menu. Americans and Europeans gather here to watch the sunset, quaff tropical drinks and swim off the dock (there's a freshwater shower for customers). Wed are *salsa* night, Sat a DJ spins and Sun features a lunch barbeque. Closed Mon.

Cartwheel Café Dame Eugenia Charles Boulevard ☎767/448-5353. Light, tropical breakfasts and flavourful curry lunch fare in a handsome stone house on the waterfront. Curry from EC$20 and a variety of sandwiches from EC$12. Closed Sun and dinner.

Cornerhouse Café 11 King George V St ☎767/449-9000. Atmospheric café on a second-floor veranda with comfy indoor sofas, a small book exchange and Internet access. The menu has a range of sandwiches (from EC$15) and Creole specials, and it's a good place to meet up with other travellers.

The Garage 15 Hanover St ☎767/448-5443. Beautifully located in a cut-stone building with modern decor and tables inside and out. This is a lively spot for a meal – fish kebabs, ribs, grilled meats – or a drink, with DJs on Fridays and sports events on the big-screen TVs.

Guiyave Restaurant and Patisserie 15 Cork St ☎767/448-2930. This bright green and yellow local café serves tasty and inexpensive breakfast and lunch upstairs, with tables on the veranda, and pastries downstairs (meat pies from EC$1.50). Closed Sun and dinner.

La Maison *Fort Land* ☎767/440-5287. One of Dominica's few expensive places to eat, this is an upmarket French restaurant with a Creole twist and a strong emphasis on seafood. Great wine list, and tables inside or up on the breezy veranda.

Natural Livity 13 King George V St ⓣ767/265-5912. Set back from the street with tables in a little courtyard, this Rasta-run restaurant offers delicious natural juices and lunches, from pizza and veggie burgers to soups and stews. On Fri, a laid-back party scene features reggae on the sound system and late opening.

La Robe Creole 3 Victoria St ⓣ767/448-2896. An intimate masonry-walled pub with an extensive wine list and good, mid-priced Creole dishes like curried conch and coconut shrimp as well as steaks. The prices reflect the food's quality; drinks are inexpensive. Reservations recommended; closed Sun. Downstairs is *Mousehole*, a take-out joint offering inexpensive rotis, meat pies, sandwiches and pastries.

South to Scotts Head

Heading south from Roseau, the coastal road winds past green hillsides on the way to the pretty fishing village of **SOUFRIÈRE**. The main attraction is **Champagne Beach**, marked by a small sign just before the town. The spot is so named because of bubbles in the offshore waters created by hot springs in the depths of nearby **Soufrière Bay**. The beach is a rocky affair of large rounded stones but there's a wooden boardwalk that runs along the beach to the far end, where the bubbles are. All you need is a snorkel mask or goggles to find the bubbles, which are just on the close side of the point; the reef is more developed and beautiful (though not bubbly)

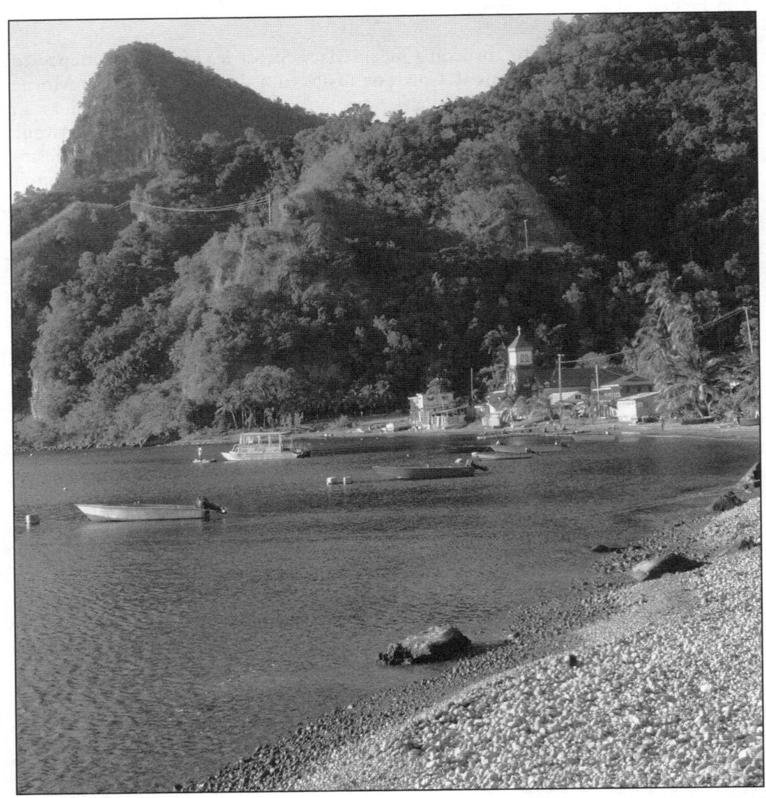

▲ Fishing village near Scotts Head

just around the point. At the entrance to the beach, Irie Safari (Ⓣ767/440-5085, Ⓦwww.iriesafari.com) offers equipment rental (US$12) and guided snorkel expeditions (US$5; around 1.5hr). They also have toilets, a changing room and a bar.

From Champagne the road continues to Soufrière Bay where the Atlantic and Caribbean meet. The bay itself has a calm cove with good snorkelling, and you can rent diving, kayaking and snorkelling gear on the village outskirts at top-notch Nature Island Dive (Ⓣ767/449-8181, Ⓦwww.natureislanddive.dm). The dive shop also rents out two lovely units in a beachfront **cottage** nearby (❻). Back in town you can grab **lunch** at the petite and lovely restaurant *Tony's*, in one of the small cottages on the left side of the main drag as you head towards Scotts Head (Ⓣ767/440-3380, is open for breakfast, lunch and dinner Mon–Sat; baked chicken lunch around EC$20).

You can check out the source of the hot springs one mile inland from Soufrière, at **Sulphur Springs** (daily 9am–5pm; EC$2). A small sulphur pool for bathing is near the parking lot and visitor centre, and a ten-minute hike uphill takes you to the springs' origin. Its barren landscape – white rocks warmed by the lava below and the overwhelming smell of rotten eggs – gives an idea of what it's like at the Boiling Lake (see p.617) for those who don't have a day (or the leg muscles) to spare for the hike.

Beyond Soufrière, the road curves around the bay to delightful **SCOTTS HEAD**, a village of brightly painted tin shacks and equally colourful fishing boats moored below a teardrop-shaped peninsula. A stroll to the tip of the headland reveals vestiges of **Fort Cachacrou**, a defence post dating from the early 1700s, and awesome coastal views. The surrounding waters shelter Dominica's best **diving** (see box above), and the **whales** that migrate here between November and April are often visible from land.

The road heading east from Scotts Head along the island's southern tip offers some gorgeous views of the dramatic coastline around the fishing village of Grand Bay. There's also an excellent place to stay at the intimate and beautifully finished *Zandoli Inn* (Ⓣ767/446-3161, Ⓦwww.zandoli.com; ❺). The appealing rooms, all with balconies, afford wonderful panoramic views of the bay and the craggy Pointe des Fous headland, and the extensive property is laced with easy walking trails; the hotel has a small pool, access to the sea for swimming and snorkelling, and great food at the restaurant.

16.2

Morne Trois Pitons National Park

Dominica's best hiking trails are found in the magnificent, 16,000-acre **MORNE TROIS PITONS NATIONAL PARK**, which spreads over the island's southern region and rises to the 4550ft **Morne Trois Pitons**. Covered with a dense canopy of primordial rainforest and sparse elfin woodland, and broken up by volcanic fumaroles and piping hot springs, this UNESCO World Heritage Site is an astonishing environment, unlike anything else in the Caribbean.

Hikes run from the easy five- to ten-minute walks to beautiful **Emerald Pool** and stunning **Trafalgar Falls**, to the more arduous treks to **Boeri Lake** and **Middleham Falls**. The latter two start from the town of **Laudat**, 3.5 miles northeast of Roseau, also the location of the trailhead to **Boiling Lake**, a fascinating geological wonder high up on the forest peaks.

Around Laudat

The park's major hikes begin at **LAUDAT**, a village 1970ft above sea level with stupendous views of the undulating countryside (for details on how to get here, see opposite). The signposted trail to one of Dominica's tallest waterfalls, the refreshing 275ft **Middleham Falls**, begins just south of town off the road into Laudat, and is a straightforward 45-minute walk through yanga palms, wild anthurium and leafy bromeliads to one of the largest waterfalls on the island. There's a visitor centre (daily 9am–5pm) with displays on mountain fauna and flora at the trailhead; you also pay your park fees here. Thirty minutes past the falls lies **Tou Santi**, a collapsed lava tube emitting warm, smelly gases, and whose crevices shelter bats and the occasional boa constrictor.

At the entrance to Laudat proper, a well-marked and groomed path heads off to the largest of Dominica's four lakes, **Freshwater Lake**, which sits at 2500ft above sea level. There's not much to see here, aside from sulphurous jets that leave rust marks on nearby rocks and greenery, so it's not one of the island's best hikes. Fifteen minutes beyond Laudat, the road ends in a cul-de-sac where you'll find the trailhead for the **Boeri Lake** hike. Though it's close to the path of the hike to Middleham Falls, this trail is on higher ground – the lake itself is at 850m above sea level – and as it goes through both montane rainforest and elfin woodland, it's well worth doing. A much more colourful area than the central rainforest, it's full of bright flowers, wild orchids and large ferns. The forty-five minute hike leads to the beautiful crater lake, enclosed by jagged boulders.

At Laudat's eastern outskirts, an unsightly centipede-like contraption funnels a forceful mountain current into the island's main hydroelectric plant. Before reaching the plant, the water rushes through unusual **Titou Gorge**, a dark passageway sheltered by solidified lava formations, about ten minutes' walk from the plant alongside the pipe. If the current isn't too rough, you can swim beneath the formations to a small waterfall; if you see brown water sputtering in the access pool it means that the current is strong and you should not go in. You can warm up afterwards by leaning against the rocks where a hot spring that feeds the pool flows.

Just past Titou Gorge is the trailhead to Dominica's ultimate hike, the full-day outing to **Boiling Lake**, an eerie 207ft-wide cauldron of bubbling greyish-blue water shrouded in vaporous cloud. A six-mile, seven-hour round-trip undertaking, the trek should only be attempted by fit hikers and with the help of a guide. Thought to be a flooded fumarole through which gases escape from molten lava below, the Boiling Lake is the largest of its kind in the world – though it's an erratic phenomena, having drained and refilled and ceased boiling several times in the last hundred or so years. It last drained in December 2004, but was full and bubbling again at the time of writing. On clear days, the hike includes vistas of both the Caribbean and the Atlantic from atop one of the highest points on the island. Traipse through thick forests of canopied chatannyé and bois bandé trees on your way to the **Valley of Desolation** – a moonscape of white-hot sulphuric rocks, steam vents, and boiling puddles: you could fry an egg in the vents, and guides often do. On the final leg of the trip, bathe in secluded turquoise hot springs and explore a landscape of colourful minerals. This area is also the most treacherous of the hike; your guide can help keep you out of hot water (literally) as you climb up and down steep, scree-covered slopes.

For those not ready to tackle a full or even partial day-hike, the new **Rainforest Aerial Tram** also leaves from Laudat. For US$64, an eight-person gondola will take you for a ninety-minute ride over the rainforest canopy (Ⓣ767/440-3267, Ⓦwww.rainforesttram.com; open on days cruise ships come in).

Practicalities

The only guesthouse this high up is the very accommodating *Roxy's Mountain Lodge* (Ⓣ & Ⓕ767/448-4845, Ⓔroxys@cwdom.dm; ③–④), where bright and simple doubles feature attractive woodwork and some have stunning views over the valley; those in the main building are a little nicer than those in the back. Its small **restaurant** packs hearty picnic lunches and serves organic Creole cuisine at night if you plan with the staff in the morning. Internet access is available.

Although Laudat is only eight miles from Roseau it's a good 35-minute drive up brutally tight hairpin turns, some with potholes and no guardrails – honk to signal your presence. To **reach** Laudat, head east on King George V Street in Roseau for 2.5 miles until you reach a fork; take the road on the left. From here the road begins its real ascent, and it's another three-odd miles to Laudat. **Buses** provide sporadic service (EC$5), departing from central Roseau every two hours after 6.30am; buses leave Laudat for the return trip starting about 45 minutes later. A **taxi** ride to Laudat costs around EC$70.

Trafalgar Falls

At the park's southwestern edge, the twin waterfalls known as **Trafalgar Falls** crash down a sheer 200ft rockface. The upper falls flow from the roiling currents at Titou Gorge while the lower are fed by the Trois Pitons River, which itself originates in the Boiling Lake region. The falls are easily accessed via a short trail that starts from the visitors' centre at the end of the road and leads along a track shaded by flowering bowers and canopied trees. While most visitors are content to enjoy the falls from a raised viewing platform, the more adventurous can forge onwards over rocks to the lower falls' base for a dip in the sizeable pool.

You can **stay** near the falls at the unique *Papillote Wilderness Retreat* (Ⓣ767/448-2287, Ⓦwww.papillote.dm; ④–⑤), a wonderful inn at a stunning location, with simple and elegantly decorated doubles, commodious suites and a teeming botanical garden with hot spas that work wonders on sore muscles. Resplendent with tree ferns, flowers and medicinal plants, the gardens are a delight. Non-guests can tour the gardens (EC$10; 1hr 15min) or soak in the pools (EC$10 for access to the small pool by the restaurant; EC$20 for the larger and more beautiful waterfall pool).

Nearby, the smaller and equally beautiful *Cocoa Cottages* (☎767/448-0412, Ⓦwww.cocoacottages.com; ❺) has colourful, creatively decorated and inviting rooms with intimate dining and living areas; the meals are excellent. Both Papillote and Cocoa are highly recommended.

The *River Rock Café* (☎767/448-3472) below the falls offers tasty local **food** on a splendid terrace overlooking the rainforest. Lunch is served à la carte, but dinner must be ordered in advance. The *Papillote Wilderness Retreat* (see above; dinner reservations required) also has a great restaurant onsite, serving such delights as dasheen or breadfruit puffs or fish steamed in banana leaves (EC$45) and a set three-course dinner (EC$80) with a nightly changing menu.

To reach the falls **by car**, take the road heading east from Roseau, taking a right fork 2.5 miles inland, following the signs to the village of Trafalgar. **Buses** are fairly regular; ask for ones for Trafalgar at the stop facing the Botanical Gardens on Trafalgar Road (EC$5). **Taxis** from Roseau cost EC$50.

Emerald Pool

Dominica's most-visited natural wonder, the deep **Emerald Pool** at the base of a 40ft waterfall is midway between Canefield and Castle Bruce and reached by an easy five-minute walk along a well-maintained jungly pathway whose paved sections date from its original use as a Carib trail. The pool itself is a wonderful spot for a swim, though it can get overly crowded on mornings when cruise ships dock.

The Emerald Pool is a 45-minute drive northeast of Canefield Airport along a steep road with hairpin turns. You can also hop aboard one of the infrequent **buses** beside Roseau's New Market (EC$2.50). **Taxis** from Roseau cost EC$50. It's an isolated area to **stay** in but it's here that you'll find Dominica's best eco-friendly lodging: twenty minutes uphill from Canefield is the signposted turn-off for the secluded and beautiful *Crescent Moon Cabins*, run by an American chef and his family who cultivate an extensive organic garden on the property, full of exotic spices (☎767/449-3449, Ⓦwww.crescentmooncabins.com; ❺; rates include breakfast). The simple but elegant cabins overlook the valley and have a private balcony with a hammock. Beyond the Emerald Pool along the same road is the turn-off for the *3 Rivers/Rosalie Eco Lodge* (☎767/446-1886, Ⓦwww.3riversdominica.com), aptly named as it is a reclaimed banana farm with at least three rivers on the premises. Maintaining an atmosphere that makes tourism seem not just sustainable but great for the environment, *3 Rivers* is the only place on the island that permits camping (US$16.50 for a site, plus US$22 to rent a tent – less for hammocks). It also has dorm rooms (US$22), cottages (❸) and some amazing cabins (❷–❸) up in the forest. The cabins range from a thatched Carib-style *mwena* roundhouse to the unique Chataniere Tree House built around the massive trunk of a living tree and with its own bathroom and kitchen; and the Gommier Lodge, with four stout gommier trees serving as cornerposts. Facilities are basic up in the forest area, with shared showers and pit toilets, and meals are taken communally in the eating area. There's also a gorgeous, deep pool in one of the rivers for swimming.

16.3

The rest of the island

Dotted with ramshackle fishing villages and graced with a couple of hiking trails around the island's highest peak, the scenery of rocky northwestern Dominica isn't nearly as compelling as the rest of the island. The Caribbean coast here has some decent black-sand **beaches** around the towns of **Mero** and **Portsmouth**, which represent your best bet for basking in the sun. In addition, the extensive ruins of **Fort Shirley** in **Cabrits National Park** and a trip up the **Indian River** are good reasons to take a day-trip to the north of the island. It's dangerous to swim on the Atlantic side of the island but the views of the crashing waves and the jungle-smothered countryside are stunning. The Atlantic-facing **Carib Territory**, the Caribbean's only modern-day Carib homeland, is another worthwhile day-trip from Roseau, with a newly opened village giving insight into the culture of the country's original inhabitants.

North to Portsmouth

The drive to Portsmouth from Roseau along the winding two-lane coastal road takes longer than one might expect – at least an hour and a half along some of the island's best roads. North of Roseau, the coastal road passes the Layou River then climbs through **St Joseph**, a rickety fishing hamlet perched on extremely steep roads, before hitting the village of **Mero**. There's little of interest here, save for the black-sand beach, which offers some good **snorkelling**. You can get a decent and inexpensive lunch at the *Mero Beach Bar*, right on the sand. Heading inland immediately north of Mero you'll arrive at Dominica's finest rum distillery, **Macoucherie** (Mon–Fri 7am–3pm), which produces rum from sugar cane grown on its estate. They don't have anything in the way of formal touring facilities, but you can have a look around, and they'll sell you some inexpensive rum. A little south of Mero, just inland of St Joseph along the banks of the Layou River is the **Wacky Rollers Adventure Park** (Ⓣ767/440-4386, Ⓦwww.wackyrollers.com; adults US$60, children US$30), where a series of treetop rope walkways has been set up between the forest canopy. Platforms link the suspension walks and zipwires, and there's also a daring "Tarzan" jump into a net, and a tamer course for children. The same company also operate jeep safaris and tubing down the Layou river (both US$60).

The vicinity has two good **hotels**, both north of the distillery and both far from either Portsmouth or Roseau but offer proximity to the beach and all-inclusive amenities. Just uphill from East Carib dive shop (see p.612), the small and lovely eco-friendly *Tamarind Tree Hotel* (Ⓣ767/449-7395, Ⓦwww.tamarindtreedominica.com; ④) sits on a cliff overlooking the Caribbean, affording lovely sunset views. The rooms are simple, new and have wireless Internet. The hotel has a small swimming pool and the restaurant serves great Swiss-German food; rates include breakfast. Further north is the appealing *Sunset Bay Club* (Ⓣ767/446-6522, Ⓦwww.sunsetbayclub.com; ⑤ including breakfast), which is on the beach and very much in the style of an all-inclusive resort – though quite small, it has its own dive shop, restaurant and bar, pool and sauna, and in addition to being on the beach, is also next to a small river. The simple rooms have neither TV or air-conditioning and you can stay on a B&B or all-inclusive basis.

Still further up the coast is the **Northern Forest Reserve**, a 22,000-acre parkland and home to the island's highest peak, the 4747ft **Morne Diablotin**.

Despite the reserve's gargantuan size, it only has two **hiking** trails, both of which begin four miles inland along a well-signposted access road hedged by banana and pineapple plantations; there's a visitor centre where you pay your park fee. The easier **Syndicate Nature Trail** is a straightforward 1.6km loop past a couple of **parrot**-viewing platforms; two endangered species – the imperial (or Sisserou) parrot and the red-necked parrot make their home here, and sightings often occur during early morning and late afternoon. The second of the hikes, a rugged and very difficult day-long outing to the summit of Morne Diablotin, should only be attempted with a guide, which can be arranged through your hotel for about US$50.

Portsmouth and the North

Dominica's second largest town, tumbledown **PORTSMOUTH**, has a picturesque location along Prince Rupert's Bay but is mostly residential. It also functions as a university centre for Ross Medical School, which is attended almost exclusively by Americans. Portsmouth was originally envisioned as the island's capital but plans went awry when the swampy, mosquito-infested environs couldn't be tamed. While there's not much to keep you in town, the **Indian River** on the southern outskirts is well worth a visit for the boat trips, in which you're rowed upriver through a breathtaking mile of the forest that stymied developers. The river is the deepest on the island, and knowledgeable Rasta guides lead tours (from 8am daily, 1hr; EC$40 for two people) whose boats are painted with their adopted names such as Macaroni Lover and James Bond. Sightings of blue herons, large iguanas and crabs are common, and you'll detour onto an overhung tributary lined with twisted tree-trunks that was used as a location in the second *Pirates of the Caribbean* movie. You also stop for a drink at an alfresco bar en route.

Portsmouth's other noteworthy attraction is the twin-peaked **Cabrits National Park** (daily 9am–5pm; US$2), a grassy headland jutting out into the Caribbean Sea 1.5 miles north of town. While the park encompasses the island's largest swamp and the shoals and coral reefs of nearby **Douglas Bay** (see box p.612), the main point of interest is **Fort Shirley**. Built between 1770 and 1815 mostly by the British to defend against the French, and completed by the latter when they took control of the island, the fort became a mammoth complex that ultimately was abandoned in 1854. The ruins closest to the entrance have since been restored and are surrounded by manicured lawns and trees, while those further afield remain cloaked in jungle overgrowth. Stop by the visitor centre at the entrance for maps of the many trails in the park area.

Practicalities

Portsmouth is not designed to cater to tourists, and recently even the nicer inns on the outskirts of town have been adjusting their accommodations to suit the medical students who make up the bulk of their customers. That said, some true beachfront **lodging** can be found just south of Ross Medical School at the *Picard Beach Cottages* (Ⓣ767/445-5131, Ⓦwww.avirtualdominica.dm/picard.htm; ❻). Its picturesque Creole cottages couldn't be closer to the water, and come with verandas and kitchenettes, though they're rather overpriced for what they offer. There's also a restaurant onsite, and a wellness centre offering massages, reflexology and other treatments. Beyond Portsmouth on the north coast of the island, the tiny town of Calibishie has another accommodation option. *Calibishie Lodges* (Ⓣ767/445-8537, Ⓦwww.calibishie-lodges.com; ❹) features eight tidy, appealing units with kitchenettes overlooking a sand beach and the Guadeloupe Channel. There's a pool on site, and a good restaurant, *Bamboo*, serving home-cooked breakfast, lunch and dinner, ranging from pizzas to seafood or Creole chicken. A laid-back tourist scene is developing in Calibishie itself, with a bevy of small hotels in and around the village and a string of good snackettes serving Creole food along the seafront. The Calibishie Information Centre (Mon–Fri 8.30–4pm, Sat & Sun 10am–4pm, Ⓣ767/445-8344, Ⓦwww.calibishiecoast.com) provides local info.

Portsmouth's limited **dining** options include the beachfront *Big Papa's* (Ⓣ767/445-6444), a homage to Jamaica serving specialities such as ackee and saltfish and jerk chicken alongside burgers and seafood; it's also lively after dark, with a reggae night on Wednesday, karaoke on Fridays and Caribbean night on Saturdays. Nearby *Blue Bay* (Ⓣ767/445-4985) is a great dinner option, serving tasty chicken and seafood dishes accompanied by a delicious breadfruit pie. Just across from the entrance to Ross Medical School is *Brothers*, which serves acceptable and reasonably priced Chinese and Thai food. A hundred metres up and across the street is a small outdoor market known to the students as "the shacks"; most of the stands have local and inexpensive food to take away for lunch. The *Purple Turtle Beach Club* is just north of the centre of town along the bay front – it's a great place to stop for a drink or a swim, and is frequented by locals, students and visitors alike.

Carib Territory

From Portsmouth, a road heads east across the island, passing towering royal palms and seemingly endless banana plantations, ending at the coast where you'll encounter dramatic vistas of the Atlantic pounding against unusual **red rock** outcroppings.

There's little to keep you in the string of villages clinging precariously to the rugged cliffs here, though they do offer some picture-postcard views before reaching **Bataka**, the northernmost village of the **CARIB TERRITORY**. This 3700-acre reserve is home to the only remaining tribe of Carib Indians in the Caribbean; a modern community, its traditions are nonetheless still evident in the intricate, handcrafted woodcarvings and baskets sold in huts along the 7.5-mile coastal road south of Bataka. The community's centre, the longhouse-shaped **Ste Marie of the Caribs Church**, overlooks the sea from **Salybia**, the main settlement. Check out the church's dug-out canoe altar framed by colourful frescoes of Carib life. It's not obviously marked from the main road so you're best to ask a local for directions. Nearby at Crayfish River, and signposted from the main road, is the **Kalinago Barana Autê** (mid-Oct to mid-April Tues–Sun 10am–5pm; mid-April to mid-Oct closed Wed & Thurs; EC$26), a full-scale reproduction of a Carib village that includes thatch-roofed *karbet* or *taboui*, still used by local Caribs for community events, and smaller dwellings for sleeping, eating and cooking. Guides show you dug-out canoes and demonstrate the preparation of cassava, and the tour ends at a small restaurant and a souvenir shop selling gorgeous Carib crafts.

Southwards, at the village of **Sineku**, a sign points seawards to the serpentine **Escalier Tête Chien** (or "dog's head stairs"), a peculiar lava formation that resembles steps climbing out of the sea. In Carib legend the outcroppings are the tracks left from the bottom of an enormous snake, the "tête chien".

The friendly *Carib Territory Guesthouse* at Crayfish River (Ⓣ767/445-7256, Ⓦwww.avirtualdominica.com/ctgh.htm; ❷), owned by current Carib Chief Charles Williams, has basic **doubles** and a communal veranda with ocean views; meals are available. Just beyond Carib Territory if you're heading south, *Beau Rive* (Ⓣ767/445-8992, Ⓦwww.beaurive.com; ❻) is a friendly, new and more luxurious inn. The eight simple and gorgeous rooms are furnished in a beautifully understated plantation style; two private cabins are built into the hillside. All have sweeping ocean views, and the inn has a swimming pool and welcoming library-cum-common room; delicious meals are available. Downhill towards Castle Bruce is the *Islet View Creole Park* **restaurant** (Ⓣ767/446-03780; open daily, call in advance for dinner), decorated with palm weavings and serving local food in thoughtful and creative ways (from EC$20).

17

St Lucia

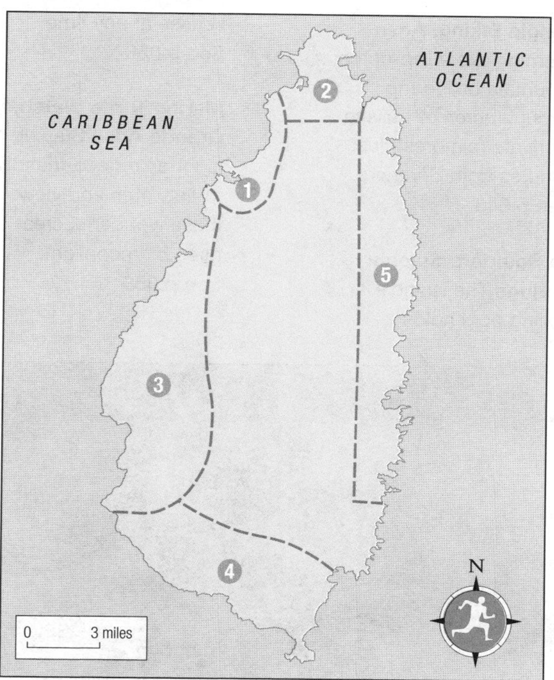

St Lucia highlights

* **Street Parties** St Lucia's famed Fish Fries at Anse La Raye and Dennery reveal the island's more raucous side – and offer great Creole cuisine. See p.647 & p.658

* **Jungle Biking, Anse Mamin** Take a top-notch mountain biking trip through acres of trails in a private rainforest, just minutes from Soufrière. See p.649

* **La Soufrière Sulphur Springs** The island's boiling pool holds bizarre, not-to-be-missed appeal. See p.649

* **The Pitons** Though best viewed at sunset with a cocktail from *Ladera Resort*, St Lucia's magic peaks are a feast for the senses at any time. See p.650

* **Marine Turtle Watch, Grande Anse** Stay up all night on an eco-friendly turtle watch and view these wonderful creatures by moonlight. See p.658

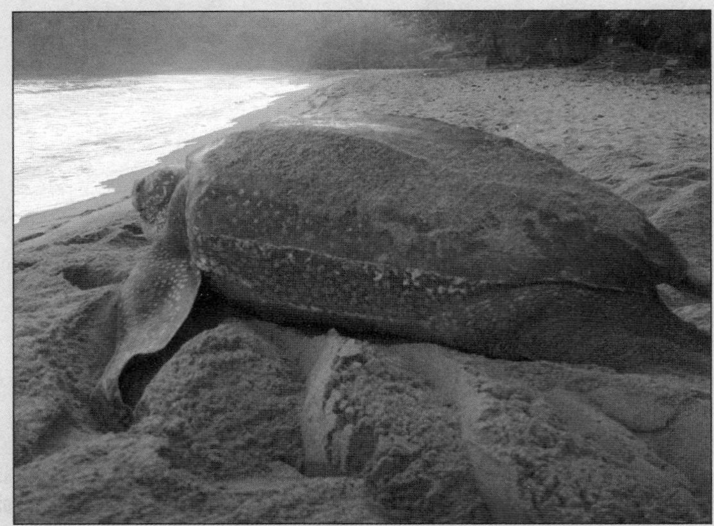

▲ Leatherback turtle

Introduction and basics

St Lucia more than lives up to the paradisiacal Caribbean stereotype: a glorious mix of honey and volcanic sand beaches, translucent waters, sheltering reefs swarming with tropical fish, lush interior rainforests, and a thriving culture encompassing literature, theatre, music and dance. The island is currently undergoing a massive expansion of tourism infrastructure, with resorts, cruise ship berths and golf courses being built aplenty. Nonetheless St Lucia's tourist boom is a recent development, and the island still has its low-key feel – one of its biggest assets.

Despite the lack of hype, St Lucia's tourist facilities are top-notch, and cater to all tastes – you can stay at luxury hotels or intimate guesthouses, dine in world-class restaurants or at roadside kiosks, and shop in duty-free malls or at open-air village markets. With little of the jaded hustle that can mar more established Caribbean destinations, St Lucia makes for a relaxed, informal and incredibly friendly place to visit.

Where to go

If it's **shopping** and **nightlife** you prefer, then you'll probably head north to the tourism stronghold of **Rodney Bay** and its lovely **Reduit Beach**. St Lucia's understated capital, **Castries**, is slowly catching up with its northern neighbour, though most visitors choose to head further south to the finer **beaches** and peaceful fishing villages of the west coast. Near the inviting town of **Soufrière** are the monolithic twin peaks of the **Pitons**, St Lucia's most famous sight. In the interior, the **rainforest**-smothered mountains are strikingly beautiful and rich in flora and fauna, while the wild and windswept east coast offers the chance to glimpse unusual wildlife, from one of the **rarest lizards** in the world to **leatherback turtles** nesting in the sand.

When to go

St Lucia's tropical climate is classically Caribbean. During **high season** (December to April), the island is pleasantly hot, with little rain and constant northeasterly trade winds keeping the nights cool. Temperatures rise during the **summer months**, which can also be wet: the rainy season lasts from June to October, with the **hurricane season** at the tail end, roughly from late August to October.

Getting there

Most visitors arrive at **Hewanorra Airport** in the south, but most connecting flights within the Caribbean land at **George F.L. Charles Airport** in the north (about an hour's drive from Hewanorra). **Ferries** from Martinique and beyond dock at Port Castries, as do **cruise lines** such as Norwegian, Celebrity, and Radisson Seven Seas, daily from October to May, while smaller lines like Sea Cloud and Star Clipper dock infrequently at Soufrière.

Money and costs

St Lucia is not cheap, and you'll pay US and European prices for restaurants and accommodation. St Lucia's official currency is the **Eastern Caribbean dollar** (EC$), which trades against the US dollar at an official rate of EC$2.68 to US$1 for travellers' cheques and EC$2.67 for cash. In the case of practically everything related to tourism, **prices** in St Lucia are quoted in both EC and US dollars, and both currencies are accepted island-wide. On the street, the exchange rate is almost always EC$2.50 to US$1, in the vendor's favour.

Major **credit cards** are widely accepted and **ATMs** are readily available at the airports, downtown Castries, Rodney Bay and Soufriére, dispensing EC dollars. US dollar **travellers' cheques** are accepted by

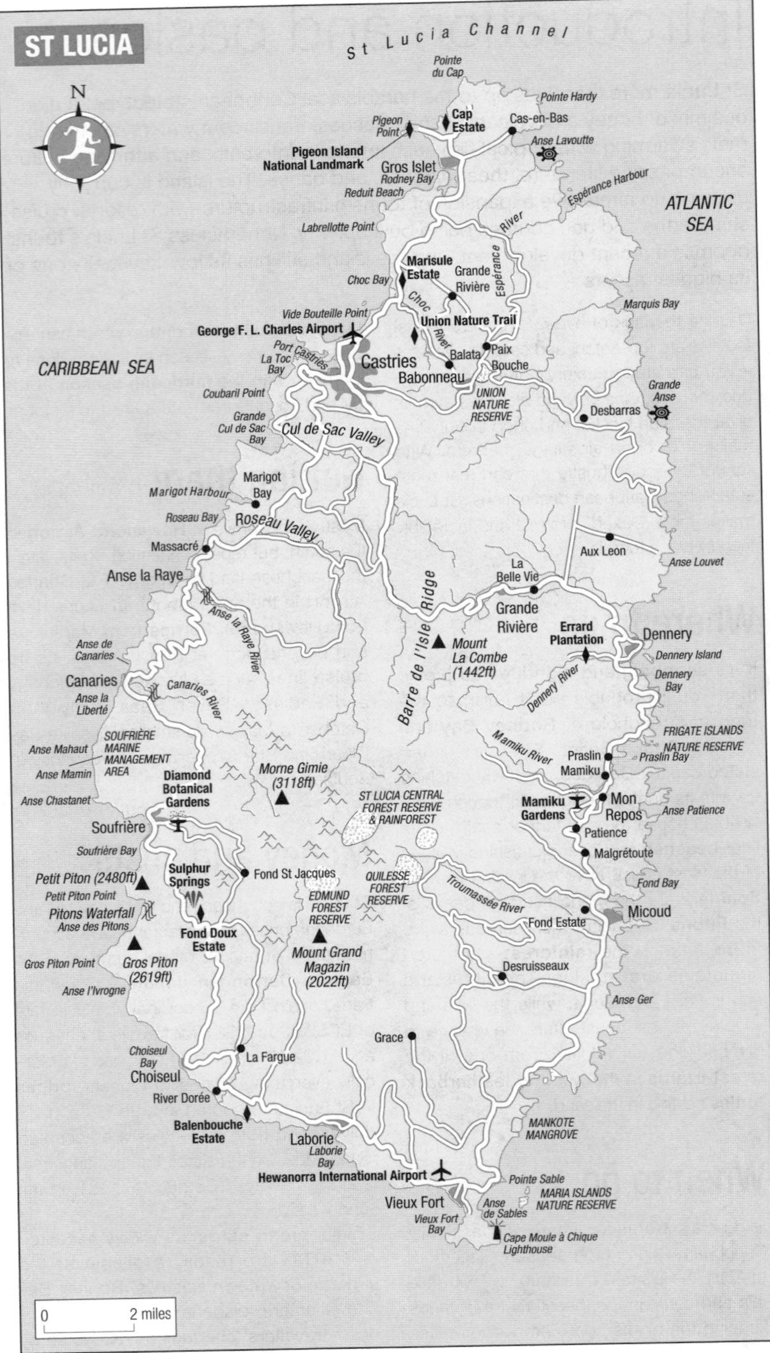
ST LUCIA
St Lucia Channel
Pointe du Cap
Pointe Hardy
Cap Estate
Cas-en-Bas
Pigeon Point
Anse Lavoutte
Pigeon Island National Landmark
Gros Islet
Rodney Bay
Reduit Beach
Espérance Harbour
ATLANTIC SEA
Labrellotte Point
River
Espérance
Marisule Estate
Grande Rivière
Choc Bay
Choc River
Marquis Bay
Vide Bouteille Point
Union Nature Trail
George F. L. Charles Airport
Port Castries
La Toc Bay
Castries
Paix Bouche
Balata
Babonneau
CARIBBEAN SEA
UNION NATURE RESERVE
Grande Anse
Coubaril Point
Desbarras
Grande Cul de Sac Bay
Cul de Sac Valley
Marigot Bay
Marigot Harbour
Roseau Bay
Roseau Valley
Aux Leon
Massacré
Anse Louvet
Anse la Raye
La Belle Vie
Barre de l'Isle Ridge
Grande Rivière
Anse la Raye River
Errard Plantation
Dennery
Mount La Combe (1442ft)
Dennery Island
Anse de Canaries
Canaries
Dennery Bay
Canaries River
Dennery River
Anse la Liberté
SOUFRIÈRE MARINE MANAGEMENT AREA
FRIGATE ISLANDS NATURE RESERVE
Anse Mahaut
Mamiku River
Praslin
Praslin Bay
Anse Mamin
Mamiku
Diamond Botanical Gardens
Morne Gimie (3118ft)
ST LUCIA CENTRAL FOREST RESERVE & RAINFOREST
Mamiku Gardens
Mon Repos
Anse Chastanet
Anse Patience
Soufrière
Patience
Soufrière Bay
Malgrétoute
Sulphur Springs
Fond St Jacques
QUILESSE FOREST RESERVE
Petit Piton (2480ft)
Fond Bay
Petit Piton Point
EDMUND FOREST RESERVE
Troumassée River
Micoud
Pitons Waterfall
Anse des Pitons
Fond Doux Estate
Fond Estate
Mount Grand Magazin (2022ft)
Gros Piton Point
Gros Piton (2619ft)
Desruisseaux
Anse l'Ivrogne
Anse Ger
Grace
Choiseul Bay
La Fargue
Choiseul
River Dorée
Balenbouche Estate
MANKOTE MANGROVE
Laborie
Laborie Bay
Hewanorra International Airport
Pointe Sable
Vieux Fort
Anse de Sables
MARIA ISLANDS NATURE RESERVE
Vieux Fort Bay
Cape Moule à Chique Lighthouse
0
2 miles
N

17 ST LUCIA

larger businesses, but it's always wise to carry cash, as taxi drivers, market stalls and most smaller restaurants and guesthouses won't accept credit cards or cheques.

Standard **bank hours** are Monday to Thursday 8am–3pm, and Friday 8am–5pm. The Bank of St Lucia at Hewanorra airport keeps somewhat later hours (Mon, Thurs, Fri & Sat 1–5pm, Tues & Wed 1–6pm, Sun 1–7pm), and branches around Rodney Bay are open Saturday mornings. Banks always offer the most favourable exchange rate.

Note that you must pay a **departure tax** of EC$54 when leaving St Lucia by air and EC$30 when departing by ferry.

Information

The **St Lucia Tourist Board** maintains several offices abroad. **On island**, the main office is in the Sureline Building, just past the roundabout on your way north from Castries (PO Box 221, Castries, St Lucia; ⓣ 758/452-4094, ⓦ www.stlucia.org). Generally, though, you'll find all the **maps** and brochures you might need at the more convenient **tourist board kiosks** located around the island at both airports, La Place Carenage and Pointe Seraphine shopping complexes, and the waterfront in Soufrière. Pick up a copy of *Visions* magazine, published yearly by the St Lucia Hotel and Tourism Association, which includes hotel and restaurant **listings** along with articles on island history and culture.

Getting around

By car and motorbike

The ideal way to get around is to rent a **car**, although it can be pricey. Rates start at US$45 per day for a compact, manual-shift or automatic vehicle without air-conditioning, and go as high as US$100 for a luxury model; **best rates** by far are from local companies, and are cheaper during low season or if you rent for three or more days. You'll need a 4WD to explore the remote parts of the island; prices range from US$65 to US$105. While mileage is often unlimited, rates don't include **petrol** – note that most petrol stations are cash-only, and it's about US$10 per gallon.

To drive on the island, visitors must purchase a temporary St Lucian **licence** (EC$30 or US$12 for one day; EC$54 or US$21 for three months), issued by rental companies, airport immigration and most police stations, on production of a valid licence from your country of origin. In St Lucia driving is on the **left side** of the road. Note that road signs are rare, so finding your way can be tricky even with a map (ask for directions), and most interior roads are unpaved and difficult to navigate. Renting a **motorbike** is not the safest way to get around due to potholed roads and erratic local drivers.

Car-and motorbike-rentals

Alto Gros Islet ⓣ758/452-0233, Hewanorra Airport ⓣ758/454-5311; ⓦwww.altorentacar.com.
Avis Castries ⓣ758/452-2700, Hewanorra Airport ⓣ758/454-6325, George Charles Airport ⓣ758/452-2046; ⓦwww.avisstlucia.com.
Budget Castries ⓣ758/452-9887, Hewanorra Airport ⓣ758/454-7470, George Charles Airport ⓣ758/452-3516; ⓦwww.budget-stlucia.com.
Candida's Rodney Bay Marina ⓣ758/452-9076, ⓦwww.candysrentacar.com.
Colly's Car Rental Gros Islet ⓣ758/452-2303 or 487-3901, ⓔchooks@candw.lc. Island's best rates, will deliver.
Cool Breeze Soufrière, Rodney Bay, and both airports ⓣ758/459-7729, ⓦwww.coolbreezecarrental.com.
Courtesy Gros Islet ⓣ758/452-8140, ⓦwww.courtesycarrentals.com.
Hertz Hewanorra Airport ⓣ758/454-9636, George F.L. Charles Airport ⓣ758/451-7351; ⓔhertz@candw.lc.
Wayne's Motorcycle Centre Castries ⓣ758/452-2059 or 384-1081.

By bus

If your schedule is laid-back enough to cope with both nonexistent schedules and frequent stops along the route, travelling by **bus** is the most economical way to get around. St Lucia's buses are private minivans of various hues, most emblazoned with colourful names like "Tempt Me" or "Redemption". Of the five main routes, route 1 links Castries and the north, route 2 Castries and Vieux Fort, route 3 Castries and Soufrière. Route 4 runs in and around Vieux Fort and route 5 serves

Castries environs. **Fares** are set by the government and range from EC$3–10; pay when you get off. Most drivers wait until the bus is full before setting off; services between major towns run every thirty to sixty minutes from 5am until 10pm weekdays; extended timetable Friday for the Gros Islet street party, reduced timetable Saturdays and very infrequent Sundays. Brightly coloured pavilions serve as **bus stops**, but it's more common to flag a bus down anywhere along a route. Once aboard, your bus will drop you anywhere; just shout "bus stop" to the driver.

By taxi

Taxis are an expensive but convenient alternative. All have "TX" on the licence plate and are unmetered; while **fares** are set by the government and there are refreshingly few unscrupulous drivers, it's always best to confirm the fare before getting in, and if in doubt, compare the price with another driver. Taxis also offer **guided tours** for negotiable rates starting around US$25/hour or US$150/day.

Water taxis are used around Rodney Bay, Castries, Soufrière and Marigot Bay, mostly for getting to nearby beaches; EC$20 upwards.

Accommodation

From spa all-inclusives to medium-sized family hotels and reasonable local guesthouses, **accommodation** runs the full range in St Lucia. Many options are bunched together in the northern region of **Rodney Bay**, with clusters around Marigot Bay and the more absorbing **Soufriére**. For even more charm and seclusion seek out one of the spots strung along the **south** or **east coasts**. There are a few truly inexpensive options, mostly rooms for rent in private houses in the smaller towns (ask around), though in high season you can expect to pay US$40 for even the most basic room.

Another option is renting a **villa**, which are available mainly in the northern Cap Estate area, with a handful of options elsewhere. Rates often include maid and cooking services; count on spending US$700–4000 per week in high season for villas with between two and 12 bedrooms. For rentals, contact Tropical Villas (Castries ⓣ758/450-8240, ⓦwww.tropicalvillas.net), Lucian Leisure (Rodney Bay ⓣ758/452-8898, ⓦwww.lucian-leisure.com), or Tropical Traveller (Castries ⓣ758/450-7827, ⓦwww.tropicaltraveller.com).

Food, drink and entertainment

St Lucia's **restaurant scene** – clustered for the most part around the tourist areas – offers the full variety, from small, unpretentious eateries to upmarket restaurants offering *haute cuisine*, which rarely disappoint. Overall, service tends to be incredibly friendly, if sometimes rather slow.

The most common culinary style is **Creole**, with chicken, seafood, or meat cooked in a variety of ways, often in a spicy tomato-based sauce (traditionally prepared in a clay "coal pot") and served with filling sides of rice, beans and local vegetables like dasheen, cassava (types of "ground provision") or breadfruit; or in a Caribbean curry sauce and served with a roti (flat bread). For a truly local experience, don't miss one of the island's **fish fries** (see p.647 and p. 658).

Piña coladas and the like are fixtures at resort bars but the local (and excellent) drink of choice is **Piton lager**, brewed in Vieux Fort and best enjoyed in view of its namesake peaks. There's also a non-alcoholic version made with molasses, the Piton Malta, but it's an acquired taste.

Though St Lucia isn't exactly the **nightlife** capital of the Caribbean, there's plenty to do after dark. Many hotels and restaurants

Room tax

When booking accommodation, remember that St Lucian hotels generally levy a 10 percent **service charge** and an 8 percent government **tax** to the bill – a hefty addition for a week's stay even at a medium-priced hotel; the prices quoted in this chapter are **exclusive** of these taxes.

in the west coast resort areas offer some sort of **live music** or **dancing** most nights of the week, and at Rodney Bay there are numerous places where you can have a drink or a meal while listening to anything from a traditional *chak-chak* group to reggae, calypso or steel-pan. The Gros Islet Friday **street lime** is the biggest local party spot. Check local newspapers and tourist publications for special events.

Mail and Communications

The General **Post Office** is on Bridge Street in Castries (Monday to Friday 8.15am–4.30pm; ⓣ758/452-5157), sub offices are located throughout the island and tend to open 1-5pm. Mail to international destinations can be a slow process so for more urgent items try **courier** services in Castries: FedEx is on Derek Walcott Square (ⓣ758/452-1320); and DHL (ⓣ758/453-1538) and UPS (ⓣ758/452-7211) are both on Bridge Street. Public **phones** take phonecards (available from pharmacies and convenience stores) but they are few and far between; if you're stuck, ask to make a call from someone's cellphone – a common occurrence in St Lucia.

Internet access is available all over the island; in **Castries** try upstairs at La Place Carenage, inside the Excelsior mall in **Soufrière**, close to the town roundabout in **Vieux Fort**, or the Cable & Wireless office at the Rodney Bay Marina; prices range EC$8–20/hr.

The **country code** for St Lucia is ⓣ758.

Opening hours, holidays and festivals

Store **opening hours** in St Lucia are generally Mon–Fri 8.30am–4pm and Sat 8am–1pm, though some stores (especially supermarkets) in Rodney Bay and the Gablewoods Mall in Castries keep extended hours and open on Sunday.

In early or mid-May, the island plays host to the two-week **St Lucia Jazz Festival** (ⓦwww.stluciajazz.org), which attracts some of the biggest names in jazz and R&B – including Herbie Hancock, Wynton Marsalis, George Benson and John Legend – who perform during the last four days of the fest at Pigeon Island. Lower-key venues – some which offer free shows – include Derek Walcott Square in Castries and Balenbouche Estate in the southwest.

A round of dancing, street masquerading and general partying, St Lucia's July **Carnival** is one of the true showcases of the island's culture, with storytelling, folk dancing and traditional music alongside more contemporary sequinned bikinis and thumping soca music.

Two **flower festivals**, La Rose in August and La Marguerite in October, hearken back to the political rivalry between the British and French during St Lucia's tumultuous colonial history. Costume parades and traditional song and dance performances take place throughout the island, although Micoud is the focal point.

Public holidays

January 1–2 New Year's
February 22 Independence Day
May 1 Labour Day
May 16 Whit Monday
May 26 Corpus Christi
August 1 Emancipation Day
October 3 Thanksgiving Day
December 13 National Day

Watersports and outdoor activities

Several local companies offer extensive **guided tours** of St Lucia's sights. Most are all-day, **all-inclusive expeditions** averaging a hefty US$100 per person, with stops at waterfalls, mountain viewing areas and banana plantations. St Lucia's mountainous terrain also offers plenty of opportunities for adventurous **hiking** and **jungle biking** – ideal to ease beach lethargy.

With dramatic coastline and miles of easily accessible sandy beaches, St Lucia is also perfect for **watersports**. Many larger resorts have in-house facilities, and together with a plethora of independent operators offer snorkelling, scuba diving, sea kayaking, windsurfing and sailing. To enjoy the water and explore the island at the same time, consider booking a trip along the west coast on one of the popular **boat cruises**.

Guided tours

Visit the **central mountains** aboard 4WD trucks with Jungle Tours in Castries (Ⓣ758/715-3438, Ⓦwww.jungletoursstlucia.com), or choose from a slew of activities (from deep-sea **fishing** to sampling rums at the local distillery) with SunLink Tours in Rodney Bay Village (Ⓣ758/456-9100, Ⓦwww.sunlinktours.com). **Helicopter tours** and airport transfers are available with SunLink and St Lucia Helicopters (Ⓣ758/453-6950, Ⓦwww.stluciahelicopters.com), costing US$120 per person for the fifteen-minute transfer from Hewanorra to Castries, and US$120 per person for a twenty–minute jaunt around the pitons and south of the island.

For more **adrenalin-oriented** pursuits, ATV Paradise Tours (Ⓣ758/455-3245; Ⓦwww.atvstlucia.com; US$120 for two people) operates an exciting and informative 3hr quadbike tour on the island's south-eastern side, while Rain Forest Sky Rides (Ⓣ758/458-5151, Ⓦwww.rfat.com) operates **aerial tram rides** through the northern forest canopy at Chassin (US$75/person, $100 with transfer), as well as guided **bird-watching** tours (US$65 including transfer and breakfast).

Diving and snorkelling

Many of St Lucia's reefs and submerged wrecks are excellent **dive sites**, though **diving** here is not as highly regarded as the region's premier scuba environments such as Saba or Bonaire. There are also plenty of good certification programmes. Dive packages are offered by hotels such as *Anse Chastanet* (see p.645), who bundle accommodation and a specified number of dives at discounted rates.

Both diving and **snorkelling** are particularly good around the pristine reefs of the island's southwest, where the protected Soufrière Marine Management Area (Ⓣ758/459-5500, Ⓔsmma@candw.lc) hugs the shoreline for nearly seven miles. Snorkelling and diving **permits** are required, available through authorized operators; the snorkelling permit costs EC$3/day and the diving one goes for EC$13/day or EC$50/year.

Local culture and language

St Lucian **culture** is archetypal Caribbean: a syncretic amalgamation of the customs, languages and religions of the island's French and British colonizers, and of the African slaves they brought over the Atlantic. Today's population of 165,000 is of predominantly African origin, and some seventy percent are Roman Catholic, with the remainder largely made up of Protestants (Anglican, Baptist and Pentecostal), as well as a small number of Rastafarians. Though Christian hymns are sung boisterously enough to raise the church roofs each Sunday, St Lucia is a society in which esoteric African traditions of magic and spiritualism are very much alive. Carnival is the best example of this fusion of Christian and African beliefs: even though the festival originated as a pre-Lenten celebration (it's now held in July), one of the costume parade's stock characters is the distinctly non-Christian moko jumbie, a wildly attired figure on stilts representing the spirit world. **Language** is another aspect that shows African influence. Though African languages were suppressed as soon as slaves arrived on the island, French planters still needed to communicate with their workers, and gradually the common language of **St Lucian Creole** (Kwéyòl) – also called Patois – evolved, heavily laced with French, West African dialects and more recently, with smatterings of English. Though **English** became St Lucia's official language in 1842, Creole is still spoken widely throughout the island, on the radio, in parliament, and many rural St Lucians speak only Creole until they start primary school, where they learn English for the first time.

Watersports operators

Action Adventures Divers *The Still Beach Resort*, Soufrière ⓣ758/459-5599, ⓦwww.aadivers.net .Scuba, snorkelling.
Dive Fair Helen Vigie Marina, Choc Bay, and Marigot Bay ⓣ758/451-7716, ⓦwww .divefairhelen.com. Scuba, snorkelling, and kayaking.
Scuba St Lucia Anse Chastanet ⓣ758/459-7755, ⓦwww.scubastlucia.com. Scuba and snorkelling.
Scuba Steve's Rodney Bay ⓣ758/450-9433, ⓦwww.scubastevesdiving.com. Diving and snorkelling.
The Reef Anse de Sables, Vieux Fort ⓣ758/454-3418, ⓦwww.slucia.com/windsurf. Windsurfing and kitesurfing.

Boat trips

Gliding up and down St Lucia's calm west coast, **sightseeing** and **party boats** offer an alternative way to view the island's bays and mountain peaks. Trips include stops for snorkelling and swimming, and a visit to a coastal village (probably Soufrière or Marigot Bay) as well as lunch and drinks; prices range from US$45 for a half-day (no lunch) to US$110 for a full day. Bear in mind that as the boats are often crowded with rowdy revellers taking advantage of the free-flowing rum, the trip may not be the quiet cruise you might anticipate; if you're looking for a more sedate excursion, ask when you book.

Endless Summer Cruises (ⓣ758/450-8651, ⓦwww.stluciaboattours.com) run full-day tours out of Rodney Bay, as well as half-day **sunset cruises** complete with a half-bottle of champagne per person. The *Brig Unicorn*, a ship featured in the film *Pirates of the Caribbean*, offers a popular family-friendly **pirate adventure** as well as a day sail (contact SunLink, see opposite). **Whale and dolphin watching** and **fishing** excursions are available with Mystic Man Tours (ⓣ758/459-7783, ⓦwww.mysticmantours.com) and Hackshaw's Boat Charters (ⓣ758/453-0553, ⓦwww .hackshaws.com) – there's a good chance you'll spot dolphins or pilot, sperm or humpback whales, many of which are year-round residents in St Lucia's waters.

Jungle biking

Jungle biking, or mountain biking through the jungle, is one of St Lucia's newer and more exciting adventure sports, accessible only by boat from the beach at *Anse Chastanet Resort*. Set in an old sugar plantation just inland from Anse Mamin, there are some 12 miles of trails suitable for all abilities, and you can expect to see anything from eighteenth-century colonial ruins and a swimming hole to hundreds of fruit trees along your chosen trail. Operated by Bike St Lucia (ⓣ758/457-1400, ⓦwww.bikestlucia .com); from US$45 per half day.

Hiking

Hiking through St Lucia's central rainforests is the best way to experience the island's fabulously beautiful **interior**; despite being laced by walkable trails, the mountains often go unexplored by beach devotees. You don't necessarily need guides for many of the hikes (though hiring one will help to identify local flora and fauna), but you do need advance permission and an inexpensive permit from the **Forestry Department** to enter protected areas such as the Edmund Forest Reserve and the Barre de L'Isle area (ⓣ758/450-2231 or 2078, ⓦwww.slumaffe.org; guides available; see also p.651). Other informative options are the inland and coastal **guided walks** offered by the **St Lucia National Trust** (ⓣ758/452-5005, ⓦwww.slunatrust .org), guided Piton and east coast hikes with **Heritage Tours** (ⓣ758/458-1454, ⓦwww .heritagetoursstlucia.org), as well as excellent (though infrequent) hikes on the eastern side of the island offered by **Mamiku Gardens** (ⓣ758/455-3729).

History

The first inhabitants of St Lucia were the Ciboney people, Amerindians who settled about 2500 years ago in caves along the coast, fishing and hunting with stone tools. The Arawaks arrived from South America 700 years later, farming cassava, sweet potatoes, corn, and cotton, and building thatched-roof houses. After a further 700 years of peace came the warlike Caribs, who ruled the island until being driven away by European settlers in the seventeenth century.

The European "discovery" of St Lucia is an ambiguous matter, though the first European to sight the island was probably a **Spaniard**. Cartographer Juan de la Cosa sailed with Christopher Columbus on his early voyages, and he listed the island as El Falcón on a map in 1500. In 1511, it appeared on a Spanish Royal Cedula of Population as St Lucia, and was included on a Vatican map of 1520.

The first European settler, however, was a French pirate by the name of François Leclerc. Also known as Jambe de Bois (Wooden Leg), Leclerc made Pigeon Island off the north-west coast his hideout around 1550 and from there terrorised passing Spanish ships. The next Europeans to arrive did so by accident: in 1605, a **British** ship called the *Oliphe Blossome* (Olive Branch) was blown off course on its way to Guyana. Tired of being at sea, 67 passengers tried their luck at settling where they were, but not long after negotiating with the Caribs for food, they were attacked. Just nineteen surviving settlers escaped in a Carib canoe.

While similar clashes between the Caribs and small bands of settlers continued, the **French** reached a **peace agreement** with them in 1660, claiming St Lucia and several neighbouring islands with little opposition – but the war for St Lucia was far from won. Over the next 150 years, bloody Anglo-French **hostilities** saw the "Helen of the West Indies" change hands between the two nations at least fourteen times. Despite the fighting, the French turned St Lucia into a money-making colony, settling along the fertile southwest coast and establishing the island's first **town**, Soufrière, in 1746. By 1765 they introduced vast **sugar cane** plantations and brought in **slaves** from West Africa to tend the hugely profitable crops.

When war broke out in 1778 between Britain and France, the British again tried to conquer the island, desiring the strategic bays in the north – all with views of the French depot Fort Royal on Martinique. After four years of fighting, Britain's **Admiral George Rodney** decimated the French navy off the coast of Guadeloupe. This British victory in the **Battle of the Saints** was the beginning of the end of French domination of the Caribbean.

The 1783 Treaty of Versailles, however, put St Lucia into French hands once again, and during the 1789–99 **French Revolution** all the towns were renamed, French nobles were executed by guillotine, and, in a radical move of solidarity, the Republicans **freed the slaves**. Sensing that the British would soon regain power, the Africans feared for their new-found freedom, many forming freedom-fighting groups known as **Brigands**, who launched terrifying attacks against the British plantations until finally surrendering in 1797. In 1814, the **Treaty of Paris** brought the conflicts to a long-overdue conclusion, with France ceding St Lucia to the British. English commercial law was introduced in 1827, and slavery was finally **abolished** on August 1, 1834 – a date recognized today by the Emancipation Day holiday.

After World War I the question of independence came to the forefront, and in 1958 St Lucia joined other British colonies in the **West Indies**

Federation, aiming for self-rule. Britain granted St Lucia self-government in 1967 and, after years of lobbying, **independence** on February 22, 1979. The island, however, remains a Commonwealth country with the British monarch as titular head of state, represented on the island by a governor general.

Sugar was the staple crop until the mid-twentieth century when the market price plummeted; by 1965, the last stalk had been cut and **bananas** became the predominant export. The banana industry heavily relied on preferential trade agreements with the European market – **competition** with large US-owned farms in Latin America was fierce. In 1997 the WTO ruled against preferential access for the Caribbean, effectively shattering the island's banana trade. While bananas farmed under the Fair Trade logo can still be found around St Lucia, since 1997 the government has been encouraging **tourism**, and large tracts of the island's coastline are under development as a result.

17.1

Castries and around

Home to some 62,000 people (more than a third of the island's total population), St Lucia's capital of **CASTRIES** on the northwest coast is a metaphor for contemporary West Indian urban culture: at times busy and congested, other times somnolent and peaceful, the town feels stuck between a centuries-old island lifestyle and a desperate push to modernize. Though the capital is easy to navigate on foot, it is not particularly blessed with museums, theatres or historical sights – your best bet to experience Castries is to enjoy its vibrant street life.

Due to extensive damage by fires between 1796 and 1948, only a few examples of colonial and Victorian architecture remain, and today's city is chiefly composed of unadorned modern concrete buildings. Despite its contemporary feel, Castries retains a certain unaffected charm, thanks to its setting more than anything else. The town wraps around the deep harbour of **Port Castries** where hundreds of cruise ships dock each year to unload tourists for a day of duty-free shopping. Recently the government unveiled plans to extend port development, which will create a vast shopping and hotel area à la Dubai or Aruba. How the rest of Castries fits into this remains to be seen, particularly **downtown** which spreads back from the harbour over a dozen or so blocks of noisy streets, shops, bus stands and general hustle and bustle of a local peoples' capital city.

Meanwhile the area **around Castries** is well worth exploring, and many sights are reachable without a car, although it takes a little effort to learn the bus system. Hills surround the capital to the east and south; the southern Morne Fortune range once provided a natural defence for the island's various occupiers, and the remains of several **forts** and **batteries** scattered throughout the area are worth a quick look. North of downtown and across the harbour is **Vigie Peninsula**, host to the island's largest duty-free complex, as well as the small **George F.L. Charles Airport** and a few waterfront restaurants.

Arrival, information and getting around

St Lucia's regional airport lies just over half a mile from downtown Castries, the island's public transport hub. Several informal bus depots are scattered around the capital. Castries' **George F.L. Charles Airport**, also known as **'Vigie'** (Ⓣ758/452-1156) on the Vigie Peninsula handles most Caribbean traffic and one or two US flights. There's an **information** booth (daily 7am–9pm; Ⓣ758/452-2596) as well as a row of **car rental** kiosks at the arrival area, while just outside is a **taxi** stand (infrequent buses also ply the adjacent road). If you've arrived from Guadeloupe, Dominica or Martinique via the **L'Express des Iles or Maritime West Indies** ferries, you'll disembark at the Ports Authority ferry terminal in Bananes Bay; downtown is a short walk east.

The administrative office of the **St Lucia Tourist Board** (Ⓣ758/452-4094, Ⓦwww.stlucia.org) is on the second floor of the Sureline Building complex in Vide Bouteille, about a mile northeast of Castries. Visitors are better served, however, by the knowledgeable and helpful staff at **information kiosks** in the Pointe Seraphine (Mon–Fri 8am–4.30pm; Ⓣ758/452-4094) and La Place Carenage (Mon–Fri 9am–5pm, Sat 9am–12.30pm; Ⓣ758/458-7194) shopping complexes.

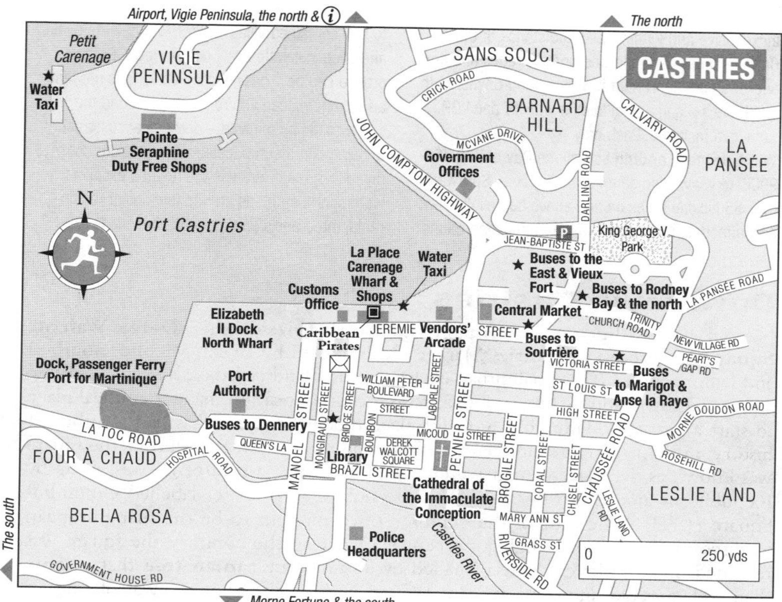

Castries is not an easy city to navigate by **car**. On weekdays in particular, the narrow streets are congested and choked with randomly parked cars and trucks. At least **parking** is easy, thanks to the municipal multistorey garage (EC$1.50/hr) behind Castries market, just off the John Compton Highway as you come into town from the north.

All the main **bus** stops are located in the downtown area. Buses to **Soufrière** (route #3D) leave from Jeremie Street in front of Castries Market. Services north to **Gros Islet** and **Cap Estate** (route #1A) leave from the Anglican School on Darling Road east of the Market, and buses to **Vieux Fort** and the south via the east coast (route #2H) leave from just up the street at the junction of Darling Road and Jean Baptiste Street. Also in the neighbourhood, buses to **Praslin** and **Mon Repos** (route #2D) head out from Julian's Supermarket off Jean Baptiste Street. Further downtown, buses to **Dennery** (route #2C) leave from the Mongiraud and Micoud Street junction, while **Marigot** and **Anse la Raye** buses (route #3C) depart from Victoria Street between Chausée Road and Chisel Street.

Accommodation

The busy streets of **downtown Castries** have little in the way of accommodation, and you'll find that most of the nearby hotels and guesthouses lie along the coast towards Rodney Bay.

East Winds Inn Labrellotte Bay ⓣ758/452-8212, ⓦwww.eastwinds.com. One of the Caribbean's top all-inclusives, *East Winds* manages to maintain the dual feat of consistently high standards and a friendly, attentive staff. The resort has a private, exclusive and relaxed feel with a predominantly 40s and upwards European clientele. Cottages scattered throughout the flower-filled gardens and along the beach are supremely attractive with their sunken stone-tiled showers a clear highlight. The restaurant is also one of St Lucia's best – the *menu du jour* and choice of wines are superb, and the king fish, mahi mahi and marlin are grilled to perfection at the twice-weekly barbeque. ⑨

Sundale Guesthouse Sunny Acres ⓣ758/452-4120, ⓔpeterkingshott@hotmail.com. This small, tightly run guesthouse on a side road near the Gablewoods Mall is basic but scrupulously clean, inexpensive and within walking distance of Choc Bay's beaches. Two one-bedroom cottages and one two-bedroom apartment have fans and private bath, and there's a communal lounge with TV and VCR. Breakfast included. Cash only. ❷

Windjammer Landing Labrellotte Bay ⓣ758/456-9000, ⓦwww.windjammer-landing.com. Sprawled over 55 hillside acres on and above Labrellotte Bay, accommodation ranges from well-appointed rooms to self-contained villas – some with private pools and chefs, all with lovely ocean views. Getting around can be a hassle since walking is not really an option; instead you're shuttled around the windy roads by minivan – perhaps accustomed to being chauffeured, celebrity guests are not unusual. A major draw is the resort's excellent watersports outfit, as are the five onsite restaurants, three pools and gorgeous beach. ❺–❾

Downtown Castries

Named after St Lucia's famous poet and Nobel Prize-winner, **Derek Walcott Square** is southeast of Castries Market and bordered by Brazil, Micoud, Bourbon and Laborie streets. This small urban centrepiece is a landscaped oasis in an otherwise congested town, and its fine architecture and central location make it an ideal place to start a city tour. Though a peaceful place today, the square has had a turbulent history: in the late eighteenth century following the French Revolution, the square was known as the Place d'Armes, and legend has it that a **guillotine** was set up by Republicans anxious to do away with the nobles. It was later labelled Columbus Square (1893) in honour of the explorer, once thought to be the first European to discover the island; in light of recent evidence to the contrary, the square was renamed in 1993. Its east side is shaded by an immense **saman tree** that is more than 400 years old, and busts of St Lucia's two Nobel Prize winners (Walcott and Sir Arthur Lewis) guard an ornate fountain in the centre.

Bordering the south side of the square, **Brazil Street** is congested and busy but showcases the city's best examples **of West Indian colonial** architecture, which miraculously escaped the hurricanes and fires of the early colonial days and the mid-twentieth century.

Cathedral of the Immaculate Conception

Nearly seventy percent of St Lucians are **Roman Catholic** – a legacy of French colonial rule – and the cornerstone of the island's faith is the imposing brick-and-mortar **Cathedral of the Immaculate Conception** dominating Derek Walcott Square's east side. With room to seat more than two thousand worshippers, the foundation of the current structure dates to 1894. In 1957, the former church was granted the status of a cathedral, and was visited by **Pope John Paul II** in 1986. Recently, though, the cathedral has been home to much less illustrious visitors. On December 31, 2000, two men claiming to be Rastafarians barged into the cathedral, setting fire to members of the congregation and killing a priest and a nun. Rastafarians throughout the island condemned the attack, denying any link to their religion. Since then, security has been greatly improved, and no further problems have arisen.

Unless Mass is in progress (in which case you are welcome to worship), you're allowed to wander inside to have a look around the ornate interior, which is bathed in rich red and diffused yellow light from ceiling portals, and busy with detailed carved wood inlay, wooden pews, iron ceiling supports and stately pillars. Note the ceiling paintings of Catholic saints and apostles, with St Lucie above the altar, and the vivid murals painted by St Lucian artist Dunstan St Omer, who also designed the country's flag.

The Central Market and around

Vividly colourful and often loud, **Central Market** (Mon–Sat 9am–5pm, Sun cruise ship days only) on Jeremie Street at the northern perimeter of downtown is one of the busiest parts of Castries, especially on Saturday mornings. Inside are rows of craft booths, with vendors selling baskets, spices, carvings, T-shirts, straw hats and tacky souvenirs. The colourful fruit and vegetable market is at the northeast corner of the complex, and adjacent to the main throughfare is a row of food stalls selling tasty **creole breakfasts and lunches** at bargain prices.

Across the John Compton Highway from the Central Market, and easily identifiable by the rust-coloured roof, is the **Vendor's Arcade** (Mon–Sat 9am–5pm, Sun cruise ship days only), another set of craft stalls selling the same rather tacky wares at slightly higher prices. For standard duty-free items like jewellery, perfume and rum, as well as for **Internet** access, visit **La Place Carenage** (Mon–Fri 9am–4pm, Sat 9am–1pm, Sun cruise ship days only) a couple blocks further west on Jeremie Street. Bring your airline tickets and passport for tax-free purchases.

Vigie Peninsula

Framing the northern half of Port Castries, the heavily developed **Vigie Peninsula** was the original site of the Castries town settlement. Then largely swampland, the area was afflicted by rampant disease, and by 1768 the town relocated to drier land across the harbour. In the twentieth century, successive government reclamation projects created the flat spit of land where the airport now sits. At the peninsula's southern end, **Pointe Seraphine** (Mon–Fri 9am–5pm, Sat 9am–2pm, Sun cruise ship days only), the island's biggest duty-free shopping complex, overlooks the bay. Two adjacent cruise-ship berths deliver disembarking tourists directly to the stores, while the **taxi stand** (☎758/452-1733) and the **water taxi** to downtown Castries (every 10min when cruise ships are docked; US$2) stand by to cater for the day-trippers.

From Pointe Seraphine, the main highway runs north to Rodney Bay. Parallel to it, between the airport runway and the sea, is the picturesque Nelson Mandela Drive, listed on maps as **Peninsular Road**; to reach it from Castries, take the first exit off the Vigie Roundabout to double back around the runway. Flanking the road is **Vigie Beach**, which, despite the occasional roar of an engine and the proximity of the town cemetery, is appealing for its uncrowded two-kilometre stretch of smooth sand, ample shade and generally calm and inviting surf.

Once clear of the airport, Nelson Mandela Drive winds uphill towards Vigie Lighthouse. The entire peninsula was once a fortification, and many of its buildings are restored military quarters, built from red brick (now painted yellow) in the late nineteenth century. On Clarke Avenue, St Lucia's **National Archives** (Mon–Thurs 9am–4pm, Fri 9am–2pm; ☎758/452-1654, Ⓦwww.stluciaarchives.org) are housed in a circa-1890 building. Inside you can browse through hundreds of old photos, lithographs, and maps – a good diversion for an hour or two if you're interested in the island's history.

North and east of Castries

The busy Castries–Gros Islet Highway runs north passing Vigie Peninsula and a string of industrial sites, shops, restaurants, hotels and schools before swinging to the coast, running parallel to sweeping **Choc Bay**. Fringed to the north by **Labrellotte Point**, a sheltered bay hosting two luxury resorts, and to the south by **Vide Bouteille Point**, Choc Bay is a handsome two-mile stretch of often deserted sand. From Vide Bouteille Point the Castries–Gros Islet Highway heads to suburban **Sunny Acres**, home to **Gablewoods Mall** which holds a post office and a good-value supermarket. Just past the mall, the winding but smooth **Allan Bousquet Highway** strikes into the interior to **Babonneau**, a farming community huddled into the central hills and worth visiting for both the sweeping views and for a taste of rural St Lucia. Several rivers flow through the hills around the settlement, and some say that Babonneau is a Patois version of the old French phrase *barre bon eau*, meaning, roughly, "mountain ridge, good water".

Set high in the hills east of Castries at Mount Pleasant, the **Folk Research Centre** (Mon–Fri 8.30am–4.30pm; by donation; ☎758/452-2279; Ⓦwww.stluciafolk.org) – or *Plas Wichès Foklò*, its Patois name – is a museum and cultural centre set in an old estate house once owned by the eminent Devaux family. Dedicated to preserving the culture heritage of St Lucia, including **Creole**, the centre houses a small **museum** whose exhibits include a reproduction of a traditional Amerindian *ti-kay* hut and examples of indigenous musical instruments. The diminutive **research library** downstairs holds one of the island's best collections of books, research papers and photographs relating to St Lucia's folklore and history.

South and west of Castries

The La Toc Road leads west from downtown Castries along the south side of the harbour, first reaching the sizeable **Victoria Hospital**, the island's largest, and a mile or so beyond, **La Toc Battery**, one of the island's best-preserved examples of British military bastions. The 2.5-acre, nineteenth-century cement fortification features mounted cannons and dim underground bunkers, tunnels and cartridge storage rooms; one of the bunkers holds a large exhibit of antique bottles. To visit the Battery, call ahead to schedule a tour (by appointment only Mon–Fri 9am–3pm; EC$20; ⓣ758/452-6039) with **Bagshaw's** silkscreening studio and shop, located about halfway between the hospital and the battery.

Regardless what road you take from Castries to get to the south of the island, you will inevitably end up winding through the suburb of **Morne Fortune**. Comprising a series of hills that flank the capital to the south, the area's elevation provides striking views of the city and the north coast – on a clear day you can see as far as Martinique – and to the south, glimpses of the conical Pitons at Soufrière. The area is reachable via Manoel Street in downtown Castries, which becomes Government House Road as it begins its snakelike ascent towards **Government House** (by appointment only; US$10; ⓣ758/452-2481), an imposing structure dating from 1895 which houses the offices of St Lucia's governor general, the Queen's appointed representative. At the small adjoining **Le Pavillon Royal Museum**, you can see artefacts and documents relating to the history of the house and St Lucia.

A few winds and turns beyond Government House, Morne Road takes you into the heart of the neighbourhood to the top of the 852-foot Morne Fortune itself (also known as "The Morne"), named "Good Luck Hill" by the French. These hills were fortified by the French in 1768 and recaptured (and renamed **Fort Charlotte**) by the British in 1803. For several years plans have been underway to restore and open some of the existing military encampments, cemeteries and batteries; however, the process is incomplete and most are in a state of disrepair. The best-preserved remnants are part of a government complex and the **Sir Arthur Lewis Community College** (ⓣ758/452-5507, ⓦwww.salcc.edu.lc), named after the St Lucian 1979 Nobel Prize-winner for economics who is buried in the grounds. The college itself comprises several nineteenth-century yellow-brick structures with weathered white columns, all of military origin. You're free to amble about and visit the buildings and the **Inniskilling monument**, which honours British soldiers who battled the French here in 1796, located on the south side of the college complex behind the Combermere Barracks.

Eating and drinking

There are only a handful of places to **eat** in the Castries area. The eateries downtown are good for grabbing a quick bite while shopping or sightseeing; by far the best of these are the stalls at Castries Central Market. For a more formal meal there are a couple of excellent options across Port Castries, where stunning views accentuate the experience. For nightlife you're best off heading north to Rodney Bay – though *Prio's Country Palace* (below) has to be seen to be believed.

Castries

Caribbean Pirates La Place Carenage ☎758/452-2543. On the waterfront and popular with locals and the cruise ship crowd alike, this stylish bar and restaurant serves moderately priced nouvelle Creole cuisine with seafood the speciality (fish from EC$25, shrimp rotis are EC$40) – if you're feeling adventurous, try the curried turtle (EC$60). Mon–Thurs 8am–7pm, Fri & Sat 8am–11pm, Sun cruise ship days only.

Castries Central Market Jeremie Street ☎758/453-1019. Market vendors, shoppers and local business people flock to eat breakfast or lunch at these dozen or so restaurant stalls in a small, crowded alleyway behind the market. Taken at unadorned plastic tables, the servings of seafood, rotis, rice and beans or meat and dumplings are hearty and delicious. Cash only (EC$5 to 25). Mon-Sat 6am–evening.

Around Castries

Coal Pot Vigie Marina ☎758/452-5566. Within the same family for over twenty years, this is one of the island's best restaurants, and dinner reservations are essential. The cuisine is a fusion of French and Creole, with choices like lobster bisque flavoured with cognac to start, and design-your-own main courses (from US$25) with your choice of fresh local seafood (such as dorado, barracuda and calamari) or meat, with sauces like coconut curry, ginger, Roquefort, or red wine and onion. On the water's edge, with an interior embellished with local artwork, this is a perfect place for a special night out. Mon–Fri lunch & dinner, Sat dinner.

Froggie Jacques Tropical Bistro Vigie Marina ☎758/458-1900. A warm and personal bar and restaurant that's big on good (if slightly overpriced) food and small on overdressed pomp. Emphasis is on hearty dishes and home-smoked fish, but vegetarians are well catered for and special requests are welcome. Mains from US$26. Mon–Sat lunch & dinner.

Prio's Country Palace Peynier Street and Jean Baptiste Street, Castries. A testament to St Lucia's current enthusiasm for country and western music, this is a giant bar/nightspot at the northern end of downtown. Booming Willie Nelson, Kenny Rogers and the like at top volume till late in the night – but with Caribbean dancing (naturally) – this is a very popular spot at weekends (cover EC$6).

The Wharf Restaurant and Bar Castries–Gros Islet Highway, Choc Bay ☎758/450-4844. This road- and beach-side joint serves decent American and Caribbean dishes at moderate prices (from EC$25), but the beach is the main draw. Lounge chairs and volleyball are available, which make it a popular spot for visitors without hotel beaches facilities, especially cruise ship passengers. Daily 10am–9pm.

17.2

Rodney Bay and the north

St Lucia's compact northern tip encompasses not just a bustling strip of coastal resorts but also the remote and arid northern shoreline between Pointe du Cap and Pointe Hardy, the lavish vacation villas of Cap Estate and the quiet village of **Cas-en-Bas** on the rugged northeast coast. On the west coast, the sweeping, two-mile-long horseshoe-shaped **Rodney Bay** is where most of the region's tourist trappings are concentrated, and as part of the push to develop, it's officially been renamed Rodney Bay Village.

Rodney Bay opens into a deep-water yacht harbour, with a marina complex to the east housing a handful of water side eateries and tour operators. Most of the area's activity, though, is focused around the restaurant-and-hotel-lined **Reduit Beach**, St Lucia's most popular strip of sand. Across the harbour channel to the north is the quiet fishing village of **Gros Islet**, a place to soak up some local flavour at small, unpretentious Creole restaurants. Just about the entire village is overtaken each Friday night for a raucous **street party** known as Jump Up when the streets are blocked off and revellers pour in for a rowdy night of roadside foodstuffs, music and alcohol.

Rodney Bay's northern half is framed by the heavily visited **Pigeon Island National Landmark**, an island that was attached to the mainland by a causeway in the 1970s. Heavily fortified by the British in the eighteenth century, the island has been transformed into a recreation park holding the restored remains of military buildings, a string of beaches and some great walking trails.

Arrival and getting around

Getting to and around St Lucia's northern reaches is relatively easy as frequent **buses** run the length of the coast between Castries, Gros Islet and Cap Estate near the island's northern tip. Marked route #1A, the buses leave near the Anglican school on Darling Road in Castries. Schedules are theoretical, for buses leave when the drivers are so inclined, but count on at least two departures every hour from 6.30am until 10pm, with more services for the Jump Up on Friday night. You'll pay around EC$3 to travel from Castries to Reduit Beach, Rodney Bay Marina or Gros Islet. If you don't have a car and would rather avoid public transport, **taxis** are readily available at hotels and along the main tourist strips. From downtown Castries to any of the resorts along the northeast coast, expect to pay around US$20–30 one-way.

Accommodation

As St Lucia's main tourist heartland, the northern region is plentifully supplied with large **resorts** and medium-sized **hotels** as well as a few inexpensive **guesthouses**, the majority located within walking distance of Reduit Beach.

Bay Gardens Beach Resort Rodney Bay/Reduit Beach ⓣ758/457-8500, ⓦwww.baygardensbeachresort.com. This newly built medium-sized resort on the beach is a cut above the nearby properties in this price range. The attractively designed rooms make up for the synthetic "plantation house" exteriors, and are fully equipped with all the usual amenities plus spacious bathrooms, kitchens and free Wi-Fi access. Friendly staff, babysitting service and private massage cabanas surrounding an extensive pool all add to the appeal. ❻

Cap Maison Pointe du Cap ⓣ758/450-8847, ⓦwww.capmaison.com. This brand new boutique property on the cliff top close to *LeSPORT* has striking views over the ocean to Martinique, and promises a level of sophistication and charm not previously found in the area. The hotel offers apartment-style rooms or villa suites with sunken pools (the largest of which are 3,000 sq ft); all have private butlers. Onsite spa, gym, multi-level pool and gourmet restaurant with walk-in wine cellar raise the allure, as does the property's private cliff-lined sandy cove. Watersports and other outdoor pursuits are easily accessed through the private facilities and two local golf-courses; staying on the hotel's 46-foot yacht with private chef is also possible. ❾

La Panache Guesthouse Cas-en-Bas Road, Gros Islet ⓣ758/450-0765, ⓦwww.lapanache.com. A wonderful inexpensive option tucked into the hillside east of Gros Islet with views south to Castries and the hills inland. This peaceful retreat has three colourful rooms (one of which sleeps four at a push) all have private baths, kitchenettes and cable TV, and there's a homey photo-festooned dining area and lounge with TV/VCR, coffee, and books to borrow. ❷

LeSPORT Cap Estate ⓣ758/457-7800, in US 800/544-2883; ⓦwww.thebodyholiday.com. One of the few all-inclusives that manages to make both singles, couples and groups feel very comfortable. Often full of stressed-out city types who perhaps don't notice the impersonal rooms and instead indulge in the (included) spa treatments, exercise classes, hikes, watersports, golf lessons and t'ai chi. The food is plentiful, healthy and well prepared, especially at the superlative *Tao* (see p.644). ❼

Villa Capri Smuggler's Cove, Cap Estate ⓣ758/450-0009, ⓦwww.capristlucia.com. A delightful nine-room guesthouse nestled in the hills above Smuggler's Cove, this is the perfect getaway for independent travellers and those who like a touch of home and camaraderie. The simply decorated rooms have lovely views of the bay, some with hammocked balconies, and there's an open-air honour bar. Spa treatments are offered in a hillside "relaxation pyramid", and yoga, t'ai chi and meditation classes are held on an outdoor wooden deck overlooking the pool and herb garden below. Rates including breakfast are available, and other meals are cooked on demand. ❹

Villa Zandoli Rodney Bay Village ⓣ758/452-8898, ⓦwww.saintelucie.com. A truly special, brightly painted guesthouse in the centre of Rodney Bay, with five cheery and comfortable rooms. It's all beautifully maintained, and the small but lush gardens are a welcome oasis in the otherwise developed streets. There's an inviting communal area, Internet access and a well-equipped kitchen (rates include breakfast). All rooms have cable TV, some share baths. ❷–❸

Rodney Bay and Reduit Beach

Named **RODNEY BAY** after eighteenth-century British commander George Brydges Rodney, the current incarnation of this former American army base is a compact but fully fledged tourist resort, sandwiched between the glorious if overcrowded Reduit Beach and yachting facilities of Rodney Bay Marina. The mangrove swamp that once separated the villages of Rodney Bay and Gros Islet has been replaced by a man-made harbour channel, which opens out into a deep-water lagoon dotted with bobbing yachts. For the main road through town, turn west off the highway at JQ's shopping mall, two hundred yards south of the marina.

The settlement itself is quite small, and most of the action takes place on the strip of land between the beach and the **yacht harbour**, considered by many to be among the finest in the Caribbean. The harbour is served by the small **Rodney Bay Marina** complex, which has full services for boaters as well as a few waterside restaurants, banks, and somewhat unappealing gift shops. **Rodney Bay Village**, at the southwest end of the harbour, is where landlubbers are likely to be found soaking up the sun at one of any number of resorts or sipping a cocktail at one of the popular bars.

Lined by private villas, the harbour is rarely visible from the village itself, but along its coastline lies the original reason for Rodney Bay's growth into a tourism epicentre: the inviting, easily accessible **Reduit** (REH-doo-ee) **Beach**. This is the most popular beach on the island, a mile long swath of wide golden sand, generally calm surf, and views of Pigeon Island to the north and the coastal hills to the south. Don't be fooled into thinking you've found a Caribbean haven, though: the beach is generally packed with the well-oiled bodies of visiting sun-worshippers – not exactly a secluded hideaway. It's also lined

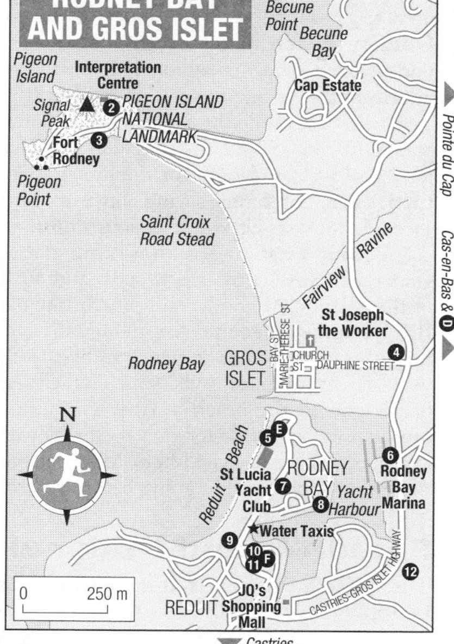

ACCOMMODATION		EATING			
Bay Gardens Beach Resort	E	Café Olé	6	The Lime	10
Cap Maison	C	Captain's Cellar Pub	2	Mojitos	4
La Panache Guesthouse	D	Charthouse	10	Razmataz	7
LeSPORT	A	The Edge	8	Rumours	11
Villa Capri	B	Jambe de Bois	3	Spinnakers	5
Villa Zandoli	F	Key Largo	12	Tao	1
				Triangle Pub	9

with places to stay, many of them large-scale but low-lying concrete blocks sitting intrusively on the beach – and adding to the general crowded feel. The beach hotels provide chairs and umbrellas for their guests, and many will rent them to visitors for about US$12/day.

Gros Islet

Just north across the channel from Rodney Bay lies **GROS ISLET** (GROZ-i-lay), a small fishing village of rickety, rust-roofed wooden homes and narrow streets lined with fruit and vegetable vendors. The beach is somewhat dirty, and generally the town holds little of interest for the visitor. Come Friday nights, though, Lucians and visitors alike pour in for the **Jump Up** street party, when everyone lets loose and parties. Much of the town is blocked off, and armies of snack vendors peddling barbecue, fried fish, hot cakes and cold beers arrive to feed the hungry masses. Bars open their doors onto the street, street corners are festooned with speakers and the music is loud. Things get going around 10pm and last till late, and it's a generally good-natured affair – though sometimes can be a bit edgy. Single women should not attend alone if they're not prepared for plenty of attention. You're also best off leaving your valuables at home and being extra cautious if walking back to your guesthouse late at night.

Cas-en-Bas

Across from the turn-off for Gros Islet just pass the Shell petrol station, the Cas-en-Bas Road strikes east off the coastal highway towards a small settlement on the east coast called **CAS-EN-BAS** (CAZ-en-bah), worth visiting for its string of **beaches** and rugged coast. Recent villa and resort developments have dismayed many locals, who used to enjoy the secluded appeal of the area (especially that of formerly isolated **Donkey Beach** to the north), but the region is still attractive and there's a few undeveloped coves remaining. Parts of the road down to the coast are a little rough, but negotiable in a sturdy car. **Horseback** is probably the best option for visiting the area; riders can wade through the water bareback when they reach the beach – Trim's Stables (Ⓣ758/450-8273) trail rides. Hand-painted signs mark a fork in the road: left for Cas-en-Bas and right for the beach at **Anse Lavoutte**, favoured by **leatherback turtles** as a spot for egg-laying between March and August. If you want to witness this spectacle for yourself, you must join a turtle watch further south at Grande Anse.

The road to Cas-en-Bas turns north at the ocean, and here you'll find a quiet, soft-sand beach with some shady spots and an outlying reef taming the rougher waters of the Atlantic. A wooden-hut beach **bar** named *Marjorie's* serves up cold drinks and BBQ. **Donkey Beach**, a five minute drive or a fifteen-minute walk along a trail that hugs the rocky, cactus-strewn coastline to the north, is worth checking out for the view. Thirty minutes' walk **south** of Cas-en-Bas along the unmarked coastal path brings you to the beach at Anse Lavoutte. Visitors to these shores should take the utmost care in the water due to the powerful Atlantic undercurrents; more than a few people have drowned here. Much of the area is deserted, so bring water and tell someone where you are going before you set off.

Pigeon Island National Landmark

The 44-acre **Pigeon Island National Landmark** (daily 9am–5pm; EC$13 or US$5; Ⓣ758/452-5005, Ⓦwww.slunatrust.org) is a handsome promontory of land jutting into the ocean just north of Gros Islet. It's one of St Lucia's most popular recreation spots, a combination concert venue, historic site and pleasant lunch stop with the added bonus of several excellent beaches, easy hiking trails and a fine pub. In the hotter months, it's best to visit Pigeon Island early in the day, as the hills provide excellent views and are well worth the climb before it gets too hot.

Having formerly hosted both Arawaks, pirates and the British Admiral Rodney's troops, Pigeon Island briefly became the base of freed African slaves known as

Brigands, who banded together to create a minor rebellion before signing a peace treaty in 1797. Since then, the island has been variously a camp for indentured East Indian labourers, a quarantine station for patients afflicted with tropical disease, and a whaling station. Protected as a National Trust landmark in the 1970s, the island's buildings were restored and a causeway was constructed; Britain's Princess Alexandra opened the park to the public in 1979, St Lucia's first day of independence.

Visiting the park

To get to the park by car, heading north from Gros Islet, take the first turn west from the highway, and continue along the causeway. You can also hop on a ferry at the southwest side of the Rodney Bay harbour (daily but unreliable schedule, hourly departures 10am–1pm, returns between 12pm and 4pm; EC$35 round-trip; ⓣ758/452-8079), which drops you off at a small dock on the south side of the park fortifications. At the park's entrance are the offices of the St Lucia **National Trust** ⓣ758/452-5005, ⓦwww.slunatrust.org), through which you can arrange tours of island highlights.

Once you've passed the main gate, paid your entrance fee and collected a map of the area, the **Pigeon Island Interpretation Centre** is on your right, located on the foundation of an old officers' mess. A mini-museum of the island's chequered past, the one-room centre is worth a brief look for its displays of Amerindian axes, clay bowls, flint and shell tools and a discussion of the infamous Battle of the Saints (see p.632); the video display is also worth a look. Just below the centre is the wonderfully cavernous *Captain's Cellar Pub*, housed in an old barracks and an ice-cold Piton is an excellent finish once you've tackled the park's hills.

Past the Interpretation Centre, the south side of the peninsula is peppered with the remains of the **military barracks** and **encampments**, including gun batteries, a powder magazine, a lime kiln and the ruins of Fort Rodney. On the south side of the island are the park's toilets, and nearby is the *Jambe de Bois* waterside café; short on service but nonetheless good for meals, snacks, drinks and live jazz on a Sunday evening.

Several prominent hillocks dominate the island north of the military buildings; of these, 319-foot **Signal Peak** is the highest. A marked trail leads right to its base, from which it takes about fifteen minutes to reach the summit, affording panoramic views south to Gros Islet and the outskirts of Castries, and north over the expanse of the St Lucia Channel to the island of Martinique.

Eating and drinking

Rodney Bay as a whole has more **restaurants** per square mile than anywhere else on the island, providing an array of choices from tandoori to steak or sushi. Nightlife generally consists of bar hopping and a few dance spots, with *The Lime* serving as a common meeting point. With little on offer in Castries many St Lucians also make the journey north at the weekend. At the Friday night **street party** in Gros Islet you'll find multitudes of vendors selling barbequed or roasted chicken, fish or meats, as well as cold beers to wash it down.

Cafes and Restaurants

Rodney Bay

Café Ole Rodney Bay Marina ⓣ758/452-8726. Italian cappuccinos, paninis, breakfast baguettes and the like are available at this friendly little café at the marina, well-patronized by both the yachtie crowd and locals.

Charthouse Rodney Bay Village ⓣ758/452-8115. At this dark-wood, marina-side restaurant (make reservations for a table on the waterside deck), steaks (from EC$80), hickory-smoked ribs and lobster are the specialities, with large portions and hearty sides – though nothing of interest for vegetarians. Top off your meal with a Cuban cigar, on sale at the restaurant. Expensive. Daily 6–10.30pm.

The Edge Harmony Suites Hotel, Rodney Bay Village ⓣ758/450-3343, ⓦwww.edge-restaurant.com. Self-styled "Eurobbean Fusion" and sushi at northern St Lucia's most exclusive eatery. The inviting menu includes scallop and shrimp mousselline, chocolate and chilli pork tenderloin, and

combined platters of duck, kingfish and jerk beef – plus lunch staples like pasta and burgers. With mains starting at around US$50 and 18-piece sushi platters a prohibitive US$70 (lunch is two-thirds the price) – you can't help feeling it's a little overpriced – especially as both food and service (though often excellent) is inconsistent.

Key Largo Castries–Gros Islet Highway ⓣ758/452-0282. Casual Italian-owned pizza place on the east side of the Castries–Gros Islet Highway at Rodney Bay, which serves the best pizza on the island, freshly cooked in a wood-fired brick oven; excellent pasta and Italian coffees also available. Meals may be accompanied by pumping music from the sports gym upstairs. Weds–Sun 9am–11pm.

The Lime Rodney Bay Village ⓣ758/452-0761. One of Rodney Bay's most popular spots for socializing and drinking with consistently good Caribbean food, including the best rotis on the island (from EC$12, although most dishes start at EC$35). Dining is indoor and alfresco (on the patio next to the road) with an in-house DJ most nights and an upstairs (aptly named "Upper Level") club on Fri and Sat, for dancing to a wide range of live music; all making *The Lime* one of the island's hottest nightlife venues. 11am–midnight, later at weekends.

Razmataz Reduit Beach Road, Rodney Bay ⓣ758/452-9800. If you're craving curry, then this popular Reduit Beach restaurant is your best bet. Specialities include spicy vindaloo, korma and tikka masala, all prepared with tandoori (grilled) chicken, lamb, beef or shrimp, from EC$35 – there are plenty of non-meat options as well, plus occasional live music. 4pm–late, closed Tues.

Spinnakers Reduit Beach, Rodney Bay ⓣ758/452-8491. Hopping beach bar and restaurant serving an international mix of steaks and grilled seafood with a family-friendly kid's menu; prices hover around EC$35. Local lobster is the most popular and expensive item at EC$120, but the ribs are tangy, tender and 1/3 the price. Come for live music Saturday nights and steel-pan group on Sundays from 2pm. Daily 9am–11pm.

North of Rodney Bay

Jambe de Bois Pigeon Point. A lovely spot for a glass of wine and a bite to eat, especially on Sun evening when there's live jazz and a good mix of people. Getting here in the dark can nonetheless be a problem if you don't know where you're going – best to find it in the daytime first.

Tao *LeSPORT*, Cap Estate ⓣ758/457-7821. Superlative East/West fusion cuisine, impeccable service and a gorgeous setting overlooking the bay make this one of the island's finest dining experiences. Booking is essential; request a table on the edge of the balcony. Choose from excellent sushi platters, tofu, duck, and wonderful seafood dishes and don't forget to leave room for dessert. Dinner daily, mains from US$30.

Bars and clubs

Mojitos Castries-Gros Islet Highway, Gros Islet ⓣ758/458-0341. Unfortunately the *mojitos* (EC$12) leave something to be desired at this otherwise enjoyable upstairs joint on the main road. A mostly upmarket local crowd here, with live music regularly at weekends.

Rumours Rodney Bay Village ⓣ758/452-9249. Close to *The Lime* and popular with a mixed crowd, this busy spot has live music or a DJ on Fri and Sat (EC$12 after 11pm), plus retro or *salsa* during the week and karaoke on Thursdays. Dancing is on a backyard wooden deck under the stars. Daily from 9pm, gets busy after 12.

Triangle Pub Rodney Bay Village ⓣ758/458-0699. Small barbecue opposite *The Lime;* live music on occasion. The main entertainment is karaoke (free) on Mon, Wed and Sat. Good, unpretentious fun with both tourists and locals, and the food's reasonable, too. Daily until late.

17.3

Soufrière and the west coast

The beautiful **west coast** of St Lucia is notable for its rich and varied attractions, pretty beaches and, in parts, its decided lack of tourist traffic. You can find isolated waterfalls, hike through astounding rainforest, swim, snorkel and scuba dive in secluded bays and visit peaceful fishing villages, all without the commercial feel of the northwest coast. The area is not without its more blatant tourist draws, and these are centred around the town of **Soufrière**, which dwells in the shadows of the imposing volcanic plugs known as the **Pitons**, and the deep and lush **Marigot Bay**. Traditionally, Marigot Bay was little more than a quiet shelter for yachts and their crews, but extensive development has made it into a busy and manicured destination for the high-end tourist market. Soufrière, despite some popular attractions and a few upmarket hotels, remains quite rustic and rural, and in 2004, the region's Pitons Management Area, including the Pitons and the malodorous **Sulphur Springs**, was named a UNESCO World Heritage Site.

Arrival and getting around

A treacherously steep and twisted – if well-paved – road snakes along the west coast, making the trip from Castries to Soufrière an entertaining drive. Once in town, **buses** returning north to Castries (route #3D) and heading south to Vieux Fort (route #4F) cluster around the town square; **taxis** can be found at the square and by the waterfront (Abraham taxi ⓣ758/519-8740 also does tours). The waterfront is also the place to hop aboard convenient **water taxis**, which traverse the area servicing all of the nearby bays, many of which are hard to access from the land. Both boat (including fishing) and land tours can be organized with Mystic Man Tours (ⓣ758/459-7783) at the end of the waterfront promenade. Roundtrip to Anse Chastenet is EC$35; arrange with your driver a good time to pick you up. Local boat owners also provide rides and can be found at the same spot or at the north end of town by Hummingbird Beach, as it's known locally; negotiate a fee before you set off.

Accommodation

Staying along the west coast between Castries and Soufrière is ideal if you want to get away from heavily trafficked tourist areas and relax in some of the finest resorts and guesthouses on the island. The beaches are inviting and relatively uncrowded, and the accommodation (the vast majority in Marigot Bay or Soufrière) tends to be less resort-like and more distinctive than those further north.

Anse Chastanet and Jade Mountain Anse Chastanet ⓣ758/459-7000, ⓦwww.ansechastanet.com and ⓦwww.jademountainstlucia.com. Hidden away above a secluded cove north of Soufrière, this single luxury property is now home to two resorts built by its architect owner Nick Troubetzkoy. Rooms at the more traditional boutique *Anse Chastanet* are either at beach or hillside level, all are airy, like very luxurious treehouses (some with trees growing through them) and have lovely views. The astonishing new addition *Jade Mountain* is among the few most exclusive hotels in the Caribbean (high season room-only rate around US$1400/night), and, depending on your taste, it's either a masterpiece of modern architecture or a serious eyesore on the Caribbean landscape. From below the Pitons *Jade Mountain* resembles an unsightly concrete fortress amidst a beautiful tropical hillside; it's a relief that once inside, the rooms are so stunning they (mostly) justify the exterior. Each one is fully open to the elements on one side, allowing for a magnificent view of the Pitons over a private infinity pool lined with stained glass. There are raised bathrooms with Jacuzzis, stone-tiled floors, luxurious but not overstated furnishings, and each "sanctuary" has its own long, drawbridge-like entrance walkway. Guests at both resorts have onsite access to a variety of watersports, tennis and a great jungle biking outfit, and with a 100-step climb to the beach, you're guaranteed some exercise. Guests say the biggest draw is the escape from modern conveniences (no TVs, radios or telephones) – not to mention the attentive staff and four good restaurants. 9

Cascara Guesthouse Soufrière ⓣ758/457-1070. The best of the three local super-basic guesthouses, this rambling old property has good views over Soufrière and a large mango tree, and is right on the main road at the town's southern end. Rooms have fans and there's a shared kitchen and living room. 1

La Haut Plantation West Coast Rd Soufrière ⓣ758/459-7008, ⓦwww.lahaut.com. Set high in the hills north of Soufrière with a spectacular and sweeping view of all the area, this tranquil and informal 52-acre working plantation is a real treat. The dozen guesthouse and cottage rooms are spacious and airy, there's two cliffside pools, one of which is a dazzling infinity pool, a good restaurant and bar, plus a cosy lounge with library, pool table and TV. Shuttles to town and beaches are complimentary. 5

Ladera Resort Soufrière–Vieux Fort Rd ⓣ758/459-7323, in US 800/738-4752, ⓦwww.ladera.com. Exquisite views are key in this highly unusual hillside resort, which looks down 1000ft to the bay and is framed by the Pitons on either side. All 25 villas and suites are open to the elements on one side to maximize both the vista and the sense of being at one with nature. The effect is spectacular, and soothing dark polished wood interiors, outdoor cliffside showers, and plunge pools may mean you never leave your room. Together with one of the island's best restaurants, a great spa and the hotel's location-sensitive design, *Ladera* is unsurpassed in St Lucia. 9

Marigot Beach Dive Resort Marigot Bay ⓣ758/451-4974, ⓦwww.marigotdiveresort.com. Ensconced on the north side of the bay just a minute or two from the road's end by ferry, the resort's location has long been its main draw. All rooms (villas and studios) come with kitchen/ettes, and the pool, beach, watersports and shops manage to keep guests plenty busy; the open-air restaurant is named *Dolittle*'s after the Rex Harrison movie filmed here in the 1960s. Studios 4, villas 6

Stonefield Estate Soufrière ⓣ758/459-7037, ⓦwww.stonefieldvillas.com. These twenty spacious villas on the well-manicured grounds of an old 26-acre plantation may be Soufrière's best-kept secret: designed and decorated with nature in mind, they rival the aesthetic of any of the area's luxury hotels for half the cost. Each airy villa has slatted wooden windows and large hammocked balconies; most have separate kitchens and wonderfully spacious and private open-air showers, with flowers trailing all around. A pool, restaurant and bar are situated for amazing views of Petit Piton, and beach shuttles are free. 6

Talk to Me Cool Spot West Coast Road, Soufrière ⓣ758/459-7437, ⓦwww.talk-2me.com. Owners Michael and Andrea Abraham make guests of this budget to mid range guesthouse feel like family, especially when eating Andrea's tasty traditional Caribbean cooking. Studio rooms are small and rustic (curtained in-room toilets and showers); doubles are more spacious and decorated with hand-painted murals. The unique view of Petit Piton and Soufrière is colourful by day and sparkling by night. Negotiate price in advance; single 2, double 4. Michael also runs a taxi and tour service and can arrange jeep rental.

Ti Kaye Village Anse Cochon (nr. Anse la Raye) ⓣ758/456-8101, ⓦwww.tikaye.com. Remote, secluded and special, *Ti Kaye*'s cottages all have garden showers, hammocked balconies and ocean views, some with private plunge pools. Perfect for a romantic retreat, but also good for families who can opt for rooms adjoined by a balcony door. The black sand beach is gloriously unspoilt and with an unobtrusive beachside bar, well worth the 167 steps to reach, but if you can't face the climb there's also a small ocean view pool. 6, rates include breakfast.

Marigot Bay and around

From Castries, the West Coast Highway scoots through winding, hilly terrain and passes the signposted turn-off for **MARIGOT BAY** about five miles south. On one side the inlet is an exquisite oasis of mangroves and palm trees with only a fistful of hotels and waterside restaurants lining its shores; on the other side, however, it's fully developed with the large, upscale hotel complex known as *Discovery,* as well as a new marina village complete with French-style bakery/café and a variety of souvenir shops and restaurants. As one of the island's best-protected natural yacht harbours, it's permanently dotted with boats and their crews. Nonetheless Marigot Bay manages to retain some of its sleepy charm, particularly along the wooden walkways that line its sheltered inner lagoon.

Arriving at the end of the road in Marigot Bay (buses and taxis will drop you here), you'll find the jetty of **The Moorings Yacht Charters**, a small **police station**, a **customs office** (☎758/458-3318, VHF 16) for incoming yachts, a **taxi stand** (☎758/453-4406), as well as a small groceries shop and First National Bank counter with **ATM**. Across the Bay, the *Marigot Beach Resort* (see opposite) and its **beach** (open to non-guests and the bay's best swimming spot) are accessible 24 hours a day via a small ferry boat (EC$5 per person return, free for the resort's guests). The beach is small but pretty, with calm surf, plenty of shade and good snorkelling to its west side. Refreshments are available from the hotel's friendly restaurant, *Dolittle's*, and there's also a dive and watersports concession.

South of Marigot Bay, the highway dips through the sharp west coast hills to the next settled area, **Roseau** (ruh-ZOH), a valley with extensive banana fields, dotted with small settlements and home to the St Lucia rum distillery. From here the road winds over another hill before reaching **ANSE LA RAYE**, famous for its Friday night "Fish Fry", a laid-back street party with sound systems and delicious roasted fish that's not to be missed (from 8pm till late). Heading further south still, **CANARIES** is another peaceful fishing community, which also holds a lively food and music-oriented event (though not as big as Anse La Raye) each Saturday.

Soufrière and around

Officially established in 1746, **Soufrière** (pronounced sou-FRAY) is the oldest town in St Lucia. While it's largest settlement of the southwest coast, it is nonetheless a quiet place, charming in its lack of polish and filled with a melange of slapped-together wooden huts and modern cement structures. Naturally framed by rainforest-smothered hills and dominated by the looming **Petit Piton** – one of the twin volcanic plugs thrusting out of the sea south of the town – Soufrière's valley and deep **bay** are extremely picturesque, particularly when viewed from the hilly coastal roads as you enter town from the north or south. This unspoiled allure has often drawn the attention of film producers: scenes from *Superman II* and the Michael Caine film *Water* were shot in and around town. Most visitors just come for a quick tour of the beaches, the Sulphur Springs and the mineral baths, all fine attractions in themselves, but make sure you save an afternoon to explore the town itself, to gain a true taste of St Lucia's southwest coast.

The Town

Soufrière is small enough to explore on foot, and the jammed and narrow streets together with the lack of signposts render driving here a confusing pastime. A good place to begin is the pretty **waterfront** walkway, decorated with ornate streetlamps, benches and poinciana trees, and framed by the two town piers where tourist party boats dock. Across the street is Soufrière's **tourist office** (Mon–Fri 8am–4pm, Sat 8.30am–noon; ☎758/459-7200), a handy source of information on local sights and attractions.

▲ Jungle biking

A block inland, hemmed in by Bridge and Church streets, is the grassy **town square**, laid out by Soufrière's settlers in the eighteenth century and, during the French Revolution, the scene of numerous **executions** by guillotine. It's a local hangout today, bordered by businesses and homes built in the classic French colonial style with second-floor balconies and intricate decorative woodwork. Dominating the east end of the square is the **Lady of Assumption Church**, built in 1953 as an expansion of the original (of which only the belfry was kept, although two years later that too had to be rebuilt after a fire that razed half the town to the ground); while it looks a bit derelict from the outside, the inside is charming. At the junction of Bridge and Fredrick Clarke streets lies Excelsior Plaza, a new mini-mall with a variety of shops and an Internet café (EC$10/hour). Just across the Soufrière River at the northern end of town, a fruit and vegetable **market** is in full force on Saturdays, with a much smaller version on weekdays.

Nearby beaches

To the immediate north of Soufrière is the popular **Anse Chastanet Beach**, presided over by the resort of the same name (see p.645). Although long and wide, it's dotted with thatched huts for use by resort guests, making it difficult for others to find a place to lay a towel. But due to the proximity of the reef to land, the spot makes for one of the best shore dives in the Caribbean and is perfect for snorkelling – visibility ranges from 60 to 120ft year-round. Scuba St Lucia (see p.631) is an excellent dive operation by the water, renting both snorkelling and scuba gear. Anse Chastanet is reachable via a poor potholed road, jutting north along the coast from the main road right at the town's entrance. The two-mile track takes about fifteen minutes by car or 45 minutes on foot. A much more pleasant option is to catch a water taxi from Soufrière (EC$35 return).

For a little more privacy, head north to one of a string of other volcanic sand beaches, most accessible only by boat. Just around the corner from Anse Chastenet is **Anse Mamin**, the starting point for a jungle biking adventure with Bike St Lucia (see p.631). Also on resort property, Anse Mamin is a slightly smaller but much less crowded version of Anse Chastanet, with more room for non-guests to spread out. Further along, spots like **Anse Jambon** and **Anse Mahaut** tend to be rocky but are secluded and untouched – be sure to secure a return trip with your water taxi, though, because there's no other way back to town.

To the south of Soufrière, a right turn leads you to **Anse Mitan**, a thin but pretty strip of sand with a couple of low-key restaurants popular with yacht crews; and a little further, edging the bay between the Pitons is **Anse des Pitons**, also known as Hilton beach – originally rocky and volcanic, it's now a stretch of golden sand imported from Guyana by the *Jalousie Hilton* resort. Like Anse Chastanet, the beach is crowded with hotel paraphernalia, but the setting is stunning.

Diamond Botanical Gardens

The **Diamond Botanical Gardens** (Mon–Sat 10am–5pm, Sun 10am–3pm; EC$13 entrance, or US$30 popular guided tour including lunch, tips expected; ⓣ758/459-7565, ⓦwww.diamondstlucia.com), about a ten-minute walk from the town square, are the main attraction at Soufrière Estate, a former sugar plantation dating from 1713 that was originally part of a 2000-acre land grant bestowed by Louis XIV to the Devaux family. Tours include trips to the gardens themselves, including a still-churning waterwheel which once provided Soufrière with its first electricity, and some small **mineral baths** and a **waterfall**; come very early or in late afternoon to avoid the crowds. You can't swim by the falls, but for EC$10 you can splash about in the slightly pungent depths of three small, rather uninviting outdoor pools fed directly by volcanic hot springs. For an additional EC$5, you can disappear into a private room with two bath-size tubs (originally dating to 1784) where the water reaches 106°F. The setting is not pristine, but the waters, comparable to Aix-les-Bains in France, are said to relieve stress and arthritis and nourish the skin.

As an alternative to the gardens, a short drive farther to the east of town are two other **bathing spots**; New Jerusalem (EC$5) is a hot bath, 5-10 minutes walk from the road, and further again, Toraille is a prettier spot, though with cold water.

La Soufrière Sulphur Springs

Misleadingly billed as the world's only drive-in volcano, **La Soufrière Sulphur Springs** (daily 9am–5pm; EC$12.50; ⓣ758/459-7686), a short drive south of town off the road to Vieux Fort, is only a small fraction of a 4.5 square-mile volcano that also includes the town of Soufrière itself. There's no crater to peer into; instead, La Soufrière is known as a caldera, having erupted and collapsed into itself some 39,000 years ago. Nonetheless, it remains active to this day – theoretically, it could erupt anywhere, anytime. As La Soufrière is now classified as a **solfatara**, meaning it emits gases and vapours rather than lava and hot ash, a molten shower is extremely unlikely.

The springs themselves are a small collection of steaming, bubbling pools of sulphur-dense water and green- and yellow-tinged rocks. Turn in at the signed road and it's quickly apparent that you're in the midst of a volcano – killed off by sulphuric emissions, the vegetation becomes sparse and an eggy odour hangs in the air. The services of an official (and informative) **guide** are included in the entrance fee (gratuities optional), and they will walk you up from the car park to the viewing platforms that overlook the boiling pools. Some years ago, visitors were allowed to walk across the field, but this practice was stopped when one of the guides fell through a fissure – though sustaining severe burns, he lived to tell the tale. Now only goats hop among the rocks, cheerfully oblivious of how close they are to becoming stew. You can, however, for no extra fee, take a **dip** in the slightly cooler pools of a stream that flows through the area, so bring along a bathing suit – but note that the hydrogen sulphide in the air can be irritating for some.

An **information centre**, reached by a steep hike up the hill from the viewing points (so steep your guide won't take you there), has a nice exhibit on Caribbean volcanic activity and a short video on the springs.

The Pitons

Also of volcanic origin, the anomalous and majestic peaks of the **Pitons** dominate the southwest coast, towering more than half a mile above sea level. Visible on a clear day from as far north as the hills of Castries, these breathtaking cones are undoubtedly St Lucia's most photographed feature. Overlooking the south side of Soufrière's harbour, the northern peak is Petit Piton; south of Petit is Gros Piton, wider at the base but similar in height. Maps and publications give various elevations for each of the peaks, some even claiming that Petit is taller than Gros Piton, but the St Lucian government figures of 2480ft and 2619ft respectively are generally accepted. Although from certain vantage points the peaks appear to be next to each other, they are actually nearly three miles apart.

Beyond their aesthetic appeal, the Pitons offer an opportunity – literally – for high adventure. Though climbing up **Petit Piton** is discouraged by island authorities due to the inherent difficulty and danger of climbing a near-vertical slab of rock, some still seem willing to clamber up. This is not, however, to be advised. **Gros Piton**, while still a challenge, is much more manageable, largely thanks to the work of the **Gros Piton Tour Guides Association** (☎758/489-0136), which maintains the trail. Managed by descendants of the freedom-fighting Brigands from the community of Fond Gens Libre at the peak's southern base (considered the first settlement of freed black people in St Lucia), this group conducts hikes to the peak and also works to promote the area's historical and ecological value. It's about a four-hour hike round-trip, and the EC$75 trail fee includes a guide, which you'll need; self-guided hikes are not allowed since the path branches off in several places, making it easy to get lost. Getting to the trail independently requires a series of turns off the main road south of Gros (ask for directions), but package tours including transportation and refreshments are available.

Eating and drinking

Soufrière and Marigot Bay hold their own against the tourism strongholds of the northwest with a wealth of **eating** establishments ranging from small cafés to more elegant restaurants for relaxed evening dining. Many spots offer varied international dishes like pastas, sushi and seafood curries but don't miss out on the local Creole fare. Note that closing times are often just an estimate.

Marigot Bay

Dolittle's Marigot Bay ☎758/451-4974. A very friendly restaurant in a romantic location with a large, sociable bar at its centre. Food ranges from lunchtime pastas, burgers and seafood to an extensive and reasonably priced evening menu of good Caribbean and international fare (from EC$40 upwards).

Rainforest Hideaway Marigot Bay ☎758/286-0511. Geared to please discriminating residents of local hotels, this intimate floating champagne bar and fusion restaurant features a menu that changes daily and has live entertainment 3–4 nights a week. Children are not allowed after 6pm when dinner mains like roast quail with cocoa and orange, and jerk shrimp and scallops with parmesan risotto, lime and ginger run from EC$85-130; reservations are strongly recommended. Sun noon–10pm, Mon & Wed–Sat noon–3pm & 6–10pm.

Soufrière and around

Above Water Flora Villa, Canaries ☎758/719-1392. Location is key at this

St Lucia's interior forest reserves

Offering an absorbing alternative to the sun-and-sand culture of coastal resorts, the 19,000-acre **St Lucia Forest Reserve** stretches across the island's interior – arrestingly beautiful and teeming with exotic flora and wildlife. Though many of the trails within the reserve were used as transportation routes in the early colonial days, today people who venture in do so for pleasure rather than necessity. All the hiking routes are maintained by the **Forestry Department** (Ⓣ758/450-2231 or 2078, Ⓦwww.slumaffe.org), who also determine public access (some parts of the interior are restricted) and provide trained **hiking guides**. For most trails, a flat fee of EC$35 covers both access and the services of a guide; it's best to call ahead to ensure guides will be on site as ranger stations often close early if no one has come by. In addition to the routes described below, it's also possible to reach the trails on a tour with a Castries-based operator such as Jungle Tours (Ⓣ758/715-3438) or SunLink Tours (Ⓣ758/456-9100).

Union Nature Trail

The short, easy **Union Nature Trail** (Mon–Fri 8.30am–4pm; EC$10) starts about ten minutes' drive from Castries, in the Forestry Department's headquarters, which also contains a medicinal herb garden, a depressing **mini-zoo** and an interpretive centre where you can learn about endangered species. The easy 1.6km **trail** loops through dry forest that was once planted as a tree nursery, returning after about an hour of walking if you don't make too many stops.

To get there, turn off the Castries–Gros Islet Highway onto the Allan Bousquet Highway (not marked; if you pass a sign denoting the boundary of Castries, you've gone too far). Along a winding 1.5km road, you'll pass three large fences on your right; turn right at the end of the third to reach the centre. Bus route #1B will bring you along the main road near to the centre from Castries.

Barre de L'Isle Trail

The "island ridge" **Barre de L'Isle Trail** (Mon–Fri 8.30am–3pm; EC$35) bisects the Central Forest Reserve and the island itself. It's a worthwhile, mildly challenging adventure that provides a good look at St Lucia's richly diverse topography and mountain flora and fauna: throughout, the trail alternates between a thick overhead cover of trees and wide-open areas with expansive vistas in all directions. The two-hour hike – three if you extend the trek and climb the ridge of Mount La Combe – is marked well enough to go it alone, though a guide will be able to identify bird, tree and plant species along the way.

The signposted start of the Barre de L'Isle trail strikes into the forest directly from the central Castries–Dennery highway, opposite the **rangers' hut** and a twenty- to thirty-minute drive or bus journey from downtown Castries. Route #2B buses leave from Manoel Street in Castries.

Enbas Saut Waterfalls Trail

Located in the **Edmund Forest Reserve** which spreads over the southwestern interior, the **Enbas Saut Waterfalls Trail** (Mon–Fri 8.30am–3pm, Sat mornings only; EC$35) offers a fairly strenuous 5km (2.5hr), guided loop down to the base of two cascading waterfalls on the Troumassée river. Bathing in the pools of rainforest water is encouraged and will rejuvenate you for the return hike back up.

The eight-kilometre drive to the Edmund Reserve takes about an hour from the west coast. From Soufrière take the inland road to Fond St Jacques, bypassing the turn-off to Morne Coubaril Estate and the south. The road to the trails is signposted off the main road, and after a very rough thirty-minute drive (requiring 4WD), a wooden forestry department **ranger station** marks the start of the trail. Relying on public transport to get here is not an option.

bar and restaurant known locally as *Del's Place*; easy to find at a bend in the main road overlooking Canaries from the north. The back terrace features one of the island's most stupendous views, and the cosy upstairs restaurant serves really tasty Creole fare like *bouillon* and stewed chicken or fish, with interesting Haitian art and local woodcarvings dotted around.

Dasheene *Ladera Resort*, Soufrière ⓣ758/459-7323. An eclectic mix of West Indian, Asian, Italian and vegetarian cuisine, the majority of it creative and artful (and pricey), though the buffet lunches can be hit-or-miss. Try the pool/bar menu for a simpler and less expensive option. Even if you don't dine here, make sure you come up for drinks at sunset; the views of the Pitons and bay below are astounding. Daily 7–10am, noon–2.30pm & 6.30–9pm.

Fedo's New Venture New Development, Soufrière ⓣ758/459-5220. A local joint at the inland end of town with a rather bland interior but a very inexpensive and appetising menu. A sizeable portion of Creole or lime butter kingfish or tuna is only EC$20, and sandwiches and rotis are under EC$10. Mon–Sat 9am–5pm.

Gee's Bon Manje La Pearl Estate, Soufrière ⓣ758/457-1418. Located on the main road just past *Still Plantation*, this popular bar and restaurant frequented by locals and tourists alike is in a smart wooden cabin raised above the ground. All the tables on its surrounding veranda have artful painted-on designs of different board games from chess to snakes and ladders, and the reasonable menu has all the Creole favourites (EC$30) plus seafood and lobster (EC$40–70). Open 7 days till 11pm.

Hummingbird Beach Resort Anse Chastanet Road, Soufrière ⓣ758/459-7232. A popular hangout for visitors at guesthouses all over town, especially for drinks at sunset by the beachside pool. It's hard to see what you're eating at the dark restaurant tables and the service is exasperatingly slow, but the seafood is excellent, with conch, king crab and octopus available seasonally. Daily 7am–11pm.

Still Beach and Plantation Resorts Soufrière ⓣ758/459-5049. A better bet for food than the neighbouring *Hummingbird*, *Still Beach* serves good Creole and international fare (EC$30 upwards) with fantastic views of Petit Piton. For a change of scene but similar (if a little cheaper) menu, have lunch at the co-owned *Still Plantation* (ⓣ758/459-7224), set on a slightly dilapidated but atmospheric 400-acre working cocoa plantation just to the east of town. Highlights at the latter include a Creole lunch buffet (EC$40) and Guyanese pepperpot; a rich and dark (normally beef) stew made with cassareep, the extracted oil from the cassava plant (EC$30).

17.4

The south coast

St Lucia's **southern coast** boasts some striking scenery: south of Soufrière, the mountain road snakes about and dips inland before swinging towards the ocean to reveal a string of coastal villages and, ultimately, the island's second largest town, **Vieux Fort**, all framed by the towering ranges of the Central Forest Reserve. This southwest corner was once an **Amerindian** stronghold, and petroglyphs found throughout the area suggest a long and fruitful habitation by the Arawaks and Caribs. After Europeans arrived, the area was home to large **plantations** producing coconuts, sugar cane and, more recently, bananas, though today these have mostly been replaced by smaller farms, fishing enterprises and light industry at the Vieux Fort Industrial Estate. Also ever-present are resort development plans, with the area's low-key nature likely to be impacted by plans for a giant *Ritz Carlton* and other resorts close to Vieux Fort.

Arrival, information and getting around

Most visitors arrive in St Lucia at **Hewanorra International Airport** in Vieux Fort, and onward transportation throughout the island is readily available from here. Once through customs, your first stop should be the helpful **tourist booth** (Mon–Fri 8am–last flight, Sat & Sun 10am–last flight; ⓣ758/454-6644), where you can pick up brochures and maps and get the low-down on the latest official taxi rates. Also lining the arrival area are a half-dozen **car rental** booths which keep limited hours (mostly noon–6pm) and may not stay open for late flights, so be sure to make prearrangements as necessary (the best rates are available from companies listed on p.627). The dispatcher at the **taxi** stand across from the rental booths can arrange official taxis. Taxis to Castries from the airport or anywhere in Vieux Fort travel the wide but pot holed East Coast Highway and turn inland towards the capital at Dennery. The **fare** to Castries is EC$175 (or US$65) and the 33-mile trip takes a little over an hour. Vieux Fort to Soufrière is the same price, and the 29-mile ride takes around 45 minutes now that the road has been predominantly paved. To travel by **bus**, you'll first need to get to Vieux Fort by taxi – about EC$10 (or, if you're patient, you can try flagging down a bus from the main road). Buses to Castries (route #2H) leave from New Dock Road and those to Soufrière (route #4F) leave from Clarke Street, next to the town traffic light and a Shell service station.

Accommodation

The area **south of Soufrière**, through the fishing villages of Choiseul and Laborie to Vieux Fort, is more residential than tourist-oriented and offers a relaxed alternative to the relentless activity of the northwest coast.

Balenbouche Estate Balenbouche Bay ⓣ758/455-1244, ⓦwww.balenbouche.com. Scattered with fruit trees, sugar factory remains and even a few Amerindian rock carvings, this family-run seventy-acre plantation just south of Choiseul is charming, low-key and different. Furnished with eclectic antiques, rooms in the estate house are clean and cosy with a shared bathroom, full of historical atmosphere but with none of the pomp; nearby cottages have fun, unique features like swinging couches and outdoor (covered) kitchens. Meals available daily, and secluded beaches are just a short walk away. House rooms ②, private cottages ④

Coconut Bay Resort and Spa Vieux Fort ⓣ758/456-9999, ⓦwww.coconutbayresortandspa.com. Currently the only resort of its kind in the south, Coconut Bay is a sprawling 85-acre all-inclusive on the beach just five minutes from the airport. Three pools, a waterpark and activities centre will keep kids happy; tennis courts, spa and jogging trails appeal to adults; though the restaurant is not one of the island's best. ⑦

Juliette's Lodge Beanfield, Vieux Fort ⓣ758/454-5300, ⓦwww.julietteslodge.com. Conveniently close to Hewanorra International Airport and Anse de Sables beach, *Juliette's* is popular amongst both airline crews and the windsurfer crowd. The 24 rooms and three apartments are comfortable and clean with a/c, cable TV and balconies with views of the Maria Islands. Mountain bikes are available for hire, and a small pool and a lively restaurant serving basic but hearty fare are onsite. Rooms ③, apartments ⑤

Mirage Beach Resort Laborie Bay, Laborie ⓣ758/455-9763, ⓦwww.cavip.com/mirage. Located right on the bay in the serene, beautiful fishing village of Laborie, this divine spot offers five comfortable rooms on the beach, all with kitchenette and terrace; the intimate beachside setting is a rarity on the island. A pristine reef not far from shore makes for excellent snorkelling. The friendly owners also have a relaxing French/Creole open-air restaurant and bar onsite. ④

The Reef Anse de Sables Beach, Vieux Fort ⓣ758/454-3418, ⓦwww.slucia.com/windsurf. Basic but comfortable beachside accommodation with private bath, aimed at the wind and kite-surfer crowd. The bargain rates include a tasty breakfast. ②

The southwest coast

South of Soufrière, the west coast road meanders through hilly inland terrain, passing several small settlements before descending abruptly towards the coast and the collection of villages known as **CHOISEUL** (shwa-ZEL). The village of Choiseul itself is a quiet place with little to do or see, especially now that the waterfront is dominated by a concrete fishing complex built by the Japanese in 2003 – but the surrounding area is best known for being the origin of most of St Lucia's crafts. Each village has its own speciality – like pottery, khuskhus grass floormats, wicker baskets, or white cedar chairs – depending on the available raw materials. The **Choiseul Arts and Craft Development Centre** (open Mon–Fri 9am–4.30pm; ⓣ758/459-9941; ⓦwww.choiseulstlucia.com), about half a mile south of the village centre in **La Fargue**, and **Crafty Creations** (open Mon–Fri 8am–6pm, Sat 9am–5pm, Sun noon–3pm, ⓣ758/717-1917), just down the road, have the best selection.

Between Choiseul and the friendly fishing village of **Laborie** a few miles southeast is **Balenbouche Estate**, an eighteenth-century plantation well worth a visit even if you're not staying there (daily 9am–6pm; EC$5, or EC$15 with guide – call ahead; see p.653 for accommodation). Dotting the serene grounds are some spectacular sugar factory ruins, including a massive sunken waterwheel.

Vieux Fort and around

Jammed with traffic, **VIEUX FORT** is St Lucia's second largest town, a busy commercial centre for businesses based around **Hewanorra International Airport**, just north of downtown. Both the town and the airport lie on a relatively flat plain that slopes gently towards the north and the south-central mountains, and as the southern tip of St Lucia comes to a point around Vieux Fort, Hewanorra's runway stretches almost entirely from the east to the west coast of the island.

Vieux Fort itself is more of a place of business than one to explore; most visitors only glimpse it on their journey to and from the airport. However, just south of town at St Lucia's most southerly point lies **Moule à Chique Lighthouse**, actually intended for Saint Lucia Cape in South Africa but brought here by mistake. It's one of the finest viewpoints on the island, reached by bearing left onto New Dock Road at the town roundabout and then left again into the hills. The **Anse de Sables Beach** stretches about a mile from the foot of the cliffs here to Pointe Sable, and is the favoured place to swim near Vieux Fort, as well as to wind- and kite surf thanks to excellent conditions and the presence of watersports operator The Reef

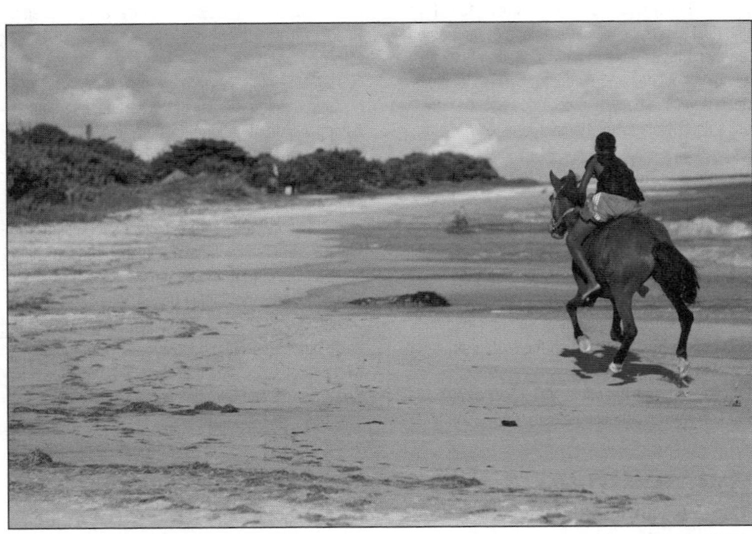

▲ Anse de Sables

(9am–7pm; ⓣ758/454-3418, ⓦwww.slucia.com/windsurf). The expansive seashore is usually windy and has few trees for shade; nor are there toilet facilities except at the restaurants – but it's a still a pretty spot. At the southern end of the beach is the **Maria Islands Interpretation Centre**, the meeting point for all visits to the Maria Islands.

Maria Islands Nature Reserve

Just over half a mile off the Anse de Sables shore are the two scrubby, windswept cays that comprise the **Maria Islands Nature Reserve**. A breeding area for numerous **sea birds** including frigates and terns, the islands are also home to two rare reptiles, one of which – the **kouwés snake** – is found nowhere else in the world. A yard long with blue eyes and dark green and brown markings, the harmless *kouwés* (cou-RESS) was eradicated on the mainland by mongooses introduced by sugar cane planters; today, they number a mere one hundred or so. The other reptile is the St Lucia's *zandoli tè*, or ground lizard, found only here and on nearby Praslin Island, where some were transferred to ensure a second habitat. At around 14 inches long with a bright blue tail, yellow belly, and black back with white spots, the male vividly displays all the colours of the St Lucian flag; females, brown with darker vertical stripes, are harder to spot.

Only the larger of the two islands, Maria **Major**, can be visited (there's not much to see on the 4 acres of Maria **Minor**), and **authorized guides** from the St Lucia National Trust are essential (three hours; EC$100 per person in a group, more for one person; contact the Trust head office at Pigeon Point ⓣ758/452-5005). Beginning at the Interpretation Centre – a one-room **museum** open only for tours with small displays on marine life and Amerindian culture (including a human skull found in the area) – trips consist of an unchallenging walking trail and stops for swimming and snorkelling (bring your own gear) at a short but comely **beach** of golden sand with a **reef** a few yards offshore.

Eating and drinking

Though there are fewer choices than along the north and west coasts, the south has its share of good places to **eat**, including a couple of excellent options near Hewanorra airport.

Debbie's Soufrière-Vieux Fort Road, Laborie ⓣ758/455-1625. A large and well-presented restaurant just off the highway where Aunty Debbie cooks up feasts of delicious seafood, lamb, pork and chicken with large portions of creamed pumpkin, mashed potatoes, fried plantains and corn cakes (mains from EC$20). The island-leading Sunday lunch buffet is a special treat with a huge choice, including home-made desert buffet with everything from profiteroles to passionfruit cake; all for a remarkable EC$50. Seven days, 7am–10pm.

Old Plantation Yard Commercial Street, Vieux Fort ⓣ758/454-6040. Local specialities prepared in an old residence dating to 1890 and served in a casual backyard patio of picnic tables located just opposite the town's fruit and vegetable market. Stewed meats and fish broths are the specialities, with a selection of local juices. Come on a Saturday morning for a traditional Creole breakfast of roast bakes (bread), cocoa tea, saltfish and smoked herring, all for only EC$10. Mon–Sat 8am–6pm.

The Reef Beach Café Anse de Sables ⓣ758/454-3418. A busy beachside restaurant and bar serving fast food fare like burgers, pizza and West Indian dishes for a predominantly young crowd of tourists and windsurfers from the attached watersports outfit and students from a nearby medical school. Inexpensive rooms also available, free Wi-Fi access throughout. Tues–Sun 8am–10pm; Mon high season only 8am–6pm.

17.5

The east coast

Churned up by the Caribbean trade winds, the pounding waters of the Atlantic have carved out a rough and jagged **east coast** on St Lucia, one that up until now has been almost entirely ignored by visitors. Still characterized for the most part by lively surf smashing against rocky and cliff-lined shores and a verdant blanket of banana plants, the area is now undergoing a dramatic condo, resort and golf course development, with concrete "reefs" put in to pacify the incoming breakers. A number of secluded oases persist, providing both a visual and atmospheric contrast to the more populated areas of the island.

St Lucia's **coastal highway** parallels the eastern shoreline from Vieux Fort to Dennery, where it cuts inland, heading up and over the rainforest to Castries. It's the preferred route for buses and taxis travelling the 33 miles between Vieux Fort and the capital, but it's still a little potholed and can make for a disconcerting drive. Along the way, east-coast **bus** stops include Micoud, Desruisseaux, Mon Repos, Praslin and Dennery, but erratic scheduling ensures that exploration by bus is not particularly easy.

Micoud and the Fond Estate

Named in honour of the French Governor de Micoud who ruled St Lucia from 1768 to 1771, the small town of **MICOUD** spreads outwards from the sheltered bay of Port Micoud. The suitability of the harbour for fishing (a rarity on the rough coast) and the ready availability of fresh water from the **Troumassée River** are the principal factors cited by archeologists as reasons for the extensive **Amerindian** presence here; some nine settlements are believed to have existed, all rapidly abandoned after the arrival of the Europeans in the eighteenth century. Aside from the quiet bay dotted with fishing boats and churches, Micoud is best known as an enthusiastic focal point for two island-wide Carnivalesque religious **festivals**: **La Rose** in August and **La Marguerite** in October; see p.629 for more on these.

Just north of town and well signposted from the main road is the **Fond Estate**, home of a new and exciting quadbike tour run by **ATV Paradise Tours** (Ⓣ758/455-3245; Ⓦwww.atvstlucia.com; no experience necessary). With the focus as much on the scenery and history as on the bikes themselves, the guided trips last three hours (US$120/bike based on two people per ATV or US$100/individual, including drinks and safety helmets) with frequent stops: in the rainforest; by a freshwater river for swimming; at a long-disused but well-preserved water-powered sugar mill; and by the beach. Taking in this full variety of environments in half a day is a rarity in the Caribbean, and well worth the effort to explore.

Mamiku Gardens and The Fox Grove Inn

Just a few minutes north of Micoud close to **Mon Repos** lies one of the most serene places in St Lucia, the beautifully landscaped fifteen-acre **Mamiku Gardens** (daily 9am–5pm; EC$20, or $25 with guide – call ahead to arrange a tour; Ⓣ758/455-3729, Ⓦwww.mamiku.com). The former plantation is teeming with brightly coloured blooms such as orchids, ginger and heliconia, as well as a variety of **birds** including white-breasted thrashers and gold-crested orielles, and there's a

Creole medicinal herb garden too. A network of short **walking trails**, each with suitably located benches, provide a shaded way to explore the gardens; one trail loops over the hilltop to the site of a former British army station where soldiers fought the **Brigands** from 1794 (see History p.632) – some interesting boards help to explain the history. Anyone interested in doing a longer walk here can join the fortnightly guided **hikes** which go deeper into the rainforest. Back at the garden's main house, you can end a pleasant afternoon's stroll with **tea** on the veranda amidst a lovely variety of tropical plants.

A ten-minute walk southwest of the gardens is the east coast's finest **dining** and **accommodation** option, the *Fox Grove Inn* (Ⓣ758/455-3800, Ⓦwww.foxgroveinn.com; ❷). The rooms are basic but charming, most with gorgeous sea-views (only partially spoilt by the new resort and golf-course development), and all have full breakfast included; two spacious two-bedroom apartments are available weekly. A pool table and a large, inviting swimming pool are onsite. The reasonably priced restaurant, open to non-guests as well, features delicately presented fresh seafood and lobster (seasonally) – and a famous garlic soup – all prepared by a chef with three decades' experience at five-star hotels in Europe. Portions are generous, the salads excellent (try the smoked king fish) and, as from the rooms, the views over acres of banana plantation to Praslin Bay and the Fregates are second to none.

Praslin Island and the Fregate Islands Nature Reserve

A haven for birdwatchers, the **Fregate Islands Nature Reserve** is centred around two tiny **cays** just a few yards offshore and named after the seagoing **frigate** (or fregate) **bird** that nests here between late March and early August. Glossy jet-black birds with forked tail feathers, male frigates have distinctive red or bright orange throat pouches which are expanded during mating time to attract females. The islands themselves are not accessible, and though the nearby peninsula was always the best spot to do a walking tour and have the best views (including up to 43 species of birds), the opening of a new condo resort and golf course has made the future of the southern section of the **Eastern Nature Trail** uncertain. It seems likely that some new, rerouted trails will be opened but in the meantime the best views of the islands are by binoculars from nearby **Praslin Island** (pronounced PRAW-lay). **Atlantic Coast Tours**, spearheaded by Peter Ernest, run tours in this area and offer a wealth of information on the local environment, including on bird species (Ⓣ758/455-3163 or 384-7056; book in advance; tours are 1 to 3 hours; from US$12/person plus an additional shared US$20 guide fee for groups fewer than four).

Praslin Island itself has a small beach perfect for swimming, wading, and for picnics; your only company is likely to be a few *zandoli tè* (see p.655) – guides are necessary only for the boat trip across. Back on the mainland, a tour around the northern section of **Praslin Bay** presents another opportunity to explore the rugged Atlantic Coast, and can easily be seen on the same day. What remains of the **Eastern Nature Trail** is still very much worth a look; offering a more active 1- to 3-mile (your preference) stroll along gorgeous craggy coastline north of the resort area, you'll see a large variety of bird and plant species, and – if you're really lucky – a St Lucia boa constrictor.

Dennery and Grande Anse

Previously known as Anse Canot (in reference to the carved canoes that once lined the bay), **DENNERY** was given its current name in the eighteenth century by the French in honour of Count D'Ennery, governor general of the Windward Islands from 1766–70. The village extends inland from a deep and protected **bay**, with uninhabited **Dennery Island** at its northern tip. Although once a major export

Turtle watching

In conjunction with the Department of Fisheries, Heritage Tours organises an annual programme of **turtle watches** at Grande Anse and Desbarras beaches, allowing around 1000 visitors each season to experience the stirring spectacle of leatherback turtles laying their eggs. The all-night watches take place Mon–Sat in leatherback season (late-March to late-August) and cost US$95, which covers transport from your hotel, tent expenses, dinner, breakfast and sleeping mats; you'll have to bring your own torch, insect repellent and warm clothing, as nights can be cool and breezy. Once at the beach, you settle into a rustic tent village and take turns patrolling the beach. Whenever a turtle is spotted, you'll be called to have a look. The watches have become very popular, so to ensure a place, it's best to contact Heritage Tours well in advance (Castries; ⓣ758/451-6058, 458-1454; ⓦwww.heritagetoursstlucia.org).

centre for agricultural produce, Dennery has become one of St Lucia's busiest **fishing** centres since the addition of the large, Japanese-funded Daito Complex and Pier processing facility; much of the local fish served in the major restaurants around the island comes from here. The **town** itself is a jumble of compact streets with a few bars but nothing much of interest save the Saturday night **fish fry** on the seafront. With a focus as much on the music and dance as on the fish, this is a pleasant, low-key affair; less developed or touristy than Gros Islet but more of a party than Anse La Raye on a Friday.

Around two miles north of Dennery is **Anse Louvet**, a remote and spectacular bay and river lagoon accessible on foot (1 hour along a straightforward path) or by 4WD from the community of **Aux Leon**, itself a turn off the main road close to Grande Riviere. Whilst the area is slated for development, including the construction of a concrete off shore reef, it may take some years for the plans to be realized; in the meantime the spot could well be the finest beach coastline in St Lucia.

Another four miles **further** north, the wide, windswept **Grande Anse beach** boasts more than a mile of blond sand set against a backdrop of cliffs and hills. Once part of a plantation estate, the bay sits in the middle of an area comprising several nearby beaches, including Anse Lavoutte to the north. As with Anse Lavoutte, the beach is a favoured nesting spot of the giant **leatherback turtles**, and turtle-watching tours are given throughout the egg-laying season (see box, above). Roads are dirt and gravel tracks that often become impassable after rains – a sedan car might make it but a 4WD is a safer bet, and it's a good idea to ask locals about current conditions. Access is easiest from the west coast at Choc Bay via the paved Allan Bousquet Highway. At Babonneau, turn off onto the gravel track that leads to Desbarras village, from where another track leads down to Grande Anse. The seven-mile ride from Choc Bay can take up to eighty minutes.

18

Barbados

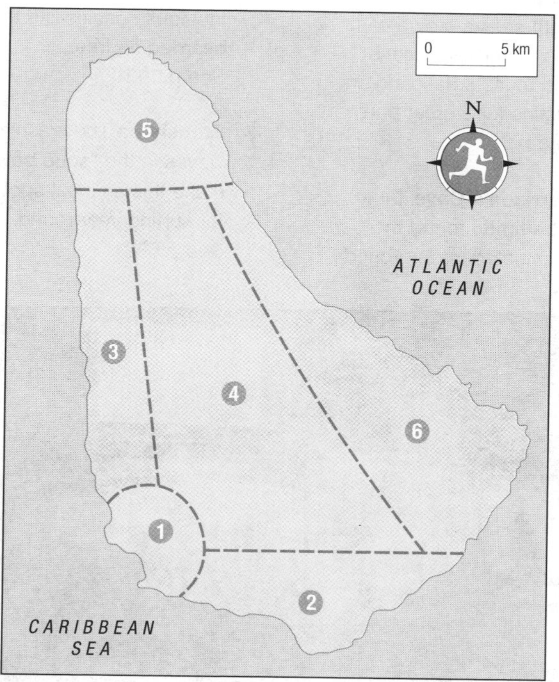

Barbados highlights

* **Crop Over** One of the most enjoyable festivals in the Caribbean, this is an extended party of calypso, dancing and rum-drinking. See p.664

* **Oistins Fish Fry** Friday night sees a crowd of young and old Bajans and tourists descend on Oistins for a great party. See p.677

* **Harrison's Cave** Take a tram ride round the illuminated underground caverns full of spectacular calcitic formations. See p.687

* **Andromeda Botanical Gardens** Probably the finest gardens in the Caribbean, packed with fabulous species like the bearded fig tree. See p.692

* **Bathsheba** The crashing waves in the "soup bowl" make this an ideal spot for surfing year-round. See p.692

▲ Oistins fish fry

Introduction and basics

Equally attractive to Caribbean first-timers and experienced travellers, **Barbados** is justifiably one of the most popular islands in the region. Certain pleasures are quite obvious – the delightful climate, the azure sea and brilliant white sandy beaches – but an engaging blend of cultures and the sheer diversity of tourist attractions help set it apart from neighbouring destinations. And while many visitors rarely stray from their hotels and guesthouses, those who make an effort find a proud island scattered with an impressive range of colonial sites and dramatic scenery in hidden caves, cliffs and gullies.

A **British colony** for over three centuries, Barbados retains something of a British feel: place names, cricket, horse-racing and polo, Anglican parish churches and even a hilly district known as Scotland. But despite the Britishness, this is a distinctly **West Indian country**, covered by a patchwork of sugar cane fields and dotted with rum shops, where calypso is the music of choice and flying fish the favourite food.

The people of Barbados, known as **Bajans**, take great pride in their tiny island of 430 square kilometres and 270,000 people which has produced writers like George Lamming, calypsonians like the Mighty Gabby, and cricket players including the great Sir Gary Sobers, who have for decades held an influence way out of proportion to the size of their home country.

Tourism inevitably plays a major part in the country's economy but revenues have generally been put to sound use and many facilities are Bajan-owned. The infrastructure and public transport are good and there are few signs of poverty. Development had, until recently, been relatively discreet but Barbados is undergoing a major construction boom that is threatening some of its natural beauty.

Where to go

Chief among the island's attractions are its **old plantation houses**, like St Nicholas Abbey and Sunbury; superb **botanical gardens** at Andromeda and the Flower Forest; and the elegant **military buildings of the Garrison area** and Gun Hill Signal Station. The prize draw, however, is Harrison's Cave and its illuminated limestone labyrinths. The capital, **Bridgetown**, is a lively place to visit with an excellent national museum and great nightlife in its bars and clubs. Small and largely untouristed **Speightstown** – once a thriving and wealthy port – is a good place to wander for a couple of hours then grab a drink on a terrace overlooking the sea. Alternatively, head over to Bathsheba to enjoy the bracing sea breezes and rugged scenery. And, of course, there are the beaches, from the often crowded strips such at **Accra Beach** and **Mullins Bay** to tiny but superb patches of palm-fringed sand in the southeast – all open to the public.

When to go

For many visitors, Barbados's tropical climate is its leading attraction – hot and sunny year-round. The weather is best during the **high season** from mid-December to mid-April with rainfall low and the heat tempered by cooling trade winds. The peak season also brings the biggest crowds and the highest prices.

In the **summer**, and particularly in September and October, the heat can become uncomfortable and the humidity oppressive. September is also the most threatening month for **hurricanes**. The season officially runs from early June to late October, but the island hasn't had a direct hit since 1955.

Getting there

All flights arrive at **Grantley Adams International Airport** located on the south coast about twelve kilometres east of Bridgetown and within easy striking distance

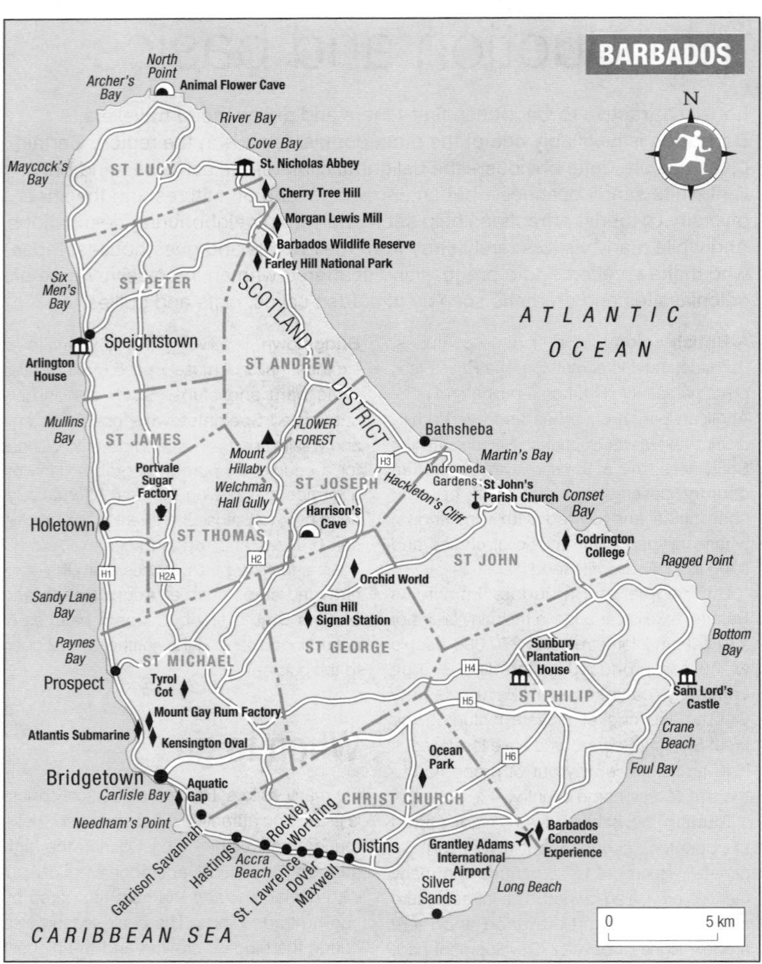

of all the main south coast resorts. **Buses** (B$1.50) between the airport and Bridgetown run every half-hour, stopping at or near most of the south coast resorts en route; services to the resorts on the west coast are less frequent. From the airport, expect to pay around B$58 for a **taxi** to Holetown on the west coast, B$73 to Speightstown in the northwest, B$30 to Crane Bay and B$40 to the resorts in the southwest.

Cruise ships arrive at Deep Water Harbour just north of Bridgetown, and taxis are always available to ferry passengers around the island.

Information

Brochures on the main attractions and events and a good road map are available from the **Barbados Tourism Authority** (BTA) which has an office at Harbour Road in Bridgetown (ⓣ427-2623, Mon–Fri 8.15am–4.30pm; ⓦwww.barbados.org) and a desk in the luggage hall at the airport and at the Deepwater Harbour. They are also available from most hotels.

While there is no detailed listings publication, the free fortnightly **magazine** *Friends* – available from the tourist office and some hotels – carries information on many events. Other useful publications, also widely available, are the handy pocket-size *Barbados in a Nutshell,* which includes an excellent map, and *Ins & Outs of Barbados.* Keep an eye also on the daily papers, the *Nation* in particular, and flyers posted up around the island.

Other worthwhile resources include the websites Ⓦwww.totallybarbados.org and Ⓦwww.funbarbados.com.

Money and costs

The island's unit of currency is the **Barbados dollar (B$)**, which comes in notes of 2, 5, 10, 20, 50 and 100 dollars, and coins of 1, 5, 10 and 25 cents and $1. The **rate of exchange** is fixed roughly at B$2 to US$1; the US dollar is also widely accepted. Prices are normally quoted in B$, with the exception of accommodation, which is almost universally quoted in US$, and we have followed this practice in this chapter.

Banking hours are generally Monday to Thursday 8am–3pm and Friday 8am–5pm. Bridgetown, Holetown and Speightstown have numerous banks, and there are branches at most of the south coast resorts. Most have **ATMs** and some allow you to make cash withdrawals on either your debit or credit card. Many hotels will also exchange money. Major credit cards are widely accepted for payment.

Barbados is one of the more expensive countries in the Caribbean with **prices** for many items comparable to what you'd pay at home. Bargaining is usually frowned upon but during the off season (May–Nov) it can be worth enquiring about reduced rates for accommodation or car rental. Many hotels and restaurants automatically add a **service charge** of 10 percent and not all advertised prices include VAT.

Getting around

While the **roads** in Barbados are mostly good and the distances short, car rental prices are fairly high, starting at around B$150 per day and B$600 per week (peak season). Mini-mokes (open-sided buggies) that you'll see all over the island are cheapest. As **car rental** companies here are all local, it can be easier to arrange rentals once you've arrived. Reliable firms include: Coconut (Ⓣ437-0297), Jones (Ⓣ426-5030), Mangera (Ⓣ436-0562) and National (Ⓣ422-0603), or for a mini-moke, Stoutes (Ⓣ416-4456).

The **bus system** in Barbados is excellent, with blue government buses and yellow privately owned smaller buses running all over the island. Fares are a flat rate of B$1.50. White **minivans** known as "route taxis" pack in passengers and stop anywhere en route, with the emphasis on speed rather than comfort. Posted with red-and-white signs, bus stops are never far apart in the more populated areas, and are marked with "to City" or "Out of City", depending on whether the bus is going to or from Bridgetown. There are two main bus terminals in Bridgetown: on Fairchild Street for the southern and eastern areas, and on Princess Alice Highway for transport north; other major bus stations are in Speightstown and Oistins. See Ⓦwww.transport.com for details of the government bus routes and timetables.

Finding a **taxi** – identifiable by the Z on their licence plates – is rarely a problem. Fares are regulated but there are no meters, so be sure to agree on the price beforehand.

Accommodation

There is no shortage of **accommodation** in Barbados with most of the pricier, swankier options on the west coast and thinning out considerably as you continue north towards Speightstown. On the south coast, where the beaches are just as good (or better – though you'll share them with more crowds), accommodation is generally much more reasonably priced, with plenty of affordable guesthouses, particularly around Worthing and St Lawrence Gap. A handful of small, long-established hotels do a light trade on the wild east coast around Bathsheba. Several resorts offer all-inclusive packages which can be good value but less so if you want to sample the myriad of great restaurants and bars around the island. The BTA website (see above) has listings of recommended accommodation options and links.

Room prices vary enormously throughout the year with some places charging double during the Christmas holiday period what they charge in September or October, when you're likely to get better deals. Off-peak, however, many hotels do most of their building or refurbishing work, which may be disadvantageous so it's advisable to check in advance.

Food and drink

The tourist market has produced a staggering variety of places to eat though options for vegetarians are limited. It's well worth sampling traditional Bajan cuisine, especially at one of the ubiquitous all-you-can-eat Sunday buffets.

Unsurprisingly **fresh seafood** is the island's speciality including snapper, tuna, dolphin fish (otherwise known as mahi-mahi), fresh prawns and lobster. Most popular of all is the flying fish – which permeates Bajan culture from the kitchen to clothing logos.

Other traditional Bajan dishes not to be missed include the national dish of **cou-cou** (a cornmeal and okra pudding), **saltfish** and pepperpot (a spicy meat-and-okra stew). If you're feeling brave you might try the Bajan weekend speciality, pudding and **souse**. It's an acquired taste: steamed sweet potato stuffed in a cleaned pig's intestine served with cuts of pork – traditionally from the head and feet, though some now use the leaner cuts – pickled in onion, lime and hot peppers.

For snacks, you'll find **cutters** (bread rolls with a meat, cheese or fish filling), coconut bake, and more substantial **rotis** (flat, unleavened bread wrapped around a filling of curried meat or vegetables).

Rum is the liquor of choice for many Bajans. An estimated 2500 rum shops dot the island, which form an integral part of Bajan social life. The popular local beer is Banks.

Mail and Communications

Barbados's **postal service** is extremely efficient. The General Post Office (GPO) is

Public holidays and festivals

Mid-January Barbados Jazz Festival ⓣ429-2084, ⓦwww.barbadosjazzfestival.com – week of international jazz artists performing at venues across the island

January 21 Errol Barrow Day

Mid-February Holetown Festival, ⓦwww.holetownfestivalbarbados – week of events showcasing local arts, crafts and Barbadian history

late Feb–mid-March Holder's Season ⓣ432-6385 ⓦwww.holders.net – international performing arts festival

Last week in April Congaline Carnival – lively music fest down at Dover (St Lawrence Gap) featuring soca, calypso, reggae and steel pan into the night.

Easter weekend Oistins Fish Festival ⓣ428-6738 – three-day extravaganza of fishing-related competitions, food stalls, music and other fun activities.

April 28 National Heroes Day

June–August Crop Over ⓦwww.barbados.org/cropover.htm – revived traditional festival celebrating the end of the sugar harvest, now involving weeks of street parades, steel pan music and calypso competitions, culminating in Kadooment Day, a full-on rum-soaked costumed street carnival.

August 1 Emancipation Day

First Monday in August Kadooment Day

November 30 Independence Day

located in Bridgetown (Mon–Fri 7.30am–5pm) and there are branches across the island, in the larger towns and villages as well as at the airport and cruise terminal (Mon–Fri 8.15am–3pm).

Calling within Barbados is simple – most hotels provide a telephone in each room and local calls are usually free. You'll also see **Bartel** phone booths all over the island, and these can be used for local and international calls. Most of the booths take phonecards only, which are available from hotels, post offices and some shops. The Barbados **country code** is ⓣ246. For **police**, ring ⓣ211; **fire**, ⓣ311; and **ambulance**, ⓣ511.

If you want to use **the Internet**, many hotels will let you use their computers for free or for a nominal charge, and Wi-Fi is increasingly available. Alternatively in St Lawrence Gap, *Bean 'n' Bagel* (see p.679) offers Internet access, as does Global Business Centre, a stall in the West Coast Mall in Holetown, and the GPO in Bridgetown.

Opening hours, holidays and festivals

Shops and businesses are typically **open** Monday to Friday 9am–5pm, with some shops open at the weekend too, typically Saturday 9am–2pm. Barbados observes the holidays and festivals listed in the box opposite.

Sports and outdoor activities

While Barbados features some fine **diving and snorkelling**, the island is also renowned for more leisurely pursuits, from golfing to cricket, the local obsession.

Diving and watersports

There's a myriad of good reef and wreck diving to be enjoyed off Barbados, including the Caribbean's top wreck site, the *Stavronikita*, a sunken Greek freighter. Barbados boasts plenty of reputable dive operators (see box overleaf), most of whom will provide transport to and from your hotel. Prices can vary dramatically between dive shops and according to season and group size – you'll also pay less if you've your own gear. Generally expect to pay between B$100–130 for a single-tank dive, B$160–220 for a two-tank dive, including use of equipment. For full open-water certification, budget around B$750. Serious divers should consider a **package deal**; some cover multiple dives while others include accommodation.

There's good **snorkelling** too, especially off the west coast, where there are plenty of good coralheads just offshore and sea turtles in the sea grass near the *Lone Star* or at *Paynes Bay*. In addition to the catamaran cruises (see box), several of the

Land-based operators

Island tours If you're without your own transport on the island or have limited time, a guided tour can be a good option. For around B$154 Island Safari (ⓣ429-5337, ⓦwww.islandsafari.bb) or Adventureland 4x4 (ⓣ418-3687, ⓦwww.adventurelandbarbados.com) can whizz you around some of the wilder, more remote parts of the island in open-sided safari vehicles, with a fair amount of off-road bumping and numerous photo stops. For similar rates, Johnson's Tours (ⓣ426-518, ⓦwww.johnsonstours.com) offers a more sedate experience, with itineraries that include a couple of major sights such as the Andromeda Gardens or Sunbury Plantation House.

Horse riding Ocean-Echo Stables (ⓣ433-6772, ⓦwww.barbadoshorseriding.com) offers fabulously scenic 2–3-hour rides round Hackleton's cliff, Codrington College and some of the tranquil coves on the east coast for around B$170–190. In St Andrew the Caribbean International Riding Centre (ⓣ422-7433) offers similar tours at comparable rates.

Biking The Highland Adventure Centre (ⓣ438-8069) organizes hugely enjoyable 90-minute mountain bike trips around Mount Hillaby and down to the east coast. The B$90 fee includes transfers.

Water-based operators

A number of operators provide access to a wealth of activities on the water.

Catamaran cruises

Catamaran cruises up the west coast are increasingly popular though whether it's a wild party or a more tranquil glide across the waters will depend to a great extent on the crowd. Most companies offer similar deals that include hotel transfer, snorkelling gear, beverages and a buffet meal for the longer trips. Cool Runnings (☎436-0911, Ⓦwww.coolrunningsbarbados.com) and *El Tigre* (☎417-7245, Ⓦwww.eltigrecruises.com) come highly recommended. Both offer five-hour lunch trips (BD$150-160) with snorkelling and swimming with turtles, and on-deck dancing on *El Tigre* during the return trip. For a potentially quieter ambience, try Small Cats (☎421-6419, Ⓦwww.smallcatscruises.com). Operating out of the Colony Club in Holetown, the smaller vessel takes a maximum of 12 people, offering three-hour snorkelling trips (B$100) and five-hour lunch cruises (B$150).

The ultimate **"booze cruise"** takes place on the multi-deck *Harbour Master* (☎430-0900, Ⓦwww.tallshipscruises.com) on Thursday evenings (B$150) and Friday lunchtimes (B$130). An all-inclusive floating party, the boat trip hosts live bands and DJs and includes a floor show complete with fire-eaters and limbo dancers. Alternatively for a mere B$45 you can join in a charter cruise, where you're more likely to be partying with Bajans but you have to purchase your own food and drinks. The highly popular pirate ship outings (previously on the *Jolly Roger*) are soon to be revived with a new state-of-the-art pirate ship due in 2008/2009. Check the same website for developments.

Deep-sea fishing

Plenty of charter boats are on the market if you fancy pursuing wahoo, dorado, tuna or barracuda (and marlin if you're lucky). Charters for up to six people start at around B$800 for a half-day, B$1400 for a full-day; rates include rods, bait, food, drink and hotel transfer. Well-known operators include Billfisher II (☎431-0741) and Blue Marlin Charters (☎436-4322) but if you hunt around the careenage, you'll find plenty of others.

dive operators also take snorkellers out on their dive trips for around B$40–50, including equipment.

Watersports have proliferated over recent years – **kayaking**, **hobie-cat** cruises, **windsurfing**, **parasailing**, **water-skiing**, **jet-skiiing** or being towed around in a **banana boat** are all possible. Most hotels will find a reputable operator for you, or you can contact them directly (see box) – many offer lessons for hefty sums. Cheaper rentals are available from guys hanging around the beach but there's no guarantee of licence, or the quality of the equipment.

Other activities

Alongside Jamaica and Trinidad, Barbados is one of the Big Three Caribbean cricketing nations and the game is *the* national passion. If you get the chance, go and catch a day of international cricket at the Kensington Oval in Bridgetown or at the Three Ws Oval up at the University of the West Indies' Cavehill Campus. Check the Barbados Cricket Association website for details Ⓦwww.bcacricket.org.

The island also has a lively **equestrian tradition**, holding races every other Saturday at the Garrison Savannah racecourse (☎426-3980, Ⓦwww.barbadosturfclub.com. The Sandy Lane Gold Cup in early March attracts the biggest crowds and prize-money. It's a great day's entertainment when you can join locals picnicking round the track but it's well worth paying the B$10 entry for a splendid grandstand view.

Barbados also has several **polo fields**, the most famous at Holder's House, which

Scuba diving

Reputable **scuba diving** operators include:

Dive Barbados ⓣ422-3133, ⓦwww.divebarbados.net

The Dive Shop in Aquatic Gap ⓣ426-9947, ⓦwww.divebds.com – Barbados's first scuba outfit on the island

Divepro Barbados ⓣ420-3337, ⓦwww.diveprobarbados.com St Lawrence Gap

Eco-dive Barbados Careenage ⓣ243-5816, ⓦwww.ecodivebarbados.com – small popular newcomer with an emphasis on reef conservation.

Submarine

An alternative way of seeing the ocean without getting wet is to board the **Atlantis submarine** (ⓣ423-6220, ⓦwww.atlantisadventures.com/barbados). The whole excursion lasts two and a half hours, though only 40 minutes are spent underwater. Your B$193 covers transfer harbour to submarine, where each passenger gets a porthole to themselves. Hotel transfer is extra.

Surfing

Surfing attracts enthusiasts from around the globe. Experienced surfers generally head for the "soup bowl" at Bathsheba although for novices and bodyboarders, the beaches on the south and south-east of the island provide adequate waves. A lot of useful info is available from the Surf Barbados website (ⓦwww.surfbarbados.com, ⓣ262-1099) including details of board rental and lessons.

Club Mistral *Silver Sands* ⓣ428-7277, ⓦwww.club-mistral.com Lessons and equipment rental in surfing, windsurfing and kite-surfing.

Watersports

Hightide Watersports, *Coral Reef Club*, north of Holetown ⓣ432-0931, ⓦwww.divehightide.com. Established initially as a dive centre, now branching out into the likes of water-skiing, parasailing, sailing, banana and biscuit rides, kayak, snorkel and windsurf rental. Not cheap.

Charles Watersports at Dover Beach, ⓣ428-2624. Cheaper rates for boogie or surfboards, kayaks, jet-skis, windsurfers, as well as hobie-cat or snorkelling trips.

hosts local and international matches in the season (Nov–March). See ⓦwww.barbadospoloclub.com for details.

You can find good public **golf courses** at the Barbados Golf Club in Durants (ⓣ428-8463, green fees B$250) and at the world-famous Sandy Lane (ⓣ444-2500, green fees B$470). Club hire is extra. There is also a decent nine-hole course at the *Club Rockley* resort (ⓣ435-7873) on the south coast. Several other courses are under construction.

Some of the best and most scenic **hiking** on Barbados is along the beaches, particularly between Martin's Bay and Bath and between Bathsheba and Cattlewash. You can also join the weekly organized hike arranged by the Barbados National Trust (BNT) which usually starts out at 6am on Sunday mornings and is free. It's a great way to see some of the less visited parts of the island and visitors are very welcome but note that even the slowest group shifts at a fair pace (ⓣ436-9033, ⓦwww.hikebarbados.com).

Attracting both locals and tourists, the Barbados National Trust's (ⓣ426-2421 or check the Totally Barbados site – see box) annual open-house season (Jan–Apr, Wednesday afternoons) treats visitors to a peek inside some of the island's more interesting private homes. The cost is B$18, with reduced rates for those with trust membership from countries with reciprocal arrangements (Scotland, England and Wales, Northern Ireland, New Zealand, Australia and heritage associations in the US and Canada) – bring your cards. Members enjoy similar discounts or free entry to other BNT sites round the island, as indicated in this chapter.

History

The earliest settlers in Barbados were Amerindians, who came to the island in dug-out canoes from the Guianas in South America. Christopher Columbus never stopped at Barbados but in the early sixteenth century, Spanish slave-traders arrived to collect Amerindians to work in the gold and silver mines of the New World.

In 1625 a party of **British sailors** landed in Barbados, claiming the island for their king, and in February 1627 eighty colonists landed at present-day Holetown. They quickly found that sugar grew well in the island soil, and the industry brought almost instantaneous prosperity – by the 1650s, Barbados was considered the wealthiest place in the New World.

As Barbados developed, a workforce was needed for the **sugar plantations**. At first, the main source of workers was indentured labourers from England, Scotland and Ireland. Later, large numbers of West African **slaves** were brought to Barbados, and the island slowly began to take on its present-day ethnic composition.

By 1700 the glory days of Barbados sugar had peaked. Huge fortunes had been made but increased competition from Jamaica and the Leeward Islands reduced profits. Many of the small planters were squeezed out, handing even more economic power to the large plantation owners. In 1807 the British government abolished the slave trade yet far more threatening to the planters was the movement for the abolition of slavery itself.

In April 1816, Barbados faced its only serious slave uprising. Named after its alleged leader, **Bussa's Rebellion** began in the southeast with attacks on property and widespread burning of sugar fields, and quickly spread to all of the island's southern and central parishes. Within three days, however, the rebellion was crushed; just a handful of whites were killed, but over a thousand slaves were either killed in battle or executed afterwards.

Nonetheless by the early 1830s the reformers in London had won the argument for the abolition of slavery and **full emancipation** took place on August 1, 1838. While some former slaves headed to the towns, particularly Bridgetown, most had little choice but to continue to work on the sugar estates. The white planters still ran Barbados, owning almost all of the farmland and controlling the Assembly that made the island's laws.

The US-sponsored construction of the **Panama Canal** in 1904 had a huge impact on the island, supplying at least 20,000 workers. Many of this huge percentage of the local workforce – which was virtually all black – returned to Barbados with sizeable savings, which they were able to invest in new businesses and in land. The white planters, who had previously refused to sell land to blacks, were now obliged to do so because of economic circumstances. Even if the amount of land bought by blacks was marginal, by the 1930s the pattern of land ownership had changed dramatically.

Alongside economic change the island saw significant political development. Black political parties formed in the 1930s and 1940s, and although executive power remained with the British-appointed governor, black politicians were appointed to the highly influential Executive Committee.

During the 1960s, **foreign investment** and tourism were actively encouraged to reduce the island's dependence on sugar. Through political movements that encouraged democratic rights for all Bajans – not just wealthy plantation owners – Barbados finally achieved **independence** from Britain in 1966.

18.1

Bridgetown and around

The nation's busy but easy-going capital, **Bridgetown**, is one of the oldest cities in the Caribbean with enough to interest the visitor for a few hours. Its architecture blends attractive, balconied colonial buildings with warehouses and brash modern office blocks. The centre of activity is the Careenage, a marina bordered by the **Barbadian parliament** (home to two small but fascinating local history museums). A number of the island's major religious buildings are located within five minutes' walk of parliament, including **St Michael's Cathedral** and a **synagogue**, both standing on the same sites since the mid-seventeenth century.

Just north of the city, a couple of **rum factories** are open for tours, while **Tyrol Cot** is an unusual nineteenth-century house that was home to two of the island's leading post war politicians, Sir Grantley Adams and his son Tom Adams. Southeast lies the historic **Garrison area** where the British Empire maintained its Caribbean military headquarters from 1780 to 1905 – its huge grassy savanna, today a racecourse and public park, was once the army's parade ground. The ranks of brightly coloured military buildings around its edge include the excellent **Barbados Museum**.

Accommodation

Though most people prefer to lodge on the west or south coast, those who wish to remain more central tend to head for the *Grand Barbados Beach Resort* (Ⓣ426-4000, Ⓦwww.grandbarbados.com; ⑥) and the *Hilton* (Ⓣ426-0200, Ⓦwww.hiltoncaribbean.com/Barbados; ⑨), both of which cater to a mixture of business travellers and holiday-makers. A recent overhaul has failed to reinvigorate the rather tired *Grand Barbados Beach Resort*. A monstrous eyesore, the *Hilton* commands spectacular views across the bay with brightly decorated rooms with all mod cons and ocean view balconies. The hotel has tennis courts, two labyrinthine pools weaving through attractive grounds and two secluded beaches popular with nesting turtles.

The City

The best place to start your tour of Bridgetown is beside the **Careenage**, a long, thin finger of water that pushes right into the city centre with expensive fishing boats and catamarans moored at its western end. The **parliament buildings**, bustling shops and a couple of smart restaurants can all be found in the immediate vicinity, with some of the latter housed in restored warehouses.

Seeing the central sights is easiest **on foot**. Bridgetown is an extremely **safe** city, even at night, though you may want to avoid the seedy area southeast of the Fairchild Street bus station, particularly around Nelson Street and Jordan's Lane, where the red-light district is located.

Independence Square, National Heroes Square and St Michael's Cathedral

On the south side of the Careenage lies the recently redeveloped **Independence Square**. Previously a car park, it's now a pleasantly landscaped fusion of fountains,

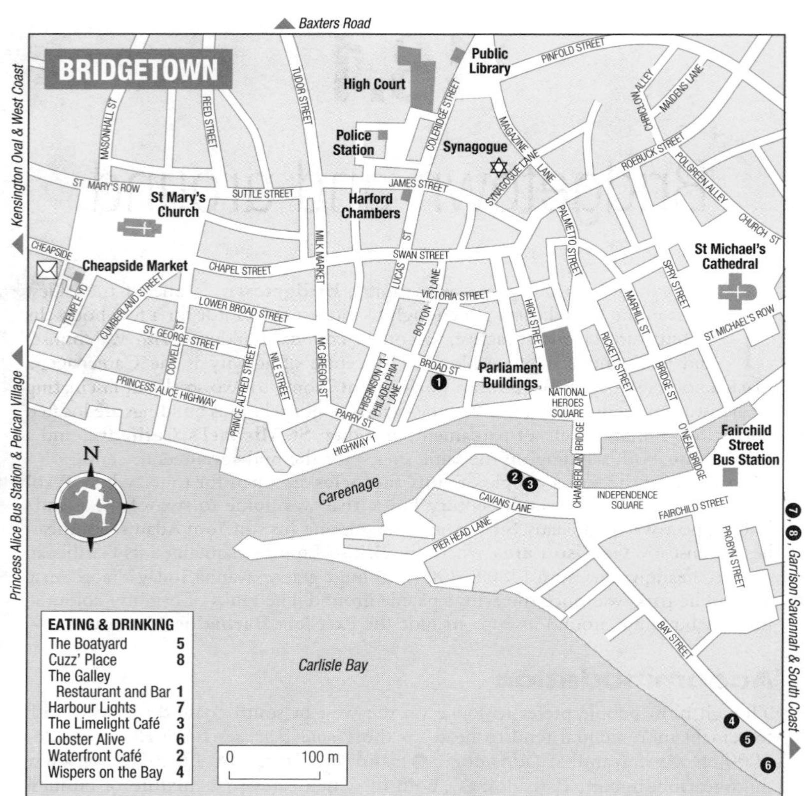

lawns and pseudo-classical half-finished temples, playfully decorated in the Bajan colours of blue and yellow. In the middle of the square stands a stately bronze statue of Errol Barrow, the country's first prime minister, his arm stretching out across the water towards parliament and **National Heroes Square**. Known for over a century as Trafalgar Square, National Heroes Square was renamed in 1999 though a bronze statue of the British Admiral Horatio Nelson controversially still stands. The square is dominated by the **parliament buildings** (open to visitors during parliamentary debates). Established in 1639, Barbados's parliament is one of the oldest in the world, though it was not until the 1870s that it settled in its current Gothic Revival home.

Parliament houses two adjoining museum collections, which are worth visiting: the **Museum of Parliament** and **National Heroes Gallery** (Mon, Wed, Thurs, Fri 9am–4pm, Sat 9am–3pm; B$14 for combined entry; ☎427-2019). The former chronicles the struggle for independence and the events and personalities that shaped the establishment of parliament. The furthest room contains the National Heroes Gallery, with informative displays on the country's ten national heroes, including assorted memorabilia. Of particular interest are the modern sculptures commissioned from Caribbean artists to represent each hero. Don't miss the Father of Barbadian Independence, Errol Barrow, portrayed as a giant colossus made from engine parts.

Along St Michael's Row, the large, red-roofed St Michael's Cathedral (daily 9am–4pm; free) is the country's principal Anglican place of worship. A stone church was first erected here in 1665, but the present building dates from 1786. The sprawling churchyard is the resting place for many of the island's most prominent figures, including Sir Grantley Adams and his son Tom.

The old city

Above the parliament buildings a network of narrow lanes links the main roads, marking the parts of the city that were first developed. Bridgetown's oldest surviving building is probably the seventeenth-century, pastel-pink **Harford Chambers**, on the corner of Lucas and James streets.

Not far away, in Synagogue Lane, stands a pink and white **synagogue** (daily 10am–4pm; free). One of the oldest in the Western hemisphere, it was first erected in 1654 and rebuilt after hurricane damage in 1833. Jews were among the earliest settlers in Barbados; many of them arrived in the 1650s to escape the Inquisition in Brazil, bringing a knowledge of sugar cane cultivation that was to prove crucial in boosting the island's fledgling agriculture. The hefty entrance fee at the adjacent **Nidhe Israel Museum** (Mon–Sat 9am–4pm; B$25; BNT) is really only worth it for enthusiasts of Jewish history but the synagogue itself merits a look inside.

Broad Street and the Pelican Village

Much of central Bridgetown is given over to shopping, with dozens of duty-free stores competing for the cruise ship dollar. The main drag is **Broad Street** which runs northwest from National Heroes Square. This has been the city's market centre since the mid-seventeenth century, and still retains some splendid colonial buildings amid the modern chaos of clothes and jewellery shops, fast-food joints and fruit vendors. It merits a stroll even if you're not planning to shop. You'll get a more authentic taste of Bajan city life if you wander along the pedestrian-only **Swan Street**, which runs parallel two streets north.

Beyond St Mary's Church, Broad Street runs into **Cheapside**, where you'll find a bustling **public market**, the **GPO**, and the **Princess Alice Bus Station**, for transport heading north. West of the bus station lies **Pelican Village**, a tourist-oriented shopping complex built on reclaimed land, with a small art gallery, a dozen or so souvenir shops, and a couple of average snack bars.

Eating, drinking and nightlife

The Boatyard Bay St ⓣ436-2622, ⓦwww.theboatyard.com. Lively beach bar/restaurant with its own jetty. Packed with tourists in high season. Live bands on Fat Tuesdays. The B$40 entry gets you free drinks from 9pm-2am. Daytime B$24 gets you an adventure beach package. Open daily.

Cuzz' Place Small brightly painted shack in the beach car park at Aquatic Gap, selling fabulous fresh fish cutters.

Harbour Lights Bay Street ⓣ436-7225, ⓦwww.harbourlightsbarbados.com. Smaller version of *The Boatyard* with a friendly atmosphere attracting locals and holiday-makers for the all-you-can-drink nightclubbing on Mon, Wed, Fri (B$40–50) until 2–3am. Mon and Wed (7–10.30pm) the place hosts tourist-oriented beach dinner shows open to all ages; B$145 covers food, drinks and dancing in the sand to a live band, a cabaret of acrobatics, limbo-dancing, fire-eating and stilt walking.

The Limelight Café The Careenage ⓣ435-9471, ⓦwww.limelightcafebarbados.com. First-floor bar/restaurant decked out with pop paraphernalia. Takes off on Fri nights with live local bands. Food is also available. Mon–Sat, 10am until late.

Lobster Alive Bay Street ⓣ435-0305. Popular beachside bistro with eclectic clientele that features fresh lobsters (B$135 for a medium serving) and other delicious seafood from B$30. Live jazz on Thurs & Sat evenings and Sun lunch. Dinner daily 6–9pm, lunch Mon–Sat noon–4pm. Closed May–July.

The Waterfront Café The Careenage ⓣ427-0093. The best ambience for eating in town, serving authentic Caribbean dishes (mains generally B$40–60) indoors or out beside the water. There's live music most evenings, with jazz the main draw. A buffet dinner accompanied by steel pan (B$65) on Tues. Mon–Sat 10am–10pm.

Wispers on the Bay ☎826-5222, Ⓦwww.wispersonthebay.com. Set back from Bay Street, the luscious tropical plants of the restaurant gardens provide a romantic backdrop for your choice from a three-course prix fixe menu (B$175 pp excluding drinks) of top-notch international cuisine with a Caribbean twist. Lunch à la carte. Mon–Sat lunch noon–2.30pm, dinner 6.30–9.30pm.

North of the city

North of the city just beyond the Kensington Oval cricket ground, the Spring Garden Highway hugs the west coast, skirting the beach almost all the way to historic Speightstown (see p.684) in the far northwest. Much of the area immediately north of Bridgetown is given over to industrial production, including a couple of **rum factories** that are open for tours. To the northeast lies **Tyrol Cot**, the former home of Sir Grantley Adams.

The Mount Gay Rum Factory and Tyrol Cot

The **Mount Gay Rum Factory** (Mon–Fri 9am–4pm; 45min tours every half-hour; B$14; ☎425-8757, Ⓦwww.mountgayrum.com), a five-minute drive north of Bridgetown on the Spring Garden Highway, is probably the pick of the rum factories (although the distillery is actually in St Lucy). It starts with a short **film** giving the history of the company, which first distilled rum on the island in 1703 and is reckoned to be the world's oldest surviving producer of the spirit. The tour covers the later stages of production, including refining, ageing, blending and bottling before you adjourn to the **bar,** where you get to sample some of the liquor.

Five minutes' northeast of Bridgetown's city centre, on several bus routes, the exquisite little house at **Tyrol Cot** (Mon–Fri 9am–5pm; B$14; BNT; ☎424-2074) was the launching pad for two of the island's most illustrious political careers. From 1929, it served as the home of Sir Grantley Adams, the first elected leader of pre-independence Barbados, and it was the birthplace of his son, Tom Adams, the nation's prime minister from 1976 until his death in 1985. The family's memorabilia is scattered about the house, including some splendid revolving mahogany bookcases and a wonderfully tacky pop-up Möet & Chandon cigarette holder in the living room. Note also the adjustable double-jalousied shutters, with sloping slats to keep the rain and sun out while letting in light and allowing air to circulate. A tiny **heritage village** lies in the grounds.

The Garrison area

By the late seventeenth century, sugar-rich Barbados had become one of Britain's most important overseas possessions, generating more wealth than all of British North America. To protect against possible invasion, defensive forts were established along the south and west coasts, with the largest of them protecting Carlisle Bay and the capital. By 1780 the British decided to make the island the regional centre for their West Indian troops, and erected more army buildings around the fort.

Today this part of the city's outer zone, just a couple of kilometres south of the centre, is known as the **Garrison area**. Chock-full of superb Georgian architecture, it remains one of Bridgetown's most evocative districts, retaining the most attractive of the island's colonial **military buildings** including, in a restored jail, the **Barbados Museum**. Also of interest is **George Washington House**, where the American founding father lodged during his stay on the island in 1751.

The Garrison Savannah, Barbados Museum and George Washington House

The centre of the Garrison area is the **savannah**, a huge grassy space that served as the army's parade ground. The military buildings – barracks, quartermaster's store and hospitals, as well as the fort itself – stand in a rough square around the savannah, flanked by coconut palms and large mango trees. The savannah includes sports grounds and play areas and is bounded by the city's **race-track** (see p.666).

To the south you can still see the thick eighteenth-century walls of **St Ann's Fort** (built in 1705 and still used by the Barbadian Defence Force and closed to visitors) while to the north stands the spectacular **Main Guard**, the area's most striking landmark with its tall, bright-red tower and green cupola.

Housed in the Garrison's old military prison on the east side of the savannah, the **Barbados Museum** (Mon–Sat 9am–5pm, Sun 2–6pm; B$11.50) is a treat. A series of galleries run clockwise around an airy central courtyard that once rang with the sound of prisoners breaking stones. A glance inside one of the spartan prison cells is a sobering reminder of the country's unsavoury colonial past. Don't rush through – the place is stuffed with interesting and informative exhibits on the island's history, culture, flora and fauna, and also showcases **prints and paintings** of old Barbados, **African crafts**, **decorative arts** from around the world and slavery-era plantation house **period rooms**.

On the northern side of savannah at Bush Hill you can find the recently restored **George Washington House** (Mon–Sat, 9am–5pm; B$25; BNT). At the age of 19, George Washington came to Barbados in 1751 to accompany his ailing brother, Lawrence, who was suffering from tuberculosis. Although George only spent two months on the island, it is argued that his sojourn had a profound effect on him, particularly his exposure to the military and new agricultural methods. Moreover he contracted smallpox on Barbados, which proved to be a blessing in disguise as it made him immune to the disease which later ravaged his troops during the American Revolution.

The elegant yellow Caribbean Georgian house with its attractive porch has been beautifully restored at considerable expense. Following a short semi-dramatised **video** presentation, a **guided tour** takes you round the downstairs rooms that contain reproduction furniture of the period, where George and Lawrence lived. Upstairs a well-presented **museum** section focuses on the restoration of the house, the evolution of the Garrison, George's time on the island, as well as on slavery in Barbados and in the US. Don't miss the opportunity to sit next to an effigy of George, who'll read extracts from his diary to you.

18.2

The south coast

The southwest of Barbados was the birthplace of tourism on the island and the area remains dominated by the holiday industry. On the whole the southwest is not as beautiful as the west coast, though the beaches are just as fine and with plenty of good restaurants and better prices, the south has much to offer. You'll find the busiest beaches at **Rockley** and **Worthing**; the liveliest restaurants and nightlife at **St Lawrence Gap**; a bustling local scene at **Oistins**; and

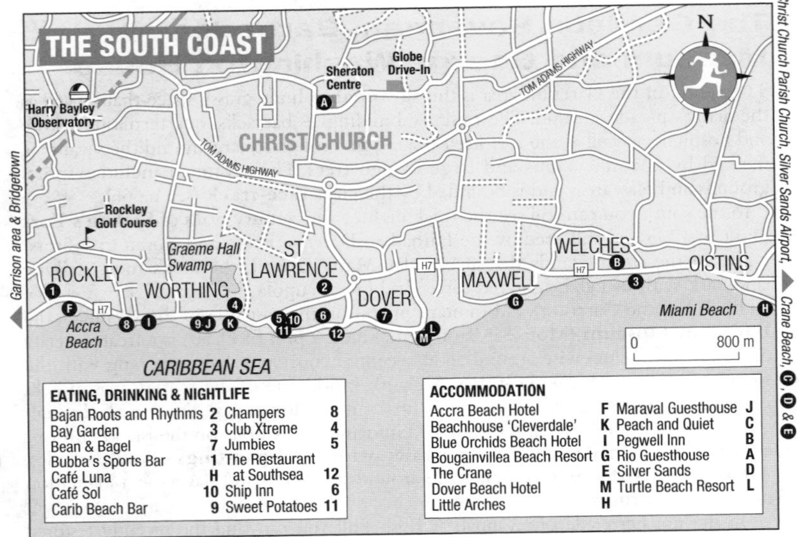

the quiet beaches at **Silver Sands** attract windsurfers and those who want to spend their holiday strolling on relatively deserted stretches of sand. On the other side of the airport, in the southeast of the island, you enter the far less developed parish of **St Philip**. While there are only a handful of hotels, the scenery is more spectacular, with the Atlantic waves lashing the rocky coast.

If you're driving, **Highway 7** runs along the coast between Bridgetown and Oistins, from where it doglegs up past the airport and on to Crane Bay. **Buses and minibuses** run from Bridgetown as far as the defunct hotel at *Sam Lord's Castle*, passing through most of the tourist zones on the coast, while route taxis go as far as Silver Sands. Service stops around midnight, so you'll need a car or a private taxi after that. Getting here from the west coast is a little harder – buses run between Speightstown and Oistins, usually bypassing Bridgetown, but they're less frequent than the ones that ply the south coast.

Although beach-life, with its dining, drinking and dancing, dominates the south-coast scene, the region holds some of the island's most rewarding attractions including the natural tranquillity of the **Graeme Hall Nature Sanctuary** and the historic **Sunbury Plantation House**.

Accommodation

Rockley and Worthing

Accra Beach Hotel & Resort Rockley ⓣ435-8920, ⓦwww.accrabeachhotel.com. Large relatively attractive resort hotel on the island's busiest beach with balconies overlooking the sea. Giant swimming pool onsite; rooms and service vary. ❻

Beachhouse "Cleverdale" Fourth Ave, Worthing ⓣ428-1035, ⓦwww.barbados-rentals.com. Spotless guesthouse just off the beach, with communal bathroom and kitchen facilities, breakfast room, living room and spacious veranda. Rooms have satellite TV, mosquito screens and fans. A/c extra in some rooms. ❷

Blue Orchids Beach Hotel Worthing ⓣ435-8057, ⓦwww.blueorchidsbarbados.com. Good-value hotel on a quiet beach for those seeking a restful sojourn. Clean, spacious bright studios or 2–3-bedroom apartments, all with a/c, and balconies with beach or ocean views. ❻

Dover and Maxwell

Bougainvillea Beach Resort Maxwell Coast Road, Maxwell ⓣ418-0990, ⓦwww.bougainvilleaeresort.com. Justifiably popular for spacious, well-appointed rooms with kitchenettes and balconies overlooking delightfully landscaped gardens. Relaxed but lively feel; kids' club, tennis, garden games, gym and watersports facilities to keep you active. 7

Dover Beach Hotel Dover ⓣ 428-8076, ⓦ www.doverbeach.com. Comfortable, laid-back place located beside a superb beach. All rooms have a/c, some have kitchenettes and there's a good-size pool. Ask for a room with a beach or pool view. 5

Maraval Guesthouse Dover ⓣ 435-7437, ⓦ www.maravalbarbados.com. Funky little place popular with European backpackers just a stone's throw from the beach. Rooms mostly en suite with shared lounge and spacious kitchen. 2

Rio Guesthouse Paradise Village, St Lawrence Gap ⓣ 428-1546, ⓦ www.rioguesthouse.hostel.com. Two minutes' walk from Dover Beach, this spotless and friendly 9-room guesthouse-cum-hostel offers good value with shared kitchen, TV room and laundry. All rooms have fans (a/c is extra); doubles and twins are en suite while single rooms share toilets/bathrooms. 2

Turtle Beach Resort Dover ⓣ 428-7131, ⓦ www.turtlebeachresortbarbados.com. Top-notch all-inclusive, with large rooms, three restaurants, two pools, good watersports facilities and a kids' club. 9

Oistins to Silver Sands

Little Arches Miami Beach (just east of Oistins) ⓣ 420-4689, ⓦ www.littlearches.com. Charming boutique hotel a short walk from delightful Miami Beach. Rooms are compact but imaginatively and luxuriously designed. There's a tiny pool and hammocks on the deck area, plus an excellent rooftop restaurant/bar (see p.680), which can generate some noise in the late evening. 8

Peach and Quiet Inch Marlow ⓣ 428-5682, ⓦ www.peachandquiet.com. This white-washed Mexican Adobe-style retreat is aimed at adults (no children allowed) who seek total tranquillity (no TVs, phones). Stone-hewn rooms are simple (no a/c) but breezy and the restaurant cuisine excellent. The natural rock-pool complete with tropical fish is a real plus and guided hikes and other activities can be arranged. 4

Pegwell Inn Welches (just west of Oistins) ⓣ 428-6150. Basic, somewhat gloomy rooms with shared small lounge and veranda offer some of the cheapest lodging in Barbados. Located on the main road next to a supermarket, it can be noisy but it's only a five-minute walk to the beach. The four rooms all have fans and private bath. 1

Silver Sands Resort Silver Sands ⓣ 428-6001, ⓦ www.silversandsbarbados.com. Pleasantly relaxed resort with two restaurants, tennis courts, a large swimming pool and over a hundred functionally designed rooms with a/c spread across a large area of landscaped grounds. 6

The southeast

The Crane Resort and Residences ⓣ 423-6220, ⓦ www.thecrane.com. On a stunning setting high above Crane Bay with its legendary pink-sand beach, this hotel exudes luxury and elegance. Its rooms, starting at US$550, are truly sumptuous; superbly appointed apartments, 3- to 4-bedroom-suite villas and two excellent restaurants (see p.680) also onsite. 9

Christ Church

Most of the island's cheaper package holiday tourism is concentrated in the parish of **CHRIST CHURCH** in the southwest between Bridgetown and the airport, with several small villages offering a variety of lodgings and places to eat. The area offers excellent white-sand beaches – though in high season some are scarcely visible beneath the tightly packed rows of sun-toasted holiday-makers – and the sea is calm pretty much all year round.

Hastings and Rockley

A short ride southeast of Bridgetown, **HASTINGS** developed as Barbados's first tourist resort, and a handful of grand old hotels still stand on the seafront to mark those glory days. Sadly, the once attractive beach has been heavily eroded.

Further along Highway 7, **ROCKLEY**'s main attraction is its magnificent beach, known locally as **Accra Beach** – a vibrant white swath of sand, popular with tourists and local families, it can get pretty crowded at peak season and weekends. The people-watching is top-notch, as hair-braiders, T-shirt and craft vendors and the odd hustler mingle with windsurfers and sun-worshippers, creating one of the liveliest beach scenes on the island but you'll need to turn a blind eye to the garish fast-food frontages that somewhat spoil the scene.

Worthing and the St Lawrence Gap

Like the Victorian seaside resort in England after which it is named, the once elegant village of **WORTHING** is now tatty and faded, but its relaxed feel and handful of decent, inexpensive guesthouses make it a popular spot for budget travellers. There's a gleaming white beach less crowded than Accra Beach further west but just as enjoyable, with a couple of laid-back bars and local guys offering boat trips and jet-ski rentals.

Just past Worthing on the left-hand side lies the **Graeme Hall Nature Sanctuary** (daily 8am–6pm; B$25; ⓣ435-9727, ⓦwww.graemehall.com). Offering welcome respite from the surrounding tourist hubbub, the reserve's main attraction is its **swamp**, containing the country's last remaining **mangroves**, which provide roosting space to an impressive number of egrets and attract numerous migratory species. Two large, attractively landscaped **aviaries** offer opportunities to enjoy closer encounters with brightly coloured birds from other parts of the Caribbean, such as parrots and flamingos and the spectacular scarlet ibis. There are helpful identification charts and an interpretive centre in addition to numerous boarded walkways and benches to enhance your birdwatching. It's also a peaceful location for a picnic though you'll need to bring your own food.

▲ Graeme Hall Nature Sanctuary

If you fancy a spot of stargazing, you should head inland, just south of Highway 6, to the **Harry Bayley Observatory** (Fri 9pm; B$15; ⓣ426-1317). Home to the Barbados Astronomical Society, the observatory opens its doors once a week to the public but you should check in advance since viewing depends on the weather.

Back on Highway 7 a few hundred metres past Graeme Hall, a right-hand turn takes you through the heavily touristed **ST LAWRENCE GAP** and **Dover** before rejoining the main road near Maxwell. As the most developed area of the south coast – with hotels, restaurants, tourist shops and vendors strung out along virtually the entire road, you'll see few Bajans here during the day, other than those who work in the industry, but at weekends the locals come to join the party-going young islanders will join the throngs. It's a laid-back place with great beaches, particularly towards the eastern end of the Gap. Most south coast buses and minibuses run through the area.

Oistins and Miami Beach

Continuing east brings you into **OISTINS**, the main town along the south coast, famous for its Friday-night fish fry, which attracts hundreds of locals and coachloads of tourists. A couple of **buses** run here from Bridgetown, as does route taxi 11, which continues to Silver Sands. The busy little town is dominated by the redeveloped fish market right by the beach, known as the Bay Garden. The community's fishing tradition is celebrated at the annual Oistins Fish Festival held over Easter weekend – an extravaganza of competitions, street food, musical entertainment and arts and crafts.

While the fish market itself is the focus during the day, the **Bay Garden** eateries take centre stage in the evening serving up fried fish straight from the boats, and on Friday nights hundreds of people descend for a "lime" – the local term for hanging out and socializing – and a dance.

As you head east of Oistins, the Enterprise Coast Road offers a fabulous drive beside the sea and leads to **MIAMI BEACH** – a lovely sheltered cove dotted with casuarina trees.. With a kids' playground, plenty of shade and a snack bar, it's a popular weekend outing for local families.

Silver Sands and Long Beach

Famous for windsurfing, **SILVER SANDS** attracts enthusiasts from all over the world, though non-surfers come here too for the quiet, easy-going vibe. Fantastic waves roll in for most of the year and there are a handful of (pretty expensive) places where you can rent a windsurfer. True to its name, Long Beach, due south of the airport, is the longest beach on the island and less busy than others because of often choppy seas. A huge stretch of crunchy white sand strewn with driftwood, it is often completely deserted.

Inland Christ Church

If you're suffering from beach-fatigue (or sunburn) it may be worth heading inland to two of the island's newest attractions. Travelling east on the airport road, turn left at the Henry Forde Roundabout, and you'll almost immediately come to **Ocean Park** (daily 9am–6pm; B$35; ⓣ420-7405, ⓦwww.oceanparkbarbados.com), also reachable by bus. A combination of indoor **tanks** and outdoor **aquariums**, the park covers a fair array of Caribbean marine life, from moray eels and sea urchins to rays and mantis shrimps. Unfortunately information placards are not always as well displayed as they might be; nor are some of the tanks as clear as you would like, while the insistent piped music provides a further niggle. The star attraction, the ocean encounter tank, containing **sharks**, barracudas and enormous rays, is suitably impressive, especially during the daily 4pm "feeding frenzy". Overall only aquarium novices are likely to feel they've had their money's worth. There's an onsite **restaurant**, and for an extra B$5 you can try your hand at pirate-themed **mini-golf**.

In an aircraft hangar directly after the airport, aviation enthusiasts can enjoy looking round the sky's most famous supersonic plane at the **Barbados Concorde Experience** (daily 9am–6pm; B$35; ⓣ253-6257, ⓦwww.barbadosconcorde.com). Since Barbados was one of only four scheduled destinations for Concorde worldwide, it is entirely appropriate that one of the planes has remained here. For your hefty entry fee you get a multi media presentation on supersonic flight and on the Concorde, followed by a clamber aboard the plane itself. You can also have a go on a flight simulator and from an observation deck overlooking the airport you can watch aircraft taking off, which of course you could see for free round the corner outside!

St Philip

The largest parish on the island, but with less than half the population of busy Christ Church, **ST PHILIP** exudes a different feel from its more touristed neighbour, with no crowds and far less development, though low-level buildings are beginning to sprout. The coastline here is rugged, with only a handful of white-sand beaches divided from each other by long cliffs and rocky outcrops. The sea is rough, too, with pounding Atlantic waves.

If you're relying on **public transport**, buses run along the south coast road as far as the closed *Sam Lord's Castle hotel*, passing the *Crane Resort and Residences* (see below), though if you're heading for any of the beaches, you'll need to walk down to them from the main road – usually a few hundred metres.

Foul Bay and Crane Bay

Three or four kilometres beyond the airport, **FOUL BAY** is the largest beach on this section of the coast – access is signposted from the main road. Gaining its inauspicious name from early sailing times when it offered poor anchorage, it is in fact a lovely, long and wide white sand beach with few tourists

Back on the main road, the rebranded **Crane Resort and Residences** (formerly the Crane Hotel) lies half a kilometre beyond Foul Bay, commanding a superb site above **CRANE BAY**. A house was first erected here in 1790 and today forms the east wing; during the 1880s the place was converted into a hotel, which boasts stunning views of the famous pink sands of **CRANE BEACH**. Public access to the beach is almost a kilometre further along the coast.

Round Six Cross Roads

Inland near Six Cross Roads, one of the island's busiest junctions, you'll find two more places of interest. First and foremost is **Sunbury Plantation House** (daily 10am–5pm; B$15; ⓣ423-6270), well signposted from the roundabout or reachable on the number 19K or 26 buses from Fairchild Street, Bridgetown. One of the oldest plantation houses, crammed with a variety of period furniture and artefacts, and the only one which has all its rooms open to the public, Sunbury is justifiably one of the island's premier attractions. Dating back from the mid-eighteenth century, the building was gutted by fire in 1995. Only the 60cm-thick coral stone walls, built to withstand hurricanes, were left standing. The excellent restoration, helped by donations of period furniture, furnishings and artefacts from around the island, has brilliantly recaptured the period feel of the rooms.

The downstairs centrepiece is undoubtedly the splendid, highly polished ball-and-claw mahogany dining table. The four upstairs bedrooms, in contrast, display a greater intimacy and include several wonderful four-poster beds, a chaise longue and an array of **Victorian clothing**. **Antique prints** on the first-floor walls provide further fascinating insights into the times. Back downstairs, the **cellars** are stuffed full of paraphernalia from plantation life, such as riding tackle, cooking utensils and a mongoose trap, as well as the largest number of **horse-drawn carriages** in the Caribbean – a collection which continues outside in the attractive grounds.

Various refreshments are available in the courtyard **café**, including high tea with the full works (B$20) and reasonably priced meals (mains B$20–40). For those who really want to sample plantation indulgence, you can splurge on a candlelit five-course formal dinner at the aforementioned dining-room table for B$187.50.

Eating, drinking and nightlife

You'll find the widest variety of **places to eat** on the south coast, particularly at the crowded **ST LAWRENCE GAP**, where street vendors flogging jerk chicken jostle with punters heading for the classy oceanfront restaurants. The Gap, as it is known, is the heart of south coast **nightlife** and offers plenty of options whether you want to see a band, hit the dance floor or just drink.

Rockley and Worthing

Bubba's Sports Bar Across from the *Accra Beach Hotel* ⓣ 435-6217. Midst a bewildering array of large and small TV screens beaming live sport from around the world you can get decent well-priced burgers, chicken and sandwiches plus Sun breakfast. Mon–Thurs 11.30am–11pm, and until 1am Fri and Sat. Sun 8am–11pm.

Carib Beach Bar next to the *Crystal Waters* guesthouse. ⓣ 435-8540. A lively place for a drink, especially during the 5pm to 6pm happy hour. Reasonably priced snacks available. Daily 11am–10pm.

Champers ⓣ 434 3463, ⓦ www.champersbarbados.com. Perched on a rocky promontory just off the eastern end of Accra Beach, this elegant two-storey establishment offers excellent fine dining. Tasty mains such as parmesan-crusted barracuda or sesame-crusted shrimp in rum sauce are on offer, generally between B$50–70, accompanied by an extensive wine list. Lunch Mon–Sat 11.30am–3pm, dinner daily 6–9.30pm.

St Lawrence Gap and Dover

Bajan Roots and Rhythms The Plantation Theatre, St Lawrence Main Road ⓣ 428-5048, ⓦ www.plantationtheatre.com. Immensely popular and unashamedly tourist-oriented, the Fri and Wed cabaret show (at 7pm) loosely recounts the history of Barbados – expect steel pans, limbo, stilt walkers and the like. B$155 covers the entertainment, a Bajan buffet dinner, drinks and hotel transport. B$90 for show only.

Bean 'n' Bagel Dover ⓣ 420-4604. Great coffee, all-day breakfasts of bagels, pancakes and omelettes, muffins and tasty lunch options at affordable prices. Daily 7am–4pm, Internet 8am–8pm.

Café Sol St Lawrence Gap ⓣ 435-9531. Lively, often crowded Mexican place with great margaritas, particularly during the 6–7pm and 10–11pm happy hours; decent and sensibly priced burritos, tacos and enchiladas are available. Daily noon–late.

Club Xtreme Dover ⓣ 228-2582, ⓦ www.clubextreme.net. Cavernous, high-energy club banging out the latest techno and dance. Attracts a very young crowd. B$45 cover, which includes drinks. Tues & Sat from 10pm.

Jumbies St Lawrence Gap ⓣ 420-7615, ⓦ www.jumbiesbarbados.com. Pumping out the loudest sounds, this double-decker bar-restaurant-club is currently the hottest spot in the Gap. The upstairs dance area offers great views across Carlisle Bay and the kitchen serves up imaginative dishes such as banana-stuffed chicken breast and citrus and brandy ceviche. Mains usually B$38–50. More happy hours than you can count including all-day Sun.

The Restaurant at Southsea St Lawrence Gap ⓣ 420-7423, ⓦ www.therestaurantatsouthsea.com. One of the island's finest dining establishments overlooking a secluded beach serving first-rate eclectic fare accompanied by a fine wine list and rum selection. Mains B$70–80. Mon–Sat 6–10pm.

Ship Inn St Lawrence Gap ⓣ 420-7447, ⓦ www.shipinnbarbados.com. Large English pub with a small dance floor and an outdoor space to mingle. Live bands and DJs every night, 10.30pm until late. *The Captain's Carvery* offers OK Bajan buffet lunches (Sun–Fri, noon–3pm) but its evening "carvery table" laden with an assortment of cut meats plus bountiful side dishes provides the main culinary draw (B$50). Thurs–Sun 6–10.30pm.

Sweet Potatoes St Lawrence Gap ⓣ 435-9638. Lively fun place that sells itself as "good old-fashioned Bajan cooking" including marinated codfish, pumpkin and spinach fritters (B$10–12) and mains of jerk pork and mango chicken (B$40–55). Daily, lunch 11am–3pm, dinner 6.30–10.15pm.

Oistins and Miami Beach

The Bay Garden Oistins Market. The island's top spot for a Friday-night lime but it can get overrun by coach loads of tourists in high season. A distinctive place that consists of a dozen or so stalls offering a variety of seafood, from conch fritters to fried kingfish to dolphin (approx BS$25). *Eric's Grill, Bar-Bq* and *Dora's & Jazzies* come recommended. Daily 5.30–10pm with dancing to high-energy soca beats continuing until the morning hours at weekends.

Café Luna *Little Arches Hotel,* Enterprise Coast Rd, Miami Beach. ⓣ420-4689, ⓦwww.littlearches.com. Idyllic, intimate rooftop restaurant offering alfresco dining. Delicious though pricey Mediterranean-style fare supplemented with weekly sushi (Thurs & Fri). Daily, 8am–9.30pm.

The southeast

L'Azure ⓣ423-6220, ⓦwww.thecrane.com. An open-air cliff top restaurant with stunning views across the bay. Caribbean seafood cuisine is excellent but the Sunday gospel buffet breakfast (B$55) featuring live music provides something a little different. Fish mains around B$50. Daily 12.30–2.30pm & 6.30–8.30pm.

Cutters ⓣ423-6220. Unmissable bright yellow deli-café on the main road just after the entrance to the Crane. 8am–5pm (closed Tues).

Zen ⓣ423-6220, ⓦwww.thecrane.com. Superlative Japanese and Thai dishes in elegant, themed surroundings (mains B$50–60). 6–9pm, (closed Tues). Reservations essential.

18.3

The west coast

Barbados's **west coast** is peppered with idyllic bays and coves along the sheltered, Caribbean side of the island. Its sandy beaches and warm blue waters have made the west coast the island's prime upmarket resort area. As a result, the coastline has been heavily built up; it holds the island's top golf courses, priciest hotels as well as the swankiest restaurants. Even so there's a smattering of reasonably priced places to stay and, as everywhere on Barbados, all of the beaches are public. Particularly those at **Prospect**, **Sandy Lane**, **Mullins** and **Paynes Bay** are well worth visiting.

Drag yourself away from the beach for a while, though, as the region possesses other attractions: **Holetown** has a fine old church; further north, **Speightstown** repays a visit with its colonial relics and picturesque old streets that recall its vanished heyday as a major port. Much of this history is entertainingly recalled in the new **Arlington House** museum.

Highway 1 runs up the coast, rarely straying far from the shoreline. **Highway 2A** runs parallel to it, some way inland, and offers a speedier road north. **Buses** and **minibuses** serve the coast road between Bridgetown and Speightstown all day, with bus stops every couple of hundred metres. Services normally stop at around midnight, after which you'll need a car or private taxi. If you're coming from the south coast, look for buses marked "Speightstown" – these usually bypass Bridgetown and save you having to change buses (and terminals) in the city.

Accommodation

Although the west coast of Barbados is renowned for **luxury hotels**, several of which are ranked among the best in the Caribbean, there are a handful of cheaper places sandwiched in between.

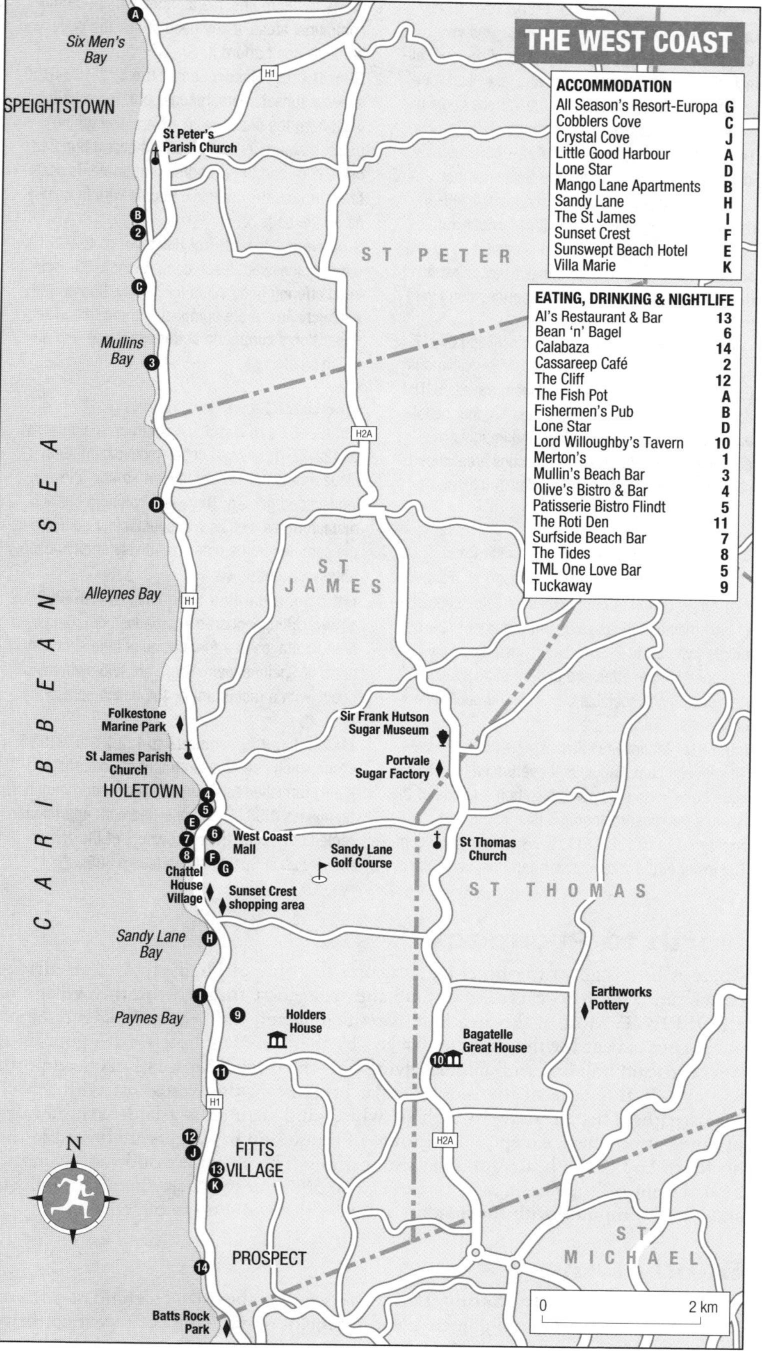

18

18.3 | BARBADOS

From Prospect to Paynes Bay

Crystal Cove Appleby, ⓣ432-2683, ⓦwww.crystalcovehotelbarbados.com. One of the best all-inclusives, with comfortable rooms, excellent food and good watersports. One of the various pools has a swim-up bar under a waterfall. 9

The St James Paynes Bay ⓣ432-0489, ⓦwww.the-stjames.com. Formerly the Beachcomber Apartments, this nicely refurbished small self-catering apartment block provides large, luxurious balconied one-or two-bedroom (sleeping up to six) apartments or studios with smaller balconies. All rooms have kitchen facilities and prices don't vary much during the year. 8

Villa Marie Lashley Rd, Fitts Village ⓣ417-5799, ⓦwww.barbados.org/villas/villamarie. Excellent value aimed at independent travellers. The double rooms and apartment suites (for four people or more) are spacious, spotless and imaginatively conceived with a large shared balcony area, superb shared kitchen facilities and garden. A/c extra. 3

Around Holetown

All Seasons Resort - Europa Sunset Crest ⓣ432-5046, ⓦwww.allseasonsresort.bb. Favourite mid-range option offering excellent value consisting of well maintained spacious one-bedroom apartments (with up to 2 extra beds), including fully equipped kitchenettes and private patio space. A sizeable pool, sociable bar area and pool table onsite. 5

Lone Star Mount Standfast ⓣ419-0599, ⓦwww.thelonestar.com. Fabulous if overpriced little boutique hotel in an old house. Also home to one of the island's trendiest restaurants (see p.685). 9

Sandy Lane ⓣ432-1311, ⓦwww.sandylane.com. The jewel of the west coast, offering spectacular luxury in the rooms, restaurants, bars and other communal areas. If you need to ask the price, you probably can't afford it. 9

Sunset Crest Resort Sunset Crest, ⓣ432-6750, ⓦwww.sunsetcrestbarbados.com. Ten minutes' walk from the beach, with several swimming pools, restaurants and bars, and over a hundred one-, two- and three-bedroom apartments scattered around the complex. Rooms vary in quality as do the beds. 4

Sunswept Beach Hotel Holetown ⓣ432-2715, ⓦwww.sunsweptbeach.com. A small, 23-room hotel offering good value for money. Rooms with full kitchenettes are compact with no frills. The upper floors command better sea views and are much quieter. 5

Around Speightstown

Cobblers Cove Hotel just south of Speightstown ⓣ422-2291, ⓦwww.cobblerscove.com. Spacious rooms (no TV) are hidden around a lovely landscaped garden. There is a splendid bar and restaurant (as well as two spectacular suites) and the complex fronts onto a relatively empty beach. Simply delightful. 9

Little Good Harbour Shermans, ⓣ439-3000, ⓦwww.littlegoodharbourbarbados.com. Gingerbread cottages in a friendly, quiet little spot just north of Speightstown. There are two swimming pools, with a restaurant by the beach across the road. 9

Mango Lane Apartments ⓣ422-2703, ⓔholli@sunbeach.net. An assortment of colourful and lightly furnished fan-ventilated two-bedroom chattel houses (US$75) and one-bedroom apartments, rented out by the friendly owners of the *Fisherman's Pub* in Speightstown (see p.685). 2

North to Prospect

There is little sign of the hotel extravaganza to come as Highway 1 clears Bridgetown and begins to carve its way up the west coast through the tiny village of **PROSPECT**. Most of the area here is residential and the beaches – largely bereft of tourists, except for the stretches backed by the area's few hotels – are popular at weekends and holidays with families living near the capital. Most visitors head north to **Payne's Bay**, one of the most popular beaches on the west coast with several access paths. This attractive stretch of white sand maintains a laid-back, family-oriented atmosphere, except when groups of cruise ship passengers are bussed to the northern end of the beach for a day's sunbathing. There's some good snorkelling to be had right off the beach, or you could swim 50m out to where the pleasure boats anchor to commune with the handful of turtles that show up to be fed.

Sandy Lane

Just north of Paynes Bay, **Sandy Lane** offers by far the island's grandest accommodation – the epitome of affluence and ostentation, with a list of repeat celebrity guests as long as your arm. The place guards its guests jealously behind high walls and security guards though if you've got the energy, it's worth striding along the sand past the tall casuarinas and manchineel trees to the bay since the sweep of gently shelving sand, backed by the elegant hotel, is quite splendid.

Holetown and around

A couple of kilometres further north lies **Holetown** the island's third-largest town and the place where English settlers first landed in 1625. It's a busy, modern hub for the local tourist industry, if somewhat lacking in character. All west-coast buses run through it, and the main highway is lined with fast-food restaurants, souvenir shops, banks and grocery stores. The reproduction chattel houses in the **chattel house village** (on the east side of the highway) and the nearby **West Coast Mall** offer some good spending opportunities. On the northern edge of town, 1st and 2nd streets, lined with trendy restaurants, lead down to the sea.

Ten minutes' walk north of the centre of Holetown, to the left of the main road, **St James' Parish Church** (daily 9am–5pm; free) is one of the most attractive on the island and is surrounded by frangipani, casuarina and mahogany trees. The church is also the oldest religious site in Barbados since Europeans arrived – the initial wooden structure was erected in 1628; the original font and church bell, both built later in the century, have survived. The graceful building with its thick pale coral stone walls has a pleasant airy countenance. Of particular interest is the modern stained-glass window in the organ apse, representing the many hues of a tropical garden, which was designed by renowned local artist Bill Grace.

The entrance to **Folkestone Marine Park** (Mon–Fri 9am–5pm; free beach access, B$1.15 for the visitor centre) lies just beyond the church. Most come for the snorkelling on the decent patches of coral reef within the protected area and on a wreck just beyond it (look for the boats). The cordon of buoys that marks the zone is a real plus in peak holiday season, ensuring that you won't be run over by jet-skis – a very real hazard elsewhere on the west coast. In addition, the park provides lifeguards, plenty of shady picnic tables and snorkel equipment rental (B$20).

A couple of kilometres inland from Holetown you can find the **Sir Frank Hutson Sugar Museum** (daily 8am–4pm; B$10 museum; B$25 museum and factory tour; ⓣ 426-2421). Signposted off Highway 2A just north of the main roundabout, the small museum has suffered a similar decline to that of the sugar industry itself. It was the brainchild of Frank Hutson, a former sugar worker who rescued a load of rusting sugar-mill machinery, cleaned it up and incorporated it into the museum, adding captions, maps and photos explaining the role of sugar on the island since its introduction in the 1640s. Many of the displays are faded and much of the machinery could do with a cleaning. It's only worth popping in between February and June when you can tour the adjacent sugar factory and view the full production process. At the end of the tour you'll be presented with a bag of sugar made at the factory.

North to Mullins Bay

Once you've passed Holetown there is little of particular interest to hold you en route north to Speightstown. A series of exclusive hotels and grand private houses, fenced in behind security gates, is interspersed with small villages of shops, fishing shacks and chattel houses, keeping a typically Bajan toehold on the increasingly developed west coast. Good snorkelling can be found offshore from the *Lone Star* hotel (see opposite), where endangered hawksbill turtles can often be spotted – look out for the buoys and other snorkellers about 200m out. Further north, **MULLINS BEACH** – a strip of sugary sand with a lively beach bar (see p.685) – is a good place to stop for a swim.

Speightstown

Small, run-down, yet utterly charming, **SPEIGHTSTOWN** (pronounced "Spikestown") is Barbados's second town. It was once a thriving port and three major forts were erected to protect it. While the place has declined precipitately over the last century, and remained largely untouched by tourist development, recent years have seen attempts to preserve some of the town's historical character. The narrow streets are lined with old-fashioned Georgian-style shops, their galleries propped up on wooden pillars, projecting over the pavements.

Buses running up the west coast normally terminate at Speightstown **bus station** at the eastern end of Church Street. From here, head down towards the sea, passing on your right **St Peter's Parish Church** (daily 9am–5pm; free). Across from the church, facing the sea, you'll find locals chatting, enjoying a bite to eat or reading the local paper in the shade of the redeveloped **esplanade**. You are now in **Queen Street**, Speightstown's main drag, which has several grand old buildings that have survived the town's decline. Midway down the street on the left-hand side stands **Arlington House** (Mon–Sat 9am–5am, B$25; BNT), a classic example of the island's early townhouses – narrow, tall and gabled, with a sharply sloping roof and balcony. The state-of-the-art interactive museum inside the house is a must, offering fascinating insights into to the town's bygone times, including audio memories and chronicles of the port's illustrious history. Up in the attic, the port's wharf has been re-created with appropriate light and sound effects, complete with imported sand and virtual fish and turtles. There are also several entertaining hands-on exhibits: steering a ship through the Caribbean, or experiencing a hurricane, or, if that all sounds too energetic, chill out on the veranda with a sandwich and a glass of wine from the adjoining *Café Mojo*.

Directly across the street from Arlington House is the **Gallery of Caribbean Art** (Mon–Fri 9.30am–4.30pm, Sat 9.30am–2pm), which features three rooms of sculpture and paintings by artists from Barbados and the Caribbean. Most pieces are for sale.

Eating, drinking and nightlife

Plenty of pricey top-notch **restaurants** line the "Platinum Coast" though there are a few less expensive options.. Particularly recommended are some of the informal stalls that appear on Friday and Saturday evenings dishing up fresh fish (accompanied by rice and peas, macaroni pie, breadfruit and various other filling favourites). You're guaranteed a full plateful for around B$25 and it's a great way to meet locals. Places like the *Fisherman's Pub* in Speightstown and *Merton's* at Half Moon Fort are worth checking out, whatever your budget. **Nightlife** tends to be pretty quiet and limited to floor shows put on by the more exclusive hotels though one or two places sometimes offer live local bands.

From Prospect to Paynes Bay

Al's Restaurant & Bar Fitt's Village (in Jordan's supermarket complex). Cheap and cheerful local eatery dishing up flying fish or chicken for B$10. Mon–Sat 8am–7pm.

Calabaza Prospect ⓣ424-4557, ⓦwww.calabazabarbados.com. Vibrant Moroccan decor and torch lit terrace on which to enoy fine "Caribblend" cuisine. Starters B$30–40, mains from B$65.

The Cliff Derricks ⓣ432-1922, ⓦwww.thecliffbarbados.com. Stunning cliff top location with first-rate service, exquisite food and fabulous cocktails. Expect some of the island's most innovative cooking and astronomical prices (B$215 for two courses; B$260 for three), not including drinks. Dec–Apr daily 6–9.30/10pm. Closed Sun May–Nov.

Lord Willoughby's Tavern Bagatelle Great House, Highway 2A ⓣ421-2121, ⓦwww.tavern-knights.com. English-style sports pub serving good-value grub (excellent chips) to mainly locals and expats for under B$40. Hours 11am–2am Mon–Thurs and 24-hours a day at weekends. Dancing with DJs most nights and occasionally live bands.

The Roti Den Paynes Bay ⓣ432-6030. Brightly painted blue shack on the corner of the turn-off to

Holder's Hill serving tasty filling rotis (B$10-15). Try the chicken and channa. Also check out the *Roti Hut* in Worthing. Mon–Sat 10am–8pm.
Tuckaway Paynes Bay ⓣ432-6140. Refreshing home-made sorbets and ice cream in authentic Caribbean flavours such as ginger, nutmeg, mango and soursop. Mon–Sat 10am–9pm, Sun 4–9pm.

Holetown

Bean 'n' Bagel West Coast Mall ⓣ432-1103. It's worth putting up with the soulless neon-lit surroundings to tuck into the excellent variety of filling breakfasts (B$22, available all day) while checking out the local papers. Inexpensive local lunches (B$23–25) are also served. Mon–Sat 8am–4.30pm, Sun 8am–2pm.
Lone Star Mount Standfast, north of Holetown ⓣ419-0599. Trendy joint in a converted beachside garage, drawing a youngish crowd and celebrities with a relaxed vibe enjoying the likes of lamb chops and mashed potato, shepherd's pie and tikka masalas; three-course Sunday roast (B$120). Mains around B$65–85. Daily 11.30am–10.30pm.
Olive's Bar and Bistro 2nd Street ⓣ432-2112. Popular eatery offering a wide choice of excellent meals. Regular starters (B$25–38) include chicken-liver parfait or chicken satay, with main courses like herb-crusted jerk pork crust or shrimp curry from around B$65. Daily 6.30–9.30
Patisserie Bistro Flindt 1st Street ⓣ432-2626. Serving tasty breakfasts (B$20–30) and light lunches on the outdoor patio; get there early for the fantastic croissants. Mon–Fri 7am–6pm, Sat 7am–2pm, Sun 7am–noon.
Surfside Beach Bar behind the Holetown police station ⓣ432-2105. A buzzing beach bar that's popular from breakfast (B$20–30) to late evening, with lunches of sandwiches, pasta or fish and chips (B$26–35) and well-priced unpretentious dishes for dinner (B$45–55). Daily happy hour 4.30–5.30pm and sports on satellite TV – though there's often a cover charge – as well as a low-key steel-pan band on a Sunday evening at 8. Daily 9am until late.
The Tides ⓣ432-8356, ⓦwww.tidesbarbados.com. One of the west coast's finest, offering fresh seafood in an elegant shore-side setting within a lush tropical garden with an amazing tree-house dining area; the desserts are particularly mouthwatering. At least B$110 for a two-course meal (B$160 for three), excluding drinks. Lunch Mon–Fri noon–2pm, dinner daily 6.30–9pm.
TML One Love Bar 1st Street. A few metal tables and chairs together with some upturned beer crates are all you need to enjoy a chilled Banks beer at a decent price (B$2.50) while enjoying a rare opportunity to converse with locals.

From Mullins Bay to Speightstown and beyond

Cassareep Café Queen Street, Speightstown (set back between *Mango's by the Sea* and the *Fisherman's Pub*). This small informal beachside café provides a handy and healthy lunchstop, serving soup and a different spicy hot dish each day as well as simple salads and sandwiches on tasty home-made bread at low prices (B$10–18). Excellent smoothies too. Mon–Sat 8am–4pm.
The Fish Pot *Little Good Harbour* ⓣ439-2604. Friendly, intimate oceanfront dining in an exquisite coral-stone house. Starters B$30–35, mains from B$50.
The Fisherman's Pub Queen Street, Speightstown ⓣ422-2703. Delightful place with a large ocean veranda, a favourite lunch spot for locals, serving up flying-fish cutters or various stews for around B$25; dinner only on Wed evenings when B$35 will buy you a Bajan feast accompanied by steel pan and limbo dancing plus DJ. Daily 11am–10pm.
Merton's Half Moon Fort. Vibrant fish-fry on a seaside veranda buzzing with life. You'll not pay much over B$25 for a large fresh piece of fish plus the usual Bajan sides. Thurs–Sat, from around 7pm.
Mullins Beach Bar Mullins Beach ⓣ422-2044. Wide ocean view veranda provides a great spot for sipping cocktails or savouring a leisurely lunch for around B$20–45 (soon to do dinners). Sun-loungers for hire. Daily from 10am, lunches 11.30am–3pm.

18.4

Central Barbados

The southern part of the central parish of **St George** possesses a mostly flat, gently rolling landscape – perfect for the sugar crop that's been cultivated here for almost four centuries. As you head north through the parish up into **St Thomas**, however, the land rises in a short series of peaks culminating in the island's highest point, **Mount Hillaby** (340m), on the border with **St Andrew**. Despite its relatively small area, central Barbados offers a number of attractions to lure you away from the beach. The parish of St George boasts the historic military signal station at **Gun Hill** while to the north, in St Thomas, lies **Harrison's Cave**, a series of weirdly beautiful underground chambers. **Welchman Hall Gully**, offers a unique glimpse of the island in its primal state while the gardens at the **Flower Forest** offer a more carefully managed look at local flora.

Getting to and from the island's interior is straightforward – **buses** from Bridgetown run to the main attractions, though services are less frequent than on the coasts; navigating cross-country from location to location, however, is more problematic. You'll save a lot of time if you rent a car for a day or two or join an organised tour (see p.665)

Gun Hill Signal Station and Orchid World

Five kilometres or so north-east of Bridgetown between Highways 3 and 4 at Charles Rowe Bridge stands **St George's Parish Church** (daily 9am–4pm; free). It's the oldest church building on the island since it was the first to be rebuilt, in 1784, after the 1780 hurricane, and merits a peek inside. Of particular note is the impressive altar painting *The Resurrection* by the renowned American artist Benjamin West, who became president of the Royal Academy. As you continue northeast and the road starts to rise sharply, the striking maroon watchtower of **Gun Hill Signal Station** (Mon–Sat 9am–5pm; B$15; BNT) can be glimpsed to the left, peering over the tree line. The turn is signposted a couple of kilometres beyond Charles Rowe Bridge. The signal station was built in 1818 following the island's first and only major slave rebellion in 1816 (see p.668). Gun Hill was one of a chain of six signal stations (see also Grenade Hall, p.688) constructed on high ground across Barbados to provide a vital chain of rapid communication in case of local rebellion or enemy invasion. Worth visiting for the view alone, the excellently restored signal station offers fabulous panoramic views across the green, gently rolling hills of central and southern Barbados and out to the ocean. Below the station, and visible from the tower, is a giant **white lion** – a British military emblem carved from a single block of limestone by soldiers stationed here in 1868.

Just over a kilometre to the north lies **Orchid World** (daily 9am–5pm; B$20; B$30 for a combined ticket to the Flower Forest, valid a week; ⓣ433-0306) which displays 20,000 of these exotic flowers among lovely coral rock gardens. It's a scenic spot but if you're not an orchid fanatic, you'll probably find the Flower Forest (see opposite) or the Andromeda Botanical Gardens (see p.692) more compelling.

Harrison's Cave and the Springvale Eco-Heritage Museum

Travelling northeast into St Thomas on Highway 2 from Bridgetown, you arrive at **Harrison's Cave** (daily 9am–3.45pm; B$40; ⓣ438-6640, ⓦwww.harrisonscave.com; 40min tours), a labyrinth of interconnecting subterranean chambers. Underground streams and dripping water have carved huge limestone caverns full of stalactites and stalagmites and other beautiful calcitic formations. Justifiably billed as Barbados's top tourist attraction, Harrison's Cave received a US$34 million face-lift in 2007, which included the valuable addition of an interpretive centre. After an informative video, you're taken underground into the various illuminated chambers on a James Bond-style electric tram. Even the guide's mechanized commentary, which rather spoils the eerie, otherwise soundless atmosphere of the place, cannot detract from the cave's spectacular beauty.

A small folk collection, the **Springvale Eco-heritage Museum** (Mon–Sat 10am–3.30pm; B$10; ⓣ438-7011) lies a few kilometres north of the caves (downhill from *Judy's Watering Hole*, a rum shop) on a former sugar plantation. Although not an essential stop, the 45-minute tour of the folk museum gives a sense of plantation life as you meander around a collection of locally made furniture, traditional cooking pots and exhibits on the mining of manjack, known as "Barbados tar", used as fuel for the sugar tayches.

Welchman Hall Gully

Signposted off Highway 2, a kilometre or so north of Harrison's Cave, the dramatic **Welchman Hall Gully** (Mon–Sat 9am–5pm; B$12; BNT) is a long, deep corridor of jungle, hemmed in by steep cliffs and abounding with local flora and fauna. The vegetation is not dissimilar to that which covered the whole island before the British arrived and the gully itself was created aeons ago when the roofs of limestone caves collapsed – a fact which becomes apparent as you follow the marked, shaded **trail**. If you visit in the early morning or late afternoon, keep your eyes out for green monkeys cavorting in the undergrowth.

The gully has two entrances – one at either end and both with parking spaces; buses from Bridgetown stop outside each one though the entry kiosk providing the trail brochure is located at the northern end. After your walk cross the road to grab a drink at the appropriately named *Viewpoint Café,* which offers splendid vistas of the East coast.

Flower Forest

As you head across the parish boundary into St Joseph, the meticulously landscaped **Flower Forest** (daily 9am–5pm, last entry 4pm; B$20 or B$30 for combine ticket with Orchid World; ⓣ433-8152) is signposted just south of Highway 2. You follow a fairly steep self-guided trail through a great variety of well-labelled indigenous and imported plants and trees including include breadfruit, coffee, Barbados cherry, avocado and a single African baobab tree, in addition to a fine collection of orchids, hibiscus and the "lobster claw" heliconias. It's a delightful spot for a picnic, especially with the spectacular views across the Scotland District. Or pick up a slice of tasty banana bread and a drink at the terrace **café**.

18.5

The north

The **north of Barbados** is the most rugged and least visited part of the island. The most popular target is the **Barbados Wildlife Reserve**, home to hundreds of green monkeys and a host of other animals. Nearby there's an old signal station and a nature trail through the forest at **Grenade Hall**, while the lovely park and desolate ruins at **Farley Hill** make a good picnic stop. Just north of here there is a working **sugar mill** at Morgan Lewis and a splendid Jacobean Great House, **St Nicholas Abbey**. The jagged coastline of **St Lucy**, at places such as **North Point,** affords dramatic cliff-top walks and contains a number of deserted coves.

Buses run through the northern parishes from both Speightstown and Bridgetown, though services are less regular than along the south and west coasts. Renting a car will make getting around much less of a hassle.

The Barbados Wildlife Reserve

Green monkeys are the chief attraction at the somewhat disappointing, though highly popular, **Barbados Wildlife Reserve** (daily 10am–5pm, last entrance 4pm; B$23, including access to Grenade Hall; ☎422-8826), just north of Highway 2 in the parish of St Peter and directly accessible by bus from Speightstown or Bridgetown. The non-profit reserve was first established as the island's leading centre for conservation of the monkeys. You'll also find brocket deer, armadillos, caiman alligators and a large breeding facility for Cuban rock iguanas. The monkeys are more easily seen at the daily 2pm feed but unless you're desperate to see them (and they're otherwise a frequent sight scampering across many of the island's roads at dawn and dusk), you're more likely to have a better wildlife experience at the Graeme Hall Nature Sanctuary (see p.676).

Grenade Hall Signal Station

The **Grenade Hall Signal Station** (daily 10am–5pm; B$25, including access to the Barbados Wildlife Reserve), was one of the chain of communication stations built in the years immediately after Barbados faced its only major slave revolt in 1816 (see p.668). While not as attractively situated as Gun Hill (see p.686), and the views from the watchtower have been stifled by the encroaching vegetation, the place is certainly worth a quick visit if you're in the area.

Below Grenade Hall a large tract of **native forest** (same hours and ticket) has been preserved and several kilometres of pathways loop down through whitewood, dogwood, mahogany and magnificent silk cotton trees.

Farley Hill National Park and Morgan Lewis Sugar Mill

Just south of the wildlife reserve on the other side of Highway 2, **Farley Hill National Park** (daily 8am–6pm; free; with car B$3.50) is a small, pleasant park at the top of a 300-metre cliff, offering commanding views over the Scotland District from an old summer house. It's a good place for a picnic, as indeed many Bajans do at the weekend. The site once had a spectacular Great House, built for a sugar baron in 1857 but destroyed in a fire a century later; the charred coral-block walls of the rather ghostly mansion now eerily form the park's focus.

Set in the midst of the crumbling ruins of an old sugar factory, a short drive northeast of Farley Hill, with a tall chimney poking defiantly from the overgrown grass, **Morgan Lewis Sugar Mill** (Mon–Sat 7.30am–3.30pm; B$10, BNT; Ⓣ 826-7075) is the only operating windmill in Barbados. The island once boasted more than five hundred mills but twentieth-century mechanization has all but eliminated them.

Though no longer in commercial use, the nineteenth-century mill is still in perfect working order. The sails, wheelhouse and machinery have been thoroughly restored, and one Sunday each month during the crop season (Feb–June) demonstrations are given. Ring ahead or contact the Barbados National Trust (Ⓣ426-2421) for dates and times.

Cherry Tree Hill and St Nicholas Abbey

Heading north from the sugar mill, the main road sweeps past sugar-cane fields before reaching a magnificent canopy of mahogany trees at **CHERRY TREE HILL**, offering one of the most spectacular views on the island.

Over the brow of the hill, a signposted right turn takes you to the splendid Great House of **St Nicholas Abbey** (Mon–Fri 10am–3.30pm; B$25; Ⓣ422-8725, Ⓦwww.stnicholasabbey.com), the oldest such house on Barbados and one of only three surviving Jacobean Great Houses in the western hemisphere – an essential stop. Dating from the 1650s, the building is a striking structure painted brilliant white with curvilinear Dutch gables and corner chimneys. It was originally owned by two of the island's largest sugar growers, John Berringer and John Yeamans, who reportedly fell out over Margaret, Berringer's wife; in fact Yeaman was so smitten that he allegedly poisoned Berringer in order to marry Margaret. How the mansion came to be called an abbey is unclear – it was possibly a nineteenth-century affectation – as are upstairs fireplaces, which are unnecessary given the Caribbean climate.

You'll get a guided tour of the ground floor (the upstairs, where the owners live, is closed to visitors) which is crammed with eighteenth-century objects of the old Barbadian aristocracy. Note also the cedar panelling in the dining room, added later and made from trees felled during the 1831 hurricane. The outbuildings at the back of the house are rather rustic, and include the original bathhouse and a four-seater toilet. The tour includes a complimentary rum punch and an evocative black-and-white **film** made in 1934 with some great footage of the boats arriving at Bridgetown harbour and of the pre-war city, and life on the plantation.

The north coast

With a sparse population, no tourist development and limited public transport, the nearly deserted northern coastline is a refreshingly isolated area affording spectacular sea views and a number of secluded coves worth exploring. Getting there without a car is tricky though not impossible.

One of the most photographed shots in Barbados, the view from the mouth of the **Animal Flower Cave** (daily 9am–4.30pm, provided the sea is not too rough; Ⓣ439-8797), provides a dramatic close-up of spray splashing up from the rocks at breathtaking proximity. It's debatable whether this sight alone is worth the B$15 entry fee since the three or four remaining tiny sea anemones (or "animal flowers") are nothing special. You can get there on the Connell Town bus from Bridgetown.

18.6

The east coast

For many the rugged, little-explored **east coast** is the most beautiful part of Barbados. The Atlantic waves crash against this wild coastline, making for superb surfing but difficult and sometimes dangerous swimming. A Sunday Bajan buffet lunch at one of the excellent restaurants in the laid-back old resort of **Bathsheba** is a must.

Although the coastal scenery is the main attraction, don't miss the delightful **Andromeda Botanical Gardens** and the dramatically located **St John's Parish Church**. Overall this is a lovely area to drive through, particularly under the steep-sided **Hackleton's Cliff**, where the road weaves through lush tropical forest, offering stunning views over the ocean. You can also walk along the beaches at **Bath** and **Martin's Bay**, watching the surf ride in.

Accommodation

A handful of small but cosy **accommodation** options on the east coast offer a change from the built-up south and west of the island. It's a wonderfully tranquil area to unwind away from the crowds. In Bathsheba you might try bed and breakfast at the *Atlantis Hotel* (Ⓣ433-9445, Ⓦwww.atlantisbarbados.com; ④ – three night minimum stay), an ancient, faded and extremely welcoming place overlooking Tent Bay with good food and eight modest rooms, without TV or telephone – ask for one with a balcony. Just above the *Atlantis* surrounded by an acre of tropical garden lies the extremely popular *Sea-U Guest House* (Ⓣ433-9030, Ⓦwww.seaubarbados.com; ⑤), offering four neat studios with kitchenettes and one guest room (all without TVs), opening out onto an excellent hammock-strewn veranda. Food available and rates include a buffet breakfast. Alternatively at the northern end of Bathsheba, the historic *New Edgewater Hotel* (Ⓣ433-9900, Ⓦwww.newedgewater.com; ④ including continental breakfast) has recently undergone large-scale renovations resulting in comfortable rooms though most have disappointing views given the superb location. Only a few pricier rooms offer good views. Nearby, the *Round House* (Ⓣ433-9678, Ⓦwww.roundhousebarbados.com; ④) has six simple (no TV) but tastefully furnished en-suite rooms, all with access to a communal roof terrace with limited sea views. Inland, the *Naniki's* restaurant (see p.692) is due to open a new eco-health spa retreat with accommodation. Call or log-on for developments.

Codrington College

Signposted on your right as you head up the east coast, Skeete Bay and Consett Bay are a quiet, pretty coves, each with fishing boats and a strip of sand. Just north of Consett Bay on the clifftop stand the handsome buildings of **Codrington College** (open 24 hours; free, donations appreciated; Ⓣ423-1140). The approach to the college is dramatic, and the buildings are pleasantly arranged around an unfinished quadrangle. The school is first degree-level institution in the English-speaking West Indies, it continues to teach theology to budding Anglican vicars, and is now affiliated to the University of the West Indies.

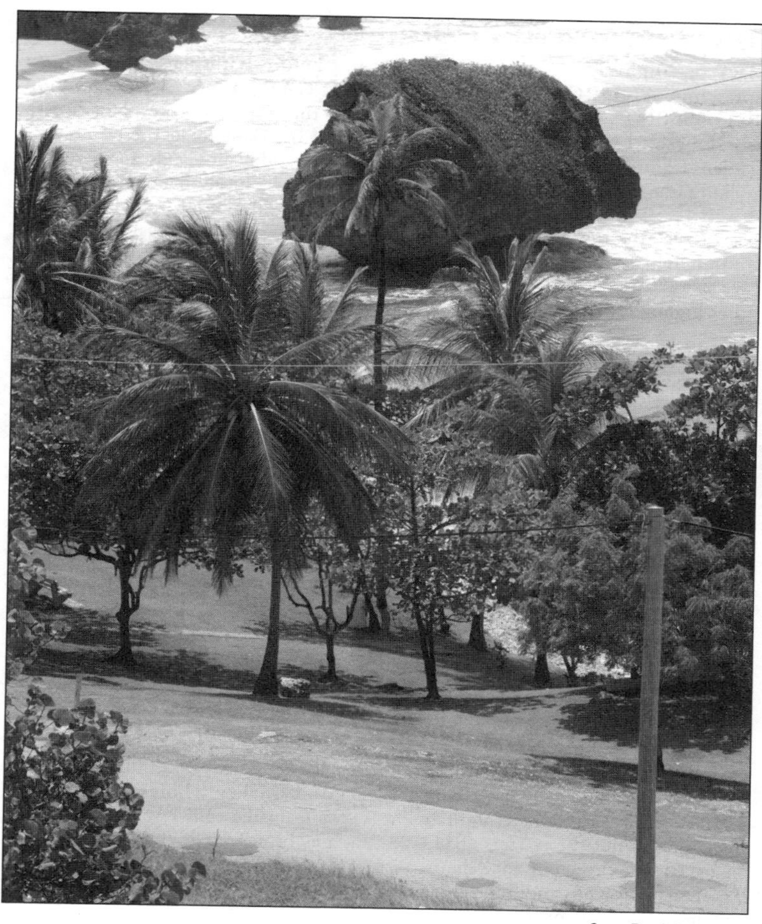

▲ Soup Bowl, Bathsheba

St John's Parish Church and Hackleton's Cliff

From Martin's Bay, a steep road climbs dramatically up through Hackleton's Cliff to the superbly situated **St John's Parish Church** (daily 9am–5pm; free). St John's was first built in the mid-seventeenth century but following damage in successive hurricanes, the present building dates from around 1836. The church's most attractive feature is the superbly hand-carved **pulpit**. Outside, the expansive **graveyard**, perched on top of the cliff, overlooks kilometres of jagged coastline.

From the church, follow the road north for about a kilometre and you'll find a sign that leads you to **HACKLETON'S CLIFF**. If you're travelling by **bus** (the Martin's Bay one from Bridgetown), you'll have a short walk to the viewpoint. This steep 300-metre coral limestone escarpment marks the edge of the Scotland District to the west and the rugged east coast. Here you can soak up the fabulous views across the craggy hills of **Scotland**, nostalgically named by early settlers for their supposed resemblance to the country of the same name, and up the sandy northeast coastline.

The Andromeda Botanical Gardens

Back on Highway 3 a bit further north, just before Bathsheba, the colourful, sprawling **ANDROMEDA BOTANICAL GARDENS** (daily 9am–5pm; B$17.50; BNT; ⓣ433-9384) make up one of the most attractive spots on the island. Created in 1954 by a local horticulturalist Iris Bannochie, these impressive gardens feature masses of local and imported shrubs and plants, landscaped around a walking trail. Informative free guided tours are given by local botanists on Wednesdays at 10.30am. On your left as you enter, the colourful hibiscus garden is the best place to see the tiny hummingbirds that frequent the place. The beautiful bearded fig tree, which appears on the national coat of arms and from which the name "Barbados" was derived, is the star attraction of the gardens, but there are plenty of other highlights. The *Hibiscus Café* at the entrance serves light lunches and snacks.

Bathsheba

The road from the gardens drops you down into **BATHSHEBA**. Picturesque, easy-going and caressed by Atlantic breezes, this has long been a favoured resort for Bajans, though surprisingly few tourists visit. Small holiday homes and the odd rum shop line the roadside as it runs along the sea and, in high season, the odd stall springs up flogging jewellery, beach towels and the like. If the bay dotted with large boulders looks familiar, it's because this is one of the most painted landscapes in Barbados. Also known as the "**soup bowl**" because of the surf that crashes here pretty much all year round, the area is a popular surfing spot and the site of several annual tournaments. Unfortunately the currents make it a dangerous place to swim, but the attractive golden beach is pleasant to walk along; alternatively, you might prefer a slightly more energetic hike north to the village of Cattlewash along the route of the old railway track below the *Round House* and the *New Edgewater Hotel,* or south to Bath Beach.

Eating, drinking and nightlife

For lunch or dinner your best bet is the *Round House Inn* (ⓣ433-9678; Mon–Sat 8.00am–10pm, Sun 8am–5pm), which offers **good-quality wholesome cooking**, a casual, family atmosphere and fabulous views from the split-level terrace. Mains are B$45–50 but the starters (B$12-28), such as breadfruit soup and the to-die-for baked brie drowning in walnut and rum, are what really catch the eye. Jazz on Wednesday evenings and Sunday lunchtimes; Saturday night musical entertainment only in the high season.

The *Atlantis Hotel* (ⓣ433-9445, daily 8am–8pm, buffet also on Wed) features a renowned Sunday buffet, which for B$60 offers you a vast Bajan feast. It's the colourful yet faded decor, lively atmosphere and fantastic terrace views that provide the real draw (book ahead).

For those on a tighter budget, you can't beat *Bonito's* (ⓣ433-9034) for lunch. Across from High Rock on the beachside road down in Bathsheba, you can watch the surfers from the pleasant first-floor veranda while tucking into some good-value fare – either a modest buffet (B$34, B$39 on Sun) or a range of salads, sandwiches and fresh fish (B$8–22), though you need to time your visit carefully to avoid the tour groups.

Slightly harder to find but well worth the effort is *Naniki's* (ⓣ433-1300, ⓦwww.lushlife.bb; Tues–Sun lunch 12.30–3.30pm), in the nearby village of Suriname (signposted off Highway 3 as the road dives down off the escarpment). It offers excellent organic Caribbean fare at reasonable rates in delightful verdant surroundings. Starters (generally B$20–27) include Jamaican beef patties and ackee, while mains (B$30–40) comprise the likes of pepperpot and veggie options such as root vegetable stew with dumplings. Sunday buffet B$65.

19

St Vincent and the Grenadines

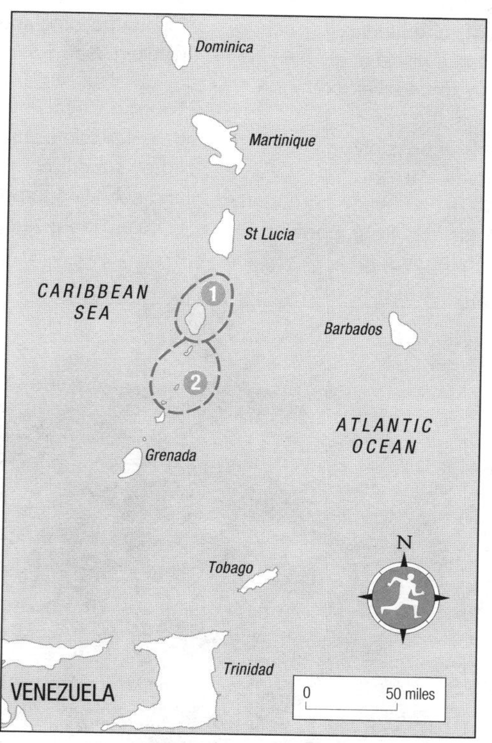

St Vincent and the Grenadines highlights

* **Inter-island ferries** A great way to see all the islands and surrounding ocean – although only recommended when the seas are calm. See p.699

* **Leeward coast drive, St Vincent** With its forests of palms and jungle-smothered hillsides giving way to undeveloped beaches, the Leeward coast is impossibly scenic. See p.706

* **La Soufrière, St Vincent** Though rugged, the strenuous two-hour trek up to the peak of this active volcano is well worth the effort. See p.708

* **Bequia** Besides glorious beaches, this laid-back island preserves its rich seafaring history through its boatbuilding and whaling. See p.709

* **Tobago Cays** Tiny deserted islets surrounded by superb coral reefs and sparkling turquoise waters. See p.718

▲ La Soufrière

Introduction and basics

Situated about one hundred miles west of Barbados and nestled between St Lucia to the north and Grenada to the south, the string of islands known collectively as St Vincent and the Grenadines may be physically close together, but vary enormously in character, terrain and appeal.

The northernmost of the islands is the mountainous St Vincent which, although far less visited than other large Caribbean islands, is the main centre of the area's activity. As well as exploring St Vincent's two distinct coastlines – the rugged windward side and the gentle leeward side – and walking the lush, interior hiking trails, don't miss the opportunity to spend time on the tiny isle of Bequia. Just a short ferry ride away, this yachters' haven is also an increasingly popular holiday destination that boasts shimmering beaches and a fascinating seafaring history. The less developed and less populated islands of Canouan, Mayreau and Union are all easily reachable by ferry and (with the exception of Canouan) still offer a taste of the unspoilt Caribbean, while Mustique, an island hideaway of the rich and famous, makes for an affordable day-trip of swimming and snorkelling – though expect to part with a good deal of money if you plan to stay overnight.

The uninhabited national park of the Tobago Cays, a cluster of islets forming the eastern point of a triangle between Union Island and Mayreau, is surrounded by coral reefs and unbelievably aquamarine waters, and offers an excellent excursion from nearby islands.

Where to go

No doubt the highlight of any trip to St Vincent and the Grenadines is making the strenuous trek through **St Vincent's lush rainforest** and volcanic ridges to the rim of **La Soufrière**, St Vincent's active volcano. Although the more than thirty islands that make up St Vincent and the Grenadines are becoming increasingly affected by tourism, they are still a superb destination for adventurous sun-seekers, snorkellers, divers and yachters. Particularly worthwhile destinations include the turquoise waters of the **Tobago Cays** for superb diving, snorkelling and windsurfing, and the delightful island of **Bequia**, whose relaxed pace of life and seafaring ways warrant a longer stay than the size of the island might suggest.

When to go

As in much of the Caribbean the best time to visit St Vincent and the Grenadines is during the **winter** – roughly January to May – when the tropical heat is tempered by the trade winds and rainfall is minimal. August to October is **hurricane season** and the wettest season, though the threat of big storms need not be a deterrent from visiting at this time of year.

Getting there

Flights touch down on St Vincent at E.T. Joshua Airport in Arnos Vale, roughly 1.5 miles southeast of the capital of Kingstown. The airport does not receive international flights from outside the Caribbean, so you'll need to fly first to Barbados, Grenada, Martinique, St Lucia, Puerto Rico or Trinidad and make a connection. It's also possible to travel to Union Island from Carriacou (one of Grenada's islands) by **boat** – see box on p.697 for details.

Information

The country has four **tourist information centres**. The main one is situated at the cruise ship terminal in Kingstown, St Vincent, with smaller offshoots at E.T. Joshua Airport and on Bequia (see p.709) and Union Island (see p.717). You can pick up **maps** of St Vincent and most of the Grenadines at all of the offices. A detailed Ordnance Survey map

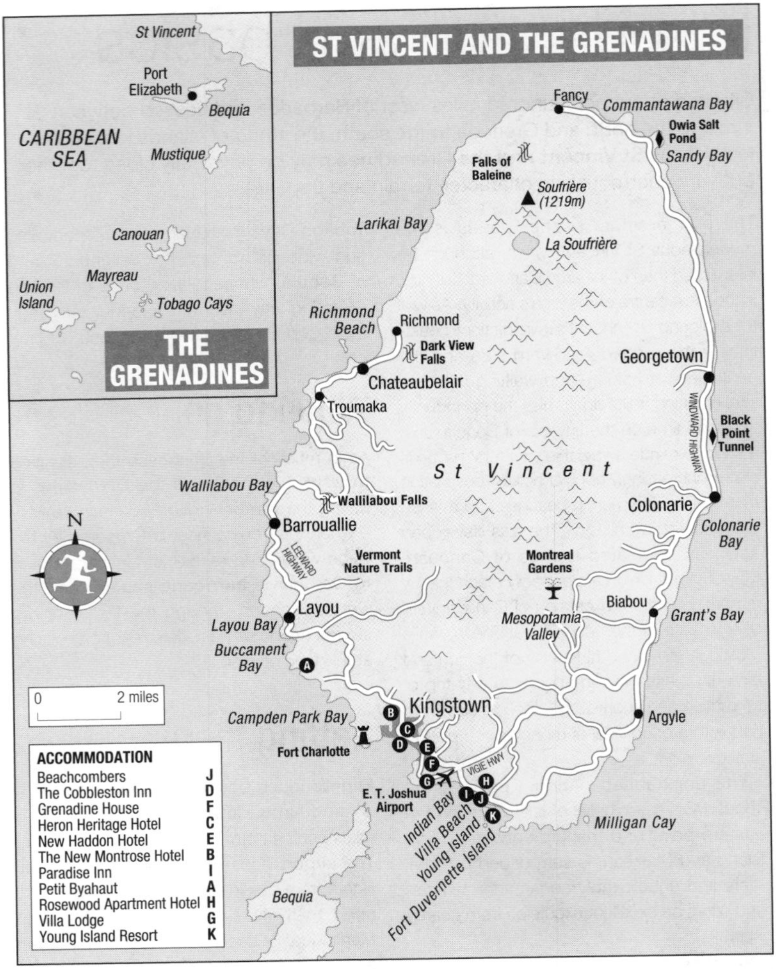

ST VINCENT AND THE GRENADINES

THE GRENADINES

St Vincent
Port Elizabeth
Bequia
CARIBBEAN SEA
Mustique
Canouan
Mayreau
Union Island
Tobago Cays

Fancy
Commantawana Bay
Owia Salt Pond
Sandy Bay
Falls of Baleine
Soufrière (1219m)
Larikai Bay
La Soufrière
Richmond Beach
Richmond
Dark View Falls
Georgetown
Chateaubelair
Troumaka
Windward Highway
Black Point Tunnel
St Vincent
Wallilabou Bay
Wallilabou Falls
Colonarie
Colonarie Bay
Barrouallie
Leeward Highway
Vermont Nature Trails
Montreal Gardens
Layou
Layou Bay
Biabou
Grant's Bay
Mesopotamia Valley
Buccament Bay
Kingstown
Argyle
Campden Park Bay
Fort Charlotte
Vigie Hwy
E. T. Joshua Airport
Indian Bay
Villa Beach
Young Island
Fort Duvernette Island
Milligan Cay
Bequia
N
0 2 miles

ACCOMMODATION

Beachcombers	J
The Cobbleston Inn	D
Grenadine House	F
Heron Heritage Hotel	C
New Haddon Hotel	E
The New Montrose Hotel	B
Paradise Inn	I
Petit Byahaut	A
Rosewood Apartment Hotel	H
Villa Lodge	G
Young Island Resort	K

of St Vincent is also available from tourist information and some tourist-oriented shops.

Money and costs

The official currency of St Vincent and the Grenadines is the **Eastern Caribbean dollar** (EC$), although the US dollar and major credit cards are widely accepted at hotels, restaurants, car rental agencies and dive and tour companies. The EC$ is divided into 100 cents. Notes come in denominations of 5, 10, 20, 50 and 100 EC dollars; coins in 1, 2, 5, 10 and 25 cents. At the time of writing, the **exchange rate** was roughly EC$2.65 to US$1.

St Vincent has plenty of **banks**, including Barclays Bank and Scotiabank on Halifax Street in Kingstown, both of which have ATMs. E.T. Joshua Airport has an **exchange bureau** which is open 8am–noon and 3–5pm on weekdays. There are also two banks on Bequia and a branch of the National Commercial Bank on Canouan and Union Island; all have ATMs. **Banking hours** are generally Monday to Thursday 9am–3pm and Friday 9am–5pm; however, some banks close at 1pm.

In St Vincent and the Grenadines a **departure tax** of EC$40 applies to stays longer than 24 hours.

Hotels and restaurants will automatically add a 7 percent **government tax** and 10 percent **service charge** to your bill. Tipping is at your discretion, but not expected.

Getting around

Details on **transport** to specific islands is covered in the individual island sections. Islands without bus services are small enough to walk around.

By bus

Buses are small minivans (known as dollar vans) that operate on the larger islands. On St Vincent, buses run from the bus terminal in Kingstown next to the New Tokyo Fishmarket from 6am to 8pm; service is much less frequent on Sundays. The terminal is organized into sections marked Leeward, Windward or Kingstown. Ask any driver if you're not sure which one you want.

Although dollar vans pack in as many people as possible, play loud music and drive very fast around the steep mountain roads, they are generally safe, fun and heavily used by locals. Though there are frequent **bus stops**, vans can be flagged down anywhere along the route – you'll always know when one is around by their incessant use of the horn. Let the conductor know when you want to get off and pay as you leave. Fares are subject to change, but from Kingstown to the airport it's about EC$1.50, EC$1.50 to Villa Beach, EC$3 to Argyle and Wallilabou, and EC$2 to Buccament; ask locals before you board. Similar bus services run on Bequia (see p.709) and Union Island (see p.717).

By car

To **rent a car** you'll need a local driving permit, available for EC$50 in Kingstown, either from the police station on Bay Street or from the Licensing Authority on Halifax Street (Mon–Fri 9am–3pm). If you have an International Driving Licence, you must get it stamped at the police station.

Avis (☎784/457-2929) is the only international car rental company on the islands and has offices at E.T. Joshua Airport. Local agencies include Rent & Drive (☎784/457-5601, ©rentanddrive@vincysurf.com), Ben's Auto Rentals (☎784/456-2907) and David's Auto Clinic (☎784/456-4026, ©dacl761@hotmail.com). Prices range from EC$140 per day for a car, and up to EC$170 for a

The Jasper

An economical way to travel between Union Island and Grenada's Carriacou is via **The Jasper**, a passenger and cargo boat that operates on Mondays and Thursdays, leaving at 6am from the jetty at Ashton village on Union Island for Carriacou and departing Hillsborough on Carriacou for the return journey to Union Island at 12.30pm. The trip takes approximately **one hour** and the **fare** is EC$20 one-way. To travel between the two islands you must go through **immigration**, either on Carriacou at the end of the Hillsborough jetty or on Union Island at the airport. It is important to keep in mind that immigration on Union Island will not be open when *The Jasper* leaves at 6am so you will need to clear immigration before 4pm the day prior to your departure.

On Union Island the **bus fare** from Ashton to the airport is EC$3 and a bus will be waiting when *The Jasper* docks to transfer passengers to the airport to go through immigration. If you are leaving on the 6am boat, it is a good idea to book a taxi to Ashton rather than rely on the bus service at this time.

Be aware that *The Jasper* is sometimes a fairly large motor-powered vessel and on other occasions it is a small, wooden boat that runs on both motor and wind power which has seen better days – expect an exhilarating ride even when the sea looks calm. Also, departure can be delayed if the boat is waiting for cargo. If you're adventurous and have good sea legs, *The Jasper* can be fun – if not, take a plane.

Websites

Ⓦ**www.grenadines.net**
Though it looks a bit ugly, this is a regularly updated, comprehensive site which features summaries of each island, articles, travel tips and promotions.

Ⓦ**www.svghotels.com**
Full of practical information on accommodation, transport, holidays and festivals, this site of the SVG Hotel and Tourism Association is a useful place to research the region before a visit.

Ⓦ**www.nbcsvg.com**
Listen to local news and sports programmes on the website of the National Broadcasting Corporation for St Vincent and the Grenadines.

Ⓦ**www.svgtourism.com**
This official site of the SVG Ministry of Tourism and Culture contains a wealth of information on each island, things to do, year-round events and the country's history.

jeep; there's little difference between local and international firms. Driving is on the left.

By taxi

Taxis are plentiful on St Vincent and tout aggressively for business around Kingstown's jetty and waterfront area. Fares are regulated but there are no meters so be sure to agree on a price before you get into the car. Fares are raised for early morning and late night journeys.

Kingstown's taxi ranks are on the corner of Upper Bay Street and South River Road and opposite the Courts store on Upper Bay Street. Main taxi companies include Sam's Taxi and Tours (Ⓣ784/456-4338) and Belford Taxis (Ⓣ784/457-9190). Fares from Kingstown to the airport cost about EC$25 and from the airport to Villa Beach EC$20.

By boat

A **ferry** ride is a wonderful way to see the islands – especially if you don't want to stay at them all – and makes for the cheapest "cruise" by far. The MV *Barracuda* and MV *Gem Star* both ply the glorious waters between St Vincent, Canouan, Mayreau and Union Island. (Be sure to keep your eyes peeled for flying fish, whales and dolphins.) From St Vincent, the single fare is EC$25 to Canouan, EC$35 to Mayreau and EC$40 to Union Island. Ferries also run frequently between Kingstown and Bequia – see p.709 for details – and less frequently to Mustique (see p.715).

By plane

Planes are a fast, convenient and relatively inexpensive option for travelling between islands. Sample one-way fares from St Vincent with SVG are around EC$70 to Mustique, EC$90 to Canouan, and EC$95 to Union Island. SVG Airways (Ⓦwww.svgair.com), Mustique Airways (Ⓦwww.mustique.com) and LIAT (Ⓦwww.liatairline.com) all provide frequent services. Tickets can be purchased online or at any of the island's airports. Universal Travel on Upper Bay Street, Kingstown (Ⓣ784/457-2779), is efficient at organizing inter-island flights.

Accommodation

St Vincent and the Grenadines offer a wide range of **accommodation**, from small hotels, guesthouses and self-catering apartments to large and at times luxurious beach resorts. **Prices** vary almost as much as the type of accommodation. Most hotels, especially those that cater for business travellers, have year-round rates, while others drop their prices during summer months (mid-April to mid-December), though not by a lot. Finding a place to stay usually isn't hard, but during the winter months it's wise to **book ahead**.

Food and drink

St Vincent grows a variety of fruit and vegetables, among them oranges, breadfruit and avocado. The island also produces 90 percent of the world's supply of **arrowroot**, a plant whose starch is used in cooking and in making glossy computer paper. Fresh **seafood** is abundant, ranging from lobster to flying fish, with conch (lambie) being particularly common.

While larger restaurants generally serve a mix of West Indian and international cuisine, you will almost always find **rotis**, curries and saltfish on offer. Vegetarians are well catered for at most large cafés and restaurants, although smaller towns and islands may not be as amenable.

The beer of choice is the Kingstown-brewed **Hairoun** (the Carib name for St Vincent) along with Guinness. Soft drinks, non-alcoholic ginger beer, tonic and soda water are also popular.

Mail and communications

The main **post office** is situated on Halifax Street in Kingstown (Mon–Fri 8.30am–3pm, Sat 8.30–11.30am). Smaller communities in St Vincent and the other islands also have branches; in addition many hotels will sell stamps and post letters.

Coin- and card-operated **phones** can be found on all the islands, and you can buy cards from Cable & Wireless on Halifax

MVs Barracuda and Gem Star ferry schedule

MV Barracuda

St Vincent to Canouan, Mayreau and Union Island
Monday and Thursday
Departs St Vincent at 10.30am
Canouan 2pm
Mayreau 3.25pm
Arrives at Union Island at 3.45pm.
Saturday
Departs St Vincent at 10.30am
Canouan 2.30pm
Mayreau 3.15pm
Arrives at Union Island at 5pm.

From Union Island to St Vincent
Tuesdays and Fridays
Departs Union Island 6.30am
Mayreau 7.30am
Canouan 8.45am
Arrives at St Vincent at noon.

MV Gem Star

St Vincent to Canouan and Union Island
Tuesdays and Fridays
Departs St Vincent 11.00am
Canouan 2.30pm
Arrives at Union Island at 4.15pm.

From Union Island to Canouan and St Vincent
Wednesdays and Saturdays
Departs Union Island 9am
Canouan 8.30am
Arrives at St Vincent at noon.

As both of these ferry services are susceptible to delays, alterations and cancellations, always check with either a tourist information centre or the port authority before travel, or call the *Barracuda* (☎784/527 6135), or the *Gem Star* (☎784/457 4157).

Street in St Vincent, as well as from tourist information centres and shops.

Kingstown has numerous **Internet cafés**, and others can be found throughout the Grenadines.

The **country code** is ⓣ784.

To contact the coastguard or the police and fire departments in an **emergency**, dial ⓣ999. **Police stations** are in Kingstown (ⓣ784/457-1211) and Bequia (ⓣ784/458-3350).

Opening hours, holidays and festivals

Business hours are generally Monday to Friday 8am–noon and 1–4pm and Saturday 8am–noon, although times can vary from store to store.

St Vincent and the Grenadines celebrate **National Heroes' Day** on March 14, **Caricom Day** on the second Monday in July, **August Monday** on the first Monday in August and **Independence Day** on October 27.

St Vincent's **Carnival**, known as Vincy Mas, is usually held on the second Tuesday of July, although festivities begin at the end of June. Like other carnivals, Vincy Mas brings the whole island onto the streets to party with parades, vibrant costumes and calypso and steel-band music. At the end of January there is also a **Blues Festival** that attracts international entertainers to St Vincent, Bequia and Mustique. Bequia hosts an **Easter Regatta**, while Union Island annually celebrates **Easterval**, a three-day festival of boat races, sports games and calypso music. Canouan's **Regatta** occurs at the end of May.

Outdoor activities

St Vincent and the Grenadines' **volcanic features** and **coral reefs** make their underwater topography ideal for diving. Breathtaking walls and spectacular drop-offs combined with large reefs and shallow coral gardens provide first-class day and night dives. Top sites include those around the coastlines of the larger islands, or the spectacular coral reefs of the Tobago Cays, reached on day-trips.

A large network of **hiking trails** weaves through St Vincent's rugged, mountainous interior; though you can follow them on your own, you'll be better off hiring a guide. The other islands are so small that walking is the easiest way to get around, but be wary of walking in the midday sun and take plenty of water.

History

Prior to European contact, the history of St Vincent and the Grenadines is hard to distinguish from that of the rest of the Eastern Caribbean. The first known inhabitants, the **Ciboneys**, were displaced by the **Arawaks** about 2000 years ago, who were in turn swept out of the territory by the **Caribs** a thousand years later. It is only when the history of the Caribs collides with that of the later arrivals (both European and African) that the history of these islands becomes distinct.

St Vincent was once densely populated, especially after it became a refuge for Caribs fleeing Europeans throughout the Caribbean. The Caribs on St Vincent aggressively fought to repulse European attempts to establish a foothold on the island – their success aided by their numbers. Of all the Europeans, the Caribs most loathed the British who were presumptuous enough to grant St

Vincent lands to royal subjects. In the end, the Caribs granted France, Britain's rival, to form the first settlement in the early eighteenth century. By this time, the Grenadines (called Los Pajaros, or The Birds, by early Spanish sailors) had all been colonized by European settlers and converted into plantation economies worked by slaves, while the native populations were eliminated, removed or marginalized.

In 1675, some years before the French settlement was established, a Dutch slave ship sank in the channel between Bequia and St Vincent. The crew and the majority of the slaves perished but many slaves managed to swim ashore and were accepted by the Caribs, forming one large community. However, within a couple generations, rifts developed and the Caribs divided along racial lines: the Black Caribs, descendants of the slave-ship survivors, and Yellow Caribs, who were of strictly native heritage. European influence increased and plantations flourished, and in 1783 Britain was granted sole control of St Vincent as part of the Treaty of Paris, which officially ended the American Revolutionary War.

In 1795 French radical **Victor Hugues** instigated a revolt that resulted in the Yellow Caribs, led by **Chief Duvallier**, and the Black Caribs, led by **Joseph Chatoyer**, sweeping across the island, burning plantations and killing settlers in their wake. Chatoyer, who believed he could not be killed by another mortal, challenged the British commander, Alexander Leith, to a duel and was killed (though under mysterious circumstances).

A year later, Carib resistance was finally crushed. Most of the surviving Caribs, some 5000, were shipped to the island of Roaton, off the coast of Honduras, and the few that were allowed to remain were settled in the northeast tip of the island at Sandy Bay. The British soon set up a plantation economy, importing 18,000 African slaves. When **slavery** was abolished in 1834, the freed slaves turned to small-plot farming, and European immigrant labour was brought in to replace them on the plantations.

However, this more expensive workforce, combined with the fact that cane was being replaced by **beet** as a main source of sugar, led to the decline of the plantation system throughout the region. What economy and politics had started, nature finished. In 1812, an eruption of **La Soufrière** on St Vincent produced major explosions which destroyed coffee and cotton crops. Another major eruption in 1902 killed 2000 people, devastated much of the northern end of the island and was the final death knell of the St Vincent's plantation economy. Nature has played its part ever since. An eruption in 1979 (the year St Vincent and the Grenadines gained independence) led to the evacuation of 20,000 people and destroyed crops and land; hurricanes in 1980, 1986 and the notorious Ivan in 2004 all damaged the agricultural industry.

Following anti-government protests in 2000, general elections were brought forward from 2003 to 2001. The long-time opposition Unity Labour Party won in a landslide victory ending almost 17 years of New Democratic Party rule under James Mitchell, and won a second term in the 2005 elections.

Known to many Vincentians as "Comrade Ralph" or "Ling Time Papa", ULP Prime Minister Ralph Gonsalves has started to implement an ambitious programme of social reform aimed at reducing poverty and the county's high unemployment rate, and increasing access to education.

19.1

St Vincent

Although some typical golden Caribbean beaches are to be found in **ST VINCENT**, the island is better known for the black stretches of volcanic sand dotting its coastline. The Leeward (western) side of the island is characterized by secluded coastal valleys and fishing villages while the dramatic Windward (eastern) side, lined with windswept beaches, is pounded by the waves of the Atlantic Ocean.

Despite these enviable assets, the main reason to visit lies in the mountainous interior which rises to an impressive 4048ft at **La Soufrière,** an active volcano that last erupted in 1979. Running through the region is a network of tranquil hiking trails through forests rich with wildlife.

Whether you choose to lie on the beach, exert yourself outdoors, or try a mixture of both, the island is small enough to take in the full range of activities in just a few days. The best place to start is **Kingstown**, the charming capital, which also makes a good jumping off point if you plan to visit St Vincent's Grenadine islands or don't want to stay in expensive resort accommodation. Just outside the capital, the main tourist areas of **Villa Beach** and **Indian Bay** and the luxury resort of **Young Island** have the most popular beaches, though more appealing swathes of sand lie in the more remote parts of the island.

Kingstown and the beach resorts

Situated in a sheltered bay on the southwest tip of St Vincent, the hard-working harbour town of **Kingstown** is the island's commercial hub. On weekdays the town moves at a frenetic pace, especially around the bustling jetty, bus station and fish market. The heat can be fierce as sea breezes barely penetrate the compact, one-way streets, lined with warehouses and dense with human and commercial traffic. Though breathtaking from a distance, Kingstown's harbour reveals the grittiness of an active port city on closer inspection. There's not much to see along the industrial waterfront, but this matters little as the town's main appeal lies in its entertaining streets. Lined with handsome **colonial-era cut-stone buildings**, the pavements are lined by the colonnaded verandas that have given Kingstown its nickname, **"City of Arches"**. Dressed in pristine white shirts and gloves, traffic officers direct vehicles through the narrow cobbled roads, lending an unexpected air of formality to this energetic, but laid-back town where tourists are barely noticed by the busy locals. Things slow down considerably in the evenings when Kingstown is a shadow of its busy weekday self; and on Saturday afternoons and Sundays when the town lies in slumber.

Accommodation

Kingstown and the Villa Beach area hold St Vincent's highest concentration of **accommodation** options, and may well be where you stay regardless of what area on the island you decide to visit – the options are better here than anywhere else. If you're looking for a real splurge, you can try the lone resort on **Young Island**, just offshore.

Kingstown

The Cobblestone Inn Upper Bay Street ⓣ784/456-1937, ⓦwww.thecobblestoneinn.com. Housed in a restored sugar warehouse, this gem of a hotel, with its cobblestone walkways and arches, is a tranquil haven. The comfortable rooms are individually decorated and come with all the amenities. ④

Grenadine House Kingstown Park ⓣ784/458-1800, ⓦwww.grenadinehouse.com. Overlooking Kingstown in a quiet residential suburb, this gorgeous new boutique hotel set in a restored great house is St Vincent's most sophisticated place to stay. Stylishly decorated and with all mod cons including wireless Internet, the elegant rooms ooze class. A lovely pool and an upmarket restaurant and bar onsite round out the experience. Rates include breakfast. ⑤

Heron Heritage Hotel Heritage Square, Kingstown ⓣ784/457-1631, ⓔinnsvg@caribsurf.com. Brilliant location right in the heart of town on bustling Heritage Square with neat, appealing rooms with a/c, TV and modern decor. Wireless Internet throughout, and a good daytime restaurant (see p.705) downstairs. ③

New Montrose Hotel New Montrose ⓣ784/457-0172, ⓦwww.newmontrosehotel.com. Modern apartment-hotel on the Leeward Highway bus route, near the botanical gardens. All rooms have cable TV, private balcony and kitchenette; a bar and restaurant are onsite. ④

Villa Beach

Beachcombers ⓣ784/458-4283, ⓦwww.beachcombershotel.com. Lovely, family-run place set in attractive gardens on the edge of Villa Beach and made up of colourfully decorated little villas with en-suite bathrooms and patios. On site facilities include a spa, a pool, a bar and a restaurant overlooking the beach. Rates include Continental breakfast. ③–⑤

Rosewood Apartment Hotel ⓣ784/457-5051, ⓦwww.rosewoodsvg.com. Friendly hotel, overlooking Villa Bay and just a few minutes from the beach, with a bus stop for Kingstown at the end of the drive. The colourful rooms come with private patios, and most have full kitchenette – a few cheaper rooms (②) only have a fridge and kettle. ④

Villa Lodge Hotel Indian Bay ⓣ784/458-4641, ⓦwww.villalodge.com. This busy little place on the headland overlooking Indian Beach offers pleasant, carpeted rooms with a/c, fan, patio and fridge; there are also some more appealing apartments with balcony and kitchen. Restaurant, bar and pool onsite. ④–⑤

Young Island

Young Island Resort ⓣ784/458-4826, ⓕ457-4567, ⓦwww.youngisland.com. The most romantic and expensive place to stay on the island, consisting of luxury cottages each with ocean view, private terrace and fresh fruit and flowers. There's also a pool, tennis courts, spa and a white-sand beach outfitted with sun loungers and hammocks. Meals at the onsite restaurant are inventive and elegantly served; rates include breakfast and dinner, and all-inclusive plans are available. ⑨

The Town

Starting at the cruise ship terminal adjacent to the port on the east side of town you'll find the **tourist information centre** (Mon–Fri 8am–4pm; ⓣ784/457-1502, ⓦwww.svgtourism.com). With little to see in this area, the best way to start exploring the town is to head west to Upper Bay Street, which runs parallel to the sea, where you'll find the **market** (Mon–Sat 8am–4pm), an ugly two-storey modernist structure crammed with stalls selling everything from fresh produce and local arts and crafts to toiletries and souvenirs. Just as busy, but twice as smelly, is the **Little Tokyo Fish Market** on the waterfront side of the road next to the bus station.

Heading west from the market's north end, Grenville Street turns into Tyrrell Street at North River Road where you will find the **St George's Anglican Cathedral**, a traditional Georgian structure with airy vaulted ceilings and exquisite stained glass. A window depicting an angel dressed in red robes was originally commissioned by Queen Victoria for London's St Paul's Cathedral; it was later bestowed as a gift to the church's bishop after the queen deemed it inappropriate for angels to wear anything but white. No visit to Kingstown is complete without a visit to the striking **St Mary's Roman Catholic Cathedral**, which stands across the street from its Anglican counterpart. Built in 1823, the cathedral was designed by local Belgian Benedictine Dom Charles Verbeke, and constructed from dark volcanic sand bricks in an eclectic mix of architectural styles including Romanesque, Moorish and Georgian.

A ten-minute walk or a short bus ride northwest along the main road towards the Leeward Highway brings you to Kingstown's superb **Botanical Gardens** (daily dawn to dusk; free), an immaculately kept 17-acre oasis and delightful place to wander or simply relax. Founded in 1765, the gardens are the oldest of their kind in the western hemisphere, and include a 50ft breadfruit tree grown from one of the original plants introduced in 1793 by Captain Bligh. Signs posted along an educational trail near the entrance explain how to identify various species of plant, and along the trail you'll spy the usual palm, bamboo, coconut and cashew trees, as well as more unusual flora such as custard apple and miraculous trees. There's also a small aviary on the grounds where St Vincent parrots are bred to help keep them from extinction. Guides wait at the gates offering informative and worthwhile tours of the gardens (EC$10), pointing out interesting features and naming the various plants and trees.

A recent addition to the gardens is a small **museum** dedicated to the life and work of local master surgeon Dr Cecil Cyrus. A working hospital until 2000, this lovingly created museum also features some items of local historical interest such as photographs of La Soufrière's eruptions in 1902 and 1979, some Carib artefacts, and photos and specimens collected by the doctor, including some of his medical innovations and squash exploits. It's open only by arrangement; call ⓣ457 8781 to make an appointment.

If you fancy a panoramic view of Kingstown and the south Grenadines, head for **Fort Charlotte**, situated on a 636ft-high ridge to the west of the town. Built by the British to protect the harbour from the French and completed in 1806, the fort holds a collection of colourful Lindsay Prescott paintings depicting scenes from Black Carib history. Exhibited in the small museum inside the old barracks, they are reason alone to visit this beautiful historic building. Fort Charlotte is about an hour's walk from Kingstown – head west along Tyrrell Street which then becomes the Fort Charlotte road, or for the less energetic, hop on a bus at any point along the route that connects it with Kingstown and ask the bus conductor for directions.

Villa Beach and Indian Bay

Four miles east of Kingstown is St Vincent's main resort area, a two-mile stretch of coast encompassing Villa Beach and Indian Bay and frequented by yachters, tourists and locals alike.

As Caribbean beaches go, **Villa Beach** is disappointingly shabby, dominated by a handful of average resorts and punctuated by the jetty that serves the far more

Young and Fort Duvernette islands

The two islands off Villa Beach – **Young Island** and **Fort Duvernette Island** – make for an interesting excursion. The private, 35-acre Young Island is an exclusive resort, (see opposite) once hired in its entirety by Bill Gates, and its gardens are a national wildlife reserve. The long golden beach offers a stark contrast to the rest of the island's lush, green foliage, and the whole place seems to float above the waters of the bay. If you want to visit the island without staying overnight, you will need to phone the resort for permission – dial 210 on the phone situated at the end of the jetty on Villa Beach. Water taxis to Young Island leave from the jetty and cost EC$2 one-way.

Tiny Fort Duvernette Island, whose steep cliffs rise to 250ft above sea level, offers splendid views of the Grenadines, as well as a crumbling fort, complete with original 24-pound guns and an eight-inch mortar. Built at the beginning of the nineteenth century to defend Calliaqua Bay from European rivals, the fort is unsafe and caution is advised when exploring its remains. Catch a water taxi from Young Island to Fort Duvernette Island and arrange a pick-up time with the driver for the return trip. The round-trip fare is approximately EC$20.

attractive **Young Island** just offshore. Although popular, the beach is not up to the quality of other, more remote beaches on the island; its thin strip of sand is ruined by two storm drains that continuously pour water into the sea. Equally unsightly are the graffiti-covered rocks separating the beach from adjacent **Indian Bay**; though tiny, the latter is cleaner, more popular with locals and excellent for snorkelling. This beach is also frequented by local vendors selling drinks and snacks at a fraction of the price of anything you'll find at Villa.

Buses from Kingstown drop passengers off at the end of the short road leading down to the jetty on Villa Beach. To reach Indian Bay ask to be dropped off at the narrow path that leads down to this beach just before the Villa Beach stop.

Eating and drinking

Eating options on the island are surprisingly limited, with again the most variety around Kingstown and Villa Beach. Prices tend to be lower in Kingstown than in Villa Beach, where you can expect to pay at least twice as much for food and drink as anywhere else on the island. In addition, many Villa Beach establishments add a 15 percent service charge, instead of the usual 10 percent. Bear in mind that most restaurants in Kingstown close on Sunday. Bars in Kingstown are mainly stalls frequented by locals.

Kingstown

Basil's Bar and Restaurant Upper Bay Street ⓣ784/457-2713. One of the most popular bars in Kingstown, *Basil's* has a tasty menu including a buffet lunch Mon–Fri for around EC$25, while the dinner menu features a range of local and international cuisine such as lobster in mornay sauce (EC$95). Closed Sun.

Bounty Restaurant Egmont Street ⓣ784/456-1776. This pleasant café overlooking the bustling heart of Kingstown doubles as a small art gallery and secondhand bookshop. It serves numerous breakfast options including saltfish and bake and fresh local fruit juices (from EC$10), and there are various rotis and curries for lunch.

Nice Foods Heritage Square ⓣ784/457-1631. Set in a colonial-era cut-stone courtyard beneath the *Heron* hotel, this is a good spot for inexpensive breakfast and lunch overlooking the buzz of the square. Local and international breakfast, and daily lunch specials from local-style chicken and fish to lasagne.

Rainbow Palace Tyrrell Street (no phone). Very popular with locals, this excellent eat-in or take-away restaurant and bar serves the best and cheapest rotis in town as well as inexpensive fish and meat lunches and a good selection of burgers and sandwiches.

The Roof Bar *The Cobblestones Inn* Upper Bay Street ⓣ784/456-1937. Open 7am–3pm this excellent, laid-back hotel bar and restaurant serves a good range of breakfast and lunch options including toasted sandwiches, salads, burgers and daily specials at reasonable prices.

Villa Beach

Beachcombers Restaurant and Bar ⓣ784/458-4283. Open from 7am for breakfast and taking the last dinner order at 10pm, this attractive beachfront restaurant commands beautiful views of Young Island and the ocean beyond. Serving a varied range of local and international dishes, lunch prices range from EC$10 for soup to EC$18 for sandwiches and the dinner menu features main courses for around EC$70. A programme of special events spice up the atmosphere throughout the year including Halloween, Christmas and Carnival parties.

Lime Restaurant and Pub Villa Beach ⓣ784/458-4227. With a wall made up of lobster traps and fishing nets draped around the ceiling, the feel of the sea permeates this waterfront restaurant. The food is excellent and the pub menu at lunch features curries from EC$40. Reservations are required for dinner, when prices range from EC$70 for dolphin fillet to EC$90 for black pepper steak. There is also a long cocktail and cigar menu.

Nightlife and entertainment

Kingstown is the centre for island **nightlife**, such as it is. For official establishments, try *The Attic* at Melville and Grenville streets (11am until late; EC$10–15 cover charge; ⓣ784/457-2559), which features a wide variety of music – live at weekends

– as well as open mic sessions and karaoke; it's also a decent and popular place to watch sports on the multi-screen TVs. *D Lime*, a semi open-air bar on the corner of Heritage Square and Bay street, is a great place for a drink, with live steel pan on the last Friday of each month, and a three beers for EC$10 deal each Friday after noon; local food is on sale, too.

At Villa Beach, the open-air *Chewee's Chill 'n' Grill* offers a pool table and a big-screen TV, and is a nice spot for a drink, as is *Xcape*, just opposite, which has live music on a Friday. The hotels in this area also often feature live entertainment in the evenings.

For more nightlife information, pick up the small weekly *What's On* guide produced by The SVG Hotel & Tourism Association and available at the tourist information centre.

Diving, sailing and island tours

Due to its volcanic origins, the underwater topography of St Vincent is breathtaking, and there is no shortage of **dive operators**. Dive St Vincent, next to the Young Island jetty at Villa Beach (Ⓣ784/457-4928, Ⓦwww.divestvincent.com) offers numerous dives, courses and packages, some of which include accommodation. Packages for seven days' accommodation, ten dives and various extras range from US$951 to US$2845 depending on where you stay; the latter is for accommodation at Young Island. They also organize an excellent snorkelling trip to the stunning 60ft Falls of Baleine (see p.709). Fantasea Tours, also based in Villa Beach at Blue Lagoon (Ⓣ784/457-4477, Ⓦwww.fantaseatours.com), offer dive packages (seven days from around US$800) and run day and night dives for both beginners and experienced divers. They also offer one-day sailing and snorkelling trips to some of the Grenadine islands; prices vary according to trip and group size. In addition to diving packages starting at US$1170, Caribbean Fun Tours (Ⓣ784/456-5600, Ⓦwww.caribbeanfuntours.com) and Barefoot Yacht charters (Ⓣ784/456-9526, Ⓦwww.barefootyachts.com) organize luxury sailing packages around the Grenadines; costs vary depending on time of year, size of boat and length of trip.

One of the best ways to explore the island is on an **organized tour**, and most companies offer similar choices. For challenging, day-long hikes to La Soufrière, expect to pay US$85–125 (including lunch) depending on how extensive the tour is. For hikes to places like Trinity Falls, expect to pay US$70–80 including lunch, and about the same for a trip and swim at Owia Salt Ponds. A light hike on the Vermont Nature Trails will cost $50–60, as will a scenic or historic tour of the island, again including lunch. Good options include the ecologically aware HazEco Tours (Ⓣ784/457-8634, Ⓦwww.hazecotours.com) who offer a wide range of boat, jeep and hiking tours, and Richmond Vale (Ⓣ784/492-4058, Ⓦwww.richmondvalehiking.com) who organize various hikes and waterfall trips.

The rest of the island

Most of the island's sights outside Kingstown and the main resort areas are accessible from the coastal highway that runs up both the island's **Leeward** and **Windward** coasts. However, except for St Vincent's southwest corner where a few roads penetrate inland, St Vincent's mountainous **interior** can be reached only via walking trails, and in one case only by boat.

The Leeward coast

On the Leeward coast the road clings to the mountainside, with little to protect you from the steep drops, and runs as far as **Richmond Beach**. The drive will take you past lush valleys (formerly the site of vast plantations but now dotted with small farms), black-sand beaches ideal for swimming and snorkelling, and peaceful communities boasting beautiful old stone churches.

A half-hour drive or bus ride from Kingstown, **Buccament Bay** is the site of a huge new resort development spreading back from the coast and up the valley. Scheduled to be opened sometime in 2009, the *Buccament Bay Beach Resort* and adjoining *Island Sanctuary* are styled as exclusive retreats offering top-notch luxury. At the time of writing, you could still see the ancient **petroglyphs** carved into the valley's cliffside by asking at the security booth; it's anyone's guess, however, as to whether access will be possible once the properties open. The curvy white petroglyphs are to the left of the valley as you approach the sea, and are accessible via a new access road to the resorts.

Less than a mile north of the pretty village of **Barrouallie**, with its quaint, ornately trimmed houses, is the tranquil beach of **Wallilabou**, famous for being transformed into the set of Jamaica's seventeenth-century Port Royal for the first incarnation of the Hollywood swashbuckler *Pirates of the Caribbean*. Here you can explore the disintegrating but photogenic remains of the set and hang out at the *Wallilabou Anchorage*, a sea-facing bar and restaurant decked out in rusting suits of armour and maritime paraphernalia, and home to models of the film's complete set. The idyllic surroundings are perfect for sunbathing and a dip in the ocean. While in the area, continue north for a mile on the inland side of the road to reach the roadside **Wallilabou Falls**, where you can escape the heat by taking a refreshing swim in the pool beneath the attractive 13ft cascade.

North of Wallilabou, the coast road swings inland through some gorgeous forest, and pitches toward the sea again at Cumberland, passing through a string of pretty villages before reaching **CHATEAUBELAIR**, from where a driveable track leads inland to **Dark View Falls**. From the car park, you negotiate a wobbly bamboo suspension bridge over the Richmond River and cross through a shady picnic area overhung with huge stands of bamboo to get to the falls themselves, an impressive cascade with a swimmable pool at the bottom. There's a trail to a second, higher, waterfall, but it was closed at the time of writing due to rockfalls.

Practicalities

If you are not staying in the main beach resorts or Kingstown, the Leeward coast offers the only other major facilities on the island. Situated about four miles north of Kingstown in a secluded bay reachable only by sea (transport provided) you'll find the private and unique *Petit Byahaut* (ⓣ784/457-7008, ⓦwww.petitbyahaut.com; ⑨). **Accommodation** comes in the form of five luxury huts with screened bedrooms, decks and solar lighting, nestled into 50 acres of gardens and set against

The petroglyphs of St Vincent

The word **petroglyph** literally means drawings on stone, and although these striking white inscriptions on St Vincent have been attributed to the Ciboneys, Arawaks and Caribs, the identity of the people who created them is still disputed. Most petroglyphs, such as those at Layou, are deeply cut into hard andesite rock, but some are carved onto agglomerate, rock made from a mass of volcanic fragments such as those near Argyle and Buccament.

Although efforts are being made to make access easier, petroglyphs take a bit of hunting out. The most popular sites are at Buccament (see above), Layou, and Barrouallie on the Leeward coast. At Layou a cluster of them can be found near the river by the Bible Camp, on the main road to the north of the town; however, they are on private land and you'll need permission from the owner to see them (EC$5 per person; ⓣ784/458-7243). At Barrouallie, petroglyphs can be found in the yard of the local secondary school.

surrounding forested peaks. This is an excellent spot to hike, swim, dive, snorkel, sail and kayak, or simply sunbathe, and rates include some of these activities, plus day-trips, all meals and airport transfer. There is also a bar, games and library onsite and five- and seven-night packages can be arranged.

In terms of **eating**, the *Wallilabou Anchorage* serves decent seafood, and has a daily happy hour (5–6pm), while the gorgeous beachfront restaurant at *Petit Byahut* serves more sophisticated (and expensive) dinners, from curried chicken with spicy beans to snapper fillet; the desserts are delicious, too.

The Windward coast

The highway on the Windward coast leads all the way up to the village of **Fancy**, at St Vincent's northern tip, and offers startling views of rugged coastline and sweeping beaches. Ten miles from Kingstown along the Windward side, you will find the very antithesis of the expected Caribbean shoreline at the windswept beach of **Argyle**, a bleak and rocky stretch reminiscent of northern Scotland (no swimming is allowed here), and the proposed site of the new international airport. To the west of Argyle spreads the rich fertile valley of **Mesopotamia**, where bananas, nutmeg, cocoa, coconuts and breadfruit grow in abundance. Further north into the valley are the unmissable **Montreal Gardens** (Dec–Aug Mon–Fri 9am–5pm; EC$5; www.montrealestgdns.f9.co.uk). The views of the river valleys and ocean are hard to match anywhere in the Caribbean, and the gardens themselves, threaded with tiny paths and bursting with exotic trees and plants, are a delight.

Most buses travel only as far as **Georgetown**, halfway up the coast – check with the drivers and conductors at the bus station in Kingstown if you want to travel further up. On the way to Georgetown, it's worth stopping off to have a look at the **Black Point Tunnel**, which was drilled by slave labour in 1815 to create a direct route for transporting sugar from the northern plantations to the wharf on the Byera side of the headland, from where it would be shipped to Kingstown. The 360ft tunnel was considered an engineering feat in its time and remains impressive today, especially as you can still see the old blast holes in the volcanic rock; the cave-like apertures to the sides were used for storing sugar. To get to the tunnel, take the signposted turn off from the main road and walk past the picnic tables and gazebos dotted along the sand to the far end of the black-sand beach. The only other point of interest on this highway is the **Owia Salt Pond**, a short distance south of Fancy, near the village of Owia – home to the remaining descendants of the Black Caribs. The lovely tidal pools, a popular spot with sightseeing tours, are sheltered from the rolling Atlantic by a huge wall of rock, and the cool, clean salt waters are a lovely place to swim.

The interior

St Vincent's **interior** can only be explored by walking trails, which are not always well marked. The **Vermont Nature Trails** on the Leeward side, signposted about five miles from Kingstown, are one of the few places where you are likely to spot the endangered St Vincent parrot, a colourful bird recognizable by its pale head, blue tail and russet wings. Here the **Parrot Lookout trail** threads its way through lush rainforest, rising approximately 500ft, and you also stand a good chance of seeing hummingbirds, black hawks and green heron along the way. The trails begin near the top of Buccament Valley and pass picnic areas along the way.

Hiking is also excellent in the north of the island around the stunning peak of **La Soufrière**. The trail to the summit leads through fertile rainforest, banana plantations and volcanic ridges, and is a rigorous one: the ascent to the crater is approximately three miles and takes around two hours. The best way to explore this area is on an organized tour as the trail is not clearly marked, and guides can also point out features along the way (see p.700).

In the remote northwest tip beyond the reach of the coastal highway you'll find the breathtaking 60ft **Falls of Baleine**, where a swim in the large rock-lined pool is unforgettable. Time spent at this stunning spot is well worth the trip. The falls are only reachable by organized tour (see p.706).

19.2

The Grenadines

THE GRENADINES consist of 32 islands and cays, some of which are reachable by plane, but most only by boat. Each island has its own distinct character, whether its the exclusive decadence of **Mustique**, the rustic appeal of **Union**, the laid-back vibe of **Bequia** or the idyllic isolation of **Mayreau**.

Bequia

Though separated from St Vincent by a mere nine miles, **BEQUIA** (pronounced "beck-way"), is the largest of the Grenadine islands, and with its aura of tranquillity and relaxed pace, it feels light years away from frantic Kingstown. No visit to St Vincent and the Grenadines is complete without a visit to this seven-square-mile island, where the beaches are breathtaking and the locals friendly. However, don't be fooled into thinking that there's no more to Bequia than a laid-back attitude and stunning scenery. The island also has a rich seafaring history with time-honoured traditions such as whaling and boatbuilding that are still practised. Bequia's proximity to the migration path of the **humpback whale** made it the most important whaling station in the area during the nineteenth and twentieth centuries.

Arrival, information and getting around

James F. Mitchell Airport, near the village of Paget Farm, is situated in the remote southwest of the island, approximately three miles from the capital of Port Elizabeth. **Ferries** run frequently, often three to four times daily, from Kingstown on St Vincent to Port Elizabeth, operated by *The Admiral* (Ⓣ784/458-3348, Ⓦwww.admiralty-transport.com) and *The Bequia Express* (Ⓣ784/458-3472). The journey takes an hour and costs EC$20 one-way, EC$35 return.

Brochures, leaflets and maps are available from the **tourist office** at the end of the ferry jetty in Port Elizabeth (Mon–Fri 8.30am–6pm, Sat 8.30am–2pm & Sun 8.30am–11am, closed on public holidays; Ⓣ784/458-3286, Ⓦwww.bequiatourism.com).

Buses ("dollar vans") depart from the end of the ferry jetty in Port Elizabeth for points around the island. Service is frequent and efficient, but the island is so small and scenic that walking is the best way to explore most of it. Fares are EC$1–3 depending on how far you travel. **Taxis** are plentiful and wait under the almond trees of Port Elizabeth's waterfront. The fare from Port Elizabeth to the airport is around EC$30 and EC$20 to Friendship Bay. If you need to call for one ahead of

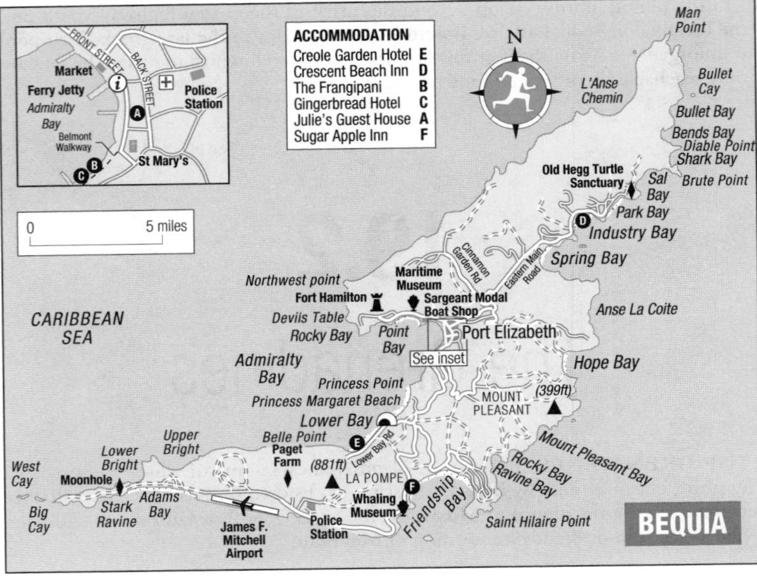

time, try Bequia Car Rentals and Taxi Service (☎784/458-3349), or Challenger Taxi 95784/458 3811). **Water taxis** ply the waters around Port Elizabeth's Belmont Walkway and the nearby beaches. They are popular, easy to hail and a quick way to travel to the beach. A one-way fare from Port Elizabeth to Princess Margaret or Lower Bay beach is EC$15.

Accommodation

There is no shortage of **places to stay** on Bequia, where options vary from basic to luxurious. The expensive choices tend to be small hotels, full of character and very comfortable. That said, most of the accommodation is of a high quality and even the budget options are excellent value for money. Although you'll find much of the accommodation concentrated around Port Elizabeth and Friendship Bay, there's plenty throughout the island.

Creole Garden Hotel Lower Bay ☎784/458-3154 Ⓦwww.creolegarden.com. Nestled in tropical gardens on a hillside surrounding Lower Bay beach, this small family-run hotel offers basic rooms with ceiling fans, mosquito nets, private bathrooms and verandas – all with sea views. Some rooms have fully equipped kitchenettes, and all are cheaper if booked by the week. There is also a good onsite bar and a beachside café. ❷–❹

Crescent Beach Inn Crescent Beach, near Industry Bay ☎784/458-3400. Situated in the northeast of the island near the Turtle Sanctuary, this secluded inn has pleasant rooms, and a bar and restaurant next door. Breakfast is included, and the beachside bar has table tennis and darts. Cash only. ❸

The Frangipani Belmont Walkway, Port Elizabeth ☎784/458-3255, Ⓦwww.frangipanibequia.com. This old family home has been converted into a hotel and is a truly special place to stay for both location and atmosphere. The five basic rooms in the main house have mosquito nets over the beds and shared bathrooms and balcony, while the cottage-like units in the back come with king-size beds and private bathrooms. An excellent and popular waterfront bar and restaurant is onsite, as well as a tennis court for guests. ❸–❼

Gingerbread Hotel Belmont Walkway, Port -Elizabeth ☎784/458-3800, Ⓦwww.gingerbreadhotel.com. This hotel, with its ornate trimmings, lives up to its name. Luxurious suites, some with four-poster beds, include kitchen, private bathroom, and a large porch overlooking Admiralty Bay. The hotel arranges tennis, kayaking, windsurfing and scuba diving for guests as well as excursions to nearby islands. ⑤–⑦

Julie's Guest House Port Elizabeth ⓣ784/458-3304, ⓔjulies@caribsurf.com. Situated on the main street near the jetty, this is an old wooden boarding house with simple, comfortable rooms with showers, toilets and fans; there's also a more modern wing, where rooms have cable TV and a porch, and there's a bar, restaurant and laundry service. ②–③

Sugar Apple Inn Friendship Bay ⓣ784/457-3148, ⓦwww.sugarappleinn.com. Set in private gardens on the opposite side of the island from Port Elizabeth near the little village of La Pompe, these spacious, individually decorated a/c apartments come with full kitchen and panoramic views of the beach – just a five-minute walk away. Amenities include DVD player, flat-screen TV and wireless Internet. ④

Port Elizabeth

Port Elizabeth, Bequia's main town, is nestled deep inside **Admiralty Bay**, the island's large natural harbour and favourite stop for yachters. This relaxed little town has lost none of its lively Caribbean character despite cosmopolitan influences brought by settlers and sailors of many nationalities. The few hours it takes to explore are time well spent, and most will find it a pleasant distraction from Bequia's main attraction – the fabulous beaches.

The centre of the town's activity is the jetty where ferries from Kingstown dock and sailboats depart for other Grenadine islands. At the end of the jetty is a small market selling fresh produce, spices and a plethora of tourist fare, including T-shirts, jewellery and locally made jams; vendors will encourage you to taste their produce,

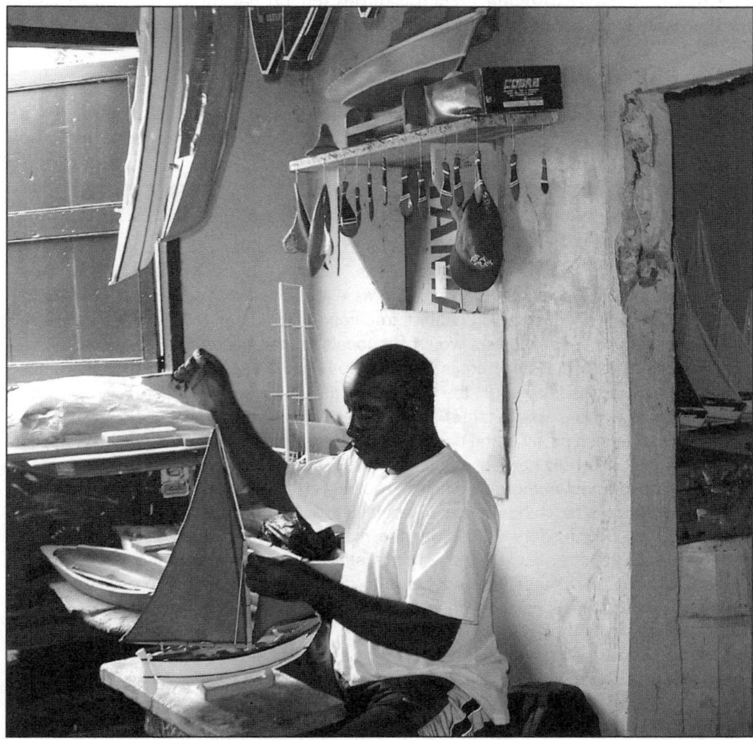

▲ Sargeant's Model Boat Builder's Shop, Port Elizabeth, Bequia

but don't feel pressured to buy once you have. Port Elizabeth's main drag, **Front Street**, with its collection of souvenir shops, yacht provisioners and restaurants, leads into **Belmont Walkway**, where most of the town's accommodation and restaurants are to be found. Don't miss the Bequia Bookshop and its large selection of Caribbean literature, maps and prints, and the Garden Boutique, with locally produced batiks.

Across the road from the Garden Boutique, just before the main street becomes Belmont Walkway, you'll find the understated **St Mary's Church**. With its profusion of wood beams painted pale blue, its pristine white, wooden pews and tall doors letting in the salty sea breeze, the church feels very much a part of the ocean it faces. Make sure to take a look at the two striking paintings near the altar by English artist John Constable.

Head northwest out of Port Elizabeth around the bay and you'll pass Mauvin and Sargeant Brothers **model boat shops**, which sell the exquisite handmade model boats for which Bequia is famed. You can go inside both shops and watch the craftsmen at work; Sergeant's is the older and more atmospheric of the two. A little way past the boat shops on the inland side of the road is the **Bequia Maritime Museum** (Mon–Fri 9.30am–5.30pm, Sat 9.30am–2pm; EC$15), established by boatbuilder Lawson Sargeant, who also offers informative guided tours of the small but intriguing collection. Exhibits include some lovely period photos of Port Elizabeth, as well as a gushing letter of thanks from England's Queen Elizabeth II thanking Sargeant for the model replica of her yacht, *Britannia*, which he presented to her when she visited Bequia in 1985.

About a mile from the docks the road winds steeply uphill to the site of **Fort Hamilton**. A few British and French cannons remain but the real reason to visit is for the panoramic views over Admiralty Bay below.

The beaches

While Bequia's beaches fulfil every expectation of a Caribbean paradise – with sparkling sands and crystal-clear waters – what makes them unforgettable is their

Whaling on Bequia

Whaling was once big business in Bequia and the island used to be one of the most important whaling stations in the Caribbean, reaching its peak in the 1920s when twenty percent of the island's working men were employed in this seasonal industry. In recognition of this longstanding cultural tradition, which dates to the early nineteenth century when American whalers would hire locals to man their ships, the International Whaling Commission allows Bequia's whalers to kill up to four animals per year. Humpback whales, which appear in the waters around the island between February and April, are the whalers' prime target. In preparation for the hunt, the whaling boats are blessed in Friendship Bay at the end of January. The traditional methods still practised here include hand-held harpoons and wooden boats, which at 25ft long, are less than half the size of most humpback whales. The whalers aren't successful every year but when they bring a catch home, all of Bequia celebrates.

Not all locals or visitors agree with the maintenance of this tradition. Hand-held harpoon attacks rarely result in quick mortal strikes, which means that a whale usually takes between 30 minutes and two hours to die from its wounds. The one exception was the year that local whaling legend, the late Athneal Ollivierre, harpooned a humpback directly in the heart, killing it instantly.

Whatever your feelings are about whaling, the small museum dedicated to preserving its history (see opposite), run by Athneal's former colleague Harold Corea, provides an insight into this important aspect of the island's history. You'll also have a fantastic view of the waters where the whales roam from the museum site.

appealing roughness. Expect to find rocky headlands, and dense palm woodland that extends to the edge of the beaches, and an aura of castaway isolation. Although the swimming is fantastic, the sea is not tame, with large waves that pound the beaches, creating a dramatic setting with some good body-surfing opportunities.

The crown jewel of Bequia's beaches is the stunning **Princess Margaret Beach** a few minutes' walk over the Princess Point headland from the end of Belmont Walkway, or a quick jaunt by road or water taxi from Port Elizabeth. The waves froth onto golden sands framed perfectly by shady palm fronds and stark rocky outcrops. Swimming, sunbathing and snorkelling along this large horseshoe bay are excellent and the beach is never crowded. By the jetty you'll find a great new restaurant and bar, Jack's (see p.714).

At **Lower Bay**, south of Princess Margaret Beach and reached via a rough trail over the headland, a short walk from Port Elizabeth along the road to the interior or by water taxi, you'll find another striking beach and more in the way of tourist amenities, including restaurants, bars and toilets.

Friendship Bay in the southwest is within easy walking distance and also served by frequent buses. Despite its clutch of hotels and restaurants, this broad sweep of Atlantic shoreline remains unspoiled. The picture-perfect beach is ideal for swimming, snorkelling and diving, and a climb up the steep hillside behind it may afford a rare glimpse of a breaching whale.

The rest of the island

On the northeast tip of the island at the end of Industry Bay is the **Oldhegg Turtle Sanctuary** (daily 9.30am–3 or 4pm; EC$10; ⓣ784/458-3245), which endeavours to save the endangered Hawksbill turtle, distinguished by its pointed bill and sleek shell. In the winter months, baby Green and Hawksbill turtles are collected from the beach soon after they are hatched and released two years later.

On the southwest tip of the island near the village of La Pompe is the **Harold Corea Whaling museum** (daily 9am–5pm; US$2), set up by a protégé of famed whaler Athneal Oliverre after the island's original whaling museum closed following Oliverre's death. Displays are somewhat limited, but include photos of local whalers in action as well as harpoons and sundry bones from whales caught on the island. The tiny museum overlooks the ocean; just offshore is Semplers Cay where whales are butchered.

Beyond La Pompe and the tiny airport, there's a swath of fabulous white-sand beach that's usually all but deserted save for guests staying at the bizarre **Moonhole** homes. Built into the limestone rock à la Flintstones, these decidedly odd residences are opened up for tours each Wednesday (1.5hr; US$22; ⓣ784/458-3086, ⓦwww.begos.com/bequiamoonhole).

Eating and drinking

Bequia has a fine selection of characterful **restaurants** and **bars** with the majority concentrated along Port Elizabeth's waterfront. The Belmont Walkway has a particularly excellent selection, but it's worth trying options further afield.

Crescent Beach Inn Crescent Beach, near Industry Bay ⓣ784/458-3400. This large shady bar by the ocean is a unique and unpretentious place, making for a perfect stop on the way to the Turtle Sanctuary or a memorable night out, especially at full moon when the owners organize a beach barbecue. At lunchtime, sandwiches start from EC$8 and starters at dinner include pumpkin soup with main courses such as curried shrimp (EC$60).

Fernando's Hideaway Lower Bay ⓣ784/458-3758. An absolute gem of a restaurant, with a few (always filled) tables set up under the home of chef Fernando. The local food – calalloo soup, steamed fish and the like – is cooked to perfection, and prices are very reasonable. Book ahead.

The Frangipani Belmont Walkway, Port Elizabeth ⓣ784/458-3255. The food and the views are first class. This restaurant is popular with yachters, especially those crewing larger vessels, which makes for a friendly and lively atmosphere. Breakfast starts at 7am, the lunch menu features numerous sandwiches, burgers and omelettes from EC$26 and seafood is a speciality in the evening, when main courses average EC$80. Thurs night is the popular "jump-up", with a buffet (around EC$75) and steel band; reservations are required.

Green Boley Belmont Walkway, Port Elizabeth ⓣ784/458-3041. This laid-back, welcoming bar is one of the few places where prices remain the same all day. You'll find budget-conscious travellers and family groups munching on tasty rotis and substantial sandwiches (from EC$8), fish and chips (EC$18) and conch curry (EC$25). There is often live music and always a good crowd.

Jack's Princess Margaret Beach ⓣ784/457-3764. Stylish, mid-priced place right on the beach, shaded by a white awning and offering sophisticated, light meals such as conch fritters, gazpacho or goats' cheese salad, as well as more substantial seafood dinners. Great cocktails from the bar, too.

Lina's Bayshore Mall, Port Elizabeth ⓣ784/457-3388. This small but popular take-away bakery and delicatessen caters primarily to yachters, selling a selection of fresh-baked breads and pastries; great for beach picnics.

Mac's Pizzeria Belmont Walkway, Port Elizabeth ⓣ784/458-3474. It's easy to see why dinner reservations are recommended at this bustling and trendy Italian restaurant. Diners eat on a large, sea-facing terrace, decorated with fairy lights and set to a funky sound system. Lobster pizza is a speciality but many cheaper and unusual options are also available, as are pastas, salads and quiches. Pizzas EC$20–80.

The Moskito Friendship Bay ⓣ784/458-3222. Lovely spot right by the sea offering good quality, mid-priced seafood lunch and dinner; go for the "Lobster Feast" on a Wed evening when there's live string band music.

Port Hole Belmont Walkway, Port Elizabeth ⓣ784/458-3458. This basic but very popular restaurant has a reasonable lunch menu featuring tasty rotis from EC$10 and sandwiches from EC$8. The evening menu includes Caribbean and international dishes starting at EC$60. A small supermarket and a large book exchange are also onsite.

Nightlife

For a small island Bequia has a fair amount of **nightlife**. In Port Elizabeth most bars and restaurants along Belmont Walkway feature **live music** on alternate nights – *The Whaleboner* (ⓣ784/458-3233) is a popular option, featuring a humpback's jawbone as over the entrance; while *New York Bar* near the jetty is a tiny little rumshop that's favoured by locals, expats and yachties. The indoor (with a/c) bar, *Salty Dog,* where Front Street meets the Belmont Walkway (ⓣ784/457-3443), is another popular spot, with a quiz night on Wednesdays and occasional live music. At weekends, an open-air party with DJs favoured by locals can be found near the Penthouse Bar; while the Devil's Table, at the Bequia Marina near the jetty, has a good Friday night reggae party. In Lower Bay, *Keegan's* beachfront bar (ⓣ784/458-3530) hosts live music nights which are popular and fun. Detailed information on what's on where can be found listed in *Bequia This Week* – a free news-sheet available at the tourist information centre.

Diving and sailing

Diving in the pristine waters around Bequia is excellent. Most sites are on the Leeward side of the island and include everything from colourful reefs to dramatic walls. Most local **dive companies** organize packages – some including accommodation. Bequia Dive Adventures (ⓣ784/458-3826, ⓦwww.bequiadiveadventures.com) offers a range of dive packages from US$60 for a single dive to US$490 for ten, while Dive Bequia (ⓣ784/458-3504, ⓦwww.dive-bequia.com) operates from the *Gingerbread Hotel* (see p.710) with similar rates.

Given the island's long seafaring history, it's no surprise that Bequia is one of the best places in the Grenadines to take a **sailing** excursion to nearby islands. Highly recommended is the romantic 80ft sailing schooner *The Friendship Rose* (ⓣ784/495-0886, ⓦwww.friendshiprose.com). The ship makes frequent trips from Port Elizabeth's jetty to Mustique and the Tobago Cays and St Vincent. Trips cost US$125 and include snorkelling, gourmet local cuisine and all drinks.

Mustique

Situated just seven miles southeast of Bequia, beautiful **MUSTIQUE** is a fantasy island for the ultra-rich. Most visitors are day-trippers drawn by the island's air of exclusivity but explorations are fairly restricted as much of place is off limits to those who aren't paying guests, and curious tourists are discouraged. Those who do spend some time here can enjoy the island's hilly terrain, its large plain to the north and seven lush valleys leading to the white-sand beaches along its coast.

Mustique's first inhabitants were European planters who arrived in the 1740s. The decline of the West Indian sugar industry led to the closing of the plantations, and prospects for the island faded. Mustique didn't regain its footing until 1958 when Scottish landowner Colin Tennant bought the 1400-acre island for £45,000 and transformed it into a holiday hot spot for the rich and famous. Now under the management of a private corporation, the island is a haven for pop stars and celebrities of the likes of Mick Jagger, David Bowie and Elton John – all of whom own properties on the island.

Practicalities

Mustique's **airport** is situated in the north of the island and receives daily flights from St Vincent and other Grenadine islands. The Mustique Company (see below) operates a scheduled flight service which departs St Vincent two or three times a day Mon–Sat. For details on sailing tour operators on other islands who organize day-trips to Mustique, see Fantasea Tours on St Vincent (p.706), and *The Friendship Rose* on Bequia (see p.714). *The Glenconner* ferry operates on Monday, Tuesday, Thursday and Friday (except public holidays), departing Mustique's Britannia Bay jetty for St Vincent at 7.30am and leaving St Vincent for the return journey at 2.30pm. The one-way fare is EC$25 and tickets can be bought at the Mustique Company offices in Kingstown or Mustique Marine, Britannia Bay on Mustique.

Accommodation and **eating** options are limited, extremely luxurious and must be booked in advance. The two hotels, *Cotton House*, between Endeavour and L'Ansecoy Bays (ⓣ784/456-4777, ⓦwww.cottonhouseresort.com; US$815–1950 including breakfast), and *The Firefly*, overlooking Britannia Bay (ⓣ784/456-3414, ⓦwww.mustiquefirefly.com; US$850–1050, including all meals and vehicle hire), have every amenity imaginable; other than the two hotels, the only other way to stay on the island is to rent one of the numerous decadent villas through the Mustique Company (ⓣ784/458-4621, ⓦwww.mustique-island.com; US$4000–48,000 weekly). To see who's who in town, head to the legendary *Basil's Bar and Restaurant* (ⓣ784/458-4621, ⓦwww.basilsmustique.com), a bamboo and thatch bar extending off the beach and on stilts in the ocean.

Canouan

In the middle of the Grenadine island chain tiny, crescent-shaped **CANOUAN** – the Carib word for turtle – consists of five square miles of lush green hills and beautiful reef-protected white-sand beaches. These beaches draw a growing number of visitors and an increasing amount of development. The construction of a large new luxury resort, 18-hole golf course, casino and holiday villas has not been without local resentment as many islanders feel increasingly squeezed out. Canuoan's growing popularity as a luxury Caribbean holiday destination means that the island is well able to caters to the needs of its visitors. The ferry docks at **Charlestown**, the island's main town, situated on one of the island's longest beaches at Charlestown Bay (also known as Grand Bay); the airport is just west of town.

The island offers more than just luxury resorts. The low, undulating hills are pleasant for walking, and you'll meet more goats than people along its peaceful pathways. The beaches are unbeatable, and the sunbathing, swimming, snorkelling and diving are all first class. With coral reefs just offshore the beaches are well protected and snorkellers needn't be apprehensive about diving in – though care should be taken to preserve these delicate organisms. The local dive company, Dive Canouan (ⓣ784/458-8044, ⓦwww.canouandivecenter.com), is located at the *Tamarind Beach Hotel* (see below) and arranges dives for beginners and experienced divers.

Practicalities

Few restaurants exist outside of Canouan's **accommodation**, and each hotel has its own facilities, with menus ranging from French cuisine and West Indian fare to pizza. The top choices include *Anchor Inn Guest House* (ⓣ & ⓕ784/458-8568; ④), a tiny guesthouse in a two-storey home near the beach at Grand Bay, with three simple rooms, and breakfast and dinner included in the room rate. Also at Grand Bay, *Casa del Mar* (ⓣ784/482-0639, ⓦwww.adonalfoyle.com/AFE_casa_del_mar.shtml; ⑥), owned by NBA basketball player and local hero Adonal Foyes, offers luxurious master suites and guest rooms in a sea-facing villa and the use of a large kitchen, spacious living room and private bar. Another Grand Bay option, the *Tamarind Beach Hotel* (ⓣ784/458-8044, ⓦwww.tamarindbeachhotel.com; ⑨), and the 156-room *Raffles Resort* (ⓣ784/458-8000, ⓦwww.raffles-canouanisland.com; ⑧–⑨) in the north of the island both offer every luxury imaginable for those who can afford it.

Mayreau

With a population of just 300, and covering only one and half square miles, **MAYREAU** is the smallest of the inhabited Grenadine islands. It almost goes without saying that the beaches, watersports and views are wonderful, but unless you want to splash out for a stay at an exclusive resort, there is little to warrant anything more than a day's exploration – a water taxi from Union Island costs about EC$130 one-way; otherwise, the *MV Barracuda* (see p.699) makes the trip from St Vincent and Canouan.

As with most of the small Grenadines, visitors come for the immaculate beaches, of which Saline Bay and Salt Whistle Bay are justly popular. The sands of **Saline Bay** in the south are nearly a mile long and completely undeveloped, though when a cruise ship visits the island this beach can get very busy. With dazzling white sand and pale-blue waters **Salt Whistle Bay**, home of a small resort (see overleaf), is both stunning and a favourite anchorage for yachts. From here, it's a short but steep walk up the newly paved road to Salt Whistle village where most islanders live and a number of local bars and restaurants can be found. The village is also home to a striking, tiny stone Catholic church whose windows and grounds provide incredible views of the Caribbean and neighbouring islands. If you visit the church during a local wedding, you'll be fortunate, as these are elabourately celebrated on Mayreau; flags are flown from relatives' houses and rum is sprinkled over graves to encourage ancestors to bless the union. A more romantic setting for a wedding would be hard to find, and if you want to get married on the island you'll need to stay more than 72 hours.

Practicalities

For those planning to stay on the island, an excellent choice is *Dennis' Hideaway*, Saline Bay (ⓣ & ⓕ784/458-8594, ⓦwww.dennis-hideaway.com; ③), a peaceful guesthouse consisting of five rooms, each with air-conditioning, private bathroom and balcony facing the sea. Downstairs, the bar and restaurant opens at 7am for breakfast (included in the room rate). Lunch starts at EC$15 and evening meals include locally caught seafood and mouthwatering spare ribs (EC$50–80). More pricey is *Saltwhistle Bay Club* (ⓣ784/458-8444, ⓦwww.saltwhistlebay.com; ⑨), a quiet beachside resort whose charming, airy bungalows made of local stone have private patios. There's an open-air restaurant too, serving standard Caribbean dishes.

Other **eating** options include the beachside *Island Paradise* (Ⓣ784/458-8941), with local favourites like callaloo soup, curried conch and red snapper; expect to pay EC$50–70 for a main course at dinner. Similar dishes such as curried conch, snapper and West Indian fruit cake can be had at *J & C Restaurant and Bar* (Ⓣ784/458-8558). Transport by boat is included in their reasonable prices. If you're after a **drink**, by far the best stop is the Rasta-run *Righteous and de Youths* bar, a kookily decorated and deservedly popular hangout.

Union Island

UNION ISLAND, the southernmost of the Grenadines, is primarily a stopoff for visitors to the Tobago Cays and a point of entry for yachters into St Vincent and the Grenadines. The terrain of this roughly three-miles-long and one- mile-wide island is not as picture-postcard perfect as some of its fellow Grenadines, but the jagged volcanic peaks are dramatic, rising from low scrubby hills to a height of 1000ft at Mount Taboi – the tallest peak in the Grenadines – and have earned the island the nickname "little Tahiti". Less built up than many of its neighbours, Union's unpolished atmosphere comes as a welcome relief from the pretentiousness of many Caribbean resorts, though there's a fair bit of tourist infrastructure nonetheless.

The commercial centre, **Clifton**, has whatever **tourist information** you might need (daily 9am–4pm). The airport, ferry jetty, banks, and numerous bars, restaurants and shops line the main street. Situated at the edge of the colourful local market with every kind of Caribbean fruit and vegetable is a 9lb cannon which once protected Clifton Harbour from American privateers during the American War of Independence.

Set in tropical gardens on the waterfront, east towards the airport, is the **Bougainville Centre**, a commercial complex catering for tourists and yatchers, with a gift shop and first class restaurant (see opposite) that's well within most budgets. Also located here are the offices of Wind and Sea Ltd (Ⓣ784/458-8678, Ⓔwindandsea@vincysurf.com), who organize numerous sailing, snorkelling, diving and sightseeing tours around the Grenadines.

Above the small village of **Ashton**, a short bus ride (EC$3 fare) or half an hour's walk inland from Clifton, a few hiking trails wend their way through the hills, offering good terrain and excellent views of the surrounding Grenadines, while the remote beaches of **Richmond** and **Big Sand** on the northern end of the island can be reached by road from Clifton. The best snorkelling is at **Lagoon Reef**, which protects the island's southern coast. Teeming with colourful marine life and rarely visited, the reef provides excellent conditions, especially around **Frigate Island**.

If you want to venture beyond Union Island, Grenadines Dive (Ⓣ784/458-8138, Ⓦwww.grenadinesdive.com) based at the *Kings Landing Hotel* in Clifton operates day-trips to the neighbouring islands of the Tobago Cays and Palm Island for EC$90–150; a filling lunch, drinks and the use of snorkelling equipment are included in the price. They also offer scuba diving, from easy to adventurous – the latter includes a dive to a 90ft volcanic valley complete with a bubbling seabed. Another option is to go on a small boat with local Mr Fabulous (Ⓣ784/492-4056) who does great beach barbecues on the Tobago Cays, and runs a water taxi between the islands hereabouts.

Practicalities

Stay at *Kingslanding Hotel* (Ⓣ784/458-8221, Ⓦwww.kingslandinghotel.com; ④), on the hill above Clifton harbour, with comfortable rooms that have good views from private patios. Down by the ocean, the relaxed *Clifton Beach Hotel* (Ⓣ784/458-8235, Ⓦwww.cliftonbeachhotel.org; ②–④) has basic rooms and cottages, plus a good restaurant and bar on the premises. On the north side of the island at Richmond Bay, the tranquil and isolated *Bigsand Hotel* (ⓣ784/485-8447, ⓦwww.bigsandhotel.com; ⑦–⑧) rents spacious and airy apartment-style rooms complete with living area, kitchen, bathroom and beachfront balcony, as well as air-conditioning, wireless Internet and cable TV; the beachside restaurant is ideal for a peaceful lunch or dinner. The lunch menu includes rotis from EC$18 and dinner options feature a mix of French and local cuisine starting at EC$34. Other **eating** options include *The Seaquarium* (ⓣ784/458-8678) located at the Bougainville Centre. Complete with its own large aquarium and wonderful sea views, this is the perfect spot to enjoy a cocktail or one of their reasonably priced and excellent fish and pasta dishes from EC$35. Located in Clifton, the elegant *West Indies Restaurant* (ⓣ784/458-8911) serves tasty salads, burgers and omelettes for lunch from EC$18 and French/Creole pasta, fish and meat dishes for dinner, EC$40–70.

Tobago Cays

Accessible only by boat, the numerous and tiny deserted islets and spectacular coral reefs of the lovely **TOBAGO CAYS** are justifiably famous for their superb snorkelling, diving, windsurfing and birdwatching opportunities, and impossibly blue, clear waters that make for simply fantastic swimming. During high season, the translucent waters of this major tourist attraction are busy with visiting yachts and local vendors touting everything from food to jewellery from their boats. The cays' popularity, however, is leading to their destruction as anchoring boats, over fishing and successive storms have caused considerable damage to the coral reefs. The islands are now a National Marine Park, and fishing, jet skis and anchoring dinghies are prohibited.

Sailing day-trips to the Tobago Cays can be organized from other Grenadine islands; try *The Friendship Rose* on Bequia (see p.714) and *Grenadines Dive* on Union Island (see p.717). Resorts also offer packages that include similar trips.

20

Grenada

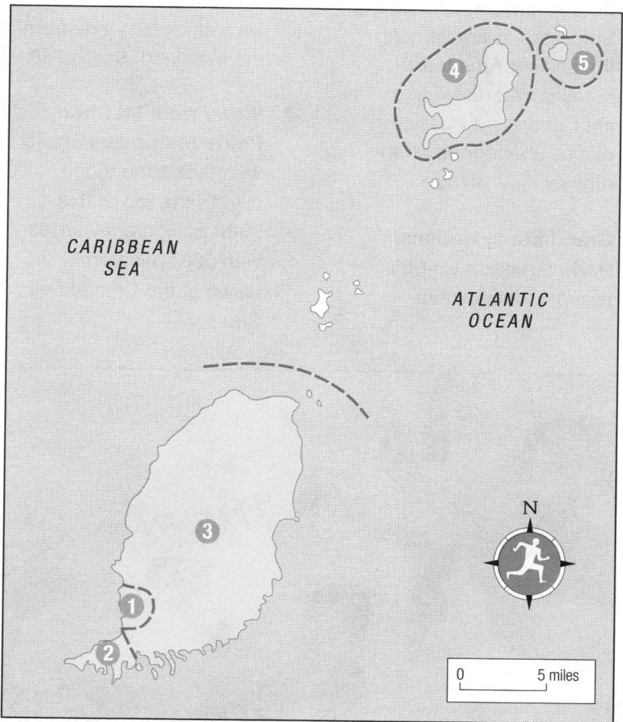

Grenada highlights

* **Grand Anse Beach, Grenada** Sunbathe on the magnificent white sands or take advantage of the many watersports options. See p.732

* **Pearls Airport, Grenada** Step back in time among the ancient Amerindian remains and rusting Cuban and Russian planes abandoned on the runway. See p.736

* **Grand Etang National Park, Grenada** Visit the island's mountainous rainforest and its waterfalls and crater lakes. See p.737

* **Carriacou** Sleepy, tiny, and with some fabulous beaches and snorkelling, Carriacou is reachable via a short ferry ride from the mainland. See p.738

* **Views from Mt Piton, Petite Martinique** Those who tackle the tough hike to the top of this 738ft peak are rewarded with 360° panoramic views of the Grenadines. See p.744

▲ Pearls Airport

Introduction and basics

The southernmost of the Windward Islands, Grenada is known as "Spice Isle" due to its production of nutmeg along with quantities of cinnamon, cloves, ginger, turmeric and mace. Though these crops were devastated, along with much of the island, by Hurricane Ivan in 2004, both the country and the plants are very much recovered, and the only remaining sign of Ivan's 125mph winds is the odd missing roof and a few bent trees high up in the rainforest.

While still largely dependent on its recovering agriculture, the tiny nation of Grenada – which includes neighbouring **Carriacou** and **Petite Martinique** – has steadily been building a reputation as a top holiday destination, and as it remains relatively unspoilt compared to many other top Caribbean destinations, Grenada and its islands can still reward any visitor with the best that the region has to offer.

All three of the main islands offer excellent **watersports** opportunities, and Grenada in particular has its share of stunning white-sand beaches, ranging from the resort-lined **Grand Anse Beach** on the southwest tip to the ruggedly spectacular **Bathway Beach** in the northeast.

Ringing the island are a variety of communities, chiefly the elegant capital of **St George's**, as well as the charming fishing village of **Goyave** on the west coast and the east coast's **Grenville**, also the country's agricultural heart. The inhabitants, 90 percent of whom live on the island of Grenada, are descended from British, French, African and West Indian settlers, and their inviting and friendly nature belies the country's turbulent history.

Much smaller and far less visited are the islands of **Carriacou** and **Petite Martinique**, appealing for their slow pace and a welcome respite from the tourist-oriented Grenada. Carriacou has a laid-back tourist scene built around its beaches, many of which offer fantastic snorkelling.

Where to go

Of Grenada's many attractions a few stand apart. The mountainous interior of the rainforest of **Grand Etang National Park** is a lush walkers' paradise, with a network of trails leading to spectacular waterfalls, fascinating crater lakes and mist-shrouded mountain peaks. Among the country's numerous white-sand beaches, by far the most stunning is Grenada's **Grand Anse**, whose long horseshoe bay of powdery sand and turquoise water is the focus of the island's tourist trade. For a taste of laid-back island life, as well as quieter beaches and secluded sunbathing, there's the smaller island of **Carriacou**, just a short ferry ride away.

When to go

Grenada's climate is warm and humid, with a **rainy season** from June to December – it rarely rains for more than an hour and lets up on some days. The coolest time of the year is November to February, which is also the island's tourist **high season**, with average temperatures in the high twenties Celsius (low eighties Fahrenheit). The official **hurricane season** lasts from June to November with September being the peak month.

Getting there

Flights arrive at Point Salines International Airport, located on the southwest tip of Grenada, approximately five miles from the capital, St George's.

Although flying is the quickest and easiest option for travelling between neighbouring islands, it is possible to travel by **boat** to Carriacou from Union Island, the most southerly of the Grenadine islands and

> When leaving, you're charged a **departure tax** of EC$50, payable in local currency only.

under the jurisdiction of St Vincent (covered in Chapter 19, starting p.693). This journey, however, is only recommended for the adventurous as the one-hour trip, which ends at the Hillsborough jetty, can sometimes be quite rough.

Information

The main visitor centre is run by the **Grenada Board of Tourism**, located at the cruise ship terminal in St George's (Ⓣ473/440-2279, Ⓦwww.grenadagrenadines.com); you'll find it well stocked with brochures and maps. There is also an **information booth** at the airport, just before immigration, and one at the Craft and Spice Market on Grand Anse Beach (see p.732). The Grenada Hotel and Tourism Association at Ocean House, Morne Rouge, in St George's (PO Box 440, Ⓣ473/444-1353, Ⓦwww.grenadahotelsinfo.com) also has a wealth of island info on its site. **Carriacou's** main tourist office is in Hillsborough on Main Street. The website of the Carriacou and Petit Martinique

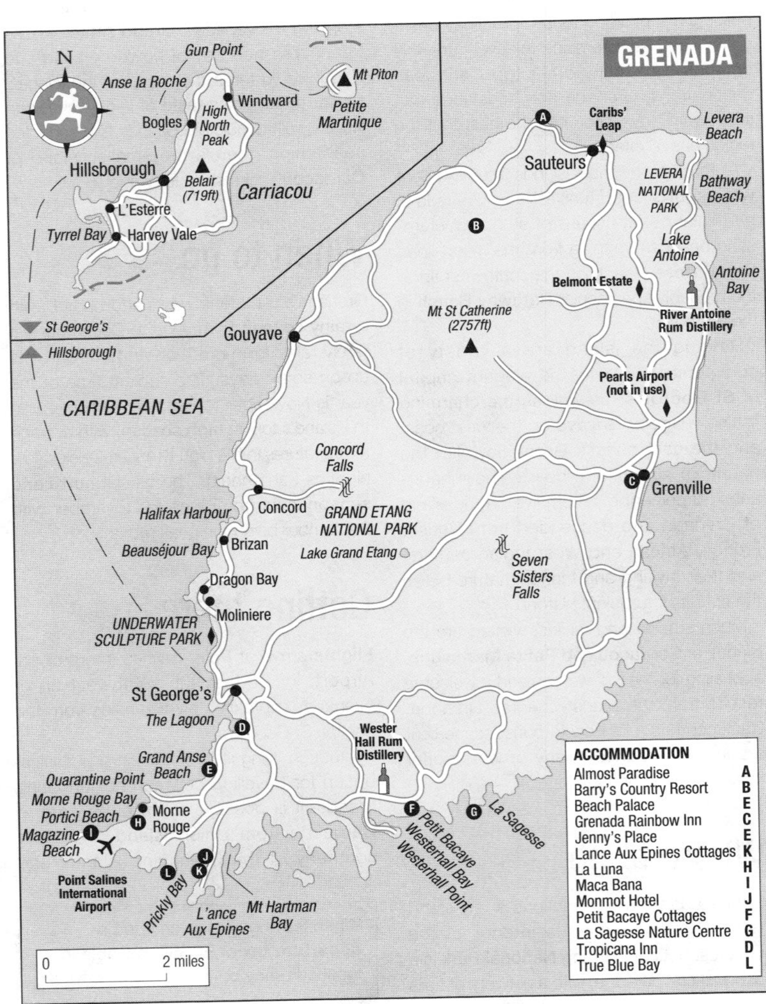

Grenada websites

Ⓦwww.grenadaexplorer.com From accommodation to eco-activities, this extensive site contains detailed travel information and features an excellent search function.

Ⓦwww.grenadaguide.com Comprehensive site with links to accommodation, restaurants, airlines, car rentals, tours and dive operators.

Ⓦwww.belgrafix.com Link to the online edition of the local weekly, which contains all the latest Grenadian news, weather and entertainment listings.

Ⓦwww.travelgrenada.com Filled with travel information and tips, as well as maps and even local recipes.

Tourist Association (Ⓦwww.carriacoupetitemartinique.com) includes plenty of info on the smaller islands.

Adequate, free **maps** – including one that details a historic walking tour of St George's – are available at tourist offices and many hotels. A detailed Ordnance Survey map can be purchased for EC$15 from hotels and tourist shops.

Money and costs

Grenada's official currency is the **Eastern Caribbean dollar (EC$)** but the US dollar is widely accepted at hotels, restaurants, shops and by taxis and car rental. The EC dollar is divided into 100 cents. Notes come in denominations of 5, 10, 20, 50 and 100 EC dollars; coins in 1, 2, 5, 10 and 25 cents. At the time of writing, the **rate of exchange** was roughly EC$2.65 to US$1.

Credit cards and major **travellers' cheques** are accepted at most hotels, restaurants and larger shops. In this chapter prices such as bus fares and admission fees have been quoted in EC$; all other prices are given in US$.

Banking hours are generally Monday to Thursday 8am–3pm, Friday 8am–5pm, with some variations. Barclays Bank, Scotiabank, Grenada Bank of Commerce and National Commercial Bank all have branches in St George's and the Grand Anse area. Most have an **ATM**, and there's also one at Point Salines Airport. Banks with ATMs can be found in Hillsborough on Carriacou, and Petit Martinique's one bank opens Tuesdays and Thursdays 9am–12 noon and has no ATM.

An 8 percent **government tax** is added at hotels and restaurants on top of a 10 percent **service charge**. Tipping is at your discretion.

Getting around

Getting around Grenada is fairly straightforward, though you'll end up travelling more miles (and taking longer) than you expect due to the hilly terrain and the narrow, winding roads.

By bus

By far the cheapest way to get around is by **bus**. These privately owned, government-regulated minivans cram in as many people as possible, drive very fast and play loud dancehall and soca. Don't be intimidated, however, as they're also great fun, friendly and safe.

Buses run 6am–8pm daily, with less frequent service on only the most popular routes on Sundays and holidays. Routes run from the main terminal on Bruce Street in St George's to destinations all over the island. You can catch a bus at stops along all routes, or you can just flag one down at any point along the way – with their constant honking, you'll always know when they are around. To get off simply rap the side of the van and pay as you leave. From St George's, expect to pay around EC$2.50 to Grand Anse, EC$3.50 to Grand Etang, EC$5.50 to Grenville, EC$6.50 to Sauteurs and EC$4.50 to Gouyave.

Although the **airport** is not on a main bus route, it is possible to get there via bus; stop any bus going to Grand Anse Beach and ask if it will take you to the airport, which is just a few miles further on. Expect to pay the **off-route fare** of EC$10–15 for this service. It's sometimes possible to pick up one of these off-route buses at the airport on its way back to the main route to St George's or Grand Anse, but don't depend on it.

By taxi

Taxis are plentiful and you will be constantly hassled by drivers seeking business. Fares from the airport to Grand Anse are around EC$35 and to St George's EC$50; expect to pay about EC$5 per mile for journeys from St George's to the rest of the island. A **surcharge** of EC$10 is added between 6pm and 6am. Taxi companies to try in St George's are the National Taxi Association (Ⓣ440 6850) right next door to the tourist information and CJs 24-hour Maxi Taxi (Ⓣ473/406-9623 or 473/414-4449), which has a stand opposite the *Nutmeg Restaurant* (see p.730) on the Carenage. Local tour guide Terry Abraham of Small Island Tours (Ⓣ473/415-0648, Ⓔtabraham11@yahoo.com) also provides an excellent, reliable and reasonably priced taxi service.

By car

To **rent a car** you will need a valid driver's licence and a local permit, available from most car rental agencies and police stations for EC$30. Dollar (Ⓣ473/444-4786, Ⓔcallistena@caribsurf.com) and David's Car Rental (Ⓣ473/444-3399, Ⓦwww.davidscars.com) have offices at the Point Salines International Airport, excellent local operators, who tend to be cheaper with a more personalized service, include Nice Services (Ⓣ473/440-7133 or 473/407-2777, Ⓔniceservices@hotmail.com) and Indigo (Ⓣ473/439-3300, Ⓦwww.indigocarsgrenada.com) while Avis (Ⓣ473/440-3936) operates out of St George's. Cars and jeeps cost US$50–70 per day. **Driving** is on the left-hand side.

By scooter and bike

To drive a **scooter** you will need a local licence available from police stations for around EC$30. Scooters can be rented from Sundance (Ⓣ473/420-1428) and cost US$35 a day. **Bikes** can be hired from Trailblazers (Ⓣ473/444-5337, Ⓦwww.adventuregrenada.com); expect to pay US$15 per day. Be warned: cycling can be tough-going on Grenada as roads are mostly hilly and the smaller ones are not always well maintained.

By boat

The **Osprey passenger ferry** (Ⓣ473/440-8126, Ⓦwww.ospreylines.com) is the most efficient and cheapest way to travel between Grenada, Carriacou and Petite Martinique. It departs from the Carenage in St George's (opposite the red fire station) for Carriacou Monday to Friday 9am and 5.30pm, Saturday 9am only and Sunday 8am and 5.30pm. It then departs Carriacou for Petite Martinique Monday to Friday 10.30am and 7pm and Sunday 9.30am and 7pm. The **return trip** leaves Petite Martinique for Carriacou Monday to Saturday 5.30am and 3pm and Sunday 3pm, and departs Carriacou to Grenada Monday to Saturday 6am and 3.30pm and Sunday 3.30pm only. The journey takes ninety minutes between Grenada and Carriacou and twenty minutes from Carriacou to Petite Martinique. The fare from Grenada to Carriacou and Petite Martinique is EC$80 one-way, EC$160 round-trip and from Carriacou to Petite Martinique EC$30 one-way, EC$60 round-trip.

By plane

St Vincent and the Grenadines Airways (Ⓣ473/444-3549m, Ⓦwww.svgair.com) **flies** daily from Grenada, Barbados, and St Vincent and the Grenadine islands to **Lauriston Airstrip**, one mile south of Hillsborough on Carriacou (see p.738).

There is no airport on Petite Martinique, and the only way to get there is by boat or ferry (see above).

Tours

Most of the island can easily be explored by bus, but if you're short on time, **organized tours** are an excellent way to see the island in a day and learn about its history and culture along the way. Local tour guide Mandoo (Ⓣ473/407-0024, Ⓦwww.grenadatours.com) has an encyclopedic knowledge of Grenada's history, politics and nature, and his selection of full- and half-day bus and trekking tours costs US$50–100 per person. Terry Abraham of Small Island Tours (Ⓣ473/415-0648, Ⓔtabraham11@yahoo.com) also offers excellent tours of attractions islandwide in a comfy air-conditioned minibus, including little-known sulphur springs and waterfalls; prices start at US$25 per hour for groups of four.

Accommodation

Most of Grenada's **accommodation** is clustered around the tourist-saturated southwest, but there are some interesting and unusual options outside this area. A variety of options are available, ranging from self-catering apartments to modern resort complexes. Villas are an excellent and often economical option if you are travelling in a large group. Spice Isle Villas (Ⓣ473/439-2486, Ⓦwww.spiceislevillas.com) rents a large selection of villas around Grenada and Carriacou, while Down Island Ltd (Ⓣ473/443-8182, Ⓦwww.islandvillas.com) specializes in Carriacou.

Prices at hotels and guesthouses are much lower during the summer months – April to December – which is also the rainy season. Accommodation rates on Carriacou and Petite Martinique are significantly lower than on Grenada, ranging from US$40 to US$125 per night; on Grenada prices vary between US$50 and US$500.

Food and drink

Grenada's Creole cuisine is invariably delicious, based on delicious local veg and fruit and laced with aromatic twists of nutmeg, cinnamon and other island spices. As you'd expect, **seafood** is plentiful, ranging from conch – known locally as lambie – to flying fish. Also widely available and unmissable are delicious rotis, fine layers of pastry folded around various fillings. Favourite starters include callaloo (similar to spinach) soup and **nutmeg ice cream** is local speciality.

The beer of choice is **Carib**, brewed on the island and available in all bars. Likewise rum produced in Grenada's distilleries is used in a wide variety of punches and cocktails. Be sure to sample the locally produced **fruit juice**. Bursting with flavour, what's on offer depends on the season; those made from passionfruit, golden apple and sorrel are delicious and well worth trying.

Grenada boasts a good range of restaurants, from basic locals diners to tourist-oriented café and restaurants, including seriously upmarket gourmet places. Most places serve a dinner menu after 7pm that is considerably more expensive than meals served during the day, and the choice of inexpensive restaurants dwindles after this time.

Mail and communications

Payphones can be found throughout the island. Some accept only phonecards, which you can buy from the main visitor centre, at the airport, in shops and from the Cable & Wireless office on the Carenage in Grenada or Patterson Street, Hillsborough on Carriacou.

The general **post office** (Mon–Fri 8am–3.30pm) is on Lagoon Road in St George's and there are smaller offices in towns and villages on Grenada and Carriacou and one on Petite Martinique (Mon–Fri 10am–noon & 2–4pm)

You'll find several **Internet cafés** in St George's and at numerous other places on Grenada and Carriacou, and one on Petite Martinique in Matthew's Shopping Centre.

The **country code** is Ⓣ473. The emergency number for **police** and **fire** is Ⓣ911.

Opening hours, holidays and festivals

Business hours are generally Monday to Friday 8am–4pm and Saturday 8am–1pm. When a cruise ship is in harbour, tourist shops in St George's will stay open later and on Sundays.

Grenada celebrates Independence Day on February 7, Corpus Christi on the ninth Thursday after Easter, Emancipation Days on the first Monday and Tuesday in August and Thanksgiving on October 25.

The biggest event in the **festival** calendar is Grenada's lively and colourful **Carnival**, held every year on the second weekend in August. Although Carriacou's Carnival is in early March, the island's main event is the **Carriacou Regatta**, which takes place in late July/early August and brings boats of all kinds from all over the Caribbean. Petite Martinique also hosts an annual **regatta** over Easter. Jazz festivals are held on Grenada and Carriacou in May and mid-June respectively.

Outdoor activities

Grenada's underwater terrain is as beautiful as the dramatic landscape rising above it, and there's no shortage of **dive operators** to help you explore it. Most dive shops operate from resorts on Grand Anse Beach in Grenada and out of Tyrrel Bay in Carriacou, and cater for all levels of experience. Though shallow reef, wall and drift dives are all on offer, the most popular site is the wreck of the *Bianca C* (see p.730) off Grenada, known locally as the "Titanic of the Caribbean". Another unmissable underwater sight is the submerged **sculpture park** at Molinere Bay, just north of St George's (see p.735).

For those who prefer to explore on dry land, numerous **hiking trails** wind through Grenada's Grand Etang National Park, while Carriacou's High North National Park has a good range too.

History

Long before Columbus espied Grenada and named it **Concepción** (the name "Grenada" was given by homesick Spanish sailors and eventually adopted by the British) on his third voyage to the Americas in 1498, Grenada had been settled by a series of migrating Amerindian peoples. Its first known residents were the **Ciboney**, who populated much of the Eastern Caribbean and left little behind but a few artefacts and petroglyphs. The Ciboney were replaced or absorbed by **Arawaks**, who came to the island by way of Venezuela and the outflow of the Orinoco River. In turn, the Arawaks were invaded and enslaved by the **Caribs**, who were making their way up through the islands from Guyana.

The **British**, in 1609, were the first Europeans to attempt to settle the island, followed in 1650 by the **French**, whose first town sank into the mouth of St George's Lagoon. These efforts were fiercely resisted by the Caribs. In 1651, the French took decisive action against the Caribs, pushing them north to **Sauteurs** where, rather than surrender to French control, they threw themselves off a cliff, now known as Caribs' Leap.

Control of Grenada passed between France and Britain as part of the settlements of various treaties, and both countries established **plantations** of indigo, tobacco, coffee, cocoa and sugar, worked by African slaves until slavery was abolished in all British colonies in 1838. Finally the French ceded the island to Britain in the Treaty of Paris in 1783, the French-brokered agreement which formally ended the American War of Independence.

In 1795 **Julian Fedon**, a mulatto planter, led a peasant rebellion based on the principles of the French Revolution and controlled most of the island for fourteen months before the rebels were crushed by British reinforcements. British rule was stable throughout the nineteenth century, a peace that culminated in 1877 with Grenada being granted crown colony status and a measure of independence.

In 1967 Grenada became a semi-independent state within the British Commonwealth and, seven years later, an independent country. By that time control of the government was firmly in the hands of **Eric Gairy**, a union leader who had led the resistance against British rule since the 1950s. During the 1970s, Gairy's rule became increasingly dictatorial and his secret police (the **Mongoose Gang**) notorious for their corruption and suppression of the opposition. Gairy was ousted from power on March 13, 1979, by a bloodless coup led by **Maurice Bishop**, the charismatic leader of the left-wing New Jewel Movement, whose father had been killed during demonstrations against Gairy's rule.

Bishop's **Revolutionary Government** became a pawn of the Cold War, supported by Cuba, Nicaragua and the Soviet Union but reviled by the United States. The period of Revolutionary Government came to an end in 1983 when Bishop was imprisoned by enemies within his own government and US forces invaded (on the pretext of evacuating American medical students from the island but having more to do with the fear of increased Soviet influence in the Caribbean). During a public demonstration for Bishop's restoration to power, he was freed from house arrest, and made his way to the army headquarters at Fort George, where he was shot dead – some say it was an execution by an army firing squad.

Grenada's first post-revolution elections were held in 1985 and won by **Herbert Blaize**, Gairy's political opponent from the 1950s and 1960s. Elections in 1995 brought **Dr Keith Mitchell** and the New National Party (NNP) to power, who, despite the shadow cast over his leadership by the investigation of alleged links to the collapse of a bank that supported him during his election campaign, won the 2003 poll by a very narrow majority. Elections are due again in 2008, with Mitchell's main opposition being Tillman Thomas, leader of the more liberal National Democratic Congress (NCC).

Grenada was dealt a severe blow on September 7, 2004 when it suffered a direct hit from the mighty **Hurricane Ivan**, which devastated ninety percent of the island as well as the tourism and agriculture infrastructure. Thanks to the help of other Caribbean nations and overseas aid agencies, recovery was amazingly swift, and today you'll see few signs of the hurricane's furore. Roofs have been replaced islandwide and crops replanted, though Ivan has had a long-term effect on Grenada's nutmeg production. Some 55,000 mature trees were destroyed, and as nutmeg saplings take some ten years to bear fruit, it will be a while before the country regains its place as one of the world's largest producers of the spice.

20.1

St George's

An attractive colonial-era town spilling down a hillside above the Carenage, with its horseshoe-shaped harbour, Grenada's capital of **ST GEORGE'S** received the full brunt of Hurricane Ivan's high winds, and the bevy of new terracotta-coloured roofs stand in testament to the power of the wind. Ivan, however, was not the first disaster to strike this picturesque town, dominated by **British colonial architecture** but with a distinctly Mediterranean feel. During the eighteenth century, the capital was partly gutted by three devastating fires, leading to legislation that restricted the height of buildings and banned the use of timber.

St George's won't take more than a day to explore, and it's worth taking time away from the beach to do so. Though the **market** is at its liveliest on Saturday morning, most shops close on Saturday afternoons, Sundays and public holidays, making the town a quiet place during those times – except when a **cruise ship** moors at the spanking new docks, in which case the town explodes into a frenzy of activity, market stalls spring up on shore, restaurants and bars fill up, street vendors and local guides come out in force, and all visitors – whether they're cruise-ship passengers or not – become the focus of a barrage of offers from taxi drivers and spice sellers.

The Town

St George's lies on two sides of a hill topped by Fort George, and is divided into the maze of streets surrounding the **Carenage** and, on the other side of the hill and connected by the Sendall Tunnel, the cruise ship dock and the commercial streets around the lively **market square**, the heart of town.

The market square and around

The site of the town's slave exchange until the trade was made illegal in 1807, the colourful **market square** on Halifax Street is now the bustling and aromatic centre of St George's, where stalls crammed with local spices and seasonal fresh produce vie for your senses alongside vendors selling barbecued corn (Mon–Sat). Clothes, shoes, music and much more are traded, and the numerous buses that pick up and drop off around its confined perimeter add to the market's sense of contained mayhem.

The streets around the market are worth exploring as they contain many architectural treasures and will give you a feel for local life – not to mention numerous stunning views of the town. Just inland above the market square on Upper Church Street is the **Cathedral of the Immaculate Conception**, still roofless and forlorn following the ravages of Hurricane Ivan.

Opposite the cathedral and home to the Houses of Parliament, the **York House** is a fine example of the town's Georgian architecture. The mace belonging to the House of Representatives is reputed to be the largest in the world.

One block south of the market on Bruce Street is the main **bus terminal** for the island. Here buses leave from clearly marked stops and arrive via the Carenage and **Sendall Tunnel**, carved through the hill in 1895 to stop horse carts from having to scramble over the headland and allowing their safe passage to the market.

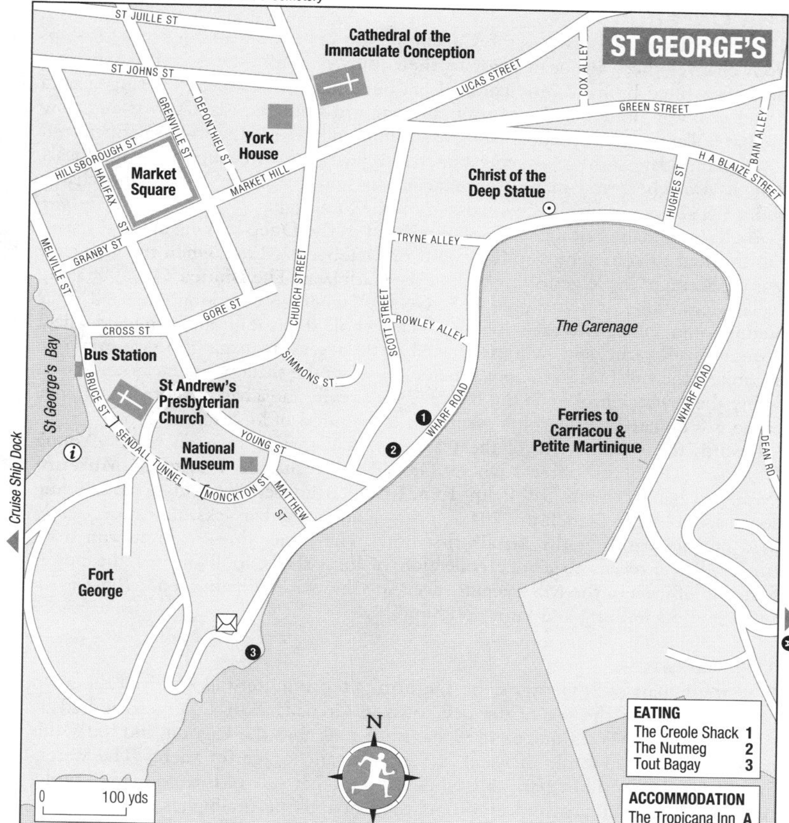

Fort George

On a hilltop at the western end of the Carenage presides **Fort George**. To reach the entrance from the market, follow Halifax Street towards the Carenage before turning right onto the steep Grand Etang Road, which climbs up to the fort. On the way you'll pass the ruins of **St Andrew's Presbyterian Church**, once a dark, imposing structure also known as Scot's Kirk. Fort George itself has splendid panoramic views of the Carenage and beyond towards Grand Anse. Built by the French in 1705 (who originally named it Fort Royal) to protect the harbour, the fort had additional defences added by the British who took control of the fort in 1763 and made it a part of their defence of the Caribbean (both the British and French used the Windward Islands as a base to raid Spanish ships). The fort has played an integral role in Grenada's history, being the focal point of every armed intervention and military coup, the most recent of which were the events surrounding the end of the Revolutionary Government in 1983. It's now home to the office of the Commissioner of Police, but you're free to wander around and explore. Behind the police compound, a tiny, dark tunnel leads through to the Parade Ground where the wall holds a plaque in memorial of former PM Maurice Bishop. Above the parade ground at the top of the fort, cannons point over the Carenage and out to sea, and there are some great views over both sides of the town.

The Carenage

The inner harbour, known as the **Carenage**, was once the meeting point for ships from all over the Caribbean prior to their journey across the Atlantic. A perfect horseshoe lined by handsome colonial-era buildings, the Carenage is ringed by a paved walkway dotted with old cannons removed from the island's forts and now used as bollards to tie up ships. Halfway around the harbour, the walkway opens out to accommodate some sea-facing benches, a favourite gathering place for locals. This is also where you may be approached by self-appointed guides, who charge about EC$20 per hour for the lowdown on the local sights.

You'll also find the striking statue of the **Christ of the Deep** looking out to sea, arms outstretched to commemorate the events of October 22, 1961, when the Carenage was the scene of the largest shipwreck in the Caribbean. The **Bianca C**, a 600ft-long Italian ocean liner, was anchored in St George's when an explosion occurred in its engine room, killing two crew members. The whole ship soon caught fire and a fleet of local boats, yachts and swimmers raced to the rescue, managing to save everyone aboard. As the still-burning ship was being towed to the shallow waters around Point Saline, the towrope broke and the *Bianca C* sank a mile and a half offshore. The bronze statue was donated by the ship's owners in recognition of local rescue efforts.

Towards the western end of the Carenage, take a right turn on narrow Young Street to Monckton Street, where Grenada's ramshackle **National Museum** (Mon–Fri 9am–4.30pm, Sat 10am–1pm; EC$5) is housed in a cut-stone building constructed by the French in 1704 as a prison and army barracks, and subsequently used by the British as the island's first hotel. The rather dusty exhibits run from Amerindian artefacts to a nice collection of local shells; look out for the poster from the officers of the MS *Lancaster* decrying shipmate William Henry Roye as an "excellent do-nothing and know-nothing".

The Lagoon

Not strictly part of St George's, the **Lagoon**, a ten-minute walk south of the town past the docks, is the site of the first town in Grenada. Fort Louis, established by the governor of Martinique in 1650, has since sunk into the Lagoon, and today this naturally protected circle of water is a popular anchorage for yachts. The waterfront is lined by scrubby parkland, while on the other side of the road you'll find a cinema, hotel, restaurants and stores, and residential properties higher in the hills.

Practicalities

As St George's is nowhere near a beach, there's little reason to **stay** in town. In terms of **eating**, there's plenty of choice around the Carenage, where options range from cafés to restaurants. Dining here is inexpensive, laid-back and a bit more authentic than at the beaches.

Restaurants

The Creole Shack The Carenage ☎473/435-7422. An attractive street-level restaurant and bar overlooking the waterfront, serving a mix of Creole and other Caribbean dishes at reasonable prices. The popular lunch menu, including saltfish and meaty oildown stew, starts at EC$10, while dinner prices average EC$45.

The Nutmeg The Carenage ☎473/440-2539. Famous for its Grenadian-style seafood dinners and nutmeg rum punch, this very popular restaurant also has sweeping views of the Carenage and beyond. Burgers and rotis (from EC$10) make up the lunch menu, while typical dinner dishes include Caribbean shrimp cocktails (EC$27) and a delicious seafood platter (EC$54).

The Tropicana Inn Lagoon Road ☎473/440-1586. Besides the mouthwatering full Grenadian breakfast (EC$16), this restaurant serves a consistently tasty and reasonably priced daily menu, including options such as curried shrimp (EC$45), grilled fish (EC$30) and T-bone steak (EC$50). Order food to go at the take-away annexe next door where large portions of fish with vegetables and rice cost around EC$15.

Shopping and entertainment

Throughout St George's you will find plenty of **arts and crafts shops**, many aimed at cruise ship passengers and varying in price and quality. Among the better ones is Art Fabrick (☎473/440-0568, Ⓦwww.artfabrikgrenada.com) on Young Street, where local **batik** artists can usually be seen at work. Just next to the museum on Monckton Street, Grenada Essentials (☎473/435-5958) is a community-based business selling lovely crafts produced in Grenada; all profits go toward local environmental projects such as turtle conservation and post-Ivan reforestation.

The town has a smattering of **entertainment** options, including the island's newest and flashiest club, *Karma* (☎473/435-2582, Ⓦwww.karmavip.com), right on the Carenage. Busiest nights are Friday and Saturday when reggae, dancehall, soca and hip-hop dominate the sound system; Wednesday is retro night. Otherwise, *The Creole Shack* (see above) is also a popular evening bar with large-screen TV, open until 10pm Monday through Thursday; on Fridays and Saturdays it's karaoke night and the bar remains open until after midnight. Opposite the *Tropicana Inn*, the Reno Cinema on Lagoon Road (☎473/440-2403) screens current mainstream films.

Cricket fans will want to catch a game at the spanking new National Stadium, a five- to ten-minute walk north of St George's, built for the 2007 Cricket world Cup with the assistance of the Chinese government.

20.2

The southwest

The southwest corner of the island is home to Grenada's most popular beaches. Only two miles from St George's is the king of them all, **Grand Anse**, whose long curve of immaculate white sand is frequented by locals and visitors alike. Further south and separated by the headland of Quarantine Point – a former leper colony – is the secluded **Morne Rouge Bay**. A favourite among wealthy tourists, the beach is excellent for swimming and it's also a popular place to snorkel. Continuing south beyond the airport are several smaller beaches and **Lance Aux Épines**, a peninsula at Grenada's southernmost point dotted with many luxury homes. **Prickly Bay** on the peninsula's west side is a popular anchorage for yachts and home to a good-sized palm-fringed beach where watersports are abundant. **Mount Hartman Bay** on the eastern side may lack beaches, but has no shortage of stunning views over the island's south coast. Be aware that while some visitors to these beaches do sunbathe topless, this practice is not permitted anywhere on the island.

Accommodation

Beach Palace Silver Sands Gap, Grand Anse Beach ☎473/439-1412, Ⓦwww.grenadabeachpalace.com. Excellent choice right on the sand, with a spread of reasonably priced, modern rooms, all with a/c, cable TV, fridge and kettle. Bar and restaurant onsite. ④

Jenny's Place Silver Sands Gap, Grand Anse Beach ☎473/405-6073, Ⓦwww.jennysplacegrenada.com. Gem of a place right on the beach, with a range of spacious, sparklingly clean and appealing a/c rooms with kitchen or kitchenette and cable TV; there's also a budget room-only option. ❷–❺

Lance Aux Epines Cottages L'Anse Aux Epines ⓣ473/444-4565, ⓦwww.laecottages.com. A ten-minute drive from the airport and right on the edge of a shady beach, these appealing, fully equipped cottages come with maid service, a/c and TV; communal games lounge onsite, and free non-motorized watersports. A good alternative to a hotel. ❺

La Luna Portici Beach ⓣ473/439-0001, ⓦwww.laluna.com. The sixteen gorgeous beach cottages of this hideaway resort are the most exclusive places to stay on the island. Each of the stylishly decorated cottages has all the usual amenities, plus its very own a plunge pool, and there's also a stunning beachfront swimming pool and free watersports. ❾

Maca Bana Magazine Beach, Point Salines ⓣ473/439-5355, ⓦwww.macabana.com. Ranged across a hillside that affords sweeping views over the ocean and down toward St George's, these beautiful and luxurious self-contained one or two-bedroom villas have been furnished with quality in mind and come with all mod cons, including a Jacuzzi on the deck. The renowned Aquarium restaurant is onsite, and there's a gorgeous infinity pool, too. ❾

True Blue Bay True Blue ⓣ473/443-8783, ⓦwww.truebluebay.com. Nestled around the waters of True Blue Bay, this friendly resort displays a certain quirkiness amidst its luxury. All of its rooms, apartments and villas are colourfully decorated and come with a/c, cable TV, wireless Internet, kitchenette and balconies with views over the bay. The onsite, waterfront restaurant and bar are both lively and feature live music some nights. ❺–❼

Grand Anse Beach and around

Most people's experience of Grenada begins and ends with the stunning **Grand Anse Beach**, a 1.3-mile stretch of white sand with a perfect view of St George's and the surrounding hills. The beach is large enough to ensure that even on busy days, pockets of peace and quiet are easy to find. The sea is exquisite, the sand powdery and soft, and there's no shortage of opportunities to water-ski, windsurf or be pulled around the bay in an inflated inner tube by speedboat. The Craft and Spice Market, selling jewellery, clothes and the ubiquitous spices (daily 8am–6pm), sits at the north end of the beach; it also has a number of small refreshment bars, as well as showers and toilets. Many vendors wander the beach touting their wares; if you're not interested, just say no.

Just south of Grand Anse on the other side of Quarantine Point lies **Morne Rouge Beach**. Having fewer resort complexes and being slightly harder to reach, this smaller, shadeless beach has an air of exclusivity and is excellent for swimming, snorkelling and private sunbathing.

The next beach along the coast, just past Petit Cabrits Point, is the even more isolated **Portici Beach**, which is accessible from the main road to the airport – just take the turn marked "Beach House Bar and Restaurant" and follow the dirt track down to the shore. The walk from the airport takes about twenty minutes, so if your plane is delayed you can while away your time on the sands rather than in the departure lounge. Here, if anywhere, you'll bump into the rich and famous who visit Grenada – the beach backs onto the exclusive resort of *La Luna* (see above). The adjacent **Magazine Beach**, another stretch of white sand, offers swimming and lovely snorkelling offshore; it's accessible to the public via the *Aquarium* restaurant (see p.733) as well as the large hotels further down the sand.

Diving

Many of the island's **dive companies** operate out of hotels or resorts in the southwest. Dive sites include the *Bianca C* shipwreck and the Molinere Reef where a wide variety of tropical fish swim around the brilliant Underwater Sculpture Park (see p.735). Operating from *True Blue Bay Resort* (see above) and with an additional store on Grand Anse beach, Aquanauts (ⓣ473/444-1126, ⓦwww.aquanautsgrenada.com) is a reliable option, offering a range of courses from US$99 for Discover Scuba to PADI Advanced Open Water courses for US$329; single tank dives cost US$55, and snorkel gear rental is US$10 per day. Another reliable outfit is Scuba

Tech, based at the *Calabash Hotel* in L'Anse Aux Epines (ⓣ473/439-4346, ⓦwww.scubatech-grenada.com), who include free Nitrox in dive prices, and charge US$48 for a single tank dive, US$135 for Discover Scuba, and US$315 for Advanced Open water. Snorkel gear is US$5, and snorkelling boat trips are also available.

Eating and drinking

The southwest is home to most of the island's **restaurants**, many of which are connected to hotels and resorts. Options range from casual pasta places to seriously upmarket restaurants of international quality; there's also a number of takeaway and fast food options around the Spiceland Mall area of Grand Anse, and in the Marquis Mall, at the southern end of the beach.

The Aquarium Restaurant Magazine Beach ⓣ473/444-1410, ⓦwww.aquarium-grenada.com. Enduringly popular with both locals and visitors, this beachfront restaurant and bar set in tropical gardens is one of the island's best options for reliable, mid-priced local and international cuisine. Lunch includes sandwiches, salads and burgers, while dinner runs from callaloo spanakopita starters to Mediterranean-style shrimp or beef Wellington entrees. Kid's menu and a good vegetarian selection; be sure to book ahead for the busy Sunday BBQ, with steaks and seafood on the grill and a delicious salad bar. Closed Mon.

La Boulangerie Marquis Mall, Grand Anse ⓣ473/444-1131. Great little place with tables under an awning, serving excellent authentic pizzas as well as tasty pasta dishes such as the the Siciliana, with eggplant and ricotta. Reasonable prices, and takeaway available.

De Big Fish Prickly Bay Marina ⓣ473/439-5265. Overlooking the marina and waters of Prickly Bay, this relaxed open-air bar and restaurant is a popular spot with yachters and non-yachters alike. Lunch options range from burgers and fish quesadillas (EC$15–25), while dinner dishes include grilled fish for around EC$40; most people, however, come for the excellent pizza. There is also a lively daily happy hour 5–6pm.

Patrick's Tamernique's Apartments, Lagoon Road ⓣ473/440-0364. Unusual and enjoyable place to sample some excellent Grenadian cooking, cooked up by the flamboyant Patrick himself. For a set price of around US$25 you get a choice of some twenty dishes, from lobster salad to curried mutton and tannia cakes with shrimp to green papaya in cheese sauce or oildown.

Red Crab L'Anse Aux Epines ⓣ473/444-4424. This popular local restaurant has a choice of indoor or outdoor seating and an extensive, moderately priced menu featuring especially good fish and seafood options. There's live music Mon and Fri evenings. Closed Sun.

Rhodes Restaurant Calabash Hotel, L'Anse Aux Epines ⓣ473/444-4334, ⓦwww.calabashhotel.com. Created by top UK chef Gary Rhodes, who designed the menu and trained all the staff, this is perhaps Grenada's most exclusive restaurant, in a formal but gorgeous, greenery-swathed setting. The food is justifiably expensive; try the shrimp and callaloo tartlet starter, or main courses from snapper with smoked salmon potatoes and gravadlax sauce to honey roasted chicken with butter beans, bacon and tomato. Desserts are appropriately delicious, too, and there's an excellent wine list. Book well ahead.

True Blue Bay True Blue ⓣ473/443-8783. This popular restaurant serves a range of Creole and international food on its enchanting terrace at the water's edge. Lunch dishes include nachos for EC$20 and salads from EC$15, and the dinner menu includes such things as callaloo and cream cheese roulade to start (EC$26) and mains such as jerked lamb and glazed duck breast for around EC$80.

Nightlife

A variety of **nightlife** options are dotted around the southwest of the island. Many hotel bars and restaurants feature live entertainment including steel bands and calypso music. *La Sirena* (ⓣ473/444-1410) and the beach bar at the *Aquarium* restaurant (see above; closed Mon) have regular live music nights. For late-night bars and clubs try *Bananas* in True Blue which has a large screen TV and a club section that stays open until 2am on the weekends, with a Latin night on Thursdays. The *Dodgy Dock* bar at True Blue hotel is good for a drink most nights and gets especially busy on Wednesdays when a DJ spins. The island's best **nightclubs** are the long-established *Fantazia*

2001 in Morne Rouge (Ⓣ473/444-2288, Ⓦfantazia2001niteclub.com), favoured by locals, and the brand-new *Karma* (see p.731) where you can dance until the small hours of the morning for a small cover charge.

The Movie Palace Cinema at Grand Anse (Ⓣ473/444-6688) shows all the Hollywood films.

20.3

The rest of the island

There is much more to Grenada than its tourist beaches and the bustle of St George's. Travelling around the island you will encounter the variety of terrain – from the mountainous rainforest of the interior to the rugged shoreline of the northeast. The three main areas to explore are the sheltered and gentle **Leeward Coast**, the weather-beaten **Windward Coast** and the dramatic, largely uninhabited **interior**.

Accommodation

Almost Paradise Sauters Ⓣ473-442-0608, Ⓦwww.almost-paradise-grenada.com. These seven cottages scattered on a hillside affording eye-popping views of Carriacou and the Grenadine islands live up to their name. Individually decorated, each comes with hammocks swaying on the private balcony, a kitchenette and a lovely outdoor shower. There's access to the sea below, and the onsite restaurant is excellent, too. 3–5

Barry's Country Resort Castlehill Ⓣ473/442-0330, Ⓦwww.barrysresort.com. Situated close to Bathway Beach in the northeast of the island, this large hotel's rooms all have a/c and cable TV. There's also a pool, tennis court and restaurant onsite. 2–3

Grenada Rainbow Inn Grenville Ⓣ473/442-7714, Ⓦwww.spiceisle.com/rainbowinn. The rooms at this friendly inn near Grenville and the outskirts of the Grand Etang National Park are basic but clean and comfortable, and come with private bathrooms and cable TV; some have balconies, and meals are available. 2

Petit Bacaye Cottages Westerhall Ⓣ473/443-2902, Ⓦwww.petitbacaye.com. These palm-thatched cottages on the edge of a small bay are the place to stay if you're seeking solitude. The rooms are simple and tastefully decorated, but don't expect to find a TV or radio. If you feel the need for company there is a small restaurant and bar on the premises, and buses to St George's pass close by. 4–5

La Sagesse Nature Centre La Sagesse Ⓣ473/444-6458, Ⓦwww.lasagesse.com. Easily accessible by public transport yet also one of the most secluded places to stay on the island, this sedate old manor house on the edge of a quiet beach has a number of elegant rooms all of which have retained their original grandeur. There are also a number of stylish new beachfront rooms and the food at the beachfront restaurant and bar is delicious. 5–6

Leeward Coast

Heading north from St George's, the **Leeward Highway** is a scenic road that twists and turns in on itself until finally reaching the north coast, where you'll find Sauteurs and the famous Caribs' Leap.

As the highway winds along it passes through a number of colourful fishing and former plantation communities such as **Beauséjour Bay**, centre of radio communication for the 1979 Revolutionary Government, and the small town of **Brizan**, once a safe haven for escaped slaves and now home to a recording studio built by pop star Billy Ocean, a native Grenadian. Just before Beauséjour, it's well worth making a detour to snorkel over the marvellous and unique **Underwater Sculpture Park** (open access; free; www.underwatersculpture.com) which features a series of sculptures set in between the teeming reef created by UK-based artist Jason de Caires Taylor. Pieces include the folklore character *La Diablesse*, a corpse-like devil woman hidden under a wide-brimmed hat; the stirring *Vicissitudes*, a circle of children holding hands; and the irreverent *Correspondent*, a typist working at his desk. There are a total of 65 individual figures, but none is marked – the beauty of the park is that you have to find them yourself (though all are within the area of Moliniere Bay). To get to the park, follow the path south from Dragon Bay along the coastline (ask locals); you can also visit as part of a snorkelling tour with one of the companies, or on any of the glass-bottom boats that ply their trade from Grand Anse.

After passing through **Halifax Harbour**, where you'll find the Grenada Dove Sanctuary, a reserve for the national bird of Grenada (also known as the invisible bird because sightings are rare), the road leads through the tiny village of **Concord**, birthplace of legendry calypsonian the Mighty Sparrow and on to **Gouyave**, a lovely old sea-weathered town whose long main street, overhung with balconies and strings of lights, belongs more to the Wild West than the Caribbean. Famous for its fishing, the town celebrates Fisherman's Birthday on June 29, the Feast Day of SS Peter and Paul during which residents head down to the beaches in the morning to bless the fishing boats and then party the rest of the day away. It's also the scene of the popular **Fish Fry** each Friday night when stalls set up on a side street around 7pm to sell delicious fresh seafood, and music blares through the speakerboxes. Gouyave is one of the main centres of the **nutmeg industry**, and a worthwhile stop is the town's nutmeg processing station (Mon–Fri 8am–4pm), where employees lead tours through the various stages of nutmeg and mace production for EC$2.70.

Situated at the end of the road is the exposed and windswept village of **Sauteurs**, dominated by its Roman Catholic and Anglican churches – symbols of the conflicts in Grenada's colonial past. The main attraction is **Caribs' Leap**: a steep cliff rising more than 100 feet out of the ocean from which the last of the island's Carib Indians threw themselves instead of surrendering to the French. From up here you'll have a stunning view of the channel where the Atlantic Ocean and the Caribbean Sea meet which is punctuated by an arch of rock known as London Bridge; you can even see as far as Carriacou. A short way from the cliff in the Catholic churchyard is the new Caribs' Leap attraction (daily 10am–5pm; EC$5), which has a small collection of Carib artefacts, a model **Carib village** and a lookout point over the ocean.

Windward Coast

Travelling south from St George's, veer left at the Spiceland Mall on Grand Anse Main Road. A sharp left at the next junction will put you on Grand Anse Valley Road, which heads east towards the affluent **Westerhall Bay**, where you can explore Westerhall Rum Distillery (Mon–Fri 8–11am & 1–3pm, Sat call to arrange; 473/443-5477; EC$5), which produces the island's best rum and the caustic Jack Iron brand. Tours take you around the remains of the colonial-era factory and water wheel, as well as a small museum on Grenadian history where you get the lowdown on rum production and can peruse an intriguing miscellany of exhibits from Grenada's first ever taxi to a German World War II machine gun.

Past Westerhall, the road clings to the island's east coast, passing the secluded and pretty beach of **Petit Bacaye**, before heading on to **La Sagesse Bay**. A signposted dirt track leads down to the sheltered beach with its straggling palm trees and small mangrove swamp, and to **La Sagesse Nature Centre** (see also p.734), formerly the home of the late Lord Brownlow, Queen Elizabeth II's cousin, who in the early 1970s built the infamous Brownlow's Gate which blocked public access to the beach. Protestors removed the gate and the Revolutionary Government nationalized the estate in 1979. A map of the walking trails in the area can be obtained from the Nature Centre, which also organizes special day-packages (EC$104) that cover transportation from your hotel, a guided nature walk, lunch and a little time on the beach.

Continuing north around the eastern side of the island, the endlessly twisting Windward Highway, in various states of repair, leads on to Grenada's second largest town, **Grenville**. Established by the French in 1763, the town is the backbone of the country's agricultural sector and home to Grenada's largest nutmeg processing station. There is little of interest in this sprawling and busy working town, and it's best to visit on a Saturday when a large colourful market selling fresh fish, fruit, vegetables and spices becomes a lively attraction. The market square is also the focus of the **Rainbow City Festival** held every year in late July and early August. Celebrating emancipation, this vibrant festival features street dancing and calypso bands.

Regardless of the time of year, the eerie **Pearls Airport**, two miles north of Grenville, is reason enough to visit the area. With a long-closed duty-free store whose specials are still posted in the window and a café that looks as if it will open at any minute, it is as if time stopped the moment the airport was abandoned in 1984 after the opening of the Cuban-built Point Salines Airport in the southwest. Two rusting Cold War relics – a Russian Aeroflot plane and a Cubana aircraft – lie just off the runway, and are slowly being dismantled by weather and vandals.

Situated a couple of miles north of Pearls Airport, and a short detour inland at the small village of Tivoli, is **Belmont Estate** (Sun–Fri 8am–4pm; EC$10; ⓣ473/442-9524; ⓦwww.belmontestate.net), a lovingly restored seventeenth-century plantation. Tours take you through the cocoa-processing warehouse, ripe with the smell of fermenting pods, out to sheds where the cocoa is dried on racks, and through gorgeous gardens where you can finish with a drink of tasty local "cocoa tea".

▲ River Antoine Rum Distillery

There's also a good restaurant (see p.737) if you fancy lunch; and if you can, try to visit on a Wednesday when, during reaping season, local farmers arrive to sell their frothing sacks of fermenting cocoa pods.

On the Windward Highway just a short distance further north is the **River Antoine Rum Distillery** (Mon–Fri 8am–4pm; EC$14; ☎473/442-7109), one of the oldest functioning water powered distilleries in the Caribbean whose water wheel has been crushing juice from locally grown sugar cane since 1785. Refreshingly casual tours led by workers take you through the fragrant factory, which still uses traditional distilling methods to produce its powerful 150-proof rum.

Another not-to-be-missed (signposted) detour from the highway north is **Lake Antoine**. Surrounded by lush agricultural land, this spectacular sixteen-acre lake inside the crater of an extinct volcano has been known to bubble when eruptions have occurred elsewhere in the region, prompting speculation that it is linked to a volcanic chain. Looking towards the coast from the lake's edge you can see rugged **Antoine Bay**, originally called Concepción by Columbus when he first sighted it in 1498.

From Antoine Bay the road continues north to **Levera National Park**. It's not difficult to understand why this remote part of the coastline attracts so many visitors: the undulating hills of this volcanic landscape are threaded with scenic hiking trails offering a beautiful excursion. On the easternmost tip of the island **Bathway Beach** is a striking, windswept stretch of sand shaded by palm trees and popular for picnics, although swimming past the reef is not permitted due to dangerous undercurrents. Visitors can buy refreshments at a roadside bar and learn more about the area at the visitor centre, situated at Bathway Beach, which has small displays explaining the region's geology; its facilities include showers, rest rooms and even an outdoor amphitheatre. Past Bathway, you can continue along a rutted dirt track to reach stunning **Levera Beach**, a completely undeveloped swath of white sand overlooked by a conical offshore island.

The interior

Grenada may be famous for its beaches but no visit to the island is complete without a trip to its dramatic rainforest at **Grand Etang National Park**. One of Hurricane Ivan's worst casualties of Ivan was the shredding of the lush, tropical vegetation that characterized the park's 3860 acres. Recovery has been swift, however, and apart from the battered trees on exposed ridges in the higher reaches of the park, few signs of Ivan's devastation remain. **Mount St Catherine** – a majestic 2757ft peak – is covered by dense rainforest and laced by a network of **walking trails**; the Park visitor centre (Mon–Sat 8am–4pm, plus Sun when cruise ships are in; ☎473/440-2452) on the main road about fifteen minutes' drive or bus ride from St George's has plenty of information on the trails; be sure to contact either tourist information or one of the island's tour guides (see p.724) in order to obtain up-to-date information on trails.

Situated 1700ft above sea level, although often shrouded in mist, is **Lake Grand Etang**. Grenada's water reservoir and an essential stop, its shores offer striking views of Mount Qua Qua and other peaks, and the surrounding rainforest; there's a small visitor centre by the entrance (same hrs as above) where you can get refreshments and information on trails around the lake.

Although some of Grenada's spectacular waterfalls are currently inaccessible, those that can be reached should not be missed. Easily accessed by road – just turn inland from the Leeward Highway at Concord – are the famous **Concord Falls**. These three waterfalls – one of which is 65ft high and has a freshwater pool large enough for swimming at its base – are one of the highlights of the Grand Etang National Park.

Eating, drinking and entertainment

If you are looking for a place to eat in the south, highly recommended is the beachfront restaurant and bar at La Sagesse Nature Centre (see p.734). A range of delicious and simple meals such as sesame seared tuna or Creole lambie (EC$50–60) are served in stylish dark-wood surroundings – one of the most romantic spots for dinner on the island. They also offer lunchtime beef, fish and veggie burgers, wraps, salads and sandwiches. Another excellent choice is the restaurant at *Almost Paradise* hotel (see p.734; lunch Thurs–Sun noon–4pm, dinner by reservation), which serves such delights as chilled vegetable soup (EC$14) to start and delicious Creole meatballs as a main, as well as great cocktails, from a killer rum punch to a cucumber gin granita. The restaurant at Belmont Estate (see p.736), on a breezy open-sided veranda atop the plantation, serves a tasty local buffet for lunch, with soup, salad, two meats, fish and side dishes, for EC$45. They also have an à la carte dinner menu Thursday through Saturday.

20.4

Carriacou

The most southerly of the Grenadine islands, **CARRIACOU** (an Arawak name meaning "island of reefs") is, at thirteen square miles, the largest of the island chain that lies between Grenada and St Vincent. Although just a short ferry hop from Grenada, the seven thousand inhabitants of Carriacou, fondly nicknamed "Kayaks" by Grenadians, enjoy a more relaxed pace of life, and the island feels more smalltown and rural. The main town of **Hillsborough**, surrounded by low, forested hills, won't detain you for long but the rest of the island, with excellent watersports and unspoilt beaches in the south and good walking trails in the north, is well worth exploring. Diving is also first class on the island, with a range of sites for all levels of experience, including the wreck of a small World War I gunboat.

Carriacou also has no shortage of **culture**. Belief systems of the African slaves remain strong and are preserved in rituals such as the powerful **Big Drum Dance**, a pre-Christian ceremony during which ancestors communicate with their descendants (see box, p.741). The Big Drum Dances, along with street parties and calypso, are the highlights of the **Carriacou Regatta** held every August, during which descendants of the island's Scottish boat builders show off their hand-built schooners. Other festivals include: **Carnival**, celebrated before the start of Lent; **May Day**; and the **Parang festival** prior to Christmas – all are opportunities to hit the streets, dance and eat, and take in some live calypso.

Arrival and information

Carriacou is easily accessible by **air**, with daily connecting flights from Barbados, Grenada, St Vincent and other Grenadine islands; flights touch down at **Lauriston Airstrip** one mile south of Hillsborough. By far the most scenic and economical way to get here from Grenada is the regular *Osprey Express* **passenger ferry** (see p.724), which arrives and departs from the Hillsborough jetty. Monday–Saturday tickets for the Osprey should be bought from their office on Patterson Street in Hillsborough (Mon–Fri 5.30–6.30am & 10.30am–4.30pm, Sat 5.30–6.30am, 10am–noon & 3–4pm; ☎473/443-8126), while on Sundays tickets can be bought

Kick'em Jenny

Directly under the waters of the ferry route from Grenada to Carriacou (although in practice the ferries veer to avoid the mile-wide exclusion zone) lies a growing underwater volcano known as **Kick'em Jenny**, whose peak is now approximately 180 metres below the water's surface. Kick'em Jenny's first known eruption, which lasted 24 hours, occurred on July 24, 1939. This produced a column of water and debris over 900ft high and caused tsunamis in Grenada and the south Grenadines. Twelve smaller eruptions have occurred since, the most recent in December 2001.

Kick'em Jenny is continually monitored by the Seismic Research Unit at the University of the West Indies in Trinidad, which issues warnings if there are signs of overactivity. There's currently a 1.5km exclusion zone around the summit of the volcano.

For details and a sonar image of the volcano, visit Ⓦwww.uwiseismic.com/KeJ/kejhome.html.

on board. A passenger and cargo boat (*The Jasper*, see p.697) also runs between Carriacou and **Union Island** in St Vincent and the Grenadines; passengers from Union Island must pass through immigration at the small office across the main road, opposite the foot of the jetty.

The **tourist office** (Mon–Fri 8am–noon & 1–4pm; Ⓣ473/443-7948) on Main Street is where you can pick up accommodation information and a map of the island. Both First Caribbean and National Commercial Bank have branches in Hillsborough on Main Street; both have **ATMs**. The lone **post office** (Mon–Fri 8am–noon & 1–4pm) is in front of the pier, while payphones can be found in front of the Cable & Wireless office on Patterson Street (Mon–Fri 7.30am–6pm, Sat 7.30am–1pm). There are several Internet cafés dotted around town.

Getting around

Buses operate from the jetty in Hillsborough and typical fares are EC$1.50 for trips up to one mile and EC$2.50 for those over one mile. A service also runs from Lauriston Airport, Tyrrel Bay and Belmont to south of Hillsborough and north to the town of Windward. **Taxis** run from the airport to Hillsborough for around EC$20 and to Belair for roughly EC$25. **Water taxis** from the jetty are the easiest way to get to the beaches. **Car rental agencies** include Sunkey's Auto Rentals in Hillsborough (Ⓣ473/443-8382); Martin Bullen (Ⓣ473/443-7204), who is based at the island's only petrol station on Patterson Street in Hillsborough; and Quality Jeeps (Ⓣ473/443-8307) in L'Esterre. All charge around EC$145 per day.

Accommodation

Despite its small size, Carriacou has a varied selection of good-value **accommodation** options.

Hillsborough

Ade's Dream Guest House Main Street Ⓣ473/443-7317, Ⓦadesdream.com. Claiming that "your best dream awaits you", this charming guesthouse with ornate balconies has a range of rooms from small with shared bathroom to larger, new rooms with a/c, cable TV, kitchenettes and private bathrooms. A grocery store is on the ground floor and the well-reviewed *New Wave Restaurant* is right across the street. ❷

Green Roof Inn Hillsborough 473/443-6399, Ⓦwww.greenroofinn.com. A ten-minute walk north of Hillsborough, this highly recommended small, family-run inn is a peaceful haven with breathtaking views. The rooms are simple but stylish and all have mosquito nets and fans, and there's wireless Internet. Bikes and snorkel equipment are available for rent and an excellent Continental breakfast and airport/jetty transfer are included in the rates. ❷–❹

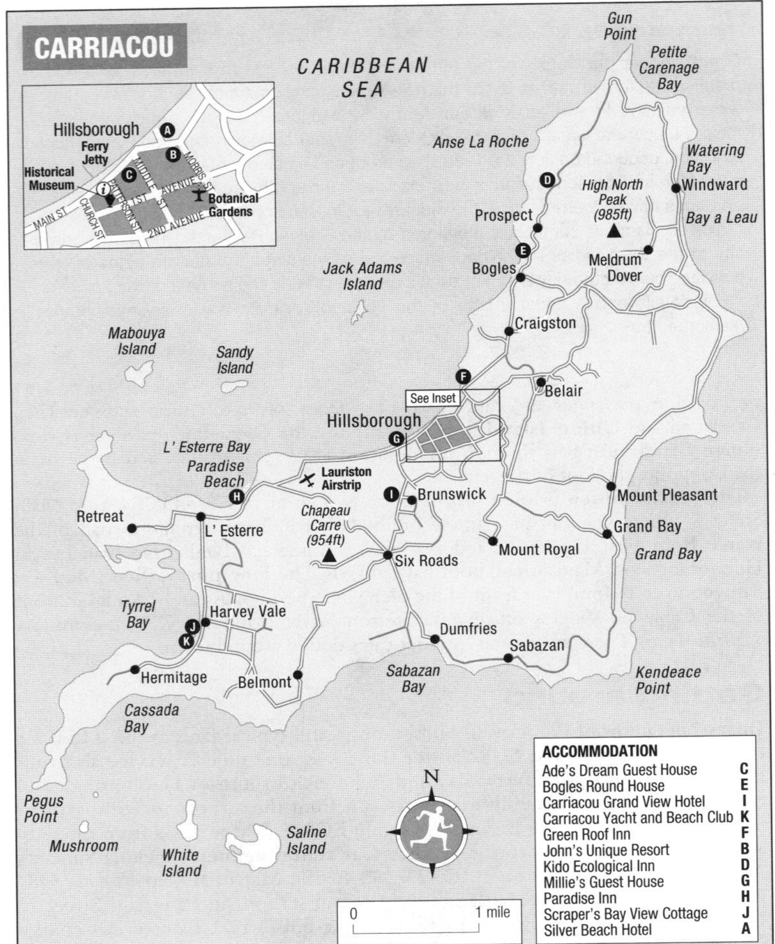

John's Unique Resort Upper Main Street ☎ 473/443-8345 ⓔ junique@caribsurf.com. All of the spacious rooms and apartments of this private hotel, located five minutes' walk from the centre of Hillsborough, are en suite and come with private balconies and cable TV; some also have a/c and kitchens. There is also an onsite restaurant and bar. ②

Millie's Guest House Main Street ☎ 473/443-7310 ⓔ millies@spiceisle.com. On the beachfront side of Main Street, this rambling hotel with covered wooden balconies is good-value budget accommodation. One room has a private bathroom and the rest share bathrooms and kitchens. ②

Silver Beach Hotel ☎ 473/443-7337, ⓔ silverbeach@caribsurf.com. Nestled by the water's edge in a secluded bay, this small resort has a range of one-bedroom suites, some with kitchenettes. Free transport is available from the airport and bus tours and sailing excursions can be arranged. One free night is offered for every seven-night stay. ③

The rest of the island

Bogles Round House Bogles ☎ 473/443-7841, ⓦ www.boglesroundhouse.com. Three lovely cottages attached to the island's best restaurant (see p.743), decorated with simple style. All have a kitchenette, fan and nets over the beds, and are just steps from the beach. ❸

Carriacou Grand View Hotel Beauséjour ☎473/443-6348, ⓦwww.carriacougrandview.com. Perched above Hillsborough harbour, this large hotel with its own pool and onsite restaurant and piano bar, commands magnificent views over the sea and surrounding countryside. All of the simple, but comfortable en-suite rooms come with private balconies, cable TV and a/c or ceiling fans. Apartments with kitchenettes are also available. ❸–❹

Carriacou Yacht and Beach Club Tyrrel Bay ☎473/443-6123, ⓔcarriyacht@spiceisle.com. Surrounded by palm trees, this self-contained complex at the water's edge is a popular haunt for yachties. The rooms are neat and comfortable and all have private bathrooms, refrigerators and coffeemakers. The resort also has its own bar and restaurant. ❷

Kido Ecological Inn Prospect ☎473/443-7936, ⓦwww.kido-projects.com. Eco-tourism is high on *Kido*'s list of priorities due to its remote location on a forested ridge on the northwestern coast. The inn is also a research station, and birdwatching, hiking, cycling, sailing and diving are all available, as is the chance to volunteer for ongoing ecological projects. Accommodation includes a two-bedroom villa and a large pagoda, and there's a well-stocked library. ❹

Paradise Inn L'Esterre Bay ☎473/443-8406, ⓔparadiseinncarriacou@yahoo.com. Right on the edge of the secluded Paradise Beach, this small inn has spacious rooms, each with private bathroom and ceiling fans. ❷

Scraper's Bay View Cottages Tyrrel Bay ☎473/443-7403, ⓔscrapers@spiceisle.com. Appealing Caribbean-style apartments whose modest rooms all have private kitchens and bathrooms. The adjoining bar and restaurant serves a range of fish and pasta dishes as well as sandwiches and burgers. ❷

Hillsborough

A small cluster of weather-worn buildings overlooking the sea, the one-street town of Hillsborough can easily be explored in an hour or two. Most of the **places to stay and eat** as well as banks and public services are found on Main Street, which runs parallel to the beach, which offers a lively scene compared to the rest of Carriacou, especially when the ferry is arriving or departing from the small pier. The beach around the jetty is narrow and a heavily used part of the working harbour, but it's also a decent place for a swim.

On Mondays the jetty is the site for a small and lively **market** where local fruit and vegetable vendors display their produce in a haphazard collection of stalls. Throughout the town old stone merchant houses serve as a reminder of the island's colonial, sugar-producing past, as does its small but interesting **Historical Museum** on Patterson Street (Mon–Fri 9.30am–4pm, Sat 10am–4pm; EC$5). Housed in the restored ruins of an old cotton gin mill, the museum features a varied collection of Amerindian utensils and pottery, and has sections devoted to the island's European and African heritage. The only other place of interest in Hillsborough is the small collection of tropical plants, flowers and trees at the **Botanical Gardens**, nestled a block inland from Main Street on First Avenue.

The Big Drum Dance

The **Big Drum Dance** is an integral part of all festivities in Carriacou. Rooted in ancestral worship and tribal identity, the tradition has survived the centuries since it came to the Caribbean with the West African slaves. The drums are made from old rum kegs and goatskin and, until independence, were banned by the British who saw them as a threat to Christianity and feared they would incite rebellion. The ritual has survived, thanks to the lack of attention of absentee European landowners and the people's determination to preserve their culture. Once reserved for special occasions, such as the launching of a boat or a funeral ceremony, the vibrant drumming and dancing is now also performed for tourists.

The rest of the island

Approximately one and a half miles southwest of Hillsborough past the airport, is the appropriately named **Paradise Beach**. A sweeping expanse of golden sand protected by two small islands, it's an ideal spot for safe swimming and snorkelling over the teeming, healthy reefs. In addition to a beachfront hotel (see p.741), facilities include a couple of bars serving snacks and hot meals and a gift shack. A short distance west from Paradise Beach is the small village of **L'Esterre**, former home of the late local artist Canute Calliste, who claimed a mermaid visited him when he was a small boy and blessed him with the gift of painting and music. The mermaid's gift was so great that Canute, who died in 2005, was known to finish sixteen paintings in one day. You can view his cheerful and vibrant works at the Historical Museum in Hillsborough.

The main road then leads south away from L'Esterre, and on to one of the most popular beaches in the area, **Tyrrel Bay**, also known as Hurricane Bay because it is a favourite anchorage for yachts during storms. The three-mile journey to this large horseshoe bay on Carriacou's western side is serviced by a frequent bus service from Hillsborough. The waters are well protected and the beaches golden, especially at the southern end of the bay around the yacht club (see p.741), after the string of bars and shops that line the road peters out.

Tyrrel Bay is also famous for its oysters, which grow in protected areas amongst mangrove roots reached by boat. Just yards inland from the bay is the pretty village of **Harvey Vale**. There's not much to explore but take time to visit an old Amerindian well, whose waters are thought to have therapeutic qualities.

Looming over Hillsborough about a mile to the north is **Belair**, a peak 719ft above sea level that commands sweeping views of the Grenadines – especially Sandy Island and Grenada. Scenic walking trails wind through the ruins of old French and British plantations nestled amongst white immortelle trees.

Further north is the small village of **Bogles**, the terminus of a bus route from the capital and the home of one of the best restaurants in all of Grenada and Carriacou (see p.743). The road becomes a track and a fifteen-minute walk, or bumpy two-minute drive if you're in a jeep, leads to the **Kido Ecological Research Station**. A short walk further along, or a water taxi ride from Hillsborough, leads to **Anse La Roche**, a peaceful beach on the northwest coast of the island where a variety of species of turtles, including green and hawksbill, swim ashore to lay their eggs at night. With its fabulous coral reefs lying just offshore, this crescent-shaped gem is one of the best places to snorkel in Grenada. It's also a pleasant spot to simply lie back and watch the yachts sail by but make sure to bring food and drink as there are currently no facilities. Unfortunately, the unspoiled seclusion is set to change as the area is earmarked for the construction of a new hotel; at the time of writing, however, the beach remained as pristine as ever.

A short walk from Anse La Roche, the northernmost tip of the island is known as **Gun Point**, so named for the cannons that used to contribute to the region's defences. On the east side of the headland is the 955ft **High North Peak**, the highest point on the island and a protected national park. Details on the network of trails that thread through this region's dry deciduous forest and the wildlife you might encounter along the way can be found at a small interpretive centre in Bogles, managed by the Kido Research Station. To fully appreciate the region, however, a guide is recommended, and Kido organizes hiking tours in the High North Park with local guides for around EC$50 per person.

Nestled on the eastern edge of the High North National Park is the tiny and picturesque fishing village of **Windward**. The windswept community's occupants are boat builders and descendants of Scottish immigrants who brought the craft here from Glasgow, back when the island was still under British colonial rule, and a small nautical museum in the village celebrates its seafaring history. Claiming to use traditions passed down through the generations, many of these craftspeople now work at Tyrrel Bay. **Petite Carenage Bay** is also nestled in the northeast corner of the island, between Gun Point and Windward, and is home to a mangrove restoration project managed by the Kido Research Station. You can explore a unique and ancient ecosystem whose dense vegetation and shallow waters are home to numerous fish, insects and birds. Kido organizes guided tours of the mangrove swamp, as well as turtle watching tours, both of which are recommended.

Ocean activities

Carriacou is especially good for **reef diving**, and is quieter than Grenada for practising other **watersports**. Diving, snorkelling, water-skiing and windsurfing are popular and can be arranged through Carriacou Silver Diving Ltd (Ⓣ473/443-7882, Ⓦwww.scubamax.com), whose office is in Hillsborough. Offering a range of day and night dives, this company caters for all levels of experience and will also arrange accommodation, island tours and even barbecues. Single dives start at US$45 and diving courses start at US$100 for a half-day Discover Scuba course. Arawak Divers in Tyrrel Bay (Ⓣ473/443-6906, Ⓦwww.arawak.de) offers a similar range of dives and runs day excursions to the Isle of Rhonde and the Tobago Cays. Also based in Tyrrel Bay, *Lumbadive* (Ⓣ473/443-8566, Ⓦwww.lumbadive.com) offers a range of dive courses including accommodation packages.

One of the most popular places to dive is **Sandy Island**, just off the coast from Hillsborough, whose stunning beaches and vibrant coral reefs have made it a popular location for filming television commercials. Sadly, its popularity has also been its undoing as dropped anchors have damaged the coral and are eroding the reef.

Turtle-watching tours, snorkelling trips and sailing excursions from a one-day whale- and dolphin-watching trip for US$160 to a two-day overnight sailing trip for US$340 can all be arranged by the Kido Research Station (see opposite).

Eating, drinking and nightlife

When it comes to **dining** and **nightlife** on Carriacou the main options are hotel bars and restaurants. There are a few independent establishments, but don't expect a lively nightlife or too much selection when it comes to finding something to eat. If you fancy a dance, *After Hours* in Tyrrell Bay has DJs at the weekends playing soca and reggae, and the occasional live band.

Bogles Round House Bogles Ⓣ473/443-7841, Ⓦwww.boglesroundhouse.com. One of the best restaurants – perhaps *the* best – in all of Grenada, this is a real treat, with delicious Caribbean/Mediterranean cuisine served up with style in a relaxed and welcoming atmosphere. You can eat prix fixe (around EC$80 for three courses) or à la carte, with mains EC$55–90. Dishes include home-made fishcakes, lobster bisque or tempura prawns to start, mains such as red snapper with mango salsa, steak or vegetarian nut roast, and gorgeous desserts, including pannacotta and key lime pie. Book ahead.

Callaloo by the Sea Main Street, Hillsborough Ⓣ473/443-8004. A quaint restaurant right on the beach, with fine views of Hillsborough Bay. Seafood is the speciality but the menu also has a range of chicken dishes, as well as chips and a selection of salads. Closed Sun. Prices range EC$40–130.

The Green Roof Inn Hillsborough Ⓣ473/443-6399. Reservations are recommended at this superb restaurant set on the veranadah, where the food is as good as the view. The menu (dinner only) varies depending on what's in season but typical dishes include smoked lobster or grilled swordfish.

New Wave Restaurant Main Street, Hillsborough Ⓣ473/443-7317. Across the road from *Ade's Dream Guest House* (see p.739) and run by the same people, this no-frills restaurant cooks up a combination of Caribbean and international dishes for breakfast, lunch and dinner, starting from EC$20. The upstairs bar is a popular late-night drinking spot with a dress code.

Turtle Dove Pizzeria Tyrrel Bay Ⓣ473/443-8322. This attractive blue and white restaurant next door to Lumbadive serves a good range of home-made Italian pizza and pasta dishes from around EC$20, and opens late (till 10pm) every night.

Twilight Restaurant & Bar Tyrrel Bay (no phone). This charming and friendly beachfront restaurant and bar serves a good range of Creole dishes such as curried lambie (EC$30) and grilled lobster. Desserts include a range of delicious ice creams, and live steel bands play into the night on Wed and Sun. There's also a daily happy hour (6–7pm).

20.5

Petite Martinique

Situated approximately three miles northeast of Carriacou, **PETITE MARTINIQUE** is a large, mile-wide hill of unspoilt forestland whose 486 acres were first settled by the French in the seventeenth century; today, its nearly one thousand inhabitants are mainly their descendants. The sea has long been the main source of income for locals who continue the tradition of seafaring, fishing and boat building – and some say, smuggling – to this day.

As the island is tiny, don't expect to find a lot to do or see, especially if the weather is bad. This is in fact a great place to do nothing at all, and most people visit on a day-trip from Grenada or Carriacou. You can easily walk around Petite Martinique via its one road, which stretches along the west coast and is dotted with houses, shops, bars and small family graveyards. At its southern end when the road stops it becomes a grassy headland with great views of the surrounding Grenadine islands. Even greater panoramic views are rewarded to those who follow the at times tough trail, which leads from the headland to the island's 738ft peak of **Mt Piton** – a walk which requires good shoes and plenty of water.

For those who prefer to lounge on the beach, the stretch of sand leading south away from the ferry jetty is your best bet. This is both a working and a tourist beach with rocky headlands at both ends, and a small boatyard with a number of traditional wooden boats in various states of repair at the far southern end.

Petite Martinique's **Carnival** is held during the two days before Lent, and at Easter the island holds its two-day **regatta**, which features the famous greasy-pole contest, in which competitors inch their way out over the water along a slippery pole to reach the prize hanging at the end.

Practicalities

As most visitors come here on a day-trip, **accommodation** and **dining options** are limited. Try *Melodies Guest House* (ⓣ473/443-9052, ⓦwww.spiceisle.com/melodies; ❷), a family-run beachside guesthouse just three minutes' walk from the main jetty, where the basic rooms come with private showers and some with verandas. The restaurant and bar serves a variety of local food and you can choose to eat either inside or under shady trees on the edge of the sea. Overlooking the harbour is *Seaside View Holiday Cottages* (ⓣ473/443-9007; ❷), an attractive collection of one- and two-bedroom self-catering beachfront cottages, all of them well maintained, whose owners also run the Sea View supermarket and gift shop, and will arrange pick-up charters from Carriacou.

The friendly *Palm Beach Restaurant* (ⓣ473/443-9103; daily 10am–10pm) is a pleasant option for **eating**. Tables under outdoor gazebos edge sea-facing gardens, and the stunning harbour view makes this a fine place to enjoy a cocktail or two as well as a meal. The lunch menu features rotis, burgers and grilled fish dishes for EC$18–47 and main courses on the dinner menu include grilled fish and BBQ chicken for around EC$50. Vegetarian options are available on request.

Other than the local bars strung out along the main road, the only other place for an evening drink and occasional live music is the bar at *Melodies Guest House*.

21

Trinidad and Tobago

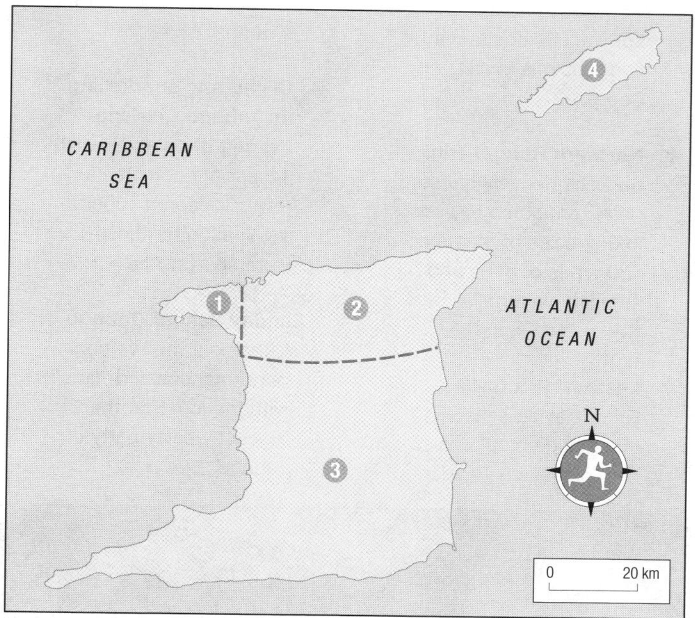

Trinidad and Tobago highlights

* **Trinidad street food** Trinidad's delicious street food includes corn soup, doubles and curry-filled rotis. See p.751

* **Carnival, Trinidad** The original West Indian carnival – now exported worldwide – features spectacular costumes and fabulous music. See p.760

* **Northern Range, Trinidad** The densely forested peaks are home to over 100 species of mammal, 430 types of birds and stunning waterfalls. See p.766

* **Leatherback turtles** During laying season these huge creatures nest nightly on Trinidad and Tobago's north coasts, providing a rare and moving sight. See pp.772 & 773

* **Caroni Swamp, Trinidad** Visit the nesting grounds of the stunning scarlet ibis on a boat trip through eerie mangrove swamps. See p.775

* **Diving and snorkelling on Tobago** Challenging drift dives and easily accessible coral reefs make Tobago a superb destination for these watersports. See p.783

* **Sunday School, Tobago** Check out the live pan performances and "lime" with the locals at the biggest weekly party on Tobago. See p.787

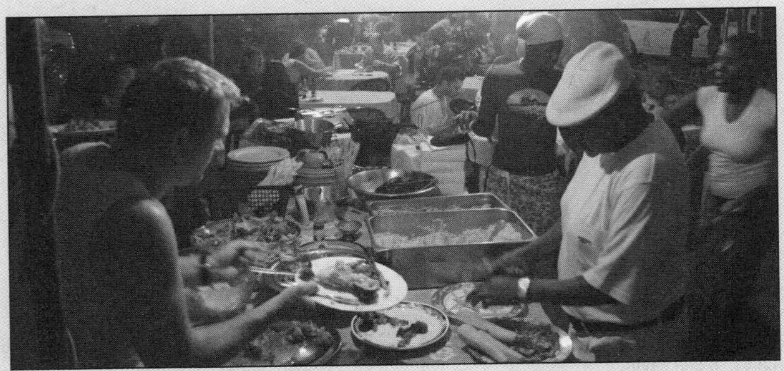

▲ Sunday School

Introduction and basics

Just off the coast of the South American mainland they were once part of, Trinidad and Tobago (usually shortened to "T&T") form the southernmost islands of the Lesser Antilles chain and the most influential republic in the Eastern Caribbean. Two of the most exciting, underexplored and uncontrived of the Caribbean islands, T&T are rich in indigenous culture. A cultural pace-maker best known as the home and heart of West Indian Carnival, the nation can also boast of having the most diverse and absorbing society in the region.

T&T remain relatively **inexpensive**, as natural gas and oil reserves have ensured economic independence and freedom from the tourist trade. Regionally they are the richest destinations for **eco-tourism**, combining the flora and fauna of the Caribbean with the wilder aspect of the South American mainland. In Trinidad you can hike through undisturbed rainforest studded with pristine waterfalls, take a boat ride through mangrove swamps and watch leatherback turtles nest on remote beaches. And with more than 430 species in an area of 4830 square kilometres, the **birdwatching** is among the world's best. Meanwhile, **Tobago** (300sq km) has glorious beaches and stunning coral reefs. Declared the "Disneyland of diving", Tobago has one of the largest brain corals in the world and sightings of manta rays are common.

Equally absorbing are T&T's dynamic **towns** and **cities**, showcases for the architectural, religious and cultural traditions of their cosmopolitan populations. The 1.3 million inhabitants hail from India, China, Portugal and Syria as well as Africa, England, France and Spain, and though racial tensions are inevitably present, Trinbagonians (as they're collectively known) co-exist with good humour, and are proud of their **multiculturalism**. The result is a highly creative culture with a lively **music scene** that rivals that of Jamaica.

Unlike its Caribbean neighbours, full-scale **slavery** was practised on Trinidad for a relatively short fifty years as the Dutch, French and British were too busy fighting over Tobago to cater to the demands of King Sugar on Trinidad. Consequently the national psyche is characterized by a strong sense of identity and a laid-back enjoyment of the good things in life, best displayed in the local propensity for "**liming**" – meeting friends for a drink and a chat. With more than a dozen public holidays, local festivals and the pre-Lenten **Carnival**, a no-holds-barred two days of dancing in the streets, the islands' reputation of knowing how to party is well deserved.

Where to go

A visit to Trinidad inevitably begins in the capital, **Port of Spain**, home to most of the island's accommodation and the centre of its transport system. The most accessible **beaches** are on the north coast, while the **Northern Range** offers excellent hiking, river and waterfall swimming and superb birdwatching. In contrast to the north, central Trinidad is dominated by flat agricultural plains with a population of primarily Indian descent. In terms of natural assets, there's the **Caroni swamp**, nesting area of the scarlet ibis, and the protected **wetlands of Nariva**, home of manatees and anacondas. The burgeoning city of **San Fernando** is a friendly base to explore Trinidad's "deep south", an area largely unvisited by tourists, where modern oil towns contrast with picturesque fishing villages and deserted beaches.

In **Tobago**, the majority of visitors stay in the hotel-dominated **western tip**. A more genuine picture of local life can be seen in the capital, **Scarborough**, and along the northern coast in friendly **Castara** or at the fishing village of **Charlotteville**.

When to go

Most travellers come to T&T between January and March, during the **Carnival** season when the **climate** is at its most

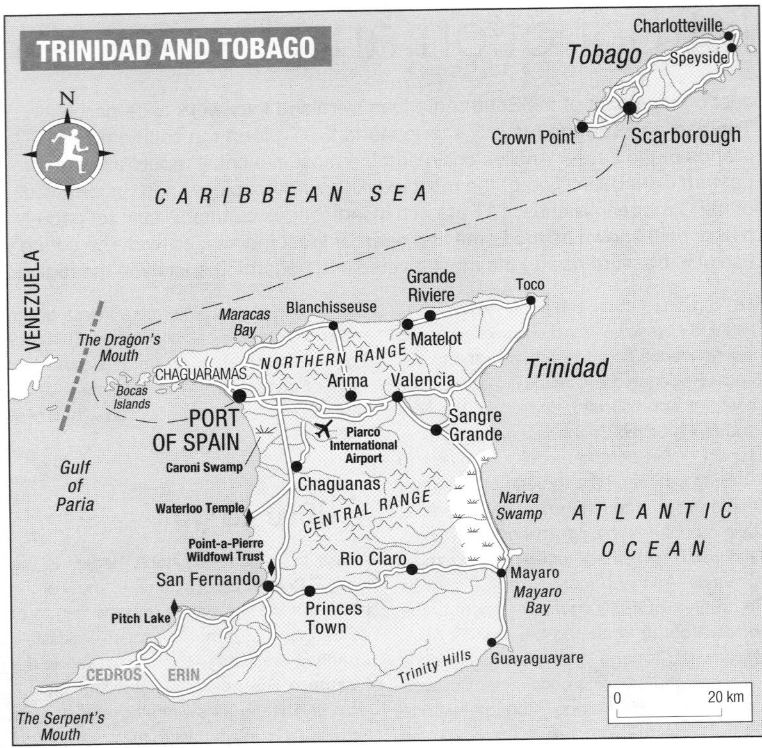

forgiving (25–30°C/72–87°F). By May, the **dry season** parches the lush landscape and bush fires often rage through the hills. The **rainy season** starts in June and lasts till December, but in September there's usually a dry spell known as the *petit carem*, an Indian summer of two to four weeks; it's an excellent time to visit, with flights at low-season rates. Tobago hoteliers hike rates during high season (mid-Dec to mid-April), as do Trinidad hotels during Carnival, but smaller hotels on both islands charge the same all year round.

Getting there

In Trinidad flights touch down at **Piarco International Airport**, a large, modern complex with numerous facilities situated approximately 32km southeast of Port of Spain on Golden Grove Road in Piarco. For details of travelling between the airport and Port of Spain see p.755. Flights into Tobago arrive at **Crown Point International Airport**, a small open-plan complex with limited facilities situated on the southeast tip of the island. For details of transport around Tobago from the airport see p.782.

Those that arrive via **cruise ship**, any other form of boat or travel between the islands by ferry will dock in Trinidad at the **King's Wharf** in Port of Spain; in Tobago all ships and ferries dock at the cruise ship and ferry terminal in **Scarborough**.

Money and costs

The local currency is the **Trinidad and Tobago dollar** (**TT$**), divided into one hundred cents. Coins come in 1, 5, 10 and 25-cent pieces, while notes come in denominations of 1, 5, 10, 20 and 100. Keep some cash in small denominations as supermarkets and bars may exchange TT$100 but taxis and street vendors often can't, and should be paid with TT$20 or less.

Traveller's cheques and **credit cards** are accepted in most restaurants, high-class shops and hotels, though in smaller establishments and rural areas they are unlikely to take anything but local currency. Most host homes do not have credit card facilities. There are ATMs in all cities and towns, and some machines (in West Mall, Trinidad, and around Crown Point, Tobago) will dispense in US dollars.

At the time of publication the **exchange rate** was around TT$6.29 to US$1, and TT$12.34 to the UK pound. For **Trinidad**, Piarco Airport Exchange Bureau (daily 24hr) has reasonable rates, although it is not as competitive as the banks in Port of Spain; there are several on Independence Square, and there is a Republic bank on Ariapita Avenue and on the Western Main Road in St James.

Travellers flying into **Tobago** can change money at the airport bureau de change or the Republic Bank opposite the terminal (Mon–Thurs 8–11am & noon–2pm, Fri 8am–noon & 3–5pm); there's also a Royal Bank on Airport Road. There are several banks in Scarborough, including Republic on Carrington Street.

Banking hours vary slightly, but are usually Monday to Thursday 8am–2pm and Fridays 8am–noon and 3–5pm. Most banks in Trinidad's larger malls open and close later (9am–6pm) with no break. Outside banking hours money can be exchanged in the larger hotels in Port of Spain (at a poor rate). Most shops and vendors will accept American dollars – pay in small denominations and be prepared to receive your change in local currency.

Trinidad and Tobago are undoubtedly one of the **cheapest** Caribbean destinations due to their low profile on the tourist market. It is possible to survive on £25/US$35 a day if you're prepared to take the least expensive accommodation, eat at low-cost cafés and travel by public transport. If you stay at tourist accommodation and eat at finer restaurants, you will need at least £65/US$95 a day. A rental car will add around £30–40/US$45–60 per day.

During **Carnival** season, all accommodation rates in Port of Spain rise by 10 to 70 percent, as do other prices, including entrance fees, drinks and taxi fares. If you want to enjoy yourself during Carnival, plan on a budget of at least £100/US$140 a day.

Upon leaving T&T, you'll be required to pay a TT$100 (US$17) **departure tax** in local currency.

Information

The T&T tourist board, known as the Tourism Development Association or TDA, has a fairly good website ⓦwww.visittnt.com, listing useful accommodation options, and includes a calendar of events. The board has information booths at Crown Point and Piarco airports with friendly, helpful staff. Tobago's main tourist advice centre is at the Tobago House of Assembly (THA) in Scarborough (ⓣ868/639-2125 or 4636, ⓦwww.visittobago.gov.tt).

The main **newspapers** include the broadsheet *Trinidad Guardian* (ⓦwww.guardian.co.tt), the tabloid *Express* (ⓦwww.trinidadexpress.com) and *Newsday* (ⓦwww.newsday.co.tt); Tobago has only one paper, *Tobago News* (ⓦwww.thetobagonews.com), published on Fridays. Though the islands have two terrestrial **TV stations** – the main local news slot is at 7pm on TV6 – cable TV is predominant. **Radio** is hugely popular, with the best stations for contemporary local music being WE FM (96.1) and Tobago's local station, Radio Tambrin (92.1 FM).

Getting around

Travelling around Trinidad and Tobago takes ingenuity and patience. **Public transport** is minimal, so a privately run system of route taxis, maxi taxis and regular taxis fill the gaps. If you want to see more than the urban areas, however, it is advisable to **rent a car**.

By bus

Though **bus** services have improved in recent years, particularly in Port of Spain, public transport remains erratic, with most buses clustered around peak hours. **Tickets** cost TT$2–10 and must be bought in advance from the Port of Spain and Scarborough bus terminals or from small general stores around

Websites

ⓦ**saucytrini.blogspot.com** The best T&T Carnival site is actually a blog, with links to all the costume bands and essential advice to prepare you for the main event.
ⓦ**www.search.co.tt** Exhaustive directory of T&T-related sites. Essential and non-essential stuff.

ⓦ**www.tntisland.com** Though it's not pretty to look at, this is one of the best of the many personal websites devoted to T&T – everything from Trinbagonian beauty queens to places to do your laundry.

ⓦ**www.trinibase.com** Fact-heavy site with local statistics and links to all things Carnival and Trinbagonian. You must register (for free) in order to access the site.

ⓦ**www.caribbeanfreeradio.com** Blogs, podcasts and links to all things Trini from a thoughtful, arty angle.

ⓦ**www.meppublishers.com/online/discover** Website of the Discover T&T tourism booklet.

the country. All buses in Trinidad leave and terminate at City Gate/South Quay in Port of Spain. In Tobago, all buses depart from the terminal on Greenside Street in Scarborough.

By car

The main hazards on the islands' roads are blind corners and potholes, and Tobago's roads are much quieter than Trinidad's. Road signs are based on the English system (although distances and speed limits are in kilometres) and you drive on the left. **Petrol stations** can be scarce outside urban areas so keep the tank full. **Car rental** starts at around US$40 per day. Thrifty is the only major international chain on both islands, though there are many local firms. Econo Cars (191–193 Western Main Rd, Cocorite; ⓣ868/669-1119, ⓦwww.trinidad.net/econocar) is the least expensive in Trinidad, while in Tobago, Sherman's (Lambeau ⓣ868/639-2292, ⓦwww.shermansrental.com) is the most reliable. All companies require you to be 25 or over, to have held a driving licence for a minimum of two years and require a credit card imprint.

By taxi

Maxi taxis are private minibuses that carry ten to twenty people and have set routes and standardized fares (TT$2–10) but no set timetables. An entertaining experience for the decor, music and conversation, maxis have colour-coded stripes along the side of the vehicle relating to the area in which they work. Yellow (Port of Spain and the west), red (east) and green (central and south) commute between Port of Spain and outlying towns, while black (Princes Town), brown (San Fernando to the southwest peninsula) and blue (Tobago) work within their own areas. Routes radiate from main centres; you can board anywhere – just stick out your hand to be picked up. **Route taxis** follow similar rules, but take a maximum of five passengers and are slightly more expensive. **Private taxis** take you directly to your destination but are more expensive; always agree on the price beforehand.

Inter-island transport

There are two ways to travel **between** Trinidad and Tobago. By **sea,** there's a fast catamaran (TT$50 one-way, 2.5hr) and a regular ferry (TT$37.50; 5–6hr) between Port of Spain and Scarborough; call ⓣ868/625-4906 or 639-2416 or visit ⓦwww.patnt.com for more schedules and ticketing. Travel by **plane** is quicker (20min) but pricier (TT$150 one-way) – call ⓣ625 7200 or visit ⓦwww.caribbean-airlines.com.

Accommodation

Most **accommodation** in Trinidad is located in Port of Spain and the larger towns, while in tourist-oriented Tobago most hotels are found in the Crown Point area on the island's western tip. Expect to pay US$40–100 for a room in Port of Spain and slightly more in Tobago. There are no high and low seasons in Trinidad but rates may increase by up to

70 percent during Carnival. In Tobago high-season rates (quoted throughout the guide) operate between December and mid-April, dropping by 25 percent in low season. We have taken room tax (10–15 percent) and service charge (10 percent) into account, but it's worth checking each time you rent a room whether these have been included.

One time of year you simply cannot count on getting a room in Trinidad is the three weeks before and after **Carnival**. Rooms must be booked months in advance. Most hotels, guesthouses and host homes offer special Carnival packages for the Friday before Carnival to Ash Wednesday; expect to pay US$100 per night for a basic room, and anything up to US$300 in the smarter hotels.

For those looking for an alternative to standard hotels, **guesthouses** are small-scale properties with fewer facilities (perhaps a shared bathroom and fan instead of air-conditioning), while private **host homes** are an excellent and inexpensive option giving you greater insight into the local lifestyle. They normally cost around US$35 per person. For host homes in Trinidad contact the Bed and Breakfast Co-operative Society (Ⓣ868/663-4413, Ⓔla-belle@tstt.net.tt), or visit the TDC website (see p.56); in Tobago, contact Ms Miriam Edwards, c/o Federal Villa, 1–3 Crooks River, Scarborough (Ⓣ639 3926). Those travelling in a group may prefer holiday **villas**, which can be quite economical when two-plus couples share. Contact Villas of Tobago Ltd (Ⓣ868/639-9600, Ⓦwww.villasoftobago.com).

Food and drink

One of the highlights of Trinidad and Tobago is the fantastic **cuisine**, a unique blend of African, Indian, Chinese and European influences. Although you may be offered insipid tourist-oriented fare in larger hotels, local cooking – meaning anything from Indian curry to Creole pelau or Spanish-style *pastelles* – still reigns supreme, and there's a great selection of restaurants in Tobago and in Port of Spain.

The national dish is the Creole staple **callaloo** – dasheen leaves cooked with okra and coconut. Other Creole favourites are pelau (rice, chicken and pigeon peas stewed in coconut milk), cowheel soup and fish broth. Wild meat, such as agouti, lappe, manicou and even iguana are a staple of Tobago's harvest festivals, while no trip to that island would be complete without tasting the delicious **coconut curried crab** and **dumpling**. Indian influences have given the country **roti** – a stretchy flat bread (called a skin) containing curried meat, vegetables or fish – the unofficial national dish.

For snacking, the best option is **street food**; doubles (a gloopy chickpea curry sandwiched between *bara*, a soft, fried bread), oysters, corn soup and a variety of pies – fish, potato (aloo) and beef. The St James district of Port of Spain offers particularly rich pickings. The ubiquitous **shark and bake** is best consumed on Maracas beach where vendors compete to produce the tastiest version of fried bread filled with seasoned shark and topped with salad and sauces made from tamarind, Chandon beni (similar to cilantro) or garlic.

Carib and Stag are light, locally produced **lagers** and Mackeson **stout** is an excellent local alternative to Guinness. The best **rum** is produced by the Trinidadian Angostura/Fernandes manufacturers, makers of the world-famous Angostura Bitters – their 1919 dark rum is delicious.

A recommended nonalcoholic thirst quencher is the vitamin- and mineral-packed **coconut water**, fresh from street vendors. Bitter **Mauby**, made from tree bark, cloves and aniseed, is a delicious but acquired taste, while **sorrel**, made from a flower of the hibiscus family, is a sweet drink enjoyed at Christmas.

Mail and communication

Public telephones take 25¢ coins but they're increasingly rare since the domination of the cellphone. Local SIM cards from Digicel or bMobile are available everywhere for around TT$100, and you can use one in your handset from home if it's tri-band. A good option for international calls from a private, hotel or public phone is a Companion **phonecard** (TT$10, $30, $60 and $100 + VAT), available in newsagents, pharmacies and supermarkets.

The **country code** is ⓣ868.

You'll find **Internet cafés** throughout Port of Spain and other larger towns in Trinidad, and in all of Tobago's resorts; access averages at TT$10 per hour. Many hotels, bars and restaurants have free Wi-Fi, too.

Festivals and public holidays

Trinbagonians have a well-deserved reputation for partying, and T&T's cultural and ethnic diversity provides plenty of occasions to celebrate.

Of T&T's thirteen **public holidays**, **Carnival** is the most famous. Held on the Monday and Tuesday before Ash Wednesday, it is a hedonistic two days of drinking and dancing in ornate and revealing costumes, preceded by at least a month of huge outdoor parties and competitions amongst pan bands, soca singers and calypsonians. In Trinidad, especially in Port of Spain, everything shuts down for two days, and increasingly three, as people use Ash Wednesday to recover. Other significant Trinidadian festivals are the altogether more serious Islamic **Hosay** (see p.761) during May and June, and the Hindu **Phagwa** festival (see p.774). The festival of **Diwali**, celebrated nationwide in late October, honours the Hindu goddess of light with *deyas* lit in every house.

In Tobago, the **Tobago Heritage Festival** occurs in the last two weeks of July and features traditional customs, storytelling and festivities. The annual **Fisherman's Fetes**, held in Castara and Charlotteville in the middle of July, are wild beach parties. On the Tuesday after Easter in Buccoo, crab and goat races are held – serious and bizarre spectacles well worth seeing. For the latest information on events and a festival calendar, visit the TDA website (see p.749).

Public holidays

January 1 New Year's Day
March/April Good Friday, Easter Monday
March 30 Spiritual Baptist (Shouter) Liberation Day
June 10 Corpus Christi
May 30 Indian Arrival Day
June 19 Labour Day
August 1 Emancipation Day
August 31 Independence Day
October Diwali
November/December Eid-ul-Fitr (celebration at the end of Ramadan)
December 25 Christmas Day
December 26 Boxing Day

Sports and outdoor activities

Unique in the Caribbean for its **environmental diversity**, T&T ranks among the world's top ten **birding** sites, with more than 430 recorded bird species per square kilometre. The most accessible birdwatching spots in Trinidad are the Asa Wright Nature Centre and the Caroni Bird Sanctuary – nesting place of the scarlet ibis. In Tobago, head for Little Tobago, also known as Bird of Paradise Island, and the protected Tobago Forest Reserve.

There is excellent **hiking** in the Trinidad forests of the Northern Range and the Chaguaramas hills – though make sure you go with a guide as it's easy to get lost in the jungle. **Snorkelling** and **scuba diving** are extremely popular in Tobago, where the water is clear and the reefs spectacular. The best dive spots are Speyside, Charlotteville and around the Sister's Rocks. Lush **waterfalls** such as Argyll in Tobago and Paria, Avocat or Salybia in Trinidad offer great freshwater swimming, while big breakers around Mount Irvine in Tobago and Toco in Trinidad make ideal conditions for **surfing**.

There are hundreds of **tour companies** in T&T offering everything from hiking, birdwatching and kayaking to more conventional driving tours. The average cost is US$50–100 per day, though the Chaguaramas Development Authority (ⓣ868/634-4364 or 4349, ⓦwww.chagdev.com) provides excellent hiking from

US$25. Two of the best outfits for hikes, birdwatching and everything eco-oriented are Caribbean Discovery Tours (Ⓣ868/624-7281, Ⓦwww.caribbeandiscoverytours.com) and Paria Springs Tours, 44 La Seiva Rd, Maraval (Ⓣ622 8826, Ⓦwww.pariasprings.com). Island Experiences (Ⓣ868/625-2410, Ⓔgunda @wow.net) provides tailor-made cultural tours including *mas* camps and panyards, as well as great night tours of Port of Spain.

Music

Trinbagonian **music** is some of the most exciting and thought-provoking in the Caribbean. The heart of T&T's music scene is **calypso**, which comments on shifting attitudes towards love, gender, race and religion. Its most eloquent proponent is **David Rudder** (Ⓦwww.davidrudder.com), Trinidad's answer to Bob Marley. The best place to hear calypso is in the "tents" at Carnival, such as Calypso Revue and Kaiso House.

Equally popular nowadays is the more souped-up, danceable **soca**, which dominates during Carnival. The Road March title – given to the song played most often during the party season – is usually captured by big names such as Machel Montano or Shurwayne Winchester. East Indians have given soca their own slant through **chutney**, mixing soca beats with sitars, dholak drums and Hindi and English lyrics. Vocalists to look out for include Rikki Jai, Rooplal Girdharrie and Heeralal Rampartap.

Invented in the impoverished Port of Spain suburb of Laventille, when oil drums brought by US troops in World War II were hammered into concave sections that produced rough notes, the **steel pan** is the national instrument. The panyard calendar revolves around **Panorama**, a nationwide competition held during Carnival, but there are smaller competitions throughout the year, and you can visit the panyards to listen to practices.

T&T's musical spectrum is wider than just these styles: at Christmas, you'll hear the Spanish-sounding **parang**, while East Indian festivals such as Hosay (see box on p.761) and Phagwa (see box on p.774) feature **tassa drumming**, and Jamaican **dancehall reggae** is ubiquitous all year round.

History of Trinidad

For a history of **Tobago**, see p.780. **Trinidad** was the first inhabited island of the Caribbean, settled by **Amerindians** from South America as early as 5000 BC. They called it "Ieri", land of the hummingbird. When **Christopher Columbus** "discovered" the island in 1498 – naming it **Trinidad** after the three peaks of the Trinity Hills – there was a population of 35,000 who had trade links to South America. Within three hundred years, the indigenous people were all but wiped out through exposure to European diseases and Spanish massacres. **Spanish settlers** arrived in 1592 but the Spanish empire had neither the desire nor the resources to develop the island. Governors of Trinidad did as they pleased and **pirate** attacks were commonplace. In 1783 Spain issued the **Cedula of Population** to encourage fellow Catholics to settle on the island. Most who did so were **French planters** and the amount of land allocated to them depended on the number of **slaves** they brought. Unusually for the region, immigrants of mixed European/African race could also receive land, opening the way for a property-owning coloured middle class.

Though Spanish-run, the island's culture became increasingly **French**, and it was during this period that **Carnival** was introduced. Things heated up politically when the British, led by **Sir Ralph Abercromby**, invaded in 1797. The

Spanish surrendered with hardly a shot fired and **Thomas Picton** became governor, beginning a reign of terror. By 1802, Picton's activities had become an embarrassment even to the British government and he was demoted.

The island became a British experiment: a **Crown colony** ruled from London but governed by French and Spanish law. Planters, forced to look for alternative sources of labour after the Act of Emancipation, introduced indentured **Indian labourers** to the island in 1845. By 1917, when the system finally ended, some 145,000 Indians, mainly from Calcutta, had arrived. Though better regulated than slavery, the working and living conditions of the labourers were indistinguishable from those of slaves. Many never returned to India, accepting land in lieu of their passage home. Known still as "East Indians", they have contributed greatly to the island's culture, especially with their food. Further adding to the ethnic mix in T&T were **immigrants** from other parts of the world, among them Africans, Portuguese labourers, Chinese, a handful of Jews and Syrians.

Several components – including the **oil industry**, an **anti-indentureship movement**, and the establishment of the *Beacon* (1931–34), a stridently anti-colonial, anti-government magazine – meant Britain faced an increasingly unruly population. **World War II** brought economic improvements as large areas, such as the Chaguaramas peninsula, were leased to the US military to establish a Caribbean base. In return the Americans improved Trinidad's infrastructure and brought oil drums to the island, which led to the invention of the **steel drum music**.

Though universal **suffrage** was granted in 1945, Britain did not hand over control until 1956 when the **People's National Movement** (PNM), under the leadership of the Oxford-educated historian Dr Eric Williams, took power. **Independence** was granted in 1962 but the colonial structure of society remained. Disillusionment led to the **Black Power** movement in the late Sixties, resulting in jobs being given to locals rather than expatriates. By 1970, Trinidad was **bankrupt** but when vast **oil reserves** were discovered just as the world was sliding into the 1974 oil crisis, the country found itself swimming in money overnight. When oil prices fell in the 1980s, the economy went into recession. As the population became increasingly dissatisfied, the political opposition unified, and in 1986 PNM was ousted for the first time in favour of the **National Alliance for Reconstruction** (NAR), led by the Tobagonian A.N.R. Robinson. Within a year the government was breaking up under the pressure of harsh economic measures imposed by the IMF. In 1990, the **Jamaat-al-Muslimeen** – a revolutionary Muslim organization – attempted to overthrow the government (see p.759). Though the coup was crushed, the government's authority was undermined, and the following year the PNM returned to power.

Over the next five years, the PNM stabilized the economy and paid off the IMF. The 1995 election split the country down the middle, with the PNM and the **Indo-Trinidadian United National Congress** (UNC) both winning exactly seventeen seats. The first Indo-Trinidadian prime minister, **Basdeo Panday**, took power in 1995. A 2000 election seemed to guarantee the UNC control but three parliamentarians switched parties, giving the PNM party an edge; **Patrick Manning**, of the PNM party, has been Prime Minister since 2000.

Trinidad and Tobago can boast the most **stable economy** in the Caribbean, thanks mainly to the continuing revenue from the oil and natural gas industries. However, rising crime rates, drug trafficking, high rates of domestic violence and HIV infection, not to mention political **corruption**, have ensured that locals have more to worry about than what to wear to next year's Carnival.

21.1

Port of Spain and the Western Tip

The hub of Trinidad's booming economy, **PORT OF SPAIN** is also the centre of Trinidad's rich **cultural life**, with countless *mas* camps (see p.760), art galleries, panyards and theatres – not to mention the endless clubs and bars that place the capital at the forefront of T&T's nightlife scene. The city is bordered by the Gulf of Paria on one side and the Northern Range on the other, providing its 51,000 inhabitants with both mountain and sea views. The mish mash of architectural styles, with tower blocks and concrete behemoths, seems rather ugly at first sight – especially **downtown** – but look closely and you'll spot many fine nineteenth-century buildings along with quaint "gingerbread" houses, so named because of their intricate fretted woodwork.

Thanks in large part to its fine natural harbour, Port of Spain was made Trinidad's capital in 1757. The downtown area is the oldest section of the city, and serves as the **shopping** and **financial centre**. Within the compact grid of streets surrounding broad Brian Lara Promenade/Independence Square and bustling Frederick Street, internationally known shops jostle for space with old Spanish warehouses, offices, shops and the paraphernalia of the docks, while the thoroughfares are jammed with

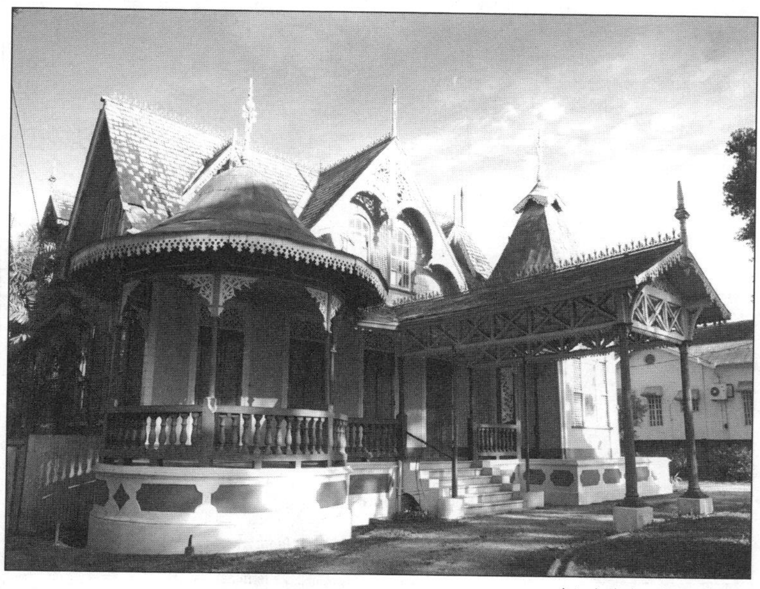

▲ A typical gingerbread house

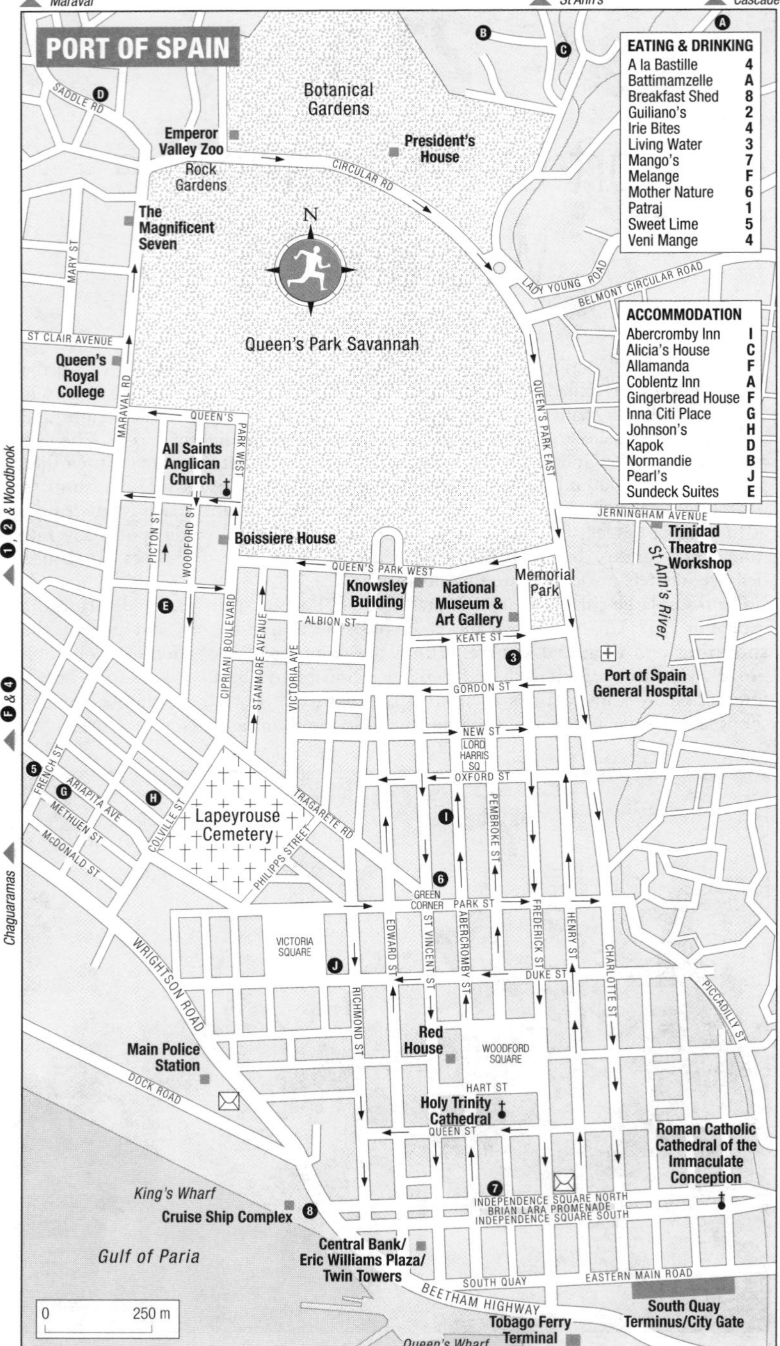

PORT OF SPAIN
Maraval
St Ann's
Cascade
EATING & DRINKING
A la Bastille 4
Battimamzelle A
Breakfast Shed 8
Guiliano's 2
Irie Bites 4
Living Water 3
Mango's 7
Melange F
Mother Nature 6
Patraj 1
Sweet Lime 5
Veni Mange 4
ACCOMMODATION
Abercromby Inn I
Alicia's House C
Allamanda F
Coblentz Inn A
Gingerbread House F
Inna Citi Place G
Johnson's H
Kapok D
Normandie B
Pearl's J
Sundeck Suites E
Botanical Gardens
Emperor Valley Zoo
President's House
Rock Gardens
Saddle Rd
Circular Rd
The Magnificent Seven
Queen's Park Savannah
Lady Young Road
Belmont Circular Road
Mary St
St Clair Avenue
Queen's Royal College
Maraval Rd
Queen's Park West
Queen's Park East
All Saints Anglican Church
Jerningham Avenue
Trinidad Theatre Workshop
St Ann's River
Boissiere House
Picton St
Woodford St
Memorial Park
Knowsley Building
National Museum & Art Gallery
Albion St
Keate St
Cipriani Boulevard
Stanmore Avenue
Victoria Ave
Gordon St
Port of Spain General Hospital
New St
Lord Harris Sq
Oxford St
French St
Ariapita Ave
Methuen St
McDonald St
Colville St
Lapeyrouse Cemetery
Tragarete Rd
Philipps Street
Pembroke St
Green Corner
Park St
Victoria Square
Edward St
St Vincent St
Abercromby St
Frederick St
Henry St
Charlotte St
Duke St
Piccadilly St
Wrightson Road
Richmond St
Main Police Station
Red House
Woodford Square
Dock Road
Hart St
Holy Trinity Cathedral
Queen St
Roman Catholic Cathedral of the Immaculate Conception
King's Wharf
Cruise Ship Complex
Independence Square North
Brian Lara Promenade
Independence Square South
Gulf of Paria
Central Bank/ Eric Williams Plaza/ Twin Towers
South Quay
Eastern Main Road
Beetham Highway
South Quay Terminus/City Gate
Tobago Ferry Terminal
Queen's Wharf
0 250 m
Churchill Roosevelt Highway & Piarco Airport
1, 2 & Woodbrook
F & 4
Chaguaramas

traffic, pedestrians and pavement vendors – all overshadowed by the sleek bulk of new government tower blocks, the oldest which are the imposing, 1970s-eque twin towers of the Central Bank. Just over the road on the bay are the modernistic blocks of the waterfront complex where pedestrian walkways (under construction at the time of writing) open up the Gulf to pedestrians.

West of the city centre lies **Woodbrook**, an elegant middle-class suburb settled in the early twentieth century. Established by Indian immigrants in the nineteenth century, the **St James** district further west still has streets named after the settlers' home towns. North of the city at the base of the Northern Range are the districts of St Ann's and Maraval, which have fast become the centre of the city's expanding hotel trade.

Arrival and getting around

Port of Spain is about 20km northwest of **Piarco International Airport**. Official **airport taxis** wait outside the main entrance and will take you to the capital for around US$30 (30min, 1–2hr during rush hour, 6–8am and 4–6pm). Alternatively, take a shared **route taxi** (they pass in front of the main entrance at regular intervals during the day; less frequently during the night) to Arouca Junction on the Eastern Main Road (TT$4). From there, catch an eastbound **red-band maxi taxi** to **City Gate**, the main transport terminus downtown (TT$5).

If **arriving by ship**, you'll pull into Port of Spain's docks. Private taxis tout for passengers coming off the boat but unless you arrive late at night, it's much cheaper to use the route and maxi taxis that run along the Wrightson Road. Note that maxis are not allowed within the city centre, and run along Wrightson Road only.

Port of Spain has a compact, grid-based city centre. **City Gate**, located east of the docks, is the main transport terminal, and many route taxi ranks are located in the city centre. Most of the sights are within walking distance of each other, but bear in mind that under the hot sun energy fades fast.

Maxi taxis operating in Port of Spain and the west – recognizable by their yellow stripes – can be caught in three locations. For **Diego Martin/Petit Valley**, the maxi rank is at the junction of South Quay and Abercromby Street. Maxis bound for **Maraval** (and sometimes **Diego Martin**) go via **St James** and start at the corner of Charlotte and Park streets. Maxis for **Carenage** and **Chaguaramas** go via **Ariapita Avenue** in **Woodbrook** and start at Green Corner (corner of St Vincent and Park streets).

Route taxis are distinguishable by the "H" numberplate. Starting points are dotted around Port of Spain, so it is best to ask a local to find the appropriate stand. From 7pm until 5am, many taxi stands relocate to Brian Lara Promenade/ Independence Square. Private taxis can be hired by phone (try Independence Square Taxi Service, ⓣ868/625-3032, or Ice House Taxi Service, ⓣ868/627-6984) or by going to their ranks at Brian Lara Promenade/Independence Square. If you prefer a female driver, call the reliable, friendly Camille (ⓣ790 4147); her prices are reasonable. There are a variety of **car rental firms** in Port of Spain if you want your own transport. Econo Cars, 191–193 Western Main Rd, Cocorite (ⓣ868/622-8072), and Convenient, Tropical Marine, Western Main Rd, Chaguaramas (ⓣ634 4017) are reputable.

Accommodation

The main areas for **accommodation** in Port of Spain are the city centre, **Woodbrook** and **St Ann's-Cascade**. The **city centre** is obviously convenient, though Woodbrook has the most inexpensive accommodation and the lion's share of the **guesthouses**; it's also excellent for Carnival activities. St Ann's-Cascade is greener and less urbanized but slightly less accessible. Another alternative is the suburb of **Maraval** outside of the city limits to the north. If you're planning to come for the festival, make sure you book well in advance; the higher price codes given below correspond to prices during Carnival season.

Hotels

Coblentz Inn 44 Coblentz Ave, Cascade ⓣ621 0541, ⓦwww.coblentzinn.com. Trinidad's only real boutique hotel, full of quirky, stylish furnishings and thoughtful touches that convey a sense of understated, chic luxury. The rooms come with all mod cons, there's wireless Internet throughout, and a shady rooftop terrace with a Jacuzzi. The hotel restaurant is also good (see p.763). Continental breakfast included, and no minimum stay for Carnival. 5–7

Kapok 16–18 Cotton Hill, St Clair ⓣ868/622-5765, ⓦwww.kapokhotel.com. Stylish, spacious rooms decorated with rattan furniture and batik, and wireless Internet throughout. There's a good restaurant and bar, a swimming pool, gym and sundeck; breakfast is included in the Carnival rate. Great location for Carnival. 6–7

Normandie 10 Nook Ave, St Ann's ⓣ868/624-1181, ⓦwww.normandiett.com. One of the city's more atmospheric hotels, with an onsite theatre, art gallery and boutiques as well as a popular restaurant and café. All rooms have a/c, cable TV, phone with voicemail and en-suite bathroom, and there's a lovely pool. Breakfast included in the room rate. 5–6

Guesthouses

Abercromby Inn 101 Abercromby St ⓣ623 5259 or 627 6658, ⓦwww.abercrombyinn.com. Right in the heart of downtown, and with a range of fairly decent rooms, from basic (fan-only, wash basin and shared bathroom) to deluxe (cable TV, telephone, microwave and fridge). Friendly atmosphere and communal sundeck; breakfast included. Five-night Carnival package. 2–3

Alicia's House 7 Coblentz Gardens, St Ann's ⓣ623 2802, ⓦwww.aliciashouse.com. Located on a quiet road close to the Savannah, all the rooms at this busy little hotel have wicker furniture, a/c, fridge, phone and cable TV; most are en suite, but a few share bathrooms, and there's a swimming pool, sundeck and Jacuzzi. Meals are available, and breakfast is included. Five-night minimum stay at Carnival. 3–6

Allamanda 61 Carlos St, Woodbrook ⓣ622 1480 or 7719, ⓔtheallamanda@yahoo.com. Airy, professionally run place with a calm and collected feel and spotlessly clean en-suite rooms; all have a/c, cable TV, ceiling fan, tea- and coffee-making equipment and fridge, and there are also a couple of studios with the same facilities plus kitchenette. All guests are lent a mobile phone, and breakfast is included. Seven-night minimum at Carnival. 2–5

Gingerbread House 8 Carlos St, Woodbrook ⓣ627 8170, mobile 792 4334, ⓦwww.trinidadgingerbreadhouse.com. Beautifully maintained gingerbread house with a wraparound veranda and a small selection of gorgeous rooms, elegantly decorated and with quirky, chic modern touches courtesy of the architect owner. All are en suite with a/c, fridge and cable TV, and there's a rather unique plunge pool out back. Full breakfast included; seven-night minimum for Carnival. 3–5

Inna Citi Place 37 Ariapita Ave, Woodbrook ⓣ625 5911, mobile 683 6132, ⓦwww.innacitiplace.com. Inexpensive, well-run and centrally located, with a balcony overlooking Ariapita Ave – perfect for watching Carnival pass by or just taking in the city scene. The appealing rooms vary; some share very clean bathrooms, en-suite ones have cable TV and a/c. Rates include breakfast. Seven-night Carnival minimum. 1–5

Johnson's 16 Buller St, Woodbrook ⓣ628 7553, ⓔjohnsonsbandb@hotmail.com. Friendly, helpful hosts and spotless, well-maintained rooms with fans and cable TV; a/c rooms with fridge cost a bit more, and the cheaper ones share bathrooms. Guests have use of a kitchen and lounge. Good value, and just 10min from the town centre; breakfast is included in all rates. Seven-night minimum for Carnival. 2–4

Pearl's 3–4 Victoria Square East ⓣ868/625-2158ⓔpeterhenry@yahoo.com. This old colonial mansion, with a veranda overlooking picturesque Victoria Square, is the best bargain in Port of Spain. The basic rooms have fans, sinks and 1960s furniture. Perfectly situated for Carnival and downtown sightseeing. 1–2

Sundeck Suites 42–44 Picton St, Newtown ⓣ868/622-9560, ⓦsundeck.co.tt. Bright, modern self-catering apartments with kitchenette, ceiling fans, a/c, en-suite bathroom and TV; some have a small balcony. There's a sundeck on the roof, and facilities for the disabled. Ten-night minimum stay for Carnival. 3–5

The Red House and the 1990 coup

The imposing neo-Renaissance **Red House**, at the edge of Woodford Square, derives its name from an earlier building on the site which was painted bright red to celebrate Queen Victoria's diamond jubilee in 1897. The present terracotta-coloured structure, completed four years after its predecessor was destroyed in the 1903 water riots, was itself attacked in a **coup** in 1990, and bullet holes still scar the stonework.

The coup, led by **Yasin Abu Bakr**, leader of the fundamentalist revolutionary group **Jamaat-al-Muslimeen**, occurred on July 27, 1990. The group stormed the Red House and took the prime minister and other government officials hostage. A **state of emergency** was declared.

Though many Trinidadians were discontented with the harsh fiscal measures of the government of the time, few supported its violent overthrow. With little public support, after a six-day siege the rebels surrendered on condition of amnesty. Bakr and 113 other Jamaat members were jailed for two years while the courts debated the amnesty's validity, and eventually set them free after a ruling by the UK Privy Council.

Many Trinidadians found it hard to believe that such events could take place in stable, democratic, fun-loving Trinidad. With characteristic humour, though, the crisis resulted in numerous amusing stories, such as those telling of wild "**curfew parties**", riffing on the common conception of Trinidadians always being up for a good time.

Downtown Port of Spain

Dating back to the 1780s, Port of Spain's **downtown** area is the oldest part of the city. For anyone arriving by boat, the first sight is the city's most unattractive area, **King's Wharf** – the hub of Trinidad's booming import–export trade – with its busy docks and jagged, industrialized skyline of cranes, gantries and containers. Nearby, adjacent to the spanking new Tobago ferry terminal, the **Cruise Ship Complex** caters to passengers during their few hours on land with an overpriced craft market. Just east of the docks, the grand Victorian stone building on South Quay – originally Port of Spain's **train station** – is **City Gate**, the hub of Trinidad's transport system. This is the terminus for all buses and maxi taxis running to all parts of the island.

The heart of downtown, just north of the docks, is **Brian Lara Promenade/Independence Square**. Consisting of two parallel streets divided by a paved area furnished with benches and chess tables, this promenade runs the width of the city centre. It's a popular after-work hangout when stalls are set up against closed offices and street food vendors do a brisk trade. During the Carnival season, the promenade hosts **free concerts** and performances, advertised in the local press and radio. The western end is dominated by the shiny **Nicholas Tower**, a 21-storey blue-and-silver office block, and the twin towers of the **Central Bank of Trinidad and Tobago** – the first and second tallest buildings on the island respectively – while the eastern end is marked by the dusty **Roman Catholic Cathedral**, completed in 1836 after sixteen years of construction. Near the cathedral on the southern side of the square, the **UCW Drag Brothers Mall** (Mon–Sat 9am–6pm) is a great place to buy handmade leather sandals and local crafts.

Bisecting the promenade, **Frederick Street** is Port of Spain's main shopping drag, crammed with clothes and souvenir shops as well as street vendors selling home-made jewellery, belts and craft items. Halfway up, the pretty, tree-shaded **Woodford Square** provides a pleasant space to escape the crowds and listen to local orators at the "University of Woodford Square" – the T&T equivalent of London's Speakers' Corner in Hyde Park. Anyone can join in – if they can get a word in edgeways. On the western side of the square is the grand **Red House**, seat of Trinidad and Tobago's parliament and site of the 1990 coup (see box above); on the square's southern side stands the city's **Anglican Cathedral**.

Uptown Port of Spain

Ranged around the broad, grassy expanse of the Queen's Park Savannah and framed by the foothills of the Northern Range, Port of Spain's **uptown** district oozes prosperity. Along the wide boulevards that ring the Savannah, the palatial mansions of the colonial plantocracy compete with the residences of the republic's president and prime minister and sundry glitzy corporate headquarters. This part of town also boasts Port of Spain's main tourist attractions: a comprehensive **museum**, an above-average **zoo** and beautiful **botanical gardens**.

The **Queen's Park Savannah** is Port of Spain's largest open space. Its grassy expanse is crisscrossed by paths and its 3.7km perimeter is shaded by the spreading branches of old samaan trees. Often deserted during the hot daylight hours, the Savannah comes to life after 4pm, with footballers, joggers and couples and families taking an early evening stroll. This is when you'll find food stalls serving tasty snacks such as roasted corn, *pholouri* and oysters.

In recent years, the Savannah has served as the centrepiece of the Carnival celebrations, with the **Panorama** competition, **Dimanche Gras**, **Parade of the Bands** and **Champs in Concert** all taking place on the stage set up between the now-departed **Grandstand** and **North Stand**, just back from the road off Queen's Park West. The ailing structures were demolished in 2007, and the plan is to replace them with a spanking new **National Carnival and Arts Centre** on the same spot – through when this will be completed is anyone's guess. Carnival events still take place on the Savannah with a series of temporary structures serving in the interim. At the top end of Frederick Street, the imposing, gabled **National Museum and Art Gallery** (Tues–Sat 10am–6pm, Sun 2–6pm; free) stands at the corner of Keate

Mas camps and playing mas

Mas camps are the headquarters of the Carnival bands, traditionally the place where the costumes are produced, and where prototypes of the designs are put on show for potential revellers to peruse. Each band will choose a **theme to portray** during Carnival. The band is then divided into different **sections**, each with its own costume (linked to the general theme) and marching position when the band assembles for the Parade of the Bands on Carnival Monday and Tuesday. If you want to participate in the Parade of the Bands or **"play mas"**, you must first register to join a band; you can do this online at the websites listed below or go directly to the *mas* camp and try your luck. All-inclusive registration packages, including costume, a place in a particular section of the band, security, and food and drink during the Monday and Tuesday parades cost anything from TT$2000 to TT$4000.

The list below represents a selection of the best-known bands with *mas* camps in Port of Spain; for a full list of bands, contact the National Carnival Bands Association, Queen's Park West (ⓣ627 1422, ⓦwww.ncbatt.com).

Brian McFarlane 49 Rosalino St, Woodbrook ⓣ625 8931, ⓦwww.macfarlanecarnival.net

Callaloo Company/Peter Minshall Building C, Western Main Rd, Chaguaramas ⓣ634 4491, ⓦwww.callaloo.co.tt

Harts 5 Alcazar St, St Clair ⓣ622 8038, ⓦwww.hartscarnival.com

Island People 11 Stone St, Woodbrook ⓣ622 5581, ⓦwww.islandpeoplemas.com

Legacy 88 Roberts St, Woodbrook ⓣ622 7466, ⓦwww.legacycarnival.com

Masquerade 19 De Verteuil St, Woodbrook ⓣ623 2161, ⓦwww.masquerade.co.tt

Pulse 8 6 Gallus St, Woodbrook ⓣ627 8330, ⓦwww.pulse8carnival.com

Tribe 20 Rosalino St, Woodbrook ⓣ625 6800, ⓦwww.carnivaltribe.com

Trini Revellers 35 Gallus St, Woodbrook ⓣ625 1881, ⓦwww.trinirevellersmas.com

Hosay

The Islamic festival of **Hosay**, commemorating the martyrdom of Mohammed's grandsons Hussein and Hassan during a *jihad* (holy war) in Persia, has been marked in Trinidad ever since the first Indian Muslims arrived in 1845. Its exposure to the island's other cultures had turned it into something carnivalesque, with lewd dancing and loud music, but local Shi'a Muslims have recently taken great pains to restore the occasion's solemnity. It's fascinating to watch but not a festival for raucous revelry.

Hosay is celebrated in Curepe, Tunapuna, Couva and Cedros, but the best place to see it is in St James. The celebrations take place over four days (ranging from Jan to Nov as dictated by the Islamic calendar). All the weekday parades start at 11pm and continue into the early hours of the morning; the parade on the Saturday takes place in daylight, from 3pm. The third night is the most spectacular. Large *tadjahs* more than two metres high are paraded through the streets accompanied by loud *tassa* drumming, while dancers carry two large sickle moons representing the two brothers. At midnight there is the ritual "kissing of the moons", as the dancers symbolically enact a brotherly embrace. The following night the exquisite *tadjahs* are thrown into the sea, a sacrifice to ensure that prayers for recovery from sickness and adversity will be answered.

Street. Albeit a bit dated in its presentation, the museum's collection is extensive and wide-ranging, covering everything from early **Amerindian history** and the technology of the **oil industry** to an excellent collection of works by **local artists** – definitely worth a couple hours of browsing.

One of the finest of the many mansions surrounding the Queen's Park Savannah is the ornately decorated **Knowsley Building**, home to the Ministry of Foreign Affairs, on the corner of Queen's Park West and Chancery Lane. Resembling a fantastical doll's house, it's one of numerous examples of the work of Glaswegian architect George Brown who introduced the mass production of fretted woodwork to the islands. **Boissiere House**, on the corner of Cipriani Boulevard and Queen's Park West, is perhaps the best example of the style, with a whimsical concoction of fretted wooden finials and bargeboards, stained glass depicting meandering strawberry vines and a small pagoda-like roof over one room.

North of Queen's Park West on Maraval Road stands a bizarre group of crumbling mansions affectionately known as the **Magnificent Seven**, a magical-realist parade of European architectural styles with a tropical slant. Constructed between 1904 and 1910, the remarkable buildings are the result of the competing egos of rival plantation owners, each of whom tried to outdo their neighbours in grandeur. Standouts among them are **Queen's Royal College**, first of the seven, built in Germanic Renaissance style and now Trinidad's most prestigious school (former pupils include authors V.S. and Shiva Naipaul); it's currently under restoration, however. At the other end of the row, the gleaming white paint of the Venetian-style palazzo of **Whitehall** gives it the air of a freshly iced birthday cake. Right at the northern end, it's worth taking a look at **Killarney**, also known as Stollmeyer's Castle, which was modelled on Queen Victoria's residence at Balmoral. Unfortunately none of these buildings is open to the public.

On the northern side of the Savannah is the **Emperor Valley Zoo** (daily 9.30am–6pm, last tickets sold at 5.30pm; TT$10, children 3–12 years TT$5; Ⓦwww.trinizoo.com). A magnet for local kids, it's worth a wander to get a close-up look at Trinidadian species that you're unlikely to see in the wild. Its collection of relatively well-kept animals includes a large selection of **monkeys** including local red howlers, aquarium fish and snakes, as well as **ocelots**, **spectacled caiman** and numerous **birds**, from parrots and toucans to scarlet ibis, the national bird.

Next door to the zoo, and spreading back from the Savannah towards the President's House, are the exquisite **Botanical Gardens** (daily 6am–6pm; free), home to one of the oldest collections of exotic plants and trees in the western hemisphere. There are no official guides, though for a small fee unofficial guides will take you round – a good idea as most of the labels have disappeared. A small **cemetery** within the gardens contains the crumbling gravestones of many of the island's governors. Behind the Botanical Gardens stands the **President's House**, a stately villa built in 1876, while behind it, hidden from view, is the **Prime Minister's Residence**, newly – and controversially expanded by current incumbent Patrick Manning at a cost of TT$148 million. Both buildings are closed to the public.

The suburbs of Port of Spain

Behind the fretwork facades of the suburbs lies the engine room of T&T's cultural life. The creative energy of **Carnival production** is concentrated in the western suburb of **Woodbrook**, while further west still, the streets of **St James** come alive with night-time revellers throughout the year. In the east, **Laventille** is the home of the Caribbean's favourite instrument, the **steel drum**. All the suburbs are a ten- to twenty-minute walk from the city centre but as the heat can quickly sap your energy, you might like to take a taxi to your destination.

The elegant old district of **Woodbrook** – between Philipps Street to the east and the Maraval River to the west – was originally a sugar estate owned by the Siegert family, creators of Trinidad's famous **Angostura Bitters**, and many of the streets still bear their names. The suburb has traditionally been a middle-class residential area, and its streets are still graced by old houses with wonderful fretwork bargeboards, delicate balustrades and finials. Though it has become increasingly commercialized in recent decades, it is a safe and pleasant area to stay, with many good restaurants and lively bars along the length of the well-lit central street, Ariapita Avenue. Woodbrook is also home to numerous **mas camps**, which burst into life during Carnival season, from November to February (see box).

At the edge of Woodbrook, on Philipps Street, is the entrance to the **Lapeyrouse Cemetery** (daily 6am–6pm), a walled burial ground dating back to 1813 and filled with Victorian and modern tombs. At the western end of Tragarete Road is the **Queen's Park Oval** (daily 8am–4pm; Ⓣ868/628 9787, Ⓦwww.qpcc.com), Trinidad's premier **cricket ground**. Hosting national and international matches between February and April, you'll pay TT$40–200 for a seat in the stands, or TT$250–300 for an all-inclusive ticket to the Trini Posse stand (food and drink included).

St James

It was in the western suburb of **St James** that the British landed in 1797. Legend has it that they fortified themselves with rum punch they found here, giving themselves the courage to capture Port of Spain. The area was settled by **Indian** indentured labourers after emancipation, and local street names – Calcutta, Delhi and Madras – bear witness to their homesickness.

Panyards

The best way to hear **pan** is live, in the open air on a warm starry night. Though there are many official events, an often more enjoyable time can be had by going to a local **panyard** when the bands are practising. Sessions are held throughout the year but are particularly good in the run-up to Carnival. The most accessible panyards to visit in Port of Spain are Invaders (147 Tragarete Rd, opposite the Queen's Park Oval, Woodbrook), Phase II Pan Groove (13 Hamilton St, off Damian St, Woodbrook) and BPTT Renegades (138 Charlotte St, Port of Spain).

Today St James is one of the capital's most cosmopolitan districts, with residents from all the country's ethnic groups. It's a bustling place, especially at night when it becomes one of the prime liming spots in Port of Spain. **Western Main Road**, which runs through the centre of St James, is a broad thoroughfare lined with shops, bars and take-aways. It's also the scene of the annual Muslim **Hosay** processions (see box on p.761).

In the weeks running up to Hosay, it's possible to watch craftsmen build the ornate minareted tombs from bamboo and coloured paper (**tadjahs**); the houses where they work have large flags planted in their yards. The task involves great financial, physical and spiritual sacrifice as the materials can cost up to TT$50,000, and the builders have to fast during daylight hours and refrain from alcohol and sexual activity for the duration. Understandably, perhaps, not many of the younger generation find the prospect appealing, and as the years pass fewer and fewer *tadjahs* are being built.

Eating

Port of Spain's **restaurant** scene has boomed in recent years. Ariapita Avenue is best for upscale establishments, and you'll most likely need to make reservations. For something more casual, there are scores of **cafés** in the downtown area, while the best **street food** is located in St James and, to a lesser extent, Independence Square.

A la Bastille Corner Ariapita Ave and DeVerteuil St ⓣ622 1789, ⓦwww.alabastille.com. Perhaps the best restaurant in Port of Spain, with a real touch of France in everything from the decor to the home-baked baguettes to the Breton cider. The cooking fuses local and imported ingredients with French culinary prowess – everything from bouillabaisse to filo pastry with crab, seaweed and avocado puree to honey-glazed leg of duck with Calvados or steak with frites. There's a three-course lunch special during the week for TT$159.

Battimamzelle *Coblentz Inn*, 44 Coblentz Ave, Cascade ⓣ868/621-0591. This Caribbean-flavoured gourmet spot is one of Trinidad's top restaurants. Dishes include barbecue kingfish, oxtail pepperpot and crab gallette, served amidst decor that's in keeping with the hotel's hip-yet-coy ambience. Closed Sun, no lunch on Sat.

Breakfast Shed Wrightson Rd, opposite Independence Square, next to the Cruise Ship Complex. Hearty, inexpensive and excellent local food served at long communal trestle tables mainly for local workers; expect to pay under TT$35. The traditional breakfast of bake and shark and cocoa for TT$25 is delicious. Breakfast and lunch only.

Guiliano's 62 Tragarete Rd ⓣ628 1236. A real gem, serving delicious Italian food at extremely reasonable prices. Proper thin-crust pizzas and calzone, as well as lovely pasta – try the penne with tomato and fish sauce – and daily fish and meat specials; kingfish in green peppercorn sauce with spinach and parmesan mashed potato is one to look out for. Well-priced wine list, and takeaway available too.

Irie Bites 68 Ariapita Ave, Woodbrook. Jamaican jerk shack painted red, gold and green that's the best of the cluster on this stretch of Ariapita Avenue. Seasoned and cooked over pimento wood, the jerk chicken, pork and fish are served with festival (a sweetish fried dumpling) for under TT$30. Lunch and dinner Mon–Sat, closed Sun.

Living Water 109 Frederick St ⓣ623 4677. The a/c canteen of this Catholic charitable organization is a popular spot for delicious, inexpensive meals (as well as offering respite from the downtown heat), and channels its profits into its good works. The menu changes daily: breakfasts range from buljol and bake to eggs, while lunches always include meat, fish and vegetarian options (including veggy gravy); Trini-style cakes and pastries are also on offer.

Mango's Corner Independence Square and Chacon St ⓣ626 2646. Right on the square, this buzzing place has seats in the indoor a/c area and the open-air balcony upstairs. Served cafeteria-style from behind a glass counter, the selection is huge, from Chinese to Creole to Indian, as well as a large range of salads and grills – all tasty and all very fresh.

Mélange 40 Ariapita Ave, Woodbrook ⓣ868/628-8687. Genteel, colonial-style decor and sophisticated international cuisine at this fine dining restaurant. Choose from seafood, steak, pork, lamb or chicken dishes or go for a mix at the lunch buffet. Lunch only Mon, lunch and dinner Tues–Sat, closed Sun.

Mother Nature Vegetarian Restaurant St Vincent St, central Port of Spain. Creative vegetarian meals and wonderfully filling fruit punches – everything from beetroot to papaya for under TT$25. Breakfast and lunch only, closed Sun.

Patraj 159 Tragarete Rd ⓣ622 6219. Hailed by many Trinis as the capital's best roti shop. Patraj consistently dishes out quality food, from the delicious morning sada roti with tomato choka to the usual array of skins and fillings for lunch and early dinner.

Sweet Lime Ariapita Ave, at French St, Woodbrook. A great spot for people-watching and moderate prices (between TT$70–150). Satay chicken, crab backs, mussels and shrimp for starters, seafood, ribs and steaks for mains. Good kids' meals available as well. Open late.

Veni Mange 67 Ariapita Ave ⓣ624 4597, ⓦwww.venimange.com. Set on the first floor of a pretty, greenery-swathed building, *Veni* is a Port of Spain institution, ably presided over by its genial owners and as good a bet for a liming spot as it is a place to eat. The mid-priced food is a happy blend of local staples with an international twist, such as steamed grouper with a shrimp stuffing and coconut tomato sauce or grilled chicken with pineapple, raisin and tamarind salsa. There's always a good veggie option, such as lentil, mushroom and cashew nut loaf, as well as hearty salads and tasty puddings.

Drinking, nightlife and entertainment

Trinidadians seem to live to party so it's no surprise that Port of Spain boasts excellent **bars and nightclubs**. Most places come alive after 10pm and are busiest from Thursday to Sunday; on Fridays, though, the after-work crowd get things going early. A stroll along Ariapita Avenue in Woodbrook will take you past most of the best places for a drink. If you're headed to a club, make sure you abide by the dress codes and wear something smart; no sneakers or shorts for men, and no flip-flops for women.

If you want an introduction to the nightlife or bar scene, Island Experiences (see p.753) offer excellent evening city tours.

51° 51 Cipriani Blvd ⓣ627 0051, ⓦwww.51degrees.biz. PoS's second most popular club, icily a/c and with DJs playing dancehall, R&B, hip-hop and dance from Thurs–Sat.

CroBar Corner Ariapita Ave and Carlos St. Reliably busy open-air drinking spot that attracts a youngish crowd. Pumping soca, dancehall, hip-hop and R&B competing with the more sedate sounds of the upmarket *Coco Lounge*, directly across the road.

Mas Camp Pub French St, at Ariapita Ave, Woodbrook ⓣ627 4042. Now renamed as the *Nu Pub*, this longstanding PoS favourite is a good bet for live calypso (Wed evening) and for a dance; weekly schedule of events is available at the door.

Shakers Ariapita Ave. Lovely location in a gingerbread former home on the Avenue, with an a/c indoor section and tables under the trees outside, and usually pretty busy. Mixed crowd and an odd 1980s playlist.

Smokey and Bunty's 97 Western Main Rd, at Dengue St, St James. This local institution draws a mixed crowd – young, old, arty, gay and straight, though the scene can feel a bit seedy at times. The bar clientele spills onto the pavement, making for some excellent people-watching. Open till 3am on weekdays, 6am at the weekends.

Zen 9–11 Keate St ⓣ625 9936, ⓦzen.tt. Set over three floors in a lavishly redecorated former cinema, *Zen* is the country's premier club, with long queues at the weekends. Best on a Wed for the all-inclusive night, and on the weekends. Look out for live shows here, too.

Listings

Embassies and high commissions British High Commission, 19 St Clair Ave, St Clair ⓣ868/622-2748, ⓦwww.britain-in-trinidad.org; US Embassy, 15 Queen's Park West ⓣ868/622-6371, ⓕ628-5462.

Hospital The Community Hospital, 767 Western Main Rd, Cocorite (ⓣ868/622-1191) and the St Clair Medical Centre, 18 Elizabeth St, St Clair (ⓣ868/628-1451).

Internet In downtown Port of Spain, Xyber Xynergy, upstairs at Town Centre Mall, Frederick St, just north of Independence Square (Mon–Fri 8am–5pm, Fri 8am–6pm, Sat 8am–3pm, TT$10 per hr); In Maraval, Rikmer Technologies, 36 Saddle Rd (Mon–Fri 10am–4pm; TT$10 per hr). In Woodbrook, there's Vega, 53 Luis St (Mon–Sat 10am–10pm; TT$6 per hour).
Laundry Ashleigh Phillip's Coin Laundry, 10 Western Main Rd, St James ⓣ628 2268; Simply Clean Laundromat, 135 Long Circular Rd, Maraval ⓣ628 1060.
Police Report crimes at the Central Police Station, St Vincent St, at Hart St (ⓣ868/625-1261); in an emergency dial ⓣ999.
Post office TT Post, 177 Tragarete Rd, next to Roxy Roundabout, Woodbrook (Mon–Fri 7am–5pm, Sat 8am–noon).

The Western Tip

The **Western Tip** encompasses satellite suburbs of Port of Spain, friendly fishing villages, the island's largest national park and local playground and an extensive marina hosting international yachters escaping the hurricane belt. Easy and accessible to explore from Port of Spain, the furthest point is thirty minutes' drive from the city centre.

Travelling west from the capital you pass the ever-expanding residential suburbs of Diego Martin, Petit Valley, West Moorings, West Mall and Glencoe. There's little of interest here for the visitor in the endless residential streets. A few kilometres beyond the Diego Martin junction and the plush entrance to the West Mall shopping emporium, you pass through the pleasantly scruffy fishing village of **Carenage**. Onwards the road sticks close to the coast offering lovely views of the offshore islands, and takes you into **Chaguaramas** (pronounced "shag-ger-*rarm*-ms"), with wide expanses of grassland and virgin forests – much of which have been set aside to form the Chaguaramas National Park. More rainforest than park, the protected area spans the low-lying mountains of the western end of the Northern Range. Tracks into the forest take you along rivers to waterfalls and spectacular mountain views. On the flatlands opposite the Chagville Beach are a series of buildings remaining from the US occupation of the area in World War II – now the location of the **Callaloo mas camp**, workshop of one of Trinidad's most famous Carnival designers, Peter Minshall – and the **Chaguaramas Military History and Aviation Museum** (daily 9am–5pm; TT$20; ⓣ868/634-4391). The museum exhibits chronicle the military history of Trinidad and Tobago from 1498 to the present and though the presentation is somewhat haphazard, it's an interesting contrast to the typical beaches-and-palms image of the Caribbean.

Leisure development in Chaguaramas has, for the most part, been sensitive and unobtrusive. The protected Chaguaramas National Park is pristine rainforest, popular with hikers and birdwatchers, whilst the strip of flatland along the south coast is the only built-up area, shelter to a scattering of restaurants and nightclubs. At weekends the area becomes busy with locals going kayaking, hiking and cycling. There is a string of **beaches** along the south coast, though the sea can be dirty and polluted here; better swimming can be had on the north coast at **Macqueripe Beach**, a delightful cove that's easily accessible by road; it's a signposted right turn from the main just past the police station. On the way you'll pass through the gorgeous Tucker Valley, with its walking trails all well signposted from the main road.

You can rent a kayak from the **Kayak Centre**, located immediately after the sign welcoming you to Chaguaramas (daily 6am–6pm; ⓣ868/633-7871), for TT$25 for a single and TT$35 for a double; both rates are per hour. Another energetic option is to rent a **mountain bike** from Bay Sports next door (Sat, Sun and public holidays 6am–6pm; ⓣ868/687-0566), costing TT$20 per hour; you can pay an extra TT$10 for a **guided ride** into the interior of the National Park. The **Chaguaramas Development Authority** (Mon–Fri 8am–4pm; ⓣ868/634-4227, ⓦwww.chagdev.com) offers well-informed tours of the local area and the Bocas (see p.766) for anywhere between TT$$30 and TT$200. The Chaguaramas **Golf** Course (daily 7am–6pm; ☎868/634-4227) is TT$60 for nine holes, TT$10–65 to use the driving range and TT$40 to rent clubs.

Back on the main road, beyond the cluster of former military buildings and newly built restaurants, a plethora of **yachting** facilities draw some three thousand vessels each month. Past the **marinas** with their extensive facilities – supermarkets, ATMs, shops, Internet cafés and banks, the road ends just past the shabby *Cove* hotel. Just before the hotel, the Island Property Owners marina is the place from which to take a boat to the **Bocas**, or "down de islands" as locals refer to them. These rocky islets are separated from the mainland by the **Bocas del Dragon** (Dragons' Mouth), a series of rocky channels connecting the Gulf of Paria with the Caribbean. The most popular destination is **Gaspar Grande** where you can find the lovely Gasparee Caves with its huge caverns filled with bats, glittering stalactites and stalagmites and a swimmable brackish pool. Otherwise there's lovely swimming at Scotland Bay (actually part of the mainland) and good snorkelling and hiking on Chacachacare. Renting a boat (with driver) from the marina will cost about TT$900 for a full day. Alternatively the CDA runs inexpensive trips to the Gasparee Caves, Chacachacare and other islands, as does In-Joy tours (☎633 4733 or 753 2775, Ⓦwww.injoytours.com), who offer excellent trips covering all the islands and taking in Scotland Bay.

21.2

The north

The north of Trinidad is an eighty-odd-kilometre stretch dominated by the **Northern Range**, a rugged spine boasting the island's highest peaks, El Cerro del Aripo and El Tucuche. Trinidad's most splendid **beaches** line the coast to the north of the range, with the enduringly popular Maracas Bay melting into the quieter, less developed beaches of Las Cuevas, Blanchisseuse and beyond. The Arima–Blanchisseuse Road – where the bird-watcher's paradise of the Asa Wright Nature Centre can be found – cuts across the mountainous spine, connecting the coast with the Eastern Main Road, offering an amazing drive through lush **rainforest**.

Away from the jungle-smothered hills, along the traffic-choked **Eastern Main Road** (EMR), known locally as the "East–West Corridor", are some of Trinidad's most densely populated areas outside of Port of Spain. Towns such as the historic **St Joseph** and **Arima** are home to the majority of the island's **African** population. Creole cooking reigns supreme and soca and Jamaican dancehall blare from from shops, bars and maxis. Inland of the EMR, river valleys cut into the Northern Range to a host of interior attractions such as the island's two most spectacular **waterfalls**, La Laja and Sombasson, and **river swimming** at Maracas Valley, Caura and Guanapo Gorge. The EMR ends abruptly just east of Arima, replaced by the winding minor roads spanning the weather-beaten northeast coast and tip. This wild and rugged peninsula, jutting some 20km into the Atlantic Ocean is Trinidad's best-kept secret. The populace is overwhelmingly friendly, and along the **Toco coast** on its northern side, **leatherback turtles** clamber up the wave-battered sandy beaches to lay their eggs.

Though parts of the north are well served by **public transport** – especially the East–West Corridor – a **car** is useful to visit the more remote north coast.

The Saddle to Maracas Bay

Saddle Road (usually called "the Saddle") makes one of the island's best scenic journeys, climbing the Northern Range and joining the **North Coast Road**. Bordered by the glittering Caribbean sea on one side and cliffs smothered with tangled jungle on the other, its first destination is Maracas; if you're going by **public transport**, route taxis make the trip along the north coast from the corner of Prince and George streets in Port of Spain's City Gate (TT$10 to Maracas, $12 to Las Cuevas, $16 to Blanchisseuse).

Gliding by St Andrew's Golf Course and the last of Maraval's grand residences, Saddle Road begins its serpentine ascent into the Northern Range. After a couple of hairpin bends, two stone pillars mark a **junction**. To the right, **Saddle Road** meanders downhill through the pastoral Santa Cruz Valley, a half-hour scenic jaunt through cattle pastures and farmland to the urban bedlam of San Juan. Cricket supremo **Brian Lara** spent his childhood in Cantaro Village, the valley's largest community. The left of the junction is the North Coast Road, one of the smoothest on the island, built by US Army engineers in 1944 as a recompense for the American occupation of the Chaguaramas peninsula (see p.754). On the way to Maracas, you can stop off at the **La Vache Scenic Area** to take in some marvellous coastal views; at weekends, vendors sell corn soup and local titbits such as mango chow and salt prunes.

Maracas Bay

A 45-minute drive from Port of Spain, **Maracas Bay**, is more than just a beach, it's an institution, and on Sundays, it is *the* place to see and be seen. On weekdays it's much quieter – the sand is almost empty and the extensive facilities look a bit out of place.

Scenically overlooked by jungle-smothered mountains, the generous 1850-metre curve of fine off-white sand is fringed with groves of palm trees and bordered to the west by the **Maracas Bay** fishing village, and to the east by *Uncle Sam's* bar – pumping out reggae and soca at weekends. Swimming out to sea, you'll get a sublime view of the beach and the cloud-tipped peaks of the Northern Range. The water is usually clear but the tides and undercurrents are often dangerously strong; stick to the areas between red and yellow flags and listen to the lifeguards (daily 10am–6pm). The extensive **facilities** include numerous tasty bake and shark vendors (*Richard's* and *Natalie's* are the best), a huge car park (TT$10; you'll get a ticket if you park anywhere else at weekends) and changing facilities (daily 10am–6pm; TT$1).

Further east of Maracas is the smaller **Tyrico Bay**, popular with the Indian community, and with slightly less wave action, it's a better choice for those travelling with children. Lifeguards are on duty daily 10am–6pm. Even quieter is the isolated beach at **Diamier Bay**, just a few minutes' drive east.

Las Cuevas Bay and around

After an inland curve that provides impressive views of the jagged double apex of Mount El Tucuche, Trinidad's second highest mountain, the North Coast Road turns back to the sea at **Las Cuevas Bay**, the north coast's second most popular strip of sand. Headlands enclose the bay in a tight horseshoe, affording protection from the wind and a relatively gentle surf – lifeguards put out yellow and red flags to mark safe bathing spots. There's a car park above the bay (free), as well as changing rooms, showers and toilets (10am–6pm; TT$1) and a bar serving inexpensive Creole food. The only drawback to the beach is the legendary **sandfly** population – take repellent and try to cover up as the day wears on.

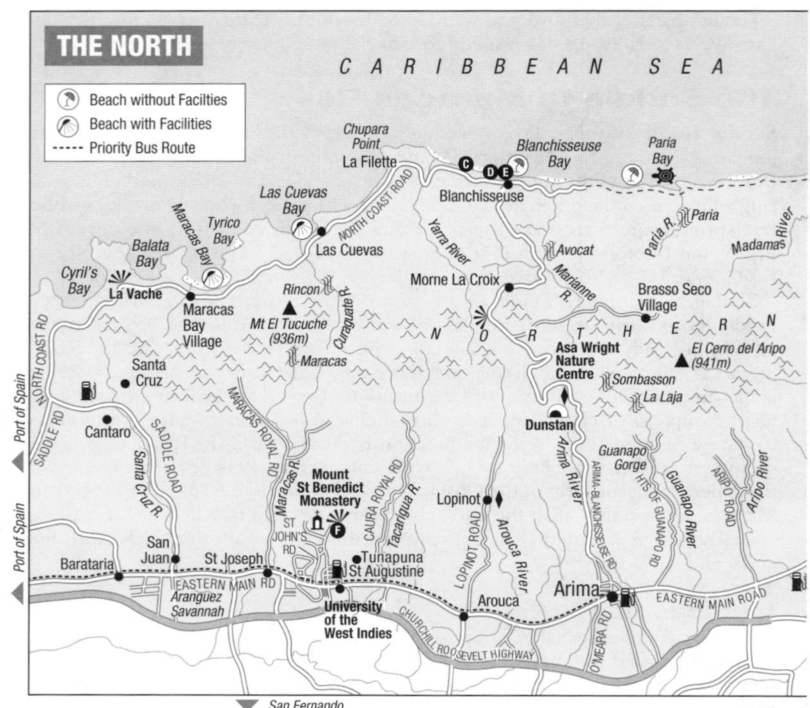

On the eastern outskirts of Las Cuevas, the secluded **One Thousand Steps Beach** is ideal for a secluded swim, but keep to a depth you can stand in – the tides can be strong even on apparently calm days. The beach is opposite Rincon Trace, which is the route to the spectacular **Rincon Waterfall**, a two-and-a-half-hour uphill walk through the bush. You'll need a guide to find this and the nearby **Angel Falls**; guides have to be arranged in advance as few tourists trek this way. Laurence Pierre (Ⓣ868/632 9746, Ⓦwww.hikeseekers.com) is recommended.

Past the tiny villages of La Filette and Yarra is **Blanchisseuse** (pronounced "blaan-she-shers"), the last village before the road tails off into the bush. With a population of around three thousand and an attractive assortment of weather-beaten board houses wreathed by rambling bougainvillea, Blanchisseuse isn't exactly a hamlet, and the clutch of ever-growing flashy holiday homes on the western outskirts are testament to its growing popularity as a retreat. The atmosphere is relaxed and supremely friendly, and there are as many local holiday-makers as there are foreign. Tourists divide their time between enjoying the succession of marvellous sandy **beaches**, hiring a local guide and hiking through the rainforest, and river-swimming in the nearby **Three Pools**, **Paria Beach** and **waterfall**, or the **Avocat Waterfall**. Local Eric Blackman, owner of *Northern Sea View Villa* (see below), is a good guide with tours including Three Pools with kayaking, hiking and swimming (TT$100 per person), Avocat Waterfall (TT$200) and a four-hour walk to Paria (TT$100). Take note that Blanchisseuse's three beaches have a reputation for rough and **treacherous waters**, particularly between November and February, so keep to a depth you can stand in (the large waves, however, are popular with local **surfers**). **Marianne** is the main beach stretching around 2km. At the eastern end the Marianne river **lagoon** is an inviting place to swim where you can also rent kayaks (TT$80 per hour) from here. It's also an excellent place for birdwatching.

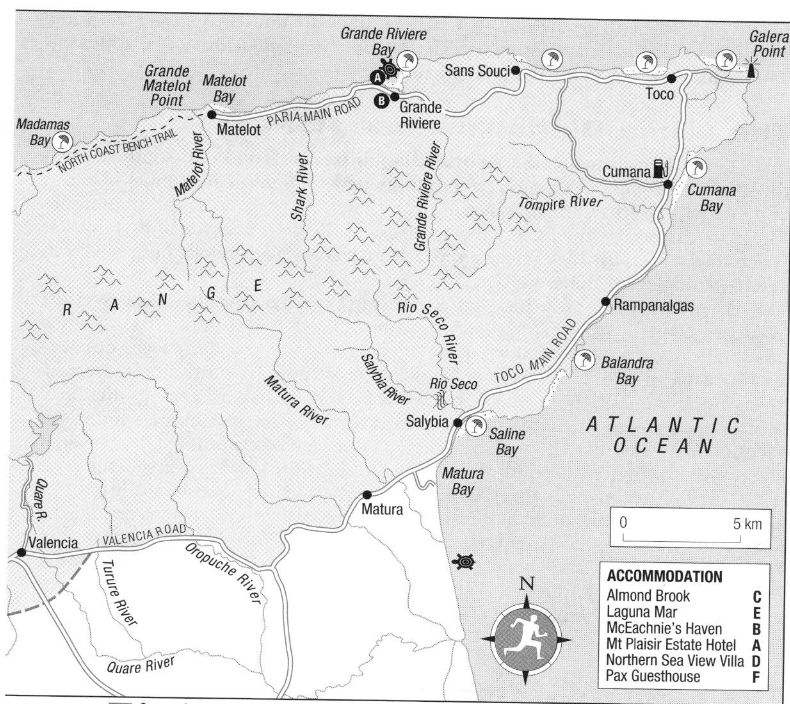

Beyond Blanchisseuse, the North Coast Road gives way to one of the few remaining stretches of **undeveloped coastline** in Trinidad. The next piece of tarmac is some 30km away in Matelot, leaving intact a sanctuary for bird and animal life, with gorgeous waterfalls and stunning beaches that are the favourite nesting sites for **leatherback turtles**. Through all this cuts the **north coast bench trail**, a two-day hike that requires camping in the bush along the way, though shorter options are available. If you prefer a solitary walk, go during the week; Saturdays, Sundays and public holidays are prime times for local hiking groups. A good local guide is Carl Fitz-James Jr (ⓣ868/669-6054, ⓔcarlfitzjames@hotmail.com).

Practicalities

The best **accommodation** options for the north coast are located in Blanchisseuse, which has a surfeit of guesthouses and host homes. *Almond Brook* (ⓣ758 0481 or 322 1762; ❷–❸) is by far the most atmospheric place in the upper village, with wood-panelled rooms decorated with shells and artefacts; all have mosquito nets, private bathroom and queen-size bed. There is a communal kitchen with fridge and microwave – though a good breakfast is included in the rates. *Laguna Mar* (ⓣ868/669-2963, or ⓣ868/628-3731, ⓦwww.lagunamar.com; ❸) is the largest and most professional of the bunch. Tucked away at the end of the road, this comfy hotel has rooms housed in blocks of six with a communal balcony; each has two double beds, fans and bathroom. There is also a three-bedroom villa to rent, and Marianne Beach is two minutes' walk away. The hotel restaurant, *Cocos Hut*, is in a converted cocoa-drying house and serves lunch and dinners consisting of excellent, local-style fish, chicken and meat. Expect to pay TT$70–100 for a meal. Vegetarians are catered for – ask in advance. For those on a budget, *Northern Sea View Villa*, North Coast Rd and Wilson Trace (ⓣ868/669-3995; ❷), is an excellent choice. These two basic apartments offer little in the way of luxury but they are directly opposite Marianne Beach and the owners are extremely friendly. Both apartments have two bedrooms with a fan, a kitchen, veranda and living room.

The Arima-Blanchisseuse Road

Inland from Blanchisseuse, the **Arima–Blanchisseuse Road** cuts south through the Northern Range, climbing high into misty peaks and through a tunnel-like road of green with overhanging canopies of mahogany, teak, poui, cedar and immortelle. There are impressive mountain views throughout the drive and you're more or less guaranteed to see **birdlife** wherever you stop; crested oropendola, hummingbirds and hawk-eagles are commonplace.

Seven miles north of Arima lies a birdwatcher's paradise, the **Asa Wright Nature Centre** (Ⓣ868/667-4655, in the US Ⓣ1-800/426-7781, Ⓦwww.asawright.org; ⑤). The 800,000-square-metre estate was established as a **conservation area** in 1967 and today is Trinidad's most popular birdwatching retreat, with hummingbirds, honeycreepers, tanagers and manakins among the forty species making frequent visits to the veranda feeders. The centre offers luxurious accommodation with rates including three meals and afternoon tea. However, if you're not staying, it's a good idea to get there before 10am to avoid the rush – the centre's on many a tour-bus route and the excited squeals of an unusual sighting and the whirr and click of paparazzi-standard zoom lenses can spoil the peaceful setting. Open daily 9am–5pm; the entrance fee (US$10) includes an hour-and-a-half tour and access to the veranda. You can have an excellent buffet **lunch** for TT$100 (Mon–Sat, TT$140 on Sun). Residents of more than three nights get a tour of **Dunston Cave**, which houses the world's most accessible colony of **oilbirds**.

The East-West Corridor

Running along the southern flank of the Northern Range, the **East–West Corridor** is traversed by the **Eastern Main Road** (EMR), a driver's nightmare; the **Priority Bus Route**, a fast-track commuter thoroughfare that's accessible only to public transport; and the **Churchill Roosevelt Highway**, a quick route connecting Port of Spain with the northeast tip. Hot and dusty as it is, the slow pace of the EMR allows you to absorb the commercial chaos, passing through the old Spanish capital of **St Joseph** and ending at **Arima**, the corridor's largest town and home to what's left of Trinidad's **Carib** community. The road is also the gateway to many a day-trip from Port of Spain, including the **Maracas Waterfall** and the **Mount St Benedict Monastery**. Beyond Arima, the buildings let up, but a few country lanes lead to the two most impressive waterfalls on the island, **La Laja** and **Sombasson**.

St Joseph

With its resplendent crescent- and star-topped main dome, the imposing **Mohammed Al Jinnah Memorial Mosque** signals your arrival into **ST JOSEPH**, Trinidad's oldest European town and first official **capital**. Lined with fretworked French and Spanish architecture, it's one of the better places along the EMR to get a flavour of the East–West Corridor. Striking uphill into Abercromby Street takes you through the town to the Maracas Royal Road, continuing north into the lush Maracas–St Joseph Valley. Eight kilometres from the EMR is the signposted Waterfall Road – the appropriately named route to **Maracas Waterfall**. A spectacular ninety-metre fall best seen during the rainy season (June–Dec), it's an excellent place for a quick dip after the sweaty twenty-minute walk it takes to get there. Route taxis run from Curepe junction, a busy public transport exchange two kilometres east of St Joseph, to Maracas Valley between 7am and 6pm; the fare is around TT$4, though you'll pay more if you go off-route along Waterfall Road.

Mount St Benedict

Back on the EMR, past the busy town of Curepe, lies the crucifix-lined, serpentine St John's Road, the route to **Mount St Benedict Monastery**. Visible from the central plains, the white-walled, red-roofed buildings dominate the hillside. Established in 1912 by Benedictine monks fleeing religious persecution in Brazil, it's a great place to go for spectacular views, peace and quiet and a spot of afternoon tea at the neighbouring *Pax Guesthouse* (daily 3–6pm). Taxis for Mount St Benedict leave from the corner of St John's Road and the EMR (TT$4).

Past the junction with the Churchill Roosevelt Highway and the entrance to the **University of the West Indies St Augustine Campus** lies Caura Royal Road, the turn-off for **Caura Valley** – one of the most popular **picnic** and **hiking spots** in the East–West Corridor.

Practicalities

Though this area is within thirty minutes' drive of Port of Spain, if you wish to find accommodation outside the hustle of the capital there is an excellent option for those seeking a more peaceful base from which to explore. The highly recommended **Pax Guesthouse**, Mount St Benedict (Ⓣ868/645-4232, Ⓦwww.paxguesthouse.com; ④) is perched adjacent to the monastery and commands magnificent views across central Trinidad. Along with an atmosphere of complete peace, the spacious rooms are furnished with antiques, some have private bathrooms and nos. 1 to 7 have great views across the central plains. The rates include breakfast, a pre-dinner rum punch and a delicious three-course evening meal (around TT$150 for non-guests). Surrounded by rainforest, the guesthouse is a popular spot with bird-lovers – hummingbirds are seen frequently on the veranda – and is an excellent, if not better, alternative to the Asa Wright Centre, for it is far less busy.

Lopinot

Further east and easily missed is **AROUCA**, notable only as the point where you turn off the EMR onto snaking Lopinot Road for an eight-kilometre drive to **LOPINOT**. This pretty hamlet is best known for the **Lopinot complex**, a former cocoa estate that has been transformed into a beautiful, secluded picnic spot (daily 6am–6pm; free). Settled by the **Comte de Lopinot**, a planter who fled Haiti following the 1791 revolution, the estate house has been carefully restored, complete with a small **museum** dedicated to the culture of local residents. The community – mainly of Spanish, African and Amerindian descent – has spawned some of Trinidad's finest parang players; they can be heard at Christmas and the annual harvest festival on May 17. The route taxi fare from Arouca to Lopinot is TT$4; cars are fairly frequent (Mon–Sat 5am–6pm), but service is reduced on Sundays.

Arima

Past Arouca the EMR takes on a more rural aspect, wreathing through Cleaver Woods up to **ARIMA**. Named Naparima by the Amerindians who were the first to settle in the area, it has a far deeper history than its commercial facade would suggest. The town is home to what's left of Trinidad's **Carib** community – most of whom live around the crucifix-strewn **Calvary Hill**. The Santa Rosa Carib Community Association, formed in 1974, has its headquarters on Paul Mitchell Street behind the cemetery, and sells good-quality traditional Amerindian craft such as woven baskets or carved calabashes. Apart from the **Santa Rosa festival** – a combination of Catholic and Carib celebration held during the last week in August – the only other compelling reason to stop in Arima is the fabulous open-air **market**, which is liveliest on Fridays and is a great opportunity to view local life. As the region's **main transport hub**, maxis to Sangre Grande (TT$4), Manzanilla (TT$4), Toco (TT$8), Mayaro (TT$8) and Grande Riviere (TT$16) leave from Raglan Street and Broadway, whilst maxis to Port of Spain (TT$5) leave from the northern end of St Joseph Street. **Taxis** to Sangre Grande (TT$4) and Valencia

(TT$2) leave from the Arima dial, and taxis to Port of Spain (TT$5) can be caught on Broadway. Alternatively, catch the ECS **bus** to the capital (TT$4) on Hollis Avenue outside Scotiabank.

Once past the outskirts of Arima, a turn-off at the WASA Guanapo Waterworks sign leads to the **Heights of Guanapo Road**. This is a fantastic hiking area but not a place to explore without a **guide**; Laurence Pierre is recommended (ⓣ868/632-9746, ⓦwww.hikeseekers.com), as are Paria Springs (see p.753). Here you'll find the breathtaking **Guanapo Gorge** – a vine-wreathed deep channel – and two waterfalls, **La Laja** and **Sombasson**, a twenty-metre and a three-tiered fifty-metre cascade respectively. You can see them all in a day's hike but you'll need to be in fairly good shape.

The Northeast Tip

Stretching from **Matura** in the east to **Matelot** in the north, the rugged coastline of Trinidad's **Northeast Tip** is a perfect escape from the bustle of the capital and the northwest corridor. At least a three-hour drive from Port of Spain to Matelot, the region seems suspended in a time warp as people and houses are few and far between and an air of hypnotic quiet pervades. The residents have the only community radio station on the island – Radio Toco 106.7 FM – which provides a unique taste of local life. **Farming** and **fishing** are the mainstays of the economy, and you'll lose count of the signs advertising shark oil, saltfish and sea moss for sale.

To explore the Northeast Tip easily you'll need your own car. Though a rural **bus** service (TT$9) runs buses – concentrated at peak periods – and you can find the occasional **maxi** and **taxi** (TT$7–20), public transport is somewhat sporadic; all options leave from Sangre Grande, fifteen kilometres southeast of Valencia and accessible by public transport from Port of Spain and Arima. The quickest way by **car** from Port of Spain is to take the Churchill Roosevelt Highway, turn left when it ends and then right onto a quiet portion of the EMR to Valencia, from where the Valencia Road swings north to the Toco coast.

After passing through the quiet town of Valencia and the one-street town of **Matura** you reach the prime nesting sites of **leatherback turtles**. If you want to visit the beach you'll need a permit (TT$10) and a guide (U$10) – restrictions imposed to protect the turtles. Both can be obtained on the main road from **Nature Seekers Incorporated** (ⓣ868/668-7337, ⓔnatseek@tstt.net.tt), a local conservation project which also arranges night visits to the beach to watch female leatherbacks nest during season (March–Aug). Past Matura, the Toco Road meets the east coast for the first time. The first safe place to swim is a beach just past the tiny village of **Salybia**. Opposite the entrance to the beach is the clearly signposted **Rio Seco waterfall trail**, a pleasant one-hour walk and the route to one of the area's more spectacular **waterfalls** (known locally as Salybia Waterfall), an eight-metre cascade surrounded by bathing pools. Approximately fifteen kilometres past Salybia is the village of Cumana, home to the last **petrol station** on this stretch of coast (Mon–Sat 8.30am–6pm, Sun 8.30am–noon).

Toco and Galera Point

The largest town in the area, **TOCO** is an attractive, quiet fishing village which retains a distinctly antiquated air and contains the highest concentration of Baptists in the Caribbean. As you enter the town, where Galera Road strikes off to the right is the **Toco Folk Museum** (open during school hours 8am–3.30pm, or ring ⓣ868/670-8261; TT$3, TT$2 children), located in the Toco Composite School. A fascinating project highlighting local history, the small museum houses Amerindian artefacts, snakeskins, butterflies and household items, including a gramophone and some rare 78rpm calypso records, which can be played if especially requested. The road continues to a good **beach** and, just beyond, **Galera Point**, the island's extreme eastern tip. Adjacent to the lighthouse is a windblown, rocky bluff, known as Fishing Rock, an atmospheric place where the Caribbean Sea and Atlantic collide in a distinct swirl of aquamarine meeting shimmering slate froth. Standing on the rock you feel as if you are on the edge of the world, which is how a group of rebellious Amerindians must have felt in 1699 when they leapt to their deaths here rather than be killed by their Spanish slave-masters.

Past Toco the road becomes **Paria Main Road** and runs perilously close to the cliffs where huge waves crash onto a wild and rugged coast. The next village, **Sans Souci**, has a safe beach and is the island's **surfing** capital.

Grande Riviere

One of the most appealing villages on the Toco coast, **GRANDE RIVIERE** is also the only place in the area with a developed tourist infrastructure. The beautiful beachside *Mount Plaisir Estate Hotel* has spurred some local residents to open up **guesthouses**, but development has remained low-key. Local people are incredibly welcoming, often throwing parties for departing guests.

The village boasts a superlative **beach** famous for nesting **leatherback turtles** – it's common for 150 or more to lay simultaneously here in season. Local residents have formed the Grande Riviere Environmental Awareness Trust to guard against poachers and provide guides, most of which work either through *Mount Plaisir Estate Hotel* or the Grande Riviere Nature Tours Guide Association (Ⓣ868/670-4257) housed in a small hut next to the hotel. As well as the beach there are hosts of **waterfalls**, **river walks** and excellent **birdwatching** – including the rare piping guan; local guides (see above) can be hired to help you explore the surrounding hiking trails. As for village life and entertainment, most of the action occurs at the *Mount Plaisir Estate* where the **bar** is a favourite liming spot. Other friendly options include the *Guy's Rec Club* and the *Lagoon Bar* on the main road.

Apart from the popular **Shark River** swimming spot, there's little reason to continue along the road past Grande Riviere which soon ends at the tiny fishing hamlet of Matelot.

Practicalities

Grande Riviere may be small but it has one of the best **hotels** in Trinidad: *Mount Plaisir Estate Hotel* (Ⓣ868/670-8381, Ⓦwww.mtplaisir.com; ❸–❹), a fantastic place to stay if you can afford it. The *Estate* overflows with easy style and is decorated with hand-crafted furniture, beautiful paintings and wall hangings; the rooms sleep four to six people – ask for one that opens directly onto the beach. They also have some basic rooms aimed at backpackers (❷). The excellent onsite *Ylang Ylang* **restaurant** equals the best in Port of Spain. Food served includes home-made bread, local-style meat, fish and imaginative vegetarian options, as well as an extensive wine list; expect to pay in excess of TT$150 for a three-course meal. The hotel will also collect you from the airport (US$85). For those on a more limited budget, *McEachnie's Haven*, at Bristol and Thomas streets (Ⓣ868/670-1014, Ⓦwww.mchaventt; ❷), makes up in friendliness for what it lacks in style. This yellow guesthouse has homey, basic rooms sleeping up to four, with fans, mosquito nets and en-suite bathroom. The owner, Ingrid, cooks delicious meals on request for both guests and non-guests (TT$50–70), and as her children are tour guides and her husband, Eric, is a well-known local musician, a stay here makes for a great opportunity to get to know a local family. The beach is just five minutes away, too.

21.3

Central and south Trinidad

Central and south Trinidad encompass an astonishing variety of landscapes. The **west coast** is gritty and industrialized, punctuated by the odd oasis of calm such as the **Caroni Swamp** – home of the scarlet ibis – and Trinidad's busy second city, **San Fernando**. On the **east coast**, there are the stunning **Manzanilla** and **Mayaro beaches** lined with coconut palms and still undiscovered by the tourist trade while inland sits the protected **Nariva Swamp**, home of endangered species such as the **manatee** (sea cow). In contrast to the northern East–West Corridor, the central and southern regions of Trinidad are populated predominantly by people of Indian descent – look for Hindu temples, prayer flags and Indian delicacies along the roadside.

Transport is no problem along the west coast, and most towns are easily accessible from the **Uriah Butler–Solomon Hochoy Highway** which runs from Port of Spain to San Fernando. Inland rural areas and the coast in the south and southwest can be more of a problem, however – **maxis** and **taxis** take long circular routes and the absence of road signs can make driving confusing. Most of the region, however, can be reached from Port of Spain in a day-trip unless you plan to spend time on the south and southeastern coast.

Central Trinidad

The region is predominantly rural, typified by the agricultural **Caroni Plains** which are bracketed between the woody Montserrat Hills and the stunning Manzanilla Beach. The exception is central Trinidad's busy and industrial main town, **Chaguanas**. The dominance of **Indian** culture is immediately noticeable upon joining the Uriah Butler–Solomon Hochoy Highway where the twelve-metre statue of Swami Vivekananda, which presides over the **National Council of Indian Culture** complex, looms into view on the eastern side of the road. And at the **Waterloo Temple** west of Chaguanas you may be forgiven for thinking you're in southern Asia, not the Caribbean.

Phagwa

A lighthearted celebration of the arrival of spring, the Hindu Holi festival – known in Trinidad as Phagwa (pronounced "pag-wah") – is held in March. Upbeat and carnivalesque, Phagwa celebrations are massive outdoor parties that represent a symbolic triumph of light over darkness. The festivities include the singing of devotional folk songs called **chowtals**, but the main focus is an intense fuchsia-pink dye known as **abir** which is squirted from plastic bottles over participants wearing white. Games add to the fun; adults participate in **makhan chor**, where teams form a human pyramid in order to grab a suspended flag, while children compete in roti-eating contests. In the north, Aranguez Savannah in San Juan has particularly lively celebrations, whereas Tunapuna Hindu School close to the Churchill Roosevelt Highway holds a slightly more restrained event. At Chaguanas, the car park of the National Council for Indian Culture is a popular location, as is the Kendra Phagwah Festival in an open space off Longdenville Old Road. None is widely publicized – you'll have to scan the newspapers or ask around for exact dates.

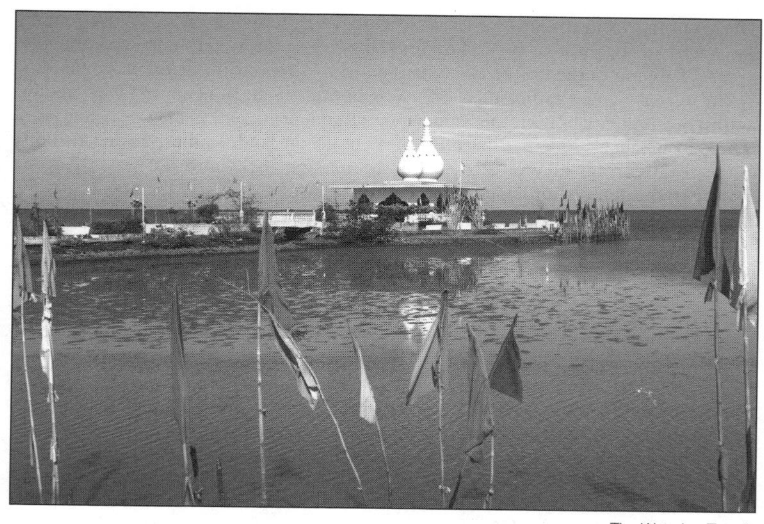

▲ The Waterloo Temple

Caroni Swamp and Bird Sanctuary

Less than an hour's drive from Port of Spain is Trinidad's most heavily promoted environmental attraction, the **Caroni Swamp and Bird Sanctuary**. This is the island's only roosting place for the **scarlet ibis**, the national bird, sporting an amazingly bright red plumage. The swamp is home to 157 species of birds, and caimans, snakes and silky anteaters inhabit its waters and mangroves. It's a quiet, mysteriously beautiful place well worth a visit. Tours, taken at dusk on small wooden boats, are available (TT$100/US$15) leaving daily at 4pm and lasting two and a half hours; advance booking is advisable. Contact Nanan (ⓣ868/645-1305, ⓦwww.nananecotours.com) or Sean Madoo (ⓣ868/663-0458) for more information and to make bookings.

It is not possible to get close to the birds' roosting spot without disturbing them so bring binoculars or a powerful zoom lens or you'll see little more than red specks against the dark green foliage. Leave Port of Spain at 3pm if you're driving, and if catching public transport take **maxis** or **route taxis** bound for Chaguanas; ask them to drop you at the Caroni Swamp exit, from where it's a five-minute walk. Lashings of insect repellent are a must during the rainy season.

The Waterloo Temple

Past the sprawling settlement of **Chaguanas** – the birthplace of the Nobel Prize winner **V.S. Naipaul** and site of the annual Phagwa celebration (see box) – and onto the Southern Main Road, you'll pass a selection of small settlements and grandiose, crumbling estate houses. About a kilometre south of Chase Village, Orange Field Road cuts west off the Southern Main Road through the **Orange Valley Estate** to join the signposted Waterloo Road down to the sea. At **Orange Field**, close to the junction of the Orange Field and Waterloo roads and surrounded by a cluster of neat bungalows built in the 1920s for sugar estate managers, stands the majestic 26-metre-high statue of Hindu deity **Hanuman** alongside its attached bright pink and ornate Hindu temple and ashram. Past here, in Waterloo village, the small yet enlightening **Indian Caribbean Museum**, Waterloo Main Rd (Wed–Sun only 10am–5pm; free; ⓣ673 7007) is the country's only permanent exhibition of artefacts and documents relating to the Indian experience

This superb drive through sugar cane plantations culminates half a kilometre down the road where, as you emerge at the sea, you'll be greeted by a remarkable scene.

The gleaming white, onion-domed **Waterloo Temple** stands on a pier overlooking the waters of the Gulf of Paria. The funeral pyres at the water's edge and the flags (*jhande*) flapping in the breeze all contribute to the impression that you are standing by the River Ganges rather than on a Caribbean island. Built in 1947 by **Seedas Sadhu**, an Indian labourer, the temple is a testament to one man's struggle against colonial bureaucracy; denied permission to build on land, Sadhu decided to build in the sea, using his bicycle to carry the foundation rocks into the water. Anyone can enter the temple, provided they remove their shoes first. Opening hours are Tues, Wed, Sat & Sun 8am–3pm, though these times depend on when the caretaker arrives; the grounds are open daily between 6am and 6pm. To get to the temple by **public transport**, take a route taxi from the Mid Centre Mall in Chaguanas to St Mary's Junction on the Southern Main Road just beyond the Orange Field Road turn-off (TT$4), where you pick up another taxi to the junction of Orange Field and Waterloo roads. Route taxis ply the lengthy Waterloo Road from Orange Field to the temple.

Pointe-a-Pierre Wildfowl Trust

After Waterloo the Southern Main Road winds its way through Trinidad's economic heartland, an area of smoke-belching sugar and oil refineries. Past Claxton Bay, an industrial suburb cloaked in dust from the nearby cement factory, stands a stunning oasis of nature, located on the extensive grounds of the Petrotrin Oil Refinery. The **Pointe-a-Pierre Wildfowl Trust** (Mon–Fri 8am–5pm, Sat & Sun 10am–5pm; TT$8; ⓣ868/658-4200 ext 2512, ⓦwww.trinwetlands.org) consists of 250,000 square metres of attractively landscaped grounds that are home to many **rare species of bird**, including the wild Muscovy duck, the red-billed whistling duck and white-cheeked pintail. Some of the rarer birds, including scarlet ibis, are caged to allow breeding programmes to continue. The well-maintained **learning centre** has good photographic displays, collections of shells, insects and Amerindian artefacts and an informative account of Trinidad's original inhabitants. To **drive** to the Trust from Port of Spain or San Fernando, leave the Uriah Butler–Solomon Hochoy Highway at the Gasparillo exit and follow the signs to the Petrotrin Oil Refinery. On **public transport**, take a Port of Spain–San Fernando maxi, route taxi or bus, and get out at the Gasparillo exit, from where the refinery is a two-minute walk. Once inside, it's another fifteen-minute walk to the Trust. The best time to visit is before 11am or after 3pm.

Manzanilla

In refreshing contrast to the smoggy, industrialized central west coast, central Trinidad's east coast features nothing more than miles of sand and endless coconut palms. South of Sangre Grande, the largest town in the east, the coast is dominated by the **Cocal**, 24km of unbroken sand, lined by grove upon grove of swaying coconut palms. The air is raucous with the calls of the **red-chested macaws**, and street vendors sell the shellfish known as chip-chip, crabs, black conch, fish and watermelon at the side of the road. So far the owners of the east coast coconut estates have declined to sell the property to hotel developers, and Manzanilla beach and the protected Nariva Swamp retain their idyllic seclusion. Deserted during the week but popular at weekends, take care while swimming as the undercurrents can be dangerous. There are changing facilities at the northern end (daily 10am–6pm; TT$1). The only hotel directly on the beach along this stretch of coast is the well-signposted **Coconut Cove** (ⓣ868/691 5939 or 868/671-7369; ❸). Beautifully located on a stretch of the beach sheltered by the Manzanilla Point headland, their smart double rooms have air-conditioning, TV, DVD and a balcony overlooking the sea. There is also a bar and restaurant onsite.

Nariva Swamp

The internationally recognized wetland of **Nariva Swamp** covers 15 square kilometres behind the coconut estates along the east coast. The area is made up of agricultural land as well as reed-fringed marshes, mangroves and **Bush Bush**

Island, bordered by palmiste and moriche palms and covered in hardwood forest. The swamp's unique freshwater ecosystem harbours large concentrations of **rare wildlife**, with some 58 species of mammals, 37 species of reptiles, and 171 species of birds. The swamp is also home to 92 species of mosquito, so remember to bring your insect repellent.

Nariva is the only place in Trinidad to see the threatened **manatee**, a peculiar elephantine mammal that can grow up to three metres in length and weigh over 900 kilograms, and which feeds off water hyacinth, moss and waterlilies. The swamp is also an excellent place to view caimans, freshwater turtles, red howler monkeys, white-fronted capuchin monkeys, silky anteaters, opossums, porcupines and a wide variety of birds including savannah hawks, dicksissels, orange-winged parrots and the yellow-capped Amazon parrot. Its most alarming inhabitants must be the **anacondas**, snakes capable of growing up to ten metres long; they're the heaviest reptiles in the world, and the largest in the Americas.

To visit the sanctuary, it's essential to have a **guide**, both to learn about the flora and fauna and to avoid getting lost; prices vary. Stephen Broadbridge of Caribbean Discovery Tours (see p.753) pioneered the tour in the early days, and still offers a marvellous Nariva trip with a walk through Bush Bush, kayaking if water levels permit and a truly excellent Indian lunch cooked by residents of Kernaham Village. Kayman Sagar at Limeland Tours (☎668 1356) in Manzanilla is extremely knowledgeable of the flora and fauna and also arranges a boat trip in rainy season, as well as helping you look for manatees in the right spots. If you're a serious ornithologist, opt for the excellent birding tours offered by Paria Springs (see p.753).

The south

Geographically, Trinidad's south presents a mirror image of the north with the low ridge of the forested **Southern Range** as its spine and a peninsula jutting out towards Venezuela. That's as far as the comparison goes because apart from Trinidad's second city, **San Fernando**, the region is the island's most sparsely populated. Although many of the inhabitants still earn a living from agriculture, the economy is based around **oil**. Ironically this is what has left the south so unspoilt; the petroleum business leases large expanses of forest from the government that remain largely undeveloped, providing homes for wildlife reserves and endangered species such as the ocelot. This calm, however, is slated to be shattered by the presence of an immensely polluting and controversial **aluminium smelter** at La Brea; construction is approved, but has yet to commence at the time of writing.

Tourists rarely venture this far south, and those who do make a beeline for **Pitch Lake**, the only proper attraction in these parts. Still, **Cedros** and **Erin** are picturesque areas, and **Mayaro** offers up a gorgeous swath of sand on the southeast coast – a popular holiday resort with Trinidadians. Consequently, there are few facilities for visitors but all of the towns and villages in the south, along with many of the beaches, are accessible by **public transport**. **Beaches** in the south are best visited during the dry season (Dec–May), as from June to November they are polluted by brackish water and litter.

San Fernando

Nestled against the base of the bizarrely shaped **San Fernando Hill**, the city of **SAN FERNANDO** enjoys the most striking location of any in Trinidad. Usually referred to as the industrial capital of T&T, it has an old-fashioned charm helped in large part by its winding lanes studded with charming gingerbread buildings. It's also the best place in the south to find **accommodation**, good **restaurants** and lively **entertainment**. Far quieter than Port of Spain, San Fernando is a friendly place, and getting to know the people here is easy enough provided you make an effort – and often the first move. There are no buses or maxis travelling within San

Fernando, and **route taxis** charge a flat fare of TT$4 for most journeys, with an added dollar or two for off-route drops; a good place to hail one is Library Corner next to the *KFC*.

Most of the historical sights and shops are located on and around the **Harris Promenade**, a broad, elegant boulevard running west from the foot of **San Fernando Hill**. At 200 metres high, the hill – with flattened, steep protruding points from quarrying activity – overshadows the town centre and makes for a pleasant recreation area with picnic tables, a children's playground and panoramic views.

High Street is San Fernando's main shopping street, lined with clothes stores and street vendors. At its southern end is Happy Corner, location of a few renovated colonial buildings and **King's Wharf**, where you can buy fresh snapper, kingfish and shark at the local fish market. On **Carib Street** stands the city's oldest building, the Carib House – an eighteenth-century Spanish colonial building – while neighbouring **Coffee Street** is home to many of the south's **steel bands**; the highly acclaimed Fonclaire have now moved one bock south to Dottin Street. San Fernando is the hub of the south's transport system, and you can catch maxis, buses and taxis to Port of Spain, La Brea, Princes Town and Point Fortin.

Accommodation

Most **accommodation** in San Fernando caters for visiting oil-industry personnel, so expect a business atmosphere.

Royal Hotel 46–54 Royal Rd ⓣ868/652-3924, ⓦwww.royalhoteltt.com. Comfortable and reasonably priced for its facilities. The bright rooms have a/c, cable TV, phone, fridge, jacks for Internet access and en-suite bathrooms, and there's a breezy open-air restaurant and pool onsite. ❺

Tradewinds Hotel 38 London St ⓣ868/652-9463, ⓦwww.tradewindshotel.net. The best-equipped hotel in the south and a friendly place in a quiet suburb. The better rooms are in the renovated building next to the pool, but all have a/c, cable TV, fridge, minibar, kettle and en-suite bathrooms. There's a popular restaurant/bar and a gym and Jacuzzi onsite, and breakfast is included in the rates. ❸

Eating and entertainment

While there are numerous **fast food** outlets in San Fernando, finding a sit-down **restaurant** is less straightforward: choices are restricted to a couple of Chinese places, hotel restaurants and a handful of other eateries. In terms of **entertainment**, San Fernando has upped its game in recent years, with a few new bars and a flashy club keeping things lively.

Atherly's by the Park 104 Gooding Village, near Cross Crossing Shopping Centre ⓣ652 0873. Roadside diner close to Skinner Park with an a/c main room and a couple of tables outside, serving inexpensive, reliable Creole and Indian dishes, principally at lunchtime. The menu changes daily and there is a buffet on Wed. In the evenings, the place becomes more bar than eatery.

Jazz & Calypso Lounge 110 Cipero St ⓣ653 9725. The newest and most sophisticated bar in town has a cool ambience and excellent selection of liqueurs. Live jazz and calypso/poetry on Sun from 6pm, and good jazz and Latin music played otherwise.

Karamat Roti Shop Coffee St, next to Willie's Ice Cream. Quite simply the best roti in town – a long history has ensured standards remain high – that is known to be better than the roti fare in the capital.

Mother Nature 58 St James St. This shop and café is known for its good range of inexpensive natural juices and vegetarian snacks, alongside "miracle" vitamin supplements. Provides a good break from the downtown Sando mayhem.

Nam Fong Lotus Restaurant 91–93 Cipero St ⓣ868/652-3356. Serves huge Chinese lunches and dinners at inexpensive prices. A relaxing, comfy and more upmarket atmosphere than the usual plastic tables. Closed Sun.

Richie's Paradise Cipero St ⓣ653 0711. A great underground club close to the centre of town with a big dance floor that attracts a more mature crowd and lots of couples (late 20s–40s); music ranges from back-in-times (retro) reggae and soul to dance. Cover charge usually TT$30.

Sting San Fernando Bypass/Gulf View, La Romaine, ⓦwww.stingnightclub.com. This new club opposite Gulf City Mall is the trendiest place to be seen for the south's younger crowd, though its large warehouse structure lacks atmosphere. Nonetheless it's in vogue and has occasional live music featuring local and international reggae, soca and chutney artists, and attracts a crowd reflecting Trinidad's diverse mix. Cover charge TT$60–80.

Swiss Grill at Club Kolumbo 34 Sutton St ⓣ657 9295. Swiss-run restaurant with a not very Swiss-like menu including steaks, jerked pork and pasta dishes, but best known for its fantastic succulent mahi-mahi steaks, grilled swordfish and barracuda, and paella. Occupying a restored colonial building, this is an upmarket but still casual liming spot.

Around San Fernando

Trinidad's **southwest peninsula**, known as the "deep south", offers a mix of gritty oil towns and marvellous drives through sleepy backwaters, forested hills and teak and coconut plantations, down to beaches of soft brown sand, backed by red-earth cliffs and lapped by calm seas. The larger towns, such as **Point Fortin** and the **Siparia-Fyzabad** conurbation, revolve around the oil industry and provide little interest to the passing visitor. The south coast, though, has a variety of excellent, deserted beaches at **Cedros** and **Erin**, while in the southeast, **Guayaguayare** and **Mayaro** beaches are popular with Trinidadian holiday-makers – quiet during the week but busy at weekends and public holidays. If you're **driving** to Mayaro from Port of Spain, the quickest route is via the Churchill Roosevelt Highway to Valencia, through Sangre Grande and down the east coast via Manzanilla. This is also the swiftest way by **public transport** – take a maxi to Arima, then one to Sangre Grande and then one down to Mayaro. If you're coming from San Fernando and the west coast, drive east along the Manahambre, Naparima and Mayaro roads. Maxis go from San Fernando to Princes Town; change here for a maxi to Mayaro. There are few places to stay on the south coast – most are basic beach houses advertised in the local press. **Azee's Guest House**, at the 3.5-mile marker on Guayaguayare Rd (ⓣ868/630-4619, ⓔazees@tstt.net.tt; ❷), is a small, friendly hotel just two minutes' walk from Guayaguayare Beach. All rooms have air-conditioning, cable TV, telephone, fridge and en-suite bathrooms, and there's a homey bar onsite as well as a restaurant, good for meals even if you're not a guest. Popular with Trinidadian holidaymakers during school holidays, it is best to book ahead.

The Pitch Lake

Roughly 25km southwest of San Fernando lies **Pitch Lake** (daily 9am–5pm; ⓣ868/651-1232), source of some of the world's finest-quality **asphalt**. The popular tourist attraction is well signposted 1.5km south of La Brea on the Southern Main Road. Locals may claim it as the eighth wonder of the world but to the sightseer it bears a remarkable resemblance to the wrinkly hide of an elephant. It is a genuine curiosity as there are only a few such lakes in the world. Five to six million years ago, asphaltic oil flowed into a huge mud volcano, developing over time into the asphalt that oozes from the lake. The material is used to pave roads all over the world, including Pall Mall leading to Buckingham Palace in London. Sadly the poor local village has yet to profit from this resource on its doorstep. Although **free** to enter, it's worth visiting with a **guide**. Authorized guides (identifiable by their badges and green shirts) operate from within the fenced compound (TT$30), and if you plan on touring wear flat shoes and be careful not to let the pitch touch your clothes – it's a nightmare to clean.

21.4

Tobago

An elongated oval just 41 by 14 kilometres, **TOBAGO** packs a surprising diversity between its craggy coastal fringes, from deserted beaches and pristine coral reefs to a wealth of lush rainforest. Though tourism has taken root with breathtaking speed – especially around the southwest tip – Tobago is hardly the typically jaded resort island. There are few all-inclusive hotels, celebrations such as the Easter **goat races** are attended by more Tobagonians than tourists, and local culture is honoured at the annual **Heritage Festival** each August. Nevertheless, tourism *is* changing Tobago. Fisherman needed to pull in seine fishing nets are still called by a resonant toot on a conch shell but nowadays the men often wait until they have a captive audience before hauling in the catch. And the African drumming that forms a major part of local Orisha and Spiritual Baptist ceremonies is now the soundtrack of many a hotel floor-show.

Geographically Tobago is breathtaking; heavy industry is confined to Trinidad, so the smaller island's beaches are clean and the landscape is largely left to its own devices. The flat coral and limestone plateau of the southwest – the **Lowlands** – is the island's most heavily developed region, with hotels clustered around powder-sand beaches such as **Pigeon Point** and **Mount Irvine**, home to excellent surfing (best between November and February). The capital, **Scarborough**, is a picturesque port town tumbling down a lighthouse-topped hillside.

The island's rugged **windward** (south) **coast** is lined with charming fishing villages; **Speyside** and **Charlotteville** in the remote eastern reaches have some fine coral reefs and scuba diving is a burgeoning industry. Tobago is an excellent and inexpensive place to learn to dive, and there's plenty of challenging drift diving for the more experienced, while the many reefs within swimming distance of the beaches make for fantastic snorkelling. The **leeward** (north) **coast** has Tobago's finest beaches; some, like **Englishman's Bay**, are regularly deserted, while at **Castara**, **Parlatuvier** and **Bloody Bay**, you'll share the sand with local fishermen.

The landscape of the eastern interior rises steeply, forming the **Main Ridge**, mountains which shelter the **Forest Reserve**, the oldest protected rainforest in the western hemisphere. Ornithologists and naturalists flock in for the bird and animal life that flourishes here; David Attenborough filmed parts of his celebrated *Trials of Life* series at **Little Tobago**, a solitary sea bird sanctuary off the coast of Speyside. For more casual visitors, the squawking, chirruping forest offers plenty of opportunities for birdwatching or a splash in the icy waterfalls.

One point worth making is that Tobago's close-knit community keeps the island pretty **safe** – especially outside the Crown Point area. Nonetheless, there have been robberies against tourists, particularly at isolated villas and far-flung beaches such as Englishman's Bay – so make sure to lock up at night, don't take unnecessary risks such as moonlit walks along deserted beaches, and don't flash wads of cash or expensive jewellery.

Some history

Control of Tobago has been hotly contested over the centuries. The original **Carib** population fiercely defended the island they called Tavaco (the name derived from the Indian word for tobacco), driving off several attempts by European colonists throughout the late 1500s and early 1600s. English sailors

(Ⓣ868/639-2292, Ⓦwww.shermansrental.com) is a recommended local operator, and Auto Rentals (Ⓣ868/639-0644, Ⓔmail@autorentals.co.tt) has one of the largest fleets in Tobago; amongst the internationals, Thrifty (Ⓣ868/639-8507, Ⓦwww.thrifty.com) is reliable. **Scooters** are available from some beach outlets and cost approximately US$25 a day.

Legions of **route taxis** ply the western portion of the island; travelling between Crown Point and Buccoo, Mount Irvine, Scarborough or Plymouth simply involves standing on the correct side of the road for your destination, sticking out your hand and asking the taxi driver where they're headed. If you're going further afield, you'll need to travel into Scarborough, where the main route taxi departure points are to be found as well as a taxi rank located by the docks.

Tobago's grey **buses** have greatly improved in recent years. From Scarborough, buses run along the windward coast to Charlotteville (seven buses Mon–Fri, four on Sat & Sun, running 4.30am–6.30pm at variable times). The leeward coast route extends from Scarborough to L'Anse Fourmi via Moriah, Castara, Englishman's Bay, Parlatuvier and Bloody Bay (seven buses Mon–Fri, four on Sat & Sun, running 4.30am–6.30pm at variable times). In the Lowlands, buses run from Scarborough to Mount Thomas via Les Coteaux and Golden Lane (five Mon–Fri, running 5.30am–6pm at variable times); they also go from Scarborough to Plymouth via Mount Irvine and Black Rock (Mon–Fri 4–8am at variable times and then hourly until 8pm). All tickets must be **pre-purchased** (fares range TT$2–8) and are available from general stores in

Scuba diving and watersports

Tobago is one of the best **diving** spots in the southeastern Caribbean, internationally recognized for its exciting, though difficult, drift dives, where you essentially let yourself be carried along by the current. The island's aquamarine seas are home to three hundred species of South Atlantic coral and a variety of spectacular multicoloured tropical fish. Tobago is best known for the enormous number of **manta rays** and the largest **brain coral** in the world. Speyside is known as "the Disneyland of diving", while Goat Island is popular for drift dives and Little Tobago is where many of the manta ray encounters occur. The island's **diving industry** has blossomed since being established in the 1980s, and many hotels, beaches and guesthouses feature their own centres. Prices for one to three dives are US$35-40 each; one-day resort courses are US$65-65; five-day PADI open-water certification courses run US$300-450; and advanced open-water start from US$265. Reliable operators include **Dive Tobago** (Ⓣ639 0202 or 2150, Ⓔcohel@tstt.net.tt) and Manta Dive Centre (Ⓣ868/639-9969 or 9209, Ⓦwww.mantadive.com). Much of the exotic plant and fish life in Tobago's waters can also be seen while **snorkelling.** Recommended sites include Pirate's Bay in Charlotteville, Arnos Vale and Englishman's and Great Courland bays. Most dive operators rent out snorkelling equipment for US$10 a day – if you plan to snorkel a lot, it's cheaper to bring your own.

Jet skis have yet to become a regular feature amid the surf (though you can rent them from R & Sea Divers Den on Pigeon Point (TT$240 per hr). **Kayak rentals** cost about TT$100 an hour at Pigeon Point, and Tobago Sea Kayak (Ⓣ868/660-6186, Ⓦwww.seakayaktobago.com) offer guided kayak excursions from US$40. Wild Turtle (Ⓣ868/639-7936, Ⓦwww.wildturtledive.com) and World of Watersports (Ⓣ868/660-7234, Ⓦwww.worldofwatersports.com) offer a variety of watersports including **water-skiing** (TT$250 for 20min), **inflatable bananas** (TT$150 for 15min), **parasailing** (TT$299 for 10–12min) and **windsurfing** (TT$250 for 1hr). The most popular local **surfing** site is Mount Irvine beach where boards can be rented for around TT$100 per hour from George, who also offers surfing lessons. Note that the water at Mount Irvine is shallow and directly over coral reef – surf fins can be badly damaged and protective footwear is prohibited to protect the reef from overeager surfers jumping in and damaging the coral.

the airport complex and throughout the island. For information on travel **between** Tobago and Trinidad, see p.750.

Organized tours

A multitude of **tour companies** offer rather sterile itineraries of Tobago's main sights costing US$60–80 per person; Frankie's Tours (Ⓣ868/639-4527, Ⓦwww.frankietourstobago.com) and Alibaba Tours (Ⓣ635 1017 or 686 7957, Ⓦwww.alibaba-tours.com) are the best of the bunch. For custom-designed **hiking** and **wildlife tours**, certified tour guide Harris McDonald (Ⓣ868/639-0513, Ⓦwww.harris-jungle-tours.com) runs half-day rainforest and birdwatching walks (US$50) as well as full-day excursions and night trips to the rainforest and turtle watching in season. Mark Puddy (Ⓣ868/639-4931) does fabulous offbeat **hiking trips** to deserted beaches and waterfalls (US$35); and **Peter Cox** (Ⓣ751 5822 or 385 3909, Ⓦwww.tobagonaturetours.com) leads brilliant nature and cultural tours of the island, particularly good for birders. One of the most popular ways to explore the brine is on a pleasure-boat cruise. Several operators work the waters – their prices for a full-day trip vary little (usually around US$50–60 per person for a 3hr trip and US$75 for a 6–8hr cruise) and usually include lunch and an open bar, snorkelling at Bon Accord Lagoon, Englishman's Bay or other similarly deserted coves; Large trimaran Natural Mystic (Ⓣ868/639-7245, Ⓔmystic@tstt.net.tt) is one of the best, while Frankie's and Ali Baba (see above) use smaller boats, making for a more intimate time. **Glass-bottom boat** tours of Buccoo Reef (US$25) leave from Store Bay, Pigeon Point and Buccoo.

Accommodation

Most of the island's **hotels** and **guesthouses** are concentrated in the tourist-oriented lowlands, meaning this is where you'll find the greatest choice and variety – from basic budget rooms to lavish, luxurious hotel complexes. Most of the accommodation is around Crown Point, but there's also a cluster of places along the coast from Buccoo to Plymouth, as well as plenty of villas (for the latter, contact Villas of Tobago (Ⓣ639 9600, Ⓦwww.villasoftobago.com). If you want something quieter, there are some lovely options in Castara, Speyside and Charlotteville.

Alibaba's Sea Breeze Little Bay Ⓣ686 7957, Ⓕ635 1017, Ⓦwww.alibaba-tours.com. Four en-suite apartments occupying the best location in Little Bay: close to the beach and immaculate views of Castara Bay. All suites have private balconies with well-equipped kitchens, fans and mosquito nets. The friendly owners are a great source of information and also run one of Tobago's most professional tour operators. ②

Banana Boat 6 Mac's Lane, Charlotteville Ⓣ868/660-6176, Ⓦwww.banana-boat-tobago.com. Quirky hotel and great budget option set on the edge of the beach. The basic en-suite rooms come with a/c or fan and banana-related decor. ②

Blue Haven Bacolet Bay Ⓣ868/660-7400, Ⓦwww.bluehavenhotel.com. This elegantly restored historic hotel – former guests include Rita Hayworth – is the best luxury accommodation on the island. The lavish rooms have four-poster or sleigh beds, a/c, TV, minibar, phone and modern artwork, along with spacious bathrooms and a balcony overlooking stunning Bacolet Bay. There's a pool, mini-gym, spa and tennis court, and an excellent – though expensive – restaurant onsite. Scarborough's a twenty-minute walk away. ⑥–⑨

Canoe Bay Beach Resort Cove Estate Ⓣ868/631-0367, Ⓦwww.find-us.net/canoebay. Set in 44 acres of beautiful landscaped gardens, each self-contained apartment at this secluded resort on the edge of a quiet beach consists of a bedroom, kitchen, bathroom and private balcony, with TV and a/c. ③

Cuffie River Nature Retreat Runnemede, near Moriah Ⓣ868/660-0505, Ⓦwww.cuffie-river.com. Nestled in the forest of an old plantation, peaceful hideaways don't come better than this. All the large, airy, comfortable en-suite rooms have a/c, radio and private balconies. There's a pool, beautiful shared lounge areas and excellent restaurant onsite. ⑤

Harris's Guesthouse Golden Grove Rd, Canaan Ⓣ868/639-0513, Ⓦwww.harris-jungle-tours.com. This fabulous guesthouse, situated on a quiet road, has two spotless double rooms with private patios and one family room, all en-suite with fans. Freshly cooked local breakfast included in the rates. ❷

Kariwak Village Store Bay Local Rd, Crown Point ⓣ868/639-8442, ⓦwww.kariwak.co.tt. A jewel in the middle of bustling Crown Point, accommodation is in thatched-roof cabanas furnished using local wood crafted on the premises; each has a/c and phone. Facilities include a pool, Jacuzzi and fabulous restaurant/bar. The only downside is intermittent airport noise. ❺

Man O' War Bay Cottages Man O' War Bay, Charlotteville ⓣ868/660-4327, ⓦwww.man-o-warbaycottages.com. Situated right on the bay in pretty landscaped gardens, the cottages are different shapes and sizes, with one to four bedrooms. All have fan, bathroom, hot water and kitchen, simple but attractive decor, books on the shelves, driftwood ornaments and an overwhelming feeling of peace. There's a small commissary onsite and the maid/cook service, which costs extra, is optional. ❷

Manta Lodge Main Rd, Speyside ⓣ868/660-5268, in US ⓣ1-800/544-7631, ⓦwww.mantalodge.com. Located opposite the bay, this hotel is colonial-style luxury catering for scuba enthusiasts. Standard rooms are small but stylish with ceiling fan and balcony; "superior" rooms provide more space and a/c, while the quirky attics have the lot plus a private sundeck on the roof. There's a good restaurant (breakfast included in the rates), pool and dive shop onsite. ❹

Miller's Guesthouse Miller St, Buccoo Village ⓣ660 8371, ⓕ631 0492 ⓦwww.millers-guesthouse.tripod.com. Pleasant guesthouse in a nice spot overlooking Buccoo Bay. The rooms are basic yet comfortable, with private bathroom, sink and fan. Dormitory accommodation is available for the budget traveller, while a self-contained beach house sleeping nine is good value for groups. Standard ❷ dormitory ❶ beach house ❺

Sandy's Robinson St, Scarborough, ⓣ868/639-2737, ⓦwww.tobagobluecrab.com. Run by the hospitable owner of the Blue Crab restaurant, this wonderful guesthouse has four pretty and spotless rooms with a/c and private bathrooms. Breakfast included. ❷

Toucan Inn Store Bay Local Rd, Crown Point ⓣ868/639-7173, ⓦwww.toucan-inn.com. This welcoming hotel is a haven of tranquillity in the middle of Crown Point's bustle. The unusual, octagonal cabana rooms are set in attractive gardens around a pool; all have a/c and fittings made from local teak and pine. *Bonkers* – the onsite restaurant – is a local institution. ❸

The Lowlands: Crown Point to Arnos Vale

Tobago's flattest, most accessible portion is focused around a crowded five-kilometre stretch of **Milford Road** from the airport and Store Bay Beach – a tiny area known as **Crown Point** – through Bon Accord, Canaan and Mount Pleasant, and 10km north along **Shirvan Road** to **Buccoo**, **Mount Irvine** and **Plymouth**. Usually lumped together as "**the Lowlands**", this is home to most of Tobago's residents as well as the vast majority of hotels, restaurants, nightclubs and the most popular beaches; you'll inevitably spend a lot of time here.

Store Bay to Pigeon Point

A two-minute walk from the airport brings you to one of Crown Point's busiest swimming spots, **Store Bay Beach** (lifeguards 10am–6pm). Close to the main hotels and with excellent, inexpensive food and crafts available, the fine, off-white sand is a favourite with Trinidadian holiday-makers. Though the cove is fairly small, the calm crystal waters and family atmosphere make it excellent for children. Facilities include a car park, showers and changing facilities (daily 10am–6pm; TT$1) with lockers (TT$10 per day), as well as a couple of bars blasting reggae and soca. Not to be missed are the row of cream-brick take-aways housing a number of famed cookshops (8.30am–8.30pm) including local institutions *Miss Jean*'s and *Miss Esmie*'s; any trip to Tobago would be incomplete without a plate of their **crab and dumplin'**.

Running north from the airport past the entrance to Store Bay, Airport Road becomes Milford Road. Here, a left-hand turn (marked by the neon constellation of the *Golden Star* bar and restaurant) leads to **Pigeon Point Beach** (daily 8am–7pm; TT$18), the only fee-paying stretch of sand in T&T and the most "resort-like" place for a swim. Its shoreline – unlike the majority of Tobago's rugged beaches – is definitively Caribbean, with powdery white sand and a turquoise sea lined with coconut palms. Pigeon Point's immensely popular strip includes Tobago's most photographed pier – a weathered wooden boardwalk with a thatched roof hut at the end – and is one of the few places in the island to suffer from overdevelopment. A series of shops selling beachwear, clothes and upmarket souvenirs nestle into the landscaped area around the busy bar, and the road leading to the beach is also lined with craft stalls and watersports outlets.

Picturesque as it is, the beach is a source of **controversy** among locals as a result of its "private" status, seen by many as a means of preventing locals from entering. As there is (theoretically) free access to all beaches in Tobago, the charge is actually for the use of the facilities and road; so you can avoid paying by simply walking along the beach at low tide into Pigeon Point. Be warned, however, that the area is patrolled by security guards who look for the wristbands that visitors are given once they've paid; if you're not wearing one, you may be asked to leave the beach. Many locals now refuse to go to Pigeon Point, especially after a fisherman was fatally shot following an altercation with security guards. This history has diminished the beach's appeal somewhat, even if its natural beauty has not suffered.

Bon Accord to Buccoo

Bisecting Tobago's low-lying southwest tip, ruler-straight **Milford Road** is the artery of the area, traversing the Bon Accord, Tyson Hall, Canaan and Friendship communities. North of the road is **Bon Accord Lagoon**, a sweeping oval of mangrove swamp and reef-sheltered shallow water which forms one of the most important fish nurseries on the island. The lagoon, despite suffering pollution in the past, is a sanctuary for conch, snails, shrimp, oysters, crab, urchins and sponges. The land is difficult to access so it's best to visit as part of a boat trip (see p.784), many of which include a barbecue on the gorgeous white sand of **No Man's Land**.

A kilometre or so before Milford Road widens into Claude Noel Highway, **Shirvan Road** strikes off to the left. This is the route to Buccoo Bay and its famous **reef**, several wide yellow-sand **beaches** and the neat coastal town of Plymouth. The road is lined with a mishmash of swanky restaurants and upmarket hotels alongside fruit stalls and simple board shacks.

▲ Goat racing in Buccoo

Sunday School

A Tobago institution, **Sunday School** at Buccoo Bay is most definitely not for the pious. A massive beach party that the whole island seemingly attends, Sunday School is the highlight of the week's nightlife. The action begins at 8pm when the Buccooneers Steel Orchestra play pan for a couple of hours. The crowd begins to thicken around 10pm when the sound system at the covered beach facilities begins to play. The music is inevitably Jamaican dancehall with the most popular soca tunes thrown in alongside hip-hop and R&B. Experienced winers – "wining" being the local name for dirty dancing – display their skills, foreigners relax and the gigolos (and tourists) scout for a partner; Sunday School is a well-known pick-up joint. The largest Sunday School of the year takes place each Easter Monday, when several more sound systems add to the cacophony and parked cars back up all the way to the Mount Irvine golf course. To avoid car parking hassles, it's a good idea to book a taxi to collect you at a prearranged time, or get a place on an organized trip which costs about US$20.

Buccoo

A cluster of tourist-oriented signposts marks the intersection of Auchenskeoch (pronounced "or-kins-styor"), Buccoo Bay Road and Shirvan Road, known as **Buccoo Junction**. A right turn climbs into one of Tobago's smartest residential districts, where opulent villas nestle next to tiny villages. The left turn takes you to **BUCCOO**, a small village haphazardly built around a calm and beautiful bay. Fishing remains a major industry but since the nearby reef has become a premier attraction, the community has embraced tourism. The annual **goat races** have been held here since 1925 and are a delightful spectacle. The event is taken very seriously by competitors – jockeys train the belligerent animals who generally refuse to obey any orders, and the result is a joy to watch. **Crab races** also take place but are taken less seriously. The quiet village atmosphere disappears every Sunday when the masses descend for **Sunday School**. A muddy seabed and its use as a urinal on Sundays make central Buccoo a terrible place to swim, but the palm-lined western fringe of the bay is appealing, with cleaner water and plenty of shells and coral fragments to collect.

Covering around twelve square kilometres of Caribbean seabed, **Buccoo Reef** is the largest and most heavily visited in Tobago. It's home to forty-odd species of hard and soft coral, which provide good feeding for the brilliantly coloured trigger, butterfly, surgeon and parrot fish. South of the reef is **Nylon Pool**, a gleaming coralline sand bar forming an appealing metre-deep swimming pool smack in the middle of the sea. The pool is said to have been named by Princess Margaret in the 1950s when she remarked that the water was as clear as her nylon stockings.

Sadly, carelessly placed anchors and removal of coral souvenirs mean that many parts bear more resemblance to a coral graveyard than a living reef. Overfishing has reduced fish and crustacean populations, and spear guns have ripped chunks from the coral. Declared a protected **national park** in 1973, scant resources have failed to enforce the law and the damage continues unabated. Today, glass-bottom boat operators are more conscientious, anchoring only on dead reef and warning visitors that touching or removing reef matter and shells is illegal, but they still hand out plastic shoes, making it possible for a single footstep to damage or kill hundreds of years' growth. Do your bit by standing on seabed only and refusing to buy any coral trinkets. **Glass-bottom boat** tours for two to three hours cost around US$25. The best leave from Buccoo and include snorkelling and a dip in Nylon Pool; the most reliable operator is Buccoo-based Johnson and Sons (ⓣ868/639-8519). Trips taken at low tide are best for snorkelling.

Mount Irvine to Turtle Beach

The shaven greens of Tobago's first **golf course** herald the outskirts of **Mount Irvine**, the next coastal village past Buccoo. The challenging course plays host to the Tobago Pro-Am tournament every January, and greens fees are US$30 for nine holes, US$48 for eighteen – there's also a weekly rate of US$264 (Ⓣ868/639-8871). Around the next bend is **Mount Irvine Bay Beach**, a busy slip of fine yellow sand with just enough room for beach tennis and volleyball, surrounded by gazebos and the ubiquitous palm and sea grape trees. The facilities (daylight hrs; TT$1) are adequate and there's a bar/restaurant onsite doling out tasty Creole food. During summer months, the water is calm enough to explore the ornate offshore **reef**, but come the winter – between December and March – Mount Irvine becomes one of the island's best **surfing** beaches when huge breakers crash upon the sand. See p.783 for info on board rental and lessons.

Nestled in the hills behind the beach along Orange Hill Road (take the right turn just past the Mount Irvine golf course then follow the signposts) is the castle-like building that holds the **Kimme Museum** (open Sun only 10am–2pm, appointments taken for other days; TT$20; Ⓣ868/639-0257, Ⓦwww.luisekimme.com). Here you'll find the private gallery of eccentric German sculptor Luise Kimme, who settled in Tobago in 1979. Her eerily beguiling wood and bronze sculptures are dotted around the artist's quirky, mural-decorated fretworked home, and a tour makes for a pleasant break from beach-related activities.

Back on the Shirvan Road past Mount Irvine is the sublime beach at **Stone Haven Bay** (also known as Grafton beach), a wide swath of sand that's backed by an all-inclusive hotel, expanding villa complexes, and the inevitable beach vendors. A few minutes' drive further north is **Turtle Beach**, a kilometre of picturesque, coarse yellow sand, again overlooked by the concrete blocks of a large hotel. Though the beach is officially called **Great Courland Bay**, it acquired its colloquial title on account of the **turtles** that lay eggs here in the dark of night. All of the hotels along this stretch organize a turtle watch during the laying and hatching seasons but if you're not staying in the area, contact Nick Hardwicke at the small *Seahorse Inn* (Ⓣ868/639-0686) or Save Our Sea Turtles Tobago (Ⓣ868/639-9669) for turtle-watching expeditions.

Plymouth and Arnos Vale

A mile or so beyond Turtle Beach, Grafton Road meets a junction; a left turn leads to **PLYMOUTH**, Tobago's first European community, settled first by Latvians, then the Dutch and finally by the British. An attractive little town, its main attraction is **Fort James**, the oldest stockade in Tobago, built in 1811 by the British. The coral-stone structure and four cannons preside over an excellent view of Turtle Beach. If you're driving up the coast, it's wise to fill your tank at Plymouth's petrol station (Mon–Sat 7am–9pm, Sun 7am–noon) as it's the only one for miles.

From the centre of Plymouth, a well-signposted but narrow road meanders through the greenery towards **Arnos Vale**, one of the few sugar estates to keep its land. The main point of access is at the old estate **water wheel** (daily 9am–10.30pm; TT$12), where new buildings constructed from natural materials house a modest **museum**, gift shop, bar and restaurant. The wheel, pump and fermenting house that once worked the sugar cane have been restored and can be viewed via a system of wooden walkways. The estate is a pretty and atmospheric spot, with lavish flowering plants and lush foliage – nice for a relaxing drink. The bay – overlooked by one of Tobago's oldest hotels – is great for **snorkelling**.

Scarborough

SCARBOROUGH, Tobago's raucous, hot and dusty capital (population 18,000), spills higgledy-piggledy down a hillside. The island's administrative centre and its main **port**, the flourishing town is devoid of touristic pretensions. As the commercial centre of the island, shopping is one of the town's main attractions. The **market**, located opposite the docks, with its fruit and vegetables display, bargain crafts and excellent fast food, is a must; main trading days are Friday and Saturday. The **Fort King George** complex, perched on the lighthouse-topped hill, also contains a local craft centre (Mon–Fri 9am–1pm) with more unusual items. This complex, at the top of the well-signposted Fort Street, is free to enter and contains a landscaped **park** as well as the largest fortification in Tobago, **Fort King George**; at 140m above sea level, it also affords excellent views along the coast. Don't miss the **Tobago Museum** (Mon–Fri 9am–4.30pm; TT$10), a small but fascinating collection that includes Amerindian artefacts, satirical colonial prints from slavery days, African drums and notes on local culture.

Away from the commercial clamour, the sweeping lawns and luscious flowers of the **botanical gardens** (daylight hrs; free) opposite the bus station on Gardenside Street offer respite from the traffic and steep climbs that can make Scarborough a bit of an ordeal; visiting on an overcast day makes sightseeing more comfortable. As Scarborough is so small, there are no bus services within the town but you can easily see all the sights by foot. For **information**, head to the tourism offices of the Tobago House of Assembly, Division of Tourism, 197 Doretta's Court, Mt Marie (Mon–Fri 8am–4pm; ⓣ868/639-2125, ⓦwww.visittobago.gov.tt). Free **parking** is available at the wharf car park on the corner of Carrington and Castries streets. Scarborough is the departure point for **route taxis** serving the whole of the island; ask a local to point you to the appropriate stand. **Maxis** to Charlotteville leave two or three times a day from outside James Park on Burnett Street (TT$10).

The leeward coast

Beyond Arnos Vale, the leeward coast feels more remote than any other part of the island. Tourist development is minimal, leaving the ravishing beaches at **Englishman's Bay**, **Parlatuvier** and **Bloody Bay** much the same as they were twenty years ago, though **Castara** has a smattering of places to stay and eat with a pleasingly laid-back scene. **Fishing** and **agriculture** are the main industries; boats with bamboo rods bob in all the bays, and you'll often see machete-wielding farmers walking to their small farms.

Though the area is accessible from Crown Point along the coast road via Plymouth, the twists and turns in the route make for a long – but very scenic – drive. If you want to travel quickly, take the **Northside Road**, which begins on the outskirts of Scarborough at Calder Hall, off the Claude Noel Highway, and then works its way across the island.

The first port of call **along the coast road** is **Castara**, an attractive fishing village that's slowly developing a nonchalant tourist-friendliness. Low-key guesthouses are scattered up the hillsides, while visitors dribble in to swim at the marvellous **beach** or splash in the nearby waterfall. Fishing remains the main industry and the beach is one of the best places to participate in the pulling of a **seine net**, still used by the supremely friendly Rasta fishermen. The village abandons its languid air each August when the beach is packed with revellers attending the **Castara Fishermen's Fete**, one of Tobago's most enjoyable festivals.

Past Castara, houses and shops melt away and the road is flanked by enormous bamboo. The next worthwhile beach, **Englishman's Bay** (look out for the blue and white sign), is utterly beautiful and completely undeveloped save for the fabulous *Eula's Café by the Sea* stall near the entrance, serving hot meals (including roti on Sundays) and drinks, and a few craft stands.

East of Englishman's Bay, the coast road climbs upwards and inland, passing through the diminutive community of **Parrot Hall** before descending to reveal one of the most arresting views on the island: **Parlatuvier Bay**, it's turquoise waters flanked by a pretty hillside scattered with palms, terraced provision grounds and the odd house. Another crescent of pearly sand, the bay makes **swimming** a vigorous experience: waves are usually quite strong and the water deepens sharply from the sand. The last accessible beach on the coast is **Bloody Bay**, another deserted shoreline; the right turn at the Bloody Bay junction takes you to the **Tobago Forest Reserve**; carrying straight on takes you to tiny L'Anse Fourmi and, ultimately, Charlotteville.

Tobago Forest Reserve

The road swinging inland through the protected **forest reserve** is known as the Roxborough–Parlatuvier Road. The route makes for a steep but beautifully quiet drive through the seemingly impenetrable rainforest canopy which in fact contains a number of managed **trails** that even the most confirmed city-dweller should find easy to explore.

The oldest protected rainforest in the western hemisphere, the Tobago Reserve is easily accessed at **Gilpin Trace**, marked by a huge slab of rock by the road in front of a forestry division hut. A trail strikes straight into the forest from here, but unless you only plan to go a few hundred yards, it's advisable to hire a **guide**; he or she will understand a lot more about forest dynamics, and you won't need to worry about getting lost. Guides are often found hanging around at Gilpin Trace, but the best bet is to book on an organized trip before you get here. Contact the operators listed on p.784, or try Shurland James (Ⓣ660 7883 or 376 5908) – the only woman of the bunch – or Fitzroy Quamina (Ⓣ660 7836). A three-hour walk will cost around TT$220.

The windward coast

Rugged and continually breathtaking, Tobago's southern shoreline is usually referred to as the **windward coast** and its languid coastal villages offer a complete contrast to the west. Narrow and punctuated by blind corners, the Windward Road spans its length and provides fantastic views of the choppy Atlantic waters. Though rip tides and strong undercurrents make some of the most attractive-looking beaches unsafe for swimming, there are plenty of sheltered bays to take a dip. Some – such as **King's Bay** – have changing facilities but mostly you'll share the sand only with fishermen. Most of the windward traffic heads for the tiny village of **Speyside** and its smattering of guesthouses and small hotels. Fifteen minutes' drive from Speyside and directly opposite on the Caribbean coast, picturesque **Charlotteville** is the last point of call on the windward route. Beyond the village, a new road to L'Anse Fourmi has recently opened, meaning that you can now drive in a circular route around the entire island.

The Windward Road

From Scarborough the Windward Road leads northeast through a string of little communities, including **Mount St George** (the island's first British capital), Goodwood, Goldsborough, Pembroke, Glamorgan and Belle Garden. Past here, the next reason to make a stop is the **Argyll Waterfall** (daily 9am–5pm, last tour at 4pm; TT$30; Ⓦwww.argylewaterfall.com), signposted from the roadside. Official guides wearing blue, green or yellow Argyll Falls shirts will take you from the car park to the falls, giving a brief history of the area and pointing out birds and flowers on the way (their services are included in the entrance fee, although a tip is expected). After a pleasant fifteen-minute walk, you're rewarded by the sight of the falls themselves; at 54m, they're the island's highest and comprise three main cascades, all of which have pools for swimming.

Turning inland past the small village of Roxborough, the Windward Road swings through the hilltop village of **Delaford**, making one almighty bend at the outskirts to reveal a breathtaking view of the spiky coconut plantation surrounding beautiful, deep-blue **King's Bay** below. The **beach** (open daylight hours; free) here is one of the few along the windward coast to provide changing facilities (TT$1).

Speyside

Past King's Bay, the coast swings out of view as the road turns inland. Constant hairpin bends and a steep incline make the going pretty treacherous, so if you're driving, don't let your surroundings become too much of a distraction. Luckily, a designated **lookout** point has been built before the descent into **SPEYSIDE** – be sure to stop, as there's an amazing view of the horseshoe **Tyrrel's Bay**, along with **Little Tobago** and **Goat Island** and an expanse of aquamarine coral reef-strewn water.

Though Speyside is slowly adjusting to its latest role as a **scuba-diving** destination, it still retains its fishing village atmosphere and small-town attitude. The main strip consists of several dive shops, a smattering of restaurants, including the well-known *Jemma's*, and a few hotels and guesthouses; *Speyside Inn* and the *Manta Lodge* are two of the better ones.

As you descend into the village, to the right is a cluster of candy floss-coloured grocery shops and snack bars surround a large playing field – the venue for local football matches. A road running between the playing field and the sea takes you to the **beach** facilities, basic changing rooms and toilets (daylight hours; TT$1). The swath of sand here is slightly wider than in the central part of the bay, and the famous **reefs**, Speyside's main attraction, are within swimming distance. Generally pristine with little sign of bleaching or human damage, the reefs boast one of the world's largest **brain corals**, a tremendous four metres high and six metres across. Apart from the regular shoals of small fish – butterfly, grunt, angel, parrot and damsel – the currents also attract a number of deep-water dwellers, including nurse sharks, dolphins and, most notably, **manta rays**. For those who wish to see more than small fish and limited portions of reef, scuba diving is excellent in this area. The most popular Speyside dive sites include Kelleston Drain (site of the brain coral), Japanese Gardens, Angel Reef, Flying Manta and Blackjack Hole, and most dives are of the drift variety (for reliable operators see p.783). **Glass-bottom boats** are a good way to see the reefs if you don't want to get wet, though you can always jump overboard for a spot of snorkelling as well. Frank's (Ⓣ868/660-5438), based at *Blue Waters Inn*, offers(US$15) drift snorkelling at Little Tobago (US$20), as well as a boat tour around St Giles Island (US$40).

On leaving Speyside, just past the *Manta Lodge* hotel, the road forks; left takes you across the interior and into Charlotteville, while the right turn is the route to the astonishingly blue waters and rich reefs of **Bateaux Bay**, site of another luxurious hotel. Beyond Bateaux Bay are the picturesque Belmont and Starwood bays, but the road is often impassable; if so, ask a local fisherman to take you aboard a pirogue. Both bays offer great snorkelling and diving.

Little Tobago and Goat Island

Of the two misshapen islets sitting five kilometres or so out of Tyrrel's Bay, **Goat Island** is the closer, though it's privately owned and closed to the public. However, birdwatchers and hikers flock to the larger island, **Little Tobago**, a kilometre further out to sea. Known as "Bird of Paradise Island", it has been a bird sanctuary since 1924. Uninhabited, it's home to one of the largest sea bird colonies in the Caribbean, including flocks of frigates, boobies, terns and the spectacular red-billed tropic bird, the latter especially prevalent between October and June. Make sure you take drinking water with you, as there are no refreshments available on the island. To get the most from your visit, hire an experienced guide such as Peter Cox (Ⓣ751 5822 or 385 3909, Ⓦwww.tobagonaturetours.com).

Charlotteville

From Speyside, the Windward Road strikes inland, climbing steeply upwards through jungle-like mountain foliage before plummeting down to the opposite shoreline. Just before the descent, there's a stunning perspective over **Charlotteville**, its houses tumbling down the hillside to the calm waters of the bay. Snugly situated under the protective cover of the two-kilometre-wide **Man O' War Bay**, Charlotteville is Tobago's foremost **fishing** community – more than 60 percent of the island's total catch is brought in by local fishermen. The town has an isolated feel, and though the tourist dollar is steadily encroaching upon this self-contained community, the atmosphere is so friendly that it's hard not to relax.

Charlotteville is actually one of Tobago's oldest communities, first settled by Caribs and then by the Dutch in 1633. Increasingly popular as a retreat, accommodation gets booked up quickly. There's little to do but arrange a **fishing** trip, while away the hours on the fine yellow sand of **Man O' War Bay Beach** (open during daylight hours; changing facilities TT$1) or enjoy the excellent snorkelling in the sublime **Pirate's Bay**, a short but steep walk from the village along a track that strikes out around the headland just beyond the pier. Benches along the sea wall, the pier and a covered pavilion are popular liming spots, great for soaking up the village scene. In July, Man O' War Bay is the site of Tobago's most popular fisherman's fete, held to celebrate **St Peter's Day**. Charlotteville's petrol station is open Monday to Saturday 6am–8pm and Sunday 6–11am & 8.15–8.30pm.

Eating, drinking and entertainment

Unlike Trinidad – where fetes and street food are a daily staple – Tobago is far more easy-going. The best budget **food** options – including the sublime curry crab and dumpling and fantastic rotis – are available from the stalls on Store Bay, and from snackshops along Milford Road. Most **restaurants** cater to tourists and are therefore located in the Lowlands area, but options are expanding further afield. If you're here in the slow season (mid-April to mid-Dec), bear in mind that many kitchens close at around 9pm. Apart from occasional concerts – look out for posters – most **entertainment** on the island revolves around bars, rum shops, the infamous Sunday School in Buccoo (see box, p.787), and the open-air *Shade* nightclub off Milford Road (Wed–Sat). *Bago's Beach Bar*, on the road to Pigeon Point, is a pretty spot for a drink overlooking the water.

Blue Crab Robinson St, at Main, Scarborough ☎868/639-2737. This friendly restaurant with a lovely shady terrace serves decently priced, excellent Creole food. Lunch weekdays, dinner by reservation only.

Bonkers *Toucan Inn*, Store Bay Local Rd, Crown Point ☎868/639-7173. This excellent and popular restaurant serves tasty Tobagonian food at moderate prices under a shady pavilion or at poolside tables. There's a good and varied wine list and a regular "limetable" of live music.

Café Iguana Store Bay Local Rd, at Airport Rd, Crown Point ☎868/631 8205. This lively bar and restaurant serves great, decently priced Caribbean cuisine and a range of cocktails, with live jazz and *salsa* on Fri & Sat. Daily from 6pm.

La Cantina Airport Rd ☎639 8242. Off the road in the little complex housing the RBTT bank, this brilliant Italian-owned pizzeria serves some fabulous pizzas baked in a proper oven, with all the toppings you'd expect. Good wine list, and daily specials too. Takeaway available.

Ciao Café King's Well, Scarborough ☎868/639-3001. This fantastic, popular Italian café and bar with outside terrace serves authentic cappuccino, over twenty different flavours of delicious home-made ice cream, fine Italian wine, good beer and colourful cocktails.

Jemma's Sea View Kitchen Main Rd, Speyside ☎868/660-4066. Popular with every island tour bus, this place lurches crazily in the boughs of a tree, and the sea view is fantastic. Serves tasty Creole-style food at relatively high prices; expect to pay $TT100–150. No alcohol. Closes Fri at 4pm, closed Sat.

Kariwak Village Store Bay Local Rd, Crown Point ☎868/639-8442. Fresh herbs and spices, inventive slants on local staples and a relaxing setting make this restaurant, attached to the hotel of the same name, one of best and most expensive places to eat in the Crown Point area. Breakfast and dinner menus are set – usually with a meat, fish or vegetarian option – and everything is supremely fresh, succulently cooked and completely delicious. Accompanied by live music, the Friday-night buffet is particularly good. Vegan food available.

Mélange 133 Shirvan Rd ☎631 0121. Popular Creole restaurant housed in a pretty multi-coloured colonial-style building. The "fusion" cooking is imaginative and delicious, and there's live music most Wed nights.

Shore Things Old Milford Rd, Lambeau ☎868/635-1072. A delightful café in a brightly painted old house with veranda overlooking the sea. Serves delicious light lunches, pizzas, *pastelles*, quiches and salads plus fresh pastries and fruit juices. High-quality regional crafts and furniture are also on sale. Closed Sun.

La Tartaruga Buccoo Bay ☎868/639-0940. Tobago's best Italian restaurant, with open-air patio near the sea. The select menu features top-class cuisine, including a selection of authentic regional Italian specialities, plus an extensive wine list. Closed Sun.

22

The ABC Islands

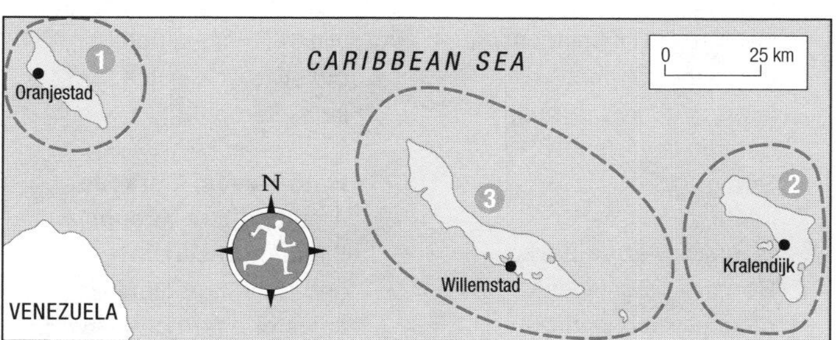

The ABC Islands highlights

* **Aruba's beach strip** Seven kilometres of unspoilt white-sand beaches line the turquoise waters of the island's west coast. See p.805

* **Arikok National Park, Aruba** Explore the Martian-like interior, home to towering stands of cacti, divi divi trees, iguanas and herds of wandering goats. See p.807

* **Pink flamingos, Bonaire** Over 10,000 flamingos grace the saltpans and lakes scattered throughout this tiny island. See p.815

* **Bonaire Marine Park, Bonaire** Magnificent coral gardens harbour vast schools of tropical fish just off the leeward coast. See p.817

* **Willemstad, Curaçao** Stroll along the picturesque waterfront of this UNESCO World Heritage Site and enjoy the city's bustling street life and entertainment scene. See p.822

* **The Kura Hulanda Museum and Hotel** The Caribbean's flagship museum houses a superb and moving collection on slavery and much more, located within a unique hotel in the style of a Dutch village. See p.823

* **Hato Caves, Curaçao** A guided tour through these mystical caves and their incredible flowstone formations will leave you breathless. See p.825

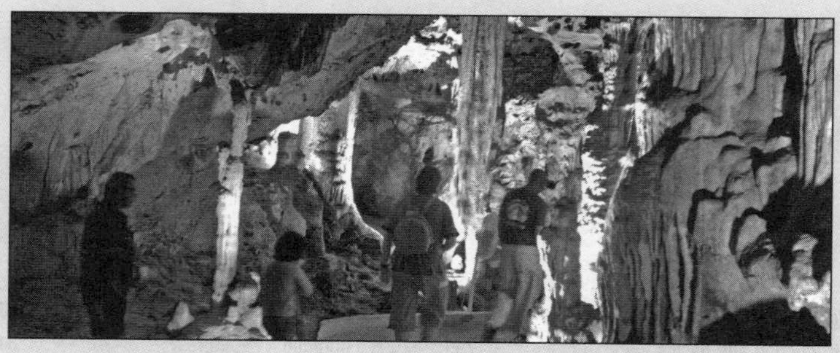

▲ Hato Caves, Curaçao

Introduction and basics

Tucked away from the main Caribbean chain of islands and just north of Venezuela lie Aruba, Bonaire and Curaçao, collectively known as the "ABC islands". Despite similar histories and their former status as part of the Netherlands Antilles, these tiny islands are surprisingly individual, each with its own distinct attractions, identity and feel.

Aruba is the priciest and most touristed of the three islands, attracting mostly American (but also European and Venezuelan) holiday-makers on package vacations and cruises to its glamorous resort complexes, flashy casinos, upscale boutiques and duty-free shops. Laid-back Bonaire, renowned for its phenomenal **diving and snorkelling**, draws a select group of visitors from around the world in search of an outdoors-oriented vacation. Less visited than its smaller neighbours, Curaçao has a more local as well as African-influenced feel, still attracting its share of travellers who come for the fantastic smaller beaches and the charms of the capital city of Willemstad, home to some of the Caribbean's most attractive **colonial architecture** and arguably its best **museum**.

Where to go

Most travellers to Aruba spend their time in the resort areas between **Eagle and Palm beaches** or in the capital of **Oranjestad**, where the casinos, nightclubs and shop-filled streets are the main diversions. Nonetheless, Aruba is not short of natural attractions, mostly based around its rugged northern coastline and the arid landscape of **Arikok National Park**. Interesting rock formations at **Casibari** and **Ayó** along with the fierce coastal *bocas* add to the extreme contrast to resort life.

Divers and snorkellers come to Bonaire to immerse themselves in colourful marine life at the **Bonaire Marine Park**, though they are increasingly tempted from beneath the surface by excellent hiking, caving, kayaking and windsurfing, some of which is found in the **Washington-Slagbaai National Park**. The island is also home to a large number of **pink flamingos** mostly concentrated around the colourful **saltpans** in the south.

Not to be missed on Curaçao is lively **Willemstad**, whose pristine Dutch colonial architecture has earned it the designation of a UNESCO World Heritage Site, and whose cultural entertainments and historical attractions hold much of interest. Away from Willemstad, the best **beaches** and hotels are in the northwest, not far from **Christoffel National Park**, which boasts a variety of flora and fauna and good hiking trails. For something different, take a guided tour of the limestone **Hato Caves** or visit the **plantation houses** scattered about the island.

When to go

The ABC islands are a year-round destination, though **peak tourist season** is mid-December to mid-April when the weather is a little cooler. Sitting outside of the **hurricane belt**, the islands do not experience major storms. The average daytime temperature is 28°C (82°F) and steady trade winds keep the humidity down.

All three islands receive very little **rainfall**, which usually comes in the form of gentle showers between October and March.

Getting there

The majority of visitors to Aruba **fly** to the state-of-the-art **Queen Beatrix International Airport** (☎297/582-4800), a few kilometres south of Oranjestad. Numerous **taxis** wait for passengers outside the arrival terminal. If you are staying at one of the smaller hotels or guesthouses in town, the ride will set you back US$12–15; fares to the hotels along the beach are US$20–30. Alternatively, De Palm Tours (☎297/582-4400) operates an efficient network of air-conditioned **motor coaches** that take visitors to the major beachfront hotels. Round-trip tickets ($20; about 30 min) can be purchased from the booth at the terminal's baggage claim. **Cruise ships** dock at the pier in downtown Oranjestad from where taxis are on hand to take you around the island.

Bonaire's principal gateway, **Flamingo International Airport**, lies 5km south of Kralendijk. The easiest way to reach the capital or your hotel is to take a taxi from outside the terminal; expect to pay around US$12–18. Several **cruise ships** also visit the island every week docking in the heart of Kralendijk, from where taxis are readily available.

On Curaçao, visitors arrive at **Hato International Airport** (☎5999/868-1719), 12km northwest of Willemstad. Numerous car rental agencies, taxis and buses wait for passengers outside. **Taxis** to downtown Willemstad usually cost US$25, while a ride to most hotels outside the city will set you back US$20–40. Most hotels provide a slightly more reasonable **shuttle bus** to and from the airport; **public buses** to Willemstad are frequent and cheap but the journey can take over an hour (US$2). There are two **cruise terminals**, both of them in Willemstad's Otrobanda district. The mega-pier is located near the Riffort by the harbour entrance, a ten-minute walk from downtown. The smaller terminal is closer to downtown in Santa Anna Bay.

Information

The **Aruba Tourism Authority** (ATA) operates a tourist information office near Eagle Beach on L.G. Smith Blvd 172 (Mon–Fri 7.30am–noon & 1–4.30pm; ☎297/582-3777, Ⓦwww.aruba.com). Grab a copy of *Aruba Nights* and *Aruba Experience*, both of which have maps and useful tips on accommodation, restaurants, activities, nightlife and beaches. Decent road maps to the island are available here and at the airport. Ⓦwww.arubatahot.com is also an excellent source of information for accommodation, transport and Aruban culture.

Tourism Corporation Bonaire has a tourist information office in the centre of Kralendijk on Kaya Grandi 2 (Mon–Fri 7.30am–noon & 1.30–5pm; ☎599/717-8322, Ⓦwww.InfoBonaire.com), where you can pick up *Bonaire Nights* and *Bonaire Affair*, two useful free magazines. Brochures and maps are also available at the airport.

The **Curaçao Tourist Board** operates a tourist information office just outside central Punda in Willemstad on Pietermaiiweg 19 (Mon–Fri 8am–5pm & Sat 9am–noon; ☎5999/434-8200, Ⓦwww.curacao.com) and manages booths at the airport and on the Punda side of Queen Emma Bridge. They distribute *Curaçao Nights* and *Curaçao Events* as well as a free guide to beaches and dive sites.

Money and costs

Given the separate political status of the three islands, different currencies are used. **Aruba's official currency** is the **Aruban Florin**, abbreviated as **Afl** and known as the **guilder,** while Bonaire and Curaçao currently use the **Netherlands Antillean Florin** (Naf, also termed guilder) – though Curaçao is currently debating whether to introduce its own Florin. Both currencies are divided into 100 cents and operate at a **fixed exchange rate** against the US$, currently 1.78 florins to US$1. All florin notes come in denominations of 10, 25, 50, 100, 250 and 500, and coins come as 5, 10, 25 and 50 cents, one florin and five florins. **US dollars** in cash are widely accepted at most hotels, restaurants and shops, as are most major credit cards. Banks are found throughout all three islands, with most ATMs located in the capital cities.

Aruba is an **expensive** destination, with all-inclusive holiday **packages** from tour operators usually offering the best value. Travelling **independently**, lodging at the major beachside resorts starts at US$175 per night, though there are a few apartment-style options to be found for US$50–70 a night. Bus travel is cheap and most beaches are free, but even if you're very conscientious you'll need around US$100 a day to get by due to high food prices.

Apart from your flight, **accommodation** and **diving lessons and gear** are likely to be your greatest expenses in Bonaire, particularly if you stay at one of the many **dive resorts** during peak season. A few small guesthouses offer rooms for US$60. If you want to do much exploring on and off the island, count on spending around US$150–200 a day; twice that if you're looking for a more luxurious vacation, less if you're just planning to hike and cycle.

With a **wide range** of accommodation and eating options in and around Willemstad on Curaçao, it's possible to squeak by on a daily budget of less than US$80 a day, though you'll pay closer to double that if you want to take part in any tours or activities.

Getting around

Getting around on all of the islands is fairly straightforward, thanks to their small size. In most cases, however, you'll need to rent a car or taxi if you want to explore beyond the capitals and resort areas. Note that there are no longer ferry services between the three islands; instead there are a good network of **flight companies**: Tiara Air (ⓣ297/582-0901, ⓦwww.tiara-air.com) operates the most comprehensive service from Aruba to both Curacao and Bonaire, while Divi Divi Air (ⓣ5999/839-1515, ⓦwww.flydivi.com) offers the best fares on the Curacao–Bonaire route.

By bus

Aruba has an inexpensive and frequent daily **bus** service linking Oranjestad with all the major areas. The main **bus terminal** is located across from the Port of Call Shopping Centre; route #10 services downtown Oranjestad and the hotel strip between Eagle Beach and Palm Beach. Tickets can be purchased directly from the driver (US$1.45 one-way; US$2.25 round-trip; local or US currencies used; limited change available).

On Curaçao, buses run to all the major towns and districts, but the system is confusing, very slow and rarely used by visitors. Bus terminals are located outside the post office in Punda and near the police station in Otrobanda.

Bonaire has no public bus system.

By car

By far the easiest way to get around all three islands is with a **rented vehicle**, and all of the major rental agencies operate booths at the airports and at some hotels.

While many of the major roads in Aruba and Bonaire are in excellent condition, you'd be wise to rent a **jeep** or **pick-up truck** (from US$350/week) if you're planning to explore either of their national parks or if you need to haul around bulky scuba equipment. Rentals are handled at the airports and they will usually deliver the car to your hotel. Bear in mind that many of the **main highways** on Aruba are labelled according to the direction you are travelling (you may be driving east on 7A, but as soon as you turn around, the same road is referred to as 7B).

By taxi

Taxis on the ABC islands are very safe and reliable, and can be hired from hotels, hailed from the street or requested by calling the central dispatch. **Rates** are fixed according to zones (there are no meters). Sightseeing tours around each island average US$30/hour on Aruba and Curaçao, and US$30 for a half-day on Bonaire; in all cases prices cover up to four passengers.

On Aruba, a ride from the capital to Eagle Beach costs US$8 and US$9 to Palm Beach for up to four people. Add an extra US$2 if you're travelling after midnight and US$4 on Sundays and holidays. For pick-up call the central dispatch (ⓣ297/582-2116 or 582-1604).

On Bonaire, expect to pay US$6 to US$12 to travel from downtown to most area hotels; US$18 to Lac Bay. A **surcharge** applies for more than four passengers and fares increase by 25 percent after 6pm and by another 50 percent after midnight. Call the central dispatch (ⓣ599/717-8100) for a pick-up.

On Curaçao a ride from the south-eastern hotels to downtown Willemstad costs upwards of US$12, and close to US$20 from the beaches further south; fares increase by 25 percent after 11pm. Call the central dispatch (ⓣ5999/869-0752) to arrange a pick-up.

By bike or scooter

Renting a **mountain bike** or **scooter** is a good option on Bonaire, where less traffic and many unpaved roads make this a

Local dishes

Aros bruin	brown rice
Funchi	cornmeal
Galina	chicken
Giambo	okra soup
Hobi duchi	cactus soup with pork, fish and/or shrimp
Kabritu	goat meat
Karni stoba	beef stew
Moro	rice and peas
Papaja stoba	papaya stew with pig's tail and corn beef
Piska kora	red snapper, usually deep-fried whole
Piska mula	wahoo, usually deep-fried
Snijboonchi	green beans
Sopi karni-piska	meat or fish soup

pleasant way to see the island's unspoilt beauty. Bike and scooter rental agencies are found in Kralendijk (see "Listings", p.818). Plan on spending US$12–20 per day for a bike or US$18–25 per day for a scooter.

Heavy traffic on Curaçao and Aruba make these islands unsuitable for scooters, though mountain biking in the national parks is still possible.

Food and drink

Dining out is a clear highlight of all three islands, where countless excellent chefs serve a wide range of international cuisines in atmospheric surroundings. Perhaps surprisingly, Bonaire has the best variety and most reasonably priced selection of the three, whereas on Aruba dining out tends to be an elegant and expensive affair, with a crop of top-class restaurants. Nonetheless, a number of good, reasonably priced options are also to be found there. Curaçao is less expensive than Aruba and caters to all tastes and budgets.

You'll find imported beer and wine at most restaurants and bars, as well as the locally produced beers – Aruba's **Balashi** and Curaçao's **Amstel Bright**. The islands' popular cocktails include the local liqueur **Curaçao Blue**, made from the peels of the Valencia orange. You'll also find delicious fruit drinks and smoothies sold at many snack stands.

Popular **local dishes** on all three islands include goat or conch stew, iguana soup, **chicken** and **beef**, as well as fried or stewed **fish** such as red snapper, wahoo and barracuda. Not-to-be-missed **Aruban specialities** include *stoba*, goat stew with vegetables; *soppi di pisca*, a fish soup made with coconut milk; freshly caught red snapper or wahoo served with plantain or *funchi* (cornmeal); and *keshi yena*, a baked mixture of Gouda cheese stuffed with beef, fish or chicken and seasoned with spices, raisins, tomatoes and olives. For dessert or for a snack try the mildly sweet *pan bati*, which is similar to a thick pancake. You'll find similar local dishes on Bonaire and Curaçao, with slight variations in their names. On Curaçao, look out for lunchtime **snack stands** and bars which serve scrumptious **local food**, always cooked on an open grill and normally costing less than US$8.

Prices at dinner will on average set you back US$20–30, though you'll pay upwards of twice that at the finer restaurants on Aruba. A 10–15 percent **service charge** is normally included your bill, though it's not uncommon to add a little extra at your discretion (especially on Aruba where this is customary). **Reservations** are recommended on all three islands, especially during high season.

Mail and communications

Payphones are located all over Aruba and Curaçao, almost all requiring **phonecards**, which are available from shops or vendors. On Bonaire there are payphones outside

Country codes

Aruba ⓣ297
Bonaire ⓣ599
Curaçao ⓣ5999

Emergency numbers

Aruba
Police ⓣ100
Fire/ambulance ⓣ115
Hospital ⓣ87 4300

Bonaire
Police ⓣ133
Fire ⓣ191
Hospital/ambulance ⓣ114

Curaçao
Police/fire ⓣ911
Ambulance ⓣ912
Hospital ⓣ910

the **TELBO office** near the tourist office (purchase phone cards from the vending machine next to the office), at the airport and elsewhere in town. Aside from these, you're likely to be stuck calling from hotels – which charge exorbitant rates.

On Aruba, international calls are best made from the **SETAR telephone office** in the Royal Plaza in downtown Oranjestad (daily 8am–9.30pm) or at the Internet call centre on Palm Beach (see Aruba listings). A few specially marked telephone booths where you can reach the international operator are available at the cruise terminal and airport.

On Curaçao, it's best to make international calls from Willemstad where there are a couple of privately run **Internet call** centres in Otrobanda and Punda, as well as a few specially designated telephone **booths** which have direct access to the international operator, allowing you to use your calling card or credit card.

The **postal systems** on all three islands are relatively efficient, and **Internet access** is available at hotels and a handful of locations in the capitals (see "Listings" sections for individual islands).

Opening hours, holidays and festivals

On all three islands, most shops and business are normally **open** Monday to Saturday 8am–noon and 2–6pm, with a few places opening on Sunday mornings if cruise ships are in port. **Banks** are generally open Monday to Friday 8am–3.30pm, and some close for lunch; the bank at Curaçao's airport is open Monday to Saturday 8am–8pm and on Sundays 9am–4pm.

Of the many festivals and celebrations on the islands, the one that all three share is **Carnival**, which on Aruba and Bonaire officially begins three days before Lent, and is celebrated with parades, steel bands, costumes and colourful floats. Curaçao's is the liveliest, with a month-long Carnival season kicking off on New Year's Day, and culminating in a grand parade on the day before Ash Wednesday. See ⓦcuracaocarnival.info if you would like to participate in the parades. Emotions run high during the four-day **Tumba festival**, a preamble to Carnival, when local musicians compete to have their piece (*tumba*) selected as the official road song.

May to October on Aruba signifies the **"One Cool Summer"** festival, which features concerts, traditional food, cultural and sporting events including: the **Hi Winds Pro-Am Windsurfing competition** in June, which draws international competitors of all ages and skill levels; **Dera Gai** on June 24, a folkloric celebration commemorating

Public holidays

The following holidays are observed on all three islands, unless specified otherwise.

January 1 New Year's Day
January 25 G.F. Croes Day (Aruba)
Monday before Ash Wednesday Carnival Monday (Aruba)
March 18 National Anthem and Flag Day (Aruba)
March/April Good Friday and Easter Monday
April 30 Queen's Birthday and Rincon Day (Bonaire)
May 1 Labour Day
May 24 Ascension Day
July 2 Curaçao Flag Day
September 6 Bonaire Flag Day
December 25 and 26 Christmas
December 31 New Year's Eve

Useful Papiamento phrases

Welcome	*Bon bini*
Good morning	*Bon dia*
Good afternoon	*Bon tardi*
Good evening	*Bon nochi*
How are you?	*Con ta bai?*
I am fine	*Mi ta bon*
Have a good day	*Pasa bon dia*
Thank you	*Masha danki*
Goodbye	*Ayo*
You're welcome	*Di nada*
Very good!	*Hopi bon*
See you later	*Te aworo*

the harvest; and the annual **Festival de las Americas** in October, a music celebration showcasing the unique rhythms of the Americas.

Outside Carnival, Bonaireans have a number of events to look forward to: the **Simadan harvest festival** in Rincon in April, when locals pay tribute to the farmers with traditional music and costumes; the week-long **Bonaire Dive Festival** in June, when activities and games focus on raising awareness of the importance of the coral reefs; and the **International Sailing Regatta** in October. The events of the preceding twelve months are recapped in song and dance during the colourful **Bari Festival** held in December.

Curaçao hosts a **regatta** (late Jan or early Feb), when sailors from around the world compete in races near Willemstad; a **Jazz Festival** in May; and a **Salsa Festival** (dates vary in summer), which attracts popular international stars.

Language

The **official language** of the ABC islands is **Dutch**, although **English** and **Spanish** are spoken by almost everyone. In the home and on the street locals speak **Papiamento**, a Creole language that developed in Curaçao in the 1500s between the African slaves and their owners. It quickly spread to Aruba and Bonaire and has evolved over time, incorporating Portuguese, Spanish, Dutch and English elements from the plethora of merchants, missionaries and colonizers who have visited the islands. Written Papiamento is now more commonplace and a strong movement exists to formalize it in place of Dutch as the school teaching language.

History

The first inhabitants of the ABC islands were the **Caiquitìos Indians**, an Arawak-speaking tribe from South America who established themselves on all three of the islands centuries before the arrival of the **Spanish** in 1499. In the years that followed, more Spaniards settled here in search of precious metals and drinking water. Not finding any gold or silver, they quickly dubbed the ABCs "las islas inutiles" or the "useless islands". (In fact, they should have looked harder on Aruba where over three million pounds of gold were discovered in the nineteenth century.)

Disappointed by the lack of natural resources, the Spanish **enslaved** many of the Amerindians and shipped them to Hispaniola to labour in the mines and plantations there. Returning in the mid-1520s to colonize the ABCs, the Spaniards introduced cattle and other livestock, and brought back many of the original slaves to work in agriculture.

During the early 1630s the **Dutch**, on a quest for a suitable Caribbean base from which to launch attacks against the

Spanish, took control of Aruba, Bonaire and Curaçao, and the next century saw a drastic increase in commerce on all three islands.

Prized for its naturally deep harbour, its strategic location and its **saltpans** (salt was an important commodity for preserving fish and meat shipped back to Europe), Curaçao quickly developed into an important Dutch naval base. Bonaire was also valued for its vast quantities of salt and tracts of agricultural land left behind by the Spaniards. The **Dutch West India Company** began exporting large amounts of salt, along with sorghum, maize, divi divi pods (used in the tanning process) and meat to Europe and to the rest of the world. They also imported livestock to Aruba for the sole purpose of feeding the many slaves and colonists living on Curaçao.

Curaçao, in fact, became the Caribbean's busiest **slave depot** during the seventeenth century, despite minimal agricultural land. The Dutch and Portuguese shipped tens of thousands of Africans to the island to work the salt fields and the so-called "**plantations**"– in fact holding houses where slaves were broken in to their new roles and troublemakers were weeded out, before they were sold on to plantation owners from across the Caribbean and Brazil. Slavery was finally abolished in the ABCs in 1863, after which the Dutch West India Company closed most of the plantations.

Economic prospects were bleak until the discovery of rich **oilfields** off the coast of Venezuela at the beginning of the twentieth century, which proved to be a boon for all three of the islands. Aruba and Curaçao both built refineries, attracting workers from Bonaire and around the world until they closed in the mid-1980s. While the oil and salt industries remain important today, it was the **tourism initiatives** of the 1990s that revived the islands' economies, providing jobs for a substantial number of their populations, particularly on Aruba and Bonaire.

The history of the ABCs is easily reflected upon today, where distinct ethnic and cultural differences between each island provide a glimpse of the changing patterns in **migration** over the centuries. Aruba is noticeably more Amerindian and European than African, for example, while Curaçao maintains a number of very African music, dance and art forms. Each island has also experienced a massive influx of Colombians, Venezuelans and other Caribbean nationals in recent years, all in search of wealth in this prosperous corner of the Caribbean, and themselves altering the islands' face once again.

22.1

Aruba

The smallest of the ABC islands – only 30km long and barely 100,000 residents – **ARUBA** receives more than one million visitors a year who come to indulge in the glitz associated with its luxurious beachside resorts, elegant restaurants, boutiques, vibrant 24-hour nightlife and casinos and enjoy its seemingly endless supply of white sandy beaches and turquoise waters. As a result, it can feel rather crowded and, at times, a little lacking in soul.

The harbourside capital **Oranjestad** attracts many of the visitors, as do resort-filled **Eagle** and **Palm beaches** just north of town. In stark contrast to these glamorous areas, the rugged interior is dotted with stands of cacti, twisted divi divi trees and herds of wandering goats. In the Mars-like landscape of **Arikok National Park**, mysterious boulders painted with ancient petroglyphs and limestone caves are sights worth catching.

Gold was discovered here in 1824, but the real economic boom began in the early 1900s when **oil** was discovered off the coast of Venezuela and a refinery was built at **San Nicolas**. After the oil supply's decline in the 1980s, the Aruban government turned to large-scale **tourism**. Seeking more independence and greater control of its finances from the Netherlands, Aruba gained *status aparte* in 1986, thus allowing Arubans to have their own parliament, flag, currency and more freedom in their internal affairs. Today more than half of the population is employed by the flourishing tourism industry and Arubans enjoy a higher standard of living than those on most other Caribbean islands.

Though not seriously rivalling Bonaire for diving, Aruba has some exciting **dive sites** scattered along its northwestern coast, including a few shipwrecks. Dive centres located at many of the hotels arrange charter boat tours. There are also excellent **windsurfing** conditions on the island at Hadicurari, and the best **snorkelling** is found still further north at Malmok and Arashi.

Accommodation

Aruba is small enough that you can pretty much base yourself anywhere and be close to all activities and attractions. Downtown Oranjestad doesn't offer much **accommodation**; the majority of resorts and hotels are located along the main **seafront strip** between Eagle and Palm beaches, and most of the affordable guesthouses and apartments are located a little further afield.

Oranjestad

Renaissance Aruba Resort & Casino L.G. Smith Blvd 82 ⓣ297/583-6000, ⓦwww.marriott.com. There is no lack of activity at this enormous resort in the heart of downtown with onsite restaurants, bars, pools, boutiques, fitness centres and a casino. The 500+ rooms are spacious and have balconies affording spectacular views. The real treat is free access to a private island just a fifteen-min boat ride away. ⑨

The beach strip and northwest tip

Amsterdam Manor Hotel Eagle Beach ⓣ297/587-1492, ⓦwww.amsterdammanor.com. This friendly 72-room hotel on excellent Eagle Beach has its own swimming pool, sports facilities and beach bar. Justifiably popular and with many repeat visitors, the hotel is known for its excellent food at onsite *Mango* restaurant and its great family rates. ⑥

Aruba Beach Villas across from Hadicurari Beach on L.G. Smith Blvd 462 ⓣ297/586-1072,

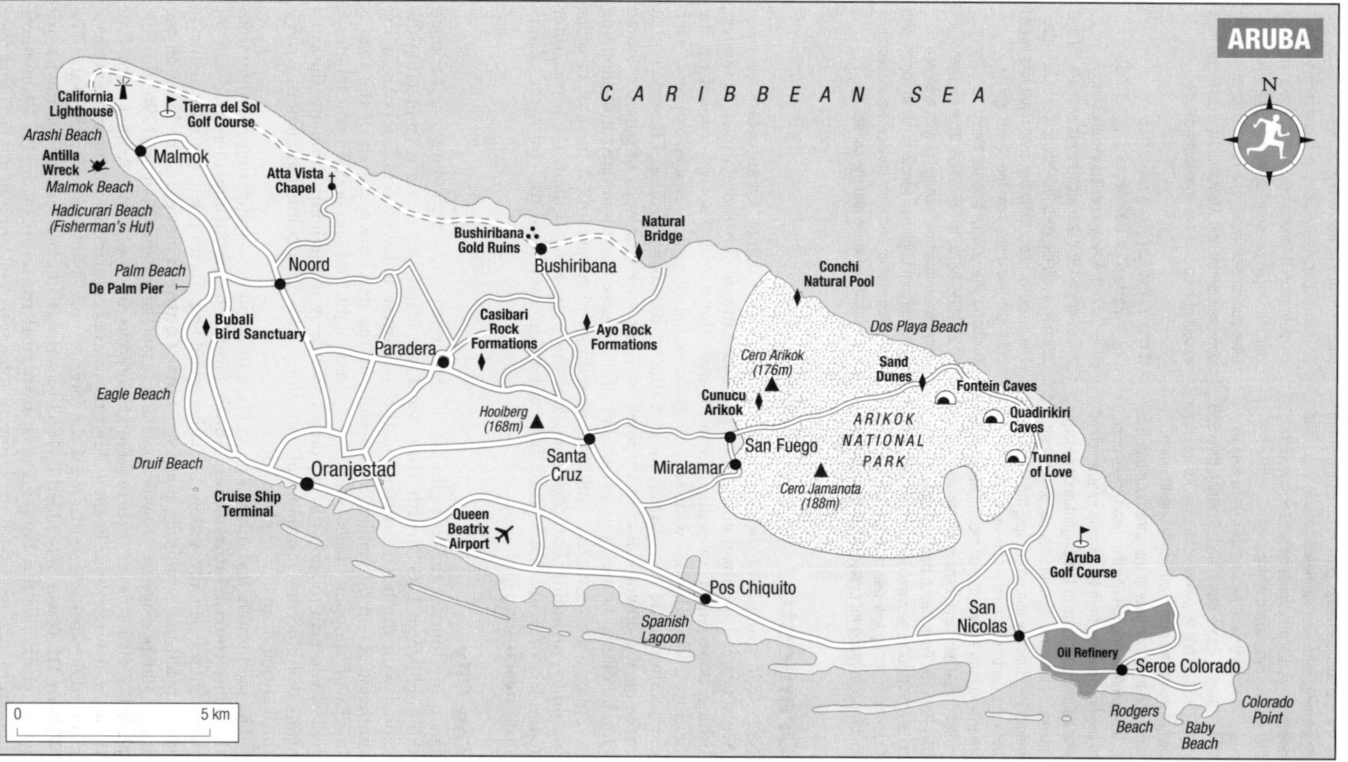
ARUBA
CARIBBEAN SEA
N
California Lighthouse
Tierra del Sol Golf Course
Arashi Beach
Malmok
Antilla Wreck
Malmok Beach
Hadicurari Beach (Fisherman's Hut)
Atta Vista Chapel
Bushiribana Gold Ruins
Natural Bridge
Bushiribana
Noord
Palm Beach
De Palm Pier
Conchi Natural Pool
Bubali Bird Sanctuary
Casibari Rock Formations
Ayo Rock Formations
Dos Playa Beach
Paradera
Cero Arikok (176m)
Sand Dunes
Fontein Caves
Eagle Beach
Cunucu Arikok
Hooiberg (168m)
Quadirikiri Caves
ARIKOK NATIONAL PARK
San Fuego
Santa Cruz
Miralamar
Tunnel of Love
Druif Beach
Oranjestad
Cero Jamanota (188m)
Cruise Ship Terminal
Queen Beatrix Airport
Aruba Golf Course
Pos Chiquito
San Nicolas
Spanish Lagoon
Oil Refinery
Seroe Colorado
0
5 km
Rodgers Beach
Baby Beach
Colorado Point

Ⓦwww.arubabeachvillas.com. Rooms range from apartments with kitchenettes to private villas with ocean views. Location popular with windsurfers; low season rates are half price. ❹

Bucuti Beach Resort and Tara Beach Suites Eagle Beach on L.G. Smith Blvd 55B Ⓣ297/583-1100, Ⓦwww.bucuti.com. An exquisite owner-managed resort with sixty one-bedroom units and a further forty in the ultra-luxurious Tara Suites annexe. Adults-only, the resort takes pride in the finer details, from the champagne welcome and helpful concierge to the elegant and modern interiors. All rooms have a/c, phone, private bath, fridge, TVs, balcony and onsite spa, fitness and business centres. The major bonus is *Bucuti's* award-winning environmental record. Rates include buffet breakfast; meal plans available. ❾

Divi Resorts Palm Beach on J.E. Irausquin Blvd 75 Ⓣ297/583-5000, Ⓦwww.diviresorts.com. These four neighbouring low-rise resorts and casinos aim to have something for everyone. An all-inclusive pass from any of the resorts allows access to all four properties, including golf and tennis with resident pros, a fitness centre, spa, pools, climbing wall, and eight restaurants and six bars. Rooms have pool or sea views. The resort's flagship *Windows* restaurant and *Mulligans* bar/restaurant have excellent food and live entertainment. ❾

The rest of the island

Perle d'Or Boegoeroei 11, Ⓣ297/587-7710, Ⓦwww.perledoraruba.com. Amazingly good-value apartments with a/c, TV and balcony, available on both a student or hotel rate. The property has a lively bar, restaurant and large pool, just two miles from the beach. ❷

Turibana Plaza Apartments Noord 124, Noord Ⓣ297/586-8872, Ⓕ586-2658. This excellent-value small apartment complex with eighteen two-bedroom units has spacious, clean rooms with a/c, kitchenettes and daily service. Near several restaurants, beaches and the capital. ❷

Oranjestad

Named in honour of the Dutch Royal House of Orange, **Oranjestad** has been Aruba's capital and main port since 1797. Today, the small harbour attracts schooners, fishing boats and cruise ships from all over the world. The tiny capital on the southwest shore bustles with activity as thousands of visitors descend upon it each day to shop, dine or try their luck at one of the many casinos. The streets that make up the downtown core are lined with modern imitations of pastel-coloured Dutch colonial houses; a good number of them have been renovated into shopping complexes, administrative buildings, museums and restaurants. A handful of older buildings, including Fort Zoutman and the lofty King Willem III Tower, offer reminders of Aruba's past. Just a hop and a skip away from the city is the island's main **beach strip** and resort area.

The City

For many tourists, the first glimpse of Oranjestad is along the busy palm-fringed thoroughfare of **L.G. Smith Boulevard**, the island's main artery, connecting the capital with the hotel district and the northwest and with San Nicholas in the southeast. Running parallel to the harbour, the downtown stretch of the road is lined with shopping malls, boutiques, casinos, nightclubs and government buildings. Unless you plan to shop till you drop or while away the hours gambling, the city's sights won't occupy too much of your time – the city's cultural attractions cover a small area and are best explored on foot.

The picturesque harbour is a good place to begin your wanderings. Starting from the white **tourist information booth** adjacent to the Atlantis Pier, head east for five minutes past the yellow parliament building. Turning left onto Oranjestraat, you'll reach the beautifully preserved **Fort Zoutman**, the oldest building on the island and perhaps the town's most important landmark. Built in 1796, the fort played a vital role in securing Dutch interests on the island. Armed with four cannons, it was originally sited along the coast; centuries of shifting currents have changed the coastline so that today the fort sits some 300m away from the water. The **Willem III Tower** was added in 1868 to serve as a lighthouse and the town's first public clock. The fort houses a small **historical museum** (Mon–Fri 10am–noon, 1.30pm to 4.30pm; US$8) displaying an interesting collection of artefacts that trace

Shopping

Duty-free **shopping** is an irresistible draw for many visitors to Aruba. Bargain-hunters crowd the heart of the shopping district, where malls, boutiques and craft shops line the main streets of L.G. Smith Boulevard, Havenstraat and Caya G.F. Betico Croes. Most stores are full of imported goods such as fragrances, linens, liquors, gold jewellery, watches, cameras, name-brand fashions and Dutch porcelain figurines. Malls of note are the **Renaissance Mall** within the luxurious *Renaissance Beach Resort and Casino*, the nearby **Royal Plaza Mall**, at the corner of Weststraat and L.G. Smith Blvd, and the open-air **Seaport Marketplace** on the east side of the harbour and across L.G. Smith Blvd. Shops are open Monday to Saturday 8am–6.30pm; many close for lunch between noon and 2pm. A small cluster of craft stalls selling typical souvenirs and wooden handicrafts can also be found at the Wharfside Market on L.G. Smith Blvd.

Aruba's history. Its open-air courtyard also hosts the weekly folkloric **Bon Bini Festival** (Tues 6.30–8.30pm; US$5), which features traditional music and dance, and is the best place to try local dishes.

One block east, on Zuidstraat 27, is the fascinating **Numismatic Museum** (Mon–Thurs 9am–4pm, Fri-Sat 9am–12pm; free), home to over 30,000 historical coins from Aruba and around the world dating back to 220 BC. Some of the many highlights include a display of Aruban Indian shells used for barter, beads used as money by Caquetios Amerindians and notes made of silk and linen.

At the north end of the city the tiny **Archeological Museum**, J.E. Irausquin Blvd 2-A (Mon–Fri 8am–noon & 1–4pm; free), has an impressive array of local artefacts and pottery, including stone tools from 2000 BC, pottery from 500 AD and skeletal remains excavated from an Indian burial site.

Back near the harbour, around the corner from the Seaport Casino, is the quiet **Wilhelmina Park**, honouring the 1955 visit of Queen Juliana of the Netherlands, a white marble statue of whom dominates the plaza. The park is especially striking when tropical plants are in bloom between June and October. Benches set amongst the shady grove of trees makes this an ideal place to rest after sightseeing or a long day of shopping.

The beach strip and the northwest tip

Easily reached from J.E. Irausquin Boulevard, which intersects L.G. Smith Boulevard, the best **beaches**, **watersports facilities** and **hotels** are found along the famous gold coast on the leeward side (northwest) of the island. Here, Aruba's best 7km of fine white sand and turquoise waters stretch between Eagle Beach and Palm Beach. Further northwest, good conditions coupled with a handful of colourful coral reefs and sunken ships attract **windsurfers**, **divers** and **snorkellers**.

Eagle Beach and Palm Beach

Eagle Beach is the largest and most popular sandy stretch along this excellent strand, offering plenty of shade and watersports activities. Several low-rise hotels allow beach-goers to eat and drink at their restaurants and bars. Divi Winds (see box, p.806) offers windsurfing and sailing lessons, and rents boards, kayaks and snorkelling gear. A few kilometres north on J.E. Irausquin Boulevard is **Palm Beach**, known for its luxurious high-rise resorts and more superb watersports. De Palm Tours operates a pier here from which many of their water-based tours and activities originate (see box, p.806). The surrounding shallow waters and long stretches of clean sand are very popular with families. It gets crowded at weekends and holidays, during which time food stalls selling local dishes are set up.

A couple of diversions are in the area if you're looking to take a break from the beach. Naturalists will delight in the more than forty species of butterfly fluttering

Watersports and activities

Aruba offers a wide selection of excellent watersports and related activities.

Snorkelling trips to coral reefs and shipwrecks can be arranged with Fun Factory Sailing Adventure (ⓣ297/586-2017), departing daily from behind the *Radisson Hotel* at 10am. The four-hour trip (US$65) includes an open bar, hot buffet lunch, snorkelling gear and visits to a couple of reefs and to the *Antilla*, a sunken World War II German freighter off the coast of Malmok.

Diving lessons and packages can be arranged with Pelican Watersports (ⓣ297/587-2302, ⓦwww.pelican-aruba.com) located next to De Palm Pier, Red Sail Sports (ⓣ297/586-1603, ⓦwww.redsailaruba.com) behind the *Hyatt Regency Resort* on Palm Beach, who also do night dives, and JADS (ⓣ297/584-6070, ⓦwww.jadsaruba.com) at Baby Beach near San Nicholas, who specialize in the less-visited reefs, cliff jump dives and 007-style underwater scooters. One-and two-tank dives cost around US$50–75; a fully certified Open Water Certification course will set you back around US$400.

Kayaking trips can be undertaken with Aruba Kayak Adventure (ⓣ297/582-5520, ⓦwww.arubakayak.com; US$99 including hotel pick-up, instruction, lunch and snorkelling gear), who offer a four-hour guided kayaking trip along the southern coast and through Spanish Lagoon, a legendary hiding place for pirates.

Deep-sea fishing for marlin, wahoo, kingfish or barracuda can be arranged by calling Pair-a-dice Charters on ⓣ297/592-9586; half-day charters run from US$300. Excellent **fly-fishing** excursions for bonefish, barracuda or tarpon are organized by local enthusiasts through ⓦwww.flyfishingaruba.com; free.

Sailing and sunset tours are offered by Jolly Pirates (ⓣ297/586-8107; ⓦwww.jolly-pirates.com), who operate a 70-ton schooner and organize great fun sailing and snorkelling trips departing from MooMba Beach (starting at US$33), while Mi Dushi Sailing Adventures (ⓣ297/586-2010; ⓦwww.midushi.com) sets sail Tuesday and Thursday on a sunset & snorkelling cruise (US$35). Both have open bars throughout the cruise.

Windsurfing lessons (US$55), sailing lessons (US$60) and board rental (US$20/hr) are offered by Divi Winds (ⓣ297/583-7841), between the *Divi* and *Tamarijn* resorts. At Hadicurari Beach, Aruba Active Vacations (ⓣ297/586-0989) also rents windsurfers at US$20 per hour or US$55 for the day; lessons are US$135/full-day. ⓦwww.kitesurfingaruba.com (ⓣ297/586-5025) offers **kitesurfing** in the same area; it's US$120 for a two-and-a-half-hour lesson.

Submarine trips on board the island's sole craft, *The Atlantis*, are an exciting way to explore Aruba's underwater realm (ⓣ297/583-7077; departing from Atlantis Pier opposite *Renaissance Resort*; adults US$89, children half price), descending to 150ft where you can view schools of tropical fish, coral reefs and the remains of the *Mi Dushi* shipwreck.

about the gardens of the **Butterfly Farm** (daily 9am–4pm; US$12, US$6 children), located on J.E. Irausquin Boulevard across from the *Divi Phoenix Beach Resort*. Around the corner, the **Bubali Bird Sanctuary** is a small oasis of marshland, sheltering hundreds of species of migratory waterfowl. A viewing platform atop a tower allows you to observe the grebes, terns, herons, cormorants and coots, among others.

The northwest tip

Further north along L.G. Smith Boulevard is **Hadicurari**, locally referred to as Fisherman's Hut Beach, a popular **windsurfing** and **kitesurfing** destination and host to the Hi Winds Pro-Am Windsurfing Challenge held each June. A couple of boardsailing companies offer windsurfing lessons and board rentals (see box above).

Superb snorkelling, diving and swimming can be had near the northern tip of the island at **Malmok** and **Arashi beaches**. Several coral reefs and offshore shipwrecks are worth checking out – you'll need a boat to get to them.

Overlooking the northwestern tip of the island is the towering yellow **California Lighthouse**, a favourite place to enjoy sunset. Built in 1914 on top of a small hill and sandwiched between sand dunes, this 125-foot lighthouse was named in honour of a British steamship, the *California*, shipwrecked off the coast in 1891. The lighthouse is operational and remains closed to the public.

From here, an off-road track continues south-eastwards along the coast to the Alta Vista Chapel (see below) and beyond, fairly easily navigable in an ATV or jeep.

The north coast and around

Leaving the beach district behind, Highway 4A heads east to Aruba's rugged north coast and its barren interior. Past the small community of Paradera, a series of road signs direct you to the mysterious **rock formations** of **Casibari** and nearby **Ayû**. Resembling something out of *The Flintstones*, nobody knows for sure how these smooth, monolithic diorite boulders came to be here, particularly because their geology is so different from that of the rest of the island. Also a mystery is the origin of the ancient **petroglyphs** found on a few of these boulders; the weathered vestiges of these paintings can be seen through protective steel bars. Both Casibari and Ayû offer well-groomed trails through the rock gardens, while steps carved into the boulders allow you to climb up for a panoramic view of the island and nearby **Hooiberg**, a 168-metre hill resembling a haystack.

Continuing north from Ayû, a gravel road leads to the **Bushiribana Gold Ruins**, the site of a gold smelter on the coast that was operational for most of the nineteenth century. Constructed with natural rock in 1825, the smelter processed over three million tons of raw material from the nearby mines before it was abandoned some ninety years later. The crumbling ruins stand as a testament to Aruba's rich gold history, but unfortunately there are no guides on hand.

A short distance away, the road turns east and follows the coast for 2.5km until it ends at the remains of a hundred-foot **Natural Bridge**, formerly the most photographed attraction on the island until it collapsed in 2007. It's still an attractive spot, however, with surf pounding a small sandy beach, accessible by a set of stairs from the parking lot. A large café and gift shop sells refreshments and snacks by the car park.

Finally, sitting on top of a hill overlooking the north coast, the charming **Alta Vista Chapel**, 5km west of the gold mine ruins, was the first Catholic chapel on the island. It was originally built by Spanish missionaries in 1750 and renovated two hundred years later. A necklace with a Spanish cross on display in the chapel dates back to the time of the original missionaries and is believed to be the oldest of its kind in the Dutch-speaking islands. To get there, head west along the coastal gravel road from the gold ruins or take Highway 2B north from the town of **Noord** for 0.5km and turn right at the narrow road which winds uphill to the chapel (3.3km).

Arikok National Park

The untamed beauty of Aruba is best experienced in **Arikok National Park**, a large protected area encompassing almost twenty percent of the island's landmass. The park's desert landscape looks more like the Australian outback than a tropical Caribbean island, and is interspersed with bizarre patches of reddish-orange rock and soil formations. The hilly interior also reveals several abandoned gold mines and traditional country homes, while Arikok's rugged coastline is littered with sand dunes, grottoes and secluded bays. Growing throughout are groves of towering cacti, contorted divi divi trees and other thorny plants, and the area is populated by burrowing owls, fruit-eating bats, lizards and herds of wandering goats.

A potholed dirt road and 34km of well-marked **hiking trails** allow visitors to see the park at their own pace. Access is via Highway 7A, which leads to the **park gate** near the town of San Fuego. Past the entrance, the highway turns into a narrow dirt road and continues to the coast before it heads south towards San Nicolas. A jeep is recommended (a car will do in fine weather), as is sunscreen, water and a hat. Guidebooks with **trail maps** can be purchased for US$15 at the gate.

Exploring the park

A sign posted shortly beyond the entrance will direct you to a **fork** in the road. Straight ahead leads to the coast, dunes and caves; heading right will bring you uphill to **Cunucu Arikok**, a small rocky garden surrounded by a stone and cactus-lined wall. A neighbouring building houses a small **museum** displaying a scant collection of photos, tools and animal specimens. Inside the enclosure a 1.5km trail guides visitors past several species of plants as well as **rock formations** similar to those found in Ayû and Casibari. A **petroglyph** of an ancient bird is painted on one of these boulders. Close to the centre of the garden is a **cas di torta**, a traditional nineteenth-century house with a typical construction out of rocks and dried cactus husks held together with layers of mud and grass.

A short drive uphill from the garden will take you to the top of **Cero Arikok** (176m), where you'll be rewarded with a spectacular panoramic view. If you want to explore the coastline, head back to the fork in the road at the main gate, and then take the road heading east for 5km. Along the way there is a 4km hiking trail (watch for signs shortly after the fork) that leads to the gold pits of **Miralamar** and the foot of **Cero Jamanota**, Aruba's highest peak (188m). Hiking conditions are relatively easy.

Gently rolling white **sand dunes** mark the beginning of the coastline. The secluded **Dos Playa** beach can be reached by turning left at the dunes and continuing along the road for 1.5km. Swimming is not recommended – the surf is too dangerous – but it's an ideal place for a picnic. Past the dunes, southeast along the cost for another 200m is a small **restaurant** (daily 10am–6pm) serving a good selection of burgers, chicken and seafood dishes and other munchies for US$10–20.

Turning right at the restaurant, the road leads to the **Fontein Caves**, a collection of small grottoes that were once occupied by native peoples. Centuries of graffiti, brownish-red Indian rock paintings and beautiful flowstone formations adorn the walls and ceilings of these limestone caves. Fruit-eating bats roost during the day and fly out at night. Free tours are offered every fifteen minutes by the park rangers; flash photography is not permitted.

Adjacent to the caves is the **Fontein Garden** (Place Hofi Fontein), the site of a nineteenth-century **plantation** run by the Gravenhorst-Croes family. This was the only place on the north coast where permanent running fresh water was available throughout the year, which helped the plantation's development.

San Nicolas and the southeast tip

Up until the late nineteenth century, **San Nicolas**, the oldest city in Aruba, existed as a fishing settlement with a few small huts scattered along the southeast coast. All that changed in 1879 when locally mined **phosphate** began to be exported to the US. Subsequent demand prompted officials to build houses for an expanding workforce, and the makings of the town began. In addition, after vast oilfields were discovered off the coast of Venezuela during the early part of the twentieth century, the Largo Oil and Transport Company announced plans to build an **oil refinery** near town. Oil giant Exxon arrived in 1927, and soon the population grew to just over 20,000 residents – twice the size of the town's current population. New luxurious suburbs of Largo Heights and Cero Colorado sprung up, and hordes of workers flocked here from all over the Caribbean, ensuring San Nicholas' status as a predominantly English speaking enclave.

When the refinery closed in 1985, the city was left in a shambles. Things brightened up a bit in 1991 when Coastal Aruba Refining reopened the refinery, but the town hasn't got much to offer – there are a few old buildings that give a glimpse of the British-Caribbean charm of the town's glory days. A handful of restaurants, snack stalls and shops selling local crafts and souvenirs can be found alongside the picturesque promenade on Zeppenfeldstraat, and a requisite stop is the legendary *Charlie's Bar*, which dates back to 1941 (see below). San Nicholas also maintains a policy of legalized prostitution in regulated gentleman's clubs which line the main street near *Charlie's*; the clubs' Colombian workers can be seen all over town.

About 6km east of San Nicolas are two small popular public **beaches**. To reach them, take Fortheuvelstraat out of town until you come to a huge cement anchor at the end of the road. Turn right on the main road and follow the signs to **Rodger's Beach**, which, despite a view of the nearby oil refinery, is a good spot with decent swimming conditions and the *Coco Bar and Grill Restaurant*. Just east of here, the sheltered waters of **Baby Beach** offer ideal swimming conditions, especially, as the name might suggest, for families with small children. There's also good snorkelling and diving; JADS Beach Store (Ⓣ297/584-6070, Ⓦwww.jadsaruba.com) rents snorkelling gear and has a good range of dive courses.

Eating and drinking

The majority of the island's finer **eateries** are in the capital along Wilhelminastraat and around Palm Beach, with a couple of good exceptions elsewhere. You can find anything from fine Brazilian steakhouses to local seafood dishes and Jamaican to French cuisines; most are open seven days in high season, though it's usually wise to make reservations – some can be made online at Ⓦwww.arubawineanddine.com.

Oranjestad

Café The Plaza Seaport Marketplace Ⓣ297/583-8826. Popular no-frills place with live music outside most nights and a very reasonable menu of steak, seafood and more starting at US$8.

Cuba's Cookin' Wilhelminastraat 27 Ⓣ297/588-0627. Genuine Cuban cuisine and lively entertainment are on offer at this traditional nineteenth-century country house. Try the lobster enchilada. Entrees US$20–30. Dinner only.

Iguana Joe's Royal Plaza Mall, second floor Ⓣ297/583-9373. Long one of Aruba's most popular restaurants. Delicious dishes include quesadillas and crispy calamari; vegetarian options also available. Don't miss out on their enormous tropical drinks like the famous Pink Iguana, a smooth, refreshing strawberry colada. Mains under US$20.

Jamaica Me Krazy Certified Mega Mall, 150 LG Smith Blvd Ⓣ297/583-4692. Excellent little Jamaican restaurant, with all the usual options like brown fish stew, ackee and saltfish and curried goat. Closed Sun.

Que Pasa Wilhelminastraat 18 Ⓣ297/583-4888. Really friendly bar & restaurant with open-air dining. A wide menu including steaks, seafood and sushi; try the fried brie in walnut and cranberry or the tenderloin with blue cheese.

Taj Mahal Wilhelminastraat 4A Ⓣ297/588-4494. The oldest and best Indian restaurant in town. Delicious authentic dishes, averaging US$15, all prepared to order.

The beach strip and the northwest tip

La Trattoria el Faro Blanco at the California Lighthouse Ⓣ297/586-0786. Fine Italian dining in a small restaurant belonging to the former lighthouse keeper. The food is expensive but excellent, and the views are stunning. Reservations recommended.

Smokey Joes Playa Linda, Palm Beach Ⓣ297/586-1000. Popular outdoor restaurant serving excellent ribs, slathered in a variety of sauces, as well as jerk chicken and fish dishes for US$12–18. Dinner only.

Texas de Brazil 382 J.E. Irausquin Blvd, Palm Beach Ⓣ297/586-4686. The best of Aruba's steakhouses, with superb grilled meats, and it's all-you-can-eat; take your pick from chicken, pork, beef and lamb, and help yourself from the excellent salad bar. Daily from 6pm.

Windows on Aruba at Divi Village, J.E. Irausquin Blvd Ⓣ297/581-4653. The best of the resort restaurants – and perhaps best islandwide – serves an imaginative selection of international and nouvelle cuisine that will delight your tastebuds, combined with a great location over the golf course. Try the scallops and lardo or the roast duck. Top musicians provide entertainment, dividing their time between *Windows* and the more informal *Mulligans Bar and Restaurant* below, which also has excellent food.

San Nicolas area

Charlie's Bar and Restaurant downtown on Zeppenfeldstraat 56 ☎297/584-5086. This popular hangout has become something of a legend. Over sixty years of mementos left here by seamen, refinery workers and scores of visitors cover the interior. Don't be turned off by all the "reserved" signs on the tables: the owners are keeping the table for you. Be sure to try the mouthwatering jumbo shrimp and *pasapalo* (delicious local-style tenderloin) served with their famous hot honeymoon sauce.

Yuwana Crijnssenstraat ☎297/584-8283. Sports bar and restaurant with twenty screens showing sports from around the world and a decent international menu. Closed Tues.

Nightlife

Rightly famous for its nightlife, Aruba has something for every taste. The dazzling lights of Oranjestad attract scores of revellers who visit as many **bars**, **nightclubs** and **casinos** as possible before daybreak. Most nightclubs are located around LG Smith Boulevard and Weststraat, a good few offering live local **bands** all through the week and all easily found on foot. Additionally, most hotels and resorts offer theme nights and activities for guests and non-guests alike, the most glitzy of which is the Las Vegas-style **dance shows** at the Crystal Theater and Casino in the *Renaissance Resort*. Many restaurants also double up as late bars (see above).

Café Chaos LG Smith Boulevard 60 ⓦwww.cafechaos-aruba.com. Lively, popular late bar with live music Mon, Thurs and Sat, and free wireless Internet in the daytime.

Crystal Theater and Casino downtown at the *Renaissance Aruba Beach Resort* on L.G. Smith Blvd ☎297/583-6000. An impressive heart-thumping "Let's Go Latin" dance show (US$45) with live music and dancers. Show times are from Mon to Sat beginning at 9pm.

Garufa Cigar and Cocktail Lounge Wilhelminastraat 63 ☎297/582-3677. Aruba's top smart spot is busy after work until late, serves an excellent range of cocktails, wines and *hors d'oeuvres*, and has live local music nightly. Smart casual dress.

Mambo Jambos Royal Plaza Mall, second floor ☎297/583-3632, ⓦwww.mambojambosaruba.com. Tables are removed on Fri and Sat for live music and dancing until very late; other nights this place is great for hanging out and listening to Latin music. Also serves sandwiches and snacks.

MooMba Beach Bar JE Irausquin Blvd 230, next to *Holiday Inn* and the *Marriott* ☎297/586-5365. King of the beach bars, *MooMba* is best known for its drinks happy hour (6–7pm) and occasional wild beach parties. Live music on Fri from 7pm is a major draw; open till 1am, food also served.

Radisson Aruba Caribbean Resort Casino at the *Radisson Caribbean Resort* on Palm Beach ☎297/586-4045. Casino surrounded by lavish drapery and Caribbean palms. The lounge and sports bar are also popular.

Sopranos Piano Bar A surprisingly good option at the high-rise hotel strip at Arawak Gardens, ☎297/586-6822. Open from 5pm until late, the highlight is the amazing pianists who can play seemingly any request.

Listings

Banks Many banks are located on Caya G.F. Betico Croes, including Aruba Bank (☎297/527-7700); Caribbean Mercantile Bank (☎297/582-3118); and RBTT (☎297/588-0101). Many ATMs are also found in shopping centres. Opening hours are normally weekdays 8am–6pm.

Car rental Alamo (☎297/583-3244); Amigo (☎297/583-8833); Bon Bini (☎297/734-1111); Budget (☎297/582-8600); Caribbean (☎297/582-2515); Hertz (☎297/582-1845); Thrifty (☎297/583-5335).

Internet access Blue Sea Internet Call Services, Palm Beach 33 (Mon–Sat 9am–7pm; US$8 for 1hr); State of the Art, Seaport Marketplace (Mon–Sat 9am–8pm, Sun 12–6pm; US$6 for 1hr); Café Chaos, LG Smith Boulevard 60 has free Wi-Fi.

Laundry Aruba Laundry & Cleaning, Hendrikstraat 30 (☎297/582-3627); Oranjestad Laundry, Arendstraat 107 (☎297/582-5656).

Pharmacies Called *boticas* in Aruba, pharmacies are open Mon–Sat 7.30am–7.30pm. A few good ones are Botica Eagle, near the hospital

(☎297/587-9011); Botica del Pueblo, Caya G.F. Betico Croes 48 (☎297/582-2154); and Botica Kibrahacha, across from the SETAR telephone office on Havenstraat (☎297/583-4908).

Post office The main post office is located across from the St Franciscus Church (Mon–Fri 7.30am–noon & 1–4.30pm). A small postal outlet is also located on the ground floor of the Royal Plaza Mall (Mon–Fri 8am–3.30pm).

22.2

Bonaire

Regarded as one of the world's premier sites for shore diving, the tiny boomerang-shaped island of **BONAIRE**, located 80km north of Venezuela, has much to offer those seeking an active tropical holiday. Beneath the clear blue waters of the island's sheltered western coast, divers and snorkellers are treated to a stunning spectacle: schools of fish of every imaginable shape, size and colour swim with sea turtles and other marine creatures in and around the delicate coral and sponge gardens. All this and more can be found in the waters of the **Bonaire Marine Park**, which surrounds the entire island and its neighbouring 1500-acre offshore cay, the uninhabited **Klein Bonaire**. The majority of sites are so close at hand, all you need to do is park your truck, grab your gear and swim a few metres to the reef.

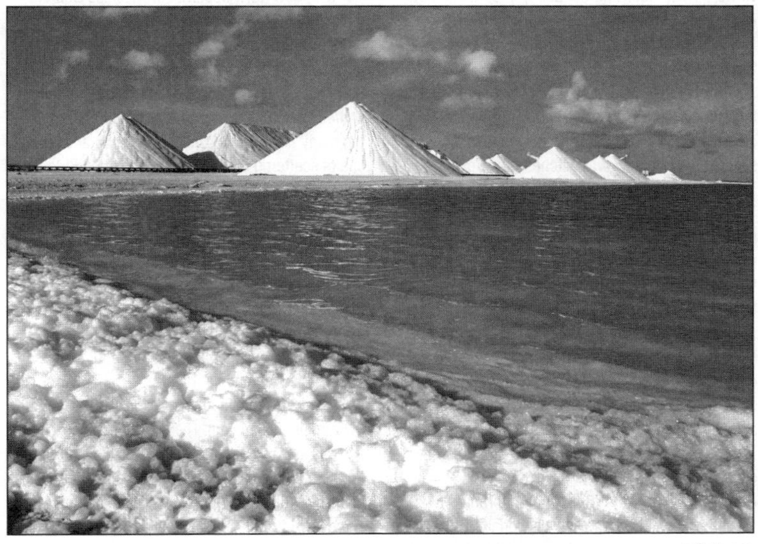

▲ Saltpans

As rugged and barren as the land may seem, the island has a different character to it depending on where you are. In the hilly north, the cactus-strewn landscape of **Washington-Slagbaai National Park** preserves remnants of the island's history along with a host of local flora and fauna. To the south, the land opens up and becomes flatter, and vast multicoloured **saltpans** attract the largest colony of **pink flamingos** in the Caribbean. If you're after more adventure, there's **windsurfing** at **Lac Cai**, on the island's rugged and windy east coast, and **kayaking** in the nearby mangrove swamps.

Outside of its natural attractions, Bonaire's appeal is low-key. In the evening you can enjoy the sunset while dining in one of the many good restaurants found in **Kralendijk**, the island's tidy capital, also home to a few cultural attractions and numerous shops.

With the break-up of the Netherlands Antilles in 2008, Bonaire voted in favour of closer ties with Holland, effectively making it a Dutch **city-state**. Unlike Curaçao, Bonaire residents were concerned that the island is too small to effectively manage its own affairs, and while not affecting tourism unduly, this decision is likely to signify greater alignment of Bonaire with Dutch and European law, and perhaps even further involvement of the Dutch in Bonaire's affairs.

Accommodation

The largest concentration of Bonaire's **hotels** and **dive resorts** is along the coast just north and south of downtown Kralendijk. Most dive resorts have a dive centre on the premises and a house **reef** just offshore. While the majority of visitors are on package deals, there has been a recent boom both in the number of independent travellers and in low-key **guesthouses** to host them.

Bellafonte Chateau de la Mar E.E.G. Blvd. 10 ⓣ599/717-3333, ⓦwww.bellafontebonaire.com. Amazingly good value from one of the most luxurious and private properties on the island, near to the airport. The rooms range from simple studios with kitchenettes to spacious suites with large kitchens and ocean views. Private pier and sundeck, rinse tanks and house reef add to the overall appeal. 4–9

Buddy Beach and Dive Resort Kaya Gobenador Nicolaas Debrot 85 ⓣ599/717-5080, ⓦwww.buddydive.com. Laid back oceanfront resort just ten min north of town. Best-known for good-value drive-and-dive packages, accommodation is in spacious apartments with kitchenette, a/c, cable TV, and patio or balcony; request an ocean view. There's also a pool, attractive bar, and *Lion's Den* restaurant onsite with nightly meal and/or drinks promotions. 4

Captain Don's Habitat Kaya Gobernador Nicolaas Debrot 103 ⓣ599/717-8290, ⓦwww.habitatdiveresorts.com. One of the first dive resorts on the island, this relaxed place next to *Buddy Dive* remains a diver's favourite. Simple but comfortable cottage-style rooms surround a pool and garden; many have kitchenettes, a/c and private bath. There's a fully equipped dive centre and the gorgeous house reef is just offshore. 5

Divi Flamingo Beach Resort J.A. Abraham Blvd 40 ⓣ599/717-8285, ⓦwww.divibonaire.com. This large resort minutes from downtown has standard rooms with terraces. There's also a dive centre, tennis court, mini-mart, spa, casino, great waterfront restaurant/bar (open to non-guests) and good snorkelling on the house reef. A weekly slide show on marine diversity alongside regular live music provides the entertainment. Good wheelchair access. 5

Eden Beach Kaya Gobernador Nicolaas Debrot ⓣ599/717-6720, ⓦwww.edenbeach.com. Standard hotel rooms and one- and two-bed apartments at this friendly resort just north of Kralendijk. The lively *Bongos Beach* bar/restaurant is the highlight, serving great seafood and attracting many non-guests. Onsite dive shop and lounge chairs scattered along the small beach add to the appeal. 4

Lagoen Hill Kaminda Lagun ⓣ599/717-2840, ⓦwww.lagoenhill.com. Ten minutes east of town, this group of villas offers comfort and good value, albeit a drive away from the beaches and restaurants. Villas range from one-bed studios to three-bedroom cottages that sleep up to eight; all have fully equipped kitchen, a/c and cable TV. There's also a small pool. 2

The Lizard Inn Kaya America 14 ⓣ599/717-6877, ⓦlizardinnbonaire.com. Their motto, "clean, cheap, and casual", just about sums up this place at the northern end of town. Set around a small courtyard with sofas, all rooms have a/c, fridge and hot water, some have full kitchen and cable TV. Wi-Fi and rinse tanks on site; breakfast extra. 2

Kralendijk

Set alongside a picturesque harbour on the west coast, the tiny capital of **KRALENDIJK** ("coral dike" in Dutch) is Bonaire's commercial centre and the first stop for anyone visiting the island. Marked by a few low-rise buildings painted in pretty pastel colours and a handful of narrow streets, the town holds most of the island's government buildings, shops, hotels, restaurants and bars. There's not much to do or see other than shop or dine at the excellent restaurants. The town's couple of historical buildings and small cultural **museum** won't take more than an hour or two to explore.

Generally quiet, the town gets busy when hordes of cruise ship passengers crowd the small streets. The best time to see the sights is late afternoon when the cruise ships have departed. It's easy enough to **walk** around, and you won't need a map to see the few attractions, many of which are found close to the coast on the main roads of Kaya Charles E.B. Helimund and Kaya Grandi.

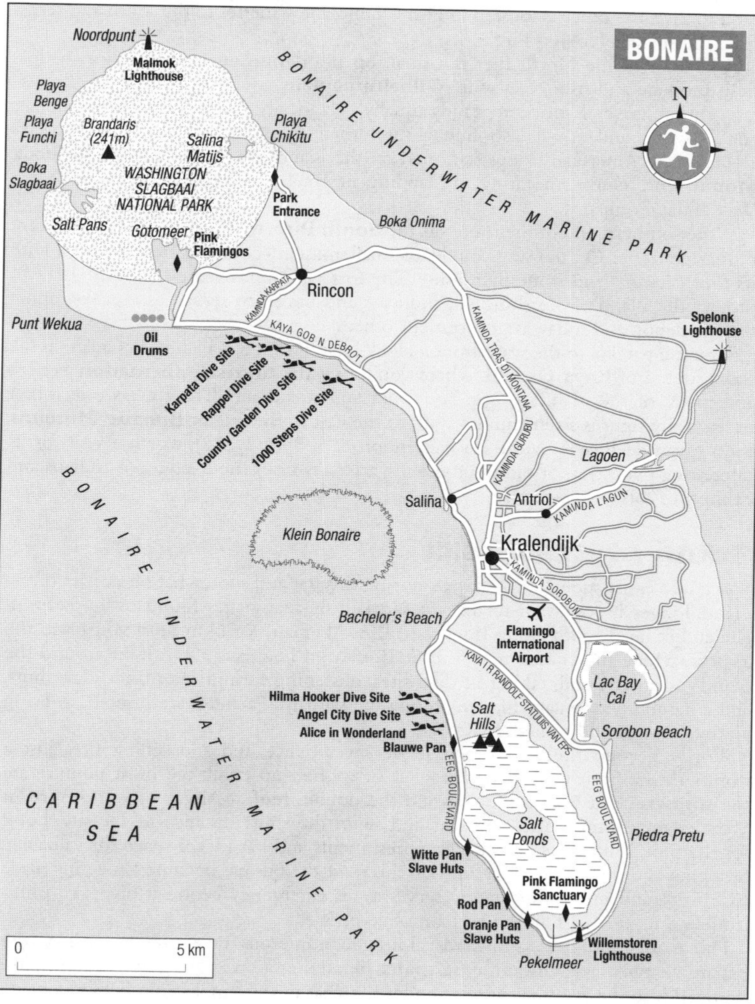

The best way to get your bearings is to follow the colourful **waterfront** thoroughfare known as Kaya Jan N.E Craane, which merges with Kaya Charles E.B. Helimund toward the south end of town. Along this route you'll find several government buildings, shops, restaurants and bars, as well as the occasional Dutch Caribbean-style building painted yellow and gold. This stretch is also a popular place to take in the tropical surroundings or catch the sunset.

On the north end of the route, **Karel's Pier** is home to a favourite watering hole for locals and tourists, as well as Pirate Cruises and the watertaxi to **Klein Bonaire**. Across the way, you can also browse through the shops, boutiques and restaurants of the **Harbourside Mall**.

Further south and closer to the centre of Kralendijk is the Town Pier, often referred to as the **North Pier**; it's a superb spot for night diving. Its underwater pillars are encrusted with sponges, corals and other sea creatures, all of which come to life after sundown. The pier is extremely busy most day times, with heavy cruise ship and boat traffic, and you must obtain permission from the harbourmaster if you wish to dive; the office is located in Fort Oranje, a few metres to the south and across from the smaller Ro-Ro Pier.

Next door to the North Pier is a small open-air **market** where vendors peddle fresh produce and fish. Nearby in **Wilhelminaplein,** a courtyard near the Protestant church, several souvenir stands usually sell locally made wooden handicrafts and artwork, and you'll also find a monument honouring Eleanor Roosevelt's 1944 visit to American troops stationed on the island, as well as the **Van Walbeck Monument**, commemorating the landing in 1634 of the director of the Dutch West India Company.

At the southern end of the route sits the **South Pier**, which receives a fair amount of marine traffic. On the way you'll pass small, mustard-coloured **Fort Oranje** with its four cannons and stone lighthouse. The fort was built by the Dutch in 1817 to protect the island's flourishing salt industry, and has since served as a prison and a storage depot, and today as government offices.

Running parallel to the waterfront a block inland from Kaya Jan N.E. Craane is the short stretch of **Kaya Grandi**, where you'll find the **tourist information centre** and many of the island's shops, boutiques and restaurants. The town's only other noteworthy sight is a ten-minute walk to the east to the quaint **Bonaire Museum**, Kaya J. van de Ree 7 (Mon–Fri 8am–noon & 1–5pm; US$2), worth a visit for its interesting collection of old photographs, artefacts from the Caiquetios Indians and exhibits of folkloric costumes.

South of Kralendijk

You could easily spend a half-day exploring this flat and somewhat bleak part of the island, longer if you want to dive or snorkel the many sites found offshore. From Kralendijk head south along Boulevard L.A. Abraham for 5km until you reach the airport, where the coastal road E.E.G. Boulevard begins a 32km loop around the island's southern end, taking in dive sites, glistening mountains of salt, slave huts, and a flamingo sanctuary hidden among the saltpans. Facilities are limited, so bring plenty of water and something to eat.

Shortly beyond the airport you'll see several dive and snorkelling sites just a stone's throw from the narrow beaches of washed-up coral; the most popular are the **shipwreck** at Hilma Hooker and the double **reef** at Angel City and Alice in Wonderland. Simply park your car and swim the short distance to the site. Look for the pink **Dive Bus**, which sells refreshments and has locker space for valuables. Stopping at different dive locations on this road, the bus has become a meeting place for divers, and more importantly serves as an emergency centre if divers run into trouble – it has a first aid kit and a mobile phone.

The road continues southwards alongside numerous dive sites as well as the expansive pink and turquoise **saltpans** belonging to Cargill Salt. Ocean water pumped into the pools evaporates under the heat of the sun, leaving behind a briny solution from which salt crystals are grown and harvested for export. The cement **obelisks** at Blauwe Pan and Rod Pan were used until 1863 as flagpoles signalling to trade boats that the salt was ready for export.

At Whitte Pan and 2km further south near Oranje Pan, you'll find clusters of small white and reddish-brown former **slave huts** atop a bluff overlooking the exposed coastline. Built in 1850, these tiny cement buildings housed slaves from the nearby salt fields, each building just waist high with a steep roof and a tiny opening for a door and window. If you look carefully in the salt fields you can still see the trails once used by these slaves.

As the road winds its way to the southern tip keep your eyes peeled for a pink haze over the salt fields. With binoculars it's possible to distinguish thousands of **pink flamingos** inhabiting Pekelmeer Sanctuary, the largest flamingo breeding ground in the western hemisphere. These tall, graceful birds are shy and easily disturbed; to protect them the government has declared the entire area off limits – even the airspace overhead. Each night many of the birds make their way to Venezuela and return to feed at dawn. Across from Pekelmeer stands the battered remains of the **Willemstoren Lighthouse**, the island's first, built in 1837.

From the lighthouse the road turns north and follows a more rugged coastline, passing **Piedra Pretu** (black stone), worth a brief stop for a wander among the large chunks of sun-bleached coral and piles of twisted driftwood, and to experience first-hand the awesome force of the waves that have shaped this side of the island.

Lac Bay and around

At the north end of the road, just before it turns back towards Kralendijk, is **Lac Bay**, a shallow stretch of water on the east coast with some of the best **windsurfing** and **kayaking** conditions in the Caribbean. Starting with *Sorobon Beach Resort* (clothing optional), you'll come upon a few locally run businesses renting boards and kayaks and offering windsurfing lessons, the most popular of which is *Jibe City* (daily 9am–6pm; ⓣ599/717-5233, ⓦwww.jibecity.com), who also have a lively afternoon spot, the *Hang Out Beach Bar*. You can rent kayaks (from US$35/day) and windsurfing boards (US$60/day) and take windsurfing lessons (US$50 for beginners and advanced; board included for beginners only). The bay's sheltered waters and steady trade winds draw surfers of all levels and ages, and each October serve as the site of Bonaire's **windsurfing regatta**.

Beyond the southern end of Lac Bay the road heads inland for 500m before splitting. The left fork, Kaya I.R. Randolf Statuuis Van Eps, takes you to the hotels on the west coast, while the right, Kaminda Sorobon, follows the western edge of Lac Bay, eventually leading back to Kralendijk. Both roads pass through desert littered with cacti and scrubby vegetation; watch out for roaming donkeys and goats.

If you take Kaminda Sorobon, follow the signs to the dirt road leading east to **Cai**, a small point on the northern tip of Lac Bay. Every Sunday afternoon locals and surfers gather here to listen to live music, drink beer and eat local food. *Lac Suid*, an occasionally open snack-hut at the end of the road is a good place for a meal; more reliably open is *Maiky Snack*, signposted off Kaminda Sorobon. This area is also the starting point for **kayaking** trips to nearby mangrove swamps (Outdoor Bonaire organizes tours; see box, p.816).

Rincon and Washington-Slagbaai National Park

Bonaire's oldest settlement, **RINCON**, is a pretty cluster of red-roofed houses nestled in a valley northwest of Kralendijk. Originally established as a Spanish settlement in the sixteenth century, Rincon became home to slave families who laboured in the nearby plantations and salt fields of the southern peninsula. The town is best visited during the annual **Rincon Day festival** (April 30), when visitors from all over the Caribbean come for traditional music and dancing, as well as local food such as goat stew served with *funchi* (cornmeal). At other times Rincon is worth seeking out for its laid-back rural setting and tasty local lunches served at the *Rose Restaurant* on Kaya Guyaba.

Washington-Slagbaai National Park

From Rincon follow the main road northwest for 3.5km to **Washington-Slagbaai National Park** (8am–5pm, no entrance after 2.45pm; US$10; Ⓦwww.washingtonparkbonaire.com), which occupies most of the island's northwestern tip. The land, which once belonged to two plantation owners who produced and exported vast quantities of aloe, goat meat and charcoal, is now a reserve protecting fascinating flora and fauna, including towering cacti (known locally as *kadushi,* a staple of soups), pink flamingos and numerous species of parrot, bats, iguanas and lizards. Other highlights include salt ponds, rocky coves, plantation houses, snorkelling spots and **Brandaris Hill**, the highest point on the island at 241m.

Once past the gate you can choose to drive along two routes that will take you through the park: the shorter 24km **green route** (2hr), traversing the hilly interior, or the longer 40km **yellow route** (4hr), which follows the coast before joining up with the green route. Stick to the coloured trail markers and follow the map, keeping in mind that you cannot backtrack – all roads lead in one direction.

Both routes start by taking you past the saltpans of **Salina Matijs**, where between December and March hundreds of flamingos arrive. From here the yellow route brings you to **Playa Chikitu**, a popular sunbathing spot, though swimming is not advisable because of the strong outgoing current. Continuing along this route, you'll pass many rugged coves (*bokas* – literally "mouths") and stunning vistas, while the green route cuts west, skipping the park's northern reaches.

Dive centres and tour operators

There's no shortage of **dive centres** on Bonaire, many of them located in hotels or resorts. All offer rentals and equipment repair and can organize boat tours to many of the dive sites, including those on Klein Bonaire. Expect to pay around US$20–25 for a shore dive, US$30–35 for a one-tank boat tour and around US$330–400 for a five-day underwater certification course, plus equipment rentals (US$10/day for regulators; US$12/day for snorkel, fin and mask; and US$15/day for tanks, including weights).

Your best bet is to arrange a **package deal** with a resort, which usually covers accommodation, equipment rental and a specified number of dives. Among the best are: *Buddy Beach and Dive Resort* (see p.812) who offer an eight-day drive-and-dive package for US$1100 upwards (based on two sharing), including accommodation, a rental vehicle and unlimited air fills for shore diving, plus six boat dives. Or try *Captain Don's* (p.812), which has a range of underwater certification and photography courses taught by highly qualified instructors.

For **underwater camera** rentals (US$25–45/day), visit Dive Friends Bonaire, *Caribbean Court*, J.A. Abraham Blvd (Ⓣ599/717-3460, Ⓦwww.dive-friends-bonaire.com). Divi Dive Bonaire, based at *Divi Flamingo Beach Resort* (Ⓣ599/790-5353) is another reputable **dive** operator who also offer snorkelling, sailing and kayaking trips.

Bonaire has many **tour operators** offering a range of activities; almost all offer hotel pick-ups, and be sure to book in advance. Two excellent choices are: Outdoor Bonaire (Ⓣ599/791-6272 or 785-6272; Ⓦwww.outdoorbonaire.com), an outfit specializing in small groups who offer an exceptional range of adventurous trips, from **kayaking** in the Lac Bay mangroves to **caving** in some of the island's remarkable complexes and **hiking**, **climbing** or **abseiling** in the Washington National Park (all priced around US$50); and Pirate Cruises on Karel's Pier in Kralendijk (Ⓣ599/717-8330), which offers guided **snorkelling** trips to Klein Bonaire for US$30, departing daily at 9.30am and 1.30pm.

At Brandaris Hill the yellow route joins the green route, and there's decent snorkelling nearby at playas Funchi and Bengé. The best place for swimming is at **Boka Slagbaai**, 1.5km south of Playa Funchi. Both routes then make their way inland; the yellow route goes by more flamingos at the larger saltpan of Gotomeer before joining the green route for the final stretch back to the park entrance.

It is worth bearing in mind that you can also see Gotomeer without entering the park; simply follow the coast road as far west as you can go then cut north past the eastern side of the park, and you should see a flock of flamingos at the lake. Continuing along the road brings you around to Rincon.

Park practicalities

To navigate the park's bumpy and narrow dirt roads, a rugged **4WD** vehicle is necessary, especially after a rainstorm; mountain bikes, scooters and camping are all strictly forbidden. The alternative is taking a hiking, climbing or kayaking **tour** led by Outdoor Bonaire, which also covers some of the park's history; highly recommended for adventurous people (see box opposite).

Before venturing in, stock up on refreshments and snacks at the **plantation house** where you pay your fee, as there are no facilities past the park gate. You can also view a small collection of Arawak artefacts and tools at the nearby **museum**. Proper footwear and a pair of binoculars are recommended.

Bonaire Marine Park and Klein Bonaire

Bonaire's pristine coral reefs and abundant marine life have been protected from development since 1979, when the government established the **Bonaire Marine Park** (Ⓦwww.bmp.org). Comprising the entire coastline of the island – and that of the neighbouring uninhabited cay of **Klein Bonaire** – down to 60m, the park is widely recognized as a model of marine conservation.

Bonaire has 86 **dive and snorkel sites**, the majority of which are on the leeward side of the island. All sites are marked with yellow stone markers or a buoy and come with colourful names such as Country Garden, Forest, Yellow Man's Reef, Ol' Blue and Bloodlet. **Boats** are not permitted to drop anchor and must instead use the mooring site. The majority of sites can be reached directly from shore, while Klein Bonaire is accessible only by boat (see box opposite). Popular dive and snorkelling spots include 1000 Steps, Karpata, Rappel, Pink Beach, Country Garden and, on Klein Bonaire, No Name. Most sites harbour magnificent stands of elkhorn and brain coral as well as sponges surrounded by an array of tropical fish and marine invertebrates. Many resorts have an onsite house reef and offer a variety of underwater certification and photography courses. A **map** available on the island (including from the tourist office) describes which of the marked sites are for divers and which for snorkellers. Bear in mind that most of the entry points to the sea are rather rocky (the pretty site at 1000 Steps is an exception), so it helps to have good footwear.

The clear waters provide excellent visibility for **snorkelling**, and though a major storm in 1999 damaged many beaches and shallow-water corals, signs of recovery are visible; snorkellers can still enjoy schools of parrotfish, trumpet fish, barracuda, moray eels and angelfish around the sponges and other numerous coral species.

Park practicalities

Rangers patrol the 6400-acre park to enforce the strict rules. Divers and snorkellers are asked to show their **Marine Park Tag** (US$25 for divers, $10 for others, valid for one year), available from dive operators or from the Marine Park's office at Barcardera. They also need to attend a warm-up dive session with an instructor, which can be arranged through any dive centre. Diving gloves and kneepads are not permitted, nor is disturbing or removing any coral, fish or marine invertebrate, dead or alive.

Eating, drinking and nightlife

Surprisingly for its small size, there is a truly excellent selection of **eating opportunities** in and around Kralendijk, most of them within walking distance of downtown. While **hotel restaurants** are generally more expensive than dining in town, Kralendijk also has a couple of grocery stores and bakeries offering a wide selection of fresh produce and imported goods. The local **snack stands** scattered throughout the island are the best place to try delicious meals like goat, fish or conch stews, and most cost under US$10.

Bonaire has a few spots with decent **nightlife**, and many of the **bars** at hotels and resorts have **live music** at weekends; check the *Bonaire Reporter*, a free bimonthly newspaper, for upcoming events.

Kralendijk

Bistro de Paris Kaya Gob. N. Debrot 46 ⓣ599/717-7070, ⓦwww.bistrodeparis.com. This may well be the best French restaurant in the Caribbean, where large portions of excellent food is combined with a small friendly atmosphere. The salads are scrumptious – as is the home-made *crème brûlée*. Good wine list. Closed Sun.

Capriccio Kaya Isla Riba 1 ⓣ599/717-7230. Classy Italian place, serving pizzas, pasta and mains like duck breast in a red wine sauce (US$12–30). The wine list is superb. Closed Sun.

City Cafe Kaya Grandi 7 ⓣ599/717-8286. A great place to grab a reasonably priced meal (from NAf$10) and have a pint or two as the sun goes down. Happy hour 5.30–6.30pm; live bands at weekends.

Imperial Harbourside Mall. Good Japanese restaurant opposite *Karel's Beach Bar*, offering fresh sushi and sashimi (US$25 for a large combo platter) as well as teppanyaki.

It Rains Fishes Kaya Jan N.E. Craane 24 ⓣ599/717-8780. This popular, friendly restaurant on a covered outdoor terrace facing the water offers delicious and affordable local seafood dishes for NAf$30. Also available are chicken, beef tenderloin and a selection of salads. Dinner only, closed Sun.

Karel's Beach Bar on a small pier across from Harbourside Mall. A favourite watering hole with good views of the busy harbour. Happy hour 5.30–8pm. Live music at weekends.

Mona Lisa Bar and Restaurant Kaya Grandi 15 ⓣ599/717-8718. Located on the main street in town, this cosy Dutch-owned establishment is a Bonaire institution, serving scrumptious seafood and smoked chicken dishes. Expect to pay NAf$40 for the catch of the day. Mon–Fri: restaurant 6–10pm, bar 4pm–2am.

North of Kralendijk

Bongos Beach at the *Eden Beach Resort* on Kaya Gobernador Nicolaas Debrot 73 ⓣ599/717-7238. Popular beachside hangout offering tasty snacks and speciality drinks. Especially lively on Fri nights. Happy hour 5.30–6.30pm.

Rose Bar Restaurant Kaya Guyaba 4, Rincon ⓣ599/562-6364. The only choice in Rincon is a great lunchtime option, serving creole cuisine such as fish or iguana soup and large portions of baked chicken or fish and rice and beans, served in an attractive courtyard.

East of Kralendijk

Jibe City Sorobon Beach, Lac Bay ⓣ599/717-5064, ⓦwww.jibecity.com. A great place to chill out with a beer in the afternoon, this trendy spot serves big sandwiches and home-made apple pie.

Maiky Snack ⓣ599/565-3804. Snack stand offering traditional Bonairean food; try the huge portions of chicken or goat served with rice or *funchi* (cornmeal). Daily 11am–3pm, closed Thurs.

Mi Banana Kaya Nikiboko Norte 42 ⓣ599/717-4472. One of the few Latin American-owned options, just east of town in a homey atmosphere. Doubles as a friendly bar in the early evening.

Listings

Banks Banco di Caribe, Kaya Grandi 22 (ⓣ599/717-8295); Maduro & Curiel's Bank, Kaya L.D. Gerharts 1 (ⓣ599/717-5520).

Bicycle rental Cycle Bonaire, Kaya L.D. Gerharts 11D (ⓣ599/717-7558), and De Freewieler, Kaya Grandi 61 (ⓣ599/717-8545). Both rent mountain and touring bikes for about US$15–25 per day.

Bookshops Bonaire Boekhandel, Kaya Grandi 50 (ⓣ599/717-8499), has a small selection of paperback books, maps and stationery supplies.

Car and scooter rental AB Car Rental, located at the airport (ⓣ599/717-8980, ⓦwww.Abcarrental.com).

Internet access Seahorse Cybercafé, Kaya Grande 6 (Mon–Sat 10am–9pm, Sun 2pm–6pm), and Chat 'n' Browse, Kaya Gob. N. Debrot 79, (Mon–Fri 9am–6pm, Sat 9am–5pm).

Pharmacies Botica Bonaire, Kaya Grandi 27 (☎599/717-8905).

Post office Bonaire's main post office is located on Plaza Wilhelmina 11, near the tourist information office (Mon–Thurs 7.30am–noon & 1.30–5pm, Fri 7.30am–noon & 1.30–4.30pm).

Supermarkets Cultimara Supermarket, Kaya L.D. Gerharts 13 (☎599/717-8278), has a large selection of fresh produce, meat and other grocery items.

22.3

Curaçao

CURAÇAO (population 130,000), the largest of the ABC islands, and from 2008 an independent country, remains relatively unknown outside of the Netherlands and the Caribbean. Encountered by the Spaniards in 1499 and taken over by the Dutch in 1634, Curaçao has been slower to develop the kind of tourist industry its neighbours are known for, though its capital city – and recently designated UNESCO World Heritage Site – **Willemstad**, rivals any in the Caribbean for picturesque charm. The island also offers decent diving and swimming possibilities, especially its secluded coves on the leeward side. More active pursuits can be had in the rugged and hilly interior; **Christoffel National Park**, in the north, is overgrown with towering cacti, scrubby vegetation and gnarled divi divi trees, and well worth a hike. Besides such flora, island inhabitants include goats, bats, lizards, iguanas and countless species of colourful birds. The various **plantation houses** that dot the island are remnants from Curaçao's history as the Caribbean's busiest slave depot in the seventeenth century; the trade was finally abolished in 1863.

Curaçao has plenty of watersports to choose from. The island has some decent **dive sites** scattered on its leeward side (the southern coast) in the twenty-kilometre **Curaçao Underwater Park** and around **Klein Curaçao**, a small deserted volcanic island to the southeast (an hour-and-a-half boat ride from Willemstad). Most sites are rich in coral formations while others have sunken ships and submerged artefacts. Some sites are easily accessible from shore but most require a **boat ride**. Good snorkelling exists at most of these locations.

Accommodation

You'll have no problem finding a **place to stay** in Curaçao. The largest concentration of hotels and dive **resorts** is within fifteen minutes of downtown Willemstad – both along the coast to the south and to the northwest near Piscadera Bay – though two of the island's best options are towards the northwestern tip. There are also a few budget and luxury options to be found in Willemstad's **Punda** and **Otrobanda** districts. Be prepared to pay a **room service charge** of 6–15 percent.

Curaçao dive centres

Though nowhere near as renowned as Bonaire, Curaçao is home to some decent **diving** and **snorkelling**. Several reputable dive centres are on the island, most of them offering a variety of services including open-water dive courses, equipment rental and charter boat services. The following are highly recommended: *Habitat Curaçao*, north of Willemstad, is the island's flagship dive resort, offering a wide selection of courses, underwater camera rental, offshore diving and chartered boat dives to surrounding reefs; the friendly Dutch owners of Scuba Do, at Jan Thiel Beach (Ⓣ5999/767-9300; Ⓦwww.divecenterscubado.com), who charge US$30 for one guided dive including weights and air, have numerous underwater courses beginning at US$250, charters to Klein Curaçao for US$65, and "The Bubblemaker", an introductory diving programme for children (US$85); and at the northwestern end of the island, Ⓦwww.oceanencounterswest.com, located at the beautiful Playa Kalki beach and with Dive Site Alice In Wonderland offshore (US$42 guided tour of house reef, US$55 boat dive).

Willemstad

Estoril Hotel Breedestraat 181, Otrobanda Ⓣ5999/462-5244, Ⓔhotelestorilcua@yahoo.com. Set on the main street in Otrobanda, this hotel offers twenty basic but clean rooms with private bathrooms, public telephone and a/c. ②

Hotel Kura Hulanda Langestraat 8, Otrobanda Ⓣ5999/434-7700, Ⓦwww.kurahulanda.com. Fabulous 80-room hotel based around the restored architecture of an eighteenth- and nineteenth-century Dutch village, with a maze of cobbled passageways and overgrown courtyards with pools and Jacuzzis. The rooms are luxurious and welcoming. Four restaurants, a spa, casino and the pre-eminent Kura Hulanda Museum (see p.823) onsite. ⑨

Hotel Otrobanda Breedestraat, Otrobanda Ⓣ5999/462-7400, Ⓦwww.otrobandahotel.com. Located in the heart of Willemstad, the *Otrobanda*'s rooms are cramped but afford terrific views; price includes breakfast. A pool and lively casino on the premises. ④

Pelikaan Hotel and Casino Langestraat 78, Otrobanda Ⓣ5999/462-3555. Popular with budget travellers; small and simple rooms with a/c and televisions, and a casino onsite. ②

Pietersz Guesthouse and Apartments Roodeweg 1, Otrobanda Ⓣ5999/462-9511. Close to the *Estoril,* the twelve pleasant rooms have kitchenettes private baths and TVs. Tucked below is the *Pietersz Coffeshop*, serving home-made snacks, cold drinks and ice cream. ②

San Marco Hotel Columbusstraat 7, Punda Ⓣ5999/461-2988, Ⓦwww.sanmarcocuracao.com. Located in the heart of Punda atop a casino, the recently renovated but small rooms come with a/c, cable TV and private bathroom, and there's a relaxing reading room with free Internet access. ②–③

Around the island

Habitat Curaçao 30 minutes' northwest of Willemstad near Rif. St Marie Ⓣ5999/864-8800, Ⓦwww.habitatdiveresorts.com. Attractive apartments set alongside a small beach and rocky cliffs. Spacious rooms come complete with kitchenettes, a/c and a large terrace or balcony. There's also a pool, excellent restaurant and bar and a professionally run dive shop with a range of courses and excursions. Friendly staff. ⑤

Kura Hulanda Lodge Playa Kalki 1, Westpunt Ⓣ5999/839-3600, Ⓦwww.kurahulanda.com. New boutique property in a gorgeous location. Offering deluxe studios or cottages with private beach, three restaurants, spa and fitness centre, this is a classy resort. Full range of activities including dive shop. Packages available with the sister property in Willemstad. ⑨

Lions Dive Hotel south of Willemstad near the Sea Aquarium complex on Bapor Kibra Ⓣ5999/461-8100, Ⓦwww.lionsdive.com. Dutch-Caribbean-style accommodation with ocean-facing rooms. Clean rooms, many with balconies. Unlimited free access to Sea Aquarium and its private beach, plus free shuttle bus to downtown. ⑥

Sunset Waters Beach Hotel Santa Martha Bay Ⓣ5999/864-1233, Ⓦwww.sunsetwaters.com. An exception among all-inclusives, this is a delightful little resort with friendly staff and a relaxed yet sociable feel. On a lovely crescent beach, with good facilities for sailing, diving (packages available), snorkelling and kayaking, a good restaurant and two lively bars. Non all-inclusive options available. ⑤–⑥

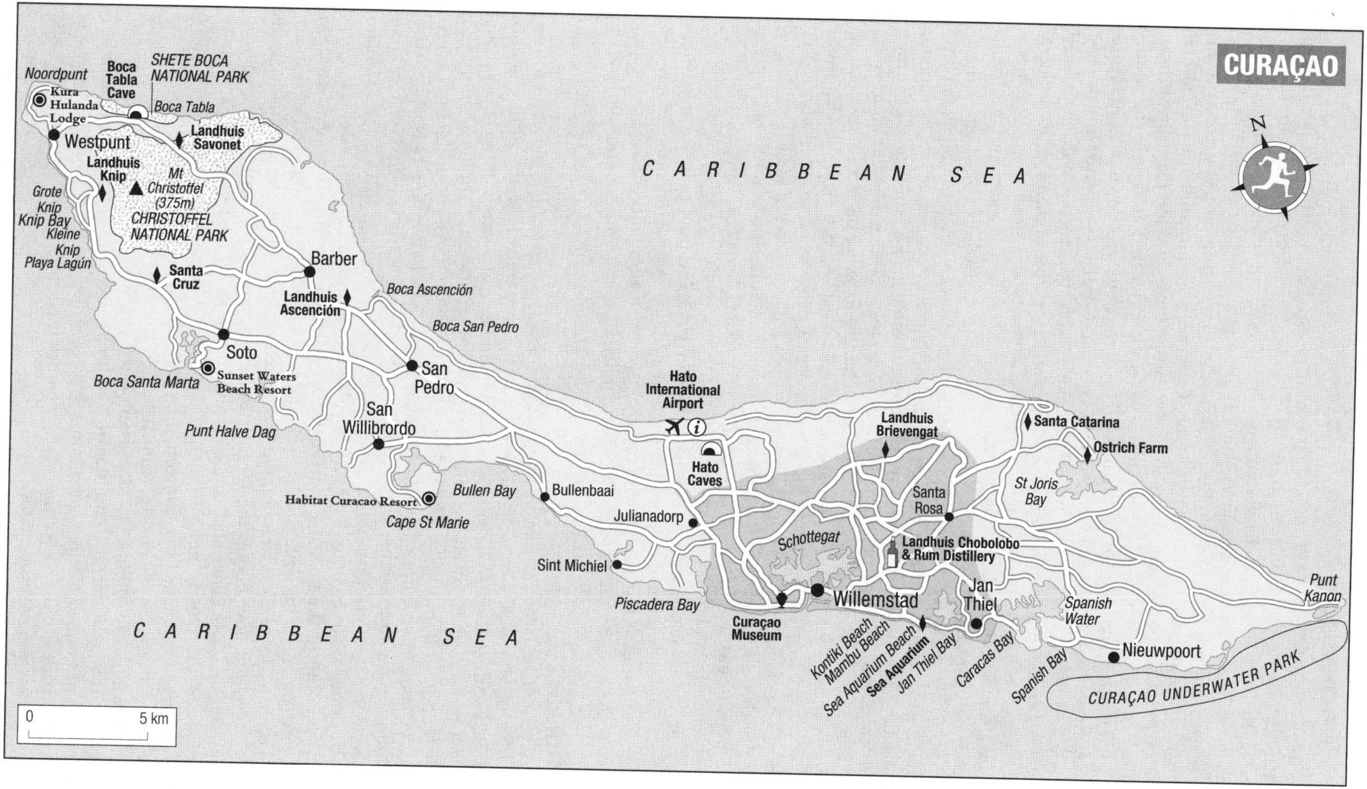

CURAÇAO

N
CARIBBEAN SEA
Noordpunt
Kura Hulanda Lodge
Boca Tabla Cave
SHETE BOCA NATIONAL PARK
Boca Tabla
Westpunt
Landhuis Savonet
Landhuis Knip
Mt Christoffel (375m)
CHRISTOFFEL NATIONAL PARK
Grote Knip
Knip Bay
Kleine Knip
Playa Lagún
Santa Cruz
Barber
Boca Ascención
Landhuis Ascención
Boca San Pedro
Soto
Boca Santa Marta
Sunset Waters Beach Resort
San Pedro
San Willibrordo
Punt Halve Dag
Hato International Airport
Hato Caves
Habitat Curacao Resort
Bullen Bay
Bullenbaai
Cape St Marie
Julianadorp
Sint Michiel
Piscadera Bay
Curaçao Museum
Schottegat
Willemstad
Landhuis Brievengat
Santa Rosa
Landhuis Chobolobo & Rum Distillery
Santa Catarina
Ostrich Farm
St Joris Bay
Jan Thiel
Kontiki Beach
Mambu Beach
Sea Aquarium Beach
Sea Aquarium
Jan Thiel Bay
Caracas Bay
Spanish Bay
Spanish Water
Nieuwpoort
Punt Kanon
CURAÇAO UNDERWATER PARK
CARIBBEAN SEA
0 5 km

Willemstad

Vibrant **WILLEMSTAD**, full of colourful colonial architecture, is the hub of activity in Curaçao. Unlike its counterpart capitals in Aruba and Bonaire, Willemstad is large enough to have retained a lively local economy and cultural scene independent of the tourist centres. You feel like a genuine guest at many of the free concerts put on in the town's squares, instead of the feeling on many other islands that events are staged for visitors alone. Curaçao is cosmopolitan, with cultural attractions, shopping and places to eat to satisfy those looking for a break from the normal Caribbean beach vacation. Magnificently sited alongside the south-eastern coast and divided by a narrow, but deep, channel known as Santa Anna Bay, downtown Willemstad is split into two main districts – **Punda** on the east side and **Otrobanda** to the west. The former, with its gorgeous waterfront lined with elaborate eighteenth-century buildings and gingerbread mansions, is distinctly Dutch in origin, home to boutiques, shops, museums and street-side cafes. Across the channel, Otrobanda, literally meaning "the other side" in Papiamentu, has had its core restored to its erstwhile elegance after a period of decline.

Both sides make for memorable wandering and are linked by two bridges: the fifty-metre-high **Queen Juliana Bridge**, a four-lane highway towering above the harbour, and the **Queen Emma Pontoon Bridge**, a floating bridge. The latter is the most remarkable and central of all landmarks in Willemstad. Designed by US businessman Leonard B. Smith in 1888, it was designed to be able to swing open for boats entering the harbour – which it still does about ten times a day. Back then, Smith charged 2¢ per person for anyone wearing shoes while allowing free access to those who walked across barefoot; today crossing the bridge is free to all regardless of their footwear.

Another district, the old Jewish neighbourhood of **Scharloo**, is north of Punda, as is **Schottegat**, a large inland lake connected to Santa Anna Bay, where many of the oil refineries and dockyards are located.

The Dutch settled the city as a naval base in 1643, and built military strongholds to defend the naturally deep channel and harbour. As the economy flourished, attracting many Dutch and Jewish merchants, construction proceeded apace creating new districts. By the nineteenth century, much of this growth fell into disrepair.

Punda

Across the pontoon bridge to the east, the scenic waterfront along the bustling street of **Handelskade** in Punda is the most photographed spot in all of Curaçao. Lined with centuries-old pastel-coloured buildings and a string of cafés, this is the best place to start a walking tour. Many of the traditional buildings found along here have been renovated (the red tiles seen on the roofs of these buildings originally came from Europe as ships' ballast) – one of the best examples is right across from the pontoon bridge at the multilevel **Penha & Sons**, a canary-yellow shop decorated with elaborate white gables, built in 1708. Close at hand is Punda's main **shopping district**, bounded by Handelskade, Madurostraat and Breedestraat.

Just south of the busy main street of Breedestraat is the large **Fort Amsterdam** complex, one of the first military strongholds, built in 1635 by the Dutch West Indies Company. Until 2008, the restored fort seated the government of the Netherlands Antilles, and now houses the Curaçao administration. If you look closely you can still see a British cannonball embedded in one of its walls (the result of a skirmish between the Dutch and British in the early 1800s). Around the corner is the renovated Protestant **Fort Church**, the oldest church in Curaçao (built in 1769).

The remains of the island's original fort, **Waterfort**, is located a block south of Fort Amsterdam. Built in 1634 and renovated two hundred years later, it was used by the US army during World War II (the laying of a steel net across the mouth of the bay prevented German submarines from entering the deep harbour). A series of **waterfront arches** east of the fort **were** once used to store gunpowder, **and** today house a string of seaside restaurants.

Situated in the heart of Punda, the **Mikvé Israel-Emanuel Synagogue**, on Hanchi Snoa at Columbusstraat (Mon–Fri 9am–4.30pm; ⓣ5999/461-1067; US$6), is one of the Caribbean's most important landmarks and possibly the oldest synagogue still in use in the western hemisphere. Members of the original Jewish community who came here from Europe dedicated the synagogue in 1732. The white sand sprinkled on the floor is said to honour Moses' leading of his people through the desert. Tucked inside is the **Jewish Cultural Museum** where you can view an impressive array of Torah scrolls, Hanukah lamps and other religious artefacts.

In the northern corner of Punda, it's worth a visit to the colourful **floating market**, which lines the canal by Sha Carpileskade. Every morning wooden boats loaded with fish, fresh tropical fruits and vegetables make their way from Venezuela to sell in Willemstad; they typically leave by noon. A few other sights exist nearby, including the popular and highly recommended **Marshe Bieu** (old market) behind the post office, where you can sample inexpensive local cuisine from charcoal grills.

Directly across the water from the market, in the former Jewish district of Scharloo, you'll find the **Maritime Museum** (Mon–Sat 9am–4pm; US$6.50), which pays homage to Curaçao's rich seafaring history. Ship models, maps and coins from sunken treasures are on display.

Otrobanda

West of the pontoon bridge, Otrobanda has a couple of attractions worth looking into. Right beside the bridge is the main square, **Brionplein**, where a statue of Pedro Brion holds sway. Brion is one of the island's most famous men, born in 1782 and a right hand man to Simón Bolívar as they fought for the independence of South American countries from the Spanish. Otrobanda's main street, **Breedestraat** (not to be confused with the street of the same name in Punda) runs perpendicular from the channel and is chock-full of small shops selling bargains as well as the odd rum shop.

Be sure to visit the magnificent and highly recommended **Kura Hulanda Museum**, just off Breedestraat to the north on Klipstraat 9 (Mon–Sun 10am–5pm; US$10), built in a restored nineteenth-century mansion. The museum boasts a splendid selection of original art and artefacts from all over Africa, as well as a superb collection of gold pre-Columbian figures from South America. The highlight, however, is the permanent exhibition on the trans-Atlantic slave trade; through documents, artefacts and models, it describes the realities and dispels myths about the experience from slave capture to the middle passage to the plantations. The reconstructed hold of a slave ship is enough to send shivers down the spine, the whole experience providing a moving portrayal of events which changed the face of the modern world.

Across town on the western outskirts of Otrobanda, the smaller **Curaçao Museum**, V. Leeuwenhoekstraat (Mon–Fri 9am–noon & 2–5pm, Sun 10am–4pm; US$5), is home to a scant collection of traditional and contemporary local art and artefacts.

Out of town attractions

One of the more popular attractions **south** of Willemstad is the **Sea Aquarium** (daily 8.30am–5.30pm; US$15, children 5–12 US$7.50; ⓣ5999/461-6666, ⓦwww.curacao-sea-aquarium.com), a short drive south of the capital. Touch tanks, aquariums and 3D movie theatre, plus a shark-feeding observatory and an option to swim with dolphins or sea lions (at a premium), all provide a good preface to getting underwater yourself. You can also swim with dolphins offshore at the entrance to the twenty-kilometre **Curaçao Underwater Park**.

A short stroll from the aquarium leads to a large stretch of man-made sandy **beach** fringed with palm trees. An entrance fee of US$3.50 will get you into Kontiki, Mambo and the nearby Sea Aquarium beaches. All three are safe for swimming and have bars, restaurants, changing room facilities and parking.

Located 4km east of the Sea Aquarium, a smaller but quieter beach can be found at *Zanzibar Beach Resort* on **Jan Thiel Bay** (US$3.50); you can snorkel, dive or swim, and beach chairs and mountain bikes are available for rent.

Many **watersports** activities, including jet skiing, kayaking and windsurfing, are offered at nearby **Caracas Bay Island**, a recreation park near the town of Jan Thiel (Ⓣ5999/747-0666).

Free tours and liqueur sampling are available **east** of town at the **Senior & Company Liqueur Distillery** (Mon–Fri 8am–noon & 1–5pm; Ⓦwww.curacaoliqueur.com), a few minutes' drive east of Punda at the Landhuis Chobolobo in Saliòa. In operation since 1896, the distillery is known for its sweet-tasting **Curaçao Blue**, a liqueur made from the peel of a bitter variant of the Valencia orange, this small factory bottles more than 20,000 gallons per week.

Christoffel National Park and the northern tip

Tucked in the northwest corner of the island is the spectacular **Christoffel National Park**, a 4600-acre wilderness protecting a diverse array of plants and animals. Located 45 minutes from Willemstad and centred around **Mount Christoffel** (375m), this former plantation is home to the tiny Curaçao deer as well as numerous species of bats, birds, non-poisonous snakes, iguanas, orchids and cacti. Several well-marked walking and driving routes allow you to explore the rugged and hilly interior at your own pace.

The **main entrance** (Mon–Sat 8am–2.30pm, Sun 6am–1.30pm; US$10) is located at the mustard-coloured **Savonet** plantation house, on the right-hand side of the main road leading to Westpunt. A local restaurant and small giftshop/museum can also be found here. From the main gate it's possible to access any of eight colour-coded **hiking trails**, which can take anywhere from twenty minutes to five hours to complete. The most strenuous is a steep ascent up Mount Christoffel, which rewards with breathtaking views, not to mention the delicate orchids visible along the path. It's also possible to drive through the interior on any one of three well-maintained dirt roads; **maps** are available at the main entrance, as is a highly recommended guidebook.

Various **tours** of the park are also on offer, including a two-and-a-half-hour one with park rangers from the main gate on Friday mornings at 10am (US$10), and horse riding and mountain-biking tours; call Rancho Alfin (Ⓣ5999/864-0535) for details.

Two kilometres north of Christoffel's main gate, the rugged north coast is best viewed from the tiny **Shete Boka National Park** (US$2). A series of walking trails on exposed sharp coral wind their way along the coast to several limestone **grottoes**, including **Boka Tabla**, where you view the waves crashing in from two viewing platforms. Keep an eye out for ancient coral formations and fossils along the path, as well as sea turtles – the park was established as a sanctuary for breeding these animals. Swimming is not allowed as the currents are far too dangerous.

A few kilometres further north, quiet **Westpunt** has just two claims to fame: *Jaanchie's* restaurant, where the menu is sung to each customer, and the new luxurious *Kura Hulanda Lodge* resort (p.820). Ten minutes south of Westpunt along a winding and hilly coastal road is **Landhuis Knip**, the island's best example of a colonial plantation house. Built in the early 1700s and rebuilt in 1830 after a fire, this was one of Curaçao's most prosperous plantations, producing wool, indigo, sorghum, beans and divi divi pods. Now an interesting museum covering aspects of plantation and colonial life, the large rooms are decorated with antique furniture and period pieces.

Some of the island's best **beaches**, **diving** and **snorkelling** are found along this northwest stretch of Curaçao. If you're coming directly from Willemstad (rather than the park) follow the road signposted to Westpunt, then turn left on the road to Santa

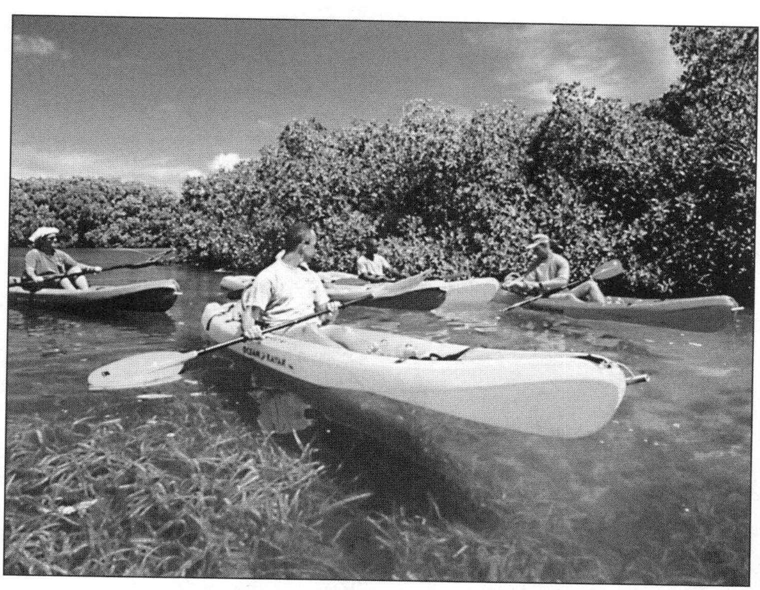

▲ Kayaking

Cruz at the town of San Pedro. The most popular spots, both on Knip Bay, are **Grote Knip** with its calm, turquoise-blue waters and beautiful sandy beach nestled in a protected cove, and the smaller **Kleine Knip**, a few kilometres south of Grote Knip. Both beaches offer superb snorkelling and are crowded at weekends and holidays; a small snack bar and changing facilities are available at Grote Knip. Watch out for the poisonous manchineel trees growing by the beach.

As you return to Willemstad stop by **Landhuis Ascension**, the oldest plantation house on the island, built in 1672. Some 5km north of the highway intersection to the beaches, it has been beautifully restored and is now used as a recreation centre for Dutch marines. There's an open house on the first Sunday of every month, with local music, handicrafts and food.

The rest of the island

The rest of the island has some scattered attractions, most along the lines of **plantation houses** (*landhuizen*), though many are in disrepair. East of the airport, however, is the lovely **Landhuis Brievengat** (Mon–Fri 9.15am–noon & 3–6pm), which has been transformed and offers a wide selection of local crafts and occasional live *salsa* music.

Just a half-kilometre south of the airport are the mysterious limestone **Hato Caves** (daily 10am–5pm; US$8), where stunning flowstone formations, stalagmites and stalactites grow in humid chambers. They can be viewed, alongside ancient rock drawings, on the 45-minute guided tours that depart every hour on the hour.

Quite the sight to see as well are the eight hundred ostriches at the **Curaçao Ostrich Farm** (Tues–Sun 9am–5pm; US$10; ⓣ5999/747-2777), situated in the remote east of the island. Tours (call for hotel pick up) offer the chance to feed these flightless creatures, hold one of the large eggs (equivalent in weight to twenty chicken eggs) and learn about their life cycle. The adjacent **Aloe Vera Plantation** also offers tours, which include an interesting demonstration of the natural uses of the plant.

Eating and drinking

Willemstad

Astrolab Observatory in the *Hotel Kura Hulanda*, Langestraat 8, Otrabanda ⓣ5999/434-7700. Superb restaurant, with starters such as lobster salad or crab cakes and entrees such as home-made duck ravioli or sesame-crusted tuna (US$25–40). Daily 8am–11pm.

Iguana Cafe on the waterfront at Handelskade (next to Queen Emma Bridge), Punda ⓣ5999/461-9866. One of the few places in Punda to enjoy a light dinner at a reasonable price, mainly sandwiches and Dutch specialities. A great place to watch the cruise ships and tankers pass by. Closed Sun.

Il Barile Hanchi Snoa 12, Punda ⓣ5999/461-3025. Don't let appearances fool you; this small street-side restaurant is the best place in Willemstad for home-made Italian food (mains US$10–25), sandwiches and cappuccinos. Sit outside on the small patio or dine upstairs. Closed Sun.

Jaipur in the *Hotel Kura Hulanda*, Langestraat 8, Otrabanda ⓣ5999/434-7700. Fine Tandoori cuisine, with chicken, fish and jumbo shrimp curries starting at US$20. Dinner only, closed Mon.

Marshe Bieu on the open-air terrace behind the post office, Punda. A popular lunch spot, this market is the best place to sample local dishes like deep-fried *kora* (red snapper), as well as Chinese and Surinamese dishes. Lunch only, closed Sun.

Plein Cafe Wilhelmina Wilhelmina Park, Punda ⓣ5999/461-0461. A pleasant downtown setting for a cold beer and a fresh baguette or "toastie" (toasted cheese sandwich). The chicken sate smothered in peanut sauce is also worth trying (mains US$15). Closed Sun.

Rijsttafel Mercuriusstraat 13–15, Salina, close to Chobolobo (home of Senior & Co.) ⓣ5999/461-2606. An elegant Indonesian restaurant decorated with shadow puppets, batiks and copper pots. Go with a group to enjoy a traditional Indonesian banquet (US$28 per person, minimum two people); a vegetarian menu is also available. Open for lunch and dinner; closed Sun.

Ska Loko Plasa Mundo Merced, Scharloo ⓣ5999/461-4685. Hidden in a small alley behind the cinema, this is a Caribbean-style tapas bar open for dinner and drinks seven days a week. A tasty array of dishes such as coconut rum chicken, camembert and guava quesedilla and excellent Haitian pumpkin and beef soup (Nfl10-20).

The rest of the island

Jaanchie's on main road in Westpunt ⓣ5999/864-0126. Delicious and very inexpensive local dishes served by friendly staff. Their speciality is wahoo served with rice, salad and plantains, but you can get soups (fish, iguana, goat or beef) or fish, shrimp and conch sandwiches. Watch for the "I Love Jaanchie's" sign on the main road. Open for lunch and dinner.

Sjalotte west of Willemstad at the *Floris Suite Hotel*, Piscadera Bay ⓣ5999/462-6111. Right on the bay, this is a fine restaurant, serving starters like snails or fried sweetbreads from US$10 and mains like bouillabaisse or vegetable lasagne from US$15. Open for lunch and dinner.

Zambezi Restaurant at the Curaçao Ostrich Farm, Groot St Joris West ⓣ5999/747-2777. Ostrich and other African dishes are their speciality (mains from US$20). Reservations recommended. Closed Mon, lunch only Tues, lunch and dinner Wed–Sun.

Nightlife

Most of the popular **bars** and **nightclubs** are located outside of downtown Willemstad, either along the beachfront or around Salina, east of town. The informative weekly entertainment guide, *K-Pasa* (ⓦwww.k-pasa.com), can be picked up at tourist offices and most hotels and cafés.

Asia de Cuba just off the ring road at Zuikertuintje shopping centre, Santa Rosa ⓣ5999/747-9009. Attractive and animated *salsa* bar with frequent live music.

De Heeren ⓣ5999/736-0491. Popular hangout on Mon and Thurs nights, attracting a fairly young crowd of Dutch locals. Great place to dance, listen to music and have a beer.

Hooks Hut Piscaderabaai ⓣ5999/462-6575. Popular Willemstad bar, with live Caribbean music on Weds. Look out for the seventeen-piece Grupo Ritmiko Karabela, who play here from time to time.

The Living Room Saliòa 129. A popular nightspot on Fri and Sat for listening to music from reggae to *salsa*.

Mambo Beach Sea Aquarium Beach, Bapor Kibra ☎5999/461-8999. Lively after-work bar offering something different every night of the week and dancing every Sat until 4am. Happy hour 5–6pm.

Wet and Wild Beach Club next door to *Mambo Beach*, Bapor Kibra ☎5999/561-2477. Young peoples' hot spot is full of energy from the daily 6pm happy hour till late. Live DJs play reggaeton to techno and everything in between.

Zanta Bapor Kibra, next to *Princess Casino* at *Breezes*. Trendy club with three dance floors playing house music, hip-hop/R&B and latin flavours, respectively. Wed is ladies night, from 10pm.

Listings

Banks Many are located in the shopping district of Punda and Otrobanda, and there's a branch of Maduro & Curiel's Bank at the airport. All ATMs dispense US cash or guilders.

Car rental Antillean (☎5999/461-3144); Hertz (☎5999/888-0088); Noordstar (☎5999/737-5616); and Thrifty (☎5999/461-3089).

Cinema An excellent seven-screen cinema is in Scharloo, five minutes' walk from the centre (☎5999/465-1000).

Internet access Wireless Internet Café at Hanchi Snoa 4, just across from the floating bridge (Mon–Sat 9am–5pm; US$3/hr; ☎5999/461-0590); in Punda at Café Internet, Handelskade 3b (Mon–Sat 9.00am–8pm; US$3/hr; ☎5999/465-5088). The Telecentre is also the best place to make international calls.

Pharmacies Botica Brion is across from the post office in Otrobanda (☎5999/462-7027); in Punda try the centrally located Botica Popular at Madurostraat 15 (☎5999/461-1269).

Post office In Punda, the post office is next to the main market on Waaigatplein 1 (Mon–Fri 7.30am–noon & 1.30–5pm; ☎5999/433-1100), while in Otrobanda the post office is located on the main floor of the large white Landskantoor building on Breedestraat (same hrs as above).

Taxis Taxi Centrale ☎5999/869-0747.

Travel store

UK & Ireland

Britain
Devon & Cornwall
Dublin **D**
Edinburgh **D**
England
Ireland
The Lake District
London
London **D**
London Mini Guide
Scotland
Scottish Highlands & Islands
Wales

Europe

Algarve **D**
Amsterdam
Amsterdam **D**
Andalucía
Athens **D**
Austria
Baltic States
Barcelona
Barcelona **D**
Belgium & Luxembourg
Berlin
Brittany & Normandy
Bruges **D**
Brussels
Budapest
Bulgaria
Copenhagen
Corsica
Crete
Croatia
Cyprus
Czech & Slovak Republics
Denmark
Dodecanese & East Aegean Islands
Dordogne & The Lot
Europe on a Budget
Florence & Siena
Florence **D**
France
Germany
Gran Canaria **D**
Greece
Greek Islands
Hungary
Ibiza & Formentera **D**
Iceland
Ionian Islands
Italy
The Italian Lakes
Languedoc & Roussillon
Lanzarote & Fuerteventura **D**
Lisbon **D**
The Loire Valley
Madeira **D**
Madrid **D**
Mallorca **D**
Mallorca & Menorca
Malta & Gozo **D**
Moscow
The Netherlands
Norway
Paris
Paris **D**
Paris Mini Guide
Poland
Portugal
Prague
Prague **D**
Provence & the Côte D'Azur
Pyrenees
Romania
Rome
Rome **D**
Sardinia
Scandinavia
Sicily
Slovenia
Spain
St Petersburg
Sweden
Switzerland
Tenerife & La Gomera **D**
Turkey
Tuscany & Umbria
Venice & The Veneto
Venice **D**
Vienna

Asia

Bali & Lombok
Bangkok
Beijing
Cambodia
China
Goa
Hong Kong & Macau
Hong Kong & Macau **D**
India
Indonesia
Japan
Kerala
Korea
Laos
Malaysia, Singapore & Brunei
Nepal
The Philippines
Rajasthan, Dehli & Agra
Shanghai
Singapore
Singapore **D**
South India
Southeast Asia on a Budget
Sri Lanka
Taiwan
Thailand
Thailand's Beaches & Islands
Tokyo
Vietnam

Australasia

Australia
East Coast Australia
Fiji
Melbourne
New Zealand
Sydney
Tasmania

North America

Alaska
Baja California
Boston
California
Canada
Chicago
Colorado
Florida
The Grand Canyon
Hawaii
Honolulu **D**
Las Vegas **D**
Los Angeles & Southern California
Maui **D**
Miami & South Florida
Montréal
New England
New York City
New York City **D**
New York City Mini
Orlando & Walt Disney World® **D**
Oregon & Washington
San Francisco
San Francisco **D**
Seattle
Southwest USA
Toronto
USA
Vancouver
Washington DC
Yellowstone & The Grand Tetons
Yosemite

Caribbean & Latin America

Antigua & Barbuda **D**
Argentina
Bahamas
Barbados **D**
Belize
Bolivia
Brazil
Buenos Aires
Cancùn & Cozumel **D**
Caribbean
Central America on a Budget
Chile
Costa Rica
Cuba
Dominican Republic
Ecuador
Guatemala
Jamaica
Mexico
Peru
Puerto Rico
St Lucia **D**
South America on a Budget
Trinidad & Tobago
Yucatán

D: Rough Guide **DIRECTIONS** for short breaks

Available from all good bookstores

Africa & Middle East
Cape Town & the Garden Route
Dubai **D**
Egypt
Gambia
Jordan
Kenya
Marrakesh **D**
Morocco
South Africa, Lesotho & Swaziland
Tanzania
Tunisia
West Africa
Zanzibar

Travel Specials
First-Time Africa
First-Time Around the World
First-Time Asia
First-Time Europe
First-Time Latin America
Make the Most of Your Time on Earth
Travel with Babies & Young Children
Travel Online
Travel Survival
Ultimate Adventures
Walks in London & SE England
World Party

Maps
Algarve
Amsterdam
Andalucia & Costa del Sol
Argentina
Athens
Australia
Barcelona
Berlin
Boston & Cambridge
Brittany
Brussels
California
Chicago
Chile
Corsica
Costa Rica & Panama
Crete
Croatia
Cuba
Cyprus
Czech Republic
Dominican Republic
Dubai & UAE
Dublin
Egypt
Florence & Siena
Florida
France
Frankfurt
Germany
Greece
Guatemala & Belize
Iceland
India
Ireland
Italy
Kenya & Northern Tanzania
Lisbon
London
Los Angeles
Madrid
Malaysia
Mallorca
Marrakesh
Mexico
Miami & Key West
Morocco
New England
New York City
New Zealand
Northern Spain
Paris
Peru
Portugal
Prague
Pyrenees & Andorra
Rome
San Francisco
Sicily
South Africa
South India
Spain & Portugal
Sri Lanka
Tenerife
Thailand
Toronto
Trinidad & Tobago
Tunisia
Turkey
Tuscany
Venice
Vietnam, Laos & Cambodia
Washington DC
Yucatán Peninsula

Phrasebooks
Croatian
Czech
Dutch
Egyptian Arabic
French
German
Greek
Hindi & Urdu
Italian
Japanese
Latin American Spanish
Mandarin Chinese
Mexican Spanish
Polish
Portuguese
Russian
Spanish
Swahili
Thai
Turkish
Vietnamese

Computers
Blogging
eBay
FWD this link
iPhone
iPods, iTunes & music online
The Internet
Macs & OS X
MySpace
PlayStation Portable
Website Directory

Film & TV
American Independent Film
British Cult Comedy
Chick Flicks
Comedy Movies
Cult Movies
Film
Film Musicals
Film Noir
Gangster Movies
Horror Movies
Sci-Fi Movies
Westerns

Lifestyle
Babies
Ethical Living
Pregnancy & Birth
Running

Music Guides
The Beatles
The Best Music You've Never Heard
Blues
Bob Dylan
Book of Playlists
Classical Music
Elvis
Frank Sinatra
Heavy Metal
Hip-Hop
Led Zeppelin
Opera
Pink Floyd
Punk
Reggae
The Rolling Stones
Soul and R&B
Velvet Underground
World Music

Popular Culture
Classic Novels
Conspiracy Theories
Crime Fiction
Cult Fiction
The Da Vinci Code
Graphic Novels
His Dark Materials
Poker
Shakespeare
Superheroes
Tutankhamun
Unexplained Phenomena
Videogames

Science
The Brain
Climate Change
The Earth
Genes & Cloning
The Universe
Weather

Small print and

Index

A Rough Guide to Rough Guides

Published in 1982, the first Rough Guide – to Greece – was a student scheme that became a publishing phenomenon. Mark Ellingham, a recent graduate in English from Bristol University, had been travelling in Greece the previous summer and couldn't find the right guidebook. With a small group of friends he wrote his own guide, combining a highly contemporary, journalistic style with a thoroughly practical approach to travellers' needs.

The immediate success of the book spawned a series that rapidly covered dozens of destinations. And, in addition to impecunious backpackers, Rough Guides soon acquired a much broader and older readership that relished the guides' wit and inquisitiveness as much as their enthusiastic, critical approach and value-for-money ethos.

These days, Rough Guides include recommendations from shoestring to luxury and cover more than 200 destinations around the globe, including almost every country in the Americas and Europe, more than half of Africa and most of Asia and Australasia. Our ever-growing team of authors and photographers is spread all over the world, particularly in Europe, the USA and Australia.

In the early 1990s, Rough Guides branched out of travel, with the publication of Rough Guides to World Music, Classical Music and the Internet. All three have become benchmark titles in their fields, spearheading the publication of a wide range of books under the Rough Guide name.

Including the travel series, Rough Guides now number more than 350 titles, covering: phrasebooks, waterproof maps, music guides from Opera to Heavy Metal, reference works as diverse as Conspiracy Theories and Shakespeare, and popular culture books from iPods to Poker. Rough Guides also produce a series of more than 120 World Music CDs in partnership with World Music Network.

Visit www.roughguides.com to see our latest publications.

Rough Guide travel images are available for commercial licensing at www.roughguidespictures.com

Rough Guide credits

Text editor: Courtney Miller
Layout: Sachin Tanwar
Cartography: Karobi Gogoi, Katie Lloyd-Jones, Ed Wright
Picture editor: Emily Taylor
Production: Rebecca Short
Proofreader: Amanda Jones
Cover design: Chloë Roberts
Photographers: Demetrio Carrasco, Sean Edghill, Lydia Evans, Roger Mapp, Martin Richardson, Polly Thomas
Editorial: **London** Ruth Blackmore, Alison Murchie, Andy Turner, Keith Drew, Edward Aves, Alice Park, Lucy White, Jo Kirby, James Smart, Natasha Foges, Róisín Cameron, Emma Traynor, James Rice, Emma Gibbs, Kathryn Lane, Christina Valhouli, Monica Woods, Mani Ramaswamy, Joe Staines, Peter Buckley, Matthew Milton, Tracy Hopkins, Ruth Tidball; **New York** Andrew Rosenberg, Steven Horak, AnneLise Sorensen, April Isaacs, Ella Steim, Anna Owens, Sean Mahoney, Paula Neudorf; **Delhi** Madhavi Singh, Karen D'Souza
Design & Pictures: **London** Scott Stickland, Dan May, Diana Jarvis, Mark Thomas, Nicole Newman, Sarah Cummins; **Delhi** Umesh Aggarwal, Ajay Verma, Jessica Subramanian, Ankur Guha, Pradeep Thapliyal, Anita Singh, Nikhil Agarwal
Production: Vicky Baldwin
Cartography: **London** Maxine Repath; **Delhi** Jai Prakash Mishra, Rajesh Chhibber, Ashutosh Bharti, Rajesh Mishra, Animesh Pathak, Jasbir Sandhu, Alakananda Bhattacharya, Swati Handoo, Deshpal Dabas
Online: **London** George Atwell, Faye Hellon, Jeanette Angell, Fergus Day, Justine Bright, Clare Bryson, Aine Fearon, Adrian Low, Ezgi Celebi, Amber Bloomfield; **Delhi** Amit Verma, Rahul Kumar, Narender Kumar, Ravi Yadav, Debojit Borah, Rakesh Kumar, Ganesh Sharma
Marketing & Publicity: **London** Liz Statham, Niki Hanmer, Louise Maher, Jess Carter, Vanessa Godden, Vivienne Watton, Anna Paynton, Rachel Sprackett, Libby Jellie; **New York** Geoff Colquitt, Nancy Lambert, Katy Ball; **Delhi** Ragini Govind
Manager India: Punita Singh
Reference Director: Andrew Lockett
Operations Manager: Helen Phillips
PA to Publishing Director: Nicola Henderson
Publishing Director: Martin Dunford
Commercial Manager: Gino Magnotta
Managing Director: John Duhigg

Publishing information

This 3rd edition published November 2008 by
Rough Guides Ltd,
80 Strand, London WC2R 0RL
345 Hudson St, 4th Floor,
New York, NY 10014, USA
14 Local Shopping Centre, Panchsheel Park,
New Delhi 110017, India
Distributed by the Penguin Group
Penguin Books Ltd,
80 Strand, London WC2R 0RL
Penguin Group (USA)
375 Hudson Street, NY 10014, USA
Penguin Group (Australia)
250 Camberwell Road, Camberwell,
Victoria 3124, Australia
Penguin Group (Canada)
195 Harry Walker Parkway N, Newmarket, ON,
L3Y 7B3 Canada
Penguin Group (NZ)
67 Apollo Drive, Mairangi Bay, Auckland 1310,
New Zealand
Cover concept by Peter Dyer.

Typeset in Bembo and Helvetica to an original design by Henry Iles.

Printed and bound in China

848pp includes index

A catalogue record for this book is available from the British Library

ISBN: 978-1-85828-819-2

The publishers and authors have done their best to ensure the accuracy and currency of all the information in **The Rough Guide to the Caribbean**, however, they can accept no responsibility for any loss, injury, or inconvenience sustained by any traveller as a result of information or advice contained in the guide.

1 3 5 7 9 8 6 4 2

Help us update

We've gone to a lot of effort to ensure that the third edition of **The Rough Guide to the Caribbean** is accurate and up to date. However, things change – places get "discovered", opening hours are notoriously fickle, restaurants and rooms raise prices or lower standards. If you feel we've got it wrong or left something out, we'd like to know, and if you can remember the address, the price, the hours, the phone number, so much the better.

Please send your comments with the subject line **"Rough Guide Caribbean Update"** to Ⓔ mail@roughguides.com. We'll credit all contributions and send a copy of the next edition (or any other Rough Guide if you prefer) for the very best emails.

Have your questions answered and tell others about your trip at Ⓦ community.roughguides.com

Acknowledgments

Robert Coates: On St Lucia, sincere thanks go to Chris, Janelle, Arlene and family; Chefs Orlando and Xavier and Shaftoe. Thanks also to Jolien and the staff of the Reef, Michael and Andrea at Talk To Me, Esther and Franz at Fox, Roger at La Panache, all at Balenbouche, and Toby at Essential Detail. On St Kitts and Nevis, thank yous go to Kevin at Rawlins, John at DanceBEAT and the Culture House, all the lovely staff at Ottley's, Vaden, John and Winston at Oualie, Rob and Liz at Dasents, and Gillian at Bananas. On the ABC Islands, thanks to Laurenz and Miriam, Mieke at AxisEuro, Rensley at Divi Resorts, Indra at Tiara Air, Shirley and Delno at Kura Hulanda, Jim and Gaynor at Sunset Waters, Germaine at Divi Air and Jan Willem at Solar.

Joe Fullman: Muchas gracias to everyone in the DR (and beyond) who took the time to talk, write, sort things out, answer my queries, recommend things, show me a good time and generally help out. These include, in no particular order, Luis in Punta Cana, Martina in Bayahibe, Ricardo in Santiago, Karla in Puerto Plata, Andrea and Lisa in Cabarete, Marleen and Aude in Las Terrenas. Big thanks too to Jane Watkins and Kara Hoffman and to Lynn Guitar for her detailed information about the country's Taino sites. And finally, much gratitude to AnneLise, Courtney and above all to Nicola for putting up with me (and my driving), and for remaining always lovely.

Sara Humphreys: Thanks to Merlyn, Sharon and Twyla at the Anguilla Tourist Board, various staff at the Barbados Tourism Authority and Saba Tourist Bureau; Roland at the Statia Tourist Office, and not forgetting Bede for the indispensable loan of a bicycle on Anguilla. In addition thanks are due to Elisa and Tom Holland on Statia; Máiréad and Adrian on Barbados; Helene & Richard West for restaurant tips; Rob for useful advice; and Courtney for her thorough editing.

Stephen Keeling: Thanks to Madeline Santiago Figueroa at the Puerto Rico Tourism Company; Jessica Almy Pagán and Miguel Ortiz at La Caleta; Jen Gold and Lauren Hatfield for their generosity and advice in Vieques; the indomitable Jim Petersen and Elias Robinson in Culebra; Mary Lee and daughter Suzie in Guánica; Courtney Miller in RG New York, and lastly Tiffany Wu, whose support, as always, made this possible.

Lesley McCave: My thanks go to Ethelyn Philips, D Annette Michael and Randy Allen, Sue McGill-Kauffman, Elise Magras, James Mitchell for constant support, and the Geographia guys.

Lisa Risher: A great many thanks to: John Brinckerhoff for his vast global connections, John & Myra Reilly's support, Silvana Rahming and The Bahamas Ministry of Tourism for their help and guidance. Countless thanks to my Bahamian family Heather & Ryan Bellot and the entire Bellot clan for their kindness, generosity, friendship, information, unending assistance, good time and "pay it forward attitude".

Rebecca Strauss: Many thanks to Joanne Gammage and Nasaria Budal at the Cayman Islands tourist board, Kayla Lightbourne of the Turks and Caicos tourist board, Harmony Turnbull and Sophie Carrera of the British Virgin Islands tourist board and Heather Carty and Chantel Hoheb at the US Virgin Islands tourist board. Thanks also to Arie Barendrecht, Peter Hillenbrand, Sandra McLeod and Kristen Boshoff among many, many others for their warm island hospitality.

Alex Robertson Textor: On Guadeloupe, thanks to the extraordinarily helpful Luigy Ssosse as well as Philipp Heinzelmann, Alain Narcisse, Jackie Cauet, Marlène Hoff, Alex Brute, and Brigitte Genet. On Martinique, huge thanks to Muriel Wiltord, Christel Coita, and Marc Martial. On Montserrat, Ernestine Cassell, Cheryse Aimer, and Rosetta West at the tourist board were amazingly helpful; thanks as well to Eustace Dyer, Scriber Daley, and fellow travel writer Jad Davenport.

Polly Thomas would like to thank everyone who assisted with research and planning, particularly: in Jamaica, Marjorie Morris; Andre McGann of Doctor's Cave Beach Hotel; Axel and Andrea at Mar Blue Villa Suites; Nell Hegarty of Riva PR; Jason and Laura Henzell; and Jenny Wood at Goldeneye. In Trinidad, Stephen Broadbridge of Caribbean Discovery Tours; Courtenay Rooks of Paria Springs; Dexter Lewis; and the Baden-Semper family. In Dominica, Maxine Alleyne of the Dominica Tourist Board; and Susie Tempest of the Saltmarsh Partnership. In St Vincent and the Grenadines, Angela Maini, Maitha Ahmed and Hannah Nicholson of BGB. In Grenada, Kate Fenton at Representation Plus; Lucille Sylvester at Indigo Cars; Terry Abraham; True Blue Hotel; and Maca Bana Villas.

The editor wishes to thank all the contributors for their valiant efforts and remarkable understanding of the bigger picture; to Sachin Tanwar, Karobi Gogoi, and everyone at RG India for thorough and exacting input; and to the RG New York and London staff for unparalleled guidance. Countless thanks to Emily Taylor for wonderful help with the photos.

Readers' letters

Thanks to all the readers who have taken the time to write in with comments and suggestions (and apologies if we've inadvertently omitted or misspelt anyone's name):

Chris Alger, Michael Bütow, Joy Charnley, Pip Chissell, Johan Dippenaar, Graham Dumas, Carol Hodgson, Anja Rudolf, David White and Katy Winter.

Photo credits

All photos © Rough Guides except the following:

Cover

Front picture: Boat on the Caribbean Sea © Saki Sakakibara/Getty
Back picture: Barbados guard house © Altrendo images/Getty
Inside back picture: Toucan at Graeme Hall Nature Sanctuary, Barbados © Martin Richardson/Rough Guides

Introduction

Trinidad Carnival, Pretty Mas © CAFerris/Cafémoka

Things not to miss

02 Trinidad Carnival © The Image Bank/Getty
03 Kayaker, Exuma © Stephen Frink Collection/Alamy
04 Boiling Lake, Dominica © George H. H. Huey/DRR.Net
05 Bonefishing, Bahamas © Tom Montgomery/Photolibrary
08 Bonaire Marine Park © Whitney Lane/DRR.Net
09 Willemstad © David Sanger/DDR.Net
10 Kura Hulanda museum, Curaçao © Rob Coates
11 Windsurfers © picturescolourlibrary.com/DDR.Net
13 Saba © Joe Viesti/DRR.Net
14 Bomba's Surfside Shack © Atlantide Phototravel/Corbis
15 Dolphins, Bimini © Islands of Bahamas Tourist Office
16 Street party, Jamaica © Debbie Bragg/www.everynight.co.uk
19 Seven Mile Beach, Grand Cayman © Macduff Everton/Corbis
21 Gorda Baths © Ron Rovtar/DDR.Net
24 Snorkelling, Long Island © Greg Johnston/Bahamas Tourist Office
25 War Memorial, Montserrat © David Sanger/DDR.Net

Parties in paradise colour insert

Carnival, Trinidad © jtb Photo/Photolibrary
Blue devil reveller © Alison Wright/Corbis
Jouvert © Grant Rooney/Alamy
Elephant Man © Redferns
Queen of Carnival © Blaine Harrington III/Alamy
Sailboat, Antigua © Onne van der Wal/Corbis
Junkanoo costume © Walter Bibikow/DRR.Net

Underwater Caribbean colour insert

French angelfish in pillar coral © Danita Delimont Agency/DRR.Net
Brain Coral, Cuba © WaterFrame/Alamy
Moray eel, Cayman Islands © Stephen Frink/Corbis
Mermaid statue © Stephen Frink/Corbis
Manta ray © National Geographic/Getty
Humpback whale © Carlos Eyles/Getty
Rhone wreck, British Virgin Islands © Carlos Villoch/Alamy
Feather star and sponge © Peter Pinnock/Jupiter Images

Black and whites

p.62 Junkanoo parade © Philip Gould/Corbis
p.75 Hairbraiding © MO/Alamy
p.90 Lucayan National Park © Charles Stirling/Alamy
p.107 Glass Window Bridge, Eleuthera © Timothy Pike/istock
p.118 Church, Long Island © Greg Johnston/DDR.Net
p.124 Providenciales © Hemis/Alamy
p.133 Queen conch © Tom Stack/DRR.Net
p.143 Salinas © Walter Bibikow/DRR.Net
p.146 Musician in Cuba © Cuba Tourist Board
p.191 Baseball, Cuba © Mark Lewis/Alamy
p.214 Stingray, Grand Cayman © Tom Stack/DRR.Net
p.228 Cayman Brac parrot © Bob Krist /Corbis
p.270 Rafting, Rio Grande © The Jamaica Tourist Board
p.275 Dunn's River Falls, Ocho Rios © Greg Johnston/DDR.Net
p.283 Damien Marley © The Jamaica Tourist Board
p.346 Festival, Dominican Republic © Ministry of Tourism of Dominican Republic
p.398 RMS Rhone © Stuart Westmorland/Corbis
p.411 Blackbeard's Castle © Danita Delimont/Alamy
p.421 St Annaberg Sugar Mill Ruins © US Virgin Islands Dept. of Tourism
p.435 Sage Mountain National Park © Stuart Westmorland/Corbis
p.451 Jost Van Dyke, British Virgin Islands © Andre Jenny/Alamy
p.458 Sailboats © Layne Kennedy/Corbis
p.468 Bankie Banx © David Sanger/DRR.Net
p.472 St Maarten regatta © Steve Arkley/Alamy
p.482 Grand Case © Danny Lehman/Corbis
p.490 Simon Doncker Historical Musuem © Bob Turner/Alamy
p.499 Iguana © Caribbean, Turks & Caicos Tourist Office
p.506 Mount Mazinga © Bob Krist/Corbis
p.508 Cannons, St Kitts © Roger Brisbane/Brisbane Productions
p.520 Horseback riding, Phinney Beach © Bob Krist/Corbis
p.524 Montserrat Volcano Observatory © Rolf Richardson/Alamy
p.533 Volcano, from Old Town © David Sanger/DRR.Net
p.562 Grand'Rivière, Martinique © Danita Delimont Agency/DDR
p.572 Colonial houses, Guadeloupe © Ingolf Pompe 8/Alamy
p.594 Guadeloupe © LOOK Die Bildagentur der Fotografen GmbH/Alamy
p.648 Mountain biking, St Lucia © St Lucia Tourist Board
p.694 Soufrière Volcano © Yann Arthus-Bertrand/Corbis
p.794 Hato caves, Curaçao © M. Timothy O'Keefe/Alamy
p.811 Salt, Bonaire © Tourism Corporation Bonaire
p.825 Kayaking, Bonaire © Tourism Corporation Bonaire

Index

Map entries are in colour.

E

F

G

M

N

O

T

U

V

W

Y